WORLDMARK

ENCYCLOPEDIA
of National
Economies

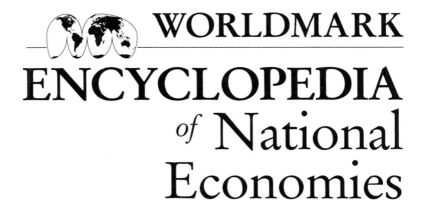

WORLDMARK
ENCYCLOPEDIA
of National
Economies

Volume 1 – Africa

Sara Pendergast and Tom Pendergast, Editors

GALE GROUP

™

THOMSON LEARNING

Detroit • New York • San Diego • San Francisco
Boston • New Haven, Conn. • Waterville, Maine
London • Munich

Jeffrey Lehman and Rebecca Parks, *Editors*
William Harmer, *Contributing Editor*
Brian J. Koski, Jeffrey Wilson, *Associate Editors*
Shelly Dickey, *Managing Editor*

Mary Beth Trimper, *Manager, Composition and Electronic Prepress*
Evi Seoud, *Assistant Manager, Composition Purchasing and Electronic Prepress*

Barbara J. Yarrow, *Manager, Imaging and Multimedia Content*
Randy Bassett, *Imaging Supervisor*
Pamela A. Reed, *Imaging Coordinator*
Leitha Etheridge-Sims, Mary K. Grimes, David G. Oblender, *Image Catalogers*
Robyn V. Young, *Project Manager, Imaging and Multimedia Content*
Robert Duncan, *Senior Imaging Specialist*
Christine O'Bryan, *Graphic Specialist*
Michelle DiMercurio, *Senior Art Director*
Susan Kelsch, *Indexing Manager*
Lynne Maday, *Indexing Specialist*

Trademarks and Property Rights

Library of Congress Control Number: 2001099714

TABLE OF CONTENTS

Countries are listed by most common name. Official country names are listed in the entries.

Preface vii

Notes on Contributors xi

Introduction xv

Algeria. 1
Angola 13
Benin 21
Botswana 29
Burkina Faso 37
Burundi 47
Cameroon. 55
Cape Verde. 67
Central African Republic 75
Chad 83
Comoros. 91
Congo, Democratic Republic of the 99
Congo, Republic of the 109
Côte d'Ivoire 117
Djibouti 127
Egypt. 135
Equatorial Guinea 151
Eritrea 159
Ethiopia 167
Gabon 179
The Gambia 187
Ghana 195
Guinea 205
Guinea-Bissau. 215
Kenya 223

Lesotho 235
Liberia 243
Libya 251
Madagascar 261
Malawi. 269
Mali. 277
Mauritania 285
Mauritius 293
Morocco. 303
Mozambique 313
Namibia 327
Niger 337
Nigeria. 347
Rwanda 365
São Tomé and Príncipe 373
Senegal 381
Seychelles 393
Sierra Leone 401
Somalia 409
South Africa 417
Sudan. 431
Swaziland. 441
Tanzania. 449
Togo 463
Tunisia. 473
Uganda. 483
Zambia. 495
Zimbabwe 505

Glossary 515

Index 523

PREFACE

The *Worldmark Encyclopedia of National Economies* joins the Worldmark family of encyclopedias and attempts to provide comprehensive overviews of the economic structure and current climate of 198 countries and territories. Each signed entry provides key data and analysis on a country's economic conditions, their relationship to social and political trends, and their impact on the lives of the country's inhabitants. The goal of this set is to use plain language to offer intelligent, consistent analysis of every important economy in the world.

It is our sincere hope that this set will open the reader's mind to the fascinating world of international economics. Contained within this collection are a number of fascinating stories: of Eastern European nations struggling to adapt to capitalist economic systems in the wake of the collapse of communism; of Pacific Island nations threatened with annihilation by the slow and steady rise of ocean levels; of Asian nations channeling the vast productivity of their people into diversified economies; of the emerging power of the European Union, which dominates economic life across Europe; of Middle Eastern nations planning for the disappearance of their primary engine of economic growth, oil; and many others. To make all this information both accessible and comparable, each entry presents information in the same format, allowing readers to easily compare, for example, the balance of trade between Singapore and Hong Kong, or the political systems of North and South Korea. Economics has a language of its own, and we have **highlighted** those economic terms that may not be familiar to a general reader and provided definitions in a glossary. Other terms that are specific to a particular country but are not economic in nature are defined within parentheses in the text.

This set contains entries on every sovereign nation in the world, as well as separate entries on large territories of countries, including: French Guiana, Martinique, and Guadeloupe; Macau; Puerto Rico; and Taiwan. The larger dependencies of other countries are highlighted within the mother country's entry. For example, the entry on Denmark includes a discussion of Greenland, the United Kingdom includes information on many of its Crown territories, and the United States entry highlights the economic conditions in some of its larger territories.

ENTRY OBJECTIVES

Each entry has two objectives: one, to offer a clear picture of the economic conditions in a particular country, and two, to provide statistical information that allows for comparison between countries. To offer comparable information, we have used some common sources for the tables and graphs as well as for individual sections. Even the most exhaustive sources do not provide information for every country, however, and thus some entries either have no data available in certain areas or contain data that was obtained from an alternate source. In all entries, we tried to provide the most current data available at the time. Because collection and evaluation methods differ among international data gathering agencies such as the World Bank, United Nations, and International Monetary Fund, as well as between these agencies and the many government data collection agencies located in each country, entries sometimes provide two or more sources of information. Consequently, the text of an entry may contain more recent information from a different source than is provided in a table or graph, though the table or graph provides information that allows the easiest comparison to other entries.

No one source could provide all the information desired for this set, so some sources were substituted when the main source lacked information for specific countries. The main sources used included: the *World Factbook 2000* and *2001,* which provided the common information on the countries' gross domestic product (GDP) at purchasing power parity, the division of labor, balance of trade, chief imports, chief exports, and population, unless otherwise noted in the text; the World Bank's *World Development Indicators,* which was a valued source for information about the infrastructure and consumption patterns of many countries; the *Human Development Report,* from the United Nations, which provided GDP per capita information on many countries; and the International Monetary Fund's *International Financial Statistics Yearbook,* which provided historical records of trade balances for most countries. Each entry also contains a bibliography that lists additional sources that are specific to that entry.

ENTRY ORGANIZATION

All entries are organized under 16 specific headings to make it easy to find needed information quickly and to compare the conditions in several different countries easily. (The sole exception is the entry on the Vatican, whose unique features necessitated the removal of several sections.) The sections are as follows:

COUNTRY OVERVIEW. This section includes information about the size of all land surfaces, describing coastlines and international boundaries. It also highlights significant geographical features in the country and the location of the capital. The size of the country is compared to a U.S. state or, for smaller countries, to Washington, D.C. Also included is information on the total population, as well as other important demographic data concerning ethnicity, religion, age, and urbanization. Where relevant, this section also includes information about internal conflicts, major health problems, or significant population policies.

OVERVIEW OF ECONOMY. This overview is meant to provide an analysis of the country's overall economic conditions, mentioning those elements that are deemed most important to an understanding of the country. It provides context for the reader to understand the more specific information available in the other sections.

POLITICS, GOVERNMENT, AND TAXATION. This section identifies the structure of the government and discusses the role the government, political parties, and taxes play in the economy.

INFRASTRUCTURE, POWER, AND COMMUNICATIONS. This section offers a description of the roads, railways, harbors, and telecommunications available in the country, assesses the modernity of the systems, and provides information about the country's plans for improvements.

ECONOMIC SECTORS. This section serves as an overview for the three more specific sections that follow, providing a general description of the balance between the country's different economic sectors.

AGRICULTURE. This section discusses the agriculture, fishing, and forestry sectors of the country.

INDUSTRY. This section discusses the industrial sector of the country, including specific information on mining, manufacturing, and other major industries, where appropriate.

SERVICES. This section concentrates on major components of the diverse services sector, usually focusing on the tourism and banking or financial sectors and sometimes including descriptions of the retail sector.

INTERNATIONAL TRADE. This section focuses on the country's patterns of trade, including the commodities traded and the historical trading partners.

MONEY. This section offers a brief description of the changes in inflation and the exchange rates in the country, and the impact those may have had on the economy. It also mentions any recent changes in the currency and the nature and impact of the central banking function.

POVERTY AND WEALTH. This section paints a picture of the distribution of wealth within the country, often comparing life in the country with that in other countries in the region. It includes governmental efforts to redistribute wealth or to deal with pressing issues of poverty.

WORKING CONDITIONS. This section describes the workforce, its ability to unionize, and the effectiveness of unions within the country. It also often includes information on wages, significant changes in the workforce over time, and the existence of protections for workers.

COUNTRY HISTORY AND ECONOMIC DEVELOPMENT. This section provides a timeline of events that shaped the country and its economy. The selected events create a more cohesive picture of the nation than could be described in the entries because of their bias toward more current information.

FUTURE TRENDS. To provide readers with a view to the future, the entry ends with an analysis of how the economic conditions in the country are expected to change in the near future. It also highlights any significant challenges the country may face.

DEPENDENCIES. This section discusses any major territories or colonies and their economies.

BIBLIOGRAPHY. The bibliography at the end of the entry lists the sources used to compile the information in the entry and also includes other materials that may be of interest to readers wanting more information about the particular country. Although specific online sources are cited, many such sources are updated annually and should be expected to change.

In addition, a data box at the beginning of each entry offers helpful economic "quick facts" such as the country's capital, monetary unit, chief exports and imports, gross domestic product (GDP), and the balance of trade. The U.S. Central Intelligence Agency's *World Factbook* (2000 and 2001) was the main source of this information unless otherwise noted. Each entry also includes a map that illustrates the location of the country. Since economic conditions are often affected by geography, the map allows readers to see the location of major cities and landmarks. The map also names bordering countries to offer readers a visual aid to understand regional conflicts and trading routes.

ACKNOWLEDGMENTS

We wish to thank all those involved in this project for their efforts. This set could not have been produced without the unfailing support of the publisher and our imaginative advisory board. At the Gale Group, managing editor Shelly Dickey and Peggy Glahn in New Product Development were especially helpful. We would also like to thank Gale editor William Harmer for his work in the early stages of the project, but special thanks must go to editors Rebecca Parks and Jeffrey Lehman who brought the set to publication. Copyeditors Edward Moran, Robyn Karney, Karl Rahder, Jennifer Wallace, and Mary Sugar must also be commended for their work to polish the entries into the form you see here.

COMMENTS

We encourage you to contact us with any comments or suggestions you may have that will benefit future editions of this set. We want this set to be a meaningful addition to your search for information about the world. Please send your comments and suggestions to: The Editors, *Worldmark Encyclopedia of National Economies,* The Gale Group, 27500 Drake Road, Farmington Hills, MI 48331. Or, call toll free at 1-800-877-4253.

—Sara Pendergast and Tom Pendergast

NOTES ON
CONTRIBUTORS

Abazov, Rafis. Professor, Department of Politics, La-Trobe University, Victoria, Australia. Author, *Formation of the Post-Soviet Foreign Policies in Central Asian Republics* (1999), and annual security and economic reports, *Brassey's Security Yearbook*, and Transitions Online.

Abazova, Alfia. LaTrobe University, Victoria, Australia. Reviewed for *Pacifica Review* and *Europe-Asia Studies.*

Amineh, Parvizi Mehdi, Ph.D. Department of Political Science, University of Amsterdam, the Netherlands. Author, *Towards the Control of Oil Resources in the Caspian Region* (New York: St. Martin's Press, 1999); *Die Globale Kapitalistische Expansion und Iran: Eine Studie der Iranischen Politischen Ökonomie (1500–1980)* (Hamburg-London: Lit Verlag).

Arnade, Charles W. Adviser. Distinguished Professor of International Studies, University of South Florida. Author, *The Emergence of the Republic of Bolivia.*

Audain, Linz, M.D., J.D., Ph.D. Staff physician, Greater Southeast, INOVA Fairfax and Southern Maryland hospitals; former professor of law, economics, and statistics at various universities; editor, *Foreign Trade of the United States* (2nd ed.), *Business Statistics of the United States* (6th ed.).

Benoit, Kenneth, Ph.D. Lecturer, Department of Political Science, Trinity College, University of Dublin, Ireland.

Bouillon, Markus R. Doctoral student in international relations with a regional focus on the Middle East, St. Antony's College, University of Oxford.

Burron, Neil. Graduate student in International Development, The Norman Paterson School of International Affairs, Carleton University, Ottawa.

Campling, Liam. Lecturer in International Politics and History, Seychelles Polytechnic (University of Manchester Twinning Programme). Editor, *Historical Materialism—Special Issue: Focus on Sub-Saharan Africa* (2002). Contributor to *West Africa* and *African Business* magazines.

Carper, Mark Daniel Lynn. Instructor of Geography, Central Missouri State University.

Cavatorta, Francesco. Doctoral candidate in the Department of Political Science, Trinity College, Dublin, Ireland. Author, "The Italian Political System and the Northern League," in *Contemporary Politics,* March 2001.

Chari, Raj. Lecturer, Department of Political Science, Trinity College, Dublin, Ireland. Author, "Spanish Socialists, Privatising the Right Way?" in *West European Politics,* Vol. 21, No. 4, October 1998, and "The March 2000 Spanish Election: A 'Critical Election'?" in *West European Politics,* Vol. 23, No. 3, July 2000.

Chauvin, Lucien O. Freelance journalist, Lima, Peru. President of the Foreign Press Association of Peru.

Childree, David L. Graduate student in Latin American Studies at Tulane University, specializing in politics and development.

Conteh-Morgan, Earl. Professor, Department of Government and International Affairs, University of South Florida, Tampa, Florida. Co-author, *Sierra Leone at the End of the 20th Century* (1999).

Costa, Ecio F., Ph.D. Post-doctoral associate, Center for Agribusiness and Economic Development, Department of Agricultural and Applied Economics, University of Georgia, Athens, Georgia. Author, "Brazil's New Floating Exchange Rate Regime and Competitiveness in the World Poultry Market," in *Journal of Agricultural and Applied Economics.*

Cunha, Stephen, Ph.D. Professor of Geography, Humboldt State University, Arcata, California. Consultant, USAID, World Bank, National Geographic Society.

Davoudi, Salamander. Graduate student in Middle Eastern economics, Georgetown University, Washington, D.C. Former aid at the Royal Jordanian Hashemite Court.

Deletis, Katarina. M.I.A. (Master of International Affairs), Columbia University, New York. International communications officer, Deloitte Touche Tohmatsu, New York.

Divisekera, Sarath. Ph.D., School of Applied Economics, Victoria University, Melbourne, Australia. Author, *Income Distribution, Inequality and Poverty in Sri Lanka* (1988).

Eames, Rory. Honors student, School of Resources, Environment, and Society, The Australian National University, Canberra, Australia.

Easton, Matthew. Independent consultant, Cambridge, Massachusetts. Author, *In the Name of Development: Human Rights and the World Bank in Indonesia* (1995).

Feoli, Ludovico. Graduate student in Latin American Studies, Tulane University, New Orleans, Louisiana. Publications director and academic coordinator, CIAPA, San José, Costa Rica.

Ferguson, James. Writer and researcher specializing in the Caribbean. Author, *A Traveller's History of the Caribbean* (1999).

Florkowski, Wojciech J. Associate professor, Department of Agricultural and Applied Economics, University of Georgia.

Foley, Sean. Ph.D. candidate, History, Georgetown University, Washington, D.C. Author of various articles and a chapter in *Crises and Quandaries in the Contemporary Persian Gulf* (2001).

Foroughi, Payam. Ph.D. student in International Relations, University of Utah. International development consultant, NGOs, USAID, and the United Nations, Central Asia; freelance writer.

Friesen, Wardlow. Senior lecturer, Department of Geography, The University of Auckland, New Zealand. Author, "Tangata Pasifika Aotearoa: Pacific Populations and Identity in New Zealand," in *New Zealand Population Review*, Vol. 26, No. 2, 2000; "Circulation, Urbanisation, and the Youth Boom in Melanesia," in *Espace, Populations, Sociétés*, Vol. 2, 1994; "Melanesian Economy on the Periphery: Migration and Village Economy in Choiseul," in *Pacific Viewpoint*, Vol. 34, No. 2, 1993.

Fry, Gerald W. Adviser. Professor of International/Intercultural Education, and director of Graduate Studies, Department of Educational Policy and Administration, University of Minnesota—Twin Cities; former team leader on major Asian Development Bank funded projects in Southeast Asia.

Gazis, Alexander. Commercial specialist, U.S. Embassy, N'Djamena, Chad. Author, *Country Commercial Guides* for Chad (Fiscal Year 2001 and 2002).

Genc, Emine, M.A. Budget expert, Ministry of Finance, Ankara, Turkey.

Genc, Ismail H., Ph.D. Assistant professor of Economics, University of Idaho, Moscow, Idaho.

Gleason, Gregory. Professor, University of New Mexico. Former director, USAID Rule of Law Program in Central Asia.

Guillen, April J., J.D./M.A. International Relations candidate, University of Southern California, Los Angeles, with an emphasis on International Human Rights Law.

Hadjiyski, Valentin, Ph.D. New York-based freelance author, former United Nations expert.

Hodd, Jack. Queen's College, Cambridge, researching graphical presentations of general equilibrium models.

Hodd, Michael R. V. Adviser. Professor of Economics, University of Westminster, London, and has worked as a consultant for the ILO and UNIDO. Author, *African Economic Handbook,* London, Euromonitor, 1986; *The Economies of Africa,* Aldershot, Dartmouth, 1991; with others, *Fisheries and Development in Tanzania,* London, Macmillan, 1994.

Iltanen, Suvi. Graduate of the European Studies Programme, Trinity College, Dublin, Ireland.

Jensen, Nathan. Ph.D. candidate in political science, Yale University, and visiting scholar at UCLA's International Studies and Overseas Programs. He is currently completing his dissertation titled "The Political Economy of Foreign Direct Investment."

Jugenitz, Heidi. Graduate student in Latin American Studies, Tulane University, New Orleans, Louisiana. Research assistant, Payson Center for International Development and Technology Transfer.

Kiyak, Tunga. Ph.D. candidate in marketing and international business, Michigan State University. Research assistant, Center for International Business Education and Research (MSU-CIBER). Curator, International Business Resources on the WWW.

Kuznetsova, Olga. Senior research fellow, The Manchester Metropolitan University Business School, Manchester, UK. Author, *The CIS Handbook. Regional Handbooks of Economic Development: Prospects onto the 21st Century,* edited by P. Heenan and M. Lamontagne (1999).

Lang-Tigchelaar, Amy. Graduate student in joint MBA/MA in Latin American Studies Program, Tulane University, New Orleans, Louisiana.

Lansford, Tom. Assistant professor, University of Southern Mississippi, Gulf Coast. Author, *Evolution and Devolution: The Dynamics of Sovereignty and Security in Post-Cold War Europe* (2000).

Lynch, Catherine. Doctoral candidate in political science, Dublin City University, Ireland. Areas of interest include the political economy of implementing peace agreements, the politics of peace building, the implementation of policy, and other aspects of comparative political science.

Mahoney, Lynn. M.A., University of Michigan. Associate director of development, director of communications, American University of Beirut New York Office; freelance writer.

Mann, Larisa. Graduate student of economic history, cultural studies, and legal studies, London School of Economics. Presented "Shaky Ground, Thin Air: Intellectual Property Law and the Jamaican Music Industry" at the "Rethinking Caribbean Culture" conference at the University of West Indies, Cave Hill, Barbados.

Mazor, John. Writer and journalist specializing in economic and political issues in Latin America and the Levant. Graduated from Boston University with a degree in literature and studied intelligence and national security policy at the Institute of World Politics in Washington, D.C.

Mobekk, Eirin. MacArthur postdoctoral research associate, Department of War Studies, King's College, London, United Kingdom.

Mowatt, Rosalind. Graduate student in Economics, Wits University, Johannesburg, South Africa. Former economist for National Treasury, working with Southern African Development Community (SADC) countries.

Muhutdinova-Foroughi, Raissa. M.P.A., University of Colorado at Denver. Journalist, Radio Tajikistan; consultant, United Nations, World Bank, and Eurasia Foundation, Commonwealth of Independent Nations; freelance writer.

Mukungu, Allan C. K. Graduate student, University of Westminster, London, and has done consultancy work for the World Bank.

Musakhanova, Oygul. Graduate, University of Westminster; economist, Arthur Anderson, Tashkent, Uzbekistan.

Naidu, Sujatha. LL.M. in Environment Law, University of Utah. Ph.D. student in International Relations, Department of Political Science, University of Utah; freelance writer.

Nicholls, Ana. Journalist. Assistant editor, *Business Central Europe,* The Economist Group. Author of three surveys of Romania.

Nicoleau, Michael. J.D. Cornell Law School, Ithaca, New York. Co-author, "Constitutional Governance in the Democratic Republic of the Congo: An Analysis of the Constitution Proposed by the Government of Laurent Kabila," in *Texas International Law Journal,* Spring 2000.

Nuseibeh, Reem. Graduate student in Comparative Politics/Human Rights, University of Maryland, Maryland. Middle East risk analyst, Kroll Information Services, Vienna, Virginia.

Ó Beacháin, Donnacha. Ph.D. Political Science from National University of Ireland, Dublin. Civic Education Project visiting lecturer at the Departments of International Relations and Conflict Resolution at Tbilisi State University and the Georgian Technical University, respectively, 2000–2002.

Ohaegbulam, F. Ugboaja. Professor, Government and International Affairs, University of South Florida. Author, *A Concise Introduction to American Foreign Policy* (1999), and *Nigeria and the UN Mission to the Democratic Republic of the Congo* (1982).

O'Malley, Eoin. Doctoral candidate in Political Science at Trinity College, Dublin, and visiting researcher at UNED, Madrid, Spain. Author, "Ireland" in Annual Review section of the *European Journal of Political Research* (1999, 2000, 2001).

Ozsoz, Emre. Graduate student in International Political Economy and Development, Fordham University, New York. Editorial assistant for the Middle East, The Economist Intelligence Unit, New York.

Peimani, Hooman, Ph.D. Independent consultant with international organizations in Geneva, Switzerland. Author, *The Caspian Pipeline Dilemma: Political Games and Economic Losses* (2001).

Pretes, Michael. Research scholar, Department of Human Geography, Research School of Pacific and Asian Studies, The Australian National University, Canberra, Australia.

Sabol, Steven. Ph.D., the University of North Carolina at Charlotte. Author, *Awake Kazak! Russian Colonization of Central Asia and the Genesis of Kazak National Consciousness, 1868–1920.*

Samonis, Val, Ph.D., C.P.C. Managed and/or participated in international research and advisory projects/teams sponsored by the Hudson Institute, World Bank, CASE Warsaw, Soros Foundations, the Center for European Integration Studies (ZEI Bonn), the Swedish government, and a number of other clients. Also worked with top reformers such as the Polish Deputy Prime Minister Leszek Balcerowicz, U.S. Treasury Secretary Larry Summers, the World Bank, and OECD Private Sector Advisory Group on Corporate Governance, and with the Stanford Economic Transition Group; advisor to the Czech government (Deputy Prime Minister Pavel Mertlik), the Lithuanian parliament, and several Lithuanian governments, international organizations, and multinational corporations; founding editor, *Journal of East-West Business* (The Haworth Press Inc).

Sezgin, Yuksel. Ph.D. candidate in Political Science, University of Washington. Former assistant Middle East coordinator at the Foreign Economic Relations Board of Turkey.

Schubert, Alexander. Ph.D., Cornell University.

Scott, Cleve Mc D. Ph.D. candidate and graduate assistant, Department of History, University of the West Indies, Cave Hill Campus, Barbados.

Stobwasser, Ralph. Graduate student in Middle Eastern Studies, FU Berlin, Germany. Worked in the Office of the Chief Economist Middle East and North Africa, World Bank, Washington, D.C.

Strnad, Tomas. Ph.D. student, Department of the Middle East and Africa, Charles University, Czech Republic. Chief editor of the *Arab Markets Magazine*; author of "The Kuwaiti Dilemma," "OPEC—Main Sinner or Sheer Scapegoat?," and "Globalization in the Arab and Muslim World" in *International Policy* and other magazines.

Stroschein, Sherrill. Assistant professor of Political Science, Ohio University. Frequent contributor to scholarly journals on East European topics and a former contributor to *Nations in Transit* (1995 and 1997 editions).

Thadathil, George. Associate professor of History, Paul Quinn College, Dallas, Texas. Author, "Myanmar, Agony of a People" in *History Behind Headlines*, 2000. His research interests include South and Southeast Asia, and Asian collective security.

Thapa, Rabi. Editor and environmentalist, France. Environment/development assignments in Nepal, 1998.

Tian, Robert Guang, Ph.D. Associate professor of Business Administration, Erskine College. Author, *Canadian Chinese, Chinese Canadians: Coping and Adapting in North America* (1999).

Ubarra, Maria Cecilia T. Graduate student in Public Policy and Program Administration, University of the Philippines, Quezon City, Philippines. Research fellow, Institute for Strategic and Development Studies; case writer, Asian Institute of Management, Philippines.

Vivas, Leonardo. M.Phil., Development Studies, Sussex University (UK); Ph.D., International Economics and Finance, Nanterre University (France); fellow, Weatherhead Center for International Affairs, Harvard University.

Viviers, Wilma. Program director, International Trade in School of Economics, Potchefstroom University, South Africa.

Zhang, Xingli. Ph.D. student, University of Southern California, Los Angeles. Author, "Brunei" in *East Asian Encyclopedia* (in Chinese).

INTRODUCTION

THE POWER OF ECONOMIC UNDERSTANDING

The economies of the world are becoming increasingly interconnected and interdependent, a fact dramatically illustrated on 2 July 1997 when the Thai government decided to allow its currency to "float" according to market conditions. The result was a significant drop in the value of the currency and the start of the Asian economic crisis, a contagion that spread quickly to other Asian countries such as the Republic of Korea, Indonesia, Malaysia, and the Philippines. Before long the epidemic reached Brazil and Russia.

In this way, a small economic change in one less-developed country sent economic shock waves around the world. Surprisingly, no one predicted this crisis, though economist Paul Krugman in a prominent 1994 *Foreign Affairs* article argued that there was no Asian economic miracle and the kind of growth rates attained in recent years were not sustainable over the long term. In such an interconnected global economy, it is imperative to have an understanding of other economies and economic conditions around the world. Yet that understanding is sorely lacking in the American public.

Various studies have shown that both young people and the public at large have a low level of literacy about other nations. A survey of 655 high school students in southeast Ohio indicated that students were least informed in the area of international economic concerns, and the number of economics majors at the college level is declining. The economic and geographic illiteracy has become such a national concern that the U.S. Senate recently passed a resolution calling for a national education policy that addresses Americans' lack of knowledge of other parts of the world.

The information provided by the media also frequently reflects a distorted understanding of world economies. During the Asian economic crisis, we often heard about the collapse of various Asian countries such as Korea and Thailand. They were indeed suffering a severe crisis, but usually companies, not countries, collapse. The use of the "collapse" language was therefore misleading. In another example, a distinguished journalist writing in a prominent East coast newspaper claimed that Vietnamese women paid more in transportation and food costs than they were earning while working in a factory manufacturing Nike shoes. Such a statement, while well intended in terms of genuine concern for these women workers, makes no economic sense whatsoever, and is actually not accurate. The wages of these women are indeed extremely low by U.S. standards, but such wages must be viewed in the context of another society, where the cost of living may be dramatically lower and where low salaries may be pooled. At other times, a fact—such as the fact that a minority of the Japanese workforce enjoys employment for life—is exaggerated to suggest that the Japanese economy boomed as it did in the 1980s *because* of the Japanese policy of life-long employment. Such generalizing keeps people from understanding the complexities of the Japanese economy.

"THINGS ARE NOT WHAT THEY SEEM." In defense of this lack of economic understanding, it must be said that understanding economics is not easy. Paul A. Samuelson, author of the classic textbook *Economics* (1995), once stated about economics "that things are often not what at first they seem." In Japan, for example, many young women work as office ladies in private companies as an initial job after completing school. These young ladies often stay at home with their parents and have few basic expenses. Over several years they can accumulate considerable savings, which may be used for travel, overseas study, or investing. Thus, as Samuelson noted in his textbook, actual individual economic welfare is not based on wages as such, but on the *difference* between earnings and expenditures. Wages are not the only measure of the value of labor: one must also consider purchasing power and how costs of living vary dramatically from place to place. Without taking into account purchasing power, we overestimate economic well-being in high-cost countries such as Japan and Switzerland and underestimate it in low-cost countries such as India and Cambodia.

Consider the following examples: The cost of taking an air-conditioned luxury bus from the Cambodian capital of Phnom Penh to its major port, Sihanoukville, is less than $2. The same bus trip of equal distance in Japan or the United States would cost $50 or more. Similarly, a (subsidized) lunch at a factory producing Nike shoes in Vietnam may cost the equivalent of 5 U.S. cents in 1998, while lunch at a student union on a U.S. college campus may cost $5. Thus a teaching assistant on a U.S. campus pays 100 times more for lunch than the Vietnamese factory worker. Who is more "poorly paid" in these situations? Add to this the reality that in many developing countries where extended families are common, members of the family often pool their earnings, which individually may be quite low. To look only at individual earnings can thus be rather misleading. Such cultural nuances are important to keep in mind in assessing economic conditions and welfare in other nations.

Various economic puzzles can also create confusion and misunderstanding. For example, currently the United States has the highest trade deficit in world history: it imports far more that it exports. Most countries with huge trade deficits have a weak currency, but the U.S. dollar has remained strong. Why is this the case? Actually, it is quite understandable when one knows that the balance of trade is just one of many factors that determine the value of a nation's currency. In truth, demand for the U.S. dollar has remained high. The United States is an attractive site for foreign investment because of its large and growing economic market and extremely stable politics. Second, the United States has a large tourism sector, drawing people to the country where they exchange their currency for U.S. dollars. Several years ago, for the first time ever, there were more Thais coming to the United States as tourists than those in the United States going to Thailand. Third, the United States is extremely popular among international students seeking overseas education. Economically, a German student who spends three years studying in the United States benefits the economy in the same way as a long-term tourist or conventional exports: that student invests in the U.S. economy. In the academic year 1999-2000, there were 514,723 international students in the United States spending approximately $12.3 billion. Thus, the services provided by U.S. higher education represent an important "invisible export." Fourth, 11 economies are now dollarized, which means that they use the U.S. currency as their national currency. Panama is the most well known of these economies and El Salvador became a dollarized economy on 1 January 2001. Other countries are semi-officially or partially dollarized (Cambodia and Vietnam, for example). As the result of dollarization, it is estimated by the Federal Reserve that 55 to 70 percent of all U.S. dollars are held by foreigners primarily in Latin America and former parts of the U.S.S.R. Future candidates for dollarization are Argentina, Brazil, Ecuador, Indonesia, Mexico, and even Canada. With so many countries using U.S. dollars, demand for the U.S. dollar is increased, adding to its strength. For all these reasons, the U.S. currency and economy remained strong despite the persisting large trade deficits, which in themselves, according to standard economic logic, suggest weakness.

SYSTEMS OF CLASSIFICATION. As in other fields, such as biology and botany, it is important to have a sound system of classification to understand various national economies. Unfortunately, the systems commonly used to describe various national economies are often flawed by cultural and Eurocentric biases and distortion. After the end of World War II and the start of the Cold War, it became common to speak of "developed" and "underdeveloped" countries. There were two problems with this overly simplistic distinction. First, it viewed countries only in terms of material development. Second, it implied that a nation was developed or underdeveloped across all categories. As an example, "underdeveloped" Thailand has consistently been one of the world's leading food exporters and among those countries that import the least amount of food. Similarly, in "developed" Japan there are both homeless people and institutions to house the elderly, while in "underdeveloped" Vietnam there are no homeless and the elderly are cared for by their families. Which country is more "developed"?

Later the term "Third World" became popular. This term was invented by the French demographer Alfred Sauvy and popularized by the scholar Irving Horowitz in his volume, *Three Worlds of Development*. "First World" referred to rich democracies such as the United States and the United Kingdom; "Second World" referred to communist countries such as the former U.S.S.R. and former East Germany. The term "Third World" was used to refer to the poorer nations of Africa, Latin America, and Asia (with the exception of Japan). But this distinction is also problematic, for it implies that the "First World" is superior to the "Third World." Another common term introduced was modern versus less modern nations. The Princeton sociologist Marion J. Levy made this distinction based on a technological definition: more modern nations were those that made greater use of tools and inanimate sources of power. Thus, non-Western Japan is quite modern because of its use of robots and bullet trains. Over time, however, many people criticized the modern/non-modern distinction as being culturally biased and implying that all nations had to follow the same path of progress.

More recently, economists from around the world have recognized the importance of using a variety of factors to understand the development of national economies. Each of these factors should be viewed in terms of a continuum. For example, no country is either completely industrial or completely agricultural. The entries in this volume provide the basic data to assess each national economy on several of these key criteria. One can determine, for example, the extent to which an economy is industrial by simply dividing the percentage of the economy made up by industry by the percentage made up by agriculture. Or one can determine how much energy national economies use to achieve their level of economic output and welfare. This provides an important ecological definition of efficiency, which goes beyond limited material definitions. This measure allows an estimate of how "green" versus "gray" an economy is; greener economies are those using less energy to achieve a given level of economic development. One might like to understand how international an economy is, which can be done by adding a country's exports to its imports and then dividing by GDP. This indicator reveals that economies such as the Netherlands, Malaysia, Singapore, and Hong Kong are highly international while the isolationist Democratic People's Republic of Korea (North Korea) is far less international.

Another interesting measure of an economy, particularly relevant in this age of more information-oriented economies and "the death of distance" (Cairncross 1997), is the extent to which an economy is digitalized. One measure of this factor would be the extent to which the population of a given economy has access to the Internet. Costa Rica, for example, established a national policy that all its citizens should have free access to the Internet. In other economies, such as Bhutan, Laos, and North Korea, access to the Internet is extremely limited. These differences, of course, relate to what has been termed "the digital divide." Another important factor is whether an economy is people-oriented, that is, whether it aims to provide the greatest happiness to the greatest number; economist E.F. Schumacher called this "economics as if people mattered." The King of Bhutan, for example, has candidly stated that his goal for his Buddhist nation is not Gross National Product but instead Gross National Happiness. Such goals indicate that the level of a country's economic development does not necessarily reflect its level of social welfare and quality of life.

Another important category that helps us understand economies is the degree to which they can be considered "transitional." Transitional economies are those that were once communist, state-planned economies but that are becoming or have become free-market economies. This transitional process started in China in the late 1970s when its leader Deng Xiaoping introduced his "four modernizations." Later, Soviet leader Mikhael Gorbachev introduced such reforms, called *perestroika,* in the former Soviet Union. With the dissolving of the U.S.S.R. in 1991, many new transitional economies emerged, including Belarus, Uzbekistan, Kyrgyzstan, and the Ukraine. Other countries undergoing transition were Vietnam, Laos, Cambodia, and Mongolia. These economies can be grouped into two types: full transitional and partial transitional. The full transitional economies are shifting both to free markets and to liberal democracies with free expression, multiple parties, and open elections. The partial

transitional economies are changing in the economic realm, but retaining their original one-party systems. Included in the latter category are the economies of China, Vietnam, Laos, and Cuba. This volume provides valuable current information on the many new transitional economies emerging from the former Soviet world.

KEY THEMES IN THE WORLD ECONOMY. In looking at the economies of countries around the globe, a number of major common themes can be identified. There is increasing economic interdependence and interconnectivity, as stressed by Thomas Friedman in his recent controversial book about globalization titled *The Lexus and the Olive Tree: Understanding Globalization.* For example, the People's Republic of China is now highly dependent on exports to the United States. In turn, U.S. companies are dependent on the Chinese market: Boeing is dependent on China for marketing its jet airliners; the second largest market for Mastercard is now in China; and Nike is highly dependent on China and other Asian economies for manufacturing its sports products. Such deep interdependence augurs well for a peaceful century, for countries are less likely to attack the countries with whom they do a vigorous business, even if their political and social systems are radically different. In fact, new threats to peace as reflected in the tragic terrorist attack of 11 September 2001, primarily relate to long-standing *historical* conflicts and grievances.

Conventional political boundaries and borders often do not well reflect new economic realities and cultural patterns. Economic regions and region states are becoming more important. The still-emerging power of the European Union can be gauged by reading the essays of any of the countries that are currently part of the Union or hoping to become a part of it in the coming years. This volume may help readers better understand which nations are becoming more interconnected and have similar economic conditions.

The tension between equity (fairness) and efficiency is common in nearly all national economies. In some economies there is more stress on efficiency, while in others there is more stress on equity and equality. Thus, as should be expected, countries differ in the nature of the equality of their income and wealth distributions. For each entry in this volume, important data are provided on this important factor. The geographer David M. Smith has documented well both national and international inequalities in his data-rich *Where the Grass is Greener* (1979).

Invisible and informal economies—the interactions of which are outside regulated economic channels—represent a growing segment of economic interactions in some countries. In his controversial but important volume, *The Other Path* (1989), the Peruvian economist Hernando de Soto alerted us to the growing significance of the informal economy. In countries such as Peru, research has shown that in some cases individuals prefer work in the informal to the formal sector because it provides them with more control over their personal lives. The Thai economist Pasuk Phongpaichit and her colleagues have written a fascinating book on Thailand's substantial invisible economy titled *Guns, Girls, Gambling, and Ganja* (1998). Thus, official government and international statistical data reported in this volume often are unable to take into account such data from the hidden part of economies.

In an increasingly internationalized economy in which transnational corporations are highly mobile and able to move manufacturing overseas quite rapidly, it is important to distinguish between real foreign direct investment and portfolio investment. At one point during Thailand's impressive economic boom of the late 1980s and early 1990s, a new Japanese factory was coming on line every three days. This is foreign direct investment, involving actual bricks and mortar, and it creates jobs that extend beyond the actual facility being constructed. In contrast foreign portfolio investment consists of a foreign entity buying stocks, bonds, or other financial instruments in another nation. In our current wired global economy, such funds can be moved in and out of nations almost instantaneously and have little lasting effect on the economic growth of a country. Economies such as Chile and Malaysia have developed policies to try to combat uncertainty and related economic instability caused by the potential of quick withdrawal of portfolio investments.

Some argue that transnational corporations (owned by individuals all over the world), which have no national loyalties, represent the most powerful political force in the world today. Many key transnational corporations have larger revenues than the entire gross national products of many of the nations included in this volume. This means that many national economies, especially smaller ones, lack effective bargaining power in dealing with large international corporations.

Currently, it is estimated by the International Labor Office of the United Nations that one-third of the world's workforce is currently unemployed or underemployed. This means that 500 million new jobs need to be created over the next 10 years. Data on the employment situation in each economy are presented in this volume. The creation of these new jobs represents a major challenge to the world's economies.

The final and most important theme relates to the ultimate potential clash between economy and ecology. To the extent that various national economies and their peoples show a commitment to become greener and more environmentally friendly, ultimate ecological crises and catastrophes can be avoided or minimized. Paul Ray and Sherry Anderson's *The Cultural Creatives: How 50 Million People Are Changing the World* (2000) lends credence to the view that millions are changing to more environmentally conscious lifestyles.

In trying to understand the global economy, it is critically important to have good trend data. In each of the entries of this volume, there is an emphasis on providing important economic data over several decades to enable the reader to assess such patterns. Some trends will have tremendous importance for the global economy. One phenomenon with extremely important implications for population is the policy of limiting families to only one child in China's urban areas. This deliberate social engineering by the world's most populous country will have a powerful impact on the global economy of the 21st century. The global environmental implications are, of course, extremely positive. Though there is much debate about the economic, political, and socio-cultural implications of this one-child policy, overall it will probably give China a tremendous strategic advantage in terms of the key factors of human resource development and creativity.

THE POWER OF UNDERSTANDING. By enhancing our knowledge and understanding of other economies, we gain the potential for mutual learning and inspiration for continuous improvement. There is so much that we can learn from each other. Denmark, for example, is now getting seven percent of its electrical energy from wind energy. This has obvious relevance to the state of California as it faces a major energy crisis. The Netherlands and China for a long period have utilized bicycles for basic transportation. Some argue that the bicycle is the most efficient "tool" in the world in terms of output and energy inputs. Many new major highways in Vietnam are built with exclusive bike paths separated by concrete walls from the main highway. The Vietnamese have also developed electric bicycles. The efficient bullet trains of Japan and France have relevance to other areas such as coastal China and the coastal United States. Kathmandu in Nepal has experimented with non-polluting electric buses. In the tremendous biodiversity of the tropical forests of Southeast Africa, Latin America, and Africa, there may be cures for many modern diseases.

We hope to dispel the view that economics is the boring "dismal science" often written in complex, difficult language. This four-volume set presents concise, current information on all the economies of the world, including not only large well-known economies such as the United States, Germany, and Japan, but also new nations that have emerged only in recent years, and many microstates of which we tend to be extremely uninformed. With the publication of this volume, we hope to be responsive to the following call by Professor Mark C. Schug: "The goal of economic education is to foster in students the thinking skills and substantial economic knowledge necessary to become effective and participating citizens." It is our hope that this set will enhance both economic and geographic literacy critically needed in an increasingly interconnected world.

—Gerald W. Fry, University of Minnesota

BIBLIOGRAPHY

Brown, Lester R., et al. *State of the World 2000.* New York: W. W. Norton, 2000.

Buchholz, Todd G. *From Here to Economy: A Shortcut to Economic Literacy.* New York: A Dutton Book, 1995.

Cairncross, Frances. *The Death of Distance: How the Communications Revolution Will Change Our Lives.* Boston: Harvard Business School Press, 2001.

Friedman, Thomas F. *The Lexus and the Olive Tree: Understanding Globalization.* New York: Anchor Books, 2000.

Fry, Gerald W., and Galen Martin. *The International Development Dictionary.* Oxford: ABC-Clio Press, 1991.

Hansen, Fay. "Power to the Dollar, Part One of a Series," *Business Finance* (October 1999): 17-20.

Heintz, James, Nancy Folbre, and the Center for Popular Economics. *The Ultimate Field Guide to the U.S. Economy.* New York: The New Press, 2000.

Horowitz, Irving J. *Three Worlds of Development: The Theory and Practice of International Stratification.* New York: Oxford University Press, 1966.

Jacobs, Jane. *The Nature of Economies.* New York: The Modern Library, 2000.

Korten, David C. *When Corporations Rule the World.* West Hartford, CT: Kumarian Press, 1995.

Levy, Marion J. *Modernization and the Structure of Societies.* 2 vols. New Brunswick, NJ: Transaction Publications, 1996.

Lewis, Martin W., and Kären E. Wigen. *A Critique of Metageography.* Berkeley: University of California Press, 1997.

Lohrenz, Edward. *The Essence of Chaos.* Seattle: University of Washington Press, 1993.

Ohmae, Kenichi. *The End of the Nation State: The Rise of Regional Economies.* London: HarperCollins, 1996.

Pasuk Phongpaichit, Sungsidh Priryarangsan, and Nualnoi Treerat. *Guns, Girls, Gambling, and Ganja: Thailand's Illegal Economy and Public Policy.* Chiang Mai: Silkworm Books, 1998.

Pennar, Karen. "Economics Made Too Simple." *Business Week* (20 January 1997): 32.

Ray, Paul H., and Sherry Ruth Anderson. *The Cultural Creatives: How 50 Million People Are Changing the World.* New York: Harmony Books, 2000.

Salk, Jonas, and Jonathan Salk. *World Population and Human Values: A New Reality.* New York: Harper & Row, 1981.

Samuelson, Paul A., William D. Nordhaus, with the assistance of Michael J. Mandal. *Economics.* 15th ed. New York: McGraw-Hill, 1995.

Schug, Mark C. "Introducing Children to Economic Reasoning: Some Beginning Lessons." *Social Studies* (Vol. 87, No. 3, May-June 1996): 114-118.

Schumacher, E.F. *Small is Beautiful: Economics as if People Mattered.* New York: Perennial Library, 1975.

Siegfried, John J., and Bonnie T. Meszaros. "National Voluntary Content Standards for Pre-College Economics Education." *AEA Papers and Proceedings* (Vol. 87, No. 2, May 1997): 247-253.

Smith, David. *Where the Grass Is Greener: Geographical Perspectives on Inequality.* London: Croom Helm, 1979.

Soto, Hernando de; translated by June Abbott. *The Other Path: The Invisible Revolution in the Third World.* New York: Harper & Row, 1989.

Stock, Paul A., and William D. Rader. "Level of Economic Understanding for Senior High School Students in Ohio." *The Journal of Educational Research* (Vol. 91, No. 1, September/October 1997): 60-63.

Sulloway, Frank J. *Born to Rebel: Birth Order, Family Dynamics, and Creative Lives.* New York: Pantheon Books, 1996.

Todaro, Michael P. *Economic Development.* Reading, MA: Addison Wesley, 2000.

Wentland, Daniel. "A Framework for Organizing Economic Education Teaching Methodologies." Mississippi: 2000-00-00, ERIC Document, ED 442702.

Wood, Barbara. *E.F. Schumacher: His Life and Thought.* New York: Harper & Row, 1984.

Wren, Christopher S. "World Needs to Add 500 Million Jobs in 10 Years, Report Says." *The New York Times* (25 January 2001): A13.

ALGERIA

Democratic and Popular Republic of Algeria
Al-Jumhuriyah al Jaza'iriyah
ad-Dimuqratiyah ash-Sha'biyah

CAPITAL: Algiers.

MONETARY UNIT: Algerian dinar (AD). One Algerian dinar equals one hundred centimes. There are coins of 20, 10, 5, 2, and 1 dinars, and 50, 20, 10, 5, and 1 centimes. Paper currency comes in denominations of AD1,000, 500, 200, 100, and 50.

CHIEF EXPORTS: Petroleum, natural gas, and petroleum products.

CHIEF IMPORTS: Capital goods, food and beverages, and consumer goods.

GROSS DOMESTIC PRODUCT: US$147.6 billion (purchasing power parity, 1999 est.).

BALANCE OF TRADE: Exports: US$13.7 billion (f.o.b., 1999 est.). Imports: US$9.3 billion (f.o.b., 1999 est.).

COUNTRY OVERVIEW

LOCATION AND SIZE. Algeria is located in North Africa, bordering the Mediterranean Sea. It shares borders with Morocco, Mauritania, Mali, Niger, Libya, and Tunisia. Taken together, Algeria, Morocco, and Tunisia form what is known as the Arab Maghreb or West. With an area of 2,381,740 square kilometers (919,595 square miles) and a short coastline of 998 kilometers (620 miles), Algeria is the second largest country in Africa after Sudan, and is slightly less than 3.5 times the size of Texas. Algeria's capital city, Algiers, is located in the north on the Mediterranean Sea. Other major cities include Annaba and Oran, both in the north.

POPULATION. The population of Algeria was estimated at 31,193,917 in July of 2000, an increase of 6.2 million from the 1990 population of 25,010,000. In 2000, Algeria's birth rate stood at 23.14 per 1,000, while the death rate was reported at 5.3 per 1,000. With a projected growth rate of 1.7 percent between 2000 and 2015, the population is expected to reach 39.8 million by the year 2015. Muslims, mostly of the Malekite Sunni tradition, make up 99 percent of the population, while Christians

and Jews make up the remaining 1 percent. A small percentage of the population are the indigenous Berbers, who speak Tamazight. Since 1995, the Berbers have been given wider autonomy and have been allowed to speak and teach their language. Arabic is the official and dominant language.

Algeria's population growth has slowed significantly since the early 1990s, reaching 2.8 percent in 1998, down from 3.06 percent in 1987. The slowdown is mostly attributable to a falling birth rate, which is now 2.15 children per family. Population growth is expected to drop even further in the coming years. The success of the Algerian government's family planning policies has ensured wider access to contraceptives and family planning education. The Comite national de la population (CNP) was established in October 1997 to oversee and coordinate national planning policies.

The population is generally young, with some 35 percent below the age of 14 and just 4 percent older than 65. Given the population makeup and the significant drop in the population growth rate, the government is faced with the daunting challenge of creating new employment opportunities, and is bracing itself for an aging population in the coming decades. Algeria's young population has also been a source of political instability, feeding an anti-government Islamic backlash that began in the early 1990s. Unemployment and limited job opportunities are largely responsible for an Islamic insurgency that has destabilized the country since 1991.

As in many developing countries, a majority of Algerians live in urban areas. In 1997, 60 percent of the population was urban, an increase of 29 percent from 1966, but the trend toward rural-urban migration is believed to have leveled off. Most of the population is

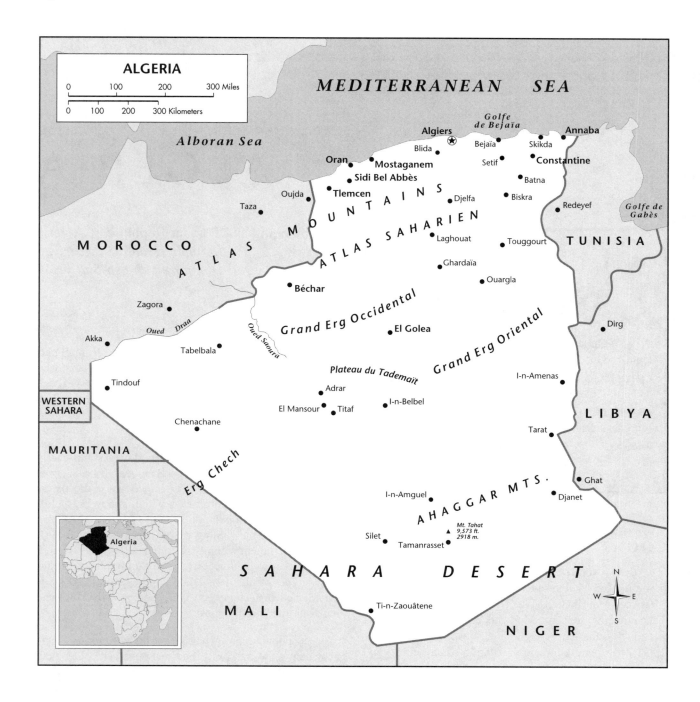

concentrated in the north, with the capital Algiers and its suburbs being home to the largest concentration of Algerians; 4 million people live in the capital.

OVERVIEW OF ECONOMY

Algeria's small- to medium-sized economy is largely dependent on the hydrocarbons sector, which accounts for about 95 percent of export earnings, 52 percent of budget revenues, and 25 percent of GDP. The second-largest natural gas exporter in the world, Algeria is home to the fifth-largest reserves of gas worldwide. Algeria also has

the 14th-largest reserves of oil in the world. The European Union is the largest market for Algerian natural gas.

The industrial sector is the largest contributor to the economy, accounting for 51 percent of GDP and employing 13.6 percent of the **labor force** of 9.1 million workers. The sector is dominated by oil-related industries. Other light industries can also be found, but their contribution to GDP is modest. The services sector is the second-largest economic sector, accounting for 37 percent of GDP and employing 13.5 percent of the labor force. The agricultural sector contributes 11–12 percent of GDP annually and employs some 22 percent of the labor force.

Algeria entered the twentieth century as a French colony heavily dependent on agriculture. Soon after the conquest of Algeria in 1830, the French created large agricultural tracts, built factories and businesses, and exploited cheap local labor. Until Algeria's independence in 1962, the bulk of its economic activity and wealth was controlled by the French colonizers, who successfully developed a small industry and a sophisticated export trade that provided food and raw materials to France in return for capital and **consumer goods**. The French also controlled about 30 percent of the total arable land, and were responsible for most of agricultural production and exports.

Since 1962, Algeria's economy has been centrally-planned, despite state efforts to **privatize** the economy and attract foreign investment. The country's huge **foreign debt**, which in 1999 reached US$30 billion according to the CIA, forced the government to launch an economic reform program in 1989. The government also concluded agreements with the International Monetary Fund (IMF) in the late 1980s and 1990s to secure international credit for its envisioned reform program.

This program has been largely successful, with the government curbing **inflation**, cutting budget spending, and preserving **foreign exchange reserves**. The adoption of the economic reforms program has also accelerated growth and succeeded in reestablishing economic stability. In the late 1980s and early 1990s, the program was coupled with austerity measures designed to reduce Algeria's **external debt**, which has proven difficult to control. In 1995, the government approved a framework for the privatization and **restructuring** of **public sector** enterprises. A financial sector reform program has also been initiated, although progress has been slow. As a result, Algeria has managed to achieve an average annual real growth rate of 5.5 percent since the mid-1990s, with the hydrocarbon sector being the main driving force of economic growth.

While the government has managed to achieve some progress toward economic recovery and reform, the country's troubled economy continues to be heavily dependent on volatile oil and gas revenues. Furthermore, the slow pace of the reform program, coupled with political turmoil, has failed to attract sufficient foreign investment or to create sufficient employment opportunities. Neither the hydrocarbon sector nor agriculture is capable of providing enough jobs to counteract long-standing unemployment problems. The rate of unemployment in 1999 was reported at 30 percent. By contrast, unemployment in the United States in 1999 was just 4.2 percent. The challenge to create new job opportunities for Algeria's young population is one of the biggest tasks facing the government.

Government bureaucracy is a major impediment to the conduct of business in Algeria. Red tape permeates all government ministries and the commercial court system, which resolves disputes between merchants and other businesspeople. Corruption is also widespread at all levels of the public sector, largely as a result of the low wages and difficult living conditions. In 1998, the government launched an anti-corruption drive, which resulted in as many as 2,000 public officials being prosecuted or awaiting trial on charges ranging from petty crime to grand larceny.

POLITICS, GOVERNMENT, AND TAXATION

After a bitter guerilla war with France (guerilla wars are fought with non-conventional methods by small units against larger, more conventional armies), which held Algeria as a colony, the country finally achieved independence in 1962. But Algeria's economy was in a state of chaos. Skilled labor was in short supply, as the French had taken with them most of the skilled personnel who ran the country. Until the late 1980s, Algeria's successive governments reacted by instituting a highly centralized **socialist** system that ensured the government a central role in the economy. Algeria's first president, Ahmad Ben Bella, moved to **nationalize** land and property previously owned by the French colonialists, which by 1963 had fallen under state control. Oil companies were nationalized in 1971, while agricultural land was placed under the control of workers. During this phase, the government placed special emphasis on the development of capital-intensive heavy industry. However, these state-led development programs and socialist policies soon proved to be a failure. The agricultural sector was particularly hit by bureaucratic mismanagement, inefficiency, and graft.

It was not until 1985 that the government came to realize the high costs associated with its socialist policies. Falling world oil prices, coupled with a high food import bill and a growing foreign debt burden, forced the government to re-evaluate its policies and abandon socialist policies. High unemployment rates, a lack of consumer goods, and shortages in basic foodstuffs threatened the country's political stability, as signs of popular unrest began to manifest themselves in protests. In 1985, President Chadli Benjedid shifted the focus of the country's development plans toward building a diversified economy by placing greater emphasis on agriculture. Benjedid's economic **liberalization** program sought to reduce central planning and decrease government control over the economy.

Since independence, Algeria has been ruled by 1 party, the National Liberation Front (FLN), which has largely used its dominance to impose heavily centralized economic structures that were justified through socialist ideology. However, the regime's priority on heavy industry and centralized management led to the neglect of the agricultural sector and the basic needs of its growing population. The decade of the 1980s laid bare the failure of the FLN to achieve either a lasting political consensus or a sustainable basis for economic growth. The sharp decline of oil prices in the mid-1980s, coupled with an intolerable debt burden and a high food imports bill, precipitated a financial crisis that accelerated the decline of the regime's appeal. Civil unrest and widespread demonstrations in 1988 sent a clear signal that the government's command of the people's allegiance had worn thin.

In an attempt to reverse the situation, the regime experimented with democracy between 1988 and 1991. In June 1990, elections for local councils resulted in an astonishing victory for Islamic fundamentalists, with the Islamic Salvation Front (FIS) winning more than half the nation's towns and cities, including the capital of Algiers. In parliamentary elections in December 1991, the FIS continued to make impressive gains and appeared poised to take control of the government in the run-off vote slated for January 1992. Before this crucial election could take place, however, the army stepped in to put an end to this democratic experiment and its unforeseen consequences, canceling the elections, banning the FIS, and imprisoning its leaders. The military's decision to abort the electoral process led to the unraveling of what little political consensus and national unity once existed. The FLN had been discredited both by its inability to defeat the Islamists at the polls and its failure to manage the country's relatively rich economic resources.

Since 1992, Islamic militants have gone underground and launched a campaign of terror against the government. More than 75,000 Algerians have been killed in the ensuing armed struggle. Islamic militants have also staged attacks against the country's **infrastructure**—including telephone exchanges, electrical stations, rail links, and the international airport—as well as multinational oil facilities. The military has responded to growing terrorist attacks with a ferocious crackdown on militants. Since 1992, thousands of Islamic rebels have been killed by security forces during routine raids and ambushes. Even so, these efforts do not appear to have lessened the militants' resolve, and the spiral of violence continues.

Presidential, parliamentary, and local elections were organized in November 1995 through October 1997. These elections were aimed at transforming the military junta (a group of military leaders who rule a country) into a democratically elected government, and thus putting an end to the Islamic rebels' claims that the regime was not legitimate. However, with the army running the country, the political scene remains riddled with problems. Under pressure from the military, Gen. Liamine Zeroual, who won the 1995 presidential elections, announced his untimely resignation in September 1998, paving the way for the 15 April 1999 election of Abdulaziz Bouteflika, a 62-year-old former foreign minister. Bouteflika's election raised hope that the 7-year civil war may come to an end, but the violence is far from over. Shortly after taking office, Bouteflika declared general amnesty for Islamic militants who give up their arms and return to the fold of the nation.

Structurally, the Algerian government is a republic, with a president directly elected for a 5-year term and a **bicameral** (2-house) Parliament. The 380 members of the National People's Assemby are popularly elected for 4-year terms, while the 144 seats in the Council of Nations are filled with either members appointed by the president or elected by indirect vote. The prime minister is appointed by the president. However, this ideal government structure has rarely been achieved in Algeria, where ongoing civil and political struggles have meant the suspension, cancellation, and rescheduling of elections, and frequent interference by the military.

Since the 1960s, Algerian politics have been dominated by the military, which has constituted the power base of the regime. The role of the military, which has traditionally also played a big role in the economy, was briefly suspended in 1989 following the restoration of democracy in the country. By 1991, the military, which forms the bulk of the security apparatus, was back into politics to counter the Islamic insurgency. Today, the military in Algeria is stronger than ever and its powers are so extensive that no president can be nominated without the consent of the generals running Algeria behind the scenes.

The major source of government revenues comes from hydrocarbon receipts and customs **duties**, in addition to corporate, salary, road, and property taxes. According to the IMF, in 1999, taxes accounted for 13.5 percent of the central government's non-hydrocarbon revenue. Tax revenues decreased from 16.2 percent in 1997 to 13.5 percent in 1999, the direct result of the 1998 tax reforms, which sought to lower tax rates across the board. Taxes come in different forms. Taxes on goods and services account for the largest proportion of tax revenues, making up 6.4 percent of the total. Customs duties, which in 1999 accounted for 3.5 percent of tax revenues, are the second largest contributor. Taxes on income and profits and on wage income together accounted for 4.5 percent of government revenues.

However, tax evasion is a major problem, costing the government an estimated AD30 billion a year. Tax revenues dropped slightly from AD329.8 billion in 1998 to AD314.8 billion in 1999. The government's plans to press ahead with plans to improve tax collection measures in line with the IMF's recommendations are complicated by economic and political uncertainties—mainly the ongoing civil war.

INFRASTRUCTURE, POWER, AND COMMUNICATIONS

Algeria enjoys an extensive though aging infrastructure that has been largely neglected since independence. The country is serviced by a network of over 104,000 kilometers (64,626 miles) of primary and secondary roads, 71,656 kilometers (44,527 miles) of which are paved. According to the EIU *Country Profile*, Algeria's poor road system claims the lives of 10 people a day, while the cost of accidents to the state is estimated at AD10 billion annually. The road system is badly in need of repairs, and repair and renovation costs are estimated at AD227 billion. Roads, especially in urban areas, are highly congested. Plans are underway to privatize the road system in 2001 to cover the renovation costs, but the process is likely to be slow, despite the availability of foreign financing for the projects. Similarly, the nations' railway system, which consists of 4,820 kilometers (2,995 miles) of track, is troubled. The state's railway company, Societe national de transport ferroviare (SNTF) is also slated for privatization, but the process has been stifled by the lack of progress in the restructuring of the industry to focus on business activities. Rail lines have more than once sustained damage as a result of sabotage attacks by Islamic militants. The SNTF has been heavily indebted for years, and the railway system is mostly used to transport cargo.

Algeria has 4 major airports, located in Algiers, Oran, Annaba, and Constantine, all of which are fairly modern. Several airlines stopped service to Algeria in December 1994, following the hijacking of an Air France airplane at Houari Boumedienne airport. Many European airlines, with the exception of Air France, have resumed flights since 1999. The national carrier, Air Algerie, serves 37 destinations in Europe, Africa, and the Middle East. It carries 3 million passengers per year. Plans are currently underway in 2001 to upgrade the country's airports and expand their capacities and privatize Air Algerie. Algeria has 9 major ports, at Algiers, Oran, Bejaia, Arzew, and Annaba. The government plans to expand the handling capacity at the ports of Algiers and Oran in 2001.

Electrical power is supplied to Algerians by the state-owned power company, Sonelgaz. Over 90 percent of Algeria's 21.38 billion kilowatt hours (kWh) of power is generated from gas, while the remaining 7 percent is generated by hydroelectric power stations in Kabylie. Over 94 percent of homes are connected, and the government is planning in 2001 to extend the power network to rural areas at the rate of 150,000 new homes annually. Like the rest of state-owned companies, Sonelgaz is slated for restructuring.

Telecommunications services in Algeria are generally aging, but are better in the north than they are in the south. Telephone service is provided by the Ministry of Posts and Telecomunications. The country had 1.17 million telephone lines in use in 1995, and some 33,500 mobile cellular phones in 1999. The Ministry of Posts and Telecommunications in 2001 is upgrading the country's phone lines using fiber optic technology and digital systems. In 1999, the country had 1 Internet service provider.

ECONOMIC SECTORS

Algeria's low- to medium-size economy is heavily dependent on natural gas and hydrocarbons, which account for about 95 percent of export earnings, 52 percent of budget revenues, and 25 percent of GDP. The industrial sector is the largest contributor to the economy, accounting for 51 percent of GDP and employing 13.6 percent of the labor force. The sector is dominated by oil-related industries. Other light industries can also be found, but their contribution to GDP is modest. The services sector is the second largest economic sector, accounting for 37 percent of GDP and employing 13.5

Communications

Country	Newspapers	Radios	TV Sets[a]	Cable subscribers[a]	Mobile Phones[a]	Fax Machines[a]	Personal Computers[a]	Internet Hosts[b]	Internet Users[b]
	1996	1997	1998	1998	1998	1998	1998	1999	1999
Algeria	38	241	105	0.0	1	0.2	4.2	0.01	20
United States	215	2,146	847	244.3	256	78.4	458.6	1,508.77	74,100
Nigeria	24	223	66	N/A	0	N/A	5.7	0.00	100
Libya	14	233	126	0.0	3	N/A	N/A	0.00	7

[a]Data are from International Telecommunication Union, *World Telecommunication Development Report 1999* and are per 1,000 people.
[b]Data are from the Internet Software Consortium (http://www.isc.org) and are per 10,000 people.

SOURCE: World Bank. *World Development Indicators 2000.*

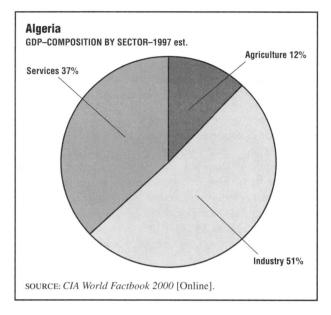

Algeria
GDP–COMPOSITION BY SECTOR–1997 est.

Agriculture 12%

Services 37%

Industry 51%

SOURCE: *CIA World Factbook 2000* [Online].

finally given way to reform. The government has embarked on an ambitious restructuring program coordinated with the IMF and its successful implementation is one of the main challenges facing the government in 2001.

AGRICULTURE

Agricultural production is a moderate contributor to the Algerian economy, accounting for 11–12 percent of GDP and 22 percent of total employment in 1997. The sector's contribution to the economy, however, has declined sharply since independence. Years of government restructuring, lack of investment, meager water resources, and dependence on rainwater for irrigation have contributed to this decline. The production of cereals as well as orchard and industrial crops has significantly dropped. As a result, Algeria today has become dependent on food imports, accounting for close to 75 percent of food needs.

Although Algeria is the second-largest country in Africa, the arable land of about 8.2 million hectares accounts for only 3.4 percent of the total land area. The vast Sahara desert, which spans much of the south central part of the country, is not available for agriculture. Between 1961 and 1987, all arable land was controlled by the state, which divided the land into state farms, known as *domaines agricoles socialistes*. State farms were dismantled in 1987 and the land was divided into smaller collective and individual farms. Despite these measures, about one-third of cultivable land in Algeria is still owned by the government, which leases the land to private investors and farmers. The remaining two-thirds of arable land (about 5 million hectares) is privately owned.

Algeria's main crops are cereals (mainly wheat and barley), citrus fruit, vegetables, and grapes. Fresh dates exports have risen sharply in the past decade and have become the second-largest export after hydrocarbons. Some 72,000 hectares are cultivated with palm trees, mainly in the Saharan oases. Algerian dates are mainly exported to France, Russia, Senegal, and Belgium. Algeria was once a major exporter of wine and associated products. Despite government efforts to revive the sector, production has fallen significantly since 1962, reaching 248,000 hectoliters (6,552,160 U.S. gallons) in 1996, down from 410,000 hectoliters (10,832,200 U.S. gallons) in 1992. Algeria is also a producer of olive oil, and production has generally averaged around 150,000 hectoliters (3,963,000 U.S. gallons) annually.

percent of the labor force. The agricultural sector contributes 11–12 percent of GDP annually and employs some 22 percent of the labor force. The sector, however, has been vulnerable to adverse weather conditions, and production has fluctuated accordingly.

Two of the greatest obstacles to growth in all of Algeria's economy are inefficiency in the state-controlled public sector and the state's central role in the economy. Recognizing these obstacles, Algeria has targeted certain sectors, mainly state-owned enterprises, for privatization. Years of inefficient state control over the economy have

The bulk of Algeria's crops are cultivated in the fertile but narrow plains around Bejaïa and Annaba in the east, in the Mitidja Plain south of Algiers, and beyond Oran from Sidi Bel Abbes to Tlemcen. The agricultural sector's dependence on rainwater for irrigation has often

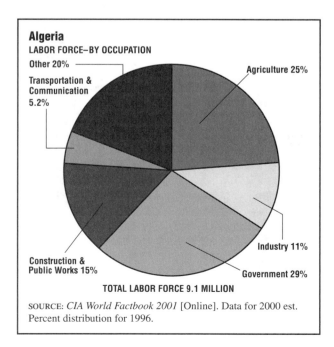

Algeria
LABOR FORCE–BY OCCUPATION

Other 20%

Transportation & Communication 5.2%

Agriculture 25%

Construction & Public Works 15%

Industry 11%

Government 29%

TOTAL LABOR FORCE 9.1 MILLION

SOURCE: *CIA World Factbook 2001* [Online]. Data for 2000 est. Percent distribution for 1996.

affected its production levels, especially during droughts. The cereal harvest, for example, was badly affected by drought conditions that plagued North Africa in 2000, producing only half of its annual yield. Hence, despite government efforts to extend funding and technical assistance to farmers and increase the productivity of the agricultural sector, Algeria imports the bulk of the food it consumes, especially cereals (mainly wheat).

FISHERIES. Though Algeria's location would suggest that the country would have a booming fishing industry, actual fishing production remains low, largely due to under-exploitation. Since the late 1990s, the government has embarked on a modernization program to increase the productivity of the sector, but most fishing activity continues to center around small boats and family-owned businesses. The government has also been trying to attract foreign investment in this sector, in the year 2000 granting some 20 Japanese fishing boats the right to fish in Algerian waters. This agreement was based on a provision that the catch does not exceed 750,000 metric tons of red tuna a year.

INDUSTRY

MINING. Hydrocarbons, mainly oil and gas, are the country's main exports. Algeria's oil and gas reserves rank 14th and 5th largest in the world, respectively. During the 1970s, Algeria was a large producer of oil, but has since lost that status as oil was replaced by gas production as the country's main source of export revenue. Oil, first produced in commercial quantities in the late 1950s, accounted for 73 percent of Algeria's hydrocarbon productions in 1980, but now accounts for about 20 percent. France, Spain, Belgium, Turkey, and the United States are the main consumers of Algeria's oil, and plans are underway to expand export activities, mainly to Europe. Although most restrictions on oil exports were removed in the 1990s and the government no longer subsidizes the sector, the state-owned company Sonatrach continues to retain full control over its activities.

The oil sector opened to foreign investment in 1991. As a result, foreign companies are now allowed to invest and even buy existing oilfields, and despite the high political risk associated with these investments, several foreign companies operate in the country in 2001. A total of 18 foreign companies operate in the oil sector, bringing in around US$1.5 billion in investments. Natural gas production began in 1961, and in 2000 represented 57 percent of total proven hydrocarbon reserves. Algeria is the second-largest exporter of liquid natural gas in the world after Indonesia. The bulk of Algeria's gas is exported to Europe through 2 major pipelines that run through Tunisia and Morocco. Since the late 1990s, the government has been engaged in efforts to upgrade and expand oil and liquefied natural gas exploration by attracting foreign investments. It has also moved to increase the production of liquefied petroleum gas as a means to diversify income from this sector.

Algeria's non-hydrocarbon mining infrastructure remains underdeveloped. In addition to oil and natural gas, Algeria mines gold in the southeast Hoggar region and diamonds near the Mali borders, and exports high-grade ore, iron pyrites, phosphates, lead, zinc, mercury, barite, and antimony. Since the late 1990s, the government has made progress in removing restrictions on foreign and private investment in the non-energy mining sector in an effort to minimize the state's control over the sector. The sand, marble, and gold sectors have received special interest from small private investors.

MANUFACTURING. The non-hydrocarbon manufacturing sector is a moderate though declining contributor to the Algerian economy. According to the EIU *Country Profile* for 2000, though manufacturing accounted for 12 percent of GDP in 1993, its contribution fell to 9 percent in 1999. The decline in manufacturing's contribution to GDP can be attributed mainly to the legacy of centralization and inefficiency that have characterized the state enterprises controlling the sector. Algeria's manufacturing industries are beset by an oversized bureaucracy and debt, and have, as a result, lost their ability to compete with imported finished products. The government's efforts since the 1980s to restructure the industrial sector into smaller state-run units and encourage **joint ventures** with the **private sector** have failed to produce the desired turnaround.

Before independence, food processing, textiles, cigarettes, and clothing constituted the main manufacturing activities in the country. Since the mid-1960s, a greater emphasis has been placed on heavy industry. Historically, Algerian companies have processed petrochemicals, steel, metals, electronics, clothing, leather, paper, timber, chemicals, and construction equipment. Petrochemicals are an important contributor to GDP. Petrochemical industries include methanol, resins and plastics, and fertilizers, and are centered in the 2 cities of Skikda and Arzew. Production in the private sector recorded a 10-percent increase in 1999, in contrast to the non-hydrocarbon industrial state sector, which saw a drop in output of 1.5 percent in 1999. The pharmaceuticals, chemicals, construction equipment, and leather industries were the leading performers.

SERVICES

FINANCIAL SERVICES. Financial services in Algeria are fairly outdated, and the lack of modern services is an obstacle to the growth of the private sector and foreign investment alike. Until 1998, the banking sector was dominated by 3 major state-owned banks. But private banks, including U.S. and French banks, have been allowed to operate in the country since 1998 as part of a government plan to reform the sector. A new money and credit law was adopted in 1990, and although the Treasury purchased most of the local banks' debt in 1994, these banks continue to suffer from **bad loans**, mismanagement, and political interference. The Algerian stock exchange was officially opened in 1999, also part of the government's plan to privatize the economy.

TOURISM. Tourism is not a major contributor to GDP, despite government efforts to encourage the sector. Its promising potential is stifled by a lack of investment and the endemic political violence in the country, although the south, where some of the government's most recent projects are located, has been spared from these problems. Potential holiday destinations are the mountains and deserts of the interior and the country's beaches. Although foreign tourists have since 1998 started returning to Algeria, the sector has a long way to go to full recovery.

RETAIL. Lacking many large commercial centers other than Algiers, Oran, and their suburbs, Algeria has a poorly developed **retail** sector. While Algiers is home to a variety of retail stores, the majority of towns in the interior of the country have small family-owned shops, farmer's markets, and temporary roadside stands.

INTERNATIONAL TRADE

Over the past several decades, Algeria has maintained a **trade surplus**, largely due to the export of hydrocarbons, which accounts for 90 percent of exports. In 1999 that surplus reached $4.4 billion on exports of $13.7 billion and imports of $9.3 billion. This surplus has endured even when oil prices dropped, as they did in 1998 when the trade surplus reached US$1.5 billion. Non-hydrocarbon exports, although minimal, have risen in the last 3 years, but much of that is believed to have come as a result of repayment of debt owed to the former Soviet Union in the form of goods.

The value of imports increased between 1987 and 1995. Merchandise imports fell between 1996 and 1998, thanks to a good harvest, but rose slightly in 1999 due to an increase in domestic demand. Capital equipment accounted for 34 percent of imports, while food has generally accounted for almost 25 percent of imports. Semi-finished products were in third position, accounting for 27 percent of total imports.

The European Union and the United States are Algeria's main trade partners. The EU, which is negotiating a new Euro-Mediterranean Partnership (EMP) agreement with Algeria, is a major importer of the country's hydrocarbons. In 1999, Italy—Algeria's largest trade

Trade (expressed in billions of US$): Algeria		
	Exports	Imports
1975	4.700	5.498
1980	13.871	10.559
1985	12.841	9.841
1990	12.930	9.715
1995	10.240	10.250
1998	N/A	N/A

SOURCE: International Monetary Fund. *International Financial Statistics Yearbook 1999.*

partner in the last decade—accounted for 17.8 percent of exports, followed by France (12.4 percent) and Spain (10.2 percent). The United States is Algeria's second-largest trading partner, accounting for 16.4 percent of exports in 1999. France is Algeria's main source of imports, accounting for 29.8 percent, followed by Italy (9.7 percent), Germany (6.8 percent), and Spain (5.9 percent). The United States comes in the fifth place, providing 5.3 percent of Algeria's total imports.

MONEY

The value of the Algerian dinar held steady until September 1994, due to the central bank's policy of setting it at a fixed rate against other widely used currencies. This policy resulted in a wide gap between the official rate and informal **exchange rates** on the **black market**, where the dinar sold as high as 6 times the official rate at the end of 1989. The dinar has since been stable, but only after the government introduced full convertibility, allowing local importers to bid for **hard currency** in the local banking system. The country's strong foreign exchange reserves have allowed the banking system to meet the currency demands of the local market. Since 1998, the dinar has averaged AD66.57 to the U.S. dollar, but had slightly **devaluated** at the end of 2000, averaging 79.14 to the U.S. dollar.

Exchange rates: Algeria	
Algerian dinars per US$1	
Jan 2001	74,813
2000	75.260
1999	66.574
1998	58.739
1997	57.707
1996	54.749

SOURCE: CIA *World Factbook 2001* [ONLINE].

POVERTY AND WEALTH

In the first 2 decades after independence, the government of Algeria made impressive gains in terms of raising living standards in the country by creating employment opportunities in the public sector and extending social benefits. However, the country's declining economic conditions since the 1980s, brought about by falling oil prices and years of inefficient state control, have had serious implications for the living standards of Algerians. High unemployment and **inflation rates** since the 1980s have led to a sharp increase in the incidence of poverty in the country. Between 1988 and 1995, the percentage of the population below the poverty line increased from 8 percent to 14 percent. According to the EIU *Country Profile* for 2000–01, **GDP per capita** in 1994 dropped by 2.5 percent over the preceding decade. While unemployment and poverty figures rose sharply in urban areas, the countryside was more seriously affected; almost 70 percent of the poor live in rural areas. Unemployment is especially serious among younger, unskilled workers.

Despite widespread poverty, however, uneven development has led to the emergence of an affluent class that controls most of the country's wealth, enjoying an elevated standard of living and visiting shopping centers featuring the best imported goods. Living in the suburbs of Algiers and Oran, the wealthy send their children to private schools and universities abroad. Yet not far from these affluent neighborhoods, a significant number of poor Algerians live in squalor, with poor and overcrowded housing, limited food supplies, and inadequate access to clean water, good quality health care, or education. The extremes are reflected in the country's distribution of income: in 1996, the wealthiest 20 percent of Algerians controlled 42.6 percent of the country's wealth, while the poorest 20 percent controlled only 7 percent of wealth. This uneven distribution of income has been exacerbated by chronic housing shortages, which have given rise to poor shantytowns in most cities. These shortages have been the result of high population growth rates and decades of rural-urban migration. This has prompted the government since the early 1980s to shift

Distribution of Income or Consumption by Percentage Share: Algeria	
Lowest 10%	2.8
Lowest 20%	7.0
Second 20%	11.6
Third 20%	16.1
Fourth 20%	22.7
Highest 20%	42.6
Highest 10%	26.8

Survey year: 1995
Note: This information refers to expenditure shares by percentiles of the population and is ranked by per capita expenditure.

SOURCE: *2000 World Development Indicators* [CD-ROM].

its spending priorities to address the housing shortages by constructing subsidized housing units and prefabricated houses at moderate cost.

The decline in living standards in Algeria continued throughout the 1990s, as the government embarked on a structural reform program to reverse economic decline, and as **subsidies** of basic foodstuffs were lifted. Unemployment numbers also continued to rise, standing at 2.3 million in 1999, and representing about 25 percent of the labor force, according to official estimates. Another 10 percent of the labor force is believed to be **underemployed**.

Algeria's mounting economic difficulties fueled public discontent that culminated in the Islamic rebellion against the state that began in 1991. The military's decision to abort the electoral process led to the unraveling of what little political consensus and national unity once existed. The FLN had been discredited both by its inability to defeat the Islamists at the polls and by its failure to manage the country's relatively rich economic resources. In the absence of viable secular parties, the Islamists claimed to represent the voice of the people.

WORKING CONDITIONS

Algeria's labor force has steadily increased in the course of the past 2 decades. In 2000, Algeria's labor force was estimated at 9.1 million, up 2.7 million since 1995. The majority of the labor force is concentrated in the public and agricultural sectors. Algerian workers are relatively poorly educated, as technical and basic education have lagged in the 1990s.

Algerian labor has a tradition of unionization, headed by the Union Generale des Travailleurs Algeriens (UGTA). About two-thirds of the labor force is unionized. UGTA has been a powerful force in negotiating public sector wages with the government, but the 1990 labor law brought collective bargaining to an end. However,

GDP per Capita (US$)					
Country	1975	1980	1985	1990	1998
Algeria	1,460	1,692	1,860	1,638	1,521
United States	19,364	21,529	23,200	25,363	29,683
Nigeria	301	314	230	258	256
Libya	N/A	N/A	N/A	N/A	N/A

SOURCE: United Nations. *Human Development Report 2000; Trends in human development and per capita income.*

UGTA still retains its power to organize public-sector strikes to protest the decline of wages. These strikes, however, have seldom succeeded in forcing concessions from the government.

The government has adopted labor rights regulating working conditions and other rights of workers. The minimum age for employment is 16 years. These regulations, however, are rarely enforced, and child labor, especially in the agricultural sector, remains widespread. The minimum wage is US$90 (6,000 dinars) per month. The standard workweek is 40 hours.

COUNTRY HISTORY AND ECONOMIC DEVELOPMENT

1830. France occupies Algeria and begins to lay down the economic foundation of its colony.

1933. Anti-French political protests begin and continue through 1956.

1950. Ahmad Ben Bella founds the Revolutionary Committee of Unity and Action (Comité Révolutionnaire d'Unité et d'Action—CRUA), later renamed the National Liberation Front (FLN).

1962. After a guerilla war, Algeria gains independence from France. The Democratic and Popular Republic of Algeria is formally proclaimed. First President Ahmad Ben Bella forms country's first cabinet since independence.

1963. President Ben Bella declares that all agricultural, industrial, and commercial properties previously operated and occupied by Europeans are vacant, legalizing their confiscation by the state.

1970. The first Four-Year Plan emphasizing capital-intensive heavy industry is adopted.

1971. President Houari Boumedienne launches an agricultural reform plan calling for the seizure of additional property and the redistribution of the newly acquired public lands to cooperative farms.

1976. Boumedienne drafts the National Charter; the constitution is promulgated.

1977. Boumedienne's death sets off a struggle within the FLN to choose a successor. Colonel Chadli Bendjedid is sworn in on 9 February 1979.

1980. The First Five-Year Plan (1980–84) and Second Five-Year Plan (1985–89) aiming at diversifying the economy are adopted.

1985. The 1985–89 Four-Year plan places greater emphasis on agriculture and decreased central planning.

1987. The Ministry of Planning is abolished.

1988. Popular protests break out; government declares state of emergency.

1989. New constitution promising pluralism is adopted. Abbassi Madani and Ali Belhadj found the Islamic Salvation Front (FIS).

1991. Government cancels national elections. FIS wages rebellion against the state.

1992. Parliament is dissolved.

1999. President Bouteflika announces national reconciliation plan to end the civil conflict.

FUTURE TRENDS

Algeria entered the 21st century under a cloud of economic uncertainty. For much of the century, state control of the economy and the government's experiment with socialism has left the economy in shambles. The economic reform program waged in the early 1990s has set the stage for partial economic recovery, however. Some progress has been achieved in terms of improving transparency, cutting budget expenditures, updating legislation, and liberalizing the telecommunications market. Wide-ranging structural reforms have also been achieved.

The pace of Algeria's economic reform program, however, has been rather slow. Despite major reform efforts, the public sector continues to be a major force in the economy. Long-term challenges include servicing the country's huge external debt, further privatizing state-owned enterprises, and attracting foreign investment. More importantly, the government is faced with the daunting challenge of improving living standards, which have steadily declined over the last few decades, and creating new job prospects for Algeria's youth, who account for over 50 percent of the population. If left unresolved, the problem of unemployment in particular may potentially become a renewed source of political instability and a credible challenge to the regime. Much work is also needed on the political front. The government will have to improve the unstable security situation in the country to attract foreign investments. To that end, it has to find a way to end the cycle of violence waged by Islamic insurgents since 1991, which has become a major obstacle to foreign investments and economic recovery.

DEPENDENCIES

Algeria has no territories or colonies.

BIBLIOGRAPHY

Economist Intelligence Unit. *Country Profile: Algeria, 2000/2001*. London: Economist Intelligence Unit, 2000.

The Embassy of Algeria in Washington, D.C. <http://www
.algeria-us.org>. Accessed August 2001.

International Monetary Fund. *Algeria: Recent Economic
Developments.* Washington, D.C.: International Monetary
Fund, August 2000.

Ruedy, John. *Modern Algeria: The Origins and Development of
a Nation.* Bloomington: Indiana University Press, 1992.

U.S. Central Intelligence Agency. *World Factbook 2000.* <http://
www.odci.gov/cia/publications/factbook/index.html>.
Accessed August 2001.

U.S. Department of State. *Country Commercial Guide: Algeria
Fiscal Year 1996.* <gopher://dosfan.lib.uic.edu:70/00ftp:
DOSFan:Gopher:12%20Business%20Affairs:04%20Country
%20Commercial%20Guides:Algeria%20Commercial%20
Guide>. Accessed June 2001.

U.S. Department of State. *1999 Country Reports on Human
Rights Practices. Algeria.* <http://www.state.gov/www/global/
human_rights/1999_hrp_report/algeria.html>. Accessed
February 2001.

—*Reem Nuseibeh*

ANGOLA

Republic of Angola
República de Angola

CAPITAL: Luanda.

MONETARY UNIT: The currency of Angola is the nova kwanza (Kzr). One Kzr equals 100 centimos. Notes are in denominations of Kzr5, 10, 50, and 100. Coins are in denominations of Kzr1, 2, 5, and 100, as well as 10, 20, and 50 centimos.

CHIEF EXPORTS: Crude oil, diamonds, refined petroleum products, gas, coffee, sisal, fish and fish products, timber, cotton.

CHIEF IMPORTS: Machinery and electrical equipment, vehicles and spare parts, medicines, food, textiles, military goods.

GROSS DOMESTIC PRODUCT: US$11.6 billion (purchasing power parity, 1999 est.).

BALANCE OF TRADE: Exports: US$5 billion (f.o.b., 1999 est.). **Imports:** US$3 billion (f.o.b., 1999 est.).

COUNTRY OVERVIEW

LOCATION AND SIZE. Angola is located in southern Africa, and borders the South Atlantic Ocean, Namibia, Zambia, and both Congos—the Democratic Republic of Congo and the Republic of the Congo. Angola has a total area of 1,246,700 square kilometers (481,351 square miles). It has a coastline of 1,610 kilometers (1,000 miles) on the South Atlantic Ocean. Comparatively, the area is slightly less than twice the size of Texas. The capital of Angola, Luanda, is located on the north-central coastline. The highest point in Angola is Morro de Moco at 2,620 meters (8,596 feet). Angola also includes the exclave of Cabinda (an exclave is an area of land that is part of another country but separated physically from that country). A province of Angola, Cabinda's size is roughly 7,300 square kilometers (2,800 square miles), and it lies south of the Republic of Congo on the Atlantic coast.

POPULATION. The population of Angola was estimated by the CIA to be a little over 10 million in July 2000, although the World Bank put the figure at 12.4 million for 1999. These organizations also believe that the annual population growth rate decreased from 3.2 percent in 1995 to 2.9 percent in 1999. The growth rate for the year 2000 was estimated at 2.15 percent. In 2000 the birth rate stood at 46.89 births per 1,000, while the death rate was 25.01 per 1,000.

The population of Angola is very young. Only 3 percent of the population is over 65 years of age. About 54 percent of the population is between 15–64 years old, and 43 percent is below the age of 15. The life expectancy at birth for women is about 39 years and about 37 years for men.

The population density in 1995 was 8.8 people per square kilometer (18.1 people per square mile). The urban population has increased slowly but steadily from 31 percent in 1995 to 33.6 percent in 1999. The illiteracy rate in Angola is very high; only 42 percent of people over the age of 15 can read and write. There is a significantly higher number of men who are literate than women (56 percent versus 28 percent).

OVERVIEW OF ECONOMY

Angola's economy is in disarray due to the near-continuous warfare that has been ongoing in the country since independence in 1975. The National Union for the Total Independence of Angola (UNITA) and the Popular Movement for the Liberation of Angola (MPLA) have struggled for control of Angola and its abundance of natural resources since Portugal relinquished its control of the nation in 1975. Although the MPLA has managed to stay in power for most of Angola's history, the effort it expends in fighting UNITA and other hostile forces prevents it from developing Angola's economy. The government is likewise hindered by the fact that UNITA controls much of Angola, including its valuable

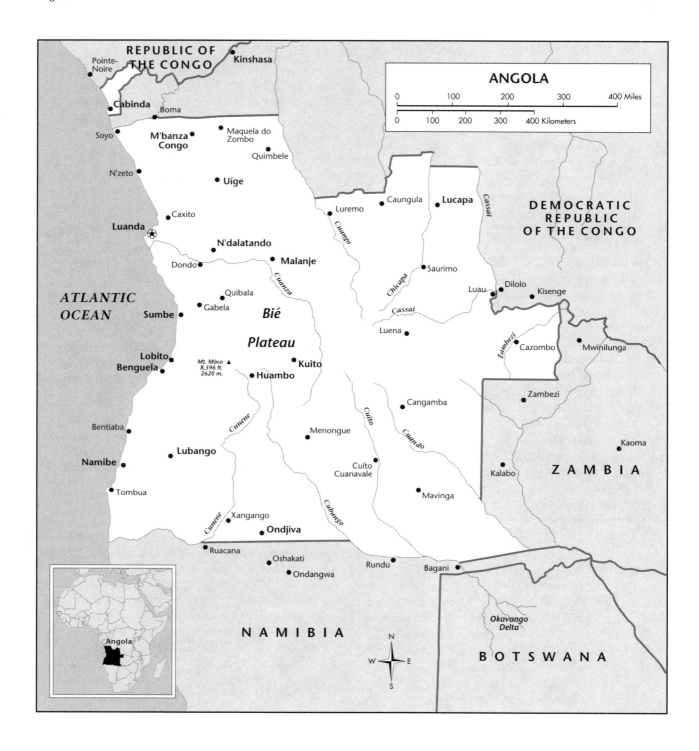

diamond mines, the profits of which go towards UNITA's military efforts rather than the development of a stable economy. The result is that Angola is among those nations with the lowest output per capita in the world. **GDP per capita** in 1999 was estimated by the CIA World Factbook at US$1030, figured according to **purchasing power parity**.

The dominant force shaping Angola's economy today is oil and oil-related activities. These are essential to the economy of the country and contribute about 45 percent to GDP and 90 percent of exports. Thanks to oil production, the economy grew by 4 percent from 1998 to 1999. U.S. oil companies have invested heavily in Angola's oil production. In 1997, the United States bought 70–80 percent of all Angola's oil. In 2000, 7 percent of all U.S. petroleum came from Angola. This is expected to rise to 10 percent within 8 years. Unfortunately, the continual warfare has stifled investment in all other sectors. Diamonds are an important export product, but

UNITA's control of this valuable resource limits its positive impact on the nation's economy.

Subsistence agriculture provides the main livelihood for 85 percent of the population, but larger-scale farming is difficult in Angola's landmine-ridden countryside. These mines remain throughout the country and hamper any development of the agricultural sector, even though the country itself is fertile. As a result, much of Angola's food must be imported. Coffee is one product that could be a large export opportunity, but the presence of so many minefields makes this development problematic.

Angola is severely indebted. The burden of debt on each Angolan is 3 times higher than the average for Africa. In 1999 the total outstanding debt was US$10.5 billion, more than two-thirds of which was owed to private creditors. In 1995 international donors (the World Bank, the European Union, and the United Nations' specialized agencies are the leading multilateral donors) pledged over US$1.0 billion in assistance to Angola. However, these funds have been held back because of the stalemated peace process between the MPLA and UNITA.

POLITICS, GOVERNMENT, AND TAXATION

MPLA and UNITA began by fighting a common enemy—Portugal—for Angola's independence in 1961. They formed a coalition government along with the National Front for the Liberation of Angola (FLNA) following Portugal's decision to grant Angola independence on 11 November 1975, but the differences between the groups resulted in the coalition's disintegration before independence was achieved. The failure of the coalition government set the stage for a civil war that continued to plague the nation into the 21st century. UNITA, backed by the United States and South Africa, fought MPLA, backed by the Soviet Union and Cuba in a Cold-War showdown. However, the MPLA forces gained the victory when they overpowered major UNITA strongholds, and earned recognition from the Organization of African Unity (OAU) as the official government of Angola in 1976.

However, MPLA's hold on the government was far from secure. UNITA continued operating from southern Angola and from Namibia to topple MPLA; both South Africa and Cuba remained involved in Angola's war-battered landscape as military presences. With so many countries and factions involved in the war, a peace agreement seemed impossible until the thawing of the Cold War in 1988 resulted in the withdrawal of South African and Cuban troops from Angola. The first free elections in 1992 gave a narrow victory to the MPLA (which then became the Government of the Republic of Angola, GRA), but UNITA alleged voter fraud and did not accept the results. Fighting broke out once more and

UNITA gained control of 75 percent of the country. However, the international community condemned UNITA's failure to honor the election results and recognized the MPLA government as the legitimate power. The 1994 Lusaka Protocol attempted to broker a peace agreement between UNITA and MPLA, but not even the 6,000 peacekeeping troops installed in Angola by the United Nations in 1995 could stop continued fighting. By 1999 the United Nations withdrew its peacekeeping force and acknowledged the failure of the Lusaka Protocol.

The governmental structure of Angola is considered to be in transition pending the settlement of the civil war. In the country's first elections following independence, Jose Eduardo Dos Santos, the head of the MPLA, was elected under a one-party system. The 1992 elections were designed to elect the president by popular vote and the 220-seat National Assembly by proportional vote, with both president and legislators to serve 4-year terms. UNITA, led by presidential candidate Jonas Savimbi, contested the 1992 elections after winning 40.1 percent of the vote. Since that time the official government has been led by the MPLA with no new elections.

INFRASTRUCTURE, POWER, AND COMMUNICATIONS

Due to the extensive warfare, most of Angola's **infrastructure** has been destroyed. Millions of land mines were laid, and efforts to remove them have so far made little progress. Not only do these vast numbers of mines hamper the building of an infrastructure of extensive road networks, but they continue to maim and kill civilians. There are 19,156 kilometers (11,903.5 miles) of paved roads and a total of 2,952 kilometers (1,834.4 miles) of rail tracks. There are 32 airports with paved runways and 217 with unpaved runways. However, the condition of these airfields varies, and mines are a problem here as well.

Transportation in general is a problem in Angola. Perhaps no sector has suffered more than transportation from the war. Roads, railways, and bridges have been severely damaged. Ports are run-down and antiquated. More than 60 percent of the paved road network needs repair. The estimation of the Angolan government is that it will take 10–15 years to restore the road network to the status prior to the war. However, this presumes an end to the fighting, without which the road infrastructure will take considerably longer to recreate. The road, railway, and bridge networks are essential for the other economic sectors to grow. They will link the main cities in the country and get the products from one end of the country to the next.

The continued political violence and fighting is the reason for the lack of external investment in Angola. However, when stability returns, the lack of an infrastructure

Communications

Country	Newspapers	Radios	TV Sets[a]	Cable subscribers[a]	Mobile Phones[a]	Fax Machines[a]	Personal Computers[a]	Internet Hosts[b]	Internet Users[b]
	1996	1997	1998	1998	1998	1998	1998	1999	1999
Angola	11	54	14	N/A	1	N/A	0.8	0.00	10
United States	215	2,146	847	244.3	256	78.4	458.6	1,508.77	74,100
South Africa	32	317	125	N/A	56	3.5	47.4	33.36	1,820
Dem. Rep. of Congo	3	375	135	N/A	0	N/A	N/A	0.00	1

[a]Data are from International Telecommunication Union, *World Telecommunication Development Report 1999* and are per 1,000 people.
[b]Data are from the Internet Software Consortium (http://www.isc.org) and are per 10,000 people.
SOURCE: World Bank. *World Development Indicators 2000.*

will be a major factor hindering economic development. Building an infrastructure is essential for the country's further development of other economic areas such as agricultural products, of which Angola used to be a net exporter.

There are about 60,000 telephone main lines in use (1995). The telephone system is limited mostly to government and business use. Radio telephones are used extensively by the military. There are 2 Internet service providers in the country (1999), but the level of personal computer ownership is very low (0.8 per 1,000 in 1998). There are also very few televisions in Angola, with only 14 sets per 1,000 people in 1998.

ECONOMIC SECTORS

Angola's total **labor force** for 1997 was estimated at 5 million, with 85 percent of the workforce engaged in agriculture, and industry and services with 15 percent. Despite the large segment of the population in agriculture, it contributed only 13 percent to GDP in 1998. Industry contributed 53 percent, and services provided 34 percent of GDP in the same year, according to the *CIA World Factbook*.

The most important industries are petroleum, diamonds, fish, and fish processing. Other significant industries are iron ore, phosphates, feldspar, bauxite, uranium, gold, cement, basic metal products, food processing, brewing, tobacco products, and sugar textiles.

Agricultural products include bananas, sugarcane, coffee, sisal, corn, cotton, manioc, tobacco, vegetables, plaintains, livestock, forest products, and fish. The most important of these agricultural products for export are coffee, sisal, timber, and cotton. However, agricultural

Angola
GDP–COMPOSITION BY SECTOR–1998 est.

Services 34%
Agriculture 13%
Industry 53%

SOURCE: *CIA World Factbook 2000* [Online].

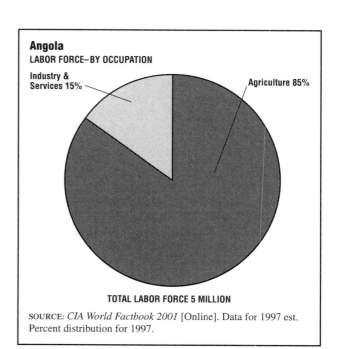

Angola
LABOR FORCE–BY OCCUPATION

Industry & Services 15%
Agriculture 85%

TOTAL LABOR FORCE 5 MILLION

SOURCE: *CIA World Factbook 2001* [Online]. Data for 1997 est. Percent distribution for 1997.

production in Angola has been severely reduced by the civil war. The majority of agriculture is now **subsistence farming**. The industrial sector has likewise been reduced, with oil as the sector's only growing industry. This is important for the economic development of Angola, but is not enough to create sustainable development, and leaves Angola's economy vulnerable to fluctuating oil prices.

AGRICULTURE

Agricultural production is the sector that contributes the least to Angola's economy, a mere 13 percent of the GDP. Prior to the civil war in 1975 Angola was self-sufficient in food production and was a major exporter of agricultural products. The two most important products for export prior to the war were coffee and sisal. Angola was the second-largest producer of coffee in Africa and the fourth-largest in the world in 1974. Today only 3 percent of all arable land is being cultivated. There are two crucial reasons for this. First, large numbers of refugees have fled the country due to constant fighting, leaving the land uncultivated. Secondly, the vast amounts of anti-personnel mines that have been buried throughout the countryside make it difficult to cultivate the land again. This is unfortunate because Angola has the potential to grow a huge range of both semi-tropical and tropical crops. With continued fighting, Angola cannot fulfill its promise as a major agricultural producer.

COFFEE. There have been attempts at coffee production during the conflict, but continued fighting has made the sector's recovery impossible. There are several advantages to focusing on coffee production in Angola. First, it is an area where Angola can compete in the global market, hence supplementing oil as a major income generator. Second, Angolans have a lot of experience in the production of coffee. Third, the fertile land is well disposed to the cultivation of coffee. Today, the coffee industry is moribund. The U.S. Department of Agriculture estimates Angola's total coffee production for 2001 will be 65,000 bags of coffee (each weighing 60 kilograms). This is up slightly from 55,000 bags for the previous year. In contrast, Mexico was expected to produce 5.8 million bags, and Kenya's production was estimated at 1.1 million for 2001. Angola is not even on the list of the top 35 suppliers of coffee to the United States.

FISH AND FISH PRODUCTS. The fishing industry in Angola prior to the war was very important, and annual catches were about 600,000 tons. This shrank to only 35,000 tons during the war, but began to rise from 1993, when the catch was 122,000 tons, and this trend has continued. Angola has been building up its fishing fleet with the support of Spain, Italy, Portugal, and the Arab Bank for African Economic Development (BADEA). The World Bank helped the Angolan government set up the

Angolan Support Fund for Fisheries Development. Angola has a long coastline which is especially rich with sardines, tuna, and mackerel. There is great potential for continued expansion in this sector.

INDUSTRY

Industry is the most important sector in Angola's economy, accounting for 53 percent of the GDP. The 3 important industrial sectors are mineral resources, energy, and manufacturing, the former two being by far the most significant. All of these were severely affected by the war, but since 1994 have increased significantly.

MINERAL RESOURCES. Angola has vast deposits of a large variety of mineral resources including diamonds, gold, iron ore, phosphates, copper, lead, and zinc. However, the most important mineral with respect to export is diamonds. Prior to 1975 Angola was the fourth-largest diamond producer in the world, but this dropped during the war because of large-scale theft, smuggling, and transportation problems. UNITA controls the majority of the diamond-producing land, which has added to the government's problems in controlling the diamond trade. In 1992 Angola exported diamonds worth $250 million. While diamond exports are increasing, they have not reached pre-war levels. With a stable peace agreement there should be no obstacles keeping Angola from reaching and exceeding former export levels.

Apart from diamonds, Angola's resources are vast, but largely untapped. The Angolan government's efforts to promote private investment led it to abolish the previously state-held **monopoly** of mineral rights. (This began on a small scale in 1986 in relation to diamonds). Mining ventures can consequently be privately held. However, the continued conflict makes it difficult to attract private investment, and these resources remain untapped.

ENERGY. Angola is a regional player in energy production. Angola co-ordinates the energy policy for the Southern African Development Co-ordination Conference (SADCC), and its energy secretariat is based in Luanda. Energy production is essential for Angola, with 90 percent of the country's total exports coming from oil. In 2000 oil contributed 45 percent to the GDP of the country. Energy is the only sector that expanded throughout the 1980s, during the war. The oil industry is run by the Angolan state oil firm Sonangol, in conjunction with foreign oil companies. Angola is the second-largest producer of oil in sub-Saharan Africa and provides 7 percent of all U.S. oil imports. The United States is the main purchaser of Angolan oil, buying some 70–80 percent of all oil exports.

New oil reserves are being discovered regularly, and faster than the country's reserves can be depleted. Foreign companies have not been deterred from investing in Angola's oil industry irrespective of the warfare. The oil industry is viewed as an attractive investment opportunity that offers the oil companies favorable geological conditions, low operating costs, and co-operation from the Angolan government. The total foreign investment in oil production in the 1980–86 period was US$2.7 billion. The investment level in the next 3 years was US$2 billion, with US$4 billion invested between 1993 and 1997.

Hydroelectric power has been a priority of the Angolan government. In 2000 75.03 percent of the electricity produced was hydro-generated. Several large rivers flow through the country and give an enormous potential for hydroelectricity. The current generating capacity exceeds demand locally and output is increasing. This makes Angola a potential regional exporter of hydroelectric energy. However the power supply has been irregular, partially due to sabotage by the warring factions, and a deteriorating infrastructure due to poor maintenance and lack of investment. However, the potential for regional export is vast when stability returns, even though Angola exported no electricity as of 1998.

MANUFACTURING. Angola had about 4,000 manufacturing enterprises before the civil war, which employed 200,000 people. However, this was significantly reduced by the onset of the war. The only products that are manufactured and exported from Angola today are cement and refined petroleum products. There is potential for establishing the pre-war levels of production, but this will require stability and outside investment. It would also necessitate the creation of an infrastructure. Hence, investment in oil and diamonds will for a long time be more interesting to outside investors than Angola's manufacturing sector.

SERVICES

Services in Angola are not very developed, again a direct consequence of the war. The government has begun to encourage investment in tourism. However, with the continued strife and breached peace agreements it is doubtful whether such projects will take place. Foreign investors will shy away from investing in tourism in such a volatile society. Not only will it take substantial time before there will be investors in tourism, but the entire infrastructure to support such an expansion is at present lacking. The willingness of tourists to go to such an area is also in doubt. Financial and human services are in a similar state of disarray.

INTERNATIONAL TRADE

In 1999 Angola exported a total of US$5 billion worth of goods and services and imported US$3 billion worth. Due to Angola's colonial past, its primary trading partner has historically been Portugal. Today, Portugal is still a primary trading partner from which 20 percent of Angola's commodities are imported. The United States and South Africa are other major sources of imports for Angola, providing 17 percent and 10 percent, respectively. However, the United States is the major source of Angolan exports with 63 percent of all exports; 9 percent of exports going to the Benelux countries (Belgium, the Netherlands, and Luxembourg), and China, Chile, and France are also important sources of exports.

MONEY

In 1990 the Angolan government changed the currency from the kwanza to the nova kwanza. This was done to reduce the money supply and force prices down in the **informal sector**, which operated parallel to the more regulated conventional market. This measure was taken to satisfy requirements of the World Bank, the IMF, and other financial institutions as part of the reforms that these institutions see as essential to higher growth and poverty reduction in Angola. A **devaluation** followed in which the official value of the kwanza was cut in half. In order to control the foreign exchange in circulation, 4 different **exchange rates** were applied in the banking system. **Privatization** was also introduced gradually because of pressure from international financial institutions. This **liberalization** process was stopped in 1992 due to resumption of the war.

Angola's financial woes heightened in 1994 and the government renewed its reform efforts. Since 1993 there has been a 25 percent decline in **real GDP**. In 1994 the government's **budget deficit** was US$872 million. The central bank attempted to address these deficits by increasing the money supply, but this raised **inflation** to 1,838 percent in Luanda in 1993, in 1995 inflation had reached 3,700 percent. In 1994 another adjustment program was attempted. However, this was made more difficult by the development of a robust informal sector with

Exchange rates: Angola	
kwanza per US$1	
Jan 2001	17,910,800
2000	10,041,000
1999	2,790,706
1998	392,824
1997	229,040
1996	128,029

Note: In December 1999 the kwanza was revalued with six zeroes dropped off the old value.

SOURCE: CIA *World Factbook 2001* [ONLINE].

its own credits and expenditures which were outside the control of the Ministry of Finance. In 1994 as much as 60 percent of the income of the state was outside treasury accounts.

There has yet to be any economic stabilization in Angola. There are 2 reasons why it might continue to be difficult to obtain even with a peace process. First, military expenditures will remain high because of the previous history of broken peace processes, in addition to the involvement of other countries in the conflict. Second, strong adjustment policies may antagonize the population, because they may want to see change come about quicker than is practically feasible.

The nova kwanza has dropped in value against the U.S. dollar for several years. In 1995, the official rate was Kzr2,750 to the dollar, and by January 2000, the rate had risen to Kzr577,304 to the US$1.

POVERTY AND WEALTH

The vast majority of Angolans live in poverty, while the political elites are very wealthy. Access to goods for the poor and the rich is very different. For years there has been a shortage of **consumer goods**, and the government sought to obtain fair distribution via *lojas do povo* (people's stores). However, only about 15 basic commodities were available, and in practice the shelves were often empty. The elites on the other hand had access to *lojas de responsaveis* (stores for high-ranking people) and *lojas francas* (free shops) where they could buy goods with foreign currency only. Economic policies were faltering and this made it more difficult for people to make ends meet both in rural and urban areas. Therefore, a parallel economy grew rapidly after independence.

An estimated three-quarters of economically active people have been involved in the informal economy. There are 2 main elements of the informal economy: rural, subsistence agricultural production (which occupies 85 percent of the population) and the urban parallel market, a system of exchange outside regulated channels. However, due to the lack of infrastructure and war conditions, there has been little integration of these two aspects of the informal sector. Therefore, the urban markets tend to rely on imports.

WORKING CONDITIONS

The working conditions in Angola are tightly connected with the war and the development of dual economies. Wages were nominal after the war began and therefore could not serve to ensure access to consumer goods. There is also vast unemployment, which affects more than half of the population. In addition, 25 percent of the population depended upon humanitarian aid for survival in 1996.

Most Angolans are active in the informal sector. This mainly consists of subsistence farming and urban markets. Since this economy is informal there are no laws to protect the workers or unions. The effect of the war has resulted in 1.5 million internal refugees. Workers in the mines in UNITA-held territories extract diamonds to sell in support of their cause.

COUNTRY HISTORY AND ECONOMIC DEVELOPMENT

1575. Portuguese settlement established at Luanda.

17TH CENTURY. Portugal controls the slave trade from its base in Angola, though the Dutch, French, and British began to establish a presence on the African continent.

1836. The export of slaves is banned.

1850s. Angola's exports are dominated by ivory, wax, and rubber.

1912. Alluvial diamond mining becomes an important industry in northeast Angola.

1930. With the Colonial Act of 1930, Portugal modernizes Angola's economy and binds it to that of Portugal by a system of protective **tariffs**.

1956. The Popular Liberation Movement of Angola (MPLA) is founded. It is supported by the Soviet Union.

1957. The National Front for the Liberation of Angola (FNLA) is founded. It is supported by the United States.

1961. A major revolt against Portuguese rule erupts in northern Angola, followed by a long guerrilla war.

1966. Political leader Jonas Savimbi breaks from the FNLA and sets up the National Union for the Total Independence of Angola (UNITA). UNITA, FNLA, and MPLA all fight a guerrilla war against Portuguese forces.

GDP per Capita (US$)					
Country	1975	1980	1985	1990	1998
Angola	N/A	698	655	667	527
United States	19,364	21,529	23,200	25,363	29,683
South Africa	4,574	4,620	4,229	4,113	3,918
Dem. Rep. of Congo	392	313	293	247	127

SOURCE: United Nations. *Human Development Report 2000; Trends in human development and per capita income.*

1975. Portugal releases its claim to Angola, and independence is declared. A government is established, consisting of the 3 nationalist groups and a Portuguese representative. However, this government collapses and civil war ensues. Over the next 25 years the MPLA acts as official government, and the coalition of UNITA/FNLA has been in rebellion. The MPLA is backed by the U.S.S.R. and Cuba, while UNITA and the FNLA are backed by the United States, the United Kingdom, and South Africa. The civil war claims a total of 500,000 lives by 2000.

1981. An undeclared war with South Africa begins. Its origins lie in the refusal of South Africa to grant independence to Namibia and South Africa's struggle against the nationalist groups in Namibia fighting against South African rule.

1989. The United Nations monitors the withdrawal of Cuban troops.

1991. The government and UNITA conclude a peace agreement.

1992. The Forcas Armadas Populares de Libertacao de Angola (FAPLA) and UNITA forces are disbanded and a new national army established. Elections are held, and the MPLA wins a narrow majority. Refusing to accept the results of the elections, UNITA forces resume fighting.

1993. The UN sponsors peace talks amidst continued fighting.

1999. It is estimated that there are 1.5 million refugees inside Angola displaced by the civil war.

FUTURE TRENDS

The future of Angola's economy depends entirely upon a cessation of hostilities and the creation of a stable and secure environment. If this does not happen, Angola will continue to have a low GDP regardless of the vast resources it possesses. However, due to the destruction of the infrastructure and the immense problem with land mines, there will be huge problems to overcome even if the war is ended. Infrastructure is necessary for expansion of the mining industry and agricultural production. The removal of mine fields will take huge resources. Both of these objectives will take a long time to achieve and have a high cost. Therefore, even with the creation of a stable and secure society it will take a long time before Angola can begin to tap its vast resources. An additional problem is that Angola is one of the most indebted countries in the world. Unless there is a substantial debt reduction the possibilities of rebuilding Angola's economy are slim, irrespective of cessation of hostilities.

DEPENDENCIES

Angola has no territories or colonies.

BIBLIOGRAPHY

"Angola History." *Newafrica.com.* <http://www.newafrica.com/history/country.asp?CountryID=5>. Accessed January 2001.

"Angola." *Jubilee 2000: Profile: Angola.* <http://www.jubileeplus.org/databank/profiles/angola.htm>. Accessed January 2001.

"Countries: Angola." *The World Bank Group.* <http://www.worldbank.org/afr/ao2.htm>. Accessed January 2001.

Economist Intelligence Unit. *Country Profile: Angola.* London: Economist Intelligence Unit, 2001.

Embassy of the Republic of Angola. "Business & Economics." *Angola.* <http://www.angola.org/business/index.htm>. Accessed January 2001.

Hodges, Tony. "Looking to Angola's Future: Rebuilding the Economy." *Africa Insight.* Vol. 23, No. 3, 1993.

James, W. Martin. *A Political History of the Civil War in Angola, 1974–1990.* New Brunswick, NJ: Transaction Publishers, 1992.

Moura Roque, Fatima. "Economic Transformation in Angola." *South African Journal of Economics.* Vol. 62, No. 2, June 1994.

Tvedten, Inge. *Angola's Struggle for Peace and Reconciliation.* Oxford, England: Westview Press, 1997.

U.S. Central Intelligence Agency. *World Factbook 2000.* <http://www.odci.gov/cia/publications/factbook/index.html>. Accessed July 2001.

—Eirin Mobekk

BENIN

Republic of Benin
République du Bénin

CAPITAL: Porto-Novo.

MONETARY UNIT: Communauté Financière Africaine franc (CFA Fr). One franc equals 100 centimes. There are coins of 1, 2, 5, 10, 25, 50, 100, and 500 CFA Fr. There are notes of 50, 100, 500, 1,000, 5,000, and 10,000 CFA Fr.

CHIEF EXPORTS: Cotton, crude oil, palm products, cocoa.

CHIEF IMPORTS: Foodstuffs, tobacco, petroleum products, capital goods.

GROSS DOMESTIC PRODUCT: US$6.6 billion (purchasing power parity, 2000 est.).

BALANCE OF TRADE: Exports: US$396 million (f.o.b., 1999 est.). **Imports:** US$566 million (c.i.f., 1999 est.).

COUNTRY OVERVIEW

LOCATION AND SIZE. Benin is a slim, rectangular country situated in West Africa. Benin has a narrow 100-kilometer (62-mile) coastline along the Bight of Benin, in the Atlantic Ocean. The country is bordered to the west by Nigeria, to the north by Niger and Burkina Faso, and to the east by Togo. Benin has a land area of 112,622 square kilometers (42,985 square miles), making it slightly smaller than the state of Pennsylvania. Both the capital, Porto-Novo, and Cotonou, the largest city, are located on the coast in the southeast of the country.

POPULATION. The population was estimated at 6.4 million in mid-2000. The relatively high population growth rate of 3.3 percent from 1992 to 1996 has led to a young population age profile, with 47 percent below the age of 15, 50 percent aged between 15 and 64, and only 3 percent 65 and over. The birth rate was 45 per 1000 in the year 2000, and the death rate was 15 per 1000.

The principal ethnic groups are the Fon (42 percent), the Adja (15.6 percent), and the Yoruba (12.1 percent) in the south, and the Bariba (8.6 percent), the Otamari (6.1 percent), and the Peulh (6.1 percent), who live fur-

ther north. Some 40 other groups are identifiable. Around 70 percent of the population follow traditional indigenous beliefs, 15 percent are Muslim, and 15 percent Christian.

Roughly 38 percent of the population live in towns (1995 estimates), double the 1990 census figure of 16 percent. Approximately 54 percent of urban dwellers have sanitation facilities. Infant mortality is high at 140 per 1000 births, but down from 205 per 1000 births in 1980 (by way of comparison, in the United States, infant mortality is 7 per 1,000).

OVERVIEW OF ECONOMY

Benin is one of the 30 or so poorest countries in the world. **Gross domestic product (GDP) per capita** measured with the **purchasing power parity** conversion (which makes allowance for the low price of many basic commodities in Benin) was estimated to be US$1,030 for the year 2000. The economy is heavily dependent on agriculture, which employs approximately 80 percent of the population. Crops are grown for export as well as domestic consumption. Industry is relatively underdeveloped and restricted mainly to simple **import substitution** products and basic agro-industrial processes.

Successive governments have struggled to tighten the country's economic and fiscal performance at the request of the International Monetary Fund (IMF) and the World Bank, while dealing with trade union pay demands. Benin entered agreements with the IMF in 1989 to introduce reforms. Though progress has been slow and is hindered by political infighting, there have been significant changes in the economy as a result of these reforms. In 1991–96 the government **privatized** or liquidated 100 state enterprises including cement, textiles, brewing, tobacco, and petroleum enterprises. The insurance sector has been **liberalized**, leading to increased

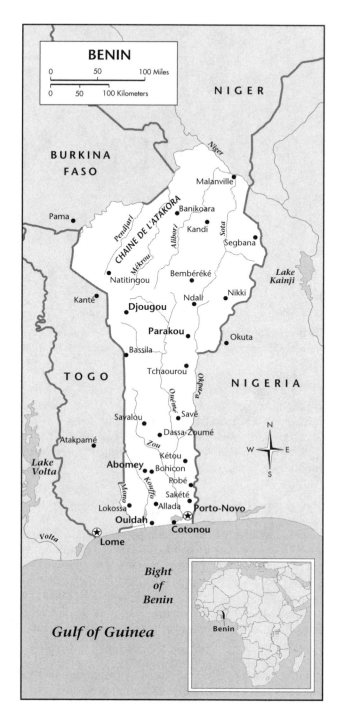

BENIN

0   50   100 Miles
0   50   100 Kilometers

NIGER

BURKINA
FASO

Malanville

Banikoara

Pama

Kandi

CHAINE DE L'ATAKORA

Pendjari

Alibori

Sota

Segbana

Mékrou

Bembéréké

Lake
Kainji

Natitingou

Ndali

Nikki

Kanté

Djougou

Parakou

Okuta

Bassila

TOGO

Tchaourou

NIGERIA

Okpara

Savalou

Savé

Ouémé

N

Dassa-Zoumé

Atakpamé

Zou

W   E

Kétou

S

Lake
Volta

Abomey

Bohicon

Mono

Pobé

Kouffo

Sakété

Lokossa

Allada

Porto-Novo

Ouidah

Cotonou

Volta

Lome

Bight
of
Benin

Gulf of Guinea

Benin

competition. There has been significant foreign investment in telecommunications. Cotton production is also opening up to private investment. However, the IMF has continued to press for further privatization's of state-run enterprises, including the major utilities such as electricity and water, as well as postal services and telecommunications. Privatization has significantly decreased the proportion of government spending. Since the collapse of the government in 1989 and the restoration of multi-party democracy with the introduction of the new con-

stitution in 1990, there has been increased investment from overseas, and a resumption of donor lending.

Monetary policy is controlled by membership of the Union Economique et Monetaire Ouest-Africaine (UEMOA,) and Benin is also a member of the African Franc Zone, which consists of those countries that use the CFA franc for their national currencies. Membership limits government borrowing and credit creation and sets interest rates as well. The UEMOA oversaw a 50 percent **devaluation** of the CFA franc in 1994, which increased the prices received by producers for exports. Local production recovered, and GDP growth rose to about 5 percent a year in the late 1990s. The other effect of the CFA franc devaluation was that it led to **inflation** rising to 38 percent in 1994 and 14 percent in 1995. Inflation then fell to 4.9 percent in 1996 and 3.5 percent in 1997. It rose once more in 1998 to 5.7 percent due to wage increases, cereal crop shortages, and the energy crisis caused by the drought in Ghana. Inflation fell again in 1999 to 3 percent.

Agriculture has been the main economic growth sector. Cotton production grew over 300 percent from 1990 to 1997. However, cotton production has been affected adversely by falling prices and management problems. Gasoline production stopped in 1998, but rehabilitation is under way due to the recent rise in world oil prices. In 1998 a drought in Ghana led to a serious setback in economic growth due to interruption of Benin's electricity supply, which caused much industry to close. Electricity supplies returned to normal in 1999.

The U.S. State Department states: "the most daunting obstacle to economic development . . . is the pervasive and increasing level of corruption throughout society. Corruption impacts virtually all aspects of social, economic, and political life in Benin. Inefficient and unmotivated government bureaucracies, even when not overtly corrupt, also make it extremely difficult for foreign businesses to conduct operations in Benin." The government agreed in 2001 to increase plans to end corruption, but the effect of these measures is not yet clear.

POLITICS, GOVERNMENT, AND TAXATION

Benin (once known as Dahomey) became a French colony in 1900 and was granted independence in 1960. Since that time it has experienced severe political turbulence. Hubert Maga, elected under a multi-party system and the country's first president, was ousted in a coup (a domestic military takeover of a government) in 1963, and regular changes of government then ensued until another coup in 1972 brought General Kerekou to the presidency. In 1974 **Marxism**-Leninism (the political and economic doctrines of Karl Marx and Vladimir Ilyich Lenin) became the country's official ideology. Major companies, banks, and offices were **nationalized**. Corruption followed and the economy contracted so sharply that the government was unable to pay wages, which led to strikes and eventually to a crisis in 1989. Kerekou convened a national conference of leading politicians, including opposition representation, later in 1989, which resulted in the creation of a multi-party democracy. A new constitution was adopted after a referendum in 1990. Legislative and presidential elections were held in 1991, and in a contest with Kerekou, Nicephore Soglo was elected president with 67 percent of the vote. Since the creation of the new constitution in 1990, Benin has, according to the U.S. State Department, been viewed as "a democratic model not only for its West African region but even for the entire continent."

Soglo became unpopular due to the persistence of economic problems—the inability of the government to pay salaries, high inflation, and shortages of basic commodities—and he succeeded in alienating his supporters such that he lost the 1996 election to Kerekou. In the meantime, Kerekou had renounced his military title, developed a new tolerance for the free market economy, and expressed his determination to combat corruption. Despite opposition from 16 other candidates, and a second round run-off (from which Soglo withdrew), Kerekou was successful at the polls in 2001 and secured another presidential term.

The 1990 constitution instituted a 5-year presidency, with the president eligible for re-election only once. The president has executive power and can suspend parliament with court approval. The members of the 83-seat assembly serve a 4-year terms. The position of prime minister (created in 1996) was dissolved in 1998 due to conflict between the president and the prime minister over executive powers.

Currently the main parties are fragmenting, leading to the formation of unstable coalitions, which has also decreased the effectiveness of the parliament. This dissension is likely to continue in the near future. Mr. Kerekou's coalition and the opposition are roughly equally represented in the assembly, meaning that the smaller parties can decide the parliamentary majority by aligning with one side or the other. Such tactical alliances have succeeded in blocking much government legislation. The trade unions are very powerful and are able to challenge the government's economic and **fiscal policies** through strikes, which also tend to lead to civil unrest and severe economic losses.

Benin raises less than 10 percent of the GDP in tax revenue and receives a further 2 percent in surpluses from state-owned enterprises, mainly **monopolies**. About 50 percent of government spending goes to social services (which includes health and education), about 14 percent on the armed forces, and the remainder is absorbed by general **public sector** administration. The military is an important influence in political life, and it has seized power though coups on several occasions. The relatively high level of spending on the military is an attempt to prevent alienation of the armed forces.

INFRASTRUCTURE, POWER, AND COMMUNICATIONS

There are 7,500 kilometers (4,660 miles) of roads and tracks in Benin, only 20 percent of which are paved. The coastal road that runs along the Lagos-Accra route is paved, and travel between Porto-Novo and Cotonou is easy. Contracts were awarded in 1998 for the construction of another motorway from Cotonou to Porto Novo. A north-south road forms a link to Burkina Faso and Niger. Development is focused primarily on rehabilitation and feeder roads to allow farmers to market their crops more effectively.

There are 635 kilometers (394 miles) of railway line, of which 579 kilometers (360 miles) are main lines. The most important route is from Cotonou to Parekou (440 kilometers, or 273 miles), which provides an important part of the link between Niger and Cotonou. The deep-water port at Cotonou handles 2 to 2.5 million metric tons per year and processes transit trade to Burkina Faso and Niger. A World Bank study showed that the port was losing a potential US$22 million per year in container operations due to poor organization by the state handling company. Management and development of Cotonou Port is due to be transferred to a private operator, while leaving equipment

Communications

Country	Newspapers	Radios	TV Sets[a]	Cable subscribers[a]	Mobile Phones[a]	Fax Machines[a]	Personal Computers[a]	Internet Hosts[b]	Internet Users[b]
	1996	1997	1998	1998	1998	1998	1998	1999	1999
Benin	2	108	10	N/A	1	0.2	0.9	0.04	10
United States	215	2,146	847	244.3	256	78.4	458.6	1,508.77	74,100
Nigeria	24	223	66	N/A	0	N/A	5.7	0.00	100
Togo	4	218	18	N/A	2	4.1	6.8	0.17	15

[a]Data are from International Telecommunication Union, *World Telecommunication Development Report 1999* and are per 1,000 people.
[b]Data are from the Internet Software Consortium (http://www.isc.org) and are per 10,000 people.

SOURCE: World Bank. *World Development Indicators 2000*.

and installations in state hands. Cotonou International Airport carries 250,000 passengers per year. There are 4 secondary airports. The private Benin Inter-Regional Airline was started in 1991 and provides local and regional flights.

In 1996 there were 30,000 telephone lines in Benin, but expansion has been underway. A 1,500 kilometer microwave network currently connects 52 exchanges, and an Intelsat station is being installed. In 1999 Alcatel (a French company) and U.S.-based Titan won a US$60 million contract for fixed and mobile phone expansion projects respectively. There are approximately 150,000 radio sets being used in Benin. Television broadcasts began in 1972, but the state monopoly over television ended in 1997. In 1998, 35 radio licenses (including 13 commercial station licenses) and 3 TV station licenses were issued. There are 13 daily newspapers.

Most of the country's energy for domestic use comes from wood fuel. Electricity is produced and imported by Communaute Electrique du Benin (CEB), Benin's state-owned electricity company. CEB relies heavily on Ghana's Akosombo dam for most of its electricity. However, this reliance produced a crisis during the 1998 Ghanaian drought, when Benin's electricity supply was severely affected. This difficulty has led to attempts to diversify electricity production facilities and moves to import generators. Togo and Benin also have a shared 65 megawatt (mw) station on the Mono River, although both are still dependent on Ghana. A second 104 mw dam is under construction on the Mono River.

ECONOMIC SECTORS

Agriculture (including hunting, forestry, and fishing) employed roughly 80 percent of the **workforce** and gen-

erated 37.9 percent of the GDP in 1999. Cotton and palm oil are the main exports, and the country is predominantly self-sufficient in foodstuffs. Industry (including mining, manufacturing, construction, and power) provided 13.5 percent of the GDP in 1999, while services contributed 48.6 percent.

AGRICULTURE

Problems in the agriculture sector arise from poor transport, inadequate storage, and the inability of farmers to provide legal evidence of land ownership as collateral for loans. Despite these difficulties, agriculture has expanded and developed since the 1994 CFA franc devaluation. In 1997 a project was started to rejuvenate the collective farms, costing US$5 million and employing 2000 people over 5 years. The project will be run by the **private sector**, with foreign management of some farms.

The oil palm is the most important tree crop in the south, and the oil it produces has a wide variety of uses in foodstuffs (especially margarine) and in industry (especially in soaps). Output in the 1970s and 1980s, however, fell due to drought, the overvalued franc, and low world prices. In 2000 a pilot project aimed to raise yields of coffee, cocoa, ground nuts (such as peanuts), and kerite (shea nuts), all grown in the south.

Cotton, the main export, is normally grown in the north. Higher producer prices after the 1994 devaluation boosted output to 15,000 metric tons of lint (unprocessed cotton fiber) in the 1997–98 season, though it fell again in the 1998–99 season due to smaller yields and a financial scandal in Sonapra (the cotton **parastatal**). The cotton price slump in 1999 means Sonapra might not be able to find growers at current prices and might face being sold to the private sector.

Food and livestock production accounts for 48 percent of the total agricultural output. **Smallholders** produce for domestic and regional markets. Maize and cassava are grown in the south and sorghum, millet, and yams in the drier north. Rice production is expanding rapidly and reached 30,900 metric tons in the 1998–99 season with help from a UN-backed program. Production was encouraged by Centre d'Action Regionale pour le Development Rural (Center of Regional Action for Rural Development), a government body set up to develop the rural economy.

In 1998 there were 1.3 million cattle, 6 million sheep, 1.1 million goats, and 5 million pigs in Benin. Cattle are kept mainly in the north, but there have been attempts to move production to the south. Livestock output meets 60 percent of the national requirements. Production is currently more competitive due to the 1994 devaluation of the CFA franc. There is a long-term plan for the country

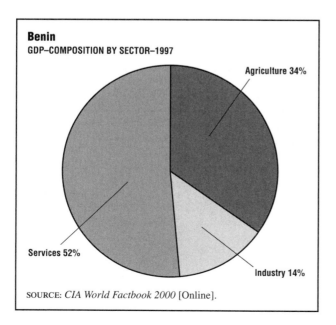

Benin
GDP–COMPOSITION BY SECTOR–1997

Agriculture 34%

Services 52%

Industry 14%

SOURCE: *CIA World Factbook 2000* [Online].

to be self-sufficient in dairy products (as of 2001 Benin imports 8,000 metric tons of dairy products each year).

The Office Nationale du Bois was established 1983 to develop timber production and to stop deforestation. Plantations, mainly teak, covered 38,000 hectares in 1989 and further planting is planned. The fish catch is mainly from inland waters, rivers, and lagoons. Fish production is currently 12,000 metric tons per year, which meets 50 percent of domestic consumption.

INDUSTRY

In Benin there is no significant mining except for limestone, which is used in cement production. Improvements in mining regulations have stimulated foreign interest in recent years. Gold mining has attracted investment from 8 foreign companies and there are also proven reserves of iron and phosphates.

In 1999 the government signed a contract with Zetal Oil to rehabilitate the Sémé oil field at a cost of US$45 million. Sémé began production in 1982 and reached its peak production in 1985 at 10,000 barrels per day. Production ended in 1998 when low world prices and dwindling reserves meant that the field was not economical. Foreign companies (especially from the United States and Canada) are exploring Benin for further viable fields.

In 1999 a US$17.9 million oil terminal opened in Cotonou Port. The oil distribution company, Sonacop (previously state-owned), was sold to the private sector in 1999. Plans for a 1,000-kilometer gas pipeline from Nigeria to Benin, Togo, and Ghana moved forward in 1999 when 2 international companies and 4 regional gas boards signed a deal on the US$400 million project.

Manufacturing focuses on the processing of agricultural products and the production of **consumer goods**. The latter sector depends on imported inputs and was hit hard by the 1994 currency devaluation. However, this impact also meant the local raw material companies found it easier to compete with imports.

Cotton led agro-industry in the 1990s. Ginning capacity expanded rapidly, and the country currently can process 462,500 metric tons per year in 10 government-owned plants and 6 private plants. Capacity could be increased to 673,000 metric tons per year if the planned expansion is carried out. **Restructuring** plans for the government-owned plants are currently underway.

Palm oil has been in decline since the 1980s. Sonicog runs 6 small palm oil mills, though only 3 have operated in recent years. The sector is being restructured with World Bank assistance for privatization. Food, drink, and tobacco processing, as well as footwear man-

ufacture and ceramics, form the basis of the import substitution sector.

SERVICES

After the collapse of several banks in 1998 and 1999, the financial sector was completely overhauled, with the liquidation of failed banks and the setting up of new private sector institutions with assistance from France and the World Bank. Benin's banks include the Banque Internationale du Benin, Ecobank, Bank of Africa-Benin, and Financial Bank.

A regional stock exchange, the Bourse Regionale des Valeurs Mobilieres (BRVM), was opened in 1998. It will help improve the capital market by attracting local savings and slowing **capital outflow** to Europe. The headquarters of the stock exchange is in Abidjan, but all UEMOA members have trading floors in their countries.

Tourism is in its infancy, and arrivals are usually French citizens or backpackers exploring West Africa. Attractions are many: the former slave towns of Porto Novo and Grand Popo, stilt villages and the lagoons around Ganvie, the northern nature reserves including the Pendjari area, and the Parc West (on the border of Burkina Faso and Niger). Hotel facilities vary in quality and availability, and outside Cotonou they provide only the basics.

INTERNATIONAL TRADE

There is a chronic international **trade deficit**, with exports in 1999 valued at US$396 million, and imports at US$566 million. However, the large number of unrecorded transactions means that assessment is difficult, mainly due to illegal cross-border trade with Nigeria.

Cotton is the most important export, followed by oil. **Re-exports** (goods that are imported into Benin and then sent to neighboring countries such as Burkina Faso and Niger) account for one-third to one-half of total exports, while food and **capital goods** account for one-quarter and one-fifth of imports respectively.

Trade (expressed in billions of US$): Benin

	Exports	Imports
1975	.032	.188
1980	.063	.331
1985	.150	.331
1990	.122	.265
1995	.414	.692
1998	N/A	N/A

SOURCE: International Monetary Fund. *International Financial Statistics Yearbook 1999.*

In 1999, France (38 percent), China (16 percent), the United Kingdom (9 percent), and Côte d'Ivoire (5 percent) were the main sources of imports for Benin. Currently, Asia supplies rice and manufactured goods for regional re-exports. Brazil (14 percent), Libya (5 percent), Indonesia (4 percent), and Italy (4 percent) are the main destination for exports, mainly cotton, in 1999.

MONEY

Benin is part of the 8-member UEMOA, and the currency is the CFA franc. The Banque Centrale des Etats de l'Afrique de l'Ouest (BCEAO) issues currency notes and regulates credit expansion. The CFA franc was pegged at a **fixed exchange rate** to the French franc at 50:1 from 1948 but was overvalued in the late 1980s and subsequently devalued to CFA Fr 100 to 1 French franc in 1994. Since France joined European Monetary Union, the CFA franc is tied to the euro at CFA Fr655.959:Euro 1.

Benin is burdened with a huge **foreign debt** of more than US$1.6 billion, although the country's major creditors are working with the Paris Club (an informal organization made of various creditor companies and countries), the IMF, and the World Bank to help it manage its obligations.

POVERTY AND WEALTH

One-third of the population live below the poverty line set by Benin, which suggests that close to 50 percent live below the dollar-a-day international poverty line. The dollar-a-day poverty line is based on the income required to provide the absolute minimum of nutrition, clothing, and shelter. Some 29 percent of children under 5 are malnourished (the figure is 1 percent for the United States), and life expectancy is 55 years (in the United States it is 77 years). Almost all those in poverty are in rural areas, relying on small-scale agriculture for their livelihoods and suffering because of poor land, inadequate rainfall, and not enough income to purchase good seeds, fertilizer, or farm machinery. In 1998 Benin was ranked 157th out of 174 countries in the UN's Human Development Index, which combines measures of income, education, and health provision.

In 1995 there was 1 doctor per 200,000 inhabitants. There was 1 midwife per 12,000 pregnant women, and just 42 percent of the population had access to health care. Several international initiatives to improve these figures have been undertaken. The constitution decrees that primary education is compulsory for all, though fees must be paid. In 1996 there was a 62 percent enrollment in primary age education, though this number dropped to 17 percent in secondary education. In 1993 almost US$1 million was set aside for a scheme for rural girls to be exempted from school fees. In 1992 adult literacy stood at 27 percent.

Exchange rates: Benin

Communaute Financiere Africaine francs (CFA Fr) per US$1	
Jan 2001	699.21
2000	711.98
1999	615.70
1998	589.95
1997	583.67
1996	511.55

Note: From January 1, 1999, the CFA Fr is pegged to the euro at a rate of 655.957 CFA Fr per euro.

SOURCE: CIA *World Factbook 2001* [ONLINE].

GDP per Capita (US$)

Country	1975	1980	1985	1990	1998
Benin	339	362	387	345	394
United States	19,364	21,529	23,200	25,363	29,683
Nigeria	301	314	230	258	256
Togo	411	454	385	375	333

SOURCE: United Nations. *Human Development Report 2000; Trends in human development and per capita income.*

Household Consumption in PPP Terms

Country	All food	Clothing and footwear	Fuel and power[a]	Health care[b]	Education[b]	Transport & Communications	Other
Benin	52	5	15	5	3	3	17
United States	13	9	9	4	6	8	51
Nigeria	51	5	31	2	8	2	2
Togo	N/A	N/A	N/A	N/A	N/A	N/A	N/A

Data represent percentage of consumption in PPP terms.
[a]Excludes energy used for transport.
[b]Includes government and private expenditures.

SOURCE: World Bank. *World Development Indicators 2000.*

WORKING CONDITIONS

Most people are very poor and earn their living through agriculture on small family farms. Most of the work is undertaken by hand, and women do most of the labor, helped by children. There are no official unemployment figures for Benin, but unemployment figures have little significance in a low-income African economy. There are very few with no work at all. There is no unemployment benefit, and those who do not work rely on support from charities or their families. Many people would like a modern sector job, but eke out an existence on family farms or in casual **informal sector** activities (such as **hawking**, portering, scavenging) in the urban areas. There was a minimum professional salary of US$38 per month in 1997. The biannual civil servant salary increase stopped in 1998, but trade unions are demanding its reintroduction. The **United Nations Development Program** estimates that 55 percent of urban dwellers earned less than US$160 per year in 1992.

The constitution of the Republic of Benin guarantees the basic rights and freedoms of citizens. Forced labor is illegal, but human rights are not enforced in a consistent manner. Children often work to supplement household income, resulting in lower school attendance figures. In 1998 it was estimated that 29 percent of children aged 10–14 had to work to supplement family income.

COUNTRY HISTORY AND ECONOMIC DEVELOPMENT

1900. Dahomey (the former name of Benin) becomes a French colony.

1960. Independence is granted, and Hubert Maga becomes the country's first president.

1963. A coup brings Colonel Christophe Soglo to power.

1963. Dahomey returns to civilian rule, with Sourou-Migan Apithey elected president.

1965. Soglo assumes power again.

1967. Major Maurice Kouandete seizes power through a coup.

1968. Emile-Derlin Zinzou is appointed president by the military, but Kouandete again assumes power.

1969. A presidential election is attempted but collapses. Maga is nominated president again.

1972. Maga is succeeded by Ahomadegbe, but Major Mathieu Kerekou seizes power.

1975. Dahomey changes its name to Benin.

1990. A new constitution is adopted, paving the way for political stability.

1991. Nicephore Soglo defeats Kerekou at the polls to become president. Soglo begins the privatization or liquidation of 100 state-run companies.

1994. The CFA franc is devalued by 50 percent, boosting exports and increasing inflation.

1996. Kerekou defeats Soglo in an election to become president again.

2001. Kerkou wins re-election to the presidency.

FUTURE TRENDS

After success in the 2001 presidential election, President Mathieu Kerekou was expected to continue with his popular poverty reduction and growth program, which is set to last to 2003. Driven by plans for increased public investment and commitments of donor support, **real GDP** growth is expected to remain at around the 5 percent a year level, allowing for steady improvements in average living standards. Cereal production still faces problems, despite recent improvements, as a result of weak **infrastructure** and delays in payments to farmers. Future growth rates are expected to be below the rate of population increase, leading to increased reliance on food imports. Sound monetary policy, implemented by the regional central bank, is projected to keep inflation at around 3 percent. The gap between international payments and receipts will be helped by increased foreign aid, expansion in cotton exports, and **debt relief** from the Heavily Indebted Poor Country (HIPC) scheme, a program instituted by the IMF and World Bank to help the poorest countries manage their foreign debt.

In politics, the multiparty system introduced in 1990 appears to be secure, with all parties prepared to accept the verdict of the ballot box. President Kerekou appears unlikely to make any major change in the style and composition of his executive team. The new anti-corruption measures, which require leaders to declare their assets, is now being implemented, and there are high expectations that they will increase honesty in public life. An interesting development is the introduction of a new electoral code in which expatriate residents are able to vote, and this move is seen as an attempt to make politics less inward-looking.

DEPENDENCIES

Benin has no territories or colonies.

BIBLIOGRAPHY

Allen, Chris, and Michael Radu. *Benin, the Congo, Burkina Faso: Economics, Politics, and Society.* New York and London: Printer, 1988.

"Benin Economy." *Newafrica.com.* <http://www.newafrica.com/profiles/economy.asp?countryid=6>. Accessed October 2001.

Economist Intelligence Unit. *Country Profile: Benin.* London: Economist Intelligence Unit, 2001.

Hodd, Michael. "Niger." *The Economies of Africa.* Dartmouth: Aldershot, 1991.

Kelly, R. C. et al., editors. *Benin Country Review 1998/1999.* Houston: Commercial Data International, Inc., 1999.

U.S. Central Intelligence Agency. *World Factbook 2001.* <http://www.odci.gov/cia/publications/factbook/index.html>. Accessed September 2001.

U.S. Department of State. *FY 2001 Country Commercial Guide: Benin.* <http://www.state.gov/www/about_state/business/com_guides2001/africa/index.html>. Accessed October 2001.

—*Jack Hodd*

BOTSWANA

Republic of Botswana

CAPITAL: Gaborone.

MONETARY UNIT: Pula. 1 pula equals 100 thebe. (Pula means "rain" and "greetings.") Notes come in 5-, 10-, 20-, 50-, and 100-pula denominations, and coins come in denominations of 1, 5, 10, 25, and 50 thebe and 1 and 2 pula.

CHIEF EXPORTS: Diamonds, vehicles, copper, nickel, and meat.

CHIEF IMPORTS: Foodstuffs, machinery and transport equipment, textiles, and petroleum products.

GROSS DOMESTIC PRODUCT: US$5.7 billion (purchasing power parity, 1999 est.).

BALANCE OF TRADE: Exports: US$2.36 billion (1999 est.). Imports: US$2.05 billion (1999 est.).

COUNTRY OVERVIEW

LOCATION AND SIZE. Botswana is a landlocked country in southern Africa, located just north of South Africa. Botswana has a total area of 602,957 square kilometers (232,802 square miles), making it about the same size as the state of Texas. The length of Botswana's border is 4,011 kilometers (2,493 miles), and its neighbors are Namibia to the west, Zimbabwe to the east, and South Africa to the south. The capital, Gaborone, has a population of about 135,000 and is located in the southeast of the country, almost on the border with South Africa.

POPULATION. Botswana's population was estimated at 1.58 million in July 2000, growing at the slow rate of .76 percent. The population was expected to reach 2 million by 2030. The birth rate was 29.63 births per 1,000 people, and the death rate was 22.08 deaths per 1,000 people. Approximately 41 percent of the population was less than 15 years old, 55 percent was 15–64 years old, and only 4 percent had lived over 64 years of age in 2000.

Botswana is one of the few countries in sub-Saharan Africa with a fairly homogeneous ethnic background. The Batswanans make up 95 percent of the population, of which the Tswana tribes constitute 60 percent. The San

people (also known as Basarwa, Khwe, or Bushmen) number 60,000. Population density is low due to the harsh climate of the Kalahari desert, at 2.6 people per square kilometer (6.7 people per square mile). The majority of Botswana's people live in the southeast of the country, where the desert gives way to the more fertile land of the Okavango river delta and swamp, and 50 percent of the total population lives within 100 kilometers (62 miles) of Gaborone. At independence in 1966 only 3 percent of the population lived in urban areas, but by 2000 this figure had risen to over 65 percent.

The rapid spread of AIDS in Botswana is a major reason that population growth is low. It is estimated that 25–36 percent of the population is infected with the virus, reflecting one of the highest rates in the world. This has caused a great number of social problems including labor shortages and a health care crisis. AIDS-related health and safety information is openly available, but cultural practices, social mobility, and the fact that Botswana lies on major trucking routes between South Africa and the north have contributed to the spread of the disease.

OVERVIEW OF ECONOMY

Botswana's economy depended primarily on the raising of livestock, especially cattle, until the early 1970s. At that time, the diamond industry surpassed cattle raising as the main source of foreign exchange. While the export of diamonds generates a great deal of money for the few who own and work the diamond mines, subsistence agriculture and cattle raising provides employment for about 80 percent of the population and supplies half of the domestic food consumption. The government of Botswana hopes to develop a more diversified economy through **ecotourism**, manufacturing, and financial services.

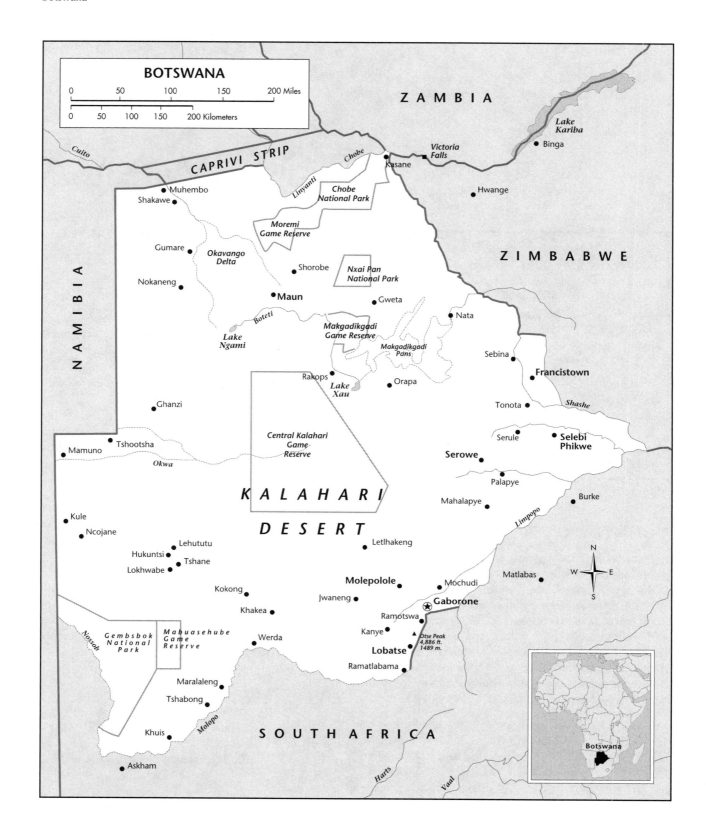

BOTSWANA

| 0 | 50 | 100 | 150 | 200 Miles |

| 0 | 50 | 100 | 150 | 200 Kilometers |

Botswana's **external debt** is small, at US$651 million (or about 10 percent of GDP in 1998). The country is one of the only African nations (with Swaziland) that contributes money to the World Bank and the International Monetary Fund (IMF). Botswana has historically favored free market policies and encourages foreign investment, although a **monopoly** in the diamond industry discourages smaller mining ventures. The South

African company De Beers, in partnership with the Botswanan government, controls virtually all of the diamond industry. In contrast, cattle are exported from smaller domestic companies. Large African companies such as Waverly Blankets (from South Africa) run manufacturing operations.

POLITICS, GOVERNMENT, AND TAXATION

Botswana was a British colony called Bechuanaland until 30 September 1966, when it received its independence. It is a republic, with a **unicameral** (single-chambered) parliament similar to that of the United Kingdom. The president of the country is elected by Parliament and then chooses the vice president. The main political parties are the Botswana Democratic Party, Botswana National Front, Botswana Congress Party, and Botswana Peoples Party. Botswana has a stable political history, with peaceful elections held every 5 years. Sir Seretse Khama was elected president of Botswana in 1966 and held office until 1980. Quett Masire took office upon the death of President Khama and remained president until 1998, when he resigned. Festus Mogae of the Botswana Democratic Party was elected president in 1998. Political opposition parties question the government about unemployment and the perception that foreigners take jobs away from locals.

Though Botswana in general practices free market policies, there is some government control over central services such as banking and telecommunications. Government policy leans towards **privatization** of publicly-owned companies. Taxes on investment are among the lowest in the Southern Africa region. Corporate taxes apply equally to foreign and domestic businesses and were lowered from 35 percent to 25 percent in 1995 in order to attract more investment. A similar tax reduction in the same year was applied to the manufacturing sector, where taxes were lowered from 35 percent to 15 percent.

INFRASTRUCTURE, POWER, AND COMMUNICATIONS

Botswana has 971 kilometers (603 miles) of rail lines, 18,482 kilometers (11,484 miles) of roads (of which only 23 percent are paved), and 92 airports, of which 12 have paved runways. The national airline is Air Botswana, which flies domestically and to other countries in Africa. Direct air service from Gaborone to London and Paris is provided by British and French airlines.

Botswana has a good **infrastructure** by African standards. The quality of infrastructure was greatly improved by the development of the mining industry, which required adequate transportation and communication networks. Botswana also benefits from its location next to South Africa. This has allowed Botswana access to South Africa's telecommunications infrastructure. Botswana's desire to become an international financial services center is a key factor driving the improvement of the country's land line and cellular telephone networks. In 1998 there were 78,000 phone lines in use.

Domestically produced coal generates 100 percent of the electricity for Botswana, which is approximately 1.619 billion Kilowatts (1998). Every other source of energy, including oil, must be imported.

ECONOMIC SECTORS

The vast majority of Botswana's people practice **subsistence farming** and cattle raising. Because subsistence farm products and livestock are primarily raised for local consumption and are not sold in the formal market, the value of this production is not included in the **gross domestic product** or formal employment figures. Although agricultural employment is estimated at 15.6 percent of the formal **labor force**, the true figure is more like 80 percent of the informal labor force. The mining and service sectors (especially government, finance, transportation, and communication) account for most of

Communications

Country	Newspapers	Radios	TV Sets[a]	Cable subscribers[a]	Mobile Phones[a]	Fax Machines[a]	Personal Computers[a]	Internet Hosts[b]	Internet Users[b]
	1996	1997	1998	1998	1998	1998	1998	1999	1999
Botswana	27	156	20	N/A	15	2.3	25.5	6.00	12
United States	215	2,146	847	244.3	256	78.4	458.6	1,508.77	74,100
South Africa	32	317	125	N/A	56	3.5	47.4	33.36	1,820
Zimbabwe	19	93	30	N/A	4	N/A	9.0	1.19	20

[a]Data are from International Telecommunication Union, *World Telecommunication Development Report 1999* and are per 1,000 people.

[b]Data are from the Internet Software Consortium (http://www.isc.org) and are per 10,000 people.

SOURCE: World Bank. *World Development Indicators 2000.*

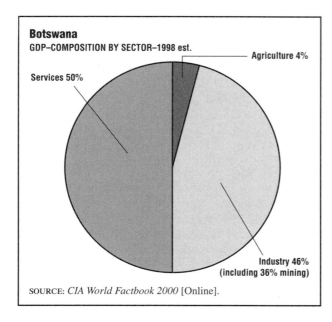

Botswana
GDP–COMPOSITION BY SECTOR–1998 est.

Agriculture 4%
Services 50%
Industry 46%
(including 36% mining)

SOURCE: *CIA World Factbook 2000* [Online].

INDUSTRY

MINING. Mining provides 86 percent of the country's export earnings, most of this from diamond sales. However, the mining sector employs only about 4.4 percent of the formal labor force. The country has 3 main diamond mines, at Orapa, Lethlakane, and Jwaneng. These are all owned and operated by Debswana, an equal **joint venture** between the South African diamond mining company De Beers and the Botswana government.

Though diamonds dominate Botswana's mining industry, the country is also rich in copper, nickel, and gold. Botswana also has sizable coal deposits.

Many of Botswana's mineral resources have not yet been discovered, but are presumed to exist given the country's geology. The area is expected to yield natural gas and crude oil; Central Botswana and the Kalahari Desert are perhaps the most likely sources of new discoveries. Though Botswana has tried to diversify its economy away from mining, the minerals sector continues to dominate the economy. Fortunately, the Botswana government saved and invested a portion of the country's mineral revenues, producing additional income for the country as well as providing investment capital for new industries.

MANUFACTURING. Manufacturing contributes only 5 percent of GDP and employs only 8.5 percent of the country's labor force. Botswana exports most of its natural resources in raw form, with minimum processing. The Botswanan government would like more manufacturing companies to locate in the country, therefore it is focusing on the natural resources that may be used in manufacturing operations. Such resources include soda ash, which is used to produce detergents and fertilizers; and copper and nickel, which are used in electrical components. Other established manufacturing products include cement, food, and beer. In 1997 the Botswana Export Development Investment Authority was established to encourage the export of goods manufactured in Botswana.

the nation's gross domestic product, but employ very few people. About 100,000 people are employed in the **public sector**, and about 245,000 in the **private sector**.

Botswana is one of the world's largest diamond producers. Debswana (an equal partnership of the South African company De Beers and the Botswanan government) controls most of the country's diamond industry. The Botswana government is currently trying reduce the country's dependence on diamonds by encouraging new manufacturing and service industries to locate in the country.

AGRICULTURE

Agriculture in Botswana is practiced primarily to feed the country, rather than for export. Yet agricultural production is not sufficient to meet domestic demand. Botswana's agricultural exports totaled US$114.2 million in 1998, while agricultural imports for the same year totaled US$348.4 million. Though the majority of people in Botswana practice agriculture (80 percent), it contributes only 4 percent to GDP and accounts for only 15.6 percent of formal employment.

Environmental factors have determined the kinds of crops and animals that can be raised in the country. Much of Botswana is part of the Kalahari Desert, with a dry and drought-prone climate. The primary crops are corn and wheat, which are grown in the wetter eastern parts of the country. The drier parts of Botswana are suitable for non-intensive cattle raising, similar to the western United States. Botswana's only important agricultural exports are meat and animal hides.

SERVICES

The services sector contributes roughly 51 percent of GDP, and employs 71.5 percent of the formal labor force. Transportation, telecommunications, and tourism are the key sectors within the services sector, as is government. Transportation is dominated by passenger air travel and cargo rail. A number of important truck routes between South Africa and central and eastern African countries pass through Botswana. The tourism sector received 734,000 tourist arrivals in 1997, generating US$184 million. The tourism industry in Botswana is characterized by ecotourism. The country has great tourism potential given its desert scenery and plentiful wildlife. Botswana also has a developing financial ser-

Trade (expressed in billions of US$): Botswana		
	Exports	Imports
1975	.142	.218
1980	.503	.692
1985	.728	.580
1990	1.784	1.946
1995	2.143	1.914
1998	1.122	1.120

SOURCE: International Monetary Fund. *International Financial Statistics Yearbook 1999.*

Exchange rates: Botswana	
pulas per US$1	
Jan 2001	5.4585
2000	5.1018
1999	4.6244
1998	4.2259
1997	3.6508
1996	3.3242

SOURCE: CIA *World Factbook 2001* [ONLINE].

vices sector. There are currently a number of commercial banks, a savings bank run through the post office (which accepts very small deposits), a development bank, and the government's central bank. Botswana is hoping to become an international financial services center.

INTERNATIONAL TRADE

During the colonial period and in the years immediately after independence, Botswana's trade was primarily with Great Britain and Western Europe. Imports from Europe declined during the 1970s while imports from other African countries, and especially with South Africa, increased. In 1999 Botswana exported a total of US$2.36 billion in goods and imported US$2.05 billion. In 1996 74 percent of exports went to EU countries, 21 percent went to South African Customs Union (SACU) countries, and 3 percent went to Zimbabwe. In the same year, 78 percent of imports came from SACU countries, 8 percent from EU countries, and 6 percent from Zimbabwe.

The South African Customs Union was formed in 1969 with Botswana as one of the founding members, along with South Africa, Lesotho, Namibia, and Swaziland. Membership in the customs union removes many of the trade barriers, such as import **duties** and taxes, between member countries, making it easier to import and export goods within the local region. South Africa especially has been a source of imports (electricity, manufactured goods, and foodstuffs) and a destination for exports (diamonds, copper, and livestock). Exports to Europe, and especially to Great Britain, have increased. The declining value of the Botswanan currency has made imports from outside the customs union more expensive, while also making it cheaper for European nations to import Botswana's products, especially diamonds.

MONEY

The Botswana pula has traditionally had a similar **exchange rate** to the South African rand, which meant that goods sold for almost the same price in both coun-

tries. During the late 1990s the pula was much stronger than the rand, resulting in South African products becoming relatively cheaper when purchased in pula. Botswana could afford to import more South African products. The stronger pula relative to the rand also meant that foreign investors found Botswana a more attractive place to invest money. However, during the same time period the pula gradually lost its value against the U.S. dollar, meaning that imports valued in U.S. dollars, such as those from the United States itself as well as from many other countries, were more expensive. But Botswana's exports, especially diamonds, were cheaper for American and European buyers.

The Botswana Stock Exchange, established in 1995, had 22 companies listed in 2001, including 6 South African companies.

POVERTY AND WEALTH

Living standards in Botswana are high by African standards, but vary considerably across the country. Ethnic minorities, such as the San, get little recognition or support from the government, and thus tend to practice a traditional lifestyle without much involvement with the formal economy. Botswana has recently come under criticism regarding alleged human rights violations against the San people, who were removed from their traditional lands in the Central Kalahari Game Reserve to develop tourism and mining. On the other hand, Botswana has

GDP per Capita (US$)					
Country	1975	1980	1985	1990	1998
Botswana	1,132	1,678	2,274	3,124	3,611
United States	19,364	21,529	23,200	25,363	29,683
South Africa	4,574	4,620	4,229	4,113	3,918
Zimbabwe	686	638	662	706	703

SOURCE: United Nations. *Human Development Report 2000; Trends in human development and per capita income.*

Household Consumption in PPP Terms							
Country	All food	Clothing and footwear	Fuel and power[a]	Health care[b]	Education[b]	Transport & Communications	Other
Botswana	24	5	12	2	7	5	45
United States	13	9	9	4	6	8	51
South Africa	N/A	N/A	N/A	N/A	N/A	N/A	N/A
Zimbabwe	20	10	21	3	15	9	22

Data represent percentage of consumption in PPP terms.
[a]Excludes energy used for transport.
[b]Includes government and private expenditures.
SOURCE: World Bank. *World Development Indicators 2000.*

been one of the most rapidly urbanizing nations in the world. With the obvious and major exception of the dramatic effect of AIDS on life expectancy in Botswana (32 years for men and women), living standards in urban centers are good. Botswana was ranked 122 on the Human Development Index in 1997, very high for an African country. In the urban centers, 91 percent of the population had access to sanitation and sewage disposal, and 100 percent had access to safe drinking water. The percentage having access to safe drinking water across the country as a whole was 70 percent.

WORKING CONDITIONS

The unemployment rate in Botswana is a debated figure, with the official estimate at 20 percent, and the unofficial rate at 40 percent. Most infrastructure developments, such as hospitals, roads, and schools, have been in urban areas and benefit urban residents. With the majority of the population (65 percent) living in urban centers, working conditions have improved. Wages in the mining sector are high, but are low in the agricultural sector. Women have poorer employment prospects, make less money, and are rarely promoted. Until 2000 education in Botswana was free, but in that year the government required students to pay fees, even for elementary schooling. In 1995 enrollment rates for males and females in primary and secondary education was between 81 and 89 percent, but this figure was expected to drop due to the new fees.

COUNTRY HISTORY AND ECONOMIC DEVELOPMENT

1885. The British government takes control of Bechuanaland.

1909. Bechuanaland is exempted from inclusion in the proposed Union of South Africa.

1966. The independence of Bechuanaland, now called Botswana.

1966. Sir Seretse Khama elected President of Botswana, holding office until 1980.

1969. Botswana helps to form the Southern African Customs Union.

1972. Botswana's first diamond mine begins production at Orapa.

1977. A political Botswana Defense Force is established because of conflict in neighboring Rhodesia.

1980. Quett Masire takes office upon the death of President Khama and remains president until 1998.

1997. The Botswana Export Development Investment Authority (BEDIA) is established.

1998. Festus Mogae is elected president.

FUTURE TRENDS

Botswana has remained peaceful and democratic since independence in 1966, and, with the opening of diamond mines in the 1970s, the country has been economically prosperous as well. Botswana has managed to invest its diamond revenues carefully, but still relies heavily on the export of diamonds for most of its revenue. This is likely to be the case for some time, though the Botswanan government is trying to diversify the economy by encouraging manufacturing industries to locate in the country. This strategy has met with mixed success. Botswana is likely to compete with South Africa for much of the manufacturing employment in the region. The Botswana government remains committed to its twin goals of economic diversification and balancing the budget.

Regional political instability, especially in neighboring Zimbabwe, but also in South Africa and Angola (where a civil war is still raging), will have an impact on Botswana, especially as refugees move into the country. However, given its political and economic history and its current policies, Botswana is likely to remain one of the most prosperous African countries.

DEPENDENCIES

Botswana has no territories or colonies.

BIBLIOGRAPHY

Botswana Central Statistics Office. *National Accounts Statistics.* <http://www.cso.gov.bw/cso/national_accts.html>. Accessed March 2001.

Botswana, Government of. *Economic Snapshot: Botswana Economy Facts and Figures.* <http://www.gov.bw/economy/index.html>. Accessed March 2001.

Economist Intelligence Unit. *EIU Country Report: Botswana.* London: Economist Intelligence Unit, 2001.

International Institute for Applied Systems Analysis. *Botswana: Currently Employed Persons by Industry, Region, and Sex.* <http://www.iiasa.ac.at/Research/POP/pde/FigTabs/bw-employ95.html>. Accessed May 2001.

Mines 2000. *Country Profiles: Botswana.* <http://www.mines2000projects.com/html/botswana.htm>. Accessed December 2000.

Newafrica. *Botswana Economy.* <http://www.newafrica.com/profiles>. Accessed March 2001.

U.S. Central Intelligence Agency. *World Factbook 2000.* <http://www.odci.gov/cia/publications/factbook/index.html>. Accessed July 2001.

—*Michael Pretes and Rory Eames*

BURKINA FASO

Republic of Burkina Faso
Burkina Faso Jamahiriya

ulation is still the largest ethnic group in Burkina Faso, accounting for nearly half of the total population. There are many other groups, but the most significant are the Gurmanche, who are related to the Mossi group and are located in various parts of the country; the Gurunsi in the South; the Bwa, Bobo, Lobi, Senufo, Marka, and the Samo in the West; and the Fulfulde (otherwise known as the Fulani) in the North. Ethnic relations are generally relaxed, with few, if any, overt ethnic hostilities.

A large number of Burkinabe work in neighboring countries, though Cote d'Ivoire (originally the most popular with migrant workers) has become less welcoming recently.

COUNTRY OVERVIEW

LOCATION AND SIZE. Burkina Faso is a landlocked West African state. With a total border length of 3,192 kilometers (1,984 miles), Burkina Faso is bordered by Mali to the north and west; Niger to the east; and Benin, Togo, Ghana, and Cote d'Ivoire to the south. It has a land area of 274,122 square kilometers (105,839 square miles), making it slightly larger than the U.S. state of Colorado. The country spans 400 kilometers (250 miles) from east to west and 200 kilometers (125 miles) from north to south. The capital, Ouagadougou, is located in the center of the nation.

POPULATION. The population was estimated at 12.3 million in 2001, with a growth rate of 2.7 percent per year. The country's population density stands at 42 people per square kilometer (109 people per square mile), but the population is unevenly distributed, with the north and east regions being sparsely populated. About 17 percent of the total population live in urban areas, but the urban population is growing at a rate of 11.3 percent per year.

The country is ethnically diverse. In pre-colonial times it was part of the Mossi Empire, and the Mossi pop-

OVERVIEW OF ECONOMY

Burkina Faso is estimated to be one of the 20 poorest countries in the world. The **gross national product (GNP) per capita**, as measured by the **exchange rate** conversion, is estimated at approximately US$240. The **purchasing power parity** conversion (which makes allowance for the low price of many basic commodities in Burkina Faso) estimates per capita income at US$1,000 (2000 est.). This amount can be compared with an average per capita income of US$36,200 in the United States in the same year.

The economy depends very heavily on agriculture, which accounted for 26 percent of the GDP in 1998. Approximately 90 percent of the population depend on subsistence agriculture, as even urban dwellers maintain strong links to the countryside. The main food crops are sorghum, millet, maize, and groundnuts. The Burkinabe economy also relies on the export of gold, cotton, and livestock. Industry, although it provides 27 percent of the GDP, is not extensive and consists mainly of mining and some manufacturing (soap, soft drinks, beer, and

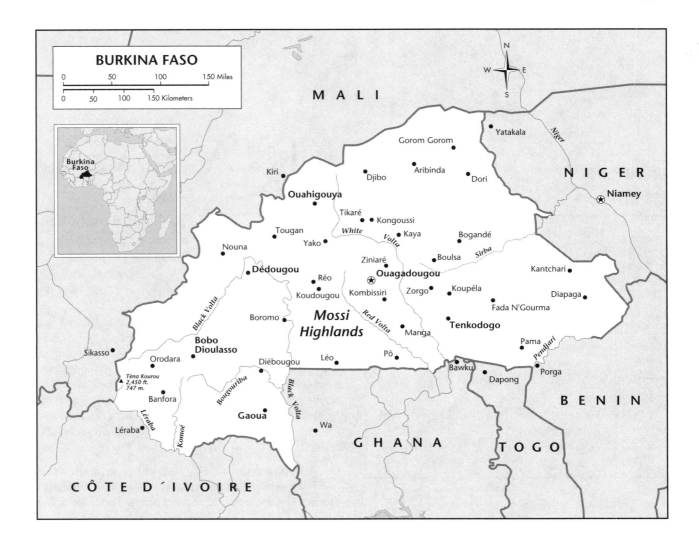

household utensils). In 1998 **retail** and wholesale trade generated about 12 percent of the GDP and transport and communications approximately 10 percent, and the total contribution to the GDP by the service sector stood at 47 percent. Despite major fluctuations, Burkina Faso's GDP growth has kept pace with population growth over the past decade. The GDP growth rate was estimated at 5 percent in 2000.

Following a coup that brought Thomas Sankara to power in 1983, Burkina Faso instituted a centralized economy. The Burkinabe government eventually succumbed to international pressure and agreed to a **structural adjustment program** with the International Monetary Fund (IMF) in 1991. This agreement led to the implementation in 1993 of the first of 3 Enhanced Structural Adjustment Facilities (ESAFs), the last of which started in 1999. The programs call for **privatization** of the state run sector, **liberalization** of the major trading sectors, reform and rationalization of banking, greater in-

centives for **private sector** development, and tighter controls on public spending and revenue collection.

The IMF has been pleased with Burkina Faso's progress. A further ESAF was granted for 1999 to 2002 to allow for more civil service **restructuring**, increased privatization, the liberalization of the cotton sector, strengthening of the judiciary, the implementation of the common external **tariff** with other West African Economic and Monetary Union (UEMOA) states, and the improvement of health-care and education provisions. By May 2000, 22 state enterprises had been privatized, 8 were up for sale, and a further 12 had been liquidated.

Burkina Faso's taxable capacity is very low due to the limited extent of commercial activity. Many past governments have tried to cut spending, but the unavoidable expenditure on development, the high cost of **debt servicing**, and rising wages have proved obstacles. Fiscal reform is thus a priority under the ESAFs, and the government will attempt to widen its tax base, rationalize **direct taxes**, reinforce **value-added tax** (VAT) collection, and reform custom **duties**. The government has pledged to stabilize current spending while improving spending on priority areas—health, education, and social services.

Burkina Faso's economic performance depends very much on agriculture, which in turn depends upon the weather, all of which means that the nation's economy tends to fluctuate. Inadequate and unreliable data also restrict proper analysis of the macro economy, although the situation is improving.

The Ministry of Finance indicated **real GDP** growth at 2.6 percent in the years 1986 to 1990, which was close to the rate of population growth. The strong economic expansion of 1991 was reversed in the years 1992 to 1994. The **devaluation** of the CFA franc in 1994 did not boost growth that year, but the economy grew by 4 percent in 1995, by 5.7 percent from 1996 to 1998, and by 5.8 percent in 1999.

Investment has been consistently high in recent years. The World Bank estimated investment to be 29 percent of the GDP in 1998, marking an increase from 17 percent since 1980. The **public sector** provides half to two-thirds of all investment, much of which is financed by aid, mostly from France. Economic aid totals 16 percent of the GDP.

Prices rose by 25 percent in 1994, but **inflation** fell rapidly the following year to 5.3 percent and remained at that rate until the end of 1998, and then dropped even further to -1.1 percent in 1999. Normally domestic price levels are determined by harvests, and import prices have been kept down by the strong CFA franc. Nonetheless higher prices for certain goods, such as medicines, have hit the population hard.

POLITICS, GOVERNMENT, AND TAXATION

The state of Burkina Faso consists of an area that was controlled by the Mossi from the 14th century until 1895, when the French took control. It was made part of the Franc Zone and it was named Upper Volta in 1919 after having been marked out from the surrounding territory. It was divided in the 1930s to form 2 states but returned to a single unit in 1947, changes which led to the border disputes with Mali. Burkina Faso became independent in 1960 under President Maurice Yameogo.

The first administration ended due to economic decline, corruption, and increasing authoritarianism. Rigged elections caused public demonstrations and led to military intervention in January 1966, when General Sangoule Lamizana became the head of a military ruling council. He remained in control for 15 years, despite some civilian power-sharing in the 1970s. Party bickering and trade union unrest led to a bloodless coup in 1980,

bringing Colonel Saye Zerbo to power. In 1982, when the constitution was suspended, political parties were banned amid corruption allegations. Army officers replaced Zerbo with Major Jean-Baptiste Ouedraogo as president. The regime that followed was an uneasy coalition of army conservatives and young radicals.

The attempted ousting of Prime Minister Thomas Sankara in 1983 led to student, labor, and young officer unrest. Sankara himself became president via a coup, and the National Revolutionary Council (CNR) was formed. The CNR championed the redistribution of wealth to rural areas. Sankara renamed the country Burkina Faso in 1984. He aimed to reduce foreign dependence, shift the economy towards the productive sectors, and expand health care and education. Internal divisions unsettled Sankara's support, and in October 1987 Sankara and 13 of his entourage were killed in a violent coup by the self-proclaimed Popular Front. The party was led by Captain Campaore, who then declared himself head of state. The continuing violence employed by his regime led to diminishing internal support and international condemnation. International concern further increased in 1989 when 2 former ministers and 2 army officers were executed for plotting a coup to overthrow the Campaore regime.

Starting in 1990 and amid protests, Campaore opened the way for the liberalization of the regime. However, the government refused to convene a national conference with the opposition and drew up a new constitution on its own terms for multiparty elections. The constitution was approved in a referendum in 1991, albeit with a poor turnout. Campaore's ODP-MT party renounced its **Marxist**-Leninist ideology and embraced free enterprise policies instead. The opposition parties boycotted the December 1991 presidential election, and Campaore stood unopposed, winning on a 25 percent voter turnout.

The ruling alliance also dominated the 1991 legislative election, with the ODP-MT party winning 78 out of 107 seats in parliament and the fragmented opposition winning only 23. In 1996, ODP-MT absorbed several smaller parties (including some opposition parties) and formed the new Congress for Democracy and Progress (CDP). With state office, large resources, and some opposition parties on their side, the CDP dominated the legislative election of 1997, winning 101 of 111 seats. Campaore was reelected in 1998 with a 56 percent turnout and 87 percent of the vote, with some of the opposition boycotting the elections.

In 1991, the constitution formally separated the state from the ruling party by creating separate executive, judiciary, and legislative branches; basing the government on a multiparty system; and ensuring freedom of the press. A civilian president would be inaugurated for a 5-year term. Although the president was only eligible to be reelected once in the original constitution, this was changed to allow a president to be reelected indefinitely. However, following public protest, this amendment was changed back in 2000 so that any president may now only be reelected once. In 2000, the Supreme Court was split into 3 High Courts, which oversee the judicial system, administration, and the audit of public finances.

The president selects the prime minister, subject to parliamentary approval. A parliament of 111 seats sits for 5 years. The constitution also allows for a 174 seat representative chamber.

Although salaried workers only account for a small percentage of the population, they exert a significant political effect due to unionization and their location near legislative centers. Students, who can also be a political influence, staged a 3-month strike in 1997 over political killings.

The presidential guard is a major force in Burkina Faso, although the transition to formal civilian rule and the loss of their uniforms has led to a reduction in their influence. However, tensions still exist in the military and the possibility of a future coup cannot be ruled out, especially in light of public protests in 1999.

Burkina Faso is a member of the Economic Community of West African States (ECOWAS) and UEMOA. The UEMOA headquarters are based in Burkina Faso. Relations with Côte d'Ivoire have become increasingly difficult, with the latter wishing to curb migration from Burkina Faso. Relations with Mali have been controlled since a brief border dispute, but Campaore's support of rebel factions in Liberia and Sierra Leone has irritated his neighbors.

There is little recent information on taxation. In the 1980s, Burkina Faso raised tax revenue equivalent to 10 percent of the GDP, mostly from import duties. A further 1 percent of the GDP was received from the surpluses of state-owned enterprises, mostly the big utilities that operated as **monopolies**. With increased privatiza-

tion, this source of revenue has diminished in importance. The government spends 30 percent of its revenue on social services (including health and education), about 30 percent on the armed forces, and the remaining 40 percent is absorbed by general administration.

INFRASTRUCTURE, POWER, AND COMMUNICATIONS

Despite recent investment, the transport system is poorly developed. Given that the country is landlocked, the nearest ports are found in Cote d'Ivoire, Benin, and Togo. The government is undertaking a US$360 million World Bank program to create a coherent policy and a regulatory framework for **infrastructure**, rehabilitate the road and rail network, and restructure the state transport system.

There are 13,200 kilometers (8,202 miles) of classified roads in Burkina Faso, of which 1,800 kilometers (1,119 miles) are paved. The former state bus company has been privatized and now runs 5 main routes throughout the country. The 1,260-kilometer (783-mile) Abidjan-Niger railway is the main transport axis, although the line has not recently operated efficiently, and rail traffic is in decline. Burkina Faso's 622 kilometers (387 miles) of line are scheduled for restructuring. In 1995 a French dominated company took control of the railroad, and the line is anticipated to be rehabilitated with a US$31 million World Bank loan.

The country has 2 international airports, and several regional carriers operate international services. The former **parastatal**, Air Burkina, has been bought by the Aga Khan's business group (the Aga Khan is the leader of the Ismailis, a Muslim sect originating in the Indian subcontinent), and is undergoing overhaul and expansion.

The main government newspaper is *Sidwaya,* but there are several private papers. Since legislation allowing opposition parties, several short-lived political newspapers have come and gone.

Communications									
Country	Newspapers	Radios	TV Sets[a]	Cable subscribers[a]	Mobile Phones[a]	Fax Machines[a]	Personal Computers[a]	Internet Hosts[b]	Internet Users[b]
	1996	1997	1998	1998	1998	1998	1998	1999	1999
Burkina Faso	1	33	9	N/A	0	N/A	0.7	0.19	4
United States	215	2,146	847	244.3	256	78.4	458.6	1,508.77	74,100
Nigeria	24	223	66	N/A	0	N/A	5.7	0.00	100
Ghana	14	238	99	N/A	1	N/A	1.6	0.06	20

[a]Data are from International Telecommunication Union, *World Telecommunication Development Report 1999* and are per 1,000 people.
[b]Data are from the Internet Software Consortium (http://www.isc.org) and are per 10,000 people.
SOURCE: World Bank. *World Development Indicators 2000.*

Radio broadcasts in French and local dialects are a major form of government communication. There are 17 FM stations, 2 AM stations, and 1 SW station that broadcast to 370,000 radio receivers. In 1997, 103,000 televisions received programs from Burkina Faso's 1 TV station.

The telephone network is very small, with only 42,000 subscribers. The state telecommunications company, Onatel, is expected to be privatized and the domestic market will be liberalized, although Onatel will have a monopoly on international calls.

Burkina Faso is predominantly dependent on thermally generated energy. The National Grid Group, a leading international electricity and telecommunications organization, only covers 4 percent of the population. Sonabel, the national electric company, produced 305 million kilowatt hours (kWh) in 1997, of which two-thirds was thermally produced and one-third was hydro-electrically produced. Construction has begun on a new dam, but the cost of electricity production is still significantly higher in Burkina Faso than in neighboring countries. Although the government is not planning Sonabel's privatization, the market will be liberalized and companies will be able to compete for production and distribution with Sonabel.

Consumption of petrol products is low, and wood fuel provides over 90 percent of domestic energy. The government is trying to promote butane in order to slow deforestation.

ECONOMIC SECTORS

The relative sizes of the main sectors of the economy—agriculture, industry, and services—have barely changed

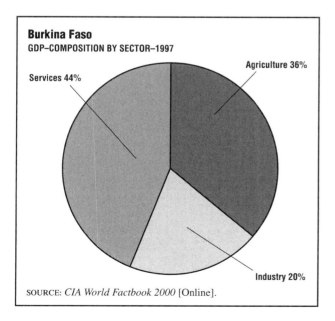

Burkina Faso
GDP–COMPOSITION BY SECTOR–1997

Services 44%
Agriculture 36%
Industry 20%

SOURCE: *CIA World Factbook 2000* [Online].

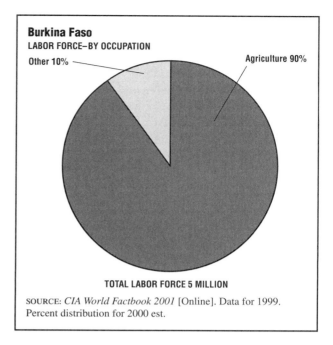

Burkina Faso
LABOR FORCE–BY OCCUPATION

Other 10%
Agriculture 90%

TOTAL LABOR FORCE 5 MILLION

SOURCE: *CIA World Factbook 2001* [Online]. Data for 1999. Percent distribution for 2000 est.

since independence in 1960. The industrial sector contracted during the period of Marxist control of the economy from 1983 to 1991, and the agriculture sector expanded as more people relied on subsistence agriculture to meet their day-to-day needs, but there has been a reversal of these trends in the past decade.

The economy is heavily dependent on agriculture to provide livelihoods for its population. Although the agriculture sector (including hunting, forestry, and fishing) provided only 26 percent of the GDP in 1998, it employed about 90 percent of the workforce. Industry (including mining, manufacturing, construction, and power) contributed 27 percent of the GDP in 1998 but occupied 2 percent of the workforce. Services contributed 47 percent of the GDP in 1998 and employed 6 percent of the population. The agriculture sector is much larger than those of most African nations, which on average generate 17 percent of GDP. Burkina Faso's industry and service sectors are smaller than average (in Africa they generally would produce 34 percent and 50 percent of GDP, respectively).

AGRICULTURE

Agriculture and livestock provide a living for approximately 90 percent of the population. However, due to the climatic variations in rainfall and because there are few permanent watercourses, irrigation is limited to only 15,000 hectares (37,067 acres) of the nation's total 3.27 million hectares (8.1 million acres). Soil quality varies, though it is generally better in the southwest of the country. Cotton, shea nuts, millet, and sorghum are grown in the central Mossi plateau. Livestock is the main source of livelihood in the north, with 18 million head and providing around 15 percent of exports in 1998.

The lack of advanced technology also hinders farming in a poor environment. Only 36 percent of farmers have links with extension services, and only 30 percent own either a plough or traction animals. Fertilizer is used almost exclusively on **cash crops**. Land holdings are also very small. An extended household may farm around 9.6 hectares (24 acres) in total, but plot sizes are small, with each plot averaging only 0.4 hectares (1 acre). This means that Burkina Faso can easily fall below self-sufficiency in food production, especially in the north where the rains may come late or there may be a drought.

The main staple crops are rain-fed millet and sorghum. Maize is grown in increasing amounts, however, and vegetables are also produced in significant quantities. Attempts to boost rice production (for example, through public irrigation) doubled its production to 94,000 metric tons in 2000. The main export, cotton, has seen a revival in recent years, reaching a high of 338,000 metric tons in the 1997–98 season. It has since fallen in both the 1998–99 and 1999–2000 seasons due to farmers' debt repayments, a depressed world market, and poor weather.

Timber production is negligible, although forest and woodland cover some 50 percent of Burkina Faso. Much deforestation has taken place as a result of firewood collection and has only been partially offset by campaigns to promote tree planting. In 1991 the government launched a long-term management program to maintain the environment.

The fish catch of 6,000 to 7,000 metric tons per year, taken from rivers, dams, and ponds, is much lower than the estimated consumed figure of 13,000 metric tons. Inland fish farms are being developed.

INDUSTRY

Primary components of Burkina Faso's industrial sector are manufacturing, mining, and construction. Construction has enjoyed a boom as a result of international and government based infrastructure development schemes. Road building and the provision of water supplies are major government priorities and provide a further stimulus to construction.

MANUFACTURING. Manufacturing focuses predominantly on food processing, textiles, and substitutes for **consumer goods** imports. It is mainly concentrated in the Ouagadougou, Bobo-Dioulasso, Koudougou, and Banfora regions. There are about 100 companies in Burkina Faso, and most are publicly owned. Manufacturing accounts for 20 percent of the GDP but only employs around 1 percent of the workforce. Growth has been limited by the lack of materials, the need to import fuel, and the small domestic market. The sector was in trouble from 1985 to 1995, with an average contraction of 5.8 percent per year but has shown some signs of recovery in food processing and metalworking since 1995. However, companies in Burkina Faso are worried they will not be able to compete as regional trade is liberalized.

The agro-industry accounts for 55 percent of **value-added** manufacturing in Burkina Faso. Sosuco (the former sugar parastatal), now owned by the Aga Khan, is the single biggest employer with 1,800 workers. The company has suffered recently from the competition of cheap imports and, due to its inability to pay wages, endured repeated union strikes in 1999. The government agreed to place a ceiling of 1,000 metric tons on any sugar or rice imports, tripled the import tax on sugar, and imposed a new **levy** on sugar imports, thereby making foreign costs equal local costs in order to help the industry.

The second largest component of the manufacturing sector is textiles (including leather goods), which contributed 21 percent of value-added manufacturing in 1998. The largest textile company in Burkina Faso, Sofitex, employs 700 people and produces mostly for the domestic market. The company also exports 25 percent of its production regionally.

MINING. Burkina Faso has large unexploited mineral deposits, as one-quarter of its land is comprised of sedimentary formations from volcanoes. In 1993 the mining code was revised to encourage private investment, and the mining institutions have been restructured. Between 1992 and 1998 the government issued 180 prospecting licenses to 30 foreign and local companies. However, interest slackened in 1999 following the dip in world oil prices.

The third largest export, gold is by far the most important commodity mined in Burkina Faso. Yet Burkina Faso's gold output has remained stagnant in recent years. Underground exploitation of the Poura gold mine, which has a 26,000-kilogram (57,300-pound) reserve, stopped in 1999. The government plans to restructure the mine before reopening and privatizing it.

SERVICES

The services sector consists mainly of wholesale and retail distribution, telecommunications, posts, transport, hotels and restaurants, repairs, financial services, tourist services, and government administration. For the most part, the service sector responds to the general growth of the economy. The size of the distribution sector has remained constant at around 12 percent of the GDP, and the transport and communications sectors have likewise remained constant at 10 percent.

BANKING AND FINANCE. Since the early 1990s banking has undergone restructuring, and the government has been limited to 25 percent participation. Of the 3 commercial banks, Banque Internationale du Burkina Faso has completed its reforms; the Banque Nationale de Developpement du Burkina is being liquidated; and Banque pour le Financement du Commerce et des Investissements du Burkina (BFCIB) has been privatized. Banking regulation is also being tightened by the Banque Centrale des Etats de l'Afrique de l'Ouest (BCEAO), the regional central bank.

TOURISM. Problems of communication and poor facilities mean mass tourism is not yet an option in Burkina Faso. However, the country does have some attractions to offer visitors; it is host of the Biennial National Culture Week, the Pan African Film Festival, and the International Handicrafts Fair. National parks are also of interest. Given its central West African position, the country has also become a common location for regional conferences. In 1997, tourism receipts reached US$22 million and accounted for 9 percent of the GDP.

INTERNATIONAL TRADE

Burkina Faso's **trade deficit** fluctuates, rising in poor harvest years. The trade deficit reached a high point in 1990 at US$262 million but was reduced to US$164 million in 1994, mainly due to the CFA franc's devaluation. As imports recovered, the gap grew again to US$330 million in 1996 before receding in 1998 to US$261 million, primarily due to improved cotton exports.

Principal exports in 1998 were cotton (66 percent), livestock (8 percent), hides and skins (6 percent), and gold (5 percent). The main destinations of exports were France (15 percent), Cote d'Ivoire (10 percent), Indonesia (6 percent), Taiwan (3 percent), and Ghana (3 percent).

Principal imports in 1998 were machinery and transport equipment (29 percent), food products (13 percent), and petroleum products (12 percent). Most of the remaining imports were other types of consumer manufactures. The main origins of imports were France (28 percent), Cote d'Ivoire (19 percent), Japan (5 percent), and Italy (4 percent).

MONEY

Burkina Faso is part of the 8-member West African economic union, UEMOA, and the currency is the CFA franc. The regional central bank, BCEAO, issues currency notes and regulates credit expansion. The CFA franc was pegged to the French franc at 50:1 in 1948 but was overvalued by the late 1980s and was devalued to CFA Fr 100:1 French franc. With this devaluation, much of the benefit coming from confidence in a stable rate of exchange with the French franc was lost. However, the devaluation raised the domestic price of export crops, which improved output and raised export revenue, and made imports more expensive and resulted in lower import expenditures. With France having joined the European Monetary Union, the CFA franc is now tied to the euro at CFA Fr655.959:1 euro. Inflation averaged less than 3 percent per year from 1996 to 2000. The **inflation rate** was estimated at 1.5 percent in 2000.

A regional stock exchange has been established, the Bourse Regionale de Valeurs Mobilieres, that serves Benin, Burkina Faso, Cote d'Ivoire, Guinea Bissau, Mali, Niger, Senegal, and Togo. There are branches in each of the 8-member countries. To date, only companies in Cote d'Ivoire and Senegal are listed on the exchange.

Trade (expressed in billions of US$): Burkina Faso		
	Exports	Imports
1975	.044	.151
1980	.090	.359
1985	.071	.332
1990	.152	.536
1995	.160	.455
1998	N/A	N/A

SOURCE: International Monetary Fund. *International Financial Statistics Yearbook 1999.*

Exchange rates: Burkina Faso	
Communaute Financiere Africaine francs (CFA Fr) per US$1	
Jan 2001	699.21
2000	711.98
1999	615.70
1998	589.95
1997	583.67
1996	511.55

Note: From January 1, 1999, the CFA Fr is pegged to the euro at a rate of 655.957 CFA Fr per euro.

SOURCE: CIA *World Factbook 2001* [ONLINE].

GDP per Capita (US$)

Country	1975	1980	1985	1990	1998
Burkina Faso	196	207	224	225	259
United States	19,364	21,529	23,200	25,363	29,683
Nigeria	301	314	230	258	256
Ghana	411	394	328	352	399

SOURCE: United Nations. *Human Development Report 2000;*
Trends in human development and per capita income.

POVERTY AND WEALTH

Burkina Faso is a low-income country, but there are no official poverty figures. However, average income per capita in the rural areas is estimated to be near the poverty level, and it can be concluded that probably more than 60 percent of the population are in poverty. The overwhelming majority of the impoverished live in the rural areas, relying on agricultural production from small family farms or herding family-based livestock for their livelihood. To be below the established dollar-a-day poverty level means that a person does not have enough income to provide the barest minimum of food, clothing, and shelter. In 1995, Burkina Faso was ranked 172 out of 174 countries in the United Nations Human Development Index, which combines measures of income, health, and education.

In 1998, 41 percent of Burkinabe children attended primary school, 10 percent attended secondary school, and only 1 percent attended schools of higher education. The pupil to teacher ratio climbed to 51:1 in 1998, and figures indicated that only 19 percent of the population over the age of 15 were literate in 1995 (30 percent of males and 9 percent of females). Health care has improved since independence, though it is still very poor. The infant mortality rate stands at 107 deaths per 1,000 live births (2001 est.), compared to a rate of 7 deaths per

Distribution of Income or Consumption by Percentage Share: Burkina Faso

Lowest 10%	2.2
Lowest 20%	5.5
Second 20%	8.7
Third 20%	12.0
Fourth 20%	18.7
Highest 20%	55.0
Highest 10%	39.5

Survey year: 1994
Note: This information refers to expenditure shares by percentiles of the population and is ranked by per capita expenditure.

SOURCE: *2000 World Development Indicators* [CD-ROM].

1,000 live births in the United States. Life expectancy is 47 years (2001 est.).

WORKING CONDITIONS

The **labor force** of Burkina Faso numbers 4.7 million and includes people 10 years of age and older. The government is the largest formal employer with about 40,000 public sector workers. A large proportion of the male labor force migrates annually to neighboring countries for seasonal employment. There are no official unemployment figures for Burkina Faso, but regardless, these figures would have little significance in such a low-income economy. Although there may be few people considered as unemployed, many of these people only live off **subsistence farming**. There are no unemployment benefits, and those who do not work rely on support from charities or their families. Many people would like a modern sector job but are forced instead to survive by working on their family farms or in casual **informal sector** activities in the urban areas (such as **hawking**, portering, and scavenging).

A labor court enforces the rights of workers as detailed in the national labor code, and trade unions are legal. The modern sector has a workforce of about 450,000, of which 40,000 are civil servants. Trade union membership is 60 percent in the public sector and 50 percent among private sector employees. Although union participation is small in relation to the total population, since there is such strong membership among workers and because the unions are strategically located in the modern sector and in the urban areas, they have considerable power when they exercise their right to strike.

The relatively high GDP growth from 1995 onwards has improved living standards only marginally. The guaranteed minimum industrial wage remained at US$0.44 per hour from 1988 to 1994. It increased by 10 percent after the devaluation of the CFA franc in 1994. Trade unions only gained a 3 to 5 percent rise in public sector salaries in 1996 and another 5 to 10 percent in 1999.

The Constitution of the Fourth Republic of Burkina Faso guarantees the collective and individual political and social rights of the country's citizens.

COUNTRY HISTORY AND ECONOMIC DEVELOPMENT

1300–1895. As Upper Volta, Burkina Faso is part of the Mossi Empire.

1895. France colonizes a broad area containing Burkina Faso.

1947. Burkina Faso becomes a recognized territory.

1960. Independence is gained from France, and Maurice Yameogo becomes the first president.

1966. Following a coup, General Sangoule Lamizana becomes president.

1970. A civilian government is elected to serve under Lamizana.

1974. The army assumes power under Lamizana.

1978. Multiparty elections are held. Lamizana is elected president.

1980. A coup brings Colonel Saye Zerbo to power.

1982. Zerbo is deposed, and Major Jean-Baptiste Ouedraogo becomes president.

1983. Prime Minister Thomas Sankara seizes presidential power.

1984. Upper Volta is renamed Burkina Faso.

1985. A 6-day war with Mali occurs.

1987. Sankara is assassinated, and Captain Blaise Campaore becomes president.

1991. A new constitution is adopted by a referendum.

1991. Campaore is reelected president in an unopposed election; the opposition boycotts the election.

1993. Enhanced Structural Adjustment Facility (ESAF) is signed with the IMF.

1994. The CFA franc is devalued, raising prices to producers of exports and raising the price of imports, thereby avoiding a period of higher inflation.

1998. Campaore is reelected as president in a contested election. The assassination of newspaper editor and popular antigovernment critic, Norbert Zongo, sparks civil unrest.

1999. There is a general 1-day strike over privatization, low salaries, and the assassination of Zongo. The government responds with a program to promote unity and national reconcilation.

2000. In all, 22 state-owned enterprises are privatized.

2001. Burkina Faso suffers severe drought.

FUTURE TRENDS

Militancy on the part of trade unions and human rights organizations is likely to continue, despite concessions announced by President Campaore in 1999. These concessions include setting up an inquiry into the death of Norbert Zongo, assuring the military that their delayed housing allowances will be paid in installments, and appointing a new prime minister who has incorporated members of the opposition into his cabinet.

The new prime minister, Paramango Ernest Yonoli, appointed in October 2000, will have to prove himself to the public, particularly with regard to the task of carrying out privatization and civil service reforms in the face of trade union opposition. Yonoli announced a new cabinet that includes figures from the moderate opposition parties. Teacher and student protests have thrown the school system into chaos, and the University of Ouagadougou has been closed since the riots that followed Zongo's death. Civic groups and opposition parties have also kept up the pressure for justice. Three presidential guards finally have been imprisoned over the assassination of Zongo, but this will hardly satisfy the opposition, who want those senior figures in the government that were behind the assassination to be brought to justice.

Despite international economic aid, GDP growth is expected to slow to 4 percent in 2001, due mainly to civil unrest, which creates a climate of political instability and discourages investment, and the impact of the drought, which has resulted in poor harvests. Prospects for cotton earnings will remain sluggish, but **debt relief** is under way under World Bank and IMF supervision. Aid from these organizations in the form of a Heavily Indebted Poor Country (HIPC) initiative should help Burkina Faso's situation.

DEPENDENCIES

Burkina Faso has no territories or colonies.

BIBLIOGRAPHY

A la découverte du Burkina Faso. <http://www.primature.gov.bf>. Accessed October 2001.

"Burkina Faso: Economy." *NewAfrica.* <http://www.newafrica.com/profiles/economy.asp?countryid=8>. Accessed September 2001.

Economist Intelligence Unit. *Country Profile: Burkina Faso.* London, England: EIU, 2000.

Embassy of Burkina Faso. <http://www.burkinaembassy-usa.org>. Accessed October 2001.

Hodd, M. "Burkina Faso." *The Economies of Africa.* Aldershot, England: Dartmouth Publishing, 1991.

Kelly, R. C., et al., editors. "Burkina Faso Country Review 1999/2000." *CountryWatch.com.* <http://www.CountryWatch.com>. Accessed September 2001.

U.S. Central Intelligence Agency. *World Factbook 2001.* <http://www.cia.gov/cia/publications/factbook/geos/uv.html> Accessed October 2001.

U.S. Department of State. *Background Notes: Burkina Faso, March 1998.* <http://www.state.gov/www/background_notes/burkina_0398_bgn.html>. Accessed October 2001.

—Jack Hodd

BURUNDI

Republic of Burundi
République du Burundi
Republika yu Burundi

CAPITAL: Bujumbura.

MONETARY UNIT: Burundi Franc (BFr). The largest Burundian note in circulation is BFr5,000 and the smallest is BFr10. There are also BFr20, 50, 100, 500, 1,000, and 5,000 notes. The only coins in circulation are BFr1, 5, and 10.

CHIEF EXPORTS: Coffee, tea, cotton, cigarettes, soft drinks, and beer.

CHIEF IMPORTS: Cement, asphalt, petroleum, fertilizer, pesticides, textiles, and vehicles.

GROSS DOMESTIC PRODUCT: US$885 million (purchasing power parity, 1998 est.). [Source: *2000 World Development Indicators*. Washington, D.C.: World Bank, 2000.]

BALANCE OF TRADE: Exports: US$56 million (1999 est.). Imports: US$108 million (1999 est.).

Approximately 99 percent of the citizens of Burundi are Rundi (or Barundi) and speak Kirundi. Kirundi and French are the country's official languages. Ethnic groups include the Hutu (85 percent), Tutsi (14 percent), and Twa (1 percent). Due to conflict between the Hutu and Tutsi ethnic groups, and among different Tutsi groups, the country experienced mass **emigration** of refugees. Many people fled to neighboring Rwanda, Tanzania, and the Democratic Republic of Congo, hoping to avoid violence. The net emigration rate was estimated to be 7.43 emigrants per 1,000 people in 2000.

Burundi has a very young population with 47 percent aged 14 or younger and just 3 percent aged 65 or older. As the younger half of the population grows to maturity and reproduces, Burundi's already high population density of 260 per square kilometer (100 per square mile) is expected to reach dangerous levels. However, the terrifying death toll of the AIDS epidemic may retard such population growth.

It is estimated that 39,000 Burundians died from AIDS in 1999 and 30 percent of all 25–29 year olds were HIV positive. The national rate of HIV infection stood at 11.32 percent. The social and economic costs of the disease are high. For example, the drawn out nature of death from AIDS requires a large amount of care and attention. As a result many of the population (mostly women) who could be employed are instead providing long-term care for the dying. In addition, by 1999 the estimated number of orphans created due to AIDS in Burundi reached 230,000.

COUNTRY OVERVIEW

LOCATION AND SIZE. Burundi is a landlocked state in Central Africa, east of the Democratic Republic of Congo, south of Rwanda, and west of Tanzania. It has an area of 27,830 square kilometers (10,745 square miles), slightly smaller than Maryland. Burundi's capital city, Bujumbura, is located on the shore of Lake Tanganyika near the country's border with the Democratic Republic of Congo.

POPULATION. The United Nations Economic Commission for Africa estimated Burundi's population at 6.97 million in 2000, growing at an annual rate of 2.5 percent. In 2000 the birth rate stood at 40.46 births per 1,000 population while the death rate was 16.44 deaths per 1,000. The population is expected to reach 10.37 million by 2015 and 16.94 million by 2050. In 1999, only 9 percent of Burundians lived in urban habitats, which was one of the lowest levels of urbanization in Africa. About 67 percent of Burundians are Christians, mostly Roman Catholics, while 23 percent hold some form of indigenous beliefs, and 10 percent are Muslims.

OVERVIEW OF ECONOMY

Agricultural production dominates Burundi's national economy. During the colonial period (1899–1962) the German and Belgian administrations forced Burundi's

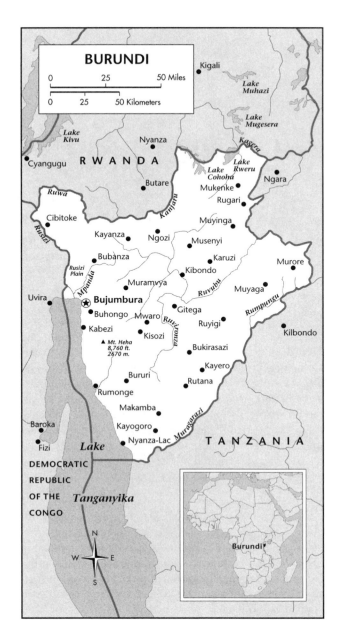

BURUNDI

0   25   50 Miles

0   25   50 Kilometers

RWANDA

Kigali

Lake Muhazi

Lake Mugesera

Lake Kivu

Nyanza

Cyangugu

Butare

Lake Cohoha

Lake Rweru

Ngara

Ruvu

Kanjaru

Mukenke

Rugari

Kayumba

Cibitoke

Muyinga

Kayanza   Ngozi   Musenyi

Bubanza   Karuzi

Rusizi Plain   Kibondo   Murore

Muramvya   Ruvubu

Muyaga

Uvira   Bujumbura   Gitega   Rumpungu

Buhongo   Mwaro

Kabezi   Kisozi   Ruyigi   Kilbondo

Mt. Heha 8,760 ft. 2670 m.

Bukirasazi

Kayero

Bururi   Rutana

Rumonge

Makamba

Baroka   Kayogoro

Fizi   *Lake*   Nyanza-Lac   Muragarazi

DEMOCRATIC   *Tanganyika*   TANZANIA

REPUBLIC

OF THE

CONGO

N   W   E   S

Burundi

workers to produce goods like coffee and tea for export to Europe. This pattern of production continues, while the mining, manufacturing, and service sectors are less developed.

Violence and political conflict between the Tutsi and Hutu ethnic groups plagued Burundi after its independence from Belgium in 1962. By the 1990s the instability caused by civil war, Burundi's landlocked status, its colonial legacy, a limited material base, and the general decline of investment in Africa throughout the 1990s led to an overall collapse of the economy. In 1986 the government agreed to a program of economic **liberalization** with the International Monetary Fund (IMF) and the World Bank. However, a brief but brutal re-

sumption of ethnic massacres in 1988, and the resumption of the conflict in 1993, halted this program of economic development.

While Burundi's **gross domestic product** enjoyed an average annual growth rate of 4.4 percent between 1980–1990, during 1990–1999 the annual growth rate declined by an average of 2.9 percent. Agricultural production fell by 2 percent, industrial production fell by 6.7 percent, and services production fell by 2.5 percent annually during the 1990s. The failing economy was aggravated by an economic **embargo** imposed by regional and Western powers in an attempt to encourage Burundi's politicians to make peace. This embargo and economic instability contributed to the national economy's **balance of payments** deficit of US$54 million in 1998 and US$27 million in 1999.

In 1980 Burundi's total **external debt** stood at US$166 million, but with a government surplus of 9.8 percent of gross domestic product (including external aid) the country was able to pay interest on its debt. By 1998 Burundi's total external debt was US$1.12 billion while the government had a deficit equal to 5.4 percent of the gross domestic product. Burundi's financing of debt as a percentage of exports rose from 20.4 percent in 1985 to 40 percent in 1998, draining the foreign capital generated from exports. Due to the national crisis, external donors were reluctant to lend money to Burundi, and external aid per capita fell from US$53.1 in 1992 to US$11.6 in 1998. The country continues to rely on a decreasing level of foreign aid while it is unable to pay off debts. The **inflation rate** was recorded at 26 percent in 1999. At the dawn of the 21st century, Burundi was a country in deep economic crisis.

POLITICS, GOVERNMENT, AND TAXATION

Burundi was ruled by a king (mwami) from the 1500s until colonization. European colonial powers Germany (1899–1916) and Belgium (1916–62) forced Burundians to cultivate crops for European consumption (such as coffee and tea), to act as porters and laborers, and to pay taxes. When Burundi achieved independence in 1962, Belgium still influenced its government and politics. When legislative elections were held in 1961, a Tutsi-dominated party which included Hutus, the Parti de l'Unité et du Progrès National du Burundi (UPRONA), won 80 percent of the votes. Prince Louis Rwagasore was appointed Prime Minister, but at the end of 1961 Rwagasore was assassinated in a plot by the Belgian-sponsored Hutu party, the Parti du Peuple (PDC).

Burundi's main political parties are the multiethnic Front pour la démocratie au Burundi (FRODEBU),

UPRONA, and the militant Hutu party Parti de la libéra-tion du peuple hutu (PALIPEHUTU). The army is also of central importance in Burundi's politics, as are mili-tia groups, which are often linked to political parties. After an extensive period of military rule, Melchior Ndadaye of FRODEBU won 1993 multiparty elections with 65 percent of the vote. However, after only a few months President Ndadaye was assassinated by the Tutsi-dominated military. This led to a series of large-scale massacres of both Hutu and Tutsi by various mili-tias and the army.

In 1996 Major Pierre Buyoya became president af-ter a military coup. In 1998 Buyoya ushered in a new constitution, which gave executive powers to an elected president and gave legislative power to the 812-member elected Assembly. He led the creation of a 10-year power sharing agreement in 2000, which brought together many of Burundi's political and military organizations. However, a full compromise remained elusive despite mediation and financial inducements by the European Union and the United States. Over 300,000 people, mainly civilians, were killed between 1993 and 2000. Hundreds of thousands more were displaced, and over 0.5 million Hutus were forcibly relocated by the army to live in camps.

The revenue collecting capabilities of the Burundian government are minimal. Tax revenue as a percentage of gross domestic product amounted to only 12.7 percent in 1999, falling from a 1990 level of 16.3 percent. The IMF estimates that in 1998, taxes on goods and services amounted to 43.2 percent of government revenue, tax on international trade was 28.6 percent, and taxes on income and profits constituted 22.6 percent. The most important individual source of revenue was taxes on the brewing industry, which provided around 40 percent of total gov-ernment tax receipts. Petroleum provided around 8 per-cent of **indirect taxes**.

INFRASTRUCTURE, POWER, AND COMMUNICATIONS

Burundi's transport **infrastructure** is very limited. A crumbling network of 14,480 kilometers (8,998 miles) of roads, of which 1,028 kilometers (639 miles) are paved, is used by only 19,000 passenger cars and 12,300 commercial vehicles. In 2000 the World Bank encour-aged a 50 percent reduction of tanker trucks bringing in fuel to Burundi to reduce the erosion of the country's roads. A 30 percent refined petrol and diesel price rise at the beginning of 2000 helped to create a fuel shortage. The majority of Burundi's trade is conducted across Lake Tanganyika with the Democratic Republic of Congo. There is no rail infrastructure. As Burundi is landlocked it relies on the sea ports of Dar es Salaam in Tanzania and Mombasa in Kenya. Burundi has 1 international air-port, which is located at Bujumbura, while another 3 air-ports exist but are unpaved. Only 12,000 people traveled by air in Burundi in 1998.

Burundi's power needs are partially supplied by the **parastatal** Regideso. It controls 4 small hydroelectric power stations that produced 127 million kilowatt hours of electricity in 1998. Burundi is also an importer of elec-tricity which is drawn from hydroelectric plants in the Democratic Republic of Congo. Most of this power is consumed within Bujumbura. With only 17,000 tele-phone main lines, 343 mobile cellular phones in use by 1995, and no Internet hosts, Burundi's telecommunica-tions system was underdeveloped.

ECONOMIC SECTORS

Because Burundi is landlocked, its exports are costly. They also lose competitiveness due to the **tariffs** imposed on them from neighboring countries. The most important and largest sector in the economy is agriculture, both for the domestic supply of food and for the provision of

Communications

Country	Newspapers	Radios	TV Sets[a]	Cable subscribers[a]	Mobile Phones[a]	Fax Machines[a]	Personal Computers[a]	Internet Hosts[b]	Internet Users[b]
	1996	1997	1998	1998	1998	1998	1998	1999	1999
Burundi	3	71	4	N/A	0	0.7	N/A	0.00	2
United States	215	2,146	847	244.3	256	78.4	458.6	1,508.77	74,100
Dem. Rep. of Congo	3	375	135	N/A	0	N/A	N/A	0.00	1
Rwanda	0	102	0	N/A	1	0.1	N/A	0.00	5

[a]Data are from International Telecommunication Union, *World Telecommunication Development Report 1999* and are per 1,000 people.
[b]Data are from the Internet Software Consortium (http://www.isc.org) and are per 10,000 people.

SOURCE: World Bank. *World Development Indicators 2000.*

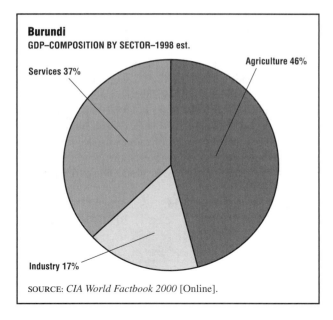

Burundi
GDP–COMPOSITION BY SECTOR–1998 est.

Agriculture 46%

Services 37%

Industry 17%

SOURCE: *CIA World Factbook 2000* [Online].

foreign currency through the export of coffee and tea. However, Burundi's dependence on agricultural commodities is a weakness since coffee and tea production are subject to the constant fluctuation of the weather, and the change of prices on international markets. The agricultural sector provided 46 percent of Burundi's GDP in 1998 and employed 93 percent of its people. Comparatively, industry contributed 17 percent of GDP and employed 1.5 percent, while services contributed 37 percent and employed 1.5 percent. Four percent of the country's workers are employed by the government.

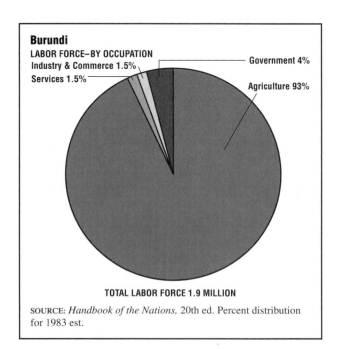

Burundi
LABOR FORCE–BY OCCUPATION
Industry & Commerce 1.5%
Services 1.5%

Government 4%

Agriculture 93%

TOTAL LABOR FORCE 1.9 MILLION

SOURCE: *Handbook of the Nations,* 20th ed. Percent distribution for 1983 est.

AGRICULTURE

Burundi's agricultural sector benefits from a mild climate due to high elevation of the land and regular rainfall. However, deforestation and poor farming methods have caused extensive soil erosion and depletion. It is estimated that there will be no more arable land left in Burundi by 2020, at current depletion rates. The agricultural sector provided 46 percent of GDP in 1998, and 93 percent of the **labor force** was employed in agricultural production. In the 10-year period from 1988–1997 Burundi produced an annual average of US$80 million of agricultural exports. The most important of these exports were **cash crops** such as coffee, tea, tobacco, and cotton.

The export of coffee accounts for around 80 percent of all export earnings. In 1992, 40,000 metric tons of Burundian coffee was sold abroad. However, due to the civil war and economic embargo, coffee exports dropped between 1993 and 1996 with an annual average export of only 18,500 tons. By 1997 the coffee sector recovered with 32,000 tons exported. Tea accounts for around 10 percent of all export earnings. Exports actually grew slightly during the civil war and economic embargo. Between 1988–1992 an annual average of 4,600 tons of dry green tea leaves were exported, yet between 1993–1997 an annual average of 5,400 tons was recorded. In 1999 the parastatal Office du Thé du Burundi raised the price of tea by 15 percent in order to encourage farmers to raise production for 2000. However, there was a price slump of both coffee and tea on international markets in 2000 and early 2001.

Burundi's major food crops consist of bananas, cassava, sorghum, rice, maize, and millet. Production of these crops was steady between 1989 and 1997 except for rice, which grew by more than 50 percent from 40,000 tons to 64,000 tons, and cassava, which grew from 569,000 tons to 610,000 tons. However, over the same 9-year period Burundi imported an average of US$16.4 million of food per year.

INDUSTRY

Industry is very limited in Burundi. The industrial sector accounted for 19 percent of GDP in 1990, but due to the instability caused by civil war this fell to 17 percent by 1998.

MINING. Burundi has extensive mineral reserves. By 2001, gold, tungsten, and cassiterite (tin ore) were mined on a small scale. One gold reserve was estimated to contain 60 tons of gold ore. It is estimated that about 5 percent of world nickel reserves are on Burundian territory, and there are significant reserves of uranium, platinum, and vanadium. Due to political instability, the country's landlocked status, and its limited infrastructure, many of these highly profitable mineral deposits remain untouched.

MANUFACTURING. Manufacturing is based in Bujumbara. Reaching a high of US$11 million of exports in 1992, manufacturing exports fell to US$1 million by 1997. Imports of manufactured goods heavily outweigh exports with US$55 million imported in 1992, falling to US$33 million in 1997.

A key manufacturing sector within Burundi's economy is the brewing of beer. In 1996, 40 percent of all government tax receipts were received from only 1 brewery, the Dutch- and government-owned company Brarudi. Due to rising **inflation** Brarudi lost money throughout 1998–1999. High inflation caused a rise in the price of raw material imports used to manufacture beer. Sales fell by 10 percent in 1999 due to the price increases that were passed on to consumers. Other products manufactured in the country include soft drinks, cigarettes, soap, glass, textiles, insecticides, cosmetics, cement, and some agricultural processing.

SERVICES

The service sector in Burundi is of minimal importance. Credit and banking services are limited and the **retail** sector is based on small trading and shops. Due to the instability caused by civil war the export of commercial services declined from US$7 million in 1990 to US$3 million in 1998.

TOURISM. Although Burundi has a great deal to offer tourists, such as rare wildlife, beautiful green mountainous landscapes, national parks, and access to one of Africa's largest lakes (Lake Tanganyika), terrible massacres and roaming militia members act as a considerable deterrent to tourists. In 1992, before the outbreak of the political crisis, 86,000 tourists arrived in Burundi (the majority from Africa and Europe), by 1996 only 26,670 were recorded entering the country.

INTERNATIONAL TRADE

Burundi's **balance of trade** showed an average annual deficit of US$39.5 million between 1985–1999. In 1999 the deficit stood at US$52 million on exports of US$56 million and imports of US$108 million. To counter this deficit the government consistently resorted to borrowing in order to maintain its spending levels. This led to greater indebtedness and a rise in annual debt repayment levels. Imports and exports were partially reduced in 1996 due to an embargo imposed by regional countries and the European Union in an attempt to force a peace agreement. However, due to smuggling to and from Burundi this embargo was soon rendered ineffective. At the outset of 1999 civil conflict had lessened in intensity, yet shortages of sugar and fuel raised the population's discontent.

Trade (expressed in billions of US$): Burundi		
	Exports	Imports
1975	.032	.062
1980	.065	.168
1985	.112	.189
1990	.075	.231
1995	.106	.234
1998	.065	.158

SOURCE: International Monetary Fund. *International Financial Statistics Yearbook 1999.*

The Economist Intelligence Unit estimated Burundi's principal imports in 1997 as US$70.4 million of **intermediate goods**, US$63.1 million of **capital goods**, US$55.1 million of food, and US$31.2 million in energy. The main origins of these imports were neighboring Tanzania which supplied 14.8 percent of the total, Kenya (14 percent), the United States (11.1 percent), Belgium-Luxembourg (8.3 percent), and Germany (5.1 percent). The import of refined petroleum products represented around 15 percent of Burundi's total imports, and took between 20–30 percent of all national foreign exchange earnings.

In 1997, Burundi's most important exports were coffee, which sold US$45.2 million, tea (US$20.7 million), hides (US$4.6 million), and cassiterite (US$3.7 million). Burundi's main export partners for these goods were based in the European Union. Belgium and Luxembourg consumed 36.1 percent of all Burundi's exports, while Germany consumed 20.6 percent. Other destinations for Burundi's exports were the Netherlands, which imported 4.1 percent, the United Kingdom (2 percent), and the United States (1 percent).

MONEY

Due to a lack of confidence in Burundi's national economy since the 1993 conflict, the Burundi franc (BFr) consistently declined in value against the U.S. dollar. In 1995, BFr249.76 bought US$1, while in 2000 a dollar was

Exchange rates: Burundi	
Burundi francs per US$1	
Jan 2001	782.36
2000	720.67
1999	563.56
1998	477.77
1997	352.35
1996	302.75

SOURCE: CIA *World Factbook 2001* [ONLINE].

the equivalent of BFr720.67. The decline in value of the Burundi franc meant that the average citizen was paying more and more in order to obtain even the most essential products. This process of inflation led to a rise in the price of **consumer goods** by 31 percent in 1997 and 17 percent in 1998. This meant that, in constant Burundi francs, the price of sugar rose from BFr230 in 1996 to BFr350 in 1999, and the price of petrol per liter rocketed from BFr165 to BFr350. In sum, inflation contributed considerably to the rise of extreme poverty between 1993 and 2000.

POVERTY AND WEALTH

With an annual average **GDP per capita** of US$730 in 1999, Burundi was one of the poorest countries in the world with 60 percent of the population living in conditions of extreme poverty. The vast majority of Burundians were farmers on small plots of land used for subsistence agriculture or for the cultivation of cash crops such as coffee and tea. The poorest 40 percent of the country controlled only 20 percent of the wealth, whereas the richest 40 percent controlled 63.7 percent. The government spent only 0.6 percent of its gross domestic product on health but 5.8 percent on military expenditures. The majority of Burundian citizens struggled to supply themselves and their families with even the most basic

GDP per Capita (US$)					
Country	1975	1980	1985	1990	1998
Burundi	162	176	198	206	147
United States	19,364	21,529	23,200	25,363	29,683
Dem. Rep. of Congo	392	313	293	247	127
Rwanda	233	321	312	292	227

SOURCE: United Nations. *Human Development Report 2000; Trends in human development and per capita income.*

Distribution of Income or Consumption by Percentage Share: Burundi

Lowest 10%	3.4
Lowest 20%	7.9
Second 20%	12.1
Third 20%	16.3
Fourth 20%	22.1
Highest 20%	41.6
Highest 10%	26.6

Survey year: 1992
Note: This information refers to expenditure shares by percentiles of the population and is ranked by per capita expenditure.

SOURCE: *2000 World Development Indicators* [CD-ROM].

health care, with only 6 doctors and 17 nurses per 100,000 people. The daily intake of calories for the average Burundian fell from 2,104 in 1970 to only 1,685 in 1997. Over the same period the daily supply of protein fell by 30.8 percent and the intake of fat by 26.7 percent.

WORKING CONDITIONS

In 1998, the minimum wage in Burundi for urban areas was US$0.37 a day and $0.24 a day for the rest of the country; this represents a considerable decline from the 1994 minimum wage of $0.63 and $0.42 respectively. Considering that inflation, nation-wide instability, and the economic embargo led to a dramatic price increase of consumer goods throughout the late 1990s, the decline of the minimum wage over the same period meant that Burundi's 4 million workers were having to pay more to survive with reduced means to do so. The very low level of organization and influence of trade unions and their division along ethnic and religious grounds meant that Burundi's workers lacked a sufficient mechanism to assert their rights against declining pay and poor working conditions.

The rate of illiteracy in Burundi gradually improved through the 1980s and 1990s. In 1985 illiteracy amongst the population aged 15 and above was 68 percent. By 1997 this had been reduced to 55 percent, but this was still 13 percent below the African average. This level of illiteracy worsened due to the civil war, which helped to reduce the level of primary school enrollment from 73 percent in 1990 to 54.2 percent in 1998. In addition, it will be difficult for a government with such limited revenue to provide sufficient education and vocational training for the large number of Burundi's youth. This has significant implications for the country's economic development as the labor force remains generally unskilled. The problem of an unskilled workforce will be accentuated by the AIDS epidemic, which hits the mature working sector the hardest.

COUNTRY HISTORY AND ECONOMIC DEVELOPMENT

1500s. Kingdom of Burundi is formed.

1885. Burundi is allocated to Germany at the Berlin Congress of European colonial powers.

1899. Burundi becomes a full military district of the German Empire.

1916. Belgium occupies Burundi in World War I.

1961. Prince Louis Rwagasore is elected president, and is assassinated less than 5 months later.

1961. Burundi gains independence and the ethnic violence begins.

1972. Massacre by the army and militias claims 200,000 lives and 150,000 Hutu flee the country.

1986. Burundi adopts a program of economic liberalization as prescribed by the IMF and World Bank.

1993. Assassination of democratically elected President Melchoir Ndadaye leads to civil war.

1996. Major Pierre Buyoya becomes president in a military coup.

FUTURE TRENDS

Even though Nelson Mandela and many others have attempted to assist Burundi's peace process it remains unlikely that a long-term solution will be found to the highly complex and tragic conflict in Burundi. This is in part due to the exclusion of certain Hutu militias from talks and the involvement of the Burundian army and Hutu militia groups in the war in the Democratic Republic of Congo. External donors such as the IMF, World Bank, and European Union are eager to provide aid to the country if it is able to properly adapt free market reforms and end the conflict. In fact, it seems likely that these donors will accept any kind of reform as an excuse to provide much needed capital in this devastated country whose crisis has negative effects on the region as a whole. If a suitable peace agreement can be reached the national economy will enjoy significant growth due to the input of promised external aid, the reconstruction of the national infrastructure, and increased economic stability.

DEPENDENCIES

Burundi has no territories or colonies.

BIBLIOGRAPHY

Africa Institute. *Africa A-Z: Continental and Country Profiles.* Pretoria, Republic of South Africa: Africa Institute of South Africa, 1998.

Amnesty International. *Burundi: Protecting Human Rights: An Intrinsic Part of the Search for Peace.* London: Amnesty International, January 2000.

Common Market for Eastern and Southern Africa (COMESA). <http://www.comesa.int>. Accessed March 2001.

Economist Intelligence Unit. *Country Report: Rwanda, Burundi.* London: Economist Intelligence Unit, 2000.

Human Rights Watch. *Burundi: Neglecting Justice in Making Peace.* New York: HRW, Volume 12, Number 2(A), April 2000.

International Monetary Fund. *Burundi: Statistical Annex, IMF Staff Country Report No.99/8.* Washington DC: IMF, February 1999.

International Monetary Fund. *International Financial Statistics Yearbook 2000.* Washington DC: IMF, 2000.

Jennings, C. *Across the Red River: Rwanda, Burundi and the Heart of Darkness.* London: Victor Gollancz, 2000.

Lemarchand, R. *Burundi: Ethnic Conflict and Genocide.* New York: Woodrow Wilson Center Press, 1996.

Mazrui, A. M. "Ethnicity in Bondage: Is Its Liberation Premature?" in *Ethnic Violence, Conflict Resolution, and Cultural Pluralism.* Geneva: United Nations Research Institute for Social Development (UNRISD), 1995.

United Nations Economic Commission for Africa. <http://www.uneca.org>. Accessed March 2001.

United Nations, *Statistical Yearbook, Forty-Third Issue, 1996.* New York: United Nations, 1998.

U.S. Central Intelligence Agency. *World Factbook 2000.* <http://www.odci.gov/cia/publications/factbook/index.html>. Accessed July 2001.

World Bank. *World Development Report 2000/2001: Attacking Poverty.* New York: Oxford University Press 2000.

—Liam Campling

CAMEROON

Republic of Cameroon
République du Cameroun

CAPITAL: Yaoundé.

MONETARY UNIT: Communauté Financière Africaine (CFA) franc. The CFA franc is tied to the French franc at an exchange rate of CFA Fr50 to Fr1. One CFA franc equals 100 centimes. There are coins of 5, 10, 50, 100, and 500 CFA francs, and notes of 500, 1,000, 2,000, 5,000, and 10,000 CFA francs.

CHIEF EXPORTS: Crude oil and petroleum products, lumber, cocoa beans, aluminum, coffee, cotton.

CHIEF IMPORTS: Machines and electrical equipment, transport equipment, fuel, food.

GROSS DOMESTIC PRODUCT: US$31.5 billion (purchasing power parity, 1999 est.).

BALANCE OF TRADE: Exports: US$2 billion (f.o.b., 1999). **Imports:** US$1.5 billion (f.o.b., 1999).

COUNTRY OVERVIEW

LOCATION AND SIZE. Located on the west coast of Central Africa, Cameroon covers an area of 475,400 square kilometers (183,695 square miles), slightly more than California. Land boundaries extend for a total of 4,591 kilometers (2,853 miles) between Nigeria to the northwest, Chad to the northeast, the Central African Republic (C.A.R.) to the east, and the Republic of the Congo, Gabon, and Equatorial Guinea to the south. The country also has 402 kilometers (249 miles) of coastline on the Bight of Biafra, part of the Atlantic Ocean. The topography of Cameroon is varied, ranging from tropical rain forests in the south to mountainous highlands in some western central regions, and semi-arid savanna in the far north.

POPULATION. The population of Cameroon was estimated at 15,421,937 in July 2000 and is growing at an annual rate of 2.47 percent. The birth rate is estimated at 36.6 births per 1,000 people and the death rate is 11.89 births per 1,000 people. If these trends continue, the population will approach 20 million in 2010. Cameroon has a very young population: 43 percent of its people are younger than 15, while just 3 percent are over 65. Though English and French are the "official" languages, there are 24 major language groups spoken by a diversity of ethnic groups. The CIA's *World Factbook* lists the religious composition as 40 percent Christian, 20 percent Muslim, and 40 percent indigenous beliefs, but these categories are not so neatly divided, as traditional animist beliefs are often mixed with Muslim or Christian beliefs.

OVERVIEW OF ECONOMY

Since gaining its independence in 1960, Cameroon's economy has swung from a long period of prosperity to a decade of **recession**, followed by a partial recovery. The economy depends on the production of various raw commodities and has therefore been vulnerable to price fluctuations for these commodities. The country remains primarily agricultural, but it has gradually diversified into the production of petroleum and lumber, and the provision of basic industries and services. Its abundant natural resources, favorable geographic position, and relative political stability have allowed Cameroon to build one of the most diverse and prosperous economies in sub-Saharan Africa.

Following independence in 1960, Cameroon enjoyed 25 years of prosperity before falling on hard times in the mid-1980s. During that period, the country developed a prosperous and diverse economy, based on agriculture, petroleum production, and some basic industries. Beginning in 1986, however, the economy shrank dramatically as low prices for oil, coffee, and cocoa reduced Cameroon's export income. Oil production also began a steady decline during the 1980s and fell from 9 million metric tons in 1986 to 5 million metric tons in 1997. Cameroon's **GDP** declined by 30 percent between 1986

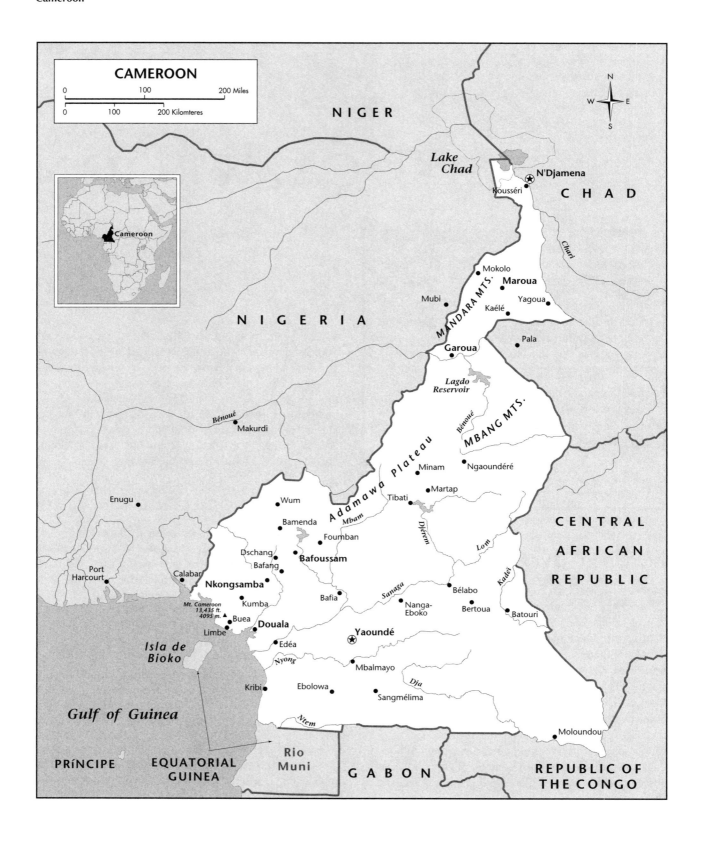

and 1995. In 1993, the government was forced to reduce civil service salaries by 30 to 50 percent in an effort to limit its spending and, throughout this period, it tried with little success to revive the country by making structural adjustments and reforms. Only during the late 1990s did Cameroon begin emerging slowly from the doldrums, averaging annual growth of almost 5 percent from 1997–1999.

Beginning in the early 1980s, petroleum became Cameroon's largest single export commodity, accounting for nearly half of export earnings. Although agriculture continues to occupy most of the country's workforce, petroleum contributes the largest share of its export earnings. Falling prices and decreasing production levels reduced oil revenues to 30 percent of export earnings in the 1990s, but a surge in oil prices doubled Cameroon's oil revenues in 1999–2000. Lumber is Cameroon's second largest export, providing an additional 20 percent of export revenues. Agricultural commodities, especially coffee, cocoa, bananas, and cotton, account for most of the remaining export earnings. Cameroon also produces a number of food crops and light industrial goods that are sold in domestic and regional markets.

Several advantages have enabled Cameroon to prosper more than its neighbors. The country is blessed with a wealth of natural resources, especially its fertile land, petroleum, and lumber. Unlike all of its immediate neighbors, Cameroon has not been damaged by any serious civil conflicts, and enjoys an advantageous geographic position between Nigeria and several central African countries that provide growing markets. Two neighboring countries, Chad and the C.A.R., rely on Cameroon's transportation system and the port city of Douala for links to the outside world.

Cameroon's long economic crisis of the 1980s and 1990s contributed to a rising debt burden estimated at nearly US$7.7 billion, or 84 percent of GDP, in 1999. **Debt service** payments have reduced the value of export earnings and consumed an excessive portion (33 percent) of government budgets. In late 2000, the International Monetary Fund (IMF) announced that Cameroon would qualify for the Heavily Indebted Poor Countries (HIPC) **debt relief** initiative, which will provide US$100 million annually to cover debt service payments. Increased oil revenues have also helped to reduce the government's debt burden.

Pervasive corruption and government mismanagement have seriously hindered Cameroon's economy by creating an unfavorable business climate and discouraging investment. Based on a poll of private companies, Transparency International rated Cameroon as the world's most corrupt country for 2 consecutive years in 1998 and 1999. The country's main port, Douala, is particularly notorious for its corruption, inefficiency, and high costs, but corruption exists throughout the government bureaucracy where civil servants routinely obstruct paperwork until they receive their "gumbo," or tip. The government has initiated high-profile attempts to fight corruption, but these practices are not widely accepted and it remains difficult to eliminate. Corruption was aggravated by Cameroon's long period of economic decline, culminating in the government's decision to cut

civil service salaries by up to 50 percent in 1993. Though Cameroon fell to 7th in Transparency International's 2000 listing, corruption has continued to have an adverse effect on Cameroon's economic expansion.

Economic figures in the 1990s indicated that Cameroon had made progress in reducing some of these problems. Four years of solid growth during the late 1990s followed a decade of decline and, in 2000, the government began a second 3-year **structural adjustment program** that aims to continue **privatization** of state enterprises and improvement of public management. The government has also revised tax laws and undertaken reforms to encourage investment, while several **infrastructure** projects should also help the business climate. During 2000–2004, the Chad-Cameroon Development project, one of the largest infrastructure projects in Africa, will provide Cameroon with a major economic boost, particularly in the construction and transportation sectors. This project will invest US$3.7 billion to build oil production facilities in southern Chad, a pipeline across Cameroon, and associated infrastructure in both countries.

POLITICS, GOVERNMENT, AND TAXATION

Cameroon was originally colonized by Germany, but was divided between England and France after World War I. Since gaining independence in 1960, Cameroon has had only 2 presidents: Ahmadou Ahidjo, who relinquished power voluntarily in 1982, and Paul Biya, the current president, who was elected to a 7-year term in 1997.

Historically, political stability has proved one of Cameroon's most vital economic assets. The country has watched civil wars and serious unrest erupt in each of its neighbors, while managing to avoid major conflict within its own borders. Cameroon's first president, Ahidjo, ruled the country by sometimes authoritarian methods, but the resulting stability allowed for the growth of a highly diverse economy.

The popularly-elected Cameroonian president presides over the **unicameral** (1-house) National Assembly, comprising 180 seats. Members are elected by popular vote to a 5-year term of office, but the president has the power to lengthen or shorten the term of a government. Though Cameroon is a stable country with ostensibly democratic institutions, political power remains concentrated in the hands of President Biya and his ruling party. Like the heads of state of many neighboring countries in sub-Saharan Africa, President Biya has developed a democratic facade while maintaining effective control of most governmental institutions. Past elections have been marred by serious fraud, leading most major opposition parties to boycott the most recent elections in 1997. President Biya will be eligible for reelection in 2004.

The ruling Democratic Rally of the Cameroon People (RDPC) has dominated Cameroonian politics and controlled its government since independence. Since 1990, many opposition parties have freely organized themselves to compete in elections, but the opposition remains divided. The most prominent opposition parties include the Social Democratic Front (SDF), led in 2001 by John Fru Ndi; the National Union for Democracy and Progress (UNDP), led in 2001 by Maigari Bello Bouba; and the Cameroonian Democratic Union (UDC), led in 2001 by Adamou Ndam Njoya. All of these parties espouse similar ideologies of free enterprise.

Cameroon is handicapped by the lack of an effective and independent judiciary. Judges are appointed by the president, and courts are subject to the influence of money and politics. In 1999, Groupement Inter-Patronal du Cameroun (GICAM), an organization representing and coordinating Cameroon's largest businesses, established a business arbitration center in order to avoid the inefficiencies and uncertainties of Cameroon's legal system. A regional commercial court is due to be established in N'Djamena in Chad. Lack of an independent court system further deters foreign companies from investing in Cameroon.

The country is gradually reducing the legacy of state involvement in economic affairs that it inherited from France. Beginning in 1997, Cameroon began collaborating with the IMF and the World Bank on a new structural adjustment program. Four previous reform programs ended in failure, but the recent program has been more successful. Reforms have sought to privatize state enterprises and improve management practices in government. The tax code has been simplified and customs rules have been partly reformed in order to bring Cameroon into harmony with regional standards established by the Central African Economic and Monetary Community (CEMAC), the economic and monetary community of Central Africa.

These measures have contributed to the recent turnaround in Cameroon's economy.

As part of its structural adjustment reforms, Cameroon is continuing the process of privatizing its state enterprises. Though the pace of this process has been slow, a state insurance company, the national railroad, the mobile telephone company, and all state banks have been privatized, as have several agro-industrial firms, including the state sugar company, a rubber company, and a palm oil company. Plans for the privatization of Cameroon Airlines and the Cameroon Development Corporation are well advanced, and the state electricity, water, and telephone companies should be privatized during the next 2 years. The privatization process has already contributed to recent economic growth by encouraging investment in developments that the state was unwilling to finance.

Cameroon's government generates revenues primarily from oil sales, customs **duties**, and taxes on businesses. Oil revenues declined from 50 percent of government revenue in the 1980s to 30 percent in the 1990s before returning to 50 percent when oil prices rose in 1999–2000. During the late 1990s, Cameroon began to revise its tax and customs codes to bring them into compliance with CEMAC standards. As part of CEMAC's regional integration plan, all 5 member-countries established a **value-added tax** and began to harmonize their customs duties.

INFRASTRUCTURE, POWER, AND COMMUNICATIONS

Cameroon's infrastructure is partially developed, but inadequate investments have allowed some resources to deteriorate and lack of adequate infrastructure has impeded economic development in certain areas. Cameroon has developed a network of hydroelectric power stations that provide most of its electricity, while the telecommunications sector, previously stifled by government

---

Communications

Country	Newspapers	Radios	TV Sets[a]	Cable subscribers[a]	Mobile Phones[a]	Fax Machines[a]	Personal Computers[a]	Internet Hosts[b]	Internet Users[b]
	1996	1997	1998	1998	1998	1998	1998	1999	1999
Cameroon	7	163	32	N/A	0	N/A	N/A	0.00	20
United States	215	2,146	847	244.3	256	78.4	458.6	1,508.77	74,100
Nigeria	24	223	66	N/A	0	N/A	5.7	0.00	100
Gabon	29	183	55	N/A	8	0.4	8.6	0.02	3

[a]Data are from International Telecommunication Union, *World Telecommunication Development Report 1999* and are per 1,000 people.
[b]Data are from the Internet Software Consortium (http://www.isc.org) and are per 10,000 people.

SOURCE: World Bank. *World Development Indicators 2000*.

---

monopoly, has recently seen a surge in investment. Privatization of the state electric, water, and phone companies is expected to stimulate further investment in infrastructure.

Cameroon's road system is partially developed, but many rural roads are heavily eroded and poorly maintained. The road network covers 34,300 kilometers (21,266 miles), only 4,300 kilometers (2,666 miles) of which are paved. Most provincial capitals are accessible through decent roads, but many rural areas are more difficult to reach, while mountainous terrain and annual torrential rains seriously degrade the road system in many areas. During 2000–2005, several major projects are expected to pave over 800 kilometers (500 miles) of roads and improve transportation links with Chad and the C.A.R. During 1999–2000, the European Union and France allocated over CFA Fr35 billion to road construction and maintenance projects. In the long term, the government has prepared a 15-year investment plan to pave 3,000 kilometers (1,860 miles) of roads.

A railroad links the port facilities in Douala to the capital city of Yaoundé and continues to the northern city of Ngaoundéré. In addition to serving Cameroon's capital city, this railway transports goods between Douala and Chad and the C.A.R. Under public management, investments were limited and the railroad experienced frequent breakdowns until 1999, when the government railroad, Fercam, was renamed Camrail and sold to 2 foreign companies, Groupe Bollore of France and Comazar of South Africa. These 2 companies planned to invest nearly US$50 million in infrastructure improvements. With increased traffic in materials for the Chad-Cameroon pipeline, Camrail hoped to raise its annual cargo from 2 million to 2.5 million metric tons.

Douala is one of Africa's largest ports, with annual traffic exceeding 5 million metric tons. In addition to serving Cameroon's interior regions, Douala also serves as a principal port for Chad, Congo, and the C.A.R. Douala has long been plagued by problems of slow, costly services and widespread corruption but, under pressure from the World Bank and the IMF, the government has begun drafting plans to reform Douala's port services. These reforms had not yet been clearly defined by 2000, but it is expected that management of certain port services will be privatized. In the longer term, Cameroon is planning to develop other port facilities in Limbe, Kribi, and Garoua. The port in Douala is not deep enough for the larger ships that are expected to carry an increasing share of sea cargo, but Kribi is more suitable for such traffic.

Cameroon has 3 international airports, in Douala, Yaoundé and Garoua, as well as 8 smaller airports with paved runways. The national airline, Cameroon Airlines, provides services between Cameroon and several neighboring countries, while Douala and Yaoundé are also served by several international airlines with connections to Paris and several cities throughout Africa.

Cameroon consumes approximately 3 billion kilowatt-hours (kWh) of electricity per year, most of which is provided by hydroelectric power. The country's electricity grid is mainly confined to urban areas and industry consumes over half of the power supply. The state electricity company, Sonel, has not invested in any infrastructure improvements for over a decade, but when Sonel is privatized its managers are expected to improve infrastructure and develop a wider customer base over coming years.

Telecommunications are quite limited, but are expected to develop more quickly as the sector is **liberalized**. In 1999, Cameroon had less than 90,000 telephone lines, giving a telephone density of less than 6 phones per 1000 people, but licenses have now been granted to several cellular telephone companies and Internet service providers. The number of cellular and Internet users is still small, but is growing rapidly. Two cellular companies, 1 French and 1 South African, have invested in cellular networks and are competing aggressively to sign up clients.

ECONOMIC SECTORS

Although primarily an agricultural economy, Cameroon has developed petroleum resources and a variety of industrial and service enterprises. Agriculture employed 70 percent of the working population and provided 42 percent of GDP in 1997. Commercial crops such

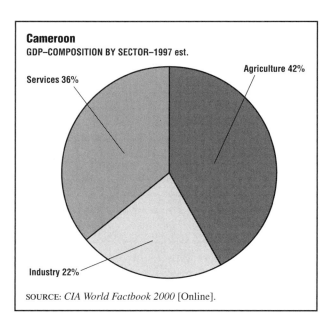

Cameroon
GDP–COMPOSITION BY SECTOR–1997 est.

Services 36%

Agriculture 42%

Industry 22%

SOURCE: *CIA World Factbook 2000* [Online].

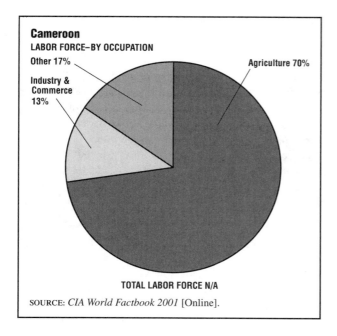

Cameroon
LABOR FORCE–BY OCCUPATION

Other 17%

Industry &
Commerce
13%

Agriculture 70%

TOTAL LABOR FORCE N/A

SOURCE: *CIA World Factbook 2001* [Online].

as coffee, cocoa, and bananas provide a significant share of Cameroon's export earnings and additional crops are produced for domestic consumption. Lumber has grown into Cameroon's second largest export, but the country's forests will probably be exhausted during the next decade.

Cameroon has developed an array of industrial enterprises that provided 22 percent of its GDP in 1997. Though oil production levels have declined since the 1980s, petroleum still provides a large share of Cameroon's export earnings. Agro-industrial enterprises produce sugar, fruit juices, pasta, powdered milk, coffee, chocolate products, corn oil, and palm oil. A textile company produces fabric from cotton grown in northern provinces, and a cement company produces cement that is sold in Chad and the C.A.R. as well as domestically. Cameroon has recently tried to encourage domestic processing of its forestry resources by banning the export of raw lumber. Additional industries manufacture matches, batteries, beer, and mineral water. Most of these products are marketed in Cameroon and its neighboring countries.

The service sector provided an additional 36 percent of Cameroon's GDP in 1997. Cameroon has profited from its geographic position by providing transportation services to several neighboring countries. The banking sector currently includes 9 commercial banks and a number of smaller financial institutions. The energy and telecommunications sectors have stagnated over the past 2 decades due to the failure of government to invest in infrastructure. Banking, telecommunications, and insurance sectors are still in the process of being liberalized and a number of state services are being privatized.

AGRICULTURE

Agriculture remains the backbone of Cameroon's economy, employing 70 percent of its workforce, while providing 42 percent of its GDP and 30 percent of its export revenue. Blessed with fertile land and regularly abundant rainfall in most regions, Cameroon produces a variety of agricultural commodities both for export and for domestic consumption. Coffee and cocoa are grown in central and southern regions, bananas in southwestern areas, and cotton in several northern provinces. In addition to export commodities, Cameroonian farmers produce numerous subsistence crops for family consumption. Principal food crops include millet, sorghum, peanuts, plantains, sweet potatoes, and manioc. Animal husbandry is practiced throughout the country and is particularly important in northern provinces.

LUMBER. The lumber industry is Cameroon's second largest source of export revenue behind petroleum, employing 25,000 workers and accounting for 7.4 percent of Cameroon's GDP. Cameroon's forest resources are concentrated in its southeastern provinces, near the borders with Congo and C.A.R. Cameroon has recently enacted laws to increase the processing of its forest resources by banning the export of raw lumber. Several foreign companies are competing in this industry and a total of 66 lumber-processing mills have been established. Annual production capacity has increased from 1.2 million cubic meters in 1994 to 2.68 million cubic meters in 1999, but lumber companies have been cutting down trees at an unsustainable rate. If the trend continues, Cameroon's forest resources will be almost exhausted by 2010. The government has enacted laws to improve the management of forest resources, but these laws have been poorly enforced.

COCOA AND COFFEE. An estimated 4 million Cameroonians depend on cocoa and coffee for their livelihood. Both commodities are produced by millions of farmers on small-scale farms. Cameroon is a major cocoa producer and exports approximately 120,000 metric tons of cocoa annually. In the late 1990s, annual coffee production has varied between 60,000 and 100,000 metric tons. Some of these commodities are processed locally, but most are exported to Europe. Coffee and cocoa prices recently fell to their lowest levels in nearly 30 years, thus reducing Cameroon's export earnings. Most of the country's coffee is produced in the western region of Moungo, while cocoa is produced primarily in central southern Cameroon. The coffee and cocoa industries were formerly under government control, but they were privatized beginning in 1995. Several hundred businesses initially jumped into the coffee exporting business, but several foreign firms have come to dominate the trade.

BANANAS AND PLANTAINS. Banana exports have risen dramatically during the past decade, increasing from 80,000 to nearly 250,000 metric tons per year. This increase is due in large part to improved farming methods that have brought greater yields. In addition to these quantities for export, Cameroonian farmers produce another 700,000 metric tons of bananas and 1,300,000 metric tons of plantains for domestic consumption. Plantains are grown by individual small-scale farmers throughout southern and western Cameroon, while banana exports are produced primarily by 2 large companies in the southwestern region, the Marseille Fruit Company, and the Cameroon Development Corporation, which is currently being privatized.

Though productivity has recently increased, Cameroon's bananas are less competitive than Central American bananas. Cameroon is one of the leading suppliers of bananas to Europe, where the European Union has long offered them preferential market access. This has provoked a well-publicized trade dispute with the United States. In 1998, the United States won a decision from the World Trade Organization (WTO) to eliminate preferential access by 2006, putting less competitive Cameroonian producers at risk. Nevertheless, some observers believe that continuing gains in productivity will allow Cameroon's bananas to compete in 2006.

COTTON. Cotton is produced in Cameroon's far northern provinces where it is the main **cash crop**. More than 300,000 farmers cultivate 172,000 hectares (424,840 acres) to produce 60–80,000 metric tons of cotton fiber a year. Cotton production is managed by a state enterprise, Sodecoton, that provides training for cotton farmers, supplies fertilizer and insecticides, and buys the crop. Sodecoton is in the midst of a slow privatization process. Cotton earnings have varied significantly according to fluctuations of rainfall in the northern provinces and prices on the international market. Prices have recovered some ground following their plunge in the 1980s and Cameroon's production has grown in recent years, but the cotton sector has not regained the profitability it enjoyed prior to the years of decline.

RUBBER. Rubber is produced primarily in the forested region of Niete, north of Yaoundé, by 3 agro-industrial companies, CDC, Hevecam and Safacam. The rubber yield plummeted from 58,000 metric tons in 1998–1999 to 32,000 metric tons in 1999–2000. The main producer, Hevecam, was purchased in 1996 by the GMG Group based in Singapore. Most of Cameroon's rubber is exported to the European Union. With average annual rubber exports valued at CFA20 billion (US$30 million), this industry provides 2 percent of Cameroon's export revenue.

SUBSISTENCE CROPS. Cameroonian farmers cultivate a variety of crops for domestic consumption, and increased their production throughout the 1990s. Cameroon has consistently been able to feed itself from subsistence crops that include plantains, corn, sweet potatoes, cassava, and millet. Farmers also grow a variety of vegetables for sale in local markets, while a number of fruits and vegetables are also exported to regional markets. In recent years, Cameroon has tried to decrease its reliance on traditional exports by encouraging the production of pineapples, avocados, plantains, and other foods for export to neighboring CEMAC countries.

ANIMAL HUSBANDRY. Approximately two-thirds of Cameroon's rural population raises animals by traditional methods, keeping cows, goats, sheep, and chickens in their compounds. Farmers raise animals as savings, to earn extra income, and for their own consumption. In rural African culture, chickens and goats are slaughtered as a gesture of hospitality for relatives and important visitors. Some semi-nomadic families raise animals as their principal occupation, particularly in several northern provinces where much of Cameroon's meat is produced. Almost all of these animals are consumed in Cameroon. Overall, animal husbandry contributes an estimated 2.6 percent of the country's GDP.

INDUSTRY

Industry employs one-eighth of Cameroon's **workforce** and contributed 22 percent of its GDP in 1997. Cameroon has gradually developed a range of industrial ventures aimed mainly at domestic and regional markets. Many of these industries are based in the port city of Douala, the country's industrial capital, and have benefited from Cameroon's geographic position and its low energy prices. The development of petroleum reserves has been accompanied by the construction of light refineries. Cameroon has also developed the manufacture of several light **consumer goods** that tend to replace more expensive imports. These include batteries, pasta, palm oil, beverages, cigarettes, and textiles. The cement industry supplies the country's booming construction sector as well as some promising neighboring markets.

PETROLEUM. Cameroon is the fifth-largest oil producer in sub-Saharan Africa and produced 100,000 barrels per day in 1999. Elf, Perenco, and Pecten International (a subsidiary of Shell) have produced crude oil from several different deposits. Petroleum production began in 1977 and reached a peak of 9 million metric tons in 1986, before declining to 6 million metric tons in 1996. Thereafter, production stabilized, and oil revenues in 1999–2000 surged from US$500 million to nearly US$900 million with the doubling of oil prices. In the late 1990s, Cameroon revised its laws to stimulate additional exploration, but has so far had limited success. One area where oil reserves hold promise is the Bakassi Peninsula, a region also claimed by neighboring Nigeria in a dispute that has been referred to the International Court of Justice. A state-owned company, Sonara, refines 1.5 million metric tons of imported crude oil and exports 40 percent of its product. Another state oil company, Société Nationale des Hydrocarbures (SNH), manages Cameroon's interests in the petroleum sector.

MINERAL PROCESSING. One of Cameroon's largest factories is an aluminum smelting plant in Douala, which produces aluminum from imported bauxite. In 1999, aluminum exports reached nearly US$100 million, representing 5 percent of the country's export revenues. Cameroon's cement company, Cimencam, operates a factory in Douala and one in Figuil, on the Chad border. In addition to the domestic market, these factories supply the entire markets of Chad and the C.A.R. Cameroon produces small amounts of gold in the eastern province near the border with C.A.R.

BEVERAGES. Beer and soft drinks are manufactured for the domestic market and are also exported to several neighboring countries. Two of Cameroon's 5 largest companies (measured in terms of annual profits in 1998–99) are beverage producers: Cameroon Breweries and Guinness. Cameroon Breweries, owned by the French company Castel, controls 70 percent of the beer market and holds licenses to produce several major international brands including Amstel, Mutzig, Castel, and Tuborg. It also produces Tanguy mineral water and Coca-Cola soft drinks. Guinness (based in the United Kingdom) holds 17 percent of the drinks market.

AGRO-INDUSTRY. Cameroon has developed a number of small industries for processing its agricultural produce. The recently privatized domestic sugar company, Socucam, produces 100,000 metric tons of sugar for the domestic market. Panzani produces 4,500 metric tons of pasta in a factory in Douala, most of which is exported to regional countries. Cameroon makes Maggi bouillon cubes for cooking, while Chococam processes some of the country's raw cocoa to produce several chocolate products for regional markets. Cameroonians use copious amounts of palm oil in their cooking, and a number of companies produce approximately 100,000 metric tons of palm oil for the local market.

TEXTILES. Cameroon has cotton and textile industries based in the northern provinces. Sodecoton gins Cameroon's raw cotton and sells 7 percent of its product to Cicam, a textile company. Cicam employs 1,500 workers at factories in Garoua and Douala, producing fabric sold on regional markets. Cicam is the largest textile producer in the Central African region, but it has experienced difficulties in competing against imports from Nigeria and East Asia. During the late 1990s, increasing imports of cheap used clothing from Europe and the United States reduced Cicam's domestic market.

SERVICES

Cameroon's service sector has begun to benefit from the ongoing privatization of banking, transportation, and telecommunications services. In 1997, services employed an estimated 17 percent of Cameroon's workforce and produced 36 percent of its GDP. During the late 1990s, the government privatized the railroad operator and a mobile telephone company, as well as several banks and insurance companies. The state telephone company, Camtel, was offered for sale in 2000. Investments in the petroleum sector are expected to stimulate further growth in Cameroon's service sector.

TRANSPORTATION. Cameroon profits from its geographical position by serving as the principal transportation link for Chad, C.A.R., and other neighboring countries. Cameroon's railroad has traditionally transported large volumes of wood from Cameroon and the northern Congo and cotton from Chad and northern Cameroon. Cargo volumes are expected to increase in coming years when rail will be used to transport pipes, fuel, and other materials for the Chad-Cameroon oil production and pipeline project.

In spite of many problems, port services in Douala have thrived along with the transportation sector. Douala handles over 95 percent of imports to Cameroon, Chad, and the C.A.R. Cargo volumes exceeded 5 million metric tons annually in the late 1990s and Douala's capacity is estimated at 7 million metric tons.

FINANCIAL SERVICES. During Cameroon's recent economic resurgence, financial services have flourished, growing by 10 percent in 1999–2000. Total market resources increased from CFA Fr646 billion in 1999 to just over CFA Fr800 billion in 2000. Banking services are dominated by branches of several multinational banking groups such as Société Genérale, Crédit Lyonnais, and Standard Chartered Bank. During the late 1990s, Cameroon's largest state-owned bank, Banque International du Cameroun pour l'Epargne et le Crédit (BICEC), was privatized and another multinational, Groupe Populaire, took a controlling share. The banking sector expects continuing growth to be fueled by further privatization and rising investments associated with the Chad-Cameroon pipeline project.

TELECOMMUNICATIONS. A recent surge in telecommunications investment is expected to continue. Since the mid-1990s, 2 companies have begun investing in the provision of cellular services, and in 1998 the government divided the state telephone company into 2 entities, Camtel and Camtel Mobile. Camtel maintained a monopoly over fixed phone services, while Camtel Mobile offered cellular services. A second cellular license was sold to an affiliate of France Telecom, and Camtel Mobile was bought by MTN, a South African cellular phone company. The government is in the process of soliciting and evaluating bids from several foreign companies interested in buying a controlling share of Camtel. When Camtel is finally freed from government management, continuing investment and increasing access to telephone services will assure continuing growth in this sector.

RETAIL. There is a vast array of **retail** businesses of varying sizes in both rural and urban areas of Cameroon. Weekly rural markets attract farmers who sell their food crops while individual traders peddle a variety of household goods. Most durable goods, such as cars and household appliances, are sold in Yaoundé, Douala, and some provincial capitals. These urban centers also have shops offering a large variety of consumer goods.

INTERNATIONAL TRADE

During the 1990s Cameroon consistently ran **trade surpluses**, though these varied according to commodity prices. In 1999, for example, exported goods totaled almost US$2 billion, while imported goods amounted to almost US$1.5 billion. A surge in oil prices contributed to a 30 percent rise in the value of Cameroon's exports during the late 1990s. At the same time, lower revenues from cocoa and rubber were offset by increased revenues from coffee, cotton, and aluminum. In 1999–2000, oil provided nearly half of the country's export revenues, while agricultural products provided an additional 25 percent, lumber 16 percent, and aluminum 5 percent.

The European Union is Cameroon's biggest trading partner. It supplies most of Cameroon's imports, while receiving over 80 percent of its exports. All of Cameroon's principal exports—including oil, coffee, cocoa, bananas, cotton, lumber, and aluminum—travel primarily to European ports. In 1999–2000, 22 percent of Cameroon's exports went to Italy and another 16 percent to France. Cameroon also exports a variety of fruits, vegetables, and manufactured goods to neighboring countries. France has historically supplied the largest share of Cameroon's imports, which include machinery, processed food products,

and a range of other consumer goods. Although Cameroon exports crude and refined oil, it also imports fuel for its domestic needs. Fuel accounted for 20 percent of imports in 1999. Most of this fuel is imported and distributed by 4 international firms: TotalFinaElf, Mobil, Shell, and Texaco, while other goods are imported by a variety of trading firms and industrial companies.

MONEY

Cameroon is part of the Central African Monetary and Economic Union (Communaute Economiquareue et Monetaire de l'Afrique Centrale, or CEMAC), a group of 5 francophone countries that use the same currency, the CFA franc. The CFA franc is tied to the French franc and can be readily exchanged at 50 CFA francs to 1 French franc. Cameroon, like all members of the CFA franc communities, has benefited from this stable currency.

As a member of the CFA zone, Cameroon was profoundly affected by the 50 percent **devaluation** of the CFA in 1994. The devaluation caused a temporary rise in **inflation** to nearly 30 percent in 1995 before descending to around 2 percent in the late 1990s. The country's economy appears to have benefited from this devaluation, which made its traditional exports more competitive on world markets. In the short term, however, devaluation lowered living standards and probably increased poverty by raising prices while most salaries remained static.

CEMAC planned to open a regional stock exchange in Libreville, Gabon, in 2001, despite the existence of a limited stock exchange in Douala.

POVERTY AND WEALTH

Though Cameroon's poverty indicators still compare favorably to other sub-Saharan countries, years of economic decline have increased the percentage of Cameroonians living in poverty. One study conducted by the

Trade (expressed in billions of US$): Cameroon

	Exports	Imports
1975	.447	.599
1980	1.384	1.602
1985	.722	1.151
1990	2.002	1.400
1995	1.651	1.199
1998	N/A	N/A

SOURCE: International Monetary Fund. *International Financial Statistics Yearbook 1999.*

Exchange rates: Cameroon

Communaute Financiere Africaine francs (CFA Fr) per US$1

Jan 2001	699.21
2000	711.98
1999	615.70
1998	589.95
1997	583.67
1996	511.55

Note: From January 1, 1999, the CFA Fr is pegged to the euro at a rate of 655.957 CFA Fr per euro.

SOURCE: CIA *World Factbook 2001* [ONLINE].

GDP per Capita (US$)

Country	1975	1980	1985	1990	1998
Cameroon	616	730	990	764	646
United States	19,364	21,529	23,200	25,363	29,683
Nigeria	301	314	230	258	256
Gabon	6,480	5,160	4,941	4,442	4,630

SOURCE: United Nations. *Human Development Report 2000;
Trends in human development and per capita income.*

United Nations Development Program (UNDP) and cited in *Marche Tropicaux* estimated that this percentage rose from 40 percent in 1983 to 50 percent in 1999. Per capita income fell from US$1,100 in the early 1980s to around US$600 in the 1990s. The government reacted to Cameroon's shrinking economy by reducing producer prices and government expenditures during the early 1990s. Farmers who sold their cotton, cocoa, or other agricultural goods to state-run businesses saw their incomes drastically reduced. In 1993, the government also reduced civil service salaries by 50 percent, while devaluation of the CFA franc in 1994 also contributed to increased poverty by raising inflation. In 1999, the UNDP ranked Cameroon as 134th out of 174 countries on its Human Development Index. The Index is a social and economic indicator which ranks poverty on the basis of statistics for life expectancy, access to clean water, adequate food, and the provision of health care, education, and public services. While Cameroon ranks high among sub-Saharan African countries, it still compares unfavorably with most Asian and South American countries.

As in most other developing countries, traditional measures indicate that poverty is most prevalent in rural areas. Studies have indicated that, in 1999, 20–30 percent of the population in Yaoundé and Douala lived in poverty compared to over 60 percent in rural areas. Nearly 80 percent of rural households lacked access to electricity compared to 20 percent of urban households. Rural house-

holds are also far less likely to have access to potable water and adequate health services, and children are less likely to continue their studies through secondary school. Nevertheless, rural families enjoy many advantages insofar as they grow their own food and build their own housing, and thus have less need for monetary income.

Different classes of varying income levels inhabit the urban areas. A large civil servant class is primarily stationed in Yaoundé, Douala, and provincial capitals. Civil service salaries have fallen from the levels enjoyed prior to Cameroon's recession, but they are still higher than the average Cameroonian income. Many urban dwellers make a living from **informal sector** activities such as shopkeeping, street vending, construction, etc. Basic foods are easily available and generally inexpensive, so famine is rarer than in neighboring countries. City dwellers usually live in cooked-brick, cement-block, or adobe housing and most have access to electricity. Cameroon's cities house the upper-class officials from both public and private enterprises, whose lifestyles are comparable to those in developed countries.

While government provides education and subsidized health services, users must also contribute certain fees for these services. Education is subsidized through the university level. Government and formal sector workers are required to participate in a state pension system. The extended family traditionally serves as a safety net in the informal sector, and children are regarded as retirement insurance since they are expected to take care of their elderly parents.

WORKING CONDITIONS

Cameroon has been called a miniature version of the African continent because of its varied topography and wide range of peoples and lifestyles. In rural regions, most of Cameroon's population cultivates food crops for their own consumption and cash crops to earn money. Farmers in different regions cultivate different cash crops: cotton in the north, coffee and cocoa in the south-

Household Consumption in PPP Terms

Country	All food	Clothing and footwear	Fuel and power[a]	Health care[b]	Education[b]	Transport & Communications	Other
Cameroon	33	12	8	2	9	8	28
United States	13	9	9	4	6	8	51
Nigeria	51	5	31	2	8	2	2
Gabon	40	3	9	3	7	4	34

Data represent percentage of consumption in PPP terms.
[a]Excludes energy used for transport.
[b]Includes government and private expenditures.

SOURCE: World Bank. *World Development Indicators 2000.*

central region, and bananas in the southwest. In the northern provinces, animal herders live semi-nomadic lives, migrating south in search of pastures during the dry season. Rural areas also host a number of small businessmen who purchase goods in rural markets and transport them for sale to urban vendors.

Most Cameroonians live the life of small-scale farmers. Their work routine is dependent on seasonal changes of weather, with different regions of the country subject to different seasonal cycles according to rainfall patterns. In all cases, farming families have annual periods for sowing their crops, laboring their fields, and reaping their harvests. All capable family members, including students and small children, usually contribute to this work, particularly during busy periods. Local schools sometimes plan their schedules to allow pupils the freedom to participate in the seasonal farm work.

Professional and civil servant classes live in urban areas, alongside unskilled workers, and the cities reflect this mix of classes whose lifestyles and living conditions vary according to their occupations and income. The majority of Cameroon's city-dwellers are involved in various informal sector activities that provide limited income. Women play a crucial role in the informal sector economy, supplementing their husbands' income through various working activities, particularly the preparation and selling of food and beverages. Like many other large African cities, Douala and Yaoundé are plagued with increasing crime problems.

Cameroon has a number of unions that represent both private and **public sector** workers, including civil servants, dock workers, and truckers. These unions have rights to organize, to bargain with employers, and to hold strikes. Some unions have engaged in political demonstrations, but they serve primarily to negotiate with employers for wage increases and prompt payments, and generally represent the interests of employees.

COUNTRY HISTORY AND ECONOMIC DEVELOPMENT

1884. Germany establishes a protectorate over the Douala region of coastal Cameroon.

1920. Cameroon is divided between England and France at the end of World War I.

1958. France grants self-rule to Cameroon and Ahmadou Ahidjo becomes its first president.

1960. Cameroon formally gains independence and joins the United Nations.

1961. British Southern Cameroon is federated with Cameroon, while British Northern Cameroon joins Nigeria.

1977. Cameroon begins to export oil.

1982. President Ahidjo resigns and is succeeded by Paul Biya.

1986. Cameroon's economy begins a decade of steep decline when prices for oil and other commodities plunge.

1990. Opposition political parties are legalized.

1994. Cameroon's currency, the CFA franc, is devalued by 50 percent.

1997. The government embarks on a program of structural reform in collaboration with the IMF and the World Bank, aimed at increased privatization.

2000. Work begins on the Chad-Cameroon Oil Production and Pipeline project.

FUTURE TRENDS

Cameroon's economic growth is expected to continue in the near future, but several long-term problems remain. During 2000–2004, Cameroon is expected to receive a boost from the Chad-Cameroon Oil Production and Pipeline project. The country remains reliant on a limited number of export commodities and needs to diversify its economy and develop new export industries in order to ensure its long-term economic security. Corruption and lack of an independent and effective judiciary remain pervasive problems that have barely been tackled, despite some high-profile government campaigns aimed at improving the situation. Future levels of foreign investment may well depend on the success of these initiatives. Further short-term growth will make it easier for Cameroon to reform its investment climate and continue a program of economic liberalization.

The Chad-Cameroon Oil Production and Pipeline project is the largest infrastructure project in sub-Saharan Africa. A consortium led by Exxon will invest US$3.7 billion to build production facilities in southern Chad and a pipeline to transport oil to the Cameroonian port of Kribi. Nearly half of this investment will go to Cameroon, where most of the pipeline will be installed. The construction and transportation sectors will be the primary short-term beneficiaries of this project. Due in large part to this project, the construction sector already registered growth of over 75 percent in 2000, and the project will also impact positively on financial services and other sectors.

Cameroon remains vulnerable to falls in commodity prices, especially for oil. In addition, the valuable exports of petroleum and lumber are threatened as these resources gradually run out. Discovery of additional petroleum reserves may offset falling production levels from current oil fields, but lumber resources will be far more difficult to replace. Cameroon will need to establish more effective institutions for managing its forests and other natural resources. In the long term, Cameroon must diversify its economy and reduce its dependency on oil and agricultural products.

DEPENDENCIES

Cameroon has no territories or colonies.

BIBLIOGRAPHY

"Cameroon" (special edition). *Marchés Tropicaux et Méditerranéens*. December 1999.

"Cameroon." *The World Bank Group*. <http://www.worldbank.org>. Accessed August 2001.

Economist Intelligence Unit. *Country Profile: Cameroon, Central African Republic and Chad*. London: Economist Intelligence Unit, 2001.

International Monetary Fund. *Cameroon and the IMF*. <http:// www.imf.org/external/country/CMR>. Accessed August 2001.

Schatzberg, Michael G., and I. William Zartman, editors. *The Political Economy of Cameroon*. New York: Praeger, 1986.

"Special Cameroon." *Marchés Tropicaux et Méditerranéens*. 12 January 2001.

U.S. Central Intelligence Agency. *World Factbook 2000*. <http:// www.odci.gov/cia/publications/factbook/index.html>. Accessed August 2001.

U.S. Department of State. *FY 2001 Country Commercial Guide: Cameroon*. <http://www.state.gov/www/about_state/business/ com_guides/cameroon.html>. Accessed December 2000.

—Alexander Gazis

CAPE VERDE

Republic of Cape Verde
República de Cabo Verde

CAPITAL: Praia.

MONETARY UNIT: Cape Verde escudo (CVE). One escudo equals 100 centavos. There are notes of 100, 200, 500, 1,000, and 2,500 escudos and coins of 1, 2.5, 10, 20, 50, and 100 escudos and 20 and 50 centavos. In July 1998 the Cape Verde escudo was pegged to the Portuguese escudo at 55:1.

CHIEF EXPORTS: Fuel, shoes, garments, fish, bananas, and hides.

CHIEF IMPORTS: Foodstuffs, industrial products, transport equipment, and fuels.

GROSS DOMESTIC PRODUCT: US$670 million (purchasing power parity, 2000 est.).

BALANCE OF TRADE: Exports: US$40 million (2000 est.). **Imports:** US$250 million (2000 est.).

ropean and African background, and an estimated 95 percent are Roman Catholics. Approximately half of the population lives on Santiago Island. In recent years, Praia and Mindelo have become urban migration magnets, accounting for much of the urban growth. In 1995 the

COUNTRY OVERVIEW

LOCATION AND SIZE. Cape Verde is an archipelago of 10 islands and 5 islets situated 483 kilometers (300 miles) due west of Dakar, Senegal, in the North Atlantic Ocean. Cape Verde's total land area is 4,033 square kilometers (1,557 square miles), which makes it slightly larger than the U.S. state of Rhode Island. The islands stretch over a distance of 350 kilometers (218 miles) north to south and 300 kilometers (186 miles) east to west. The terrain is mountainous and there is limited rainfall, making the islands very arid. The capital, Praia, is on Santiago Island, located in the south of the archipelago. The second largest town, Mindelo, is situated in the northwest of the archipelago on the island of Sao Vincent. The islands have a total coastline of 965 kilometers (600 miles).

POPULATION. The high rate of **emigration** and recent famines have limited population growth in Cape Verde. In 2001 the population was estimated at 405,163, with a very low growth rate of 0.92 percent. At least 500,000 Cape Verdeans are living abroad in Europe, the United States, and Africa. Most Cape Verdeans are of mixed Eu-

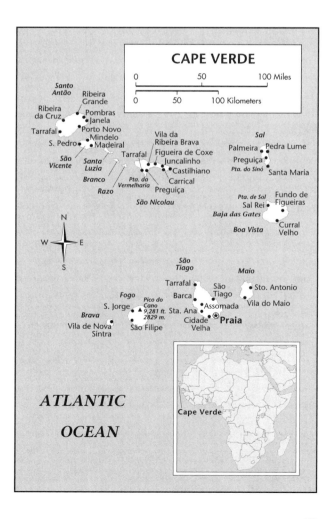

United Nations (UN) estimated the urban population to be 54 percent of the total.

OVERVIEW OF ECONOMY

Cape Verde's economy is limited by the difficulties of accessing the islands, the nation's small size in terms of both population and geographical area, the absence of any mineral resources apart from some salt deposits, and a chronic shortage of rainfall. The rocky terrain and lack of rainfall hamper agricultural production. Most employment is in the services sector, which is sustained by **remittances** from Cape Verdeans living overseas (amounting to 16 percent of **gross domestic product** [GDP], in 1998), economic aid (mainly from Portugal and 29 percent of the GDP in 1998), and some tourism (3 percent of GDP in 1996).

However, in comparison to other African nations, Cape Verde is one of the more financially stable countries. It is considered to be on the margin between low-income and lower-middle income status. Nevertheless, living standards are still very low by comparison to the industrialized countries of the West. Per capita **GNP** measured by the **exchange rate** conversion, was $1,060 in 1998. The **purchasing power parity** conversion (which makes allowances for the low price of many basic commodities in Cape Verde) estimates per capita income at $1,700 in 2000. This amount can be compared with an average per capita income of $36,200 in the United States in the same year.

Insufficient food production and the lack of resources have resulted in a high dependence on imports, foreign investment, and aid. Since 1988 the government has tried to diversify and **liberalize** the economy in the hope that foreign investors might expand small-scale industry and develop the fishing and tourism sectors. Foreign investment and the development of local entrepreneurs are seen as the key to future growth.

The government has also started a program of **privatization**. Twenty-six **parastatals** were privatized by 1998, and a further 23 should be privatized by 2002, including utilities and financial institutions. The program of privatization has earned $80 million for the government and was expected to boost foreign investment to $11 million by 1999. The **budget deficit** grew from 6 percent of GDP in 1991 to 14 percent in 1994 due to expansion in public investment, stimulated by a massive boost in external aid. Although 32 percent of public revenue comes from external grants, the government has increased domestic revenue by higher **tariffs** and better taxation. Combined with a range of austerity measures, the budget deficit has now fallen to sustainable levels (4 percent in 1998).

Under the budget for 2000, expenditures were expected to grow by only 0.4 percent to $232 million. This estimate still indicates that government spending was much higher than expected (51 percent of GDP in 2000), due to the fact that expenditures grew by 17 percent in 1999. In accordance with the government's current National Development Plan (NDP), social expenditures were expected to be the largest expenditure item in the budget.

In 1998 the government started to implement its fourth NDP, which runs until 2001. As the main aim of the NDP is to alleviate poverty, it has the support of international donors. Under the NDP, powers are to be devolved to local councils to control spending, taxes, and investment at a local level. The NDP also aims to develop the **private sector**, provide vocational training programs, reform the education and health care systems, cut public spending, and reduce imports.

Since the pegging of the Cape Verde escudo to the Portuguese escudo, the government has committed itself to greater fiscal discipline and has sought to meet European Monetary Union (EMU) targets. These goals include a general government deficit of less than 3 percent of the GDP, public debt of less than or equal to 60 percent of the GDP, and an **inflation rate** that is less than 1.5 percent higher than those of the 3 EMU member states with the lowest inflation rates that year.

Despite its handicaps, the economy has grown steadily since independence in 1975 due to favorable loans and remittances from expatriates. World Bank figures indicate that the GDP grew by 8 percent per year from 1974 to 1985 and 4 percent per year from 1986 to 1992, comfortably faster than the population growth rate. Since 1994 the GDP growth rate has been 5.7 percent per year, and this has led to a per capita GNP that is among the highest in the West African region.

Unemployment is one of the biggest problems in Cape Verde with 25 percent of the **labor force** unable to find formal work. Although public investment in productive, export-oriented sectors is likely to increase, it will not grow quickly enough to absorb the expanding workforce. Therefore, many seek work in foreign countries, despite increasing U.S. and European barriers to **immigration**.

The government has abolished some **price controls**, while retaining a food aid distribution network. Average consumer **inflation** has fluctuated since 1989, averaging 6.5 percent between 1995 and 1999. Despite erratic inflation, interest rates remained stable.

POLITICS, GOVERNMENT, AND TAXATION

The Portuguese colonized Cape Verde in 1456 and populated the islands with slaves brought from West Africa. Cape Verde achieved independence in 1975 after peaceful negotiations with Portugal, which had itself changed government in 1974. The African Party for the Independence of Guinea-Bissau and Cape Verde (PAIGC) was the only political party recognized during the transition. Aristedes Pereira, the first president, was reelected in 1981 and 1986. The same party ruled in both Guinea-Bissau and Cape Verde, and there were plans for the political unification of the countries. However, the Cape Verde arm of the party abandoned unification in 1980 following a coup in Guinea-Bissau. The new African Party for the Independence of Cape Verde (PAICV) was then formed.

Constitutional changes in 1991 allowed Cape Verde to be the first sub-Saharan one-party state to hold multi-party elections. The Movement for Democracy (MPD) was voted in, bringing to office Prime Minister Carlos Alberto Wahnon de Carvalho Veiga and President Antonio Mascarenhas Monteiro. In 1992 the MPD established a new constitution defining Cape Verde as a sovereign, unitary, and democratic republic and included provisions for the protection of democratic rights and freedoms. The president stands as head of state and must be elected by two-thirds of the voters. Legislative power resides in the **unicameral** parliament, the Assembleia Nacional, which nominates the prime minister. The prime minister is the effective head of government and nominates his ministers. In July 1999, the parliament made further reforms, allowing the president to dissolve parliament and creating a constitutional court. It also established an Economic and Social Advisory Council, and gave Crioulo, a blend of Portuguese and West African speech, official status as a national language.

The 2 major forces in Cape Verde's political scene are the MPD party and PAICV. The MPD was formed in opposition to PAICV's one-party state and has implemented economic and constitutional reform to change Cape Verde to a democracy with a market economy. The MPD has attracted foreign aid to the nation and has built confidence in Cape Verde's economic and political stability both at home and abroad.

The PAICV, under a new leader, Pedro Pires, has retained its leftist orientation, but its ideals are losing favor with the younger members of the party. The PAICV has tended to be popular with emigrants, particularly those who live in the United States. The only party other than the PAICV and the MPD to win seats in the 2001 legislative election was the Democratic Alliance for Change (ADM), which earned 2 seats by garnering 6 percent of the vote.

The MPD won a convincing victory in the 1995 legislative election, and Veiga was returned as prime minister. Monteiro was reelected to the presidency in 1996, when he stood unopposed. The 2001 presidential election was closely fought, with Pedro Pires of the PAICV narrowly defeating Carlos Veiga of the MPD. Pires beat the former prime minister for the presidency by a margin of 12 votes.

Cape Verde has maintained an internationally non-aligned status, while strengthening its ties with both Portugal and Brazil. Cape Verde is a member of the Organization for African Unity (OAU), the Economic Community of West African States (ECOWAS), and the Lomé Convention.

Cape Verde raises about 9 percent of the GDP from income and corporation taxes, 13 percent from import **duties**, and 7 percent from **indirect taxes**. Grants from overseas add the equivalent of 18 percent of the GDP. Education receives 19 percent of government expenditure, 21 percent goes to social security, and 19 percent is spent on health care. Cape Verde has a small armed force of 1,100 men, and less than 2 percent of government spending goes to the military.

INFRASTRUCTURE, POWER, AND COMMUNICATIONS

While the **infrastructure** of Cape Verde is adequate, the government is committed to improving its ports and roads. About 600 kilometers (373 miles) of the 2,250 kilometers (1,398 miles) of roads are paved. The irregularity of maritime transport has hindered exports, but the government has tried to set up regular links to Africa and Europe. There are regular ferry services between most islands, and the main port is the newly enlarged Porto Grande in Mindelo. Praia port has recently been modernized, and a new port to the north of the capital is under construction.

The main international airport on Sal Island handles some 300,000 passengers per year. The national airline, TACV, has several international routes to Africa, Europe, and the United States, as well as providing domestic flights. A new international airport has been opened near the capital on Santiago Island.

Since Portugal Telecom acquired a 40 percent share of Cabo Verde Telecom in 1995, it has increased the number of telephone lines by 70 percent and also has provided fiber optic links between the islands, as well as Internet access. It was estimated that the nation had 45,644 telephone main lines in use in 2000. In 1998 Telemovel became the country's first cellular network. Portugal Telecom pledged $100 million for the modernization of telecommunications up until 2001.

There are only 2 weekly papers published in Cape Verde; one is state-owned and the other is run by the opposition. State television and radio merged in 1997 to form the new RTC company, and in 1998 the government allowed the resumption of private radio broadcasts. RTPi and Canal France International began broadcasting 24-hour television and radio in 1995.

Communications

Country	Telephones[a]	Telephones, Mobile/Cellular[a]	Radio Stations[b]	Radios[a]	TV Stations[a]	Televisions[a]	Internet Service Providers[c]	Internet Users[c]
Cape Verde	45,644 (2000)	19,729	AM 0; FM 11; shortwave 0	73,000	1	2,000	1	5,000
United States	194 M	69.209 M (1998)	AM 4,762; FM 5,542; shortwave 18	575 M	1,500	219 M	7,800	148 M
Nigeria	500,000 (2000)	26,700	AM 82; FM 35; shortwave 11	23.5 M	2 (1999)	6.9 M	11	100,000
Guinea-Bissau	8,000	N/A	AM 1; FM 2; shortwave 0	49,000	2	N/A	1	1,500

[a]Data is for 1997 unless otherwise noted.
[b]Data is for 1998 unless otherwise noted.
[c]Data is for 2000 unless otherwise noted.
SOURCE: CIA *World Factbook 2001* [Online].

Cape Verde has no known oil or gas deposits and imports all it needs from Africa and Europe. The privatized Empresa Nacional de Combustives and Shell Cabo Verde distribute fixed-price fuel. The parastatal Electra (which went up for sale in February 1999) is the primary electricity provider. There are plans to develop the country's thermal capacity, and the government is seeking to improve access to electricity in rural areas. Total electricity production in 1999 reached 40 million kilowatt hours (kWh).

ECONOMIC SECTORS

In 1998 the contribution to the GDP by sector was agriculture, 13 percent; industry, 19 percent; and services, 68 percent. The economy has also been bolstered by expatriate remittances, which are equivalent to 16 percent of the GDP, and grants from donors, equivalent to 18 percent of the GDP. In 1993, agriculture employed an estimated 24 percent of the working population, industry employed 25 percent, and services engaged 51 percent of the workforce. Approximately 24 percent of the labor force was unemployed in 1999.

AGRICULTURE

Although agriculture and fishing only accounted for 13 percent of GDP in 1998, it was still a significant source of employment. However, flooding and droughts make agricultural production extremely unsteady. The most important crops are sugarcane, maize, and beans, while **cash crops** like bananas, pineapples, and coffee are being encouraged. Currently bananas are the only exported crop.

Agriculture has been affected by an unequal landholding system, overpopulation of cultivable land, and the excessive subdivision of plots. Since independence the government has worked to reform the landholding system and more recently has turned its attention to maximizing water usage. Estimates suggest there is enough water available to cultivate 8,600 hectares (21,251 acres), compared to the present cultivation of only 3,000 hectares (7,413 acres).

Fishing (including lobster and tuna fishing) accounted for 2 percent of GDP in 1998 and is an important source of foreign currency. Cape Verde's **Exclusive Economic Zone** (EEZ) covers 734,265 square kilometers (283,500 square miles) and contains one of the last under-used fishing grounds in the world. In the long term Cape Verde expects to expand its fishing industry, with the island of Sao Vicente having the greatest potential. A recent deal was signed with Senegal and Guinea that opens their waters to Cape Verdean fishermen.

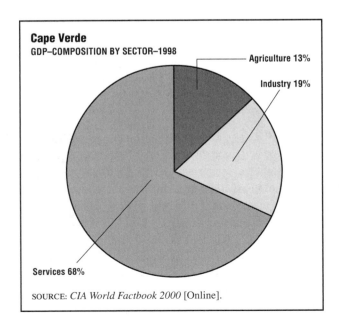

Cape Verde
GDP–COMPOSITION BY SECTOR–1998

Agriculture 13%
Industry 19%
Services 68%

SOURCE: *CIA World Factbook 2000* [Online].

INDUSTRY

Mining makes a negligible contribution to the economy. Salt is the most important mined resource in Cape Verde, and current production stands at only 7,000 metric tons per year. On the island of Santo Antao there has been intermittent exploitation of pozzolana, a volcanic ash used in making hydraulic cement.

Manufacturing, though slowly expanding, is quite small and underdeveloped. The main areas of manufacturing are in shoemaking, fish canning, rum distilling, textiles, and beverage bottling. There are about 120 small to medium-sized privately owned manufacturing companies, mostly located in Praia and on Sao Vicente. The government believes the nation's geographical position, relatively skilled labor force, and low wages make it suitable for light industry. Since 1993 a **free zone** enterprise law has provided custom and tax duty exemptions in an attempt to attract foreign investment. As a result, industrial exports quadrupled from 1994 to 1998.

SERVICES

Cape Verde's services sector is small and widely dispersed. The majority of the income produced in this sector comes from port-related services, including fueling and repair services. The Banco de Cabo Verde, the central bank, is expected to gain additional autonomy under the 1999 constitutional reforms. Banco Comercial do Atlântico (BCA) and Caixa Económica de Cabo Verde (CECV) are the only commercial banks, both of which are in the process of being privatized. Two Portuguese banks have opened in Cape Verde and should raise the availability of credit. Reforms in the financial sector have allowed the government to offer tax-free government bonds and high yield savings accounts. A stock exchange opened in Praia in 1999.

Tourism contributed only 3 percent to the GDP in 1998 but has been identified as having significant potential growth. The government aims to attract 400,000 visitors per year by 2008, a big expansion from the 57,000 visitors in 1998. Several new hotel developments are underway, and since the mid-1990s tourist arrivals have grown by 11 percent per year, with tourists coming mainly from Europe (especially Portugal).

INTERNATIONAL TRADE

Cape Verde has little to export, and total export revenues were only $40 million in 2000. In 1994 the primary exports were foodstuffs (50 percent) and manufactured items (mostly leather goods and garments, 46 percent). Exports in 1994 went to Portugal (59 percent),

Trade (expressed in billions of US$): Cape Verde		
	Exports	Imports
1975	.002	.040
1980	.004	.068
1985	.006	.084
1990	.006	.136
1995	.009	.252
1998	N/A	N/A

SOURCE: International Monetary Fund. *International Financial Statistics Yearbook 1999.*

Spain (14 percent), the United Kingdom (14 percent), and France (5 percent).

Cape Verde relies heavily on imports, which totaled approximately $250 million in 2000. Primary imports in 1994 were foodstuffs (28 percent), fuels (4 percent), machinery and transport equipment (37 percent), construction materials (16 percent), and other consumer manufactures. Imports come mainly from Portugal (36 percent), France (14 percent), Netherlands (8 percent), Japan (5 percent), Denmark (4 percent), Germany (4 percent), Sweden (4 percent), Belgium (3 percent), and Brazil (3 percent).

Cape Verde has recorded large merchandise **trade deficits** on a regular basis since independence, and the deficit worsened in the 1990s. Initiatives backed by the International Monetary Fund (IMF) have lessened the trade gap, but it still remains high. The balance of trade deficit stood at $210 million in 210, which was over 30 percent of GDP.

MONEY

The Cape Verde escudo has been pegged to the Portuguese escudo at a rate of 55:1 since 1998 and, therefore, is fairly stable. In January 1999 the pegged currency was transferred to the euro at CVE 110.265:1 euro. The Banco de Cabo Verde, the central bank, gained additional

Exchange rates: Cape Verde	
Cape Verdean escudos per US$1	
Dec 2000	123.080
2000	115.877
1999	102.700
1998	98.158
1997	93.177
1996	82.591

SOURCE: CIA *World Factbook 2001* [ONLINE].

autonomy in constitutional reforms made in July 1999. Its main functions are to control the money supply through the issue of currency and to regulate the commercial banks. However, most capital for development has had to come from foreign investment and aid, which the ruling MPD party has been consistently successful at attracting. The continuing high rate of inflation in Cape Verde is problematic, since it is higher than that of its main trading partner, Portugal, and thus raises Cape Verde's export prices, making them noncompetitive. Inflation stood at 4 percent in 2000.

POVERTY AND WEALTH

Only a small proportion of the population of Cape Verde (7 percent) are below the dollar-a-day poverty line (to be below this line means not having enough income to obtain the barest minimum of food, clothing, and shelter). Those in poverty include families that rely on agriculture for their livelihoods, whose farms may suffer from poor soil and inadequate rainfall, and urban dwellers without formal sector jobs and no family support, who exist by casual **hawking**, portering, and scavenging. Although average incomes are comparable to the average elsewhere in Africa, many Cape Verdeans are still very poor.

According to the **United Nations Development Program**'s (UNDP) Human Development Index (which combines measures of income, health, and education), Cape Verde climbed from 117th in 1995 to 106th in 1999 out of 174 total countries. In sub-Saharan Africa it now ranks third out of 43 countries, placing Cape Verde firmly in the medium development bracket, reflecting not only its economic development, but also its progress in health and education since independence.

Life expectancy was estimated at 69 years in 2001 (up from 52 years in 1960), which is the highest in sub-Saharan Africa, and this is partly due to a well-developed health care system. Infant mortality stood at 53 per 1,000 live births in 2001 (better than the 65 per 1,000 average for developing countries). There is 1 doctor for every 4,270 people (according to 1992 estimates). There are plans for a new hospital to be built in the capital.

GDP per Capita (US$)					
Country	1975	1980	1985	1990	1998
Cape Verde	N/A	N/A	1,039	1,120	1,354
United States	19,364	21,529	23,200	25,363	29,683
Nigeria	301	314	230	258	256
Guinea-Bissau	226	168	206	223	173

SOURCE: United Nations. *Human Development Report 2000; Trends in human development and per capita income.*

Clean water and sanitation have been a problem for Cape Verde, leading to intermittent outbreaks of cholera. However, the government has implemented a scheme to bring clean water to all its citizens by 2005. The 1999 budget allocated $15.5 million to health care.

Literacy stood at 71 percent in 1997 (compared to 36 percent in 1970). There is universal primary school enrollment, secondary school enrollment is 27 percent, and 3 percent go on to higher education. Improving education at all levels in Cape Verde is a key priority for the UNDP. Education accounted for 19 percent of government expenditure in 1999.

WORKING CONDITIONS

The constitution guarantees respect for human dignity and recognizes the inviolable and inalienable rights of humanity, peace, and justice. It recognizes the equality of all citizens before the law, without distinction of social origin, social condition, economic status, race, religion, political convictions, or ideologies. The constitution promises transparency for all citizens in the practicing of fundamental liberties and guarantees the equality of citizens in all fields. Forced labor is illegal. However, Cape Verde lacks the legislation and implementation machinery to ensure that the requirements of the constitution are upheld. Despite this, Cape Verde is a tolerant society, and the multiparty democratic process and the rule of law are well established.

A major problem in Cape Verde is unemployment, with 24 percent of the economically active population unable to find formal work. Although public investment in productive, export-oriented sectors is likely to increase, it will not grow quickly enough to make major reductions in the unemployed workforce. Therefore, many will continue to seek work in foreign countries, despite the increasing legal problems of immigration to the United States and Europe. There is no set minimum wage. Trade unions exist in Cape Verde but are not particularly aggressive.

Social Security is available through the Instituto Nacional de Previdencia Social (INPS), established in 1991. The INPS provides a range of benefits, including retirement and disability pensions. In 1995 the scheme covered 23,000 workers, who contribute 23 percent of their earnings.

COUNTRY HISTORY AND ECONOMIC DEVELOPMENT

1456. Cape Verde is colonized by the Portuguese.

1500s. Cape Verde thrives as center for the transatlantic slave trade.

1951. Portugal changes Cape Verde's status to that of an overseas province, granting more local control.

1975. Cape Verde becomes independent following a 1974 revolution in Portugal. Aristedes Pereira is elected as the first president and the first National Assembly is elected.

1980. The Cape Verde arm of the African Party for the Independence of Guinea-Bissau and Cape Verde (PAIGC) abandons its goal of unification with Guinea-Bissau and forms the African Party for the Independence of Cape Verde (PAICV).

1981. Pereira of the PAICV is reelected president.

1986. Pereira is reelected president.

1990. Opposition political groups form the Movement for Democracy (MPD) in April and campaign for the right to take part in elections.

1991. The first multiparty elections are held in January, with the MPD winning a majority in the National Assembly and electing Antonio Monteiro as president.

1992. A new constitution is adopted.

1996. Monteiro is reelected president.

2001. Pedro Pires, of PAICV, is elected president by a narrow margin of 12 votes.

FUTURE TRENDS

Cape Verde's isolation, lack of important minerals, and inadequate rainfall are expected to limit progress in the immediate future. There are, however, 2 causes for cautious optimism. The first is that Cape Verde has good prospects for expanding its tourism sector: it is relatively close to Europe for a tropical destination, and it has the priceless benefit of a secure regime and political stability. Cape Verde is aiming for an 8-fold increase in tourism over the next 8 years, and with suitable foreign investment, this is quite achievable. If successful, this growth will provide a major boost to the nation's economy. The second encouraging feature is that Cape Verde has managed to establish manufacturing and exports in leather goods and garments. The low wage rates in Cape Verde, the good educational level of the Cape Verdean workforce, and the proximity to the markets of Europe sug-

gest that this sector of the economy can undergo significant expansion.

As for the foreseeable future, the 2000 budget was approved, but spending exceeded projections in 1999. The World Bank backed a loan to support administrative reform. Inflation has fallen but remains above target. Ties with the Azores have strengthened and the current account deficit doubled between 1997 and 1998. GDP growth estimates have been lowered slightly from 6 percent to 5.5 percent from 2000 to 2001, due to lapses in policy reform. The reduction in the growth rate can be expected to persist until the new government reveals its commitment to the liberalizing process. The election of Pedro Pires as president is unlikely to affect the overall policy of economic liberalization, although the privatization process may be slowed.

DEPENDENCIES

Cape Verde has no territories or colonies.

BIBLIOGRAPHY

Assembleia Nacional de Cabo Verde. <http://www.parlamento.cv>. Accessed October 2001.

"CapeVerde: Economy." *NewAfrica.* <http://www.newafrica.com/profiles/economy.asp?countryid=11>. Accessed September 2001.

Economist Intelligence Unit. *Country Profile: Cape Verde.* London: Economist Intelligence Unit, 2001.

Hodd, M. "Cape Verde." *The Economies of Africa.* Aldershot, England: Dartmouth Publications, 1991.

Kelly, R. C., et al., editors. *Cape Verde Country Review 1998/1999.* Commercial Data International, Inc., 1999.

U.S. Central Intelligence Agency. *World Factbook 2001.* <http://www.odci.gov/cia/publications/factbook/index.html>. Accessed September 2001.

U.S. Department of State. *Background Notes: Cape Verde, May 1998.* <http://www.state.gov/www/background_notes/cape_verde_0598_bgn.html>. Accessed October 2001.

U.S. Department of State. *FY 2001 Country Commercial Guide: Cape Verde.* <http://www.state.gov/www/about_state/business/com_guides/2001/africa/index.html>. Accessed October 2001.

—Jack Hodd

CENTRAL AFRICAN REPUBLIC

CAPITAL: Bangui.

MONETARY UNIT: Communauté Financière Africaine franc (CFA Fr). There are 100 centimes to 1 CFA Fr and 100 CFA Fr equal 1 French franc. Coins are in denominations of 5, 10, 25, 50, 100 and 500 CFA Fr, and bills of 500, 1,000, 2,000, 5,000 and 10,000 CFA Fr.

CHIEF EXPORTS: Diamonds, timber, cotton, coffee, and tobacco.

CHIEF IMPORTS: Food, textiles, petroleum products, machinery, electrical equipment, motor vehicles, chemicals, pharmaceuticals, consumer goods, and industrial products.

GROSS DOMESTIC PRODUCT: US$6.1 billion (purchasing power parity, 2000 est.).

BALANCE OF TRADE: Exports: US$166 million (f.o.b., 2000). Imports: US$154 million (f.o.b., 2000).

COUNTRY OVERVIEW

LOCATION AND SIZE. The former French colony of Ubangi-Shari, now the Central African Republic (CAR), is well named; it is a landlocked country in the center of the African continent. Land boundaries extend for 5,203 kilometers (3,233 miles) connecting Cameroon to the west, Chad and Sudan to the north, and the Republic of Congo and the Democratic Republic of Congo to the south. The country covers an area of 622,984 square kilometers (240,534 square miles), slightly smaller than Texas. The CAR is covered with tropical rainforest in the southern and western regions and dryer savanna in the north and east. The capital city, Bangui, is in the southwest, on the border of the Democratic Republic of the Congo. The other main towns are Bambari and Bossangoa.

POPULATION. The population of the Central African Republic was estimated at 3,576,884 in July 2001. It was growing 1.85 percent annually. The birth rate is estimated at 37.05 per 1,000 people and the death rate is 18.53 per

1,000 people. If current trends continue, the population, of which 43 percent are younger than 15, will surpass 4.2 million by 2010. These figures may change, however, because of the devastating effects of AIDS, which was prevalent in nearly 14 percent of the population in 1999, and the small percentage of people over 65 years. Some estimate that deaths caused by AIDS may be the most disruptive economic problem that the CAR will have to face in the coming years.

According to some sources, there are as many as 75 ethnic groups in the CAR but the Banda predominate, with the Baya, Sara and Mandjia people also prominent. There are 6,500 Europeans in the country, of which 2,500 are French. Approximately 24 percent of the population subscribe to indigenous religious beliefs, 50 percent are Christians (25 percent Protestant, 25 percent Roman Catholic), and 15 percent Muslim, with 11 percent after other faiths. Two-thirds of the people live in rural areas, with most of the remaining third residing in the capital, Bangui.

While French is the official language of the CAR, the national and most widely spoken language is Sangho. Other African languages, notably Hunsa and Swahili, are also spoken, as is Arabic.

OVERVIEW OF ECONOMY

The Central African Republic's economy is based primarily on subsistence agriculture, with important mining and timber industries the main source of export earnings. Diamonds are the country's most profitable export, while agriculture occupies most of its working population. Farmers grow cotton, coffee, and tobacco for export and crops for local markets, but economic development is handicapped by the CAR's landlocked position, limited **infrastructure**, and the low education of its **workforce**. Poor government management and political instability have further weakened the CAR's economic condition. The **informal sector** is important in the CAR, accounting for most economic activity and a large share of the diamond trade.

The CAR has had a turbulent economic history. Since gaining independence in 1960, the economy has endured intermittent periods of economic decline caused

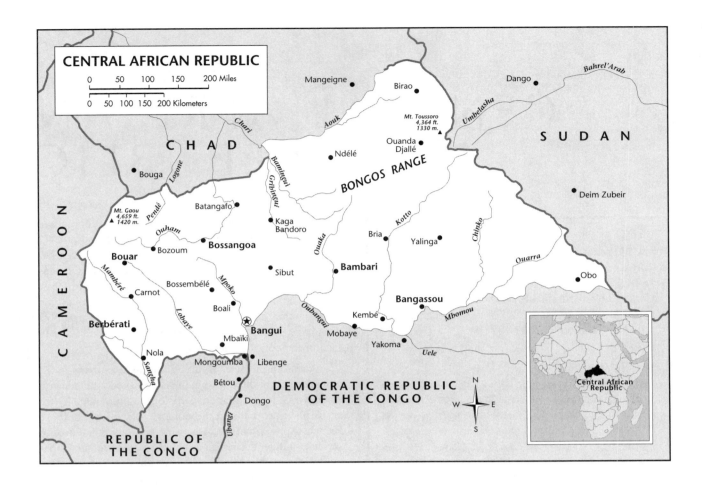

CENTRAL AFRICAN REPUBLIC

in part by poor management. Between 1960 and 1990, the CAR's first 3 presidents pursued authoritarian policies that often impeded economic growth. **Gross domestic product** (GDP) declined at an average annual rate of 2.5 percent between 1985 and 1995, partly due to self-proclaimed Emperor Jean Bedel Bokassa's **nationalizing** several industries during the 1970s. During the 1980s, government mismanagement and corruption and low commodity prices accentuated this decline. During the 1990s, the CAR pursued economic and democratic reforms with some success, but several army mutinies in 1996 and 1997 degenerated into looting and destruction of property in Bangui. These events weakened the government and damaged the economy.

Agriculture is the primary occupation for four-fifths of the population in the CAR. During the colonial era, the French introduced cotton and coffee. They have served as the main **cash crops** for rural families ever since. Small amounts of tobacco are also grown for both the export and domestic markets. Cassava (manioc) is by far the biggest staple food crop and is produced primarily for home consumption. Millet, sorghum, corn, peanuts, and yams are also grown by farmers, who consume most of these foods themselves and sell excess harvest in the local markets.

While crop farming is the main work activity, diamonds and timber provide most of the CAR's export earnings. Diamonds are especially important, accounting for 54 percent of export revenues in 1999, while timber earned an additional 16 percent. For the domestic market, the CAR has developed a few industries that produce **consumer goods**.

Poor transport links are obstacles to economic development. An estimated 90 percent of the CAR's commercial traffic passes through the port of Douala in Cameroon, where services are notoriously inefficient and costly. Poorly maintained dirt roads link the country to Cameroon's northern railway terminal in Ngaoundere.

Government mismanagement and political instability are 2 additional factors that have hindered economic growth. Many nationalized companies have suffered under government mismanagement, thus contributing to the CAR's long decline. The resulting chronic budgetary problems, with the government unable to collect sufficient revenue to pay salaries, have fueled social tensions and political instability. To address these problems the CAR has collaborated with the World Bank (WB) and the International Monetary Fund (IMF) to **privatize** several state companies and made efforts to stimulate growth. While there has been progress, the problem of chronic financial mismanagement continues. The CAR's economic woes are also exacerbated by the scarcity of jobs, rampant diamond smuggling, the large informal economy, and low levels of private investment.

Despite many problems, the CAR has valuable economic assets that could be profitably exploited. Fertile land and consistent rainfall are favorable to agriculture, there is the potential to export more mineral resources, and the country has abundant hydroelectric power that provides cheap electricity. But any growth is reliant on political stability and peace in the country.

POLITICS, GOVERNMENT, AND TAXATION

Politically, the CAR is an emerging democracy, whose population has the vote from age 21. The Republic's head of state is elected by popular vote for a 6-year term. He or she is responsible for appointing a prime minister as head of government, the council of ministers (cabinet), and the judges who serve the supreme and constitutional courts. The legal system is based in French law. The parliamentary structure is a 109-seat **unicameral** National Assembly, whose members are elected by the people and serve for 5 years. The National Assembly is advised by the Economic and Regional Council. The 2 bodies, when deliberating together, are known as the Congress. Local government is administered by 14 departments called prefectures, plus 2 economic prefectures, while the capital, Bangui, is designated as a commune.

There are 11 political parties, which field candidates for the National Assembly, but only a handful win representation. Until the mid-1990s, however, the country was run as a 1-party state, the party of the president. After the adoption of a constitution in January 1995, the system became more democratic and representative. By 2000, there were 12 political parties operating in the country.

An army officer, Jean Bedel Bokassa, stands as a potent symbol of the corruption and excess that characterizes many African leaders. Bokassa seized power in a military coup in 1965 and ruled for 14 years until 1979. In 1977, he crowned himself emperor-for-life in a lavish ceremony and began nationalizing the CAR's few industries. Under Bokassa's management, the economic steadily declined. The country's 3 other presidents since independence (David Dacko, Andre Kolingba, and Ange-Felix Patasse), they have proved unable to manage the CAR's economy.

After many decades of stability, army mutinies in 1996 and 1997 destabilized the political institutions and damaged the economy of the CAR. The mutinies began after soldiers, students, and civil servants protested over not being paid for months. The protest widened into widespread looting and destruction in the capital. After 3 years, a regional military force and a United Nations (UN) peacekeeping force reestablished political stability, allowing the CAR to organize democratic elections. The UN force was removed in 2000, but the budgetary problems—if not the open hostility—that caused the mutinies remain. Unable to reduce widespread tax evasion, the Central African government remains unable to raise enough revenue to pay its employees.

INFRASTRUCTURE, POWER, AND COMMUNICATIONS

Infrastructure in the CAR is underdeveloped, poorly maintained, and inadequate. The CAR has no railroads, and only 450 kilometers (280 miles) of the 25,000 kilometers (15,535 miles) roads are paved. Dirt roads are poorly maintained and deteriorate in the rainy season. No organized public transport is available because the country's poor infrastructure drives up the cost, thereby discouraging commerce and investment.

The CAR suffers economically from its inadequate links to port facilities. Some of Bangui's commercial cargo has traveled down the Ubangi River to Brazzaville and by rail to Point Noire. Civil unrest in the Congos has forced the CAR to divert its commercial traffic towards the Cameroonian port of Douala. The CAR has over 4,000 kilometers (2,485 miles) of waterways; over 1,000 kilometers (621 miles) are navigable.

The country has abundant hydroelectric resources that provide reliable and inexpensive power to the capital city. About 80 percent of the CAR's electricity is provided by hydroelectricity, most of which is generated north of Bangui, with fossil fuels providing the rest. Besides these hydroelectric generators, Bangui has oil-powered generators to supplement power during peak periods and to use as backup. The state-owned enterprise, Enerca, supplies the electricity. The potential exists to harness more water resources and export energy to neighboring countries.

The CAR's telephone service is limited to a small percentage of Bangui's population but operates efficiently. The state phone company, SOCATEL, has invested little capital in improving or expanding the system and customers regularly wait up to 6 months to have new phone lines installed. A SOCATEL subsidiary began providing Internet services in 1996, but subscribers remain low. During the late 1990s, several mobile phone companies began operations, but their infrastructure was initially confined to Bangui. When SOCATEL is privatized and other companies are allowed to compete, investments are expected to increase coverage.

Communications									
Country	Newspapers	Radios	TV Sets[a]	Cable subscribers[a]	Mobile Phones[a]	Fax Machines[a]	Personal Computers[a]	Internet Hosts[b]	Internet Users[b]
	1996	1997	1998	1998	1998	1998	1998	1999	1999
Central African Republic	2	83	5	N/A	0	0.1	N/A	0.00	1
United States	215	2,146	847	244.3	256	78.4	458.6	1,508.77	74,100
Dem. Rep. of Congo	3	375	135	N/A	0	N/A	N/A	0.00	1
Chad	0	242	1	0.0	0	0.0	N/A	0.00	1

[a]Data are from International Telecommunication Union, *World Telecommunication Development Report 1999* and are per 1,000 people.
[b]Data are from the Internet Software Consortium (http://www.isc.org) and are per 10,000 people.

SOURCE: World Bank. *World Development Indicators 2000.*

The CAR has only 1 international airport (near Bangui) and a few dirt airstrips. Several international airlines offer weekly flights between the capital and Paris, and to several regional capitals.

ECONOMIC SECTORS

Though production levels vary annually, agriculture has been the bedrock of the Central African economy, employing most of its workforce and accounting for half of the GDP for years. Agricultural output varies by product but has remained strong. Cotton production suffered from declining prices in the late 1990s, but this decrease was compensated for by increased food production. Lumber production also increased during the late 1990s as new timber companies entered the market. The CAR could produce far more agricultural exports, but it has been constrained by the lack of modern methods and poor access to regional markets.

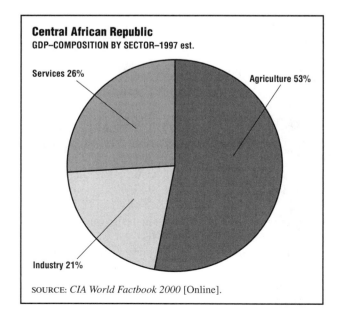

Central African Republic
GDP–COMPOSITION BY SECTOR–1997 est.

Services 26%
Agriculture 53%
Industry 21%

SOURCE: *CIA World Factbook 2000* [Online].

The industrial sector is focused on diamond mining, in which 80,000 members of the labor force are employed, and which accounts for most of Central Africa's export revenue. Production figures have been difficult to estimate because of widespread diamond smuggling, but production grew during the late 1990s. During 2000, evidence was found of world-class deposits of iron ore, offering hope of expanded mining activities. In addition, oil exploration in the northern part of the country has begun. The construction of a pipeline between Douala and southern Chad will make oil production more feasible in the CAR. There are also several basic industries producing beverages and footwear and assembling bicycles for the domestic market. The industrial sector accounted for 20 percent of GDP in 1999.

The service sector includes a few companies and a thriving informal **retail** trade. Although small (27 percent of the GDP in 1999), the service sector has been strengthened by the privatization of several state enterprises during the 1990s. As the government sells its industrial companies, private ownership increases the demand for banking and other services. Nevertheless, the World Bank estimates indicate that services fell from a high of 32 percent of the CAR's GDP during the late 1990s.

AGRICULTURE

Agriculture employs four-fifths of the CAR's labor force and accounts for more than half of the total GDP (53 percent in 1999). The country's largest agricultural export, timber, is harvested by several foreign companies. Farmers also produce cotton, coffee, and tobacco for export. **Subsistence farmers** grow cassava, millet, corn, and bananas for their own consumption and for sale on domestic markets. Individual small-scale farmers using traditional agricultural methods produce these crops. Small amounts of palm oil and sugar are produced for the domestic market.

Timber is acquired in the southwestern regions bordering on Cameroon and the Congos and is logged and exported by several foreign firms. Production has risen from 200,000 to 300,000 cubic meters in the early 1990s to nearly 500,000 cubic meters. Forests covered nearly half of the country in the late 1990s, but this area has been reduced since timber companies do not replace the trees they have cut down.

Coffee and cotton are the most important agricultural exports after timber. Introduced by the country's French colonizers, cotton is grown in the northern provinces bordering on Chad. The CAR usually produces about 50,000 tons of raw cotton, which is purchased and ginned by the state cotton company, SOCOCA. Cotton production suffered when prices fell during the 1980s, but it partially rebounded during the 1990s. Coffee farmers in central and southern regions produce 10,000 to 15,000 tons annually.

Cassava (manioc) is by far the biggest subsistence crop in the CAR. Farmers produce about 500,000 tons of cassava annually, greater than the combined output of millet, sorghum, rice, and corn. Peanuts, yams, and sesame are also cultivated for the domestic market. In addition, almost all farm families raise livestock, partly for family consumption and to provide extra income. An assortment of cattle, goats, sheep, pigs, and poultry are owned by most rural households across the country. Individual families using traditional methods produce these commodities. Some farmers harness cattle to plow their fields and transport their crops, but most plow, hoe, and harvest by hand. The entire family, regardless of age, helps in the long, hard work of farming.

INDUSTRY

The industrial sector makes up about 20 percent of GDP. Mining is the most significant part of this sector. Mining is conducted by individual miners who use simple equipment. CAR has deposits of gold, uranium, iron ore, manganese, and copper. Lack of infrastructure, which makes it difficult to find and to transport mined minerals, has impeded further mineral exploration, but the CAR has over 400,000 square kilometers (154,440 square miles) of unexplored terrain with high geological potential for diamonds and other mineral deposits.

Diamonds provide about half of the CAR's export earnings. An estimated 80,000 independent miners officially produced 415,000 carats of diamonds in 1999. The official numbers are well below the actual amount of diamonds mined because there is a great deal of diamond smuggling in the country. Legitimate miners sell their products to 160 certified agents who sell to purchasing agents in Bangui. But one respected French economic journal, *Marche Tropicaux*, estimated total exports in 1997 at 1.5 million carats, more than 3 times the official total.

Besides mining, the CAR has several industries that process products for export as well as producing goods for domestic markets. Though most lumber is exported as raw logs, some of it is processed in sawmills and exported as boards. As in many African countries, breweries are one of the country's oldest and largest industries, brewing beer primarily for domestic consumption. Several other small companies assemble bicycles and motorcycles. In recent years, the country's textile factory has become inactive because it was unable to compete against cheap imports and the second-hand clothing market.

SERVICES

The small banking sector remains plagued by past management problems and offers only limited services. A report by the Central Bank of Central Africa (BEAC) estimated in 1999 that only one of the CAR's 3 commercial banks was financially sound, but the other 2 were at least making progress with internal reforms. Several banks have been privatized during the 1990s, and 2 of these have joined the large European banking groups, Société General and Groupe Belgolaise.

The government telecommunications company, SOCATEL, holds a **monopoly** over most telephone services (excluding cellular services). In 1996, the government agreed to sell 40 percent of SOCATEL to the French company France Radio et Cable (FRC) and plans to sell its remaining 60 percent stake in the coming years.

Small informal vendors dominate retail services. A few modern shops are centered in Bangui's commercial district, but most retail sales are conducted by unregistered street vendors or those operating from one-room stores or roadside stalls. Informal trade is difficult to quantify, but it is clear that most retail commerce is conducted within the informal economy.

INTERNATIONAL TRADE

France is the largest trade and investment partner for the CAR and supplies 35 percent of its imports. French companies have invested in most major local industries as well as in banking and telecommunications services. Other European countries, particularly the Benelux countries (Belgium, the Netherlands, and Luxembourg) and Spain, import many of CAR's exports. Within Africa, the Ivory Coast and Cameroon are major trading partners, while trade with neighboring countries such as Chad, Cameroon, and Nigeria is probably far higher than official estimates because much of it evades customs.

The CAR generally has a **trade deficit** because it imports more than it is able to export, although the 2000 figures registered a surplus, with US$166 million in exports against US$154 million in imports. Export revenues

Trade (expressed in billions of US$): Central African Republic

	Exports	Imports
1975	.047	.069
1980	.116	.081
1985	.092	.113
1990	.120	.154
1995	.171	.174
1998	N/A	N/A

SOURCE: International Monetary Fund. *International Financial Statistics Yearbook 1999.*

are dependent on diamond production levels, but these are difficult to estimate because most of the diamond trade goes unrecorded by customs agents. Exports, especially of diamonds, coffee, cotton, and timber, rose after the 1994 **devaluation** of Central Africa's currency, but were later affected by political unrest in 1996 and 1997. The most important imports include petroleum products, machinery, and different consumer goods, which became more costly to purchase after the currency was devalued.

MONEY

The CAR is part of the Central African Monetary and Economic Union (Communaute Economiquareue et Monetaire de l'Afrique Centrale, or CEMAC), a group of 5 francophone countries that use the same currency, the CFA franc. The CFA franc is tied to the French franc and can be readily exchanged at 50 CFA francs to 1 French franc. The CAR, like all members of the CFA franc communities, has benefited from this stable currency.

As a member of the CFA zone, the CAR was profoundly affected by the 50 percent devaluation of the CFA in 1994. This had some positive short-term effects, though, in promoting exports of diamonds, timber and

cotton because it doubled the value of these exports in CFA francs, boosting revenue. The devaluation caused a temporary rise in **inflation** and lowered living standards temporarily and probably increased poverty by raising prices while most salaries remained static.

In the long term, results were more mixed. The devaluation made imported products relatively more expensive. One of the most significant price increases was of petrol, which was priced beyond the reach of many and severely curbed the use of petrol-powered transport, effectively stopping bus service, for example.

POVERTY AND WEALTH

Unemployment, given the lack of work opportunities in the CAR, is low at 6 percent, but poverty is high. In 1998, life expectancy was estimated at less than 45 years and less than half of the population could read. Per capita income levels have remained among the lowest in the world. Though most Central African families have limited income, they benefit from climatic conditions that enable them to produce enough food to survive. Most Central African people live under similar rural conditions, where food is available but money and consumer goods are more difficult to obtain. Social services, such as health care and education are seriously lacking.

GDP per Capita (US$)

Country	1975	1980	1985	1990	1998
Central African Republic	454	417	410	363	341
United States	19,364	21,529	23,200	25,363	29,683
Dem. Rep. of Congo	392	313	293	247	127
Chad	252	176	235	228	230

SOURCE: United Nations. *Human Development Report 2000; Trends in human development and per capita income.*

Exchange rates: Central African Republic

Communaute Financiere Africaine francs (CFA Fr) per US$1

Jan 2001	699.21
2000	711.98
1999	615.70
1998	589.95
1997	583.67
1996	511.55

Note: From January 1, 1999, the CFA Fr is pegged to the euro at a rate of 655.957 CFA Fr per euro.

SOURCE: CIA *World Factbook 2001* [ONLINE].

Distribution of Income or Consumption by Percentage Share: Central African Republic

Lowest 10%	0.7
Lowest 20%	2.0
Second 20%	4.9
Third 20%	9.6
Fourth 20%	18.5
Highest 20%	65.0
Highest 10%	47.7

Survey year: 1993
Note: This information refers to expenditure shares by percentiles of the population and is ranked by per capita expenditure.

SOURCE: *2000 World Development Indicators* [CD-ROM].

The urban population centered in Bangui is diverse, encompassing many different occupations and classes. However, as in several other countries in the region, the wealthy share their fortune with poorer relatives who live in rural areas, who frequently send gifts of produce in exchange for money. Many urban dwellers make their living through small-scale commerce. Women are particularly active in buying, processing, and selling different food commodities in local markets.

WORKING CONDITIONS

Working conditions in the CAR are similar to those encountered throughout rural Africa. Subsistence farmers use labor-intensive traditional farming methods to produce food and cash crops. Agricultural work varies seasonally, with fields plowed and crops sown in the early rainy season around May and June. The fields are worked during the rainy season, and the harvest is gathered between September and December. Most work is done by hand, but some farmers harness oxen to plough their fields.

A small portion of the population works in the diamond and lumber industries. Diamond miners are self-employed prospectors, whose earnings vary according to their luck in finding diamonds.

Most of the working population centered in Bangui is employed in the informal sector. Women often buy and sell different foods for meager profits, while men typically work in trades such as carpentry, masonry, and tailoring. Women have little access to education or to jobs and suffer from lesser protection under the law.

Members of the small civil service normally constitute a middle class elite, but this class has endured periods without salary because of the government's chronic budgetary problems.

COUNTRY HISTORY AND ECONOMIC DEVELOPMENT

1894. French forces occupy Central Africa (the current CAR).

1905. The CAR is joined to Chad under French colonial control.

1910. The CAR and Chad are joined with Gabon and the Congo to form French Equatorial Africa.

1928–31. Congo-Wara rebellion against forced labor on coffee and cotton plantations breaks out and is eventually crushed.

1946. A rebellion in the CAR forces France to grant the territory a legislative assembly and representation in the French parliament.

1958. The CAR achieves self-government as a part of French Equatorial Africa.

1960. The CAR gains its own independence. David Dacko is elected the country's first president.

1965. Army commander Jean-Bedel Bokassa takes power in a coup d'état.

1977. Bokassa crowns himself "emperor for life."

1979. Dacko overthrows Bokassa with the help of France in a bloodless coup.

1981. A bloodless coup led by General Andre Kolingba overthrows Dacko and establishes military rule.

1993. Ange-Felix Patasse is elected president.

1996–97. Several army mutinies break out over unpaid salaries and quickly degenerate into widespread looting of the capital city of Bangui. Patasse flees.

1997. Bangui accords are signed in January to reconcile political factions; France withdraws its troops in October.

1998. The UN sends a peacekeeping force to help maintain order throughout the legislative and presidential elections.

1999. Patasse is reelected president.

2001. More mutinies disrupt the political and economic stability of the country.

FUTURE TRENDS

The CAR has a great deal of economic potential. The country's fertile land and abundant water resources offer hope in the agricultural sector, while rich mineral resources offer an opportunity to expand the export of commodities other than diamonds. The current construction of the pipeline project will also increase the feasibility of petroleum exploration by making it easier and cheaper to export oil reserves through Cameroon. The potential is great, but all depends on the CAR's ability to conquer its past demons.

Despite the CAR's vast natural resources, several obstacles impede the CAR's future prosperity: deforestation, poor infrastructure, the AIDS epidemic, and political instability. Deforestation is an unfortunate result of the heavy logging industry. New strategies must be developed for the timber industry to thrive economically. Deforestation adds to the problems of frequent flooding as well as to the country's vulnerability to **desertification**. The poor quality and lack of adequate infrastructure throughout the country also hampers economic development, making it difficult to get products to market or to explore new deposits of valuable minerals. With AIDS cases reaching epidemic proportions, the lack of health-care coverage and education threaten the well-being of the country. Some estimate that the CAR will lose an increasing number of its labor force to AIDS. Finally, and to some—most importantly—the government needs to overcome its budgetary problems. Internal budgetary mismanagement has deprived civil servants and others of their salaries and has bred political unrest. The government's ability to manage successfully will determine political stability, the essential precondition for foreign investment and consequent economic growth.

DEPENDENCIES

Central African Republic has no territories or colonies.

BIBLIOGRAPHY

"Central African Republic and the IMF." *International Monetary Fund.* <http://www.imf.org/external/country/CAR/index>. Accessed January 2000.

"Central African Republic (CAR)." *Mbendi: Information for Africa.* <http://www.mbendi.co.za/land/af/cr/p0005.htm>. Accessed February 2001.

"Central African Republic." *World Bank.* <http://www.worldbank.org/>. Accessed January 2000.

Central African Republic Page. <http://www.sas.upenn.edu/African_Studies/Country_Specific/CAR.html>. Accessed October 2001.

Economist Intelligence Unit. *Country Report: Cameroon, Central African Republic and Chad, 2nd Quarter, 1999.* London: Economist Intelligence Unit, 1999.

U.S. Central Intelligence Agency. *World Factbook 2001.* <http://www.odci.gov/cia/publications/factbook/index.html>. Accessed October 2001.

U.S. Department of State. *Background Note: Central African Republic.* <http://www.state.gov/r/pa/bgn/index.cfm?docid=4007>. Accessed October 2001.

U.S. Department of State. *FY 2001 Country Commercial Guide for Chad.* <http://www.state.gov/www/about_state/business/com_guides/CAR>. Accessed December 2000.

—*Alexander Gazis*

CHAD

Republic of Chad
République du Tchad

CAPITAL: N'Djamena.

MONETARY UNIT: Central African franc (CFA Fr). 100 CFA Fr equals 1 French franc. There are coins of 5, 10, 25, 50, 100, and 500 CFA Fr. In the local marketplace, money is expressed in terms of "riyal," a unit equal to 5 CFA Fr. Thus 500 CFA Fr equals 100 riyal.

CHIEF EXPORTS: Cotton, cattle, textiles, gum arabic.

CHIEF IMPORTS: Machinery and transportation equipment, industrial goods, petroleum products, foodstuffs, textiles.

GROSS DOMESTIC PRODUCT: US$8.1 billion (purchasing power parity, 2000 est.).

BALANCE OF TRADE: **Exports:** US$172 million (f.o.b., 2000 est.). **Imports:** US$223 million (f.o.b., 2000 est.).

COUNTRY OVERVIEW

LOCATION AND SIZE. The former French colony of Chad, a landlocked country located in northern Central Africa, is more than 3 times the size of California. The country has an area of 1,284,000 square kilometers (495,755 square miles), with a land boundary length of 5,968 kilometers (3,708 miles). Neighboring countries are Niger, Nigeria, and Cameroon to the west; Libya to the north; Sudan to the east; and the Central African Republic (C.A.R.) to the south. Lake Chad in the southwestern part of the country is the largest body of water in the Sahel region. Chad also has the Tibesti mountain range in the far north, some smaller mountains in central Chad, and a few hills near the southern and western borders. Most of the country is desert or savanna with limited rainfall, although there are moderately temperate areas in the south. Chad's capital, N'Djamena, is in the southwestern part of the country.

POPULATION. In July 2001, the population of Chad was estimated at 8,707,078, an annual growth rate estimated of 3.29 percent. The birth rate is estimated at 48.28 per

1,000 people and the death rate at 15.4 per 1,000 people. Most of the population, half of which is under the age of 15, lives in several southern provinces where high rainfall makes farming and animal husbandry easier. About 1 percent lives in the arid upper half of the country extending into the Sahara desert. Population density varies between 0.15 persons per square kilometer (0.39 per square mile) in the northern province and 61.7 persons per square kilometer (154 per square mile) in the Logone Occidental province.

OVERVIEW OF ECONOMY

Chad's economy is primarily agricultural. Most of the population engages in **subsistence farming** and animal husbandry, producing food mainly for their own consumption. Chad depends on 3 commodities—cotton, cattle, and gum arabic (a gum from different African trees, used as an emulsifier in pills and candies)—for its export revenues. During the past 30 years, Chad's economy has been seriously damaged by chronic political instability. Its development has also been hindered by high energy and transport costs due in part to its geographic position. The beginning of a major oil project in southern Chad in 2000 offers an opportunity for Chad to diversify its economy and stimulate further growth.

The country's export commodities are subject to fluctuations in production and price levels. Cotton and cattle have been Chad's main exports before independence in 1960, but during the 1990s gum arabic emerged as a third major export commodity, making Chad the world's second biggest exporter after Sudan. Chad's economy has been vulnerable to swings in cotton prices, and when these fell during the 1980s, the economy suffered. Prices recovered during the 1990s, but production levels continue to vary according to the annual rainfall.

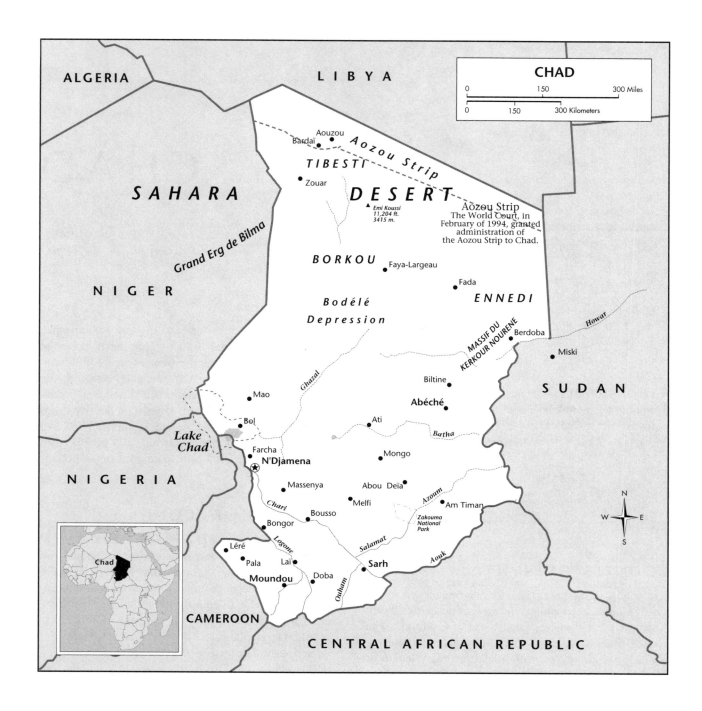

Armed conflicts and continuing tensions between ethnic, religious, and regional groups have severely damaged the economy. After independence in 1960, Chad was governed by the authoritarian leader, Francois Tombalbaye, until he was assassinated in 1975. Tombalbaye's death was followed by a decade of turbulence as several armed groups from different regions vied for control. The situation reached a climax in 1979 when a truce broke down between 2 principal armies stationed in N'Djamena, leading to further conflict and increased tensions between Muslim and Christian southerners. By the early 1980s, Hissein Habre, a ruthless northern dic-

tator, managed to consolidate his power. He ruled until 1990, when he was ousted by Idriss Deby, a former deputy. These years of violence and political instability have damaged Chad's **infrastructure** and seriously impeded its economic development.

Economic progress has also been hindered by several other constraints. Chad is seriously handicapped by its landlocked position; exports and imports must pass through Cameroon where widespread corruption inflates transport costs. Energy prices in Chad are among the highest in the world, and variable rainfall causes frequent deficits in food production. Heavy taxes, corruption, and the lack of an independent judiciary have discouraged foreign investment. These issues continue to limit commercial opportunities in Chad.

Like other poor countries with limited resources, Chad must import many goods and is dependent on foreign aid. Although the country's overall burden of debt is low by the standards of developing nations, the government relies on foreign donors to finance most investment projects. The European Union (EU), notably France, provides the largest share of foreign aid aimed toward health, education, and transport. Multilateral lending agencies, the United Nations (UN), the International Monetary Fund (IMF), and the World Bank also supply assistance to encourage improvements in government management and social services. Chad has a small industrial sector that produces paint, fruit juices, roofing, and a few other products mainly for domestic consumption, and depends on foreign suppliers for fuel and **consumer goods**.

As in many other developing countries, Chad's economy includes a thriving **informal sector**. Many entrepreneurs conduct commercial activity without official structure or permits and do not use organized accounting. Informal commerce ranges from individual vendors peddling their wares on the streets of N'Djamena to major business entrepreneurs transporting thousands of tons of gum arabic. Many businesses neglect to register their companies to avoid the high taxes imposed on formal businesses. The informal sector is hard to measure, but many observers estimate that most of Chad's economic activity is conducted by informal businesses.

During the late 1990s, Chad collaborated with the World Bank and the IMF to implement **structural adjustment programs** aimed at **liberalizing** the economy and improving government management. These programs have had some success. By 2000, most of Chad's state enterprises had been **privatized** and opened up to competition. In the rural water supply sector the former state-owned **monopoly** was converted into a private company and the water supply business opened to other competitors. The government has also managed to limit spending and meet some of its budgetary targets.

Chad's economy will receive a huge boost from the Chad-Cameroon Development project. A consortium (businesses working together) led by Exxon will invest US$3.7 billion in building production facilities, a pipeline, and associated infrastructure to export over 1 billion barrels of crude oil reserves in southern Chad. The World Bank has played a role in providing financing for the governments of Chad and Cameroon to invest in this project. In return for this financing, the World Bank has obtained agreements from the 2 governments that they will closely monitor environmental conditions and revenue management, issues of serious concern in the region. When oil starts flowing in 2004, the project is expected to double Chad's government revenue. More importantly, this project may stimulate investment in food processing and other promising sectors as local businesses satisfy demands created by the project.

POLITICS, GOVERNMENT, AND TAXATION

Chad's government continues to be dominated by a powerful president and his Patriotic Salvation Movement (MPS) party. After decades of civil war and regional clashes, Chad made some progress in increasing political freedoms and establishing democratic institutions during the 1990s. Nevertheless, elections have been marred by irregularities, and power remains concentrated in the president and his ruling Zaghawa clan. Chronic corruption and human rights abuses have contributed to a resurgence of armed conflict in the far north. These problems have seriously dampened Chad's economic climate and have forced the government to divert scarce resources into military expenditure.

To explain local politics, Chadian political observers have coined an often-quoted dictum: "A man's strength lies in his cooking pot." In such a poor country, vulnerable to famine, politicians ally themselves to the party that can best fill their "cooking pot." The ruling MPS has thus used its control over highly coveted civil service jobs to co-opt many rival parties and develop a nationwide membership. Some opposition parties support a more decentralized federal structure, but most parties rely on regional and ethnic loyalties and do not espouse ideology.

Chad is gradually trying to overcome a legacy of **socialism** inherited from France. Until recently, state companies enjoyed monopolies over major sectors, and lack of competition encouraged mismanagement and corruption in these companies. The government has privatized Chad's 2 largest banks, its rural water supply company, and its meat packing plant, as well as many other companies. State enterprises continue to control the cotton, electricity, and telecommunications companies, but these companies are due for privatization. The IMF and the World Bank have been helping the government to reduce its direct involvement in the economy.

High taxes and customs **duties** are another handicap to private business. Because there are so few formal businesses from which tax can be raised, the government must tax these firms heavily to acquire a modest amount of revenue. Corruption is also a major problem in tax collection and customs agencies. The government has, however, made efforts to reduce certain taxes and harmonize its tax and customs system with those of other countries in the Central African Economic Community (CEMAC).

Communications

Country	Newspapers	Radios	TV Sets[a]	Cable subscribers[a]	Mobile Phones[a]	Fax Machines[a]	Personal Computers[a]	Internet Hosts[b]	Internet Users[b]
	1996	1997	1998	1998	1998	1998	1998	1999	1999
Chad	0	242	1	0.0	0	0.0	N/A	0.00	1
United States	215	2,146	847	244.3	256	78.4	458.6	1,508.77	74,100
Nigeria	24	223	66	N/A	0	N/A	5.7	0.00	100
Central African Republic	2	83	5	N/A	0	0.1	N/A	0.00	1

[a]Data are from International Telecommunication Union, *World Telecommunication Development Report 1999* and are per 1,000 people.
[b]Data are from the Internet Software Consortium (http://www.isc.org) and are per 10,000 people.

SOURCE: World Bank. *World Development Indicators 2000.*

INFRASTRUCTURE, POWER, AND COMMUNICATIONS

Chad's infrastructure is exceptionally poor even by standards in other developing countries. Decades of civil war have taken their toll, and improvements have proceeded slowly. The road system is unpaved and vulnerable to erosion. Mismanagement of government-run power and communications monopolies slowed the development of infrastructure in these essential sectors. Chad's people have limited access to power, electricity, telecommunications, water, and other modern services fundamental in developed societies. Nevertheless, some improvements are expected as the government liberalizes energy and telecommunications sectors and gradually improves the transport infrastructure.

Transport costs are high, and most of Chad's roads are unpaved dirt or laterite (red soil found in humid tropical and subtropical areas) that can become impassable during the rainy season and make some regions inaccessible. According to the U.S. State Department's *2001 Country Commercial Guide* for Chad, less than 10 percent of 6,200 kilometers (3,853 miles) of roads in Chad were paved in 2000. Road conditions can vary widely according to the seasons.

Electricity and water services are confined to the capital, N'Djamena, and a few regional capitals. Even in these limited areas, electricity is extremely expensive and services are often cut off. Urban electricity and water supplies have long been provided by a state company, Société Tchadien d'Eau et d'Electricité (STEE), that has suffered from chronic corruption and mismanagement. As this company is privatized, there is hope that utility services will improve and prices will be lowered. In rural areas, most people rely on traditional wells with little or no protection against surface water contamination. Because of the absence of latrines and other human waste disposal systems in rural areas, there is a high incidence of water-borne diseases.

Chad ranks with those countries in the world that have the lowest density of telephones, televisions, and Internet users. According to the *World Development Indicators for 2000,* Chad has 1 television set per 1,000 people. Advertisements from the telephone company, Soteltchad, at the end of 2000 estimated that Chad had 10,260 telephones and 1,020 Internet subscribers. The country has 1 television station that is run by the state and a governmentally-run radio station which broadcasts from several regional capitals. Both the television and radio stations provide information from the government's perspective. Although there are several newspapers circulating in the city of N'Djamena that offer differing political views, the news does not reach Chad's mostly rural and illiterate population.

ECONOMIC SECTORS

Agriculture is the backbone of Chad's economy. In 1998, the *World Factbook* estimated that agriculture, fishing, and herding accounted for nearly 40 percent of the GDP and occupied 80 percent of the workforce. Agriculture continues to dominate Chad's economy, account-

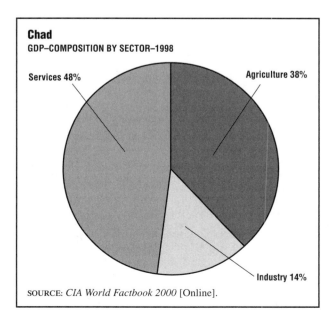

Chad
GDP–COMPOSITION BY SECTOR–1998

Services 48%
Agriculture 38%
Industry 14%

SOURCE: *CIA World Factbook 2000* [Online].

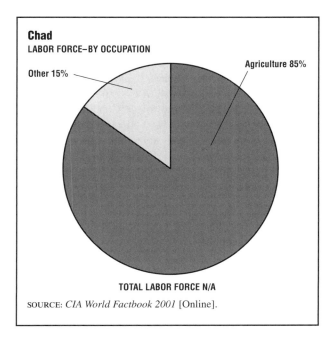

Chad
LABOR FORCE–BY OCCUPATION

Other 15%

Agriculture 85%

TOTAL LABOR FORCE N/A

SOURCE: *CIA World Factbook 2001* [Online].

ing for 44 percent of the GDP, but this figure alone does not convey the importance of agriculture and animal husbandry to the society. An estimated 85 percent of Chad's population relies primarily on these activities for its livelihood. In the agricultural sector, cotton accounts for half of Chad's export earnings and cattle provide most of the remainder. In addition, Chadians produce several crops and animals for their own consumption.

Chad has developed a small industrial sector that produces electricity, beverages, soap, oil, paint, and construction materials. Most of these goods are consumed domestically, while further industrial ventures have been impeded by high production costs and Chad's limited market. Industry accounted for 14 percent of GDP in 1998, according to the *World Factbook*. The petroleum sector is expected to grow dramatically in coming years as proven oil reserves of over 1 billion barrels are exploited in southern Chad.

The service sector is limited in size and in different services, although it accounted for 46 percent of GDP in 1998. According to the U.S. State Department's *Country Commercial Guide*, the banking sector had an estimated US$100 million in total deposits in 2000. The cost of credit is high, reflecting the risk to bankers. Medical services are rudimentary, limited by scarcities of human and material resources.

AGRICULTURE

Agriculture and animal husbandry employs 85 percent of the country's workforce but only contributes 44 percent to the GDP. While cotton, cattle, and gum ara-

bic provide most of Chad's export revenue, farmers also produce several subsistence crops for domestic consumption.

Farming methods are traditionally simple, and irrigation and mechanical equipment are rarely used. Farmers work their fields by hand or use cattle to till the soil. Competition for land between farmers and cattle-herders has caused conflicts in rural areas.

Cotton employs an estimated 2.5 million Chadians and provides half of Chad's export revenue. Over the past decade, production of raw cotton has varied between 94,000 tons and 260,000 tons. Production levels depend primarily on variations in annual rainfall, and the cotton sector has been affected by fluctuations in world prices. During the 1980s, low cotton prices caused the state cotton company, Cotontchad, to lose money for several years until it modernized its ginning factories and prices recovered. In addition to ginned cotton, Cotontchad produces oil and soap from cottonseed.

Chad's second leading export is cattle, most of which travel overland to Nigeria. Cattle-herders lead a semi-nomadic lifestyle, migrating north during the rainy season and traveling south in search of green pastures during the dry season. These migrations often bring them into conflict with farmers when cattle damage crops. Cattle-herders travel in small groups but are well armed to defend against hostile farmers. Camels, donkeys, goats, and sheep are also farmed, primarily for domestic use or consumption. These animals also represent savings and a measure of wealth in rural areas where money is scarce.

The country's main subsistence crops include grains, oilseeds, tubers, and several leafy vegetables (legumes). Millet and sorghum are the major staples of the local diet. These grains are also widely used to produce bili-bili and arghi, 2 popular alcoholic beverages. Chad produces between 600,000 and 1,100,000 tons of grain per year, most of which is consumed locally. Peanuts, groundnuts, and sesame are Chad's principal oil seeds and are also primarily for local consumption. Farmers grow several tubers, including manioc and sweet potatoes.

In the 1990s, gum arabic production soared, and Chad solidified its position as the world's second largest producer of this commodity. Chadian gum arabic production rose from fewer than 6,000 tons in the early 1990s to approximately 18,000 tons in 2000. Gum arabic is exported to Europe, the United States, and other industrialized nations, where it is used in soft drinks, pharmaceuticals, and many other products. Chadian gum is tapped by small-scale harvesters from wild acacia trees throughout the semi-arid Sahel region.

INDUSTRY

Chad has a small industrial base that mainly supplies its domestic market and contributed 14 percent of GDP in 1998. Industries manufacture construction materials, beverages, and a few other products for the local market. A textile mill produced fabric for several decades but was unable to compete with foreign imports. A consortium of oil companies is investing in a major oil project in southern Chad, which is expected to provide a boost to the economy. The high costs of energy and transport have impeded new industrial ventures, yet if these constraints can be eased and improved access found to Nigeria's market, the potential exists to process more raw commodities.

MANUFACTURING. Based in Moundou, Chad's most important industrial company, Cotontchad, gins cotton and manufactures soap and oil from cottonseed. Cotontchad also has ginning operations in several large southern towns. In addition to Cotontchad, Moundou has a cigarette company and a firm that assembles agricultural equipment. In N'Djamena, several companies produce paint, metal roofing, fruit drinks, mineral water and cookies. Chad's third largest city, Sahr, hosts a sugar production factory and an idle textile mill.

PETROLEUM. Chad's petroleum industry will be extremely important in the short-term future. There are plans to exploit 2 known petroleum deposits: a small reserve of high-grade oil north of Lake Chad and a much larger deposit of heavy crude oil in the Doba Basin of southern Chad. A consortium led by Exxon will employ up to 4000 workers and invest US$3.7 billion to exploit over 1 billion barrels in the Doba basin. Further exploration is planned to determine whether more reserves can be exploited.

MINING. A South Korean company, AFKO, recently began building a factory to extract gold reserves near the southern town of Pala. Chad is known to hold deposits of bauxite, iron ore, uranium, tin, and tungsten, but further research is necessary to determine whether these resources can be extracted.

SERVICES

Chad's service sector is limited, although it contributes an estimated 49 percent of the GDP, up from 46 percent in 1998. Privatization and improved management practices have strengthened financial services, but they remain limited in size and in the services they offer. **Retail** sales are conducted primarily in the informal sector. Chad holds some potential for tourism, but instability and lack of infrastructure have prevented the development of this sector. Some firms in the capital, N'Djamena, have seen a proliferation of computer service firms, offer insurance, accounting, and computer services. Several international firms offer accounting services, tax advice, and business consultancy services, but the market for these services remains limited as long as most Chadian entrepreneurs remain in the informal sector.

FINANCIAL SERVICES. Chad's banking sector is small by international standards. With US$100 million in deposits and limited capital investment, Chadian banks have little money to lend. Much of their capital finances the cotton-buying season for Cotontchad. For other businesses, credit is expensive and difficult to obtain. Short-term credit can cost 18 to 26 percent and long-term credit is rarely available.

RETAIL. The retail business is conducted primarily in the informal sector. Thousands of vendors wander in Chad's urban streets searching for buyers for their wares. In addition, thousands of small stores and roadside stands sell limited varieties of household goods. In rural and urban areas, many vendors gather in a network of small markets where perishable goods are sold.

TRANSPORTATION. Transport of goods is managed by many informal sector operators. Small vehicles and large semis carry passengers and merchandise between N'Djamena and different regional centers. Most vehicles are old and break down often.

INTERNATIONAL TRADE

Chad's principal trading partners are the EU countries and neighboring CEMAC countries. France has been Chad's largest trading partner, accounting for 41 percent of imports. Nigeria and Cameroon are probably Chad's next biggest trading partners, although much of this trade goes unrecorded by customs officials. The 2 countries export many consumer products to Chad. Cotton exports usually go to Portugal and other EU countries, while most beef exports go to Nigeria. Gum arabic has traditionally been exported to France and other EU countries, but increasing volumes now go to the United States.

For decades, Chad has run large **trade deficits**, importing far more than it exports. In 1999, exports were estimated at US$288 million against imports of US$359

Trade (expressed in billions of US$): Chad		
	Exports	Imports
1975	.048	.133
1980	.071	.074
1985	.062	.166
1990	.188	.286
1995	.277	.250
1998	N/A	N/A

SOURCE: International Monetary Fund. *International Financial Statistics Yearbook 1999.*

Exchange rates: Chad	
Communaute Financiere Africaine francs (CFA Fr) per US$1	
Jan 2001	699.21
2000	711.98
1999	615.70
1998	589.95
1997	583.67
1996	511.55

Note: From January 1, 1999, the CFA Fr is pegged to the euro at a rate of 655.957 CFA Fr per euro.

SOURCE: CIA *World Factbook 2001* [ONLINE].

GDP per Capita (US$)					
Country	1975	1980	1985	1990	1998
Chad	252	176	235	228	230
United States	19,364	21,529	23,200	25,363	29,683
Nigeria	301	314	230	258	256
Central African Republic	454	417	410	363	341

SOURCE: United Nations. *Human Development Report 2000; Trends in human development and per capita income.*

million. By 2000, the *World Factbook* estimated that exports had reached US$172 million and imports, US$223 million. When money flows out of Chad to purchase these exports, foreign donors compensate for this flow by sending money back into Chad for investment in development programs. In 1997, Taiwan promised US$125 million and the African Development Bank, US$30 million.

MONEY

As a member of the Central African Franc Zone, Chad underwent a 50 percent **devaluation** of its currency in early 1994. Unlike other CFAF countries, however, Chad benefited little from this devaluation, which raised **inflation** for two years but failed to stimulate export volumes. Chad has otherwise benefited from a stable currency.

In Chad's domestic markets, inflation and **deflation** are seasonal occurrences. Food prices fall during the harvest season and usually rise by at least 100 percent during the rainy season. Chad's markets are volatile, and prices vary from day to day and week to week. At the end of each month when civil servants are paid, prices for prized consumable goods such as fish and chicken rise for a short while as suppliers take advantage of a brief rise in demand.

POVERTY AND WEALTH

In the **United Nations Development Program**'s World Development reports, Chad's Human Development Indicator has increased from 0.29 in 1990 to 0.393 in 1999, placing it among the 10 poorest countries in the world. In the benchmarks used to measure poverty (literacy rates, access to health care, access to clean water, etc.) Chad has ranked among the poorest countries in Africa.

Chad's population can be divided into rural and urban classes. In rural areas, farmers and animal herders construct their own housing and produce most of their own food but earn little monetary income. In urban ar-

eas, small business people practice an array of trades. The civil service constitutes Chad's upper class, though its employees are poorly paid by international standards. A small class of diplomats, international aid workers, high-ranking government officials, and a few **private sector** managers occupy topmost wage scale.

Urban and rural classes are closely linked by Chad's extended family traditions. Poor rural farmers will often send children to live with comparatively wealthy urban relatives to study in urban schools. And wealthy urbanites often send money in return for foodstuffs as a means of helping out less fortunate rural relatives. Given the lack of social security programs, the poor, the elderly, and the handicapped usually depend on members of their extended family for support.

WORKING CONDITIONS

Working conditions, too, differ between rural and urban areas. Farmers rely on family members, including small children, to help labor in the fields and harvest the crops. Animal herders have a different lifestyle, migrating seasonally between northern and southern pastures. Monetary wages are low for unskilled workers, averaging less than a dollar per day. More educated workers can earn substantially more, but the scarcity of jobs tends to drive down wage rates. Chad's labor code is adapted from French laws that are protective of workers, but workers in the informal sector are not covered by these rules. Several unions have been formed to represent different workers, but their influence is limited.

COUNTRY HISTORY AND ECONOMIC DEVELOPMENT

1891. France begins colonizing Chad.

1900. Decisive battle between France's Major Lamy and Chad's Rabah marks the French victory over the Chadian leader. Both Lamy and Rabah die during the battle.

1960. Chad gains its independence from France. Francois Tombalbaye becomes Chad's first president.

1975. Tombalbaye is assassinated.

1979. Civil war erupts in N'Djamena.

1982. Hissein Habre consolidates power in N'Djamena.

1990. Idriss Deby takes power by military force.

1996. Constitution is voted on by referendum. Presidential elections are held.

2000. The Chad-Cameroon oil production and pipeline project begins.

FUTURE TRENDS

Provided Chad's civil unrest is resolved, Chad's economy could improve. The boost expected by the oil production project in the southern Doba Basin region will help in the service sector as well, creating transportation jobs in particular. The construction phase began in October 2000 and is due to finish by 2004. Once production begins, this Exxon-led project will double current government revenue. The increased revenue will allow Chad to invest in social programs and reduce its dependency on foreign donors. Chad should experience improvement in other parts of the economy as well, especially in the cotton industry, which is scheduled to be privatized over the next several years. Despite the improved economic prospects for Chad, political stability remains the most important factor for economic progress in the country.

DEPENDENCIES

Chad has no territories or colonies.

BIBLIOGRAPHY

Economist Intelligence Unit. *Country Report: Cameroon, Central African Republic and Chad, 2nd Quarter, 1999.* London: Economist Intelligence Unit, 1999.

"Chad at a Glance." *World Bank Group.* <http://www.worldbank .org/data/countrydata/aag/tcd>. Accessed January 2000.

"Chad Country Brief." *World Bank Group.* <http://www .worldbank.org/data/countrydata/aag/tcd>. Accessed January 2000.

"Chad Data Profile." *World Bank Group.* <http://www.worldbank .org/data/countrydata/aag/tcd>. Accessed January 2000.

Embassy of Chad in the United States. <http://www.chadembassy .org>. Accessed October 2001.

International Monetary Fund. <http://www.imf.org/external/ country/TCD/index>. Accessed January 2000. "Tchad." *Marché Tropicaux Special Edition.* May 28, 1999.

U.S. Central Intelligence Agency. *World Factbook 2001.* <http:// www.odci.gov/cia/publications/factbook/index.html>. Accessed October 2001.

U.S. Department of State. *FY 2001 Country Commercial Guide: Chad.* <http://www.state.gov/www/about_state/business/ com_guides/chad>. Accessed December 2000.

—Alexander Gazis

COMOROS

Federal Islamic Republic of the Comoros
République Fédérale Islamique des Comores
Jumhuriyat al-Qumur al-Ittihadiyah
al-Islamiyah

CAPITAL: Moroni.

MONETARY UNIT: Comoran franc (KMF). One Comoran franc equals 100 centimes. There are notes with denominations of 25, 50, 100, 1,000, 5,000, and 10,000 francs. Coins come in denominations of 1, 2, 5, 10, and 20 francs and 20 centimes. French francs are also commonly used. The Comoran franc is currently pegged to the euro at KMF 492 = 1 euro.

CHIEF EXPORTS: Vanilla, ylang-ylang, cloves, perfume oil, and copra.

CHIEF IMPORTS: Rice and other foodstuffs, consumer goods, petroleum products, cement, and transport equipment.

GROSS DOMESTIC PRODUCT: US$419 million (purchasing power parity, 2000 est.).

BALANCE OF TRADE: Exports: US$7.9 million (f.o.b., 1999 est.). **Imports:** US$55.1 million (f.o.b., 1999 est.).

COUNTRY OVERVIEW

LOCATION AND SIZE. Comoros is comprised of 3 islands that are part of a 4-island archipelago in the Mozambique Channel. The fourth island, Mayotte, is still a dependency of France. The islands lie between the northern tip of Madagascar and the African mainland. The archipelago, formed by the tips of a volcanic mountain range rising from the Mozambique Channel, stretches over 300 kilometers (186 miles) from north to south. Comoros has a land area of 2,170 square kilometers (838 square miles), making it slightly larger than 12 times the size of Washington, D.C. The main island, Grande Comore (locally known as Ngazidja but also called Njazidja), is geologically the youngest. It measures 60 kilometers (37 miles) from north to south and 20 kilometers (12 miles) from east to west. Its most prominent geographical feature is Mount Kartala (2,361 meters/7,746 feet), an active volcano which smokes and bubbles continuously on Grande. The capital, Moroni, is located on Grande Comore. The other 2 smaller is-

lands are Anjouan (Nzwani) and Mohéli (Mwali). Anjouan is the most topographically varied, with steep coastlines and deep valleys. Its highest peak, Mount Ntingui, rises 1,595 meters (5,233 feet). Mohéli, on the other hand, is the smallest, least populated, and least developed island. The total coastline of the islands is 340 kilometers (211 miles).

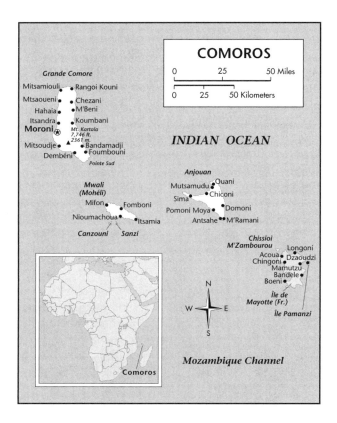

POPULATION. The population of Comoros was estimated at 596,000 in July 2001, up from 479,600 in 1994. The nation has a young population; the proportion of older people (65 years of age and above) was estimated at 2.9 percent in 2001, while the 0–14 age group was 43 percent in the same year. Comoros is steadily becoming more urbanized, with the proportion of the population living in towns having increased from 29.9 percent in 1994 to 32.1 percent in 1998. The population consists almost entirely of persons of mixed-race, mostly of African, Malagasy, and Arab descent.

French, Comoran, and Arabic are the official languages. Comoran, the main spoken language, is akin to Swahili but has elements borrowed from Arabic. Other languages spoken include Malagasy and Swahili.

Islam, the state religion, is followed by 98 percent of Comorans. Almost all Comorans are Sunni Muslims. There are small numbers of Christians, mostly Roman Catholics of French Malagasy descent.

OVERVIEW OF ECONOMY

The economy of Comoros is limited by low incomes, high unemployment, an inadequate transport system, the nation's isolated location, the absence of any mineral resources, and a heavy dependence on foreign aid. Most of the population relies on small-scale family agriculture for their livelihoods. The industrial sector is very small and relies mostly on construction and electricity and water distribution. The industrial sector also is supplemented by some processing of ylang ylang (a flower used to make perfume) and vanilla. The services sector comprises mostly government employees, with some employment in the tourism sector.

Comoros has suffered continuous political instability since independence in 1975, which has impeded economic progress. Local and foreign businesses are unwilling to invest in the current volatile (unstable) political and business climate. Falling world prices and increased competition in the international market for the principal export commodities of Comoros have contributed to economic decline. Emphasis is currently on containing **public sector** wage costs to reduce domestic **inflation** and speeding-up **privatization** of state-owned enterprises.

The per capita **gross national product** (GNP) of Comoros was estimated at $370 in 1998 by the **exchange rate** conversion. Per capita GNP declined in real terms from 1990 to 1997 at an average annual rate of -3.1 percent. Output grew at an almost negligible rate of 0.1 percent per year in the last half of the 1990s, much less than the population growth rate, which was estimated at 3 percent in 2001.

POLITICS, GOVERNMENT, AND TAXATION

The 3 islands that form the present state of Comoros were French protectorates at the end of the 19th century and were proclaimed colonies in 1912. Following a referendum in December 1974, the Comoran Chamber of Deputies unilaterally declared the islands' independence on 6 July 1975. Mayotte, the fourth island in the group, opted to remain a French dependency.

Since 1975 there has been continuous political instability characterized by coups and undemocratic regimes. Recent years have been marked by internal political disruptions, and the islands of Anjouan and Mohéli have attempted to secede.

The constitution of 1 October 1978 was amended in 1983, approved in a referendum, and Comoros became a Federal Islamic Republic. Mayotte was permitted the right to join when it so chose. A new constitution was adopted on 20 October 1996. The constitution stipulates that each of the islands has a council and a governor who is appointed by the president. The president is elected by direct universal suffrage for an unlimited number of 5-year terms.

The president appoints the prime minister, who heads the Council of Ministers. There is a **bicameral** legislative branch, consisting of a 43-member Federal Assembly, the members of which are directly elected for 5-year terms, and a 15-member Senate, made up of 5 members from each island who are selected by regional councils.

Colonel Azali Assoumani staged a bloodless coup on 30 April 1999. He introduced a new constitutional charter giving himself full legislative and executive powers. The Federal Assembly has not met since the coup. Azali promised that he would serve for 1 year at the time he came to power, but the elections promised for spring 2000 were not held. Assoumani has pledged that elections will take place before the end of 2001, and it is expected that this will herald a reopening of the Federal Assembly.

Comoros had a 1,500-man national army in 1997, the Force Comorienne de Defense (FCD), which was supported by a French military contingent. The size of the armed forces has not changed since the coup. The role of the French has been to exert pressure for a return to democratic rule.

The main political forces are continually fragmenting and reforming, and alliances are based mainly on opportunism. The party of government prior to the 1999 coup was the National Union for Democracy in Comoros (NUDC). Other parties are the Republican Party of Comoros (PRC), the Democratic Front (DF), and the Movement for Socialism and Democracy

(MSD). These parties are now dormant. They are expected to come to life only when the military government **sanctions** campaigning for the elections expected in late 2001.

Previously the island governors undertook tax collection, but it became a federal responsibility under a 1983 constitutional revision. Wage and salary earners were taxed at a maximum rate of 15 percent in 1987; however, only government employees appear to pay tax, and there has been no attempt at **income tax** reform in subsequent years. Tax rates have ranged from 17 percent on **consumer goods** to 60 percent on building materials and cars to 200 percent on luxury goods. Import and export licenses are required but are usually limited to a few favored firms. Tax revenue as a share of expenditure increased from 33 percent in 1994 to 54 percent in 1998, implying an improved ability to meet public sector expenses without relying on aid from overseas. The total tax revenue share of the **gross domestic product** (GDP) also increased from 13 percent in 1994 to 15 percent in 1998.

The overall **budget deficit** in 1998 was estimated at US$8.4 million, equivalent to 4 percent of the GDP. The nation's **external debt** at the end of 1997 totaled US$197.4 million, and the cost of **debt servicing** was about 10 percent of the value of exports in 1998, or slightly below the 15 percent average for African nations. The relatively low debt-servicing ratio means that Comoros has a greater availability of foreign exchange with which to purchase imports.

Comoros is a member of several international organizations. These include the Indian Ocean Commission (IOC), which is dedicated to regional cooperation; the Common Market for Eastern and Southern Africa (COMESA), which aims at reducing barriers to trade and the movements of labor and capital; and the Franc Zone, which pegs the currency to the French franc.

INFRASTRUCTURE, POWER, AND COMMUNICATIONS

Comoros has poorly developed **infrastructure**. The transport system is particularly limited. In 1996, it was estimated that there was a total of 880 kilometers (547 miles) of highways, 673 kilometers (418 miles) of which were paved. There are no railways. Prince Said Ibrahim Airport is the international air terminus near Moroni. In 1996, it handled 92,000 passengers.

There were 75,000 telephone main lines in 1997 and 100 fax machines in 1995. There were 36 post offices in 1993. Comoros does not have any local newspapers; the few that are read are circulated from Madagascar. The U.S. State Department noted that there were about 5 independent local television stations in 1998. The CIA *World Factbook* estimated that the country only had 1,000 televisions in 1997. There were 90,000 radios in the country by 1997, with 1 government-run station, Radio Comoros; an opposition station, Tropique; and about 20 other regional stations. The government introduced Internet service in 1998 and there were 800 Internet users by 2000.

In 1981, Comoros had 236 primary schools, 1 teacher training college, and 2 technical schools. In 1998, there were no universities, and the public schools on Grand Comore were closed for most of the year because of civil unrest.

Work began in 1985 on a 4,500-kilowatt hydroelectric dam on Anjouan. In 1998, 15 million kilowatt hours (kWh) were generated. Fossil fuels currently generate 87 percent of electricity, with the remaining 13 percent provided by hydroelectricity.

Communications

Country	Telephones[a]	Telephones, Mobile/Cellular[a]	Radio Stations[b]	Radios[a]	TV Stations[a]	Televisions[a]	Internet Service Providers[c]	Internet Users[c]
Comoros	6,000	N/A	AM 1; FM 2; shortwave 1	90,000	0 (1998)	1,000	1	800
United States	194 M	69.209 M (1998)	AM 4,762; FM 5,542; shortwave 18	575 M	1,500	219 M	7,800	148 M
South Africa	5.075 M (1999)	2 M (1999)	AM 14; FM 347; shortwave 1	13.75 M	556	5.2 M	44	1.82 M
Mauritius	223,000	37,000	AM 5; FM 9; shortwave 2	420,000	2	258,000	2	55,000

[a]Data is for 1997 unless otherwise noted.
[b]Data is for 1998 unless otherwise noted.
[c]Data is for 2000 unless otherwise noted.

SOURCE: CIA *World Factbook 2001* [Online].

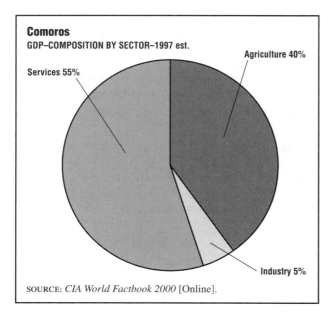

Comoros
GDP–COMPOSITION BY SECTOR–1997 est.

Services 55%
Agriculture 40%
Industry 5%

SOURCE: *CIA World Factbook 2000* [Online].

ECONOMIC SECTORS

Agriculture (including hunting, forestry, and fishing) contributed 40 percent of the GDP in 2000. About 74 percent of the workforce are employed in this sector. Agriculture accounts for more than 98 percent of total exports. The principal **cash crops** are vanilla, ylang ylang, cloves, and copra (dried coconut flesh).

Industry (including manufacturing, construction, and power) contributed 4 percent of the GDP in 2000. The industrial sector employs 6 percent of the workforce. The manufacturing sub-sector is the largest contributor to the industrial share of the GDP. Manufacturing in Comoros

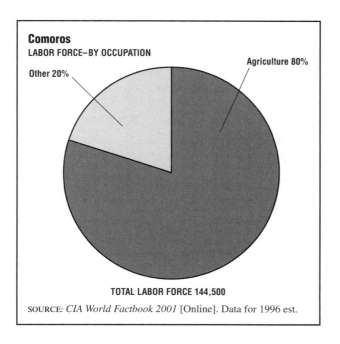

Comoros
LABOR FORCE–BY OCCUPATION

Other 20%
Agriculture 80%

TOTAL LABOR FORCE 144,500

SOURCE: *CIA World Factbook 2001* [Online]. Data for 1996 est.

is primarily comprised of agro-processing industries, with vanilla and essential oils as their main products. Energy is derived from woodfuel (78 percent) and thermal installations.

The service sector contributed 56 percent of the GDP in 2000 and employs approximately 20 percent of the workforce. Despite political instability, there has been some growth in tourism leading to expansion in retailing, catering, and hotel activities.

AGRICULTURE

The chief agricultural export product used to be sugar, but now vanilla, copra, maize, cloves, and essential oils (citronella, ylang-ylang, and lemon grass) have gained increasing importance. Crops that are mainly for domestic consumption include cassava, taro (a tropical root crop), rice, maize pulses, coconuts, and bananas. Almost all agricultural production takes place on small family farms, with tilling, weeding, and harvesting undertaken by hand. The success of the harvests heavily relies on rainfall, which is generally adequate and regular. From 1990 to 1996, the **real GDP** of the agricultural sector declined at an average annual rate of -0.7 percent, mainly as a result of political instability that discouraged investment and poor progress with economic reforms.

In 1995, 9,000 hectares (22,240 acres) of Comoros was forestland, or about 4 percent of the total land area. The shortage of cultivable land, the pressure to increase ylang-ylang production, and the demand for woodfuel are all contributing to deforestation at a rate of 6 percent a year. At present the government has no policies to combat deforestation.

Fishing is small-scale and is accomplished without modern equipment. The catch was estimated at 13,200 metric tons in 1995.

INDUSTRY

Industry comprises mostly construction and the provision of electricity but also includes the processing of spices and extraction of perfume from flowers. The construction sector consists of **private sector** enterprises and is very reliant on conditions elsewhere in the economy. Spurts in tourist activity, for example, lead to increased hotel and dwelling construction. International construction companies undertake most large construction projects (such as highways, ports, and modern hotels). The amount of agricultural processing has not expanded in recent years, mainly because low prices offer little incentive to growers to invest in new planting and increase output.

Owing mainly to a sharp rise in construction activity, industrial GDP increased at an average annual rate of 5.7 percent from 1990 to 1996. Industry's contribution to the GDP has subsequently contracted, providing 4 percent of GDP in 2000, down from 6.0 percent in 1994.

SERVICES

Service is now the largest sector of the economy in terms of output, contributing an average of 48 percent of the GDP from 1994 to 1998 and 56 percent by 2000. However, only 20 percent of the workforce is employed in services. The service sector generates the highest incomes in Comoros, and earnings are particularly high in government service and tourism.

The tourism industry was undeveloped at independence and still has made only modest progress towards its potential. The major hindrance has been the lack of political stability, which clearly has discouraged visitors. Fortunately, the regular unconstitutional changes of government have not resulted in any serious problems for tourists who have visited the islands. The bigger issue is that foreign investment in hotels and resorts has been discouraged. Nevertheless, a number of development projects have been completed, and there has been some recent rise in tourism receipts. In 1996, there were 23,775 tourist arrivals by Air Comoros and receipts totaled $9.1 million.

INTERNATIONAL TRADE

Comoros has had persistant **trade deficits**, which are covered by foreign aid, most of which comes from France. Merchandise export earnings in 1999 were $11 million. (The *World Factbook* estimated that exports reached US$7.9 million that same year.) The bulk of the exports were ylang-ylang essence, other essential oils, vanilla, cloves, copra, and other agricultural produce. The most important export earner is vanilla, although there is yearly variation depending on the success of the harvests. Most exports go to France (35 percent) with Germany, the United States, Singapore, and Mauritius also providing important export markets.

Exchange rates: Comoros	
Comoran francs per US$1	
Jan 2001	524.41
2000	533.98
1999	461.77
1998	442.46
1997	437.75
1996	383.66

Note: Prior to January 1999, the official rate was pegged to the French franc at 75 Comoran francs per French franc; since January 1, 1999, the Comoran franc is pegged to the euro at a rate of 491.9677 Comoran francs per euro.

SOURCE: CIA *World Factbook 2001* [ONLINE].

Imports include rice and other foodstuffs, petroleum products, consumer manufactures, and motor vehicles. In 1999, imports were valued at $48 million. (The *World Factbook* estimated that imports reached US$55.1 million that same year.) Most imports come from France with Pakistan, South Africa, Kenya, the United Arab Emirates, and Belgium also supplying significant quantities.

MONEY

Comoros is a member of the Franc Zone, which it joined in 1976. The national currency, the Comoran franc (KMF), is pegged to the French franc and is fully convertible. This arrangement has provided considerable advantages in terms of exchange rate stability and low inflation, but the Franc Zone has also placed restrictions on public sector budget deficits. Some of the stability associated with Franc Zone membership was undermined by a 50 percent currency **devaluation** that took place in January 1994. Now that France is a member of the European Monetary Union (EMU), the peg to the French franc also implies a peg to the euro.

POVERTY AND WEALTH

With the low price of basic commodities in Comoros taken into account, per capita GDP was estimated at

Trade (expressed in billions of US$): Comoros		
	Exports	Imports
1975	.010	.023
1980	.011	.029
1985	.016	.036
1990	.018	.052
1995	.011	.063
1998	N/A	N/A

SOURCE: International Monetary Fund. *International Financial Statistics Yearbook 1999.*

GDP per Capita (US$)					
Country	1975	1980	1985	1990	1998
Comoros	N/A	499	544	516	403
United States	19,364	21,529	23,200	25,363	29,683
South Africa	4,574	4,620	4,229	4,113	3,918
Mauritius	1,531	1,802	2,151	2,955	4,034

SOURCE: United Nations. *Human Development Report 2000; Trends in human development and per capita income.*

$1,398 (**purchasing power parity** (PPP), 1998 est.). By 2000, the *World Factbook* estimated that the **GDP per capita** (PPP) had sunk to US$720. Together with a life expectancy of 60 years, an adult literacy rate of 80 percent, and an enrollment ratio in all levels of education of 39 percent, Comoros was placed by the United Nations (UN) in the group of countries with medium human development. Comoros, however, is close to the bottom of the ranking of those in this group.

There are no figures for the percentage of the population below the dollar-a-day poverty line, which is defined as not having enough income to provide the barest minimum of food, shelter, and clothing. The indicator for children judged underweight at age 5 would suggest that around 30 percent of the population are below the poverty line. Most of those in poverty are members of rural families who must rely on small-scale family farms for their livelihoods. These families are unable to increase their incomes as they are unable to afford investments in mechanization, fertilizers, insecticides, and improved seeds that would boost their output. Even in the main towns, electricity and the piped water supply is erratic. In the rural areas electricity and plumbing are practically non-existent; lighting is by small paraffin lamps with wicks, and water is obtained from wells. There is some septic tank sewage disposal in the towns, but in the rural areas people rely on pit latrines.

WORKING CONDITIONS

The workforce in 1996 numbered 286,000. About 74 percent of this labor was engaged in agriculture. The unemployment rate was 20 percent in 1996. Comoros has a national labor union, the Union des Travailleurs des Comores (Union of Comoran Workers, UTC), which negotiates to regulate the working conditions. Implementation, however, is very ineffective. There are no official welfare programs, despite the high level of unemployment. Those without employment rely on support from their families or charity, and in the urban areas many try to earn what they can from casual **hawking**, portering, and scavenging.

COUNTRY HISTORY AND ECONOMIC DEVELOPMENT

1841. France begins the process of occupation and colonization of the islands, which were formerly an autonomous sultanate.

1909. The islands are made a dependency of Madagascar (also a French colony).

1940. With France occupied by Germany, Britain assumes administration of the islands.

1946. Comoros is returned to France and granted administrative autonomy as an overseas territory.

1973. France agrees to independence within 5 years.

1974. In a special referendum, all of the islands except for Mayotte (which remains as a dependency of France) vote for independence.

1975. The Chamber of Deputies votes a unilateral declaration of independence and proclaims the Republic of Comoros, with Ahmed Abdallah as president.

1975. President Abdallah is overthrown in a coup led by French mercenary Bob Denard, who installs Ali Soilih, the leader of a 4-party coalition known as the National United Front (NUF).

1975. The National Assembly is dissolved.

1975. Island of Mayotte rejects union with Comoros in 2 referenda.

1975. French estates in Comoros are **nationalized**, and French officials are **repatriated**.

1976. Comoros joins the Franc Zone, with its currency fully convertible and pegged at a fixed rate to the French franc.

1978. Soilih is ousted in a coup led by Denard. Former president Ahmed Abdallah is installed as leader of the new government and is endorsed as president by an election. The band of 50 mercenaries, headed by Denard, forms a presidential guard and controls the administration. The mercenary presence infuriates other African nations, and Comoros is expelled from the Organization for African Unity (OAU). A new constitution is drafted and approved by 99 percent of the votes. Diplomatic relations with France are resumed. The newly elected Federal Assembly approves the formation of a one-party state. The mercenaries leave and OAU readmits Comoros.

1984. Abdallah is elected for a second 6-year term.

1989. Abdallah is assassinated. Said Muhammad Djohar is named interim president.

1990. Djohar is elected president.

1995. Djohar is ousted by a coup. An interim government rules until scheduled elections.

1996. The election is won by Taki Abdoulkarim's National Union for Democracy in Comoros (NUDC), and Taki is elected president. In May, Taki dissolves parliament and calls for new elections in October. The NUDC obtain 36 of the 43 seats at stake in the elections, which are boycotted by the opposition.

1997. In August, a secessionist movement headed by Abdallah Ibrahim calls for the independence of Anjouan Island.

1998. In March, over 99 percent of Anjouan citizens vote for independence in a referendum. Mohéli Island declares independence. Troops are sent to restore status quo (the normal order).

1998. President Taki dies amid rumors of a political assassination. An interim government is formed under Tadjidine Ben Said Massoude.

1999. Colonel Azali Assoumani takes power through a coup and imposes military rule.

2001. A new constitution and new national government are established.

FUTURE TRENDS

The future of Comoros is clouded by uncertainty. There is little doubt that the 2 smaller islands, Anjouan and Mohéli, would like to enjoy the prosperity and stability of Mayotte, the fourth main island in the archipelago, which has remained a French dependency. Mayotte is administered by France, and the island sends deputies to the French National Assembly. Mayotte's population benefits from social security and general development support from France, which has substantially improved the island's income levels. Such status would significantly improve conditions on Grande Comore. However, it would be a bitter blow to the pride of the ruling elite on Grand Comore and to the Organization for African Unity (OAU). Local politicians see more to their advantage in hanging on to power and accumulating wealth through corrupt practices. It remains to be seen whether the OAU will continue to oppose the democratically expressed wishes of the 2 smaller islands for independence and a possible return to French rule.

The economy is totally dependent on agriculture and tourism for the foreign exchange that it requires to import manufactures and fuels. Agricultural output has been stagnant due to soil degradation, and producers of export crops are discouraged by declines in export prices. Tourism is the most promising sector for expansion. With political stability, perhaps secured by a return to French rule, there is little doubt that foreign investment in tourism would expand, and the islands would progress toward the levels of income enjoyed by their French-ruled neighbors in the Indian Ocean, Reunion and Mayotte. The most likely outcome, however, is that there will be some reconciliation between the other islands and Grande Comore, and Comoros will continue to stagnate.

DEPENDENCIES

Comoros has no territories or colonies.

BIBLIOGRAPHY

"Comoros." *World Yearbook.* London: Europa Publications, 2000.

Economist Intelligence Unit. *Country Profile: Comoros.* London: EIU, 2000.

Economist Intelligence Unit. *Country Profile: Comoros.* London: Economist Intelligence Unit, 2001.

Hodd, M. "Comoros." *The Economies of Africa.* Aldershot, England: Dartmouth Publications, 1991.

U.S. Central Intelligence Agency. *World Factbook 2001.* <http://www.odci.gov/cia/publications/factbook/index.html>. Accessed October 2001.

U.S. Department of State. *Background Notes: Comoros, April 1997.* <http://www.state.gov/www/background_notes/comoros_0497.html>. Accessed October 2001.

World Bank. *The Comoros: Problems and Prospects of a Small Island Economy.* Washington, D.C.: World Bank Group, 1979.

World Bank. *World Bank Africa Database 2000.* Washington D.C.: World Bank Group, 2000.

—Allan C.K. Mukungu

CONGO, DEMOCRATIC REPUBLIC OF THE

CAPITAL: Kinshasa.

MONETARY UNIT: Congolese franc (FC). One Congolese franc equals 100 makuta. Due to the unstable nature of the currency it is impossible to predict which notes and coins are available in the country.

CHIEF EXPORTS: Diamonds, copper, coffee, cobalt, crude oil.

CHIEF IMPORTS: Foodstuffs, mining and other machinery, transport equipment, fuels.

GROSS DOMESTIC PRODUCT: US$35.7 billion (purchasing power parity, 1999 est.). [Because most economic activity in the Democratic Republic of Congo is in the informal sector and difficult to track, different world agencies provide very different estimates of GDP. For example, the World Bank listed GDP in 1998 as US$7.0 billion, while the International Monetary Fund listed GDP as US$34.9 billion in the same year.]

BALANCE OF TRADE: **Exports:** US$530 million (f.o.b., 1998 est.). **Imports:** US$460 million (f.o.b., 1998 est.).

COUNTRY OVERVIEW

LOCATION AND SIZE. The Democratic Republic of the Congo (DRC; the country is often simply called the "Congo" or "Congo-Kinshasa" to distinguish it from the neighboring Republic of the Congo) is located in Central Africa. The Congo is the third-largest country in Africa. It shares borders with the Central African Republic (1,577 kilometers, or 980 miles), Sudan (628 kilometers, or 390 miles), Uganda (765 kilometers, or 475 miles), Rwanda (217 kilometers, or 135 miles), Burundi (233 kilometers, or 145 miles), Tanzania (473 kilometers, or 294 miles, all on Lake Tanganyika), Zambia (1,930 kilometers, or 1,199 miles), Angola (2,511 kilometers, or 1,560 miles), and the Republic of the Congo (2,410 kilometers, or 1,498 miles), and has a small coastline of 37 kilometers (23 miles) on the South Atlantic Ocean. The Congo is

2,345,410 square kilometers (905,563 square miles), slightly less than one-fourth the size of the United States.

Kinshasa is the capital of the Congo. The Congo's other major cities are Lubumbashi, Mbuji-Mayi, Kolwezi, Kisangani, and Matadi.

POPULATION. As of July 2000 the population of the Congo was estimated at 51,964,999, making it the third-most populous country in Africa. The birth rate was 46.44 per 1,000 persons and the death rate was 15.38 per 1,000 persons according to 2000 estimates. Congolese women on average bore 6.92 children in 2000. As of the year 2000, the Congo's estimated infant mortality rate was 101.71 deaths per 1,000 live births. Males have a life expectancy of 46.72 years while females have a life expectancy of 50.83 years. Some 48 percent of the population is under age 15, while only 3 percent of the population is older than 65 years.

The Congo is made up of more than 200 tribes. The 4 largest tribes in the Congo are the Mongo, Luba, Kongo, and Mangbetu-Azonde. Approximately 700 local languages and dialects are spoken in the Congo. The majority of Congolese speak one of the following languages: Kikongo, Lingala, Tshiluba, Swahili, and French. Most of the Congolese population lives in rural areas, while one-third of the population is urban.

About 80 percent of the Congolese population is Christian. Most non-Christians have traditional African religious beliefs.

OVERVIEW OF ECONOMY

The Democratic Republic of Congo (DRC, or the Congo) is a nation rich in natural resources, including diamonds, cobalt, and copper. The DRC also has vast onshore oil reserves which it has yet to exploit. Despite its potential wealth, however, the Congo's economy has drastically declined since the 1950s. Prior to a bitter war in 1998, the Congolese government had tightened **fiscal policy** and managed to curb the country's runaway **inflation** and the drastic depreciation of its currency. Most recently, however, those gains have been erased

as a result of the war that began in the summer of 1998. The Congo's economic plight is exacerbated by the reduction of foreign business operations as a result of the war. The war, however, is not the only reason for the Congo's economic woes. The country's poor **infrastructure**, inoperative legal system, corruption, and lack of openness in economic policy and financial operations continue to be further obstacles to investment and growth. Although there have been a number of meetings between the Congolese government and the International Monetary Fund (IMF) and the World Bank to develop a coherent economic plan, most reforms are on hold.

During the Cold War, the Congo (then known as Zaire) was a key figure in the United States' African policy because of its strategic location in the center of the continent. Approximately half of all U.S. aid designated for Africa went to Zaire. Under the dictatorship of Mobutu Sese Seko, who controlled the country for more than 35 years, widespread corruption blossomed and the diversion of public resources for personal gain hindered economic growth. The United States supported Mobutu from the 1960s until 1990. After the collapse of the Soviet Union in 1989, however, the Congo declined in importance in U.S. policy and U.S. financial backing was greatly reduced.

Mobutu ran the Zairian economy like his personal piggy bank. From 1965 through 1997, Mobutu and his associates stole billions of dollars from the Zairian economy. Because of this kleptocracy (government institutionalized theft), Zaire's infrastructure crumbled. In 1971 Mobutu legalized his plunder of the Zairian economy under the guise of "Zairianization," a law which effectively turned over to Mobutu and his associates ownership of over 2,000 foreign-owned businesses. These businesses ranged from medium-sized grocery stores to huge billion-dollar mining conglomerates, and were the mainstay of the Zairian economy. As a result of inexperience and mismanagement, many of these **nationalized** companies became bankrupt, and the Zairian economy came to a halt. Realizing that the Zairian economy was in a tailspin, Mobutu returned many of the businesses to their rightful owners. The Zairian economy, however, never rebounded.

Mobutu and his associates further crippled the Zairian economy by openly flouting and discouraging the application of the rule of law (a term which refers to a broad system of laws and regulations that keep social and economic order). Instead of the rule of law, Mobutu installed a system of patronage which had at its pinnacle Mobutu and his family. Mobutu's system of patronage replaced the Zairian judicial system as the true arbiter of disputes. By 1997, at the time of his ouster, Mobutu's corrupt government and his system of patronage had laid waste Zaire's economy and social fabric.

Mobutu's regime began to crumble following the collapse of the Soviet Union in 1989. Not only did the United States withdraw aid, but the Congo fared no better with the World Bank and the International Monetary Fund (IMF). Both international aid organizations cut off aid to the Congo in early 1990. As a result, the country was incapable of servicing its **external debt** and by 1993 both the IMF and the World Bank suspended the country's borrowing rights. Further compounding the Congo's economic malaise was the promulgation (to make known by open declaration) of a new currency, the "new zaire." The new zaire was not only overvalued against foreign currencies, but inflation rose to a dizzying 9,000 percent by early 1994. In 1993, 5 new zaires could buy a British pound. Four years later, it took 200,000 new zaires to buy 1 pound. In 1997, following Mobutu's removal, a new currency called the France Congolese was introduced, but it too faced real instability. There were, in the late 1990s, many informal **exchange rates** in the country, and the only currencies of real value came from outside the country.

In May 1997 Laurent Kabila, an unknown rebel supported by Rwanda and Uganda, toppled the Mobutu regime. As the head of the Alliance des Forces Démocratiques pour la Libération du Congo-Zaire (AFDL), Ka-

bila renamed the country the Democratic Republic of Congo and made attempts to reform the tax system and the police force, and repair the decrepit road system. Unfortunately, President Kabila's attempts were too little and came too late to solve the Congo's economic and social problems.

By August 1998 the coalition of armed militias which had supported Kabila fell apart, plunging the nation into a bloody war that further damaged an already broken economy. Warring forces with ethnic ties to Uganda and Rwanda soon brought these and most of the remainder of Congo's neighbors into the conflict. Much of eastern Congo was a battleground for warring forces from these surrounding nations, some of whom are fighting against each other on Congolese soil. The country is now divided into regions under rebel control and regions ruled by the Kabila regime. Commerce between these regions has come to a halt.

In January of 2001 Laurent Kabila was assassinated by one of his bodyguards, but his son, Joseph Kabila, stepped in to continue his father's disastrous regime. Joseph Kabila has suggested that he would like to **liberalize** the economy, and hopes to capitalize on diminished fighting within the country. However, he has inherited a country whose major economic engines—the mining companies—are held by powerful government-run agencies to whom Kabila owes his political power. Bringing these companies back into private hands, and bringing anything like normal economic order back to this shattered country, will be Kabila's great challenge.

POLITICS, GOVERNMENT, AND TAXATION

On May 17, 1997, with the clandestine support of Rwanda, Uganda, and the United States, Laurent Kabila toppled President Mobutu. Mobutu had been at the helm of the Congo for more than 3 decades. For the most part, Zairians (as the Congolese were then called) welcomed Kabila and even embraced the idea of renaming Zaire the Democratic Republic of the Congo. Even so, peace in the Congo was fleeting.

Kabila imposed rule by decree. All governmental powers were vested in the executive branch, which even had the power to appoint and to dismiss members of the judiciary. Not surprisingly, Kabila filled his 26-member cabinet with loyalists from his political party, the Alliance of Democratic Forces for the Liberation of Congo-Zaire (AFDL). By Kabila's decree, the AFDL was the only political party that could engage in political activities.

At the inception of his rule, Kabila lowered the **inflation rate** and improved internal security. However, some armed groups remained beyond his control, including the

Hutu/Interahamwe, Mai-Mai soldiers, and the Tutsi Banyamulenge. Upon taking command, Kabila promised reform. At first, Kabila claimed that his government was one of transition and would lead to a new constitution and elections by 1999. During his tenure in power, however, elections were never held and a 1998 constitution was not finalized. Although Kabila's stated aim in toppling the Mobutu regime was restoring democracy to the Congo, his rule resembled that of his predecessor more so than a democracy. When Kabila banned every political party save his own, protests grew both domestically and internationally.

In the summer of 1998, Kabila attempted to gain autonomy from Rwanda and Uganda, which led to war. Kabila's first move was to expel the Rwandan and Ugandan troops that helped him topple the Mobutu regime. This war eventually embroiled the rest of the countries in the region. On the one side fighting against the Kabila government were the Rally for Congolese Democracy and the Movement for the Liberation of the Congo, which are supported by Rwanda, Uganda, and Burundi. Fighting on the side of the Kabila government were Angola, Namibia, Chad, Zimbabwe, the Congolese army, and the Interhamwe (the former Rwandan-Hutu army exiled in the Congo). All the belligerents in this war had their own separate reasons for intervening. Rwanda, Uganda, and Angola wanted to protect their borders. Zimbabwe wanted to maintain the balance of power in the region. But all of them wished to participate in the bounty of the Congo's vast riches.

The warring parties reached a cease-fire in Lusaka, Zambia, in July 1999. The parties memorialized the terms of their cease fire in the Lusaka Peace Accord, which called for a cessation of war, a peacekeeping force comprised of international troops mostly from Africa, and the commencement of a "national dialogue" on the Congo's future. Unfortunately, the Peace Accord was not implemented and only lip-service was devoted to the national dialogue.

President Laurent Kabila was assassinated on January 16, 2001, in Kinshasa by one of his own soldiers. His son, Major General Joseph Kabila, was appointed as interim president on January 26, 2001. At the beginning of his rule, Joseph Kabila made valiant efforts to rekindle the Lusaka Peace Accord, and Rwanda and Uganda have begun removing their troops from the Congo. In March 2001, the UN inserted peacekeeping troops in areas where Rwandan and Ugandan forces had withdrawn. It remains to be seen, however, if peace will come to the Congo and if Joseph Kabila will engage the country in a national dialogue.

During the rule of Laurent Kabila, U.S.-Congolese relations soured. In fact, the United States and other western nations largely blamed Kabila for the perpetuation of the war. However, relations between the Congo and the United States seem to be improving since Joseph Kabila has come to power, as demonstrated by the meeting between Joseph Kabila and U.S. Secretary of State Colin Powell early in the new Bush administration.

The government collects taxes primarily from businesses. Tax collection is arbitrary and many charge that harassment from tax authorities has lately reached unprecedented levels. Moreover, taxes have served to enrich corrupt government officials.

INFRASTRUCTURE, POWER, AND COMMUNICATIONS

The Congo's infrastructure is virtually non-existent and is a major impediment to economic improvement. Though there are an estimated 157,000 kilometers (97,560 miles) of roads in the country, most of them are poorly maintained and there are no major paved roads connecting the regions of the country. Most goods are transported by air. The Congo has 6 major airports located in Kinshasa, Lubumbashi, Kinsangani, Goma, Mbuji-Mai, and Gbadolite, and hundreds of small landing strips elsewhere in the country. There were 5,138 kilometers (3,193 miles) of railways in 1995, but most

Communication									
Country	Newspapers	Radios	TV Sets[a]	Cable subscribers[a]	Mobile Phones[a]	Fax Machines[a]	Personal Computers[a]	Internet Hosts[b]	Internet Users[b]
	1996	1997	1998	1998	1998	1998	1998	1999	1999
Dem. Rep. of Congo	3	375	135	N/A	0	N/A	N/A	0.00	1
United States	215	2,146	847	244.3	256	78.4	458.6	1,508.77	74,100
Nigeria	24	223	66	N/A	0	N/A	5.7	0.00	100
Sudan	27	271	87	N/A	0	0.6	1.9	0.00	5

[a]Data are from International Telecommunication Union, *World Telecommunication Development Report 1999* and are per 1,000 people.
[b]Data are from the Internet Software Consortium (http://www.isc.org) and are per 10,000 people.

SOURCE: World Bank. *World Development Indicators 2000.*

of these were destroyed or damaged during the wars of the late 1990s.

The production of electricity contributes merely 1 percent of the country's GDP. Yet, the Congo's hydroelectric potential is extraordinary. During the 1970s, Congolese and foreign investors, principally from the United States, invested heavily in the Inga-Shaba hydroelectric facility, but today the dam is operating at only a small fraction of its capacity. In 1998 the country produced 5.74 billion kilowatt-hours of total electric power, the vast majority of which was consumed domestically.

The Congo's telecommunications infrastructure, like its roads, is also virtually non-existent. There were 36,000 main lines and 10,000 cellular phones in use in 1995. There are only about 0.7 telephones for every 1,000 Congolese. Even the few telephones that exist are often inoperable because the telecommunications infrastructure is so poorly maintained. Cellular telephones, such as those provided by the American company TELECEL, are replacing wire-based telephone networks, and the numbers of cellular phones in use have risen dramatically in the last several years.

ECONOMIC SECTORS

In 1997 agriculture represented about 58 percent of the Congo's GDP. The country's primary **cash crops** include coffee, palm oil, rubber, cotton, sugar, tea, and cocoa. The Congo's primary food crops include rice, groundnuts, maize, plantains, and cassava. Two-thirds of the Congo's **labor force** works in the agricultural sector.

In 1997, the industrial sector represented approximately 17 percent of GDP and employed 16 percent of

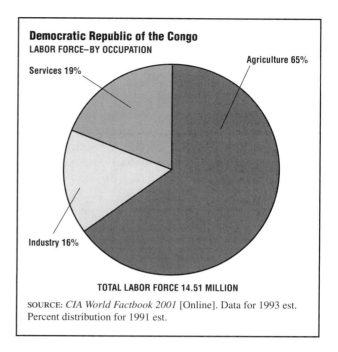

Democratic Republic of the Congo
LABOR FORCE–BY OCCUPATION

Agriculture 65%
Services 19%
Industry 16%

TOTAL LABOR FORCE 14.51 MILLION

SOURCE: *CIA World Factbook 2001* [Online]. Data for 1993 est. Percent distribution for 1991 est.

the workforce. Industrial diamonds alone account for 52 percent of exports. The Congo's abundant reserves of copper and cobalt present enormous potential to its economy. However, this potential has not been met because the Congo's mining companies have failed to keep up with general improvements in mining technology. Also, the war has had a great effect on production in the industrial sector. Services account for just 25 percent of the economy and employ 19 percent of the workers.

AGRICULTURE

The Congo's economy is largely based on subsistence agriculture. However, 99 percent of the Congo's land is not under cultivation. Nearly 70 percent of the population lives in the countryside and continues to cultivate individual tracts of land by traditional methods for personal consumption. Coffee, cocoa, sugar, palm oil products, rubber, tea, and quinquina are produced on plantations and by small farmers. Food crops include plantains, maize, cassava, groundnuts, and rice. The Congo's agricultural sector has declined since independence because the government has imposed low producer prices, encouraged the importation of cheap foodstuffs, implemented policies that hampered the access of credit to rural areas, and neglected the country's transportation and energy infrastructure. The Kabila governments promised, as part of their development policy, upgrades in rural roads and agricultural mechanization, so far without much success.

Although the Congo's agricultural sector is full of promise, the Congo still remains dependent on imports,

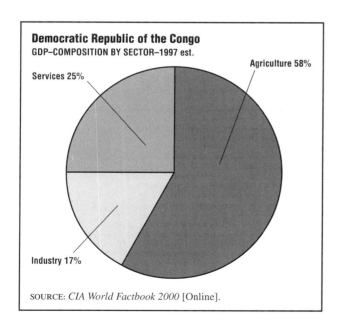

Democratic Republic of the Congo
GDP–COMPOSITION BY SECTOR–1997 est.

Agriculture 58%
Services 25%
Industry 17%

SOURCE: *CIA World Factbook 2000* [Online].

despite having been a net exporter prior to its independence. In the 1980s, the Congo experienced a 2 percent growth in the agricultural sector. But since the early 1990s, the agricultural sector has been stagnant, experiencing zero or negative growth rates. Livestock production was decimated by fighting in 1996–97, and fish production on interior rivers has decreased dramatically. Finally, income from timber sales can hardly be considered part of the Congolese economy, as the timbered areas remain under rebel control in 2001.

INDUSTRY

MINING. Since the colonial era, mining has been and continues to be the Congo's main source of exports and foreign exchange. The Katanga region of the Congo contains some of the world's richest deposits of copper and cobalt. The national copper mining company, GECAMINES, which had been struggling in the 1980s, collapsed in 1991 and has had little success in expanding production since then, thanks again to the wars of the late 1990s. Recovery in this sector will occur only if the Congo enjoys sustained political stability and the mines receive massive technological improvements.

As recently as the 1980s, the DRC was the world's fourth leading producer of industrial diamonds. It also has an abundant reserve of gem-quality diamonds. The Congo exports its diamonds mainly to Belgium, Israel, and India. Two-thirds of the Congo's industrial diamond production is realized through artisanal (skilled worker) diamond diggers. In the 1990s the state granted to one company, IDI Diamonds, a **monopoly** on the sales and export of diamonds. This move—meant to bring order to the diamond industry—in fact forced most diamond sales into the **black market** as artisanal diamond diggers sought the highest prices for their diamonds.

The Congo also produces gold. However, production has suffered as a result of both the current and previous wars. Currently, the Congo's main gold mines are in regions governed by rebel forces. Like industrial diamonds, gold production takes place mostly through artisanal panning and is not significant.

PETROLEUM. Compared to other sub-Saharan African oil producers, the Congo produces very little crude oil. However, offshore oil fields remained one of the government's few stable sources of revenue in the 1990s. The country produces about 22,000 barrels per day of oil. U.S.-owned Chevron and Mobil dominate the Congo's crude oil sector. SOCIR, the national refinery, is unable to process the country's crude oil so it must be processed externally, limiting the economic benefits of this natural resource.

MANUFACTURING. The Congo's primary manufacturing regions are Kinshasa and Lubumbashi, and they produce batteries, tires, shoes, food products, plastics, beverages, autos, textiles, and other **consumer goods**. Agricultural processing is one of the few relatively healthy industries, thanks to its ability to benefit from the mass of Congolese who are involved with agriculture. Although the Congo's locally-produced goods are far more expensive than imports, local manufacturers have been able to withstand import competition ironically because of the Congo's poor transportation system.

SERVICES

The service sector represents one-fourth of GDP and employs 19 percent of the labor force. The primary services are banking, communications, government, and transportation, yet each of these subsectors are plagued by inefficiency, corruption, and the stresses from war. The public health and education systems are, in the words of the U.S. Department of State, "defunct" and most health and education services are now provided by international aid agencies. Transportation services are rudimentary and inefficient. The state-run transport firm Office National des Transports (ONATRA) has a difficult time competing with private transporters, the majority of whose activities go unreported in economic statistics. Tourism in the past decade has been virtually non-existent.

Congo's banking system includes the central bank, Banque Central du Congo, 10 commercial banks, and a development bank, as well as a variety of smaller financial institutions. In the 1990s, however, most of these banks were insolvent, their assets demolished by runaway inflation, massive defaults on loans, and the government's misuse of central bank funds. Most Congolese avoid formal banks and participate in a cash economy.

INTERNATIONAL TRADE

As with GDP, there is immense difficulty in determining accurate statistics for international trade for the Democratic Republic of Congo, thanks to the difficulty

Trade (expressed in billions of US$): Democratic Republic of the Congo

	Exports	Imports
1975	.275	.300
1980	.544	.278
1985	.950	.792
1990	.999	.888
1995	.438	.397
1998	N/A	N/A

SOURCE: International Monetary Fund. *International Financial Statistics Yearbook 1999.*

of assessing the contributions of the **informal economy**. The CIA World Factbook reports exports of US$530 million and imports of US$460 million in 1998. The World Bank estimated 1999 exports of US$1.94 billion and imports of US$549 million, comparable to the Banque National du Congo's most recent figures of US$1.546 billion in exports and US$936 million in imports in 1995.

According to the CIA World Factbook, the country's primary export partners in 1998 were the Benelux countries (52 percent), the United States (14 percent), South Africa (9 percent), and Finland (4 percent). The Congo's primary import partners in the same year were South Africa (25 percent), Benelux (14 percent), Nigeria (7 percent), Kenya (5 percent), and China.

MONEY

The local currency in the Congo is the Congolese franc. The Congolese franc replaced the new zaire and was issued in 1997 for the first time. The official exchange rate, set by the Banque Central du Congo, was widely ignored as the value of the Congolese franc plummeted against every world currency. No foreign currency is available at the official exchange rate, so most foreign currency must be traded on the black market. The drop in the value of the currency has led to high inflation, which has been a chronic problem in the DRC. Inflation rates in the last decade were as high as 8,828 percent in 1993, dropping to 6 percent in 1997 before climbing again to 333 percent in 1999. Because wages have not kept up with inflation, most Congolese cannot afford many goods and resort to **bartering** to obtain basic necessities.

POVERTY AND WEALTH

Independence from Belgium, gained with little trouble in 1960, has had the unintended effect of increasing the gap between rich and poor in the Congo. The Congo lacks a middle class. The wealthy Congolese—usually tied to those in power by patronage—live in the city in

GDP per Capita (US$)					
Country	1975	1980	1985	1990	1998
Dem. Rep. of Congo	392	313	293	247	127
United States	19,364	21,529	23,200	25,363	29,683
Nigeria	301	314	230	258	256
Sudan	237	229	210	198	296

SOURCE: United Nations. *Human Development Report 2000; Trends in human development and per capita income.*

modern houses and apartment buildings and drive expensive cars. The urban poor, who make up the majority of the population, live in overcrowded slums lacking even the basics of life, such as running water and basic health care. Congolese who live in the rural parts of the country live in thatched huts and survive on subsistence agriculture. Though any estimates of income are questionable, it is estimated the per capita GDP is as low as US$100.

Since independence, the Congo has made efforts to provide its citizens with access to primary and secondary schooling. About 80 percent of the males and 65 percent of females aged 6 to 11 were enrolled in a mixture of state- and church-run primary schools in 1996. At higher levels of education, males greatly outnumber females. The country's elite continue to send their children abroad to be educated, primarily in Western Europe.

Taxes are very burdensome for Congolese, and rural dwellers are subjected to a variety of coercive measures by officials to extract payments, fines, and other financial penalties. The health care system, roads, and school system have virtually collapsed, and the government has focused its meager resources in the urban areas, leaving rural citizens with nothing but high taxes, low prices for their agricultural products, and much suffering.

WORKING CONDITIONS

The DRC has a sizable labor force of some 14.51 million workers, but working conditions for the average Congolese are abysmal. Most Congolese work in the agricultural sector. The average income of a Congolese worker does not provide a sufficient income to sustain a family. In fact, most Congolese earn less than $40 a month. Most workers supplement their income by doing odd jobs besides their usual work and depend heavily on the assistance of their extended families. The government has established minimum wage scales for workers, but wages have not kept pace with inflation, making such wage scales nearly meaningless.

The country created the 1967 Labor Code to provide guidelines for labor practices, including the employment

Exchange rates: Democratic Republic of the Congo	
Congolese francs per US$1	
Jan 2001	50
2000	4.5
1999	4.02
1998	1.61
1997	1.31
1996	0.50

Note: On June 30, 1998 the Congolese franc was introduced, replacing the new zaire.

SOURCE: CIA *World Factbook 2001* [ONLINE].

of women and children, anti-discrimination laws, and restrictions on working conditions. The collapse of the economy and the corruption in the government have destroyed the enforcement of most such laws. Several of the limited number of larger employers, however, pay for benefits for their employees and may even provide roads, schools, and hospitals for the local community.

The employment of children of all ages is not uncommon in the informal sector and in subsistence agriculture, which are dominant portions of the economy. Such employment is often the only way a child or family can obtain money for food. Neither the Ministry of Labor, which is responsible for enforcement, nor the labor unions make an effort to enforce child labor laws.

COUNTRY HISTORY AND ECONOMIC DEVELOPMENT

1885. The Congo is colonized as a personal fiefdom of Belgian King Leopold II and is called the Congo Free State.

1907. The administration of the Congo Free State is transferred to the Belgian government, which renames the country the Belgian Congo.

1960. The Congo gains independence from Belgium. Shortly after, the army mutinies and the Katanga province secedes. The United Nations sends troops to protect Europeans and maintain order. Joseph Desire Mobutu, the army's chief of staff, intervenes militarily to resolve a power struggle between President Joseph Kasavubu and Prime Minister Patrice Lumumba. Mobutu has Lumumba arrested.

1961. Mobutu returns power to President Kasavubu. Lumumba is handed over to Katanga rebels and soon murdered.

1964. The country is renamed the Democratic Republic of the Congo.

1965. Mobutu stages a military coup amid a political crisis, appointing himself president for 5 years and canceling scheduled elections.

1970. Mobutu establishes his Popular Movement of the Revolution as the sole political party and all Congolese are forced to join the party. Mobutu is also re-elected as president in a one-candidate election.

1971. Mobutu begins reform under his "Zairianization" policy. Under this policy he changes the country's name to the Republic of Zaire, and Zairians are forced to use their African names (as opposed to their Christian names) and adopt African dress.

1973. Under "Zairianization," the government appropriates over 2,000 foreign-owned businesses. These

businesses are mostly distributed to Mobutu and his associates.

1977. Former Katangan secessionists invade Katanga from Angola, where they had been living in exile. Mobutu suppresses the rebellion with the help of Moroccan troops and military assistance from his Western allies.

1982. Dissidents of Mobutu's one-party rule form the Union for Democracy and Social Progress (UDPS). UDPS leaders are harassed and imprisoned.

1990. Mobutu announces the creation of a multiparty democratic system. However, a national multiparty conference to draft a new constitution is suspended. The United States, which had supplied Mobutu with hundreds of millions of dollars annually, ends direct military and economic aid because of corruption and human rights abuses by the Mobutu regime.

1991. As a result of mounting domestic and international pressure, Mobutu agrees to form a coalition government with UDPS leader Etienne Tshisekedi.

1992. The multiparty constitutional conference resumes amid squabbling and continued unrest. Conference members name Tshisekedi as Prime Minister to head a transitional government. Later, the Conference adopts a draft constitution to incorporate a **bicameral** parliament and a system of universal suffrage to elect a president.

1994. Rwandan ethnic Hutus massacre over 500,000 Rwandan ethnic Tutsis. Shortly thereafter, an outside Tutsi rebel force takes over Rwanda. Fearing retribution, over 1.3 million Rwandan Hutus flee into eastern Zaire. Accompanying these refugees are many of the Hutus responsible for the Tutsi massacre.

1996. Zairian Tutsi in eastern Zaire revolt because they are threatened with expulsion by Hutus. Uganda and Rwanda seize upon this revolt to secure their borders from the Hutus responsible for the massacre and select veteran guerrilla fighter Laurent Kabila to invade eastern Zaire. Hundreds of thousands of Hutu refugees return to Rwanda.

1997. Kabila's army, composed mostly of Rwandans and Ugandans, takes Kinshasa, and Mobutu flees into exile. Kabila appoints himself as president and changes the country's name back to the Democratic Republic of the Congo.

1998. Kabila kicks out his Rwandan supporters, which sparks a war supported by Rwanda and Uganda against him. Rebel activity unofficially divides the Congo into 3 regions.

1999. The Lusaka Peace Accord is signed by Kabila and representatives of Rwanda and Uganda. Pursuant to the Accord, the parties agree to a cease-fire, the installation of U.N. peacekeeping troops in the Congo, and a "national dialogue" to chart the country's future. All parties continue to violate the Accord.

2001. President Laurent Kabila is assassinated by one of his bodyguards. His son, Major General Joseph Kabila, is appointed as interim president. Rwanda and Uganda begin removing their troops and the U.N. sends peacekeeping forces.

FUTURE TRENDS

The outbreak of war in August 1998 caused the collapse of the Congo's already frail economy. Since the outbreak of war, the country has been divided into Rwandan/Ugandan rebel-governed areas, and areas controlled by the government. Commerce between these regions has ceased and the Congo's economy has suffered even more.

As a result of this war, the Congolese government's revenues went from bad to dismal. Customs revenues have declined because the flow of imports has dried up. Tax revenues have also substantially declined because of the fall in business activity. Further compounding the problem is the fact that unpaid government bills owed to private businesses have increased to the point that some businesses have been forced to close.

On January 16, 2001, President Laurent Kabila was assassinated by one of his bodyguards. Ten days later Major General Joseph Kabila was appointed as interim president. At the inception of his presidency, Joseph Kabila has demonstrated a sincere interest in re-establishing peace in the Congo. Thus far, he has revived the Lusaka Peace Accord, and both Rwanda and Uganda have begun removing their troops from the Congo. Additionally, the U.N. began sending peacekeeping troops to the Congo. There are also signs that Joseph Kabila will adopt a less

hard-line approach to governing the Congo than his father. He has already replaced his father's hard-line cabinet with appointees with a more liberal outlook on governance. Joseph Kabila has also engaged in extensive travel to meet heads of state of many of the Western nations to reintegrate the Congo into the international community. It remains to be seen how he intends to reinvigorate the Congo's decrepit economic state.

DEPENDENCIES

The Congo has no territories or colonies.

BIBLIOGRAPHY

Economist Intelligence Unit. *Country Profile: Democratic Republic of Congo.* London: Economist Intelligence Unit, 2001.

Leslie, Winsome J. *Zaire: Continuity and Political Change in an Oppressive State.* Boulder, CO: Westview Press, 1993.

"Making a Mint From the Zaire Shambles." *Electronic Mail and Guardian* (Johannesburg, South Africa). <http://www.mg.co.za/mg/news/97apr2/21apr-zaire.html>. Accessed July 2001.

U.S. Central Intelligence Agency. *World Factbook 2000.* <http://www.odci.gov/cia/publications/factbook/index.html>. Accessed July 2001.

U.S. Department of State, Bureau of African Affairs. *Background Notes: Democratic Republic of the Congo.* <http://www.state.gov/r/pa/bgn/index.cfm?docid=2823>. Accessed April 2001.

U.S. Department of State. *1999 Country Reports on Human Rights Practices: Democratic Republic of the Congo.* <http://www.state.gov/www/global/human_rights/1999_hrp_report/congodr.html>. Accessed April 2001.

U.S. Department of State. *FY 2001 Country Commercial Guide: Democratic Republic of the Congo.* <http://www.state.gov/www/about_state/business/com_guides/2001/africa/index.html>. Accessed April 2001.

—*Michael David Nicoleau and Raynette Rose Gutrick*

CONGO, REPUBLIC OF THE

CAPITAL: Brazzaville.

MONETARY UNIT: Communauté Financière Africaine franc (CFA Fr). The CFA franc is tied to the French franc at an exchange rate of CFA Fr50 to Fr1. One CFA franc equals 100 centimes. There are coins of 5, 10, 50, 100, and 500 CFA francs, and notes of 500, 1,000, 2,000, 5,000, and 10,000 CFA francs.

CHIEF EXPORTS: Petroleum, tropical and other woods, diamonds, sugar, coffee, and cocoa.

CHIEF IMPORTS: Petroleum products, machines and appliances, construction materials, chemical products, transportation equipment, foodstuffs, textiles, and paper products.

GROSS DOMESTIC PRODUCT: US$4.15 billion (purchasing power parity, 1999 est.).

BALANCE OF TRADE: Exports: US$1.7 billion (f.o.b., 1999). Imports: US$770 million (f.o.b., 1999).

COUNTRY OVERVIEW

LOCATION AND SIZE. The Republic of the Congo (ROC) is located in Western Africa and has an area of 342,000 square kilometers (132,000 square miles). It has a modest coastline of 169 kilometers (105 miles) along the Atlantic Ocean in the southwest and shares land borders with Gabon, Cameroon, and the Central African Republic on the west and north. The country is sometimes referred to casually as simply Congo or the Congo, or even Congo Brazzaville, to designate that it is the Congo with Brazzaville as its capital, distinguishing it from the Democratic Republic of the Congo (or Congo Kinshasa), which has its capital at Kinshasa. The Democratic Republic of the Congo lies along Congo's eastern border, with Angola's Cabinda Province sharing a small section of the southeastern border. The Congo is slightly smaller than Montana. The capital city of Brazzaville is located in the southeast of the country, directly across the Congo River from Kinshasa.

POPULATION. Congo's population was 2,830,961 and growing at an annual rate of 2.23 percent annually in 2000. The birth rate and the death rate in 2000 were estimated at 38.61 and 16.35 per 1,000 population, respectively. Life expectancy in Congo is only about 47 years of age, with women living to age 50 and men on average to age 44. One contributing factor to this short life span is the AIDS epidemic, which has in recent years swept across much of sub-Saharan Africa (that part of the African continent that is south of the Sahara desert).

The Congo is one of the most urbanized countries in Africa. Eighty-five percent of the population lives in Brazzaville, Pointe-Noire, or one of the smaller cities found along the railway which connects Brazzaville and Point-Noire. The official language is French. However, there are many dialects spoken in the Congo of which Lingala and Monokutuba are the most widely spoken.

The population of the Congo is made up of 4 major ethnic groups: the Kongo, the M'Bochi, the Sangha, and the Teke. Only 12,000 pygmies (or the Baka people, a collection of tribes who dwell in African forests in the region occupied by Congo and its neighbors) remain in the country.

OVERVIEW OF ECONOMY

The Congolese economy depends on agricultural production for personal consumption and the exploitation of natural resources. Because the country provides a key port and other transport facilities for neighboring countries such as Chad, Gabon, and the Central African Republic, commercial activities also play an important role in the economy. In 1997, the Congo's government had US$302 million in revenues and US$468 million in expenditures, with a major share of its revenues derived from oil drilling. In the 1980s rising oil revenues provided the Congolese government with the ability to finance large-scale development projects by borrowing against a large share of its future oil income. But this has resulted in shortages in current government revenues. In the late 1990s, oil prices fell and this further reduced government revenue and the country's economic progress.

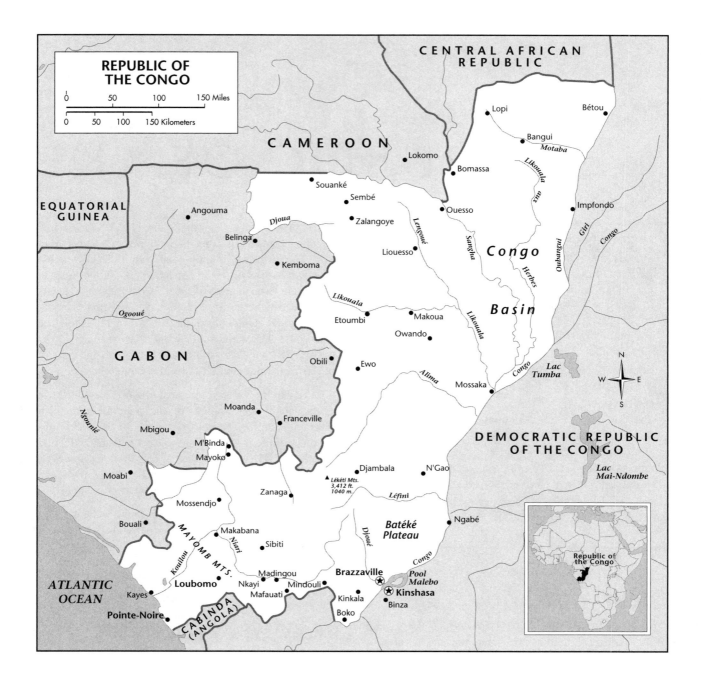

Further, the Congo suffered another setback due to a civil war that broke out in 1997.

By the end of the 1990s the Republic of the Congo was in a state of disarray. The country's **external debt** in 1997 was estimated at a huge US$5 billion. Added to this burden of debt was a highly overvalued CFA franc, which made it difficult to export goods; a 5-month civil war in 1997 that cost thousands of lives, wreaked havoc on the capital city of Brazzaville, and sent hundreds of thousands of refugees into the countryside and out of the country; a volatile oil market; and a bloated bureaucracy that is unable to quickly shift economic policies for the better.

POLITICS, GOVERNMENT, AND TAXATION

The Congo's 1992 constitution states that the Congo is a multiparty democracy, and that the president is head of state. Legislative power is apportioned between a 125-member National Assembly and a 60-member Senate. The constitution also stipulates that the president and members of the national assembly are to be elected every 5 years, while senate members are to be elected every 6 years. In 1997, however, the constitution was suspended by former President General Denis Sassou-Nguesso, who overthrew the popularly-elected government of President Pascal Lissouba. To his credit, President Sassou installed a cabinet composed of individuals from various political parties in order to build a broad consensus. In addition, he created a **unicameral** 75-member National Transitional Council to act as a legislature until the time that elections are held again. He has failed, however, to make good on his promise to restore democratic rule to the Congo by 2001.

The Republic of Congo gained its independence from the colonial power of France in 1960, and was led in its first years by a Catholic priest named Abbé Fulbert Youlou, who created a single-party state and aligned the nation with the **socialist** nations led by the Soviet Union. General Sassou-Nguesso first seized power in 1979. He transformed himself into a civilian leader, and continued the country's socialist policies. However, with the collapse of the Soviet Union in the late 1980s the country made the difficult transition to market economic practices and created a new constitution that paved the way for democratic elections. Sassou-Nguesso lost the presidency in the Congo's first universal elections in 1993 to Pascal Lissouba. In 1997, as the next presidential election loomed, conflict broke out between supporters of President Lissouba and Sassou-Nguesso. A 5-month civil war erupted, and troops from neighboring Angola intervened on Sassou-Nguesso's behalf. General Sassou-Nguesso's forces won, and he declared himself president. However, the peace was short-lived, and fighting broke out once more. The war reached its zenith in 1998 during the battle to control Brazzaville, which substantially destroyed the city and resulted in the deaths of thousands and the flight of 250,000 of its inhabitants. Since that time there have been several attempts to negotiate an end to the conflict, but as of 2001 no settlement has been agreed upon and Sassou-Nguesso remains in power.

The war has had a devastating impact on the Congo's economy, due in part to the severing of the main rail line between Brazzaville and Pointe-Noire, which disrupted trade. Oil revenue is the only reason the Congo has not experienced a total collapse of its economy. In 1998, as a result of the war, the country's **budget deficit** increased to 30 percent. It was reduced to 10 percent in 1999.

INFRASTRUCTURE, POWER, AND COMMUNICATIONS

Two major rivers—the Congo (the fifth largest in the world) and the Ubangi—carry commercial shipping in the Congo, and comprise a vital mode of economic activity. A 534-kilometer (332-mile) railroad links many of Congo's villages and the 2 major cities of Brazzaville and Pointe-Noire; however, this railway was badly damaged in the civil war of 1997–98. Congo's road system consists of a total of 12,800 kilometers of highways (7,954 miles), of which only 1,242 kilometers (772 miles) are paved. The Congo has 2 international airports in Brazzaville and the port city of Pointe-Noire.

Six newspapers are published in the Congo daily. Congolese sources report that there are 4 AM and 1 FM radio stations, while the *CIA World Factbook* lists 1 AM, 5 FM, and 1 short-wave station. Very few people in the Congo have telephones, international calls are possible, and the telephone system is highly unreliable. In 1998, there were only 8 telephone lines per 1,000 people. Internet service is provided on a limited basis by the government's Ministry of Post and Telecommunications, as well as by a small number of providers in the neighboring Democratic Republic of the Congo.

The Congo's potential for hydroelectric power generation is substantial, but is not fully exploited. Even though hydroelectric plants provide some 99 percent of the country's power, the Congo must still purchase roughly one-fourth of its electricity requirements from its neighbor, the Democratic Republic of the Congo. Altogether, the total electricity produced in 1998 amounted to 503 million kilowatt hours (kWh). Wood is the primary source of fuel for most people living in rural areas.

Communications

Country	Newspapers	Radios	TV Sets[a]	Cable subscribers[a]	Mobile Phones[a]	Fax Machines[a]	Personal Computers[a]	Internet Hosts[b]	Internet Users[b]
	1996	1997	1998	1998	1998	1998	1998	1999	1999
Rep. of Congo	8	124	12	N/A	1	N/A	N/A	0.00	1
United States	215	2,146	847	244.3	256	78.4	458.6	1,508.77	74,100
Dem. Rep. of Congo	3	375	135	N/A	0	N/A	N/A	0.00	1
Gabon	29	183	55	N/A	8	0.4	8.6	0.02	3

[a]Data are from International Telecommunication Union, *World Telecommunication Development Report 1999* and are per 1,000 people.
[b]Data are from the Internet Software Consortium (http://www.isc.org) and are per 10,000 people.

SOURCE: World Bank. *World Development Indicators 2000.*

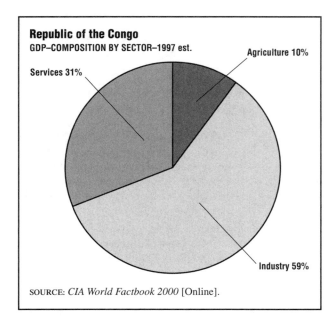

Republic of the Congo
GDP–COMPOSITION BY SECTOR–1997 est.

Agriculture 10%

Services 31%

Industry 59%

SOURCE: *CIA World Factbook 2000* [Online].

ECONOMIC SECTORS

Agriculture contributes to 10 percent of the GDP and employs approximately 60 percent of the **workforce**, indicating the real inefficiency of this sector. Most participants in the agricultural sector produce food for their own consumption only. Industry and services represents 59 percent and 31 percent of GDP, respectively. Petroleum produced from offshore oil fields and crude oil represent 75 percent of the Congo's annual exports. Additionally, the Congo exports natural gas, lead, gold, and copper.

The Congolese state bureaucracy is a major employer. At the beginning of the 1990s the state employed some 80,000 people, an enormous number for a country of its size. Since that time government efforts to **privatize** state-run industries have lessened state employment, but the still large and corrupt government bureaucracy acts as a drag on economic growth.

AGRICULTURE

Agriculture and forestry comprised 12 percent of GDP in 1995, and just 10 percent in 1999. Reliable statistics for a country such as the Congo are difficult to obtain, as most agricultural labor takes place outside of official channels, but most estimates put the percentage of the workforce engaged in agriculture between 60 and 75 percent. In 1998, agricultural exports totaled US$15.3 million, while agricultural imports totaled US$130 million. Cassava is the principal food crop. Other major crops include manioc, plantains, bananas, peanuts, sugarcane, cocoa, coffee, and palm kernels. Agricultural commodities that are exported include tropical and other woods, sugar, coffee, and cocoa. The Congo also pro-

duces beef and veal, chicken, lamb, game, and pork. Less than 2 percent of the country's land is cultivated.

Forest products from the Congo's lush rainforests represent 10 percent of export earnings, and once led exports until the country developed its oil industry. But due to high transportation and wage costs as well as low productivity, the forest industry has suffered severe declines in recent years.

INDUSTRY

MANUFACTURING. The Congo's manufacturing sector plays a small role in the economy, consisting of around 100 factories in Brazzaville and Pointe Noire, mostly engaged in the processing of agricultural and forest products. There are a number of companies engaged in manufacturing **import-substitution** products such as footwear, soft drinks, chemicals, cement, and metal-working products. The less significant sectors of the manufacturing industry produce textiles, footwear, cement, and soap.

OIL. Oil is Congo's main export and the major support for a faltering economy. In 1998, the Congo exported more than 257,000 barrels of oil daily, and petroleum comprises some 50 percent of exports. In sub-Saharan Africa, the Congo is the fourth-largest oil producer, and has an estimated 1.5 billion barrels in reserve.

In 1994, the Congo took steps to **deregulate** the oil industry by offering production-sharing agreements with major foreign oil companies. This initiative is intended to regularize the flow of income to the government. Despite these steps, declining oil prices in 1998 badly hurt the Congo's economy. The French oil company Elf-Aquitaine, which accounts for 70 percent of Congo's annual oil production, is the major producer, along with the Italian oil firm Agip, and Chevron and Exxon from the United States. Rising worldwide oil prices in 2001, together with new discoveries and production, are expected to increase export revenues in the coming years.

OTHER INDUSTRIES. The Congo has the third-largest natural gas reserves in sub-Saharan Africa, estimated at over 3 trillion cubic feet. As of 2001, however, there was no development of a natural gas industry. The Congo has substantial reserves of copper, lead, zinc, gold, and platinum, but these metals are mined in small quantities.

SERVICES

Services provide a major portion of GDP, making a 37 percent contribution in 1997, second only to industry's 59 percent (largely composed of oil production).

One major services area in the Congo is the public bureaucracy. In the early 1990s, the Congolese government was the biggest employer in the country, with a payroll in excess of 80,000. This was a severe drain on the country's resources. Due to pressure from the World Bank and other institutions, the government made major cuts in the number of civil servants as well as their salaries. Since the mid-1990s, the payroll has been cut in half and nearly 8,000 government employees have been let go.

Figures for other aspects of the service sector such as banking are sketchy. Most of the service industry is located in Pointe-Noire and Brazzaville. As of 2001, the government was engaged in intensive talks with the World Bank, the IMF, and other bodies in an effort to renegotiate aid packages and rebuild the banking system.

INTERNATIONAL TRADE

With exports of US$770 million and imports of US$1.7 billion, the Congo has a severe trade imbalance of nearly US$1 billion. The Congo conducts considerable trade with other Central African countries such as Cameroon, the Central African Republic, and Gabon, which are part of the Customs and Economic Union of Central Africa. However, it exports the majority of its goods—primarily oil—to Western countries. The United States purchased 23 percent of the country's exports in 1998, while the Benelux countries took 14 percent, followed by Germany, Italy, Taiwan, and China. France was the major source of goods imported into the Congo, with 23 percent; the United States provided 9 percent; Belgium, 8 percent; and the United Kingdom, 7 percent.

Although the Congo has a bilateral investment treaty with the United States and a new investment code intended to bring in more **foreign direct investment**, it has been unable to attract meaningful foreign investment. According to the U.S. Department of State Background Notes, "High costs for labor, energy, raw materials, and transportation; militant labor unions; and an inadequate transportation **infrastructure** are among the factors discouraging investment. The recent political instability, war damage, and looting also will undermine investor confidence."

Exchange rates: Republic of the Congo

Communaute Financiere Africaine francs (CFA Fr) per US$1

Jan 2001	699.21
2000	711.98
1999	615.70
1998	589.95
1997	583.67
1996	511.55

Note: From January 1, 1999, the CFA Fr is pegged to the euro at a rate of 655.957 CFA Fr per euro.

SOURCE: CIA *World Factbook 2001* [ONLINE].

MONEY

The Republic of the Congo is part of the Central African Monetary and Economic Union (Communauté Economiquareue et Monetaire de l'Afrique Centrale, or CEMAC), a group of 5 francophone countries that use the same currency, the CFA franc. The CFA franc is tied to the French franc and can be readily exchanged at 50 CFA francs to 1 French franc. Congo, like all members of the CFA franc communities, has benefitted from this stable currency.

As a member of the CFA zone, Congo was profoundly affected by the 50 percent **devaluation** of the CFA in 1994. The currency had been overvalued prior to the devaluation, making it difficult for the country to export its goods. The devaluation has made its traditional exports more competitive on world markets. In the short term, however, devaluation lowered living standards and probably increased poverty by raising prices while most salaries remained static.

CEMAC planned to open a regional stock exchange in Libreville, Gabon, in 2001, despite the existence of a limited stock exchange in Douala.

POVERTY AND WEALTH

The lack of proper monitoring makes it difficult to determine the actual income levels of the Congolese people, the majority of whom are involved in subsistence agriculture and trade their labor for the goods that they need. World Bank estimates indicate that the per capita GDP was just US$670 per year in 1999. According to the Congolese government, only 30 percent of the population has access to health care, and they estimate that CFA44 billion is needed to rebuild the medical services sector. Further, there are over 120,000 HIV/AIDS victims in Congo, and only 14 percent of the people live in "healthy" environments.

Trade (expressed in billions of US$): Democratic Republic of the Congo

	Exports	Imports
1975	.275	.300
1980	.544	.278
1985	.950	.792
1990	.999	.888
1995	.438	.397
1998	N/A	N/A

SOURCE: International Monetary Fund. *International Financial Statistics Yearbook 1999.*

GDP per Capita (US$)

Country	1975	1980	1985	1990	1998
Rep. of Congo	709	776	1,096	933	821
United States	19,364	21,529	23,200	25,363	29,683
Dem. Rep. of Congo	392	313	293	247	127
Gabon	6,480	5,160	4,941	4,442	4,630

SOURCE: United Nations. *Human Development Report 2000; Trends in human development and per capita income.*

For children ages 6 through 16, schooling is compulsory and free. The CIA and World Bank estimate that 79 percent of Congolese over the age of 15 are literate. The country's only university, Universite Marien-Ngouabi, is located in Brazzaville and has an enrollment of 12,000 students annually.

WORKING CONDITIONS

The lack of proper monitoring agencies makes it impossible to estimate the total workforce or unemployment figures for the Congo; moreover, the existence of a large **informal economy** and subsistence agricultural practices would distort any figures that were available.

The government calls for a monthly minimum wage of about US$85, a sum insufficient to afford a worker and his or her family a decent standard of living. The lack of proper protections for workers has led to the rise of a number of militant labor unions, including the Congolese Trade Union Congress, the General Union of Congolese Pupils and Students, the Revolutionary Union of Congolese Women, and the Union of Congolese Socialist Youth.

COUNTRY HISTORY AND ECONOMIC DEVELOPMENT

1879. Pierre Savorgnan de Brazza of France explores the area of today's Congo. He signs treaties with its

leaders and declares the area to be subject to France's protection. Subsequently, this territory becomes known as the Middle Congo.

1910. The Middle Congo officially becomes one of France's federated colonies. Brazzaville becomes the principal city of the Middle Congo and head of the Federation's government.

1924–34. The Congo-Ocean Railway is completed, which paves the way for the development of the port city of Point-Noire and the numerous townships along the ocean.

1944. Major reforms in France's colonial policy take place as a result of the Brazzaville Conference, including the end of compulsory labor, French citizenship for colonial members, and the right to limited self-rule.

1960. France grants Middle Congo its independence; the country is renamed the Republic of the Congo.

1963. Fulbert Youlou becomes the Congo's first president and prohibits all political parties except his own. He is overthrown by Alphonse Massamba-Débat 3 years later. President Massamba-Débat introduces **communism** to the Congo and establishes strong ties with communist states, including the People's Republic of China.

1968. Marien Ngouabi becomes head of state after overthrowing Massamba-Débat. Ngouabi's 9-year rule is even more leftist than that of his predecessor.

1970. A new constitution is ratified, renaming the country the People's Republic of the Congo.

1977. General Joahim Yhombi-Opango assumes power after Ngouabi is assassinated. The Congo continues its close ties with France, despite its ideological affiliation with communism.

1979. President Yhombi-Opango is succeeded as president by Colonel Denis Sassou-Nguesso.

1981. The Congo signs a treaty with the Soviet Union establishing cooperation and friendship between the 2 nations.

Household Consumption in PPP Terms

Country	All food	Clothing and footwear	Fuel and power[a]	Health care[b]	Education[b]	Transport & Communications	Other
Rep. of Congo	34	2	12	3	3	11	36
United States	13	9	9	4	6	8	51
Dem. Rep. of Congo	N/A	N/A	N/A	N/A	N/A	N/A	N/A
Gabon	40	3	9	3	7	4	34

Data represent percentage of consumption in PPP terms.
[a]Excludes energy used for transport.
[b]Includes government and private expenditures.

SOURCE: World Bank. *World Development Indicators 2000.*

1991. A new constitution is ratified making the Congo a multi-party democracy. The country's name is changed back to the Republic of the Congo and the country adopts a new national flag and anthem.

1992. Sassou-Nguesso is defeated in the presidential elections by Pascal Lissouba. Subsequently, Lissouba is accused of ethnic favoritism and armed factions supporting Sassou-Nguesso rise against him.

1997. Civil war breaks out in Brazzaville, which results in Brazzaville's destruction. Later that year, Sassou-Nguesso overthrows Lissouba with help from Angola.

FUTURE TRENDS

One of the major impediments to improvements to the Congo's economy is the service on the Congo's external debt. The Congo is one of Africa's most indebted countries, with its **foreign debt** totaling about 250 percent of its GDP. As a result, too large a share of the government's revenues goes to servicing that debt and very little remains for building infrastructure and maintaining the social services of the country. To solve this problem, the International Monetary Fund agreed to an Interim Post-Conflict Reconstruction and Rehabilitation Program which provides for **debt relief** based on the Congo's implementation of economic reforms. If these measures are undertaken, and debt relief is begun, this will free up much needed resources that can be channeled to infrastructure building. Improvements in infrastructure are essential if the country wishes to draw any foreign investment and build its underdeveloped manufacturing and industrial base.

The Congo's economic progress had been hampered by poor oil prices in 1998, which resulted in a decline in government revenue. The government also experienced a slump in revenue as a result of the war. Both of these factors contributed to the major decline in the Congo's economy, which experience -3.0 percent annual GDP

growth in 1999. Subsequent increases in world oil prices in 2000 and 2001 were certain to aid the economy, though the destruction of the country's infrastructure by the 1997–98 civil war may make it difficult for the country to prepare its goods for export.

In the long term, the Congo must rebuild political stability and commit itself to the dual projects of paying down public debt and rebuilding its infrastructure. Should it solve its political problems the country is likely to gain the assistance of international lending agencies, but even with such assistance the Congo faces a long and difficult road to economic well-being.

DEPENDENCIES

The Republic of the Congo has no territories or colonies.

BIBLIOGRAPHY

Congo Brazzaville Report. <http://www.brazzaville-report.com>. Accessed July 2001.

CongoWeb. <http://www.congoweb.net/english.html>. Accessed July 2001.

Economist Intelligence Unit. *Country Profile: Republic of the Congo.* London: Economist Intelligence Unit, 2001.

"Republic of Congo." *The World Bank Group.* <http://wbln0018 .worldbank.org/AFR/afr.nsf/3b04e45cded3efce852567cf004d4 c6b/ce353f161c2b36ef852567d1004790b5?OpenDocument>. Accessed August 2001.

U.S. Central Intelligence Agency. *World Factbook 2000.* <http:// www.odci.gov/cia/publications/factbook/index.html>. Accessed August 2001.

U.S. Department of State. *Background Notes: Congo.* <http:// www.state.gov/www/background_notes/congo-ro_0002_bgn .html>. Accessed August 2001.

—*Michael David Nicoleau and Raynette Rose Gutrick*

CÔTE D'IVOIRE

Republic of Côte d'Ivoire
République de Côte d'Ivoire

CAPITAL: Yamoussoukro has been the official capital since 1983. However, Abidjan remains the administrative center, and most countries maintain their embassies there.

MONETARY UNIT: Communauté Financière Africaine franc (CFA Fr). 1 franc equals 100 centimes. Coins exist in 5, 10, 50, 100, and 500 CFA Fr. Paper currency denominations are of 500, 1,000, 2,000, 5,000, and 10,000 CFAF.

CHIEF EXPORTS: Cocoa, coffee, tropical timbers, petroleum, cotton, bananas, pineapples, palm oil, cotton, and fish.

CHIEF IMPORTS: Food, manufactured consumer goods, heavy machinery, fuel, and transport equipment.

GROSS DOMESTIC PRODUCT: US$26.2 billion (purchasing power parity, 2000 est.).

BALANCE OF TRADE: Exports: US$3.8 billion (f.o.b., 2000 est.). **Imports:** US$2.5 billion (f.o.b., 2000 est.).

COUNTRY OVERVIEW

LOCATION AND SIZE. Côte d'Ivoire (which means "Ivory Coast") is a West African country bordering the North Atlantic Ocean between Ghana and Liberia. It has an area of 322,460 square kilometers (124,502 square miles) of which 318,000 square kilometers (122,780 square miles) are occupied by land while water occupies the remaining 4,460 square kilometers (1,722 square miles). Its boundaries are 3,110 kilometers long (1,932 miles). These borders include 716 kilometers (445 miles) with Liberia in the west, 610 kilometers (379 miles) with Guinea in the northwest, 532 kilometers (330 miles) with Mali in the north, 584 kilometers (363 miles) with Burkina Faso in the north, and 668 kilometers (415 miles) with Ghana in the east. The country's coastline is 515 kilometers (320 miles) long.

Located on the Gulf of Guinea, Côte d'Ivoire has 2 major natural divisions. Its topography is a mix of plains and low hills containing a small mountainous area, with Mont Nimba rising to 1,752 meters (5,748 feet) above sea level in the Man region to the west. The south's equatorial rainforest (much of which has been logged) changes into woodland savanna to the north. The south has heavy rainfall and lush rain forests where foreign investors have large plantations of crops like coffee, cocoa, and bananas while the north is a granite plain characterized by savannas, where small landowners raise sorghum, corn, and peanuts. Côte d'Ivoire has one of the fastest rates of deforestation in the world.

POPULATION. The population was estimated to be 15.9 million in 2001, up from 13.9 million in 1995, and 11.8 million in 1990. The population density is 50 people per square kilometer (129 per square mile), up from 43.6 in 1995 and 37.1 in 1990. The population growth rate has been 3.1 percent a year in the period 1990–98, and the fertility rate is correspondingly high. The average number of children per woman is 5.1. Urban population has been growing, rising from 40 percent in 1990 to 46 percent in 1999. The structure of the population is youthful, with only 2 percent aged 65 and over, while 52 percent are aged between 15 and 65, and 46 percent are under 15 years. Life expectancy at birth has been decreasing from 50 in 1990 to 46 in 1999, and the incidence of AIDS has been one of the main factors in this decline, with more than 1 million Ivorians affected.

The population includes 5 major ethnic groups: the Kru, Akan, Volta, Mande, and Malinke, inhabiting both the savannas and rain forests, subdivided into approximately 80 smaller groups. Nearly two-thirds of the population follow traditional African religions, while 23 percent are Moslems, and 12 percent are Christians. French is the official language, but there are many other local languages. The most widely spoken are Diula in the north, Baule in the center and west, and Bete in the southeast.

The net out-migration rate was estimated in July 2000 to be 1.6 migrants per 1,000 of the population. After Liberia's civil war started in 1990, more than 350,000 refugees fled to Côte d'Ivoire, but by the end of 1999 almost all the Liberian refugees had returned.

OVERVIEW OF ECONOMY

Côte d'Ivoire has benefited since independence in 1960 from considerable political stability, and to no small measure this has been due to the close relationship with the former colonial power, France, and the presence of French troops in the country. These provided a secure platform for economic development and an encouraging environment for foreign investment. This state of affairs was disturbed by a military coup (a domestic overthrow of a government) in 1999, but international pressure led to a return to constitutional civilian government in 2000.

Most people in the economy (more than half) depend on agriculture for their livelihoods, and they are the poorest section of the community. Farming is undertaken on small family plots, and much of the output is consumed by the producing family. The economy depends heavily on exports of tropical agricultural products to generate the foreign exchange that Côte d'Ivoire requires to purchase the manufactured goods it does not have the capacity to produce itself. The main exports are cocoa and cocoa products, coffee, and fish. Exports generate 40 percent of the GDP. However, the heavy reliance on tropical agricultural exports makes the economy very vulnerable to changes in international commodity prices and the weather. In 1994, the currency was devalued by 50 percent which resulted in higher prices to producers of export crops who have responded with higher output, but much of the benefit has been eroded by declining world prices, particularly for coffee. Sparked by the **devaluation**, in the 1994–98 period the **real gross domestic product** (GDP) growth averaged 5.5 percent providing the first sustained improvement in per capita GDP since the late 1970s. During this period, the external current account deficit (including grants) was lowered from 11 percent of the GDP in 1993 to 4 percent in 1998, and the **external debt** burden was reduced.

Despite the positive economic results of devaluation, the government is aware of its economy's vulnerability due to its heavy reliance on cocoa and coffee. To safeguard the economy, the government is doing its best to encourage other agricultural exports, such as pineapples and rubber, and exploring for offshore deposits of oil and gas. Since 1986, Côte d'Ivoire has been undertaking a program of economic **liberalization**, which has involved ending state **monopolies**, particularly in agricultural marketing, and **privatizing** state-owned enterprises in an effort to make these sectors more efficient.

The economic situation was further boosted by an increase in grants and low interest rate loans, mainly from France, between 1994 and 1998. Significant progress was made in consolidating public finances during this period with the overall **budget deficit** declining from about 12 percent of the GDP in 1993 to 2.5 percent in 1998. The 50 percent devaluation of CFA franc in January 1994 caused a single jump in the **inflation rate** to 26 percent in 1994, but the rate fell sharply to 9.4 percent in 1996 and 1.3 percent in 1999.

The sharp downturn in the terms of trade, with cocoa prices falling by 40 percent below their end-of-1998 level as well as a significant slowdown in disbursement of external assistance have given rise to problems. Economic growth has slowed, and investment has slipped with the **private sector**'s adoption of a more cautious stance in the uncertain political environment following the 1999 coup.

POLITICS, GOVERNMENT, AND TAXATION

In pre-colonial times, the territory of present-day Côte d'Ivoire was inhospitable to the sea-borne European traders because of the dense, thinly populated tropical forest stretching hundreds of kilometers inland from the At-

lantic Ocean. There was little European interest in the interior before the mid-19th century. Northern Côte d'Ivoire, largely savanna and populated by Muslims, was historically controlled by the Guinean kingdoms, which periodically exerted influence over much of modern Mali, Guinea, and Niger. The French presence grew after 1893 when the colony of Côte d'Ivoire was officially established. The potential of the country's agricultural and forestry resources came to be realized with the building of the railway through Côte d'Ivoire into present-day Burkina Faso, and by the late 1940s, Côte d'Ivoire had replaced Senegal as France's richest colony in West Africa.

Côte d'Ivoire became independent in August 1960, with Felix Houphouet-Boigny, a successful cocoa farmer and former minister in the French government, as president. Close ties to France have characterized the period since independence, and trade and investment links have expanded, as well as the number of French expatriates working in Côte d'Ivoire.

Capitalizing on his carefully cultivated personal relations with successive French governments as well as his skillful economic and political management, Houphouet-Boigny dominated the country's political life for more than 3 decades. Houphouet-Boigny's party, Parti Democratique de Côte d'Ivoire (PDCI), became the only legal political party in Côte d'Ivoire. In the 1960s and 1970s, he presided over Côte d'Ivoire's emergence as one of Africa's few stable and economically successful countries. With the introduction of multiparty politics in 1990, his PDCI remained in control. There was remarkably little internal strife and no significant external threat, leading to a resolution not to develop a costly and possibly untrustworthy army, and instead entrusting national defense to France.

However, Côte d'Ivoire faced serious social and economic problems in the 1980s with the fall in world commodity prices. As Houphouet-Boigny slipped into old age and popular dissent grew in the beginning of the 1990s, demonstrations and strikes became commonplace. The first multiparty elections were held in 1990 and were won by Houphouet-Boigny's PDCI amid accusation from the opposition of vote rigging.

Flamboyant Laurent Gbagbo, leader of the Front Populaire Ivorienne (FPI), defiantly led thousands of protesters through the streets of Abidjan in 1992, resulting in widespread rioting in the commercial capital and attracting a stern reaction from the authorities. Many protesters, including Gbagbo, were arrested and charged under legislation rushed through parliament, although many were freed 6 months later.

Mr. Houpouet-Boigny's death in 1993—which was feared would lead to social chaos and dash hopes of a return to economic prosperity—resulted in a controversial power transfer to Konan Bedie, formerly president of the Assemble Nationale.

In the October 1995 presidential elections Konan Bedie won 95 percent of the vote amid protests from the opposition against a PDCI-dominated parliament's passing of a law that barred Alassane Dramane Ouattara, a World Bank-schooled economist who had been prime minister since 1990, from participating. The law excluded anyone who was considered not born to Ivorian parents, or who had been resident abroad in the preceding 5 years, and Ouattara was deemed to fall into both categories. A pro-Ouattara party, the Ressemblement des Republicans (RDR), was formed by defectors from the reformist wing of the PDCI. Whereas the presidential elections were marred with violence, the parliamentary elections were more peaceful, resulting in a PDCI victory with 149 of the 175 available seats while the rest were split between the FPI and the RDR.

In December 1999, a military coup—the first ever in Côte d'Ivoire's history—overthrew the government and installed military rule under General Robert Guei. The presidential elections in October 2000 were contested by Guei and Laurent Ggagbo of the FPI. Ouattara of the RDR was prevented from running. The results were unclear, and Guei attempted to hijack the process by announcing himself the elected president. Demonstrations and protests and pressure from the international community prevailed, however, and on the basis of the available electoral results, Gbagbo was declared president.

Côte d'Ivoire has a republican (constitutional) government with a multiparty presidential regime established in 1990. It is a country with 50 administrative departments (or districts), with a constitution that was first drawn up in November of 1960 but has been amended on numerous occasions, the last time being in July 1998. The constitution recognizes universal adult suffrage at 21 years of age. The legal system is based on French civil law and customary law with judicial review in the Constitutional Chamber of the Supreme Court. There is a **unicameral** (1-chamber) National Assembly of 175 seats to which members are elected by direct popular vote to serve 5-year terms.

Côte d'Ivoire has a more effective tax revenue collection system than most of sub-Saharan Africa. It includes a wide range of taxes on personal income, capital gains, **value added** on economic activities, exports, and imports. Tax revenues as a share of GDP were 20 percent in 1999. Taxes on international trade are around 40 percent of total government revenue. Income, profits, and capital gains taxes were 21 percent, taxes on goods and services were 5 percent, and the remaining 34 percent came from other taxes, licenses, and the surpluses of state-owned enterprises. There has been a steady rise in revenue collection, which has favorably affected the fiscal situation from 1994 to 1996. Tax revenue increased by an average annual rate of 24 percent in this period, reflecting the impact of the devaluation, strong GDP growth and the effects of improved tax measures. Tax revenues have increased because of the government's efforts to reintroduce an export tax on cocoa and coffee in 1994 and to build the capacity of its revenue departments by implementing strategies to curb fraud and tax evasion.

INFRASTRUCTURE, POWER, AND COMMUNICATIONS

By 1996, Côte d'Ivoire had a fairly well-developed network of 50,400 kilometers (31,317 miles) of roads, of which 4,889 kilometers (3,038 miles) were paved; about 6,000 kilometers (3,728 miles) were primary roads; and 7,000 kilometers (4,350 miles) are secondary roads. A fall in railway traffic has increased the burden on the road network. The government plans to develop the system further, for instance, by extending the country's main highway from Abidjan to Yamoussoukro and to Grand-Bassam, southwest of Abidjan.

The only railway line in Côte d'Ivoire was built by the French, and it links Abidjan with Ouagadougou, the capital city of neighboring Burkina Faso. The Ivorian side is 660 kilometers (410 miles) of meter gauge railway. The rail company, Societe Ivoirienne des Chemins

Communications

Country	Newspapers	Radios	TV Sets[a]	Cable subscribers[a]	Mobile Phones[a]	Fax Machines[a]	Personal Computers[a]	Internet Hosts[b]	Internet Users[b]
	1996	1997	1998	1998	1998	1998	1998	1999	1999
Côte d'Ivoire	17	164	70	0.0	6	N/A	3.6	0.25	20
United States	215	2,146	847	244.3	256	78.4	458.6	1,508.77	74,100
Nigeria	24	223	66	N/A	0	N/A	5.7	0.00	100
Ghana	14	238	99	N/A	1	N/A	1.6	0.06	20

[a]Data are from International Telecommunication Union, *World Telecommunication Development Report 1999* and are per 1,000 people.
[b]Data are from the Internet Software Consortium (http://www.isc.org) and are per 10,000 people.
SOURCE: World Bank. *World Development Indicators 2000.*

de Fer (Ivory Society of Railroads, SICF), saw the number of passengers decline by 75 percent to about 760,000 by 1993, owing in part to the poor condition of the rolling stock.

There are 980 kilometers (609 miles) of navigable rivers and canals, as well as numerous coastal lagoons. There are also 4 major ports: Abidjan, Aboisso, Dabou, and San-Pedro. The Port Autonome d'Abidjan (PAA) is the busiest in Francophone West Africa (the former French colonies in West Africa, in which there is still a legacy of French civil law and language) and earns revenue from transit traffic to and from the country's landlocked neighbors, particularly Burkina Faso and Mali. Petroleum products account for approximately 40 percent of its tonnage. Côte d'Ivoire's second largest port, San Pedro, handles smaller volumes of timber and cocoa.

In 1999, there were an estimated 36 airports in the country, 7 of which had paved runways. Côte d'Ivoire has an important stake in the multinational Air Afrique, which provides most international connections.

Although an estimated 64 percent of the country's electricity is generated from hydroelectric plants, gas power stations are becoming more important with fossil fuels constituting 36 percent of the country's electric energy production. Total electric energy production in 1998 was estimated to be 3.36 billion kilowatt hours (kWh) against a consumption demand of 3.2 billion kWh. Oil is refined for domestic use but is also exported to the region, including to Nigeria where a dismal downstream oil industry has led to persistent oil shortages.

There were 182,000 telephone land lines and more than 60,000 mobile cellular phones in use in 1998. By June 1999 the telephone system was well-developed by African standards but operating far below capacity. Domestic needs are met by land lines and microwave radio relays, 90 percent of which are digitalized. Two Intelsat satellite earth stations and 2 coaxial submarine cables serve international demand. The government sold 51 percent of the national telecommunications company, CI-Telcom, to France Telecom in 1997, which renamed the company Côte d'Ivoire Telecom. At the time of privatization, CI-Telcom was operating 120,000 lines, but the government intended to have 400,000 lines in use by 2002. The long waiting list has enabled many Ivorian companies to benefit from the scramble for market share after liberalization of the industry.

Radiodiffusion-Television Ivorienne (Ivorian Radio Broadcasting-Television, RTI) is a government-owned corporation but is in most respects independent. It is partly funded by advertising and operates 2 television channels and a national radio service, broadcasting in French and local languages. Radio Espoir is owned and operated by the Roman Catholic Church. In 1999 there were a total of 2 AM, 8 FM and 3 short-wave stations, as well as 14 television stations. In 1997 there were 900,000 television sets.

While there were a number of new publications as a consequence of the 1990 political liberalization, many disappeared during Konan Bedie's tenure, and at least 20 journalists have been jailed since 1994. Nonetheless, there remains a healthy opposition press which includes the daily *Notre Voie* and *Nouvel Horizon*, owned by the pro-FPI Nouvel Horizon media group. This alternative coverage provides a counterweight to the dominance of the pro-government press, mainly the daily *Fraternite Matin* founded in 1964 and its evening sister paper, *Ivoire Soir*, with a circulation of about 50,000 and 40,000 respectively.

ECONOMIC SECTORS

For many years after independence from France in 1960, Côte d'Ivoire was the jewel of West Africa, with a strong economy—initially based on agriculture, particularly coffee and cocoa—that attracted many thousands of workers from neighboring countries. Sizeable French and Lebanese communities established themselves in the capital, Abidjan. In 1998, agriculture contributed 32 percent of the GDP, industry 18 percent, and services 50 percent. Agriculture remains based on 2 major crops—cocoa and coffee, which together provided 45 percent of export revenue in 1998. The industrial sector's share of the GDP increased in 1999, and this trend is likely to continue in the coming decade as the country develops food processing. Services, 50 percent of the GDP in 1998, are led mostly by trade and transport, the latter accounting for 30 percent of the GDP.

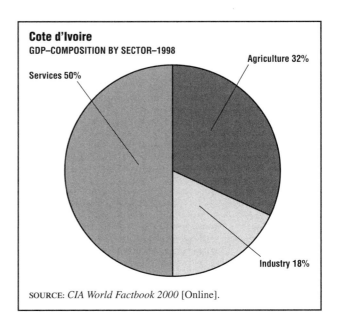

Cote d'Ivoire
GDP–COMPOSITION BY SECTOR–1998

Agriculture 32%

Services 50%

Industry 18%

SOURCE: *CIA World Factbook 2000* [Online].

AGRICULTURE

Agriculture (including forestry and fishing) is a very significant sector of Côte d'Ivoire's economy. It contributed an estimated 32 percent of the GDP and employed about 51 percent of the **labor force** in 1998. However, the disparity between share of the GDP and share of the labor force indicates that agriculture generates much lower incomes than the other 2 major sectors, industry and services. Exports of cocoa and related products contributed an estimated 37 percent of total export earnings in 1998. Export taxes on cocoa and coffee contributed more than 10 percent of government revenue in each year since 1996.

Production of cocoa beans doubled between 1970 and 1979, making Côte d'Ivoire the largest exporter in the world. The country has been the world's largest cocoa producer since 1977–78, when its level of production overtook that of Ghana. Overall output continued to rise, with some fluctuations, reaching a record 1.1 million metric tons in 1995–96 and an estimated 1 million metric tons in 1996–97, up from an annual average of 750,000 metric tons over the 1990–94 period. This increase, however, was attributed to the government incentives program of the 1980s as well as the resultant switching of resources from coffee production. Until 1989, both coffee and cocoa attracted virtually the same producer prices, although coffee was more heavily taxed and is more difficult to grow.

The total land area is distributed among different uses as follows: arable land 8 percent, permanent crops 4 percent, permanent pastures 41 percent, forests and woodland 22 percent, and others 25 percent. In 1993 only 680 square kilometers (262 square miles) of land was under irrigation. Agricultural production increased by an average of 2.4 percent annually between 1990–98. There were 2.44 million hectares of arable land in 1994, 1.27 million hectares of permanent cropland, and 13 million hectares of meadow and pasture. The other major **cash crops** include cotton, rubber, bananas, and pineapples. The principal subsistence crops are maize, yams, cassava, plantains, and, increasingly, rice, as demand continues to outstrip local production of rice. In 1996, it was estimated that there were 1.28 million cattle, 1.31 million sheep, 1.0 million goats, 290,000 pigs, and 27 million chickens.

With about two-thirds of the total export earnings provided by the sale of coffee and cocoa, which are both highly vulnerable to fluctuations in international prices, the government has sought to diversify agricultural production. Since the 1960s, Côte d'Ivoire has become a major producer of palm oil, and local processing of palm products has developed. Cotton production has done particularly well in recent decades, enabling Côte d'Ivoire to compete—alongside Sudan, Mali, and Benin—for the position of Africa's second largest producer of cotton af-

ter Egypt. Most of the cotton is processed locally in 8 ginning complexes both for export (some 80 percent of total production) and the local textile industry.

The rubber industry has also shown growth since the mid-1980s with output increasing by more than 50 percent between 1990 and 1994 in response to government plans for Côte d'Ivoire to become Africa's leading rubber producer. Côte d'Ivoire is also a significant producer of pineapples and bananas with exports mostly directed to European markets.

In recent years, the government has stressed the need to increase output of basic food crops such as rice in which Côte d'Ivoire is not self-sufficient. A deficiency in the sugar supply and the need to save foreign exchange on sugar imports led the government to initiate a sugar program in the 1970s. By the 1980s, the 2 schemes could supply most of internal demand, then estimated at 80,000 metric tons a year, but production costs were twice the world price, leading to cancellation of further sugar projects.

Livestock is not a significant sector, comprising mostly small herds, which can supply only about one-third of the nation's demand for livestock products. On the other hand, fishing is a significant activity, and Abidjan is the largest tuna-fishing port in Africa with an annual catch of more then 90,000 metric tons. However, most of this catch is by foreign vessels, and the only benefits to Côte d'Ivoire are the license fees. Ivorian participation in this sector is still low, with the domestic fishing fleet numbering only 38 vessels and most traditional fishing being undertaken by non-Ivorians. Domestic production meets only about 40 percent of local demand.

Forestry has always been a significant source of export revenue, from both logs and sawn timber. Boosted by enhanced price competitiveness since 1994, timber has displaced both coffee and petroleum products as the country's second highest earner of foreign exchange earnings, after cocoa. Most of the production is carried out by large integrated foreign-owned firms. The area of exploitable timber has fallen to only about 1 million hectares in 1987 compared with some 15.6 million hectares in 1960 because of logging and the encroachment of agriculture into forest areas. Progress in reforestation has been disappointing, and the government is committed to a ban on exports of timber once the country's foreign payments position has improved.

The main current environmental issue is deforestation. Some 94 percent of the country's forests—once the largest in West Africa—have been cleared by the timber industry since independence. Water pollution from sewage, industrial plants, and agricultural effluents is also causing concern.

INDUSTRY

Industry includes agricultural processing, mining, manufacturing, construction, and power. It comprises mostly foodstuffs, beverages, wood products, oil refining, automobile assembly, textiles, fertilizer, construction materials, mining, and electricity. It contributed an estimated 18 percent of the GDP in 1998 and employed about 12 percent of the labor force in 1994.

MINING. Mining contributed only an estimated 0.3 percent of the GDP in 1998. This sub-sector's contribution, however, is expected to increase considerably following commencement in the mid-1990s of commercial exploitation of important offshore reserves of petroleum and natural gas. Gold and diamonds are also produced, although the illicit production of the latter has greatly exceeded formal commercial output. There is believed to be a significant potential for the development of nickel deposits, and there are also notable reserves of manganese, iron-ore, and bauxite.

MANUFACTURING. The manufacturing sub-sector contributed about 14.6 percent of the GDP in 1998. It is dominated by agro-industrial activities such as processing of cocoa, coffee, cotton, palm kernels, pineapples, and fish. Crude petroleum is refined at Abidjan while the tobacco industry uses mostly imported tobacco leaf. In 1998 almost two-thirds of Côte d'Ivoire's electricity was derived from thermal sources while the rest was from hydro-generation. Through exploitation of natural gas reserves, the country is expected to generate sufficient energy for its own requirements by 2000 and for regional export thereafter. Imports of petroleum products including crude oil accounted for 14.9 percent of the total value of imports in 1998.

Manufacturing output expanded in real terms at an average rate of 8.9 percent per year between 1965 and 1974, easing to 5.4 percent per year in the following decade after the main industrial opportunities had been exploited. However, this sector continues to be sustained by the high rate of growth in domestic demand, arising mainly from the rapid increase in the country's population and the boost in competitiveness to domestic industry resulting from the 1994 devaluation of the CFA franc. Between 1990 and 1998, industrial GDP increased by an average of 5.1 percent per year, while the industrial production growth rate was estimated to be about 15 percent in 1998.

SERVICES

A major economic feature of the 1990s has been the expansion of the services sector. It contributed about 50 percent of the GDP in 1998 and employed about 37 percent of the labor force in 1994. The transformation of Abidjan's stock market into a regional exchange for the member states of the Union Economique et Monetaire Oeust-Africaine (UEMOA) together with the hosting of the headquarters of the Africa Development Bank is expected to enhance the city's status as a center of financial services.

Emphasis was also placed on the revival of tourism as a major source of foreign exchange. Tourism developed strongly in the 1970s with a newly created ministry stimulating diversification both in location (away from the Abidjan area) and in type of visitors (aside from business travelers) who previously accounted for almost two-thirds of arrivals. Special tax incentives and guarantees were offered for hotel construction, and by 1984 the number of hotels was 452, about 5 times the 1972 level. The number of tourists increased from 93,000 in 1974 to 198,900 in 1979 with business visitors accounting for 40 percent of arrivals. Since then, visitor arrivals have fluctuated in the range of 200,000–290,000 per year, broadly reflecting trends in tourism. The government's target is for 500,000 arrivals by 2000.

Abidjan is also central to regional communications and trade. The service sector's contribution to the GDP increased at an average rate of 3.5 percent per year from 1990 to 1998.

INTERNATIONAL TRADE

Côte d'Ivoire had very rapid economic growth between 1950 and 1975, with fewer problems with the **balance of payments** than most African countries. Exports increased at a faster rate than the GNP and they remain the main factor contributing to economic growth in the new millennium. Côte d'Ivoire's balance of trade has always been in surplus because of the strength of its exports, which have largely been determined by the level of earnings from sales of coffee and cocoa. In recent years, the surplus has also been boosted by the 1994 devaluation of the CFA franc, affecting both cocoa and timber exports, although increases in export earnings from

Trade (expressed in billions of US$): Côte d'Ivoire		
	Exports	**Imports**
1975	1.181	1.127
1980	3.135	2.967
1985	3.198	1.749
1990	3.072	2.098
1995	3.645	2.945
1998	N/A	N/A

SOURCE: International Monetary Fund. *International Financial Statistics Yearbook 1999.*

logs and sawn wood have been limited owing to the impending exhaustion of the country's forestry resources. Other exports that have responded favorably to the currency adjustment are canned fish, natural rubber, bananas, and other fruits. The CIA *World Factbook* estimated the country's exports to be US$3.8 billion in 2000.

Despite the government's wish to diversify the direction of trade, the existing pattern reflects Côte d'Ivoire's historical ties with European colonial powers. In 1998, the EU absorbed an estimated 58 percent of all its trade, with France accounting for 21 percent. Trade with African countries is increasing and represented 28 percent of total trade in 1998, and the government is eager to promote closer trade links with the 8-member Francophone Union (UEMOA), of which Côte d'Ivoire is a member. UEMOA countries are in the process of reducing import **duties** on their goods, and the government hopes that West Africa will provide a market for 50 percent of total exports early in the 21st century. Meanwhile, exports to Asia continue to increase, reaching 15 percent of total exports in 1998. The CIA *World Factbook* estimated Côte d'Ivoire major export partners to be France (15 percent), United States (8 percent), Netherlands (7 percent), and Germany and Italy (both at 6 percent) in 1999.

Imports are mainly food, manufactured **consumer goods**, heavy machinery, transport equipment, and fuel. In 2000, the total value of imports was estimated to be US$2.5 billion. Imports are sourced from France (26 percent), Nigeria (10 percent), China (7 percent), Italy (5 percent), and Germany (4 percent).

MONEY

The unit of account is the West African CFA franc. There are no restrictions on the import of local currency. **Monetary policy** in Côte d'Ivoire is set by the regional central bank, the Central Bank of West African States (BCEAO). The Bank aims to conduct a prudent policy

GDP per Capita (US$)					
Country	1996	1997	1998	1999	2000
Côte d'Ivoire	4,300	1,700	1,680	1,600	1,600
United States	28,600	30,200	31,500	33,900	36,200
Nigeria	1,380	N/A	960	970	950
Ghana	1,530	2,000	1,800	1,900	1,900

Note: Data are estimates.

SOURCE: *Handbook of the Nations*, 17th, 18th, 19th and 20th editions for 1996, 1997, 1998 and 1999 data; CIA *World Factbook 2001* [Online] for 2000 data.

consistent with the **fixed exchange rate** to the French franc, which since January 1999 has implied a fixed exchange rate to the euro, the new common currency of the European Union. In January 2000 the **exchange rate** was 647CFA Fr = US$1, a depreciation in the value of the CFA franc of 23 percent from 499CFA Fr = US$1 in 1995.

The BCEAO controls monetary policy in the Côte d'Ivoire, and a cautious rate of increase in the money supply has kept the inflation rate low in since 1995. In 1999 **inflation** was estimated at 0.8 percent a year.

POVERTY AND WEALTH

In 1998, it was estimated that 17.5 percent of the population lived below the dollar-a-day poverty line (this line is based on the income required to provide the absolute minimum nutrition, clothing, and shelter). It means that 24 percent of the children under 5 years of age are malnourished (the figure is 1 percent in the United States), and life expectancy is 47 years (in the United States it is 77 years). However, poverty levels are markedly better in Côte d'Ivoire than nearby Senegal, which has almost exactly the same level of average income per head but has 34 percent below the dollar-a-day

Exchange rates: Côte d'Ivoire	
Communauté Financière Africaine francs (CFA Fr) per US$1	
Jan 2001	699.21
2000	711.98
1999	615.70
1998	589.95
1997	583.67
1996	511.55

Note: From January 1, 1999, the CFA Fr is pegged to the euro at a rate of 655.957 CFA Fr per euro.

SOURCE: CIA *World Factbook 2001* [ONLINE].

Distribution of Income or Consumption by Percentage Share: Côte d'Ivoire	
Lowest 10%	3.1
Lowest 20%	7.1
Second 20%	11.2
Third 20%	15.6
Fourth 20%	21.9
Highest 20%	44.3
Highest 10%	28.8

Survey year: 1995
Note: This information refers to expenditure shares by percentiles of the population and is ranked by per capita expenditure.

SOURCE: *2000 World Development Indicators* [CD-ROM].

Household Consumption in PPP Terms

Country	All food	Clothing and footwear	Fuel and power[a]	Health care[b]	Education[b]	Transport & Communications	Other
Côte d'Ivoire	30	7	4	1	18	8	32
United States	13	9	9	4	6	8	51
Nigeria	51	5	31	2	8	2	2
Ghana	N/A	N/A	N/A	N/A	N/A	N/A	N/A

Data represent percentage of consumption in PPP terms.
[a]Excludes energy used for transport.
[b]Includes government and private expenditures.

SOURCE: World Bank. *World Development Indicators 2000.*

poverty line. Almost all those in poverty are in the rural areas, relying on small-scale agriculture for their livelihoods, and suffering because of poor land, inadequate rainfall, and not enough income to purchase good seeds, fertilizer, or farm machinery.

The **GDP per capita** was at US$1,730 in 1998, relatively high for the region. Nevertheless, this placed Côte d'Ivoire in the low-income category of countries and is put in perspective by the US$29,340 level of the GDP per head for the United States. As with most developing countries, there is considerable income inequality, with the poorest 10 percent of the country's population sharing only 2.8 percent of the country's household income while the share for the richest 10 percent is 28.5 percent.

The UN's Human Development Index (HDI), which attempts to measure the quality of life on the basis of real GDP per head, the adult literacy rate, and life expectancy at birth, placed Côte d'Ivoire at 154 out of 174 countries in 1999, firmly in the low human development category.

WORKING CONDITIONS

The workforce in 1998 was estimated at 6 million, of which 33 percent were women. Of children aged 10 to 14, about 20 percent were engaged in full-time work. There are no official unemployment figures for Côte d'Ivoire, but unemployment figures have little significance in a low-income African economy. There are very few with no work at all. There are no unemployment benefits, and those who do not work rely on support from charities or their families. Many people would like a modern sector job, but eke out an existence on family farms or in casual **informal sector** activities (such as **hawking**, portering, and scavenging) in the urban areas.

The National Union of Côte d'Ivoire was formed in 1959 but was replaced in 1962 by the General Union of Côte d'Ivoire Workers (Union Generale des Travailleurs de Côte d'Ivoire), controlled by the PDCI. In mid-1980s, it had some 190 affiliated unions and 100,000 members. A labor inspection service supervises conditions under

which foreign workers are employed. The greater prosperity of Côte d'Ivoire has led to considerable migrations of workers from Mali and Burkina Faso, many of them illegal workers, and the inspection service tries to prevent them from being unfairly exploited by employers.

Labor legislation is still based on the French overseas labor code of 1952 which provides for collective agreements between employees and trade unions, the fixing of basic minimum wages by the government, and a 40-hour week for all except agricultural workers for whom longer working hours are permitted. The average annual wage was estimated by the IMF to be US$4,545 in 1999, up from about US$4,200 in 1993 with government employees earning on average better than those in the private sector. Legislation also provides wage earners with paid annual leave and children's allowances. The government has the power to impress persons into public service for up to 2 years.

COUNTRY HISTORY AND ECONOMIC DEVELOPMENT

1893. Côte d'Ivoire becomes a French colony.

1944. Felix Houphouet-Boigny founds Syndicat Agricole Africain (SAA) to protest the colonial authorities' preferential treatment of French planters in the recruitment of farm labor.

1960. Republic of Ivory Coast is proclaimed with Felix Houphouet-Boigny elected president. A new constitution is adopted.

1963. A plot against the government is uncovered, and hundreds are arrested, including members of the National Assembly and cabinet ministers.

1969. Street clashes between Ivorians and immigrant workers are followed by student demonstrations. Diplomatic relations with the Soviet Union are broken.

1970. The government restricts **immigration** of foreign workers and suppresses a group of Bete rebels led by Gnabe Opadjele.

1973. A coup attempt by 12 army officers is foiled.

1990. Opposition parties are legalized. First multiparty elections are held. Houphouet-Boigny is re-elected president.

1993. Felix Houphouet-Boigny, Côte d'Ivoire's president since independence in 1960, dies in December. Henry Konan Bedie, president of the National Assembly, succeeds him.

1994. The CFA franc is devalued in January by 50 percent, preparing ground for further economic reforms and a sustained period of economic growth.

1995. In October, Konan Bedie wins 95 percent of the vote in the presidential elections in the face of a widespread opposition boycott.

1998. The constitution is amended in August strengthening the powers of the president and barring Ouattara from standing in the 2000 presidential election.

1999. Bedie is ousted in a coup, and a military government under General Robert Guei is installed.

2000. The presidential elections between General Guei and Laurent Ggagbo of the FPI occurs. After an attempt by Guei to announce himself elected, Gbagbo is declared president.

FUTURE TRENDS

There is no question but that the 1999 coup was a severe setback to the image of Côte d'Ivoire as a secure and stable civilian-led country where the rule of law was respected and the business environment was encouraging for domestic and foreign investment alike. It is fortunate that the matter was speedily settled, but the subsequent elections were resolved only by civilian demonstrations and international pressure. A major task for the new government is to reestablish the strength of democratic procedures and ensure the support of the armed forces.

The strong rebound in Côte d'Ivoire's economic performance following the 1994 devaluation permitted sustained improvement in per capita incomes after several years of decline. This performance was marked by a return to low inflation and a sizeable reduction in external debt, as well as the substantial progress with the extensive economic reform program. However, growth was expected to slow down in 2000 because of the country's difficulty in meeting the conditions of international donors, continued low prices of key exports, and post-coup uncertainty.

The authorities recognize that the private sector is the engine of growth and employment and seem inclined to strengthen the climate for private sector activity through continued enterprise reform. If the governance issues can be addressed and the management of the **public sector** improved, Côte d'Ivoire should be able to realize its growth potential and bring about a sustained reduction in poverty.

DEPENDENCIES

Côte d'Ivoire has no territories or colonies.

BIBLIOGRAPHY

"Côte d'Ivoire." *Europa World Yearbook.* London: Europa Publications, 2000.

"Côte d'Ivoire: Selected Issues and Statistical Appendix." *International Monetary Fund.* <http://www.imf.org/external/pubs/cat/longres.cfm?sk=3657.0>. Accessed February 2001.

Economist Intelligence Unit *Country Profile: Côte d'Ivoire.* London: Economist Intelligence Unit, 2000.

Hodd, Michael. "Côte d'Ivoire." *The Economies of Africa.* Dartmouth: Aldershot, 1991.

U.S. Central Intelligence Agency. *World Factbook 2001.* <http://www.cia.gov/cia/publications/factbook/geos/iv.html#Econ>. Accessed October 2001.

U.S. Department of State. *Background Notes: Côte d'Ivoire, July 1998.* <http://www.state.gov/www/background_notes/cote_d_ivoire_0798_bgn.html>. Accessed October 2001.

—Allan C. K. Mukungu

DJIBOUTI

Republic of Djibouti
République de Djibouti
Jumhouriyya Djibouti

CAPITAL: Djibouti.

MONETARY UNIT: Djiboutian franc (Dfr). One Djiboutian franc equals 100 centimes. There are notes of 1,000, 5,000, and 10,000 francs and coins of 10, 20, 50, 100, and 500 francs. Since 1973 the Djiboutian franc has been tied to the U.S. dollar at a rate of Dfr177.72:US$1.

CHIEF EXPORTS: Reexports, hides and skins, and coffee (in transit).

CHIEF IMPORTS: Foods, beverages, transport equipment, chemicals, and petroleum products.

GROSS DOMESTIC PRODUCT: US$574 million (purchasing power parity, 2000 est.).

BALANCE OF TRADE: Exports: US$260 million (1999 est.). **Imports:** US$440 million (1999 est.).

COUNTRY OVERVIEW

LOCATION AND SIZE. Djibouti is situated in the Horn of Africa, at the southern entrance to the Red Sea, bordering the Gulf of Aden. To the north lies Eritrea with a shared border of 113 kilometers (70 miles); to the north, west, and southwest lies Ethiopia, with a border length of 337 kilometers (209 miles); and to the southeast lies Somalia, with a border length of 58 kilometers (36 miles). Djibouti has a land area of 23,000 square kilometers (8,880 square miles), making it slightly smaller than the U.S. state of Massachusetts. It has 314 kilometers (195 miles) of coastline. The city of Djibouti, located on the coast, is the nation's capital and only major urban center.

POPULATION. The U.S. Central Intelligence Agency estimated the population of Djibouti at 460,000 in July 2001, though the accuracy of this figure is uncertain. The uncertainty arises because there are an unknown number of expatriates and refugees, and sensitivity over the ethnic composition of Djibouti makes the government unwilling to produce definitive figures. The population is comprised of 2 main ethnic groups. The Somali are estimated as 60 percent of the population, and the Afar are estimated at 35

percent. The remaining 5 percent are mostly French, Arabs, Ethiopians, and Italians. Both the Somali and the Afar are Muslim groups and speak related Cushitic languages. French and Arabic are the official languages. There is an Arab minority population that numbers 12,000 and is mostly people of Yemeni descent. The European population in Djibouti (including French troops) was estimated at 8,000 in 1997. The Somalis are divided into clans, of which the Issa, Gadburs, and Issaqs are the largest.

The population was estimated to be growing at a rate of 2.6 percent per year in 2001, with 43 percent of the population less than 15 years of age. In the 1980s a survey showed that 75 percent of the population were urban (with around half living in the capital), and the rest primarily lived nomadic lives. The urban population has increased significantly in recent years as people have fled from the civil war in the north, the Eritrea-Ethiopia border clash, and the conflicts in Somalia.

OVERVIEW OF ECONOMY

Djibouti is a small country both in terms of geographical size and population, with an economy that depends on the provision of port services for goods in transit to and from Ethiopia. The only other links between the coast and Ethiopia pass through Eritrea. However, since the start of the border dispute and the subsequent war between Ethiopia and Eritrea that took place from 1988 to 2000, Ethiopia has not been inclined to use the Eritrean routes. Thus Ethiopian use of Djibouti's port facilities has expanded.

The structure of the economy has not changed much since Djibouti achieved independence from France in 1977. The economy is mostly based on services, and this sector accounted for 75 percent of **gross domestic product** (GDP)

eign assistance led to GDP growth that averaged only 1 percent per year from 1989 to 1991. Growth became negative following the outbreak of civil war (1991–94), which was instigated by dissidents from the minority Afar group. **Informal sector** activities, which evade both tax and customs, flourished in the mid-1990s, resulting in the apparent 5.5 percent per year decrease in the GDP from 1991 to 1994 as reported by the **UN Development Program**. Since 1992 the port has registered a fall in the number of imports for domestic use, leading to the closure of many outlets. The reduced use of the French garrison since 1999 will also decrease growth, though the increased provision of services for the transit trade with Ethiopia due to its war with Eritrea is expected to provide some compensation.

In the 1980s attempts to improve **infrastructure** and reduce structural problems in the economy had little impact. A program for the decentralization of the economy, the development of **free trade zones**, and agricultural and livestock programs all depended on foreign aid, which was terminated in 1991 following the outbreak of the civil conflict. In 1992 the depth of the crisis led to the suspension of government investment which resulted in the crumbling of infrastructure, most notably of electric power.

Djibouti has had a stable government since independence under the ruling People's Progress Assembly (RPP), namely the presidencies of Hassan Gouled and his successor Ismael Gouleh. Nonetheless, government policy since 1991 has consisted of a series of short-term responses to both external donor pressure (particularly from France) and internal demands (especially during the civil war). The government controls the major sectors of the economy—the port facilities, railway, and utilities—but there are currently plans for **privatization** of these enterprises.

In the period from 1991 to 1994, the civil war upset an already limited tax base, and budget controls disappeared as income dwindled. Expenditures rose, causing major deficits—although the extent was hidden by irregular accounting—and the government built up debts in salary **arrears** with private creditors.

In 1996 proposed budget cuts caused a general strike and civil unrest, which led to a policy reversal. A more comprehensive package was then drafted in 1996 with the International Monetary Fund (IMF), World Bank, and French help. This culminated in an IMF US$6.2 million standby credit, which started in April 1996, and the resumption of limited French budget assistance. A donor conference in 1997 secured limited funds for reforms, especially for the demobilization of the army after the civil war, which had been the single biggest cause of the **budget deficit** in recent years.

In the period from 1999 to 2000, the government launched plans for the privatization of all the major utilities (including water, electricity, post, railway, telecom-

in 1998. The significance of the service sector is connected to the country's strategic location and its free trade status in Northeast Africa. The primary components of the sector are the port and railway service, the civil service, and the French garrison stationed in Djibouti. Public administration is the largest sector in the economy. Djibouti has no significant mineral resources, and farming is constrained by the poor quality of the land and limited water availability.

Uncertainty over the size of the population makes estimates for per capita **gross national product** (GNP) rather tentative, but using the **exchange rate** conversion the figure is approximated at US$750. The United Nations (UN) provides a figure using **purchasing power parity** conversion (which makes allowances for the low price of some basic commodities in Djibouti) of $1,300 in per capita GDP in 2000. Both of these estimates place Djibouti in the low-income category of nations.

After modest growth enjoyed during Djibouti's first decade of independence, poor planning and reduced for-

munications, and port facilities). The government also hopes to attract private capital in free-trade zone projects.

POLITICS, GOVERNMENT, AND TAXATION

The French first took control of the small coastal settlement of Obock in 1859. The completion of the Franco-Ethiopian railway in 1917 established the town of Djibouti and began a period of economic growth as the port facilities were developed. Djibouti was known as French Somaliland until 1967 when it was renamed the French Territory of the Afars and the Issas; it became Djibouti at independence in 1977.

Ethnic tension between the Afars and Somali has always been high. In 1967 the people of Djibouti voted in a referendum to maintain an association with France, despite claims of expulsions of pro-Somali politicians and vote rigging favoring the Afars in the first election supervised by the French. Growing pressure from the Organization for African Unity (OAU) led to the peaceful progression towards independence in 1977, and Hassan Gouled (an Issa) became the first president. Within one month, Somalia and Ethiopia began the Ogaden war, which had severe economic effects for Djibouti since the fighting, ranging over the rail link between Ethiopia and Djibouti, closed rail links to Addis Ababa, Ethiopia, for a year and cut port traffic.

Despite the resignation of 5 Afar members from the cabinet in 1977, the president managed to contain ethnic strife for most of the 1980s. Political stability was maintained through patronage dispensed through the RPP, the sole political party. Despite winning the elections in 1982 and 1987, the government became extremely unpopular in the late 1980s, and there were calls for a multiparty political system. The government's suppression of Afar civil unrest in Djibouti caused an insurgency in the north.

The Afar rebellion, led by former Prime Minister Ahmed Dini, spread rapidly, and 3 rebel groups came together to form the Front for the Restoration of Unity and Democracy (FRUD). However, the government was able to deflect French pressure for compromise, and with Arab funding regained control of the north, defeating the insurgents. The government signed a cosmetic peace accord with the minority group of the now divided rebels in 1994 and gave 2 of its leaders cabinet posts. The presidential adviser Ismail Omar Guelleh consolidated his position during president Gouled's long illness and became president himself in the 1999 election. The change of president is not expected to lead to a change in policy, as Guelleh headed the cabinet for 20 years and has proved ruthless in dealing with opposition. Guelleh has retained most of the previous cabinet, but power essentially lies with him and his personal advisers.

The constitution is largely French in structure, and provides for universal suffrage. The president is elected for a 6-year term and the members of the 65-member Chamber of Deputies for 5-year terms. At the height of the civil war in 1992, a constitution endorsed by a referendum brought in a multiparty system, though it only recognized 4 political parties. However, formal government institutions have been severely disrupted since 1991. The judicial system has been undermined by political pressure, and most actual power resides in the hands of the security services, which are under the direct control of the president.

The 2 opposition parties are divided and—despite large support—the Party for Democratic Renewal (PRD) and the National Democratic Party (PND) failed to gain any seats in the 1992 or the 1997 elections, mainly due to infighting. In the 1999 presidential election they presented a united candidate, Moussa Ahmed Idriss, who gained a quarter of the votes in a 15 percent voter turnout.

Internationally, Djibouti has remained politically non-aligned, though it has been watchful of its larger neighbors and has been active in promoting the regional developmental organization, the Intergovernmental Authority on Development (IGAD).

The border dispute in 1998 between Ethiopia and Eritrea brought economic benefit to Djibouti, since most international trade with Ethiopia then had to come through Djibouti's ports. This situation strengthened Djibouti's trade ties with Ethiopia, which have remained strong after the cessation of the border dispute. Djibouti broke off diplomatic links with Eritrea and forged solid links with the ruling Ethiopian party in 1998.

Unrest in neighboring Somalia, which began in 1991, could have been destabilizing for Djibouti, but the establishment of the stable, but unrecognized, Somaliland Republic adjacent to the border has limited the impact. French military presence in the form of a naval base has protected Djibouti from international threats both before and after independence, although French presence is currently being scaled down. Despite having an Arab minority, Djibouti declares itself an Arab state and plays an active role in the Arab League.

Djibouti succeeded in raising 31 percent of the GDP as government revenue in 1997. About 19 percent of this money was raised by **income taxes** on individuals and corporations, 20 percent from other **direct taxes** (mostly property taxes), 46 percent by **indirect taxes** (mostly customs **duties**), and 15 percent came from license fees and property sales. Grants received from abroad (mostly from France) are about 3 percent of GDP. Administration made up 41 percent of government recurrent expenditure, 28 percent was spent on defense, education accounted for 12 percent, transfers were 10 percent, 5 percent was spent on health care, and **subsidies** to state-owned enterprises was 4 percent. Government capital expenditure was about 5 percent of the GDP. Defense spending in 1997 was about twice its normal level as a result of demobilization payments made to reduce the size of the defense forces at the conclusion of the civil war.

INFRASTRUCTURE, POWER, AND COMMUNICATIONS

Transport in Djibouti is geared towards international trade, with local transport being only of secondary concern. The port facilities are central to the economy. Djibouti's use as a naval base by French, British, Italian, and U.S. fleets that operate in the Gulf may be lucrative but is not a basis for growth. Improved port efficiency was needed for the 1998 increase in Ethiopian trade, with traffic up 333 percent to 1.2 million metric tons. Only 10 percent of the 2,800 kilometers (1,740 miles) of roads in Djibouti are paved, and the railway, jointly owned with Ethiopia, is in desperate need of an overhaul.

The capital of Djibouti houses the nation's only international airport, which is serviced by Air France, Ethiopian Airlines, and Yemenia. Several small companies fly to Somalia. Djibouti Air was relaunched in 1997 with private investment and flies to Ethiopia, Yemen, Saudi Arabia, and the United Arab Emirates.

The international telephone exchange has a radio link with Saudi Arabia and Yemen, 2 earth satellite stations, and a submarine fiber optic link to Sri Lanka and Europe. Domestic and international telephone exchanges are being **restructured** to attract foreign investment. There were 8,000 telephone main lines in use in 1997. The country's international telecommunications company offers a range of Internet services. In 1992 Japan provided a TV studio for Djibouti. The only newspaper printed in Djibouti is state-owned.

Energy resources are very limited. The population has no access to trees for wood fuel and must import charcoal and all petroleum products. The Boualos diesel electricity generator is in urgent need of repair, and power cuts are frequent. In 1999 the country produced a total of just 180 million kilowatt hours (kWh) of electricity, 100 percent of which was generated from fossil fuels.

ECONOMIC SECTORS

Agriculture, though it engaged 75 percent of the working population in 1991, provides very low incomes and generated only 3 percent of the GDP in 1998. Industry contributed some 22 percent of the GDP in 1998 and engaged 11 percent of the working population in 1991. The largest sector by far in terms of contribution to the GDP is the services sector, which accounted for 75 percent of the GDP in 1998 and engaged 14 percent of population in 1991. The services sector is strongly dependent on the reexporting of goods.

AGRICULTURE

Official figures suggest that 75 percent of employment was in agriculture in 1991 and that the sector pro-

GDP per Capita (US$)					
Country	1975	1980	1985	1990	1998
Djibouti	N/A	N/A	N/A	N/A	742
United States	19,364	21,529	23,200	25,363	29,683
Egypt	516	731	890	971	1,146
Eritrea	N/A	N/A	N/A	N/A	175

SOURCE: United Nations. *Human Development Report 2000; Trends in human development and per capita income.*

Communications

Country	Telephones[a]	Telephones, Mobile/Cellular[a]	Radio Stations[b]	Radios[a]	TV Stations[a]	Televisions[a]	Internet Service Providers[c]	Internet Users[c]
Djibouti	8,000	203	AM 2; FM 2; shortwave 0	52,000	1 (1998)	28,000	1	1,000
United States	194 M	69.209 M (1998)	AM 4,762; FM 5,542; shortwave 18	575 M	1,500	219 M	7,800	148 M
Egypt	3,971,500 (1998)	380,000 (1999)	AM 42; FM 14; shortwave 3 (1999)	20.5 M	98 (1995)	7.7 M	50	300,000
Eritrea	23,578 (2000)	N/A	AM 2; FM 1; shortwave 2 (2000)	345,000	1 (2000)	1,000	4	500

[a]Data is for 1997 unless otherwise noted.
[b]Data is for 1998 unless otherwise noted.
[c]Data is for 2000 unless otherwise noted.

SOURCE: CIA *World Factbook 2001* [Online].

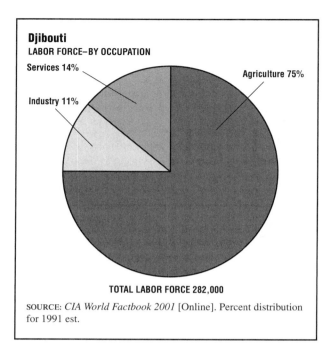

Djibouti
LABOR FORCE–BY OCCUPATION

Services 14%

Agriculture 75%

Industry 11%

TOTAL LABOR FORCE 282,000

SOURCE: *CIA World Factbook 2001* [Online]. Percent distribution for 1991 est.

INDUSTRY

No minerals are mined in Djibouti, despite the fact that perlite (on the Ergelaba plateau), limestone, gypsum (located at Ali Sabieh), and high magnesium content diatomites (present at Lake Assal) have been found by surveys. In 1997, a U.S. company received a license to prospect for gold, although it is unclear if deposits exist.

Manufacturing is small, providing only 5 percent of the GDP, with only 13 companies employing more than 10 people in 1989. The most important producers in the industrial sector are the water bottling plant, the dairy plant, the Coca-Cola plant, the flour mill, and the ice factory. All of them closed during the civil war, however, and many remain idle. Privatization of **parastatal** enterprises is being discussed as part of economic reforms.

Construction has been depressed by low industrial activity and by the fact that most people in Djiboutian towns live in shanty areas, despite some state housing and donor-funded sanitation schemes. The reconstruction of the port and the airports will be major projects in the near future.

SERVICES

The main high-income activities in Djibouti are located in the services sector, in port and transportation services, government administration, and in providing services for the considerable contingent of French troops and their dependents.

The port and transportation services are, however, particularly vulnerable to political developments in the region. The French were aware of the strategic importance of Djibouti—located at the mouth of the Red Sea and in a position to control access to the Suez Canal—when they took possession of the territory in 1859. The importance of Djibouti to France was enhanced when a French company constructed the railway from Djibouti to Addis Ababa, the capital of Ethiopia. Ethiopia is a large country, both in terms of population and geographical area, and the railway through Djibouti was for many years the only practical link Ethiopia had with the coast. When the Italians occupied Ethiopia in 1935, they constructed a road from Asab in Eritrea (an Italian colony) to Addis Ababa, which ended Ethiopia's near total reliance on the railway. This road proved to be a sound strategic move on the part of the Italians since Italy and France found themselves on opposite sides during World War II. The existence of the road led to neglect of the railway, and, in turn, a stagnation of the services provided by the port and the railway. This slow down was exacerbated by the paralysis of the Ethiopian economy under the **Marxist** regime in the 1970s and 1980s. The demand for

duced 3 percent of GDP in 1998. These figures are somewhat deceptive in that almost everyone over the age of 10 in the rural areas is considered to be involved in agricultural production, though many of them are not engaged in such work full time. However, this also indicates that incomes in agriculture are very much lower than in the industrial and the service sectors. Given the aridity of the area, barely 6,000 hectares (14,827 acres) can be farmed even with irrigation, though only 500 hectares (1,236 acres) are under permanent cultivation. Crop production is mostly limited to fruit and vegetables. Several market garden plots have been established and are provided with water by 50 wells (18 of which were provided by Saudi Arabia since independence), though many of these wells have fallen into disrepair.

Livestock has always been more important than farming in Djibouti, but animal husbandry is highly susceptible to droughts. Droughts in the 1970s and 1980s cost some of the nomads their entire herds. The Food and Agriculture Organization (FAO) estimates the number of animals in Djibouti at 200,000 cattle, 500,000 sheep, 500,000 goats, and 62,000 camels.

Djibouti has a short coastline, but there is an estimated fish catch of 7,000 to 9,000 metric tons per year. Most of the catch is caught by large-scale industrial trawlers, many of which are foreign owned. Only 500 metric tons per year are caught by traditional methods by approximately 140 small vessels. About two-thirds of the fish catch is exported, with Djiboutian fish consumption at 3.5 kilograms (7.7 pounds) per person per year. The fishing port is being upgraded with African Development Bank money to try to raise the catch.

Djibouti's port services began to recover with the fall of the Ethiopian Marxist regime in 1991 and the resulting restoration of economic growth and external trading links. When Eritrea became independent in 1993, Ethiopia became landlocked and entirely dependent on surface transport links through either Djibouti or Eritrea. The outbreak of the border war between Eritrea and Ethiopia in 1998 led to a complete reliance of Ethiopia on Djibouti, and this business has been a big boost for the Djibouti port and railway sectors. There will undoubtedly be some reconciliation between Eritrea and Ethiopia at some stage in the future, so the task for Djibouti is to establish a level of efficiency in their port and railway services so that they can be competitive with the road link through Asab when Ethiopia eventually resumes use of this route.

Likewise, the income generated by the French troops and their families is dependent on how the French see their role as a world power and, particularly, the nature of their involvement in Africa. The reduction in French forces stationed in Djibouti is a reflection of the reduced emphasis that France is currently placing on its role in Africa.

Djibouti is effectively a city-state; there is little banking outside of the capital. A number of banks have been established in Djibouti, most of which are French-owned or backed. The central bank is the Banque National de Djibouti. The formal **retail** and wholesale sectors are in private hands, and the role of French companies in the economy is in decline. Since 1997 there has been an increase in Ethiopian business near the port. The potential for tourism in Djibouti has not been exploited.

INTERNATIONAL TRADE

Merchandise exports, including reexports, were valued at $260 million in 1999, and merchandise imports, including goods for reexport, at $440 million. Excluding the reexport trade, Djibouti exported $16 million of domestically produced goods and imported $24 million of goods for domestic use in 1998. The trade gap is met by the receipts from the port and transport services supplied by Djibouti and the earnings from the presence of French troops.

Locally produced merchandise exports are limited to livestock and hides (21 percent), miscellaneous manufactures (20 percent), and coffee products (11 percent), with all the other exports (48 percent) not classified according to category. The reexports are predominantly coffee from Ethiopia, fish caught by foreign fishing fleets, livestock, meat products and hides from Somalia, and manufactured goods reexported to Ethiopia. The main destinations of domestically produced exports are Somalia (53 percent), Yemen (23 percent), and Ethiopia (5 percent).

Imports for domestic use consist mainly of foods and beverages (39 percent); machinery, metals, and vehicles (20 percent); fuels (13 percent); and qat (13 percent). Qat is a mild but legal stimulant that is chewed. Official trade statistics do not reflect the level of the informal trade with Ethiopia and Somalia, much of which involves the smuggling of qat. In 1998, the main sources of imports for domestic use were France (13 percent), Ethiopia (12 percent), Italy (9 percent), Saudi Arabia (6 percent), the United Kingdom (6 percent), and Japan (4 percent).

MONEY

The Djiboutian franc has been tied to the U.S. dollar since 1973 at Dfr 177.72:US$1, which allows for considerable stability, although the Djiboutian franc has experienced a steady climb against the French franc. Foreign reserves have been steady during the 1990s and stood at $66 million in 1998. **Devaluation** of the Djiboutian franc seems unlikely in the foreseeable future. The Banque Nationale de Djibouti, the central bank, controls the money supply through the issue of currency and regulates the commercial banks.

Trade (expressed in billions of US$): Djibouti		
	Exports	Imports
1975	.015	.140
1980	.012	.213
1985	.014	.201
1990	.025	.215
1995	N/A	N/A
1998	N/A	N/A
SOURCE: International Monetary Fund. *International Financial Statistics Yearbook 1999.*		

Exchange rates: Djibouti	
Djiboutian francs per US$1	
Jan 2001	177.721
2000	177.721
1999	177.721
1998	177.721
1997	177.721
1996	177.721
Note: Djibouti currency has been at a fixed rate since 1973.	
SOURCE: CIA *World Factbook 2001* [ONLINE].	

GDP per Capita (US$)					
Country	1975	1980	1985	1990	1998
Djibouti	N/A	N/A	N/A	N/A	742
United States	19,364	21,529	23,200	25,363	29,683
Egypt	516	731	890	971	1,146
Eritrea	N/A	N/A	N/A	N/A	175

SOURCE: United Nations. *Human Development Report 2000;*
Trends in human development and per capita income.

POVERTY AND WEALTH

Per capita GDP, using the purchasing power parity conversion, was estimated at $1,300 in 2000. There are wide disparities between those who are engaged in modern sector activities in the town of Djibouti and the rest of the population, which mainly consists of shanty-dwellers relying on the informal sector, rural farmers, and nomadic shepherds. Perhaps 80 percent of the people who rely on agriculture for their livelihood are below the US$1 per day poverty line, meaning that approximately 60 percent of the total population live in poverty. Of an estimated **labor force** of 282,000 in 2000, formal unemployment stands at 50 percent, although many of the unemployed are engaged in informal sector activities

In 1987, government statistics indicated that 66 percent of the population were able to read, but in 1995 a new estimation measured the literacy rate of the population over 15 years of age as 46 percent (males 60 percent; females 33 percent). In the period from 1991 to 1992 there were 33,500 pupils, 66 schools, and 707 teachers in primary education. In 1996, the total enrollment at primary and secondary schools was equivalent to 26 percent of the school-age population. Education is limited primarily to urban areas, where teacher strikes are frequent. There is no university in Djibouti, and technical skills are often found lacking.

Life-expectancy estimates are 49 years for males and 53 years for females in 2001. Infant mortality stands at 102 per 1,000, which marks an improvement from the past but is still a long way from what can be achieved (the U.S. rate is 7 per 1,000). There is a 600-bed hospital in the capital and a 60-bed maternity and pediatric hospital in Balbala. There are 6 medical centers and 21 dispensaries cover the interior of the country. Virtually all medicines can be obtained, but since they must be imported they are expensive. The large prostitute population, attracted by the French troops stationed in Djibouti, leads to a high incidence of sexually transmitted diseases, including HIV.

WORKING CONDITIONS

The labor force in 1991 was estimated at 282,000. However, 50 percent of the labor force was thought to be unemployed in 2000. Of those who had employment, around 75 percent were engaged in agriculture, almost entirely on small family farms or in family-based cattle herding. The largest single employer in the formal sector is the civil service, with an estimated 10,000 employees. The rest of the state-owned sector (which includes the port, railway, posts, telecommunications, and utilities) employs an estimated 16,000 people. Many people seek work in the government sector since it entails considerable job security, family medical benefits, and a pension. Forced labor is illegal in Djibouti.

There is a social insurance scheme in Djibouti with benefits, which depend on whether the worker is employed in the **private sector**, the civil service, or the army. Employees receive benefits in case of accidents at work and are allocated retirement pensions after the age of 55 years.

Trade unions and workers can be militant, as was shown in 1996 when proposed budget cuts caused a general strike and civil unrest. The government also has often built up salary arrears that have led to discontent among the workforce.

COUNTRY HISTORY AND ECONOMIC DEVELOPMENT

1859. The French first take possession of the coastal settlement of Obock.

1917. The Franco-Ethiopian railway from Djibouti to Addis Ababa is completed.

1977. Djibouti becomes independent. Hassan Ghouled becomes the first president.

1977–1988. The Ogaden War between Somalia and Ethiopia adversely affects Djibouti's economy.

1981. Ghouled is returned as president in an uncontested election.

1987. Ghouled is returned as president in an uncontested election.

1991. Civil war with the Afars commences in the North. The rebel group FRUD is formed.

1992. Multiparty elections under a new constitution return Ghouled and his RPP party.

1994. A peace accord is signed, ending the 3-year uprising by Afar rebels.

1996. Proposed budget cuts cause a general strike and civil unrest.

1997. Multiparty elections return the FRUD-RPP alliance with Ghouled as president.

1998. A border dispute between Ethiopia and Eritrea leads to an increase in trade through Djibouti.

1999. The successor to Ghouled, Ismael Guelleh, wins the presidential election.

FUTURE TRENDS

The key factors for the Ethiopian economy are the amount of Ethiopian trade passing through the port and the size of the French garrison. Despite the interim settlement between Ethiopia and Eritrea, almost all of Ethiopia's trade still flows through Djibouti, and this situation is likely to continue for the foreseeable future. Domestic political pressure to maintain employment levels in the **public sector** is likely to limit the pace of economic reform through privatization, despite IMF pressure. Delegation visits by the IMF have not resolved concerns over the lack of financial transparency and the poor availability of data, and this will impair the prospects for financial assistance from the donor community. The economy is not expected to show much significant growth in the near future, with the expansion of the use of port facilities by Ethiopia being offset by the scaling-down of the presence of French troops.

In politics, Guelleh received praise for having convened the Somali peace conference. Full relations have been restored with Eritrea, and there is now the prospect of more stable relations in the area. If peace comes to Somalia, it will reduce tensions caused by the influx of Somali refugees as the refugees begin to return home.

DEPENDENCIES

Djibouti has no territories or colonies.

BIBLIOGRAPHY

"Djibouti and the IMF." *International Monetary Fund.* <http://www.imf.org/external/country/DJI/index.htm>. Accessed October 2001.

"Djibouti: Economy." *NewAfrica*.com. <http://www.newafrica.com/profiles/economy.asp?countryid=18>. Accessed September 2001.

Economist Intelligence Unit. *Country Profile: Djibouti.* London, England, 2001.

Hodd, M. "Djibouti." *The Economies of Africa.* Aldershot, England: Dartmouth Publications, 1991.

Ministère de l'Economie, des Finances et de la Planification Chargé de la Privatisation. <http://www.mefpp.org>. Accessed October 2001.

République de Djibouti. <http://www.republique-djibouti.com>. Accessed October 2001.

Tholomier, Robert. *Djibouti, Pawn of the Horn of Africa.* Metuchen, NJ: Scarecrow Press, 1981.

U.S. Central Intelligence Agency. *World Factbook 2001.* <http://www.odci.gov/cia/publications/factbook/index.html>. Accessed September 2001.

U.S. Department of State. *Background Notes: Djibouti, March 1996.* <http://dosfan.lib.uic.edu/ERC/bgnotes/ef/djibouti9603.html>. Accessed October 2001.

—Michael Hodd

EGYPT

Arab Republic of Egypt
Jumhuriat Misr al-'Arabiyah

CAPITAL: Cairo.

MONETARY UNIT: Egyptian Pound. One hundred piastres equals one Egyptian pound. Notes are in denominations of 1, 5, 10, 20, 50, and 100 pounds, and coins in denominations of 5, 10, 20, 25, and 50 piastres.

CHIEF EXPORTS: Crude oil and petroleum products, cotton, textiles, metal products, and chemicals.

CHIEF IMPORTS: Machinery and equipment, foodstuffs, chemicals, wood products, and fuels.

GROSS DOMESTIC PRODUCT: US$200 billion (purchasing power parity, 1999 est.).

BALANCE OF TRADE: **Exports:** US$4.6 billion (f.o.b., 1999 est.). **Imports:** US$15.8 billion (f.o.b., 1999 est.).

COUNTRY OVERVIEW

LOCATION AND SIZE. The Arab Republic of Egypt is located in North Africa, bordering on the Mediterranean Sea to the north, Libya to the west, the Gaza Strip to the east, and Sudan to the south. With an area of 1,001,450 square kilometers (386,659 square miles) and a coastline of 2,450 kilometers (1,522 miles), Egypt is slightly more than 3 times the size of New Mexico. Egypt's capital city, Cairo, is located in the north of the country.

POPULATION. The population of Egypt was estimated at 69,359,979 in July of 2000, an increase of 17,115,079 from the 1990 population of 52,244,000. In 2000, Egypt's birth rate stood at 25.38 per 1,000, while the death rate was reported at 7.83 per 1,000. With a projected annual growth rate of 1.5 percent between 2000 and 2015, the population is expected to reach 92 million by the year 2030.

Egypt's population is the largest in the Arab world, and is generally young, with 35 percent below age 14 and just 4 percent older than 65. Almost 50 percent of the population is below 20 years of age and 39 percent under 15, presenting a real challenge to government in creating job opportunities. The vast majority of the population—94 percent—is Sunni Muslim. Coptic Christians, and other smaller religious groups represent 6 percent of the population, while smaller minorities—primarily Nubians, Armenians, and other Europeans—make up approximately 1 percent of the population.

A large number of Egyptians—44.9 percent in 1998—live in urban areas. The capital city of Cairo and its suburbs is home to the largest concentration of Egyptians, with a population of almost 7 million. Other major cities include Alexandria, which has a population of 3.3 million, and Port Said, with 469,000 inhabitants. Migration from rural to urban areas presents a serious problem for policy planners due to the heavy stress it places on services in major cities. Egypt is over-populated and continuing population growth places a major strain on land and resources alike. Most Egyptians are concentrated in the Valley and Delta of the Nile River, areas that account for only one-third of the entire land surface of Egypt. The rest of the country is largely uninhabited desert.

Family planning policies were first adopted in the 1950s, but it was not until the mid-1980s that a government family planning body, the National Population Council (NPC), was established. The country's population policy has addressed multiple issues, focusing on the promotion of primary health care, encouragement of family planning in rural areas, and the reduction of infant and maternal mortality. The annual population growth rate has dropped dramatically in recent years, reaching 1.9 percent in 1998. The drop can be credited to carefully designed and well-financed family planning policies adopted since the mid-1990s by the government of President Mubarak. In 1995, the Family Planning Association (FPA) was formed to complement government health services and to provide family planning services through its clinics and voluntary organizations. In conjunction

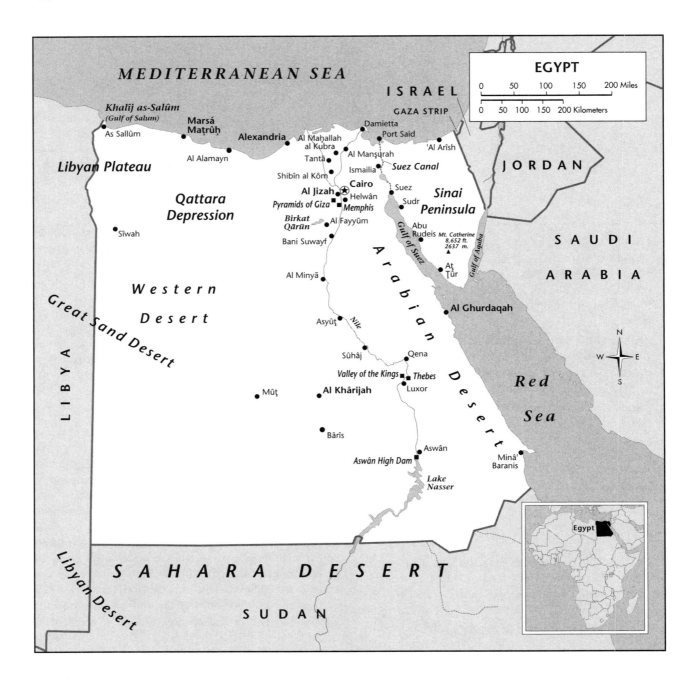

with the ministries of health and social affairs, the FPA also carries out programs to educate the general public about reproductive issues.

OVERVIEW OF ECONOMY

Egypt's economy improved dramatically in the 1990s as a result of several arrangements with the International Monetary Fund (IMF) and the move by several, mainly Arab, countries to relieve a large proportion of its debts. These decisions were primarily to reward Egypt for its stand with the U.S.-led coalition against Iraq in the 1990–91 Gulf War. Since that time, Egypt has managed to maintain positive growth rates. **Inflation** has been

kept down, the country's **budget deficit** decreased, and its foreign reserves increased, while **gross domestic product** (GDP) has averaged annual growth of 4–5 percent. Despite the slow pace of **privatization** and new business law enactment mandated by the IMF reform program, the country has succeeded in attracting foreign investment by moving towards a market-based economy. Having successfully stabilized the economy since 1995, the government embarked on a privatization plan in 1997 aimed at expanding the role of the **private sector**.

In spite of this considerable economic progress, the Egyptian government continues to face serious challenges. Egypt's economic growth has slowed down since

1998, partly due to the economic crisis in Asia, but also as a result of huge government investment in large-scale **infrastructure** projects. The **recession** that affected Gulf economies in 1998 and 1999 also impacted Egypt's economy, with lower oil prices causing a drop in **remittances**—traditionally a major source of foreign currency—sent home by Egyptian workers in the Gulf region. Tourism receipts also fell in reaction to the wave of terrorist acts waged by Islamic militants in Egypt, thus causing a further decline in the levels of foreign exchange. The government's reluctance to relinquish its shares in state enterprises has further contributed to the slowdown in the Egyptian economy since 1998. Little progress has been made in **deregulating** the largely state-run economy, or in bringing about legislative reforms and structural overhaul, ranging from **tariff** reduction to wholesale reform of the collapsing education system.

Egypt entered the twentieth century as a British protectorate, heavily dependent on agriculture—mainly cotton production—which accounted for 90 percent of its exports in 1914. The British fostered the development of a small industrial base, mainly concerned with processing raw materials, but further industrial development was stifled by a British trade policy that focused on selling British products at the expense of local goods. Although Egypt was granted independence in 1922, Britain continued to control the country in an alliance with the Egyptian monarchy until 1952, when a group of young army officers overthrew King Farouk. In 1954, Gamal Abdel Nasser ousted the first president Muhammad Maguib and became a popular and influential leader.

Since gaining independence from Britain, Egypt has struggled to rid itself of the feudal economic system left behind by the British and to create an independent economy capable of standing on its own. By the end of the twentieth century, Egypt had not yet achieved a vibrant economy and remained heavily dependent on foreign aid and imported goods.

Today, Egypt is primarily a free-market economy with some state control. Despite occasional outbreaks of political violence, it has a reasonably stable multiparty system and is strongly supported by the United States and the European Union. The economy's main exports are crude oil and petroleum products, cotton, textiles, metal products, and chemicals. Agriculture today accounts for 17 percent of GDP, industry for another 32 percent, while the services sector provides 51 percent.

Egypt is the world's largest exporter of cotton and its textile industry is large. Other industries include the production of cement, iron and steel, chemicals, fertilizers, rubber products, refined sugar, tobacco, canned foods, cottonseed oil, small metal products, shoes, and furniture. Although the agriculture sector continues to employ almost one-third of the **workforce**, most of the

arable land is used to cultivate cotton, and Egypt must import about half of its food requirements. Unemployment in 1998 was reported at 20 percent, and the income disparity between the highest and lowest strata of society remains high. By contrast, unemployment in the United States in 1999 was just 4.2 percent.

Since the 1950s, foreign aid has played a major role in Egypt's development processes. As a **socialist** country, Egypt received much financial and military assistance from the former Soviet Union between 1952 and 1970, but this ended in the 1970s after Egypt signed a peace treaty with Israel. Following Egypt's defeat in the 1967 war with Israel, the Arab states of Kuwait, Saudi Arabia, and Libya provided Egypt with US$221 million annually, increasing to a total of US$1 billion annually between 1973–1979. Arab support, mainly from the Gulf states, was frozen in 1979 because of Arab opposition to Egypt's 1978 peace treaty with Israel.

From 1979, the United States emerged as Egypt's main source of economic aid. This was seen, in large part, as a reward for Egypt's warmer attitude toward Israel, as well as to assist the country in meeting the demands of the extreme economic and political challenges it was facing. Between 1979 and 1998, Egypt received US$815 million annually from the United States. Since 1999, the level of U.S. aid has gradually decreased, reaching US$727 million in 2000 and US$695 million in 2001. Aid levels are expected to decrease further, to US$400 million over a 10-year period. U.S. aid to Egypt has come in the form of development assistance for infrastructure programs, job creation, education, democracy and governance, and in incentives for enlarging the private sector.

Arab aid to Egypt resumed in 1987 with the restoration of diplomatic relations. In 1990, Egypt was rewarded for its pro-Kuwait stand during the Gulf War with the write-off of its US$7 billion in debt to the United States. Although support from Arab sources has declined since the end of the Gulf War in 1991, U.S. and European aid has increased in support of the Euro-Med **free-trade zone**, to be set up by the year 2010.

According to the U.S. State Department *Country Commercial Guide* for 2001, government bureaucracy is a major impediment to the conduct of business in Egypt. Red tape permeates all government ministries and the commercial court system. Corruption is also widespread at all levels of the **public sector**, largely as a result of low wages and difficult living conditions.

POLITICS, GOVERNMENT, AND TAXATION

Egypt has had 3 presidents since the 1954 revolution that brought popular president Gamal Abdel Nasser to power. Between 1954 and 1970, Nasser attempted to institute socialist economic principles on the Soviet model, and actively sought to industrialize an agriculture-based economy. Internally, Nasser dismantled the political and economic power of the landed class by **nationalizing** land previously owned by rich feudal landlords and distributing it to the poor. During those years, the government spearheaded a campaign to improve the lot of the working class and the peasants, who were offered free education and employment opportunities. Although the economy grew at an acceptable rate in the initial years, the failure of Nasser's socialist policies became evident toward the end of his rule, especially after the 1967 war in which Egypt lost parts of the Sinai desert to Israel. Military expenditure consumed about 25 percent of **gross national product** (GNP) under Nasser, while a rapidly growing population began to place additional pressures on the state.

Under President Anwar Sadat (1970–81), Egypt began its move toward a market-based economy. In April 1974, Sadat announced a new economic policy that came to be known as "infitah," or open-door policy. This policy brought the relaxation of currency regulations and led to a remarkable increase in foreign investment and a larger economic role for the private sector. In 1977, acting on the advice of the World Bank, Sadat lifted **subsidies** on flour, rice, and cooking oil and canceled bonuses and pay increases. These actions, in the face of growing disillusionment at the infitah policy, which allowed only a handful of people to accumulate wealth, led to a wave of popular protest across the country on 17 January 1977. As a result of the 2-day clashes in which 800 people were killed and several thousands more wounded, the government was forced to back down on the price increases while retaining 10 percent wage increases and other benefits for public sector employees.

In 1981, President Sadat was assassinated by fundamentalists of the Islamic Jihad group, who disagreed violently with his policies. He was succeeded by his vice-president, Hosni Mubarak, who was still holding office in 2001. The threat of growing popular dissatisfaction explains the economic reforms chosen by the Egyptian government since 1990. In 1991, Islamic groups began pressing for a strict Islamic state that would shun Western values and lifestyles. Their quest to overthrow the government includes demands for restrictions on freedom of expression, liberal education, and secular laws. These groups have resorted to violent means to overthrow the government, and have mostly targeted government installations and the tourism sector. The government has cracked down hard on the Islamists since 1994 but, although the threat from many of these groups has abated since 1998, they nevertheless have continued to be a source of much concern to the government and a serious impediment to foreign investment.

Since taking office in 1981, President Mubarak has demonstrated commitment to the program of economic reform that President Sadat charted for the country in the mid-1970s. At the time Mubarak came to power, the economy was faltering under the weight of massive **foreign debt**. Unable to meet its payments, the Mubarak government was forced to reschedule US$6.5 billion in debts to the IMF and the Paris Club (an informal group of official creditors comprising the world's largest countries) in 1987. It was not, however, until 1991 that the government, faced with a growing Islamic threat, began concentrating all its efforts on economic reform. The results of the reform program have been promising. According to the U.S. State Department *Country Commercial Guide* for 2000, the public debt has fallen from $40 billion to $30 billion, the Egyptian pound is stable, and inflation is under control. Further, foreign reserves reached an all-time high in 1997 and the budget deficit was slashed. Egypt's heavy debt burden accumulated during the 1980s had been reduced from $31 billion to $19 billion by 1998.

Politically, Mubarak allowed parliamentary elections in 1984. However, for most of the last 25 years, Egypt has been governed by a single party, the National Democratic Party. Although the national constitution describes Egypt as a "democratic, socialist state," in reality it is not much of either. While it is not a dictatorship, the government is an authoritarian one, given legitimacy by being elected. Egyptian voters elect a 448-member *Majlis al-Sha'ab* (People's Assembly), which, in turn, elects a president who wields wide powers during a 6-year term. The president appoints the vice-president and all ministers, and can be re-elected for additional terms. However, given that emergency powers—first put into effect shortly after the assassination of President Anwar Sadat—were extended for a further 3 years in February 2000, the current regime and the security forces behind it have far more power than the constitution allows.

There are a total of 13 legal political parties, the most important of which include the New Wafd (Delegation) Party, the Socialist Labor Party, the Umma Party, and the Socialist Liberal Party. However, since its creation by Sadat in 1978, the New Democratic Party (NDP) has maintained an unequaled nationwide party machine and an iron grip on the Assembly, and thus on the presidency. The ruling NDP won an overwhelming majority in the 1996 and 2000 parliamentary elections, as well as in the April 1997 local and municipal elections, although opposition candidates and many foreign observers alleged vote rigging and intimidation at the ballot boxes.

Since the late 1990s, the Islamic movement known as the Ikhwan al-Muslimin (The Muslim Brotherhood) has made substantial inroads into the political establishment, but is largely held at bay by the NDP. The Brotherhood is officially banned by Egyptian law, which prohibits political parties founded on a religious basis. However, Islamist candidates do campaign under the auspices of legal opposition parties, such as the Socialist Labor Party, a practice quietly **sanctioned** by the government. Although the official presence of the Brotherhood is still minor, it maintains a powerful grassroots movement and has captured control of nearly every professional organization in the country, including the influential Lawyers' Association.

The judicial system in Egypt has been fairly independent from the executive branch of government. Although freedom of expression is to some extent tolerated, the media—including newspapers, magazines, and periodicals—are subject to censorship. The government owns all domestic television and radio stations.

Between 1952 and the mid-1970s, the military emerged as the strongest institution in Egypt and, as a result, played a major role in its politics and economy. Egypt's large professional army, which numbers 450,000 personnel, was created in the 1950s as a deterrent force against Israel and today represents 1 percent of the population. However, unlike other developing countries, the military's role in Egypt has not been politically disruptive. Its political role, in fact, greatly diminished over the last 2 decades of the twentieth century, particularly as the country moved toward political **liberalization** in the mid-1980s. Although the military has opted to stay out of the government's confrontation with Islamic militants opposing the state, it continues to form the backbone of the regime and enjoys great privileges. Since the early 1990s, however, the military's economic involvement has expanded into 4 major areas: military industries and arms production, civilian industries, agriculture, and national infrastructure.

Taxes are a major source of state revenue, contributing approximately one-third of the government budget, and 16.6 percent of GDP. Taxes come in a variety of forms, including **income tax**, which accounts for 22

percent of the total tax revenue, and taxes on goods and services, which account for another 17 percent. Tax increases are expected in the coming years, but, aware of the potentially disruptive political implications of such a course, the government has been reluctant to burden the Egyptian populace with further taxes.

INFRASTRUCTURE, POWER, AND COMMUNICATIONS

Egypt's infrastructure is relatively underdeveloped. The country is serviced by a network of over 64,000 kilometers (39,769 miles) of primary and secondary roads, 49,984 kilometers (31,060 miles) of which are paved. Despite the modernization of the road system in the 1980s, most roads remain in poor condition or under construction. With growing numbers of licensed automobiles in the 1990s, the road system, especially in urban areas, has become highly congested, and is a major safety concern. According to the EIU *Country Profile,* "Egypt reports the highest incidence of traffic fatalities in the world: 44.1 deaths per 100,000 kilometers driven in 1994." Egypt's aging state-owned railway system, which has 9,400 kilometers (5,841 miles) is old by regional standards and in need of upgrade. The sector is slated for privatization. Cairo's new metro system, opened in 1987, is one of the most heavily used systems in the world, carrying some 1.4 million passengers a day.

Egypt has a total of 90 airports. Egypt Air, the country's official airline, carries some 4.6 million passengers, roughly 25 percent of international air traffic, and an estimated total of 87,240 metric tons of freight annually, but has a poor service record and is generally unreliable. Egypt has 3 major ports, at Alexandria, Port Said, and Suez, and 3,500 kilometers (2,175 miles) of waterways, divided between the Nile and the canals.

Electrical power is supplied to Egyptians by the state-owned Egyptian Electricity Authority (EEA), which

Communications

Country	Newspapers	Radios	TV Sets[a]	Cable subscribers[a]	Mobile Phones[a]	Fax Machines[a]	Personal Computers[a]	Internet Hosts[b]	Internet Users[b]
	1996	1997	1998	1998	1998	1998	1998	1999	1999
Egypt	40	324	122	N/A	1	0.5	9.1	0.28	200
United States	215	2,146	847	244.3	256	78.4	458.6	1,508.77	74,100
Saudi Arabia	57	321	262	N/A	31	N/A	49.6	1.17	300
Nigeria	24	223	66	N/A	0	N/A	5.7	0.00	100

[a]Data are from International Telecommunication Union, *World Telecommunication Development Report 1999* and are per 1,000 people.
[b]Data are from the Internet Software Consortium (http://www.isc.org) and are per 10,000 people.

SOURCE: World Bank. *World Development Indicators 2000.*

has the capacity to produce 15,000 megawatts of power, 80 percent of which are from natural gas. Plans are underway to expand power production by an additional 1,950 megawatts by 2002. Power consumption has been growing at the rate of 5.6 percent year, and EEA plans to invest some US$4.5 billion in the coming years to boost the country's power generation capacity.

Telecommunication services in Egypt are thoroughly modern. Telephone service is provided by the state-owned Telecom Egypt. According to the EIU *Country Profile* for 2000/2001, the country has some 6.5 million lines, and has been adding new ones at the rate of 1 million per year. In 2000, Egypt had over 60 local Internet service providers.

ECONOMIC SECTORS

Egypt's economy is the second largest in the Arab world (after Saudi Arabia) and its economic sectors reflect its size. The service sector is by the far the largest and fastest-growing economic sector and accounts for almost 51 percent of GDP. Tourism, trade, banking, and shipping services on the Suez Canal constitute the main sources of service sector revenue. Both tourism and the Suez Canal were hit hard by Islamic violence in the 1990s, with tourism in particular suffering badly after the 1997 Luxor attack, in which 58 foreigners were killed by Islamic militants. The massacre is estimated to have cost the tourism sector 50 percent of its annual US$3.7 billion revenues in 1998, when foreign visitors stayed away from the country. The government has moved to aggressive promotion of domestic tourism to compensate for the loss of foreign tourism, and managed to restore more than 60 percent of the pre-1997 tourist traffic by late

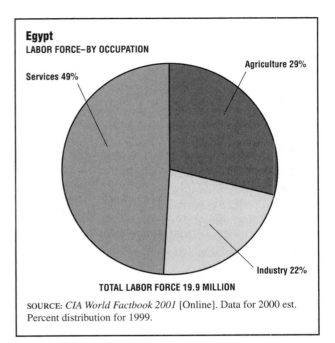

Egypt
LABOR FORCE–BY OCCUPATION

Services 49%
Agriculture 29%
Industry 22%

TOTAL LABOR FORCE 19.9 MILLION

SOURCE: *CIA World Factbook 2001* [Online]. Data for 2000 est. Percent distribution for 1999.

1999. The sector's performance improved dramatically in the first 2 quarters of 2000, growing by 43 percent on the previous year. The prospects of recovery in the Suez Canal sector, however, have been less promising, with growth in that area rather slow, despite government plans to revive it.

Industry is the second-largest economic sector in Egypt, and accounted for 32 percent of GDP in 1999. Some 13 percent of the total labor force is employed in industrial activity, which is concentrated in Cairo and the Nile delta. Major industries include the production of petroleum and petroleum products, accounting for roughly 7 percent of GDP and providing a major source of foreign currency. The sector's contribution is heavily dependent on the performance of the world's oil markets, and fluctuates accordingly. The growth in domestic energy demands in the 1990s has placed constraints on Egypt's petroleum exports, leading to a downturn in net revenues. The construction industry has become one of the fastest-growing sectors of the economy, thanks in large part to huge government infrastructure and modernization projects. Overall, the industrial sector's contribution has increased as a result of the government's efforts towards privatization.

Even though arable land accounts for only 3 percent of the country's overall land area, agriculture remains one of the most important sectors of the economy, employing roughly 40 percent of the labor force. However, agriculture's contribution to GDP declined from 20 percent in 1986–87 to 17 percent in 1999, and the number of workers in the sector decreased steadily during the 1990s.

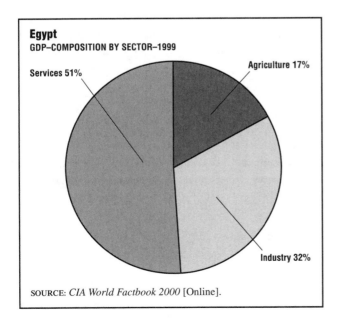

Egypt
GDP–COMPOSITION BY SECTOR–1999

Services 51%
Agriculture 17%
Industry 32%

SOURCE: *CIA World Factbook 2000* [Online].

AGRICULTURE

Even though its contribution to GDP has declined considerably in the last 15 years, from 25.6 percent in 1985–86 to 17 percent in 1999, agriculture remains a significant contributor to Egypt's economy, accounting for 20 percent of commodity exports. In 1998, according to the CIA *World Factbook* for 2000, 40 percent of the labor force was employed in the agriculture sector.

Cotton has been the country's largest agricultural export product for many years. The proportion of land cultivated with cotton has dropped significantly over the last 4 decades, from 924,000 hectares in 1962 to 227,000 hectares in 2000–01. For most of the century, cotton has been heavily subsidized by the government. These subsidies, however, were lifted in the mid-1990s and, as a result of higher cultivation costs, cotton exports have dropped from 121,500 metric tons in 1993–94 to only 45,000 metric tons in 1996–97.

In an attempt to reverse this trend, the government moved to raise the purchase price of cotton above international market levels. This was coupled with a move to import lower-grade cotton in March 1996 to allow for the export of better-quality cotton, and the full liberalization of the cotton trade in 1998–99. Higher price incentives have led to increased production and higher export deliveries, but the cotton trade is threatened by dwindling acreage.

Wheat and rice outputs have grown dramatically since the early 1990s, particularly since 1994 when all subsidies for fertilizers, seeds, and pesticides were lifted. The result has been self-sufficiency in several important commodities. Today, 95 percent of the wheat and rice crops are used to satisfy domestic consumption but, despite increased output, Egypt continues to be a large importer of food, especially agricultural products. Imports of wheat rose by 8 percent in 1996–97 and have generally accounted for more than a quarter of total imports.

Egypt's agricultural sector remains one of the most productive in the world, despite the small area of arable land and irregular and insufficient water supplies. Farmers do not have to pay for water used in irrigation. Since the construction of the Aswan Dam on the Nile river, the sector's development has been hindered by the problems of waterlogged soil and soil with a high salt content. Drainage efforts have proved insufficient to counter the harmful effects of these 2 factors to the sector's performance. Since the mid-1980s, the government has attempted to reclaim the desert for cultivation, and has managed to successfully reclaim some 1 million acres of desert. Plans are underway to reclaim an additional 3.5 million acres by the year 2017 with the South Valley Development project near Lake Nasser. These efforts, however, are countered by the fast pace of urban and industrial expansion, which has been claiming an average of 31,000 acres a year.

INDUSTRY

MINING. Egypt's main mining activity revolves around the extraction of crude oil. The country is not a major producer of oil, and its reserves are small by regional standards. According to the EIU *Country Profile* for 2000–01, oil reserves were estimated at around 3.8 billion barrels in July 2000; in comparison, Saudi Arabia has over 260 billion barrels of proven and unproven reserves. Until 1998, Egypt produced an average of 880,000 barrels a day of crude oil, the majority of which was refined domestically, but production has steadily declined since 1998, mainly due to the depletion of the main oil fields. In July 1998, production reached 840,000 barrels a day, but had declined to 787,660 barrels a day in 1999.

Despite declining production, however, oil remains a significant source of government revenue and export earnings. The decline in crude oil exports in recent years has been mainly due to rising domestic demand and depressed world oil prices in 1998. As a result, crude oil exports, which accounted for 55 percent of overall export earnings in 1992–93, accounted for only one-quarter of overall export earnings in 1998–99.

Most oil production is concentrated in the Gulf of Suez, which produces 79 percent of Egypt's oil. Oil exploration activity is also taking place in the Western Desert near the Libyan border, offshore in the Mediterranean, and in the Sinai Desert. Unlike their neighboring Arab countries, where the state maintains full control of the oil industry, Egypt's oil production is dominated by foreign companies, working in conjunction with the state-owned Egyptian General Petroleum Corporation. The bulk of oil exploration activity is undertaken by large foreign companies, mainly British Petroleum and the Italian company AGIP. In recent years, the government has awarded exploration rights to a number of small local companies, but their presence is minimal in comparison to the foreign giants.

According to the EIU *Country Profile* for 2000–01, Egypt is one of the largest producers of refined oil goods in Africa, producing 35 million tons of refined goods annually. Refineries are based in Suez and Sidi Keir. Output in the sector has increased since 1994, when the private sector was allowed to enter the refineries business.

In addition to the extraction of crude oil, Egypt has natural gas reserves estimated at 45 trillion cubic feet, while potential reserves were estimated at a further 75 trillion cubic feet in year 2000. So as to increase oil exports, the government has adopted a policy of promoting the use of natural gas for domestic consumption. Gas production is mostly concentrated in the Nile delta region and the Western Desert, and is mostly used for power generation. Natural gas production is expected to rise in the coming years as the government concludes several agreements with its neighbors, mainly Israel, Jordan, and the Palestinian Authority. In July 2000, the government signed an agreement with the Spanish electricity company Union Fenosa to supply almost 25 percent of Spain's annual natural gas consumption.

Most of Egypt's coal reserves are located in Sinai and are estimated at 50 million tons. Egyptian coal, however, is of poor quality, and previous plans to increase production have been abandoned due to the sector's lack of economic viability. Egypt also produces limestone and phosphates, which are mined near Bur Safaga and Quseir on the Red Sea, and iron ore is extracted at the Baharia oasis in the Western Desert. Other minerals, such as manganese, gold, zinc, tin, lead, copper, potash, sulphur, and uranium, can also be found in Egypt, but their mining is limited because of the high cost involved in their exploitation and transportation.

MANUFACTURING. The manufacturing sector is an important and growing contributor to the Egyptian economy, with production dominated by large state-owned enterprises. Industrial activity grew rapidly in the 1970s and early 1980s as a result of the oil boom in the Gulf and the influx of large Arab investments in Egypt, recording an annual growth rate of 10 percent or more. Growth, however, has since slowed down, although the private sector has expanded since 1996, and its contribution has increased dramatically as a result of economic liberalization. By contrast, growth in the public sector's industrial production has declined sharply, mainly thanks to the legacy of centralization and inefficiency that characterizes state-controlled manufacturing industries. One example is textile manufacturing, once one of the largest industries in Egypt. The sector, which continues under state **monopoly**, has been largely inefficient, and beset by problems ranging from the lack of modern machinery to over-employment of workers. By contrast, the privately owned ready-made garment industry has been booming.

Egyptian companies produce a wide range of goods. Textiles and food processing account for the largest share of Egypt's manufacturing revenue. Other manufactured goods include furniture, ceramics, and pharmaceuticals. The termination of public sector monopoly over the production of automobiles in 1991 has led to a considerable growth in the car assembly sector. Egypt has a fledgling computer software industry that the government has encouraged. Heavy industries, including iron and steel production, are based in Helwan, outside Cairo, and in Dikheila, near Alexandria. Aluminum production is based in Nag Hammadi, while the production of chemi-

cals is concentrated in Aswan. Since the 1970s, the government has attempted to encourage industrial production in non-agrarian regions in order to relieve the congestion in the main cities. As a result, 7 free zones (areas within which goods are received and stored without payment of **duty**) have been established throughout the country, and industrial production in those areas is subject only to minimal regulations.

The country's large defense industry employs around 75,000 workers. The sector assembles arms for export, mainly to the United States, and manufactures industrial goods for consumption in the civilian sector. Egypt has attempted to capitalize on one commodity where it maintains a significant advantage: cheap labor. The government has moved in recent years to develop an information technology industry, which has been growing at the rate of 35 percent annually. Plans were underway in 2001 to train software engineers and programmers to increase the fledgling industry's potential and to boost computer software export over a 3-year period from US$15 million to US$1 billion.

CONSTRUCTION. The construction sector is a major contributor to the Egyptian economy and one of its fastest-growing sectors. This growth, estimated at an average of 20 to 22 percent annually since the 1980s, is fueled by the ever-increasing demand for housing and by the state's large infrastructure projects. Among these projects are the Greater Cairo Wastewater Project, considered one of the largest sewerage developments in the world, and the US$88.5 billion South Valley Development project, which aims to create an alternative delta along the Nile and relocate urban communities so as to ease the severe congestion in the major cities.

Most of the material required for the construction sector is produced locally. Local cement production, amounting to 24 million tons annually and meeting more than 70 percent of domestic demand, is expected to increase over the coming decade due to heavy government investment in the sector. Private companies have also been allowed to compete in the production of cement, which continues to be dominated by state-owned companies. The construction industry is expected to continue its upward trend in the coming years as a result of continued government and private business expenditure, anticipated to reach 20 billion Egyptian pounds annually.

SERVICES

TOURISM. Despite the drop in revenue as a consequence of political violence, tourism remains a significant contributor to Egypt's economy and the premier source of its foreign exchange earnings. The sector has huge potential, owing to the country's rich archeological heritage, such as the pyramids and other major attractions, as well as attractive tourist destinations on the Red Sea. The majority of visitors to Egypt, almost 61 percent, come from Western and Southern Europe. Tourists from other parts of the Middle East, especially from the Arab Gulf region, account for 19 percent of the total number, while Americans and Eastern Europeans each represent 6 percent of the total, and Asian visitors make up 5 percent.

The sector's growth has been stifled by periodic Islamic political violence, the absence of adequate facilities, and poor government management of state-owned tourist enterprises. The tourism industry suffered a sharp decline from October 1992, when the militant Islamic movements waged their war to discredit the state. The sector began to recover in 1995, with a record 4 million tourists visiting the country in 1996–97 and generating some US$3.7 billion in tourist receipts. This upward trend was reversed after the November 1997 massacre in which 58 tourists were killed while visiting the Luxor archeological site. The sector has managed to recover quickly, with some 4.8 million tourists visiting the country in 1999, spending some US$4 billion. According to the EIU *Country Profile* for 2000–01, tourism revenue is believed to have risen by 33 percent in 1999–2000, generating a record US$4.3 billion. Plans are underway to achieve a 12 percent growth in the tourism sector by the year 2005 by attracting some 9.5 million tourists annually over the next 5 years. The sector employs some 2.3 million people.

Major international hotels have a presence in Egypt. These include the Four Seasons, Sheraton, Hilton, and Marriott chains, among others, and there are major resort complexes, especially on the Red Sea. The most visible growth area of the tourist industry is the operation of Nile cruises. Dozens of cruise ships, many owned and operated by foreign companies, and particularly popular with British visitors, ply the river between Aswan and Luxor, stopping to take visitors ashore to the major cultural sites of Ancient Egypt. These cruises are accompanied by teams of licensed and highly qualified Egyptian guides.

THE SUEZ CANAL. The other major component of Egypt's service industry is the Suez Canal, which links the Red Sea to the Mediterranean. The canal generates revenue from fees charged for shipping to pass through the canal. Some 13,490 ships passed through the Suez Canal in 1999. Twenty-five percent of the tankers that pass through the canal carry petroleum and petroleum products from the Gulf region to the United States, while the remaining 75 percent carry dry goods. According to the EIU *Country Report* for 2000, revenue from the canal has declined steadily since 1994, down to US$1.7 billion in 1998, from US$2.1 billion in 1994. Despite the government's efforts to promote the Suez Canal, receipts have remained sluggish, largely due to competition from alternative routes and the effects of the economic slowdown in Asia. The government is currently attempting to deepen the canal to accommodate huge tankers, and has changed its pricing policies to make usage of the canal more lucrative to international traffic.

FINANCIAL SERVICES. For an economy of its size, Egypt's banking system is underdeveloped. Most of the services provided by the banking sector remain basic, with the majority of transactions in the country still conducted using cash. Regulatory controls are inefficient, and the banking sector in general is not only overstaffed, but also suffers from a lack of well-trained or experienced employees. State-owned banks suffer from low capitalization and a high percentage of poorly performing loans.

The roots of the banking sector's inefficiency can be found in the nationalization policy implemented by President Nasser between 1957 and 1974. In that period, private banking was banned and only state banks were allowed to operate. State-owned banks still dominate the banking market, even though private banks were once again allowed to operate in 1974. In 1992, foreign banks were allowed to engage in local operations, reversing a policy that had restricted them to foreign currency business since 1974. But it was not until 1995 that foreign banks were allowed a majority ownership in local banks, a right denied them under the previous 1974 regulations. Efforts to reform banking and raise it to international standards are ongoing, with reform focused on improving the regulatory and institutional aspects of the sector. The government, however, has thus far been reluctant to cede control of the financial sector for both financial and political reasons. The privatization of the 4 state-owned commercial banks has been delayed on the pretext of popular opposition to such a move. The commercial banks provide banking and credit services to remote areas, and are profitable partners in the government's large development projects.

The banking sector is controlled by the Central Bank of Egypt, which sets banking and **monetary policies** through the control of interest rates, **liquidity**, and **reserve ratios**. The central bank also sets fees charged for the various transactions conducted in the sector. According to the EIU *Country Report* for 2000–01, there are currently 81 banks operating in Egypt, including 28 commercial banks, 32 investment banks, 2 real estate banks, 18 agricultural banks, and 3 specialized banks. The commercial banks are by far the most important, providing more than 75 percent of loans and accounting for more than 90 percent of deposits. As a result of the excessively large number of banks operating in the market, the Central Bank has placed a ceiling on the entrance of new banks, both Egyptian and foreign, into the market. The banking sector has been hit by a liquidity crisis that has affected the market since 1998, mainly as a result of indirect pressure from the government to limit credit to importers in order to control currency fluctuation.

Interest rates have, as a result, remained high, averaging over 10 percent in the first 6 months of 2000.

Egypt has one of the oldest stock markets in the Middle East. Established in 1906, the Cairo and Alexandria stock exchanges were forced to close in 1961 as a consequence of President Nasser's nationalization drive. The 2 markets re-opened in 1986 in line with President Mubarak's privatization program. A 1992 law paved the way for the reorganization of the stock markets in Egypt, granting the Capital Markets Authority wider regulatory powers. A 2 percent capital gains tax was abolished in 1996 to encourage investment in the stock market. The 2 markets are now open to foreign investors, but interest in trading has declined over the last few years as a result of government mismanagement and eroding confidence in the country's political environment. According to the EIU *Country Profile* for 2000–01, the market grew by 157.9 percent in 1994, following the passage of the Capital Markets Law. The market's inconsistent performance since 1994 has been largely determined by the pace of the government privatization program.

INSURANCE. Egypt has a large domestic insurance market, dominated by 4 state-owned companies that control almost 90 percent of the insurance market. Since May 1995, the lifting of restrictions that prevented foreign companies from being majority holders in domestic insurance companies has encouraged foreign activity in the Egyptian insurance market. The government is currently reviewing the viability of privatizing the 4 state-owned companies.

RETAIL. The absence of large commercial centers other than Cairo and Alexandria has resulted in a poorly developed retail sector. While Cairo and Alexandria are home to a variety of retail stores, including fast food franchises such as KFC and McDonald's, the majority of towns in the interior of the country rely on small family-owned shops, farmer's markets, and temporary roadside stands.

INTERNATIONAL TRADE

Egypt has grown increasingly reliant on imports over a very long period of time, and has, as a result, maintained an external trade deficit for most of the past 6 decades. The deficit, however, grew considerably between 1974 and 1984 as a result of President Sadat's open-door policy that encouraged imports, and reached US$4.86 billion in 1980. This sharp rise was fueled by the infusion of large amounts of foreign aid following the signing of the Camp David peace accords with Israel in 1978 and the rise in oil revenue. Imports dropped for a brief period between 1984 and 1986, due to the shortage of foreign exchange coupled with debt repayments. Since 1986, imports have been on the rise, increasing from US$11.74 billion in 1995 to US$15.8 billion in 1999,

Trade (expressed in billions of US$): Egypt		
	Exports	Imports
1975	1.402	3.751
1980	3.046	4.860
1985	1.838	5.495
1990	2.585	9.216
1995	3.435	11.739
1998	N/A	N/A

SOURCE: International Monetary Fund. *International Financial Statistics Yearbook 1999.*

when exports totaled US$4.6 billion. Thus, with exports remaining steady at around US$4.5 billion, Egypt has continued to maintain its trade deficit. Since 1998, the government has attempted to discourage imports by tightening trade financing and controlling the amounts of foreign currency in the country. Coupled with higher oil prices, the policy of lowering imports succeeded in reducing the deficit in 2000. However, imports are likely to continue outpacing exports due to the widespread lack of most raw materials, especially those needed by the construction and industrial sectors.

Egypt imports a wide variety of goods, especially **capital goods** such as machinery and equipment, necessary for its economic and infrastructure development. Food has traditionally accounted for 20 percent of Egypt's imports, but chemicals, wood products, and fuels are also imported. Before 1973, one-third of Egypt's imports came from the former Eastern European bloc, or Comecon countries, as part of Egypt's alliance with the Soviet Union. After the signing of the Camp David accords, Egypt's new pro-Western orientation was coupled with a shift in trading partners. Today, the European Union, especially Germany, Italy, and France, supplies more than 40 percent of Egypt's imports, while the United States accounts for 15–20 percent of total imports.

Between 1960 and 1980, agricultural products made up the bulk of exports, accounting for 71 percent of the total. That percentage dropped significantly in the 1990s, reaching 20 percent of total exports in 1995, according to the EIU. On the other hand, the export of fuel, minerals, and metal rose sharply over that same period, from 8 percent in 1960 to 41 percent in 1995. The export of manufactured goods has also risen since the 1990s, from US$2.9 million in 1993 to US$3.4 million in 1998. This increase has been mainly the result of the growth in clothing and textile production, which accounted for 14 percent of total exports in 1998. The value of exports has been steady since 1997, reaching US$4.6 billion in 1999. The failure to expand exports has been blamed on a number of factors: state bureaucracy and red tape, lack of competitiveness in the **exchange rate** market, the shortage of modern technology, and low industrial capacity. Additionally, the inadequate marketing experience of Egyptian exporters has left them ill-equipped to compete successfully in the export business.

Egypt's main export partners are the European Union—chiefly Italy, the United Kingdom, and Germany—and the United States. Before 1973, Egypt exported some 55 percent of its goods to **communist** countries then in the sphere of influence of the Soviet Union. Since the early 1990s, Egypt has gradually regained its influential role in the region, which it had lost after the signing of the 1978 Camp David Accords, and its exports to neighboring Arab countries have increased.

Egypt has been a member of the World Trade Organization (WTO) since 1995. The effects of the implementation of membership requirements remain unclear. While the agreement secures better access to developing markets, there is rising concern about its impact on the protected sectors of the economy, namely the industrial and agricultural sectors. The lifting of state protection might make these sectors more competitive, but could also lead to a huge increase in the country's import bill.

MONEY

The value of the Egyptian pound has been fairly stable since 1991, thanks to the government's efforts to maintain a stable exchange rate against the U.S. dollar. Traditionally, the government's policy has rested on the principle of defending the Egyptian pound against the U.S. dollar and increasing the country's foreign reserves. However, since 1998, a policy designed to keep the supply of U.S. dollars tight by removing them from the market led to a 10–12 percent **devaluation** of the Egyptian pound against the dollar in the last 6 months of the year 2000. This setback occurred despite government assurances that the pound would not be devalued. As a result, the Egyptian pound's exchange rate has fluctuated since the beginning of 2000, moving from EP 3.4 to the dollar in January 2000 to EP 3.8 to the dollar by the end of the year.

The banking sector is expected to continue suffering from foreign currency shortages in 2001, as the supply of U.S. dollars remains tight. For the time being, the government appears to have allowed market forces to determine the exchange rate of the pound as a means of relieving the pressure caused by tight foreign currency supplies. The government is hoping that in the longer term, the tight foreign currency supply will be offset by a rise in foreign currency receipts from the tourism sector, a lower budget deficit, and decreased imports.

POVERTY AND WEALTH

Living standards in Egypt are low by international standards, and have declined consistently since 1990. According to United Nations figures, some 20 to 30 percent of the population live below the poverty line. Despite widespread poverty, however, uneven development has led to the emergence of an affluent class that controls most of the country's wealth and enjoys an elevated standard of living that includes shopping at centers that feature the best imported goods. Living in such Cairo suburbs as Garden City, al-Zamalek, and Nasr New City, the wealthy send their children to private schools and to universities abroad. Yet not far from these affluent neighborhoods, a significant number of poor Egyptians live in squalor, with poor and overcrowded housing, limited food supply, and inadequate access to clean water, good quality health care, or education. The extremes are reflected in the country's distribution of income: in 1996, the wealthiest 20 percent of Egyptians controlled 39 percent of the country's wealth, while the poorest 20 percent controlled only 9.8 percent of wealth.

Uneven development in Egypt has not only affected the urban population. Inequality in the distribution of wealth is dictated by geographical regions. Historically, the north of Egypt has been more prosperous and received more government attention than the predominantly rural south, which stretches from Beni Suef, 120 kilometers (75 miles) south of Cairo to the border with Sudan. The central government, which retains great power over the country, has always been based in the north, and has

Exchange rates: Egypt	
Egyptian pounds per US$1	
Jan 2001	3.8400
2000	3.6900
1999	3.4050
1998	3.3880
1997	3.3880
1996	3.3880
SOURCE: CIA *World Factbook 2001* [ONLINE].	

GDP per Capita (US$)					
Country	**1975**	**1980**	**1985**	**1990**	**1998**
Egypt	516	731	890	971	1,146
United States	19,364	21,529	23,200	25,363	29,683
Saudi Arabia	9,658	11,553	7,437	7,100	6,516
Nigeria	301	314	230	258	256
SOURCE: United Nations. *Human Development Report 2000; Trends in human development and per capita income.*					

Distribution of Income or Consumption by Percentage Share: Egypt

Lowest 10%	4.4
Lowest 20%	9.8
Second 20%	13.2
Third 20%	16.6
Fourth 20%	21.4
Highest 20%	39.0
Highest 10%	25.0

Survey year: 1995
Note: This information refers to expenditure shares by percentiles of the population and is ranked by per capita expenditure.

SOURCE: *2000 World Development Indicators* [CD-ROM].

therefore based major economic activity in that area. According to the EIU *Country Profile* for 2000–01, almost one-half of economic and social establishments in the country are based in the northern cities of Cairo and Alexandria. This uneven development has fueled a cycle of rural-urban migration from south to north that has only started to abate since the mid-1990s. Migration has only served to aggravate the state of underdevelopment prevailing in the south.

The economic reforms launched by the Egyptian government in the early 1990s have been double-edged, severely affecting the lower classes and threatening to further erode popular support for the government. Both the rural and urban poor have suffered from the long decline in the quality of social services provided to Egyptians. A lack of adequate resources for schools and hospitals has meant that these services have declined in quality over the years. Despite this deterioration, 93 percent of primary level students are enrolled in schools, and a government-funded health-care system ensures that all Egyptians have access to some form of health care.

As a result of high inflation, which, at its peak, reached 28.5 percent in 1989, the middle and lower classes have seen their living standards erode since the 1980s. The problem has been compounded by the government's reduction of subsidies on basic foodstuffs and certain budget controls on public services since 1991. The government's awareness of the political implications of the complete lifting of subsidies has slowed down the implementation of IMF-mandated price deregulation. In 1991, to soften the impact of these measures on the poor and those affected by privatization, the government established the Social Fund for Development, a US$613 million project funded by the European Union, the World Bank, and the **United Nations Development Program** (UNDP). The fund is a job creation project aimed at training and finding jobs for workers displaced as a result of privatization. However, poverty remains endemic in Egypt despite these efforts.

WORKING CONDITIONS

Since the 1970s, the Egyptian labor force has been growing at the rapid rate of 500,000 (2.7 percent) per year. In 2000, Egypt's labor force stood at 19 million. The official unemployment rate for 1999 was 7.4 percent. However, Egypt's unemployment rate is believed to be higher than the official figures. Independent estimates put unemployment at about 10 percent. Almost one-third to one-half of the labor force is believed to be under-employed.

Egypt's labor force generally lacks secondary education and proper job training, which explains why much of the younger workforce cannot expect high pay. Despite higher rates of school enrollment since the 1960s, illiteracy is still high, at 35 percent for men and 58 percent for women. The educational sector remains overburdened and understaffed, and shortages in technical skills are viewed as a major impediment to business operations.

Unemployment remains especially high among women and workers under 20 years of age. The government is hard-pressed to meet its commitment to create

Household Consumption in PPP Terms

Country	All food	Clothing and footwear	Fuel and power[a]	Health care[b]	Education[b]	Transport & Communications	Other
Egypt	44	9	7	3	17	3	17
United States	13	9	9	4	6	8	51
Saudi Arabia	N/A	N/A	N/A	N/A	N/A	N/A	N/A
Nigeria	51	5	31	2	8	2	2

Data represent percentage of consumption in PPP terms.
[a]Excludes energy used for transport.
[b]Includes government and private expenditures.

SOURCE: World Bank. *World Development Indicators 2000*.

jobs for the thousands of university graduates entering the workforce every year, a major challenge since the 1980s. The average waiting period for a job in the public sector is estimated to be 11 years.

Egypt has a long tradition of trade unions. Workers' unions have existed in Egypt since the British mandate and, although repressed by the British government, workers routinely organized strikes to protest working conditions. By 2001, the workers' movement was less effective. Workers have the right to join trade unions, but are not required to do so by law. Some 27 percent of union members are state employees. There are 23 general industrial unions and some 1,855 local trade unions; all of them are required by law to be members of the Egyptian Trade Union Federation (ETUF). Although semi-independent, the ETUF maintains close ties with the ruling National Democratic Party and has traditionally avoided confrontations with the government. The close connection between the ETUF and the ruling party has meant less protection for state-sector employees, but the federation has been far more successful in bargaining on behalf of private sector employees.

The Egyptian government supports workers' rights promoted by the International Labor Organization (ILO) and has set conditions governing industrial and human relations and established minimum-wage standards. The 6-day, 42-hour working week is the standard. The government-mandated minimum wage in the public sector is approximately US$33 a month, although the actual income a worker takes home is triple that amount, due to a complex system of added benefits and bonuses. The minimum-wage law is also observed in the private sector. In addition, the government provides social security benefits that include a retirement pension and compensation for on-the-job injuries. Wages have increased steadily over the last few years and are expected to increase again, since the 2001–02 budget has allocated US$10 billion for public sector workers' salaries and bonuses. However, it is only recently that the rate of increase in public wages has exceeded the rate of inflation.

Egypt has had a history of child labor problems. Poverty has driven many children younger than the minimum working age of 14, to join the labor force. Official estimates indicate that children under the age of 14 make up 1.5 percent of the total labor force. The number, however, is believed to be much higher, and it remains difficult to gauge the real extent of the child labor problem. The majority of working children (78 percent) work in agriculture. Children are also employed in craft shops, as domestic servants, and in the construction industry. The problem of child labor is worsened by poor enforcement of the law and the inadequacy of the education system.

The current labor laws make it difficult for employers to dismiss workers. Despite the protection offered by unions and the labor laws, however, working conditions are not ideal. Workers do not have the right to strike, and although strikes occur, they are considered illegal. The abundance of available labor has meant that workers are generally underpaid and are usually forced to work in overcrowded and often unsafe conditions. Government health and safety standards are rarely enforced, resulting in many workers seeking extra income through a second job or work in the **informal sector**, perhaps as street vendors. Thousands of Egyptians also seek employment opportunities in other countries, mainly in the Arab Gulf region. According to the latest census by the Egyptian government, 1.9 million Egyptians live and work abroad, and their remittances are a major source of foreign currency.

COUNTRY HISTORY AND ECONOMIC DEVELOPMENT

1798. The Emperor Napoleon Bonaparte invades and occupies Egypt, bringing Western influences to the country for the first time in its very long history, during which it has been variously under the rule of Greeks (Alexander the Great, 332 B.C.), Macedonians, Persians, Romans, Mamelukes, and Turks.

1801. An alliance of British and Turkish Ottoman Empire forces invades Egypt and expels the French. Ottoman army officer Muhammed Ali takes over control of the country, organizing the economy, the military, and the educational system according to Western standards.

1854. French engineer Count Ferdinand de Lesseps is granted the right by the Egyptian government of Mohammed Said to dig the Suez Canal, which will become one of the world's most strategically significant waterways.

1869. The Suez Canal is opened under the reign of the Khedive Ismail. Khedive enters into agreements with Britain which pave the way for British control of Egypt.

1882. Egypt enters a long period of British rule, and becomes dependent on imports of British manufactured goods and exports of Egyptian cotton.

1914. Egypt is formally incorporated into the British Empire as a protectorate during World War I.

1922. Egypt gains independence from Britain under monarch King Fuad.

1935. Fuad's son, King Farouk, assumes the Egyptian throne and signs the Anglo-Egyptian Treaty allowing the British to retain rights to the Suez Canal Zone.

1947. Egypt joins a joint Arab invasion of the newly created State of Israel, but Israel wins the war.

1952. Clashes break out between Egyptians and British in the Suez zone. Revolutionaries led by army officers Gamal Abdel Nasser and Muhammad Naguib lead an insurrection that forces the abdication and exile of King Farouk.

1953. Egypt is declared a republic in June, with Maguib as president. Nasser takes over as president in 1954 and ushers in an era of Socialism, during which Egypt allies itself with the Soviet sphere of influence.

1956. Nasser nationalizes the Suez Canal in July. In October, the Suez War breaks out as Britain, France, and Israel attempt unsuccessfully to seize control of the Canal.

1967. Egypt loses the Six-Day war against Israel.

1970. President Nasser dies and is succeeded by Anwar Sadat.

1973. Syria launches an attack on Israel, leading to the October War between Israel and an alliance of Arab States, including Egypt. Israel triumphs.

1974. President Sadat introduces his "infitah," or open-door economic policy, but the lifting of subsidies on basic foodstuffs leads to countrywide rioting.

1978. Sadat pays a historic visit to Jerusalem, and Israel's prime minister Menachem Begin pays a reciprocal visit to Cairo. In the United States in September, the 2 leaders meet for peace discussions brokered by President Jimmy Carter and sign the Camp David Accord, under which the Sinai, captured by Israel in the war, is returned to Egypt.

1981. Sadat is assassinated by Islamic extremists. He is succeeded by President Hosni Mubarak, who introduces new economic policies emphasizing the free market. The first parliamentary elections take place, and the government launches a program of economic reform.

1990–91. Egypt allies itself with the United States and Great Britain in the Gulf War against Saddam Hussein of Iraq. The United States rewards Egypt's support by canceling its massive debt.

1997. Mubarak's government begins a program of privatization, but the economy is badly affected when 58 foreign tourists are massacred by Islamic terrorists at the Luxor tourist site.

FUTURE TRENDS

Egypt entered the 21st century under a cloud of economic uncertainty. For much of the 20th century, Egypt's experiments with socialism left the economy in a shambles. The open-door policy, begun in the 1970s, set the stage for partial economic recovery, but it was not until the 1990s that the government embarked on a real reform and privatization program to address the country's woes. The economic reform program has been successful, with Egypt's business climate continuing to improve. The government appears committed to the path of reform started in the early 1990s, and if the longer-term structural reforms, especially privatization, are accelerated and fully implemented, then Egypt will be able to position itself as a leading economy in Africa and the Middle East.

Despite major reform efforts, however, economic growth has slowed down considerably since 1998. The public sector continues to be a major force in the economy. According to the EIU *Economic Profile* for 2000–01, the Egyptian government today accounts for one-third of total GDP, two-thirds of non-agricultural GDP, and two-thirds of manufacturing. In addition to the need to reduce its dominant role in the economy, the government is hard-pressed to meet several serious challenges that are crucial to the success of its economic reform program and, more importantly, its long-term political stability. These include addressing the unemployment problem and achieving social stability. To achieve that goal, Egypt will have to sustain a **real GDP** growth of about 6 percent, which would require dealing with the low levels of domestic savings and investment, increasing competition in the domestic economy, and stimulating export performance, as well as reducing dependence on foreign sources of income, primarily remittances and foreign assistance. Although aware of the possible political repercussions associated with its economic program, the government has done little to alleviate its impact on the majority of Egyptians, whose living standards have continuously deteriorated over the last decades. And it remains to be seen whether popular support for the government's economic reforms will outlast Egypt's enduring economic difficulties.

DEPENDENCIES

Egypt has no territories or colonies.

BIBLIOGRAPHY

Bush, Ray. *Economic Crisis and the Politics of Reform in Egypt.* Boulder, Colorado: Westview Press, 1999.

Economist Intelligence Unit. *Country Profile: Egypt, 2000–01.* London: Economist Intelligence Unit, 2000.

Handy, Howard, et al. *Egypt: Beyond Stabilization, Toward a Dynamic Market Economy.* Washington, D.C.: International Monetary Fund, 1998.

Marr, Phebe, ed. *Egypt at the Crossroads: Domestic Stablity and Regional Role.* Washington, D.C.: National Defense University Press, 1999.

U.S. Central Intelligence Agency. *World Factbook 2000.* <http://www.odci.gov/cia/publications/factbook/index.html>. Accessed July 2001.

U.S. Department of State. *FY 2001 Country Commercial Guide: Egypt.* <http://www.state.gov/www/about_state/business/com_guides/2001/nea/index.html>. Accessed July 2001.

Waterbury, John. *The Egypt of Nasser and Sadat: The Political Economy of Two Regimes.* Princeton, N.J.: Princeton University Press, 1983.

—Reem Nuseibeh

EQUATORIAL GUINEA

CAPITAL: Malabo.

MONETARY UNIT: Communauté Financière Africaine franc (CFA Fr). One CFA Fr equals 100 centimes. There are coins of 1, 2, 5, 10, 25, 50, 100, and 500 CFA Fr and notes of 50, 100, 500, 1,000, 5,000, and 10,000 CFA Fr. [The country is part of the "Franc Zone," which includes a number of former French colonies in Africa that share a common currency that is pegged to the French franc. The Communauté Financière Africaine franc was introduced in 1985.]

CHIEF EXPORTS: Petroleum, timber, cocoa.

CHIEF IMPORTS: Petroleum, manufactured goods, and equipment.

GROSS DOMESTIC PRODUCT: US$960 million (purchasing power parity, 1999 est.).

BALANCE OF TRADE: Exports: US$555 million (f.o.b., 1999). **Imports:** US$300 million (f.o.b., 1999).

Republic of Equatorial Guinea
República de Guinea Ecuatorial

COUNTRY OVERVIEW

LOCATION AND SIZE. Equatorial Guinea is a small West African nation of 28,051 square kilometers (10,830 square miles), roughly the same size as Maryland. It consists of a mainland enclave called Río Muni, on the west coast of Africa bordering Cameroon and Gabon, and 5 small islands off the coast of Cameroon in the Bight of Biafra: Bioko, Annobón, Corisco, and the 2 small islands known together as Islas Elobey. Total boundary length of Equatorial Guinea equals 835 kilometers (519 miles). The capital city, Malabo, is on the island of Bioko.

POPULATION. Estimated at 472,214 in July 2000, the population is growing at a rapid rate of 2.47 percent, which will result in the population increasing to over 600,000 by 2010. This fast rate of growth is attributed to the very high fertility rate of 4.94 children per woman, although this is combined with a very high infant mortality rate of 111 per 1,000. The high rate of population

growth is reflected in the age distribution of society where over 43 percent of the population is under the age of 14 years old. Equatorial Guinea residents have an average life expectancy of 50 years. The health problems limiting many residents' lives are preventable diseases, including malaria, parasitic disease, upper respiratory infections, gastroenteritis, and pregnancy-related problems.

Decades of economic stagnation have prevented urbanization. There has been some population movement towards the capital in recent years due to the search for jobs in the booming oil industry, although a considerable amount of the population still resides in rural areas.

Although French and Spanish are the official languages, Europeans make up a very small percentage of the population. The primary ethnic groups include Bioko (Bubi and Fernandinos) and Río Muni (Fang) and languages associated with these groups are commonly spoken.

Equatorial Guinea has a literacy rate of 78.5 percent, much higher than the Sub-Saharan African average of 55 percent. Unfortunately, the economic collapse of the 1970s and 1980s left many workers with little skills and very few individuals with high levels of education. The first university in the country was established in 1999 and prior to that very few individuals could afford to study at overseas universities.

OVERVIEW OF ECONOMY

The economic mismanagement of the rule of Francisco Macias Nguema left the economy of Equatorial Guinea in very sad shape by the 1990s. Commercial cocoa production was essentially destroyed and most families in rural areas survived through **subsistence farming** and through the relatively high levels of foreign aid. But many charities and international lending agencies

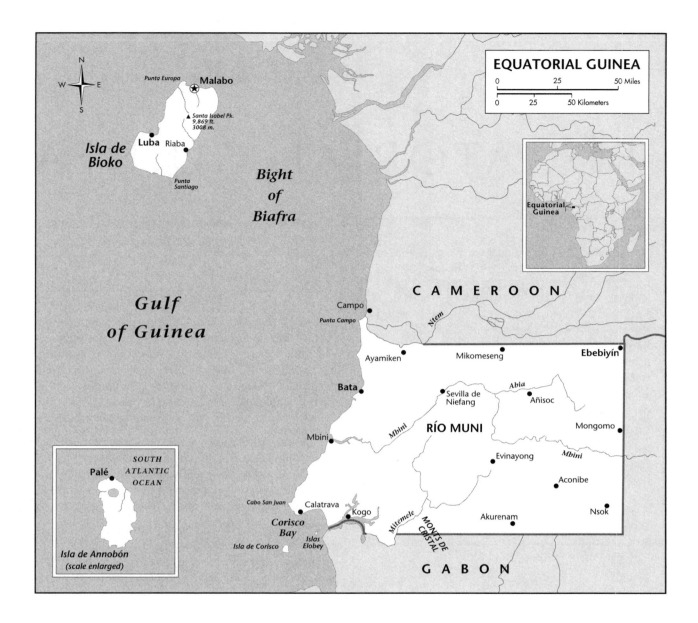

have ceased providing new funds to the country due to the high level of corruption. With little manufacturing, forestry has been one of the few promising industries which thrived in the early and mid-1990s.

The country is rich in natural resources, specifically oil, gold, titanium, iron ore, manganese, and uranium, although the country has been slow to exploit them. Specifically, the country has only just begun to produce and export oil after finding enormous deposits off Bioko Island in 1991. These oil deposits have attracted a number of **multinational corporations**—the first significant foreign investments into the country.

Although the discovery of oil can be a blessing to a developing country, the government has recognized some of the problems associated with allowing the economy to be based on oil production and hosted a United Nations

Conference concerning the proper governance of such an economy. Besides the obvious potential problems of environmental damage and the difficulty of negotiating with powerful multinational corporations, a number of countries in Africa have recognized the political and economic problems associated with natural resource dependent economies. Economically, reliance on oil makes the economy very susceptible to the extremely volatile oil prices and may lead to the lack of incentive to develop other aspects of the economy such as manufacturing and services. Politically, the profits from natural resources can inspire new levels of corruption in the government, both in filling the pockets of politicians and supporters and in helping the ruling elite to maintain power. The issue of corruption is especially striking in Equatorial Guinea. In 1993 the IMF and World Bank suspended a number of loans and grants due to the discovery of high levels of corruption. Although some of these loans have been reinstated in recent years, levels of corruption have not improved dramatically.

POLITICS, GOVERNMENT, AND TAXATION

In the early 1990s a wave of democracy swept through Eastern Europe, the former Soviet Union, and much of the African continent. While hopes were high that democracy would take hold across the globe, many nations made little progress towards real democracy. In many cases the dictators of the former regimes became the central political figures in supposed multi-party democracies. Unfortunately, Equatorial Guinea was one of these countries.

After the Spanish departed in 1968 and made way for Equatorial Guinean independence, the country suffered harsh political and economic times. The country was ruled by Francisco Macias Nguema, who quickly established a one-party state. Nguema contained any possible opposition, declaring himself president for life and the "Unique Miracle of Equatorial Guinea." Nguema cut off ties to the West and aligned the country with the **socialist** bloc countries.

The Partido Democrático de Guinea Ecuatorial (PDGE), the country's only political party prior to 1991, was created by Teodoro Obiang Nguema Mbasogo after a successful coup in 1979. After the brutal Nguema regime, internal and external pressure forced the ruling elite to reform the constitution and hold democratic elections. Even after a movement towards multi-party democracy along with much of Africa in the early 1990s, the PDGE remained the central political party, retaining the vast majority of parliamentary seats and Obiang the powerful presidency. In the 1999 elections, the PDGE won over 80 percent of the vote and gained 75 out of the 80 seats in the parliament.

Outside of the formal systems of political parties, clan networks complicate the transition to democratic rule. Some groups, such as the minority Bubi population, have been all but left out of politics. These marginalized groups have become more active in recent years. The militant Movimiento para la Autodeterminacion de la Isla de Bioko (MAIB), for example, has been accused of attacking government installations throughout the country.

Obiang's rule continues to be centered on personality, not ideology. Obiang and the PDGE have maintained tight control over the economy, although they have begun to allow higher levels of international investment.

Equatorial Guinea has been a target of human rights activists in recent years. The current regime has been accused of harassing political opponents, limiting freedom of expression, limiting the development of new political parties, and inhumane conditions in the country's prisons. In 1999 Amnesty International, an international human rights organization, issued reports on the arrest of 3 citizens for "insults against the government and the Armed Forces" stemming from their activities with Amnesty International and their attempt to establish a political party.

INFRASTRUCTURE, POWER, AND COMMUNICATIONS

Fueled by both the revenues from natural resources and the increased demands for power, roads, and harbors to continue the production of natural resources, the country has made large improvements in the vastly underdeveloped **infrastructure**. This includes upgrading the port at Luba, the airport at Malabo, and many roads linking major cities. The telecommunications revolution has

Communications

Country	Telephones[a]	Telephones, Mobile/Cellular[a]	Radio Stations[b]	Radios[a]	TV Stations[a]	Televisions[a]	Internet Service Providers[c]	Internet Users[c]
Equatorial Guinea	4,000 (1996)	N/A	AM 0; FM 2; shortwave 4	180,000	1	4,000	1	500
United States	194 M	69.209 M (1998)	AM 4,762; FM 5,542; shortwave 18	575 M	1,500	219 M	7,800	148 M
Nigeria	500,000 (2000)	26,700	AM 82; FM 35; shortwave 11	23.5 M	2 (1999)	6.9 M	11	100,000
Cameroon	75,000	4,200	AM 11; FM 8; shortwave 3	2.27 M	1 (1998)	450,000	1	20,000

[a]Data is for 1997 unless otherwise noted.
[b]Data is for 1998 unless otherwise noted.
[c]Data is for 2000 unless otherwise noted.

SOURCE: CIA *World Factbook 2001* [Online].

slowly been introduced with a new digital network, public phone booths, a cellular system, and even some limited Internet access.

Most of the country's power is generated by a number of oil-fired power plants and a few large dams. The country's power generation capacity will be doubled when a new gas-fired power plant is completed on Bioko. The gas for this power station will be supplied domestically.

These investments in infrastructure have helped increase the attractiveness of the country to foreign investors and have a positive impact on economic development. Unfortunately, the prior political regime left the country's infrastructure in a horrible state. Even with these vast improvements, the lack of developed infrastructure is still a major hindrance to economic development. The country currently has no rail system, few paved roads, and an inefficient communications system. Especially troubling is the lack of physical infrastructure in rural areas.

ECONOMIC SECTORS

The oil industry dominates all economic activity in Equatorial Guinea. The oil industry draws most the country's foreign investment, provides most of the exports, and provides the central government with a tremendous amount of revenue. Unfortunately, this industry has not provided a significant amount of jobs. Most citizens survive through subsistence agricultural production on small family plots.

In recent years the timber industry has played more of an important role in the economy and has contributed to country exports, mostly to Asia. Cocoa and coffee pro-

duction, once the mainstay of the economy, has declined in importance since the 1970s. Today this sector plays a very small role in the economy. The manufacturing and service sectors also have very little impact on the national economy and provide very few jobs.

AGRICULTURE

Although agriculture employs the majority of the population, it contributed to less than 20 percent of **gross domestic product** (GDP) in 1998. Most agricultural production is done through subsistence farming. Only a few cocoa and coffee plantations produce agricultural products for sale on the open market. The only efficient agricultural sector is the production and export of timber and timber products. Unfortunately, many environmentalists believe that the level of production may be unsustainable.

COCOA AND COFFEE. The once thriving cocoa and coffee industry were devastated by years of economic mismanagement under authoritarian rule. Cocoa and coffee production in 1969 stood at an impressive 36,161 tons and 7,664 tons, respectively. By the mid-1990s cocoa production had plummeted to less than 3,000 tons (1993) and coffee production to under 200 tons (1996). Obscured in these numbers is the decline in the quality of the products, which has been especially glaring in the quality of cocoa. With only a few large and inefficient plantations still producing coffee and cocoa, coupled with declining cocoa prices due to the European Union's (EU) loosening of regulations on the percentage of cocoa needed for chocolate production, the future of these 2 industries is bleak.

TIMBER. Timber exports have been increasing rapidly in recent years due to government promotion of the industry and available capital from oil revenues. By 1997 trade in tropical wood exports alone amounted to almost 6 percent of GDP. The economic success of this industry has been a mixed blessing, increasing economic growth and employment, but threatening serious environmental damage. While environmentalists have become increasingly active on this issue, the most serious challenge to this industry remains the weakening of markets in Asia due to the recent financial crisis. This crisis has both reduced exports to the region and, with the weakening of the Asian currencies, has been followed by a drop in the price of timber from other exports in Asia. The *Economist Intelligence Unit* argues that the competition from Asian timber exports was felt as early as 1998, decreasing sales substantially. Even with this competition, the recent investments in infrastructure (especially the roads and port systems) may greatly help the timber industry.

FISHING. The small island of Annabón is situated in the midst of one of the richest fishing areas in the Atlantic Ocean. The 300,000-square-kilometer area around the island is an exclusive maritime fishing zone, although the

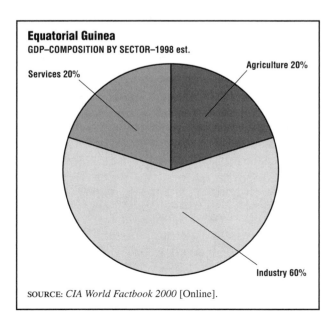

Equatorial Guinea
GDP–COMPOSITION BY SECTOR–1998 est.

Services 20%
Agriculture 20%
Industry 60%

SOURCE: *CIA World Factbook 2000* [Online].

government of Equatorial Guinea has granted concession to the EU for the use of this zone. Few reliable figures exist on the size of current production, but it is clear that the rich fishing waters offer a substantial opportunity for the development of a large domestic fishing industry.

INDUSTRY

MANUFACTURING. The manufacturing industry of Equatorial Guinea contributes only a 0.6 percent of GDP. Manufacturing is limited to the mainland processing of timber and a water-bottling plant at Bata. The *Economist Intelligence Unit* paints a gloomy picture for the prospects of developing a manufacturing industry: "Despite the high overall growth rates, the lack of skills and capital, the small size of the local market, and the weakness of national infrastructure make any significant growth in the manufacturing sector unlikely."

OIL. In the late 1980s and early 1990s the economy of Equatorial Guinea was fueled by international aid; it is now fueled by oil. The country has emerged as the sixth largest oil producer in sub-Saharan Africa, an amazing feat for such a small country. This sector has attracted a number of significant international investments. These investments have ranged from a **joint-venture** between local producers and a U.S. partner to produce diesel and methane gas, to contracts for foreign firms to explore for oil offshore, to the pumping of crude oil from existing oil deposits. Oil remains the largest export and is the potential key to further economic development. Profits from the oil industry have been used for the upgrading of the country's infrastructure.

MINING. The country is believed to have large deposits of gold, diamonds, uranium, bauxite, iron ore, titanium, manganese, and copper. Little domestic production has occurred in this sector, but new mining codes were issued in 1995 to attract investments in the sector. Efforts to negotiate mining contracts with multinational corporations has been much more complex than expected. The lack of infrastructure, less severe for the development of oil resources, is especially damaging to this sector due to the need to ship produces through rural areas to coastal ports. At the very least, the mining sector will take years to develop.

SERVICES

TOURISM. The pristine environment and rare animals offer the country a tremendous amount of potential for tourism. To date, tourism has made very little contribution to the local economy, although investments in infrastructure and the recent establishment of Mt. Alen National Park may help attract tourists. The recent construction of a number of hotels in Malabo offers some sign of the future significance of tourism to the economy.

Trade (expressed in billions of US$): Equatorial Guinea		
	Exports	Imports
1975	.026	.020
1980	.014	.026
1985	.017	.020
1990	.062	.061
1995	.086	.050
1998	N/A	N/A

SOURCE: International Monetary Fund. *International Financial Statistics Yearbook 1999.*

INTERNATIONAL TRADE

The international trade position of the country has improved dramatically. Prior to the discovery of oil, exports were dominated by agricultural production, which declined dramatically under the period of authoritarian rule. The trade balance in the late 1980s and early 1990s was in constant deficit, only to improve with the explosion of oil production in the early 1980s. With a depreciation of the CFA Fr, the price of timber from Equatorial Guinea is less expensive relative to timber from other countries. This depreciation has led to a dramatic increase in timber exports. These 2 industries propelled the country into a surplus in the mid-1990s.

With no real manufacturing base, almost every manufactured good has to be imported. The increased activity in the oil sector has led to a surge in imports to service this industry's needs.

The country's main trading partner is the United States, consuming 62 percent of the country's exports and providing 35 percent of the imports. France, Spain, China, Cameroon, and the United Kingdom are also important trading partners.

MONEY

In 1985 the country abandoned the national currency, the bikwele, and joined a number of former French colonies in pegging their own national currencies to the French franc and adopting the CFA Fr. The CFA Fr is supported by the French Treasury and is fully convertible. With this financial arrangement and the competent **monetary policy** of the regional central bank, the Bank of the Central African States, Equatorial Guinea has greatly helped reduce the levels of **inflation** from almost 40 percent in 1994 to a range of 6 to 12 percent in 1994–1999. Given the extremely fast economic growth of almost 20 percent in recent years, this inflation-fighting performance is impressive.

Attempts to establish a commercial banking sector following the 1979 coup failed miserably. Only the Banque centrale des Etats de l'Afrique centrale (BEAC) offers commercial financial services, although there are some prospects for new entrants in the commercial center of Malabo.

POVERTY AND WEALTH

Even though Equatorial Guinea is one of the wealthiest countries in Africa, with **GDP per capita** estimated at more than US$2,000 in 1999, the bulk of the citizenry lives in poverty. Official unemployment stands at almost 30 percent, and the government's social safety net does not adequately provide for the unemployed. The massive economic growth rates have been fueled by the production of oil offshore, an industry that has not substantially increased the number of jobs in the country. Timber, on the other hand, has made some contribution to increasing living standards, although this industry currently remains too small to make a significant contribution to the average worker's standard of living. The bulk of the population remains poor and makes a living off subsistence farming. The majority of Equatorial Guineans live without electricity, basic education, adequate health care, or safe drinking water.

GDP per Capita (US$)					
Country	1975	1980	1985	1990	1998
Equatorial Guinea	N/A	N/A	352	333	1,049
United States	19,364	21,529	23,200	25,363	29,683
Nigeria	301	314	230	258	256
Cameroon	616	730	990	764	646

SOURCE: United Nations. *Human Development Report 2000; Trends in human development and per capita income.*

WORKING CONDITIONS

Few studies have examined the working conditions in rural areas. Most people work on small farms for family consumption. Hours can be long and conditions can be harsh due to the lack of advanced farming equipment and farming techniques.

The United States Department of State Human Rights Report (1999) argues that working conditions for employees are substandard in Equatorial Guinea. The current minimum wage, roughly equivalent to US$41 a month does not provide for a sufficient standard of living for families. Labor standards, while officially codified into law, are seldom enforced. Laws declare women to have the same rights as men, but discrimination continues.

COUNTRY HISTORY AND ECONOMIC DEVELOPMENT

1963. Provinces of Fernando Po (Bioko Island) and Río Muni (3 small islands and the mainland) are joined under Spanish rule.

1968. Country gains independence from Spain.

1979. Macias is overthrown by Brigadier-General Teodoro Obiang Nguema Mbasogo in a violent coup.

1985. Country joins the Franc Zone.

1991. Obiang declares the end of one-party rule.

1991. Large oil and natural gas deposits are discovered.

1994. Investment by Mobil in the oil sector is followed by a number of multinationals over the next couple of years.

1996. Multi-party elections in 1996 are won by Obiang with 98 percent of the vote. This election is widely contested as unfair.

1997. French becomes second official language.

1997. The government claims an attempted coup in May and doubles the size of the military to 2,000.

1998. Attacks on government installations in January. Government blames a militant group for the attacks.

1999. The ruling PDGE increases its majority in parliament.

1999. Border dispute with Sao Tomé and Príncipe is settled by negotiation.

1999. First university established.

FUTURE TRENDS

The future is mixed for the country and the people of Equatorial Guinea. The aggregate growth prospects for the economy remain fairly bright, with high levels of economic growth being forecast for the future. These growth forecasts are dependent on the recent high prices of oil, which historically have been subject to tremendous price fluctuations. A drop in world oil prices could be disastrous for these future growth prospects.

Perhaps even more troubling is the uneven level of development in the country. While the oil sector has been booming in recent years, the bulk of the population remains dependent on subsistence farming for their livelihood. This large part of the population has been relatively untouched by recent economic successes and most likely would be untouched by further economic growth fueled by the oil sector.

On the positive side, Equatorial Guinea has shown some ability to develop the timber industry and has great potential for development in the mining and tourism sectors. The challenge for the country is to find the means to further develop these sectors.

In recent years the country has made some progress in investing in telecommunications, roads, and rail systems. This is one means of using the government revenues from the economic boom in the oil sector to finance economic development in other parts of the country. While this exhibits some positive signs, much more needs to be done.

In many ways, Equatorial Guinea suffers from the same problems as many other African countries. The country is rich in natural resources, yet poor in essentially all other aspects of economic development. The problems ahead will revolve around issues of how to use these resources to stimulate even economic development.

DEPENDENCIES

Equatorial Guinea has no territories or colonies.

BIBLIOGRAPHY

Amnesty International. "Equatorial Guinea. No Free Flow of Information. June 2000." <http://www.amnesty.it/ailib/aipub/2000/AFR/12400400.htm>. Accessed February 2001.

Economist Intelligence Unit. *Country Profile: Ghana, Equatorial Guinea.* London: EIU, 2000.

Energy Information Agency. "Country Analysis Briefs: Equatorial Guinea October 2000." <http://www.eia.doe.gov/emeu/cabs/eqguinea.html>. Accessed February 2001.

U.S. Central Intelligence Agency. "CIA World Factbook 2000: Equatorial Guinea." <http://www.odci.gov/cia/publications/factbook/geos/ek.html>. Accessed February 2001.

U.S. Department of State. "1999 Country Reports on Human Rights Practices: Equatorial Guinea." <http://www.state.gov/www/global/human_rights/1999_hrp_report/eqguinea.html>. Accessed February 2001.

—Nathan Jensen

ERITREA

State of Eritrea
Hagere Ertra

CAPITAL: Asmara.

MONETARY UNIT: Nakfa (Nkfa). One nakfa equals 100 cents. There are coins of 1, 5, 10, 25, 50 and 100 cents, and notes of 1, 5, 10, 20, 50, and 100 nakfa.

CHIEF EXPORTS: Livestock, sorghum, textiles, food, small manufactures.

CHIEF IMPORTS: Processed goods, machinery, petroleum products.

GROSS DOMESTIC PRODUCT: US$2.9 billion (purchasing power parity, 1999 est.).

BALANCE OF TRADE: Exports: US$26 million (1999 est.). **Imports:** US$560 million (1999 est.). [The *CIA World Factbook* lists exports of US$52.9 million (f.o.b., 1997 est.) and imports of US$489.4 million (c.i.f., 1997 est.).]

COUNTRY OVERVIEW

LOCATION AND SIZE. Eritrea is an eastern African country occupying an area of 121,320 square kilometers (46,841 square miles), which makes it slightly larger than the state of Pennsylvania. It borders Sudan to the north and west, Ethiopia and Djibouti to the south, and the Red Sea to the east. Its land borders extend for 1,630 kilometers (1,012 miles), while its total coastline is 2,234 kilometers (1,388 miles). Eritrea's capital, Asmara, and its 2 other major cities, Assab and Massawa, are in the southeastern and eastern parts of the country.

POPULATION. Eritrea's population was estimated to be 4,135,933 in July 2000. The population increased from 2.1 million in 1975 to 3.6 million in 1998, indicating a growth rate of 2.4 percent. The estimated birth rate in 2000 was 42.71 births per 1,000, and the estimated death rate 12.3 deaths per 1,000, contributing to a 3.86 percent growth rate in 2000. The population is expected to increase to about 5.5 million by 2015. Because of drought and a war with Ethiopia, about 1 million Eritreans lived

abroad (mostly in Sudan) in 2000, while at least 955,000 were internally displaced.

The major ethnic groups of the predominantly African population of Eritrea are the Tigrinya (50 percent), Tigre and Kunama (40 percent), Afar (4 percent), and Saho (3 percent). There are a variety of religions in the country, with Muslims, Coptic Christians, Roman Catholics, and Protestants dominating. There are also a variety of Cushitic languages spoken in the country. The population is young, with 43 percent under the age of 15 and only 3 percent above the age of 65.

Most Eritreans live in rural areas. In 1998 urban dwellers accounted for only 18 percent of the population, but this figure is expected to reach 26.2 percent by 2015. Asmara is the largest city with 480,000 inhabitants. Other major urban areas include Assab (70,000), Keren (70,000), Mendefera (65,000), and Massawa (35,000).

OVERVIEW OF ECONOMY

Eritrea gained independence from Ethiopia in 1991 and declared statehood in 1993, but its underdeveloped economy had suffered greatly from the 30-year war of independence with its neighbor. Conditions were worsened by a serious drought in the late 1990s, and the outbreak of a new war with Ethiopia that arose over a territorial dispute in 1998 and reached an uneasy, internationally brokered peace in mid-2000. This combination of adverse conditions further destroyed Eritrea's already limited agricultural and industrial capabilities and exhausted its inadequate financial resources, leaving the economy in ruins. Consequently, the country's **foreign debt** rose from $76 million in 1997 to $142 million in 1998, and to $242 million in 1999.

Eritrea is in transition from a deteriorating **socialist** economy to a market economy. The government has

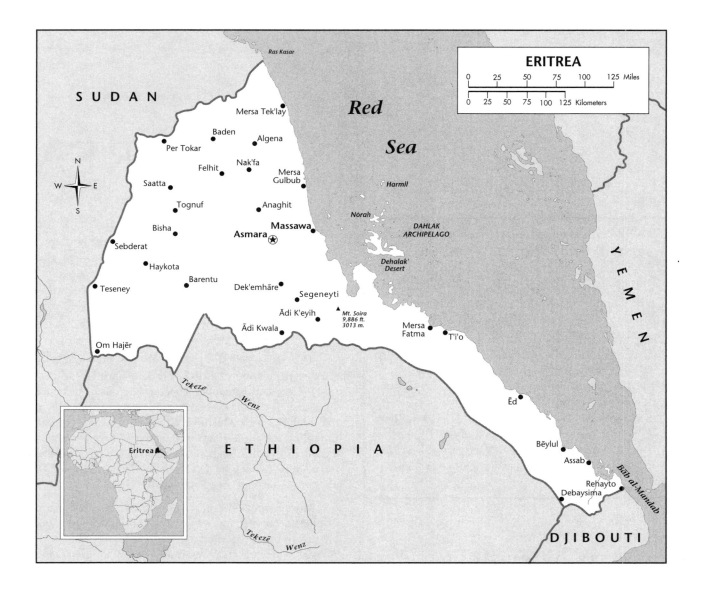

taken steps to end state **monopolies** and foster the growth of a **private sector**. It has encouraged domestic and foreign investments by beginning the **privatization** of state enterprises and passing laws to open trade and investment to market forces. Measures such as the lowering of business taxes have created some incentive for investment, but the emerging private sector is still too weak and foreign investment too small to make an impact on Eritrea's severe underdevelopment. The private sector is limited to the importation and distribution of goods.

The country's industrial, agricultural, and service sectors are small-scale and underdeveloped. Exports are limited and the country relies heavily on imports, including foodstuffs. Unsurprisingly, the **balance of trade** has recorded a large annual deficit since independence—$534 million in 1999. Since 1952, Eritrea has depended on 2 strands of economic activity to provide employment and revenue: port services at Assab and Massawa and

agricultural exports. Landlocked Ethiopia conducted most of its international trade through these ports until the outbreak of war in 1998. Agricultural exports to a few African and Middle Eastern countries have been a major source of income for Eritrea.

The Eritrean economy grew during the first few years of independence. However, since this growth was due to its earnings from port services, it proved unsustainable as a consequence of hostilities with Ethiopia. Ethiopia placed an **embargo** on Eritrea's ports, while the heavy cost of war between the 2 countries and a sharp decline in agricultural production caused by war and drought have since damaged the economy. Economic contraction began in the late 1990s, with the growth of Eritrea's **gross domestic product** (GDP) falling from 7 percent in 1997 to 4 percent in 1998, and to nil in 1999 and 2000. This disaster has made Eritrea dependent on foreign assistance for its survival. The Persian Gulf countries, Italy, Japan, the United States, the

World Bank, the African Development Bank (ADB), and the European Union (EU) have collectively been the country's main source of loans, grants, and food aid. Eritreans who have dispersed to live in other countries have become the main **hard-currency** providers since 1998.

POLITICS, GOVERNMENT, AND TAXATION

Eritrea has enjoyed internal political stability since its independence. In 1993, a splinter group of senior members of the Eritrean Liberation Front (ELF) joined the Eritrean People's Liberation Front to become a political party, the People's Front for Democracy and Justice (PFDJ), which has ruled the country ever since. The Eritrean constitution provides for a multiparty political system, but the reality is a one-party system dominated by the PFDJ, which, while so far unable to rescue the economy, keeps a tight rein on internal order, sometimes by measures such as the restriction of press freedom, that ensures domestic political stability. The opposition groups are all in exile (in Sudan) and include the Eritrean Islamic Salvation party and dissenting ELF factions, but they have no impact on Eritrea's economy.

Despite its **liberalization** policies, the government still dominates the economy. However, corruption is enviably low by the standards of many third world countries, and the government encourages industrial growth and exports. It has introduced low customs **duties** (2 percent in 2000) on **capital goods**, intermediate industrial spare parts, and raw materials, side by side with high **tariffs** (50–200 percent) on luxury goods (liquor and tobacco). Nevertheless, by 2001, efforts to create a viable free-enterprise economy and stimulate sustainable growth had not yet succeeded. The major barriers to meeting these objectives include limited financial resources, the absence of adequate **infrastructure**, lack of expertise and management, and a high illiteracy rate. These factors, with an environment made unattractive by war and drought, have conspired to discourage investment.

It is difficult to gather accurate statistics regarding revenues obtained by the Eritrean government, but it is evident that taxes and tariffs contribute little. In 1996, when the economy showed some growth, taxes contributed 30 percent of national income. However, the worsening economic situation and low international trade figures do not yield sufficient taxable profits or incomes, and the 1996 figure undoubtedly took a sharp fall in 1999 and 2000 when economic growth halted. From 1998, the war with Ethiopia and the drought proved disastrous to the economy. With drastic reductions in port fees and exports, the share of port-generated revenue dropped from 16 percent of revenues in 1996 (about $32 million) to almost nil in 1999 and 2000, while export earnings decreased from about 48 percent in 1996 ($95 million) to about 12 percent in 1999 (just under $26 million).

The gap between Eritrea's annual income and its expenditures is enormous (expenditures outstripped income by more than half in 1996), thus forcing the government to finance its deficit through foreign loans and grants and money from expatriates. In 1999 expatriate purchases of government bonds generated $400 million. Eritrea has been mostly successful in securing favorable loans, enabling it to keep its foreign debt low ($242 million in 1999).

INFRASTRUCTURE, POWER, AND COMMUNICATIONS

Eritrea suffers from seriously inadequate infrastructure. An extensive road and rail network built by

Communications

Country	Telephones[a]	Telephones, Mobile/Cellular[a]	Radio Stations[b]	Radios[a]	TV Stations[a]	Televisions[a]	Internet Service Providers[c]	Internet Users[c]
Eritrea	23,578 (2000)	N/A	AM 2; FM 1; shortwave 2 (2000)	345,000	1 (2000)	1,000	4	500
United States	194 M	69.209 M (1998)	AM 4,762; FM 5,542; shortwave 18	575 M	1,500	219 M	7,800	148 M
Egypt	3,971,500 (1998)	380,000 (1999)	AM 42; FM 14; shortwave 3 (1999)	20.5 M	98 (1995)	7.7 M	50	300,000
Djibouti	8,000	203	AM 2; FM 2; shortwave 0	52,000	1 (1998)	28,000	1	1,000

[a]Data is for 1997 unless otherwise noted.
[b]Data is for 1998 unless otherwise noted.
[c]Data is for 2000 unless otherwise noted.

SOURCE: CIA *World Factbook 2001* [Online].

the Italians in the 1930s was destroyed during the long war of independence. It is now estimated that there are 4,010 kilometers (2,491 miles) of roads, of which 874 kilometers (543 miles) are paved, but they are poorly maintained. The country's Italian-built, narrow-gauge railway, owned by the state, is almost defunct, with only 317 kilometers (196 miles) accessible. The few road and rail reconstruction projects are proving to fall far short of what is required.

Eritrea has 21 airports and airstrips, 3 of which have paved runways. Asmara International Airport was damaged during the war. Assab has a small airport and another is being built in Massawa. Eritrea's 2 major ports, Massawa and Assab, require upgrading.

Energy production is limited in Eritrea. According to 1997 estimates, the country generates and consumes 177.6 million kilowatt hours (kWh) of electricity, powered by fossil fuel, and many parts of the country, particularly the rural areas, lack electricity. Saudi Arabia, Kuwait, and the United Arab Emirates (UAE) have funded the construction of an 84-megawatt power station, and the European Development Bank has pledged a loan for the restoration of war-damaged power infrastructure. Eritrea has a limited oil production (0.55 million tons in 1998), but its main refinery is closed and thus it must import all refined oil products. Imports of petroleum products amounted to 100,000 tons in 1998.

Eritrea's telecommunications system is old and inadequate. In 2000 there were only 23,578 telephone lines in the entire country. The Eritrean government has installed a digital system to improve and expand the service. There is 1 Internet service provider and a growing number of e-mail stations. The country has 1 state-run television channel and 5 radio stations. In 1997 there were only 345,000 radios and 1,000 television sets in use.

ECONOMIC SECTORS

At the time of independence, Eritrea lacked the basic infrastructure and resources to address its many economic problems. Efforts to improve the infrastructure and develop its backward agriculture, industry, and services have had limited success, despite foreign assistance. Drought devastated agriculture, and war further damaged the inadequate infrastructure, destroyed many farms, and exhausted financial resources. The result was a massive internal displacement of civilians and the flight of large numbers of Eritreans to neighboring Sudan. Thus, by 2000, the country was unable to meet the basic needs of its population. In the wake of such devastation, Eritrea has had to depend on foreign aid and a large quantity of imports for its survival, and most of its limited developmental projects have been placed on hold.

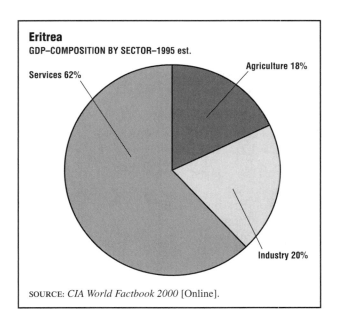

Eritrea
GDP–COMPOSITION BY SECTOR–1995 est.

Services 62%
Agriculture 18%
Industry 20%

SOURCE: *CIA World Factbook 2000* [Online].

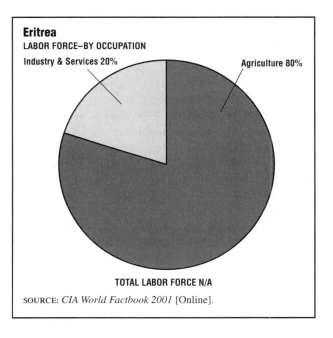

Eritrea
LABOR FORCE–BY OCCUPATION

Industry & Services 20%
Agriculture 80%

TOTAL LABOR FORCE N/A

SOURCE: *CIA World Factbook 2001* [Online].

AGRICULTURE

Subsistence agriculture shapes Eritrea's economy and employs about 80 percent of its population, but its contribution to the economy is small. Agriculture's share of the GDP was only 9 percent in 1998 (equal to $261 million), while its contribution to exports was only $8 million. Major exports are livestock, sorghum, and food products exported to Ethiopia (before the war), Sudan, Yemen, the UAE, and Saudi Arabia. In the absence of statistics, one can assume with some certainty that the 1998–2000 war and drought have lowered the contribution of agriculture to Eritrea's economy. The main agricultural products (sorghum, lentils, vegetables, corn, cotton, tobacco, coffee, sisal, and livestock) are insufficient to meet domestic needs, and these must be satisfied through foreign aid and large imports of foodstuffs ($63 million in 1998). The sharp fall in production during the crisis period between 1998 and 2000 led to price increases in food. The production of sorghum fell from 120,000 tons in 1994 to 62,000 tons in 1998. Eritrea can only become self-sufficient in food production if it is able to address its major handicaps: lack of money, poor irrigation, extensive soil erosion, and outdated technology.

The Red Sea coastline of Eritrea is rich in lobster, shrimp, and crab and offers the potential for a valuable export-oriented fishing industry. However, the lack of adequate investment, modern fishing boats, and technology have prevented any development, and fishing represents a negligible economic activity with a low annual catch (5,000 tons in 1999). Fishery projects are focused on privatization and the creation of storage and processing facilities funded by the **United Nations Development Program** (UNDP) and Japan.

INDUSTRY

Industry is the second largest sector after the service sector. Its main activities, manufacturing and mining, accounted for 29.5 percent of the GDP in 1998, valued at $855 million.

MANUFACTURING. The manufacturing industry is unable to meet domestic needs, while its exports are insignificant. Exports earned a paltry $4 million in 1998, while imports of industrial goods ran to $250 million. Manufacturing consists of Asmara-based small and medium size establishments producing consumer products such as glass, leather, processed foods, cotton, textile, liquors, and other beverages. New factories produce marble, recycled plastics, metals, and rubber goods. Low investment and management capacity, outdated machinery, and poor infrastructure have prevented growth, and the Eritrean government has privatized some of its industries while ending **subsidies** to others to stimulate development. It has also lowered taxes and tariffs on industrial exports and imports and offered other incentives to foreign investors.

MINING. Eritrea's mining industry is small but has growth potential. Its mineral resources include substantial reserves of barite, feldspar, kaolin, gold, potash, rock salt, gypsum, asbestos, and marble. If mining developed, Eritrea's proximity to the Middle East and Europe would be favorable to the export of minerals to those markets. In the absence of domestic investments, companies from Australia, Canada, France, South Korea, and the United States have operated or now operate limited mining operations there. Mineral exports accounted for $12 million

in 1998. Eritrea has sought foreign investment for the exploration and development of offshore oil and gas reserves, but Anadarko, an American company, stopped drilling operations in 1999 after disappointing results.

SERVICES

The most important services in Eritrea are tourism, **retail**, and financial. Services form the largest economic sector, accounting for 61.2 percent of the GDP and 20 percent of the workforce in 1998. However, like the rest of the country's economic sectors, services suffer from underdevelopment.

FINANCIAL SERVICES. Eritrea has a small state-run financial system. It consists of a central bank, the National Bank of Eritrea (NBE), 4 other banks, dominated by the Commercial Bank of Eritrea (CBE), and an insurance company, the National Insurance Corporation of Eritrea. The NBE accounted for over 60 percent of Eritrean banking assets in 2000. Except for the Housing and Commerce Bank of Eritrea, owned by the ruling party, all other financial institutions are state-owned, and the government licensed several private exchange offices in 1997 to liberalize the industry. No foreign financial institution operates in Eritrea, but the CBE has arrangements for money transfers with 40 foreign banks.

TOURISM. With its long warm-water coastline and an abundance of historical, archaeological, and natural sites, Eritrea has much to offer as a tourist destination. However, the development of tourism is constrained by the lack of basic infrastructure. There are only 11 hotels, all in Asmara, all of which require renovation. The government has privatized 3 hotels but has failed to find buyers for the rest. Thanks to some success in attracting foreign investment, in 2000 the first foreign hotel, the Inter-Continental, was opened in Asmara. In that year the government negotiated the construction of a casino and several hotels on the Dahlak archipelago by U.S. and Saudi Arabian companies.

RETAIL. The retail sector of Eritrea is poorly developed. It consists of small-scale traditional shops that are unable to ensure the accessibility of goods and services to either the rural or the urban populations. The emerging middle class is encouraging the establishment of modern retail outlets in major urban areas, but the economic devastation of the country has delayed the creation of a viable retail sector.

INTERNATIONAL TRADE

Eritrea's international trade is characterized by its deficit. The 1998 deficit of $499 million rose to $534 million in 1999, as the value of exports dropped to $26 million against imports of $560 million. Large trade deficits are a clear sign of Eritrea's underdeveloped economy in which the necessity for large-scale imports does not begin to be matched by its output of exportable goods. Imports accounted for a huge 89.7 percent of the GDP in 1998, the same year that an epidemic of cattle disease stopped major livestock exports to Saudi Arabia and Yemen, while drought and the outbreak of war with Ethiopia further decimated local productivity. Although that war ended in June 2000, Eritrea's exports are likely to remain low for a long time because of its devastated farms and infrastructure, its depleted financial resources, and the massive displacement of its population.

The country's main export products are salt, livestock, flour, sorghum, foodstuffs, small manufactures, and textiles. Major imports include foodstuffs, fertilizers, fuel, machinery, spare parts, construction materials, and military hardware. The war brought a sharp increase in military hardware imports, causing state expenditures on defense to jump from 9 percent of the GDP in 1997 to about 44 percent in 1999.

Ethiopia was Eritrea's largest trading partner until 1998, taking 65.8 percent and 64 percent of its total exports in 1996 and 1997. Ethiopia's share dropped to 26.5 percent ($28 million) in 1998 when the countries went to war, but their bilateral trade did not resume when the war was over. Eritrea's other main trading partners are Sudan, Italy, Japan, Saudi Arabia, the United States, Yemen, and the UAE. Sudan was Eritrea's second largest export destination in 1997, taking 17 percent of exports, rising to 27.2 percent in 1998. In 1996 and 1997, Eritrea's main source of imported goods was Saudi Arabia, followed by Italy and the UAE; in 1998, Italy was the most important supplier of imports, followed by the UAE and then Germany.

MONEY

Eritrea shared the Ethiopian currency, the birr, until November 1997 when it introduced its own currency, the nakfa. The NBE adopted a **fixed exchange rate** for the first 6 months and then switched to a **floating exchange rate**, that is, a rate determined by supply and demand. There are no exchange restrictions for the Eritreans or foreigners. The nakfa remained stable between 1997 and 2000, during which time it depreciated slowly against the U.S. dollar, declining from 7.2 to 9.5 nakfas to US$1. This minor fluctuation had no noticeable impact on the pace of economic activity or on the purchasing power of the population.

POVERTY AND WEALTH

Eritrea is one of the world's poorest countries. Poverty is rampant, and the severity of the war, compounded by the effects of drought, forced the migration of about 1 million people (1998 est.) to neighboring Sudan, decreasing the resident population to 3.5 million. In 2000 about half of this population faced a serious humanitarian emergency as their dismal situation gave rise to epidemics of diarrhea, malaria, and respiratory infections.

Basic necessities for dealing with the crises of homelessness, want, and disease are worse than inadequate. In 1997 access to sanitation was available to a mere 13 percent of Eritreans, while only 22 percent had access to safe water. Widespread malnutrition and a poor health-care system lead to high infant mortality (70 per 1,000 live births) and low life expectancy (50.8 years) in 1998. The inadequate medical services are barely available outside the capital.

A high illiteracy rate, estimated at between 49 and 80 percent, demonstrates the weakness of the educational system. Over half of the children of school age do not study because of poverty and a lack of educational facilities. There is only one small university in Asmara with 1,300 students. Solutions to these many social problems are unlikely so long as Eritrea lacks domestic resources and foreign aid remains relatively low.

WORKING CONDITIONS

Eritrea's workforce consists of unskilled workers, over 80 percent of whom are involved in agriculture. The

Exchange rates: Eritrea	
nakfa per US$1	
2001	N/A
Jan 2000	9.5
Jan 1999	7.6
Mar 1998	7.2
1997	N/A
1996	N/A
SOURCE: CIA *World Factbook 2001* [ONLINE].	

GDP per Capita (US$)					
Country	1975	1980	1985	1990	1998
Eritrea	N/A	N/A	N/A	N/A	175
United States	19,364	21,529	23,200	25,363	29,683
Egypt	516	731	890	971	1,146
Djibouti	N/A	N/A	N/A	N/A	742
SOURCE: United Nations. *Human Development Report 2000; Trends in human development and per capita income.*					

country suffers from a shortage of skilled or educated labor. There are no unemployment statistics, but one must conclude that, given the state of the economy, it must be high. Unions are legal and The National Federation of Eritrean Workers consists of 129 unions representing over 23,000 workers, and public and private company employees. The labor code prohibits child labor, discrimination against women, and anti-union regulations. Regulations permit the right to strike and endorse equal pay for equal work for women. However, in the absence of mechanisms for enforcement, the labor laws exist in principle rather than in practice. About half of children work and women face discrimination. The working week is 44.5 hours, but many work less than that due to limited employment opportunities. There is no minimum wage, and the market determines wages.

COUNTRY HISTORY AND ECONOMIC DEVELOPMENT

16TH CENTURY. Eritrea falls under the rule of the Ottoman Empire but claims to the region are disputed by the Ottomans, Italians, Ethiopians, and Egyptians.

1889. Italy signs the Treaty of Wechale with the king of Ethiopia to establish the borders of its colonial state of Eritrea.

1941. Italy loses Eritrea to Britain during World War II (1939–45), and Eritrea falls under a British mandate until 1952.

1948. The United Nations (UN) is mandated to determine the future of Eritrea.

1950. The UN adopts Resolution 390 A (V) to provide for the creation of a federation of Eritrea and Ethiopia with Eritrea to retain autonomy under the Ethiopian crown.

1952. The Federation of Eritrea and Ethiopia is ratified.

1961. The Eritrean Liberation Front (ELF) begins an armed struggle against Ethiopia.

1962. Ethiopia formally annexes Eritrea in violation of international law.

1973. A splinter group of the ELF forms the Eritrean People's Liberation Front (EPLF).

1991. Ethiopia's military junta is overthrown. The EPLF defeats the ELF and establishes control over Eritrea. The 2 new governments agree to discuss Eritrea's independence.

1993. In a referendum held in April, almost 100 percent of voters demand independence for Eritrea, and the country declares its independence on May 24.

1994. The EPLF reorganizes itself as a political party, renamed the People's Front for Democracy and Justice (PFDJ).

1997. In May, Eritrea's constitution is promulgated. In November, the Ethiopian currency (the birr) is replaced by the Eritrean nakfa.

1998. In May, a territorial dispute between Eritrea and Ethiopia leads to a new and devastating war.

2000. In June, Eritrea and Ethiopia conclude a peace accord, and refugees who have fled to Sudan begin to reenter the country.

FUTURE TRENDS

War and drought have devastated the Eritrean economy. Eritrea requires large investments in infrastructure as a first step for an overhaul of its economy, and extensive foreign assistance is essential in tackling urgent problems such as malnutrition, and to help revive and expand the economy. The expansion of fishery and tourism could make a major contribution to Eritrea's economic growth, but there is little interest on the part of international donors to help Eritrea achieve these objectives. In the absence of foreign resources, the outlook for the Eritrean economy, at least in the future, would appear bleak.

DEPENDENCIES

Eritrea has no territories or colonies.

BIBLIOGRAPHY

Economist Intelligence Unit. *Country Profile: Eritrea.* London: Economist Intelligence Unit, 2001.

Eritrea: A New Beginning. London: United Nations Industrial Development Organization, 1996.

Government of Eritrea External Affairs Office. *Birth of a Nation.* Asmara, Eritrea: Government of Eritrea, 1993.

Tesfai, Alemseged, and Martin Doornbos, editors. *Post-Conflict Eritrea: Prospects for Reconstruction and Development.* Lawrenceville, NJ: Red Sea Press, 1999.

United Nations. *Human Development Report 2000.* New York: Oxford University Press, 2000.

U.S. Central Intelligence Agency. *World Factbook 2000.* <http://www.odci.gov/cia/publications/factbook/index.html>. Accessed August 2001.

U.S. Department of State. *FY 2000 Country Commercial Guide: Eritrea.* <http://www.state.gov/www/about_state/business/com_guides/2000/africa/index.html>. Accessed September 2001.

—Hooman Peimani

ETHIOPIA

Federal Democratic Republic of Ethiopia
Ityop'iya Federalawi Demokrasiyawi Ripeblik

COUNTRY OVERVIEW

LOCATION AND SIZE. Located in the Horn of Africa— the pointy peninsula-like landmass that emanates out of the eastern part of the continent—Ethiopia has a total area of 1,127,127 square kilometers (935,183 square miles), rendering it slightly less than twice the size of Texas. A landlocked country completely surrounded by other states, Ethiopia has a total border length of 5,311 kilometers (3,300 miles). Ethiopia is bordered by Kenya to the south, Somalia to the east, Djibouti and Eritrea to the northeast, and Sudan to the west. The capital of Ethiopia, Addis Ababa, is located in the heart of the country.

POPULATION. In 1975, the population of Ethiopia was approximately 32.2 million. With a relatively high growth rate of 2.7 percent between 1975 to 2000, the population of Ethiopia doubled during this period, reaching a total of 64,117,452 by July 2000. Currently, the population growth rate remains high (2.76 percent), and it is forecasted that the population will reach 90.9 million by 2015 (July 2000 est.). In order to restrain the growth process, the Ethiopian government recently included a population control component in its overall development program. The death rate was estimated at 17.63 deaths per 1,000 people, and the birth rate was 45.13 births per 1,000 people (2000 est.). In terms of the age structure of the population, 47 percent of Ethiopians are younger than 15 years of age, 50 percent are between the ages of 15 to 64, and only 3 percent are older than 65 years of age. Only 16.3 percent of the population live in urban areas.

Ethnically, the population of Ethiopia is extremely heterogeneous (diverse). The country's principal ethnic groups are the Oromo (40 percent), the Amhara and Tigre (32 percent), Sidamo (9 percent), Shankella (6 percent), Somali (6 percent), Afar (4 percent), and Gurage (2 percent). The remaining 1 percent belong to various other ethnic groups. In total, there are more than 80 different ethnic groups within Ethiopia. Islam is the predominant religion with 45 to 50 percent of the population identifying as Muslim, 35 to 40 percent as Ethiopian Orthodox (a distinct denomination of Christianity), and 12 percent as animist (a term used to delineate a wide range of native African religious belief systems). The remaining 3 to 8 percent are adherents of various other religions.

Many languages are spoken by the inhabitants of Ethiopia, including Amharic, Tigrinya, Orominga, Guaraginga, Somali, and Arabic. Numerous other local languages and dialects also are spoken. Many of the languages are from the Semetic or Cushtic linguistic groups. Amharic is the country's only official language, while English is the major foreign language taught to Ethiopians in the educational system.

Like many African countries, one of the most daunting prospects that Ethiopia faces is a massive HIV/AIDS epidemic. By the end of 1997, conservative estimates stated that 2.6 million Ethiopians were living with HIV/AIDS, while the adult prevalence rate was 7.4 percent. In addition to causing considerable suffering,

HIV/AIDS places a large burden on health care expenditure and diminishes the ability of the poor to save and invest, due to the high cost of treating the disease. According to the **United Nations Development Program** (UNDP), the efficacy of the government's plan to curb the epidemic will depend on its ability to address the structural factors that facilitate the spread of the disease, such as poverty and gender inequality.

OVERVIEW OF ECONOMY

The Ethiopian state consists, territorially, of the only area in Africa that was never colonized by a European power, with the exception of a brief Italian occupation from 1936 to 1941. Indeed, Ethiopia—or Abyssinia, as the area was once called—is one of the oldest independent countries in the entire world. Modern Ethiopia, char-

acterized by political centralization and a modern state apparatus, emerged in the mid-19th century. Throughout much of the 20th century, Ethiopia was presided over by the emperor, Haile Selassie, who ruled the state autocratically (single-handedly and dictatorially), until he was overthrown and subsequently executed in the revolution of 1974.

Under Selassie's rule, the Ethiopian economy relied primarily on agriculture, particularly coffee production. During this time, agricultural production resembled a feudal system since land ownership was highly inequitable, and the vast majority of Ethiopians were obliged to till the fields of the wealthy landowners. Much of the marginal amount of industry that did exist was concentrated in the hands of foreign ownership. For example, by 1962, the Dutch H.V.A. Sugar Company, which commenced operations in Ethiopia in the early 1950s, employed 70 percent of the Ethiopian **workforce** involved in the industrial food-processing sector. The food-processing sector, in turn, employed 37 percent of all workers involved in manufacturing and industry.

Spouting anti-feudal and anti-imperialist (anti-foreign dominance) rhetoric, an administrative council of soldiers, known as the Derg, overthrew Selassie in 1974, ushering in a lengthy period of military dictatorial rule. The Derg regime, in turn, vocally promoted a **Marxist**-Leninist system, though according to Ghelawdewos Araia, author of *Ethiopia: The Political Economy of Transition,* it was only ostensibly (superficially) based on **socialist** principles. The Derg introduced substantial land reform and **nationalized** almost all of the country's important industries. The Derg regime, however, known for its particularly brutal suppression of opposition forces, failed to solve Ethiopia's many economic problems. In 1991, massive discontent led by the student movement, declining economic conditions caused by drought and famine, and provincial insurrections led by ethnic separatist groups forced the Derg chairman and Ethiopian president, Mengistu Haile Mariam, to flee the country. Following a period of transitional rule by the Transitional Government of Ethiopia, free elections were held in 1995, resulting in a victory for the Ethiopian's People's Revolutionary Democratic Front (EPRDF).

Since its democratic assumption of power, the EPRDF has supported a process of economic reform based on the **privatization** of state-owned enterprises, promotion of agricultural exports, and **deregulation** of the economy. By 1999, the Ethiopian Privatization Agency had already overseen the privatization of more than 180 **parastatals**, including most state-owned **retail** shops, hotels, and restaurants.

Since the fall of the Derg regime, the economy has experienced several positive economic developments. In 1992, for example, the International Monetary Fund's (IMF) *Staff Country Report No. 98/6* stated that 62,941 persons were registered as unemployed, whereas in 1996, the figure of officially unemployed fell to 28,350 persons. Of course, for both years, many unemployed Ethiopians, and perhaps even the majority, did not register themselves as such. Nonetheless, it would be fair to deduce that a considerable amount of formerly unemployed Ethiopians have found jobs throughout the 1990s. At the same time, however, the UNDP estimates that the annual growth rate in **gross national product** (GNP) per capita between 1990 to 1998 was 1.0 percent, while the average annual rate of **inflation** during the same period was 9.7 percent. This means that Ethiopians were having an increasingly difficult time purchasing the commodities, such as food, that are essential for human existence.

The Ethiopian economy remains highly dependent upon coffee production, with 25 percent of the population deriving its livelihood from the coffee sector. Indeed, from 1995 to 1998, coffee accounted for an average of 55 percent of the country's total value of exports. Gold, leather products, and oilseeds constitute some of the country's other important exports. Major export partners include Germany, Japan, Italy, and the United Kingdom, while import partners include Italy, the United States, Japan, and Jordan. Ethiopia's imports include food and live animals, petroleum and petroleum products, chemicals, machinery, and motor vehicles.

Since Ethiopia mostly exports agricultural products and imports higher valued **capital goods**, the country runs a severe **balance of trade** deficit. This deficit, in turn, means that Ethiopia must borrow heavily to finance its imports, a factor that has led to the development of a significantly sized **external debt** (owed to both foreign-owned banks and international financial institutions, such as the World Bank and the IMF). In 1997, the total debt stood at US$10 billion. The frequent droughts that plague the country also prevent the creation of a self-sufficient agricultural economy. Consequently, as many as 4.6 million people rely on annual food assistance provided by the wealthy industrial countries. Indeed, Ethiopia is the largest recipient of U.S. aid in sub-Saharan Africa. Notwithstanding (not including) emergency food aid, in 1996 Ethiopia received a total of US$45 million in Official Development Assistance (ODA) from the United States alone.

POLITICS, GOVERNMENT, AND TAXATION

The executive branch of the Ethiopian government consists of both an elected president, who is the chief of state, and a prime minister, who is the head of government. Cabinet ministers are selected by the prime minister and approved by the House of People's Representatives, the lower chamber of the **bicameral** parliament. Members of the lower chamber are directly elected by popular vote, while members of the upper chamber, the House of Federation, are chosen by the various state assemblies. The president and vice president of the Federal Supreme Court, the chief institution of the judicial branch of government, are recommended by the prime minister and appointed by the House of People's Representatives.

In June 1994, the first democratic multiparty elections in Ethiopia's history took place, ending a 3-year transitional period that commenced following the overthrow of the Derg regime. During the transitory phase, the Eritrean People's Liberation Front (EPLF) assumed control of Eritrea and established a provisional government in the Ethiopian province. In April 1993, the EPLF administered a separatist referendum under the auspices of the United Nations (UN), which subsequently formed the basis of a declaration of independence at the end of that month. Thereafter, Eritrea was recognized internationally as an independent sovereign nation. Since 1998, Ethiopia and Eritrea have officially been engaged in a border war as a result of territorial disputes.

The June 1994 national elections resulted in an overwhelming victory for the Ethiopian People's Revolutionary Democratic Front (EPRDF), a coalition of numerous ethnically based Derg-opposition movements led by the Tigrayan Peoples' Liberation Front (TPLF). The TPLF initially entered politics as a Marxist guerrilla movement bent on overthrowing the Derg regime. As the leading party in the EPRDF, however, the TPLF has officially adopted a pro-democracy and pro-free market stance, as its economic and political policies clearly make manifest. Nonetheless, the U.S. Department of State argues that the EPRDF displays certain residual (left-over) control-oriented tendencies, which result from the party's quasi-authoritarian guerrilla past (during the insurgency, the TPLF was directed necessarily as a military unit). The recently held 2000 national elections saw the EPRDF return to power, and Meles Zenawi, the leader of the party, is serving his second term as prime minister. Most observers have agreed that Zenawi's government has pursued sound policies, which have contributed to economic growth and reductions in unemployment.

Several other parties also add to the plurality of Ethiopian political life, including the Coalition of Alternative Forces for Peace and Democracy (CAFPD); the Ethiopian Democratic Union (EDU); The Ethiopian Movement for Democracy, Peace, and Unity (EMDPU); the Ethiopian National Democratic Party (ENDP); the Oromo Liberation Front; and the All-Amhara People's Organization (AAPO), not to mention dozens of other smaller parties. While most parties are more or less pro-democracy and pro-free market, several Ethiopian parties, including the last 2 listed above, represent the specific interests of particular ethnic groups.

Import **duties**, which ranged from 0 to 50 percent and averaged approximately 20 percent in 1997, are the most significant contributor to government tax revenue. **Income tax** on employment, in turn, is the second most important source of tax revenue, while taxation of business profits is the third most important. There are 5 income tax brackets, with the highest marginal tax rate set at 40 percent for monthly incomes above 3,301 birr, and the lowest marginal tax rate set at 10 percent for monthly incomes between 121 to 600 birr. The profits of incorporated businesses are taxed at a uniform rate of 35 percent. **Excise taxes** are also quite important, and the tax rates of many products, including pure alcohol (150 percent), perfumes and automobiles (100 percent), dishwashers (80 percent), and tobacco and tobacco products (75 percent), are set at exceptionally high rates. Since most of these items are luxury products, the high tax rates do not affect poor consumers. However some of the more essential commodities, such as petroleum and petroleum products (20 percent), are also taxed quite heavily. The government's total revenue stood at US$1 billion in 1996.

INFRASTRUCTURE, POWER, AND COMMUNICATIONS

According to the U.S. Department of State's *Country Commercial Guide 2000,* Ethiopia's surface and transport **infrastructure** is exceedingly poor and underdeveloped. Indeed, the country has the lowest road density in the world, and only 13.3 percent of all roads are paved (1999 est.). There are few interconnecting links between nearby regions and large parts of the country are isolated and dependent upon pack animals for transportation. The main highway route is from Addis Ababa to the port of Djibouti, which Ethiopia uses extensively since it is a landlocked country without ports and harbors of its own. The only train network consists of the 681-kilometer (423-mile) long segment of the century old Addis Ababa-Djibouti railroad.

Communications

Country	Newspapers	Radios	TV Sets[a]	Cable subscribers[a]	Mobile Phones[a]	Fax Machines[a]	Personal Computers[a]	Internet Hosts[b]	Internet Users[b]
	1996	1997	1998	1998	1998	1998	1998	1999	1999
Ethiopia	1	195	5	N/A	0	0.0	N/A	0.01	8
United States	215	2,146	847	244.3	256	78.4	458.6	1,508.77	74,100
Dem. Rep. of Congo	3	375	135	N/A	0	N/A	N/A	0.00	1
Eritrea	N/A	91	14	N/A	0	0.4	N/A	0.01	1

[a]Data are from International Telecommunication Union, *World Telecommunication Development Report 1999* and are per 1,000 people.

[b]Data are from the Internet Software Consortium (http://www.isc.org) and are per 10,000 people.

SOURCE: World Bank. *World Development Indicators 2000.*

Since May 1998, Ethiopia has expended considerable effort to repair and maintain the railroad lines. Moreover, with the help of various donors, including the World Bank, the European Union (EU), and the African Development Bank (ADB), the government has implemented a US$3.9 billion Road Sector Development Plan designed to expand the road network by 80 percent for 2007. In 1998, the World Bank approved a US$309 million loan to be used for the project, a welcome contribution even though the loan will contribute significantly to Ethiopia's overall debt.

As for air transport, there are a total of 85 airports in Ethiopia, 11 of which have paved runways. All passenger and cargo flights are provided by Ethiopian airlines. The airlines' international services link the country with 43 cities on 3 continents, while domestic services link 38 airfields and 21 landing strips with Addis Ababa.

The government-owned Ethiopian Telecommunications Corporation (ETC) provides the population with telephone services. However, with only 3.1 telephone mainlines per 1,000 people, very few Ethiopians actually have telephone access (1999 est.). The situation compares unfavorably with most other sub-Saharan African nations, to say nothing of the wealthier industrialized nations of the world. In the United States, for example, there are 640 phone lines per 1,000 people (1996 est.).

Almost 90 percent of Ethiopia's electricity is derived from hydropower, which is exclusively provided by the parastatal Ethiopian Electric Power Corporation. In 1999, the country's total electric capacity was 400 megawatts. Over the next several years, the government plans on tripling this capacity to reach 1,200 megawatts. Although doing so would satisfy current electrical needs, Ethiopia has an untapped natural potential to generate over 30,000 megawatts of hydroelectric power. Ethiopia neither exports nor imports electricity, though it does heavily import oil.

ECONOMIC SECTORS

Like most of the countries of the African continent, Ethiopia's economy is dominated by agricultural production. For many similar countries, this dominance is the direct result of the colonial period, which encouraged policies of agricultural exportation at the expense of industrial development. African territories were forced to export primary crops to their colonizing countries and to import higher **value-added** manufactured commodities. For Ethiopia, however, which was never a European colony, the agricultural predominance is in part a historical legacy of the feudalistic policies that prevailed throughout most of 20th century. These policies consisted of onerous (oppressive) obligations on the part of the peasantry, who were expected to provide high taxes and

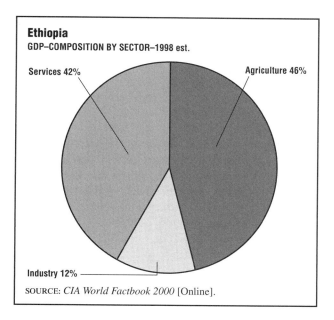

Ethiopia
GDP–COMPOSITION BY SECTOR–1998 est.

Services 42%
Agriculture 46%
Industry 12%

SOURCE: *CIA World Factbook 2000* [Online].

agricultural surplus to sustain the livelihoods of the ruling classes (consisting of the royal family, government officials, and lords and nobles). In this system, which lasted until the mid-1970s, the government was more concerned with maintaining the rule of the status quo (the existing order) than in fostering industrial development, which resulted in the foreign domination of industry.

Industry still remains a relatively small aspect of the Ethiopian economy, though there is potential for growth in both manufacturing and mining. The service sector, which has become extremely important in terms

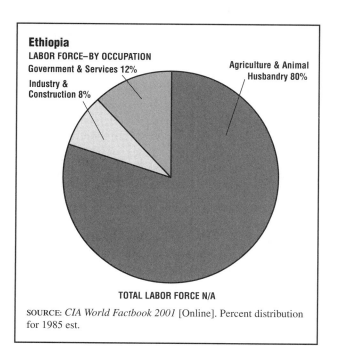

Ethiopia
LABOR FORCE–BY OCCUPATION
Government & Services 12%
Industry & Construction 8%
Agriculture & Animal Husbandry 80%

TOTAL LABOR FORCE N/A

SOURCE: *CIA World Factbook 2001* [Online]. Percent distribution for 1985 est.

of contribution to the **gross domestic product** (GDP), is characterized by a strong financial system. Tourism is one area of the service sector that is currently marginal, though there is significant potential for commercial development.

AGRICULTURE

Agriculture, which constituted 46 percent of GDP and more than 80 percent of exports in 1998, is by far the most important economic activity in the Ethiopian economy (1998 est.). An estimated 85 percent of the population are engaged in agricultural production. Important agricultural exports include coffee, hides and skins (leather products), pulses, oilseeds, beeswax, and, increasingly, tea. Domestically, meat and dairy production play an integral role for subsistence purposes.

Socialist agricultural reforms conducted by the Derg included land reforms that led to relatively equitable patterns of land tenure. The state maintained complete ownership of land, and state marketing boards were created with **monopolistic** rights to purchase and sell agricultural commodities. Currently, the government retains the right of ultimate land ownership in the agricultural sector, though most marketing boards have been abolished. While marketing boards enabled farmers to sell their crops to the highest bidder, they also required the dissolution of minimum prices for agricultural commodities. Since the government normally purchased agricultural commodities at low prices, however, the abolition of marketing boards may prove to be a positive development.

With 25 percent of all Ethiopians—approximately 15 million people—gaining their livelihoods from coffee production, the coffee sector is the most important agricultural activity. According to the U.S. Central Intelligence Agency *World Factbook 2000,* coffee production, Ethiopia's largest source of foreign exchange, contributed US$267 million to the economy in 1999, with export volumes equaling 105,000 metric tons. Coffee has long held a central role in Ethiopia's export economy and, as early as the mid-1970s, about 55 percent of the nation's total export earnings derived from coffee exports. This percentage share remained more or less constant until the mid-1990s, when it increased to an average of 63 percent of total export earnings between 1995 to 1998.

With the export economy so heavily dependent upon the exportation of a single crop, the Ethiopian economy is structured into a precarious (insecure and dangerous) position. If annual production declines as a result of a bad harvest (due to natural factors, such as drought—a constant threat), export earnings will suffer considerably, exacerbating (making worse) the country's already negative balance of trade. Similarly, if all coffee producing countries produce large amounts of coffee in a given year—resulting in an excessive supply—international prices for coffee will decline and Ethiopia's export economy will accordingly suffer. Such was the case in 1998, when a **glut** in the world supply of coffee reduced Ethiopia's coffee earnings by 22 percent from the previous year.

With 75 million heads of livestock, Ethiopia has the largest concentration of livestock on the African continent. According to the *Country Commercial Guide 2000,* however, it is difficult to calculate the cattle sector's exact value, since a substantial amount of meat and dairy production is for subsistence consumption. In certain regions, such as the highlands, livestock is utilized only to support farming. Still, hides and leather products are Ethiopia's second most important export, though the *Commercial Guide* states that the sector's huge potential remains largely untapped, as a result of weather conditions (drought), diseases, and the lack of a coherent government plan for the development of the sector. In 1996, Ethiopia produced 8,500 metric tons of leather and leather products for exportation, thereby earning a total of US$6.5 million.

Ethiopia is also the continent's leading producer and exporter of beeswax and honey. The country has approximately 7 million bee colonies. Other important agricultural activities include tea production, which has reached approximately 4,000 metric tons of output in recent years, and cotton and sugar production. Moreover, there are opportunities for expanding cultivation and export of dried fruits, cut flowers, and canned vegetable products.

While the agricultural export economy is constantly subjected to the caprices (whims) of the weather, so too is agricultural production geared towards domestic consumption. In 1992, for example, IMF statistics indicate that Ethiopia produced 51,850 quintals of cereals, mostly for domestic consumption, whereas the following year the cereals output dropped to 47,404 quintals—a decline of 8.6 percent. The decrease was largely the result of drought. The fact that Ethiopia has an extremely poor infrastructure for agricultural production does not help the matter. Though there is the potential for Ethiopia to become self-sufficient in grain production, the country must currently continue to import grains in addition to receiving food aid in order to feed the population.

Like many African countries, Ethiopia confronts several environmental issues that are particularly problematic for the agricultural sector of the economy. Such issues include deforestation (depletion of forests), overgrazing (depletion of pastures), soil erosion (depletion of quality soil), and **desertification** (extensive drying of the land). Since only 12 percent of all Ethiopian land is arable, 1 percent is used for permanent crops, and 40 percent is comprised of permanent pastures, it is essential for Ethiopia to address these environmental problems in order to maintain the land so fundamental for agricultural activities. Moreover, according to Girma Kebbede, the author of *The State and Development in Ethiopia,* it is precisely these environmental problems—rather than just the shifting weather patterns—which contribute primarily to the chronic famines that so frequently plague the country. Quite simply, limited arable land as a result of soil erosion and other environmental difficulties mean that in times of drought, there are very few available methods to prevent widespread famine.

INDUSTRY

Ethiopian industry, including both mining and manufacturing, constitutes approximately 12 percent of the GDP, while providing employment for 8 percent of the country's labor force (1998 est.). Under the Derg regime, almost all of the major industries were owned exclusively by the state. With a marginal average annual growth rate of 3.8 percent between 1980 and 1987, the state's policies of industrial control did not fare well. According to Kebbede, the failure of such policies can be attributed to "bureaucratic mismanagement, inefficiency, and corruption." State bureaucracies were costly and wasteful because they were not held responsible to any section of the society and because political and ideological questions took precedence over questions of efficiency or practicality. At the same time, however, one must remember that for many impoverished African countries fearful of foreign domination and eager to create more or less equitable societies, state control of industry seemed to be the most reasonable form of economic organization throughout the 1960s and 1970s. The country's first democratic government, formed in the early 1990s, made privatization of Ethiopia's industrial sector a major objective to promote economic growth, but progress remained slow at the beginning of 2000.

MINING. Regarding the exploitation of natural resources, gold, marble, limestone, and small amounts of tantalum are the major minerals mined in Ethiopia. Of these minerals, gold, which provided US$12.5 million to the economy in 1996, is the most significant contributor to export earnings. Gold mining output has oscillated (wavered) considerably throughout the 1990s, fluctuating, for example, from 3,500 metric tons in 1992 to 1,800 metric tons in 1994 and 5,100 metric tons in 1996. Traditionally, the mining industry, which remains under state domination, has played a marginal role in Ethiopia's economy. Resources with potential for future commercial development include potash (recently found in large deposits), natural gas, iron ore, and possibly coal and geothermal energy.

MANUFACTURING. Manufacturing as a percentage of the GDP only marginally increased throughout the 1990s.

In 1992, for example, manufacturing constituted 3.9 percent of the GDP, whereas its percentage share had slightly increased to 4.3 percent by 1998.

The manufacturing sector of the Ethiopian economy produces construction materials, metal, and chemical goods, in addition to basic **consumer goods** such as food, beverages, clothing, and textiles. Despite massive privatization campaigns, the industrial sector remained dominated by the state, with 150 public (state) enterprises accounting for more than 90 percent of the entire sector's value in 1999. Production by state-owned enterprises is centered on food and beverages, textiles, clothing, leather products, tobacco, rubber, plastic and cement. In 1999, there were also 165 **private sector** manufacturing firms involved in producing goods such as bakery products, textiles, footwear, and furniture.

Though certain areas of manufacturing are now open to participation by foreigners with permanent residence status as a result of legislation passed in 1998, still other areas, such as garment factories, are restricted from foreign participation. In 1998, there were a total of 163 foreign investment projects with total projected capital investment of US$1.2 billion. Of these projects, 90 were wholly foreign owned while 73 were **joint ventures** with local partners. Major foreign investors include the United States, with investments worth US$9 million in 1999, as well as Saudi Arabia, South Korea, Kuwait, and Italy. U.S.-based manufacturing companies that have a significant presence in Ethiopia include Pepsi-Cola, Coca-Cola, Caterpillar, General Motors, Xerox, and John Deere. Numerous other U.S. firms also operate in Ethiopia, albeit in different sectors of the economy.

SERVICES

Accounting for 42 percent of the GDP, services are an extremely important component of Ethiopia's economy (1998 est.). At the same time, however, with only 12 percent of the labor force engaged in services and government employment, a relatively small percentage of Ethiopians work in the service sector. The large contribution of services to the GDP stems mostly from the government and the strong financial sector.

TOURISM. According to the aforementioned *Country Commercial Guide 2000,* the tourism industry in Ethiopia is negligible, though there is great potential for commercial development. With many unique indigenous plant, bird, and mammal species, the country has an enormous diversity of wildlife, exotic landscapes, and architectural ruins of prehistoric, historical, and religious significance. As such, Ethiopia is an ideal location for foreign and local visitors embarking upon historic, cultural, or **ecotourism** expeditions.

FINANCIAL SERVICES. Following the 1974 revolution, the banking and financial sector in general came under the domination of the state. In 1994, legislation was passed that permitted the establishment of private banks and insurance companies but prohibited foreign ownership of such companies.

Ethiopia's central bank, the National Bank of Ethiopia (NBE), seeks to foster monetary stability and a sound financial system by maintaining credit and exchange conditions perceived to be conducive to the balanced growth of the economy. All transactions in foreign exchange must be carried out through authorized dealers under the control of the NBE. The Commercial Bank of Ethiopia (CBE), whose assets totaled over US$3 billion in 1996, is a government-owned bank with 167 branches in operation and over US$1.5 billion on deposit (1996 est.). The CBE, the largest bank in Ethiopia, offers credit to investors on market terms, though the 100 percent collateral requirement limits the ability of small entrepreneurs with limited resources to capitalize upon business opportunities.

Ethiopia's first private bank, Awash, commenced operations in 1994 and now boasts 6 branches in Addis Ababa and 2 in the Oromiya Regional State. In addition to Awash, 5 other private banks now operate in Ethiopia, including Dashen Bank (with a total of 12 branches), the Bank of Abyssinia (2 branches), and Wegagen Bank (5 branches). The 2 newest private banks in operation are NIB International and United Bank. Since the banking and financial reforms of 1994, there are also 7 private insurance companies in operation—United, Africa, Nile, Nyala, Awash, National, and Global. Ethiopia does not have a securities market, although the U.S. Department of State reported that a private sector initiative to establish a mechanism for buying and selling company shares was expected to begin by the year 2000.

RETAIL. Ethiopia's retail sector consists mostly of small shops, local markets, and roadside stands, many of which are part of the **informal sector** of the economy, which remains unregulated and untaxed. Investment legislation passed in September 1998 also allows foreigners with permanent resident status to participate in retail and wholesale trade.

INTERNATIONAL TRADE

Ethiopia has chronically run a negative **balance of payments**, rendering the country highly dependent upon foreign aid and loans to finance imports. Throughout the 1990s, the situation has shown little sign of improvement. Indeed, the balance of trade deficit was US$829.4 million in 1992 and—despite a brief amelioration in 1994 when the deficit declined to US$609.5 million—it remained approximately the same in 1998, when it

Trade (expressed in billions of US$): Ethiopia		
	Exports	Imports
1975	.240	.313
1980	.425	.716
1985	.333	.993
1990	.298	1.081
1995	.423	1.145
1998	.560	N/A

SOURCE: International Monetary Fund. *International Financial Statistics Yearbook 1999.*

reached US$830.0 million. The constant deficit ensures Ethiopia's perpetual indebtedness to the commercial banks of the rich industrial countries and international financial institutions, such as the IMF, the World Bank, and the ADB. In 1997, Ethiopia's total external debt stood at US$10 billion.

Ethiopia's major exports include coffee, gold, leather products, beeswax, canned vegetables, tea, sugar, cotton, and oilseeds. Purchasing approximately 22 percent of Ethiopia's exports in 1997, Germany is Ethiopia's largest trading partner. Along with many other countries of EU—such as Italy, France, and the United Kingdom—Germany has steadily increased its quantity of Ethiopian imports. In 1992, for instance, the countries of the EU purchased approximately Br203.3 million worth of Ethiopian exports, whereas this figure increased dramatically to Br1,351.5 million in 1996. Similarly, the United States has increased its quantity of Ethiopian imports from Br19.6 million in 1992 to Br169.9 million in 1996. This major increase in trade with the Western countries can be explained primarily by the fall of the Derg and the subsequent **liberalization** policies pursued by the EPRDF. Other major importers of Ethiopian products include Saudi Arabia, China, and Japan, the latter of which purchased 12 percent of all Ethiopian exports in 1997. Ethiopia's largest trading partner in Africa is Djibouti, a neighboring country through which Ethiopia must conduct all of its importing and exporting since Ethiopia is landlocked and thus lacks a port of its own.

Ethiopia's major imports include food and live animals, petroleum and petroleum products, chemicals, machinery, civil and military aircraft, transport and industrial capital goods, agricultural machinery and equipment, and motor vehicles. Ethiopia's imports have followed the same pattern as its exports in the 1990s, with the percentage of imports from the countries of the EU and the United States steadily increasing. In 1991, imports worth Br364.7 million were purchased from the countries of the EU, while this figure increased to Br2,006.7 million in 1995. In the same year, a similar value (Br2,300.7 million) of imports came from various countries of Asia and the Middle East, including Japan, Saudi Arabia, and China. With imports to Ethiopia equaling Br146.8 million in 1995, Djibouti is Ethiopia's number-one regional exporter, while Kenya is second.

Ethiopia's balance of trade deficit can be largely explained by the unequal terms of trade between agricultural commodities (the country's major exports) and capital goods (Ethiopia's major imports). International markets accord a higher price to commodities that are manufactured—or "value-added"—than to those that are in their raw form. Recognizing the uneven terms of international trade, many countries, including Ethiopia, pursued policies of protectionism throughout the 1960s and 1970s to develop national industrial capacity or **import-substitution**. In many cases, where the state pursued policies of complete industrial control, they failed miserably. For others, however, such as the economies of Southeast Asia, the policies were more successful, enabling these countries to eventually partake in liberalized free trade at the global level.

Ethiopia's policies of import substitution were largely disastrous. This does not mean, however, that the country should necessarily abandon all forms of protection in favor of free trade, which is theoretically designed to increase the efficiency of national industries through competition with the outside world. Instead, such liberalization may lead to the inability of Ethiopian industries to compete at all, thereby further assuring the dominance of the agricultural sector. To date, Ethiopia has proceeded with the liberalization process relatively cautiously, maintaining an average **tariff** rate of approximately 20 percent (1997 est.), though there are plans to reduce this figure to 17 to 18 percent. Ethiopia is considering application to the World Trade Organization (WTO), and it is already a member of the Common Market for Eastern and Southern Africa (COMESA). Regional trading arrangements such as the latter may offer member countries the opportunity to profit from increased trade while competing from a more level playing field. There has been little trade increase between the members of COMESA, however.

MONEY

Prior to 1993, the official rate of the Ethiopian birr was pegged (fixed) to the U.S. dollar at US$1:Br5.000. Since a pegged **exchange rate** does not necessarily represent a currency's true market value, the EPRDF replaced the **fixed exchange rate** system with a **floating exchange rate** system. The value of the birr is thus determined in an inter-bank market where the national bank sells foreign currency to private banks, the Commercial Bank of Ethiopia, and large corporations at weekly auc-

Exchange rates: Ethiopia	
birr (Br) per US$1	
Dec 2000	8.3140
2000	8.3140
1999	8.1340
1998	7.5030
1997	6.8640
1996	6.4260

Note: Since May 1993, the birr market rate has been determined in an interbank market supported by weekly wholesale auction.

SOURCE: CIA *World Factbook 2001* [ONLINE].

tions. In this way, the official exchange rate is auction-determined. The purchasers of foreign exchange, in turn, are free to establish their own exchange rates.

The value of the birr in relation to the U.S. dollar has steadily depreciated since the implementation of the floating exchange system. In 1995, for instance, the exchange rate was set at US$1:Br6.3200 while, 3 years later in 1998, the rate had decreased to US$1:Br7.5030. As of January 2000, the rate was determined at US$1:Br8.2.

According to the *Country Commercial Guide 2000,* the Ethiopian currency has remained relatively stable, especially in comparison to the currencies of most other sub-Saharan African nations, as a result of conservative **monetary policies** and considerable **foreign exchange reserves**. Nonetheless, the steady depreciation of the currency means that it takes a growing amount of Ethiopian birr to purchase imports from abroad. While this can help the export economy, since fewer U.S. dollars are needed to purchase Ethiopian exports, it also renders valuable imports, such as food for the population, more expensive. In 1998, incidentally, food imports constituted 14 percent of all merchandise imports.

POVERTY AND WEALTH

Under the rule of Haile Selassie, Ethiopian society was characterized by gross inequality between the largely aristocratic elite—consisting of landowners, lords, nobles, the royal family, government officials, and elements of the clergy—and the impoverished peasantry. Indeed, according to Kebbede, the massive famines of the 1960s could have been avoided if the obligations on the part of the peasantry towards the elite (in terms of providing agricultural produce) had not been so oppressive. The Derg regime subsequently abolished feudal obligations and titles of privilege, even going to the extreme of executing numerous members of the high-ranking nobility (the so-called "red terror"). Despite the egalitarian rhetoric of the Derg, however, high-ranking government officials

GDP per Capita (US$)

Country	1975	1980	1985	1990	1998
Ethiopia	N/A	N/A	91	100	110
United States	19,364	21,529	23,200	25,363	29,683
Dem. Rep. of Congo	392	313	293	247	127
Eritrea	N/A	N/A	N/A	N/A	175

SOURCE: United Nations. *Human Development Report 2000; Trends in human development and per capita income.*

retained privileged economic positions. Today, Ethiopia's elite continues to consist of government officials, in addition to a small upper class of highly skilled managers and professionals.

Like all the countries of Sub-Saharan Africa, poverty is rampant in Ethiopia. The UNDP's Human Development Index (HDI) listings, which arranges countries according to their overall level of human development, ranks Ethiopia 171st out of a total of 174 nations. The HDI is a composite index (one that assesses more than one variable) that measures life expectance at birth, adult literacy rate, school enrollment ratio, and the **GDP per capita**. It is indicative of a country's general social and economic well-being. As such, Ethiopia's HDI ranking demonstrates that the country is one of the poorest and least developed in the world. Fortunately, the situation has shown small signs of improvement, and the Ethiopian HDI score increased from a dismal 0.265 in 1985 to a slightly better 0.309 in 1998 (the highest possible rank is 1.0, and Canada—the highest ranking HDI country—scored 0.935 in 1998).

The Ethiopian government spends relatively little on education and health. In 1998, for example, public expenditure on health and education as percentages of the GDP equaled 1.6 percent and 4.0 percent respectively. Though these expenditures displayed marginal increases,

Distribution of Income or Consumption by Percentage Share: Ethiopia

Lowest 10%	3.0
Lowest 20%	7.1
Second 20%	10.9
Third 20%	14.5
Fourth 20%	19.8
Highest 20%	47.7
Highest 10%	33.7

Survey year: 1995
Note: This information refers to expenditure shares by percentiles of the population and is ranked by per capita expenditure.

SOURCE: *2000 World Development Indicators* [CD-ROM].

they are nowhere near the percentage level of industrialized countries, such as the United States, which spent 5.4 percent of the GDP on education and 6.5 percent on health in 1998. Moreover, the Ethiopian government spends a significant amount on military expenditure, largely as a result of the border war with Eritrea, though such expenses have decreased substantially from 10.4 percent of the GDP in 1990 to 3.8 percent in 1998. The fact that the Ethiopian government must continually service a large debt does not help the social expenditure cause.

The vast majority of Ethiopians spend their meager incomes on the basic necessities of life, such as food, rents, clothing, fuel, and transportation. Very little is spent on entertainment and recreation, which are considered luxuries for those that live in considerable poverty. To make matters worse, in the past 10 years, the increase in the GNP per capita has been grossly outweighed by mounting inflation, which means that Ethiopians are having an increasingly difficult time purchasing the commodities essential for human existence. The UNDP estimates that the annual growth rate in GNP per capita between 1990 to 1998 was 1.0 percent, while the average annual rate of inflation during the same period was 9.7 percent.

WORKING CONDITIONS

Since 85 percent of Ethiopia's workforce engages in **subsistence farming** in the countryside, only a very small percentage of the population is involved in wage labor. The Ethiopian constitution and the 1993 labor law provide wage laborers with the right to form and belong to unions, though employees of the civil and security services (where most wage earners work), judges, and prosecutors are denied these rights. The Confederation of Ethiopian Trade Unions (CETU), established after the fall of the Derg regime in 1993, includes 9 federations organized by industrial and service sector. There is no requirement that unions belong to the CETU. Approximately 250,000 Ethiopian workers are unionized.

Workers who provide an "essential service," such as those who work in air transport, railways, bus service, police and fire services, post and telecommunications, banks, and pharmacies, are denied the right to strike. Other workers are granted the right to strike, though the unions involved must follow certain detailed procedures before doing so. The same applies for the right of an employer to lock out workers. Both sides must make efforts at reconciliation and provide at least 10 days notice to the government before the commencement of an action.

The minimum age for wage labor is 14 years, and various laws protect children between the ages of 14 to 18 years, including restrictions that they may not work more than 7 hours per day. The U.S. Department of State maintains that there are some efforts to enforce such regulations within the formal industrial sector, though there are large numbers of children of all ages that grow and harvest crops outside government regulatory control in the countryside or work as street peddlers in the cities. The harsh reality is that many impoverished parents depend on the work contributions of their children to ensure the survival of the household.

While there is no minimum wage in the private sector, a minimum wage in the **public sector** has been in effect since 1985. According to the U.S. Department of State, however, the minimum wage in the public sector, which equaled about US$16 per month in 1996, is insufficient to provide a decent standard of living for a worker and family. The Office of the Study of Wages and Other Remunerations, for instance, reports that a family of 5 requires a monthly income of US$61 in Ethiopia. Even with 2 minimum wage earners, therefore, a family receives only about half the income needed for adequate subsistence. These factors result in the family's reliance upon the children to contribute to the household income.

Most employees in Ethiopia work a 40-hour week, and the government, industry, and unions negotiate occupational health and safety standards. The Inspection Department of the Ministry of Labor and Social Affairs cannot enforce these standards effectively, however, due to a lack of human and financial resources.

COUNTRY HISTORY AND ECONOMIC DEVELOPMENT

5TH CENTURY B.C. Ethiopia becomes one of the first countries in Africa. Ethiopia is described by the Greek historian Herodotus, and the Old Testament records a visit by the Ethiopian Queen of Sheba to Jerusalem.

4TH CENTURY. Missionaries from Syria and Egypt introduce Christianity to the country.

1493. The Portuguese establish contact with Ethiopia, prompting a lengthy conflict between Roman Catholic converts and adherents of Ethiopian Coptic Christianity.

1630s. All foreign missionaries are expelled from Ethiopia, and the country subsequently remains isolated from the West until the mid-19th century.

MID-19TH CENTURY. Under the Emperors Theodore (1855–68), Johannes IV (1872–89), and Menelik II (1889–1913), Ethiopia becomes a modern state characterized by political centralization.

1930. Adopting the throne name Haile Selassie, Ras Tafari Makonnen is crowned emperor, commencing a lengthy period of rule that witnesses the perpetuation of a quasi-feudal system, albeit with marginal reforms.

1936–42. The Italians occupy Ethiopia despite Selassie's plea to the League of Nations for intervention. The Italians are expelled by British and Ethiopian forces, and Selassie returns to rule after a period of forced exile.

1974. Following a period of civil unrest, Selassie is deposed, and a military administrative council known as the Derg declares a military dictatorship supposedly based on socialist principles. The Derg, which pursues abhorrent policies of political repression (the "red terror"), nationalizes the land and most of the economy.

1991. Ethnic insurrection, a collapsed economy, and recalcitrant (rebellious) students cause the final collapse of the Derg regime. The Ethiopian People's Revolutionary Democratic Front (EPRDF) is democratically voted into office.

1993. Eritrea establishes its independence under a UN-monitored referendum. Ethiopia and Eritrea commence a border war that continues to restrain the development of both countries.

FUTURE TRENDS

Despite the pervasive poverty, marginal growth rates, and tumultuous political and economic history of Ethiopia, there are several signs indicative of hope and improvement. For the first time in the country's history, for instance, an effective democracy has been institutionalized. While this will most certainly not solve Ethiopia's deeply embedded economic difficulties overnight, it is, if nothing else, a huge step forward in the direction of the establishment of a responsive and stable government. Moreover, the economy has experienced an unprecedented degree of stability since the mid-1990s, though this is, admittedly, counterbalanced by a precarious agricultural dependence and a chronic balance of payments deficit.

While there are undeniably positive developments, there remain severe impediments that prevent the assurance of a sustained path towards economic development. Perhaps the most significant question that the Ethiopian government must address is the specific policy framework that must be implemented over an extended period of time to surmount these impediments. Privatization and the absolute rule of the free market currently reign supreme in the international neo-**liberal economic** environment. Rather than accepting the virtues of neo-liberal ideology at face value, however, Ethiopia must adopt policies that are relevant to its particular circumstances. To its credit, this is precisely what the EPRDF seem to be doing. Though the government has pursued policies of trade liberalization, they have not promoted unobstructed free trade. Similarly, while many state-owned enterprises have been privatized, the government retains a considerable role in certain areas of the economy, such as telecommunications, infrastructure provision, and electricity. Moreover, foreign dominance, which can be nationally unprofitable, has been entirely excluded from certain segments of the economy, such as the finance sector. The EPRDF must continue along this path, withstanding international pressure to create a complete free market economy that may not be appropriate at this stage of Ethiopia's economic development.

DEPENDENCIES

Ethiopia has no territories or colonies.

BIBLIOGRAPHY

Araia, Ghelawdewos. *Ethiopia: The Political Economy of Transition.* Lanham, Maryland: University Press of America, 1995.

Hansson, Gote. *The Ethiopian Economy 1974–1994: Ethiopian Tikdem and After.* London: Routledge, 1995.

International Monetary Fund. "IMF Staff Country Report, Ethiopia: Statistical Appendix." <http://www.imf.org>. Accessed May 2001.

Kebbede, Girma. *The State and Development in Ethiopia.* New Jersey: Humanities Press, 1992.

United Nations Development Programme. *Human Development Report 2000.* New York: Oxford University Press, 2000.

U.S. Central Intelligence Agency. *World Factbook 2000.* <http://www.odci.gov/cia/publications/factbook/index.html>. Accessed May 2001.

U.S. Department of State. *Background Notes: Ethiopia.* <http://www.state.gov/www/background_notes/ethiopia_0398 _bgn.html>. Accessed May 2001.

U.S. Department of State. *FY 2000 Country Commercial Guide: Ethiopia.* <http://www.state.gov/www/about_state/business/com_guides/ 2000/africa/ethiopia00_08.html>. Accessed May 2001.

World Bank Group. *Ethiopia: Competitiveness Indicators.* <http://wbln0018.worldbank.org/psd/compete.nsf/1f22456200 75540d85256490005fb73a/74c17aa2249b1b70852564e40068d b3c>. Accessed May 2001.

—Neil Burron

GABON

Gabonese Republic
République Gabonaise

CAPITAL: Libreville.

MONETARY UNIT: Communauté Financière Africaine (CFA) franc. The CFA franc is tied to the French franc at an exchange rate of CFA Fr50 to Fr1. One CFA franc equals 100 centimes. There are coins of 5, 10, 50, 100, and 500 CFA francs, and notes of 500, 1,000, 2,000, 5,000, and 10,000 CFA francs.

CHIEF EXPORTS: Crude oil and natural gas, timber and wood products, manganese, uranium.

CHIEF IMPORTS: Machinery and equipment, foodstuffs, chemicals, petroleum products, construction materials.

GROSS DOMESTIC PRODUCT: US$7.9 billion (purchasing power parity, 1999 est.).

BALANCE OF TRADE: Exports: US$2.4 billion (f.o.b., 1999 est.). **Imports:** US$1.2 billion (f.o.b., 1999 est.).

COUNTRY OVERVIEW

LOCATION AND SIZE. The Gabonese Republic lies along the equator on the west coast of Africa with a border length of 2,551 kilometers (1,585 miles) and a coastline of 885 kilometers (550 miles). Gabon is bounded to the west by the Atlantic Ocean, to the north by Equatorial Guinea (350 kilometers/218 miles) and Cameroon (298 kilometers/185 miles), and to the east and south by the Republic of the Congo (1,903 kilometers/1,183 miles). The drainage basin is comprised of the westward flowing Ogooue River, together with several smaller coastal rivers such as the Nyanga and the Como. Gabon covers an area of 267,667 square kilometers (103,346 square miles), of which land comprises 257,667 square kilometers (99,484 square miles) and water occupies 10,000 square kilometers (3,861 square miles). Comparatively, the area occupied by Gabon is slightly smaller than the state of Colorado. It has a tropical climate, which is always hot and humid. The terrain is comprised of a narrow coastal plain, savannah grassland in the east and south, and a hilly interior. The major rural areas are found in Woleu Ntem in the north, where coffee and cocoa are the main **cash crops**, and around Lambaréné, located inland from the central coastal belt, where palm oil and coffee are important. The highest point is Mount Iboundji, which stands at a height of 1,575 meters (5,168 feet). The capital city of Libreville is located on the country's northwestern coast.

POPULATION. At the July 1993 census, the population of Gabon numbered 1,014,976 and in mid-1998 the United Nations (UN) estimated a total of 1,188,000, giving an average density of 4.4 inhabitants per square kilometer. The population estimate for 2000 was 1,208,436. The population growth rate was estimated at 1.08 percent in 2000, with a life expectancy at birth of 48.94 years for males and 51.26 years for females in the same year. The infant mortality rate was 96.3 deaths per 1,000 live births while the fertility rate was 3.73 births per woman. The birth rate (per 1,000 population) was 27.6 while the death rate was 16.83 in 2000. The slow population growth takes into account the effects of mortality due to AIDS. AIDS results in lower life expectancy, higher infant mortality and death rates, and a lower population growth rate than would be expected under normal conditions. The distribution of population by age and sex is also affected, with those in the sexually active age groups and women being more vulnerable to the disease.

The population is more urbanized than most of Africa, with 53 percent living in the towns in 1988. It is mostly a young population with only 6 percent above 65 years of age and over 33 percent below 15 years. The country's principal ethnic groups are the Fang (30 percent) and the Eshira (25 percent), who reside primarily in the north, followed by the Bapounou and Bateke. French is the official language.

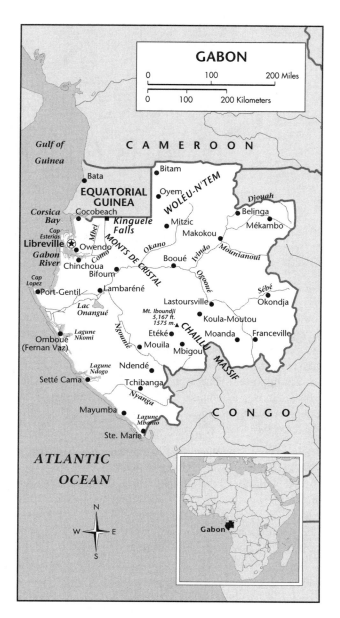

GABON

| 0 | 100 | 200 Miles |
| 0 | 100 | 200 Kilometers |

growth has fluctuated widely in recent decades. While growth in GDP averaged 9.5 percent per year between 1965 and 1980, the average growth rate declined to 0.8 percent from 1985 to 1990 following the collapse of the petroleum prices in 1986. When the Rabikonga oil fields were developed in the 1990s, however, there was some improvement, reaching an average growth rate of 3.2 percent per year from 1990 to 1997. But due to steeply falling petroleum prices and a downturn in Asian demand for timber, the economy contracted by approximately 4 percent in 1998 and only saw a modest recovery in 1999 with an estimated 2 percent rise in GDP.

The petroleum boom of the mid-1970s and the expectation that oil prices would remain high led to government investment spending and borrowing, which left the country with a heavy debt burden. Consequently, in the mid-1980s the government had to undertake a series of economic adjustment programs designed to reduce debt while promoting the development of non-petroleum activities. Programs of **privatization**, rationalization, and retrenchment (cutting expenses) of **public sector** enterprises were undertaken.

Progress was limited in the areas under reform and the non-petroleum economy failed to expand as hoped. However, in January 1994 the government adopted a program for economic recovery supported by the International Monetary Fund (IMF). The objectives of this program were broadly achieved by the end of 1998. A number of major privatizations have taken place (the power utility and railway companies, for example), while others pending include the telecommunication services and the national airline. Some significant tax reforms have been introduced, notably the extension of the **value-added tax** (VAT) to forestry companies, removal of tax exemptions, and introduction of an investment code consistent with IMF recommendations.

OVERVIEW OF ECONOMY

The combination of a small population and plentiful petroleum resources has given Gabon one of the highest incomes per capita in sub-Saharan Africa. The 1999 per capita **gross domestic product** (GDP) was a comfortable US$6,500. It therefore ranks as an upper middle-income country, a rarity among African nations.

Gabon's economy depended on timber and manganese until oil began to be exploited in significant quantities offshore in the early 1970s. The oil sector now accounts for 50 percent of GDP. Gabon continues to face fluctuating prices for its oil, timber, manganese, and uranium exports. The dominance of the petroleum sector is reflected in the economy's vulnerability to changes in world prices for this commodity, and the rate of economic

POLITICS, GOVERNMENT, AND TAXATION

Formerly part of French West Africa, Gabon was granted internal autonomy in 1958 and became fully independent on 17 August 1960. Leon M'Ba, president of the new republic, established Gabon as a one-party state by inviting the opposition to join the government. There was a coup in 1964, but M'Ba was restored by French troops. Following his death in November 1967, M'Ba was succeeded by his vice-president, Albert Bernard (later Omar) Bongo. Bongo organized a new ruling party, the Parti Democratique Gabonais (PDG), which became the sole legal party in 1968. Gabon enjoyed relative stability in the 1970s and joined the Organization of Petroleum Exporting Countries (OPEC) after the discovery of oil deposits. But in the early 1980s, social and political strains began to emerge led by the Mouvement pour le Redressement National (MORENA), a moderate opposition group. This group accused Bongo of corruption and personal extravagance and demanded restoration of political pluralism. But Bongo resisted and maintained the single-party system.

A series of strikes and demonstrations by students and workers in the early 1990s culminated in a constitutional amendment that led to the creation of a multiparty system and formation of an interim government. Bongo was elected president in 1990 and reelected in 1993 and 1998. Elections for the National Assembly were held in December 1996, and the PDG gained 89 of the 120 seats. At the Senate elections in early 1997, the PDG won 53 of the 91 seats.

The 1991 constitution provides for an executive president directly elected for a 5-year term (renewable only once). The head of government is the prime minister, who appoints the Council of Ministers. The **bicameral** legislature consists of the 120-member National Assembly and the 91-member Senate. Both houses are directly elected for 5-year terms. Local governments exist in each of Gabon's 9 provinces, and are administered by a governor appointed by the president. There are also 37 smaller divisions, or departments, each administered under a prefect.

Total government revenue in 1997 was US$1.565 billion. Of this, US$301 million was from international trade, with import **duties** contributing US$254 million. In addition, the government gains substantial royalties from the oil sector. Corporate and capital gains taxes are levied at 40 percent, but if companies make small profits or suffer losses, they are taxed at 1.1 percent of **turnover**. There is a withholding tax of 20 percent on dividends remitted overseas.

INFRASTRUCTURE, POWER, AND COMMUNICATIONS

Despite substantial investment in the Trans-Gabonais railway and foreign backing for road develop-

ment in the 1990s, the surface transportation system is still inadequate and inconsistent with Gabon's high per capita income level. Until 1979, there were no railways except for the cableway link between the Congo border and the Moanda Manganese Mine. The main rivers are navigable for only the last 80 to 160 kilometers (50 to 100 miles) of their course to the Atlantic Ocean. The road network is poorly developed and much of it is unusable during the rainy seasons. In 1996 there were an estimated 7,670 kilometers (4,766 miles) of roads, of which only some 634 kilometers (394 miles) were paved. The government's aim is to surface some 1,400 kilometers (870 miles) of the road network in the next few years, with an eventual target of 3,580 kilometers (2,225 miles).

By 1989 the railway line linking Libreville and Franceville, which is located in the southeast area of the country, was fully operational. The main port for petroleum exports is Port Gentil, which also handles logs (floated down the Ogooue River). Owendo, the principal mineral port, also handles timber. A third deepwater port operates at Mayumba, in the south.

Air transport plays an important role in the economy, particularly because of the dense forest that covers much of the country and makes other modes of transport impracticable. There are international airports at Libreville and Port-Gentil and scheduled internal services link these to a number of domestic airfields. Gabon has a total of 61 airports within its borders, 11 of which have paved runways. The national carrier, Air Gabon, is 80 percent state owned.

In 1997 there were 37,300 telephone lines, 4,000 cellular phone subscribers, 6,000 PCs, and 400 fax machines. The domestic telephone system combines the use of cable, microwave radio relay, radiotelephone communication stations, and a domestic satellite system with 12 earth stations. For international links it operates 3 Intelsat satellite earth stations. There were also 4 television broadcast stations in 1997. In 1998 there were approximately 400 Internet users and 1 Internet service provider.

Communications									
Country	Newspapers	Radios	TV Sets[a]	Cable subscribers[a]	Mobile Phones[a]	Fax Machines[a]	Personal Computers[a]	Internet Hosts[b]	Internet Users[b]
	1996	1997	1998	1998	1998	1998	1998	1999	1999
Gabon	29	183	55	N/A	8	0.4	8.6	0.02	3
United States	215	2,146	847	244.3	256	78.4	458.6	1,508.77	74,100
Nigeria	24	223	66	N/A	0	N/A	5.7	0.00	100
Cameroon	7	163	32	N/A	0	N/A	N/A	0.00	20

[a]Data are from International Telecommunication Union, *World Telecommunication Development Report 1999* and are per 1,000 people.

[b]Data are from the Internet Software Consortium (http://www.isc.org) and are per 10,000 people.

SOURCE: World Bank. *World Development Indicators 2000*.

There was a range of radio broadcast stations, with 6 AM, 7 FM, and 6 short-wave stations in 1998.

The installed capacity for electricity production was 1.02 billion kilowatt hours (kWh) in 1995. Power generation is both hydroelectric and thermal (gas fired), with 72 percent of total capacity hydroelectric. There are proven crude petroleum reserves estimated in 1997 at 1.34 billion barrels. Production in 1996 was 135 million barrels. Natural gas production in 1995 was 102 million cubic meters.

ECONOMIC SECTORS

Agriculture (including forestry and fishing) contributed an estimated 10 percent of GDP in 1999, and employed about 41 percent of the **labor force**. The forestry sector alone accounted for an estimated 3 percent of GDP in 1997 and engaged an estimated 15 percent of the working population in 1991. The exploitation of Gabon's forests (which covers about 75 percent of the land area) is a principal economic activity. Although Gabon's territorial waters contain important fishing resources, their commercial exploitation is minimal.

Industry (including mining, manufacturing, construction, electricity, and water) contributed an estimated 60 percent of GDP in 1999, and about 12 percent of the working population were employed in the sector. Industrial GDP increased at an average annual rate of 2.7 percent from 1990 to 1997. Mining alone (including oil) accounted for an estimated 46 percent of GDP in 1997. Gabon is among the world's foremost producers and exporters of manganese. Gabon's manufacturing sector is relatively small, accounting for an estimated 6 percent of GDP in 1997. A substantial part of this is represented by

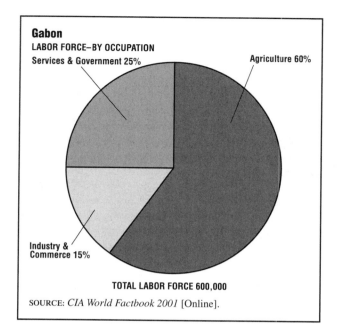

Gabon
LABOR FORCE–BY OCCUPATION
Services & Government 25%
Agriculture 60%
Industry & Commerce 15%
TOTAL LABOR FORCE 600,000
SOURCE: *CIA World Factbook 2001* [Online].

oil refining and timber-processing. Electricity and water are produced and distributed by the Societe d'Energie et d'Eau du Gabon (SEEG).

Services engaged 47 percent of the economically active population and provided an estimated 30 percent of GDP in 1999. The GDP of the service sector increased at an average annual rate of 3.3 percent over the period from 1990 to 1997.

AGRICULTURE

Owing to the density of the tropical rain forest, only a small proportion of land area is suitable for agricultural activity and only 2 percent is estimated to be under cultivation. With over 50 percent of the population living in towns and with a poor road **infrastructure**, the contribution to GDP of the agriculture, forestry, and fishing sector is very modest by African standards at approximately 10 percent in the 1990s. The country lacks self-sufficiency in staple crops and over half of food requirements must be imported. Cocoa, coffee, palm oil, and rubber are cultivated for export. The principal subsistence crops are plantains, cassava, and maize. Coffee and cocoa were once relatively significant cash crops with a small amount available for export, but outputs for both have been falling since the 1980s.

Animal husbandry was for many decades hindered by the prevalence of the tsetse fly (a bloodsucking fly that causes disease in cattle), until the first tsetse-resistant cattle were imported in 1980. Livestock numbers have since risen, with 1998 estimates standing at 39,000 head of cattle, 208,000 pigs, 259,000 sheep, and 24,000 goats. The Societe Gabonaise de Developpement d'Ellevage (an

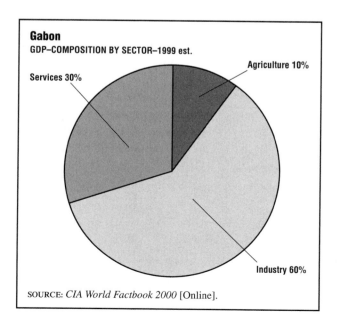

Gabon
GDP–COMPOSITION BY SECTOR–1999 est.
Services 30%
Agriculture 10%
Industry 60%
SOURCE: *CIA World Factbook 2000* [Online].

offshoot of AgroGabon) manages 3 cattle ranches covering 14,000 hectares (34,595 acres). Poultry farming is mainly on a **smallholder** basis. The fishing catch, at 45,000 metric tons, falls well below total demand. Industrial fleets account for about 25 percent of the catch, and about half of the total catch comes from marine waters.

FORESTRY. The exploitation of Gabon's forests (which cover some 85 percent of the land area) is a principal economic activity and the second leading source of exports, with 14 percent, behind petroleum. According to the U.S. State Department, commercial wood reserves cover 50 million acres and contain 400 million cubic meters of wood. Production levels reached 2.77 million cubic meters of lumber in 1997, declined in 1998 thanks to the Asian financial crisis, and rebounded again in 1999. The sector is the second largest employer, behind the government, and there is some potential for further growth. The major problem facing the industry is the fact that most forestry exports are in raw lumber. **Value-added** processing occurs abroad. Should foreign investment allow for more milling and processing of logs at home, the industrial sector would be boosted substantially.

INDUSTRY

Industry is the largest of the 3 major sectors in terms of GDP, but the smallest in terms of employment. This sector provides its employees with the highest average incomes.

OIL AND MINING. Oil and its related industries has been the main source of Gabon's economic growth since the 1970s. In 1997, the petroleum industry was still the dominant sector of the economy, contributing 42.5 percent of GDP when all subsidiary industries are factored in. Petroleum and petroleum products accounted for an estimated 77 percent of total export earnings. Oil reserves are declining, however, and there have been no major new discoveries in recent years.

Mining holds great potential for further economic growth. Gabon is one of the largest producers and exporters of manganese in the world. Gabon holds 25 percent of the world's manganese reserves, and the main manganese mining operation, COMILOG, produces about 2.5 million metric tons a year of finished ore. Uranium has also been a major source of export income, though uranium reserves are nearly depleted. There is potential for the mining of phosphates, niobium, iron, gold, and diamonds; foreign investment is needed for these mineral deposits to prove profitable.

MANUFACTURING. The manufacturing sector contributed an estimated 6 percent of GDP in 1997. The principal activities are the refining of petroleum and processing of other minerals, the preparation of timber, and other agro-industrial processes. The chemical industry is also significant. Electric energy is derived principally from hydroelectric installations. Imports of fuel and energy comprised an estimated 21 percent of the total value of imports.

SERVICES

The services sector is the biggest employer in Gabon, with the government being the single largest employer in the nation, and incomes earned in this sector are significantly higher than average. The mineral and forestry sectors drive the economy, and services expand to support these activities. The production of the service sector increased at an average annual rate of 3.3 percent from 1990 to 1997. Due to the poor infrastructure and the dense forests, tourism is limited.

The telecommunications sector has been identified by the U.S. State Department as a prime area for growth. The **parastatal** Office des Postes et Telecommunications du Gabon (OPT), which has a **monopoly** on telecommunications services in the country, is slated for privatization. This development is expected to encourage foreign investment and create jobs as the country is opened to modern telecommunications networks and cellular services.

INTERNATIONAL TRADE

Gabon has sustained a considerable surplus in its foreign trade, even through periods of quite marked fluctuations in petroleum prices, because the import demand of its small population has remained relatively modest. Exports are normally 2 to 3 times the value of imports and most investment spending is directed toward generating increased earnings from the export of petroleum, timber, and manganese. In 1999, exports stood at US$2.4 billion, while imports were US$1.2 billion.

The main export markets in 1998 were the United States (68 percent), China (9 percent), France (8 percent),

---

Trade (expressed in billions of US$): Gabon

	Exports	Imports
1975	.983	.469
1980	2.173	.674
1985	1.951	.855
1990	2.204	.918
1995	2.713	.882
1998	N/A	N/A

SOURCE: International Monetary Fund. *International Financial Statistics Yearbook 1999.*

and Japan (3 percent). Imports come mostly from France (39 percent), the United States (6 percent), and the Netherlands (5 percent). Despite high per capita income levels and the foreign investments its petroleum sector attracts, Gabon receives a significant amount of aid (US$38 per capita in 1998). This has helped to support both the budget and **balance of payments**.

While Gabon has traditionally enjoyed a **trade surplus**, it has also tended to have a balance of payments deficit. This deficit is a result of high outflows on interest payments on the **foreign debt** and on **remittances** on profits and dividends by the petroleum industry. Foreign debt was US$4.213 billion in 1996. However, high per capita GDP and a poor record of compliance with commitments to the IMF mean that Gabon is not a priority candidate for **debt relief**.

MONEY

Gabon is part of the Central African Monetary and Economic Union (Communaute Economiquareue et Monetaire de l'Afrique Centrale, or CEMAC), a group of 5 francophone countries that use the same currency, the CFA franc. The CFA franc is tied to the French franc and can be readily exchanged at 50 CFA francs to 1 French franc. Gabon, like all members of the CFA franc communities, has benefitted from this stable currency.

As a member of the CFA zone, Gabon was profoundly affected by the 50 percent **devaluation** of the CFA franc in 1994. The devaluation caused a temporary rise in **inflation**. The average annual **inflation rate** during the period from 1990 to 1996 was 9.8 percent. However, inflation declined through the late 1990s, reaching a rate of 2.9 percent in 1999. The country's economy appears to have benefitted from this devaluation, which made its traditional exports more competitive on world markets. In the short term, however, devaluation lowered living standards and probably increased poverty by raising prices while most salaries remained static.

CEMAC planned to open a regional stock exchange in Libreville, Gabon, in 2001.

POVERTY AND WEALTH

The population of Gabon earns a per capita income 4 times that of most other sub-Saharan African nations. Although the relative strength of Gabon's economy has led to a decline in the sharp poverty that is familiar to these other African nations, much of the population remains poor and income inequality is high. The portion of the population that does suffer from poverty is almost all in the 40 percent of the population that relies on agriculture for its income.

Exchange rates: Gabon

Communaute Financiere Africaine francs (CFA Fr) per US$1

Jan 2001	699.21
2000	711.98
1999	615.70
1998	589.95
1997	583.67
1996	511.55

Note: From January 1, 1999, the CFA Fr is pegged to the euro at a rate of 655.957 CFA Fr per euro.

SOURCE: CIA *World Factbook 2001* [ONLINE].

GDP per Capita (US$)

Country	1975	1980	1985	1990	1998
Gabon	6,480	5,160	4,941	4,442	4,630
United States	19,364	21,529	23,200	25,363	29,683
Nigeria	301	314	230	258	256
Cameroon	616	730	990	764	646

SOURCE: United Nations. *Human Development Report 2000;* *Trends in human development and per capita income.*

Household Consumption in PPP Terms

Country	All food	Clothing and footwear	Fuel and power[a]	Health care[b]	Education[b]	Transport & Communications	Other
Gabon	40	3	9	3	7	4	34
United States	13	9	9	4	6	8	51
Nigeria	51	5	31	2	8	2	2
Cameroon	33	12	8	2	9	8	28

Data represent percentage of consumption in PPP terms.
[a]Excludes energy used for transport.
[b]Includes government and private expenditures.

SOURCE: World Bank. *World Development Indicators 2000.*

Social security, based on the French system, was introduced in 1956. Under this program, family allowances are paid to all salaried workers. There is a national fund for state insurance, which provides medical care.

The UN's Human Development Index (HDI), which attempts to measure the quality of life on the basis of **real GDP** per capita, the adult literacy rate, and life expectancy at birth, placed Gabon at 123 out of 174 countries in 1999, in the medium human development category.

WORKING CONDITIONS

The workforce in 1996 numbered 519,000, 56 percent of which are males. The unemployment rate in 1997 was estimated at 21 percent. There is a standard 40-hour working week. However, around 40 percent of the economically active population engages in agriculture, which is poorly regulated. Due to the small population, much of the labor is imported from the neighboring countries.

COUNTRY HISTORY AND ECONOMIC DEVELOPMENT

1470. The Portuguese, French, Dutch, and English begin trading along Gabon's coast.

1839. First French settlement established.

1910. Gabon becomes part of French Equatorial Africa.

1958. Gabon granted internal autonomy by the French.

1960. Gabon is formally proclaimed an independent nation, with Leon M'Ba as prime minister.

1961. M'Ba is elected president and heads a government of National Unity with his opponent, Jean Hilaire Aubame, serving as foreign minister.

1963. Aubame is fired from his position in the Department of Foreign Affairs.

1964. Aubame leads a successful coup; French troops respond to M'Ba's appeal, intervene, and restore him to office. Aubame is sentenced to 10 years in prison.

1967. M'Ba is reelected president but dies a few months later. Vice-President Albert Bernard (later Omar) Bongo succeeds M'Ba as president.

1968. Parti Democratique Gabonais (PDG) is proclaimed as the sole legal political party in the country.

1973. Bongo is reelected president.

1979. As the only candidate in the national presidential elections, Bongo is reelected for a second 7-year term.

1980. In national, municipal, and legislative elections, independents are permitted to run against official candidates.

1981. Over 10,000 Cameroonians are expelled from Gabon following a riot against a Gabonese soccer team at Douala, Cameroon.

1982. Members of the opposition Mouvement pour le Redressement National (MORENA) are arrested for insulting the president and are sentenced to harsh prison terms.

1983. The Owendo-to-Booue section of the Trans-Gabonais Railway is opened by French and Gabonese presidents.

1984. France agrees to supply Gabon with a 9,300-megawatt nuclear power plant, the first in an African nation under black rule.

1986. The Chernobyl accident in the Soviet Union results in the cancellation of the nuclear power plant. MORENA political prisoners are freed.

1990. After much social unrest, President Bongo legalizes opposition to his government. In the country's first multiparty election, Bongo's PDG wins 65 seats in the legislature while opposition parties take the remaining 55 seats.

1993. Multiparty elections are held in December, and Bongo wins with slightly more than 50 percent of the vote. The main opposition leader, Paul Mba Abbesole, claims the process was flawed.

1994. Devaluation of the CFA franc by 50 percent.

1995. The National Assembly election held in December results in a seat distribution of PDG 89, opposition parties 31.

1996. Senate elections are held in January and result in a seat distribution of PDG 53, opposition parties 38.

1998. Bongo is reelected president with 67 percent of the vote.

FUTURE TRENDS

Despite the abundance of natural wealth, the Gabonese economy is hobbled by poor economic management. In 1992, the fiscal deficit widened to 2.4 percent of GDP, and Gabon failed to settle **arrears** on its debt, leading to a cancellation of rescheduling agreements with official and private creditors. Devaluation of the currency by 50 percent in January 1994 sparked a one-time inflationary surge to 35 percent, but the rate dropped to 6 percent by 1996 and 2.9 percent by 1999. In 1997, an IMF mission to Gabon criticized the government for overspending on off-budget items, over-borrowing from the central bank, and slipping on its schedule for privatization and administrative reform. The IMF is expected to continue to support Gabon as long as progress is made on privatization and fiscal discipline. The rebound of oil prices in 1999 helped growth, but drops in production hampered Gabon from fully realizing potential gains. Gabon's potential for economic growth is based upon its considerable mineral and forestry resources. It is a country with high potential and with support from higher oil prices, reinforced by better economic management, Gabon can be expected to make steady progress.

DEPENDENCIES

Gabon has no territories or colonies.

BIBLIOGRAPHY

Economist Intelligence Unit. *Country Profile: Gabon.* London: Economist Intelligence Unit, 2001.

"Gabon." *MBendi: Information for Africa.* <http://www.mbendi .co.za/land/af/ga/p0005.htm>. Accessed September 2001.

Hodd, Michael. *The Economies of Africa.* Aldershot, England: Dartmouth, 1991.

U.S. Central Intelligence Agency. *World Factbook 2000.* <http:// www.odci.gov/cia/publications/factbook/index.html>. Accessed August 2001.

U.S. Department of State. *FY 2001 Country Commercial Guide: Gabon.* <http://www.state.gov/www/about_state/business/ com_guides/2001/africa/index.html>. Accessed September 2001.

World Bank. *World Bank Africa Database 2000.* Washington, DC: World Bank, 2000.

—*Allan C.K. Mukungu*

THE GAMBIA

Republic of The Gambia

CAPITAL: Banjul.

MONETARY UNIT: Dalasi (D). One dalasi equals 100 bututs. Dalasi notes come in denominations of 5, 10, 25, and 50, and coins are in denominations of D1 and 1, 5, 10, 25, and 50 bututs.

CHIEF EXPORTS: Ground nuts, fish and fish products, palm kernels, cotton.

CHIEF IMPORTS: Food, machinery, transport equipment, manufactured goods, fuels.

GROSS DOMESTIC PRODUCT: US$1.5 billion (purchasing power parity, 2000 est.).

BALANCE OF TRADE: Exports: US$125.8 million (f.o.b., 1999). **Imports:** US$202.5 million (f.o.b., 1999).

The Mandinka people constitute 42 percent of the total population, followed (in descending order of population) by the Fula, Wollof, Jola, and Savaluli. There is also a community of Akus (Creoles) descended mainly from African slaves freed in the 19th century. About 90 percent of the population is Muslim and the rest are mostly Christians. There are also traditional religions practiced. English is the official language with Mandinka extensively used in the provinces while Wollof is widely spoken in Banjul.

OVERVIEW OF ECONOMY

The Gambia's economy is closely tied to its command of the Gambia river system, which gives it considerable potential in trade, depending on the level of development in the hinterland. At present, it is an economically disadvantaged country, hampered by its small size, geographical and climatic difficulties, lack of mineral or other natural resources, and rudimentary **infrastructure**. The economy is driven by agriculture (especially groundnut production) and tourism. Agriculture production suffered during the droughts of the last 2 decades, although the Gambia is less vulnerable than its Sahel (a semi-arid region just south of the Sahara desert) neighbors.

Tourism is the most important source of foreign exchange revenue. It suffered in the wake of an abortive coup in 1981 and again after the successful coup of 1994. It has since recovered and in 1996 and 1998 the number of tourist arrivals had overtaken pre-coup levels.

Foreign aid has been key to the development of infrastructure as well as general budgetary support. An economic recovery program, launched in August 1985, later renamed the Programme for Sustained Development, introduced austerity measures which controlled **inflation** and produced significant **real GDP** growth in the latter

COUNTRY OVERVIEW

LOCATION AND SIZE. The Republic of The Gambia measures 11,295 square kilometers (4,361 square miles) and consists of a long narrow ribbon of land sitting astride the river Gambia, one of the major waterways in West Africa. Apart from the 50-kilometer (31-mile) stretch of coastline on the Atlantic ocean, it is entirely surrounded by Senegal. At the estuary of the river Gambia, the northern and southern boundaries are only 45 kilometers (28 miles) apart and the belt of land narrows to about 20 kilometers (13 miles) inland. Banjul is the coastal capital located on the southern side of the estuary.

POPULATION. The population of The Gambia was estimated at 1.026 million in the 1993 census and 1.169 million in 1997. The estimated population in 2000 was 1.367 million, growing at a rate of 3.2 percent a year with a fertility rate of 5.2 children per woman. It is a young population with about 45 percent under 14 years of age, 52 percent between 15 and 64 years, and 3 percent 65 and over. Population density is 117 per square kilometer (1997) with 30 percent of the people living in urban areas. Life expectancy was estimated at 47 years in 1997, up from 36 years in 1970.

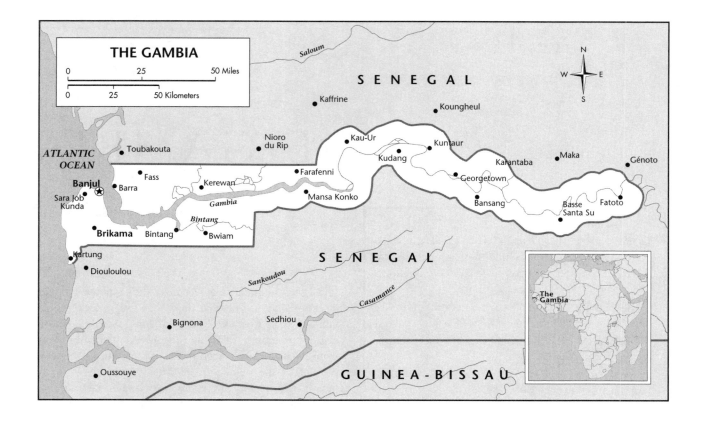

THE GAMBIA

part of the 1980s. Real GDP grew at 3.6 percent annually between 1980 and 1990 and 2.2 percent annually between 1990 and 1997. The economy grew in real terms by 5.3 percent in 1996, 4.9 percent in 1997, and 4.7 percent in 1998. The Gambia has continued to implement market-oriented reforms which won it praise from the International Monetary Fund (IMF) in 1992, and its policies have been broadly continued by the post-1994 government.

The Gambian economy is strongly affected by the health of CFA franc because of its close relationship with Senegal. The Gambia has enjoyed a successful **re-export** trade, and the success of Banjul port has been the result of its ability to undercut the port charges of Dakar in Senegal . When the CFA franc was devalued by 50 percent in 1994, the position changed abruptly, affecting the Gambia-Senegal cross-border trade in groundnuts. Nuts grown in the Gambia were sold in Senegal because of the higher prices there, with Gambia losing on the processing and shipping revenues.

The Gambia had US$37.8 million of international debt in 1998, and this was 9.1 percent of GDP, and US$31 per head. **Debt service** took up 9.7 percent of the export earnings on goods and services. The levels of debt in relation to GDP and per person are significantly higher than the African average, but the debt servicing requirement from export earnings is lower.

POLITICS, GOVERNMENT, AND TAXATION

Gambia did not receive administrative autonomy from the British until 1963. Two years later, on 18 February 1965, they achieved full independence and joined the British Commonwealth. Until the military coup of 1994, the Gambia had been governed under a republican constitution by an executive president and a **unicameral** legislature, with the House of Representatives elected for 5-year terms. Until 1996, the House of Representatives had 36 members elected by universal adult suffrage, 5 chief's representative members elected by head-chiefs, plus the attorney general and 8 non-voting nominated members.

A new constitution was approved by referendum on 7 August 1996. It provides for a unitary republican democracy with a president, vice-president, and secretaries of state responsible to parliament. Five members are nominated by the president, and 45 elected. There is an ombudsman and an independent judiciary. The constitution allows for declaration of a state of emergency and convening of special courts to try cases of corruption. A two-thirds majority in parliament is required to change the constitution.

Dawda Jawara, founder of the Peoples Progressive Party (PPP) who dominated Gambian politics from the 1960s, won the election in 1970 when the country was proclaimed a republic. In 1994, a military coup led by

Yahaya Jammeh overthrew president Dawda Jawara, ending his long political leadership of the country. In September 1996, Jammeh—up to then chief of the Armed Forces Government Junta—became the Gambia's second elected president. Since August 1997, the government has lifted restrictions which limited political activity.

In 1995, central government revenue was 20 percent of GDP. The most recent year for which data is available is 1987, when taxes in income, profits, and capital gains generated 16 percent of government revenue, domestic taxes on goods and services 10 percent, export **levies** and import **duties** 66 percent, other taxes 1 percent, and non-tax revenue 7 percent.

Corporation tax is 25 percent, or 2 percent of **turnover**, whichever is the greater. Many charities and non-government organizations are exempt from tax, and the Ministry of Finance has considerable discretionary powers to grant tax relief to new investors.

INFRASTRUCTURE, POWER, AND COMMUNICATIONS

There are over 2,700 kilometers (1,678 miles) of road in the Gambia, 35 percent of which are paved. Roads in and around Banjul are mostly sealed. Unsealed roads are impassible in the rainy season. The road network is being improved, particularly north of the river with a view to linking up with routes in Senegal. There are plans to build more roads and bridges across the river, replacing the ferry crossings for freight at Banjul and Fawafeni. In 1996 there were 15 motor vehicles, including 8 passenger cars, per 1,000 people, and 7 motor vehicles per 1 kilometer of road.

The Gambia river runs the entire length of the country east to west, providing a vital communications link for cargo and passengers. It is navigable by ocean-going vessels up to Kuntaar (240 kilometers—149 miles—upstream) and by shallow draught vessels up to Basse Santa Su (418 kilometers or 260 miles). The principal sea port is Banjul,

serving the international and river trade, and Gambia's exports, mainly groundnuts, are shipped from there.

Banjul International Airport is situated at Yundum, 29 kilometers (18 miles) southwest of Banjul, and has a new terminal. Gambia Airways is jointly owned by the government and British Airways. Several international airlines provide air links to the country.

There are 2 English daily newspapers: *The Gambia* and *The Daily Observer*. There is also a weekly, *The Point*. There are 3 radio stations (2 of which are private). A national television service (Gambia TV) became operational in 1995. There were 164 radios, 4 TV sets and 2.6 PCs per 1,000 people in 1996–97. The country has an automatic telephone system and a good international connection in the Banjul area via satellite pick-up at Abuko. Telecommunications are run by Gambia Telecom (Gamtel), a **private sector** company. Fax facilities are available at Gamtel offices in Banjul, some open 24 hours a day. There were 21 main telephone lines and 4 mobile phones per 1,000 people in 1997.

Resources for energy production are extremely limited. Electricity supply is entirely reliant on diesel generators. All petroleum products are imported. Wood is used for domestic fuel supplies, but government policy emphasizes conservation of the forest reserves. Alternative energy sources are being developed. The use of groundnut shells for fuel and solar energy output is expanding. Various donors are assisting with the rehabilitation of electricity-generating stations, and a program of rural electrification began in 1998. Prospecting for off-shore oil was active in the early 1990s, and although the exploration is continuing off-shore in Gambian waters, no exploitable oil reserves have yet been found.

ECONOMIC SECTORS

Without minerals or other natural resources, and economically small in size with an under-developed

Communications

Country	Newspapers	Radios	TV Sets[a]	Cable subscribers[a]	Mobile Phones[a]	Fax Machines[a]	Personal Computers[a]	Internet Hosts[b]	Internet Users[b]
	1996	1997	1998	1998	1998	1998	1998	1999	1999
Gambia	2	168	3	N/A	4	1.0	2.6	0.02	3
United States	215	2,146	847	244.3	256	78.4	458.6	1,508.77	74,100
Nigeria	24	223	66	N/A	0	N/A	5.7	0.00	100
Guinea-Bissau	5	44	N/A	N/A	0	0.4	N/A	0.13	2

[a]Data are from International Telecommunication Union, *World Telecommunication Development Report 1999* and are per 1,000 people.
[b]Data are from the Internet Software Consortium (http://www.isc.org) and are per 10,000 people.
SOURCE: World Bank. *World Development Indicators 2000.*

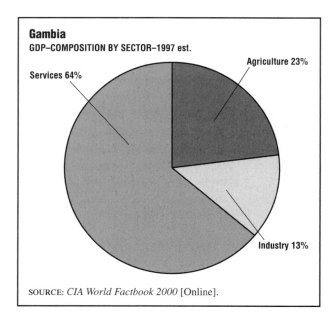

Gambia
GDP–COMPOSITION BY SECTOR–1997 est.

Services 64%

Agriculture 23%

Industry 13%

SOURCE: *CIA World Factbook 2000* [Online].

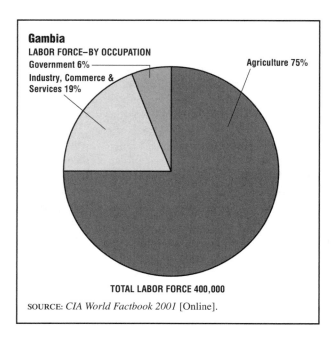

Gambia
LABOR FORCE–BY OCCUPATION

Government 6%

Industry, Commerce & Services 19%

Agriculture 75%

TOTAL LABOR FORCE 400,000

SOURCE: *CIA World Factbook 2001* [Online].

cent from 1980–90 and 0.6 percent from 1990–97, a particularly disappointing performance as the population was increasing at 3.2 percent a year. It is the mainstay of the economy, directly supporting about three-quarters of the population, with production mostly undertaken by small-scale farmers, but generating very low incomes.

The main crop and export is groundnuts which takes up 45 percent of the total planting area. Production has generally remained at 80,000 metric tons annually in the 1990s (83,700 in 1998). Exports of groundnuts and related products accounted for an estimated 63 percent of domestic export earnings in 1998. However, a significant proportion of the crop is frequently smuggled for sale in Senegal. Cotton, citrus fruits, mangoes, avocados, and sesame seed are also cultivated for export.

Other crops are sorghum, millet, maize, rice, cotton, and palm kernels. Rice is the staple food, and is cultivated under 3 systems—swamp, upland, and irrigated—but the country is not self-sufficient in food, and large quantities of rice are imported. Livestock production is an important contributor to GDP and includes sheep, cattle, goats, and pigs. Cattle are exported to other West African countries.

The fishing industry has been developed with the assistance of the EU and the African Development Bank and other donors. It has 8 factories and some 15 Gambia-registered vessels. Fish is exported to other West African countries, and the Gambia has agreements with Guinea, Guinea-Bissau, Cape Verde, Senegal, and Mauritania on fisheries protection and management, including protection of the ecosystem. A program for updating fishing facilities and equipment, supported by the African Development Bank, is running during 2000–05.

INDUSTRY

Industry (including manufacturing, construction, mining, and power) in the Gambia is quite limited. It contributed an estimated 14 percent of GDP in 1998 and about 10 percent of the total labor force was employed in the industry at the 1993 census. Industrial GDP increased at an annual average rate of 1.0 percent a year in 1990–98, with growth estimated at 5.2 percent in 1998.

Manufacturing is a significant sub-sector of industry. It contributed an estimated 6 percent of GDP in 1998 and employed about 6 percent of the labor force at the 1993 census. It is dominated by agro-industrial activities, most importantly the processing of groundnuts and fish. Manufacturing GDP increased at an annual average rate of 1.1 percent between 1990–98, and the sector's GDP increased by an estimated 2.4 percent in 1998. Beverages and construction materials are also produced for the domestic market. Although seismic surveys have suggested

infrastructure, the Gambia's economy depends heavily on agriculture, tourism, and the re-export of imported goods to neighboring countries through the port at Banjul. The 1998 estimates for the contributions of each sector to GDP were: agriculture 22 percent, industry 14 percent, and services 64 percent.

AGRICULTURE

Agriculture (including forestry and fishing), acounted for 22 percent of GDP and employed 75 percent of the **labor force** in 1998. Agriculture grew annually at 0.9 per-

existence of petroleum deposits, the Gambia's mineral resource base is economically unviable and deposits of kaolin and salt are to date unexploited.

SERVICES

The services sector is very important to the Gambia's economy. It contributed about 64 percent of GDP in 1998, but engaged only 15 percent of the labor force. The tourist sector is second only to the groundnut industry as the most important source of foreign exchange. Tourism contributed about 10 percent of annual GDP in the early 1990s and employed about one-third of the workers in the formal sector at the same time.

The tourist industry took off in the 1970s and focused mainly on the promotion of beach holidays. The highest levels of growth were recorded in the 1980s and 1990s when the number of visitors rose to 100,000 a year. The international response to the coup of 1994 and its aftermath had a severe impact on the sector, although it recovered strongly from 1996 onwards. The industry registered 80,000 tourists and generated US$22 million (9.6 percent of exports of goods and services) in 1997, and 92,000 tourists in 1998. The industry is centered in Banjul where there is a 5-star hotel with conference facilities, and several other high-quality hotels. The majority of the tourists are from Northern Europe.

The government has expressed intentions of further exploiting the country's potential as a transit point for regional trade and also as a center for regional finance and telecommunications. According to IMF figures, re-exports contributed about 84 percent of the value of total merchandise exports in 1998. The GDP of the services sector increased at an annual average rate of 3.7 percent between 1990–98 and growth in 1998 was estimated at 5.8 percent.

INTERNATIONAL TRADE

The main export of the Gambia is groundnuts. Other exports include fish (and its products) and some cotton. The largest international trade activity by far is the import of food, machinery, transport equipment, manufactured goods, and fuels—some of which are re-exported to the neighboring countries. The chief export partners are Belgium-Luxembourg, Japan, the UK, Germany, and France, and the chief import partners are Côte d'Ivoire, China, the United Kingdom, and the Netherlands.

The CFA **devaluation** of 1994 resulted in a reduction in regional re-exports, export earnings, and import expenditures. While exports have recovered slowly, imports have risen more quickly to pre-1994 levels. In 1998 total exports were worth US$132 million and imports US$201 million.

Trade (expressed in billions of US$): Gambia		
	Exports	Imports
1975	.044	.060
1980	.031	.165
1985	.043	.093
1990	.040	.199
1995	.016	.140
1998	.019	.245

SOURCE: International Monetary Fund. *International Financial Statistics Yearbook 1999.*

Exchange rates: Gambia	
dalasi (D) per US$1	
Jan 2001	15.000
Q3 1999	12.729
1999	11.395
1998	10.643
1997	10.200
1996	9.789

SOURCE: CIA *World Factbook 2001* [ONLINE].

MONEY

The dalasi (D), the unit of account, was pegged to the pound sterling until 1984, when the peg was relaxed. The currency was floated in 1986, depreciating steadily against the dollar during the 1990s. It exchanged at D9.64=US$1 in 1995, D11.8=US$1 in 1999, and in mid-2001, D16.3=US$1. This depreciation of the Gambian currency increases the prices of imported products, encouraging the use of locally-produced substitutes when these are available. It also reduces the prices of Gambian goods and services to foreigners, particularly visitors, making Gambian holidays cheaper and increasing tourism.

POVERTY AND WEALTH

The Gambia is classified as one of the least developed countries and is a low-income country. Real GNP per capita growth in the 1990–97 period averaged -0.6 percent a year, so average living standards were falling.

In 1999 it was estimated that 57 percent of the population were below the US$1 per day poverty line. The families in poverty do not have enough income to provide the barest minimum of food, shelter, and clothing. Most of those in poverty are rural families relying on small-scale family farms for their livelihoods, and unable to increase their incomes as they are unable to afford investments in mechanization, fertilizers, insecticides, and

GDP per Capita (US$)

Country	1975	1980	1985	1990	1998
Gambia	356	376	378	374	353
United States	19,364	21,529	23,200	25,363	29,683
Nigeria	301	314	230	258	256
Guinea-Bissau	226	168	206	223	173

SOURCE: United Nations. *Human Development Report 2000;
Trends in human development and per capita income.*

Distribution of Income or Consumption by Percentage Share: Gambia

Lowest 10%	1.5
Lowest 20%	4.4
Second 20%	9.0
Third 20%	13.5
Fourth 20%	20.4
Highest 20%	52.8
Highest 10%	37.6

Survey year: 1992
Note: This information refers to expenditure shares by percentiles of the population and is ranked by per capita expenditure.

SOURCE: *2000 World Development Indicators* [CD-ROM].

improved seeds that would boost their output. In the main towns, electricity and the piped water supply is generally available, but in the rural areas it is rare, and lighting is by small paraffin lamps with wicks, and water is from wells. Some mains and septic tank sewage disposal are available in the capital, but in the rural areas people rely mainly on pit latrines.

The UN's Human Development Index, which combines income, health, and education indicators, places the Gambia at 161 out of 174 countries in 1998, putting Gambia firmly in the low development category.

WORKING CONDITIONS

The labor force was estimated to comprise of some 500,000 people in 1997, of which 45 percent were female and 36 percent aged between 10 and 14 years (an improvement compared with 1980, when 44 percent were estimated to be in this category). The labor force was estimated to have grown at an annual average rate of 3.6 percent in the period 1980–97. Agriculture is significant to the Gambian economy; about 75 percent of the people work on small farms for a livelihood, with a relatively small number employed in the manufacturing, tourism, and fishing industries. In agriculture, incomes are very low, and there is no regulation of working conditions.

COUNTRY HISTORY AND ECONOMIC DEVELOPMENT

1200. The Ghana empire establishes its authority over the area.

1400. Europeans begin to explore and settle on the coast and river areas.

1588. The Portuguese sell rights to the Gambia River to British merchants.

1783. Treaty of Versailles gives the British possession of the Gambia, with the French retaining a small enclave on the north bank at Albreda.

1816. The British establish a military post on Banjul Island (then called Bathurst) to suppress the slave trade on the River Gambia.

1857. The French cede Albreda to the British.

1888. Downstream Gambia becomes a colony and the upstream section becomes a protectorate.

1889. Britain and France reach agreement as to the boundaries of their respective colonies.

1906. Slave trade outlawed in the Gambia and other surrounding areas.

1962. Dawda Jawara and the Peoples Progressive Party (PPP) win elections but fail to assume office due to a vote of no confidence by the opposition.

1963. After further constitutional changes, the country obtains administrative autonomy from British, Jawara becomes the prime minister, and the PPP forms government.

1965. On February 18, Gambia achieves full independence.

1970. Gambia proclaimed a republic with a presidential system of government. Dawda Jawara wins election again.

1972. The dalasi is introduced as the Gambia's national currency.

1973. In national elections, the ruling PPP wins 28 of the 32 seats in the House of Representatives and Jawara is re-elected president.

1975. The success of Alex Haley's book *Roots* turns Gambia into an important tourism center.

1981. Muslim dissidents attempt to overthrow Jawara but are foiled with the help of Senegalese troops.

1982. The Senegambian federation established, a loose arrangement to benefit both countries, with Abdion Diouf of Senegal as its first president.

1989. The confederation of Senegambia is dissolved after Gambian resistance to closer union.

1994. A military coup overthrows Jawara. Captain Yahya Jammeh assumes presidency.

1996. Elections return Yahya Jammeh as president.

1998. IMF approves 3-year Enhanced Structural Adjustment Facility of US$27 million.

1999. Poverty Reduction and Growth Facility US$4.5 million loan from IMF is approved.

2000. Gambia receives US$91 million in **debt relief** under the Highly Indebted Poor Countries scheme.

FUTURE TRENDS

The Gambia's overriding dependence on the groundnut sector, which lags behind other sectors in terms of modernization and productivity, remains an obstacle to growth. International debt and poor infrastructure are among the factors limiting Gambia's progress. It is hoped that the IMF-supported Enhanced Structural Adjustment Facility (ESAF) for 1998–2000 will reduce fiscal deficits, encourage further private sector development, and form the basis for future development.

DEPENDENCIES

The Gambia has no territories or colonies.

BIBLIOGRAPHY

The Commonwealth Secretariat. "Gambia." *The Commonwealth Yearbook 2000.* Birmingham: Stationery Office, 2000.

Economist Intelligence Unit. *Country Profile: Gambia.* London: EIU, 2000.

"Gambia." *Africa South of the Sahara.* London: Europa Publications, 2000.

Hodd, M. "Gambia." *The Economies of Africa.* Aldershot: Dartmouth, 1991.

U.S. Central Intelligence Agency. *CIA World Factbook 2000.* <http://www.cia.gov/cia/publications/factbook/geos/ga.html>. Accessed July 2001.

U.S. Central Intelligence Agency. *CIA World Factbook 2001.* <http://www.cia.gov/cia/publications/factbook/geos/ga.html>. Accessed September 2001.

World Bank. *World Bank Africa Database 2000.* Washington D.C., 2000.

—Allan C. K. Mukungu

GHANA

Republic of Ghana

CAPITAL: Accra.

MONETARY UNIT: The cedi (¢). One cedi equals 100 pesewas. There are coins of 1, 2, 5, 10, 20, and 50 pesewas, and 1, 5, 10, 20, 50, and 100 cedis. There are notes of 1, 2, 5, 10, 20, 50, 100, 200, 500, and 1,000 cedis. By the end of 2001, US$1 was worth more than ¢7,500. With the decline in the value of the cedi, use of the pesewa has ceased.

CHIEF EXPORTS: Gold, cocoa, timber, tuna, bauxite, aluminum, manganese ore, diamonds.

CHIEF IMPORTS: Capital equipment, petroleum, foodstuffs.

GROSS DOMESTIC PRODUCT: US$7.932 billion (1999 est.). [CIA World Factbook lists GDP as US$35.5 billion in 1999, using the purchasing power parity conversion.]

BALANCE OF TRADE: Exports: US$1.7 billion (f.o.b., 1999). Imports: US$2.5 billion (f.o.b., 1999).

COUNTRY OVERVIEW

LOCATION AND SIZE. The Republic of Ghana, formerly the Gold Coast, is a West African country lying on the Gulf of Guinea. It has a total border of 2,093 kilometers (1,300 miles), including 548 kilometers (341 miles) with Burkina Faso to the north, 688 kilometers (428 miles) with Côte d'Ivoire to the west, and 877 kilometers (545 miles) with Togo to the east. It has a coastline on the Gulf of Guinea, part of the Atlantic Ocean, measuring 539 kilometers (335 miles). It has an area of 239,540 square kilometers (92,486 square miles), making it about the size of the state of Oregon. Water occupies 8,520 square kilometers (3,290 square miles) of the country, primarily Lake Volta. The capital of Accra is located along the southeastern coast.

Ghana has a tropical climate, warm and comparatively dry along the southeast coast, hot and humid in the southwest, and hot and dry in the north. Its terrain is mostly low plains with a plateau in the south-central area. Its highest point is Mount Afadjato, which rises to 880 meters (2,887 feet). Lake Volta, its largest lake, is the world's largest artificial lake. Ghana has 10 regions: the Northern, Upper West, Upper East, Volta, Ashanti, Western, Eastern, Central, Brong-Ahafo, and Greater Accra.

POPULATION. The population of Ghana was estimated at 19,533,560 in July 2000, an estimate that takes into account the impact of HIV/AIDS. It was estimated at 17,832,000 in 1996, with a density of 81 people per square kilometer (210 per square mile). About 37 percent of the population lived in urban areas and 10 percent in urban agglomerations of more than a million people. The population grew at 2.8 percent a year between 1970 and 1990, and 2.9 percent between 1990 and 1997. The fertility rate in 1997 was 4.9 children per woman.

Ghana has a young population, with more than 42 percent of the people below 15 years of age in 2000 and 55 percent in the 15–65 year bracket. Those over 65 constitute only 3 percent of the population. Life expectancy was estimated at 57 years overall, with 56 and 58 years for men and women, respectively.

The population is predominantly of African origin, with the Akan tribe comprising 44 percent of the population, the Moshi-Dagomba 16 percent, the Ewe 13 percent, the Ga-Adangbe 8 percent, the Yoruba 1.3 percent, and European and other nationalities less than 1 percent. Most people (38 percent) hold traditional beliefs, while 30 percent follow the Islamic faith, 24 percent are Christians, and 8 percent have other beliefs. English is the official language, with the other main languages being Akan, Moshi-Dagomba, Ewe, and Ga.

OVERVIEW OF ECONOMY

Ghana's formerly strong economy has been the victim of instability resulting from a series of military coups

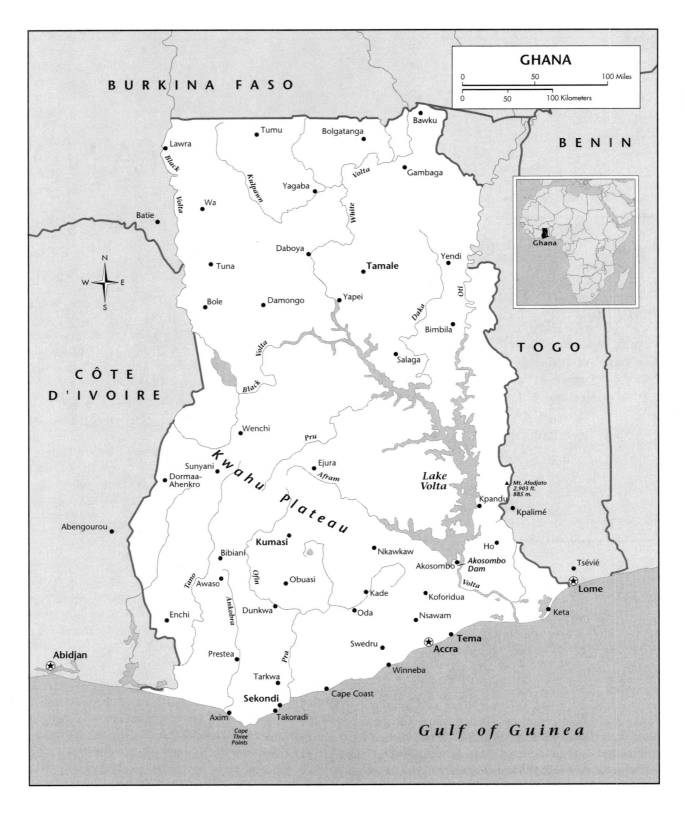

and economic mismanagement in the period from independence in 1958 to 1983. A highly protected economy and substantial government investment created a large but inefficient manufacturing sector by the mid-1980s. Over the last 15 years, economic reforms, including sub-

stantial **privatizations**, have resulted in a small but viable industrial sector.

Ghana has a considerable endowment of natural resources (timber, fertile agricultural land and fishing grounds, and minerals). Agriculture constituted about 40 percent of GDP in 1999 and employed 60 percent of the **labor force**. The main export crop is cocoa. Coffee, palm products, and tropical fruits are exported in smaller quantities. Other crops include cassava, yams, corn, sorghum, and rice, while goats and sheep are the principal livestock reared. Timber is also an important export. Fishing is important to the domestic market, with some exports of tuna.

Industry contributes about 30 percent of the GDP and employs 15 percent of the labor force. Ghana's industries include mining, lumbering, light manufacturing, aluminum, and food processing. Mineral exports—mainly gold, manganese, diamonds, and bauxite—account for a large part of the country's earnings. Petroleum is extracted in small quantities offshore between Saltpond and Cape Coast, and exploration in other areas is under way. Manufacturing is dominated by **import substitution** industries, producing food products, beverages, tobacco, textiles, timber and wood products, refined petroleum, vehicles, chemicals and pharmaceuticals, cement, and metals. Electricity is generated almost entirely from hydroelectric plants, mainly the Akosombo Dam on the Volta River.

Services contribute 30 percent of GDP and employ only 25 percent of the labor force. Trade, transportation, financial services, and public administration are the main activities.

POLITICS, GOVERNMENT, AND TAXATION

Ghana is a former British colony. Kwame Nkrumah set up the Convention Peoples Party (CPP) to campaign for independence in 1949. Elections took place in 1951 and the following year Nkrumah became the leader of the executive council and the legislature. Full independence followed in 1957, with Ghana becoming the first country in Africa to achieve this feat. Ghana became a republic on 1 July 1960, with Nkrumah as president.

In 1964 Nkrumah introduced legislation to make Ghana a one-party state. In 1966 Nkrumah was removed by military coup, making way for army leadership under the umbrella of the National Liberation Council (NLC), headed by 3 army officers. Political activity was permitted again in 1969, elections were held, and the Progress Party (PP) won a majority of seats. The leader of the PP, Dr. Kofi Busia, was invited to form a government and became prime minister. A 3-man commission of Emanuel Kotoka, Akwasi Arifa, and John Harley from the NLC acted as head of state.

In 1972 there was another military coup led by Col. Ignatius Acheampong, and he set up a National Redemption Council (NDC). In 1978 Gen. Fredrick Akuffo replaced Acheampong as head of what was now the Supreme Military Council (SMC), and in 1979 political activity began in preparation for elections scheduled for June. Two weeks before the election, however, a military coup led by Flight Lt. Jerry Rawlings ushered in the leadership of the Armed Forces Revolutionary Council (AFRC). Elections were held as scheduled, and Dr. Hilla Limann of the Peoples National Party (PNP) took office as president in September 1979.

Another coup, in 1981, put Rawlings back in power. He suspended the constitution and banned political activity. From December 1981 to November 1992 a Provisional National Defence Council (PNDC), with secretaries in charge of the ministries and the regions, ruled Ghana. A new constitution was approved by a national referendum in April 1992, based on the U.S. model. The PNDC formed a new party, the National Democratic Congress (NDC), and successfully contested the elections in December 1992 with Rawlings emerging as the president. In the 1996 elections, NDC and Rawlings were again returned to office. Rawlings stood down for the 2000 elections, and the New Patriotic Party, with John Kufuor as presidential candidate, was victorious.

The 1992 constitution makes Ghana a unitary republic with an executive president and a multiparty political system. The national legislature is the **unicameral** parliament, whose 200 members are elected by universal adult suffrage every 4 years. The president, who is the head of state and commander-in-chief of the armed forces, is elected by universal adult suffrage for a maximum of 2 4-year terms.

The president appoints the vice president and nominates a council of ministers, subject to approval by parliament. The constitution also provides for 2 advisory bodies to the president: a 25-member Council of State and a 20-member National Security Council. There are 110 administrative districts, each having a District Assembly.

In 1996 government revenues amounted to 21 percent of GDP and expenditures were 22 percent of GDP. The **budget deficit** was 1.2 percent of GDP, well within the 3 percent guidelines. The most recent year for which tax revenue data is available is 1993, when taxes in income, profits, and capital gains generated 17 percent of government revenue, domestic taxes on goods and services 40 percent, export **levies** and import **duties** 27 percent, and non-tax revenue 23 percent.

The general rate of corporation tax is 35 percent, and there is a capital gains tax of 5 percent. Hotels are subject to a 25 percent corporation tax, manufacturing companies in the regional capitals are subject to 26.25 percent, elsewhere at 17.5 percent. Interest and dividends are subject to a 10 percent withholding tax. Non-agricultural exports are subject to an 8 percent levy.

INFRASTRUCTURE, POWER, AND COMMUNICATIONS

There are 39,409 kilometers (24,490 miles) of roads, of which 11,653 kilometers (7,241 miles) were paved in 1997. In 1997 there was a 953-kilometer (592-mile) railway network (currently undergoing major rehabilitation) of narrow gauge. The railway connects Accra, Kumasi, and Takoradi, the major mining areas, to the sea ports. The railway network also provides passenger services from the interior of Ghana to the main sea ports at Tema (near Accra) and Takoradi.

The main waterways include the Volta, Ankobra, and Tano Rivers, which provide 168 kilometers (104 miles) of year-round navigation, and Lake Volta, which provides 1,125 kilometers (699 miles) of arterial and feeder waterways. The main ports are at Takoradi and Tema. There were 12 airports in 1999, 6 of which had paved runways.

Growth in electricity production averaged 4.2 percent a year between 1980 and 1996. In 1998 electricity production was 6.206 billion kilowatt-hours (kWh), 99.9 percent of which was from hydroelectric sources. In the same year, electricity consumption was 5.437 billion kWh and exports were 400 million kWh, while 65 kWh of electricity were imported. Hydroelectricity is generated at the Akasombo and Kpong power plants, which traditionally supply virtually all of the country's electricity needs, as well as provide exports to Benin and Togo.

Total dependence on hydroelectricity makes Ghana vulnerable to variations in rainfall, and power shortages reached crisis-point in 1998. This has stiffened resolve to provide alternative sources of electric power, including a recently built oil- and gas-fired power station. There are also plans for a number of gas-fired plants, using imported gas and gas from the Tano fields. The Tama oil refinery was being expanded and prepared for privatization in 1997–99. The U.S. Export-Import Bank is to provide guarantees to cover drilling in the Tano off-shore natural gas fields and construction of pipelines, plus loan financing for operations and maintenance work.

The Ghana Broadcasting Corporation provides radio services, supplemented by 36 private companies which were granted authorization to operate radios and TV networks in 1999. Broadcasters comprised 3 short-wave, 18 FM radio stations, and 11 television stations in 1999. There were 238 radios, 109 TV sets, and 1.6 PCs per 1,000 people in 1999.

Ghana has a modest telephone system which is Internet accessible, and although many rural communities are not yet connected, expansion of the services is underway. There were 200,000 main lines in use in 1998 and an estimated 30,000 cellular phones in use. Domestically the telephone system comprises a microwave radio relay, and a local wireless loop has also been installed. International communication is through 4 Intelsat satellite earth stations, and a micro-wave radio relay which links to the Panaftel system connecting Ghana to its neighbors.

International direct dialling is available to major cities. Fax facilities are available around the clock in Accra. There are also several privately-owned and operated cellular phone networks with 1 mobile phone per 1,000 people. There were 2 Internet Service Providers (ISPs) in 1999.

ECONOMIC SECTORS

In 1995 agriculture (including forestry and fishing) was the largest sector and the biggest employer of the working population. The chief agricultural export is cocoa, and it occupies more than half of the country's cultivated land.

Mining contributes a big proportion of foreign exchange earnings through the export of gold, diamonds, and bauxite (used in the production of aluminum). The

Communications									
Country	Newspapers	Radios	TV Sets[a]	Cable subscribers[a]	Mobile Phones[a]	Fax Machines[a]	Personal Computers[a]	Internet Hosts[b]	Internet Users[b]
	1996	1997	1998	1998	1998	1998	1998	1999	1999
Ghana	14	238	99	N/A	1	N/A	1.6	0.06	20
United States	215	2,146	847	244.3	256	78.4	458.6	1,508.77	74,100
Nigeria	24	223	66	N/A	0	N/A	5.7	0.00	100
Cote d'Ivoire	17	164	70	0.0	6	N/A	3.6	0.25	20

[a]Data are from International Telecommunication Union, *World Telecommunication Development Report 1999* and are per 1,000 people.
[b]Data are from the Internet Software Consortium (http://www.isc.org) and are per 10,000 people.

SOURCE: World Bank. *World Development Indicators 2000.*

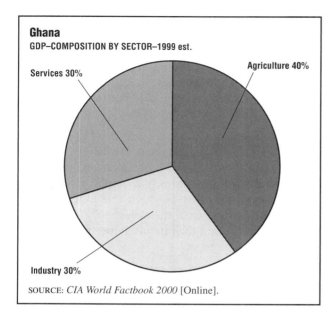

Ghana
GDP–COMPOSITION BY SECTOR–1999 est.

Services 30%

Agriculture 40%

Industry 30%

SOURCE: *CIA World Factbook 2000* [Online].

country is among the world's largest producers of manganese. Manufacturing contributed 9 percent of GDP in 1998. However, the economic recovery program of the late 1990s hit the industry through high interest rates and the lifting of restrictions on some imports.

The tourist sector, while so far not rated amongst the main economic sectors, is the fastest growing sector in the economy. The government's main priority is to privatize the state-owned enterprises to relieve government of the heavy burden on national resources. The government, with the help of the IMF, plans to diversify its exports to avoid its vulnerability to the fluctuating prices

of cocoa on the world market. The government also plans to attract more investment to achieve the diversification of exports as well as to meet local needs.

AGRICULTURE

Agriculture accounted for more than 40 percent of GDP in 1999 and employed three-fifths of the workforce. However, despite its importance, sectoral growth has lagged behind other sectors of the economy and has been unpredictable, as most farming is reliant upon rainwater. Agricultural output (including forestry and fishing) grew at just 1.0 percent per year between 1980 and 1990, and 2.7 percent between 1990 and 1997. Agricultural growth increased to 5.3 percent in 1998. Ghana is one of the world's leading producers of cocoa, mostly grown on small farms. In 1998–99 cocoa production reached 400,000 metric tons.

Although most of the year-to-year trends are attributable to weather patterns, the longer term improvement in performance can be attributed to public policy changes. As part of the broader **macroeconomic** reforms (reforms which affect the whole economy, such as changing the **exchange rate**, altering controls on interest rates, and adjusting the money supply) the government has removed food **price controls**, raised cocoa prices paid to producers, and boosted extension services, which help increase farmer productivity.

Other **cash crops** are coffee, bananas, palm oil, coconuts, and kola nuts. The chief food crops are cassava, maize, yams, coco yams, plantain, millet, corn, fruit, rice, and vegetables. Cattle are raised in the north. Yields of food crops, however, have shown disappointing growth with only cassava and millet yields improving in the past decade. This seems to be a result of low investment and poor technology. The removal of **subsidies** on fertilizers and other agricultural inputs has also had an effect on several crops.

Cocoa is Ghana's most important agricultural export crop, normally accounting for 30–40 percent of total exports. Most cocoa is produced by around 1.6 million small farmers on plots of less than 3 hectares in the forest areas of the Ashanti, Brong-Ahafo, Central, Eastern, Western, and Volta regions. In the 1960s Ghana was the world's largest producer of cocoa but it has since been overtaken by neighboring Côte d'Ivoire.

Livestock farming is restricted to the Northern region and the Accra plains. Production of meat is, however, insufficient to meet local annual demand of about 200,000 tons. The shortfall has been met by imports of livestock from neighboring countries, although imports have been constrained by dwindling **foreign exchange reserves**. As part of the revitalization effort, the government undertook to rehabilitate and restock the 6 cattle stations at Pong-Tamale, Ejura, Babile, Kintampo, Amrahia, and Nungua, but these efforts have yet to bear fruit.

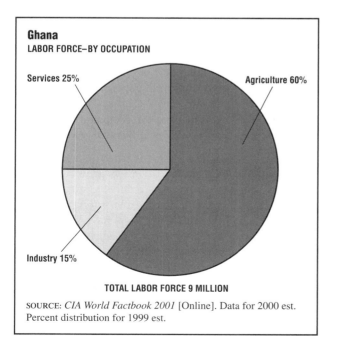

Ghana
LABOR FORCE–BY OCCUPATION

Services 25%

Agriculture 60%

Industry 15%

TOTAL LABOR FORCE 9 MILLION

SOURCE: *CIA World Factbook 2001* [Online]. Data for 2000 est. Percent distribution for 1999 est.

More than one-third of Ghana's total land area is covered by forest, although not all of it is suitable for commercial exploitation. Commercial forestry is concentrated in the Western region in Southern Ghana, and has been the third largest foreign exchange earner in recent years (accounting for about 10 percent of exports).

Since 1983, the forestry industry has undergone substantial changes, attracting aid and commercial credits which have focused on forestry management, research and equipment for logging, saw-milling, and manufacture. Since 1989 the government has banned the export of certain timbers to avoid deforestation. River and sea fishing are important, although domestic fisheries (in the ocean and Lake Volta) supply only about one-half of the country's total annual demand of 600,000 tons.

INDUSTRY

Industry contributed about 30 percent of the GDP in 1999, when it employed about 15 percent of the workforce. A policy of industrialization has resulted in the establishment of a wide range of manufacturing industries, producing food products, beverages, tobacco, textiles, clothes, footwear, timber and wood products, chemicals and pharmaceuticals, and metals, including steel and steel products. Almost all of them began as state-owned enterprises, but now are mostly privatized.

Ghana possesses substantial bauxite reserves, though the output, all of which is exported, is less than half of capacity. High-quality sand in the Tarkwa mining area provides the basis for a small but important glass industry. Cement factories have been developed at Tema and Takoradi. The development of export zones (areas where raw materials can be imported without customs duties, provided the products are for export) and industrial estates (areas with good transport links, electricity, and water supplies, for groups of enterprises able to provide services for each other) is underway.

Apart from traditional industries such as food processing, Ghana also has a large number of long-established large and medium-sized manufacturing enterprises. The large-scale manufacturing sector includes textiles, drinks, food, plastics, vehicle assembly, and aluminum processing. Much of it is owned and managed by the Lebanese community, but multinational companies such as Unilever and Valco also run factories. Various state-owned enterprises also used to be involved in manufacturing, but since **liberalization** opened up the market to foreign competition in the 1980s, many factories have been closed, leading to substantial job losses.

Gold remains central to the Ghanaian economy, although diamonds, manganese, and bauxite are also mined. The privatization of the Ashanti Goldfields Cor-poration, the largest producer of gold in the country, has been regarded as a great African success story, as it has been managed by Ghanaians and was one of the first indigenous companies to be listed on the international stock market. From a 15 percent share of export earnings in the mid-1980s, gold now vies with cocoa as the largest source of Ghana's export earnings.

Ghana's diamond sector is smaller and has struggled to survive its legacy of corruption. Production is mainly industrial grade. Structural adjustment ended the state's control over large-scale extraction but the private businesses now involved have not been able to restore official production to even a quarter of the 1970s level. Smuggling is rife, and the official figures do not reflect the actual level of output.

Ghana is also one of the world's largest exporters of manganese. There is considerable potential for expansion of bauxite extraction in conjunction with Ghana's relatively abundant supply of cheap hydro-electricity for aluminum smelting.

SERVICES

Financial services have improved in recent years with the introduction of a stock market, the Ghana Stock Exchange (GSE) in 1990, and several new financial institutions. Since 1992, privatization and the arrival of 4 new commercial banks have brought increased dynamism to the sector. The government has sold off **equity** in several wholly or partly state-owned banks. After some difficulty finding an active investor for the Social Security Bank (SSB), a consortium of fund managers led by the UK-based Blakeney Asset Management built up a controlling 51 percent stake in 1997 and hired a technical partner, Allied Irish Bank, to enhance SSB's management and services.

Competition has brought some benefits, with commercial banks introducing new products, including automatic telling machines and credit-card services, and a significant turnaround in check-clearing and cashing. However, the banks still have little appetite for lending to small and medium-sized local businesses, which has caused some concern.

The rest of the financial sector is growing and diversifying, although it remains relatively small. Ghana has 2 discount houses, and since the setting up of the stock exchange, several stock brokers have set up shop. Legislation introduced in 1999 is expected to open way for unit trusts and more varied financial instruments. There are now 17 insurance companies, up from fewer than 9 in 1993, although the industry remains dominated by 2 state firms. There are mortgage companies, building societies, at least 1 venture capital company, and 3 leasing companies.

Although **retail** facilities remain limited, urban areas are served by a range of outlets, and there are a growing number of foreign-owned stores in Accra with many more new investments expected in the coming years. Rural areas typically have mainly informal markets or modest general stores.

The tourist sector is the fastest growing sector and it has overtaken timber as a foreign exchange earner. Revenue from tourism has increased gradually, with most of the tourists coming from Nigeria, the United Kingdom, Côte d'Ivoire, the United States, and Germany. The Ghana Tourist Board and the Ghana Tourist Development Company supervise the regulation, financing, and development of the tourist industry. Tourism is being revamped through up-grading of hotels and the rehabilitating of tourist attractions. Hotels are located at Accra, Tema, Takoradi, and Kumasi, and there is a hotel at Akosombo overlooking Lake Volta. There were 325,438 tourist arrivals in 1997, including some 83,000 Ghanaians who live abroad, generating receipts of US$266 million, comprising 16 percent of foreign exchange earnings.

INTERNATIONAL TRADE

Ghana is essentially an exporter of primary products, mainly gold, cocoa, and timber, and an importer of **capital goods**, foodstuffs, and fuels. Merchandise exports amounted to $1.7 billion in 1999, of which cocoa contributed the largest share. The other main exports were aluminum, gold, timber, diamonds, and manganese. Imports were $2.5 billion in 1999. Export partners included the United Kingdom, Togo, Germany, Italy, the Netherlands, the United States, and France. Import partners were Nigeria (supplying most of Ghana's oil requirement), the United Kingdom, Italy, Germany, the United States, Spain, France, Côte d'Ivoire, and the Netherlands.

MONEY

The unit of currency, the cedi, was valued at ¢7,325:US$1 in mid-2001. Under the Economic Recovery

Exchange rates: Ghana	
new cedis per US$1	
Jan 2001	6,895.77
2000	5,321.68
1999	2,647.32
1998	2,314.15
1997	2,050.17
1996	1,637.23
SOURCE: CIA *World Factbook 2001* [ONLINE].	

Program (ERP) Phase One (1983–86), backed by the IMF and the World Bank, the cedi was allowed to depreciate rapidly from October 1983 to March 1986. Valued at ¢2.75 to the dollar in 1982, it fell to ¢90 to the dollar by 1986. Market forces currently determine the exchange rate and the depreciation has continued, making it easier for Ghana to export its goods. Travellers to Ghana are allowed to bring with them any amount of foreign exchange into the country which can be changed into cedis in commercial banks or the foreign bureau. Previously travellers were required to declare the amount of foreign currency they were carrying, and forced to exchange it at highly unfavorable rates with official foreign exchange dealers, and this served to provide a significant discouragement to tourists.

Inflation has been a persistent problem in Ghana, thanks in part to its depreciating currency. Over the period from 1997 to 1999, however, inflation declined from 20.8 percent to 15.7 percent to 9.5 percent. In 1999 the **inflation rate** rebounded to 12.8 percent.

POVERTY AND WEALTH

It was estimated in 1992 that 31 percent of the population of Ghana was below the poverty line of US$1 a day. People below this line do not have enough income to meet the barest minimums of food, clothing, and shelter. Almost all those in poverty were located in the rural areas, and rely on agricultural production from small family farms or herding family-based livestock for their

Trade (expressed in billions of US$): Ghana		
	Exports	Imports
1975	.809	.802
1980	1.257	1.129
1985	.617	.731
1990	N/A	N/A
1995	1.724	1.907
1998	1.885	N/A
SOURCE: International Monetary Fund. *International Financial Statistics Yearbook 1999.*		

GDP per Capita (US$)					
Country	1975	1980	1985	1990	1998
Ghana	411	394	328	352	399
United States	19,364	21,529	23,200	25,363	29,683
Burkina Faso	196	207	224	225	259
Nigeria	301	314	230	258	256
SOURCE: United Nations. *Human Development Report 2000; Trends in human development and per capita income.*					

Distribution of Income or Consumption by Percentage Share: Ghana

Lowest 10%	3.6
Lowest 20%	8.4
Second 20%	12.2
Third 20%	15.8
Fourth 20%	21.9
Highest 20%	41.7
Highest 10%	26.1

Survey year: 1997
Note: This information refers to expenditure shares by percentiles of the population and is ranked by per capita expenditure.

SOURCE: *2000 World Development Indicators* [CD-ROM].

livelihood. Income in 1992 was very unevenly distributed, with the poorest 10 percent of the population receiving only 3.4 percent of total household income while the richest 10 percent received 27.3 percent.

While Ghana is considered to be among the least developed countries in the world, it is rated as one of the fastest growing economies in Africa. It is a low-income economy; using the **purchasing power parity** conversion (which allows for the low price of many basic commodities in Ghana) GDP per head was US$1,900 in 1999. The rate of per capita income growth during the years between 1985 and 1995 averaged 1.4 percent per year, rising to 1.7 percent per year between 1996 and 1997, and this performance has brought about a significant increase in living standards. The growth in GDP per head experienced by Ghana is vitally important in reducing poverty, with every 1 percent of GDP per head growth reducing those in poverty by 2 percent. Thus the 1.7 percent per year rate of GDP per head growth shifts over 200,000 people out of poverty each year.

The UN Human Development Index, which combines indicators for income, health, and education, placed Ghana at 129 out of 174 countries in 1998, making Ghana one of the few African countries to achieve a medium level of human development. This means that Ghana is placed among those countries with levels of income, health provision, and educational facilities that are midway between the high human development countries of Europe, North America, and Australasia, and the very poorest and most deprived countries, mostly in Africa, where many people do not have enough food to meet minimum nutritional levels, and have no access to health or educational services.

WORKING CONDITIONS

It was estimated in 1999 that the labor force comprised 4 million people, of which 60 percent worked in agricul-

ture, 15 percent in industry, and 25 percent in services. The unemployment rate was estimated at 20 percent in 1997. However, the unemployment rate has little meaning in Africa. Many people work in some form of **subsistence farming**, which is not counted in employment figures. There are no social security provisions, and those without work or support from families or charities cannot survive. For much of the year in subsistence farming there is relatively little work to do, and this work is shared among family members. During planting and harvesting, there is more work to be done, and everyone is more fully occupied, but even in these periods, there may be more than enough labor to do the tasks, and the work is again shared. Everyone sharing the work appears to have an occupation in agriculture, but because workers are not engaged full-time the whole year, there is some "disguised unemployment."

Trade unions are governed by the Industrial Relations Act (IRA) of 1958, as amended in 1965 and 1972. Organized labor is represented by the Trades and Union Congress (TUC), which was established in 1958. The IRA provides a framework for collective bargaining and protection against anti-union discrimination.

The law prohibits civil servants from joining or organizing a trade union. However, in December 1992, the government enacted legislation allowing each branch of the civil service to establish a negotiating committee to engage in collective bargaining for wages and benefits in the same fashion as trade unions in the **private sector**. While the right to strike is recognized in law and practice, the government has on occasion taken strong action to end strikes, especially in cases involving vital government interests or public order. The IRA provides mechanisms for conciliation and arbitration before unions can resort to industrial actions or strikes.

The law prohibits forced labor and it has not been reported to be in practice. There is a minimum employment age of 15 and night work and certain types of hazardous labor are prohibited for those under 18. The violation of this law, however, is common, and young children of school-going age can often be found during the day performing menial tasks in the agricultural sector or in the markets.

In 1991 a Tripartite Commission comprising representatives of government, organized labor, and employers established minimum standards for wages and working conditions. The daily minimum wage combines wages with customary benefits such as a transportation allowance. The current daily minimum wage, ¢2,900—about US$0.40—however, does not permit a single-wage earner to support a family and frequently results in multiple-wage earners and other family-based commercial activities. By law the maximum working week is 45 hours but collective bargaining has established a 40-hour week for most unionized workers.

COUNTRY HISTORY AND ECONOMIC DEVELOPMENT

1470. Portuguese traders arrive on the coast of what is now Ghana, then known as the Gold Coast, and begin to establish trading settlements.

1553. The British begin trading along the coast, to be joined in due course by German, Danish, and Dutch traders.

1821. The British take control of all the forts along the coast.

1844. Britain signs agreement with local chiefs, which enables Britain to establish the colony of the Gold Coast.

1868. Dutch possessions are transferred to the British, and the British begin conquest of the interior. British occupation is fiercely resisted, particularly by the Fante Confederation (an alliance of coastal kingdoms) and the Ashanti.

1900. The British finally defeat the Ashanti and war ends.

1920. A number of political parties begin to emerge, dedicated to regaining African independence. Representing different regions, these parties are not nationally based.

1947. The United Gold Coast Convention (UGCC) is formed, but without representatives from some key areas in the north.

1948. Kwame Nkrumah, general secretary of the UGCC, breaks away to found the Convention People's Party (CPP), which quickly becomes a voice for the nation and for the first time draws the northern people into politics.

1949. Exasperated by the slow progress towards self-government, Nkrumah calls for a national strike. Seeking to contain the situation, the British haul Nkrumah before the courts and sentence him to jail.

1951. The CPP wins elections for Legislative Assembly while Nkrumah is in jail. He is released to become leader of the Executive Council and the Legislature.

1957. On March 6, Ghana becomes the first African country to gain independence from European control, with Nkrumah as prime minister.

1958. The Constitution Act and the Preventative Detention Act are passed, giving Nkrumah wide extra-constitutional powers to suppress opposition. Regional assemblies are dissolved.

1960. Ghana approves a republican constitution with Nkrumah as president.

1961. Ghana becomes a one-party state, with the CPP as the sole political party.

1965. The cedi is introduced as a unit of currency, replacing the Ghana pound. In the first elections, the CPP wins all parliamentary seats with an unchallenged slate.

1966. The Akosombo dam, built over the Volta river at a cost of US$414 million, is completed. Nkrumah is overthrown while on a visit to Peking by a military coup led by Emanuel Kotoka, Akwasi Arifa, and John Harley. The National Liberation Council (NLC) assumes power.

1967. The new cedi is introduced with a devalued rate of exchange. Kotoka is killed in an abortive counter-coup. Ghana joins the West African Economic Community.

1969. The constitution of the second republic is adopted. In national elections, the Progress Party (PP) led by K.A. Busia wins absolute majority; a 3-man presidential commission consisting of Harley, Arifa, and A.K. Okran is appointed to serve as head of state.

1970. The presidential troika is abolished; Edward Akufo-Addo is elected president.

1972. The Busia government is overthrown by military coup under Ignatius Acheampong. The National Redemption Council (NRC) assumes supreme power and **nationalizes** mining and textile firms.

1974. Agreement is reached with creditor nations, giving Ghana a liberal repayment schedule.

1975. The Supreme Military Council (SMC) is created as the highest legislative and administrative body in the state, with a reconstituted NRC as a subordinate cabinet.

1977. Acheampong promises return to civilian rule by 1979.

1978. Fredrick Akuffo, Acheampong's deputy, assumes power in a bloodless coup. Local assembly elections are held and the National Assembly is established.

1979. A 6-year ban on political parties is lifted. Flight Lt. Jerry Rawlings leads a coup of junior officers, and the Armed Forces Revolutionary Council (AFRC) takes power. A new constitution is adopted as a prelude to return to civilian rule. In presidential elections Hilla Limann, candidate of the People's National Party (PNP), is elected.

1981. Rawlings seizes power for second time in a bloodless coup, suspends the National Assembly, political parties, and Council of State. He sets up a Provisional National Defence Council (PNDC) with himself as chairman.

1983. Nigeria expels over 1.5 million Ghanaian residents. The government devalues the cedi by over 1,400 percent in line with IMF requirements.

1990. A pro-democracy organization, the Movement for Freedom and Justice, demands a national referendum to establish a multi-party system.

1992. A draft constitution is approved in a referendum. Political associations are allowed and 6 opposition movements are granted recognition. In November, presidential elections return Rawlings with 58.3 percent of the vote. The December parliamentary elections return the NDC with 189 out of 200 seats.

1995. Riots in Accra in February over the introduction of **value-added tax** (VAT) lead to 4 deaths and the withdrawal of the tax.

1996. Rawlings wins re-election and the NDC retains a majority in parliament.

1999. Fall in gold prices upsets Ghana's economic recovery.

2000. John Agyekum Kufour of the New Patriotic Party (NPP) is elected as president, and the NPP gains a majority in parliament.

FUTURE TRENDS

Well endowed with natural resources, Ghana has twice the per capita output of the poorest countries in West Africa. Even so, Ghana remains heavily dependent on aid and foreign investment.

Gold, timber, and cocoa production will continue as the major sources of foreign exchange. The domestic economy continues to revolve around agriculture, which accounts for 40 percent of GDP and employs 60 percent of the workforce, mainly small landholders, most of whom are very poor. It is difficult to envisage anything other than very slow progress in the agricultural sector, where so much of the work is devoted simply to providing for subsistence.

Between 1995 and 1997, Ghana made steady progress under a 3-year **structural adjustment program** in cooperation with the IMF. On the minus side, **public sector** wage increases and regional peacekeeping commitments have led to continued inflationary deficit financing, depreciation of the cedi, and rising public discontent with Ghana's austerity measures. A rebound in gold prices will provide a substantial boost to the economy.

DEPENDENCIES

Ghana has no territories or colonies.

BIBLIOGRAPHY

Commonwealth Secretariat. "Ghana." *The Commonwealth Yearbook 2000*. Birmingham: Stationery Office, 2000.

Economist Intelligence Unit. *Country Profile: Ghana.* London: Economist Intelligence Unit, 2001.

"Ghana." *Africa South of the Sahara.* London: Europa, 2000.

Ghana Embassy. <http://www.ghana-embassy.org>. Accessed September 2001.

Hodd, Michael. "Ghana." *The Economies of Africa.* Aldershot: Dartmouth, 1991.

Leite, Sérgio Pereira, et al. *Ghana: Economic Development in a Democratic Environment.* Washington, D.C.: International Monetary Fund, 2000.

The Republic of Ghana. <http://www.ghana.gov.gh>. Accessed September 2001.

U.S. Central Intelligence Agency. *World Factbook 2000.* <http://www.odci.gov/cia/publications/factbook/index.html>. Accessed August 2001.

U.S. Department of State. *FY 2000 Country Commercial Guide: Ghana.* <http://www.state.gov/www/about_state/business/com_guides/2000 /africa/index.html>. Accessed September 2001.

—Allan C.K. Mukungu

GUINEA

Republic of Guinea

République de Guinée

CAPITAL: Conakry.

MONETARY UNIT: Guinea franc (GF). One franc equals 100 centimes. There are notes of 25, 50, 100, 500, 1,000, and 5,000 francs.

CHIEF EXPORTS: Bauxite, alumina, diamonds, gold, coffee, fish, agricultural products.

CHIEF IMPORTS: Petroleum products, metals, machinery, transport equipment, textiles, grain and other foodstuffs.

GROSS DOMESTIC PRODUCT: US$10 billion (purchasing power parity, 2000 est.).

BALANCE OF TRADE: Exports: US$820 million (f.o.b., 2000). **Imports:** US$634 million (f.o.b., 2000).

areas. The capital is home to 1.1 million people, and a further 9 towns have populations of between 25,000 and 100,000.

The population is composed primarily of 3 indigenous ethnic groups: the Peuhl (40 percent), Malinke (30 percent), and Soussou (20 percent). Fully 85 percent of the population are Muslim, while 5 percent are Roman Catholic and the rest follow traditional beliefs. The population is quite young, with 43 percent between the ages of 0 and 14, and 54 percent between the ages of 15 and 64. The life expectancy in the country is 45.91 years (43.49 for men and 48.42 for women).

COUNTRY OVERVIEW

LOCATION AND SIZE. Guinea lies on the West African coast, bordered by Sierra Leone and Liberia to the south, Guinea-Bissau and Senegal to the north, and Mali and Côte d'Ivoire inland to the east. It has 320 kilometers (199 miles) of coastline, and a land area of 245,857 square kilometers (94,925 miles). Comparatively, the country is slightly smaller than Oregon. The capital of Conakry is on the coast of the Atlantic Ocean and has the only international airport.

POPULATION. The population was estimated to be 7,613,870 in July of 2001, a figure which includes up to half a million refugees from the neighboring countries of Sierra Leone and Guinea-Bissau. According to the United Nations, Guinea is the largest provider of shelter for refugees in the region, with an estimated 650,000 refugees in 2000, and the pattern has been for refugees to drift to the capital, putting pressure on municipal services. The population growth rate in 2001 was estimated at 1.96 percent. The majority of the population is rural, with just 29.6 percent of the population living in urban

OVERVIEW OF ECONOMY

Guinea is a small economy in terms of the total value of its output. The population is small, at around 7.6 million, and not very productive: the amount of output produced per person is very low at US$540 a year (by way of comparison the U.S. figure is US$29,340 per person, per year). This low output level, combined with poor educational prospects and inadequate access to health care and other human services, has earned Guinea a place near the bottom of the United Nations (UN) Human Development Index, with a ranking of 162 out of 174 countries. The population is growing fairly rapidly, at 1.96 percent a year, with the average woman giving birth to 5.5 children during her lifetime, and this rate adds to the problems of generating higher incomes. Most people— 80 percent—depend on agriculture for their livelihoods, mainly on small family farms. Despite these limitations, in the last several decades Guinea's economic output has increased more rapidly than its population, and average living standards have improved. The agriculture and services sectors have performed better, with industry doing less well.

Following independence from France in 1958 all opposition was ruthlessly crushed, and Guinea pursued a **Marxist** development strategy, which continued until 1984. Inefficient public companies controlled all economic activity, discouraging all private enterprise, and the economy was centrally planned. Vestiges of the old system remain, despite 15 years of support from the International Monetary Fund (IMF) for economic reforms. Only the mining sector remained productive over this entire period, as it operated mainly in enclaves isolated from the rest of the economy.

Some liberal policies were brought in towards the end of President Ahmed Sékou Touré's First Republic, but his death in March 1984 brought a fundamental change in policy. The new government embarked on an economic and financial reform program with IMF support and foreign creditor banking. Phase One of the pro-

gram concentrated on removing the worst distortions in the economy. This task involved a massive **devaluation** of the Guinean franc; the **privatization** or liquidation of government-owned enterprises; trade **liberalization** and the removal of **price controls**; the abolition of state marketing boards; the creation of a commercial banking system; and the review of civil service employment. The initial success of the program won Guinea partial debt rescheduling in 1986 and further IMF funding in 1987.

A second phase of reforms was designed to change attitudes in the public and **private sectors**. It included reorganizing the Customs Service, widening the tax net, and introducing stricter budgetary controls. Guinea failed to secure an extension to the 1987 loan, however, because of budgetary overspending, inadequate revenue generation, privatization delays, and a failure to cut **public sector** employment. Some of the more serious structural problems were addressed in the early 1990s on the signing of a new loan agreement which brought further support and **debt relief** from the donor community.

In 1992 the IMF had again to address the government's inability to reach targets, and in 1994 it extended its lending for 12 months while it constructed a new package. Performance was good in early 1995 but fell again later in the year. An army mutiny in February 1996 compromised donor aid and business confidence and caused the government to be unable to balance the budget after it gave in to the mutineers' demands for pay increases.

When Sidya Touré, an economist by profession, became prime minister in mid-1996, he led a sustained attempt to stick to IMF targets, especially in the field of budgetary shortfalls, public expenditures, and revenue collection. Thus, the structural adjustment loan was renewed in 1997, and lenders rescheduled Guinea's debts on exceptionally generous terms. However, the appointment of a new prime minister, Lamine Sidime, in 1999 led to further IMF and donor problems because, despite allowances being made for the exceptional circumstances of the period, the reform program had drifted off-track and had been suspended. By late 1999 the donor community felt that the situation had improved enough to release further funds to Guinea, under tight conditions. By the turn of the century, however, Guinea had labored for twenty years to improve the structure of its economy and had little to show for its efforts. Despite millions of dollars of foreign aid and loans, the government is still unable to stick to budgetary schemes, unemployment remains high, and the country remains overly dependent on the mining sector.

Agriculture accounted for 22 percent of the GDP in 1998, but it offered employment to 80 percent of the population. Most people involved in the agricultural sector are engaged in some form of subsistence agriculture, which means that they are producing goods for their own consumption or for **barter**. Mining provides the largest source of foreign exchange earnings and government revenue, but its share in the economy is declining due to under-investment and falling world prices. Due to the poor state of the government-owned industries, there has been little interest in the government's privatization program, and only 4 percent of the GDP is generated by formal manufacturing. Altogether, industry provided 35.3 percent of the GDP in 1998. There has, however, been large growth in services, with banking reforms stimulating the financial services sector and external financing bringing a boom in trading and utilities. Services contributed 42.4 percent to the GDP in 1998. Together, industry and services employed 20 percent of the workforce in 2000. The **informal sector**, comprising small-scale manufacturing and services operating from no permanent premises, is also thriving.

Consumer **inflation** has run in single figures since 1992, after hitting a high of 72 percent in 1986. This rate is mainly due to low price rises for local goods and necessities, a fall in the price of imported rice, and the tight **monetary policy** of the government.

POLITICS, GOVERNMENT, AND TAXATION

European traders settled on the coast of Guinea in the 1600s, and the French military laid claim to Guinea in the 19th century after defeating tribal chieftains in the region. Guinea became a colony in 1891, though French forces took until 1898 to consolidate the interior of the country.

Ahmed Sékou Touré led Guinea to independence at the head of the Democratic Party of Guinea (PDG), which he founded in 1947. In 1958 Guinea rejected joining the French African community, and on being granted independence in October 1958, it severed all links with France. Touré set up a Marxist state with a 1-party dictatorship; it is known as the First Republic. Touré's regime quickly became oppressive and totalitarian, and by the time of his death in 1984, about 1 million Guineans lived abroad, while the ruling party enjoyed no popular support. On Sékou Touré's death in 1984, the military seized power, led by Lansana Conté.

Lansana Conté has dominated the political scene in Guinea since 1984. He directed the economy away from **socialism**. Under Conté, the military government sought to decrease the size of the public sector and increase private ownership and investment in a program of sweeping economic changes. Conté invited prominent exiles back into government. However, Conté's early years retained the pattern of eliminating opponents and engaging in frequent coups, along with regularly changing the cabinet.

In 1989, Conté paved the way for democratic political institutions. The Third Republic began in 1991 with the adoption of a new constitution, under which the president is elected to a 5-year term by popular vote. Conté and the PUP have dominated the New Republic, winning all elections by large majorities. However, questions about how the elections were conducted led to controversy. In February 1996 a group of officers opposed to Conté's regime tried to seize power. Conté was held for some hours until he agreed to certain concessions, including doubling army salaries and conferring amnesty on those involved in the mutiny. In 1998 the presidential election was marred by the arrest of the main opposition party leader, Alpha Condé, on charges of trying to overthrow the government. Local elections in 2000 brought a landslide victory for the PUP and widespread condemnation of how the elections were held.

Cabinet reshuffles have followed every election and the 1996 mutiny. The 1996 mutiny also led to budgetary problems and the cessation of IMF support. Following the mutiny political appointees were replaced with **technocrats**, and the prime minister became head of government. Prime Minister Sidya Touré, who had restored donor relations, was replaced by Lamine Sidime in March 1999.

Guinea has 40 registered political parties, with 9 being represented in parliament. The PUP has its stronghold in the Soussou-speaking coastal areas, although through patronage, it holds influence in most towns as well. Most other parties have strong regional support, but little else. The main opposition to PUP comes from its own reformers and the traditional political elite.

The 1982 constitution, which was suspended in 1984, was replaced in 1991 by the "Loi Fondamentale." The president is elected by universal suffrage and serves a renewable 5-year term. The president appoints the Council of Ministers to share executive power. Their decisions are subject to approval by the Legislative Assembly, though opposition from the Legislative Assembly may be overruled by decree.

The 114-member People's National Assembly is elected in a complicated way. One-third of the parliament is elected by a simple majority, and two-thirds by **proportional representation**. The legal system in Guinea is based on French civil law, but with local additions, and may be modified by decree. Guinea was originally supported by the Soviet bloc, but in 1975 Guinea's attitudes changed with the signing of the Lomé Convention (a European Union aid scheme), joining the Economic Union of West African States (ECOWAS), and repairing strained relations with the West, particularly France. Conté has politically realigned the state and has now fully restored Western ties. He is active regionally, and his troops often skirmish with neighbors, as political unrest in Guinea-Bissau, Liberia, and Sierra Leone have created refugees and rebel groups that operate across Guinea's borders.

Mining revenue accounts for 20 percent of government income (including taxes, royalties, and export **duties**), but this figure has fallen with falling world prices since 1987. Guinea has also significantly widened its tax net on incomes and profits, goods and services, and trade; in fact, this source of revenue has multiplied tenfold from 1989 to 1999, though this amount has not been enough to offset the reductions in mining revenue and the increased state wage bill. Overall government expenditures have been reduced since 1991, though not enough to consistently balance the budget.

INFRASTRUCTURE, POWER, AND COMMUNICATIONS

There has been a great improvement since the mid-1980s to Guinea's transport **infrastructure**. The road network has quadrupled in size and several projects are under way to further expand it. In 1996, about 16.5 percent of the country's 30,500 kilometers (18,953 miles) of main routes were paved. Most routes link urban areas to mining areas, and access to the remainder of Guinea is difficult. Half of the 80,000 vehicles on Guinean roads provide public transport.

The only functioning railway links the ports to the mines and carries no passengers. The Kamsar to Kankan railway line no longer operates. Renovation of the railway system is under consideration.

Conakry port is operating at near saturation levels, handling 94 percent of imports. Plans are afoot to build an inland container terminal and reactivate Benty port. The country has 1 international airport, with Air Guinea operating an erratic regional schedule and internal flights to a dozen airstrips around the country.

Telecoms are handled by Sotelgui, which has been managed by Telekom Malaysia since 1995. The number of telephones increased to 25,000 by 1998, up from 19,000 in 1996. Sotelgui was scheduled to introduce a mobile cellular network in late 1997. The number of tele-

Communications

Country	Newspapers	Radios	TV Sets[a]	Cable subscribers[a]	Mobile Phones[a]	Fax Machines[a]	Personal Computers[a]	Internet Hosts[b]	Internet Users[b]
	1996	1997	1998	1998	1998	1998	1998	1999	1999
Guinea	N/A	47	41	0.0	3	0.4	2.6	0.00	5
United States	215	2,146	847	244.3	256	78.4	458.6	1,508.77	74,100
Nigeria	24	223	66	N/A	0	N/A	5.7	0.00	100
Guinea-Bissau	5	44	N/A	N/A	0	0.4	N/A	0.13	2

[a]Data are from International Telecommunication Union, *World Telecommunication Development Report 1999* and are per 1,000 people.
[b]Data are from the Internet Software Consortium (http://www.isc.org) and are per 10,000 people.

SOURCE: World Bank. *World Development Indicators 2000.*

phones is set to double by the end of 2000, although most are still only used in the capital. However, the system is still inadequate, and most companies continue to rely on their own communication services.

A vigorous independent press competes with a state-run newspaper. However, the broadcast media, especially influential in rural areas, are controlled largely by the state.

Guinea has no proven fossil fuel reserves but enormous hydro-electric potential. Nevertheless, firewood accounts for 85 percent of domestic energy needs, and petroleum products are imported. Of the 320 megawatts of installed energy production capacity, 40 percent is privately owned. Only 6 percent of the population receive grid electricity, and this group is mainly in the capital. Several projects are underway to increase electricity production.

ECONOMIC SECTORS

Agriculture generated 22.3 percent of the GDP in 1998, and the major products are rice, coffee, pineapples, and palm kernels. Industry provided 35.3 percent of the GDP. The most important part of the industrial sector is mining, providing approximately 20 percent of GDP. Guinea has major mineral resources and is the world's second largest bauxite producer (bauxite is used to produce aluminum). Services were estimated to provide 42.4 percent of the GDP in 1998.

AGRICULTURE

Agriculture provided 22.3 percent of GDP in 1998, and 80 percent of the employment of the economically active population. Guinea has a climate that allows for a range of activities, but only 15 percent of cultivable land

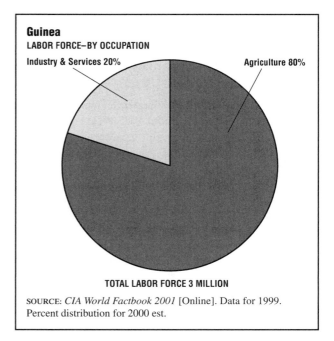

Guinea
LABOR FORCE–BY OCCUPATION
Industry & Services 20% Agriculture 80%

TOTAL LABOR FORCE 3 MILLION

SOURCE: *CIA World Factbook 2001* [Online]. Data for 1999. Percent distribution for 2000 est.

is farmed, and most production is for subsistence. After independence in 1958, agricultural production stagnated, and growth in production did not meet growth in population as many **cash crop** plantations were abandoned. Self-sufficiency in food production is still elusive, despite the end of Marxist economic policies in 1984.

There are projects in hand to improve rice production, which is the main staple and covers 50 percent of cultivable land. However, around 40 percent of the national consumption of rice is still imported. The country is self-sufficient in most other foodstuffs and is even able to export some vegetables and fruit to Europe. Oil palm, rubber, and cotton plantations have received foreign investment.

Approximately 30 percent of rural families own livestock, mainly in the Kankan and Labe regions. The UN estimates that there are 2.4 million cattle, 1.5 million sheep, 54,000 pigs, and 9 million chickens in Guinea. Guinea imports 1,500 tons of meat and 10,000 tons of dairy products for urban use every year, though several projects designed to increase production in these items are under way.

Fishing provides less than 1 percent of the GDP, but 6 percent of exports. Industrial fishing provides half of the 120,000 ton catch, and 65 percent of the industrial catch is caught by foreign-registered boats. A lack of infrastructure reduces the domestic market for fish.

INDUSTRY

MINING. Mining is the most important sector in the economy, providing approximately 20 percent of GDP,

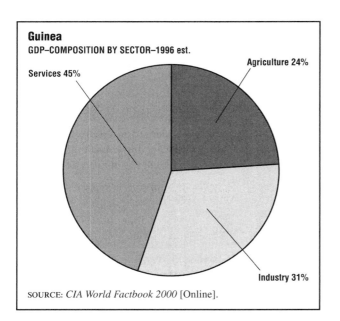

Guinea
GDP–COMPOSITION BY SECTOR–1996 est.
Services 45% Agriculture 24%
Industry 31%

SOURCE: *CIA World Factbook 2000* [Online].

90 percent of recorded exports, and 70 percent of government revenue, though world commodity price declines in the 1990s have hurt the industry. A new mining code has been an incentive to investors, and foreign companies are now responsible for 85 percent of new developments.

Guinea has 30 percent of the world's known reserves of bauxite and is the world's second largest producer of the ore. The biggest company in the sector is owned by the U.S. company, Alcoa, and produces 12.5 million tons per year, and through further investment this figure should rise to 13 million. A Soviet-backed company has had erratic production since the downfall of the Soviet system and produced only 1.5 million tons in 1998, though its capacity is 5 million tons per year. There is also a **joint venture** with Iran, though production has yet to start, as it is still waiting for improvements of the rail links with the capital to make the venture viable.

The **parastatal** Frigvia has the capacity to produce 700,000 tons per year of alumina (the processed form of bauxite), though heavy losses in the years 1991–96 and internal disputes have caused the French advisers to pull out. The privatization sale of Frigvia to a U.S. company is well advanced, and other nations have also shown interest in other smelting ventures elsewhere in the country.

Small-scale gold-mining takes place throughout the country, and several large ventures are planned or have recently come into production. Gold generates about 13 percent of export revenues according to the official figures, but the amount of small-scale mining and smuggling means that much gold production goes unrecorded, and the importance of gold to the economy is significantly greater than the statistics indicate.

The 1985 ban on small-scale diamond mining, which was designed to encourage large-scale foreign investors, was lifted in 1992, and small-scale operators are now responsible for the bulk of the national production of an estimated 80,000 to 125,000 carats per year. Official diamond exports are about US$40 million a year, but because only 15 percent of diamond mining goes through official channels, the real benefit to the economy is closer to US$250 million. The new mining code has sparked considerable international interest.

Guinea has 6 percent of the world's iron-ore, though plans to exploit the deposits have been held back due to their location near Liberia during a period of regional tension. Other reserves include chrome, cobalt, copper, lead, zinc, manganese, molybdenum, nickel, platinum, titanium, uranium, chalk, graphite, and granite. Guinea almost certainly has undiscovered deposits of commercial minerals as only one-third of the country has been surveyed.

MANUFACTURING. Formal manufacturing is small and has fallen from 4.3 percent of the GDP in 1993 to 3.9 percent of the GDP in 2000. The majority of production is in the agro-industry sector, although manufacturing in Guinea also includes brewing, soft drinks, cement, and metal manufacture. The cigarette producer, Entag, closed following a fire in 1999, and most state-run enterprises have closed, and no major enterprise opened in the 1990s. Most manufacturing is concentrated around the capital.

Publicly-funded construction accounts for one-half of total construction, and most of it was concentrated on improving the infrastructure. However, recently the private sector has become more active.

SERVICES

Guinea's financial sector includes the Central Bank, 7 deposit-taking banks, 4 insurance companies, a social security institution, 2 small co-operative banks, and 50 *bureau de change* (currency exchanges). Most banking is in the capital, and the banking system is slowly gaining in public confidence, and more people are prepared to hold their money in the form of bank deposits.

Interest rate controls were lifted as part of monetary reforms in 1993, which also reinforced banking supervision. Banks may set lending and deposit rates, subject to a maximum spread about the **Treasury bill** rate. Short-term loans accounted for 83 percent of the US$170 million credit distribution to the private-sector in 1998, with 55 percent going to trading activities. The increasing funding needs of mines and the increase in deposits have led to an increase in medium-term lending.

Guinea's small tourism industry collapsed after independence and is unlikely to be rejuvenated in the near future. Despite government efforts, only 17,000 people visited in 1998, and most of those were for business. Tourism is mainly limited to wealthy locals and expatriates. A new ministry has been set up to deal with hotels and tourism. The capital has 4 international standard hotels.

INTERNATIONAL TRADE

Guinea's trade balance varies, depending on the output of the mining sector and prices in the international commodity markets. Guinea enjoyed a **trade surplus** in 1998 of US$135 million, on exports of US$695 million and imports of US$560 million. That surplus jumped to US$186 million on exports of US$820 million and imports of US$634 million in 2000. Bauxite and alumina have contributed approximately 70 percent of official export earnings in recent years, with diamonds and gold contributing 20–25 percent. All other exports come from agriculture and fishing. The main destinations for exports in 1999 were the United States, the Benelux countries (comprised of the Netherlands, Belgium, and Luxembourg), Ukraine, and Ireland; major importers were France, Belgium, the United States, and Côte d'Ivoire.

The lack of oil deposits and significant manufacturing means that imports are largely fuels, heavy machinery, transport equipment, and consumer manufactures. The increase in mining is reflected in the increase in machinery imports since 1995. Semi-finished goods have also increased, due to the boost in the construction industry.

Developing countries now provide one-third of Guinea's imports, whereas before industrialized countries supplied more than 80 percent. This change is mainly due to the forging of new links and a shift towards new inexpensive suppliers, predominantly the Côte d'Ivoire and China.

MONEY

Guinea is a member of the Economic Community of West African States (ECOWAS). Unusual for a former French colony, Guinea did not join the Franc Zone at independence. The **exchange rate** remained virtually unchanged from independence in 1958 until 1985 at around GF20–25:US$1 but had depreciated substantially to GF1,940:US$1 in 2001.

Since 1985, economic liberalization measures and a tight monetary policy have been undertaken, as advocated by the IMF and World Bank, and by the late 1990s Guinea had succeeded in reducing the rate of inflation, increasing **foreign exchange reserves**, and raising private investment. Fiscal reform and the elimination of administrative inefficiency and corruption are ongoing concerns.

Consumer inflation has run in single figures since 1992 (but stood at 72 percent in 1986) and this fact is mainly due to low price rises for local goods and necessities, a fall in the price of imported rice, and the tight monetary policy of the government. The **inflation rate** was estimated to be 4.5 percent in 1999.

POVERTY AND WEALTH

Guinea is a poor country by any measure. The **GDP per capita** (according to the **purchasing power parity** conversion, which allows for the low price of many ba-

GDP per Capita (US$)					
Country	1975	1980	1985	1990	1998
Guinea	N/A	N/A	N/A	532	594
United States	19,364	21,529	23,200	25,363	29,683
Nigeria	301	314	230	258	256
Guinea-Bissau	226	168	206	223	173

SOURCE: United Nations. *Human Development Report 2000; Trends in human development and per capita income.*

sic commodities in Guinea) stood at US$1,300 in 2000. A 1994 survey indicated that 40 percent of the population was below the US$1 per day poverty line. About 80 percent of the **labor force** is employed in agriculture, most of which is **subsistence farming**, and the greatest incidence of poverty is in the rural areas.

Education was severely disrupted after independence in 1958, with teachers being one of the first groups to seek exile. The change of government in 1984 brought a greater emphasis on primary education, which, although it is universally compulsory, achieved only 48 percent enrollment in 1996. Secondary education enrollment stood at 12 percent in 1996. Guinea devotes 25 percent of its budget to education and is backed by the IMF and World Bank, with the aim of achieving 60 percent primary enrollment by the end of 2000. Male literacy stands at 50 percent, but the female figure is much lower at 22 percent, according to a 1995 estimate.

Guinea's health statistics are amongst the worst in sub-Saharan Africa. Life-expectancy in 2000 at birth was 46 years. This estimate is an increase from the 1965 figure of 35, although it is far below the sub-Saharan average of 51 years. Moreover, 1 in 6 live births die before the age of one year, and 12 percent die in infancy (between the ages of 1 and 5). Only 45 percent of the population has access to medical care.

Exchange rates: Guinea	
Guinean francs per US$1	
Oct 2000	1,855.0
2000	1,572.0
1999	1,387.4
1998	1,236.8
1997	1,095.3
1996	1,004.0

SOURCE: CIA *World Factbook 2001* [ONLINE].

Distribution of Income or Consumption by Percentage Share: Guinea	
Lowest 10%	2.6
Lowest 20%	6.4
Second 20%	10.4
Third 20%	14.8
Fourth 20%	21.2
Highest 20%	47.2
Highest 10%	32.0

Survey year: 1994
Note: This information refers to expenditure shares by percentiles of the population and is ranked by per capita expenditure.

SOURCE: *2000 World Development Indicators* [CD-ROM].

Household Consumption in PPP Terms

Country	All food	Clothing and footwear	Fuel and power[a]	Health care[b]	Education[b]	Transport & Communications	Other
Guinea	29	18	5	2	9	16	21
United States	13	9	9	4	6	8	51
Nigeria	51	5	31	2	8	2	2
Guinea-Bissau	N/A	N/A	N/A	N/A	N/A	N/A	N/A

Data represent percentage of consumption in PPP terms.
[a]Excludes energy used for transport.
[b]Includes government and private expenditures.

SOURCE: World Bank. *World Development Indicators 2000.*

WORKING CONDITIONS

Wages are fixed according to the Government Labor Code. The official maximum working week for industrial workers is 48 hours, but there is little enforcement.

Guinea has a total labor force of some 3 million workers, and according to official 1995 statistics, some 50 percent of the workers had no formal employment. However, estimates that include participation in the informal economy and subsistence agriculture indicate an unemployment rate of between 8 and 11 percent. Unemployment figures have little significance in Guinea. There are very few with no work at all.

The civil service is the largest formal employer, engaging 3.6 percent of the population. An estimated 16.4 percent of the population earns wages from industry, commerce, and services, with 80 percent of the population employed in agriculture, of which most are engaged in subsistence farming. There is no unemployment benefit, and those who do not work rely on support from charities or their families. Many people would like a modern sector job but eke out an existence on family farms or in casual informal sector activities (such as **hawking**, portering, scavenging) in the urban areas.

The Confederation des Travailleurs de Guinée (Confederation of Guinea Workers, CTG) is the main trade union in Guinea. However, it has done little to improve working conditions and has generally lacked the ability to confront the government or large employers.

COUNTRY HISTORY AND ECONOMIC DEVELOPMENT

1600. European traders settle on the West African coast.

1891. Guinea becomes a French colony.

1898. French troops consolidate the Guinean interior.

1947. Sékou Touré forms the Democratic Party of Guinea (PDG) party.

1958. Guinea rejects joining the French African community and becomes independent, with Sékou Touré as the first president.

1984. Sékou Touré dies. Colonel Lansana Conté leads a military takeover of the government.

1984. The constitution is suspended.

1991. The constitution is replaced by the Loi Fondamentale. Multi-party politics are introduced.

1993. Conté is elected as head of state in presidential elections.

1996. A group of officers attempt a military coup but are unsuccessful.

1998. Conté is re-elected as president.

FUTURE TRENDS

It is very difficult to have economic progress without a platform of political stability, as both domestic and foreign investors are unwilling to risk resources which may not be secure. Conté has improved the domestic environment for business, but conflict with rebels on Guinea's borders with Sierra Leone and Liberia continues to dominate the political scene, though most regional leaders are expected to work together to try to restore stability. Rebel groups from Liberia have destroyed several towns in Guinea. Refugee transfer has started, with the aid agencies struggling to cope with the numbers. ECOWAS troop deployment in the region is attempting to restore order.

Most of the population of Guinea will continue to depend on agriculture for their livelihoods, and progress in this sector is expected to be slow. Guinea's undoubted mineral wealth has created income for only a small section of the community and does little to improve living standards or reduce poverty.

The IMF has pledged further support, and as a highly indebted poor country Guinea is expecting further debt relief. Aluminum companies are showing renewed interest in the country, but realization of investment plans will depend on improving regional stability. The United Nations has asked for stricter diamond controls to keep gems out of the hands of rebel groups in Sierra Leone who are looking for sources of income.

DEPENDENCIES

Guinea has no territories or colonies.

BIBLIOGRAPHY

Economist Intelligence Unit. *Country Profile: Guinea.* London: Economist Intelligence Unit, 2001.

"Guinea and the IMF." *International Monetary Fund.* <http://www.imf.org/external/country/GIN/index.htm>. Accessed October 2001.

La Guinée. <http://www.guinee.gov.gn>. Accessed October 2001.

Hodd, Michael. "Guinea." *The Economies of Africa.* Aldershot: Dartmouth, 1991.

U.S. Central Intelligence Agency. *World Factbook 2001.* <http://www.odci.gov/cia/publications/factbook/index.html>. Accessed September 2001.

U.S. Department of State. *Background Notes: Guinea, December 1999.* <http://www.state.gov/www/background_notes/guinea_9912_bgn.html>. Accessed October 2001.

U.S. Department of State. *FY 2001 Country Commercial Guide: Guinea.* <http://www.state.gov/www/about_state/business/com_guides/2001/africa/index.html>. Accessed October 2001.

—Jack Hodd

GUINEA-BISSAU

Republic of Guinea-Bissau
República da Guiné-Bissau

CAPITAL: Bissau.

MONETARY UNIT: Communauté Financière Africaine franc (CFA Fr). The CFA franc is tied to the French franc at an exchange rate of CFA Fr50 to Fr1. One CFA franc equals 100 centimes. There are coins of 5, 10, 50, 100, and 500ÊCFA francs and notes of 500, 1,000, 2,000, 5,000, and 10,000ÊCFA francs.

CHIEF EXPORTS: Cashew nuts, shrimp, peanuts, palm kernels, and sawn lumber.

CHIEF IMPORTS: Foodstuffs, machinery and transport equipment, and petroleum products.

GROSS DOMESTIC PRODUCT: US$1.1 billion (purchasing power parity, 2000 est.).

BALANCE OF TRADE: Exports: US$80 million (f.o.b., 2000 est.). **Imports:** US$55.2 million (f.o.b., 2000 est.).

COUNTRY OVERVIEW

LOCATION AND SIZE. Guinea-Bissau lies on the west coast of Africa, with Senegal to the north and Guinea to the east and south. With a total area of 36,120 square kilometers (13,946 square miles), the country is a bit less than 3 times the size of the U.S. state of Connecticut. It has about 300 kilometers (186 miles) of coastline along the Atlantic Ocean. Guinea-Bissau also controls a set of islands, named Bolama, about 50 kilometers (31 miles) off the coast. The capital and largest city, Bissau, is located on the coast and has the only international airport in the country.

POPULATION. The United Nations estimated that in 1997 the population stood at 1.1 million. As of July 2001, the *World Factbook* estimated the population to be 1,315,822. United Nations estimates put population growth at 2.7 percent in the years 1975 to 1997. By 2001, the *World Factbook* had estimated population growth to have dropped to 2.23 percent. The average woman in Guinea-Bissau has more than 5 children.

The population is composed of many ethnic groups, with the largest being the Balanta (30 percent), followed by the Fula (20 percent), Manjaca (14 percent), and Mandinga (13 percent). Other groups include Cape Verdean expatriates, Syrian Lebanese, and some Portuguese. Nearly half (45 percent) of the population is Muslim, and the Muslim community dominates the commercial sector and, increasingly, the government.

About 20 percent of the population was estimated to live in or near Bissau. The rest of the population lives as agriculturists in 8 mainly rural regions.

OVERVIEW OF ECONOMY

Guinea-Bissau has one of the least developed economies in the world. The economy relies mostly on agriculture. Nearly 80 percent of the workforce is engaged in agriculture; most work on small family farms and some work as laborers on cotton or cashew nut plantations. The production of cashew nuts is vital to the economy, making up 70 percent of the country's total exports. The **gross domestic product** (GDP) grew by 4.7 percent per year in between 1995 and 1997, compared to 2.6 percent between 1993 and 1994. However, the civil war caused output to fall by 28 percent in 1998, with the industry and services GDP output falling by 40 percent. This decline was a serious setback, as Guinea-Bissau was already one of the 15 poorest countries in the world.

The economy of Guinea-Bissau has not performed well in recent years. Output has increased less rapidly than population, and average living standards have fallen. But development in its widest sense involves more than just income, and in that sense Guinea-Bissau also suffers. The United Nations (UN) includes education and health as well as income in its Human Development Index, for which Guinea-Bissau was ranked 169 out of the 174

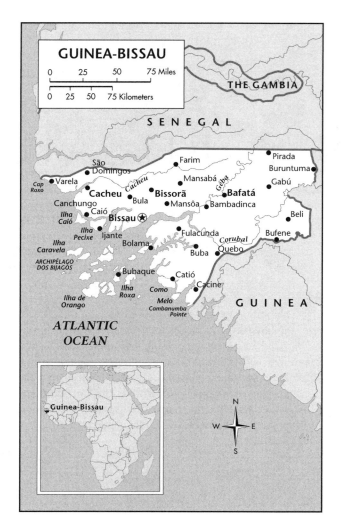

output in the country's main economic sector: agriculture. Without these resources, Guinea-Bissau is also unable to exploit its abundant fish reserves, due to its lack of a modern fleet and port facilities. Hence, fishing is contracted out to foreign fleets. Manufacturing is also small, and mining is undeveloped.

After the decline caused by the **centrally planned economy** that was introduced after independence in 1974, the government began **liberalizing** the economy in the late 1980s. Since 1987, the World Bank and the International Monetary Fund (IMF) have had almost complete control of Guinea-Bissau's economic policy, and **structural adjustment programs** (SAPs) have aimed at removing **price controls**, increasing private enterprise, and reforming the **public sector**. However, the programs have been suspended periodically due to the government's inability to meet fiscal targets, and only after 1994 did the situation start to improve, mainly due to a $15 million 3-year IMF loan. The GDP growth was restored, **inflation** fell, and the **trade deficit** was reduced. The civil war also disrupted the plans, but by 2000 the programs were getting started again, and Guinea-Bissau was aided by the receipt of US$790 million in **debt relief**.

Guinea-Bissau's 1997 entry into the Franc Zone meant that the country adopted the CFA franc as its official currency and required the membership of the regional central bank, the Union Economique et Monetaire Ouest-Africaine (West African Economic and Monetary Union, UEMOA). UEMOA demanded expenditure cuts and higher tax collection. A comprehensive tax reform in 1997 involved the introduction of a generalized sales tax, streamlined custom **tariffs**, and reformed **excise tax**. The government also began eliminating 4,000 civil service posts. However, government expenditure rose due to reform costs and the re-capitalization of Banco Central de Guinea-Bissau. In addition, the rise in prices following Guinea-Bissau's entry into the Franc Zone led to a 50 percent pay raise for civil servants in late 1997. Inflation, which ran at 107 percent per year (1992–96), was chronically high before Guinea-Bissau entered the Franc Zone due to a rise in credit to the economy and the depreciation of the peso (the country's old currency). With the adoption of the CFA franc the government was able to reduce inflation to 17 percent at the end of the year, and, despite the civil war, it fell to 8 percent in 1998 and is estimated to have been 6 percent in 1999 and 3 percent in 2000.

The outbreak of civil war in June 1998 created turmoil in the reform program and put an end to US$10 million of the IMF loan. During the civil war, most economic activities were disrupted, especially in urban areas where most of the fighting took place. The government requested US$138 million in post-war assistance in May 1999. However, only in September 1999 did the IMF give

countries listed in 1998. The **gross national product** (GNP) per capita (converted using the **exchange rate** method) was low at US$160 per year. The **purchasing power parity** conversion (which makes allowance for the low prices of many basic commodities in Guinea-Bissau) puts GNP per capita at US$616. The *World Factbook* estimated the **GDP per capita** (based on purchasing power parity) to be US$850 per capita in 2000. These measures place Guinea-Bissau near the bottom of the low human development and low income categories.

The reasons for such poor economic performance stem from the country's tumultuous political situation. At the end of the 1990s, Guinea-Bissau weathered corruption, a devastating civil war, a coup d'etat, near destruction of Bissau, and displacement of more than 250,000 people. The problems in the country can be traced back to the end of the colonial period in 1974. Since independence, the economy and **infrastructure** has been poorly managed, leading to a reliance on international aid and imports. Weak infrastructure, the lack of equipment, and unskilled labor are the major obstacles to increasing

US$3 million, which was designed to help prepare Guinea-Bissau for another 3-year loan program to support economic reforms. At the same time, the IMF urged Guinea-Bissau to increase tax revenue, control expenditure, **restructure** public enterprise, and re-capitalize the financial sector. This action led to a US$25 million Economic Rehabilitation and Recovery Credit (ERRC) loan in November, and in conjunction with other loans, this should help with the rebuilding of Guinea-Bissau.

POLITICS, GOVERNMENT, AND TAXATION

Guinea-Bissau was first colonized by Portugal in the 15th century, but later incursions met with resistance which culminated in a series of wars (1878–1936). However, during the colonial period Guinea-Bissau remained undeveloped. After a 10-year guerrilla war, Guinea-Bissau unilaterally declared independence in 1973, and Guinea-Bissau's independence was recognized by Portugal in 1974, following a military coup. A new government was formed by the African Party for the Independence of Guinea-Bissau and Cape Verde (PAIGC), which wished to unite Guinea-Bissau with Cape Verde. In 1980, Commander Joao Vieira overthrew the government and severed Guinea-Bissau's link with Cape Verde. The political situation remained unstable in the 1980s, with many attempted coups and much civil unrest.

Since 1991, the country has been a multi-party republic. The president is elected to a 5-year term by popular vote and appoints a prime minister after consultation with the leaders of the **unicameral** National Assembly, the country's legislature. Legislators are elected to 4-year terms. The court system ranges from a Supreme Court, whose members serve at the pleasure of the president to 9 regional and 24 sectoral courts.

Although Vieira forcibly took control of the government in 1980, he had agreed in principle to the implementation of a multi-party democracy in the early 1990s. Predominantly due to a fragmented opposition, PAIGC won the first election, but Vieira won a disputed presidential election in the second round in 1994. The change in government did not erase its economic ineptitude, however. The bad handling of the country's entry into UEMOA in 1997 led to strikes, and although a change of prime minister restored some confidence, corruption scandals soon struck the government. In June 1998, Vieira dismissed the army chief Brigadier Ansumane Mane, for alleged involvement in supplying arms to separatists from the Senegalese region of Casamance, which sparked a civil war. Despite a peace accord, tensions continued until Vieira was ousted in May 1999.

In November 1999, in a multi-party election, PAIGC was defeated, and Kumba Iala (also spelled Yala), the head of the Social Renovation Party (PRS), was elected president in January 2000.

The country implemented a constitution in 1984, which has been amended 5 times, the latest change approved in 1996. The original constitution of 1984 allowed a 1-party state and reforms, instituted by Vieira. The document put all power in presidential hands. In 1990, reforms led to a multi-party state. A crisis was narrowly averted in 1997, when the president unconstitutionally dismissed the prime minister without consulting the Assembly, which was later revoked after referral to the Supreme Court, with Prime Minister Correira reappointed in October with the full support of the main opposition parties. Later electoral organizational problems culminated in civil war and unrest that ended with the dismissal of Vieira.

After the problems of 1997, a committee was set up to revise the constitution and reinforce the judiciary's independence. In 1999, the Assembly passed the new constitution with a two-thirds majority. The constitutional amendments specified that any president could only be elected twice, with each term lasting 5 years, it abolished the death penalty, and it specified that only nationals born in Guinea-Bissau of parents born in Guinea-Bissau may hold high offices of state. The constitution still requires President Iala's approval, but this point is problematic because several incumbents (including Fadul and Brigadier Mane) are not of local descent. Also, the military junta's future plans are uncertain, as it has announced that it would rule alongside the new government for the next 10 years.

Since 1999, 2 parties have dominated the National Assembly—the PRS and the Resistance Ba-Fata Movement (RGB-MB)—and these 2 parties are likely to form a coalition. PAIGC's representation in the Assembly has dropped, despite its change from **socialist** ideals to those of democracy and market economics. The infighting between the new and old guard in Guinea-Bissau was responsible for the expulsion of Vieira and others and has continued. Since the civil war, for example, there has been a rift in the army between the old guard and the new professional soldiers. Because the military is underpaid and promotion is an arbitrary process, the rift could cause military problems in the long term. Some think the political situation in Guinea-Bissau remains very unstable.

Since the civil war, Guinea-Bissau has had intermittent security concerns along its border with Guinea and Senegal. Vieira had requested the assistance of Senegalese and Guinea troops to protect his administration during the civil war, which turned the coup into a regional conflict. In addition, Guinea-Bissau had also been a haven for Senegalese rebels. However, since the end of the war, the new government has sought to mend relations with Guinea and Senegal, and relations with Gambia are good.

INFRASTRUCTURE, POWER, AND COMMUNICATIONS

Guinea-Bissau does not have a very developed or well-maintained infrastructure. Since the early 1980s, one of the country's main goals has been to develop its infrastructure. The 4,400 kilometers (2,734 miles) of roads in Guinea-Bissau, of which about 10 percent (453 kilometers, 281 miles) are paved, has attracted foreign aid in the form of sealing the main road to the northern border and constructing a major bridge at Joao Landin. About 85 percent of the population lives within 20 kilometers (12 miles) of a navigable waterway. Guinea-Bissau has many rivers that could be accessible to coastal shipping, but water transport needs vast improvement. Bissau is the main port, and there are plans for a European Union-sponsored deep-water port that will specialize in minerals and will be linked to Guinea by rail. (As of 2000, the country had no railways.)

Since the liquidation of the **privatized** national airline, Guinea-Bissau has had to rely on foreign-owned carriers. The civil war severely disrupted flights and the main airport only reopened in July 1999. In 2000, the country had about 29 airports, but only 3 had paved runways.

The government has announced its intention to liberalize the telecom industry, which is at present dominated by Portugal Telecom, which has a 51 percent stake in Guinea-Telecom. The government has also announced the extension of telecommunications to the whole country and the introduction of a cellular network, while US-AID will provide Internet access. In 1997, there were 8,000 telephones in the country. By 2000, there was 1 Internet service provider and about 1,500 Internet users.

An experimental television service was started in 1989; by 1997 there were 2 television stations. The country's 3 private radio stations broadcast to nearly 49,000 radios in the country in 1997. Since 1991, a number of private newspapers and magazines have been launched, though all depend on the state printing house for publication. In 1998, there were several newspapers: 1 government biweekly, 1 private daily newspaper, and 3 private weeklies. The national printing press had difficulty maintaining enough raw material to print all the newspapers during the civil war, and publication was sporadic. By the end of the war, more regular publication had returned.

Guinea-Bissau has one of the lowest electrification rates in Africa, mostly because of corruption and inefficiency. The country is completely dependent on petroleum products, despite its own high energy potential, especially in hydroelectric power. Construction of a dam at Saltinho could eventually supply the whole country and provide excess electricity for export. After the development of an offshore upstream oil industry had been delayed by border disputes with Senegal, the United Kingdom's Monument Oil and Gas company and the Chilean company, Sipetrol, agreed to acquire the 3,500 square kilometer block with Guinea-Bissau receiving 22.5 percent of the output. In 1998, the state-owned electricity company was put up for a long-term lease to a private company, but little progress has been made.

ECONOMIC SECTORS

Although all economic sectors in Guinea-Bissau were damaged by the civil war, agriculture remained the most dominant economic sector. Agriculture (including forestry and fishing) contributed 62 percent of the GDP in 1998 and 83 percent of the **labor force** were employed in the sector in 1994. The *World Factbook* reported that agriculture contributed 54 percent of the GDP and employed 78 percent of the workforce in 1997. Industry (including mining, manufacturing, construction and power) employed an estimated 4 percent of the economically active population in 1994 and provided around 13 percent of the GDP in 1998, down from the

Communications

Country	Newspapers	Radios	TV Sets[a]	Cable subscribers[a]	Mobile Phones[a]	Fax Machines[a]	Personal Computers[a]	Internet Hosts[b]	Internet Users[b]
	1996	1997	1998	1998	1998	1998	1998	1999	1999
Guinea-Bissau	5	44	N/A	N/A	0	0.4	N/A	0.13	2
United States	215	2,146	847	244.3	256	78.4	458.6	1,508.77	74,100
Nigeria	24	223	66	N/A	0	N/A	5.7	0.00	100
Guinea	N/A	47	41	0.0	3	0.4	2.6	0.00	5

[a]Data are from International Telecommunication Union, *World Telecommunication Development Report 1999* and are per 1,000 people.
[b]Data are from the Internet Software Consortium (http://www.isc.org) and are per 10,000 people.

SOURCE: World Bank. *World Development Indicators 2000.*

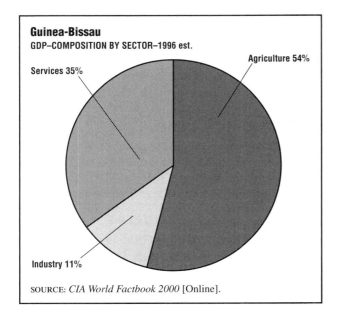

Guinea-Bissau
GDP–COMPOSITION BY SECTOR–1996 est.

Services 35%

Agriculture 54%

Industry 11%

SOURCE: *CIA World Factbook 2000* [Online].

15 percent reported by the *World Factbook* for 1997. According to World Bank figures, the industrial GDP contribution increased in real terms by an average of 2.7 percent per year from 1990 to 1997, although it rapidly decreased by 12.7 percent in 1998 during the civil war. Services employed an estimated 19 percent of the economically active population in 1994 and provided an estimated 25 percent of the GDP in 1998, down from the 31 percent reported by the *World Factbook* for 1997. Despite the disruptions caused by the civil war, the economic sectors were not and still are not able to sustain the country. The economy of Guinea-Bissau is truly reliant on international aid.

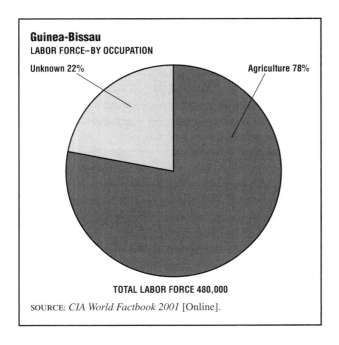

Guinea-Bissau
LABOR FORCE–BY OCCUPATION

Unknown 22%

Agriculture 78%

TOTAL LABOR FORCE 480,000

SOURCE: *CIA World Factbook 2001* [Online].

AGRICULTURE

Agriculture is the most important sector in the economy, providing well over half of the GDP. Food self-sufficiency has been the target of several governments, with the main products being rice, cassava, beans, potatoes, yams, sugar-cane, and tropical fruits. Rice production covers 30 percent of the arable land. The livestock population has recovered after the war, with the number of cattle reaching 550,000 in 2001, which is high in relation to a population of just over 1 million people. The changes in the agriculture sector have sparked much debate about land tenure issues as a result of the conflict between traditional village-based farms (*Tabancas*) and the encroaching large-scale commercial sector (*Pontas*). Even though the first development plan calling for self-sufficiency in food supplies was created in 1983, by the late 1990s foodstuffs remained the largest portion of imports.

The legacy of the Portuguese colonial period lives on in Guinea-Bissau because **cash crops** grown on vast plantations remain the largest export products for the country. Cashew nuts are the most important cash crop (cashew nut output has quadrupled since 1988). Despite suffering setbacks during the civil war, cashew nut production is expected to reach 60,000 metric tons in 2001 from 38,000 metric tons in 1997.

Forestry resources are abundant but under-used. The 2.35 million hectares of forest could produce 100,000 metric tons per year without disturbing the ecology. Under privatization the former **parastatal**, Socotram, has become 4 separate private companies, with a view to increasing competition and raising timber production.

The coastline is rich in fish and shellfish, and joint fishing ventures have been set up with Russian, Algerian, and Portuguese companies (with licensing for this fishing accounting for 40 percent of government revenue [1992–96]). However, over-fishing and lax controls have led to a drop in fishing potential and the introduction of a European Union-backed modernization program, with a quota system and more maritime patrols. In 1996, Guinea-Bissau also signed agreements to cross-monitor fishing zones with 6 other West African nations. Estimated catches of 0.25 to 0.3 million metric tons are possible if illegal fishing can be eliminated.

INDUSTRY

Industry is very small, providing only 13 percent of the GDP in 1998 and 4 percent of employment in 1994. Apart from construction, output consists largely of **consumer goods** for the domestic market. A brewery opened in 1997 and was the only large venture with international investment. Mostly there is little investment due to the poor power supply situation, the unskilled labor force, and the small market size. What little industry existed was heavily affected by the war. The mining sector is completely undeveloped, though prospecting is under way for bauxite, petroleum, and phosphate.

SERVICES

The banking system was radically reformed in 1989 to reflect economic liberalization and again in 1997 with Guinea-Bissau's entry into UEMOA. There are 2 private commercial banks in Guinea-Bissau, and an investment bank was launched with Portuguese capital. All banks were closed during the civil war and only re-opened in July 1999. Loan repayments are difficult due to the effects of the war, and credit availability is also set to contract due to reduced savings. The central bank was replaced by the Banque Centrale des États de l'Afrique de l'Ouest (Central Bank for West African States, BCEAO) when Guinea-Bissau joined UEMOA, and BCEAO has taken over part of the former central bank's assets and liabilities.

INTERNATIONAL TRADE

Since independence Guinea-Bissau has been internationally non-aligned, in order to solicit aid from all available quarters. While trading mostly with Western countries, it has also courted the other countries (including China and Brazil). In March 1997, Guinea-Bissau joined UEMOA as a full member and also became a full member of ECOWAS.

Since independence, trade has experienced many years of deficit. In 1999, imports were US$101 million. The *World Factbook* estimated that by 2000 imports had dropped to $55.2 million. Government efforts to diversify exports and to reduce export taxes have improved exports from US$27 million in 1998 to US$48 million in 1999, but this growth still left a trade deficit of US$53 million. Port closures during the war hindered exports, but the IMF expects exports to reach previous levels of

Exchange rates: Guinea-Bissau	
Communaute Financiere Africaine francs per US$1	
Jan 2001	699.21
2000	711.98
1999	615.70
1998	589.95
1997	583.67
1996	26,373

Note: Rate for 1996 is in Guinea-Bissauan pesos per US dollar. As of May 1, 1997, Guinea-Bissau adopted the CFA franc as the national currency; since January 1, 1999, the CFA franc is pegged to the euro at a rate of 655.957 CFA francs per euro.

SOURCE: CIA *World Factbook 2001* [ONLINE].

60,000 metric tons per year from 1999 onwards. By 2000, exports had risen to US$80 million, according to the *World Factbook*, giving the country a small surplus. Exports go mainly to India, Singapore, Italy, and Portugal, with imports mostly coming from Portugal, France, Senegal, and the Netherlands.

MONEY

Guinea-Bissau since 1997 has been a member of the 8-member UEMOA, and the currency is the CFA franc. The BCEAO issues currency notes and regulates credit expansion throughout the region. Since 1999, the CFA franc has been tied to the euro at 655.959:1 given that France has joined the European Monetary Union.

POVERTY AND WEALTH

Guinea-Bissau is one of the poorest countries in the world, and its population suffers. According to 1991 estimates, 50 percent of the population lives below the poverty line. The GDP per capita was estimated to be US$850 at purchasing power parity in 2000. Although the *World Factbook* estimated in 1991 that the poorest 10 percent of the population controlled 0.5 percent of the GDP and the richest 10 percent controlled 42.4 percent

Trade (expressed in billions of US$): Guinea-Bissau		
	Exports	**Imports**
1975	.007	.038
1980	.011	.055
1985	.012	N/A
1990	.019	.068
1995	.044	.133
1998	N/A	N/A

SOURCE: International Monetary Fund. *International Financial Statistics Yearbook 1999.*

GDP per Capita (US$)					
Country	**1975**	**1980**	**1985**	**1990**	**1998**
Guinea-Bissau	226	168	206	223	173
United States	19,364	21,529	23,200	25,363	29,683
Nigeria	301	314	230	258	256
Guinea	N/A	N/A	N/A	532	594

SOURCE: United Nations. *Human Development Report 2000; Trends in human development and per capita income.*

Distribution of Income or Consumption by Percentage Share: Guinea-Bissau

Lowest 10%	0.5
Lowest 20%	2.1
Second 20%	6.5
Third 20%	12.0
Fourth 20%	20.6
Highest 20%	58.9
Highest 10%	42.4

Survey year: 1991
Note: This information refers to expenditure shares by percentiles of the population and is ranked by per capita expenditure.

SOURCE: *2000 World Development Indicators* [CD-ROM].

of the wealth, there are few reliable figures for the distribution of wealth.

Economic development has been hampered by both low quality and poor coverage of education. Although education is compulsory between the ages of 7 and 13, barely half of the children in that age group attend school regularly. Primary enrollment stood at 60 percent, and secondary enrollments stood at 6 percent in 1997. Most students also supplement family income and frequently miss school. Education has also been hit by strikes over reforms and was badly disrupted by the war. According to 1997 estimates, male literacy was estimated to be 67 percent and female literacy 41 percent.

Health in Guinea-Bissau is in a state of crisis. About 90 percent of the needed funding comes from abroad, though this money is often diverted through corruption and does not reach its intended recipients. There are 1,300 hospital beds in Guinea-Bissau, and Bissau Hospital was badly affected during the war. The spread of disease and endemic malnutrition with resultant high death rates have made the level of health care in Guinea-Bissau the lowest in West Africa. Infant mortality stood at 138 per 1,000 before the war, but this figure has dropped to an estimated 112 deaths per 1,000 live births in 2000. Only a quarter of the population has access to clean water, sanitation, and health care, leading to frequent outbreaks of cholera and meningitis. HIV is also spreading, with an estimated 14,000 adults having been infected by the end of 1999.

WORKING CONDITIONS

The constitution of Guinea-Bissau makes little provision for workers and that which exists is not necessarily heeded. Forced labor is prohibited, and the economy is run along centralized lines, although this is changing under IMF and World Bank pressure. However, most of the population is employed in **subsistence farming** and the formal employment sector is small. There is no formal minimum wage. Children often work to help the

household, leading to poor school attendance figures. Unions in the formal sector have been active, as was shown in strikes following the poorly handled entry into UEMOA in 1997.

COUNTRY HISTORY AND ECONOMIC DEVELOPMENT

1878. Portugal begins the colonization of Guinea-Bissau.

1973. Guinea-Bissau declares independence.

1974. Guinea-Bissau becomes independent from Portugal. Luis Cabral becomes president.

1980. Joao Vieira overthrows Cabral and assumes the presidency.

1997. Guinea-Bissau joins UEMOA.

1998. Civil war breaks out after Vieira dismisses the army chief.

1999. Government of national unity is installed. The Senegalese and Guinean troops who had come to aid Vieira withdraw.

1999. Vieira is ousted. Multi-party elections are held.

2000. Kumba Iala is elected president.

FUTURE TRENDS

It is very difficult to have economic progress without a platform of political stability. Given the fragile peace in Guinea-Bissau, both domestic and foreign investors hesitate to risk their resources. The damage of the civil war and the continuing role of the military have been major concerns for international donors and the business community. Until confidence is restored, Guinea-Bissau cannot expect to make progress in improving the living standards of its people.

On the positive side, the general election was held without major incident and the opposition party gained the majority. It is expected that the former ruling party will continue to be a minority in the Assembly and that the military junta will struggle to reposition itself in the new political landscape. (The political parties have refused to endorse the military junta's proposed pact, which would allow it to participate in government for 10 more years.) Internal security could be unstable as demobilization of the armed forces begins. With the resumption of aid, the economy is expected to continue to recover, but long-term progress will depend on political stability and commitment to economic reform programs.

DEPENDENCIES

Guinea-Bissau has no territories or colonies.

BIBLIOGRAPHY

Economist Intelligence Unit *Country Profile: Guinea-Bissau.* London: EIU, 2000.

Forrest, Joshua. *Guinea-Bissau: Power, Conflict, and Renewal in a West African Nation.* Boulder: Westview Press, 1992.

"Guinea-Bissau." *World Yearbook.* London: Europa Publications, 2000.

Hodd, M. "Guinea-Bissau." *The Economies of Africa.* Aldershot: Dartmouth, 1991.

U.S. Central Intelligence Agency. *World Factbook 2001.* <http://www.cia.gov/cia/publications/factbook/geos/pu.html>. Accessed October 2001.

U.S. Department of State. *Background Notes: Guinea-Bissau, April 1994.* <http://www.state.gov/>. Accessed October 2001.

U.S. Department of State. *Guinea-Bissau: Country Reports on Human Rights Practices, 2000.* <http://www.state.gov/>. Accessed October 2001.

—Jack Hodd

KENYA

Republic of Kenya
Jamhuri ya Kenya

> **CAPITAL:** Nairobi.
>
> **MONETARY UNIT:** Kenyan shilling (KSh). There are 100 cents in KSh1. The Kenyan shilling includes denominations of 5, 10, 20, 50, 100, and 200.
>
> **CHIEF EXPORTS:** Tea, coffee, horticultural products, and petroleum products.
>
> **CHIEF IMPORTS:** Machinery and transportation equipment, petroleum products, iron, and steel.
>
> **GROSS DOMESTIC PRODUCT:** US$45.1 billion (purchasing power parity, 1999 est.).
>
> **BALANCE OF TRADE:** **Exports:** US$2.2 billion (f.o.b., 1999 est.). **Imports:** US$3.3 billion (f.o.b., 1999 est.).

COUNTRY OVERVIEW

LOCATION AND SIZE. Located in east Africa, Kenya has a total area of 582,650 square kilometers (224,962 square miles), rendering it slightly larger than twice the size of Nevada. With a coastline of 536 kilometers (333 miles), Kenya borders the Indian Ocean to the east, Somalia to the northeast, Ethiopia to the north, Sudan to the northwest, Uganda to the west, and Tanzania to the south. Nairobi, the capital of Kenya, is situated slightly south of the center point of the country.

POPULATION. Between 1975 and 1997, the population of Kenya, which more than doubled from 13.7 million to 28.4 million, increased at an exceedingly high average growth rate of 3.4 percent. In July 2000, the CIA *World Factbook* estimated that the population stood at 30,339,770. With a current annual growth rate of 1.6 percent, it is expected that this figure will increase to approximately 37.6 million by 2015. The birth rate in Kenya is 29.35 births per 1,000 persons, while the death rate is 14.08 deaths per 1,000 persons. In terms of age structure, the population of Kenya is relatively young, with 43 percent of all Kenyans aged between 0 to 14 years, 54 percent aged between 15 to 64 years, and only 3 percent aged 65 years and over. In 1997, only 30.4 percent of the

population lived in urban areas, though this figure is expected to expand to 44.5 percent by 2015.

The population of Kenya is highly heterogeneous (diverse). Some of the major ethnic groups include the Kikuyu (comprising 22 percent of the population), the Luhya (14 percent), the Luo (13 percent), the Kalenjin (12 percent), the Kanmba (11 percent), the Kisii (6 percent), and the Meru (6 percent). There are also several other African groups (15 percent), in addition to a small population of Arabs, Asians, and Europeans. With 38 percent of Kenyans adhering to one denomination or another of Protestantism, and 28 percent practicing Roman Catholicism, the majority of Kenyans are Christian. An additional 26 percent of the population follow an indigenous religious system unique to east Africa, while another 7 percent are devoted to Islam. A plethora (a large amount) of indigenous languages are spoken in Kenya, though the only 2 official languages are English and Kiswahili. The latter, which acts as the *lingua franca* (common language) in east Africa, is a Bantu-based language with strong Arabic influences.

Like many sub-Saharan African nations, Kenya currently confronts an HIV/AIDS epidemic of massive proportions. At the end of 1997, conservative estimates by the World Health Organization (WHO) placed the total population living with HIV/AIDS at approximately 1,600,000. The United Nations Development Programme (UNDP) argues that HIV/AIDS is inextricably interrelated to issues of poverty. Poor women in urban areas, for example, are often forced out of economic necessity to engage in prostitution in order to survive. Prostitution, in turn, exposes sexual workers and their clients to high risks of HIV contraction. As such, any effective HIV/AIDS strategy on the part of the Kenyan government will have to address the dynamics of poverty in addition to gender inequality.

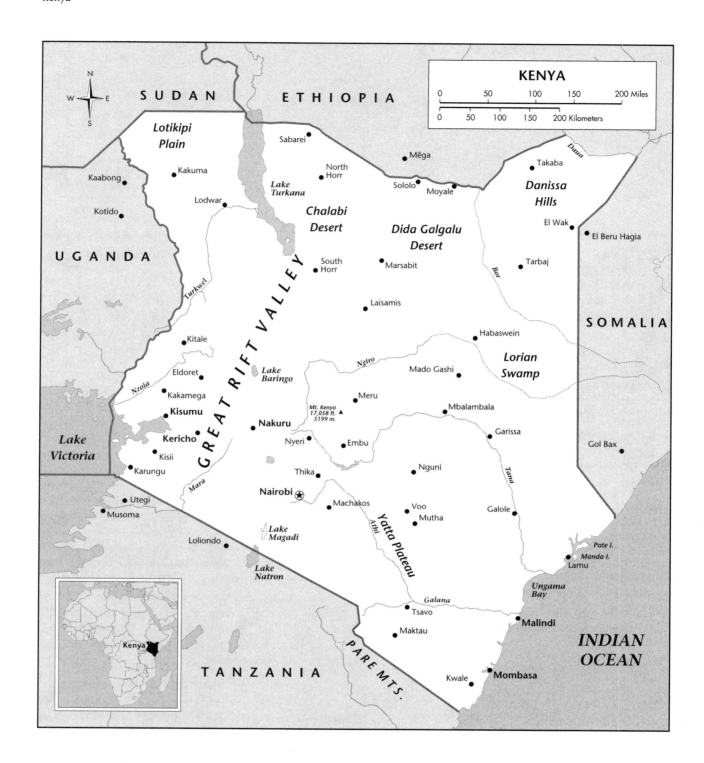

OVERVIEW OF ECONOMY

The area that now comprises Kenya came under British domination in the 1890s, though it was not declared an official Crown colony until 1920. Under British hegemony (complete domination), a racially stratified economy was created, with European settlers controlling a large segment of the fertile land and managing nascent industries, while the African indigenous population worked as laborers on **cash-crop** plantations and in fac-

tories. Indians, occupying a status somewhere between the Europeans and Africans, formed a petty-capitalist class of artisans, clerks, and merchants. By and large, the colonial economy was characterized by settler control of farming lands (settler-economy), with tea and coffee acting as the major export crops designated for sale in European markets abroad.

Following the emergence of various nationalist movements throughout the 1950s, in addition to a series of rebellions (the Mau Mau) against British rule, Kenya was granted independence in December 1963. Under the subsequent rule of the Kenya African National Union (KANU), headed by President Jomo Kenyatta, Kenya experienced significant economic growth throughout the 1960s. Although KANU, a self-proclaimed African **socialist** party, pursued various socialistic policies—including government control of agricultural marketing boards, state ownership of certain industries, and **import-substitution**—the economy under Kenyatta was more or less mixed.

In 1980, a growing **balance of payments** deficit caused by declining terms of trade (international prices for agricultural commodities greatly outweighed by prices for **capital goods**) and high international oil prices, compelled Kenya to borrow heavily from the World Bank. The latter issued a second large-scale loan to Kenya in 1982, with both the first and second loans being subjected to numerous conditionalities (requirements). Such conditionalities centered on increasing the role of the **private sector** in the economy while concomitantly decreasing the role of the government. In particular, the conditionalities—collectively labeled Structural Adjustment Packages (SAPs)—emphasized trade **liberalization** and gradual dissolution of government marketing boards that controlled purchasing and selling of agricultural commodities.

Kenya's slow progress towards implementing agricultural conditionalities, in addition to the widespread use of public resources by government and **parastatal** officials for private gain (corruption), prompted many bilateral donors and the major international financial institutions to severely criticize KANU throughout the early 1990s. Inefficient and corrupt parastatals were singled out as being particularly draining to the country's treasury, and thus a major factor behind deficit and debt problems. Economic performance in the 1990s declined severely, and the average annual GDP growth rate, which stood at 6.5 percent between 1960 to 1980, fell to 2 percent between 1990 to 1999. In August 1993, **inflation** temporarily reached a record high of 100 percent. Five years later, in 1998, the unemployment rate soared to 50 percent.

Both the IMF and the World Bank suspended **structural adjustment programs** in 1997, as a result of KANU's failure to implement governance conditionalities designed primarily to curb corruption and promote sound economic policy. In July 2000, however, Kenya signed a long-awaited 3-year Poverty Reduction and Growth Facility (PRGF) with the IMF, a development that is expected to normalize relations with the World Bank and various bilateral donors. The PRGF, a direct relative of the SAPs, sets out some of the most detailed conditions ever agreed to by a national government.

The Kenyan economy continues to be dominated by agriculture, with tea, coffee, horticultural products, and petroleum products acting as the country's major exports. Export partners, in turn, include Uganda, Tanzania, the UK, Egypt, and Germany. Tourism is the second largest contributor to foreign exchange, while agriculture is the first. Kenya's major imports include machinery and transportation equipment, petroleum products, and iron and steel, most of which are imported from the UK, the United Arab Emirates, the United States, Japan, Germany, and India. Due, in large part, to the uneven terms of trade between Kenya's agricultural exports and higher **value-added** imports, the country runs a significant **balance of trade** deficit. This means that Kenya must borrow heavily to finance imports, hence the various SAPs. In 1998, Kenya's total **external debt** stood at US$7 billion. In addition to commercial loans, the country also receives large amounts of economic aid from various international organizations and bilateral donors. In 1997, for instance, Kenya received a total of US$457 million in aid.

POLITICS, GOVERNMENT, AND TAXATION

The legislative branch of the Kenyan government consists of a **unicameral** National Assembly (bunge), whose representatives are elected by popular vote to serve 5-year terms. The executive branch consists of a chief of state who is both president and head of government. The president is elected by popular vote by members of the National Assembly. The president, in turn, selects a cabinet. The judicial branch comprises a Court of Appeal, a chief justice appointed by the president, and a High Court. The legal system is a complex hybrid of English common law, tribal law, and Islamic law. The military is more or less apolitical, and Kenya boasts one of the most stable political histories in all of east Africa. This record was slightly marred in the early 1990s, when serious ethnic clashes killed thousands and left tens of thousands homeless.

Although KANU, dominated mostly by the Kikuyu and Luo ethnic groups, initially claimed to be socialist, it has long since abandoned this pretense. Indeed, according to Vincent B. Khapoya, author of the *African Experience,* even in the earliest years of Kenyan independence, KANU promoted capitalist policies. During this period, KANU, which replaced the ethnic federalism of the original post-independence constitution with centralization, banned its major opposition party, the Kenya People's Union (KPU), thereby creating a *de facto* (in practice) one-party state. In 1982, KANU constitutionally declared a *de jure* (on paper) one-party state, claiming that this was needed to decisively avoid the effects of "tribalism" (ethnic conflict), supposedly engendered by multiparty politics. Despite the reintroduction of multiparty politics in 1992, the government of Kenya has been headed by the KANU leader, Daniel arap Moi, since the death of Kenyatta in 1978. Moi is currently serving his last constitutional term in office, which is scheduled to end in January 2003.

Some of the other major political parties represented in the National Assembly include the Democratic Party of Kenya (DP), the Social Democratic Party (SDP), the National Development Party (NDP), Forum for the Restoration Democracy-Kenya (FORD-K), and SAFINA. The CIA *World Factbook 2000* states that most opposition parties in Kenya are divided along ethnic lines, a factor which enabled KANU to win the 1997 elections despite its failure to garner the majority of votes.

Tax revenue, which accounted for 86.6 percent (KSh129,230) of government revenue in 1997, is the largest source of government income. The 3 largest sources of tax revenue, in turn, are taxes on goods and services, taxes on income and profits, and taxes on international trade. Each respectively accounted for 37 percent (KSh55,279), 33 percent (KSh49,266), and 15.3 percent (KSh22,773) of government revenue in 1997. Non-tax revenue only accounted for 13.4 percent of government income in the same year.

Taxes on companies in Kenya are set at the relatively high rate of 32.5 percent for resident companies and 40 percent for nonresident companies, though certain deductions and exemptions do apply. The **income tax** system is based on an annual pay-as-you-earn (PAYE) scheme in which a person is taxed progressively on sums of KSh90,240, beginning at 10 percent on the first KSh90,240, and ending at 32.5 percent on the sixth sum of KSh451,200. Those that make less than KSh90,240 are effectively exempted from income taxation. Moreover, a second pro-poor taxation policy includes the exemption of unprocessed agricultural products and processed foodstuffs from the standard **value-added tax** (VAT) rate of 17 percent on all goods. Some **excise tax**

rates, however, such as the rate of 135 percent on cigarettes and tobacco products, and the 95 percent rate on light beer, are set at extremely high rates. Consequently, these commodities are confined to the enjoyment of the wealthy.

INFRASTRUCTURE, POWER, AND COMMUNICATIONS

Kenya has an extensive road network of approximately 95,000 miles connecting most parts of the country. According to the U.S. Department of State *Country Commercial Guide 2000*, however, the current state of most roads is deplorable. Of the total 63,800 kilometers of highway, for example, only 8,868 kilometers are paved (1996 est.). In collaboration with various donors, the Kenyan government recently launched the ambitious 'Roads 2000' project, designed to create links between all major and minor roads, in addition to rehabilitating 20,000 kilometers of roads in 6 urban centers. The project, which will span approximately 3 years, is expected to cost US$245 million. The road network accounts for over 80 percent of Kenya's total passenger and freight transport.

The state-owned Kenya Railways Corporation (KR) manages Kenya's single-track railway system, which runs from Mombasa through Nairobi to the Ugandan border. As a result of heavy operational losses, there has been a steady deterioration in the KR's services. The World Bank and the British Overseas Development Administration are currently funding a railway rehabilitation project to make KR commercially viable, while the government has made plans to open up the railways to private-sector participation by limiting the KR's role to owning and regulating lines. Accordingly, the KR would lease locomotives to private-sector operators.

Kenya's port of Mombasa, which has an annual average freight throughput of about 8.1 million tons, is the country's main seaport and serves most East and Central

Communications

Country	Newspapers	Radios	TV Sets[a]	Cable subscribers[a]	Mobile Phones[a]	Fax Machines[a]	Personal Computers[a]	Internet Hosts[b]	Internet Users[b]
	1996	1997	1998	1998	1998	1998	1998	1999	1999
Kenya	9	104	21	N/A	0	N/A	2.5	0.19	35
United States	215	2,146	847	244.3	256	78.4	458.6	1,508.77	74,100
Dem. Rep. of Congo	3	375	135	N/A	0	N/A	N/A	0.00	1
Tanzania	4	279	21	0.0	1	N/A	1.6	0.05	25

[a]Data are from International Telecommunication Union, *World Telecommunication Development Report 1999* and are per 1,000 people.

[b]Data are from the Internet Software Consortium (http://www.isc.org) and are per 10,000 people.

SOURCE: World Bank. *World Development Indicators 2000*.

African nations. The deep-water port, boasting 21 berths, offers specialized facilities, including cold storage, warehousing, and container terminal.

The international and domestic air transport **infrastructure** is relatively well-developed in Kenya. There are 3 international airports; the largest is Nairobi's Jomo Kenyatta International Airport, which serves more than 30 airlines providing scheduled services to cities around the world. In total, Kenya has 230 airports, including 21 that are paved. Wilson airport in Nairobi, the busiest airport in Africa, handles light aircraft and general aviation.

In 1999, the Communications Commission of Kenya was established to regulate telecommunications and radio communications in the country. In the same year, the state-owned Kenya Posts and Telecommunications Corporation was split into 2 separate parastatals—Telkom Kenya, a telecommunication corporation, and Postal Corporation of Kenya, a postal services corporation. Kencell, a **joint venture** between Vivendi France and Sameer of Kenya, won the second cellular license bid in 1999 to provide cellular services in competition with the Telkom subsidiary, Safaricom. The government plans to sell up to 49 percent of Telkom Kenya through the Nairobi Stock Exchange. As of 1998, there were 290,000 main telephone lines in use, or approximately 9.9 telephone lines per 1,000 people. The United States, in comparison, boasted 640 phone lines per 1,000 people in 1996.

Kenya's electricity services are mostly provided by the state-owned Kenya Power and Lighting Company (KPLC), though an Electricity Regulation Board was appointed in 1998 to manage the opening up of the power sector to independent private producers. Since 82.74 percent of the power supply comes from hydroelectricity, power outages and blackouts have become increasingly common as a result of chronic drought. In 1999–2000, Kenya experienced its worst drought in 40 years, a development that forced the KPLC to introduce an emergency rationing program in July 2000 under which electricity supplies have been cut off for 12 hours a day. Further adding to the problem, hydro equipment tends to be outdated and poorly maintained. Consequently, the government is eager to further develop both thermal and geothermal sources of power. Two international companies were licensed at the beginning of 1997 to respectively produce 43 MW of power from a thermal plant in Mombasa and 45.5 MW from a diesel plant in Nairobi. In 1998, total electricity production in Kenya equaled 4.23 billion kWh. Only 8 percent of the Kenyan population is connected to the national grid.

ECONOMIC SECTORS

As in most of Africa, the legacy of colonialism has ensured the predominance of agriculture in the Kenyan

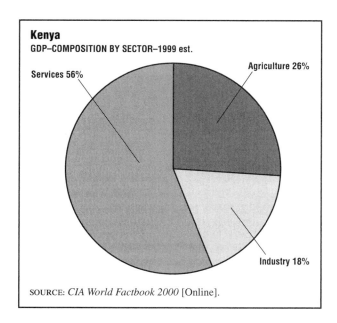

Kenya
GDP–COMPOSITION BY SECTOR–1999 est.

Services 56%

Agriculture 26%

Industry 18%

SOURCE: *CIA World Factbook 2000* [Online].

economy at the expense of industry. According to Norman Miller and Roger Yeager, authors of *Kenya: The Quest for Prosperity,* the colonial-settler-dominated economic system carried with it an explicit discouragement of indigenous **capitalism**. Policies directed towards these ends had the effect of guaranteeing African labor for colonial farmers while simultaneously preventing Kenyans from accumulating capital wealth. Perhaps even more importantly, Kenyan independence leaders accepted the unequal patterns of land tenure and private land ownership that developed in the colonial period, with the caveat that large estates were taken over by emerging African elites (so-called "Africanization"). As Miller and Yeager assert,

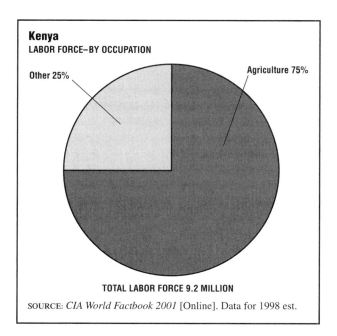

Kenya
LABOR FORCE–BY OCCUPATION

Other 25%

Agriculture 75%

TOTAL LABOR FORCE 9.2 MILLION

SOURCE: *CIA World Factbook 2001* [Online]. Data for 1998 est.

this committed Kenya to a potentially dangerous course of unbalanced economic growth, as the politically powerful landowners maintained a system of agro-export domination that engendered deep class inequality and stymied (frustrated) industrial development. Today, the industrial sector remains relatively small, though many manufacturing sub-sectors have experienced considerable growth in recent years. The service sector, for its part, forms a vital part of the economy, with financial services and tourism predominating.

AGRICULTURE

With 75 percent of the 9.2 million person **labor force** engaged in farming, the agricultural sector is the mainstay of the Kenyan economy. The sector contributes an estimated 26 percent of GDP, and generates 60 percent of the total foreign exchange earnings (1998 est.). The major agricultural products in Kenya include tea, coffee, horticulture, corn, wheat, sugarcane, dairy products, beef, pork, poultry, and eggs.

Tea production, which netted US$520 million in 1998, is Kenya's largest single foreign exchange earner. Coffee and horticulture are the other major agricultural export foreign exchange earners. With the economy so heavily dependent upon the exportation of agricultural commodities for its foreign exchange, however, Kenya is in a considerably vulnerable position. Adverse weather conditions, for instance, can completely affect the economy as a result of decreased production in any given year. Over the past 10 years, IMF statistics indicate that annual tea exports have fluctuated unpredictably, according, in large part, to weather conditions. In 1992, the total volume of tea exports equaled 169,000 tons; in 1996, this figure increased to 229,000 tons, though, in the following year, the total decreased to 206,000 tons. The Economist Intelligence Unit (EIU) November 2000 Report on Kenya estimated tea output declined by 5.3 percent from the year before, leading to a 6 percent decline in the value of exports. The cause of this decline relates to the debilitating drought that the country experienced at the close of the twentieth century.

Coffee production has similarly followed varied patterns of output according to weather conditions. In 1991, 83,900 tons of coffee were produced for exportation, with this figure increasing to 113,500 tons in 1995, and declining to 83,200 tons in 1996. To add to the problems of production instability, revenue acquired from agricultural commodity exports depends heavily upon international prices for a given commodity in a given year. For instance, if there is a considerable coffee yield by most coffee-producing countries of the world, international prices will accordingly decline as a result of a **glut** (excessive supply). The EIU estimated that coffee export

production in 1999 would reach 85,000 tons, a considerable improvement on the 1998 output of 68,100 tons resulting from the improvement in the weather of the coffee-growing regions of the Central Highlands. At the same time, coffee revenue in 1999 showed little increase due to depressed world coffee prices. Coffee export earnings fell to US$125 million in the 12 months prior to the end of August 2000, compared with US$149 million in the same period of the previous year.

Horticulture—primarily the production of flowers, fresh fruits, and vegetables—is the fourth largest earner of foreign exchange and the fastest-growing activity in the Kenyan economy. Unfortunately, the recent drought led to a 6.4 percent decline in horticultural output in 2000 and a fall of 3.6 percent (US$188 million) in export earnings.

As a result of the scarcity of arable land, in addition to the tendency to use valuable land for the cultivation of export crops, Kenya must import large amounts of food in order to feed the population. The latter factor is inextricably related to the domination of large farms producing export crops in the agricultural sector. Such farms are more concerned with producing crops for profit than in producing food for local subsistence consumption. Kenya normally produces only 35 to 40 percent of its domestic wheat requirements, which are estimated at 650,000 tons per year. Adverse weather conditions in 1997 led to a drastic reduction in domestic wheat production, thereby necessitating 465,000 tons of wheat imports. Similarly, in the same year a deficit in maize production had to be rectified with 1.1 million tons of imported maize.

In 1993, Kenya's total arable land was estimated at 8 percent, while permanent pastures and forests and woodland respectively occupied 37 percent and 30 percent of the land. Several environmental problems currently threaten this land, including deforestation (erosion of forests), soil erosion, and **desertification** (drying of the land). Other environmental problems include water pollution from urban and industrial wastes and degradation of water quality from increased use of pesticides and fertilizers.

INDUSTRY

With industry contributing 18 percent of GDP (1998 est.), the industrial sector in Kenya is a relatively small, albeit important one. Some of the major industries include small-scale **consumer goods** producers (plastic, furniture, batteries, textiles, soap, cigarettes, and flour), agricultural products processing, oil refining, and cement. Industrial production is confined exclusively to the urban centers, such as Nairobi and Mombasa.

Until the early 1990s, the Kenyan government pursued a strategy of import-substitution industrialization

(ISI) in the manufacturing sector. ISI seeks to stimulate local manufacturing capacity by blocking manufacturing imports from abroad. Although ISI has been effective in certain contexts, the neo-liberal (the ideology of the complete free market) international financial institutions have criticized it severely for facilitating the development of inefficient firms that do not have to compete with their foreign counterparts. The result is higher prices and poorer quality goods for domestic consumers. In accordance with the conditions delineated in the various SAPs, therefore, the government of Kenya has replaced ISI with a strategy of export-oriented industrialization (EOI). The latter is premised on the idea of stimulating manufacturing industries by engaging in competition and free trade. It has been criticized for not taking into account the possibility that highly competitive foreign manufacturers will depress nascent Kenyan firms if they are granted access to Kenya's markets through trade liberalization.

Aggregately (in total), the value contribution of manufacturing in the Kenyan economy has steadily increased over the past 10 years, rising from KSh6,833 million in 1991, to KSh11,976 million in 1994, and KSh23,490 million in 1996. As other economic sectors have also increased in their value contributions, however, the percentage increase of manufacturing in GDP contribution has not changed significantly. In 1991, manufacturing contributed 3.1 percent of GDP, while this figure only marginally increased to 4.6 percent in 1996. In the same year, the manufacturing sector provided employment for 210,500 Kenyans.

The production output of many manufacturing subsectors has also increased considerably throughout the 1990s. From 1991 to 1996, for instance, output of rubber products increased annually on average by 16 percent, plastic products by 12.3 percent, petroleum and other chemicals by 3 percent, metal products by 5.38 percent, electrical machinery by 7.11 percent, and, finally, clay and glass products by a whopping 46.85 percent. The cement industry, one of Kenya's most valuable, increased the value of its exports from US$15.2 million in 1992 to US$43.3 million in 1997. Other sectors did not fare so well, and annual average output for many actually declined. Beverages and tobacco declined on average by 0.13 percent, textiles by 6.9 percent, and clothing by 12.11 percent.

Although the Kenyan government does not maintain data on the value of **Foreign Direct Investment** (FDI), the U.S. Investment Promotion Center estimated that FDI totaled more than US$1 billion in 1994. Many foreign firms are located within Export Processing Zones (EPZs)—designated areas in which foreign firms are granted **tax holidays** and other concessions in order to attract their investment. There are a total of 14 EPZs in Kenya, and manufacturers are enticed with a ten-year corporate tax holiday and a 25 percent tax rate thereafter. Some of the major foreign manufacturers in the Kenyan economy include Bayer AG (German pharmaceuticals), British Petroleum, Cadbury Schweppes (UK confectionery/beverages), Coca-cola (U.S.), General Motors (U.S.), Colgate Palmolive (U.S. hygiene products), Mitsubishi (Japanese motor vehicles), and Mobil (U.S. petroleum products). While many praise FDI for creating needed investment and facilitating transfers of technology, others argue that it allows foreign firms to operate in isolation from the rest of the economy and that their profits are often expatriated (returned to the investor country).

The mining sector in Kenya, as a sub-component of the industrial sector, is negligible, though there are small deposits of gold, limestone, soda ash, salt barites, rubies, flourspar, and garnets. In 1991, mining only accounted for 0.1 percent of GDP, with this figure remaining exactly the same in 1996.

SERVICES

Accounting for approximately 56 percent of GDP, the service, or tertiary sector, is the most valuable area of economic activity in the domestic economy. The service sector consists mainly of 2 major areas: tourism and financial activities. **Retail**, which includes a significant number of restaurants in the urban centers, is dominated by small-scale street vendors, many of whom form part of the **informal sector**. In total, 144,300 Kenyans were involved in retail in 1996, not counting those that were engaged in the informal sector. The informal sector itself, known in Kenya as "jua kali," employs approximately 64 percent of all Kenyan urban workers. It is also the most dynamic sector in the economy in terms of job creation, accounting for about 90 percent of new jobs outside the **smallholder** farm sector. Informal sector activities, such as carpentry, motor vehicle repair, tailoring, **hawking**, and selling various fruits, vegetables, and other commodities, are largely service-based. Though the government recognizes the value of the informal sector, the U.S. Department of State *Country Commercial Guide 2000* argues that it could do more to develop needed infrastructure.

TOURISM. With its beautiful coastal beaches, wildlife, unique scenery, and history of relative stability, Kenya is the tourist hub of east Africa. Indeed, tourism is the country's second-largest foreign exchange earner, next to the agricultural sector as a whole. In 1995, Kenya received an estimated 785,000 tourists with earnings of about US$486 million, a slight decline from the US$501 million in earnings and 807,600 tourists of the previous year. Earnings from tourism further declined to US$448 million in 1996, though this figure still equaled about 65 percent of the combined revenues from tea and coffee exports. Europeans account for more than 50 percent of Kenya's tourists, while Americans account for less than 10 percent.

According to the U.S. Department of State *Country Commercial Guide 2000,* the relative decline in Kenya's tourism sector can be attributed to a high level of crime, disintegrating infrastructure, the eruption of ethnic violence in the early 1990s, and growing competition from neighboring countries. Reassuringly, political stability has returned and the government has offered various fiscal incentives to firms operating in the tourism sector, thereby counterbalancing the negative trends. Several **multinational corporations** are involved in the tourist sector in Kenya, including the Hilton International (British), the Intercontinental Hotel (Japanese), and Safari Park Hotel (South Korean).

FINANCIAL SERVICES. The financial sector has grown considerably in importance throughout the 1990s, increasing its value contribution to the economy from KSh7,069 million in 1991 to KSh9,843 million in 1996. In terms of GDP contribution, the financial sector accounted for 8.2 percent of GDP in 1991 and 10.1 percent in 1996. In the same year, approximately 81,000 Kenyans worked in the financial sector.

As of the beginning of 1998, the highly diversified financial sector in Kenya consisted of the Central Bank of Kenya, 53 domestic- and foreign-owned commercial banks, 15 non-bank financial institutions, 2 mortgage finance companies, 4 building societies, and numerous insurance companies and other specialized financial institutions. The banking sector is dominated by 4 large banks, which aggregately control 50 percent of all bank assets and 52 percent of bank deposits. The largest bank, the state-owned Kenya Commercial Bank, accounts for 17 percent of bank assets and 18 percent of bank deposits. The multinational Barclays Bank, with 16 percent of bank assets and 15 percent of bank deposits, is next in line, followed by the state-owned National Bank of Kenya and the multinational Standard Chartered Bank, each respectively boasting 8 percent of bank assets and 9 percent of bank deposits.

The Nairobi Stock Exchange, which handles 61 listed firms, was established in 1954. In January 1995, the stock market, including stock-brokerage, was opened up for foreign direct participation, although there is a 40 percent limit on foreign ownership. **Market capitalization** has recently manifested considerable growth, increasing from US$1.89 billion in 1995 to US$2.08 billion in 1998.

INTERNATIONAL TRADE

As an agricultural exporting and capital goods importing nation, Kenya routinely runs a balance of trade deficit that renders it highly dependent on loans and aid

Trade (expressed in billions of US$): Kenya		
	Exports	Imports
1975	.606	.945
1980	1.245	2.125
1985	.958	1.436
1990	1.032	2.124
1995	1.879	2.949
1998	1.993	3.280

SOURCE: International Monetary Fund. *International Financial Statistics Yearbook 1999.*

to finance needed imports. The balance of trade deficit varies widely, depending upon, among other things, the market success of agricultural export commodities in a given year (as we have seen, this in turn, depends on both weather conditions and international commodity prices). In 1996, for instance, the deficit stood at US$73.5 million, while this figure increased dramatically to US$251.7 million in 2000—a year of endemic drought. With a large amount of **foreign exchange reserves**, however, which equaled US$875 million in 2000, Kenya has been able to reduce its total external debt significantly, from US$6.9 billion in 1996 to US$5.7 billion in 2000.

Kenya's principal exports include tea, coffee, horticultural products, and petroleum products. Exports designated to Western Europe, particularly the United Kingdom and Germany, have increased considerably from US$437 million in 1992 to US$672 million in 1997. This increase is dwarfed, however, in comparison to the increase of exports designated to African economies. In 1992, Kenyan exports to Africa equaled US$330 million, 5 years later, in 1997, this figure exploded to US$971 million. This phenomenal increase is largely the result of the East African Cooperation (EAC) economic treaty signed with Uganda and Tanzania in 1996. The EAC promotes regional economic integration through policies geared towards eventually harmonizing inter-territorial **tariffs**, removal of trade barriers, and, in the longer-term, currency alignment.

Kenya's major imports include machinery and transportation equipment (capital goods), petroleum products, and iron and steel (**intermediate goods**). In 1996, the total value of Kenyan imports equaled US$2,928 million, US$727 million of which came from capital goods and US$1,719 million of which derived from intermediate goods. Imports from Western Europe, once more particularly Germany and the United Kingdom, have increased significantly from US$715 million in 1994 to US$1,048 million in 1997. Imports from African countries only increased marginally from US$59 million in 1994 to US$136 million in 1997. The balance of trade surplus with

Africa signifies Kenya's relative economic strength in the continent. Japan and the United States are also important exporters to Kenya, with each respectively exporting goods and services equaling US$245 million and US$261 million in 1997.

The Kenyan government has promoted policies of trade liberalization throughout the 1990s, reducing, for instance, the maximum tariff rate from 45 percent in June 1994 to 25 percent in June 1997. While the international financial institutions and Western governments in general tend to support trade liberalization, it may have negative effects for a country like Kenya that depends on agricultural exports in exchange for higher value-added capital imports. If Kenyan manufacturing firms cannot compete with their foreign counterparts, reduction of trade protection measures, such as tariffs, will simply lead to the retardation of the Kenyan industrial sector. The result would be further entrenchment of the agricultural sector in the economy, and thus the prolonging of the unequal trading patterns that sustain the country's severe balance of trade deficit. In such a context, the pro-trade idea that all countries benefit when each focuses on producing and exporting that in which they have a comparative advantage and on importing that in which they do not, seems hardly relevant.

Regional trading arrangements (RTAs), such as the EAC, may offer the benefits associated with trade, while providing a more level playing field since member countries are more likely to be at a similar level of development. Still, more relatively developed countries might benefit disproportionately, which seems to be the case with Kenya and the EAC. Kenya is also a member of the 21-country RTA, the Common Market for Eastern and Southern Africa (COMESA).

MONEY

SAP-induced reforms in the first quarter of 1994 instituted a free-**floating exchange rate** policy in Kenya, with the value of the Kenyan shilling thereafter being determined by its supply and demand in international money markets. Prior to the reform, the Kenyan government followed a fixed exchange regime in which the shilling was pegged to the U.S. dollar at a specific rate, subject to alterations only to rectify substantial distortions. Since the introduction of the free-floating exchange regime, the shilling has generally depreciated in relation to the U.S. dollar, meaning it takes increasingly greater quantities of shillings to equal the value of 1 U.S. dollar. In 1995, the **exchange rate** was averaged at KSh51.430 per US$1, with the rate depreciating to an average of KSh70.326 per US$1 in 1999, and an average of KSh76.93 per US$1 in 2000. The EIU expects that the rate will average at KSh80 per US$1 in 2001, and KSh84 per US$1 in 2002. While

Exchange rates: Kenya	
Kenyan shillings (KSh) per US$1	
Dec 2000	78.733
2000	76.176
1999	70.326
1998	60.367
1997	58.732
1996	57.115
SOURCE: CIA *World Factbook 2001* [ONLINE].	

currency depreciation is positive for the exporting sectors of the Kenyan economy, since less foreign money is needed to buy Kenyan exports which thereby renders them more attractive, it has the adverse effect of increasing the prices of imports. For a drought-effected food-importing nation like Kenya, increases in the prices of essential imports can have negative consequences on the poorest segments of the society.

POVERTY AND WEALTH

Kenya is a country characterized by abject poverty on the one hand and conspicuous wealth on the other. According to Miller and Yeager, the roots of inequality stem, in large part, from the colonial heritage that bestowed upon the nation highly unequal patterns of land tenure. Since the KANU regime has done very little to rectify the situation of land ownership in the post-independence era, a small segment of the population—now African instead of European—continues to own large tracts of land at the expense of the largely small-holding and landless peasantry. This landed elite, often absentee (having mangers run their estates so that they can live elsewhere) and centered in the urban centers, controls much of the industrial and commercial sectors. In addition to the elite landowners (though the groups are not always mutually exclusive), there exists a small class of politicians and parastatal managers that exercise extensive access to public resources. As Miller and Yeager assert, politics in Kenya are synonymous with the pursuit

GDP per Capita (US$)					
Country	**1975**	**1980**	**1985**	**1990**	**1998**
Kenya	301	337	320	355	334
United States	19,364	21,529	23,200	25,363	29,683
Dem. Rep. of Congo	392	313	293	247	127
Tanzania	N/A	N/A	N/A	175	173
SOURCE: United Nations. *Human Development Report 2000; Trends in human development and per capita income.*					

Distribution of Income or Consumption by Percentage Share: Kenya

Lowest 10%	1.8
Lowest 20%	5.0
Second 20%	9.7
Third 20%	14.2
Fourth 20%	20.9
Highest 20%	50.2
Highest 10%	34.9

Survey year: 1994
Note: This information refers to expenditure shares by percentiles of the population and is ranked by per capita expenditure.

SOURCE: *2000 World Development Indicators* [CD-ROM].

of profit, and the Kenyan political elite is particularly notorious for its high degree of corruption.

David Himbara, author of *Kenyan Capitalists, the State, and Development,* observes that cutting across the axis of class inequality in Kenya is a second axis of ethnic inequality. Thus, throughout the Kenyatta era, a large portion of the political elite consisted of members of the Kikuyu ethnic group. Indeed, Himbara states that Kenyatta's policy of Africanization was in fact a policy of "Kikuyization." Since the beginning of the Moi era, however, the Kalenjin ethnic group has displaced the majority of the Kikuyus from the most senior echelons of state power.

In contrast to the tremendous wealth of the politically- and agriculturally-based economic elite, the vast majority of the Kenyan population lives in poverty. The United Nations Development Programme's (UNDP) human development index (HDI) listings, which arranges countries according to their overall level of human development, ranks Kenya 138th out of a total of 174 nations. The HDI, a composite index (one that assesses more than one variable) that measures life expectancy at birth, adult literacy rate, school enrollment ratio, and **GDP per capita**, is indicative of a country's general social and economic well-being. As such, Kenya's HDI ranking demonstrates that the country is considerably underdeveloped, though it does fare better than many of its sub-Saharan African neighbors.

The Kenyan government spends relatively little on health, though it does spend a considerable, albeit declining, amount on education. In 1998, for example, public expenditure on health and education as percentages of GDP respectively equaled 2.2 percent and 6.5 percent, as opposed to 1.7 percent and 7 percent in 1990. Comparatively, the United States spent 5.4 percent of GDP on education and 6.5 percent on health in 1998. The vast majority of Kenyans, for their part, spend their meager incomes on the basic necessities of life, such as food, rents, clothing, fuel, and transportation. As a result of a declining economy and a deepening of poverty, however, Kenyans consume less food calories on a daily basis then they did thirty years ago. In 1970, the average Kenyan consumed 2,187 calories per day, with this figure declining to 1,976 calories per day in 1997. Americans, in contrast, consumed on average 2,965 calories per day in 1970 and 3,699 calories per day in 1997. This is not surprising, considering the increase in the GNP per capita has been grossly outweighed by mounting inflation in the past 10 years. The UNDP estimates that the annual growth rate in GNP per capita between 1990 to 1998 was 0.3 percent, while the average annual rate of inflation during the same period was 10.6 percent.

WORKING CONDITIONS

In 1997, an estimated 1.2 million males and 473,400 females engaged in formal wage employment. Women work overwhelmingly in services, while men work in education, manufacturing, building and construction, trade, and transport. The highest percentage of females working in male-dominated areas of the formal sector is in education, where women constitute 40 percent of the workforce. Women almost exclusively staff several textile factories, reflecting their overall lower status in the economy. More-

Household Consumption in PPP Terms

Country	All food	Clothing and footwear	Fuel and power[a]	Health care[b]	Education[b]	Transport & Communications	Other
Kenya	31	9	21	2	8	3	26
United States	13	9	9	4	6	8	51
Dem. Rep. of Congo	34	2	12	3	3	11	36
Tanzania	67	6	5	4	12	6	0

Data represent percentage of consumption in PPP terms.
[a]Excludes energy used for transport.
[b]Includes government and private expenditures.
SOURCE: World Bank. *World Development Indicators 2000.*

over, women tend to suffer from a double-work day, being forced out of economic necessity to engage in income-earning activities during the day, and then being responsible for the domestic work activities at night.

There are at least 33 unions representing 350,000 workers in Kenya—approximately 20 percent of the country's industrial workforce. With the exception of the National Union of Teachers, which represents 150,000 teachers, all unions are affiliated with the Central Organization of Trade Unions (COTU), an organ not known for its vigorous pursuance of workers' rights. Created by the government in 1965, COTU's leadership is comprised of the leadership of affiliated unions, though it is common for KANU to provide funding and other support for the election of senior officials.

The Trade Disputes Act permits workers to strike, provided that 21 days have elapsed following the submission of a written letter to the Minister of Labor. At the same time, however, the Ministry of Labor has the right to determine the legality of any strike, a power that was abused in 1994 when several strikes were declared illegal despite the requisite warnings. The government's response to wildcat strikes is usually severe, a problem which has been raised by various workers' rights organizations with the International Labor Organization (ILO). Members of the military services, police, prison guards, and members of the National Youth Service are legally forbidden to strike. Also, labor laws protecting workers, such as the right to organize and bargain collectively, are subject to numerous exceptions in the Export Processing Zones (EPZs).

Children under the age of 16 years are prohibited from working in the industrial sector, and the government has put forward concerted efforts to ensure this regulation is followed. Children often financially assist their parents by working as domestic servants in private homes, partaking in the informal sector, and working in family business and agriculture. Given the high levels of adult unemployment and **underemployment**, the employment of children in the formal industrial sector rarely occurs.

According to the U.S. Department of State Kenya Country Report on Human Rights Practices for 1998, the minimum wage, which has 12 separate scales according to location, age, and skill level, is insufficient to meet the daily needs of a worker and family. Consequently, most workers rely on second jobs, **subsistence farming**, informal sector opportunities, or the extended family for additional support. The legal limitation of a workweek for workers in the non-agricultural sector is 52 hours, while employees are entitled to 1 rest day per week. There are also provisions for one-month annual leave and sick leave. The Factories Act of 1951 sets forth detailed health and safety standards, which have been increasingly enforced since the early 1990s with the dramatic growth of

factory inspections. Still, many workers who find themselves in hazardous conditions are reluctant to file complaints for fear of illegal dismissal.

COUNTRY HISTORY AND ECONOMIC DEVELOPMENT

8TH CENTURY. Arab and Persian settlements begin sprouting along the Kenyan coast. The Kiswahili language develops as a *lingua franca* for trade between the newcomers and the Bantu inhabitants.

16TH CENTURY. Arab dominance along the coast gives way to Portuguese ascendancy, following the first Portuguese contacts made in 1498.

19TH CENTURY. The United Kingdom establishes its influence in the Kenyan region with the arrival of various explorers, commercial representatives, and missionaries.

1895. The government of the United Kingdom establishes the East African Protectorate and subsequently opens the fertile highlands to white settlers. The settlers are allowed a voice in government even before Kenya is officially made a colony in 1920, though Africans are denied any form of political participation until 1944.

1952–1959. The so-called Mau Mau rebellion erupts against British colonial rule, and African participation in the political process increases rapidly.

1963. Kenya becomes an independent nation with Jomo Kenyatta of the Kikuyu ethnic group and Kenya African National Union (KANU) party as president. KANU, which claims to be socialist, promotes many capitalistic practices, though the state creates many parastatals in so-called strategic areas of the economy.

1969. With the banning of the major opposition party, the Kenya's People Union (KPU), Kenya becomes a *de facto* one-party state.

1978. Following the death of Kenyatta, Daniel arap Moi succeeds as president. Moi continues to be the president of the country.

1980. Kenya receives its first conditional World Bank loan, marking the commencement of a lengthy period of international financial institution-sponsored structural adjustment programs designed to increase the role of the free market in the economy.

1982. Amendments to the constitution make Kenya a *de jure* one-party state.

1992. The Kenyan government re-introduces multi-party politics.

2000. Kenya signs a long-awaited 3-year Poverty Reduction and Growth Facility (PRGF) with the IMF.

The PRGF is expected to normalize relations with the World Bank and various bilateral donors, which had soured in the mid-1990s as a result of government corruption and resistance to implementing reforms.

FUTURE TRENDS

Kenya represents an excellent example of the general economic and political trends that have prevailed, in varying degrees, throughout most of sub-Saharan Africa in the 1990s. On the political front, significant liberalization has occurred, with the various SAPs forcing the Kenyan government to deal with major issues of corruption and mismanagement. Moreover, the reintroduction of multiparty politics in 1992 certainly represents a positive development in terms of the elaboration of a democratic system. Yet, all the while, the widespread outbreak of ethnic violence in the early 1990s demonstrates that political stability is precarious, especially in an environment characterized by rampant poverty and deep inequality.

Economically, the various SAPs that have been implemented have yet to usher in an age of sustained growth, a factor that may be attributed, in part, to certain inappropriate policies, such as major trade liberalization. Indeed, the general economic situation seems to be worsening, as indicated by the low GDP growth rates and the consistently declining GNP per capita. At the same time, there is no denying that certain major economic reforms are needed, as the inefficiency and commercial failure of most parastatals clearly suggests. The experience of state-led development in Southeast Asia also indicates that the state cannot altogether remove itself from the arena of economic activity. In the words of Himbara, "there can be no substitute for the state in capitalist development. Nor is it likely that international financial institutions, which are currently attempting to reconstruct elements of the Kenyan state and force the adoption of reforms, can become a surrogate for a national interventionist state that conceives and implements a consistent program of development."

DEPENDENCIES

Kenya has no territories or colonies.

BIBLIOGRAPHY

Himbara, David. *Kenyan Capitalists, the State, and Development.* Boulder: Lynne Rienner Publishers, 1994.

International Monetary Fund. *IMF Staff Country Report, Kenya: Statistical Appendix: 1998.* <http://www.imf.org>. Accessed May 2001.

Khapoya, Vincent B. *The African Experience.* New Jersey: Prentice Hall, 1998.

Miller, Norman, and Roger Yeager. *Kenya: The Quest for Prosperity.* Boulder: Westview Press, 1994.

United Nations Development Programme. *Human Development Report 2000.* New York: Oxford University Press, 2000.

U.S. Central Intelligence Agency. *The World Factbook 2000: Kenya.* <http://wwww.CIA.gov/CIA/publications/factbook/geos/tz.html>. Accessed May 2001.

U.S. Department of State. *Background Notes: Kenya: 1998.* <http://www.state.gov/www/background_notes/kenya_0008_bgn.html>. Accessed May 2001.

U.S. Department of State. *FY 1999 Country Commercial Guide: Kenya: 1999.* <http://www.state.gov/www/about_state/business/com_guides/1999/Africa/Kenya99.html>. Accessed May 2001.

U.S. Department of State. *Kenya Country Report on Human Rights Practices for 1998.* <http://www.state.gov>. Accessed May 2001.

World Bank Group. *Kenya: Competitiveness Indicators.* <http://wbln0018.worldbank.org/psd>. Accessed May 2001.

—Neil Burron

LESOTHO

Kingdom of Lesotho
Muso oa Lesotho

CAPITAL: Maseru.

MONETARY UNIT: Loti (L) (the plural form is maloti). One loti equals 100 lisente. Notes include denominations 2, 5, 10 , 20, 50, 100, and 200 maloti. Coins include denominations of 2, 5, 10, 25, 50, 100, 200, and 500 lisente. The South African Rand is also accepted as legal currency on par with the loti.

CHIEF EXPORTS: Textiles (clothing and footwear), raw wool and mohair, agricultural produces (corn, wheat, pulses, sorghum, barley), livestock (cattle, sheep, and goats).

CHIEF IMPORTS: Food, building materials, vehicles, machinery, medicines, fuels.

GROSS DOMESTIC PRODUCT: US$5.1 billion (purchasing power parity, 2000 est.).

BALANCE OF TRADE: Exports: US$260 million (2000). **Imports:** US$780 million (2000). [The CIA *World Factbook 2001* estimated exports at US$175 million f.o.b. and imports at US$700 million f.o.b. for 2000.]

COUNTRY OVERVIEW

LOCATION AND SIZE. Formerly called Basutoland, Lesotho is a small, landlocked, and mountainous state in southern Africa. The total area of 30,355 square kilometers (11,718 square miles) is a geographic enclave completely surrounded by the Republic of South Africa. There are no large lakes or direct access to the sea. This is the only country in the world where all the terrain is 1,000 meters (3,300 feet) above sea level. The westward tilting highland plateau descends from steep basaltic ridges into deep gorges and treeless rolling lowlands. The confluence of the Orange and Makhaleng Rivers form the lowest point (1,400 meters/4,593 feet), while Thabana Nitlenyana is the highest peak (3,482 meters/11,424 feet). The 3 large rivers, the Orange, the Caledon, and the Tugela, all rise in the mountains. Most of the population lives in a fertile 30 to 65 kilometers (18 to 40 miles) strip of lowland adjacent to the Caledon River in northwest

Lesotho, where the capital of Maseru (population 386,000) is located.

Positioned in the Southern Hemisphere, the kingdom enjoys a temperate climate with 300 days of annual sunshine and well marked seasons that vary significantly with elevation. The cool lowland winters last from May to July and become very cold in the mountainous center of the country where freezing temperatures occur most evenings. Summer extends from November to January, when the lowland daytime temperatures frequently exceed 37°C (100°F). About 85 percent of the rain falls from October to April, when snow blankets the highlands. Periodic droughts, lowland flooding, and deadly lightning strikes are the main climate hazards.

POPULATION. The 2000 population of 2.1 million was an increase of 6.5 percent since 1990. There are 33.4 live births per 1,000 population, countered by a death rate average of 12.7 per 1,000 population. The gap between these 2 rates explains why the United Nations is projecting an annual growth rate of 2.07 percent to the year 2015. The population is expected to reach 2.4 million by the year 2025. In 2000, the life expectancy at birth was 44.6 years for the total population and slightly higher for women. This dropped from 52.4 years in 1995 and reflects the devastating effects of the HIV/AIDS and tuberculosis epidemics. The total fertility rate of 4.15 children per woman is among the world's highest and is nearly double that of fully industrialized countries. Outmigration in search of employment and the HIV/AIDS epidemic will likely curb population growth during the next 50 years. This "demographic fatigue" (a declining growth rate for negative reasons) is common in developing African countries.

The population is overwhelmingly "Basotho" (99.7 percent). Europeans, Asians, and other Africans comprise

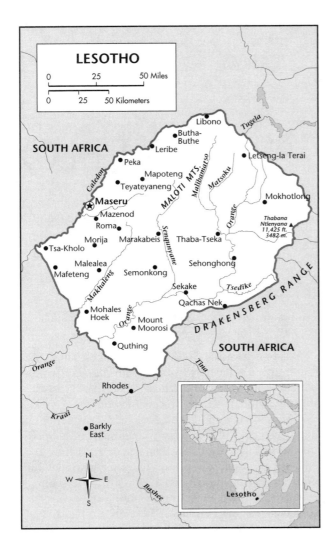

LESOTHO

0   25   50 Miles

0   25   50 Kilometers

SOUTH AFRICA

Libono
Butha-Buthe
Leribe
Peka
Mapoteng
Teyateyaneng
Maseru
Mazenod
Roma
Morija   Marakabeis
Tsa-Kholo
Malealea
Mafeteng   Semonkong
Mohales
Hoek
Mount
Moorosi
Quthing

Letseng-la Terai

Mokhotlong

Thabana
Ntlenyana
11,425 ft.
3482 m.

Thaba-Tseka

Sehonghong

Sekake
Qachas Nek

SOUTH AFRICA

Orange

Rhodes

Kraai

Barkly
East

N
W   E
S

Lesotho

OVERVIEW OF ECONOMY

Subsistence agriculture, livestock, manufacturing, and the paycheck **remittances** of "migratory" laborers employed in South Africa dominate the economy of Lesotho. Fresh water is the only important natural resource and is being exploited under the multi-year, 30 billion dollar, Lesotho Highlands Water Project (LHWP). This massive scheme provides employment, domestic energy needs, and revenue from selling both water and hydropower to South Africa. The country also depends on foreign development assistance to meet much of its current food and **infrastructure** needs.

Since the 1950s, fixed-length migratory contracts to work gold and diamond mines in South Africa have been the most important source of income for Lesotho. Under present employment terms, a percentage of the salary is remitted directly to the National Bank in Lesotho. These earnings support the farms and families back home. In the 1990s, 70 percent of households had at least 1 migrant worker, and 35 percent of households used migratory earnings as their primary income. However, the Economist Intelligence Unit reports that from 1995 to 1999, the number of migrant mine workers hired in South Africa declined from 104,000 to an estimated 65,000, adding to a growing unemployment problem.

Subsistence agriculture accounts for 75 percent of domestic employment and production and about 14 percent of the GDP. However, land shortages, international aid, and government initiatives to increase credit and implement seed-fertilizer machinery are not keeping pace with population growth and decreasing migratory work in South Africa. Since 1987, population increase has doubled the growth of agricultural productivity.

A small but growing manufacturing sector produces woolen items and machine parts, and an expanding service industry accounts for the remaining 25 percent of domestic production.

Tourism in this "Rooftop of Africa" attracts South Africans and other foreigners to hike, pony-trek, and bird watch. The hospitable Basotho villages afford excellent opportunities to observe subsistence agriculture and transhumance (the seasonal migration of livestock and the people who herd them from lowlands to mountainous regions). This sector is expanding rapidly.

Foreign assistance to Lesotho in support of the struggle against apartheid (the legal separation of races) in South Africa increased during the 1970s. This aid quickened the pace of modernization and urban development, and there were significant improvements in infrastructure, education, and communications. Since 1995, the **real GDP** growth rate averaged an impressive 7 to 10 percent. However, population growth, political conflicts,

the remaining small minority (0.3 percent). The **dependency ratio**—the number of people under 15 and over 65 years of age, compared with those who fall between—is a very high, 72.5 percent. Approximately 80 percent are Christians, while 20 percent follow indigenous faiths. A total of 81 percent of the males and 62.5 percent of females are literate. Sesotho (southern Sotho), English (official language), Zulu, Xhosa, and Afrikaans are spoken throughout the kingdom.

The overall population density is 70.2 persons square kilometer (181 per square mile). However, since 85 percent are **subsistence farmers**, the rural population density of 461 persons per square kilometer (176 per square mile) of arable land clearly reveals a critical land shortage. This expanding population is pushing settlements, grazing, and cultivation into the marginal higher elevations and more arid eastern parts of the kingdom. The resulting overgrazing and soil erosion accompanying this land use is perhaps the most serious problem facing Lesotho.

and the shrinking demand for mine workers in South Africa now jeopardize these gains.

From 1988 to 1998, the annual GNP growth averaged 3.7 percent, and the per capita GNP increased US$47, from US$649 to US$696 (in constant 1995 U.S. dollars). Civil unrest following an unsuccessful coup in 1998 eroded Lesotho's economy and destroyed nearly 80 percent of the commercial infrastructure. The CIA *World Factbook* estimated the rate of GDP growth to be 2.5 percent in 2000 and **GDP per capita** was estimated at US$2,400.

POLITICS, GOVERNMENT, AND TAXATION

Khoisan-speaking hunter-gatherers first settled this region 10,000 years ago. They were overwhelmed in the 16th century by sedentary farmers who evolved into the Sotho nation of today. By the mid-19th century internecine (struggle within a nation) conflict, competition from Boer trekkers for the Cape Colony, and British intervention finally resulted in Basutoland—a British Protectorate that lasted from 1871 until independence in 1966.

Today, Lesotho is a multi-party constitutional monarchy. There is a **bicameral** National Assembly composed of a lower house of directly elected representatives, and an Upper House (Senate) comprised of 22 non-elected principal chiefs and 11 other members appointed by the king. The legal system is modeled after English common law and Roman-Dutch law. The High Court and Court of Appeal exert judicial review of legislation.

During the 1970s, discord over apartheid in South Africa destabilized all of southern Africa. The conservative South African regime accused Lesotho of accepting refugees and harboring African National Congress operatives. South African troops attacked Maseru in 1982. About 4 years later their border blockades severed the kingdom from the outside world. A pro-South African military faction within Lesotho reacted by removing

Chief Jonathan and establishing military rule. The king became a figurative head of state.

In 1993, Lesotho returned to democracy after 23 years of authoritarian rule. The current head of state is King Letsie III, and the head of government is Prime Minister Pakalitha Mosisil. The Lesotho Congress for Democracy (LCD), Basotho Congress Party (BCP), Basotho National Party (BNP), and Maramatlou Freedom Party (MFP) are the largest of 12 to 15 political parties. The political system remains very fragile and prone to disruption. The last general election on May 1998, was disputed and triggered civil tension that is still present. An Interim Political Authority will oversee the next elections.

The government consumes 21.5 percent of the GDP. The top **income tax** rate is 35 percent, and the average taxpayer pays a 25 percent marginal tax rate. The top corporate tax rate is 35 percent.

INFRASTRUCTURE, POWER, AND COMMUNICATIONS

Printed and electronic media are available from 3 sources. South African newspapers, magazines, radio and television are the most numerous and widespread. Of these independent publications, the *Mopheme* (Survivor) and *The Mirror* are the most popular. Catholic and Evangelical church newspapers that appear on a weekly and bi-weekly schedule are a second source. Finally, the Lesotho News Agency (LENA) provides government-**sanctioned** perspectives on all issues. One organ of this, the Lesotho National Broadcasting Service, offers programs in English and Sesotho. There are 2 FM radio stations and 1 AM radio station. LENA plans to establish an Internet news service in the next few years. The government tolerates criticism from independent media.

There is no national airline, but South African Airways offers direct flights from Johannesburg to Maseru. The 31 other airstrips scattered throughout the country

Communications

Country	Newspapers	Radios	TV Sets[a]	Cable subscribers[a]	Mobile Phones[a]	Fax Machines[a]	Personal Computers[a]	Internet Hosts[b]	Internet Users[b]
	1996	1997	1998	1998	1998	1998	1998	1999	1999
Lesotho	8	49	25	N/A	5	N/A	N/A	0.08	1
United States	215	2,146	847	244.3	256	78.4	458.6	1,508.77	74,100
South Africa	32	317	125	N/A	56	3.5	47.4	33.36	1,820
Dem. Rep. of Congo	3	375	135	N/A	0	N/A	N/A	0.00	1

[a]Data are from International Telecommunication Union, *World Telecommunication Development Report 1999* and are per 1,000 people.
[b]Data are from the Internet Software Consortium (http://www.isc.org) and are per 10,000 people.

SOURCE: World Bank. *World Development Indicators 2000.*

service private aircraft and occasional charter flights. The South African railroad stops near Maseru and connects to points within Southern Africa.

In 2000, 18.3 percent (800 kilometers/480 miles) of the roads were paved. The remaining 1,600 kilometers (960 miles) vary between high quality gravel corridors and rough dirt tracks. Road upgrades since 1970 were designed to unite the country, improve commerce, and reduce the dependence on peripheral South African roads.

TELECOMMUNICATIONS. Adequate telephone service exists in and around Maseru and in settlements adjacent to the major roads. Many remote areas still await electrification. In 2000 there were approximately 30,000 telephones in use (about 1.4 per 100 people), and connections increase 13 percent each year. In 1995, a consortium (a cooperative group) of public and private telecommunications corporations combined to offer cellular service in Lesotho for the first time. Service will increase over the next decade so that remote areas will likely leap into the cellular age. There is 1 satellite Earth station for international calls. Personal computers are almost unknown, and the 1 Internet Service Provider appeared only recently.

ECONOMIC SECTORS

Lesotho's principle economic sectors are agriculture (18 percent), mining and manufacturing (38 percent), and **retail**/tourism/services (44 percent) in 1999, according to the CIA *World Factbook*. Although politically autonomous, Lesotho's economy is almost totally dependent on trade and cooperative development with the Republic of South Africa. Several reasons explain this dependence. First, South Africa completely surrounds

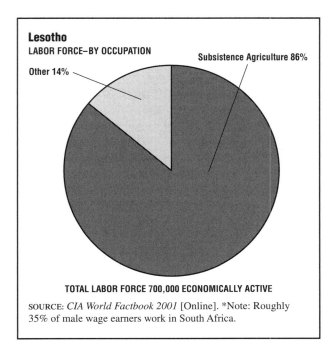

Lesotho
LABOR FORCE–BY OCCUPATION

Other 14%

Subsistence Agriculture 86%

TOTAL LABOR FORCE 700,000 ECONOMICALLY ACTIVE

SOURCE: *CIA World Factbook 2001* [Online]. *Note: Roughly 35% of male wage earners work in South Africa.

mountainous Lesotho in the same manner that water surrounds an island. Thus, all commerce and travelers to and from Lesotho must pass through their wealthier neighbor which is also their dominant trading partner. Second, 75 percent of Lesotho families rely on wages earned in South African mines for at least some of their income. Any fluctuation in mine productivity affects Lesotho. Finally, political changes in South Africa greatly alter foreign aid and investment in Lesotho. In the past, the international donor community (wealthy industrialized nations) viewed this small mountain kingdom as an island of racial freedom surrounded by a South Africa locked in apartheid. When Nelson Mandela spearheaded majority rule, South Africa became a more important recipient of international development dollars.

AGRICULTURE

Agriculture employs a modest 57 percent of the **labor force**, mostly on subsistence farms. This figure is lower than similar developing countries as the mountain environment offers less terrain for growing crops and many adult males work in South African mines. While the CIA *World Factbook* estimates that 35 percent of the male wage earners do work in South African mines, it also estimates that 86 percent of the resident population is involved in subsistence agriculture, a much higher number.

Most crops and livestock are produced in small villages distant from the major roads. The products are consumed locally with the surplus shipped for sale and profit in outside markets. Maize, wheat, and sorghum predom-

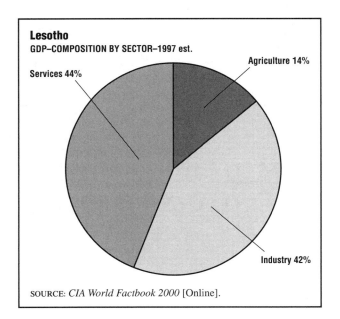

Lesotho
GDP–COMPOSITION BY SECTOR–1997 est.

Services 44%

Agriculture 14%

Industry 42%

SOURCE: *CIA World Factbook 2000* [Online].

inate. As a percentage of the GDP, farming has declined from 50 percent in the 1970s, to just 18 percent in 2000. During the 1990s, about 13 percent of the country was cultivated. This amount is shrinking as soil erosion, droughts, and the destruction of farm equipment during civil unrest in 1998 take a cumulative toll. To stimulate exports to South Africa, the government is **liberalizing price controls**, improving roads, and encouraging monocropping of cut flowers, asparagus, and fruits.

Most farmers also raise livestock to supplement crops and maintain "food security" during drought years when crop yields are low. Animal husbandry is important everywhere and is often the only revenue source in the higher elevations. Sheep and goats that produce meat, milk, and very high quality wool and mohair are the most important animals. Cattle are also increasing because they fetch more lucrative contracts.

Lesotho's forest cover is very fragmented as neither the arid lowlands nor the colder highlands favor tree growth. The best stands are in riparian sites (located on the bank of a natural watercourse) and in sheltered mountain hillsides. Aggressive wood collection for cooking, warmth, and home construction prevents trees from attaining commercial stature. The Ministry of Agriculture manages one 874-hectare (2,518-acre) forest reserve of mostly rapidly growing eucalyptus. Fishing resources are also minimal in this landlocked country with no significant lakes. There is sport fishing for river trout, and village cooperatives are experimenting with fishponds (mostly carp) to boost protein in the local diet.

INDUSTRY

MINING. Local mining and migratory labor to South African mines are essential to Lesotho's economic fortune. Diamond is the principal commercial mineral. Clay for manufacture into bricks and ceramic ware is also important. Deposits of coal, quartz, agate, galena, and uranium have been identified but are not yet commercially viable. Domestic mining and migratory mine wages account for 24 percent of total income in Lesotho. This amount exceeds comparable developing countries and stems from the unusual migratory labor pattern.

Traditional diamond mining from small and independent diggings averaged only 9,000 carats per year until 1977, when South African mining giant De Beers opened the Letseng-la-Terae open-cast mine. Production surged to 105,200 carats in 1980, so that high quality gemstones accounted for 55 percent of Lesotho's exports. The oscillating global diamond market produced many periods of boom and bust, and in 1983 De Beers ceased the Letseng-la-Terae operation. It was recently reopened under a new private/government partnership, and the ris-

ing demand for raw diamonds may also stimulate foreign investment in additional mines within Lesotho.

The "fixed contract" (or circular) migration of mostly 20- to 40-year-old male workers from Lesotho to South African mines is integral to the economy. It is also subject to market forces, and since the late 1990s, falling output from South African mines has reduced the need for foreign labor. In 2001 this demand dropped to its lowest level since the early 1970s. Still, 25 percent of Lesotho's total labor force engages in what are typically fixed-term contracts of 12 months. Remittances from mine employment accounted for 45 percent of Lesotho's GNP from 1983–91 (30 percent of each paycheck is now "deferred" until the worker returns home). If this downward spiral continues, Lesotho will face severe unemployment and a staggering loss of outside earnings that have been the primary source of family support and economic development since independence.

MANUFACTURING. Manufacturing as a percentage of the GDP rose from 8 percent in 1980 to 18 percent in 2000. This rapidly expanding sector employs 24,000 people. Basotho workers produce clothing, footwear, leather goods, handicrafts, furniture, pottery and tapestries from mostly imported raw materials. Finished goods are exported primarily to South Africa and the United States. This sector will continue to improve if the political situation remains stable.

Increasing both output and employment is an important government objective, although achieving these goals has proved contentious. Prior to 1965 the industrial base was small because geographic isolation, poor infrastructure, and no access to major commerce routes restricted growth. In 1967 the government founded the Lesotho National Development Corporation (LNDC) to attract foreign investment. The effort succeeded but hurt "indigenous" enterprise that lacked the entrepreneurial capacity and financial resources to compete with government/foreign partnerships. Basotho workers resented some foreign operations, especially those under Chinese ownership, for their demeaning labor practices (low compensation, unpaid overtime, gender bias), and apparent bribing of local officials to skirt labor laws. From 1992 to 1998, repeated strikes, walkouts, and political rallies diminished productivity. Teachers, manufacturing workers, and even those staffing the Highlands Water Project participated. Moreover, the protests coincided with the transition to majority rule and erasure of economic sanctions against South Africa, which opened their larger labor force and excellent infrastructure to the same outside investors.

ENERGY: WATER. Begun in 1986, the Lesotho Highlands Water Development Project (LHWDP) has been the most important economic and resource development project in Lesotho. Water exports started in 1998 and are now a reliable source of foreign income. Much of the water is bound for South Africa. Leadership from the World Bank and a consortium of public and private sources financed the project that provides Lesotho with 4,000 jobs, water, and energy. More hydropower stations are under construction so that the kingdom will soon export power to South Africa. The government is also investigating the possibilities of solar and LHWDP power for its rural areas.

SERVICES

TOURISM. When compared to South Africa, traveling in Lesotho is very inexpensive. Commercial accommodation and food are available in the larger towns. Elsewhere, Basotho farmers and herders accept tourists into their homes for a small fee or **bartered** item. Tourists choose to hike, pony trek, bird watch (over 300 species), and observe a rural subsistence way of life. A pony trekking cooperative offers highland routes that overnight in villages. The cool upland air and a fine reputation for local hospitality also explain why tourism is flourishing. Lesotho offers free entry visas and compared with much of Africa, risk of crime and disease is low.

FINANCIAL SERVICES. Despite pervasive state involvement in the financial sector, state control is shrinking, as are revenues from state-owned enterprises and government property ownership. The government plans to **privatize** the state-owned Lesotho Bank that formulates and implements **monetary policy** and advises on **fiscal policy**. Foreign banks operate in the kingdom. Procuring credit for investment and land purchases remains beyond financial reach for most Basotho.

RETAIL. Maseru offers the only significant hotel, dining, and retail enterprise with department stores and specialty shops marketing Basotho handicrafts. Teyateyaneng is the center of traditional arts and crafts industries such as tapestries, tribal wool products, and handcrafts.

INTERNATIONAL TRADE

Lesotho joined the Southern African Development Community (SADC) in 1994. The organization promotes economic growth and cooperation among its 14 member states. The kingdom also participates with South Africa, Botswana, Namibia, and Swaziland, in the South African Customs Union (SACU) to encourage free trade and economic exchange. Unfortunately, most SACU members are similarly underdeveloped. In 2000 the import of goods and services equaled approximately US$780 million. The net **foreign direct investment** was US$196 million.

The main exports are textiles (clothing and footwear), raw wool and mohair, agricultural produce (corn, wheat, pulses, sorghum, barley), livestock (cattle, sheep, and goats, and building materials (especially ceramics). The

Exchange rates: Lesotho	
maloti per US$1	
Jan 2001	7.78307
2000	6.93983
1999	6.10948
1998	5.52828
1997	4.60796
1996	4.29935

Note: The Lesotho loti is at par with the South African rand which is also legal tender; maloti is the plural form of loti.

SOURCE: CIA *World Factbook 2001* [ONLINE].

SACU accounts for 65 percent of export trade, with North America (34 percent), and the European Union (.07 percent) following. The primary imports include cereals, food ingredients, machinery, medical supplies, and oil and petroleum products. As with exports, the major import trading partners are the SACU (90 percent), Asia (7.4 percent), and the European Union (1.5 percent). There are no export controls except for diamonds, which require a license.

MONEY

The loti is pegged with the South African rand; both currencies are legal tender in Lesotho. Those wanting to exchange maloti for convertible currency (dollars, marks, francs, etc.) usually exchange inside Lesotho, or change for South African rand, which is then convertible worldwide. Lesotho's currency is convertible internationally but is very uncommon outside of Southern Africa. In January 2000, US$1=6.125 maloti, a rate that has remained stable in the last 3 years. There is no domestic **exchange rate** policy, and there are no controls on regional exchange flows. The average **inflation rate** is approximately 8.5 percent.

POVERTY AND WEALTH

Despite significant economic progress, Lesotho remains one of world's poorest countries. The average cit-

GDP per Capita (US$)					
Country	1975	1980	1985	1990	1998
Lesotho	220	311	295	370	486
United States	19,364	21,529	23,200	25,363	29,683
South Africa	4,574	4,620	4,229	4,113	3,918
Swaziland	1,073	1,046	1,035	1,446	1,409

SOURCE: United Nations. *Human Development Report 2000;
Trends in human development and per capita income.*

Distribution of Income or Consumption by Percentage Share: Lesotho

Lowest 10%	0.9
Lowest 20%	2.8
Second 20%	6.5
Third 20%	11.2
Fourth 20%	19.4
Highest 20%	60.1
Highest 10%	43.4

Survey year: 1986–87
Note: This information refers to expenditure shares by percentiles of the population and is ranked by per capita expenditure.

SOURCE: *2000 World Development Indicators* [CD-ROM].

izen survives on less than 2 dollars per day. Half the population exists below the United Nations poverty line. Only 14 percent of the urban residents have good access to water. The most telling statistic is that 16.5 percent of children under 5 years of age suffer from malnutrition, a figure that swells during droughts.

In comparison to the majority of African nations the overall health of the population is good. The mountainous climate and southern latitude preclude tropical diseases that devastate developing regions elsewhere. Public health expenditures amount to only 3.7 percent of the GDP in 1990–98, yet 80 percent of the population has access to health services even though many medicines are unavailable. Those with money can use South Africa's excellent health system. There are 50 doctors and 33 nurses per 10,000 people. Only 23 percent use birth control.

The AIDS epidemic that is pervasive throughout Africa is evident in Lesotho. In 2001, 25 percent of those between the ages of 15 and 49 were infected with HIV/AIDS, and the rate grows each year. Tuberculosis also strains the health-care system to capacity. The government is sponsoring aggressive prevention, control, and screening programs for both diseases. In 2000, the World Bank issued a US$6.5 million credit to improve access to quality preventive, curative, and rehabilitative health care services.

WORKING CONDITIONS

The World Bank estimates that approximately 35 percent of the labor force is unemployed or **underemployed**. Another 50 percent are fully or partially employed in South Africa. About 86 percent of the population is rural subsistence farmers and herders. As is the case throughout sub-Saharan Africa, this cohort lives in "roundavels" (circular mud and thatch huts) with outdoor plumbing, oil lamps, and wood heat. Many villages are

not connected to roadways. Fewer than 10 percent of the population works in the service and retail industry where wages are low and mistreatment by foreign-owned manufacturing plants resulted in mass civil unrest during the mid-1990s. There are no labor unions.

COUNTRY HISTORY AND ECONOMIC DEVELOPMENT

1600s. Sotho people arrive in present-day Lesotho, intermarry with the Khoisans, and establish trade links in Southern Africa.

1800. White traders introduce cattle. Boer pioneers usurp Sotho.

1820. Basotho emerge as Moshoeshoe the Great unites Sotho.

1860s. Boer wars and British intervention cost Basotho much of the western lowlands.

1880. The British gain control and prevent Lesotho's inclusion into the newly formed Union of South Africa, which spares Lesotho from apartheid.

1966. Basotholand becomes independent "Lesotho."

1970. The first prime minister, Chief Jonathan, is defeated at the 1970 poll; he suspends the constitution, expels the king, and bans the opposition.

1983. South Africa closes Lesotho's borders after Jonathan criticizes South African apartheid, strangling the country economically.

1984. Lesotho Highlands Water Development Project (LHWDP) initiated.

1986–97. A period of political unrest, coups, and skirmishes between rebel troops and government loyalists. Moshoeshoe II eventually gains power then dies in a car accident.

1994. Lesotho joins the Southern African Development Community (SADC).

1998. Elections are held under alleged cheating. Fearing violence the government calls on SADC treaty partners (Botswana, South Africa, and Zimbabwe) to help restore order. South African troops enter the kingdom and heavy fighting engulfs Maseru. Eighty percent of the shops and other businesses are severely damaged.

2000. Government promises to call new elections and privatize more enterprise.

FUTURE TRENDS

As with many developing nations, Lesotho must reconcile population growth with limited agricultural, infrastructure, and monetary resources. An isolated geographic location lacking access to the sea, overgrazing, and soil erosion are other severe problems. Failure to reverse these trends will impose severe economic hardship.

The AIDS epidemic, political unrest, and declining migrant remittances from South Africa also cloud the future. Ironically, South Africa's adroit transition to majority rule made that country more attractive to foreign investment and ended Lesotho's role as an island of racial freedom. As a result, foreign assistance was reduced and, in many cases, redirected to healing wounds in South Africa.

There are 3 phenomena that will largely determine Lesotho's future. First, the Highlands Water Project must continue expanding to generate more profit, domestic power and reliable employment. Second, sustaining political stability to attract additional foreign enterprise is critical to grow employment and domestic capital. Finally, achieving zero population growth through family planning (instead of HIV/AIDS and outmigration) will reduce pressure on agricultural and grazing lands. Accomplishing these objectives will situate this tiny nation in an excellent position to prosper when Africa begins to fully industrialize later this century.

DEPENDENCIES

Lesotho has no territories or colonies.

BIBLIOGRAPHY

Economist Intelligence Unit. *Country Profile: Lesotho.* London: Economist Intelligence Unit, 2001.

Lundahl, Mats, and Lennart Petersson. *The Dependent Economy: Lesotho and the Southern African Customs Union.* Boulder, CO: Westview Press, 1991.

Mochebelele, Motsamai T., and Alex Winter-Nelson. "Migrant Labor and Farm Technical Efficiency in Lesotho." *World Development.* Vol. 28, No. 1, 2000.

Murray, C. *Families Divided: The Impact of Migrant Labour in Lesotho.* Cambridge: Cambridge University Press, 1981.

U.S. Central Intelligence Agency. *World Factbook 2001.* <http://www.odci.gov/cia/publications/factbook/index.html>. Accessed October 2001.

U.S. Department of State. *Background Notes: Lesotho, August 1999.* <http://www.state.gov/www/background_notes/lesotho_9908_bgn.html>. Accessed October 2001.

World Bank Group. "Countries: Lesotho." *World Bank.* <http://www.worldbank.org/afr/ls2.htm>. Accessed May 2001.

—*Stephen F. Cunha*

LIBERIA

Republic of Liberia

CAPITAL: Monrovia.

MONETARY UNIT: Liberian dollar (L$). One dollar equals 100 cents. The dollar is equivalent to the U.S. dollar. There are coins of 5, 10, 25, and 50 cents and 1 and 5 dollars. No Liberian notes are in circulation, and U.S. notes are used as the paper currency.

CHIEF EXPORTS: Diamonds, iron ore and concentrates, natural rubber and gum, timber, coffee, cocoa.

CHIEF IMPORTS: Machinery and transport equipment, manufactures, food and live animals, mineral fuels, lubricants.

GROSS DOMESTIC PRODUCT: US$3.35 billion (purchasing power parity, 2000 est.).

BALANCE OF TRADE: Exports: US$55 million (f.o.b., 2000). Imports: US$170 million (f.o.b., 2000).

During the war about 1 million Liberians fled abroad, some of whom returned during the lulls in fighting, often to flee again as violence intensified in 1992, 1994, and 1996. Since the end of the war, further tensions have meant the refugees in neighboring countries have been reluctant to return, and an outflow has continued. In 1997, with international help, the government began resettling refugees.

The vast majority—95 percent—of Liberia's people are members of indigenous African tribes, with descendants of U.S. immigrants and Congolese both making up 2.5 percent of the population. Forty percent of the people practice indigenous religious beliefs, 40 percent are Christians, and 20 percent are Muslims.

COUNTRY OVERVIEW

LOCATION AND SIZE. Liberia is situated on the West African coast, bordered by Sierra Leone to the northwest, Guinea to the north, and the Côte d'Ivoire to the east. Liberia also has 300 kilometers (186 miles) of coastline on the Atlantic Ocean. Its land area is 111,370 square kilometers (43,000 square miles). The capital, Monrovia, is on the Atlantic coast.

POPULATION. Liberia's population was estimated at 3,255,837 in July of 2001, and in normal circumstances the country has had a high population growth rate of 3.3 percent (1980–87). However, the most recent estimate puts the figure at 2.3 percent for 1990–96 and just 1.92 percent for 2001, as war has lowered the birth rate and raised the mortality rate. An estimated 5 percent of the population died in the civil war of 1989–96.

Even before the war, the urban population was high at 40 percent, but during the conflict it rose to 46 percent, as people sought refuge in the towns. In early 1995, the capital's population stood at 1.3 million, a tripling of its size compared with 1986.

OVERVIEW OF ECONOMY

Liberia has traditionally relied on mining (of iron-ore, gold, and diamonds), rubber, timber, and shipping registration revenues as its major sources of income. Nearly 8 years of war ending in the mid-1990s destroyed much of the country's **infrastructure** and has brought mining to a halt. Most of the country's inhabitants are engaged in agriculture. Apart from small farmers producing rubber, however, almost all agriculture is **subsistence farming**. The government has not produced systematic data since 1989, and such information that is available has come from limited surveys by prospective aid donors.

Liberia's economic boom in the late 1960s and early 1970s was due to strong rubber and iron exports, with the **real gross domestic product** (GDP) growing at 9 percent a year. In the late 1970s, with a general slowdown in the world economy, growth slowed to 1 percent. In the 1980s the economy declined. Real GDP was 10 percent lower in 1986 than in 1979, as companies cut back on investment. The civil war—which lasted from 1989 to 1996—displaced

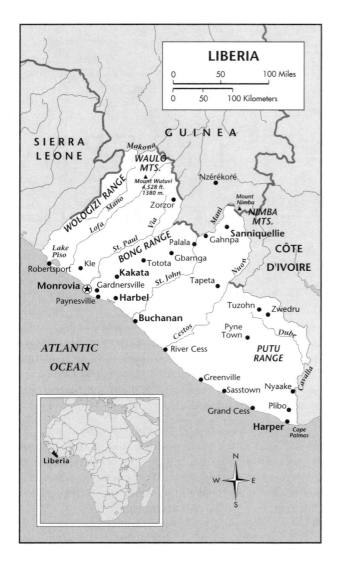

much of the population and destroyed the productive infrastructure. Iron ore output ceased relatively early on in the hostilities, although other resources, particularly diamonds, continued to be exploited by the various factions. The formal economy came to a standstill as the population turned to subsistence production for survival. Since the end of the war in 1997, the formal sector has started up again in the major towns, but the lack of reliable data makes it difficult to be confident about the extent of the recovery. According to the International Monetary Fund (IMF), domestic production has rebounded strongly, though it still only stands at one-third of its pre-war level. The GDP is thought to have doubled in 1997 and grew at 25–30 percent in 1998 due to increases in agricultural output. The *CIA World Factbook* estimates that the GDP grew at the rate of 15 percent in 2000, reaching US$3.35 billion at **purchasing power parity** in that year.

The abrupt stop in formal economic activity at the start of the war produced a drastic fall in revenues and substantial **capital flight**. The rise in military spending took an increasing share of government revenues. A string of interim governments relied principally on funds from the Liberian maritime shipping registry, which was largely unaffected by the war. In 1999 agriculture and reconstruction were allocated funds far below the levels required to revive the economy. Alleged human rights abuses and allegations of Liberian government support for destabilizing forces in neighboring Sierra Leone caused some donors to be reluctant to resume aid.

In Liberia, unlike most of Africa, a high proportion of revenue comes from **direct taxation** on incomes and profits, particularly from iron ore mining and shipping registration fees. However, revenues have invariably been inadequate to meet spending plans, and until a return to budgetary control in 1999, the government failed to pay salaries, accumulated debts, and financed **budget deficits** by printing money.

From January to June 2000, the Liberian government operated an IMF-monitored program to improve the country's fiscal position, **liberalize** import controls, and reform the civil service and the state-owned enterprises. The initial response by the government to this program has been encouraging, but the task facing the government in reforming the economy is considerable, and it will take several years to improve tax revenues, re-structure the civil service, and **privatize** the state-owned enterprises.

POLITICS, GOVERNMENT, AND TAXATION

Liberia is the only West African state never to have been formerly colonized. The country was formed in 1820 when U.S. philanthropists negotiated rights to settle freed slaves from the United States in the area. Liberia was declared a republic in 1847 and operated with political institutions modeled on those of the United States.

For the next 133 years the True Whig Party, which mostly consisted of the descendants of freed slaves, was the only significant political force. The party's rule ended in 1980 when President William Tolbert was assassinated. Following Tolbert's death Sergeant Samuel Doe took power as head of the ruling 15-member military People's Redemption Council (PRC).

The following decade was marked by growing opposition to the military regime, with many alleged or actual coup attempts resulting in executions. Rigged multi-party elections in 1985 brought Doe back to power as president with a tiny majority. In the next month a coup led by Brigadier General Quiwonkpa was put down, 600 people died, and reprisals were taken against Quiwonkpa's ethnic group, the Gio, adding further to the tensions.

On 24 December 1989, Charles Taylor, a former government employee, invaded the country with a small armed force from Côte d'Ivoire. Taylor's National Patriotic Front of Liberia (NPFL) gained popular support, and by June 1990 only Monrovia remained under Doe's control. The fight for the capital became a 3-way contest with the Armed Forces of Liberia (AFL), the NPFL, and a splinter group from the NPFL, the INPFL, vying for control.

The Economic Community of West African States (ECOWAS), anxious about regional destabilization, sent in a 6,000-strong monitoring group, ECOMOG, to take control of the capital. ECOMOG was made up of many nations, but the main constituent was Nigerian. Despite ECOMOG also offering Doe protection, Doe was kidnapped and killed. A cease fire was signed in November 1990, but the NPFL refused to recognize the interim government.

By March 1991, fighting had resumed, spilling over into Sierra Leone, with the NPFL backing a Sierra Leonian rebel group, the Revolutionary United Front (RUF). The Sierra Leone army was backed by the new United Liberation Movement for democracy in Liberia (Ulimo), who went on to attack the NPFL in north-west Liberia.

Amid this shifting chaos of armed rebel groups and failed peacemaking, diplomatic efforts continued. Finally, in June 1995, Charles Taylor visited Nigeria, and all sides agreed to a peace accord in August. The accord set out plans for elections in 1996, with an interim 6-man Council of State that included representatives of the main factions and civilians. Renewed violence in April 1996 threw this initial agreement off track, but a second peace agreement, again signed in Nigeria, called for disarmament and elections, with the threat of **sanctions** if this was not achieved. Disarmament started slowly but in early 1997 was completed, and the militias were formally disbanded.

Elections took place in July 1997, which allowed time for preparations and campaigning and were undertaken in a calm and relatively peaceful atmosphere. Taylor won 75 percent of the vote, and Taylor's National Patriotic Party (NPP) won a majority in both Houses. However, prospects for a viable multiparty system receded by 1998 with all the main opposition leaders in exile. Currently the country is not completely secure, as witnessed by invasions from armed bands in 1999 and 2000.

Liberia's political history has been dominated both by the struggle between American Liberians and ethnic Liberians (which was resolved in the 1980 coup with the ethnic Liberians gaining the upper hand) and conflicts between ethnic groups within Liberia (both to gain power and avenge past wrongs). Ethnically motivated killings and harassment were undertaken by all sides during the civil war, and reconciliation has proved to be slow and

difficult. Taylor was initially seen as a welcomed alternative to Doe but was later seen as preventing stability by not honoring the peace agreements. The murder of Samuel Dokie, a former member of the NPFL, and the intimidation of other opposition leaders led to greatly reduced opposition power and to fears of Liberia becoming a de facto 1-party state, with all power in the hands of the president.

Under the 1986 constitution, the president and vice-president have executive roles, and legislative power rests in Congress and the House of Representatives. Both houses were elected for 6 years, although this was reduced to 4 years before the 1997 elections. New legislation has endorsed the 1986 constitution, although the rebuilding of democratic institutions has been hampered by limited funding and enduring tensions.

The links with Sierra Leone's rebel RUF and the allegations of material support for the group have caused significant problems for Taylor's regime. Taylor has used his influence over the RUF in constructive ways, for example, by helping to negotiate the release of captured United Nations troops. However, renewed violence in May 2000 prompted the United Kingdom to accuse Liberia of supplying arms for diamonds and led to the suspension of a US$60 million European Union (EU) aid package for Liberia. Recently, government forces have reinforced the Sierra Leone border, and the Liberian government has accused the United Kingdom of trying to destabilize Taylor's regime.

Relations with Guinea, in the light of reports of armed incursions being launched from there as well as from Sierra Leone, have improved little despite the president of Mali's attempts to broker a reconciliation. Relations with the United States have got better since 1998, but Liberia's oldest ally is critical of civil rights abuses.

There is little recent information on government finances. In 1988 total government revenue was 18 percent of the GDP, with taxes on income of individuals and corporations raising 33 percent of government income, **indirect taxes** 25 percent, customs **duties** and export **levies** 34 percent, and other sources contributing 8 percent. General administration accounted for 24 percent of expenditure, defence 10 percent, health 5 percent, economic activities 28 percent, and other expenditures (including social services) 33 percent.

Extensive corruption and a near complete lack of respect for the law makes Liberia an extremely unfriendly place for foreigners to do business. According to the U.S. State Department, corruption and lawlessness permeates every level of the government: requests for bribes, red tape, and a lack of enforcement for legal contracts has kept investment to a minimum. The government has done little to address these problems.

INFRASTRUCTURE, POWER, AND COMMUNICATIONS

Liberia has a limited infrastructure that was severely damaged by the country's long civil war. Roads in Liberia are in poor condition due to poor maintenance and heavy rains. Only 6 percent of the national road network of 10,600 kilometers (9,942 miles) is paved. There are no passenger rail services, and the iron ore rail transport links are in need of serious repair as large sections of the rail network were dismantled and sold for scrap during the civil war.

The country's 5 ports of Monrovia, Buchanan, Greenville, Harper, and Robertsport handle 200,000 tons per year in general cargo (80 percent of which is iron-ore deposits) and 400,000 tons a year of petroleum products. Ports in the south-east of the country handle timber exports.

Robertsport had an international airport until it was destroyed by fighting in 1990. It now carries some regional commercial flights but will need major repairs to carry international flights. Harbel, 56 kilometers (35 miles) from Monrovia, remains the only international airport.

Liberian state television, ELTV, was off the air for most of the war but has resumed broadcasts as a largely commercial station. There are 2 private TV stations broadcast for a proportion of the day, and there are 6 FM radio stations and 4 shortwave stations. Independent newspapers emerge from time to time, but invariably fail to establish themselves. There were only 6,000 telephone main lines in the country in 1997 and no cellular phones.

In 1999 Liberia produced 432 million kilowatt hours (kWh) of electricity, but much of the electricity-generating infrastructure has been destroyed or damaged. Two-thirds of electricity is generated from diesel and one-third from hydro-electric sources. Access to electricity is very restricted, and those who can afford it use private diesel generators. Poor provision of electricity is a major cause of criticism of the new government. All petroleum products are imported, and so far surveys have shown no local oil reserves. 38 percent of diesel consumed in Liberia is used to produce electricity, and most domestic energy needs are provided by charcoal and wood.

ECONOMIC SECTORS

Agriculture (including fishing and forestry) employed an estimated 70 percent of the **labor force** in 1999 and contributed 60 percent of the GDP in 2000. Industry

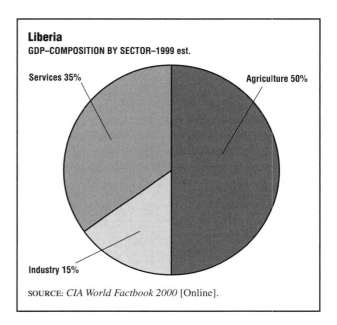

Liberia
GDP–COMPOSITION BY SECTOR–1999 est.

Services 35%

Agriculture 50%

Industry 15%

SOURCE: *CIA World Factbook 2000* [Online].

Communications

Country	Telephones[a]	Telephones, Mobile/Cellular[a]	Radio Stations[b]	Radios[a]	TV Stations[a]	Televisions[a]	Internet Service Providers[c]	Internet Users[c]
Liberia	6,000	0 (1995)	AM 0; FM 6; shortwave 4 (1999)	790,000	2 (2000)	70,000	1	300
United States	194 M	69.209 M (1998)	AM 4,762; FM 5,542; shortwave 18	575 M	1,500	219 M	7,800	148 M
Nigeria	500,000 (2000)	26,700	AM 82; FM 35; shortwave 11	23.5 M	2 (1999)	6.9 M	11	100,000
Sierra Leone	17,000	650 (1999)	AM 1; FM 9; shortwave 1 (1999)	1.12 M	2 (1999)	53,000	1	2,000

[a]Data is for 1997 unless otherwise noted.
[b]Data is for 1998 unless otherwise noted.
[c]Data is for 2000 unless otherwise noted.

SOURCE: CIA *World Factbook 2001* [Online].

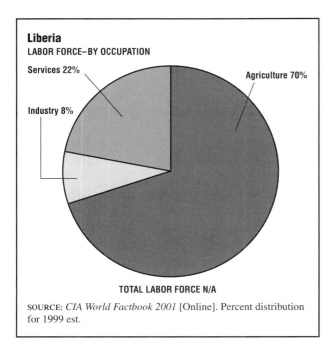

Liberia
LABOR FORCE–BY OCCUPATION

Services 22%

Industry 8%

Agriculture 70%

TOTAL LABOR FORCE N/A

SOURCE: *CIA World Factbook 2001* [Online]. Percent distribution for 1999 est.

tion of the plantations and production fell to a fifth of its pre-war level. Recovery has been steady, reaching 28,000 tons of production in 1997 with some reports suggesting output is now more than 50,000 tons. Depressed world prices have hampered recovery.

Liberia has large forest reserves, with estimated production of 317,000 cubic meters of commercial production in 1997, and 4.8 million cubic meters consumed as fuelwood. There is considerable possibility for expansion. Some Asian companies involved in the logging operations have been criticized for their poor environmental practices, and it has been suggested that they have been able to ignore environmental considerations because of involvement by key figures in the government, or their relatives, in the companies concerned.

INDUSTRY

In the 1960s Liberia was one of the biggest exporters of iron-ore, with deposits of 800 million tons of 35- to 67-percent purity ore, and new deposits of 1 billion tons of high grade ore had been discovered. Many international companies were exploiting the ore from Liberia, but in the 1980s the industry suffered from depressed steel prices and the **parastatal** NIOC closed in 1985. Other companies made cutbacks, leading to a reduction in production to only 1 million tons in 1989, from a high of 15 million tons in the mid-1980s. All production halted early in the war, and no figures have been produced since 1992, when production was estimated at 145,000 tons. Revival of the sector will take huge investments to repair mines and replace equipment, though several international companies have appeared interested.

Diamonds and gold are produced by small-scale mining, though reliable figures have never been available due to smuggling. In 1988, diamonds accounted for US$9 million of exports officially, and gold production yielded an estimated US$6 million a year in the mid-1980s. The illicit mining and export of diamonds remains widespread. In early 1999, the government estimated that there were 5,000 unlicensed and 1,000 licensed mines in Liberia. The government does not have the resources to tackle the problem of unlicensed mines. Official diamond exports tripled between 1998 and 1999, but this is almost entirely due to smuggling of diamonds from Sierra Leone now that there are restrictions on Sierra Leone diamond export to prevent the proceeds supporting the rebel movement there.

(including mining, manufacturing, construction, and power) employed an estimated 8 percent of the workforce in 1999 and provided just 10 percent of the GDP in 2000. The services sector employed 22 percent of the workforce in 1999, and contributed an estimated 30 percent of GDP in 2000. Each sector of the economy was impacted by the civil war, and each is still recovering from the damage done by that war.

AGRICULTURE

The devastation caused by Liberia's civil war has helped to make agriculture the dominant sector in the economy. That dominance, however, reflects not the strength of the agricultural sector but rather the complete failure of the other sectors. Liberia's agricultural production is primarily aimed toward subsistence—providing enough food for individual farmers to survive. Liberia's main staple food is rice, but the country has low yields despite improvements arising from new varieties. Taylor's government has given high priority importance to the sector. In 1998 the FAO reported that rice and cassava production reached 70 percent and 90 percent of pre-war levels respectively, and the IMF estimates indicate good growth in the 2000 harvest.

Rubber is the most important **cash crop**, though cocoa, coffee, and palm oil are also produced. The U.S.-based Bridgestone company is a major producer in Liberia's rubber sector and owns 30 percent of rubber plantations. Despite falling world prices, rubber production rose to 106,000 tons in 1989 and was high throughout the 1980s, though the coming of war brought deser-

Before the civil war manufacturing and construction accounted for around 20 percent of the GDP; that figure dropped to 10 percent by 2000. Manufacturing was dominated by iron-ore production and rubber processing, but domestic and industrial consumption goods were also produced. The size of the local market in Liberia is very small (the United States market is 15,000 times larger in terms of purchasing power), and this makes investment to produce goods for domestic consumption in Liberia unattractive. Political instability has further discouraged investment, particularly from foreign sources. Looting during the civil war means substantial investment is needed to revive the sector. Construction should be stimulated in the post-war period due to reconstruction.

SERVICES

The services sector consists mainly of wholesale and **retail** distribution, telecommunications, postal service, transport, hotels and restaurants, repairs, financial services, tourist services, and government administration, but all such services are quite limited. For the most part, these services support the other sectors of the economy. The main exception is the charges made for the use of Liberian registration by merchant ships owned by private shipping companies from other countries, the so-called "flag of convenience."

Liberia's standing as the second largest flag of convenience was scarcely affected by the war, with revenue amounting to about US$20 million in 1995, providing the interim government with virtually its only source of income. Registration fees were collected by the International Trust Company of Liberia (ITC) on behalf of the Washington, D.C.-based Liberian Maritime Programme, which has controlled the Liberian registry since 1948. In 2000 the registry was taken over by the Liberian International Ship and Corporation Registry.

The financial sector is made up of 12 banks, but 8 were closed in 1996 when fighting erupted in Monrovia. By the end of 1997, about 80 percent of the loans held by Liberian banks were non-performing (that is, borrowers were not making interest payments or repaying the principle). Only 17 percent of the notes and coins in circulation in the country were thought to be in the banking system in 1995, implying a great lack of confidence in the banking system and reducing the ability of the banks to make loans. In April 2000 the Central Bank of Liberia stepped in to administer a leading bank, LUBI, due to **liquidity** problems and insolvency.

INTERNATIONAL TRADE

In normal times, Liberia was highly dependent on external trade; trade generated some 44 percent of the GDP in 1989. But the civil war severely limited Liberia's ability to produce goods for export and led to huge deficits in the trade balance. In 2000 the value of exports stood at US$55 million, compared to US$170 million in imports. However, there is a substantial unrecorded trade in diamonds, which in part explains the financing of Liberia's apparent **trade deficit**.

Trade (expressed in billions of US$): Liberia		
	Exports	Imports
1975	.394	.332
1980	.589	.535
1985	.436	.284
1990	N/A	N/A
1995	N/A	N/A
1998	N/A	N/A

SOURCE: International Monetary Fund. *International Financial Statistics Yearbook 1999.*

In 1999, Belgium took 53 percent of Liberia's exports, followed by Switzerland (9 percent,) the United States (6 percent), and France (4 percent). Imports in 1999 came from South Korea (30 percent), Italy (24 percent), Japan (15 percent), and Germany (9 percent).

MONEY

The Liberian dollar and the U.S. dollar are the 2 legal currencies and are officially interchangeable (that is, the official **exchange rate** is L$1:US$1). However, it is not possible for the public to purchase U.S. dollars at this rate, and in 1999 the actual exchange rate stood at L$40:US$1. Huge volumes of capital flight (the movement of money out of the country) after the coup in 1980 caused the government to mint new coins to fill the resulting gap. In 1989, coins were replaced by notes, but due to the theft of notes from the banks during the civil war, the notes were replaced by the liberty dollar in 1992. This attempt to restore monetary stability was also designed to undermine the position of the rebel leaders, whose wealth was mainly in the old currency. Hence the liberty dollars were not allowed by the rebels in rebel territory, and old notes became illegal in government territory. During the 1997 election campaign, the successful candidate, Charles Taylor, announced that he wanted U.S. dollars to be the only cur-

Exchange rates: Liberia	
Liberian dollars (L$) per US$1	
Dec 2000	39.8100
2000	41.0483
1999	41.9025
1998	41.5075
1997	1.0000
1996	N/A

Note: From 1940 until December 1997, rates were based on a fixed relationship with the US dollar; beginning in January 1998, rates are market determined.

SOURCE: CIA *World Factbook 2001* [ONLINE].

rency in Liberia, but a commission in 1998 argued that a new family of notes and coins, which entered circulation in 2000, would allow the government to benefit, on the new issues, from seigniorage (the situation that occurs when increased amounts of new notes and coins are allowed to enter circulation, allowing the issuer to make a profit to the extent that the face value of the notes and coins is greater than their cost of production).

In October 1999 the ineffective National Bank of Liberia was replaced by the Central Bank of Liberia with Mr. Saleeby, the former finance minister, at its head. The Central Bank of Liberia is pledged to a tight **monetary policy** by limiting the supply of base money to cover replacement only, and will not lend to the government to monetize budget deficits (budget deficits are monetized when the central bank prints money to lend to the government to meet its budget deficit, sparking off an increase in **inflation**). Inflation in 1999 averaged 4 percent, one of the best inflation performances in Africa.

POVERTY AND WEALTH

Using the exchange rate conversion, the GDP per head was around US$175 in 1999, with the purchasing power parity conversion (which allows for the low price of many basic commodities in Liberia) setting the GDP per head at around US$1,000. Both these measures place Liberia among the poorest 20 or so countries in the world. It was estimated in 1999 that 80 percent of Liberia's population was living below the poverty line, most of them engaged in subsistence agriculture, farming small plots of land.

Before the war there were 1,635 schools, 8,804 teachers, and 303,168 pupils. Primary and secondary education was free, though only 50 percent of the primary school age groups attended school. Although most education provision broke down during the war, new efforts to rehabilitate schools and pay wages to teachers have brought about some recovery. The adult literacy is still low at 48 percent, compared to the sub-Saharan average of 58 percent.

Life expectancy at birth was 41 years in 1960, 39 during the war, and 47 in the post-war period. Infant mortality stands at 194 per 1,000 live births (as compared with 7 per 1,000 in the United States). The good health care and nutrition levels of the pre-war period have fallen, and disease is rife. In 1995 clean water was available to 79 percent of urban dwellers and 13 percent of rural dwellers, and sanitation was available to 56 percent of urban dwellers. About half the pre-war medical centers have been rehabilitated since the war.

WORKING CONDITIONS

The government is the largest employer in Liberia, but it is a sad truth of Liberia's decimated economy that there is little formal employment. In 1999, estimates indicated that large-scale agriculture engaged 8 percent of the labor force, industry 8 percent, and services 22 percent, with the remaining 62 percent of the working population engaged in small-scale, family, mostly subsistence, agriculture. However, it was also estimated that 70 percent of the country's workforce was unemployed. Clearly, the majority of the population of Liberia works outside the formal economy, most likely in subsistence agriculture, **bartering**, illegal mining, and other **informal economy** activities.

What little legislation there is for the protection of workers is often ignored. The civil war in Liberia has seen a collapse in government services, and regulation of employment conditions is not seen as a priority by the government. There is no minimum wage, and children are often made to work in agriculture on small family farms from the age of 5 upwards, contributing to low attendance figures at schools. Slavery is officially banned in Liberia, but the civil war has produced a situation where it has been possible for people to be intimidated or coerced into working without any payment or the right to leave. Recent regimes in Liberia have given international observers great cause for concern over human rights, particularly over employment conditions and the plight of children.

COUNTRY HISTORY AND ECONOMIC DEVELOPMENT

1820. U.S. philanthropists establish a settlement for U.S. freed slaves in Liberia.

1847. Liberia becomes a republic and adopts governmental institutions similar to those in the United States.

1945. William Tubman becomes president.

1971. Tubman dies, and William Tolbert succeeds him as president.

1980. After Tolbert is assassinated, Sergeant Samuel Doe rules through a military council.

GDP per Capita (US$)					
Country	1996	1997	1998	1999	2000
Liberia	N/A	1,000	1,000	1,000	1,100
United States	28,600	30,200	31,500	33,900	36,200
Nigeria	1,380	N/A	960	970	950
Sierra Leone	980	540	530	500	510

Note: Data are estimates.

SOURCE: *Handbook of the Nations*, 17th, 18th, 19th and 20th editions for 1996, 1997, 1998 and 1999 data; CIA *World Factbook 2001* [Online] for 2000 data.

1989–96. Civil war hurts the country. In 1989, Doe is returned to power in multi-party elections, but the elections are widely considered to be flawed. Violence between ethnic and political factions begins a civil war.

1990. A coup led by Brigadier General Quiwonkpa is crushed, and 600 are killed in post-coup violence. Samuel Doe is kidnapped and killed as violence worsens.

1991. Forces led by Charles Taylor invades from Côte d'Ivoire, and the civil war becomes more violent and concentrated. For a time, fighting spills over into neighboring Sierra Leone.

1995. After many failed attempts, a peace accord is signed in Nigeria calls for future elections.

1997. The disarmament of the various military forces is completed, and Charles Taylor is elected president in multi-party elections.

1998. Opposition leaders are sent into exile. Taylor continues his support for rebel forces in Sierra Leone.

FUTURE TRENDS

Though the long civil war that so devastated Liberia's economy ended in 1996 and economic growth has increased since that time, Liberia still faces real obstacles to economic stability and recovery. With the Liberia-backed Revolutionary United Front (RUF) continuing to destabilize Sierra Leone in 2001, international donors have remained reluctant to extend aid to Liberia, and UN sanctions are a possibility. Border confrontations can be expected to continue to hinder development. This ongoing situation makes for negligible economic progress in Liberia, and the misery of most people there will continue. In 2001, it was estimated that 80 percent of the people do not have enough income to meet the barest minimum requirements for food, shelter, and clothing.

Economically, President Taylor has demanded more control over strategic commodities, there have been calls for an **embargo** on timber exports, and oil exploration permits for foreign companies have been withheld. These measures, while increasing the power of the government over the economy, are not calculated to improve the conditions of ordinary people. The government has announced plans to privatize the main public utilities, which, when implemented, should introduce improvements in electricity, water, and telecommunication services. However, it will be many years before economic stability returns to Liberia, and prosperity remains a distant dream.

DEPENDENCIES

Liberia has no territories or colonies.

BIBLIOGRAPHY

Economist Intelligence Unit. *Country Profile: Liberia.* London: Economist Intelligence Unit, 2001.

Hodd, Michael. "Liberia." *The Economies of Africa.* Aldershot: Dartmouth, 1991.

Kelly, R. C., et al., eds. *Country Review, Liberia 1998/1999.* Commercial Data International, Inc., 1998.

Liberia: Embassy of the Republic of Liberia, Washington D.C. <http://www.liberiaemb.org>. Accessed October 2001.

U.S. Central Intelligence Agency. *CIA World Factbook 2000: Liberia.* http://www.cia.gov/cia/publications/factbook/geos/li.html

U.S. Department of State. *FY 2000 Country Commercial Guide: Liberia.* <http://www.state.gov/www/about_state/business/com_guides/2000/africa/index.html>. Accessed September 2001.

—Michael Hodd

LIBYA

Socialist People's Libyan Arab Jamahiriya
*Al-Jamahiriyah al-'Arabiyah al-Libiyah ash-
Sha'biyah al-Ishtirakiyah*

CAPITAL: Tripoli.

MONETARY UNIT: Libyan dinar (LD). One Libyan dinar equals 1,000 dirhams. Coins come in denominations of 1, 5, 10, 20, 50, and 100 dirhams. Paper currency comes in denominations of .25, .50, 1, 5, and 10 dinars.

CHIEF EXPORTS: Crude oil, refined petroleum products, and natural gas.

CHIEF IMPORTS: Machinery, transport equipment, food, and manufactured goods.

GROSS DOMESTIC PRODUCT: US$39.3 billion (purchasing power parity, 1999 est.).

BALANCE OF TRADE: Exports: US$6.6 billion (1998 est.). **Imports:** US$7 billion (1998 est.).

COUNTRY OVERVIEW

LOCATION AND SIZE. Libya is a North African country, which shares a border with the Mediterranean Sea to the north, Egypt and Sudan to the east, Niger, Chad and Sudan to the south, and Algeria and Tunisia to the west. With 1,759,540 square kilometers of area (679,358 square miles), it is slightly larger than the State of Alaska. The length of its land border and its coastline is 4,383 kilometers (2,723 miles), and 1,770 kilometers (1,099 miles), respectively. With the exception of Sabha, located in the south, all its major cities—including the capital city of Tripoli—are along its coastline.

POPULATION. Libya's population of roughly 5,115,450 (est. July 2000) has seen an annual growth rate of 3.5 percent since 1975, when it was 2,400,000. With a predicated annual growth rate of 2.1 percent, the population will reach 7,600,000 in 2015. In 2000, the birth and death rates were 27.68 births per 1,000 population, and 3.51 deaths per 1,000 population, respectively.

The Arabic-speaking Berbers and Arabs constitute 97 percent of Libya's population. Greeks, Maltese, Italians, Egyptians, Pakistanis, Turks, Indians, and Tunisians are the significant minority groups.

The Libyan population is relatively young, with 64 percent of the population between the ages of 15 and 64. Only 4 percent of Libyans are over the age of 64. (In contrast, almost 13 percent of the population in the United States is over the age of 64.) In 1998, 86.8 percent of the population was living in urban areas, particularly in Tripoli and Benghazi; this percentage marks a significant growth in urban population since 1975, when it accounted for 60.9 percent of the population. Urban dwellers will constitute roughly 90 percent of the population by 2015.

OVERVIEW OF ECONOMY

After about 5 centuries of colonization by the Ottoman Empire, Italy, Britain, and France, Libya became an independent monarchy in 1951. In 1969, Colonel Muammar Qadhafi staged a coup (an internal military uprising against a government) and established a republic. During its first decade, the new regime **nationalized** all foreign businesses and weakened the **private sector** through nationalization, confiscation, and "spontaneous" seizures of private factories by workers. The private sector was confined to **retail** trade, but the shortage of investments in the late 1980s forced the Libyan government to ease laws restricting its activities. Nevertheless, the private sector is still limited to small-scale activities in agriculture, retail trade, and manufacturing. Various legal and practical restrictions have prevented its rapid expansion, including the absence of respect for private property reflected in the periodic arrest of merchants and shopkeepers, and confiscation of their businesses.

Libya has a single-product economy, which survives on exports of hydrocarbons (oil, gas, and their refined products), accounting for 94 percent of exports in 1998. Thanks to these exports, since the 1960s Libya has had **trade surpluses** and a small **foreign debt** (US$3.9 billion

in 1999) compared to its **foreign exchange reserves** (US$7.28 billion in 1999). However, the economy is highly vulnerable to fluctuations in oil prices, which directly affect government revenues. The Libyan government has been successful to a great extent in creating an **infrastructure**, but it has failed to establish viable industry, agriculture, and service sectors. In particular, it has failed to diversify the economy through establishing desired heavy industries. As a result, the Libyan economy is still an oil-based economy.

Internal and external factors have prevented the economic growth of Libya. Inconsistent planning, frequent changes in government economic policies, and the government's weakening of the private sector have been the major internal factors. External factors include periodic low oil prices, which have deprived the Libyan government of financial means needed to implement fully its development plans. In addition, the imposition of American **sanctions** in the late 1970s, 1980s, and 1990s on Libya for its alleged involvement in terrorism has limited

Libya's income and its access to foreign technology and investment. Additionally, the UN-imposed sanctions on Libya in the 1990s over Libya's refusal to hand over for trial 2 Libyan suspects implicated in the 1988 bombing of a Pan American jetliner further worsened its economic situation. Libya's improving relations with Europe following the suspension of UN sanctions in 1999, and high oil prices have eased pressure on its economy as reflected in a jump from a 2 percent growth rate in 1998 to 5.4 percent in 1999, and to an estimated 6.5 percent in 2000.

POLITICS, GOVERNMENT, AND TAXATION

As explained in his manifesto *The Green Book,* published in the 1970s, Colonel Qadhafi's ideology has shaped the Libyan political system and economy since 1969. As an "alternative" to **capitalism** and **Marxism**, this ideology draws on Arab nationalism and Islam, but its economic program is primarily **socialist**. Accordingly, the state controls the economy, and the private sector assumes a negligible role. The situation has remained the same despite the relaxation of some restrictions on the private sector.

Libya has a peculiar political system known as the *Jamahiriya* or the "republic of the masses." In theory, this means that the Libyans rule their country directly through a series of popular entities that function as local governments, which are called Basic People's Congresses (BPCs). Each BPC chooses a secretary to represent it in Libya's highest legislative organ, the General People's Congress (GPC). The GPC chooses "the secretaries of the secretariat," (cabinet ministers) who form the cabinet called the General People's Committee, and also the head of the Committee, who presides over the cabinet as the prime minister.

The system has undergone changes in form, but the theoretical concept of running the country through popular entities has been kept. In 1992, Colonel Qadhafi divided Libya into 1,500 *mahallat* (communes or neighborhoods) and granted each of them its own budget as well as executive and legislative powers. As part of his decentralization policy, in 2000 he transferred most central government executive functions excluding its defense, trade, social security, health, education, and infrastructure to 26 municipal councils represented in the GPC.

Having the title of "Brother Leader and Guide of the Revolution," Colonel Qadhafi does not hold any official government position. Theoretically, he has no power and defers to the GPC. However, in practice, the GPC is a rubber stamp for the colonel, who appoints all influential figures and ensures the docility of all security and political organs through the revolutionary committees (associations of pro-Qadhafi young men led by the

colonel's appointees). They function as a political police force with the power of arrest and summary execution, although their power has been curtailed to some extent since the late 1980s to appease the growing popular dissatisfaction with their abuses. Since mid-1996, the newly formed "purification committees" have also operated on Colonel Qadhafi's behalf to combat corruption and **black-market** activities. In short, Libya is run by Qadhafi and a small circle of his close allies.

There is no legal opposition group inside the country with an alternative economic view or with any impact on the economy whatsoever. The government has suppressed various secular and religious political groups and turned them into ineffective political forces based mainly in exile. They include the National Front for the Salvation of Libya, the Militant Islamic Group, and the Libyan Martyrs' Movement.

Fossil-energy exports have been the major contributor to government revenues since the 1960s, accounting for more than 70 percent of these revenues. The Libyan government has failed to reduce its heavy reliance on such exports by increasing its revenue from taxes due to the limited tax base and insignificant private sector activities. In absence of such activities, salaried government employees are the main tax payers, although they make little income that can be taxed. Heavy dependency on energy exports affects government revenues, since world oil prices tend to fluctuate. Due to this vulnerability on energy prices, the Libyan government makes every effort to balance its budgets and avoid deficit spending. While accurate budget figures are difficult to obtain from a relatively closed society, it is estimated that in 1999, government revenues roughly equaled expenditures of US$10.88 billion, of which the share of exports was over US$7 billion.

INFRASTRUCTURE, POWER, AND COMMUNICATIONS

Libya has a good infrastructure thanks to its development projects since the 1970s. Its fossil-fuel generators produced electricity at the rate of 16.92 billion kilowatt hours (kWh) in 1998, which was well above consumption (15.736 billion kWh in 1998). There are large-scale plans for their expansion—which will prepare Libya for increasing consumption—valued at about US$6 billion.

Libya's land communication system is confined to an extensive road network estimated at 83,200 kilometers (51,700 miles) in 1996 of which 47,590 kilometers (29,572 miles) are paved. They provide adequate access to most of its major rural and urban areas. There is no train service, but there are plans for building north-south and east-west railway lines.

Communications

Country	Newspapers	Radios	TV Sets[a]	Cable subscribers[a]	Mobile Phones[a]	Fax Machines[a]	Personal Computers[a]	Internet Hosts[b]	Internet Users[b]
	1996	1997	1998	1998	1998	1998	1998	1999	1999
Libya	14	233	126	0.0	3	N/A	N/A	0.00	7
United States	215	2,146	847	244.3	256	78.4	458.6	1,508.77	74,100
Egypt	40	324	122	N/A	1	0.5	9.1	0.28	200
Algeria	38	241	105	0.0	1	0.2	4.2	0.01	20

[a]Data are from International Telecommunication Union, *World Telecommunication Development Report 1999* and are per 1,000 people.
[b]Data are from the Internet Software Consortium (http://www.isc.org) and are per 10,000 people.

SOURCE: World Bank. *World Development Indicators 2000.*

Sea and air connections are facilitated through several ports and airports. Major ports include Tripoli, Benghazi, Marsa el-Brega, Minsurat and El-Sider (Sidra), and 3 new ports are under construction. There are also 5 major oil terminals at Zuetina, Ras Lanuf, Marsa el-Hariga, Marsa el-Brega, and El-Sider. Libya has 59 airports with paved runways and 83 with unpaved runways. UN sanctions stopped international flights to and from Libya, and lack of spare parts caused by other sanctions grounded about 80 percent of its civilian air fleet in the 1990s. The 1999 suspension of UN sanctions paved the way for the resumption of international flights and for purchasing new aircraft and modernizing the airports.

The state-owned General Post and Telecommunications Company (GPTC) dominates the Libyan telecommunications system. It provides fixed telephone services; a private company (El Mada) in which the GPTC has a 20 percent stake provides cellular telephone services. There are at least 318,000 fixed telephone lines (1995 est.) and 20,000 cellular telephones (2000 est.) in use.

All Libyan radio and television programs are state-run. There were 24 AM, FM and short wave radio programs, and 12 television programs in the late 1990s, but many people in urban areas had access to satellite television programs. There were also 1.35 million radios and 730,000 televisions in use. Internet access is provided by the GPTC.

ECONOMIC SECTORS

After a decade of growth in the 1970s, the state-dominated Libyan economy has suffered from over 2 decades of sanctions. Additionally, the practical exclusion of the private sector from major economic activities has limited the growth and diversification of the 3 economic sectors. Agriculture is the smallest sector with limited farming activities and underdeveloped fisheries; it is unable to feed the population. Industry is the largest sector, almost exclusively because of the large hydrocarbon

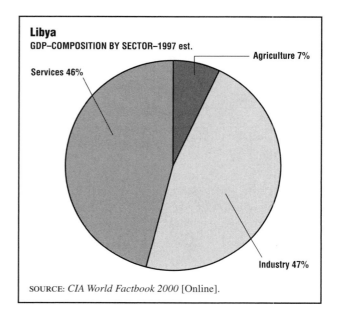

Libya
GDP–COMPOSITION BY SECTOR–1997 est.

Agriculture 7%
Services 46%
Industry 47%

SOURCE: *CIA World Factbook 2000* [Online].

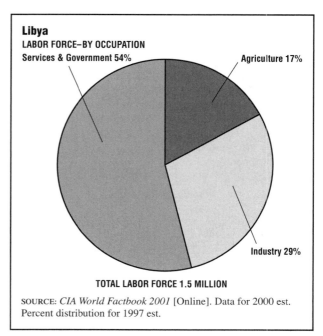

Libya
LABOR FORCE–BY OCCUPATION

Services & Government 54%
Agriculture 17%
Industry 29%

TOTAL LABOR FORCE 1.5 MILLION

SOURCE: *CIA World Factbook 2001* [Online]. Data for 2000 est. Percent distribution for 1997 est.

industry. Oil exports make industry the largest contributor to the economy, and fluctuations in oil prices expand and contract both the sector and the entire economy. The service sector is not underdeveloped, but lacks viable tourist and retail industries. Financial services and transportation, however, make service a significant part of the economy.

AGRICULTURE

Libya has sought to expand its agriculture since the early 1970s. Its success in this regard has been limited despite heavy investments that equaled 30 percent of government expenditures in the 1970s. For example, production of cereals in 1998 (207,000 metric tons) met only 15 percent of the country's needs. Therefore, Libya has remained dependent on large agricultural imports, estimated at about 75 percent of its annual needs.

Libyan agriculture is a small contributor to the workforce (about 17 percent), and to GDP (about 5.6 percent in 1997). Major barriers to its growth are limited arable land (1.7 percent of Libya's area) and water resources, over-use of arable land and fertilizers, and a shortage of labor. Apart from a limited production of barley and wheat, major agricultural products are mostly fruits and vegetables such as dates, almonds, grapes, citrus fruits, watermelon, olives, and tomatoes, which constitute about 80 percent of annual agricultural production. Agricultural activities take place mainly along the coastline. Inland farming is very limited because of water shortages. Rapid urbanization has resulted in a severe shortage of agricultural workers, forcing Libya to rely on foreign farm laborers.

Libya's animal husbandry has suffered from the sanctions, limiting imports of animal feed on which it depends heavily. For example, the production of beef and veal dropped from 22,100 metric tons in 1994 to 2,100 metric tons in 1998.

The low annual catch (34,500 metric tons in 1997) demonstrates the underdeveloped nature of Libya's fisheries, despite the richness of its waters in exportable fish (e.g., tuna and sardines). Low investments in fishing boats, ports, and processing facilities are major obstacles to its growth. The country has 1 major fishing port (Zlitan), 1 tuna plant, and 2 sardine factories with small processing capacities (1,000 metric tons per year each). Libya is planning to build 24 fishing ports in addition to the one under construction at Marsa Zuaga.

INDUSTRY

While its share of GDP is only 52.8 percent (est. 1994), industry is by far the most important segment of Libya's economy, since it encompasses the oil industry, which is vital to the country's economic survival.

OIL. As the main export item, oil dominates Libya's mining industry. Estimated at 29.5 billion barrels in 1998, Libya's oil reserves ensure exports until 2053 at the 1999 export level of 1,137,000 barrels per day (b/d). The Libyan government owns 5 oil refineries in Libya as well as a network of oil refineries in Italy, Switzerland, and Germany in partnership with European oil companies.

Libya's oil production has decreased significantly since the 1970s. In 1975, the Libyans reduced their production from 3.32 million b/d to 1.48 million b/d, for fear of drying up their resources. Managerial problems, OPEC quotas, and sanction-created shortages of spare parts and investments have further lowered production. Sanctions have also resulted in a decrease or stoppage in production of certain oil products (e.g., gasoline), which then had to be imported. American sanctions are still in force, but the 1999 suspension of UN sanctions opened the way for Europe's involvement in Libya's oil industry.

MINING. With estimated gas reserves of 1.5 trillion cubic meters, Libya is also rich in natural gas, but most of its reserves are undeveloped. The Libyan government has tried to develop them to increase the life of its oil reserves by replacing oil with gas for domestic consumption, and also to increase its gas exports. Development projects include 2 gas pipelines to connect 4 new gas-powered electricity generators to the national grid, and a US$5.5 billion project with Italy for the development of onshore and offshore gas reserves and the construction of an undersea pipeline to export gas to Italy. On average, 20 to 25 percent of annual gas production (6.4 billion cubic meters in 1998) is exported mainly to Italy and Spain.

Iron ore and salt are other major resources that play a role in Libya's economy. The iron ore resources are estimated at 700 million metric tons and are located in southern Libya far from its iron and steel complex. Their development has been delayed due to the absence of financing for building the required rail link. Libya's salt mines—located mainly around Tripoli and Benghazi—produce 30,000 metric tons annually. There is also a limited extraction of construction materials (e.g., limestone, clay, and stone).

MANUFACTURING. Libya's manufacturing industry is not well-developed. Ambitious projects in heavy industries (e.g., aluminum and fertilizer complexes) have been partially realized at best, as various sanctions have limited funds, denied foreign investments, and severely restricted transfer of technology and sale of required equipment. Manufacturing establishments suffer from a shortage of spare parts and poor maintenance, which lower their production. The current share of this industry of GDP must be well below its 1994 share of about 10 percent.

Besides a few **joint ventures** (mainly with Italy), most manufacturing establishments are Libyan. They are mostly small- and medium-sized factories producing light and **consumer goods** (e.g., foodstuffs, wood, paper, textiles, and VCRs). The limited heavy industries include an iron and steel complex, a petrochemical complex, and a pharmaceuticals plant. Libya produces about 3,000 cars a year, and assembles trucks in joint venture with Italy. The manufacturing products are far short of domestic demand, making Libya very dependent on imports.

CONSTRUCTION. Thanks to extensive hydrocarbon supplies and water projects, construction is a major industry. Two long-term major projects are the construction of the Great Man-Made River to transfer water from Libya's southern water resources to its major urban and farming areas in the north. It has received an average of 10 percent of government annual expenditures since 1984. Another project is a large gas development and pipeline construction with Italy. There have been modernization projects in major cities including Tripoli since the suspension of UN sanctions.

SERVICES

Services form a growing economic sector, which accounted for about 40 percent of GDP in 1994. Given the suspension of the UN air **embargo** against Libya in 1999, the expected growth in tourism in the first decade of the 21st century should strengthen the role of this sector in the Libyan economy.

FINANCIAL SERVICES. The Libyan government controls the financial system, including banking, insurance, and investment activities. In 1970, it nationalized all financial institutions, but economic problems forced it to allow the operation of private banks in 1993. With one exception in Misurata, no private bank has been established yet. Nor is there any foreign bank, excluding the Arab Banking Corporation, a Baharini bank partly owned by Libya. The banking system consists of the Central Bank of Libya and 8 major banks: the Agriculture Bank, the Jamahiriya Bank, the National Commercial Bank, the Savings and Real Estate Investment Bank, the Umma Bank, the Wahda bank, the Sahara Bank, and the Libyan Arab Foreign Bank. The last 2 are among the top 1,000 banks of the world. State-run companies provide insurance and business services. The Libyan finance ministry conducts foreign investments through the Libyan Arab Foreign Investment Company, which has invested US$500 million in 45 countries.

TOURISM. Libya has an underdeveloped tourist industry, although it has the potential to grow. As a Mediterranean country with long warm beaches and historic sites, Libya could attract many Europeans who currently vacation on the inexpensive warm coastlines of Libya's North African neighbors Egypt and Tunisia. The industry, however, lacks an adequate infrastructure such as hotels. Furthermore, the sanction-related fall of tourism has turned many Libyan beaches into garbage dumps. Anticipating an upsurge in the tourist trade in the wake of the lifting of UN sanctions, a tourist center, including a large hotel and entertainment facilities, is being built in Tripoli.

TRANSPORTATION. The Libyan transportation industry is significant, but has suffered a great deal from sanctions. Its merchant fleet consists of 27 vessels and is oriented towards oil and gas exports. Libya's civilian air fleet, under-utilized from the sanctions, will be expanded by the purchase of 24 Airbuses as part of a government plan announced in 2000.

INTERNATIONAL TRADE

Libya's international trade has been characterized by a positive balance since the 1960s. One estimate put its 1999 balance as US$7.01 billion in exports, and US$4.21 billion in imports, creating a trade surplus of US$2.79 billion, according to the Economist Intelligence Unit. Oil and gas and their refined products accounted for about 95 percent of Libya's exports in 1999. Its major imports are food, **capital goods**, transport equipment, and iron and steel products.

Libya has reduced its trade with the ex-socialist countries since 1991, while expanding trade with North African and Western countries. The suspension of UN sanctions removed barriers to trade with most Western countries. Italy, Germany, Spain, Turkey, France, Sudan, the UK, and Tunisia have been the major destinations of exports for Libya since 1990. With 40.1 percent, 17.8 percent, and 11.3 percent share of exports, the first 3 countries were the largest destinations in 1998. In that year, Italy, Germany, the UK, France, Tunisia, Belgium, Luxembourg, Spain, and Japan were the major exporters to Libya. The first 3 were the largest exporters in 1998 with 22.9 percent, 12.2 percent, and 9.1 percent share of exports, respectively.

Trade (expressed in billions of US$): Libya		
	Exports	Imports
1975	6.834	3.542
1980	21.910	6.777
1985	10.929	4.101
1990	13.225	5.336
1995	N/A	N/A
1998	N/A	N/A

SOURCE: International Monetary Fund. *International Financial Statistics Yearbook 1999.*

MONEY

To ensure the stability of its currency, the Libyan government pegged the Libyan dinar (LD) to the U.S. dollar at a **fixed exchange rate** in 1973. In 1986 it switched to a new system: pegging the dinar to an SDR (special drawing right) at a fixed rate. The SDR is an artificial "basket" of 5 currencies selected and used by the International Monetary Fund for internal accounting purposes. The SDR method allows greater flexibility in stabilizing the value of the dinar as world economic conditions change.

There is a significant difference between official **exchange rates** and those of the black market. In 1996, the black market rate for the U.S. dollar was 10 times as much as the official one. The government has sought to narrow the gap between the 2 rates by selling dollars to push the black market rate down. This policy showed some success in 1999 when that rate dropped to 3 times the official rate (LD 0.45 = US$1).

There are currency restrictions for Libyans and foreigners. Libyans travelling abroad may purchase a certain amount of currency (about US$6,000 in 2000) while foreigners entering Libya have to declare their currencies and leave the country with no more than the declared amount.

In absence of reliable statistics on fluctuations of price changes, it is difficult to determine **inflation rates** in Libya. The existing rates for the second half of the 1990s are therefore estimates. The inflation rate was estimated at 18 percent in 1999, a significant decrease from the average annual rate of 28.5 percent for the period 1995 to 1998. A major reason for such high rates is the heavy government **subsidies** for domestic foodstuffs, which it has kept despite their huge cost for an economy heavily dependent on large food imports. Scarcity of many consumer goods provoked rising prices, which further worsened **inflation**. Economic sanctions, with their limiting effects on trade, and the closure of many retail stores in the second half of the 1990s as part of a government crackdown on the black market, were 2 major

contributing factors. The suspension of UN sanctions in 1999 improved the availability of consumer goods and paved the way for a higher oil- and natural gas-generated income as European oil companies began to return to Libya. These factors, and lower spending by the Libyan government, helped reduce the inflation rate to 18 percent in 1999. Various government subsidies (e.g., free education and medical services and low-priced foodstuffs) helped the Libyans cope with the impact of Libya's high inflation rates without a sharp decline in their living standards.

POVERTY AND WEALTH

The living standards of Libyans have improved significantly since the 1970s, ranking the country among the highest in Africa. Urbanization, developmental projects, and high oil revenues have enabled the Libyan government to elevate its people's living standards. The social and economic status of women and children has particularly improved. Various subsidized or free services (health, education, housing, and basic foodstuffs) have ensured basic necessities. The low percentage of people without access to safe water (3 percent), health services (0 percent) and sanitation (2 percent), and a relatively high life expectancy (70.2 years) in 1998 indicate the improved living standards. Adequate health care and subsidized foodstuffs have sharply reduced infant mortality, from 105 per 1,000 live births in 1970 to 20 per 1,000 live births in 1998. The government also subsidizes education, which is compulsory and free between the ages of 6 and 15. The expansion of educational facilities has elevated the literacy rate (78.1 in 1998). There are universities in Tripoli, Benghazi, Marsa el-Brega, Misurata, Sebha, and Tobruq. Despite its successes, the educational system has failed to train adequate numbers of professionals, resulting in Libya's dependency on foreign teachers, doctors, and scientists.

Many direct and indirect subsidies and free services have helped raise the economic status of low-income families, a policy which has prevented extreme poverty. As part of its socialist model of economic development,

---

Exchange rates: Libya

Libyan dinars (LD) per US$1

Jan 2001	0.5101
2000	0.5081
1999	0.4616
1998	0.3785
1997	0.3891
1996	0.3651

Note: Libya currently has two rates for foreign trade; one for government operations and foreign companies and one for Libyan individuals (0.45 dinars per US dollar in December 1998).

SOURCE: CIA *World Factbook 2001* [ONLINE].

GDP per Capita (US$)

Country	1996	1997	1998	1999	2000
Libya	N/A	6,700	6,700	7,900	8,900
United States	28,600	30,200	31,500	33,900	36,200
Egypt	2,900	4,400	2,850	3,000	3,600
Algeria	4,000	4,000	4,600	4,700	5,500

Note: Data are estimates.

SOURCE: *Handbook of the Nations*, 17th, 18th, 19th and 20th editions for 1996, 1997, 1998 and 1999 data; CIA *World Factbook 2001* [Online] for 2000 data.

---

the Libyan government has weakened the private sector and confined it to mainly small-scale businesses. While this policy has damaged the Libyan economy significantly, it has also prevented the accumulation of wealth by a small percentage of the population. While the ruling elite (i.e., top civil servants, military officers, and politicians), enjoys much higher living standards compared to average Libyans, and corruption exists within its ranks, Libya is not a highly polarized society divided between extremes of wealth and poverty.

WORKING CONDITIONS

The Libyan labor law provides for wages and pensions, but prohibits independent trade unions. The government-created National Trade Unions' Federation is the only legal workers' organization. The labor law does not provide for the right to strike, but Qadhafi has confirmed its existence. Collective bargaining is not allowed, since the government must approve all labor agreements. The minimum age of labor is 18, the maximum work week is 48 hours, and the average monthly wage is roughly 270 dinars. At the official exchange rate, this works out to roughly US$750 a month, but is only US$100 at the unofficial (and more realistic) rate. The labor law provides for the equality of women with men, but traditional social restrictions on women's activities outside the home limit the practical effects of the law, and therefore create barriers to full participation of women in the workforce. Foreign workers may be denied rights provided for Libyan workers, and there are restrictions on their **repatriation** of income.

Libya's workforce is about 1.2 million strong as estimated in 1997. There are also 1 to 2 million foreign workers. The majority of the workforce are government employees. Unemployment was estimated at about 30 percent in 2000. The high unemployment rate is the result of years of sanctions as well as Qadhafi's efforts at preventing the emergence of a viable and growing private sector. Sanctions have been particularly effective in harming Libya's oil and gas exports, thus constraining economic security for many Libyans who directly or indirectly rely on these industries. Large infrastructure projects, financed by the government, also depend on export revenues. Thus, a decline in the activities of the oil and gas industries and large governmental projects has reduced employment opportunities, resulting in a large unemployment rate. This situation will likely change in the near future. In the aftermath of the 1999 suspension of UN sanctions, the growing interest of the European oil companies in the Libyan energy industry will increase its exports, which in turn will generate funds to be invested in the expansion of the industry and also in many other government projects. In short, the revival of the energy industry will surely help reduce unemployment in Libya.

COUNTRY HISTORY AND ECONOMIC DEVELOPMENT

643. The Arabs invade Libya and rule over it until the 1500s when the Ottoman Empire conquers it.

1911. Italy replaces the Ottoman Empire as the colonizer of Libya.

1945. Libya is divided between Britain and France at the end of World War II.

1951. Libya becomes independent, and King Idris establishes a monarchy.

1959. The first commercially viable oilfield is discovered at Zelten.

1960s. Libya emerges as a major oil-producing country.

1969. Colonel Muammar Qadhafi stages a *coup* and overthrows the monarchy.

1977. Libya was renamed as the Great Socialist People's Libyan Arab Jamahiriya. Inspired by Colonel Qadhafi, workers assume control of the private manufacturing sector.

1978. The United States imposes sanctions on Libya for its alleged state terrorism.

1982. The USA bans Libyan crude oil imports.

1992. The United Nations imposes sanctions on Libya for its refusal to hand over suspects implicated in the 1988 bombing of a Pan American airliner.

1993. UN sanctions expand to freeze Libyan financial assets abroad.

1996. The United States imposes secondary sanctions, the "Iran and Libya Sanctions Act," targeting non-American companies wishing to invest more than US$40 million a year in the Iranian and Libyan oil industries.

1999. UN sanctions are suspended as Libya, the United Kingdom, and the United States agree on the trial of the 2 suspects in the Netherlands.

FUTURE TRENDS

The suspension of UN sanctions in 1999 has paved the way for large foreign investments in the Libyan hydrocarbon industries, a necessity for its full operation, expansion, and modernization. The Italian oil companies have been eager to embark on major projects in Libya. Libya will likely further expand its economic ties with European countries in energy and non-energy areas, while American sanctions will exclude American businesses, including oil companies, from investment in that country. The expansion of the Libyan private sector will likely gain momentum, since the **liberalization** of Libya's centralized economy is a necessity for its development and diversification. In the absence of any significant opposition, there is no serious challenge to the Libyan political system and the authority of Colonel Qadhafi. For the foreseeable future, the Libyan political system led by Colonel Qadhafi will likely remain stable.

DEPENDENCIES

Libya has no territories or colonies.

BIBLIOGRAPHY

Economist Intelligence Unit (EIU). *Country Risk Service Libya.* London: EIU, 16 January 2001.

EIU. *Country Profile: Libya, 2000–01.* London: EIU, 2000.

EIU. *Country Report: Libya.* London: EIU, December 2000.

EIU. *Country Report: Libya.* London: EIU, February 2001.

Economic Research Institute. "Libya—Compensation and Benefit Legislation." http://www.erieri.com/codes/LIBYA.htm. Accessed June, 2001.

Gurney, Judith. *Libya: The Political Economy of Oil.* Oxford: Oxford University Press, 1996.

United Nations Development Program. *Human Development Report 2000.* New York: Oxford University Press, 2000.

United States Central Intelligence Agency. "The World Factbook 2000: Libya." http://www.odci.gov/cia/publications/factbook/geos/er.html. Accessed January 2001.

United States Department of State. "1999 Country Reports on Human Rights Practices-Libya." http://www.state.gov/www/global/human_rights/1999/eritrea.htm. Accessed January 2001.

—Dr. Hooman Peimani

MADAGASCAR

CAPITAL: Antananarivo.

MONETARY UNIT: Malagasy franc (FMG). One franc equals 100 centimes. Coins come in denominations of 1, 2, 5, 10, 20, 25, 50, 100, and 250. Paper currency includes denominations of 500, 1,000, 2,500, 5,000, 10,000, and 25,000 FMG.

CHIEF EXPORTS: Coffee, vanilla, cloves, shellfish, sugar, petroleum products, clothing and textiles.

CHIEF IMPORTS: Manufactured and consumer goods, petroleum, food.

GROSS DOMESTIC PRODUCT: US$11.5 billion (purchasing power parity, 1999 est.).

BALANCE OF TRADE: **Exports:** US$600 million (f.o.b., 1998 est.). **Imports:** US$881 million (c.i.f., 1998 est.).

Democratic Republic of Madagascar
République Démocratique de Madagascar
Repoblika Demokratika n'i Madagaskar

COUNTRY OVERVIEW

LOCATION AND SIZE. Madagascar lies in the southern Indian Ocean some 400 miles off Africa's eastern shore. With a land area of 587,039 square kilometers (226,656 square miles) Madagascar is a little less than twice the size of Arizona. It is also the world's fourth largest island, with a coastline of 4,827 kilometers (3,000 miles). Madagascar's capital is Antananarivo (population 2 million), located on its central plateau 1,468 meters (4,816 feet) above sea level. Other major cities include Fianarantsoa (population 440,000), inland in the southern part of the island; Taomasina (population 330,000), the principal port, located on the eastern seaboard; Antsiranana (population 320,000), at its northern-most tip; and Mahajanga (population 295,000), site of the country's second international airport. Madagascar's highest point is a mountain called Maromokotro (2,876 meters or 9,436 feet), located in the Tsaratanana Massif region along the island's central spine.

POPULATION. Demographic statistics for Madagascar are scarce and often unreliable, but a mid-2000 estimate by the U.N. Population Fund places its population at around 15.9 million. Although relative to its size this figure is below the average of its sub-Saharan neighbors, growth is brisk. With an annual birthrate estimated at 42.92 per 1,000 of population—around 3 percent per annum for the years 1995 to 2000—the fragility of Madagascar's environment makes this expansion a significant concern. The average life expectancy at birth of 54.95 years is relatively high by sub-Saharan standards, but poverty and malnutrition are nevertheless endemic, sanitation is very poor, and disease (especially cholera and malaria) is an ever-present threat. Some 27 percent of Malagasy (the people of Madagascar) lived in urban areas in 1998, a population segment which was growing at the rapid rate of 5.6 percent a year as rural inhabitants quit the countryside for the cities.

Ethnically, Madagascar is an unusual mix. Its 2 largest ethnic groups are the Indonesian-descended Merina (26 percent) and Betsileo (12 percent), who are historically concentrated in the central highlands, including the capital. Other groups include the Arab-African Betsimisaraka (15 percent) and Tsimehety (7 percent) of the east and north, respectively; and the Antandroy, of more purely (Bantu) African origin, in the south (5 percent). The prevalence of a unified language, the Malay-Indonesian Malagasy, has tended to work against sharp ethnic divisions, though there is some on-going chafing against Merina political domination. Religiously, 52 percent of Madagascar's people hold indigenous beliefs, 41 percent are Christian and 7 percent Muslim.

OVERVIEW OF ECONOMY

Although possessed of a temperate climate and variety of natural resources, Madagascar remains one of the poorest countries in the world. Its economic problems are daunting, and have been compounded by many years of

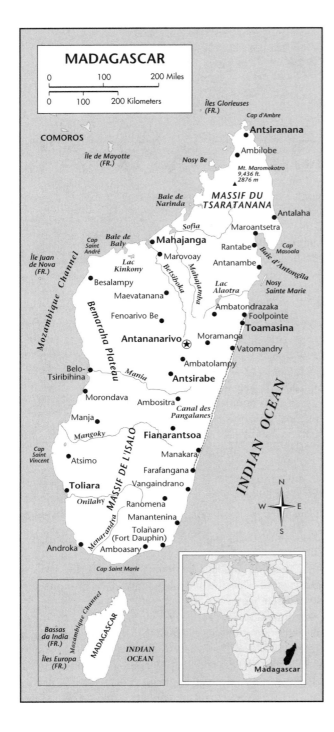

MADAGASCAR

and one-third of GDP. But population pressure combined with poor resource management has caused serious damage to Madagascar's ancient and highly delicate ecosystem, and deforestation and soil erosion are pressing concerns. By the late 1980s it was estimated that only 1 percent of the original wilderness remained.

Agriculture also suffers from droughts, locust plagues, and cyclones. A series of 3 particularly savage cyclones in early 2000 affected more than a million people and caused damage estimated by the World Bank to be near US$137 million. Growth, which had been forecast at 5.3 percent for 2000 (after a 4.7 percent rate in 1999), only reached 4.8 percent, leaving the country still crucially dependent on foreign aid and **debt relief**. The cyclones' devastating economic consequences, especially on **cash crops** such as coffee and vanilla, will be felt for years to come.

Other challenges include a limited and badly antiquated road system and rail network that are wholly unequal to the challenges of Madagascar's weather and terrain. The difficulty of transport, which in the monsoon months can leave large parts of the country inaccessible, is a major obstacle to commercial activity. But also inadequate is Madagascar's bureaucratic **infrastructure**. The civil service tends to be unresponsive and inefficient. And poor policing and corruption in the judiciary continue to render property and contract rights insecure. These factors are formidable disincentives for much-needed investment in the economy.

Madagascar's hope rests on energetic **restructuring** of its economy to reduce the **national debt**, stimulate the **private sector**, and encourage foreign development. Industries targeted as strategically central to this mission are Madagascar's fledgling manufacturing sector (especially garments and textiles) and its unique environment, with "**eco-tourism**" showing signs of real revenue promise.

POLITICS, GOVERNMENT, AND TAXATION

Colonized by France in the 1890s, Madagascar gained its independence on 26 June 1960 after a violent separatist struggle. Its first president, Philibert Tsirinan, was toppled in May 1972. In the 3 years of military rule that followed, Tsirinan's foreign minister, Didier Ratsiraka, emerged as the principal strongman and took the presidency officially in June 1975. Declaring the Democratic Republic of Madagascar, Ratsiraka closed all foreign military bases, **nationalized** the country's major industries, and opened relations with the Soviet Union and China. A drastically worsening economic situation forced Ratsiraka's Avant-garde de la révolution malagache (Arema) government in the 1980s to seek international help and institute a new monetarist reform agenda. Al-

stagnation and decline. From 1971 to 1991 Madagascar dropped from the world's 30th poorest nation to its 10th poorest, with a fall in **GDP per capita** across the same period of 40 percent. Only in the late 1990s has Madagascar really begun to turn this trend around, but progress is expected to be slow, and major set-backs can still be expected.

Still predominantly agrarian, agriculture accounts for four-fifths of the workforce (mostly at subsistence level)

though re-elected in March 1989, popular agitation for political **liberalization** had reached the point that, by 1992, Ratsiraka was forced to accede to a new pluralist, democratic constitution (pluralist societies are characterized by a variety of opinions voiced in a democratic context). In the first elections, under the constitution adopted later that year, he was voted out of office. He returned in 1996, however, after his successor, Albert Zafy, was impeached by parliament. The next presidential election is scheduled for 2001, and remains largely up in the air. Although the president's opposition is fragmented, and his IMF (International Monetary Fund)-sanctioned policies enjoy broad support, Ratsiraka himself is not especially popular; and he is also now very old. Madagascar has yet to resolve its unstable, and sometimes violent, political situation.

Madagascar's republic's laws are based on the French civil law system and traditional Malagasy rule, and a new constitution was adopted in 1998. The president of Madagascar is the chief of state and elected by direct vote for a 5-year term. The country now has a two-chamber legislature: the National Assembly and the Senate. The National Assembly is directly elected. The president and his cabinet appoint a prime minister. The country has nearly 30 active political parties.

Although the political consensus in Madagascar has generally favored fiscal discipline, it is only in the last 4 or 5 years that economic liberalization and monetary stabilization have been consistently and rigorously applied. Current policy is committed to minimizing **inflation**, servicing the national debt, stimulating the private sector, and diversifying the country's export base. The effects have been encouraging, with an average growth rate since 1995 of 3.2 percent.

Other initiatives include the divestment of state enterprises, with more than 40 slated for **privatization**, and the devolution of certain government powers to local councils, a measure to make government more efficient and accountable. Longer-term plans include reforming

the justice system to combat corruption, and re-investing in education, which has become badly neglected in the last 20 years (falling from 4.4 percent of GNP in 1980 to 1.9 percent in 1998).

With tax evasion widespread, part of the new regime of fiscal reform has also been a more aggressive approach to taxation and revenue collection. This has seen revenues increase to 10 percent of GDP in 2000, but in an economy that is largely informal, the burden has tended to fall on the fragile business sector. Vocal protests from the Malagasy business community in 1999 forced the government to soften its stance and exposed the limits of fiscal reform. To bolster industry, plans are now afoot to reduce trade-based **levies**, currently the source of 60 percent of government tax revenue. Some of this shortfall will be picked up by the 20 percent **value-added tax**.

INFRASTRUCTURE, POWER, AND COMMUNICATIONS

Underdeveloped and poorly maintained, Madagascar's inadequate infrastructure is a major obstacle to economic progress, restricting the exchange of goods and limiting development opportunities. The problem has been made even worse by an actual deterioration of the infrastructure in the 1970s and 1980s. As of 2000, only just over 11 percent of its 49,828 kilometers (30,968 miles) of roads are paved. During the rainy season, many of these are completely impassable, isolating large parts of the country. Rail is also in a perilous state, with a mere 885 kilometers (550 miles) of track, in 2 unconnected systems, and most of it in very poor repair. The introduction of private trucking licenses and the planned sale of the national railroad company should help, but the problem remains a fundamental one.

The poor condition of the land transport system has placed special emphasis on air and sea traffic. Madagascar has 15 ports, of which Tonmasina, Mahajanga, and Antsiranana are the most important. In theory, there are

Communications									
Country	Newspapers	Radios	TV Sets[a]	Cable subscribers[a]	Mobile Phones[a]	Fax Machines[a]	Personal Computers[a]	Internet Hosts[b]	Internet Users[b]
	1996	1997	1998	1998	1998	1998	1998	1999	1999
Madagascar	5	192	21	N/A	1	N/A	1.3	0.12	8
United States	215	2,146	847	244.3	256	78.4	458.6	1,508.77	74,100
South Africa	32	317	125	N/A	56	3.5	47.4	33.36	1,820
Mozambique	3	40	5	N/A	0	N/A	1.6	0.09	15

[a]Data are from International Telecommunication Union, *World Telecommunication Development Report 1999* and are per 1,000 people.
[b]Data are from the Internet Software Consortium (http://www.isc.org) and are per 10,000 people.
SOURCE: World Bank. *World Development Indicators 2000.*

211 airfields, but only 30 of these are paved. There is an international airport at Ivato, outside Antananarivo. **Deregulation** of the air market has seen considerable expansion, with the appearance of competitors pushing down prices and increasing volumes, especially between Europe and Asia. The first half of 2000 saw an 11 percent jump in European passenger numbers over the same period in 1999, and a 69 percent increase in Asian passengers. Deregulation plans include the eventual privatization of Air Madagascar.

Telecommunications in Madagascar are currently inadequate. The landline network has barely been extended since 1960, and the vast majority of telephones are concentrated in the capital. With foreign aid, the country has installed a new digital switching system, however. Privatization of the national telecommunications **monopoly**, Telma, is underway, but is unlikely to generate the investment capital necessary to expand radically the customer base. The mobile telephone market, however, is highly competitive, with 4 operators active. Thanks to the USAID-funded Leland Initiative, Internet services can now boast 10 Internet service providers (ISPs).

Madagascar has 7 hydro-electric power stations and together these contribute two-thirds of its power output. But electricity makes up only 5 percent of total energy production; 82 percent of primary energy supply comes from bagasse (sugar cane residue), firewood, and charcoal, the use of which carries a high environmental cost. The development of Madagascar's extensive coal reserves has so far been frustrated by the poor road and rail system. Oil exploration is underway, but the country remains import-dependent.

ECONOMIC SECTORS

Madagascar remains a firmly agrarian society, with agriculture generating about 32 percent of GDP and 70 percent of export earnings (1999). But the industry is limited by the prevalence of subsistence production and its orientation towards the domestic market, whereas its traditional export-focused crops, such as coffee, cotton, and spices, have been hurt by waning international prices. While there has been fruitful diversification into newer crops such as cassava (tapioca) and bananas, as well as fishing and aquaculture, agriculture alone cannot sustain future growth. Sectors which have become increasingly important are manufacturing and tourism, whose potential to generate foreign exchange earnings have made their development a government priority. But while innovative and productive steps have already been taken to encourage these sectors, and economic liberalization has helped to stimulate competitiveness, the shortage of investment capital has made progress tentative and halting.

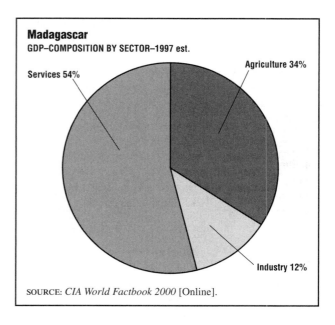

Madagascar
GDP–COMPOSITION BY SECTOR–1997 est.

Services 54%
Agriculture 34%
Industry 12%

SOURCE: *CIA World Factbook 2000* [Online].

AGRICULTURE

Agriculture forms the livelihood of the overwhelming majority of Malagasy. And yet, although agriculture is a vital export earner, the industry remains underdeveloped, accounting for only one-third of GDP—a level below that of its agrarian neighbors. Despite half the country being cultivable, only 5 percent is currently used for crop production, and only 16 percent of this is irrigated; most farmers eke out a subsistence living on small family plots. Poor transport systems and highly limited access to credit have also inhibited commercial development and discouraged investment in cash crops.

The main staple crop is rice, occupying about two-thirds of all available cropland. Despite a long-standing government goal of rice self-sufficiency, however, Madagascar remains a net importer. Traditional cash crops—most of which were introduced by the French in the 19th century—include coffee, cotton, sugar cane, vanilla, and cloves. But pressure from other producing countries has undermined Madagascar's market share in these commodities and cut into export earnings. Coffee continues to hold its own, accounting for around 8 percent of exports (US$42.5 million, est. 1998), as does cotton (4.1 percent), traditionally the second most important export crop. But vanilla and cloves have been badly hit by sagging world prices, shrinking from a traditional one-third export share to around 5 percent in 1999. Non-traditional crops have fared better and include cassava (the second major crop in terms of land used), corn, sweet potato, and bananas.

With some 50 percent of all Malagasy land used for herding, livestock farming (especially Zebu beef cattle) is another important export earner, though ownership patterns and social imperatives inhibit full commercialization. Timber is also significant. Although Madagascar's native reserves have been largely cleared for farming, there is heavy international pressure to conserve what is left; about 260,000 hectares of pine and eucalyptus forests are currently under cultivation.

Fishing is growing in importance and shows considerable promise. Prawn and tuna exports in particular are valuable export earners, and production is expected by 2001 to have increased by 25 percent over its 1995 levels, with 20 percent more jobs created. Shrimp farming is also taking off; other products include tilapia, black bass, trout, and lobster.

INDUSTRY

Industry is a fledgling sector in Madagascar, providing only 13.6 percent of GDP (1998), but one showing definite potential. Mineral deposits are substantial and largely unexploited. Gold and chromite are both mined extensively, as are, on a smaller scale, graphite, mica nickel, ilmenite, and marble. Iron and bauxite, as well as semi-precious stones (especially sapphires) are being developed, and have a combined export potential of up to US$380 million. The industry is not without its problems, however. Many of Madagascar's deposits are inside national parks and hence off-limits to development. Low investment is also a hindrance, as is—in the case of gold and gemstones—chronic smuggling.

Manufacturing is an area of some success, greatly stimulated by the formation of the export processing zone (EPZ) in 1996, which offers tax exemptions for export-focused industries. The project has grown to include 150 companies and has generated 80,000 jobs, producing 37.4 percent of Madagascar's foreign trade revenue. Its main products are clothing (48 percent), handicrafts (13 percent), and agro-processing (9 percent). Textiles are another important export, supported by Madagascar's cotton industry and low wage rates, and accounts for 15 percent of manufacturing production. Other products include plastics, pharmaceuticals, leather goods, footwear, and tobacco.

SERVICES

TOURISM. Madagascar's climate, beaches (4,827 kilometers—or 3,000 miles—of them), and unique ecology (Madagascar is home to many endangered species of flora and fauna) make tourism one of its most dynamic and promising sectors. The industry has the potential not only to create jobs and wealth, but to turn Madagascar's unusual and endangered environment into a productive asset. Interest is great, and two-thirds of the country's visitors come for eco-tourism. In 1998, tourists brought in US$92.2 million. But although visitor numbers are rising steadily (doubling since 1994), volume is still low.

In 1997 Madagascar attracted less than a fifth of neighboring Mauritius's 536,000 visitors. Further development of the industry also faces significant difficulties. Air links to Europe and Asia are few and expensive, hotel facilities are sparse and inadequate, and investment is scarce. Government attempts to meet these obstacles have included rationalizing (removing inconsistencies and streamlining) the relevant laws, creating a coordinated tourist authority, and liberalizing the airline market.

FINANCIAL SERVICES. Limitations in the financial sector continue to impede growth. The nation's assets are controlled by the central bank and 5 commercial banks, the largest of which, BNI-Credit Lyonnais, has a total asset base of US$200 million. Few Malagasy, however, qualify for these banks' services. The problem is especially acute in the rural areas where only 1.5 percent of small farmers have access to credit; the agriculture sector itself receives only 5 percent of total lending. High interest loan rates and fees have also discouraged business borrowing. The lack of a stock exchange and shareholding culture have further restricted financing options.

RETAIL. Few in Madagascar can afford more than the bare essentials, and steady depreciation of the currency has eroded purchasing power even further. This combined with the poor condition of the country's transport network means that trade tends to be localized and retailing minimal. However, the opening of the economy has expanded the range of goods available somewhat, especially in the main urban centers like Antananarivo.

INTERNATIONAL TRADE

Trade continues to run heavily in Madagascar's disfavor, with imports exceeding exports by more than US$200 million. Although there are signs the situation may be improving, the disparity remains debilitating.

The main trading partner is Madagascar's old colonial patron, France, which in 1998 took 39.6 percent of its total exports, at a value of US$349 million. France in turn supplied 24.1 percent of its imports, mostly machinery

Trade (expressed in billions of US$): Madagascar

	Exports	Imports
1975	.302	.366
1980	.401	.600
1985	.274	.402
1990	.319	.571
1995	.368	.499
1998	.241	.514

SOURCE: International Monetary Fund. *International Financial Statistics Yearbook 1999.*

Exchange rates: Madagascar

Malagasy francs (FMG) per US$1

Nov 2000	6,656.3
2000	N/A
1999	6,283.8
1998	5,441.4
1997	5,090.9
1996	4,061.3

SOURCE: CIA *World Factbook 2001* [ONLINE].

GDP per Capita (US$)

Country	1975	1980	1985	1990	1998
Madagascar	364	344	277	276	238
United States	19,364	21,529	23,200	25,363	29,683
South Africa	4,574	4,620	4,229	4,113	3,918
Mozambique	N/A	166	115	144	188

SOURCE: United Nations. *Human Development Report 2000;
Trends in human development and per capita income.*

(25.7 percent), textiles and clothes (16.1 percent), chemicals (13.2 percent), and transport equipment (10.6 percent). Other buyers of Malagasy goods are Mauritius (6.9 percent), the United States (5.9 percent), and Germany (4.4 percent). Germany was also the source of 7.3 percent imports, while Iranian oil accounted for a further 7.1 percent.

Under the Lomé Convention, Madagascar enjoys preferential entry to European export markets. It is also a member of the 20-nation Common Market for Eastern and Southern Africa trade group (COMESA), whose long-term plans include monetary union and a common central bank. Madagascar has also applied to join the similarly aimed Southern African Development Community (SADC).

MONEY

Madagascar's **external debt** stands at over US$3.3 billion, its annual deficit at around 4 percent of GDP (1999). This is some improvement over the previous 6 years, when the deficit had averaged in excess of 6 percent per annum, but it remains a heavy economic burden, and has put considerable pressure on its currency. Inflation has long been a problem, with an average of 60 percent as recently as 1994. But while efforts by Madagascar's central bank have seen this fall in 1998 to 6.4 percent, further progress is hindered by the high world oil price; and increased government spending saw this bounce back up to 14.4 percent in 1999.

Since the Malagasy franc was first floated in 1994 it has lost about half its value against the U.S. dollar. Although this has made imports more expensive, it has also enhanced Madagascar's export competitiveness. The Malagasy franc now sits at about 7,000 to the U.S. dollar.

POVERTY AND WEALTH

Chronic poverty is Madagascar's foremost burden. Its wage rates are amongst the lowest in the world, and, according to a 1993–94 survey, 70 percent of the coun-

**Distribution of Income or Consumption by Percentage
Share: Madagascar**

Lowest 10%	1.9
Lowest 20%	5.1
Second 20%	9.4
Third 20%	13.3
Fourth 20%	20.1
Highest 20%	52.1
Highest 10%	36.7

Survey year: 1993
Note: This information refers to expenditure shares by percentiles of the
population and is ranked by per capita expenditure.

SOURCE: *2000 World Development Indicators* [CD-ROM].

try lived below even Madagascar's own baseline poverty level, and conditions had not improved by the end of the century. Average per capita GDP sits at US$250 per annum (1999), low even for sub-Saharan economies, and one-hundredth of France's GDP per capita. Although the economy continues to grow, the effects remain unfelt by the majority of the population, for whom disease and famine are continual blights.

Poverty levels are not helped by skewed distribution. Traditional Malagasy society is highly hierarchical, with a rigid ranking system according to ethnicity, age, and gender. The effect has been to rigidify social structures and to leave Madagascar's richest 10 percent controlling 35 percent of the country's wealth. Corruption and patronage too tend to concentrate wealth in the hands of the elite, though the planned devolution of governmental power to the regions may go some way to expanding the political class.

WORKING CONDITIONS

The Malagasy workforce is estimated to be around 7 million strong. Unemployment is officially low— around 2.8 percent in rural areas, 6.6 percent in the cities—but these figures are likely to be significantly underestimated. Although the rate has been slowly falling,

Household Consumption in PPP Terms

Country	All food	Clothing and footwear	Fuel and power[a]	Health care[b]	Education[b]	Transport & Communications	Other
Madagascar	61	8	4	2	2	5	18
United States	13	9	9	4	6	8	51
South Africa	N/A	N/A	N/A	N/A	N/A	N/A	N/A
Mozambique	N/A	N/A	N/A	N/A	N/A	N/A	N/A

Data represent percentage of consumption in PPP terms.
[a]Excludes energy used for transport.
[b]Includes government and private expenditures.

SOURCE: World Bank. *World Development Indicators 2000.*

more than half the workforce is still **underemployed**. At least in the short-term, the down-sizing of the **public sector** is likely to see more jobs lost. Hardest hit are the young; 22 is the average age of the unemployed.

Despite Madagascar's poverty and falling government investment in education, literacy remains relatively high (by sub-Saharan standards). More than 90 percent of children enroll in primary school, and 16 percent go on to secondary school. The literacy rate is 72 percent for men and 52 percent for women. The result is a generally adaptable workforce.

COUNTRY HISTORY AND ECONOMIC DEVELOPMENT

c. A.D. 300–800. The first humans arrive in Madagascar, from Indonesia.

1642. French presence established.

1890. European powers recognize Madagascar as a French protectorate.

1944. Madagascar receives French overseas territory status.

1958. Madagascar becomes a self-governing republic within the French Community.

1960. Independence from France.

1972. Philibert Tsirinan, Madagascar's first president, is forced to resign after mass demonstrations.

1975. Didier Ratsiraka becomes Madagascar's second president.

1992. New Constitution enacted; Ratsiraka defeated in elections by Albert Zafy.

1996. Zafy impeached by parliament; Ratsiraka returns to office.

1999. Madagascar becomes eligible for U.S. debt relief.

FUTURE TRENDS

Madagascar remains desperately poor, and its people afflicted with malnourishment, endemic poverty, and disease. And yet there are signs that some cautious optimism may be in order. Progress has been slow and painful, but real. After many years of government control, new free market policies have been implemented and the government is slowly putting the productive sectors of the nation into private hands. And while climatic factors remain a wild-card threat, on-going attempts to diversify the economy and address poverty levels will help to reduce exposure. But much will depend on continued international support.

DEPENDENCIES

Madagascar has no territories or colonies.

BIBLIOGRAPHY

Brown, Mervyn. *Madagascar Rediscovered: A History from Early Times to Independence.* Hamden, Connecticut: Archon Books, 1979.

Covell, Maureen. *Madagascar: Politics, Economics, and Society.* New York: Frances Pinter, 1987.

Economist Intelligence Unit. "Country Profile: Madagascar, Mauritius, Seychelles, Comoros." <http://db.eiu.com/report_dl.asp?mode=pdf&valname=CPAMGB>. Accessed December 2000.

Economist Intelligence Unit. "Country Report: Madagascar." <http://db.eiu.com/report_dl.asp?mode=pdf&valname=CRAMGC>. Accessed December 2000.

U.S. Department of State. *Country Commercial Guide: Madagascar.* Washington DC: U.S. Department of State, 2001. <http://www.state.gov/www/about_state/business/com_guides/2001/africa/madagascar_ccg2001.pdf>. Accessed December 2000.

U.S. Library of Congress. "Country Studies: Madagascar (1994)." <http://lcweb2.loc.gov/frd/cs/mgtoc.html#mg0006>. Accessed December 2000.

—*Alexander Schubert*

INTRODUCTION TO WORLD CURRENCY

The following insert contains color photographs of paper currency from around the world. Where possible, the most recent issue and lowest denomination was selected to show the bank notes of the countries represented in this encyclopedia. As of the year 2002, approximately 169 countries issued their own paper money.

Bank notes are more than a measuring system for value to be used as payment for goods and services. In many instances a banknote is a graphic reflection of a country's history, politics, economy, environment, and its people. For example, many bank notes depict plant life such as flowers and trees, as well as birds and other animals native to that geographic region. The 5-lats note of Latvia has a giant oak tree on the front, while the 25-rupee note of Seychelles and the 5-guilder note of Suriname both show flowers from the homeland. Birds adorn notes from São Tomé and Príncipe, Papua New Guinea, and Zambia. Large animals such as the mountain gorillas on the 500-franc note from Rwanda, the white rhinoceros on the 10-rand note from South Africa, and the bull elephant on the 500-shilling note of Uganda are commonplace.

Famous rulers and political figures from history are prevalent. Sir Henry Parkes, a famous 19th-century statesman, graces the front of the 5-dollar note from Australia; and Canada's Sir John Alexander MacDonald, a noted Canadian prime minister from the same time period, appears on the front of the 10-dollar Canadian note. Mieszko I, a medieval prince credited with being the founder of Poland in 966, is on the 10-zloty note from that country. Bank notes also reflect the power of more contemporary rulers, as exemplified by the image of Iraq's current president, Saddam Hussein, on that country's 50-dinar note, issued in 1994. Malaysia's paramount ruler and first chief of state, Tunku Abdul Rahman, is on the front of that country's 1-ringgit note and all notes of all denominations issued since 1967.

Architectural vignettes are common on world notes. Islamic mosques with minarets can be found on the 5000-afghani note from Afghanistan, as well as the 25-piaster note from Egypt, indicating the prevalent Islamic religious influence in those 2 countries. The 5-pound 1994 regular issue note from Ireland shows the famous Mater Misericordiae Hospital in Ireland, where Sister Catherine McAuley, founder of the Sisters of Mercy religious order, served in the area of health care. The depiction of religious figures is common on European notes. Examples include St. Agnes of Bohemia on the 50-koruna note of the Czech Republic, St. John of Rila on the 1-lev note of Bulgaria, and the Archangel Gabriel on the 50-denar note of Macedonia.

Artists, authors, scientists, and musicians are also honored on many bank notes. James Ensor (1860–1949), an innovative painter and etcher, is shown on the 100-franc note from Belgium, while Baroness Karen Blixen (pen name Isak Dinesen), the famed Danish author of *Out of Africa* is found on the 50-krone note of Denmark.

Several notes commemorate the new millenium, significant local events, or anniversaries. The front of the 2000-leu commemorative note from Romania has an imaginative reproduction of the solar system as a reference to the total solar eclipse of 11 August 1999. Another example of a commemorative note is the 200-rupee note from Sri Lanka. The note was issued 4 February 1998 to commemorate the 50th anniversary of independence as a self-governing Dominion of the British Commonwealth.

As of 2002, 15 countries did not issue or use their own paper currency, but allowed the bank notes of neighboring countries as well as U.S. currency to circulate freely in their local economies. Many of these countries are relatively small in size with economies to match. Countries such as San Marino, Monaco, Liechtenstein, and Vatican City are tourist-oriented and do not see a need to issue their own homeland currency. Five of these fifteen countries—namely Marshall Islands, Micronesia, Palau, Panama, and Puerto Rico—all use the U.S. dollar as their monetary unit of exchange. As of March 2001, Ecuador and El Salvador had joined the above-mentioned countries in adopting the U.S. dollar. Countries struggling with hyperinflation (uncontrolled inflation marked by the sharp devaluation of the homeland currency) may choose to use the U.S. dollar in place of their own currencies in an attempt to stabilize their economy by linking it directly to the strength and stability of the

U.S. economy. Countries that use U.S. dollars in conjunction with sound economic policies can usually expect to control and/or minimize inflation. The complete adoption of the U.S. currency has been more successful than the practice of pegging the value of local currency to the U.S. dollar according to a fixed ratio, an approach attempted recently by Argentina to disastrous effect. Even those countries that have not completely adopted the U.S. dollar as their currency often have economies operating freely with both their own national and the U.S. currencies. The strength of the U.S. dollar has also made it the currency of choice in the global black market.

Another trend that will probably continue into the future is the joining together of several neighboring countries to form a central bank issuing a common currency. The primary objective of these economic and monetary unions is to eliminate obstacles to free trade, creating a single unified marketplace. This grouping together tends to strengthen the economy and currency of the member countries as well as providing a cost savings in currency production. While such economic partnerships have occurred throughout history, more recent examples began in the early 1950s with the union of the East Caribbean States, followed by the Central African States, French Pacific Territories, and West African States. The most recent and highly publicized example is the European Monetary Union (EMU), composed of 12 European member countries—namely Austria, Belgium, Finland, France, Germany, Greece, Ireland, Italy, Luxembourg, the Netherlands, Portugal, and Spain. On 1 January 2002, the EMU, through its newly formed central bank, replaced the participating countries' homeland currencies with a new common currency called the *euro*. An example of the 10-euro note is shown on the following currency insert pages. Those countries that had pegged their currencies to an EU member's currency prior to the euro's adoption (as several Francophone countries in Africa did with the French franc) now peg their currency to the euro.

It should be mentioned that, in contrast to this recurring trend of country unification for economic and monetary purposes, there are several countries with isolationist governments that have done just the opposite in order to limit the influence of the international community on their economies and populations. For example, Iraq and Syria have made it illegal to use or export their currency outside of their homelands. Several other nations embraced this isolationist attitude through the use of trade voucher and tourist certificates in place of currency, thus keeping their national circulating bank notes from being used or exported by visitors to their country. China, Bulgaria, and Poland are examples of countries that issued what they termed "foreign exchange certificates" for this specific purpose. However, this practice has largely been discontinued, with the exception of Cuba, which still uses a similar certificate first issued in the mid-1980s.

So what does the future have in store for the economies of the world? Trends indicate most countries in the world want free, open, and balanced trade with a strong, stable, and growing economy, free of hyperinflation. More countries are achieving this goal by unifying in regional economic partnerships such as the European Union, or by clearing the barriers to free trade through agreements such as NAFTA (North American Free Trade Agreement). As the use of the U.S. dollar increases throughout the Americas, some economists predict that this region will follow in the footsteps of Europe in terms of establishing a common currency under a central bank. The Asian and Middle-Eastern regions are also likely candidates for similar regional economic partnerships given the prevalence of established trade agreements already in existence among those countries. As the globalization of trade necessitates closer economic ties between countries, it is not inconceivable that a single central bank and common currency will eventually unite the countries of the world. While that development is still only a remote possibility at this point, there is little doubt that nations' increased dependence on international trade for economic prosperity will promote a currency policy conducive to closer trade ties and cross-border partnerships.

—*Keith S. Bauman, professional numismatist*
International Bank Note Society
American Numismatic Association
Professional Currency Dealers Association

Afghanistan

Albania

Algeria

Andorra
(used both Spanish and French currency until the
adoption of the euro in January of 2002)

Angola

Antigua and Barbuda
(shares currency with other East Caribbean States)

Argentina

Armenia

Aruba

Australia

Austria
(adopted the euro as of January 2002)

Azerbaijan

The Bahamas

Bahrain

Bangladesh

Barbados

Belarus

Belgium
(adopted the euro as of January 2002)

Belize

Benin
(shares currency with other West African States)

Bhutan

Bolivia

Bosnia and Herzegovina

Botswana

Brazil

Brunei Darussalam

Bulgaria

Burkina Faso
(shares currency with other West African States)

Burma (Myanmar)

Burundi

Cambodia

Cameroon
(shares currency with other Central African States)

Canada

Cape Verde

Central African Republic
(shares currency with other Central African States)

Chad
(shares currency with other Central African States)

Chile

China

Colombia

Comoros

Democratic Republic of the Congo

Republic of the Congo
(shares currency with other Central African States)

Costa Rica

Côte d'Ivoire
(shares currency with other West African States)

Croatia

Cuba

Cyprus

Czech Republic

Denmark

Djibouti

Dominica
(shares currency with other East Caribbean States)

Dominican Republic

Ecuador

Egypt

El Salvador

Equatorial Guinea
(shares currency with other Central African States)

Eritrea

Estonia

Ethiopia

European Union (EU)

Fiji

Finland
(adopted the euro as of January 2002)

France
(adopted the euro as of January 2002)

French Guiana, Martinique, and
Guadeloupe
(used the Fench currency until the adoption of the
euro in January 2002)

French Polynesia

Gabon
(shares currency with other Central African States)

The Gambia

Georgia

Germany
(adopted the euro as of January 2002)

Ghana

Greece
(adopted the euro as of January 2002)

Grenada
(shares currency with other East Carribbean States)

Guatemala

Guinea

Guinea-Bissau
(shares currency with other West African States)

Guyana

Haiti

Honduras

Hong Kong

Hungary

Iceland

India

Indonesia

Iran

Iraq

Ireland
(adopted the euro as of January 2002)

Israel

Italy
(adopted the euro as of January 2002)

Jamaica

Japan

Jordan

Kazakhstan

Kenya

Kiribati
(uses the Australian currency)

North Korea

South Korea

Kuwait

Kyrgyzstan

Laos

Latvia

Lebanon

Lesotho

Liberia

Libya

Liechtenstein
(uses the Swiss currency)

Lithuania

Luxembourg
(adopted the euro as of January 2002)

Macau

Macedonia

Madagascar

Malawi

Malaysia

Maldives

Mali
(shares currency with other West African States)

Malta

Marshall Islands
(uses the U.S. currency)

Mauritania

Mauritius

Mexico

Micronesia
(uses the U.S. currency)

Moldova

Monaco
(used the Frency currency until the adoption of the
euro in January 2002)

Mongolia

Morocco

Mozambique

Namibia

Nauru
(uses the Australian currency)

Nepal

The Netherlands
(adopted the euro as of January 2002)

Netherlands Antilles

New Zealand

Nicaragua

Niger
(shares currency with other West African States)

Nigeria

Norway

Oman

Pakistan

Palau
(uses the U.S. currency)

Panama
(uses the U.S. currency)

Papua New Guinea

Paraguay

Peru

Philippines

Poland

Portugal
(adopted the euro as of January 2002)

Puerto Rico
(uses the U.S. currency)

Qatar

Romania

Russia

Rwanda

San Marino
(used the Italian currency until the adoption of the
euro in January of 2002)

São Tomé and Príncipe

Saudi Arabia

Senegal
(shares currency with other West African States)

Seychelles

Sierra Leone

Singapore

Slovakia

Slovenia

Solomon Islands

Somalia

South Africa

Spain
(adopted the euro as of January 2002)

Sri Lanka

St. Kitts and Nevis
(shares currency with other East Caribbean States)

St. Lucia
(shares currency with other East Caribbean States)

St. Vincent and the Grenadines
(shares currency with other East Caribbean States)

Sudan

Suriname

Swaziland

Sweden

Switzerland

Syria

Taiwan

Tajikistan

Tanzania

Thailand

Togo
(shares currency with other West African States)

Tonga

Trinidad and Tobago

Tunisia

Turkey

Turkmenistan

Tuvalu
(uses Australian currency)

Uganda

Ukraine

United Arab Emirates

United Kingdom

United States

Uruguay

Uzbekistan

Vanuatu

Vatican City
(used the Italian currency until the adoption of the
euro in January of 2002)

Venezuela

Vietnam

Yemen

Yugoslavia

Zambia

Zimbabwe

MALAWI

Republic of Malawi

CAPITAL: Lilongwe.

MONETARY UNIT: Malawian kwacha (MK). One kwacha equals 100 tambala. Paper currency includes MK5, 10, 20, 50, and 100. Coins come in denominations of MK1, as well as 1, 2, 5, 10, 20, and 50 tambala.

CHIEF EXPORTS: Tobacco, tea, sugar, cotton, coffee, peanuts, wood products.

CHIEF IMPORTS: Food, petroleum products, semi-manufactures, consumer goods, transportation equipment.

GROSS DOMESTIC PRODUCT: US$9.4 billion (1999 est.).

BALANCE OF TRADE: **Exports:** US$510 million (1998 est.). **Imports:** US$512 million (1998 est.).

COUNTRY OVERVIEW

LOCATION AND SIZE. Malawi is located in southeast Africa, landlocked between Mozambique to the east and south, Zambia to the west, and Tanzania to the north. Malawi is separated from Mozambique and Tanzania to a large extent by Lake Malawi, which lies on the country's eastern edge. The immense extent of this lake (the third largest in Africa), which accounts for 20 percent of Malawi's 118,480 square kilometers (45,745 square miles) of total area, means that despite Malawi's inland location, the country has a sizeable coastal area.

Slightly smaller than Pennsylvania in area, Malawi's long, narrow shape was determined in part by the elongated plateau on which it sits and in part by British imperial whim. Mt. Sipitwa, the country's highest point, reaches 9,850 feet. The capital of Malawi is Lilongwe (pop. 442,000, 1999 est.); other urban centers include Blantyre (pop. 486,000, 1999 est.) and Mzuzu (pop. 88,000, 1999 est.).

POPULATION. A mid-2000 estimate of Malawi's population placed it at 10,385,849. Malawi's demographics, however, are complicated by the AIDS pandemic, which

tends radically to skew its statistics. Hence the life expectancy at birth of the average Malawian is a very low 37.58 years. The proportion of the population under age 20 is 57 percent, and infant mortality runs to 122.28 deaths per 1,000, one of the worst in the world (the birth rate is 38.49 per 1,000). Despite a fertility rate of 5.33 children born per Malawian woman, population growth is only 1.61 percent per annum. Not all of this is attributable solely to AIDS, as disease and chronic malnutrition are also major causes of mortality. The scale of AIDS' impact can be understood, however, if Malawi's population figures are set against those, for example, of Madagascar, where the average lifespan is nearly 50 percent longer, the death rate is a mere third as high, and overall population growth is doubled. The United Nations estimated in 1999 that around 16 percent of all Malawians between the ages of 15 and 49 were HIV/AIDS infected. In the same year, the disease claimed 70,000 lives, with urban areas worst affected. The economic fall-out has been disastrous.

With 90 percent of Malawi's population living in rural areas, cities and towns have traditionally played a small part in the nation's life. This, however, is showing signs of changing, and between 1987 and 1998 the urban population grew by 4.7 percent.

Ethnically, Malawi is a tribal federation principally of Chewa, Tumbuka, Yao, and Ngoni peoples, and to a lesser extent Nyanja, Lomwe, Sena, Tonga, and Ngonde tribes, as well as various Asian and European groups. The national language (besides English) is Chichewa, with Chitumbuka predominating in the north. Religiously, 55 percent are Protestant, 20 percent Roman Catholic, 20 percent Muslim, with the remainder holding various indigenous beliefs.

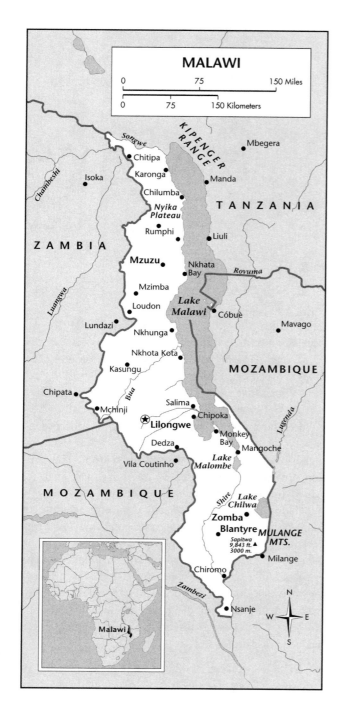

MALAWI

0   75   150 Miles

0   75   150 Kilometers

will be difficult, due to a variety of problems that plague the country, including inadequate **infrastructure** and Malawi's dependence on fuel sources such as coal and firewood.

An overwhelmingly agrarian (farm-based) nation, at 44 people per square mile Malawi is also one Africa's most densely populated countries, and pressure to use available land is intense. This has not only led to serious deforestation as new land has been cleared for cultivation, but ever greater subdivision of existing farming plots. In 1986–87 the World Bank calculated 55 percent of rural households survived on less than 1 hectare of land; by 1993, estimates put this number at 78 percent. The consequences have included decreasing incomes and long-term environmental degradation. Since most of Malawi's agricultural income comes from its independent smallholders (individual farmers), this poses a serious problem.

Over-dependence on agriculture also leaves Malawi exposed to the region's erratic rainfall pattern, as well as to fluctuating world markets. Malawi's primary **cash crop** is tobacco, and without diversification, it will continue to be exposed to changes in the world tobacco market. Growth has therefore been irregular as Malawi's economic fortunes have bounced up and down. Although hitting annual GDP growth levels as high as 10 percent (1995), long-term growth has been considerably slower, averaging 3 percent between 1980 and 2000. Disciplined budget planning is difficult, and the resulting economic instability deters foreign and **private-sector** investment. Further, the country faces a substantial **foreign debt**, which continues to hold back efforts at prioritizing infrastructure improvements that are required for Malawi to achieve the 6 percent growth that, according to World Bank estimates, is necessary if poverty levels are to be reduced.

POLITICS, GOVERNMENT, AND TAXATION

Malawi became a British colony as the protectorate of Nyasaland in 1891. In 1964, after a decade of concerted anti-colonial activity, Malawi was granted its independence. Its prime minister at that time, Hastings Kamuzu Banda, remained the country's leader for the next 30 years, becoming successively president (1966) and president-for-life (1970), as his rule shifted from benign despotism (an authoritarian leader who respects human rights and rules in the best interests of his or her people) to dictatorial repression. Mounting political pressure in the late 1980s—leading to widespread strikes, demonstrations, and riots in 1992—eventually forced the 89 year-old president to concede elections in 1994, in which

OVERVIEW OF ECONOMY

One of the least developed countries in the world, Malawi remains fundamentally dependent on international aid, of which it receives about US$400 million annually. Attempts to turn its economy towards greater productivity and self-sufficiency face heavy obstacles at almost every level. The World Bank and the International Monetary Fund (IMF) are working with the Malawian government to improve economic growth through a program of **privatization** and other reforms. But progress

he was defeated by Bakili Muluzi, leader of the free-market-promoting United Democratic Front.

The transition from Banda's one-party autocracy to a multi-party democracy has been relatively smooth. Under the U.S.-style 1994 constitution, the president still wields considerable power, appointing the 28-member cabinet and senior judges, but he is kept in check by an independent judiciary and legislature. The presidency and the 193 seats of the National Assembly are decided by direct popular election, and all Malawians over 18 years of age have the right to vote. The basic soundness of the new system was affirmed in 1999 when Malawi successfully conducted its second-ever elections (in which Bakili Muluzi was re-elected).

Nevertheless, Banda's long rule and his authoritarian and eccentric style of government have left a burdensome legacy. Challenges facing Malawi's new government have been to repair the country's strained diplomatic relations with its neighbors (Banda was ostracized in the region for his long-standing support of South African apartheid—a political and economic system based on the dominance of whites at the expense of African blacks), to restore the badly rundown economy, and to foster confidence in the political system, corrupted by years of Banda intrigue and cronyism. Progress has been slow. Corruption scandals are becoming more frequent, not only undermining the public's faith in democracy, but alienating Malawi's foreign donors.

The Muluzi government, however, is committed to the program of structural reform drawn up by the World Bank and the IMF, which is aimed at poverty reduction and economic growth. In addition to a renewed emphasis on education and health, the program includes tightening fiscal management, opening up domestic markets, privatizing public utilities, reducing the civil service (non-military government organizations), and improving conditions and opportunities for smallholder farmers by **liberalizing** the agricultural sector.

Tax reform has also been targeted, with more emphasis placed on **direct taxation**, in keeping with Malawi's traditional sources of revenue—**duties**, excises, and **levies**. But in an economy in which so much of the population lives at subsistence level, and in which so much trade is conducted informally, tapping this source of revenue is very difficult, and the burden of the new tougher stance has tended to fall disproportionately on the private sector.

INFRASTRUCTURE, POWER, AND COMMUNICATIONS

Malawi's infrastructure is in urgent need of attention. Its road and rail networks are inadequate both in their quality and extent, a problem made more serious by the country's reliance on land transport to compensate for its lack of sea access. While the road system has been expanded by 44 percent since independence in 1964, Malawi's population in the same period has doubled; of its 28,394 kilometers (17,647 miles) of road, only 5,833 kilometers (3,265 miles) are paved (18.5 percent). The poor condition of the roads has contributed to Malawi having one of the worst road accident rates in the world—despite its very low car-to-person ratio of 2 per 1,000. Rail, too, is in considerable disrepair, having been very badly affected by Mozambique's long civil war in the 1980s and 1990s, which closed off Malawi's access to the Indian Ocean ports of Nacala and Beira, once the distribution hubs of 95 percent of all Malawian trade. Starved of this traffic, on which it relied heavily, Malawi's national railroad was forced into bankruptcy in 1993. However, the company's sale in 1999 to a U.S.-African consortium is aimed at bringing new investment and reviving services. Malawi has 788 kilometers (490 miles) of track, all of which is narrow gauge.

Malawi has 2 international airports—at Lilongwe and Blantyre—and is served by a variety of international carriers. Malawi has 44 total airports, only 5 of which

Communications

Country	Newspapers	Radios	TV Sets[a]	Cable subscribers[a]	Mobile Phones[a]	Fax Machines[a]	Personal Computers[a]	Internet Hosts[b]	Internet Users[b]
	1996	1997	1998	1998	1998	1998	1998	1999	1999
Malawi	3	249	2	N/A	1	0.1	N/A	0.00	10
United States	215	2,146	847	244.3	256	78.4	458.6	1,508.77	74,100
Dem. Rep. of Congo	3	375	135	N/A	0	N/A	N/A	0.00	1
Zambia	12	121	137	N/A	1	0.1	N/A	0.48	15

[a]Data are from International Telecommunication Union, *World Telecommunication Development Report 1999* and are per 1,000 people.
[b]Data are from the Internet Software Consortium (http://www.isc.org) and are per 10,000 people.

SOURCE: World Bank. *World Development Indicators 2000.*

have paved runways. Between 100,000 and 200,000 passengers typically pass through each airport annually. The government plans to privatize Air Malawi and the introduction of a second airline is also being discussed.

Malawi's principal source of energy—providing an estimated 90 percent of all its energy needs—is wood fuel (firewood and charcoal), about 44 percent of which comes from non-sustainable sources. Demand is growing too, at a rate of some 6 percent per year, placing severe pressure on Malawi's already depleted forests. Electricity generation comes mostly from the 4 hydroelectric power stations on the Shire River begun in 1989. But irregular water flow on the river, especially in the dry season, and problems with silting (build up of sediment) often make power supplies unreliable, a problem particularly damaging to industry. Coal is imported to supplement local production, which because of underinvestment is mined below capacity. All petroleum stocks are imported.

Telecommunications is also an underdeveloped sector, with a mere 45,000 landlines, or 1 for every 230 Malawians. There are hopes, however, to triple the number of lines by 2005 with the proceeds of the sale of the state-owned Malawi Telecom in 2001. A cellular system was launched in 1996, and the licensing of more networks is planned. Malawi had 1 Internet service provider as of 1999.

ECONOMIC SECTORS

Despite government hopes to expand the country's economic base, Malawi remains overwhelmingly dependent on agriculture, especially its primary cash crop, tobacco. But international movements to discourage ciga-

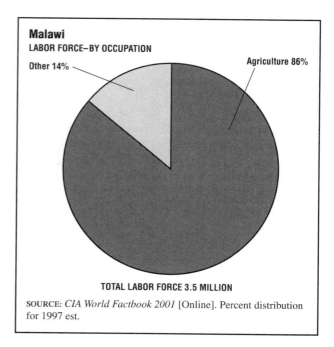

SOURCE: *CIA World Factbook 2001* [Online]. Percent distribution for 1997 est.

rette smoking can only hurt this industry further, and its viability as a long-term vehicle of growth is unclear. In 1999 agriculture supplied 38 percent of GDP. Tourism, mining, and manufacturing have also been prioritized, but infrastructure problems make development difficult. Nevertheless, industry accounts for 19.2 percent of GDP (14 percent of this in manufacturing), and services 42.8 percent.

AGRICULTURE

A lush climate and rich soil make Malawi well suited for agriculture, which is central to the country's economy and national life, occupying 86 percent of its workforce, and making up 38 percent of its GDP and 90 percent of its export earnings.

The main staple crop is maize, grown by smallholder farmers mostly at the subsistence level. Production varies, and depending on climate conditions, maize may be imported or exported. Sorghum, millet, pulses, root crops, and fruit are also grown. Another staple, as well as an important source of protein, is fish from Lake Malawi. The fishing industry accounts for about 200,000 jobs, but problems with pollution and over-fishing threaten to reduce yields.

Malawi's commercial farming sector is concentrated on large estates in the south and around Lilongwe. Its main product is tobacco, which typically accounts for between 50 percent and 70 percent of Malawi's export earnings. Formerly held back by government **price controls** and grower regulations, the liberalization of the industry in the 1990s has seen steady increases in profits for grow-

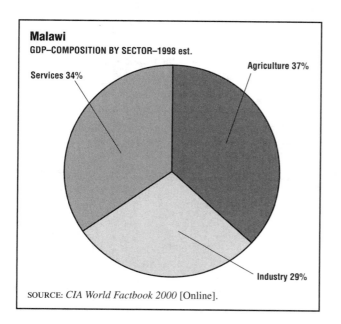

SOURCE: *CIA World Factbook 2000* [Online].

ers and a sharp rise in smallholder tobacco production, making Malawi one of the leading tobacco producers in the world. Nevertheless, the industry as a whole has been hard hit by the drop in world tobacco prices, which has cut tobacco export revenues from US$332 million in 1998 to US$218 million in 2000. As a consequence, Malawi's growers are being encouraged to concentrate on other traditional cash crops, such as tea and sugar, or diversify into new crops, such as paprika, macadamia, citrus fruits, vegetables, and cut flowers. Tea is Malawi's second most important cash crop, and Malawi is Africa's second largest producer of it. In 2000 tea accounted for about 10 percent of exports, or about US$44 million. Sugar is also significant, and made up about 6 percent of exports, or US$27 million.

INDUSTRY

Although a small and under-developed sector in Malawi, industry is nevertheless an important contributor to the country's GDP. But the burdens it struggles under are substantial. Hampered by the variability of the agricultural sector on which it is based, high transport costs, a small domestic market, and a poorly skilled workforce increasingly undermined by HIV/AIDS, Malawi's industries must also contend with a dependence on imported resources. This dependence largely robs the industrial sector of any benefit from successive depreciations of the kwacha and means Malawi's goods, despite low wage rates, often do not fare well against regional competitors.

The majority of Malawi's industrial activity (85 percent) comes from manufacturing, a sector that in 2000 generated around 14 percent of GDP. Malawian manufacturing is carried out by about 100 companies involved in agricultural processing, textiles, clothing, and footwear production. The concentration of this activity is another legacy of Hastings Banda's accumulation of wealth and power during the 30 years of his rule. The Press Corporation Limited (PCL), founded by Banda, is an example of how this legacy continues to distort Malawi's economic structure. A hugely diverse syndicate of brewing, clothing, oil, pharmaceutical, banking, and agricultural concerns with a total revenue equivalent to about 10 percent of GDP, PCL's **monopolies** in many industries further undermine competitiveness. **Nationalized** in 1997, the company is scheduled for dismantling and sale, although few of its assets are likely to attract the necessary interest.

Mining remains small-scale, and Malawi has no precious metals or oil, but ruby mining began in the mid–1990s, with Malawi the only source of rubies in Africa. Malawi also has deposits of bauxite, asbestos, graphite, and uranium. After the establishment in 1985 of a government mines department and a national min-

ing agency to explore the feasibility of exploiting various minerals, bauxite and titanium reserves in the south were singled out for development. Although the supporting infrastructure is weak, some foreign investment has been attracted.

SERVICES

TOURISM. Malawi's ongoing battles against disease, poor sanitation, and infrastructure deficiency make it an unlikely tourist destination. And yet its tropical climate and scenic landscape have seen rapid gains in the industry, with visitor numbers climbing to 215,000 in 1999, a 20 percent increase from 1995. Although visitors do come from Europe and North America, most are South African and Zimbabwean, and most come for Lake Malawi. Efforts are being made to expand facilities and boost numbers, but without the injection of significant investment, there will be little impact. Negative publicity over the presence of the potentially fatal bilharzias bacteria in Lake Malawi and fears that the region may not be safe for travellers have also proved handicaps.

FINANCIAL SERVICES. In addition to its central bank, the Reserve Bank of Malawi, Malawi has 5 commercial banks. Although newer operators have begun to extend services, the sector remains basic and highly limited, with the 2 largest banks having no foreign shareholders or strategic foreign links. Lack of competition has kept charges high and most lending tends to be to government agencies, to the exclusion of private borrowers. A stock exchange was founded in 1994, and by 2000, there were 8 companies listed on it. But its small size and the absence of a speculative trading culture have kept activity to a minimum, and the exchange has not proved a source of business financing.

RETAIL. Because of Malawi's rural and subsistence-dominated economy, the purchasing power of most Malawians is minimal, hence retailing is sparse. Urban areas are better served, with a variety of small traders selling fabrics, shoes, paper and pens, and imported electrical equipment, and with a large contingent of informal street vendors. Most of the stores are operated by Malawi's minority Asian population, estimated to control of 30 percent of commercial activity.

INTERNATIONAL TRADE

Malawi's **balance of trade** has always been precarious. With 90 percent of its receipts coming from agricultural commodities, export accounts are highly sensitive to fluctuations in production levels and shifts in world market prices. Malawi is also vulnerable on its import side. The expense of freighting all of its imports overland is a continual drain (adding as much as 30

Trade (expressed in billions of US$): Malawi		
	Exports	Imports
1975	.140	.253
1980	.295	.439
1985	.249	.285
1990	.417	.581
1995	.405	.475
1998	N/A	N/A

SOURCE: International Monetary Fund. *International Financial Statistics Yearbook 1999.*

Exchange rates: Malawi	
Malawian kwachas (MK) per US$1	
Dec 2000	80.0946
2000	59.5438
1999	44.0881
1998	31.0727
1997	16.4442
1996	15.3085

SOURCE: CIA *World Factbook 2001* [ONLINE].

percent to the import bill), while droughts, which periodically force the government to mass-import basic foods, are a regular source of balance-of-trade shortfalls. Additional problems stem from Malawi's complete dependence on imported oil, which has caused particular difficulty as oil prices have risen. The net effect, despite government prioritization of a balanced budget, is a pattern of significant trade deficits. In 1999, however, the shortfall was only $2 million on exports of $510 million and imports of $512 million.

Of Malawi's exports in 1999, 15 percent went to South Africa, 9 percent each to the United States and Germany, and 7 percent to the Netherlands. Of Malawi's imports, 38 percent came from South Africa, 18 percent from Zimbabwe, 8 percent from Zambia, and 4 percent from Japan.

In 2000, Malawi joined 8 other African nations in the free-trade area of the Common Market for Eastern and Southern Africa (COMESA). Having removed its 30 percent import duty on goods from those 8 countries, it plans to remove all trade barriers by 2004. Free movement of labor and residency is scheduled for 2014, with full monetary union and a common central bank by 2025.

MONEY

Malawi's heavy trade imbalance is the source of its consistently high deficits and mounting debt. By the end of 1999 Malawi's total **external debt** stood at US$2.6 billion, a rise of 86 percent from the previous decade. Servicing this debt cost Malawi US$105 million in 1999, cutting drastically into the government's available funds for social services and development, and further widening the budget and **balance-of-payments** gaps. The instability that such over-runs cause in the Malawian economy has seen the value of the kwacha tumble and **inflation** soar. Riding at 45 percent in 1999, inflation is expected to remain above 30 percent until mid-2001, dropping to a hoped-for 15 percent by 2002. The kwacha is also expected to stabilize after a long period of free-

fall since its floating in 1994. From around MK15 per U.S. dollar in 1995, the rate dropped to MK43 in 1998 and MK80 in 2000; forecasts are for around for MK106 in 2002. Reducing the deficit and attacking the debt are top priorities for the government.

POVERTY AND WEALTH

Malawi is one of the poorest countries in the world, its poverty severe and deeply-rooted. According to the 1998 census, 78 percent of the economically-active population were **subsistence farmers**. Even by African standards, the plight of these farmers is grave, with literacy low, access to water and sanitation poor, and disease and malnutrition endemic. Malawi's National Economic Council estimated in 2000 that 65.3 percent of Malawians were below the poverty line, "unable to meet their basic needs."

Yet Malawi also has pockets of considerable wealth. The Banda regime's policy in the 1970s and 1980s of large-scale agricultural and industrial development focused government resources on commercial enterprises. This consolidated the country's tiny political-entrepreneurial elite and further widened the gulf between it and Malawi's subsistence sector. Post-Banda politics are more open, but the political class remains small—President Muluzi, for example, was a former cabinet minister of Banda's—and recent corruption scandals suggest that patronage and favoritism are still inherent in the system.

GDP per Capita (US$)					
Country	1975	1980	1985	1990	1998
Malawi	157	169	161	152	166
United States	19,364	21,529	23,200	25,363	29,683
Dem. Rep. of Congo	392	313	293	247	127
Zambia	641	551	483	450	388

SOURCE: United Nations. *Human Development Report 2000; Trends in human development and per capita income.*

Household Consumption in PPP Terms

Country	All food	Clothing and footwear	Fuel and power[a]	Health care[b]	Education[b]	Transport & Communications	Other
Malawi	50	13	7	2	6	9	13
United States	13	9	9	4	6	8	51
Dem. Rep. of Congo	N/A	N/A	N/A	N/A	N/A	N/A	N/A
Zambia	52	10	8	2	11	3	14

Data represent percentage of consumption in PPP terms.
[a]Excludes energy used for transport.
[b]Includes government and private expenditures.

SOURCE: World Bank. *World Development Indicators 2000.*

Attempts to equalize the economic imbalance include the establishment the Land Reform Commission in 1996. The commission's report, issued in 1999, has recommended the replacement of freehold land ownership with 99-year leases, and the return of customary land from government control to tribal chiefs. A US$25 million land redistribution scheme was begun in 2001, which aims to resettle between 17,000 and 21,000 people on 14,000 hectares of land.

WORKING CONDITIONS

Malawi's workforce numbers around 3.5 million, but most of these are subsistence farmers. Given the informality of most employment, it is impossible even to estimate unemployment and **underemployment** rates in the country. The proportion of wage and salary earners is a low 14 percent, and threatens to fall further as civil service down-sizing and privatization lay-offs take effect.

Growth and job creation are severely hindered by poor standards of education and low literacy levels. Only 58 percent of the adult population is able to read and write, and only 4.5 percent of primary school children advance to secondary level, a figure low even by the standards of Malawi's neighbors. The Muluzi government is committed to improving education, but the massive increases in enrollments it has spurred (in particular by removing school fees in 1994) have swamped the schools and eroded educational quality. The result is a workforce poorly adapted to most industrial and manufacturing jobs, and unsuited even for certain types of commercial farming.

Disease is another significant problem, intensified by the over-loading of the health system by the HIV/AIDS crisis. In 1999–2000 government spending on health care accounted for 2.8 percent of GDP—or US$5 spent per Malawian—a level which was radically insufficient. Poor sanitation (only 45 percent of the population has access to clean water) and malnutrition are also fundamental problems, and until they can be properly addressed—which

will only be done with foreign help—the productivity of the Malawian workforce will remain badly crippled.

COUNTRY HISTORY AND ECONOMIC DEVELOPMENT

1891. The British establish Malawi, then called Nyasaland, as a protectorate.

1953. Formation of the Central African Federation of Nyasaland and Northern and Southern Rhodesia (now Zambia and Zimbabwe, respectively).

1962. Hastings Kamuzu Banda becomes prime minister.

1963. Malawi leaves the Central African Federation.

1964. Malawi gains independence from Britain.

1966. Malawi becomes a republic.

1970. Hastings Banda declared president-for-life.

1994. A new democratic, pluralistic Malawian constitution enacted (based on the U.S. Constitution); multiparty elections held for the first time; Bakili Muzuli ousts Hastings Banda.

1999. Bakili Muzuli re-elected as president in second free elections.

FUTURE TRENDS

Although Malawi has made important strides towards political openness and economic reform, its future remains troubled. Progress has been painfully slow, marred by corruption scandals in the government, and punctuated by economic crises that have upset the reform process. Finding itself in a delicate situation, the government is obliged to impose tough austerity measures to satisfy donors, but knows that doing so will carry a heavy political cost at home. Regionally, too, the uncertainty that Malawi faces—with Zimbabwe, the Democratic Republic of Congo, and Angola in various stages of turmoil—will require careful negotiation. However, despite some voter disenchantment, the transition to democracy (still ongoing) has been smooth, and Malawi's political situation is secure. The government has established an Anti-Corruption Bureau to ensure tighter standards of accountability, and launched its "ten point" plan in 2000, promising more consistent adherence to reform measures. If agricultural yields continue to be good, if international aid donors continue to offer their support, and if the Malawian government continues to prioritize poverty reduction, Malawi's economic future holds some promise of hope.

DEPENDENCIES

Malawi has no territories or colonies.

BIBLIOGRAPHY

Economist Intelligence Unit. *Country Profile: Malawi.* London: Economist Intelligence Unit, 2000.

Economist Intelligence Unit. *Country Report: Malawi.* London: Economist Intelligence Unit, January 2001.

Harrigan, J. *From Dictatorship to Democracy.* Aldershot, United Kingdom: Ashgate Publishing, 2000.

Lwanda, John Lloyd. *Promises, Power Politics, and Poverty: Democratic Transition in Malawi (1961 to 1999).* Glasgow, Scotland: Dudu Nsomba Publications, 1996.

Mkandawire, P. Thandika. *Agriculture, Employment, and Poverty in Malawi.* Geneva: International Labour Organization, 1999.

National Statistics Office of Malawi. *The Web Site of Malawi Official Statistics.* <http://www.nso.malawi.net>. Accessed March 2001.

Towards Vision 2020: United Nations Development Assistance for Poverty Eradication in Malawi. Lilongwe: The Framework, 1998.

U.S. Central Intelligence Agency. *World Factbook 2000.* <http://www.odci.gov/cia/publications/factbook/index.html>. Accessed July 2001.

U.S. Department of State. *Country Commercial Guide, FY 2001: Malawi.* <http://www.state.gov/www/about_state/business/com_guides/2001/africa/malawi_ccg2001.pdf>. Accessed March 2001.

World Bank Group. *Countries: Malawi.* <http://www.worldbank.org/afr/mw2.htm>. Accessed March 2001.

—Alexander Schubert

MALI

Republic of Mali
République du Mali

CAPITAL: Bamako.

MONETARY UNIT: Communauté Financière Africaine Franc (CFA Fr). CFA Fr1 equals 100 centimes. Notes include denominations of 500, 1,000, 2,500, and 10,000. Coins include 1, 5, 10, 25, 100, 250, and 500 denominations.

CHIEF EXPORTS: Cotton, livestock, gold, hides and leather, shea-nuts, fish.

CHIEF IMPORTS: Heavy machinery, transport equipment, construction materials, petroleum, foodstuffs, textiles, chemical products, consumer manufactured goods.

GROSS DOMESTIC PRODUCT: US$8.5 billion (purchasing power parity, 1999 est.).

BALANCE OF TRADE: Exports: US$640 million (f.o.b., 1999 est.). Imports: US$650 million (f.o.b., 1999 est.).

COUNTRY OVERVIEW

LOCATION AND SIZE. Mali is a landlocked country in West Africa covering an area of 1.24 million square kilometers (478,764 square miles), of which 1.22 million square kilometers (471,042 square miles) is occupied by land and 20,000 square kilometers (7,722 square miles) is occupied by water. Its border is 7,243 kilometers (4,500 miles) long. Of this, 1,376 kilometers (855 miles) in the northeast is shared with Algeria; 2,237 kilometers (1,390 miles) with Mauritania in the northwest; 419 kilometers (260 miles) with Senegal in the west; 858 kilometers (533 miles) with Guinea in the southwest; 532 kilometers (330 miles) with Côte d'Ivoire in the south, 1,000 kilometers (621 miles) in the south by Burkina Faso; and 821 kilometers (510 miles) in the southeast by Niger. The lowest point is at the Senegal river which lies 23 meters (75 feet) above sea level, while the highest point is at Hombori Tondo standing at 1,155 meters (3,789 feet) above sea level.

The northern half of Mali consists of desert, while the southern half is rain-fed land where most agriculture is undertaken without irrigation. Between these 2 areas lies the Sahel zone, where cultivation depends largely on the flooding of the river Niger which flows through the heart of the country, providing a vital waterway and source of fish. As the seasonal floods retreat, they leave behind pasture, on which thousands of livestock depend, desperate for food and water after a dry season lasting 8 months, as well as land for cultivation in an otherwise arid environment.

POPULATION. July 2000 estimates reported the population at 10.69 million, up from the April 1998 census figure of 9.79 million. The current rate of population growth is estimated at 3 percent per year, and this is particularly high, implying a fertility rate of 6.9 children per woman. Mali has a young population with only 3 percent estimated in 2000 to have been over 65 years while the 47 percent and 50 percent were under 15 years and between 15 and 65 years, respectively. Only 26 percent of the population lived in towns in 1998.

The main ethnic group is the Bambara, while minority groups include Songhai, Mandinka, Senoufo, Dogon, and Fula. The north is populated mainly by the nomadic Tuareg. By composition, the Mande (who include Bambara, Malinke, and Soninke) comprises 50 percent of the population, Peul 17 percent, Voltaic 12 percent, Songhai 6 percent, Tuareg and Moor 10 percent and others 5 percent. About 90 percent of the population are Muslim, 1 percent Christian and 9 percent follow traditional beliefs. French is the official language, although Bambara is spoken by 80 percent of the population.

OVERVIEW OF ECONOMY

Mali is among the 10 or so poorest countries in the world. The economy is a heavily dependent on agriculture, but the country's land is more than half desert or semi-arid. Most of the agriculture is restricted to the area irrigated by the floodwaters of the river Niger. About 80 percent of the **labor force** is engaged in farming and fishing and about 10 percent of the population is nomadic. The industrial activity in Mali is concentrated on agricultural processing and gold mining.

Economic planning since independence from France in 1960 has generally been incoherent and unsuccessful. Problems have been compounded by the fact that export prices fell relative to import prices between 1985 and 1994. But even though Mali remained heavily dependent on foreign aid (mostly from France), the economy was starting to show signs of improvement by 1997 from **lib-**eralization efforts suggested by the International Monetary Fund (IMF).

Mali is already sub-Saharan Africa's leading cotton producer, and cotton is the country's main export, which makes its economy particularly vulnerable to fluctuations in world prices for cotton. To reduce the economy's heavy dependence on cotton, the government has implemented an IMF-recommended **structural adjustment program** which aims to liberalize the economy and to make it more dependent on markets than on planning and state-owned enterprises.

The success of Mali's economic reforms and the 50 percent **devaluation** of the CFA franc in January 1994 led to an economic recovery in the late 1990s. Several **multinational corporations** increased gold mining operations between 1996 and 1998, and the government anticipates that Mali will become a major African gold exporter in the near future. At the beginning of the 21st century, economic growth in Mali is expected to be faster than population growth, leading to steady improvements in living standards.

POLITICS, GOVERNMENT, AND TAXATION

In 1895, the territory called the Sudan (now known as Mali) became part of the French colony of French West Africa, and the local population began producing **cash crops**, mainly groundnuts, cotton, and gum arabic. The colony merged with Senegal in April 1959 to form the Federation of Mali, which became independent from France on June 20, 1960. When Senegal withdrew after only a few months, the Sudanese Republic was renamed Mali on 22 September 1960. President Modibo Keita declared the country a 1-party state, under the Union Soudanaise-Ressemblement Democratique Africain (US-RDA).

Keita's **Marxist** regime severed links with France and developed close relations with the Eastern bloc countries, especially the USSR. A coup in 1968 led to a military regime under Lieutenant (later General) Moussa Traoré. Traoré's dictatorship ended in 1991. By 1992, Mali's first democratic elections were held, and Alpha Oumar Konare, the leader of the Alliance pour la Démocratie au Mali (Alliance for Democracy in Mali, ADEMA), was elected president. Despite political difficulties, including several new prime ministers over the next few years and the disruption of several strikes, Konare won re-election in 1997. President Konare continued to push through political and economic reforms and to fight corruption but indicated in 1999 that he would not run for a third term.

There are 8 administrative regions: Gao, Kayes, Kidal, Koulikoro, Mopti, Segou, Sikasso, Tombouctou. The constitution was adopted on 12 January 1992, providing for 3 branches of government: executive, legislative, and judiciary. The executive is headed by the president elected by popular vote for a 5-year term. The legislature is a **unicameral** National Assembly of 147 seats to which members are elected by popular vote to serve 5-year terms. The legal system is based on the French civil law system and customary law, with judicial review of legislative acts in Constitutional Court (which was formally established on 9 March 1994).

Mali's level of government expenditure was 25 percent of the GDP in 1998, and revenues were 22 percent. This financial flow resulted in a **budget deficit** of just under 3 percent of the GDP, within the IMF guidelines, and in normal circumstances (that is, in the absence of a drought), the **inflation rate** should remain below 5 percent a year. Since the creation of a democratic government in 1992, the military has withdrawn from politics. In 1996, military expenditures were only 2 percent of the GDP.

Corporate profit tax rates are moderate at 35 percent, while smaller enterprises such as partnerships pay only 15 percent. Agricultural enterprises pay 10 percent, but small-scale family farms are not taxed. In cases of low profits or losses, a corporation tax of 0.75 percent of **turnover** is levied. There is an employment tax of 7.5 percent of the wage bill. A withholding tax of 18 percent is levied on interest and dividends paid abroad.

INFRASTRUCTURE, POWER, AND COMMUNICATIONS

Mali's large geographical area and low income status makes maintenance of its **infrastructure** a major challenge. For an area of 1.24 million square kilometers (480,000 square miles), the country has a total 15,100 kilometers (9,383 miles) of roads of which only 1,827 kilometers (1,135 miles) are paved. About 729 kilometers (453 miles) of meter-gauge railway link Bamako to Senegal's railway through Kayes. Nearly 1,815 kilometers (1,127 miles) of waterways are navigable. In 1998, there were 28 airports, 6 of which had paved runways. The 1 major port is at Koulikoro on the river Niger.

Communications

Country	Newspapers	Radios	TV Sets[a]	Cable subscribers[a]	Mobile Phones[a]	Fax Machines[a]	Personal Computers[a]	Internet Hosts[b]	Internet Users[b]
	1996	1997	1998	1998	1998	1998	1998	1999	1999
Mali	1	54	12	0.0	0	N/A	0.7	0.01	10
United States	215	2,146	847	244.3	256	78.4	458.6	1,508.77	74,100
Nigeria	24	223	66	N/A	0	N/A	5.7	0.00	100
Mauritania	0	151	91	N/A	0	1.7	5.5	0.00	13

[a]Data are from International Telecommunication Union, *World Telecommunication Development Report 1999* and are per 1,000 people.
[b]Data are from the Internet Software Consortium (http://www.isc.org) and are per 10,000 people.
SOURCE: World Bank. *World Development Indicators 2000.*

In 1998, approximately 62 percent of the country's electricity was obtained from hydro-sources while the remaining 38 percent was from fossil fuel with total production of about 310 million kilowatts hours (kWh). All the power generated was for domestic consumption, and none was imported.

The domestic telephone system is poor but improving. The domestic network consists of microwave radio relays, land-lines, and radio telephone communications stations. Expansion of the microwave radio relay is in progress. There are 2 Intelsat satellite earth stations for international communication. In 1995, there was no mobile cellular phone system in the country, while there were only 17,000 land lines. In 1998, there were 7 shortwave, 14 FM and 1 AM radio broadcast stations. There was also 1 television broadcast station with 2 repeater stations in the country. There was only 1 Internet service provider in 1999.

ECONOMIC SECTORS

Mali's economy, although potentially rich in natural resources, is still underdeveloped with poor infrastructure and almost 80 percent of its workforce engaged in the rural sector. In 1998, agriculture was the most important sector, providing 46 percent of GDP, with industry 21 percent, and services 33 percent. The sectors rely on narrow bases: agriculture on cotton and livestock; industry on gold; and services on the financial sector. The country has suffered frequent shortages of grain, and the droughts of 1969–74 and 1981–83 devastated the cattle herds in the north. Most of the agricultural production takes place in the south, with cotton production dominating, accounting for 39 percent of total export revenues

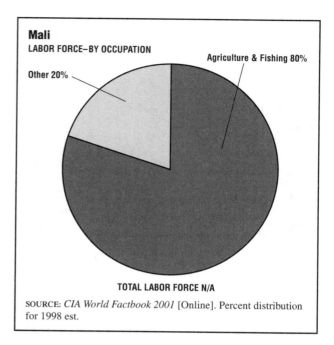

SOURCE: *CIA World Factbook 2001* [Online]. Percent distribution for 1998 est.

in 1997. Industry is dominated by gold mining, which, together with diamonds, accounts for 31 percent of exports. Gold mining has expanded rapidly under a liberal investment code and industry's share of the GDP is expected to rise significantly in the immediate future.

AGRICULTURE

Agriculture and livestock husbandry have long been the backbone of the economy, accounting for about 45 percent of the GDP in 1998 and providing the bulk of export revenue. Arable land comprises of only 2 percent of which permanent pastures comprise 25 percent, forests and woodland 6 percent, and the rest other uses. Only 780 square kilometers (301 square miles) was irrigated in 1993. There are no permanent crops. The most disruptive natural hazard is drought. But despite drought, Mali has produced agricultural surpluses for many years. Other significant environmental issues include deforestation, soil erosion, **desertification**, inadequate supplies of drinkable water, and poaching.

Cotton is Mali's most significant crop; Mali is one of the largest producers of cotton in Africa, after Egypt and Sudan. Cotton production is almost all based on small-scale family farms, with village cooperatives in the south-east being coordinated by the highly influential **parastatal** Compagnie Malienne pour le Developpement des Textiles (CMDT), in which the French Compagnie Francaise pour le Developpement des Textiles (CFDT) owns a 40 percent share. While the World Bank has pressed for liberalization of the sector with a view to increasing farmers' returns, the CMDT has countered by

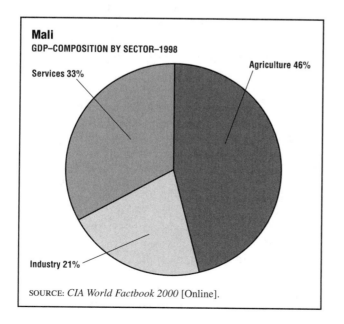

SOURCE: *CIA World Factbook 2000* [Online].

arguing that under the current system production has more than doubled since 1993.

Most Malian households depend on wood and charcoal for fuel, making the forestry sector of economic and ecological significance. With increasing population, the issue of deforestation will take on an increasing importance. Tree crop products, produced mostly by small-scale gatherers, include fruits (mainly mangoes), a wide range of traditional medicines, and shea-nut butter (karite). Export potential is considerable but is hampered by lack of investment in processing and packaging.

Fishing is mostly artisanal (small-scale) and is vulnerable to drought as well as changes brought about by dam construction and urban pollution run-off into rivers. It is mostly undertaken on the river Niger. The annual catch has amounted to roughly 100,000 metric tons in recent years, of which about 20 percent is exported mostly to urban centers in the Côte d'Ivoire, where a number of Malian fishermen and fish distributors have settled over the years.

Towards the end of the century, Mali has benefitted from a much more stable food supply than during the crisis years of the 1970s and 1980s, when Mali experienced 2 severe droughts. Since the late 1980s the government's role has been reduced to a regulatory one, but crises and slowdowns in supply remain a potential threat in a country as vulnerable to sudden climatic reverses as Mali.

Large-scale animal husbandry takes place mostly in the north and around the Niger inland delta, whereas most food and cash crops are produced in the southern regions. Livestock production is principally by **small-holders** and is thought to account for about 20 percent of the GDP in an average year. Livestock and meat product exports have suffered since the mid-1980s, mostly from unrestrained dumping by European Union countries of highly subsidized beef on West African coastal markets. Harassment from customs officials and a lack of refrigeration and bulk transport infrastructure have also constrained the sector.

INDUSTRY

Industry is becoming a significant sector of the economy consisting of mostly minor **consumer goods** production for local use and food processing, construction, and phosphate and gold mining. Natural resources also include kaolin, salt, limestone, uranium, and hydropower. There are known, but not exploited, deposits of bauxite, iron ore, manganese, tin, and copper. Industry contributed about 21 percent of the GDP in 1998. Artisanal mining and panning for gold and diamonds has been practiced in the south-west of the country for hundreds of years.

Before 1992, infrastructural weaknesses and corruption discouraged foreign investment in the sector. With the demise of the military Traore administration in 1991, a new mining code was adopted to encourage investment. Under the current tax regime, government reserves the right to take a stake of up to 20 percent in enterprises, tax profits at 35 percent, and **levy** royalties at 6 percent. Nevertheless, Mali's gold production has increased at one of the world's fastest rates, with output increasing almost 4-fold between 1994 and 1998.

Manufacturing remains comparatively unimportant, having declined throughout the 1980s and accounting for an average 3 percent of the GDP towards the end of the century. From the 1960s, inefficient parastatals produced basic consumer goods, and the **private sector** preferred to invest in trade. The sector was further handicapped by intensified competition from Côte d'Ivoire and by a flood of cheap smuggled consumer goods from Guinea and Nigeria in the years preceding the 1994 devaluation of the CFA franc.

Since the devaluation, efforts to attract manufacturing investment have had little success, although there have been signs of a move towards manufacturing among the leading local commercial families. The textiles sector has shown signs of revival, but it still faces stiff competition from industries in neighboring countries. A significant drawback to investment in the manufacturing sector is the higher production costs in Mali than in neighboring countries, owing to antiquated equipment and underdeveloped infrastructure.

SERVICES

While services have on average accounted for 43 percent of the GDP in the last decade, the service sector remains comparatively less diversified than Mali's other economic sectors. The service sector is dominated by financial services and tourism. The Dakar-based Banque Centrale des l'Afrique de l'Ouest (Central Bank of West Africa, BCEAO) acts as the central bank for Mali and 7 other West African Franc zone countries. The commercial banks include Banque Malienne de Credit et de Depots and the highly successful Bank of Africa-Mali. In this sector Mali faces the challenge of diversifying credit instruments in favor of small- and medium-sized enterprises which have historically relied on informal sources for loans.

Tourism has contributed little to the services sector, despite Mali's undisputed potential attraction for culture, adventure, and **eco-tourism**. Its attractions include Djenne, a UNESCO site of world heritage; Timbuktu, which although dilapidated still retains international allure; and the Bandiagara escarpement which is home to the Dogon. The Dogon are said to be one of the most ethnologically exotic and visually spectacular of all African traditional cultures.

Trade (expressed in billions of US$): Mali		
	Exports	Imports
1975	.053	.176
1980	.205	.438
1985	.123	.299
1990	.358	.601
1995	.441	.770
1998	N/A	N/A

SOURCE: International Monetary Fund. *International Financial Statistics Yearbook 1999.*

GDP per Capita (US$)					
Country	1975	1980	1985	1990	1998
Mali	268	301	271	249	267
United States	19,364	21,529	23,200	25,363	29,683
Nigeria	301	314	230	258	256
Mauritania	549	557	511	438	478

SOURCE: United Nations. *Human Development Report 2000; Trends in human development and per capita income.*

INTERNATIONAL TRADE

Mali's trade balance has been in chronic deficit, although there has been an overall improvement since the early 1970s when exports typically represented only half of the value of imports. By 1985 the **trade deficit** was equivalent to over 85 percent of merchandise exports compared with an estimated 5 percent in 1999. In 1997, Mali for the first time achieved a slight trade surplus, although the trade balance slipped back into deficit in 1998. The problem seems to be low export-oriented investment outside the extractive (the withdrawal of natural resources by extraction with no provision for replenishing) sector. Furthermore, Mali remains heavily dependent on imports for machinery and **capital goods**. In 1997, the major export partners included Thailand (20 percent), Italy (20 percent), China (9 percent), Brazil (5 percent), while the main import sources included Côte d'Ivoire (19 percent), and France (17 percent).

MONEY

The unit of currency is the Communaute Financiere Africaine franc (CFA) which is equivalent to 100 centimes. It exchanged at CFAF647.25 for US$1 in January 2000 a depreciation from CFAF499.15 in 1995. Since 1 January 1999, the CFA franc has been effectively pegged to the euro at a rate of CFAF655.957 per euro. Mali left the CFA franc zone in 1962 and established its own currency, the Malian franc (Mfr), at par with CFA franc and its own central bank. However, smuggling and speculation rapidly undermined the new Malian franc forcing it to rejoin the CFA franc zone in 1967. It did not, however, rejoin the sub-regional monetary organization, the Union Monetaire Ouest-Africaine (West African Monetary Union, UMOA) until 1984.

POVERTY AND WEALTH

Mali's GNP per head, converted to U.S. dollars by using **exchange rates**, was US$250 in 1998. The **purchasing power parity** (PPP) method of conversion to U.S. dollars (which makes allowance for the low price of many basic commodities and services in Mali), put the level of the GNP per head at US$720. The CIA *World Factbook* estimated the **GDP per capita** at PPP at US$820 in 1999. All these measures place Mali among the poorest countries in the world.

In the period 1989–98, it was estimated that 73 percent of the population were below the US$1 per day poverty line—this is the second most severe incidence of poverty among the 174 countries for which data have been collected by the United Nations (UN). The Human

Exchange rates: Mali	
Communauté Financière Africaine francs per US$1	
Jan 2001	699.21
2000	711.98
1999	615.70
1998	589.95
1997	583.67
1996	511.55

Note: From January 1, 1999, the CFA Fr is pegged to the euro at a rate of 655.957 CFA Fr per euro.

SOURCE: CIA *World Factbook 2001* [ONLINE].

Distribution of Income or Consumption by Percentage Share: Mali	
Lowest 10%	1.8
Lowest 20%	4.6
Second 20%	8.0
Third 20%	11.9
Fourth 20%	19.3
Highest 20%	56.2
Highest 10%	40.4

Survey year: 1994
Note: This information refers to expenditure shares by percentiles of the population and is ranked by per capita expenditure.

SOURCE: *2000 World Development Indicators* [CD-ROM].

Household Consumption in PPP Terms

Country	All food	Clothing and footwear	Fuel and power[a]	Health care[b]	Education[b]	Transport & Communications	Other
Mali	53	15	7	4	5	2	15
United States	13	9	9	4	6	8	51
Nigeria	51	5	31	2	8	2	2
Mauritania	N/A	N/A	N/A	N/A	N/A	N/A	N/A

Data represent percentage of consumption in PPP terms.
[a]Excludes energy used for transport.
[b]Includes government and private expenditures.

SOURCE: World Bank. *World Development Indicators 2000.*

Development Index developed by the UN, combines income per head (using the PPP method), education, and health (as indicated by life expectancy). Mali ranks 165 out of 174 countries, firmly in the low human development category.

For most people in the rural areas, who herd family cattle or work small family farms, living conditions are barely subsistence level. Houses are made of wood frames with mud walls and hard earth floors. Their diet consists primarily of cooked cereals and milk, and is essentially meatless. They wear secondhand clothes which originate in Europe and are shipped to local markets. Water comes from wells; cooking is done over wood fires; lighting is from small kerosene wick lamps; and sanitation is provided by pit latrines. Children are unlikely to go to school, and there are no local health centers.

In the towns, for those with employment, conditions tend to be better. Lower middle-class individuals live in cement block, tin-roofed houses with concrete floors. There is electricity and water some of the time, and schools and dispensaries are nearby. The poor live in slums where their shelter is made of throw-away bits of cloth, cardboard, or plastic. They use pit latrines and communal water taps. In the city the poor may have better access to medical care and schools for their children, but these services are in high demand and may cost too much for poor people to use.

WORKING CONDITIONS

Agriculture and fishing occupy 82 percent of the labor force. Most of the labor force is engaged in production for small family farms or fishing enterprises which generate low incomes. Most working in this sector are below the dollar-a-day poverty line. Those in the industry and services sector are comparatively well off, having incomes more than 3 times the national average.

There is no minimum wage or working hours legislation that is applicable to agriculture and fishing, and the legislation for the rest of the economy has either been rendered irrelevant by **inflation** or is not enforced.

COUNTRY HISTORY AND ECONOMIC DEVELOPMENT

300. Mali becomes part of the great Ghana empire of West Africa.

1076. Muslim Almoravids from Mauritania invade the Ghana empire and set up a capital at Kumbi 200 kilometers (124 miles) north of present-day Bamako.

1350. Sundiata Keita, leader of the Mandinka people, founds the Mali empire and converts to Islam as a gesture to his northern neighbors and trading partners.

1464. The Songhai, an Islamic empire originating in western Sudan, makes raids, eclipses the empire of Mali, and embarks on a systematic conquest of the Sahel.

1591. The Songhai empire collapses after an invasion from Morocco and an ensuing revolt by its subject peoples.

1880. French begin to subjugate the interior of Mali, then called Sudan.

1893. French appoint a governor to Sudan.

1959. Former French colony of Sudan merges with Senegal to form the Federation of Mali.

1960. Federation of Mali attains independence from France. Two months later, Senegal secedes. The Republic of Mali is proclaimed on 22 September led by President Modibo Keita with a single political party, Union Soudanaise-Ressemblement Democratique Africain (US-RDA). Keita's Marxist regime severs links with France.

1962. Mali withdraws from CFA franc zone.

1967. Agreement is reached with France for Mali's return to the CFA franc zone.

1968. Keita dissolves National Assembly. Young officers stage successful coup d'etat in November, suspending the constitution and banning all political activity. Lieutenant Moussa Traoré assumes the presidency.

1974. New constitution is approved by referendum providing for the establishment, after 5-year transition period, of a 1-party state.

1976. Union Democratiqe du Peuple Malien (UDPM) is announced as the new ruling party and the only legal party.

1977. Keita dies in detention. Hostile demonstrations from supporters of the old regime and proponents of multiparty democracy occurs.

1979. Presidential and legislative elections are held in June, with Traoré as sole candidate for presidency, winning 99 percent of the vote cast while a single list of UPDM candidates are elected to the legislature.

1981. Constitutional amendment increases the president's term from 5 to 6 years and decreases that of national assembly from 4 to 3 years. The Traoré government undertakes a program of economic liberalization in cooperation with the World Bank and western donors.

1982. Legislative election occurs in June with a single list of UDPM candidates.

1983. Severe drought occurs.

1985. Traoré is re-elected president as sole candidate with 98 percent of the vote cast.

1992. In January the Alliance pour la Démocratie au Mali (ADEMA) wins the country's first multiparty elections. In April Alpha Oumar Konare, ADEMA's leader, is elected president, and a cross-party government is formed.

1994. In January the CFA franc is devalued by 50 percent, raising prices of imports in local currency and reducing import quantities, while at the same time increasing the local revenue from sale of exports and increasing export quantities.

1997. First round of the legislative elections are won by ADEMA but annulled by the constitutional court because of badly organised ballotting, with ballot papers not available, polling stations not open at the designated times, and voters unsure of where they should vote. In the face of a widespread opposition boycott, Konare is re-elected in May. ADEMA wins the re-run of the legislative elections in August. The radical opposition comes together under the umbrella of the Collectif des Partis Politiques de l'Opposition (Collective of Political Opposition Parties, COPPO).

1999. Konare convenes a national forum which is boycotted by the opposition. ADEMA wins the majority of the country's seats in the second round of municipal elections, which are also boycotted by the opposition.

2000. Mali is granted **debt relief** under the Highly Indebted Poor Countries program.

2001. Railway from Bamako to the coast at Dakar in Senegal reopens. Dam at Tallo in central Mali to improve irrigation for rice cultivation is opposed by local and environmental groups.

FUTURE TRENDS

Much of Mali remains unsurveyed in any detail. Besides gold, the country is known to contain deposits of bauxite, manganese, zinc, copper, and lithium. Uranium in the north is not thought to be commercially viable, and the same might be true of iron-ore deposits near the Senegalese border. Surveys for viable diamond sources are underway in western Mali. Mali Diamond Exploration, owned by Ashton Mining of Australia and Mink Mineral Resources of Canada, is under license to explore for, and extract, diamonds in 36,000 square kilometers (13,900 square miles) of territory. With the right investment code and inflows, the mining sector is likely to be a significant driving force of the country's economic growth in the medium and long term.

Sound economic policies and cautious **monetary policy** look likely to ensure Mali will make progress. However, it is difficult to see how an expansion of the mining sector can **trickle down** to make a marked improvement in the prospects for the 80 percent of the population engaged in agriculture and fishing.

DEPENDENCIES

Mali has no territories or colonies.

BIBLIOGRAPHY

Economist Intelligence Unit. *Country Profile: Mali.* London: EIU, 2000.

"Mali." *Africa South of the Sahara.* London: Europa Publications, 2000.

Hodd, M. "Mali." *The Economies of Africa.* Aldershot: Dartmouth, 1991.

U.S. Central Intelligence Agency. *World Factbook 2000: Mali.* <http://www.cia.gov/cia/publications/factbook/geos/ml.html>. Accessed September 2001.

World Bank. *World Bank Africa Database 2000.* Washington DC: World Bank, 2000.

—Allan C. K. Mukungu

MAURITANIA

Mauritanian Islamic Republic
Al-Jumhuriyah al-Islamiyah al-Muritaniyah
République Islamique de Mauritanie

CAPITAL: Nouakchott.

MONETARY UNIT: Ouguiya (UM). One ouguiya equals 5 khoums. There are coins of 1 khoum and 1, 5, 10, and 20 ouguiyas, and notes of 100, 200, 500, and 1,000 ouguiyas.

CHIEF EXPORTS: Fish and fish products, iron ore, gold.

CHIEF IMPORTS: Machinery and equipment, petroleum products, capital goods, foodstuffs, consumer goods.

GROSS DOMESTIC PRODUCT: US$4.9 billion (purchasing power parity, 1999 est.).

BALANCE OF TRADE: **Exports:** US$425 million (f.o.b., 1997). **Imports:** US$444 million (f.o.b., 1997).

COUNTRY OVERVIEW

LOCATION AND SIZE. Located in northwestern Africa, bordered by Western Sahara (occupied by Morocco) and Algeria on the north, by Mali on the east and south, by Senegal on the southwest, and by the Atlantic Ocean on the west, the country has an area of 1,030,700 square kilometers (398,000 square miles), making it slightly larger than 3 times the size of New Mexico. Its total estimated boundary length is 5,828 kilometers (3,622 miles), including 754 kilometers (469 miles) of coast on the Atlantic Ocean. The capital, Nouakchott, is situated on the Atlantic coast in the southwest.

POPULATION. The population of Mauritania was 2,667,859 in 2000. Its average population density was 2 inhabitants per square kilometer (5.18 per square mile) in 1994, or the third lowest in the world. Deserts occupy 90 percent of the territory; 90 percent of the population lives in the south, along the Senegal River and the Atlantic Ocean. In 2000, the birth rate was 43.36 per 1,000 population, while the death rate equaled 13.97 per 1,000. With a fertility rate of 6.29 children born per woman, the population growth rate was 2.94 percent. The rapidly growing population is very youthful, with 46 percent below the age of 15 and 2 percent 65 or older.

Arabic-speaking Moors of Arab and Berber ancestry form 30 percent of the population, Arabic-speaking descendants of former slaves of mixed Moor and black African stock comprise 40 percent, and black Africans of the Wolof, Toucouleur (Peul), and Soninke groups constitute 30 percent. While the Moors are traditionally nomadic herders, the black Africans are engaged mostly in agriculture along the Senegal River. Communities are organized in some 150 distinct clans or tribes. Virtually all Mauritanians are Sunni Muslims. Arabic is the official language, though French and several African languages are also widely spoken. Sixty percent of the people lived in urban areas in 2000. The population of Nouakchott, the capital, was 1,070,000 in 1999; other major cities include Nouadhibou, Zouérat, and Kaédi.

OVERVIEW OF ECONOMY

Mauritania is among the world's poorest developing countries with a **gross domestic product (GDP) per capita** of just $478 in 1998, according to the **United Nations Development Program**. Since attaining independence from French colonial rule in 1960, primitive and low-productivity **subsistence farming** and herding continue to provide livelihood for the majority of the people. However, most nomads and many farmers have fled to the cities since the 1970s due to the spreading **desertification** of the land, caused by water depletion and locust attacks. Mauritania has deposits of iron ore, which contribute nearly half of its exports, and also copper ore, gypsum, and phosphates. The decline in demand for those products, however, has led to a decline in mining output and income in the 1990s. The coastal Atlantic has a rich fishing area but it is exploited by foreign interests.

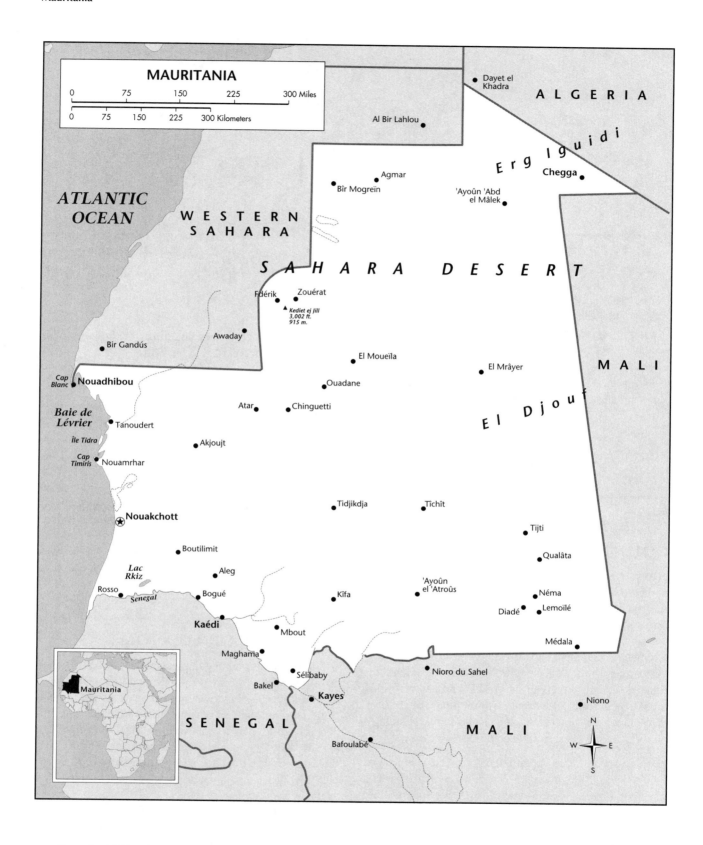

Over the 1990s, drought, mismanagement, and waste of resources have contributed to the amassing of a large **foreign debt** (US$2.5 billion in 1997, or 226 percent of 1996 GDP) and the country remains dependent on for-eign aid (US$227.9 million in 1995) and assistance. **Debt service** is a heavy burden; Mauritania has been qualified by the international community for **debt relief** as a heav-ily indebted poor country and seeks cancellation of

US$620 million of its debt. Foreign investment is scarce; France and Arab countries (mainly Algeria) are its largest sources. Since 1998, the government has pursued a reform initiative to cut budgetary costs, reduce the waste of resources, and reform the tax system. In 1999, the International Monetary Fund (IMF) approved a US$57 million enhanced structural adjustment loan to support its program.

POLITICS, GOVERNMENT, AND TAXATION

Mauritania won independence from France in 1960, and is now ruled under a republican constitution of 1991 which resembles that of France, with elements of Islamic sharia law. The constitution legalized opposition parties, but the 2 presidential elections since 1991 were flawed. Mauritania remains under an authoritarian, single-party regime. The president (Colonel Maaouya Ould Sid Ahmed Taya, in office since 1984, and reelected in 1997), is elected by popular vote for a renewable 6-year term. He appoints the prime minister and Council of Ministers (cabinet), who are subject to control by a **bicameral** parliament. The parliament consists of a 56-seat Senate, or Majlis al-Shuyukh, whose members are elected by municipal leaders to 6-year terms, and a National Assembly, or Majlis al-Watani, whose 79 members are elected by popular vote to 5-year terms.

The ruling party, the nationalist and formerly **socialist** Democratic and Social Republican Party (PRDS) of President Taya, controls 71 of the 79 seats in the National Assembly (as of early 2001), and 8 deputies represent other parties. The Union of Progressive Forces (UFP) is the most important opposition group but domestic politics is still tribally based. Mauritania experiences tensions between its black African minority and the Arabic-speaking Moor majority and has a generally ambivalent attitude towards neighboring black Africa.

The government's role in the economy is significant; economic growth and poverty reduction are key objectives of its policy, including **privatization** and reform in the banking sector, **liberalization** of the **exchange rate**, and reduction of trade and investment barriers. Since 1998, the government has also stressed market liberalization, sustainable development, poverty alleviation, education, and health improvement. It plans to modernize the administration, attract foreign investments, increase exports, and develop agriculture, mining, and fishing. Some state-owned companies (such as fish export marketing, petroleum, and insurance) have been privatized, and private initiative has been encouraged. Corruption is still a major problem, particularly in taxation, bank loans, government **procurement**, project management, traffic and vehicle control, and administrative services.

Given the poverty of the population, taxes on businesses form the bulk of the government's revenue. Since 1999, the number of taxes has been reduced from 5 to 4, with the introduction of a law that replaced 2 existing taxes that applied to imports. Customs formalities have been simplified, but the tax system is reckoned business-unfriendly. The import tax rate varies between 9 percent and 43 percent, and imports **value-added tax** (VAT) rates are from 5 percent to 14 percent. Importers consider import taxes high in comparison to other countries.

INFRASTRUCTURE, POWER, AND COMMUNICATIONS

Mauritania's **infrastructure** is poor compared to its neighbors. The roads are dilapidated, particularly in the countryside; long distances and the difficult desert climate make their maintenance difficult. There are about 7,660 kilometers (4,760 miles) of roadways, 866 kilometers (538 miles) of which are paved, and 704 kilometers (460 miles) of railroad line for carrying iron ore from Zouérat to Nouadhibou. Several roads are under construction, and land conversion and road construction are a top priority for the government.

Communications

Country	Newspapers	Radios	TV Sets[a]	Cable subscribers[a]	Mobile Phones[a]	Fax Machines[a]	Personal Computers[a]	Internet Hosts[b]	Internet Users[b]
	1996	1997	1998	1998	1998	1998	1998	1999	1999
Mauritania	0	151	91	N/A	0	1.7	5.5	0.00	13
United States	215	2,146	847	244.3	256	78.4	458.6	1,508.77	74,100
Nigeria	24	223	66	N/A	0	N/A	5.7	0.00	100
Morocco	26	241	160	N/A	4	0.7	2.5	0.28	50

[a]Data are from International Telecommunication Union, *World Telecommunication Development Report 1999* and are per 1,000 people.
[b]Data are from the Internet Software Consortium (http://www.isc.org) and are per 10,000 people.
SOURCE: World Bank. *World Development Indicators 2000.*

The Chinese-built seaport in Nouakchott receives 85 percent of the country's imported goods. The second seaport in the northern center of Nouadhibou serves fish and iron exports. Other ports include Bogué, Kaédi, and Rosso on the Senegal River; there is ferry traffic on the Senegal River.

The air transport company, state-run Air Mauritanie, provides domestic and international services between Nouakchott, Casablanca, Dakar, Las Palmas, Bamako, and Banjul. With international airports in Nouakchott, Nouadhibou, and Néma, Mauritania is served by Air France, Air Afrique, Moroccan, Tunisian, Algerian, and Senegalese carriers.

Electricity production was 152 million kilowatt-hours (kWh) a year in 1998, with 80 percent coming from thermal plants and 20 percent from hydropower installations. Most companies have their own generators. Electricity consumption is 141 million kWh (1998). **Public-sector** energy output increased 25 percent between 1993 and 1997 to meet demand in Nouakchott and Nouadhibou. Mauritania relies on imports of fuel; alternative energy production, such as solar, is limited but growing. It receives 15 percent of electricity output from the Manantali dam on the Senegal river. The Societe Nationale d'Eau et d'Electricite, the state-run electricity and water **monopoly**, is improving its management, and the government plans to privatize it and has hired a consortium headed by the Hong Kong and Shanghai Banking Corporation to prepare the process. Power projects under construction include the extension of the Nouakchott electricity grid. Firewood fulfills one-half of household fuel demand but the European Union (EU) is promoting the distribution of gas bottles and burners to encourage people to convert to gas. To satisfy its demand for potable water, the government plans to renovate the sanitation network, encourage new well drilling in the countryside, and increase of Nouadhibou and Nouakchott's reservoir capacity.

Mauritania has a poor telecommunications system with only 9,000 main lines in use in 1995, but it has undergone considerable expansion in the late 1990s. The first GSM wireless telephone system with 50,000 lines covering the Nouakchott and Nouadhibou areas was launched in 2000. The system operator, Mauritel—a **joint venture** between the Tunisian Telecommunications Company and local companies—won the $28 million license in competition with France Telecom and Spanish Starcelle. Privatization of the former state monopoly OPT (postal and telecommunications company) was launched in 1999 with the intention to create 3 separate units run by private operators. The Canadian company Sogema has been hired to reorganize telecommunications, and French Alcatel has captured market share with the installation of a new 10,000-line phone exchange in Nouakchott worth US$4.5 million. In 2000,

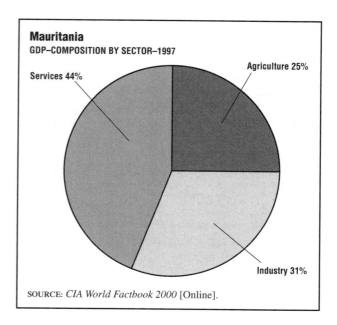

Mauritania
GDP–COMPOSITION BY SECTOR–1997

Services 44%

Agriculture 25%

Industry 31%

SOURCE: *CIA World Factbook 2000* [Online].

the World Bank approved a US$10.8 million loan to the government for assistance in privatization and expanding access to communications.

ECONOMIC SECTORS

Mauritania's GDP composition by sector in 1997 was as follows: agriculture, 25 percent; industry, 31 percent; and services, 44 percent. The relative stability of the various sectors over the years, however, disguises significant changes within those sectors. In agriculture, for instance, there was a 30 percent rise in crop output

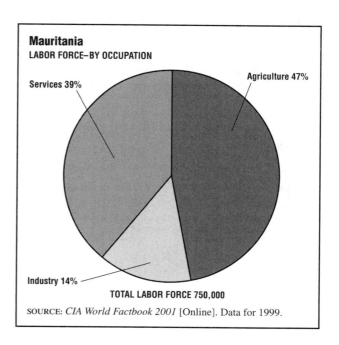

Mauritania
LABOR FORCE–BY OCCUPATION

Services 39%

Agriculture 47%

Industry 14%

TOTAL LABOR FORCE 750,000

SOURCE: *CIA World Factbook 2001* [Online]. Data for 1999.

between 1993 and 1997, while livestock and fishing declined by 40 percent. Mining production peaked in 1994 and has since dropped back to the 1993 level. Mining and fisheries contribute for 99.7 percent of the exports. The low population density does not support a diversified manufacturing sector, and industrial activities are located almost solely in Nouakchott and Nouadhibou, where the production growth rate was 7.2 percent in 1994. Growth in commerce, transport, and communications in the late 1990s compensated for declines in public sector services.

AGRICULTURE

Agriculture and herding employ 47 percent of the workforce, although its contribution to GDP is 25 percent due to its inefficiency. Most farmers are engaged in subsistence agriculture and never buy food outside their households. Farms produce dates, millet, sorghum, and root crops, while herders raise cattle and sheep. Fishing is the second largest foreign revenue source after mining. Along its 754 kilometer (469 mile) Atlantic coast, Mauritania has some of the richest fishing grounds in the world. The sector, however, is harmed by the lack of effective government policy, mismanagement, and limited technical ability to monitor and control the resources. In 1997, the government launched a reform to strengthen its control, increase the fishing areas, and encourage joint ventures with foreign companies.

There is very little arable land in Mauritania, while permanent pastures occupy 38 percent of the territory and forests and woodland cover just 4 percent. Mauritania's cereal production covers 35 percent of the country's needs (527,297 metric tons) and the food situation in 1999 called for massive imports and donor aid. The Senegal River valley has attracted local investors to regional dam projects relevant also to navigation, power generation, and distribution. The World Bank supports an irrigation program aimed at rehabilitating 11,000 hectares along the Senegal River and diversifying the crops. In 1998, the government adopted a long-term development strategy to guarantee food security and conserve natural resources by promoting private investment and introducing irrigation.

INDUSTRY

The mining of iron ore and gypsum and fish processing form the backbone of Mauritanian industry. In 1998, mining exports equaled $214 million, or 56 percent of total exports, a 23 percent increase from 1997, making the state-run mining company the largest foreign exchange generator. Mining is of greatest interest to foreign investors, and suppliers of mining equipment and services. Mauritania is trying to develop new natural resources, notably gold and oil. In 1998 and 1999, research contracts were signed with Canadian Rex Diamond Mining Corporation and Australian Ashton West Africa Property. Researchers have confirmed the presence of gold, phosphate, aluminum, and copper in several regions, and Australian Woodside Petroleum has reported positive results at its offshore drilling in Mauritanian waters.

The domestic market's lack of scale, skilled labor, and infrastructure, and its high utility costs and poor credit make Mauritania unattractive for foreign manufacturers. Manufacturing and handicrafts accounted for 4.4 percent of GDP in 1998 and are concentrated in Nouakchott and Nouadhibou. They include food processing, chemicals and plastics, building materials, and paper and packaging materials. Six companies account for 57 percent of investment and 40 percent of the 1,100 jobs in the sector. Of the 10 companies established in the 1980s in fish processing, 8 have failed due to high water and electricity costs, skilled labor shortages, poor infrastructure, and low hygiene standards.

SERVICES

Mauritania's financial sector is underdeveloped, although it has been **restructured** and privatized over the 1990s. It includes the Banque centrale de Mauritanie (the central bank, which issues currency and oversees **monetary policy**), and 5 commercial banks, the Banque nationale de Mauritanie, the Banque mauritanienne pour le commerce et l'industrie, the Banque al baraka mauritanienne Islamique, Chinguetti Bank, and the Generale de banque de Mauritanie. All banks are burdened by bad (irrecoverable) loans in the struggling fishing sector. The Saudi Al-Baraka firm, owning 85 percent of Al-Baraka Bank, and Belgium's Belgolaise bank, holding a stake at Generale, are the largest foreign shareholders in local banks. Government participation in the other banks is significant, but 2 of them are negotiating partnerships with foreign investors. There is 1 bank specialized in housing construction, 3 credit Agencies (Credit Maritime, Credit Agricole, and Mauritanie Leasing), and 2 private insurance companies. Since 1997, the government has encouraged popular saving agencies to diversify the sector and mobilize small savers' assets to promote investment.

Mauritania's **retail** trade is mostly traditional, represented by small family enterprises. It has a good tourist potential as the Banc d'Arguin reserve and ancient towns such as Chinguetti were declared World Heritage Sites by the United Nations Educational, Scientific and Cultural Organization. There are, however, very few facilities and the only international hotels are in Nouakchott.

Trade (expressed in billions of US$): Mauritania		
	Exports	Imports
1975	.176	.161
1980	.194	.286
1985	.374	.234
1990	.447	.220
1995	N/A	N/A
1998	N/A	N/A

SOURCE: International Monetary Fund. *International Financial Statistics Yearbook 1999.*

Exchange rates: Mauritania	
ouguiyas (UM) per US$1	
Dec 2000	250.870
2000	238.923
1999	209.514
1998	188.476
1997	151.853
1996	137.222

SOURCE: CIA *World Factbook 2001* [ONLINE].

INTERNATIONAL TRADE

Mauritania imports food, fuel, vehicles and spare parts, building materials, and clothes, and exports mainly iron ore, fish, and some gold. Its exports amounted to US$425 million in 1997, and are shipped mostly to Japan (24 percent), Italy (17 percent), France (14 percent), and Spain (8 percent). Imports in 1997 worth US$444 million, mostly machinery and equipment, petroleum products, **capital goods**, foodstuffs, and **consumer goods**, were purchased from France (26 percent), Spain (8 percent), Germany (7 percent), and the Benelux countries (7 percent). Mauritania's economic ties to black Western African countries have lost relative importance over the 1990s compared to those with the Arab countries of Northern Africa.

Mauritanians benefitted in the 1990s from the abolition of import monopolies on rice, wheat, flour, sugar, tea, and powdered milk, which improved the accessibility of food throughout the country. Credit restrictions, import taxes, and interest rates still hinder most importers. Mauritania is trying to promote trade, particularly with Arab countries. A **trade deficit** of 6.6 billion ouguiyas is growing, however, and reflects not only the weakness of the domestic economy but also increased debt repayments and the decrease in money transfers from Mauritanian workers abroad.

MONEY

Banking supervision has been strengthened during the 1990s to encourage bank **solvency** and the stability of local currency (with the support of the World Bank and the IMF) but interest rates have discouraged private investment. The government pursues price stability through fiscal and monetary restraint, promotes private credit agencies and institutional reform, encourages domestic and foreign investment, and encourages poverty reduction through higher wages. The foreign exchange system was liberalized in the 1990s and currencies can be obtained freely, but the central bank fixes exchange rates through a basket of currencies of the principal trading partners. In 1998, the central bank introduced incentives to encourage fish exporters to bring back their foreign currency and change them for ouguiyas, increasing the availability of foreign currencies, mainly U.S. dollars and French francs, in the market.

POVERTY AND WEALTH

Mauritania ranks among the least developed countries in the world with widespread chronic poverty among the nomadic herders, subsistence farmers, and the unemployed urban masses. Poverty is manifested not only in low income but also in limited access to basic services such as safe water, health care, and education. In 1990, it was estimated that 57 percent of the population lived below the poverty line and the country's **Gini index** (measuring economic equality, with 0 standing for perfect equality and 100 for perfect inequality) was close to 39, lower than the one in the United States but higher than in Europe. With the lowest 10 percent of earners responsible for 0.7 percent of the consumption and the highest 10 percent for 30.4 percent in 1988, Mauritania is still more equal than many of its African neighbors. The **inflation rate** was 9.8 percent in 1998. The country is heavily dependent on foreign aid and poverty reduction programs while corruption creates some large illicit fortunes. Economic inequality adds to interethnic and intertribal tension to

GDP per Capita (US$)					
Country	1975	1980	1985	1990	1998
Mauritania	549	557	511	438	478
United States	19,364	21,529	23,200	25,363	29,683
Nigeria	301	314	230	258	256
Morocco	956	1,114	1,173	1,310	1,388

SOURCE: United Nations. *Human Development Report 2000; Trends in human development and per capita income.*

Distribution of Income or Consumption by Percentage Share: Mauritania

Lowest 10%	2.3
Lowest 20%	6.2
Second 20%	10.8
Third 20%	15.4
Fourth 20%	22.0
Highest 20%	45.6
Highest 10%	29.9

Survey year: 1995
Note: This information refers to expenditure shares by percentiles of the population and is ranked by per capita expenditure.

SOURCE: *2000 World Development Indicators* [CD-ROM].

produce a very low level of human development, according to United Nations sources.

WORKING CONDITIONS

The **labor force** was estimated at 465,000 in 1981, but only 45,000 wage earners were reported in 1980, indicating that a vast number of people are employed in subsistence agriculture. By occupation, agriculture employed 47 percent, services 39 percent, industry 14 percent. Mass exodus to cities, low economic growth, and a growing uneducated young population are generating unemployment while there is a shortage of skilled workers, technicians, and managers in most sectors. The unemployment rate was officially 23 percent in 1995. But fully 50 percent of high school and university graduates are unemployed due to government hiring restraints and the stagnating **private sector**.

Workers have the right to associate and strike, but strikes are rare. There are 3 union confederations, Union of Mauritanian Workers (UTM), General Confederation of Mauritanian Workers (CGTM), and Confederation of Free Mauritanian Workers (CLTM). An employer-employee agreement, the 1974 Collective Labor Convention, establishes many employee benefits, including paid maternity leave. The workweek is 40 hours and the minimum wage is revised periodically by the unions, the employers, and the government. In 1998, the minimum wage was US$54 per month but in the private sector it was US$81.

COUNTRY HISTORY AND ECONOMIC DEVELOPMENT

c. 1–1000 A.D. Berber nomads conquer the indigenous black population, dominating trade with the African kingdom of Ghana across the trans-Saharan trade routes.

c. 1100–1674. Almoravid Dynasty controls the trade in gold, slaves, and salt.

1674. Muslim Arabs conquer the country, becoming the upper class of society. Arabic becomes the official language.

1905. Mauritania becomes a French protectorate and later colony; slavery is legally abolished.

1958. The Islamic Republic of Mauritania is proclaimed.

1960. Mauritania gains independence from France; M. Ould Daddah is elected president.

1960s-70s. The economy expands thanks to newly discovered iron and copper deposits.

1975. Spain cedes the Western Sahara to Morocco and Mauritania, sparking a continuing conflict over the status of the region.

1978. President Daddah is toppled in a coup, and in 1979 Mauritania withdraws from the Western Sahara. Prime minister, later president, Mohamed Ould Haidalla institutes strict enforcement of Islamic law.

1984. Haidalla is deposed by Colonel Taya.

1989. Mauritania joins the Union of the Arab Maghreb, a North African political and economic union whose members include Morocco, Libya, Tunisia, and Algeria.

1989. Tensions with Senegal over agricultural rights along their border result in the **repatriation** of 100,000 Mauritanians from Senegal and the expulsion of 125,000 Senegalese from Mauritania.

1991. A new constitution is adopted, and opposition parties are legalized.

1997. President Taya is reelected president in a landslide election victory.

FUTURE TRENDS

Improving economic management is expected to gradually bring about positive developments in the economy, the infrastructure, and in the alleviation of poverty. The ruling PRDS party will likely win the October 2001 parliamentary elections and **real GDP** is expected to grow in 2001 at an annual rate of 6 percent. Mauritania's economic ties will be further redirected from West Africa to the Union of the Arab Maghreb (Algeria, Libya, Morocco, and Tunisia). Economic policies oriented toward liberalization and additional bank reforms are expected to improve the investment climate. The success of the telecom privatization is expected to attract new private funds and new businesses. Good relations with the IMF and the World Bank will continue to bring in international funds for poverty reduction and development projects and strengthen the economy.

Prospects for increased mining output capacity, along with an increase in iron ore prices and the development of new mineral resources, may bring steady growth in mineral exports. The health of the fisheries industry depends to a large extent on market conditions in East Asia, particularly Japan, and may suffer from economic **recession** in that country. Domestic food production may benefit from occasional good seasons of rains but is still in jeopardy due to active desertification processes and will require extensive international aid. Environmental degradation, poor water supply and health services, unemployment, and a lack of basic education will continue to pose the most serious problems to the government in the foreseeable future.

DEPENDENCIES

Mauritania has no territories or colonies.

BIBLIOGRAPHY

Economist Intelligence Unit. *Country Profile: Mauritania.* London: Economist Intelligence Unit, 2001.

Embassy of the Islamic Republic of Mauritania. <http://www.isa-africa.com/amb-mauritanie/index1.htm>. Accessed August 2001.

Handloff, Robert E. *Mauritania: A Country Study.* 2nd ed. Washington, D.C.: Library of Congress, 1996.

"Mauritania." *MBendi: Information for Africa.* <http://www.mbendi.co.za/land/af/mu/p0005.htm>. Accessed August 2001.

United Nations Development Program. *Human Development Report, Mauritania.* New York, 2000.

U.S. Central Intelligence Agency. *World Factbook 2000.* <http://www.odci.gov/cia/publications/factbook/index.html>. Accessed August 2001.

U.S. Department of State. *Country Commercial Guides for FY2000: Mauritania.* <http://www.state.gov/www/about_state/business/com_guides/2000/africa/mauritania00_02.html>. Accessed August 2001.

—Valentin Hadjiyski

MAURITIUS

CAPITAL: Port Louis.

MONETARY UNIT: Mauritian rupee (R). One Mauritian rupee equals 100 cents. There are coins of 1, 2, 5, 10, 25, and 50 cents and 1 rupee, and notes of 5, 10, 20, 50, 100, 200, 500, and 1,000.

CHIEF EXPORTS: Clothing and textiles, sugar, cut flowers, molasses.

CHIEF IMPORTS: Manufactured goods, capital equipment, foodstuffs, petroleum products, chemicals.

GROSS DOMESTIC PRODUCT: US$12.3 billion (purchasing power parity, 1999 est.).

BALANCE OF TRADE: **Exports:** US$1.7 billion (f.o.b., 1999). **Imports:** US$2.1 billion (c.i.f., 1999).

COUNTRY OVERVIEW

LOCATION AND SIZE. Mauritius is an island in the Indian Ocean, located 2,400 kilometers (1,491 miles) off the southeast coast of Africa. It has a total area of 1,860 square kilometers (781 square miles), and a coastline of 177 kilometers (110 miles). The Republic of Mauritius also includes the barely populated Agalega Islands and the Cargados Carajos Shoals, as well as Rodrigues (population 35,000). The capital, Port Louis, is situated on the west coast of the island, and has a population of approximately 136,000.

POPULATION. The population of Mauritius was estimated to be 1,179,368 in July 2000, with a population growth rate at 0.89 percent. The population is relatively young, with 26 percent of the population under 14 years of age, 68 percent between 15 and 64, and just 6 percent over the age of 65. The life expectancy for the population is 70.98.

Mauritian society is a heterogeneous one. The 2 main population groups are the ethnic Indians, who make up 68 percent of the population, and the Creoles, mixed race descendants of African slaves and colonial settlers, who comprise 27 percent. Other groups include Chinese (3

percent) and white Franco-Mauritians (2 percent). The ethnic Indians are further divided into Hindus and Muslims, with the Hindus being the majority. Nevertheless, the inhabitants of the island tend to view themselves as Mauritians first and foremost.

Given that Mauritius has such a small land surface, population growth and **immigration** are discouraged by the government. Population density is already very high, with 571 people per square kilometer (1,479 per square mile), compared with an average of 45 per square kilometer (117 per square mile) for the world as a whole.

OVERVIEW OF ECONOMY

From the 17th century, the Mauritian economy depended almost exclusively on sugar. Slaves were imported from Africa to work on the sugar plantations. After the abolition of slavery in the 19th century, plantations came to rely more on indentured Indian labor, whose ancestors today form the largest portion of the islands' population.

By the 1960s, Mauritius was still a monocultural economy (dependent on a single crop), and had to import many goods for local consumption. Unemployment was high, which created social tensions. In the mid-1960s, the Mauritian government began to follow a 2-pronged strategy of **import substitution** and export-oriented development.

Import substitution was promoted through the use of high **tariff** barriers to protect local industry from overseas competition. To encourage the production of goods for export, Export Processing Zones (EPZs) were established in 1971, following the successful Taiwanese model. The principle behind EPZs was to import semi-finished goods **duty**-free, to complete the manufacturing process in the EPZs, and then to **re-export** these goods. Clothing and textiles were the main manufactures produced by the EPZ sector.

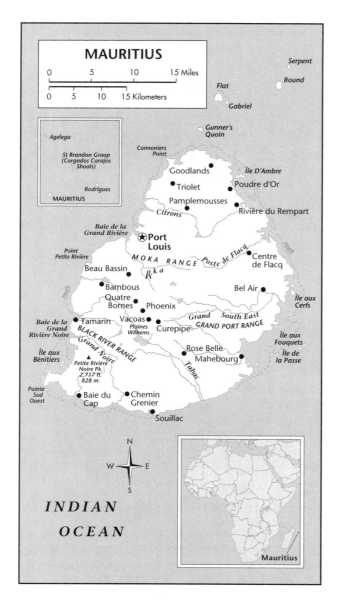

MAURITIUS

0   5   10   15 Miles

0   5   10   15 Kilometers

Agelega

St Brandon Group
(Cargados Carajos
Shoals)

Rodrigues

MAURITIUS

Serpent

Round

Flat

Gabriel

Gunner's Quoin

Cannoniers Point

Goodlands

Triolet

Poudre d'Or

Pamplemousses

Île D'Ambre

Citrons

Rivière du Rempart

Baie de la Grand Rivière

★Port Louis

Point Petite Rivière

MOKA RANGE

Poste de Flacq

Centre de Flacq

Beau Bassin

Moka

Bambous

Bel Air

Quatre Bornes

Phoenix

Île aux Cerfs

Baie de la Grand Rivière Noire

Vacoas

Plaines Wilhems

Tamarin

BLACK RIVER RANGE

Grand Noire

Grand   South East
GRAND PORT RANGE

Curepipe

Île aux Fouquets

Île aux Béniters

Petite Rivière Noire Pk.
2,717 ft.
828 m.

Rose Belle

Mahebourg

Île de la Passe

Tabac

Pointe Sud Ouest

Baie du Cap

Chemin Grenier

Souillac

N
W   E
S

INDIAN

OCEAN

Mauritius

The EPZ sector grew rapidly since its inception and attracted large amounts of foreign investment. This allowed for the rapid industrialization of the country. Nowadays, only 25 percent of export earnings come from sugar, while 40 percent are derived from manufacturing. Over the past twenty years, the economy has consistently achieved high rates of growth, resulting in a quadrupling of **GDP per capita** between 1970 and 1997. According to the World Bank, the economy of Mauritius has sustained a growth rate of about 5.5 percent since independence in 1968, and the country is currently classified among middle-income earners.

Besides manufacturing and sugar, the nation's other important economic sectors are tourism and financial services. With its white sands, coral reefs, and subtropical climate, Mauritius is an island paradise for tourists. Visitors come mainly from Europe and from South Africa.

The hospitable nature of the Mauritian people also contributes to the island's attraction.

The island of Rodrigues has not seen the same level of development as Mauritius has—which is perhaps not so surprising when one considers that the 2 islands are 600 kilometers (373 miles) apart. Subsistence agriculture is the main economic activity on Rodrigues, with the principal crop being maize instead of sugarcane.

By the late 1990s in Mauritius, only about 5 percent of the population was living below the poverty line. However, challenges such as tariff reductions, rising wages, and limited growth prospects for the almost-saturated tourism industry have contributed to an increase in unemployment on the island, which in mid-2000 stood at 8 percent. This is rather disturbing for a country that had had **full employment** only a few years before.

A major factor which should not be overlooked in Mauritius's success is the political climate, which is characterized by stability and ethnic tolerance. Ordinary Mauritians have also demonstrated a strong work ethic, which has resulted in a highly productive **labor force**.

The debt levels both in terms of GDP and exports are manageable, hence Mauritius is not considered a highly indebted country. In June 1999, **external debt** was around 30 percent of GDP. There is a healthy balance between local and **foreign debt** positions, with local debt comprising over 80 percent of total public debt and the residual being foreign.

With respect to donor assistance, the World Bank notes that, due to the country's access to capital markets, official development assistance has declined considerably since 1990 and has become increasingly selective. Although donor assistance is important to supplement private capital flows, Mauritius is not dependent on foreign aid.

POLITICS, GOVERNMENT, AND TAXATION

Mauritius earned its independence from Britain in 1968, which had controlled the islands since 1810, and the Mauritians have continued to follow the British model of government. Mauritius is a parliamentary democracy based on the Westminster model, with elections being held once every 5 years. There is a 66-seat National Assembly, 62 of whose members are elected by direct popular vote, while 4 are appointed to represent minority interest. The National Assembly elects the president, who in turn selects the prime minister.

Although Mauritius is in general a peaceful society, its politics are somewhat capricious. In spite of the small size of the country, there are a fair number of political parties. Most governments over the past twenty years have been coalitions, comprising 2 or more political parties. The major political parties are the Militant Movement of Mauritius (MMM), the Mauritian Social Democrat Party (PMSD), the Mauritian Labor Party (MLP), and the Militant Socialist Movement (MSM). Voting is based to a certain extent along ethnic lines. Although there are few significant differences among the major parties, the MMM tends to be more **socialist** in outlook and is favored especially by the Creoles, while the MLP's support-base is mainly Indian.

The elections in September 2000 resulted in a victory for an alliance of Anerood Jugnauth's Militant Socialist Movement and Paul Bérenger's Militant Movement of Mauritius. The alliance ousted Navin Ramgoolam's Mauritian Labor Party, which had gained power in 1995. Jugnauth, in power from 1982–1995, presided over the country's transformation from dependence on sugar to a modern, diversified economy. The MSM/MMM alliance has promised to tackle corruption and mismanagement of public finances (said to be the downfall of the Labor Party), but otherwise will continue with broadly similar policies to those implemented. The voter participation rate in the 2000 elections was high, with over 80 percent of registered voters turning up at the polls.

Taxation in Mauritius is relatively low, with tax revenue comprising only 17.7 percent of GDP in 1998. The highest **income tax** rate for individuals is 25 percent (recently reduced from 30 percent), while the corporate rate is 15 percent for manufacturing companies. Special tax incentives are available to certain kinds of companies, notably those classified as "offshore businesses" and those locating in the Export Processing Zone.

INFRASTRUCTURE, POWER, AND COMMUNICATIONS

Infrastructure in Mauritius is well-developed. Roads are maintained in very good condition, with 1,834 kilometers (1,139 miles) out of a total of 1,910 kilometers (1,186 miles) of roads being paved. As of the year 2000, the road system is sufficient to hold the country's traffic volume. Less than one-tenth of the population own cars. Meanwhile, several road projects have been planned such as the extension of the roadway from Nouvelle France to Plaine Magnien, the implementation of the South Eastern Highway Project, and the construction of bypasses in areas such as Flacqs, Goodlands, and Triolet. There are no railways in Mauritius. Public transport by bus is reliable and efficient, however.

The harbor of Port Louis was provided with extra capacity in the late 1990s and has been repositioned to handle high traffic and goods volume. The country operates an efficient freeport, which handles about R9 billion worth of trade per year. In volume terms, this is estimated at around 13,000 tons. Mauritius aims to become a major transshipment center, given its location between Africa, Asia, and Australia.

There are currently 5 airports, with 2 of them having paved runways. The main airlines flying to and from Mauritius are Air Mauritius (the national carrier), British Airways, Air France, and South African Airways.

The country has a modernized telecommunications infrastructure. This will be further upgraded with the forging of a partnership with French Telecom. The latter took up a 40 percent (R6.6 billion) shareholding in the local Mauritius Telecoms in the year 2000. This public-private partnership is the first step towards a full **liberalization** of the industry, in accordance with standards set out by the WTO reform plan of the sector by 2004.

Internet access is reasonably widespread. At present the country has only 6 Internet providers, and over 534 Internet hosts. Countrywide, Internet use is available to about 40,000 people.

Mauritius is a net importer of oil and petroleum. These imports are in refined form and come through the State Trading Corporation. Despite its lack of natural resources, Mauritius is adequately provided for in terms of electricity. About 25 percent of its electricity is derived

Communications

Country	Newspapers	Radios	TV Sets[a]	Cable subscribers[a]	Mobile Phones[a]	Fax Machines[a]	Personal Computers[a]	Internet Hosts[b]	Internet Users[b]
	1996	1997	1998	1998	1998	1998	1998	1999	1999
Mauritius	75	368	226	N/A	53	24.5	87.1	4.56	55
United States	215	2,146	847	244.3	256	78.4	458.6	1,508.77	74,100
South Africa	32	317	125	N/A	56	3.5	47.4	33.36	1,820
Zimbabwe	19	93	30	N/A	4	N/A	9.0	1.19	20

[a]Data are from International Telecommunication Union, *World Telecommunication Development Report 1999* and are per 1,000 people.
[b]Data are from the Internet Software Consortium (http://www.isc.org) and are per 10,000 people.

SOURCE: World Bank. *World Development Indicators 2000.*

from hydro-electricity schemes, and the rest from a combination of diesel-powered thermal stations and burning bagasse (sugarcane residue). For its energy, the country is dependent on supplies afforded by the government **parastatal** called the Central Electricity Board. Electricity production in the late 1990s stood at 34 million kilowatt-hours.

The government is currently looking for substitutive methods of generating energy using woody bio-mass, ethanol from sugarcane, and solar, wind, and sea wave power. Elsewhere efforts are in progress in the development of a renewable fuel plant near Port Louis. Commercial energy is derived from electricity (10.5 percent), coal (5.4 percent) and oil-derived products (84.1 percent).

ECONOMIC SECTORS

The importance of agriculture in the Mauritian economy has been declining over the past 3 decades. Agriculture made up 16 percent of GDP in 1970, declining to 12 percent in 1980, and finally to 9 percent in 1998. This reflects the decreasing dependence of Mauritius on sugar. Furthermore, the share of the labor force in agriculture is much smaller now than it was twenty years ago—29 percent of males and 30 percent of females worked in the sector in 1980, while only 15 percent of males and 13 percent of females did so in 1998. The industry is plagued by excess labor demand. According to reports by the Mauritius Cooperative Agricultural Federation, the reasons are that young unemployed people are not eager to work in the fields, and the population is aging.

Industry comprised 33 percent of GDP in 1998, up from 26 percent in 1980. More significantly, 25 percent of GDP came from manufacturing in 1998, compared

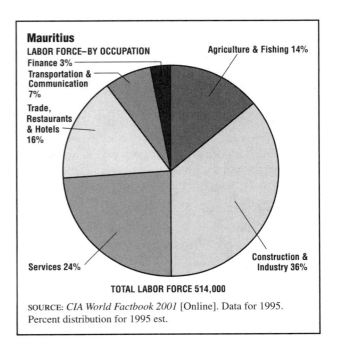

Mauritius
LABOR FORCE—BY OCCUPATION
Finance 3%
Transportation & Communication 7%
Trade, Restaurants & Hotels 16%
Agriculture & Fishing 14%
Construction & Industry 36%
Services 24%
TOTAL LABOR FORCE 514,000
SOURCE: *CIA World Factbook 2001* [Online]. Data for 1995. Percent distribution for 1995 est.

with 15 percent in 1980. Much of this growth can be attributed to the expansion of the Export Processing Zone sector. The percentage of the male labor force working in industry has increased significantly, from 19 percent (1980) to 39 percent (1992–97). The increase has not been so large for females, however—40 percent in 1980 to 43 percent over the period 1992–97. This may in part reflect a diversification away from the textile industry, which tends to employ more females, towards more high-tech industries such as information technology.

Services made up 62 percent of GDP in 1980, but declined to 58 percent in 1998. The proportion of men working in the service sector has not changed much—46 percent in 1992–97, down from 47 percent in 1980. More females are now working in the service sector, however—45 percent in 1992–97, compared with 31 percent in 1980.

AGRICULTURE

SUGAR. Sugarcane is still the dominant crop, extending over 90 percent of the cultivated land surface of the country. Twenty-five percent of export earnings come from sugar cane. Per annum sugar production amounts to approximately 630,000 tons. Due to a bad drought, this figure shrunk to 580,000 tons in 1999. As a result the agricultural sector as a whole registered a growth rate of minus 25 percent during this year. The government stepped in to help assist sugar farmers badly hit by low harvest in 1999. It provided a grant of R5,000 per hectare to farmers who experienced losses due to drought and paid a premium for sugar purchase. Mauritius is prone to recurrent cyclonic weather, which can impact the sugarcane crop, and consequently economic growth.

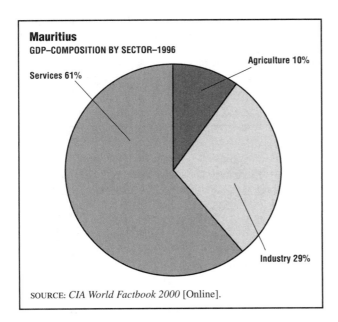

Mauritius
GDP–COMPOSITION BY SECTOR–1996
Services 61%
Agriculture 10%
Industry 29%
SOURCE: *CIA World Factbook 2000* [Online].

Other sources of export revenue in the agricultural sector include tea, coffee, and tobacco. Tea production and exports decreased dramatically over the period 1995–2000, however. The production of onions, potatoes, maize, poultry, cattle, fish, pulses, bananas, and venison occurs on a small scale, largely for local consumption. Government is also supporting the development of biotechnology and hydroponics.

INDUSTRY

Mauritius's so-called "economic miracle" is largely due to the growth of the manufacturing sector since the inception of the EPZs. The EPZs attracted significant investment from abroad as foreign companies looked for cheaper locations for production. The reduction in unemployment experienced by Mauritius over the last 20 years can generally be attributed to the rapid growth of the EPZs.

The EPZs offer duty-free imports, lower tax rates, subsidized rates on electricity and other utilities, access to credit, favorable transport costs, and institutional support facilities.

Clothing and textiles still form the mainstay of Mauritian industry and dominate the EPZ sector. Mauritian clothing and textiles are competitive, both in terms of price and quality, in foreign markets such as Europe, United States, Japan, Australia, South Africa, and Scandinavian countries.

Growth in the EPZ sector has been slowing since the early 1990s, however, in terms of employment, new investment, and the number of enterprises operating in the sector. Most of the capital in the EPZs is now locally-owned, reflecting declining foreign interest. This is partly due to the fact that wages have risen as a result of full employment, and this in turn has pushed up production costs. Many Mauritian clothing and textile companies are re-locating to cheaper production locations, notably to the nearby island of Madagascar, with which it shares a common language (French) and, to some extent, culture. The focus is also shifting towards high fashion garments as competition in the global market becomes stiffer.

The Mauritian government is also trying to promote a shift towards more high-tech industries, such as electronics, software development, and light engineering. As of the late 1990s, however, Mauritius had not been able to attract the level of foreign investment into these sectors that it had been hoping for. Other industries in Mauritius include food processing (mostly sugar milling), chemicals, metal products, transport equipment, and non-electrical machinery.

SERVICES

TOURISM. Tourism is a big foreign exchange earner for Mauritius, which has marketed itself as an "exclusive" destination. About 5 percent of GDP is derived from the tourism sector, and revenues currently amount to US$100 million per annum. Most visitors come from Europe— 66 percent of the market—with France and the UK providing 175,400 and 58,700 tourists, respectively. Africa's market share is 27 percent, with tourists coming mainly from South Africa and Reunion Island. About 17,111 people are employed in the tourism sector, 65 percent of these in the hotel industry. There are signs that growth in this sector is slowing: in 1999 the sector grew by just 6 percent, compared to double-digit figures prior to that.

FINANCIAL SERVICES. Over the past few years, the financial services sector has really stepped up its role in the economy, partly due to government support of the industry. To stimulate the development of the financial sector, the government provides tax incentives for financial institutions under the Pioneer Financial Services Scheme. To date, the industry has grown by over 62 percent, and comprises 13 percent of GDP. The aim is to develop the sector as a major financial center of international repute. Currently there are eleven **offshore banks**, which offer merchant banking, insurance, fund management, and securities services. Non-residents are the main customers of this sector, often U.S. companies with investments in India. A tax treaty between Mauritius and India creates tax advantages to companies with investments in India that channel their funds through Mauritius.

INFORMATION TECHNOLOGY. In early 2001, the government set out its National Information Technology Strategy Plan of establishing the information technology sector as a **free trade zone** with "digital parks." These parks will consist mainly of sophisticated telecommunications and IT infrastructure as well as enabling hassle-free access to the Internet. According to this plan, it is estimated that IT-penetration will increase to 50 percent and increase PC home ownership to 40 percent by 2005. The government still has to unveil its proposed package of financial incentives that will be offered in this regard.

INTERNATIONAL TRADE

Being a small island economy with few natural resources, trade is extremely important for Mauritius. Trade comprised 80 percent of GDP in 1970, increasing to 130 percent in 1998.

Mauritius's main export markets are the European Union (notably the United Kingdom, France, and Germany)

Trade (expressed in billions of US$): Mauritius

	Exports	Imports
1975	.298	.330
1980	.431	.609
1985	.436	.523
1990	1.194	1.618
1995	1.538	1.976
1998	1.734	2.183

SOURCE: International Monetary Fund. *International Financial Statistics Yearbook 1999.*

and the United States. Its imports come mainly from South Africa, India, the European Union, and China.

TRADE AGREEMENTS. Up to the year 2000, Mauritius's major exports, sugar and textiles, have benefitted substantially from preferential trade agreements under which exports from Mauritius face lower duties than those goods from other countries. Most of Mauritius's sugar is now exported to the European Union (EU) under the Sugar Protocol of the Lomé Convention, which allows the country an export quota of 300,000 metric tons, at a price which is generally quite a lot higher than that paid on the world market. Mauritian textiles have also benefitted from preferential access to EU markets, and from the Multi-Fibre Agreement.

However, the Lomé Convention expired in 2000, and the EU has decided to level access to its markets for developing countries, which will erode the preferential treatment received by former EU colonies such as Mauritius. The annual quota assigned to the African, Caribbean, and Pacific (ACP) countries will now be reduced and it is expected that the price received for sugar exports will also fall. This move is expected to hit Mauritius hard, as it is among the top 3 sugar exporters to the EU.

The Multi-Fibre Agreement is being phased out and will come to an end in 2005. The agreement works on a bilateral quota system designed both to protect clothing and textile manufacturers in developed countries and facilitate market access for developing countries. The impact on Mauritius will depend on whether the developed countries continue to try to protect their textile industries. In any event, the termination of the Multi-Fibre Agreement (MFA) is expected to result in intensified global competition in the clothing and textiles industries. As mentioned above, Mauritian clothing and textile companies are already moving to cheaper production locations in order to enhance their competitiveness. The U.S.'s Africa Growth and Opportunities Act is expected to benefit the Mauritian clothing and textile industry, and may mitigate the impact of the phasing out of the MFA.

In the 1970s, Mauritius followed a policy of import substitution, which involved protecting certain domestic industries from outside competition by keeping tariffs at high levels. This policy reduced the country's reliance on outside imports. However, following the global trend, Mauritius began to open up its markets for imports in the 1980s. Mauritius is a member of the World Trade Organization (WTO), and is therefore committed to certain WTO agreements, designed to promote free trade among nations. Mauritius is a member of the Common Market of Eastern and Southern Africa (COMESA), the Southern African Development Community (SADC), and the Indian Ocean Commission.

MONEY

The country's central bank is the Bank of Mauritius, while the commercial banking system is dominated by 2 banks, the Mauritius Commercial Bank and the State Bank of Mauritius. There are a number of other, smaller, banks in operation, however. There is an extensive ATM network across the island, and ATM-sharing mechanisms are now in place. Progress has also been made with regard to developing a better, electronically-based, national payment system.

The Mauritian Rupee has decreased in the value relative to the U.S. dollar, with the decline being fairly marked over the period 1996–98, where it depreciated by an average of 10.5 percent per year. There have been no dramatic **devaluations** or currency crises in the history of the country, however. **Inflation**, too, has remained at manageable levels, averaging 7.6 percent between 1990 and 1999.

There are no exchange controls in Mauritius, which means that both foreigners and locals can take an unlimited amount of money out of the country if they wish to do so.

The Stock Exchange of Mauritius (SEM) has been in operation since 1989. Its **market capitalization** is currently around US$1,643 million, with 48 listed companies. There are a further 80 companies listed on the "over-

Exchange rates: Mauritius

Mauritian rupees per US$1

Jan 2001	27.900
2000	26.250
1999	25.186
1998	22.993
1997	21.057
1996	17.948

SOURCE: CIA *World Factbook 2001* [ONLINE].

GDP per Capita (US$)

Country	1975	1980	1985	1990	1998
Mauritius	1,531	1,802	2,151	2,955	4,034
United States	19,364	21,529	23,200	25,363	29,683
South Africa	4,574	4,620	4,229	4,113	3,918
Comoros	N/A	499	544	516	403

SOURCE: United Nations. *Human Development Report 2000; Trends in human development and per capita income.*

the-counter" market. The trading activity taking place has increased substantially over the years, although it is still low by international standards.

POVERTY AND WEALTH

All Mauritians have benefitted from the country's prolonged economic growth, particularly from the significant reduction in unemployment. A 1992 national survey found that 10.6 percent of the population was living below the poverty line. World Bank estimates put the poverty rate in 1999 at about 5 percent, however. These figures are difficult to compare across countries, since different countries have different definitions of poverty. Primary school enrolment is now close to 100 percent, up from 79 percent in 1980. Education and health care are free, and all Mauritians have access to safe water and sanitation. Life expectancy has also increased from 66 years in 1980 to 71 in 1998. According to the CIA *World Factbook*, life expectancy is now 75 years for females and 67 years for males.

However, poverty and wealth are still delineated to some extent along racial lines. Descendants of the French plantation owners still control a major portion of the economy, in spite of the fact that they only comprise 2 percent of the population. The Creoles, on the other hand, are the ethnic group which faces the greatest hardships. The recent increase in unemployment may rekindle the racial tensions which seemed to disappear during Mauritius's prosperous years.

WORKING CONDITIONS

Trade unions are permitted in Mauritius and trade union membership stood at 106,000 in 1995, representing about 29 percent of wage and salary earners. Trade union activity has decreased as the population has become wealthier and unemployment has declined. Over the period 1990–1995, there were between 4 and 9 strikes annually.

The steady rise in unemployment between 1996 and 1999 signifies that much still has to be done to improve the skills profile of the workforce. As of 2000, the demand for skilled workers outstripped the supply, especially in fields such as marketing, management, accounting, and computing.

Women make up about 27 percent workforce, a relatively low proportion by international standards, although female labor force participation has increased since 1980. Women earn on average about half of what their male counterparts earn. The state provides welfare payments for the unemployed, and there is a social aid scheme for poor families. There is also a national pension scheme.

COUNTRY HISTORY AND ECONOMIC DEVELOPMENT

1510. Portuguese visit Mauritius, then an uninhabited island.

1598. Dutch settle on the island, introducing sugar cane.

1710. Dutch leave the island for the Cape of Good Hope in South Africa.

1715. French occupy the island. The building of the harbor of Port Louis, which then becomes the capital, takes place.

Household Consumption in PPP Terms

Country	All food	Clothing and footwear	Fuel and power[a]	Health care[b]	Education[b]	Transport & Communications	Other
Mauritius	21	8	13	3	13	10	32
United States	13	9	9	4	6	8	51
South Africa	N/A	N/A	N/A	N/A	N/A	N/A	N/A
Comoros	N/A	N/A	N/A	N/A	N/A	N/A	N/A

Data represent percentage of consumption in PPP terms.
[a]Excludes energy used for transport.
[b]Includes government and private expenditures.

SOURCE: World Bank. *World Development Indicators 2000.*

1810. British conquer the island.

1814. Mauritius formally ceded to the British in the Treaty of Paris. However, most of the French settlers remain on the island and are allowed to keep their customs, religions, and laws. The French plantation aristocracy retain their economic prominence and few British people come to the colony.

1835. Britain abolishes slavery (slaves had mainly come from Madagascar, Senegal, and Mozambique), amid much resistance from French plantation owners. This leads to importation of about 500,000 Indian indentured laborers to work in the sugar cane fields. The rapid development of infrastructure takes place and the British begin to provide free primary education.

1860s. The sugar economy begins to decline, due to increased sugar production in other countries and resultant lower prices. The opening of the Suez Canal in 1869 shifts trade routes away from the Indian Ocean.

1917. Indenture system formally ends.

1959. First elections under universal suffrage are held.

1968. Mauritius achieves independence. The country adopts a constitution based on British parliamentary system. A few weeks before independence, violence between Creoles and Muslims leaves 25 people dead and hundreds injured.

1970. Enactment of the Export Processing Zones Act.

1971. The Militant Movement of Mauritius (MMM) calls a number of debilitating strikes. A coalition government led by the Mauritius Labor Party (MLP; headed by Sir Seewoosagur Ramgoolam) promulgates the Public Order Act which bans many forms of political activity. A state of emergency lasts until 1976.

1982. MMM-led government gains power in elections, with Anerood Jugnauth as Prime Minister and Paul Bérenger as Finance Minister.

1983. Ruling coalition breaks up and new elections are held. Jugnauth's new party, the Militant Socialist Movement (MSM), joins with the MLP and the Mauritian Social Democrat Party to win the election comfortably.

1991. A coalition between the MSM and MMM wins the elections.

1992. The constitution is amended to make Mauritius a republic with the British Commonwealth.

2000. Anerood Jugnauth is reelected president as head of a coalition between the MSM and MMM.

FUTURE TRENDS

The World Bank notes that Mauritius faces several challenges in the near future due to rising unemployment and increasing external competition for export markets. These are: to improve the economic growth rate through higher productivity, to raise skill levels through better education, to encourage investment in new industries, and to reform the civil service. Reform of the education system in particular is a priority, since an increasing number of young people are entering the job market without the requisite qualifications. At the same time, the government is focusing on small and medium-sized enterprises as a strategy for promoting economic growth and unemployment.

The recent setback in economic growth has spurred an internal campaign against poverty on the island, resulting in the establishment of the Mauritius Trust Fund. The Trust will use its US$1.5 million budget to fund over 270 projects across the island and also in the neighboring Rodrigues Island. These projects are directed at infrastructure, education, social cohesion through social and cultural programs, as well as coordination of different programs of action. Also, the combined efforts of the Mauritian Women and Family Welfare Ministry are spreading a message to women to end poverty through education.

For business, however, the mood is optimistic. It is estimated that close to 53 percent of the population expects the volume of production and services to increase in the year 2001, according to local surveys.

DEPENDENCIES

Mauritius has no territories or colonies.

BIBLIOGRAPHY

Businessmap. *SADC Investor Survey: Complex Terrain.* Johannesburg, South Africa: Businessmap, 2000.

Economist Intelligence Unit. *Country Profile: Mauritius.* London: Economist Intelligence Unit, 2001.

International Labor Organization. *World Labor Report.* Geneva, Switzerland: ILO, 1997.

Library of Congress. *Mauritius: A Country Study.* <http://lcweb2.loc.gov/frd/es/mutoc.html>. Accessed August 2001.

Maurinet. "Mauritian History." <http://www.maurinet.com/history.html>. Accessed August 2001.

"Mauritius: Overview." *Mbendi: Information for Africa.* <http://www.mbendi.co.za/land/af/mr/p0005.htm>. Accessed August 2001.

Pochun, Jairaz. "Policies to Facilitate Trade and Investment in Southern Africa." In International Monetary Fund/Friedrich Ebert Stiftung, *Regional Economic Integration and the Globalisation Process.* Windhoek, Namibia: Gamsberg Macmillan, 1998.

South African National Treasury. *Regional Economic Review.* Pretoria, South Africa: FISCU, 2000.

U.S. Central Intelligence Agency. *World Factbook 2000.* <http://www.odci.gov/cia/publications/factbook/index.html>. Accessed August 2001.

U.S. Department of State. *FY 1998 Country Commercial Guide: Mauritius.* <http://www.state.gov/www/about_state/business/ com_guides/1998/africa/mauritius98.html>. Accessed August 2001.

World Bank. *The World Bank Group Countries: Mauritius.* <http://www.worldbank.org/afr/mu2.htm>. Accessed August 2001.

—Rosalind Mowatt

MOROCCO

Kingdom of Morocco
Al-Mamlakah al-Maghribiyah

CAPITAL: Rabat.

MONETARY UNIT: Moroccan dirham (Dh). One Moroccan dirham equals 100 centimes. There are coins of 1, 5, and 10 dirhams, and 10, 20, and 50 centimes. Notes come in denominations of 10, 20, 50, 100, and 200 dirhams.

CHIEF EXPORTS: Phosphates and fertilizers, food and beverages, minerals.

CHIEF IMPORTS: Semi-processed goods, machinery and equipment, food and beverages, consumer goods, fuel.

GROSS DOMESTIC PRODUCT: US$105 billion (purchasing power parity, 2000 est.).

BALANCE OF TRADE: **Exports:** US$7.6 billion (f.o.b., 2000 est.). **Imports:** US$12.2 billion (f.o.b., 1999 est.).

COUNTRY OVERVIEW

LOCATION AND SIZE. Morocco is located in the north-western corner of the African continent. It is bordered by the Atlantic Ocean to the west, the Mediterranean Sea to the north, and Algeria to the east and southeast. The Strait of Gibraltar separates it from Spain at its northern tip. Its southern border is the Sahara Desert. With an area of 446,550 square kilometers (172,413 square miles) and a coastline of 1,835 kilometers (1,140 miles), Morocco is slightly larger than California. Morocco's capital city, Rabat, is located in the northwest of the country overlooking the Atlantic Ocean. Other major cities are Casablanca on the Atlantic Ocean, Marrakech (the business capital) in the center, and Tangier in the north, on the Strait of Gibraltar.

POPULATION. Morocco's population was estimated at 30,122,350 in July of 2000, an increase of 1.2 percent from the 1990 population of 24,043,000. In 2000, Morocco's birth rate stood at 24.6 births per 1,000, while the death rate was reported at 6.02 per 1,000. The majority of the population are Muslim. Almost one-third of the population are Berbers, who are mostly concentrated in the Rif and Atlas mountains. Morocco has a sizeable community (1.7 million) of expatriates living abroad, mostly in France, Spain, and Italy.

The growth rate of Morocco's population has slowed down since the 1990s, averaging 1.6 percent between 1995 and 1999, down from 2.5 percent in the preceding decade. With a projected growth rate of 1.4 percent between 2000 and 2015, the population is expected to reach 41 million by 2029. The population is generally young, with some 23 percent under the age of 15. Like people in many developing countries, a majority of Moroccans live in urban areas. The population of urban areas has grown significantly since the 1960s. Casablanca, Marrakech, and other major urban centers are home to some 54.5 percent of the country's people.

OVERVIEW OF ECONOMY

Morocco's domestic economy is relatively diversified. The agricultural sector plays an important role, accounting for 15 to 20 percent of the GDP, depending on weather conditions. In 1999, the sector accounted for 15 percent of the GDP and employed some 50 percent of the **labor force**. The sector's output, however, varies from one year to another, due to its dependence on rainwater for irrigation. The largest contributor to the GDP is the services sector. The well-developed tourism and services sectors accounted for 52 percent of the GDP and employed 35 percent of the labor force in 1999. The expanding industrial sector has also become a major contributor to the GDP in recent years, accounting for 33 percent of the GDP in 1999. Industrial exports include textiles, clothing, shoes, and, most important, raw phosphates and processed products, including phosphoric acid and fertilizers. Morocco is the world's largest exporter of

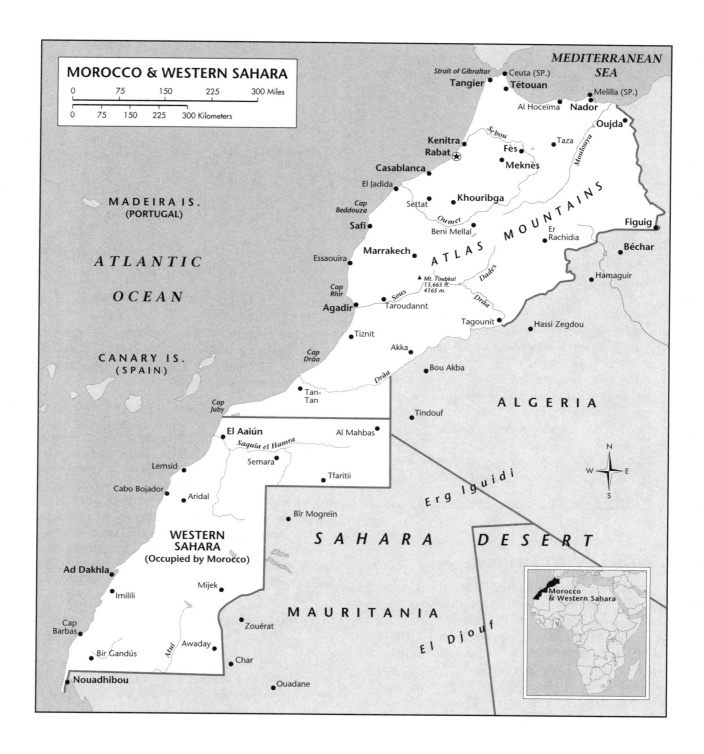

MOROCCO & WESTERN SAHARA

0   75   150   225   300 Miles

0   75   150   225   300 Kilometers

MEDITERRANEAN SEA

Strait of Gibraltar
Ceuta (SP.)
Tangier
Tétouan
Melilla (SP.)
Al Hoceima   Nador
Oujda
Kenitra
Rabat
Fès   Taza
Casablanca   Meknès
El Jadida
Settat   Khouribga
Cap Beddouza
Safi   Beni Mellal
Er Rachidia   Figuig
Marrakech   ATLAS MOUNTAINS
Essaouira   Béchar
Cap Rhir   Mt. Toubkal 13,665 ft. 4165 m.   Hamaguir
Agadir   Taroudannt
Tiznit   Tagounit   Hassi Zegdou
Akka
Cap Drâa   Bou Akba
Drâa
Tan-Tan   ALGERIA
Tindouf
El Aaiún   Al Mahbas
Saquia el Hamra
Lemsid   Semara
Cabo Bojador   Tfaritii
Aridal
Bîr Mogreïn   Erg Iguidi
WESTERN SAHARA (Occupied by Morocco)   SAHARA DESERT
Ad Dakhla
Imilili   Mijek
Cap Barbas   Zouérat   MAURITANIA
Bir Gandús   Awaday   El Djouf
Atui   Char
Nouadhibou
Ouadane

MADEIRA IS. (PORTUGAL)

ATLANTIC OCEAN

CANARY IS. (SPAIN)

Sebou
Moulouya
Oumer
Sous
Dades
Drâa

N   W   E   S

Morocco & Western Sahara

raw and processed phosphates, but the phosphates sector contributes only 3 percent to the GDP. The fishing sector is also important, employing some 300,000 people.

Morocco entered the 20th century as a colony divided between France and Spain, with France dominating the larger area. It continued to be under French control during World War II, and its demands for independence were not recognized until 1956, when Sultan Mohammed V was declared king of Morocco. Spain

relinquished its claims over Morocco around the same time but retained a small number of cities and territories. Mohammed's son, Hassan II, who succeeded his father in 1961 and ruled until 1999, is considered the father of modern Morocco.

Morocco is primarily a free-market country with some state control. The government has significantly reduced its role in the economy since the 1990s, removing trade barriers and selling several state-owned enterprises.

Despite occasional political violence, it has a fairly stable, multiparty political system headed by the king, and it enjoys the strong political and economic support of the United States and the European Union. Economic growth has been sluggish since the 1990s, partly as a result of dependence on agriculture, which has been affected by recurring droughts. The GDP real growth rate was estimated to be 0.8 percent in 2000. Mining, mostly of phosphates, is concentrated in Khourigba, Youssoufia, and the Western Saharan mine of Boucraa. Manufacturing, **retail** trade, and services are centered in urban centers, mostly Rabat and Casablanca.

Neither the agricultural sector nor the emerging industrial sector is capable of providing enough jobs to counteract Morocco's long-standing high unemployment rate. The problem of unemployment especially high among university graduates is exacerbated by the rapid population growth. Unemployment reached 19 percent in 1998; by contrast the unemployment rate in the United States in 1999 was 4.2 percent. Unemployment in urban areas is estimated to be higher than 22 percent. Although the government has made it a priority issue, unemployment will present a serious challenge for some time to come.

Morocco's **foreign debt** in 1999 was estimated at US$18.7 billion. About 50 percent is owed to state creditors within the Paris Club, a group of developed countries that extends credit and loans to developing countries, 30 percent is owed to international institutions, and 15 percent is owed to commercial banks, while the remaining 15 percent is owed to other creditors. The largest fraction of the Paris Club debt is with France (48 percent), followed by Spain and the United States, who each account for 15 percent. **Debt service** represents 24.5 percent of exports of goods and services. The country's debt burden has declined steadily since the mid-1990s: In 1992, Morocco rescheduled its debt to the Paris Club, and in 1996, the French and Spanish governments agreed to relieve part of the country's debts by converting them into investments.

Morocco's economic difficulties—trade imbalance and high unemployment—are offset by tourism receipts, **remittances** from its migrant workers abroad, and foreign investments. Some 2.35 million tourists visited the country in 1999, an 18-percent increase over the preceding year. Also in 1999, Moroccan workers, mostly in Europe, contributed some US$1.94 billion, a decline of 1.6 percent over the preceding year. Income from foreign investments tripled that year, mostly as a result of the sale of a mobile-phone license to a Spanish company.

Government bureaucracy is a major impediment to the conduct of business in Morocco. Bureaucratic inefficiencies permeate all government ministries and the commercial court system. Corruption is widespread at all levels of the **public sector**, largely as a result of low wages and difficult living conditions.

POLITICS, GOVERNMENT, AND TAXATION

After independence from France in 1956, a hereditary monarchy was established, which is now headed by King Mohammed VI, who succeeded his father and ruler of 38 years, King Hassan II, in July 1999. The country has had a multiparty system and an elected legislature since the 1970s. Morocco has more than a dozen legal political parties. The Constitutional Union (UC) Party and the National Rally of Independents (RNI) are the 2 largest. Both are conservative and pro-monarchy and together traditionally provide a near majority in parliament to back the government. Although the king tolerates the opposition, he is quick to suppress groups on the political fringe. Even members of legal political groups, such as the small, leftist Party of Progress and Socialism (PPS), have been targeted periodically for crackdowns by security forces.

Ultimate power rests with the king, who is chief of state and appoints the prime minister, all cabinet ministers, and all supreme-court judges. A new constitution, designed by the late King Hassan II in 1996 and approved by a public referendum that same year, established a **bicameral** parliament, replacing the previous system in which two-thirds of a 333-member **unicameral** parliament (Majlis Anouwab) were elected by popular vote. Under the new constitution, all members of parliament are now elected.

A program to reform the economy was launched in 1992 with the help of the World Bank. The objective was to **privatize** state-owned companies, enhance the country's economic management, raise productivity, and reduce its soaring **budget deficit**. The program gained new momentum under the government of Abderrahmane Youssoufi, who has served as prime minister since 1998. The current government, a coalition of **socialist**, left-of-center, and nationalist parties and, for the first time in years, opposition parties, has launched a campaign to reform business laws and regulations and draft a new labor law. The judicial system and intellectual property rights legislation have already been revamped. Overall, however, the pace of Morocco's privatization program has been rather slow; only 60 out of 114 state companies identified for privatization in 1993 had been privatized by 2001. Plans are underway to sell off the government's shares in Maroc Telecom and Banque Centrale Populaire, the largest bank, primarily to a group of foreign investors.

Taxes and custom **duties** are a major source of government revenue, accounting for 42 percent of income. Customs duties account for 14 percent of revenue, while

direct taxation accounts for the remaining 28 percent. Morocco's tax system, reformed in 1984, consists of a wide variety of taxes including the 20 percent **value-added tax** (VAT), which was instituted in December 1985, a 35 percent corporate tax, general **income tax** and return-on-shares tax, effective since December 1986.

One of the major items on Morocco's international agenda is its claim to the Western Sahara. The region is a vast stretch of inhospitable land containing large phosphate reserves. Ever since former colonial power Spain abandoned the region in 1975, it has been the site of an insurgency led by the pro-independence Popular Front for the Liberation of Saquia Al Hamra and Rio De Oro (Polisario). A United Nations vote on the future of the territory, originally scheduled for January 1992, has been repeatedly deferred due to unresolved arguments over voter eligibility and registration.

INFRASTRUCTURE, POWER, AND COMMUNICATIONS

Morocco enjoys one of the most highly developed infrastructures in Africa. The country is served by a network of 57,847 kilometers (35,946 miles) of primary and secondary roads, of which 30,254 kilometers (18,800 miles) are paved. With growing numbers of licensed automobiles, the road system, especially in urban areas, has become highly congested. According to official statistics, road accidents claim up to 3,000 lives annually. Plans are currently underway to modernize the country's railway system, which plays an important role in the transport of phosphates and their derivatives.

Morocco has 70 airports, 11 of which are major and quite modern, and efforts are underway to modernize all of them in 2001. The largest of them, an international airport just south of Casablanca, offers flights to several destinations in Europe, the United States, Canada, the Middle East and Africa. It is serviced by more than 50 airlines that bring in most of the country's tourists. Rabat has 24

ports, which handle 98 percent of the Morocco's foreign trade. The port of Casablanca is a world-class port and the second largest in Africa. In addition to goods, Morocco's ports also service tourist ferries to and from Spain and France.

Electrical power is provided by the state-owned Office National de L'électricité (National Office of Electricity, ONE). Despite the recent discovery of modest amounts of oil reserves in Morocco, most electricity is produced from imported fuels, mainly from Saudi Arabia. Morocco's total power capacity is estimated at 13.16 billion kilowatts, 124 million of which are imported, mainly from Spain. Power shortages are common. The government is planning to build additional power plants and boost electric capacity by the end of 2010 to meet the increasing demands of industrial projects and extend electric services to currently unserved rural areas. About 80 percent of Morocco's rural areas are not electrified, and it is estimated that some 12 million rural inhabitants live without electricity.

Telecommunications services in Morocco are thoroughly modern and have greatly improved since the mid-1990s. Most telephone service is provided by the state-owned Maroc Telecom and Meditel, the country's two largest telephone companies. The country had 1,455,853 phone lines at the end of 1999. Mobile service is also available. In 1999, Morocco had 27 Internet Service Providers.

ECONOMIC SECTORS

Morocco's economic sectors reflect the diversified and growing base of the economy. Its economy depends on output from the agricultural sector, rich fisheries, growing tourist and manufacturing industries, and a dynamic telecommunications sector.

In 1999, the agricultural sector accounted for 15 percent of the GDP and employed some 50 percent of the

Communications

Country	Newspapers	Radios	TV Sets[a]	Cable subscribers[a]	Mobile Phones[a]	Fax Machines[a]	Personal Computers[a]	Internet Hosts[b]	Internet Users[b]
	1996	1997	1998	1998	1998	1998	1998	1999	1999
Morocco	26	241	160	N/A	4	0.7	2.5	0.28	50
United States	215	2,146	847	244.3	256	78.4	458.6	1,508.77	74,100
Egypt	40	324	122	N/A	1	0.5	9.1	0.28	200
Algeria	38	241	105	0.0	1	0.2	4.20	0.01	20

[a]Data are from International Telecommunication Union, *World Telecommunication Development Report 1999* and are per 1,000 people.
[b]Data are from the Internet Software Consortium (http://www.isc.org) and are per 10,000 people.

SOURCE: World Bank. *World Development Indicators 2000.*

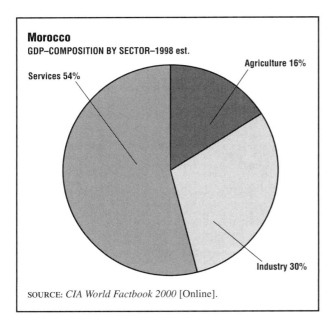

Morocco
GDP–COMPOSITION BY SECTOR–1998 est.

Services 54%

Agriculture 16%

Industry 30%

SOURCE: *CIA World Factbook 2000* [Online].

and processed products, including phosphoric acid and fertilizers, but Morocco also exports textiles, clothing, and shoes. Although Morocco is the world's largest exporter of raw and processed phosphates, the phosphates sector overall contributes only 3 percent to the GDP. The fishing sector is also an important sector of the economy, employing some 300,000 people.

Despite its diverse and vibrant economic base, Morocco's economic growth has been sluggish since the mid-1990s, mainly due to its dependence on rain-fed agriculture and other structural problems that affect economic performance, such as bureaucratic red tape and a soaring budget deficit. Recognizing these structural problems, the government has moved to **deregulate** the telecommunications sectors and to privatize several state-owned companies.

AGRICULTURE

FARMING. The labor-intensive agricultural sector is largely underdeveloped and inefficient, as a result of the high cost of energy, credit, and land, and a scarcity of investment. Only 1 million hectares of a total of 8.7 million hectares of cultivated land are irrigated. About 90 percent of the land, mostly comprised of small land holdings, is dependent on rainwater. A small fraction of the cultivated land, some 1 million hectares is comprised of modern export-oriented farms that produce 80 percent of Morocco's citrus and wine production, 33 percent of its vegetable output, and 15 percent of its cereals production. These irrigated farms, concentrated in the Gharb plain around Fez and Meknes, the Doukkala plain around Casablanca, and the Beni Mellal and Berkane areas, also produce tomatoes, potatoes, and beet and cane sugar, as well as oil and olive oil for export. In addition to legal agricultural products, Morocco is a major producer and exporter of cannabis (marijuana), which is mostly concentrated in the northern Rif region.

labor force. The sector's output varies from one year to another due to its dependence on rainwater for irrigation; in a good year, it can account for 20 percent of total the GDP. The largest contributor to GDP is the services sector. The well-developed tourism and services industries accounted for 52 percent of the GDP and employed 35 percent of the labor force in 1999. The expanding industrial sector has also become a major contributor to GDP in recent years, accounting for 33 percent of the GDP and employing 15 percent of the workforce in 1999. The most important industrial exports are raw phosphates

Major agricultural products include dairy products, meat, fruit, and vegetables, in which Morocco is self-sufficient. Morocco is also a producer of grains, which are grown on 68 percent of the cultivated land, plus sugar, oils and tea, but production is rarely sufficient to meet domestic demand. As a result, and depending on annual winter rainfall, Morocco imports the bulk of its cereals. According to the EIU, harvests range from around 10 million to under 2 million metric tons annually and have averaged 5.8 million metric tons since 1990. Agriculture production has dropped significantly since 1998, due to drought conditions, prompting the government to increase customs duties on wheat imports to protect local farmers.

FISHERIES. The fishing industry is also a major contributor to the economy, accounting for an average of

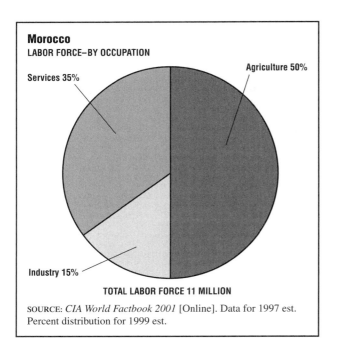

Morocco
LABOR FORCE–BY OCCUPATION

Services 35%

Agriculture 50%

Industry 15%

TOTAL LABOR FORCE 11 MILLION

SOURCE: *CIA World Factbook 2001* [Online]. Data for 1997 est. Percent distribution for 1999 est.

US$600 million in export earnings. Morocco's fishing industry is underdeveloped and is forced to compete with European companies. It is also overexploited, which has prompted the government to impose periodic bans on the harvesting certain types of fish. Since 1997, the government has been attempting to revamp and upgrade the fishing industry. Several new ports, at Dakhla, Boujdour and Layoun, among other places, are to be built as part of the plan, and the government is reportedly seeking **joint ventures** with foreign investors, mainly in Japan and France, to replace the government's fisheries agreement with the European Union, which expired at the end of 1999.

INDUSTRY

MINING. Phosphates account for 95 percent of Morocco's output by volume. mining. Phosphates, raw and manufactured, are the country's main exports, managed by the state-owned Office Cherifien des Phosphates. The export of phosphates and phosphate products accounted for US$1.4 billion in 1999, or about 18.5 percent of total earnings from exports. With three-quarters of the earth's phosphate reserves after the United States and Russia (11 billion metric tons of known reserves and 58 billion metric tons of probable reserves), Morocco is the world's third largest producer of phosphates and the largest exporter of phosphate rock. Phosphates are mined in Khouribga, Youssoufia, and the Western Saharan mine of Boucraa and Benguerir. A new mine at El Gantour, south of Rabat, will soon start production. Phosphate revenue has increased steadily since 1996, the first profitable year for the industry, reaching US$44 per metric ton in 1999, up from US$33–35 per metric ton in 1993–95. Mining and processing capacity have increased steadily over the past years, and a 30-percent expansion is planned in 2001. Since 1996, the government has shifted focus toward marketing its phosphate products through joint ventures with foreign companies, mainly French and Belgian.

In addition to phosphates, Morocco is a major producer and exporter of industrial minerals and base metals. It produces silver, zinc, cobalt, copper, fluorine, lead, barite, iron, and anthracite. In contrast to the state-controlled phosphate sector, the extraction and processing of most of these minerals is in private hands, and efforts are currently underway to privatize the rest, especially the silver and lead mines, by 2002. A comprehensive survey of minerals across the country is also underway with the help of French, British, South African, and Canadian companies

MANUFACTURING. The manufacturing sector is an important and growing contributor to the Moroccan economy. The sector has steadily grown by an average of 1.9 percent a year between 1994 and 1998. Production increased by 2.8 percent in 1999 and is likely to maintain that upward trend in 2001. The government adopted a new investment law in 1981 to encourage domestic and foreign investment in the industrial sector. These efforts gained added momentum with the launch of the privatization program in the early 1990s. A plan to modernize the sector and upgrade existing companies to meet European standards was launched in 1997. These efforts have been largely successful in attracting foreign investment. Major U.S. companies, such as Microsoft, Compaq, and Oracle, have a presence in the country.

Manufacturing industries are mainly concentrated in Casablanca, Fez, Rabat, Tangier, and Settat. In recent years, considerable investment has been made in cement works and sugar factories to meet the major part of local demand. Plans are also underway to develop steel production in the city of Nador and the production of chemicals and fertilizers in the El Jadida region. Morocco's industrial base consists mostly of food processing, textiles, pharmaceuticals, and the processing of phosphate rock into phosphoric acid and fertilizers. Since the early 1980s, the output of textile production, mostly done under contract with European companies, has grown by 5 times, from US$120 million in 1980 to US$570 million in 1990. Growth in the clothing sector slowed down in the late 1990s, due to declining domestic purchasing power and lower world demand, but the sector is expected to continue to grow in the future. The pharmaceutical industry, which mostly relies on imported raw material, is also a growing sector, although most of its output is consumed domestically.

SERVICES

TOURISM. Tourism is important to the health of the Moroccan economy, generating approximately US$1.98 billion and employing some 600,000 people in 2000. Tourism is Morocco's second greatest foreign-currency earner after remittances by Moroccan expatriates and has been identified as the second most important growth sector in the country. The tourism sector's growth, however, has been stifled by a combination of factors, including the lack of investment in hotel capacity and personnel training. Regional events, such as the civil war in neighboring Algeria, have also adversely affected the sector, as evidenced in the decline in the number of tourists in 1991 out of concerns about the spillover of the conflict into Morocco.

Since the mid-1990s, however, the government has moved to revitalize the sector by attracting foreign capital, rescheduling part of hotel debts, and reducing the tax burden. The government also plans to set up a special tourist police force to insure safety. Several state-owned hotels were sold to private investors, mainly foreign companies from France and the United Kingdom. Worldwide hotel chains, such as the Sheraton, Hilton and Intercontinental, have a presence in Morocco, but the majority of hotels are locally owned. The government has been actively encouraging the development of tourism, mainly in the cities of Agadir and Marrakech. As a result, a 10 percent increase in the number of tourists visiting the country was recorded in 1998. Plans are currently underway to double the number of tourists to 4 million and raise gross revenue to US$6 billion by 2005.

FINANCIAL SERVICES. Morocco's banking system is comprehensive. Despite government efforts since the early 1990s to reform the financial sector and improve banking regulations, restrictions continue to be in place, especially on the movement of capital. The conversion of the dirham into a **fully convertible currency**, originally set for 1997, has also been delayed. Morocco requires the majority shares in commercial banks to be owned by Moroccans. Most of the country's 14 commercial banks are partly owned by European banks. Since 1996, foreign banks have been able to buy and sell foreign currency at market rates, due to the new interbank foreign exchange market set up that same year.

Morocco has a single stock exchange, the Bourse Valeurs de Casablanca, which is the third largest in Africa after South Africa and Cairo. The market, managed by 13 brokerage companies, was privatized in 1996 and has been regulated by an independent commission since. Although full foreign participation in the market is allowed, foreign investments constitute only 10 percent of overall investment. At the end of 1999, the Casablanca stock exchange recorded a 5.2 percent correction, largely due to previous overvaluation. Efforts were underway in 2001 to attract foreign investment by upgrading its **infrastructure**.

CONSTRUCTION. The construction sector is one of the fastest growing sectors of the economy. Growth in this sector has been fueled by public works (construction by the government) and the private construction of affordable housing units to alleviate the chronic shortages in housing, especially in urban areas. In 1994, the government launched an ambitious construction project to build 200,000 housing units. Although the program has failed to reach its target, the construction activity is likely to continue. New internationally funded initiatives were announced in 1999. These include a US$80 million project funded by the U.S. Agency for International Development to construct new housing to replace shantytowns in major cities and a US$75 million construction project to rehabilitate the city of Fez.

RETAIL. Morocco has a poorly developed retail sector. While the major cities sport a variety of retail stores, including fast-food franchises such as McDonald's, which operate alongside souks (traditional markets), most towns in the interior of the country have small family-owned shops, farmers' markets, and temporary roadside stands.

INTERNATIONAL TRADE

Over the past several decades, Morocco has relied more and more on imports, and has maintained a steady trade balance as a result. The value of imports in 1999 was estimated US$12.2 billion, but exports were estimated to be only US$7.6 billion in 2000. **Capital goods** (industrial and semi-finished products) account for well more than half of Morocco's imports, followed by food and beverages, **consumer goods**, and fuel. Morocco's export base is diversified, with phosphates and phosphate byproducts being the largest contributor, accounting for one-third of exports. Textiles and leather items come in second place, followed by fish and fish products.

Morocco exports and imports most of its goods from the European Union, with France being its largest trade partner, providing one-fifth of total imports and accounting for one-quarter of exports. Spain comes in second place, followed by the United States, Italy, and Saudi Arabia. Morocco initialed a free-trade accord with the European Free Trade Association in 1997, which stipulates the elimination of trade barriers in industrial goods by 2010.

The substantial and growing trade imbalance that Morocco endured over the years has been partially offset by tourist receipts and remittances sent home by Moroccans working abroad. Morocco is a member of the World Trade Organization, which has stipulated that **tariffs** on goods be lifted. The government has moved to gradually reform the trade sector and remove barriers to export by approving a new foreign trade law that minimizes the state's role in the export of goods and that **liberalizes** import practices. The government's dependence on tariffs largely explains its reluctance to proceed with the implementation of trade reform. As a result, Morocco continues to run a **trade deficit** that forces it to borrow heavily to pay for its consumption.

Trade (expressed in billions of US$): Morocco

	Exports	Imports
1975	1.543	2.567
1980	2.493	4.164
1985	2.165	3.849
1990	4.265	6.800
1995	6.881	10.023
1998	7.219	10.262

SOURCE: International Monetary Fund. *International Financial Statistics Yearbook 1999.*

Exchange rates: Morocco

Moroccan dirhams per US$1

Jan 2001	10.590
2000	10.626
1999	9.804
1998	9.604
1997	9.527
1996	8.716

SOURCE: CIA *World Factbook 2001* [ONLINE].

Distribution of Income or Consumption by Percentage Share: Morocco

Lowest 10%	2.6
Lowest 20%	6.5
Second 20%	10.6
Third 20%	14.8
Fourth 20%	21.3
Highest 20%	46.6
Highest 10%	30.9

Survey year: 1998–99

Note: This information refers to expenditure shares by percentiles of the population and is ranked by per capita expenditure.

SOURCE: *2000 World Development Indicators* [CD-ROM].

MONEY

The value of the Moroccan dirham has remained relatively stable since 1990, trading at an average of 8.54 against the U.S. dollar between 1990 and 1996. Until 1996, the central bank, Bank Al-Maghrib, set the **exchange rate** of the dirham against a group of currencies of its main trading partners. Since 1996, the government has allowed the exchange rate to fluctuate within certain limits based on the same group of foreign currencies. European currencies in the mix carry a larger weight than other currencies. This arrangement makes the dollar more volatile than the European currencies against the dirham. As a result of a stronger dollar, the value of the Moroccan dirham has depreciated by an average of 19 percent against the dollar, while the euro has fallen more than 27 percent against the dollar since January 1999. The government has refused to **devaluate** the dirham. In January 2000, the exchange rate was 10.051 dirhams to US$1.

POVERTY AND WEALTH

Living standards in Morocco are low by international standards and have declined continually since the early 1990s. As a result, the number of Moroccans living below the poverty line has risen sharply in the last decade. Although poverty levels dropped to 13 percent in 1991, some 19 percent of the population lived below the poverty line in 2000. Despite widespread poverty, uneven development has led to the emergence of an affluent class that

controls most of the country's wealth and enjoys an elevated standard of living. In 1998, the wealthiest 20 percent of Moroccans controlled 46.6 percent of the country's wealth, while the poorest 20 percent controlled only 6.5 percent of wealth.

Poverty is more widespread in rural areas than in urban areas. Some 36 percent of Moroccans living in rural areas are poor, while poverty affects 24 percent of urban dwellers. Children under 15 are the most heavily impacted by poverty. Inequality in the distribution of wealth coincides with geographical regions. Historically, the Casablanca-Rabat axis has been more prosperous and has received more government attention than the predominantly mountainous northern provinces and the Western Sahara region. Although the latter region has received government attention since the 1990s because of its phosphate deposits, the northern provinces, which include the Rif Mountains, home to 6 million Moroccans, have been largely neglected. This region is a haven for the cultivation of cannabis. In 1998, the government launched a program to develop the northern region, largely with international help. Spain has shown particular interest in the development of the region, since its underdevelopment has fueled illegal **immigration** and drug trafficking across the Strait of Gibraltar.

The uneven development among Morocco's regions has also fueled a cycle of rural-urban migration that has shown no signs of slowing down. Currently, an estimated 60 percent of population live in urban areas, 35 percent higher than the urban population of 1971. Low standards of living have also forced many young Moroccans to seek employment opportunities abroad, especially in Spain and other parts of Europe.

Both Moroccan rural and urban poor have suffered from a long decline in the quality of social services, especially educational and medical. Despite this deterioration, 50 percent of primary-level students are enrolled in

GDP per Capita (US$)

Country	1975	1980	1985	1990	1998
Morocco	956	1,114	1,173	1,310	1,388
United States	19,364	21,529	23,200	25,363	29,683
Egypt	516	731	890	971	1,146
Algeria	1,460	1,692	1,860	1,638	1,521

SOURCE: United Nations. *Human Development Report 2000; Trends in human development and per capita income.*

Household Consumption in PPP Terms

Country	All food	Clothing and footwear	Fuel and power[a]	Health care[b]	Education[b]	Transport & Communications	Other
Morocco	33	11	16	5	15	6	16
United States	13	9	9	4	6	8	51
Egypt	44	9	7	3	17	3	17
Algeria	N/A	N/A	N/A	N/A	N/A	N/A	N/A

Data represent percentage of consumption in PPP terms.
[a]Excludes energy used for transport.
[b]Includes government and private expenditures.
SOURCE: World Bank. *World Development Indicators 2000.*

schools, and a government-funded system insures that all Moroccans have access to adequate health care.

Although the government continues to subsidize basic consumer goods and health products, the middle and lower classes have seen their living standards erode since the 1980s. The government's awareness of the political implications in a complete lifting of **subsidies** has slowed down the pace of the implementation of IMF-mandated price deregulation.

WORKING CONDITIONS

In the last few decades, Morocco's labor force has been growing at the very fast rate of 300,000 per year. In 1999, Morocco's labor force stood at 11 million, up from 8.9 million in 1990. The official unemployment rate for 1998 was 19 percent, a figure that is believed to be higher than unofficial figures. The CIA *World Factbook* estimated that the unemployment rate was 23 percent in 1999. Unemployment rates have risen in recent years as a result of the **restructuring** of the economy, which has forced many companies to reduce the number of employees.

Morocco's labor force generally lacks proper job training and secondary education, which explains why much of the younger workforce cannot expect high-paying jobs. Despite higher rates of school enrollment since the 1960s, illiteracy in Morocco is one of the highest in the Arab world, standing at 56.3 percent in 1998 (69 percent for women and 43.3 percent for men). The educational sector remains overburdened and under-staffed, and shortages in technical skills are viewed as a major impediment to business operations. The official unemployment rate in urban areas for 1999 was 22 percent, up from 17 percent in 1997. Unemployment remains especially high in urban areas, especially for women and for all workers under 34 years of age. Unemployment is also higher for university graduates and diploma holders.

Moroccan trade unions played a crucial role in the independence movement. Approximately 450,000 workers are unionized, mostly in the public sector, representing 5 percent of the labor force. The influence of the Moroccan labor union movement has shrunk considerably since independence. The once powerful movement is comprised of 17 trade-union federations, but real political clout is in the hands of 3 unions only. Although labor laws protecting the right of workers have been in place for decades, regulations are rarely enforced, and working conditions in Morocco are far from ideal. Labor actions, strikes, slowdowns, and protests frequently disturb work life, and are often met with repressive governmental actions and police brutality.

The government of Morocco supports workers' rights promoted by the International Labor Organization (ILO) and has set conditions governing industrial and human relations and established minimum-wage standards. The 5-day 48-hour workweek is the standard. The government-mandated minimum wage in the public sector is approximately US$165 a month. The government provides social-security benefits that include a retirement pension and pay for on-the-job injuries. Wages have increased steadily over the last few years and are expected to increase again, as the 2001–02 budget has allocated US$10 billion for public sector workers' salaries and bonuses. However, it was not until the late 1990s had the rate of increase in public wages has exceeded the rate of **inflation**.

COUNTRY HISTORY AND ECONOMIC DEVELOPMENT

1904. France and Spain conclude a secret agreement that divides Morocco into zones of French and Spanish influence, with France controlling almost all of Morocco and Spain controlling the small southwestern portion, which became known as Spanish Sahara.

1906. Algeciras Conference takes place. The sultan of Morocco maintains control of his lands, and France's privileges are curtailed.

1912. The sultan of Morocco, Moulay Abd al-Hafid, permits French protectorate status.

1953. Sultan Mohammed V is deposed by the French and replaced by his uncle.

1955. Sultan Mohammed V returns to power as a result of popular pressure.

1956. France and Spain recognize Morocco's independence.

1961. Sultan Mohammed's son, Hassan II, ascends to the throne.

1976. Spain withdraws from Western Sahara.

1979. Mauritania withdraws from the rest of the Western Sahara. The rebellious Polisario Front wages a war for independence and clashes with Moroccan police.

1981. King Hassan agrees to a ceasefire in Western Sahara.

1992. Government launches economic reform program.

1996. Association Accord is signed with the European Union.

1997. Parliamentary elections take place.

1998. King Hassan appoints a new leftist government headed by Prime Minister Abderrahmane Youssoufi.

1999. King Hassan II dies; his son, Prince Sidi Mohammed is crowned King Mohammed VI.

FUTURE TRENDS

Morocco entered the 21st century in economic decline. For much of the last century, state control of the economy had reduced the economy to shambles. However, the economic reform programs of the early 1990s have set the stage for partial economic recovery. Some progress has been achieved as the government has curtailed spending, increased privatization, reduced trade barriers, and stopped direct credit and foreign exchange allocation. In addition, Morocco's trade position should improve as its major trade partners in Europe experience growth and the economic recovery in Asia.

The pace of Morocco's economic reform program, however, has been rather slow. Despite major reform efforts, the public sector continues to be an important force in the economy. Long-term challenges include servicing the country's **external debt**, further privatizing state-owned enterprises, and attracting foreign investment. More important, the government is faced with the daunting challenge of improving living standards, which have steadily declined over the last few decades, creating new job prospects for the youth, who account for over 50 percent of the population. If left unresolved, the problem of unemployment may potentially become a source of political instability and a credible challenge to the regime.

DEPENDENCIES

Morocco has no territories or colonies.

BIBLIOGRAPHY

Economist Intelligence Unit. *Country Profile: Morocco.* London: Economist Intelligence Unit, 2000.

Horton, Brendan. *Morocco: Analysis and Reform of Economic Policy.* Washington, DC: World Bank, 1990.

"Morocco." *Tradeport.* <http://www.tradeport.org/ts/countries/morocco/trends.html>. Accessed February, 2001.

U.S. Central Intelligence Agency. *World Factbook 2001.* <http://www.cia.gov/cia/publications/factbook>. Accessed October 2001.

U.S. Department of State. *FY 2001 Country Commercial Guide: Morocco.* <http://www.state.gov/www/issues/economic/trade_reports/neareast98/morocco98.html>. Accessed February 2001.

—Reem Nuseibeh

MOZAMBIQUE

Republic of Mozambique
República de Moçambique

COUNTRY OVERVIEW

LOCATION AND SIZE. Located in southeast Africa, Mozambique has a total area of 801,590 square kilometers (309,493 square miles)—an expanse which is slightly less than twice the size of the state of California. The coastline of the country, which spans 2,470 kilometers (1,535 miles) along the entire eastern frontier, borders the Mozambique Channel and the Indian Ocean. To the north of Mozambique lies Tanzania, to the northwest Malawi and Zambia, to the west Zimbabwe, and to the southwest South Africa and Swaziland. Maputo, the capital of Mozambique, is situated at the pointy southern tip of the country's territory, not far from the South African and Swaziland border.

POPULATION. From 1975 to 1998, the population of Mozambique grew at an average annual rate of 2.6 percent, increasing substantially from approximately 10.5 to 18.9 million. With a current annual growth rate of 1.7 percent, the population should reach 25.2 million by 2015. In order to restrain this growth, the government announced a population control policy in 1997. Among other things, the plan seeks to disseminate information on different forms of birth control. One of the major impediments, however, is that most people in rural areas must have large families in order to have more workers to till the family plots. According to a 1997 census, approximately 70.8 percent of the population live in rural areas, where poverty is rampant and birth control limited.

The current birth rate in Mozambique is 37.99 births per 1,000 persons, while the death rate is 23.29 deaths per 1,000 persons (2000 est.). The high death rate reflects, in part, a growing HIV/AIDS epidemic. The Health Minister Aurelio Zihao, for example, estimated that approximately 250,000 Mozambicans died as a result of AIDS in 1999, though most of these deaths were not registered as HIV/AIDS related. Zihao states that the major causes behind the HIV/AIDS epidemic are poverty, unemployment, illiteracy, and the low status of women. The educational campaign sponsored by the Health Ministry targets vulnerable groups, such as soldiers, long-distance truck drivers, students, poorly educated women, street children, migrant mineworkers and their wives, and prostitutes. The government at large has been criticized for not taking an active role in the HIV/AIDS campaign.

With 43 percent of the population aged 14 years and younger, 54 percent aged between 15 and 64 years, and only 3 percent aged 65 years and over, the population of Mozambique is relatively young. A young population may offer opportunities in terms of an expanding **labor force** and thus a potentially expanding economy. If economic decline accompanies labor force growth, however, the results will be higher unemployment and exacerbated poverty.

Approximately 99.66 percent of the Mozambican population belong to one of the many indigenous (local) ethnic groups, such as the Shangaan, Chokwe,

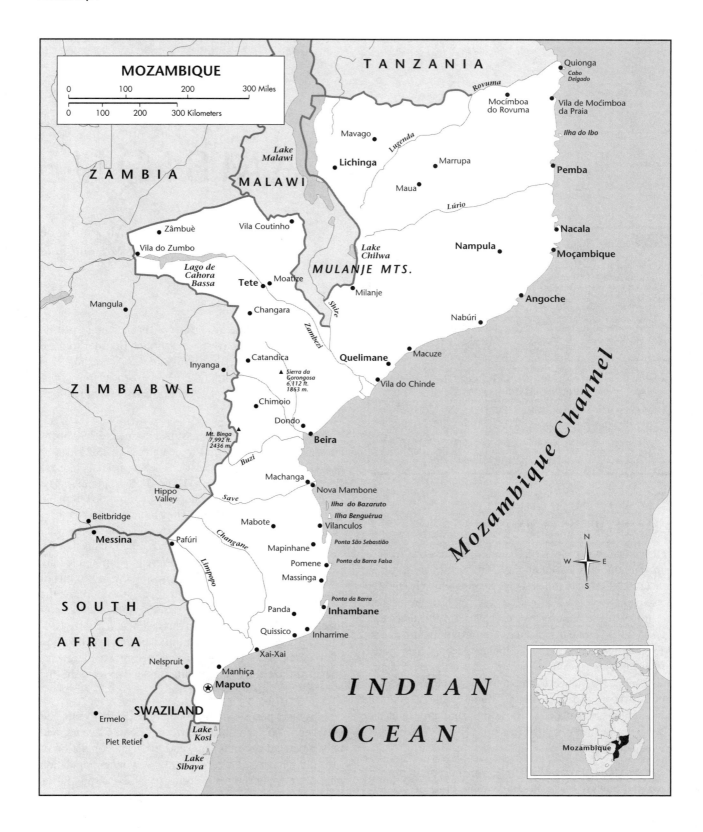

Manyika, Sena, and Makua. Europeans comprise a marginal 0.06 percent of the population, while Euro-Africans and Indians respectively account for 0.2 percent and 0.08 percent. In terms of religion, 50 percent of Mozambicans are adherents of indigenous religious systems, 30 percent are Christians, and 20 percent are Muslims. The official language of Mozambique is Portuguese, though most Mozambicans express themselves primarily in one of the numerous local languages that are spoken.

OVERVIEW OF ECONOMY

Although the Portuguese participated in the trading networks of southeastern Africa as early as the 16th century, they did not establish hegemonic (total) colonial dominance over the territory that now comprises Mozambique until the early 20th century. By the mid-1920s, the Portuguese succeeded in creating a highly exploitative and coercive settler economy, in which Africans were forced to work on the fertile lands taken over by Portuguese settlers. African peasants mainly produced **cash crops** designated for sale in the markets of the colonial metropole (the center, i.e. Portugal). Major cash crops included cotton, cashews, and rice. The little industrial development that did occur throughout the 1950s and early 1960s was based primarily on British and South African capital.

In 1975, a coup in Portugal led to the overthrow of the fascist dictatorship that governed the nation, and thus an end to the colonial wars that raged in the various Portuguese African colonies since the early 1960s. Mozambique became an independent nation and the Frente de Libertacao de Mocambique (FRELIMO), the **socialist** guerrilla organization that had fought the colonial war against Portugal, assumed power. Over the next several years, FRELIMO pursued numerous socialist policies, including **nationalization** of land and large industries, centralized planning, and heavy funding for the educational and health sectors. At the same time, the government encouraged the large network of cantinas (tiny shops), which were owned by Portuguese settlers, to remain in the hands of the **private sector**. The exodus (mass departure) of the Portuguese following independence facilitated the takeover of the cantinas by Mozambicans. Unfortunately, the exodus, which totaled 250,000 Portuguese, also led to a huge loss of professionals, productive machinery, and skilled workers.

By the early 1980s, Mozambique became what Joseph Hanlon—author of *Peace Without Profit: How the IMF Blocks Rebuilding in Mozambique*—called a "Cold War battlefield." The term refers to the situation in which socialist Mozambique was forced to fight a lengthy civil war against a counterinsurgency movement of opportunistic Mozambicans named RENAMO, funded and directed by the neighboring capitalist economies of South Africa and Zimbabwe. (The cold war was defined by animosity between capitalist and socialist world powers, and though there was never an outright military conflict between the former and the latter, each respectively funded counterinsurgency movements against governments they disfavored.) The racist governments of South Africa and Zimbabwe feared that a successfully ruled African socialist system might send a message of revolution and self-rule to blacks in contemporaneous white-ruled African countries, such as their own. Under the socialist paranoia of the Reagan administration, the United

States also provided support to RENAMO, which sustained a brutal civil war against FRELIMO until a Peace Accord was signed in October 1992.

According to Hans Abrahamsson and Anders Nilsson, authors of *Mozambique The Troubled Transition: From Socialist Construction to Free Market Capitalism*, RENAMO's methods of recruiting soldiers consisted mainly of coercing peasants to join their forces through threats, torture, and killing. RENAMO's war against the government led to the death of more than 1 million Mozambicans, not to mention a total loss of the economic and social gains that had been achieved in the late 1970s. In 1989, UNICEF estimated that the country's **GDP** was only half of what it would have been without the war.

The political pressure of the ideologically charged civil war, in conjunction with the excruciating need for aid and funds to finance imports, compelled FRELIMO to negotiate its first structural adjustment package (SAP) with the World Bank and the International Monetary Fund (IMF) in 1986 (commonly referred to as the Bretton Woods Institutions or International Financial Institutions—IFIs). The series of SAPs that followed thereafter, required **privatization** of major industries, less government spending, **deregulation** of the economy, and trade **liberalization**. The SAPs, therefore, have essentially focused on the implementation of an unfettered free market economy.

Today, the economy of Mozambique continues to be dominated by agriculture. Major exports include prawns, cotton, cashew nuts, sugar, citrus, copra and coconuts, and timber. Export partners, in turn, include Spain, South Africa, Portugal, the United States, Japan, Malawi, India, and Zimbabwe. Imports, such as farm equipment and transport equipment, are **capital goods** that are worth more than agricultural products, hence Mozambique's large **trade deficit**. The country also imports food, clothing, and petroleum products. Import partners include South Africa, Zimbabwe, Saudi Arabia, Portugal, the United States, Japan, and India. In the past several years, the value of imports outweighed the value of exports by 5 to 1 or more—a factor that obliges Mozambique to depend heavily on foreign aid and loans by foreign commercial banks and the Bretton Woods Institutions (BWIs). In 1995 alone, Mozambique received $1.115 billion in aid. In 1999, the total **external debt** stood at $4.8 billion. Fortunately, in the same year significant economic recovery did occur, as the **real GDP** growth rate reached 10 percent.

POLITICS, GOVERNMENT, AND TAXATION

The legislative branch of the Mozambican government consists of a **unicameral** Assembly of the Republic, whose members are elected by popular vote to serve 5-year terms. The executive branch includes an elected cabinet and both a president, elected by popular vote to serve a 5-year term, and a prime minister, appointed by the president. Judges of the Supreme Court are also appointed by the president.

Since independence, Mozambique has been governed exclusively by FRELIMO. The ruling party formally abandoned its **Marxist** ideological orientation in 1989 and a new constitution in 1990 provided for multiparty elections and a free market economy. RENAMO entered the political life of the nation as a legitimate political party following the UN-negotiated peace accord in 1992. Despite its ignominious (shameful) political origins, RENAMO has been able to draw upon strong internal dissatisfactions with FRELIMO, caused by extreme poverty and unemployment, to garner a considerable amount of support from the local population. Since the establishment of the peace accords and subsequent development of RENAMO from a military force into a political party, there is little ideological difference between the 2 major parties, with both adhering to a free market and pluralistic orientation. In the most recent elections of 1999, FRELIMO won 133 of the 250 seats in the Assembly. In the same elections, RENAMO formed a coalition with several smaller parties, each of which did not respectively receive the 5 percent of the popular vote needed to win parliamentary seats by themselves, thereby acquiring the 117 remaining Assembly seats. Since 1986, the FRELIMO leader Joaquim Alberto Chissano has presided as president. Presidential elections are scheduled to be held in 2004.

The vast majority of government revenue comes from taxation. In 1999, for example, tax revenue accounted for a total of 92.4 percent of government income—14.0 percent derived from taxes on income and profits, 58.6 percent from taxes on goods and services, and 16.9 percent from taxes on international trade (**tariffs**). Businesses in Mozambique are taxed at rates of 35

percent, 40 percent, or 45 percent on annual net profits, depending upon their size. In terms of **income tax**, there are 4 tax brackets in Mozambique. All those that make less than Mt600,000 are exempted from taxation, persons who make between Mt600,001 and Mt2,400,000 are taxed at 10 percent, those that make between Mt2,400,001 and Mt9,600,000 are taxed at 15 percent, and all those that make more than Mt9,600,001 are taxed at 20 percent. All goods and services with a few exceptions, such as medical services and drugs, are taxed at a rate of 17 percent. Although the income taxation system is progressive, the high taxation on goods and services is retrogressive as it affects the poor much more than the rich, who can afford to pay such fees. Moreover, in addition to the general taxes on goods and services, there are also certain **excise taxes** levied on specific products, such as alcohol and fuel. Excise taxes are set at 20 percent, 35 percent, 50 percent, and 75 percent, depending upon the particular product.

INFRASTRUCTURE, POWER, AND COMMUNICATIONS

Infrastructure in Mozambique is generally poor and inadequate, especially in the many areas heavily affected by the war. The country has approximately 30,400 kilometers of highways, 5,685 kilometers of which are paved. Large sections of the remaining 24,175 kilometers of highway are virtually impassable during the rainy season. The World Bank is currently implementing an $850 million program to rebuild the road network, along with the coastal port system.

In addition to the road network, there is a total of 3,131 kilometers of railway, as well as 170 airports, although only 22 have paved runways (est. 1996). Major rail lines connect to South Africa, Malawi, and Zimbabwe. The latter 2 countries are dependent upon railway links with Mozambique since they are landlocked and must access Mozambican ports to send exports and receive imports.

Communications

Country	Newspapers	Radios	TV Sets[a]	Cable subscribers[a]	Mobile Phones[a]	Fax Machines[a]	Personal Computers[a]	Internet Hosts[b]	Internet Users[b]
	1996	1997	1998	1998	1998	1998	1998	1999	1999
Mozambique	3	40	5	N/A	0	N/A	1.6	0.09	15
United States	215	2,146	847	244.3	256	78.4	458.6	1,508.77	74,100
South Africa	32	317	125	N/A	56	3.5	47.4	33.36	1,820
Tanzania	4	279	21	0.0	1	N/A	1.6	0.05	25

[a]Data are from International Telecommunication Union, *World Telecommunication Development Report 1999* and are per 1,000 people.
[b]Data are from the Internet Software Consortium (http://www.isc.org) and are per 10,000 people.
SOURCE: World Bank. *World Development Indicators 2000.*

Recently, the Caminhos de Ferro de Mocambique (CFM), a government **parastatal** that formerly had **monopolistic** control of all ports and the railway, announced a private management concession to be awarded for management of the central railroad system. The system includes a link from Beira to Zimbabwe and the Sena line. The latter, which is critical to the development of the Zambezi River as it facilitates the export of cooking coal from Moatize in Tete Province, is in complete disrepair. As much as $500 million may be needed to reconstruct the Sena line.

There are a total of 6 ports and harbors in Mozambique, with the largest being the port of Beira. The port came under the control of the Dutch company Cornelder in 1999 following a **joint venture** concession with the CFM, and has undergone considerable reparation in recent years. Unfortunately, the port has suffered a decline in business activity due to the failing Zimbabwean economy. Moreover, the selling of ports and other means of production and infrastructure to foreign companies means that large portions of profits will be exported out of the country. At the same time, however, the country is in a bind because it does not have the money to pay for reparations and renovations itself (hence the privatization of the Sena line). Additionally, as Joseph Hanlon emphasizes in his book *Peace Without Profit,* there is also a considerable amount of pressure being exerted upon Mozambique to privatize by the IFIs.

Mozambicans consume a total of 1.018 billion kWh of electricity, 385 million kWh of which are imported from abroad. A full 75 percent of internal electricity production comes from hydro, while the remaining 25 percent is derived from fossil fuel. Located exclusively in the major cities, there is no electricity in the smaller towns and villages. The parastatal Electricidade de Mocambique (EDM) maintains a monopoly on the management of the backbone of the national grid. The EDM, which also controls the water supply system, however, has recently awarded a concession for the private management of the water supply system in 5 major cities. Privatization of the water supply can lead to decreased accessibility, as there is no governmental guarantee of fair pricing. As such, if rates to access water increase, the poor will have to cut their water intake.

Privatization has also characterized recent developments in the telecommunication sector, which has traditionally been monopolized by the government-owned national telephone company (TDM). The introduction of legislation legalizing the privatization of the telecommunication sector in 1999 led to the transformation of the TDM into a public enterprise with 100 percent of the shares owned by government. The government is currently selecting a strategic private investor to whom it can sell a 30 percent share, with the most likely candi-

date being the Portuguese firm Telecom. In 1999, there were only 4.0 telephone mainlines per 1,000 people, a dismal contrast to the United States where there were 640 mainlines per 1,000 people in 1996.

ECONOMIC SECTORS

Like most African countries, the economy of Mozambique was decisively shaped in the colonial period. As Allen Isaacman—author of *Cotton is the Mother of Poverty: Peasants, Work, and Rural Struggle in Colonial Mozambique, 1938–1961*—states, the Portuguese

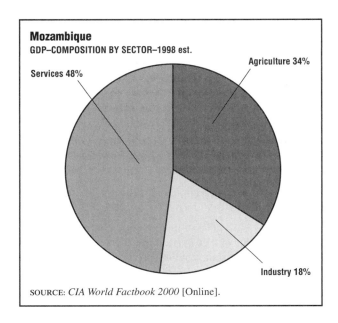

Mozambique
GDP–COMPOSITION BY SECTOR–1998 est.

Services 48%
Agriculture 34%
Industry 18%

SOURCE: *CIA World Factbook 2000* [Online].

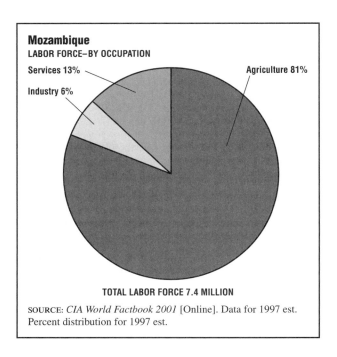

Mozambique
LABOR FORCE–BY OCCUPATION

Services 13%
Industry 6%
Agriculture 81%

TOTAL LABOR FORCE 7.4 MILLION

SOURCE: *CIA World Factbook 2001* [Online]. Data for 1997 est. Percent distribution for 1997 est.

relationship with Mozambique was determined by its need for a large labor force to produce raw materials. Consequently, Portuguese colonial policies coerced peasants into exporting agricultural products to the mother country, while preventing them from developing their own forms of manufacturing and industry. Today, the Mozambican economy remains structurally locked into the position of agricultural exporter, with the manufacturing sector holding a limited, albeit increasingly important, economic role. With increased urbanization, the service sector has become the most important contributor to GDP, though the vast majority of Mozambicans continue to labor in the agricultural sector of the economy.

AGRICULTURE

In 1998, the agricultural sector engaged approximately 81 percent of the Mozambican labor force and contributed 34 percent of GDP. Mozambique's major agricultural products include cotton, cashew nuts, sugarcane, tea, cassava, corn, rice, tropical fruits, beef, and poultry. Agricultural exports include prawns, which are a type of shellfish similar to large shrimp, cashews, cotton, sugar, copra (a coconut product), citrus, coconuts, and timber.

As part of FRELIMO's socialist legacy, all land is owned by the state. The latter, in turn, leases parcels of land to individuals and companies for up to 50 years, with an option to renew. The system is designed to protect the small family farm sector, which provides employment for 90 percent of the agricultural population. According to the *IMF Country Report Number 01/25,* 98.9 percent of the rural poor in Mozambique own land, with an average of 2.5 hectares per household. Many **small holder** farmers can only produce enough for subsistence (survival) purposes, while others are able to produce a surplus to sell on the market. Land tenure is a highly politicized issue and it is unlikely that FRELIMO will privatize land ownership any time soon. Estate production is confined mostly to the sugar sector, though there are some large agro firms maintaining commercial operations of cotton, copra, citrus, and maize production.

Though the vast majority of Mozambicans work in the production of cash crops, prawns from the fishing industry have become the country's single most important export (1998 est.). According to the U.S. Department of State *FY 2000 Country Commercial Guide,* prawns, which comprise 40 percent of all export revenue, have contributed an average of $70 million per year to the economy over the past several years. Commercial fisheries involved in catching and exporting prawns usually boast large-scale operations, many of which are foreign-owned. A small amount of local unlicensed fishers also engages in selling prawns, though the government is seeking to crackdown on such illegal operations.

Until very recently, cashews were Mozambique's most important agricultural export. Indeed, throughout the colonial period, Mozambique was the world's leading cashew producer. Although cashews continue to play an essential role in the economy, with exports increasing, for example, from 33.4 thousand tons in 1994 to 58.7 thousand tons in 1998, the cashew sector has suffered severely from declining prices on the international market. International prices for agricultural products are determined by world supply and demand in a given year, factors over which Mozambican farmers have no control. In January 2001, international prices for cashews plummeted to US$2/lb., their lowest level in over a decade.

Cotton-producing farmers have also been seriously affected by declining international prices in recent years. Cotton, which is currently Mozambique's third most important agricultural export, reached a post-war peak production of 117,000 tons in the 1998 crop season. One of the major factors promoting increased cotton production was the advent of the out-grower scheme, in which large agro-industries provided small farmers with advice and productive inputs and bought their crops. According to the Economist Intelligence Unit's April 2001 *Country Report,* a sharp fall in international prices in 1999 led to a 52 percent decline in cotton production as many small holder producers exited the market. On the positive side, production in 2001 is estimated to rebound significantly to 80,000 tons or more, though there is no telling how stable production will remain, given the inherent instability of international agricultural pricing.

International pricing is not the only factor that affects the stability of the agricultural sector. Weather conditions are a second, albeit just as important, element determining productive output. In 2000, for example, production of corn—Mozambique's most important crop produced for domestic consumption—fell to 1,019,000 tons from 1,246,000 tons the year before. The productive decline related largely to devastating floods, which lasted from January to March. Conversely, debilitating droughts also frequently afflict the country, and 2 crippling droughts in the post-war period alone led to severe declines in agricultural production. Such weather imbalances lead to oscillating (fluctuating) patterns of production, which, in addition to destabilizing export revenue, severely restrict the country's ability to gain self-sufficiency in food production. Further exacerbating the problem, only 4 percent of all land in Mozambique is arable. As a result of these problems, the country must import large amounts of rice and wheat every year.

INDUSTRY

Although only 6 percent of the Mozambican labor force is engaged in the manufacturing sector, industry accounted for 18 percent of GDP in 1998. Major industries in Mozambique include food, beverages, chemicals (fertilizer, soap, paints), petroleum products, textiles, cement, glass, asbestos, and tobacco. Virtually all manufacturing is located in the major urban areas of Maputo, Beira, and Nampula.

The value of the manufacturing sector as a whole has increased impressively throughout the past several years. In 1995, for instance, the sector was valued at Mt2,059,608, whereas this figure more than doubled to Mt4,584,352 in 1999. The food-processing and beverage industries have been of paramount importance to this increase, with each respectively growing in value from Mt573,660 and Mt348,064 in 1995, to Mt1,189,610 and Mt1,604,142 in 1999.

As the U.S. Department of State's *Background Notes on Mozambique* points out, most manufacturing industries have either recently been privatized or are currently undergoing privatization under the guidance of the SAPs. While the World Bank and the IMF argue that privatization will lead to increased efficiency since enterprises formerly-dependent upon government **subsidies** will have to become viable competitors, Mozambicans generally lack the credit necessary to purchase such enterprises and replace their highly outdated equipment. Consequently, foreign firms rich in capital have taken over many enterprises, though they have not always been successful in revamping productivity. Indeed, the inability to increase the productivity of many manufacturing industries prompted several multi-national companies, including the Portuguese Barbosa e Almeida, which took over parts of the glassmaking industry, to recently sell shares back to the Mozambican government. On the whole, however, the record of foreign takeovers has been more or less positive for the investors.

In 2000, **foreign direct investment** (FDI) in Mozambique, which is mostly in the manufacturing sector, equaled $730 million. South Africa and Portugal, respectively accounting for 63 percent and 14 percent of all FDI, are the largest foreign investors. The United States, the Netherlands, and Hong Kong are also significant investors. Major U.S. firms with a strong market presence in Mozambique include Coca-Cola and Colgate-Palmolive.

A second development that has severely affected the manufacturing sector is trade liberalization. While liberalization may offer Mozambican industries increased access to foreign markets, it may also force them to compete with more efficient foreign counterparts in the domestic economy. The so-called recent "cashew wars" exemplifies this latter possibility. The metaphorical wars centered on the elimination of tariff barriers blocking the exportation of unprocessed cashews. Such tariffs have existed in order to ensure protection for industries involved in processing cashews—high tariffs on exportations of unprocessed cashews means that cashews will inevitably be processed before leaving the country. The World Bank, however, has argued that the cashew-processing industry is inefficient and that it must face competition from abroad. As part of its SAP, the World Bank forced Mozambique to begin phasing out tariffs in 1996, despite the protests of the government, the World Bank's major adversary in the cashew wars. The results of the liberalization process were disastrous. According to the Integrated Regional Information Network (IRIN), a United Nations humanitarian information unit, by 2000, half of the cashew-processing industry's 12,000 workers were laid off, while 10 of the largest cashew-processing factories were closed due to a lack of supplies. The cashew-processing sector, which, in 1987, accounted for 31 percent of Mozambique's export earnings and employed about 25 percent of the country's workforce, has diminished in annual productive capacity from an average of Mt200,000 during the 1980s, to a current low of Mt50,000.

Despite some natural reserves of coal and titanium, mining in Mozambique is negligible. The one exception is the massive Mozal aluminum smelter outside of Maputo, which reached a full production capacity of 250,000 tons per year in December 2000. Mozal, a subsidiary of the South African company Billiton, employs 1,000 Mozambicans and represents the country's largest economic project to date. Mozal has created beneficial spillover effects (positive links) in the Mozambican economy, mainly in the form of new port facilities needed to handle the import of alumina and export of aluminum ingots. Once more, however, the profits earned by Mozal are lining the pockets of foreigners rather than the Mozambican populace. In his book, *Peace Without Profit*, Joseph Hanlon maintains that many observers are referring to the escalating foreign domination of the economy as the "recolonization" of Mozambique. On February 13, 2001, workers at the Mozal smelter, angered at the superior terms offered to foreign managers, engaged in an illegal one-day strike.

SERVICES

Accounting for approximately 48 percent of GDP, the service, or tertiary sector, is the most valuable area of economic activity in the Mozambican economy. Approximately 13 percent of the labor force is engaged in the service sector (est. 1998), though this figure does not take into consideration the many people that work in the **informal sector**. The largest contributor to the service sector is business, which constituted 19.5 percent of GDP alone in 1999. The business class consists of a small elite, whose main activities are trading and distribution. Other important service activities include finance, tourism, transport, communication, and **retail**. The latter, which includes a small number of restaurants and stores in the urban centers, is dominated by small-scale street vendors, many of whom form part of the informal sector. Informal sector activities include carpentry, motor vehicle repair, tailoring, **hawking**, and selling various fruits, vegetables, and other commodities. Recent studies, such as those conducted by researchers of the Centro de Estudos Africanos of the University Eduardo Mondlane in Mozambique, indicate that informal activity has increased substantially as a result of SAP-related cuts to the social sector, unemployment and rising food prices. Unfortunately, the burden caused by these developments has been shouldered unequally by women, who have taken the responsibility of ensuring the survival of the family. In 1994, as much as 75 percent of all women in Maputo were forced to participate in the informal sector in order to earn their chief incomes. Such women make as little as $0.20 a day, plus food.

As a result of the destruction caused by the civil war, there is a massive lack of shops and service activities in the rural areas. Moreover, the rebuilding of the retail sector in the rural areas has been slowed by a banking sector that is reluctant to provide capital to prospective entrepreneurs with very few assets. Though there are many international donor agencies funding rural service-related income-generating projects, the pace of reconstruction remains protracted (delayed).

On the whole, tourism is a relatively marginal component of the Mozambican economy. Indeed, restaurants and hotels accounted for a meager 1.2 percent of GDP in 1999—a slight increase from 1995, when they constituted 0.7 percent of GDP. At the same time, however, there is a strong potential for the development of the tourism sector, given the country's long coastline with superb beaches, the existence of several attractions of historical interest, and the great diversity of flora and wildlife.

FINANCIAL SERVICES. There are a total of 8 banks in Mozambique, in addition to the central bank, the Bank of Mozambique. All of these banks, many of which were controlled by the government prior to mid-1990s, are now part of the private sector. The Banco Comercial de Mocambique (BCM), which has a considerable presence across the country, dominates commercial banking. The government controlled BCM until 1996, when it was sold to a consortium led by the Portuguese Banco Portugues Mello. The government still retains a 49 percent share in the BCM, though it plans on selling its shares. Despite these plans, the government was forced to authorize the issuing of $39 million in **treasury bills** as part of an effort to recapitalize the BCM, along with the Banco Austral, to prevent each from becoming insolvent. Both banks have large loan portfolios that have proved unrecoverable. The Banco Austral, Mozambique's second largest

bank, was sold to a consortium led by Southern Berhad Bank of Malaysia in 1997, though the government retains a 40 percent share, which it also plans on selling.

With a share capital of $30 million, the Banco Internacional de Mocambique (BIM) is the third largest bank in the country. In January 2000, the Banco Comercial Portugues, the parent company of BIM, acquired Grupo Mello, the parent company of BCM. Consequently, 2 of the largest banks in Mozambique are now controlled by 1 bank in Portugal. Other important banks include the Portuguese-owned Banco Comercial e de Investimento and the Portuguese-South African Banco Standard Totta.

In addition to the network of banks, there are also several investment agencies operating in the Mozambican financial market, including the International Finance Corporation and the Commonwealth Development Corporation. Moreover, in 1999, a small stock exchange was established in Maputo with the assistance of the Lisbon stock exchange.

INTERNATIONAL TRADE

Like most countries in sub-Saharan Africa, Mozambique's international economic transactions are based on the exportation of agricultural commodities in exchange for capital goods. Since the international terms of trade accord higher value to the latter, Mozambique routinely suffers from a **balance of payments** deficit, hence, in part, its constant need to borrow money from the IFIs and wealthy foreign governments. The balance of trade deficit varies widely, depending upon, among other things, the market success of agricultural export commodities in a given year (as we have seen, this, in turn, depends on both weather conditions and international commodity prices). In 1995, for instance, the deficit stood at $552.7 million, while this figure increased dramatically to $930.9 million in 1999. In 2000, the gap between the value of imports vis-à-vis exports increased even more, with the latter outnumbering the former by more than 5 to 1.

Trade (expressed in billions of US$): Mozambique		
	Exports	Imports
1975	.198	.411
1980	.281	.800
1985	.077	.424
1990	.126	.878
1995	.168	.784
1998	N/A	N/A

SOURCE: International Monetary Fund. *International Financial Statistics Yearbook 1999.*

Mozambique's principal exports include prawns, cashews, cotton, sugar, copra, citrus, coconuts, and timber. The value of exports designated to the wealthy countries of the Organization of Economic Cooperation and Development (OECD), including Japan, the Netherlands, Portugal, Spain, the United Kingdom, and the United States, decreased considerably throughout the second half of the 1990s, dropping from $60.7 million in 1995, to $37.3 million in 1999. This decrease in export value, reflects, in large part, declining terms of trade and the market exit of peasant producers resulting therefrom (as was recently the case in the cotton sector). Conversely, the value of exports designated to African countries, mainly South Africa and Zimbabwe, increased somewhat during the same period—from $23.6 million in 1995, to $26.2 million in 1999. Increased trade between the countries of southern Africa has been facilitated by a rehabilitation of transportation infrastructure in Mozambique. With 16 percent of exports reaching the South African market, that country is Mozambique's second largest export partner, second only to Spain (17 percent).

Mozambique's chief imports include food, clothing, farm equipment, petroleum, and transport equipment. The value of imports from the OECD countries has also decreased considerably, falling from $46.7 million in 1995, to $27.2 million in 1999. This precipitous decline may reflect increased trade diversion (a redirecting of trade) towards South Africa, which increased its share of imports designated to Mozambique from $25.9 million in 1995, to $57.2 million in 1999. In 2000, South Africa accounted for 55 percent of all Mozambican imports.

As part of the country's structural reforms, the Mozambican government has promoted significant trade liberalization in recent years, simplifying its tariff structures and applying an average tariff of 13.8 percent to countries accorded most-favored nation status. Mozambique's tariffs are among the lowest import **duties** in southern Africa. While the international financial institutions and Western governments in general tend to support trade liberalization, it may have negative effects for a country like Mozambique that depends on agricultural exports in exchange for higher **value-added** capital imports. If Mozambican manufacturing firms cannot compete with their foreign counterparts, reduction of trade protection measures, such as tariffs, will simply lead to the retardation of the Mozambican industrial sector. The disastrous effects of tariff reduction on the cashew-processing industry is a case in point. The results of such negative developments might be further entrenchment of the agricultural sector in the economy, and thus the prolonging of the unequal trading patterns that sustain the country's severe balance of trade deficit. In such a context, it is hardly likely that Mozambique will benefit from the pro-trade idea of specializing in exporting products it produces comparatively better than other nations, and in importing those that it does not.

Mozambique is a member of the World Trade Organization (WTO) and the Southern African Development Community (SADC)—a regional trading agreement among 14 countries in southern Africa designed to lower tariff barriers between member countries. While it is difficult to justify completely free trade between wealthy and poor countries since they cannot compete from a level playing field, some argue that free trade between developing countries can be beneficial. The argument is based mainly on the idea that free trade between developing countries enables them to benefit from economies of scale in a more equitably competitive context. Still, more *relatively* developed countries, such as South Africa in the SADC, the most powerful economy in all of Africa, might benefit disproportionately due to their more competitive positioning.

MONEY

SAP-induced reforms in 1992 instituted a free **floating exchange rate** policy in Mozambique, with the value of the metical thereafter being determined by its supply and demand in international money markets. Prior to the reform, the Mozambican government followed a fixed exchange regime in which the metical was pegged to the U.S. dollar at a specific rate, subject to alterations only to rectify substantial distortions (severe imbalances between the market value of the metical against the U.S. dollar and the official value of the metical against the U.S. dollar).

Since the introduction of the free floating exchange regime, the metical has consistently depreciated vis-à-vis the U.S. dollar, meaning it takes increasingly greater quantities of meticais to equal the value of 1 U.S. dollar. In 1995, the **exchange rate** averaged Mt9,024.3 per US$1, with the rate depreciating to an average of Mt12,775.1 per US$1 in 1999, and an average of Mt13,392.0 per US$1 in 2000. The EIU expects that the rate will average at Mt16,225 per US$1 in 2001, and

Exchange rates: Mozambique	
meticais (Mt) per US$1	
Jan 2001	17,331.0
2000	5,199.8
1999	12,775.1
1998	11,874.6
1997	11,543.6
1996	11,293.8
SOURCE: CIA *World Factbook 2001* [ONLINE].	

Mt17,280 per US$1 in 2002. The substantial **devaluation** that occurred in 2001 reflects, in large part, a weakening economy affected by flooding and declining agricultural productivity.

While currency depreciation may be positive for the exporting sectors of the Mozambican economy, since less foreign money is needed to buy Mozambican exports which thereby renders them more attractive, it has the adverse effect of increasing the prices of imports. Imports become more expensive since more meticais are needed to purchase them. For a food-importing nation like Mozambique, increases in the prices of essential imports, such as wheat, can have negative consequences on the poorest segments of the society, who cannot afford to pay increased prices. In their zeal for export-led economic growth, however, the IFIs, which routinely apply pressure on sub-Saharan governments to continuously devalue their currencies, fail to take this negative affect into account.

POVERTY AND WEALTH

Though the vast majority of Mozambicans live in abject poverty, a small elite consisting of traders, politicians with business ties, foreign managers, and professionals working in the financial sector enjoy a life of luxury in the urban centers. This elite has benefited from the privatization and liberalization reforms associated with the SAPs, as they have largely displaced the state in the ruling positions of the economy. Unfortunately, policies such as the liberalization of the foreign exchange market, which enables business executives to easily acquire foreign currency, have increased the propensity of the elites to buy most of their commodities from sources abroad. Indeed, the Mozambican elite is particularly notorious for spending its money on the importation of luxury goods, rather than reinvesting in and supporting the local economy. As Joseph Hanlon notes, the elite travel extensively and identify more with the wealthy of western countries than they do with the Mozambican poor.

In contrast to the tremendous wealth of the small elite, the majority of Mozambicans find it difficult to provide for their basic needs. The **United Nations Devel-**

Distribution of Income or Consumption by Percentage Share: Mozambique	
Lowest 10%	2.5
Lowest 20%	6.5
Second 20%	10.8
Third 20%	15.1
Fourth 20%	21.1
Highest 20%	46.5
Highest 10%	31.7

Survey year: 1996–97
Note: This information refers to expenditure shares by percentiles of the population and is ranked by per capita expenditure.
SOURCE: *2000 World Development Indicators* [CD-ROM].

opment Program's (UNDP) human development index (HDI) listings, which arranges countries according to their overall level of human development, ranks Mozambique 168th out of a total of 174 nations. The HDI, a composite index (one that assesses more than one variable) that measures life expectancy at birth, adult literacy rate, school enrollment ratio, and **GDP per capita**, is indicative of a country's general social and economic wellbeing. As such, Mozambique's HDI ranking demonstrates that the country is one of the least developed in the entire world.

Although there are no recent statistics for public expenditure on education, UNDP statistics on support for the health sector indicate that the Mozambican government has considerably reduced its already meager health expenditure. In 1990, for instance, the government spent 3.6 percent of GDP on the health sector, whereas this figure dropped to 2.1 percent in 1998. Such cuts reflect so-called austerity measures induced by the SAPs, designed to decrease government spending to "free" revenue for **debt-servicing**. Comparatively, the United States spent 6.5 percent of GDP on health in 1998. The vast majority of Mozambicans, for their part, spend their meager incomes on the basic necessities of life, such as food, rents, clothing, fuel, and transportation. As a result of a declining economy and a deepening of poverty, however, Mozambicans consume somewhat less food calories on a daily basis then they did thirty years ago. In 1970, the average Mozambican consumed 1,896 calories, with this figure declining to 1,832 calories in 1997. Americans, in contrast, consumed on average 2,965 calories in 1970 and 3,699 calories in 1997. This is not surprising, considering the increase in the **gross national product** (GNP) per capita has been grossly outweighed by mounting **inflation** in the past 10 years. The UNDP estimates that the annual growth rate in GNP per capita between 1990 to 1998 was 3.5 percent, while the average annual rate of inflation during the same period was 41.1 percent. Fortu-

GDP per Capita (US$)					
Country	1975	1980	1985	1990	1998
Mozambique	N/A	166	115	144	188
United States	19,364	21,529	23,200	25,363	29,683
South Africa	4,574	4,620	4,229	4,113	3,918
Tanzania	N/A	N/A	N/A	175	173

SOURCE: United Nations. *Human Development Report 2000; Trends in human development and per capita income.*

nately, inflation stabalized at 3.8 percent in 1998, though the GNP per capita in **purchasing power parity** (adjusted to compensate for the different pricing of goods and services in Mozambique in relation to the United States) the same year leveled at a paltry US$740.

WORKING CONDITIONS

In 2000, the total working population of Mozambique was estimated at 8 million. Since most Mozambicans work in the uncertain conditions of the agricultural sector, however, only 17 percent of this total earn regular wages. In terms of gender differences in the division of labor, women tend to work overwhelmingly in service-based activities, particularly in the informal sector. Furthermore, women tend to suffer from a double work-day, being forced out of economic necessity to engage in income-earning activities during the day, and then being responsible for the domestic household tasks at night.

There are 2 major trade union federations in Mozambique, collectively representing approximately 200,000 workers and 13 unions. The largest federation, the Organization of Mozambican Workers (OTM), was established following independence. The OTM was directly controlled by the government until 1994, at which time it officially declared itself free of any political party affiliation. Legislation passed in 1991 broke the OTM's legal monopoly over trade union activity. Immediately thereafter, a separate federation, the Free and Independent Union of Mozambique (SLIM), was established by 3 OTM-breakaway unions.

The Constitution permits workers to strike, with the exception of government employees, police, military personnel, and employees engaged in other essential services (which include sanitation, firefighting, air traffic control, health care, water, electricity, fuel, post office, and telecommunications). Numerous strikes have occurred over the past several years, many of which, according to the U.S. Department of State, are centered on issues related to privatization, salaries, and increases in wage levels. In accordance with the 1991 Labor Law, there are no known instances of employers seeking retribution against striking workers.

Children under the age of 16 years are prohibited from working in the wage economy. Since there is such a high adult unemployment rate—estimated at 50 percent—there are few violations of this law. Children often work on family farms and in the informal sector, however, in order to financially assist their parents. The harsh reality is that if children do not engage in activities to assist their parents in generating income, the family will not have enough money to eat.

Although Mozambique has a minimum wage, which averaged at $40 per month in 2000, it is not adequate to support even a small family of 3. Consequently, most workers rely on earning additional income in the informal sector, in addition to growing corn and vegetables on small plots of land for personal consumption. The legal limitation of a workweek for workers in the non-agricultural sector is 44 hours, while employees are entitled to 1 rest day per week. Despite detailed legally defined health and safety standards, reports indicate that violations of such standards are commonplace. In 1995 alone, 524 major accidents occurred in the building, timber, and mining sectors.

COUNTRY HISTORY AND ECONOMIC DEVELOPMENT

11TH CENTURY. Arab and Swahili traders settled along the coast of present-day Mozambique. The Kiswahili language developed as the most used language for trade between the newcomers and the Bantu inhabitants of the interior. Sofala became a particularly important gold and ivory exporting center.

16TH CENTURY. Following Vasco da Gama's visit to Mozambique in 1498, the Portuguese began extending their influence along the coasts of East Africa. Though they succeeded in establishing their commercial dominance on the coast of Mozambique, their presence in the interior was severely limited. Portuguese traders engaged in selling gold, ivory, and slaves.

17TH CENTURY. Several Portuguese adventurers eventually founded feudal kingdoms in the interior, where they created large estates called *prazos* on which Africans were forced to work. Though the *prazeros*—the owners of the estates—were theoretically subordinate to the Portuguese crown, they ruled their kingdoms ruthlessly and autonomously.

1752. Mozambique became a separately administered Portuguese territory, under the head of a captain-general.

1820s. The Portuguese were displaced from southern Mozambique by groups of Nguni-speaking people from South Africa, though they still retained nominal colonial control.

1880s. The ignominious scramble for Africa commenced among the European powers, and Portugal's claims to Mozambique were officially recognized. The British and the Portuguese subsequently established treaties demarcating colonial zones in southern and eastern Africa.

1890–1920. Portugal forcefully established its hegemony over the entire Mozambique region in a series of wars against the African populace. Thereafter, a coercive economy was established in which Africans were forced to labor on lands taken over by whites in the production of export crops.

1950–1975. Throughout the 1950s, a nationalist anti-colonial sentiment developed, eventually crystallizing in the united-front movement called FRELIMO. The latter commenced a guerrilla war against the Portuguese in 1964, which, in conjunction with a coup d'etat in Portugal that placed an anti-colonial regime in power, enabled Mozambique to achieve independence in 1975 under the leadership of Samora Machel. A massive exodus of Portuguese settlers followed, leaving the country with a complete lack of professional expertise and productive machinery.

1975–1992. FRELIMO implemented a socialist economy based on extensive nationalization of industry, state-controlled land reform, and a heavily supported social sector. By the 1980s, Mozambique became a "Cold War battlefield" in which RENAMO, a counter-insurgency organization funded by the racist regime in South Africa, waged war against the government. After much destruction and the complete dissolution of the economy, a truce was implemented between RENAMO and FRELIMO in 1992. The former subsequently became a legitimate political party and was integrated into a newly created multi-party democratic system.

1990s. Under the leadership of Joaquim Chissano—Machel's successor—FRELIMO abandoned its Marxist orientation. The World Bank and the IMF, which had established limited control over Mozambique as early as 1984, fully imposed their **structural adjustment programs**, emphasizing mass privatization, trade liberalization, currency devaluation, foreign investment, and stabilization policies. Though a certain amount of economic growth has occurred throughout the "SAP era," there has also been an increase in poverty and a foreign take-over of the economy.

FUTURE TRENDS

The economic and political trends that have characterized Mozambican development since the peace accords of 1992 are symptomatic of the larger trends that have prevailed throughout most of sub-Saharan Africa. In the main, SAPs have failed to solve the longstanding problems of unemployment, mass poverty, balance of payments deficit, insecure informal employment, debt, inequality, and lack of access to essential social services. In many cases, these problems have actually been exacerbated by inappropriate policies, such as reckless privatization and trade liberalization. Although the country experienced a considerable rate of growth throughout the 1990s, much of this growth has disproportionately benefited a small minority of business elites, and can be at-

tributed to the termination of the civil war and the massive increase in foreign investment. As for the latter factor, it is debatable how beneficial a role FDI will play in the development of the Mozambican economy.

Politically, the cessation of the civil war and the more or less successful integration of RENAMO into the political system represents a positive development. If the economic situation as experienced by the vast majority of the Mozambican populace continues to deteriorate, however, the sustainability of the democratic process might be jeopardized. Already, the U.S. State Department has warned that political unrest and discontent are increasing in the country. The IMF and World Bank's recently touted Heavily Indebted Poor Countries (HIPC) initiative—which substantially reduces the debt and debt-servicing obligations of severely poor nations—is a first step in the reformation of the largely negative role that the IFIs have played in sub-Saharan economies. It will take much more than this initiative, however, to dramatically alter the course of development of African countries. True development will not occur until free-market panaceas (cure-alls) are discarded and a more contextual development scheme—one which possibly includes a strong role for the state—is promoted by the international community.

DEPENDENCIES

Mozambique has no territories or colonies.

BIBLIOGRAPHY

Abrahamsson, Hans, and Anders Nilsson. *Mozambique, The Troubled Transition: From Socialist Construction to Free Market Capitalism.* London: Zed Books, 1995.

Economist Intelligence Unit. *Country Profile: Mozambique, Malawi, April 2001.* London: Economist Intelligence Unit, April 2001.

Hanlon, Joseph. *Peace without Profit: How the IMF Blocks Rebuilding in Mozambique.* London: Villiers Publications, 1996.

Integrated Regional Information Networks (United Nations humanitarian information unit). *Mozambique: Government Commits US$47 million to Reviving the Cashew Sector.* <http://www.reliefweb.int/IRIN/sa/countrystories/Mozambique/20010706.phtml>. Accessed August 2001.

International Monetary Fund. *IMF Staff Country Report, Mozambique: Selected Issues and Statistical Appendix.* <http://www.imf.org>. Accessed July 2001.

Isaacman, Allen. *Cotton is the Mother of Poverty: Peasants, Work, and Rural Struggle in Colonial Mozambique, 1938–1961.* Portsmouth, NH: Heinemann, 1996.

Khapoya, Vincent B. *The African Experience.* New Jersey: Prentice Hall, 1998.

United Nations Development Programme (UNDP). *Human Development Report 2000.* New York: Oxford University Press, 2000.

U.S. Central Intelligence Agency. *The World Factbook 2000: Mozambique.* <http://wwww.CIA.gov/CIA/publications/factbook/geos/tz.html>. Accessed July 2001.

U.S. Department of State. *Background Notes: Mozambique.* <http://dosfan.lib.uic.edu/ERC/bgnotes/af/mozambique9607.html>. Accessed July 2001.

U.S. Department of State. *FY 2000 Country Commercial Guide: Mozambique.* <http://www.state.gov/www/about_state/business/com_guides.html>. Accessed July 2001.

U.S. Department of State. *Mozambique Country Report on Human Rights Practices for 1996.* <http://www.state.gov>. Accessed July 2001.

World Bank Group. *Mozambique: Competitiveness Indicators.* <http://wbln0018.worldbank.org/psd/d8feca9e97dacc08852564e40068dc2f?opendocument>. Accessed July 2001.

—*Neil Burron*

NAMIBIA

Republic of Namibia

CAPITAL: Windhoek.

MONETARY UNIT: Namibian dollar (NAD). One dollar equals 100 cents. There are coins of 1 and 5 dollars, and bills of 10, 50, 100, and 200 dollars. The Namibian dollar is linked on an equal basis to the South African rand, which is also accepted as currency in Namibia.

CHIEF EXPORTS: Diamonds, copper, gold, zinc, lead, uranium, cattle, fish products, karakul skins.

CHIEF IMPORTS: Foodstuffs, petroleum products and fuel, machinery and equipment, chemicals.

GROSS DOMESTIC PRODUCT: US$7.1 billion (purchasing power parity, 1999 est.).

BALANCE OF TRADE: **Exports:** US$1.4 billion (f.o.b., 1999 est.). **Imports:** US$1.5 billion (f.o.b., 1999 est.).

COUNTRY OVERVIEW

LOCATION AND SIZE. The Republic of Namibia lies across the Tropic of Capricorn in the south of Africa and covers an area of 824,292 square kilometers (318,259 square miles), making it slightly more than half the size of Alaska. It is bordered by South Africa to the south and southeast, Botswana and Zimbabwe on the east, Angola on the north, and the South Atlantic Ocean on the west. The Caprivi Strip, a narrow extension of land in the extreme northeast, connects it to Zambia and Zimbabwe. The country is divided into 3 broad zones: the Namib desert to the west; the Kalahari desert to the east; and the Central Plateau. The plateau—made up of mountains, rocky outcrops, sand-filled valleys, and undulating upland plains—covers over 50 percent of the land area. The plateau includes Windhoek, the capital, and slopes eastwards to the Kalahari basin and northward to the Etosha pan, the largest of Namibia's saline lakes.

POPULATION. Namibia's population was estimated to be 1.771 million in 2000, with a birth rate of 35.23 per 1,000 people in 2000 (down from 43 in 1970). The av-

erage annual growth rate was about 2.7 percent between 1970–90, falling to 2.5 percent between 1990–97. Population density is extremely low overall, at about 2 people per square kilometer (5.18 per square mile), and 35 percent of the population lives in urban areas. The urban growth rate averaged 5.7 percent annually between 1980–96. Life expectancy in 1997 was estimated at 56 years (up from 48 years in 1970). The population was young, with 43 percent below the age of 15 and just 4 percent above the age of 65.

The Ovambo and Kavango people together constitute over 60 percent of the population. Other groups are the Herero, Damara, Nama and the Caprivians. The San (Bushmen)—who are among the world's oldest surviving hunter-gatherers—have lived in this territory for over 11,000 years. The Basters who settled in Rehoboth in 1870 stem from marriages between white farmers and Khoi mothers in the Cape area. The "Cape Coloreds," immigrants from South Africa, tend to live in urban areas. Of the white group of approximately 90,000, about 50 percent are of South African and 25 percent of German ancestry, about 20 percent of the latter Boer "sudwesters" (longer established immigrants) with a small minority of British ancestry. The population is mostly Christian. English is the official language but is first or second language to only about 20 percent of the population.

OVERVIEW OF ECONOMY

With a **gross domestic product (GDP) per capita** of US$1,940 in 1998 (**purchasing power parity** of US$4,300 in 1999), Namibia is relatively prosperous in the African context, where the average is US$480 per head. This comparative wealth reflects a large and fairly diversified mining sector. Namibia's economy is export-driven, focussing mainly on mining and fish processing. Since independence, exports of diamonds, uranium, zinc, and fish products have grown significantly.

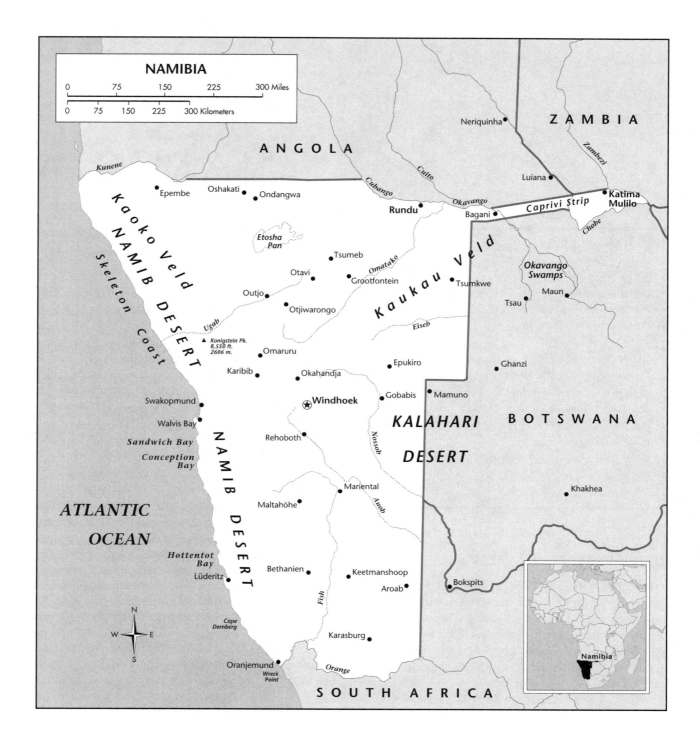

NAMIBIA

0	75	150	225	300 Miles
0	75	150	225	300 Kilometers

Rural people, however, remain largely unaffected by the growth of modern economic activities in their country and generally support themselves through subsistence agricultural activities and herding. According to UN reports, Namibia has one of the most uneven distributions of income in the world, meaning that the average income for the white minority is significantly higher than that for the majority black population. The reason for this imbalance lies in the economic structure that was imposed by colonial history. Ranches were established as white

settlers displaced Africans on two-thirds of the viable farmland, an outcome that is beginning to concern the government following the land-issues explosion in Zimbabwe. The government's current objectives are to raise per capita income, to develop the **private sector**, and to encourage manufacturing activities and tourism. It is also committed to restraining growth in public spending.

The economy remains narrowly based, growth being determined largely by mining and agriculture, especially fishing. The mining sector generates high incomes but is not well integrated with the rest of the economy. About 90 percent of the goods produced in Namibia are exported, and about 90 percent of the goods used in the country, including about one-half of the food, are imported. Despite frequent drought, large ranches generally provide significant exports of beef and sheepskins.

During the early 1980s, Namibia experienced a deep economic **recession**, intensified by war, severe drought, and low world prices for the country's mineral products and for sheepskins. In real terms, output declined by more than 20 percent over the period 1977–84, representing a fall of about one-third in real purchasing power. From the mid-1980s there was a modest economic recovery. The GDP increased by 3 percent in 1986 compared with a decline of 0.8 percent in 1995, and there were further increases in the following year until 1989 when it declined by 0.6 percent. This sluggish rate of growth was due to a number of factors, including depressed international prices for the country's mineral products, a corresponding decline in mining production, and poor performance of the South African economy, to which the Namibian economy is closely linked.

The 1990s have been better. The **real GDP** increased by 5.1 percent in 1991 and 3.5 percent in 1992 owing primarily to higher diamond output and increases in the output of the fishing and construction sectors. The GDP grew by 6.6 percent in 1994 after a decline of 2.0 percent in 1993, by 3.3 percent in 1995, and 2.9 percent in 1996. It slowed down to 1.8 percent in 1997 largely due to the impact of adverse climatic conditions on agriculture and fishing. The government estimated the GDP growth of 2.6 percent in 1998, with considerable advancement in the fishing and manufacturing sectors partially offset by the adverse impact of the Asian economic crisis on the mining sector.

POLITICS, GOVERNMENT, AND TAXATION

At the end of World War II South Africa set out to make Namibia into a South African province, initiating a decades long struggle on the part of people living in Namibia to claim independence. The fight for independence was led by the South West Africa People's Organization (SWAPO). In 1977, a UN contact group comprising the 5 western members of the security council—the United Kingdom, France, the United States, Canada, and West Germany—began to negotiate for Namibia's independence directly with South Africa and SWAPO. In 1978, South Africa announced its acceptance of the contact group's settlement proposal. However, in May of that year, South African forces attacked SWAPO's refugee transit camp at Cassing in South Angola, leaving 600 dead, and the settlement was abandoned.

Independence discussions continued for 10 years and, during this period, South Africa began to ease its grip on Namibia, allowing a transitional government of national unity (a coalition of 6 parties) to take control of internal affairs from June 1985. In November 1989, UN-supervised elections were held, and Dr. Sam Nujoma was elected and inaugurated as the president of Namibia in February 1990. One month later, on 21 March 1990, Namibia attained independence. Nujoma has been re-elected in 1995 and 1999. SWAPO has continued to have an overall majority of seats in National Assembly, with 55 seats in 1999 compared to the opposition's 17. The largest opposition party is the Congress of Democrats (COD) with 7 seats. In the National Council SWAPO has 21 seats, and 6 seats are held by the 2 opposition parties. The largest opposition party in the National Council is the Democratic Turnhalle Alliance of Namibia (DTA) with 5 seats.

The constitution provides for a multiparty democracy in a unitary state. The president is head of state and government and commander-in-chief of the defence forces. Elected by direct universal adult suffrage at intervals of not more than 5 years, the president must receive more than 50 percent of the votes cast.

The president appoints the government, the armed forces chief of staff, and members of a public service commission, but the National Assembly may revoke any appointment. The president may dissolve the National Assembly and may also proclaim a state of emergency and rule by decree, subject to the approval of the National Assembly.

There is a bi-cameral legislature. The National Council with 26 members is chosen from the elected regional councils. The National Assembly has 72 elected members and up to 6 nominated but non-voting members serving for a maximum of 5 years. The National Assembly can remove the president from office by passing an impeachment motion with a two-thirds majority. The prime minister is leader of government business in the National Assembly.

The constitution includes 25 entrenched clauses regarding fundamental human rights and freedoms. There is no death sentence nor detention without trial, and the practice and ideology of apartheid is expressly forbidden. Private property rights are guaranteed. Amendments to the constitution can only be made by two-thirds majorities in both houses.

Namibia raises most of its government revenue from trade taxes (customs **duties** and export **levies**), and 30 percent of the public income came from these sources in 1993. Sales taxes and taxes on incomes each raised 29 percent of the total, and the remaining government revenue (12 percent of the total) came from surpluses on government-owned enterprises (10 percent) and other taxes (1 percent).

INFRASTRUCTURE, POWER, AND COMMUNICATIONS

Namibia has an immense network of 64,800 kilometers (40,267 miles) of roads but only 7,800 kilometers (4,847 miles) are paved. A 4,600 kilometer (2,858 mile) tarred highway network links most of the economically-significant areas and neighboring countries. The Trans Caprivi Highway and the Trans Kalahari Highway were 2 long-haul road projects completed in the late 1990s to run through Botswana to South Africa. These arteries enable Namibia to provide land-locked central African countries with an outlet to the sea, as well as reducing journey times to Johannesburg, South Africa.

The 2,382-kilometer (1,480-mile) railway network was established under German colonial rule and much-needed upgrading was underway by the mid-1990s. A total of 1.8 million tons of freight were transported by rail in 1996–97, of which 70 percent was national traffic. Rail passenger numbers dropped from 159,000 in 1992 to 82,000 in 1994 but recovered to 124,000 in 1996 as a result of more investment and better services.

Namibia Shipping Lines was established in 1992 under the transport **holding company** Trans-Namb in a **joint venture** with South Africa's Unicorn line. The Namibia Port Authority in 1996 launched a 4-year (US$77 million) plan to modernize and extend the facilities at Walvis Bay and Lüderitz. Walvis Bay, the nation's only deep-water port, is the main export outlet, handling around 2 million tons of cargo a year, 20 percent of which is containerized. Petroleum products constitute the largest import category, salt the largest export category. Use of Lüderitz, Namibia's second operating port, has also increased, due to a rise in fishing activities. A third harbor is planned for Mowe Bay, north of Walvis. This would also serve the fishing fleet.

Air transport is important because of Namibia's size. Air Namibia, the national carrier, is another subsidiary of Trans-Namib. Since independence, a regional and international flight network has been set up, in addition to already established domestic routes. There are more than 135 airports, 22 of which have paved runways, including the international airport outside Windhoek.

Namibia in 1999 was a net energy importer, obtaining half its electricity from South Africa. It produced 1.198 billion kilowatt-hours of electricity in 1999, about 98 percent of which came from hydroelectric plants, but the country had to import over 600 million kWhs of electricity to supply its needs. Mining is a heavy energy consumer but most households still have no access to commercial energy supplies. Commercial energy is mainly obtained from imported oil and South African coal. The larger population centers in the north and northeast are being connected to the national electricity grid.

Drilling by Shell in the offshore Kudu gas field confirmed the presence of very significant reserves that would make the country a net exporter of energy. Development of the field began in 1998 with the first gas scheduled for production in the early 2000s.

Namibia maintains a free press. There were 19 newspapers, including the pro-government, but independent, daily newspaper in 1996. There are 9 radio stations which cover 80 percent of the population, and the 1 television network covers 45 percent of the population, all under the control of the Namibia Broadcasting Corporation. There is growing competition from South Africa. TV broadcasts are in local languages as well as English. There were 143 radios, 32 TV sets, and 19 PCs per 1,000 people in mid-1998.

There is an efficient postal service. The telephone system was upgraded and extended under a US$31 million investment program in 1993–97. There were some 80,000 telephone and 5,000 fax subscribers in 1997. A fully automated digital network was in operation by 1997.

Communications

Country	Newspapers	Radios	TV Sets[a]	Cable subscribers[a]	Mobile Phones[a]	Fax Machines[a]	Personal Computers[a]	Internet Hosts[b]	Internet Users[b]
	1996	1997	1998	1998	1998	1998	1998	1999	1999
Namibia	19	144	37	N/A	12	N/A	18.6	11.73	6
United States	215	2,146	847	244.3	256	78.4	458.6	1,508.77	74,100
South Africa	32	317	125	N/A	56	3.5	47.4	33.36	1,820
Angola	11	54	14	N/A	1	N/A	0.8	0.00	10

[a]Data are from International Telecommunication Union, *World Telecommunication Development Report 1999* and are per 1,000 people.
[b]Data are from the Internet Software Consortium (http://www.isc.org) and are per 10,000 people.

SOURCE: World Bank. *World Development Indicators 2000.*

Telecom Namibia has set up a GSM standard cellular telephone network, in conjunction with 2 Swedish companies. There were 58 main telephone lines and 8 mobile phones per 1,000 people in 1997.

ECONOMIC SECTORS

The economy remains narrowly-based, growth being determined largely by mining and agriculture, with the fishing sub-sector of agriculture being particularly important. Agriculture accounted for 12 percent of the GDP and 47 percent of employment in 1998, industry

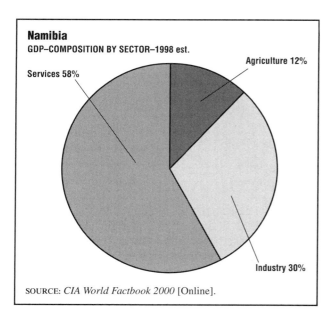

Namibia
GDP–COMPOSITION BY SECTOR–1998 est.

Services 58%
Agriculture 12%
Industry 30%

SOURCE: *CIA World Factbook 2000* [Online].

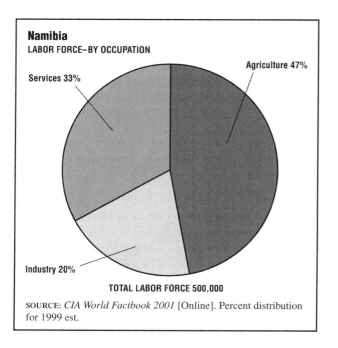

Namibia
LABOR FORCE–BY OCCUPATION

Services 33%
Agriculture 47%
Industry 20%

TOTAL LABOR FORCE 500,000

SOURCE: *CIA World Factbook 2001* [Online]. Percent distribution for 1999 est.

30 percent of the GDP (of which mining was 13 percent) and 25 percent of employment, with services providing 58 percent of the GDP and 28 percent of employment.

AGRICULTURE

Agricultural output (including fishing) grew by 1.8 percent a year in the 1980s and by 4.0 percent a year between 1990 and 1997. Agriculture and fishing together contributed 12 percent of the GDP in 1998, but animals and meat products contribute 16 percent of export earnings (1998), and around 70 percent of the population are directly or indirectly dependent on farming for their livelihood. In 1997, about 227,000 cattle and 954,000 sheep and goats were produced. The food crops are millet, sorghum, maize and some wheat. Namibia imports up to 50 percent of its food needs.

Since independence, the government has planned to combat the inequitable system of land ownership, with huge ranches co-existing with marginal communal **subsistence farming**. A commercial land reform act passed in 1994 allows the buying-up of empty or underused commercial farms for redistribution to communal farmers. The droughts of 1991–92 and 1994–95 severely affected cattle grazing and cereal production, necessitating widespread food relief.

Fishing contributed 4 percent of the GDP in 1998 while fish and fish products comprised over 30 percent of Namibia's export earnings. The main fish species are pilchard, mackerel, and hake. A 370-kilometer (230-mile) **exclusive economic zone** has been established, halting over-fishing of deep-water species by foreign trawlers. Despite the growth in fish export value, the fish catch declined after 1993's record 784,000-tonne haul to 488,000 tonnes in 1997.

INDUSTRY

Overall, the industrial sector—which includes mining, manufacturing, construction, electricity, water, and gas—generated 34 percent of the GDP in 1998.

Mining contributed 13 percent of the GDP and is the largest source of export earnings. Namibia has great mineral wealth including diamonds, uranium, copper, zinc, gold, and silver. Diamond production was about 1.4 million carats in 1998, contributing more than a third of foreign exchange earnings.

Before the country's independence in 1990 large areas of Namibia were opened to oil and gas prospecting, but as yet there have not proved to be major reserves of either fuel source. On-shore reserves are becoming depleted but off-shore output has risen quickly, helped by new mining technology.

Uranium production grew by 45 percent in 5 years to 1998, with 3,257 tons of uranium oxide mined in 1998. It is estimated that the large Rossing uranium mine has deposits to last until 2020. Copper production fell from 30,000 tons in 1994 to 8,000 tons in 1998, but a new copper mine at Haib started production in 1999 with a projected output of 115,000 tons annually. Moreover, sea salt is produced from coastal brine pans at Walvis Bay and Swakopund.

Although large zinc deposits were discovered in 1976, the technique needed to extract the metal from the ore has only recently been developed. Zinc production has been rising from the mid-1990s. It was confirmed in November 1998 that the Skorpion mine and refinery were to be developed with a projected output of 150,000 tons of refined zinc and an expected contribution to the GDP of 5 percent.

In 1998, manufacturing generated 17 percent of the GDP, and it was mostly located in the capital, Windhoek, and in some of the coastal towns. The sector comprises mainly processing of agricultural products for export and for domestic consumption. Fish processing is particularly important, and it makes up a quarter of the output of the manufacturing sector. Other important activities include the processing of meat and dairy products, beer and soft-drink production, metal fabrication (particularly the production of cans for fish), wood products, chemicals (particularly paints and plastics), and garment and leather goods manufacture.

Electricity is generated from a hydroelectric installation at Ruacana and from a coal fired station in Windhoek. When Ruacana water levels are high, electricity is exported to South Africa, and when the water levels are low, electricity is imported. There are some off-shore gas reserves at Kudu, and it is hoped these can be developed to diversify Namibia's sources of electricity generation

SERVICES

This sector contributed up to 58 percent of the GDP in 1998. The sector comprises business services and financial services, government services, community and personal services, and other services.

The financial sector includes the central bank, the Bank of Namibia, whose role is to issue notes and coins, act as banker for the commercial banks and the government, hold the country's reserves of gold and foreign exchange, regulate the financial sector, and act as lender of last resort to the banks when they run short of cash. Bank Windhoek, Commercial Bank of Namibia, First National Bank of Namibia, City Savings and Investment Bank, Namibia Post Savings Bank, and Standard Bank of Namibia are commercial banks, taking deposits from the public and lending to individuals and businesses. The Agricultural Bank of Namibia specializes in lending to the farm sector. Electronic and automatic banking are very advanced, and Namibia has benefitted from South African expertise in these areas in the period prior to independence.

Wholesaling and retailing and personal services depend on the general growth of the economy and have grown steadily in recent years. One feature is the prevalence and efficiency of large-scale supermarkets and department stores, all of which are managed by South African companies. Such stores only exist in the very largest of the cities, however.

Tourism has grown strongly during the 1990s, generating receipts of US$210 million in 1997 (12 percent of exports of goods and services) from 410,000 visitors, mainly from South Africa and Germany. Tourist attractions include wildlife parks and nature reserves (comprising in all 102,000 square kilometers or 12 percent of the land area in 1994), such as the famous Etosha Park, and spectacular desert scenery.

INTERNATIONAL TRADE

Namibia's economy is export-driven. Exports comprise 45 percent of the GDP by value and totaled US$1.4 billion in 1999. Exports of goods and services grew at 2.5 percent annually between 1965 and 1997. The main exports are diamonds, uranium, copper, zinc, gold, fish, fish products, cattle, sheep, goat and meat products. The principle destinations of exports are the United Kingdom (43 percent), South Africa (26 percent), Spain (14 percent), France (8 percent), and Japan (3 percent).

Namibia relies heavily upon imports to meet its needs, with 48 percent of the GDP being spent on goods produced outside Namibia and imports totaling US$1.5 billion in 1999. The principle imports are beverages, food, tobacco, fuel, vehicles, transport equipments, machinery, electrical goods, clothing, footwear and industrial raw materials. Imports are sourced primarily from South Africa (84 percent), with some goods coming from Germany (3 percent), the United States (2 percent), and Japan (2 percent).

The trade balance is continually in deficit, by somewhere between US$270 million in 1997 to US$100 million in 1999. There is also a deficit on the services account on the **balance of payments**, and these 2 deficits combined equal between US$60 million and US$140 million a year. These 2 deficits are covered by receipts from foreign investment in Namibia and from aid, the latter equivalent to about 5 percent of the GDP, or about US$155 million in 1997.

Exchange rates: Namibia

Namibian dollars per US$1

Jan 2001	7.78307
2000	6.93983
1999	6.10948
1998	5.52828
1997	4.60796
1996	4.29935

SOURCE: CIA *World Factbook 2001* [ONLINE].

MONEY

The Namibian dollar (NAD) is at par with the South African rand and has been affected by the rand's decline in value on the world currency exchanges. The rand was approximately at par with (equal in value to) the U.S. dollar in 1982, but by 2001 the rand (and the Namibian dollar) had depreciated to NAD8.224=US$1. The Namibian dollar is part of a de facto rand area of countries which peg the value of their currencies to the rand; this rand area includes Swaziland and Botswana. The **inflation rate** has been showing gradual improvement as the country settles into independence, with the rate falling steadily from 10 percent a year in 1995 to around 5 percent in 2000.

Namibia had a stock exchange founded in the early 1900s, in the southern town Lüderitz. It quoted companies that were established in the great diamond rush, reached a peak in 1910, but closed when the diamond rush was over. During the period of administration by South Africa, companies in Namibia were quoted on the Johannesburg Stock Exchange. At independence in 1990, it was decided to establish a stock exchange, and it finally opened in 1992, growing from 4 listed companies and 1 stockbroker at inception, to 36 listed companies and 7 stockbrokers in 2000.

POVERTY AND WEALTH

The GDP per capita (according to the purchasing power parity conversion which allows for the low price of many basic commodities in Namibia) stood at $4,300 in 1999, which places Namibia near the top of the lower middle-income countries in the world ranking. In the mid-1990s surveys indicated that 35 percent of the population were below the US$1 per day poverty line. About 49 percent of the **labor force** is employed in agriculture, most of which is subsistence farming, and the greatest incidence of poverty is in the rural areas. The high incidence of poverty, despite the relatively high levels of income per head, is an indication of the considerable inequality between the (mostly white) workers in the mining sectors and the rest of the workforce.

The rural poor work by tending family cattle or caring for small family-owned farms under harsh living conditions. They live in wood frame houses with mud walls and hard dirt floors. Mostly they eat cooked cereals and drink milk from their livestock, and rarely, if ever, eat meat. Their clothes are secondhand pieces which came from Europe and were bought in local markets. Water comes from wells, with some piped water in villages; cooking is done over wood fires and lighting is from small kerosene wick lamps, although there is electricity in the larger villages. Sanitation is provided by pit latrines. Still, there is primary education for 90 percent of the children, and dispensaries in villages provide basic health care.

In the towns, for those with employment, conditions tend to be better. Lower middle-class people may live in cement block houses with tin roofs and concrete floors. They have electricity some of the time, and water. Schools and hospitals are nearby. The poor live in slums where they have created rude shelters out of throw-away cloth, cardboard, or plastic. They use pit latrines and communal water taps.

WORKING CONDITIONS

The labor force comprised around 500,000 people in 1997, of which 41 percent were female and 20 percent were aged 10–14 (34 percent in 1980). The labor force grew at 2.4 percent a year between 1980 and 1997. Around 16,500 people enter the labor market each year. A high proportion of the workforce remains illiterate and unskilled. Agriculture provides employment for nearly half the workforce. Excluding subsistence farmers, the government is the biggest employer, accounting for over 70,000 jobs (18 percent of the workforce). There were 8,000 employed in the armed forces in 1995 (1.3 percent of the labor force).

In the colonial period a stream of African migrant workers came from the rural areas of Namibia and nearby countries such as Angola, Botswana, and Zambia. The development of the early mines and ranches depended on these sources of cheap labor. In the diamond and uranium

GDP per Capita (US$)

Country	1975	1980	1985	1990	1998
Namibia	N/A	2,384	2,034	1,948	2,133
United States	19,364	21,529	23,200	25,363	29,683
South Africa	4,574	4,620	4,229	4,113	3,918
Angola	N/A	698	655	667	527

SOURCE: United Nations. *Human Development Report 2000; Trends in human development and per capita income.*

mines, where profits have been high and the wage bill a small proportion of costs, the situation has changed, and these enterprises now pay the highest wages in the country. Elsewhere, particularly on the ranches, wages remain extremely low.

Unemployment figures have little significance in Namibia. There are very few with no work at all. Estimates in 1977 indicated that those who are unemployed or **underemployed** make up between 30 percent to 40 percent of the workforce, but this is almost all underemployment. There is no unemployment benefit, and those who do not work rely on support from charities or their families. Many people would like a modern sector job, but eke out an existence on family farms or in casual **informal sector** activities (such as **hawking**, portering, and scavenging) in the urban areas.

COUNTRY HISTORY AND ECONOMIC DEVELOPMENT

1884. South West Africa (SWA) is declared a German protectorate.

1915. South African troops defeat Germans and occupy SWA during World War I (1914–18).

1920. SWA is mandated to South Africa by the League of Nations.

1925. South Africa grants limit self-government to the territory's white inhabitants.

1945. The United Nations (UN) calls for Namibia to become a UN Trusteeship but is rebuffed by South Africa.

1950. The International Court of Justice (ICJ) rules that SWA remain under an international mandate.

1957. The Ovamboland People's Congress (OPC) is formed, with its main objective being the securing of independence for Namibia.

1958. OPC is renamed Ovamboland's People's Organization (OPO) and in 1960 becomes the South West Africa People's Organization (SWAPO) under the leadership of Sam Nujoma.

1966. The UN General Assembly terminates South Africa's mandate over SWA, placing it under UN control. South Africa ignores this and extends its apartheid laws to SWA. SWAPO launches an armed struggle against the South African regime in Namibia.

1968. The United Nations renames the country Namibia.

1971. The ICJ rules that South Africa's claims to Namibia are invalid.

1973. The UN General Assembly recognizes SWAPO as the sole legitimate representative of the Namibian people.

1978. The Democratic Turnhalle Alliance of Namibia (DTA) wins elections boycotted by SWAPO and a South African-backed internal government is established. The UN Security Council adopts Resolution 435, which calls for Namibia's independence.

1988. The terms of Resolution 435 are finally set in motion as part of a tripartite agreement formally signed by Angola, Cuba, and South Africa.

1989. In UN-supervised elections held in November SWAPO wins 41 seats in a 72-member Constituent Assembly; the DTA wins 21 seats. In December the Constituent Assembly introduces proposals for a draft constitution.

1990. On 9 February, the constitution is formally adopted. Sam Nujoma is elected as the country's first president, and SWAPO forms a government. On 21 March, Namibia becomes independent, the Constituent Assembly becomes the National Assembly, and the president assumes executive powers. In March, Namibia becomes a full member of the Southern Africa Customs Union (SACU), the UN, Organization of African Unity, and the Commonwealth.

1995. Sam Nujoma is elected president for a second term, and SWAPO forms government.

1999. Sam Nujoma elected president for a third term, and SWAPO forms government.

FUTURE TRENDS

Namibia's economic fortunes will continue to be dominated by neighboring South Africa for the foreseeable future. It is part of the Common Monetary Area (CMA) with Lesotho, South Africa, and Swaziland, and a member (with Botswana, Lesotho, South Africa, and Swaziland) of the Southern Africa Customs Union (SACU). CMA membership provides stability of **exchange rates** between the member countries and encourages trade between them, and SACU, by abolishing **tariffs** and other trade restrictions between members, also encourages trade. Its abundant mineral reserves and rich fisheries are expected to form the basis for Namibia's future economic prosperity.

The economy is expected to expand in the coming years owing to factors such as expanded output of offshore diamond mining, resumption of copper mining, and increased fish catches. Economic advancement has hitherto been accomplished primarily by the extractive (the withdrawal of natural resources by extraction with no provision for replenishment) industries and these benefits have yet to filter to the wider economy in terms of increased employment and more equitable income distribution.

Namibia has moved from colonial rule to independence with relatively little economic or social upheaval and has introduced public economic policies and physical **infrastructure** that should lead to long-term development and growth. The democratic process is well established, the government is secure, and the stability of the political process and the business environment is well established.

DEPENDENCIES

Namibia has no territories or colonies.

BIBLIOGRAPHY

"Countries: Namibia." *Africa South of the Sahara.* <http://www-sul.stanford.edu/depts/ssrg/africa/namibia.html>. Accessed September 2001.

Economist Intelligence Unit. *Country Profile: Namibia.* London: Economist Intelligence Unit, 2001.

Hodd, Michael. "Namibia." *The Economies of Africa.* Aldershot: Dartmouth, 1991.

"Namibia." *The Commonwealth Yearbook 2000.* Birmingham: The Stationery Office, 2000.

Permanent Mission of the Republic of Namibia to the UN. <http://www.un.int/namibia>. Accessed September 2001.

The Republic of Namibia. <http://www.grnnet.gov.na/intro.htm>. Accessed September 2001.

U.S. Central Intelligence Agency. *World Factbook 2000.* <http://www.odci.gov/cia/publications/factbook/index.html>. Accessed August 2001.

U.S. Department of State. *Background Notes: Namibia, April 1995.* <http://dosfan.lib.uic.edu/ERC/bgnotes/af/namibia9504.html>. Accessed September 2001.

U.S. Department of State. *FY 2001 Country Commercial Guide: Namibia.* <http://www.state.gov/www/about_state/business/com_guides/2001/africa/index.html>. Accessed September 2001.

—Allan C. K. Mukungu

NIGER

Republic of Niger
République du Niger

CAPITAL: Niamey.

MONETARY UNIT: Communauté Financiaire Africaine Franc (CFA Fr). One franc equals 100 centimes. CFA franc notes are in denominations of 500, 1,000, 2,500, 5,000, and 10,000 notes, and coins of 1, 5, 10, 25, 50, 100, and 250 francs.

CHIEF EXPORTS: Uranium, livestock and animal products, cowpeas, and onions.

CHIEF IMPORTS: Consumer goods (cereals, petroleum products), and intermediate and capital goods.

GROSS DOMESTIC PRODUCT: US$10 billion (purchasing power parity, 2000 est.).

BALANCE OF TRADE: Exports: US$385 million (f.o.b., 1999). Imports: US$317 million (f.o.b., 1999).

COUNTRY OVERVIEW

LOCATION AND SIZE. Niger is a landlocked West African country. It is bordered by Algeria and Libya to the north, Nigeria and Benin to the south, Mali and Burkina Faso to the west, and Chad to the east. Niger is about 600 kilometers (373 miles) from east to west at its widest point and about 400 kilometers (248 miles) north to south, and it extends into the Saharan desert. Niger's land area is 1,267,000 square kilometers (48,919 square miles), almost twice the size of Texas. Naimey, the capital city, is in the southwest, and both it and Agadez have international airports.

POPULATION. The population is estimated at 10,355,156 in July 2001. Of Niger's 10 main ethnic groups, the Hausa accounted for 56 percent of the population in 1998. They were followed by the Djerma-Songhai (22 percent), the Fula (8.5 percent), the Tuaregs (8 percent), the Kanouri (4 percent), with Toubous, Arabs and Gourmatche making up 1 percent of the population. About 80 percent of Nigeriens are Muslim. The official language is French, but Djerma and Hausa are also spoken.

The vast majority of the population lives in rural areas (81 percent), but urban populations are growing at a rate of 5.7 percent per year. The population is estimated to be growing at 3.2 percent per year, and the United Nations estimates the population in 2025 will be 22.4 million. This figure is mainly due to the high fertility rate of 7 children born per woman (2000 estimate), although this rate is falling.

OVERVIEW OF ECONOMY

Niger has a predominantly rural and poorly diversified economy, which is very vulnerable to outside factors (including swarms of locusts, drought, the exhaustion of natural resources, and world prices). Some improved prosperity was experienced in the 1970s due mainly to revenue from uranium. The decline in world uranium prices, the lack of rainfall, poor governance, and economic turmoil in a major trading partner, Nigeria, led to an economic decline in the 1980s. In the 1990s there was a modest improvement, with the **gross national product** (GNP) per head rising at 0.8 percent a year.

Niger is one of the 20 or so poorest countries in the world. The GNP per head measured by the **exchange rate** conversion is US$190 (in the United States, by way of comparison, it is US$29,340 per head). The **purchasing power parity** conversion (which makes allowance for the low price of many basic commodities in Niger) estimates the GNP per head at US$830. Similarly, the **gross domestic product** (GDP) per head was estimated at US$1,000 in 2000.

The economy depends heavily on agriculture, which accounted for 40 percent of the GDP in 1998. More than 90 percent of the population depends on subsistence agriculture (even urban dwellers maintain strong links to the countryside) and on the export of uranium. The main food

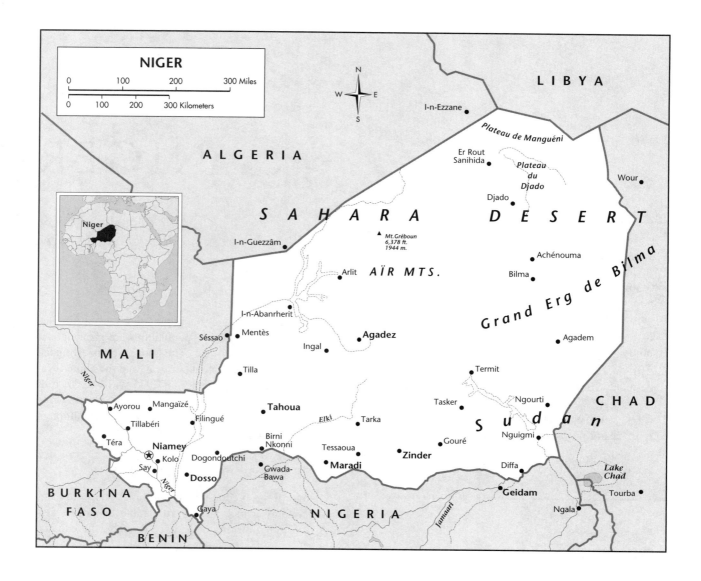

crops are groundnuts, millet, sorghum, cassava, rice and cowpeas, and cotton is grown for industrial use. Livestock reared includes cattle, sheep goats, and poultry. Industry, which provides 18 percent of the GDP, is small and consists mainly of uranium mining, the manufacturing of construction materials, textiles, the processing of agricultural products and brewing and soft drinks. In 1998 **retail** and wholesale trade, hotels and restaurants generated 17 percent of the GDP, transport and communications 5 percent, and with the rest of the services sector 20 percent.

Such low income means that 84 percent of total expenditure in Niger goes to consumption. Saving is very low at 3 percent, and, even with international aid, this in turn limits investment to 10 percent of the GDP—barely enough to maintain the capital stock at its current level. This means that worn-out machinery can be replaced and buildings, roads, ports, and airports kept in repair, but no increase in these can be made available. As more ma-

chinery and **infrastructure** are necessary for economic growth, production stagnates.

The major challenges are to restore flows of foreign aid (which have been cut as a result of the period of military rule from 1998 to 1999) and to implement the **liberalizing** reform program demanded by the international donors. The major demands on the public purse are to pay 40,000 civil servants and service the country's **external debt**. The government has pleaded for the early resumption of aid, and although some bilateral aid has been forthcoming, institutional and multilateral aid has been far more problematic. The prime minister has sought to reassure donors that poverty is the government's main concern, and the revival of the $580 million poverty eradication policy has won support from some key donors.

The government has instituted a series of economic reforms, mainly in the area of public finances, by streamlining the civil service, accelerating **privatization**, and increasing revenue collection. The government has also introduced many redundancies (duplication designed to prevent failure of the entire economic system because of the failure of one component). A weakness is the narrowness of the tax base, which extends to no more than a third of the country's economic activities. Most trade is dominated by a dozen families, who are widely suspected of avoiding taxes. Despite more than a decade tax reforms backed by the International Monetary Fund (IMF), little has improved, with fiscal revenue less than 10 percent of the GDP. But with the threat of civil unrest, the government finds it difficult to increase taxes while decreasing public wages. Thus deficits have been covered by creating **arrears**, putting a strain on donor relations.

Only 3 out of 12 major public companies have been sold in the period from 1996 to 1999, but to appease the IMF the government has declared that it is determined to continue to privatize. Sonitextil (textiles) has been sold to a Chinese corporation; Olani (milk production) has been sold to a private Nigerian company; Société Nationale de Ciment (SNC) (cement) has been sold to a Norwegian company. However, the disposal of further services (including the post service, petrol, and electricity) looks to be held up by a lack of external funding to prepare these sectors for privatization.

Niger has never suffered the same high rates of **inflation** as some of its neighbors, due to its membership of the Franc Zone (the use of a **fully convertible currency**, the CFA franc, pegged to the French franc) and the tight monetary and fiscal rules imposed by the Banque Centrale des États de l'Afrique de l'Ouest (BCEAO). However, the **devaluation** in 1994 of the CFA franc was a major inflationary problem for Niger, which imports most of its manufactured **consumer goods**. The government struggled to bring remuneration in the **public sector** under control, which delayed a new agreement being signed with the IMF. However, the government's efforts to curb inflation were successful in bringing inflation down to 36 percent , rather than seeing it reach the feared 100 percent. Inflation began to slow in 1995 and became negative in 1999 due to an excellent harvest.

POLITICS, GOVERNMENT, AND TAXATION

France took little interest in developing Niger during its colonial rule from the start of the 20th century until 1959, when uranium deposits were discovered. Independence was gained a year later and Hamani Diori became the first president. Widespread political corruption and drought in 1968 and 1969 brought civil disorder, at which point the army intervened. Lieutenant Colonel Seyni Kountche then ruled through the Conseil Militaire Supreme (CMS). Shortly before his death in 1987, he tried to create a legitimate face for the CMS by

introducing a National Charter. His successor, Aly Saibou, proposed a single-party constitution, that was passed in a 1989 referendum. The only legal party was then the National Movement for Developing Society (MNSD).

Internal social and political pressure built up in 1990–91 with demands for a multi-party state. Aid donors also began exerting force to move Niger towards democracy. Saibou eventually heeded the calls, and in 1991 a national conference was called, leading to a multi-party constitution. Legislative elections were held in 1993, and the MNSD gained 29 of the 83 seats, while the opposition Alliance de Forces de Changement (AFC) won 50 seats and formed the new government. Mahamane Ousmane, the AFC's candidate, was elected president the following month. However, the government soon ran into problems. Unrest, following the 1994 devaluation of the CFA franc led to the prime minister's resignation, fresh elections in 1995, and a period of limited cooperation between the MNSD leader, the prime minister and the president. Although achieving little in this period, the government did manage to sign a peace agreement with the Tuareg (a nomadic trading people, operating across Niger, Nigeria, Burkina Faso, Senegal, and Mali, with whom there had been armed conflict) to prevent further insurgencies.

In 1996 the army chief of staff, Colonel Ibrahim Mainassara, seized power. A new multi-party constitution was introduced, followed by an election, which Mainassara won amid malpractice protests. The opposition boycotted the legislative election and formed the Front pour la Restauration et la Defense de Democratie (FRDD) to denounce Mainassara's manipulation of the electoral process and to demand new elections. In 1997 and 1998 there were union and student demonstrations, which resulted in violent clashes with the government. Unrest in the armed forces and Tuareg insurgency created further problems for the new government.

It was hoped that the participation of FRDD in the 1999 local elections would usher in a new era of reconciliation. However, administrative muddle and indecisive results marred the election. President Mainassara was shot and killed 2 months later by members of the presidential guard. A new military council was formed by the chief of the presidential guard, Major Daouda Wanke, who became president. This military coup cost Niger much international goodwill, and many donors froze payments. Wanke was forced to announce elections and a new constitution in 1999 and stepped down with constitutional immunity from the law.

Presidential and legislative elections were held in late 1999. The new president, Mamadou Tandja, a retired colonel, won 60 percent of the vote in the second round of elections, and his MNSD, together with the Convention Democratique et Sociale (CDS), holds a majority of

seats in parliament. Elections were deemed to be satis-
factorily free and fair, leading to the resumption of donor
aid, although political stability is still very fragile. General army discontent over wages and conditions could
well lead to a mutiny or coup. In addition, social unrest,
spurred by union protests over the non-payment of
salaries, has continued. The European Union, whose aid
is frozen, is backing demands for an inquiry into assas-
sinations which implicate Major Wanke.

A referendum on the present constitution (the fifth
in recent years) received 90 percent of the vote on a 30
percent turnout in 1999. The constitution seeks to share
power between the president and the prime minister, and
the president is elected for a period of 5 years. The parliament is also elected for 5 years. The president may dissolve the assembly once in a year and picks the prime
minister from a choice of 3 selected by a parliamentary
majority. The constitution allows for a 7-member constitutional court, which interprets the constitution and val-
idates electoral results; an electoral commission to supervise and organize elections; an economic, social and
cultural council (which is in charge of examining relevant bills) and a media watchdog, the Communication
Council. In May 2000 a high council of national defence
was created to run the armed forces.

The discontent of the Tuareg and other communities
has died down, following the deal that was brokered in
1995. The rebellion cost hundreds of lives, affected infrastructure, and stopped promising tourism in the desert
town of Agadez. By mid-1999, most Tuaregs had turned
in their weapons, in return for jobs in the armed forces or
other sectors. Following these developments tourism has
picked up in Tuareg areas. However, the government now
faces problems from the Toubou community in the east.

Most of the 11 privately-owned papers suffered harassment, closures, and arrests under the Mainassara
regime. The only private FM radio station also reported
harassment. The state controls most radio and television

broadcasts. But a more moderate press law was enacted
in 1998.

Niger raises less than 10 percent of the GNP in tax
revenue and received a further 2 percent in surpluses from
state-owned enterprises, mainly **monopolies**. About 25
percent of government spending goes on social services
(which includes health and education), about 15 percent
on military equipment and the armed forces, with the remainder absorbed by general public sector administration.

INFRASTRUCTURE, POWER, AND COMMUNICATIONS

Despite much donor funded improvement, the transport system remains inadequate, with only 8 percent of
the 6,800 kilometers (4,225 miles) of roads being paved,
although international road transport has improved with
the completion of the Zinder-Agadis Road (part of the
Trans Sahara highway). Although there remains no railway network in Niger, there is an emphasis on increasing access to the sea via waterways through neighboring
states to the south.

There are international airports at Naimey and
Agadez, and 25 other towns have airports or landing
strips. Naimey is the busiest airport and is served by several regional and international carriers.

There are about 14,000 telephones in Niger, and most
main towns have public telephones. The international
telephone service links Naimey to Nigerian and French
installations. There are an estimated 38,000 televisions
and 500,000 radios in use in Niger.

In the energy sector there have been substantial rises
in fuel prices, by more than 20 percent, in 2000. This rise
has increased prices throughout the economy by making
transport and electricity more expensive, although output
is these sectors has remained more-or-less unchanged.
Domestic electricity is mainly thermally generated, with
some rural solar energy. Electricity consumption rose to

Communications

Country	Newspapers	Radios	TV Sets[a]	Cable subscribers[a]	Mobile Phones[a]	Fax Machines[a]	Personal Computers[a]	Internet Hosts[b]	Internet Users[b]
	1996	1997	1998	1998	1998	1998	1998	1999	1999
Niger	0	69	27	N/A	0	N/A	0.2	0.03	3
United States	215	2,146	847	244.3	256	78.4	458.6	1,508.77	74,100
Nigeria	24	223	66	N/A	0	N/A	5.7	0.00	100
Chad	0	242	1	0.0	0	0.0	N/A	0.00	1

[a]Data are from International Telecommunication Union, *World Telecommunication Development Report 1999* and are per 1,000 people.
[b]Data are from the Internet Software Consortium (http://www.isc.org) and are per 10,000 people.

SOURCE: World Bank. *World Development Indicators 2000.*

268 million kilowatt hours (kWh) in 1998, but production, due to poor maintenance of installations was a mere 28 million kilowatt hours. The rest is bought from Nigeria, but the country has suffered frequent power cuts due to rationing of the supply from Nigerian. A new hydroelectric dam has been proposed 180 kilometers from Naimey. The government petrol company, Sonidep, and the state electricity company, Nigelec, have been slated for privatization.

Sonichar (a **parastatal**) began opencast coal mining in Anou Arraren in 1981 to provide fuel for the local power plant and provide energy for the uranium mines and industry near Arlit, as well as the towns of Agadez and Tchirozine. Reserves stand at 6 million metric tons, and production has been 150,000 metric tons per year since 1983.

ECONOMIC SECTORS

Niger depends most on agriculture, for both output and employment, and this fact reflects Niger's low level of development. Agriculture (including hunting, forestry, and fishing) employed 90 percent of the population in 1998 and provided 40 percent of the GDP. This is a much higher reliance on agriculture for production than is general in Africa, where, on average, 17 percent of the GDP comes from farming. The involvement of the **labor force** in agriculture, too, is well above the African norm, where on average 68 percent of the workforce are engaged in farming.

Industry (including mining, manufacturing, construction and power) employed 4 percent of the population (in Africa generally, it is 9 percent) and produced 18

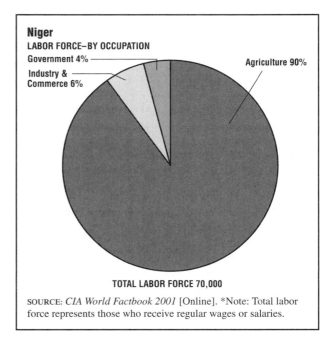

Niger
LABOR FORCE–BY OCCUPATION

Government 4%
Industry & Commerce 6%
Agriculture 90%

TOTAL LABOR FORCE 70,000

SOURCE: *CIA World Factbook 2001* [Online]. *Note: Total labor force represents those who receive regular wages or salaries.

percent of the GDP (the all-Africa figure is 34 percent). Services generated 42 percent of the GDP in 1988 (compared with Africa generally at 50 percent) and employed 6 percent of the working population (whereas the all-Africa figure was 23 percent).

AGRICULTURE

Niger's food supply problems have eased due to excellent harvests from 1998 to 2000. Food crop production (mainly millet, sorghum, paddy rice, and pulses) has benefitted from regular rains and has helped keep consumer price inflation low. However, production is very vulnerable to rainfall, disease, and pests. Famines are a constant fear and are exacerbated by poor food storage, despite measures taken since the droughts of the 1970s and 1980s.

Cereal imports vary between 10 percent and 40 percent of yearly requirements, although in millet and sorghum Niger is self-sufficient. About 44,000 metric tons of rice and 39,000 metric tons of wheat are imported to meet needs every year. with rice coming from Asia and other cereals coming from the West African region.

Most cultivating farms are family **smallholdings**. Livestock rearing is undertaken in arid areas and provides 10–15 percent of the GDP. After uranium, live cattle is the largest export, mainly to Nigeria. Niger's other export crops (cotton, ground nuts, and cowpeas) are also mainly exported to Nigeria but have suffered with the collapse of world oil prices and the consequent downturn of the Nigerian economy (Nigeria's exports are more than 95 percent oil) since 1985.

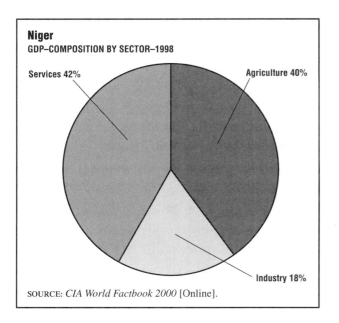

Niger
GDP–COMPOSITION BY SECTOR–1998

Services 42%
Agriculture 40%
Industry 18%

SOURCE: *CIA World Factbook 2000* [Online].

INDUSTRY

Modern manufacturing accounts for less than 1 percent of the GDP, and mainly consists of soaps and detergents, bottled drinks, and the processing of agricultural products. Two Chinese companies purchased an 80 percent stake in the textiles company, Sonitex, in 1997, and output of Sonitex fabrics totalled 5.6 million meters in 1998. Niger also has a 35,000 metric ton capacity cement plant, and several smaller factories supply local markets with metal goods and construction materials.

Uranium mining began in 1971 in the open desert near Arlit. In 1998 output was 3,561 metric tons per year, making Niger the third largest producer in the world. Mines are operated by Cominak and Somair (two private companies), though the government maintains an interest through the national mining office, Oranem. Technical support is provided by the French company, Cogema, which has a contract until 2003. New agreements from 1995 allow Somair to exploit new reserves at Takriza and Toumou, which total 15,000 metric tons. Cominak and Somair produce roughly 2,000 and 1,000 metric tons per year respectively, but both have suffered from reduced revenue due to the fall in the world price of uranium. As a result Somair has more than halved its workforce to 400, and Cominak is also expected to introduce retrenchments

After positive exploration surveys, gold production is expected to stimulate the mining sector. Revision of the mining code in 1993 to offer a 5-year **income tax** break for larger companies and no import **duty** on mining equipment makes a very appealing package for foreign investors, and several companies have moved into the Liptako area. Recent seismic surveys for copper, lithium and molybdenum also produced promising results. Cassiterite is also currently mined at a few small sites.

SERVICES

Between 1988 and 1992 4 banks collapsed: the development bank, Banque de Developpement de la Republique du Niger (BDRN), and commercial banks. Remaining are 2 development banks along with 10 other banks and financial sector institutions. The development banks borrow on international capital markets and lend to large scale business enterprises and public sector projects. The commercial banks and savings banks take deposits from the public and lend to individuals and smaller business enterprises. The commercial banks are also engaged in foreign exchange dealing.

The transport sector is very underdeveloped. There is no railway, and the Niger River is only navigable for 3 months of the year when rain increases the water level. Almost all freight travels by road along the borders with Nigeria, Benin, Burkina Faso, and Mali. The most

northerly point reached is Agadez, 300 kilometers (186 miles) from the Nigerian border, with minimal transport in the northern half of the country. There are 27 airports, of which 9 have paved runways.

Retail and wholesale distribution is undertaken by small traders predominantly in open-air markets where a wide range of foodstuffs, second-hand clothing imported from Europe, and household utensils fabricated from scrap metal, are on sale.

Niger has considerable tourism potential which was starting to expand in the 1980s. Then Tuareg rebellion closed the main attractions, such as Agadez, the capital of the desert zone. Since the peace agreement with the Tuareg in 1995, the number of tourists has begun to increase, mainly to the Tenere Desert, the Air Mountains and the Niger River, reaching 55,000 in 1999. The tourist experience focuses on the attractions of desert life and the exotic nomadic groups, such as the Tuareg, who inhabit the arid regions.

INTERNATIONAL TRADE

Niger runs a continuous deficit in merchandise trade, with exports in 1997 at US$300 million and imports at US$441 million. This deficit is met by international aid, mostly from France.

Niger's exports in 1995 were mainly uranium (49 percent), livestock and meat products (17 percent), and cowpeas (7 percent). Most of Niger's exports, mainly the uranium, went to France (74 percent), Côte d'Ivoire (8 percent), and Nigeria (3 percent).

Imports in 1995 were dominated by consumer manufactures (62 percent), machinery and vehicles (20 percent), cereals (10 percent), and fuels (8 percent). France provided most of Niger's imports with 19 percent of the total, and other sources of imports were Cote d'Ivoire (12 percent), Germany (2 percent), and Japan (2 percent).

In 1994 devaluation of the CFA franc enhanced the profitability of exports and discouraged imports. Conse-

Trade (expressed in billions of US$): Niger		
	Exports	Imports
1975	.091	.101
1980	.566	.594
1985	.259	.369
1990	.283	.389
1995	.287	.374
1998	N/A	N/A

SOURCE: International Monetary Fund. *International Financial Statistics Yearbook 1999.*

Exchange rates: Niger

Communaute Financiere Africaine francs (CFA Fr) per US$1

Jan 2001	699.21
2000	711.98
1999	615.70
1998	589.95
1997	583.67
1996	511.55

Note: From January 1, 1999, the CFA Fr is pegged to the euro at a rate of 655.957 CFA Fr per euro.

SOURCE: CIA *World Factbook 2001* [ONLINE].

Distribution of Income or Consumption by Percentage Share: Niger

Lowest 10%	0.8
Lowest 20%	2.6
Second 20%	7.1
Third 20%	13.9
Fourth 20%	23.1
Highest 20%	53.3
Highest 10%	35.4

Survey year: 1995
Note: This information refers to expenditure shares by percentiles of the population and is ranked by per capita expenditure.

SOURCE: *2000 World Development Indicators* [CD-ROM].

quently the **trade deficit** fell to half its 1980 level, and in 1997 it stood at US$141 million. Trade with Nigeria, which is Niger's biggest regional trading partner, has improved greatly since the 1994 devaluation. However, much of this trade, as in the case of other neighbors, is smuggled across unsecured land borders and goes unrecorded.

MONEY

Niger is part of the 8-member UEMOA, and the currency is the CFA franc. Niger's Central Bank (BCEAO) holds the monetary reserves of all member states and is obliged to hold 65 percent of foreign reserves at the French treasury. France in turn guarantees convertibility of the CFA franc within UEMOA. The BCEAO issues currency notes and regulates credit expansion throughout the region. The CFA franc was pegged to the French franc at 50: 1 from 1948 but because it was overvalued in the late 1980s it was devalued to CFA franc 100:1 French franc. With France having joined the European Monetary Union, the CFA franc is now tied to the euro at 655.959:1.

POVERTY AND WEALTH

Rural people eke out a slim, almost life-threatening existence tending their herds or their small farm plots.

GDP per Capita (US$)

Country	1975	1980	1985	1990	1998
Niger	298	328	242	235	215
United States	19,364	21,529	23,200	25,363	29,683
Nigeria	301	314	230	258	256
Chad	252	176	235	228	230

SOURCE: United Nations. *Human Development Report 2000; Trends in human development and per capita income.*

Their houses are made of wood with dirt. They eat mostly cooked cereal and milk, but they rarely eat meat. Their clothes are secondhand, sent from Europe to be sold in local markets. Water comes from wells, cooking is done over wood fires, and lighting is from small kerosene wick lamps. Sanitation is provided by pit latrines. Children are unlikely to go to school, and there are seldom operating health facilities close-by.

In the towns, for those with employment, conditions tend to be better. The lower middle class lives in housing made of cement blocks with tin rooftops and concrete floors. There is electricity and water some of the time. Moreover, schools and dispensaries are close. The poor live in slums where they construct their shelters from scraps of material, plastic, and rusty metal sheets. They use pit latrines and communal water taps. Urban poor have better access to medical care and schools for their children, but there are shortages of these facilities, and often the charges are too high for a poverty-stricken family to afford.

Niger is a low income country, and 61 percent of the population were below the US$1 per day poverty line in 1992, with the incidence of poverty greatest in the rural areas. Niger is ranked 173 out of 174 countries in the United Nations Human Development Index.

Average life expectancy is estimated at 47 years, and this age is a significant improvement on the 1970 figure of 38 years. Infant mortality is estimated at 125 deaths per 1,000 births (in the United States the rate is 7 per 1,000) and 320 children out of every 1,000 will die before the age of 5. There are 3 doctors and 70 nurses per 100,000 people.

AIDS is a growing problem, and the Ministry of Health estimated that there were 93,008 sufferers in 1998, with 5,378 deaths attributed to the disease. A National Commission to combat AIDS was set up in 1987. However, Islamic groups still oppose the promotion of condoms.

Niger's educational provision outside towns is rudimentary, and class sizes are universally large. There is 1 university at Naimey, as well as several small colleges. However, they are very under-funded, and close frequently due to student or teacher strikes over grants and salaries. Adult literacy was 14 percent in 1997, primary school enrollment was 24 percent, and secondary was 9 percent. There is also a large disparity between men and women in terms of access to education, with almost twice as many males enrolled as females.

WORKING CONDITIONS

The total labor force in 1998 was estimated at 5 million, of which 44 percent were women. Most children aged 10–14 have to work, and 45 percent of children in this age group were in the labor force. Children start helping with farm work from as early as 5 years of age. The public sector employs 39,000 (and is the only significant formal employer), while small shops and industry account for a few thousand jobs, as does mining. The rest of the population makes a living in agriculture, on small family farms, or in herding livestock. Gender disparities are high: while 41 percent of women work, only 8 percent hold administrative or managerial positions, and they account for only 8 percent of professional and technical workers.

The unemployment rate has little meaning in Africa. There are no social security provisions, and those without work or support from families or charities cannot survive. For much of the year in **subsistence farming** there is relatively little work to do, and this is shared among the family members. During planting and harvesting, there is more work to be done, and everyone is more fully occupied, but even in these periods, there may be more than enough labor to do the tasks, and the work is again shared. Since people share the farm work it appears that all of them have occupations in agriculture, but these workers are not engaged full time for all the year, and hence there is some "disguised unemployment." In the urban area those without formal sector jobs and any family or charitable support survive by casual **hawking**, portering, and scavenging.

The number of people earning regular wages or salaries is 70,000. There is a formal minimum wage. The government, under IMF pressure, has been streamlining the civil service, and government employees have lost their jobs, which will undoubtedly bring the government trade union trouble.

Trade unions in Niger are strong, with around 70 percent of public sector workers and more than 50 percent in the **private sector** unionized. The unions are militant, and strikes, which often lead to civil unrest, are not uncommon and have brought down governments. The present government, much like those of the past, faces much pressure from the public sector unions, which as well as protesting over pay arrears, have also opposed privatization, with support from students.

COUNTRY HISTORY AND ECONOMIC DEVELOPMENT

1900. Niger becomes a French colony.

1958. Niger is allowed internal self-government.

1959. Uranium deposits are discovered.

1960. Niger becomes fully independent with Hamani Diori as the first president.

1969. Drought and civil disorder disrupt the country, and the army takes control under Lt-Col. Seyni Kountche.

1987. Kountche dies, and Col. Aly Saibou assumes the presidency.

1989. Single-party constitution is passed by a referendum.

1991. Multi-party constitution introduced.

1993. Mahamane Ousmane is elected president.

1994. CFA franc is devalued, raising the domestic prices received for exports and increasing export volumes, while at the same time increasing import prices and reducing import volumes, these 2 factors combining to reduce the trade deficit.

1996. Col. Ibrahim Mainassara seizes power.

1999. Mainassara is shot and Major Dauda Wanke becomes president. Later, Wanke steps down, and Mamadou Tandja is elected president.

FUTURE TRENDS

On the political front, President Tandja faces militant unions who are demanding a year's salary arrears, and the opposition has become increasingly confrontational. A fashion fair has provoked Islamic fundamentalism. Political stability is still under threat as Tandja's government moves towards strong-arm tactics to clamp down on protests and civil disorder in 2001. Civil unrest serves to discourage both domestic and foreign investment, and strikes and demonstrations seriously impair economic progress.

Niger continues to participate in regional developments, such as the free trade initiatives of the Economic Community of West African States (ECOWAS) and UEMOA, but they will have limited impact as so little of Niger's trade is with neighboring countries.

The economy depends heavily on the fortunes of the agriculture sector and on the volume of the output of uranium, and the price received for it. With drought a chronic problem and minimal investment, it is to be expected that agriculture will continue to stagnate. There are no immediate prospects that the world will increase its demand for nuclear power, and the prospects are for a continuation of the depressed price for uranium and no significant increase in production from Niger's uranium sector. Niger faces the prospect of continuing economic stagnation and greater reliance on the international community for aid to maintain living standards at even their depressed current levels.

The IMF is hoping to approve new loans, but the government will struggle to meet the required conditions. The World Bank has approved a $35 million loan to help fiscal reforms and to cover the trade deficit. Inflation pressures will grow due to the increases in petroleum prices. Electricity cuts have been less frequent, but lack of rain may lead to food shortages following the 2000–01 season. In terms of international aid, the European Union has started disbursement of $48 million worth of loans, and other European countries have also begun significant disbursement of funds in Niger.

DEPENDENCIES

Niger has no territories or colonies.

BIBLIOGRAPHY

Economist Intelligence Unit. *Country Profile: Niger.* London: EIU, 2000.

Ewing, D., et al., editors. *Niger Country Review 1999/2000.* Houston: Country Watch.com, 1999.

Hodd, M. "Niger." *The Economies of Africa.* Aldershot: Dartmouth, 1991.

"Niger Economy." *Newafrica.com.* <http://www.newafrica.com/profiles/economy.asp?countryid=37>. Accessed July 2001.

"Niger." *World Yearbook.* London: Europa Publications, 2000.

U.S. Central Intelligence Agency. *CIA World Factbook 2000: Niger.* <http://www.cia.gov/cia/publications/factbook/geos/ng.html>. Accessed July 2001.

U.S. Central Intelligence Agency. *CIA World Factbook 2001: Niger.* <http://www.cia.gov/cia/publications/factbook/geos/ng.html>. Accessed September 2001.

—Jack Hodd

NIGERIA

Federal Republic of Nigeria

CAPITAL: Abuja.

MONETARY UNIT: Naira (N). 1 naira equals 100 kobo. Coins in denominations of 1, 5, 10, 25, and 50 kobo, and notes in denominations of 5, 10, 20, and 50 naira are issued.

CHIEF EXPORTS: Petroleum and petroleum products, cocoa, rubber, lumber, and peanuts.

CHIEF IMPORTS: Machinery, chemicals, transport and electronic equipment, manufactured goods, food, and live animals.

GROSS DOMESTIC PRODUCT: US$110.5 billion (purchasing power parity, 1999 est.).

BALANCE OF TRADE: Exports: US$13.1 billion (f.o.b., 1999). Imports: US$10 billion (f.o.b., 1999).

COUNTRY OVERVIEW

LOCATION AND SIZE. Nigeria is located in Western Africa, and borders the Gulf of Guinea, between Benin on the west and Cameroon on the east. It has a compact area of 923,768 square kilometers (356,376 square miles). The country's land mass extends from the Gulf of Guinea in the south to the Sahel (the shore of the Sahara Desert) in the north. Comparatively, Nigeria is slightly more than twice the size of California, or the size of California, Nevada, and Arizona combined. Abuja, the capital city of the Federal Republic of Nigeria, replaced the former capital city, Lagos, in December 1991, because of its more central location, among other reasons. Lagos remains Nigeria's commercial capital. Other major Nigerian cities include Ibadan, Kaduna, Kano, Maiduguri, Jos, Port Harcourt, Enugu, Calabar, and Aba.

POPULATION. Accurate population counts for Nigeria are difficult to obtain because such figures are tied directly to representation in the National Assembly and distribution of national wealth; therefore, they are often skewed by groups vying for political or economic advantage. In the absence of an accurate census, it is im-

possible to determine how many people live in Nigeria beyond rough estimates. The population of Africa's largest country was estimated at 123,337,822 in 2000. This figure represents an increase of 39.36 percent over the 1991 population census figure of 88.5 million, which was hotly debated and widely believed to have been an undercount. In the year 2000, the birth rate was estimated at 40.12 per 1,000, while the death rate was estimated at 13.72 per 1,000. With a projected annual population growth rate of 2.67 percent between 2000 and 2015, Nigeria's population is expected to increase to 156,269,020 in the year 2015. Excess mortality due to AIDS, lower life expectancy, and higher infant mortality and death rates might reduce this projected figure.

The density of population in Nigeria is among the highest in Africa. It ranges from 100 persons per square kilometer in the northeastern and west-central regions to more than 500 persons per square kilometer in the south and northwestern regions. The population is largely young. According to a 2000 estimate of the age structure, the largest segment of the population (53 percent) comprised individuals who are between 15 and 64 years old. This percentage included 33,475,794 males and 32,337,193 females. The second largest segment (44 percent) were between 0 and 14 years old and included 27,181,020 males and 26,872,317 females. The smallest segment (3 percent) were individuals 65 years and older, including 1,729,149 males and 1,722,349 females. The estimated sex ratio of the total population in 2000 was 1.02 males to 1 female while life expectancy at birth for the total population was 51.56 years: 51.58 years for males, and 51.55 years for females. The government hopes that the expansion of education, especially among women, and the availability of birth control information, including family planning, will help to control the population growth. Nigeria has received assistance from the United States Agency for International Development (USAID) to develop and implement its

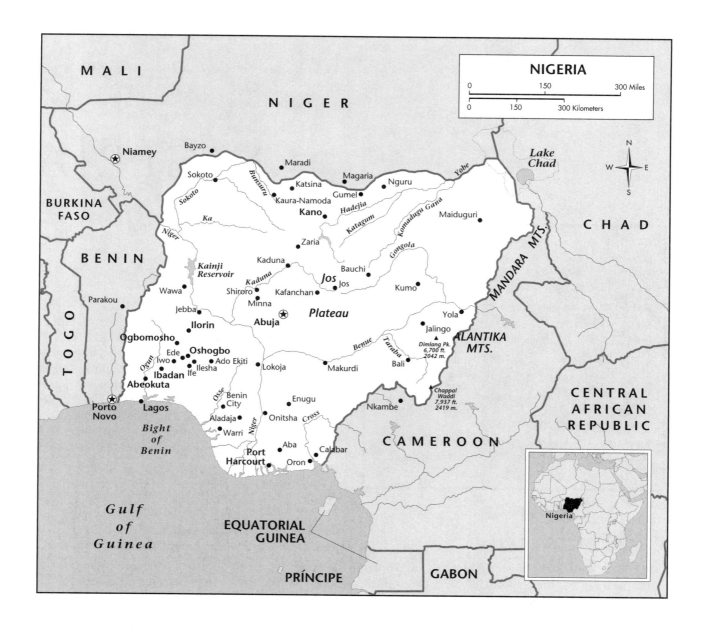

programs on family planning and child survival. In 1992, Nigeria added an HIV/AIDS prevention and control program to its existing health activities.

Nigeria is a plural or multinational state, with 250 ethnic or nationality groups. The most populous and politically influential of the nationality groups include the Hausa-Fulani (29 percent) in the north, the Yoruba (21 percent) in the southwest, the Igbo (18 percent) in the southeast, and the Ijaw (10 percent) in the Niger Delta. This characteristic ethnic composition gives Nigeria a rich diversity in customs, languages, religious and cultural traditions. It also compounds Nigeria's political and economic problems. Although the people are primarily rural dwellers, Nigeria, like other post-colonial African countries, has been urbanizing rapidly. In the year 2000, nearly 25 percent of the Nigerian population were urban dwellers. At least 24 cities have populations of more than

100,000. Lagos, the largest city, had a population of 9.8 million in 1995, 12.5 million in 2000, and is projected to have a population of 25 million in 2015.

OVERVIEW OF ECONOMY

As of 2001, the most conspicuous fact about Nigeria's economy is that the corruption and mismanagement of its post-colonial governments has prevented the channeling of the country's abundant natural and human resources—especially its wealth in crude oil—into lasting improvements in **infrastructure** and the construction of a sound base for self-sustaining economic development. Thus, despite its abundant resources, Nigeria is poorer today than it was at independence in 1960. Still one of the less developed and poorer countries of the world, it has the potential to become a major economic power if the leaders resolve to learn from past mistakes and to harness the country's rich natural and human resources for a productive and sustained effort to promote economic development.

Before the country was colonized by Britain, during the second half of the 19th century, the various nationality groups that currently make up Nigeria were largely an agricultural people. They were food self-sufficient and produced a variety of commodities that were exported overseas. British colonial administrators amalgamated (joined together) the nationality groups in 1914 into a larger economy for exploitation for the benefit of British industrial classes. Under colonial rule, Nigeria remained an agricultural country, exporting raw materials to Britain and importing from it finished goods. Therein lay the origins of the dependence of Nigerian economy on commodity markets of the industrialized Western world for its foreign exchange. While the industrialization of the country was discouraged, rudimentary foundations for a modern Nigerian economy, however, were laid. Colonial economic policies shaped future independent Nigeria's economy, particularly in marketing, labor supply, and investment. The process of colonial rule and formal economic exploitation ended in 1960 but left Nigeria a relatively strong but undiversified economy. Thereafter, Nigerians were poised to remedy this defect and to build a self-sustaining Nigerian economy comprising agricultural, industrial, and service sectors.

From independence in 1960, the state took up the direction and planning of economic growth and development. Education was progressively expanded at all levels to reduce the rate of illiteracy and to provide the requisite skills and **labor force** for development. Infrastructure of roads and communication networks were constructed far beyond what was inherited from colonial rule. Hydroelectric dams were built to generate electricity. Secondary industries and automobile assembly plants were established to create more employment opportunities. Because of the paucity (small number) of indigenous (native or local) private capital, these activities were undertaken and financed by the government, often with foreign assistance from such countries as Britain and the United States. Foreign oil companies, such as Shell-BP, Exxon-Mobil, Chevron, Agip, and Texaco, operate in partnership with the government in the oil sector, the mainstay of Nigeria's economy. The capital-intensive oil sector provides 95 percent of Nigeria's foreign exchange earnings and about 65 percent of its budgetary revenues.

Because the established, government-owned industries and businesses were often inefficient and corrupt, productivity was low at best. In particular, mismanagement and corruption were endemic (characteristic of) in the successive governments and throughout the nation. However, the gravest problem was caused by the gov-

ernment's decision to stress the industrial sector above all others. Caught in a web of competing demands for scarce resources, the officials took the path of rapid, large-scale industrialization at the expense of the agricultural sector, as well as light manufacturing. They directed the bulk of investment capital towards the promotion of what Western advisers captioned "industrial take off." This decision to abandon the known—agriculture—for the unknown—rapid large-scale industrialization—was a fundamental error. The capital and the skill needed for rapid, large-scale industrialization were not sufficiently available. Thus, an unskilled workforce and insufficient funds severely handicapped the industrial sector. Also, Nigeria's neglect of the agricultural sector aggravated already problematic food shortages. Nigeria had raised enough food to meet domestic needs during its colonial period and in the decade following independence. However, it experienced food shortages in the 1970s and 1980s, which necessitated the importation of food from foreign countries. Among the imports were palm oil (from Malaysia), of which Nigeria had been the world's largest producer and exporter, and rice (from the United States) which was considered less nutritious than Nigerian brown rice. Once Africa's largest poultry producer, Nigeria lost that status because of inefficient corn production and a ban on the importation of corn. Furthermore, it is no longer a major exporter of cocoa, peanuts, and rubber.

Several forces compounded the problems of the agricultural sector. The migration of labor from the rural areas to the urban centers reduced the traditional agricultural labor force. Ecological constraints such as poor soil, erosion, drought, and the absence of agricultural research added to the problem. Other constraints on agricultural production include the use of antiquated technology due to a lack of capital, the low status given to agriculture in the education of the youth, inefficient marketing, an inadequate transportation infrastructure, lack of refrigeration, trade restrictions, under-investment due to unavailability of credit, low prices, and unstable pricing policies which resulted in farmers literally subsidizing urban dwellers and other sectors of the economy. In addition to these handicaps, import constraints limit the availability of many agricultural and food-processing plants. In general, land tenure discourages long-term investment in technology and modern production techniques.

The problem of food shortages and imports was addressed in the late 1970s and early 1980s. In the late 1970s the military government of Olusegun Obasanjo embarked upon "Operation Feed the Nation." His civilian successor, President Shehu Shagari, continued the program as the "Green Revolution." Both programs encouraged Nigerians to grow more food, and urged unemployed urban dwellers to return to the rural areas to grow food crops. The government provided farmers with fertilizers and loans from the World Bank. The food situation has stabilized, although Nigeria still imports food. A related problem which has not been completely resolved is the pollution of water in the Delta region and Ogoniland by oil companies. Water pollution disrupts farming efforts and has been a source of friction between farmers on one side and the national government and the oil companies on the other.

The oil boom which Nigeria experienced in the 1970s helped the nation to recover rapidly from its civil war and at the same time gave great impetus to the government's program of rapid industrialization. Many manufacturing industries sprang up and the economy experienced a rapid growth of about 8 percent per year that made Nigeria, by 1980, the largest economy in Africa. The growth, however, was not sustained. The new oil wealth did little to reverse widespread poverty and the collapse of even basic infrastructure and social services. The iron and steel industry, started with the help of the Soviet Union, still has not achieved a satisfactory level of production. The oil boom also provoked a shortage of labor in the agricultural sector as members of the rural workforce migrated to jobs in the urban construction boom and a growing **informal sector**. When the price of crude oil fell and corruption and mismanagement still prevailed at all levels, the economy became severely depressed. The urban unemployment rate rose to 28 percent in 1992, and crime also increased as 31.4 percent of the population lived below the poverty line.

Nigeria's debts mounted as administrators engaged in external borrowing and subsidized food and rice imports and gasoline prices. In the 1980s, economic realities forced Ibrahim Babangida's military regime to negotiate a loan with the World Bank and to reschedule Nigeria's **external debts**. His regime undertook an economic **structural adjustment program** (ESAP) to reduce Nigeria's dependence on oil and to create a basis for sustainable non-inflationary growth. However, external borrowing to shore up the economy created more problems than it alleviated. Much of the borrowed money never reached Nigeria. The portion that reached the country often went towards abandoned or nonperforming **public sector** projects. External loans escalated Nigeria's debts to US$30 billion during the Babangida regime and consumed external earnings in **debt servicing**. Similarly, the ESAP prescribed by the International Monetary Fund (IMF) failed to advance the economy, and aggravated the problems of **inflation** and unemployment. It caused a reduction of state spending on education and health care. Continuing political instability due to Babangida's annulment of the presidential election results in June 1993 and the subsequent authoritarian rule of Sani Abacha (1993 to 1998) made the general economic situation worse. The gross corruption by the Abacha regime and its violations of people's fundamental rights turned Nige-

ria into an international pariah for 6 years, and thus discouraged foreign investment in the economy. Many industries and manufacturing companies could not obtain raw materials and closed down. Others operated under severe handicaps, including rampant power outages and refined petroleum scarcity. Not enough had been done in the years of plenty to diversify the economy or to sustain the development. Military coups (military overthrow of civilian governments) and political instability worsened the situation.

There was considerable optimism in May 1999 when Oluseguan Obasanjo became Nigeria's civilian president. Many hoped that he would lift Nigeria from the verge of economic bankruptcy. One of Obasanjo's objectives to that purpose was to secure **debt relief** from Nigeria's foreign creditors. However, these creditors insisted that Nigeria's wealth of untapped resources provided the means for the country to pay off its debts, and refused to cancel its debts of US$30 billion.

In spite of some opposition, Obasanjo embarked upon a program of **privatizing** some **parastatals** in order to reduce corruption, promote efficiency, and raise productivity. He introduced an anti-corruption bill which passed through the legislature, and recovered some of the revenues that had been stolen from the country and deposited in Western banks. The **inflation rate**, which was estimated at 12.5 percent at the start of his administration, was estimated at 6.6 percent in 2000. Significant exports of liquified natural gas started in 1999, and increased crude oil prices in 2000 provided his administration with additional revenues. So far, however, he has been unable to bring about economic recovery. Industrial capacity utilization appears to have diminished. Worse still, infrastructural facilities, including the National Electric Power Authority (NEPA), continue to be in a state of disrepair. Expected massive inflow of foreign investment, on which the government had hinged its economic revival program, failed to materialize. This is in part because of the high cost of doing business in Nigeria and a lack of transparency in economic decision-making in the country. In addition to these realities, the unemployment situation in the country remains unchanged months after the restoration of civilian government. In fact, it has worsened among university graduates and ranged from 30 to 40 percent in 2000. Political uncertainties due to ethnic and religious conflicts between Muslims and Christians, and constant feuding between the president and the legislators aggravate the economic climate. Widespread armed robbery and a crime syndicate known locally as 419 prey on foreign nationals, further hindering foreign investment and tourism. The country's economy needs the collective efforts of the president and the National Assembly as well as more definite measures to address its ills in order to foster its recovery and growth. Currently, funds available to the government are insufficient to meet the needs of all sectors of the economy at once. External investors can contribute through long-term investment and **joint ventures** in Nigeria's large national market. Crude oil, the price of which rose sharply recently, remains a very considerable asset. Properly managed, it could provide a solid platform for more sustained Nigerian development and prosperity in the 21st century and beyond.

POLITICS, GOVERNMENT, AND TAXATION

Nigeria is a federal republic currently under a strong presidential administration, a National Assembly made up of 2 chambers—a Senate and a House of Representatives—and a judiciary. It has 36 administrative divisions known as states. Each of the states is divided into local governments. Thus, Nigeria has 3 tiers of government: national, state, and local.

Nigeria emerged from British colonial rule with a multi-party system deemed essential to democratic governance. However, those political parties were not differentiated or distinguished from each other by any political or economic ideology. Rather, they were essentially ethnic and regionally based, and were preoccupied with promoting ethnic and regional interests. Two of the largest parties, the Northern Peoples Congress (NPC) and the Northern Elements Progressive Union (NEPU), represented and championed the interests of the predominantly Muslim Northern Nigeria. The other leading parties, the National Council of Nigerian Citizens (NCNC) and the Action Group (AG), pursued the interests of the southeast and southwest where they were respectively based. The primary interest of the political parties was thus to use Nigeria's constitutional set up, together with the country's national wealth and power, to promote ethnic and regional security and well-being rather than a national end. Thus, upon independence from Britain in 1960, the 4 leading political parties preoccupied themselves with acquiring control of Nigeria's national wealth and power rather than distributing the nation's power and resources equitably among its nationality groups. This issue continues to dominate Nigerian politics in spite of the formation of more comprehensive national parties in the late 1970s and early 1990s.

The politics of ethnic and regional security play a key role in Nigeria's political and economic development as well as its role in Africa and the world in general. It is the major source of growing political crisis in Nigeria. It undermines the selection of responsible and responsive national leadership by politicizing ethnicity. National leaders are recruited on the basis of their ethnicity and region, rather than their ability, experience, and vision. Hence, Nigeria's political and economic performance falls below par in comparison with other countries of comparable size and resources. The primacy of ethnicity has resulted in periodic outbreaks of violence between Nigerian people groups; this violence, in turn, supports military governments that rule with an iron fist in order to maintain order in Nigeria's tense political climate. Census enumeration for economic planning and electoral representation has fallen victim to the same ethnic politics as people groups claim bloated population numbers in order to secure more government funding and representation. It is also often the factor that determines the location of industries and development projects rather than feasibility studies or viability of the location.

Nigeria has been under 3 civilian administrations and 7 military regimes since its political independence from Britain in 1960. After the independence elections in 1959, an NPC-NCNC coalition ruled the country with Sir Abubakar Tafawa Balewa of the NPC (the senior partner) as the prime minister. In mid-January 1966, Sir Abubakar and a few of his associates were killed in a poorly executed but popular military coup after a succession of political crises, violence, and repression which Sir Abubakar could not or refused to stop. The leader of the coup, Major Kaduna Nzeogwnu, portrayed the deposed leaders as corrupt individuals who sought to keep Nigeria permanently divided so they could remain in office.

The 15 January 1966 military coup established Nigeria's first military government under General John T.U. Aguiyi-Ironsi. Like most of the leaders of the coup that overthrew Abubakar's government, Aguiyi-Ironsi was an Igbo from southeastern Nigeria, which immediately raised the suspicions of the Muslim leaders and soldiers of northern Nigeria. They saw the coup as a plot to impose Igbo-domination on Nigeria, and resentment in northern Nigeria against Aguiyi-Ironsi grew fast. His corrective policy of centralization of power became an excuse for a counter-coup by northern soldiers that put a northerner, Yakubu Gowon, in power on 29 July 1966. Initially, Gowon's regime was uncertain and unstable. It witnessed an orgy of ethnic bloodletting in which about 30,000 Igbo residents in northern Nigeria were slaughtered. Attempts to **restructure** Nigeria into a confederation failed. In May 1967 as Colonel Obumegwu Ojukwu, governor of Eastern Nigeria, contemplated the breakaway of the region, Gowon issued a decree dividing Nigeria into 12 states—6 in the North, 3 in the East, and 3 in the West and Midwest. On 30 May 1967 Ojukwu declared the Eastern region the Sovereign Republic of Biafra. Consequently, a 30-month Nigeria-Biafra War began in July 1967. The war ended in January 1970 when Nigeria forced Biafra's surrender.

Achievement of post-war reconciliation and reconstruction goals was remarkably smooth, facilitated by the oil boom of the early 1970s. However, Gowon suspended the country's normal political activities beyond his promises and the expectations of eager politicians. In addition, he was unable to curb widespread corruption as well as a scandalous and excessive import of cement that clogged the port of Lagos (then Nigeria's capital). Consequently, he was overthrown in a bloodless coup on 29 July 1975 by General Murtala Muhammad.

In February 1976 Muhammad, who had already initiated a plan for a return to civilian rule over a period of 4 years, was himself assassinated in an attempted coup later that year. He was succeeded by his second-in-command, General Olusegun Obasanjo. In the same year, 7 additional states were created, bringing the total to 19. By 1996, 17 others were carved out. Meanwhile, Obasanjo strictly observed the set schedule for a return to civilian rule. An assembly elected to draft a new constitution completed the task in 1978. The constitution was published on 21 September 1978. On the same day the ban on political activity was lifted, leading to the formation of 5 political parties. In 1979, the political parties competed in a series of elections for state and national offices. Shehu Shagari, a northern Muslim and member of the National Party of Nigeria (NPN), was elected as president. Thus, after a transition period of 3 years Obasanjo transferred political power in October 1979 to a civilian administration led by Alhaji Shehu Shagari.

President Shagari's administration marked the beginning of Nigeria's Second Republic. His administration was a coalition of 2 political parties—the National Party of Nigeria (NPN, senior partner) and the Nigerian Peoples Party (NPP). Under the administration, the characteristic politics of ethnic and regional security that ruined the First Republic re-emerged. The coalition collapsed in 1981. Internal dissension, corruption, and abuse of power by the administration became manifest and weakened the moral authority of the government.

Senior military officers overthrew Shagari's government on 31 December 1983. The officers accused the government of widespread corruption, waste, and mismanagement of the economy, making Nigeria a "beggar nation." From 1984 to 1998, Nigeria experienced socioeconomic and political subjugation under 3 successive military dictators: Muhammadu Buhari (1984 to 1985), Ibrahim Badamosi Babangida (1985 to 1993), and Sani Abacha (1993 to 1998). The series of dictators caused further decline in the Nigerian economy as unprincipled, unproductive, corrupt, and weak political elites partnered with the military to smother any opposition and banish all democratic liberties and opportunities in the country. A planned return to civilian government in 1993 did not take place. On 23 June 1993 Babangida nullified the election of Moshood Abiola, a Yoruba businessman from southwest Nigeria as president on 12 June. Faced with riots, in which 100 people were killed, and lack of sup-

port from the military, Babangida stepped down on 26 August and installed a military-backed interim government headed by another southwestern Nigerian businessman, Ernest Shonekan. Shonekan, who received little or no public support because he was perceived as a strategic tool of the military, was to rule until new elections, scheduled for 1994. He was unable to deal with Nigeria's ever-growing economic problems and was removed on 17 November 1993 by Sani Abacha, who then assumed full political authority.

Abacha quickly dissolved all democratic political institutions and replaced all elected governors with military officers. He promised to return the government to civilian rule but refused to disclose a timetable. Faced with domestic and external criticism for his measures, Abacha called for elections for delegates to a Constitutional Conference. Most Nigerians boycotted the elections which were held in May 1994. Leaders of the major opposition group, the National Democratic Coalition (NADECO), were arrested when they attempted to reactivate disbanded democratic institutions. In 1997 Abacha inaugurated a period of transition to civilian rule and promoted the emergence of 5 political parties. Soon, however, he decided instead on a program of self-succession; he created and financed a youth movement and other paid political sycophants (flatterers) to advocate his self-succession. He manipulated the 5 political parties to adopt him as their candidate for the presidency. Thus, the national election that had been planned for August 1998 was to become a referendum (a decision by the general population) on Abacha's self-succession. Every measure of opposition against the plan was foiled, while lavish national resources were spent to promote it. The referendum on Abacha's self-succession did not take place, however. On 7 June 1998, Abacha died suddenly, the nation was told, from natural causes. While he ruled, Abacha had committed human rights abuses, significantly impaired the authority and independence of the judiciary, imprisoned his critics, looted the national treasury, and failed to tackle the nation's economic problems.

Upon Abacha's death, General Abdulsalami Abubakar was selected by the military leadership to succeed him. Abubakar worked to calm the tempers of an agitated nation and promised to end military dictatorship through a genuine transition to civilian rule by the end of May 1999. He proceeded to release Abacha's political prisoners, including journalists and human rights activists. He reached an understanding to release Moshood Abiola—the presumed winner of the 12 June 1993 presidential election annulled by Babangida—from detention. However, Abiola died of a heart attack in August before he could be released. In a further move, Abubakar dissolved the 5 Abacha-regime political parties. In their place emerged 15 others, only 3 of which—People's Democratic Party (PDP), All People's Party (APP), and the

Alliance for Democracy—were certified to contest the elections at local, state, and national levels. The elections were completed at all levels by February 1999. The PDP won a majority of the seats in both chambers of the National Assembly as well as 21 of the country's 36 governorships. Olusegun Obasanjo, a former military head of state and a PDP candidate, won the presidential election. On 5 May 1999, Abubakar proclaimed by decree a constitution which went into effect on 29 May 1999. On the same day Obasanjo was inaugurated as the president of the Third Republic of Nigeria.

His administration faces formidable political and economic problems. Leaders of the southern states persistently demand a sovereign national conference to restructure the federation. The governors, especially those of the oil-producing states, demand a new formula for revenue allocation. Leaders of the northern states complain of neglect and inadequate allocation of resources and national offices to their region. Infrastructure of roads, especially in the south, is in disrepair. There is a growing income disparity, and a constant shortage of electricity and gasoline. Lax security and widespread armed robbery have triggered demands for regional control of security and resources. Ethnic and religious clashes discourage foreign investment and worsen the enormous rate of unemployment. Critics have described Obasanjo's government as unimaginative in dealing with these issues.

From independence in 1960 to the present, Nigerian governments, whether civilian or military, have not differed substantially on their economic policy. Each supported the concept of a mixed economy—a public sector controlled by the state and a **private sector** or free enterprise—and state intervention in such social sectors as education and health. This was in accord with the system of economy inherited at independence from Britain. In 1962, 2 years after independence, Sir Abubakar's government inaugurated a 6-year development plan. The plan mapped Nigeria's transition from an agricultural economy to a mixed economy whose bases were agricultural expansion and limited industrial growth.

Broad in its scope, the economic development plan sought to achieve national economic objectives, such as faster growth and higher levels of average material welfare. The plan included economic forecasts, policies towards the private sector, and a list of proposed public expenditures. Nigerian political leaders determined the general objectives and priorities of the plan, but the main authors of the actual document were foreign (Western) economists. The national government became heavily involved in carrying out the plan because it was unable to generate local private investment to raise sufficient capital for development. The Western advisors discouraged increased taxes on the wealthy and called for foreign as-

sistance—about 50 percent of the public-sector investment—in carrying out the plan.

After the civil war, the military regime of Yakubu Gowon instituted a second development plan for the years 1970 to 1975. The plan sought to promote reconstruction after the civil war, to restore the nation's productive capacity, and to achieve a measurable degree of self-reliance. In 1972 the government issued the first of Nigeria's indigenization decrees that forbade aliens to invest in specified enterprises and reserved participation in certain trades to Nigerian citizens. At that time, about 70 percent of commercial firms operating in Nigeria were foreign-owned. In 1975, as a follow-up to the indigenization decree, the federal government bought 60 percent of the **equity** in the marketing operations of the major oil companies in Nigeria. It rejected full **nationalization** as a means of promoting its program of indigenization. After the overthrow of Gowon in 1975, a third development plan (1975 to 1980) was begun. Stimulated by the oil boom of 1974, the plan sought to expand agriculture, industry, transport, housing, education, health facilities, water supply, rural electrification, and community development. These objectives were not fully achieved because of inflation in minimum wage and administrative salaries awarded by the Udorji Commission and decline in projected oil revenue.

The slump in oil revenue caused the civilian administration of Shehu Shagari to delay the start of the fourth development plan (1981 to 1985). Falling oil revenues, cost of increased food imports, and the inability of the local governments to carry out their responsibilities threatened and undermined the plan. The overthrow of the civilian government of Shagari by Muhammadu Buhari in 1985 delayed the fifth development plan. In 1989, General Babangida, who had overthrown Buhari in 1985, abandoned the idea of a 5-year national development plan. In its place he introduced a 3-year "rolling plan" between 1990 and 1992, anticipating a more comprehensive 15- to 20-year plan. Because of rapid change and economic uncertainty, such rolling plans were to be revised at the end of each year and new estimates, targets, and projects were to be added. Babangida's rolling plan sought to reduce inflation and naira **exchange rate** instability, achieve food self-sufficiency, maintain infrastructure, and reduce the adverse effects of economic structural adjustment he had imposed on the nation. His rolling plan did no better than previous 5-year plans to promote Nigeria's economic development. The current civilian administration of Obasanjo is emphasizing a private-sector-led economy and "market oriented" economy. So far, it has done little to create a solid enabling environment in spite of its anti-corruption campaign aimed at injecting transparency and accountability into economic decision-making.

Nigeria derives its budgetary revenues primarily from petroleum profit taxation, import and excise **duties**, and mining rents and royalties. Petroleum taxation accounts for 65 percent of the budgetary revenues. As of May 2000 the tax rate for assessable petroleum profit was 85 percent. In March 1995, the government established a new **tariff** structure levying taxes on imported goods, ranging from 5 to 60 percent. Import tax is non-preferential and applies equally to all countries. Import duties are either specific or *ad valorem* (**value-added tax**, VAT) depending on the commodity. In 2000 the VAT rate was 5 percent. Import duties are collected by the Nigerian Customs Service in association with government-appointed accounting/auditing firms and paid into the federal treasury through selected banks, such as First Bank of Nigeria, Public Limited Company (PLC); Union Bank of Nigeria, PLC; and United Bank for Africa, PLC.

Other sources of revenue include: companies' **income tax** (30 percent of assessable profit), capital gains tax (10 percent of capital gains), various types of licenses, and personal income tax. Employees "pay as they earn." Such taxes are deducted at monthly pay periods by employers for the federal treasury. In 2000 the tax rate varied from 5 to 25 percent of cumulative or total taxable income. Prior to the 1970s, self-employed people, including well-to-do traders and business people, paid virtually no income taxes. The government sought to collect the taxes by introducing tax clearance certificates. Individuals had to produce such certificates, proving that they had paid their taxes, before receiving government benefits, holding public office, or receiving passports for foreign travel.

INFRASTRUCTURE, POWER, AND COMMUNICATIONS

Nigeria has a fairly extensive infrastructure of roads, railroads, airports, and communication networks. The road system is by far the most important element in the country's transportation network, carrying about 95 percent of all the nation's goods and passengers. Currently, many of the roads are in disrepair because of poor maintenance and years of heavy traffic.

ROADS. The road system was started in the early 1900s under British colonial rule essentially as a feeder network for newly completed railroads. Two trunk roads running from Lagos (southwest) and Port Harcourt (southeast) to Kano (north central) were built. These were followed by the construction of several east-west roads, 2 north and 2 south of the natural division created by the Niger and Benue Rivers. The major purpose was to transport goods from the interior to the coast for export.

After independence in 1960, expansion of the road system to facilitate access to state capitals and large towns became one of the major areas of government investment. In 1978, an expressway was constructed from Lagos to Ibadan. Later, a branch of the Lagos-Ibadan expressway was extended to Benin City. By 1980 another expressway connected Port Harcourt to Enugu. Similar expressways connected major cities and commercial centers in the north. Thus, by 1990 Nigeria had 108,000 kilometers (67,112 miles) of roads. Of this total, 30,000 kilometers (18,642 miles) were paved, 25,000 kilometers (15,535 miles) were gravel, and 53,000 kilometers (32,935 miles) were unimproved earth.

Much of the road system is in disrepair and barely useable. Massive traffic jams are very common in the large cities. There are also long delays in the movement of goods. Highway accidents and deaths are frequent, and number more than 30,000 and 8,000, respectively.

RAILROADS. Railroads provide Nigeria's second means of transportation. The rail system consists of 3,500 kilometers (2,175 miles) route of 1.067 meters (3.5 feet)

Communications								
Country	Telephones[a]	Telephones, Mobile/Cellular[a]	Radio Stations[b]	Radios[a]	TV Stations[a]	Televisions[a]	Internet Service Providers[c]	Internet Users[c]
Nigeria	500,000 (2000)	26,700	AM 82; FM 35; shortwave 11	23.5 M	2 (1999)	6.9 M	11	100,000
United States	194 M	69.209 M (1998)	AM 4,762; FM 5,542; shortwave 18	575 M	1,500	219 M	7,800	148 M
Dem. Rep. of Congo	21,000	8,900	AM 3; FM 12; shortwave 1 (1999)	18.03 M	20 (1999)	6.478 M	2	1,500 (1999)
Cameroon	75,000	4,200	AM 11; FM 8; shortwave 3	2.27 M	1 (1998)	450,000	1	20,000

[a]Data is for 1997 unless otherwise noted.
[b]Data is for 1998 unless otherwise noted.
[c]Data is for 2000 unless otherwise noted.

SOURCE: CIA *World Factbook 2001* [Online].

gauge. Two main lines of the single-track railroad system connect the coast with the interior. One line runs from Lagos (southwest) to Kano (north). The Lagos-Kano line was extended to Nguru, a cattle-raising region, in 1930. The other line runs from Port Harcourt (southeast) to Kaduna (north). A branch line runs from Zaria to Kaura Namoda, an important agricultural area in the northwest. The Port Harcourt-Kaduna line was extended to Maiduguri (northeast) in 1964. The rail system is operated by the Nigeria Railway Corporation. The system suffered a progressive decline because of inadequate funding, poor maintenance, and declining profit.

INLAND WATERWAYS. Inland waterways totaling 8,575 kilometers, (5,329 miles) and consisting of Niger and Benue Rivers and smaller rivers and creeks, provide Nigeria's third internal transportation network. Water transportation of goods and services using boats and canoes is essential and common in riverine areas of Nigeria where road construction is difficult. In the 1980s the government invested funds in building river ports, hoping that increased passenger traffic on the nation's inland waterways would relieve the strained highway system. A major problem involves the fluctuations in the water level during the dry season, which hinder the movement of canoes.

PORTS. Ports provide facilities for exports and imports. The port in Lagos handles the majority of cargo flowing in and out of the country by ship; other important ports include Port Harcourt, Calabar, and the delta port complex of Warri, Sapele, Koko, and Alesa Eleme. In addition to these port complexes, 2 specialized tanker terminals at Bonny, near Port Harcourt, and Burutu, near Warri, handle crude oil exports.

AIR TRAVEL. Nigeria has 72 (1998 estimate) airports, 36 of which have paved runways. Three major international airports—Murtala Muhammad International at Lagos, Aminu Kano International at Kano, and another at Port Harcourt—offer regularly scheduled international flights. Nigeria Airport Authority manages the airports. Nigeria Airways provides domestic service between the international airports and other Nigerian cities. On 26 August 2000, Nigeria and the United States signed an "Open Skies Agreement" to expand and enhance the overall aviation partnership between the 2 countries. Among others, the agreement provides for a direct flight between Lagos and John F. Kennedy Airport in New York. It is hoped that the direct flight will boost Nigeria's tourism sector and develop Lagos as a gateway to Africa.

ELECTRICAL POWER. Electrical power for industrial and household purposes is supplied by Nigeria's National Electric Power Authority (NEPA). The state-owned corporation, nicknamed "Never Expect Power Always" by Nigerians, is very unreliable, with daily shortages and blackouts. In 1998 its production of 14.75 billion kilowatts from fossil fuel (61.69 percent) and hydropower

(38.31 percent) was highly inadequate to meet the nation's industrial and household needs. As a consequence, businesses and manufacturers operate well below capacity, while thousands of Nigerians in urban centers and rural areas buy their own power generators.

TELECOMMUNICATIONS. Telecommunications services provide high quality links internally and to the rest of the world. The government is pursuing an ambitious telecommunications expansion program. It plans to increase Nigeria's mobile and wire lines from year 2000 numbers of 700,000 to over 4 million functional telephone lines by 2002. Nigerian Telecommunications Limited (NITEL) was the nation's sole carrier until 1993 when 8 private firms were approved to be connected to its switching system so as to provide services to various Nigerian zones.

Virtually all Nigerian localities receive broadcasts from one of 65 AM radio stations, and more than a dozen cities from FM radio stations. Shortwave broadcasts from overseas and 6 local transmitters are received throughout the country. Television services are available to most urban areas as well as rural areas with rural electrification. According to World Development Indicators (2000), 223 per 1,000 Nigerians owned radios (1997), while 66 per 1,000 owned television sets (1998). While there were 5 Internet service providers, less than 20 percent of the Nigerian urban population used the Internet in 1999.

ECONOMIC SECTORS

Despite the availability of natural resources, population, and domestic markets, all sectors of the Nigerian economy performed below their potential during the nation's first 40 years of independence. The structure of

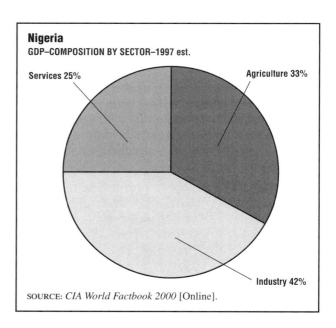

Nigeria
GDP–COMPOSITION BY SECTOR–1997 est.

Services 25%

Agriculture 33%

Industry 42%

SOURCE: *CIA World Factbook 2000* [Online].

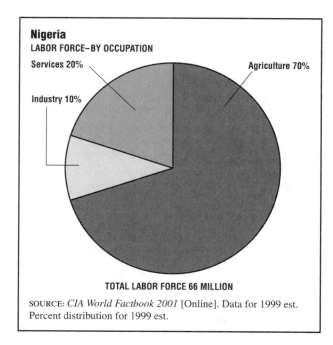

Nigeria
LABOR FORCE–BY OCCUPATION

Services 20%

Industry 10%

Agriculture 70%

TOTAL LABOR FORCE 66 MILLION

SOURCE: *CIA World Factbook 2001* [Online]. Data for 1999 est.
Percent distribution for 1999 est.

use as industrial raw materials for export. Other areas of high priority include manufacturing industries, solid minerals, oil and gas, small and medium enterprises, and tourism. Also, the industrial policy includes partial privatization of government-owned enterprises in such sectors as telecommunications, electricity generation and distribution, petroleum refining, coal and bitumen production, and tourism, in which citizens as well as foreigners may freely participate.

AGRICULTURE

Although it depends heavily on the oil industry for its budgetary revenues, Nigeria is predominantly still an agricultural society. Approximately 70 percent of the population engages in agricultural production at a subsistence level. Agricultural holdings are generally small and scattered. Agriculture provided 41 percent of Nigeria's total **gross domestic product** (GDP) in 1999. This percentage represented a normal decrease of 24.7 percent from its contribution of 65.7 percent to the GDP in 1957. The decrease will continue because, as economic development occurs, the relative size of the agricultural sector usually decreases.

Nigeria's wide range of climate variations allows it to produce a variety of food and **cash crops**. The staple food crops include cassava, yams, corn, coco-yams, cowpeas, beans, sweet potatoes, millet, plantains, bananas, rice, sorghum, and a variety of fruits and vegetables. The leading cash crops are cocoa, citrus, cotton, groundnuts (peanuts), palm oil, palm kernel, benniseed, and rubber. They were also Nigeria's major exports in the 1960s and early 1970s until petroleum surpassed them in the 1970s. Chief among the export destinations for Nigerian agricultural exports are Britain, the United States, Canada, France, and Germany.

A significant portion of the agricultural sector in Nigeria involves cattle herding, fishing, poultry, and lumbering, which contributed more than 2 percent to the GDP in the 1980s. According to the UN Food and Agriculture Organization 1987 estimate, there were 12.2 million cattle, 13.2 million sheep, 26.0 million goats, 1.3 million pigs, 700,000 donkeys, 250,000 horses, and 18,000 camels, mostly in northern Nigeria, and owned mostly by rural dwellers rather than by commercial companies. Fisheries output ranged from 600,000 to 700,000 tons annually in the 1970s. Estimates indicate that the output had fallen to 120,000 tons of fish per year by 1990. This was partly due to environmental degradation and water pollution in Ogoniland and the Delta region in general by the oil companies.

the economy remained stagnant (unchanged) and over-dependent on the oil sector. The largely subsistent agricultural sector failed to keep up with rapid population growth, forcing the one-time food exporter to import food. Inter-sectoral linkages remain weak, and the rate of unemployment remains high and problematic.

Most observers of the Nigerian scene—domestic as well as foreign—attribute the poor performance and the over-reliance on the oil sector to a variety of reasons, including political instability, prolonged authoritarian rule by the military, poor **macroeconomic** management, inadequate infrastructure, and external financing. In November 1996, the military ruler Abacha set up the VISION 2010 Committee which looked into the general situation and recommended targets for year 2010. No tangible progress has so far been made.

The civilian administration of Obasanjo has proposed substantial reform in its economic policy for 1999 to 2003. The main thrust of the reform is to **deregulate** the economy and to disengage the state from activities which are private-sector oriented, leaving the state to act as a facilitator. The plan also concentrates on the provision of incentives, policy, and infrastructure essential to the private sector's role as the engine of growth. The administration's industrial policy seeks to generate productive employment and raise productivity, increase export of locally manufactured goods, create a wider geographical dispersal of industries, attract foreign investment, and increase private sector participation. The policy places highest priority on the agricultural sector—to achieve both poverty reduction, especially in rural areas, and sufficiency in food production and surplus for

Decline in agricultural production in Nigeria began with the advent of the petroleum boom in the early 1970s. The boom in the oil sector brought about a distortion of the labor market. The distortion in turn produced adverse effects on the production levels of both food and cash crops. Governments had paid farmers low prices over the years on food for the domestic market in order to satisfy urban demands for cheap basic food products. This policy, in turn, progressively made agricultural work unattractive and enhanced the lure of the cities for farm workers. Collectively, these developments worsened the low productivity, both per unit of land and per worker, due to several factors: inadequate technology, acts of nature such as drought, poor transportation and infrastructure, and trade restrictions.

As food production could not keep pace with its increasing population, Nigeria began to import food. It also lost its status as a net exporter of such cash crops as cocoa, palm oil, and groundnuts. According to U.S. Department of State FY2001 *Country Commercial Guide,* Nigeria's total food and agricultural imports are valued at approximately US$1.6 billion per year. Among the major imports from the United States are wheat, sugar, milk powder, and consumer-ready food products.

Efforts since the late 1970s to revitalize agriculture in order to make Nigeria food self-sufficient again and to increase the export of agricultural products have produced only modest results. The Obasanjo administration, however, has made agriculture the highest priority of its economic policy.

INDUSTRY

MINING. The oil industry dominates Nigeria's mineral development, making petroleum the most important sector of the Nigerian economy. Nigeria produces 2.3 million barrels of crude oil per day (2000). It is Africa's largest oil producer, contributing 3.0 percent to the global production, and is the world's sixth largest oil exporter. Its proven reserves are estimated at 20 billion barrels, enough to last 40 years at the current rate of production. Continuing exploration is expected to raise the total to more than 25 billion. Nigeria is a member of the Organization of Petroleum Exporting Countries (OPEC).

The state-owned Nigerian National Petroleum Corporation (NNPC) cooperates with foreign oil companies such as Shell, Mobil, Elf, Agip, Chevron, and BP in its oil industry. The parastatal was recently restructured as part of a general policy to commercialize state concerns and encourage private-sector participation in them.

Crude oil (11 percent of production) is refined in Nigeria in 4 refineries which seldom meet the country's demands. Hence, there is constant shortage of fuel. Crude oil is also the nation's largest export to such countries as the United States and Japan. Petroleum products accounted for two-thirds of Nigeria's energy consumption in the 1990s. Domestic consumption of crude oil was 250,000 barrels per day.

During the process of oil exploration, vast reserves of natural gas—estimated at 100 billion standard cubic feet—were discovered. They are the largest reserves found so far in Africa. In 1988, Nigeria produced 21.2 billion cubic meters per day with 2.9 billion cubic meters used by National Electric Power Authority and other domestic customers, 2.6 billion cubic meters used by foreign oil companies, and 15.7 billion cubic meters wasted through flaring. In 2000 Nigeria began to export Liquefied Natural Gas (LNG), an increasingly important sector which is expected at some point to surpass oil as the nation's major source of revenue. Nigerian Liquefied Natural Gas Ltd., a subsidiary of the NNPC, had signed agreements in 1992 with 4 countries—United States, France, Italy, and Spain—for supplies of LNG.

Nigeria's emphasis on the oil industry resulted in the neglect of other sectors of the mining industry. Recently, however, interest has rekindled in solid minerals such as coal, tin, iron, columbine, gold, uranium, tantalum, marble, and phosphates. Many other commercially-viable solid minerals have yet to be exploited. All solid minerals are owned by the federal government. Prospecting licenses, mining leases, quarrying licenses, and leases are granted by the Ministry of Solid Minerals Development, established early in 1995 to boost non-oil exports. The National Fertilizer Company of Nigeria operates a fertilizer complex at Onne (Rivers State). Coal production had declined as industries and trains shifted to the use of oil, gasoline, and diesel, but in 1991 2 joint ventures began operations for its mining and export. A total of 60,000 tons were exported to England in 1991. The solid minerals are attracting foreign interest for potential exploitation. In addition to the development of the solid minerals noted, Nigeria engages in processing industries for such products as palm oil, peanuts, rubber, wood, hides, and skins.

MANUFACTURING. The manufacturing sector in the Nigerian economy is dominated by **import substitution**—light industries designed to produce goods that previously had been imported. The Nigerian Enterprises Promotion decrees (1972, 1977, and 1981) shifted the manufacturing sector from foreign majority ownership in the 1960s to indigenous (local) majority ownership in the mid-to-late 1970s by limiting foreign ownership shares in various industries. As a result, a few civil servants, military leaders, business people, and professionals became considerably wealthy through the purchase of the relinquished foreign-owned shares. The third development plan (1975 to 1980) envisaged a rapid phase of industrialization, emphasizing heavy industries such as iron, steel, and petrochemicals, as well as such consumer durables as automobiles. Automobile assembly plants were established in 1978 by Leyland, Peugeot, Volkswagen, Fiat, and Daimler-Benz. Major industrial projects during the third development plan included 3 new oil refineries, 2 pulp and paper mills, an iron and steel complex, 2 liquefied natural gas plants, 3 sugar refineries, and 3 new cement factories. Their productivity was low. The iron and steel complex remained incomplete.

The fourth development plan (1981 to 1985) placed high priority on the manufacturing sector in order to promote rapid development and transformation of the economy. The extant manufacturing industries concentrated on **consumer goods**: food products, mineral distillation and beer brewing, textiles, cement, building materials, glass, footwear, furniture, chemical products, ceramics, and small appliances. They produced a range of goods but did not substantially increase employment or industrial growth.

Manufacturing industries are among the Obasanjo administration's priority areas of industrial investment. The administration favors industries which can rapidly be supported by locally-produced raw materials. The government also hopes to support food-production programs through local manufacture of chemicals, equipment, and light commercial vehicles. It will also focus on industries with multiplier effect such as flat-sheet mills and machine tools industry, including foundries and engineering industries for spare-parts production. The administration invites local and foreign investors in the priority areas.

The manufacturing sector suffers from a number of constraints including low demand for locally-made goods such as textiles and footwear, and the poor state of social and economic infrastructure typified by power and water shortages. However, Nigeria's manufacturing capacity utilization rose from 34 percent in 1998 to 36 percent in 1999.

SERVICES

TOURISM. Tourism in Nigeria is highly undeveloped, considering the West African nation's available tourist resources: land, climate, vegetation, people and their festivals, abundant art treasures, national monuments, ports, traditional sports, and music. Recognizing the potential revenue the nation could generate from tourism, the government decided in 1991 to develop and promote tourism into an economically viable industry. The thrust of its policy was to "make Nigeria a prominent tourism destination in Africa, generate foreign exchange, encourage even development, promote tourism-based rural enterprises, and generate employment."

An institutional framework was put in place, namely the Federal Ministry of Commerce and Tourism, to pursue the objectives and maintain links with the state governments on funding and monitoring of a nation-wide tourism infrastructure. The government provided incentives to encourage domestic and foreign investors to par-

ticipate in the venture. For example, the sector was accorded preferred-sector status, qualifying it for **tax holidays** and import-duty exemption on tourism-related equipment. Upon the inauguration of the Third Republic, President Obasanjo accorded the industry an additional boost by creating a separate Ministry of Tourism and Culture with Chief Ojo Madueke as its minister.

The boost notwithstanding, many impediments stand in the way of a tourist industry in Nigeria. Warnings issued by foreign governments on the dangers of travel to Nigeria scare tourists. Violent crime by individuals in police and military uniforms, as well as by ordinary criminals, is an acute and constant problem. Frequently, harassment and shakedowns of foreigners and Nigerians by uniformed personnel and others occur throughout the federation. Fake business and other advance-fee scams target foreigners worldwide and pose dangers of financial loss and potential physical harm. Other barriers to a successful tourist industry include inconsistent regulations, widespread corruption and crime, crumbling roads and bridges, erratic telephone service, frequent shortages of fuel, electricity and water, and social unrest in some parts of the country.

FINANCIAL SERVICES. Regular banking services in Nigeria began in 1892 when the country's first bank was established. By 1952 there were 3 foreign-owned banks (the Bank of British West Africa, Barclays Bank, and the British and French Bank) and 2 indigenous banks (the National Bank of Nigeria and the African Continental Bank). A central bank, demanded by members of the Nigerian Federal House of Assembly in 1952 to help promote economic development, was established and operational on 1 July 1959. Similar to central banks in Western Europe and North America, the Central Bank of Nigeria establishes the Nigerian currency, controls and regulates the banking system, serves as banker to other banks in Nigeria, and carries out the government's economic policy in the monetary field.

Despite the tendency of Nigerians to prefer cash to checks for business and debt settlements, the banking system has expanded to include 90 banks in 2000 in 3 categories: commercial, merchant, and industrial or development banks. In addition to these categories, there are many mortgage and community banks, insurance companies, pension funds, and finance and leasing companies active in Nigeria. A drastic decline in the number of financial houses, commercial banks, and mortgage and community banks began in 1995 because of distress in the financial sector.

RETAIL. Nigeria has one of the best-developed and most extensive **retail** industrial sectors in sub-Saharan Africa. This is due to its large population located in many large commercial centers, such as Lagos, Ibadan, Kano, Port Harcourt, Aba, and Onitsha, in addition to hundreds of smaller towns with more than 200,000 inhabitants. There are also hundreds of trading corporations, financial institutions, and a great variety of small business enterprises, many in the informal sector, along with thousands of large market (and roadside stands) in urban as well as rural areas.

The commercial centers house a variety of retail stores, restaurants, and secular and Christian bookshops that cater to the commercial and household needs of traders and residents. Nigerians now dominate the wholesale and retail trade which in colonial days had been virtually controlled by foreign companies from metropolitan Western Europe, Lebanon, Syria, and India. Nigerian women are playing an increasing role in the retail and distribution sector.

INTERNATIONAL TRADE

Nigeria exports primarily petroleum and other raw materials such as cocoa, rubber, palm kernels, organic oils, and fats. It imports secondary products such as chemicals, machinery, transport equipment, manufactured goods, food, and animals. The dependence on oil and a few other commodities for export caused Nigeria to become especially vulnerable to world oil price fluctuations.

During the colonial years, Britain was Nigeria's leading trading partner. After independence, Nigeria diversified its trading partners. It now trades worldwide with about 100 countries. The United States replaced Britain as the primary trading partner in the 1970s. However, Britain remains Nigeria's leading vendor, selling the former colony more than 14 percent of its imports in the 1990s. Other major trading partners are Germany, France, the Netherlands, Canada, Japan, Italy, and Spain. Nigeria's meager trade with Eastern Europe and the former Soviet Union declined even further after the collapse of Euro-**Communism** and the breakup of the Soviet Union in the early 1990s. Nigeria's trade with sister African countries—mainly with other West African members of the Economic Community of West Africa (ECOWAS,

created in 1975)—was only about 4 percent of its total trade in 1990.

Prior to 1966, Nigeria had a persistent **trade deficit**. The rapid growth of petroleum as an export commodity reversed the trend between 1966 and 1977. Sluggish international demand for Nigerian crude oil renewed the trade deficit from 1978 to 1983. Severe import restrictions and an economic structural adjustment program (ESAP) adopted to address the economic breakdown brought about trade surpluses from 1984 to 1986, and again in 1990. Monies sent home by Nigerian residents overseas helped to cushion the drastic effects of the deficit and the ESAP-induced decreased government spending on the population.

MONEY

The naira, Nigeria's currency, declined rapidly after the military deposed the civilian administration of Shehu Shagari on 31 December 1983 at the time of depressed oil prices. In 1981 N1.00 was worth US$1.67. By 1986 the value of N1.00 had tumbled to US$0.64 (N1.56 equals US$1.00). It declined further in 1987 and has continued a downward spiral. In 1995, under the Babangida regime's policy of "guided deregulation" of the foreign exchange market, the official rate—N22.00 to US$1.00—became available only to the government. All individuals and organizations had to meet their foreign exchange needs from an Autonomous Foreign Exchange Market (AFEM).

The prevailing AFEM rate in 1999 was N100.00 to US$1.00. Obasanjo abolished the parallel official rate of N22.00 to US$1.00 upon his inauguration in May 1999. Since then the exchange rate has risen to N120.00 to US$1.00 (October 2000).

POVERTY AND WEALTH

Despite Nigeria's enormous resources and potential, poverty is widespread throughout the nation. Its basic indicators place it among the 20 poorest countries of the

Trade (expressed in billions of US$): Nigeria		
	Exports	Imports
1975	7.845	6.041
1980	25.968	16.660
1985	12.548	8.877
1990	13.670	5.627
1995	34.179	34.488
1998	37.029	43.798

SOURCE: International Monetary Fund. *International Financial Statistics Yearbook 1999.*

Exchange rates: Nigeria	
nairas (N) per US$1	
Jan 2001	110.005
2000	101.697
1999	92.338
1998	21.886
1997	21.886
1996	21.884

SOURCE: CIA *World Factbook 2001* [ONLINE].

GDP per Capita (US$)

Country	1975	1980	1985	1990	1998
Nigeria	301	314	230	258	256
United States	19,364	21,529	23,200	25,363	29,683
Dem. Rep. of Congo	392	313	293	247	127
Cameroon	616	730	990	764	646

SOURCE: United Nations. *Human Development Report 2000; Trends in human development and per capita income.*

Distribution of Income or Consumption by Percentage Share: Nigeria

Lowest 10%	1.6
Lowest 20%	4.4
Second 20%	8.2
Third 20%	12.5
Fourth 20%	19.3
Highest 20%	55.7
Highest 10%	40.8

Survey year: 1996–97
Note: This information refers to expenditure shares by percentiles of the population and is ranked by per capita expenditure.

SOURCE: *2000 World Development Indicators* [CD-ROM].

world. Nigeria has been in stagnation and relative decline since 1981, from a per capita GDP of US$1,200 in 1981 to about US$300 in 2000. In 1992, 34.1 percent of the population was below the poverty line, according to the CIA *World Factbook 2000*; about 70 percent fell below that line in 2000, according to the World Bank.

For many Nigerians the quality of life has declined rather than improved since independence 40 years ago. By contrast, the standard of living for a few privileged Nigerians—military officers and their civilian associates, corrupt politicians, and big contractors—has improved substantially. The average salaried worker cannot earn

enough to support a family because of inflation and rises in food prices and transportation costs. The national minimum wage of N5,500 (about US$55.00) per month, adopted by the federal government but rejected by most of the states, falls far short of what is needed to cover housing, food, education, health care and transportation. The material condition of women, who comprise 50 percent of the population, is even worse than that of men because the welfare of women in general, including education, political participation, and workforce, had been neglected over the years until recently. The incidence of prostitution of Nigerian women within and outside the country has therefore increased. It is no wonder, given these prevailing conditions, that hypertension has become a major sickness among Nigerians since the 1980s.

Housing and living facilities for the wealthy are very similar to those available to their counterparts in countries of the western world. Middle and lower-level income groups in the urban and rural areas live in individual houses or crowded flats (apartments). Rural dwellers live in cement or mud block houses with tin or thatched roofs, and have no running water for the most part. Water and electricity services in the major cities are erratic. Water supplies in many rural areas are infested with disease-carrying worms, while electricity services, under government auspices, are seldom available.

There is, therefore, much despair throughout Nigeria, a situation that has led to a "brain drain" from the country to other nations of the world. Much of the despair can be linked to the abysmal quality of life of the average Nigerian, and also to the huge income disparity between the poverty-stricken masses and the few well-to-do Nigerians. Mismanagement and corruption on the part of the government squandered the nation's wealth, and fostered an atmosphere of violence and instability that makes it very difficult to attract foreign investors. Unfortunately, the legislative and executive arms of the present civilian rule include leaders from the corrupt and wasteful regimes of Babangida and Abacha who helped create that climate. Their presence casts doubt over the

Household Consumption in PPP Terms

Country	All food	Clothing and footwear	Fuel and power[a]	Health care[b]	Education[b]	Transport & Communications	Other
Nigeria	51	5	31	2	8	2	2
United States	13	9	9	4	6	8	51
Dem. Rep. of Congo	N/A	N/A	N/A	N/A	N/A	N/A	N/A
Cameroon	33	12	8	2	9	8	28

Data represent percentage of consumption in PPP terms.
[a]Excludes energy used for transport.
[b]Includes government and private expenditures.

SOURCE: World Bank. *World Development Indicators 2000*.

nation's ability to rise above its tumultuous past into a brighter future.

The economic situation—the abject poverty and the high rate of unemployment especially—has not improved since Obasanjo became president in May 1999, despite his administration's Poverty Alleviation Program. His critics argue that the program consists merely of direct cash transfer to politically selected beneficiaries. The gap between the rich and the poor continues to widen. Segments of the nation continue to complain about their marginalization (being left at the margin or neglected), while others are favored. Armed robbery and wide-spread insecurity persist.

WORKING CONDITIONS

Nigeria had an estimated labor force of 42.844 million in 1999. Women comprised 36 percent of that force, which included talented and well-educated entrepreneurs. The estimated unemployment rate in 1992 was 28 percent. In 2000 the estimated unemployment rate increased to 32 percent. Secondary school graduates and women make up the largest proportion of the unemployed. The unemployment rate among the urban youth had hovered around 40 percent since the 1990s. Many college graduates have remained without **full employment** since the late 1980s. The government, including federal, state, and local units, is the largest employer outside the agricultural sector.

With the exception of employees classified as essential—members of the armed services, the police force, firefighters, Central Bank employees, and customs and excise staff—Nigerian workers may form or join trade or labor unions. They may strike to obtain improved working conditions and benefits and bargain collectively for higher wages. In 1999 about 3.5 million non-agricultural workers belonged to 42 recognized trade unions under a single national labor federation.

The first labor union—the civil service union—emerged in 1912. By 1950 the number had grown to 144 with more than 144,000 members, and 300,000 in 1963 affiliated with 5 central labor associations. Because of a series of labor problems and the meddling of politicians between 1963 and 1975, the military government dissolved the central unions and decreed only 1 central unit, the Nigerian Labor Congress, in 1976. In 1977 11 labor union leaders were banned from further union activity. A 1978 labor decree amendment reorganized more than 1,000 previously existing unions into 70 registered industrial unions under the Nigerian Labor Congress. In addition to the recognized trade unions, women's organizations, mostly professional and social clubs, collectively seek to improve women's conditions and participation in the economic and political life of the nation. Journalists, university professors, and students have their own organizations also as interest groups.

Nigerian labor laws prohibit forced or compulsory labor. They also prohibit the employment of children under 15 years of age in commerce and industry and restrict other child labor to domestic or agricultural work. Many children, however, **hawk** goods in markets and junctions of major roads and streets in the cities and assist their parents in trade and commerce. In 1974 the military government changed the work week from 35 to 40 hours by decree and stipulated payment for extra work done over the legal limit. Employers are required by law to compensate employees injured at work and dependent survivors of those who died in industrial accidents.

Strikes or industrial actions by workers tend to be frequent in Nigeria. Although plagued by leadership struggles, ideological differences, and regional ethnic conflicts, the Nigerian Labor Congress has been able to organize or threaten nationwide workers' strikes, demanding the retention of government **subsidies** on petroleum products, minimum wages, and improved working conditions. Public health doctors organized in 1985; several labor unions in 1998 protested the austerity measures of the Structural Adjustment Program. Similar actions were taken by the Academic Staff Union of Nigerian Universities (1986, 1988), the National Union of Nigerian Students (1986, 1989, 1990s), and the National Union of Petroleum and Natural Gas Workers (1997).

Conditions for workers in Nigeria are far from ideal. Civil servants and employees of private companies (foreign) have relatively good offices and facilities, health care, and wages, but that is not the case for most of the others. Conditions in the pre-collegiate schools and the universities have deteriorated markedly because of repression, underfunding, and irregular payment of salaries. Protests or industrial actions by trade union leaders often resulted in detention. A number of university students were killed by the police, and the universities shut down following students' protests and riots. Some doctors and professors lost their jobs because of industrial action. In addition, income inequalities between the rulers and bureaucrats on the one hand and masses of workers on the other, poor wages, and late payment of salaries demoralize workers. Furthermore, they adversely affect their standard of living, health, and work productivity. The poor conditions contribute to the pervasive corruption in Nigeria and the use of the country as a conduit for drug trafficking.

COUNTRY HISTORY AND ECONOMIC DEVELOPMENT

1861. King Dosumu of Lagos cedes the territory to Britain which becomes a British Crown colony.

1865. The British establish a consulate at Lokoja.

1887–1900. Various parts of what later became Nigeria are brought under British colonial rule as protectorates of Southern Nigeria and Northern Nigeria.

1903. The Sokoto-based Fulani Empire becomes part of the British Protectorate of Northern Nigeria.

1906. The colony of Lagos merges with the Protectorate of Southern Nigeria.

1914. For budgetary and administrative convenience, the Colony of Lagos and Protectorate of Southern Nigeria are merged with the Protectorate of Northern Nigeria as the Colony and Protectorate of Nigeria.

1922. The Clifford Constitution allows for Africans to be elected into the Legislative Council in Lagos.

1936. Nigerian Youth Movement emerges as precursor of political parties.

1937. Shell Oil Company begins oil exploration in Nigeria.

1939. Governor Bourdillion divides Southern Nigeria into Eastern and Western provinces, later to become Eastern and Western regions.

1944. The National Council of Nigeria and Cameroon emerges (becomes National Council of Nigerian Citizens in 1961).

1946. Sir Arthur Richards' Constitution goes into effect.

1949. The Northern People's Congress is formed.

1950. The Action Group (Party) is formed.

1951. Macpherson Constitution goes into effect.

1954. The Lyttleton Constitution, establishing Nigeria as a federation of 3 regions—Eastern, Western, and Northern—goes into effect.

1959. Elections, in preparation for independence, are held; an NPC-NCNC coalition government is formed with Sir Abubakar as prime minister.

1960. Nigeria becomes independent (1 October).

1963. Nigeria becomes a republic (1 October).

1966. Military overthrows Abubakar government. Major-General Ironsi is installed and is later assassinated and succeeded by Lt. Colonel Yakubu Gowon.

1966–79. Military rule; Gowon (overthrown 29 July 1975), Murtala Muhammed (assassinated 1976), succeeded by Olusegun Obasanjo.

1967–70. Eastern Region declares independence as Republic of Biafra, precipitating Nigeria-Biafra War which ends January 1970 with the defeat of Biafra.

1979–83. Second Republic with civilian rule under Shehu Shagari.

1983–93. Prolonged military rule; Muhammed Buhari overthrows the Shagari administration; is ousted (1985) by Ibrahim Babangida.

1993. Presidential election (won by M.K.O. Abiola) is annulled by Babangida (23 June) who retires and appoints businessman Shonekan as interim ruler. Abacha ousts Shonekan (17 November) and inaugurates a brutal regime.

1998. Abacha dies of natural causes. His successor, General Abubakar, inaugurates transition to civilian rule. Local government elections are held.

1999. Gubernatorial elections are held 9 January, National Assembly elections are held 20 January, and presidential elections follow 27 February. Obasanjo is inaugurated 29 May as president of the Third Republic.

FUTURE TRENDS

Nigeria's prospects for sustainable economic growth are mixed. Despite current hardships, Nigeria represents an important market in Africa with its vast human and natural resources. Its revenues from both the recent and ongoing recovery in oil prices and the export of liquified natural gas should help to rebuild the nation's shattered socio-economic infrastructure. The anti-corruption legislation, rigorously enforced, should help to restore transparency and accountability into economic decisions, which would boost national and international investor confidence in the nation. The **liberalized** rules for foreign investment and initiatives by the Obasanjo government to privatize some state-owned enterprises and promote tourism should help the nation move steadily towards targeted growth.

Nigeria has many impediments on its road to sustainable development. Earnings from non-oil exports are unlikely to improve significantly because of the high cost of production. Acrimony between the executive and legislative arms of the government continue relentlessly to the detriment of collective and decisive action. Painful and costly fuel shortages, caused by the inability of Nigeria's dilapidated refineries to produce anywhere near capacity, immobilize the nation. Inter-ethnic and religious conflicts continue to take their tolls in human lives and physical assets of the nation. Unemployment, especially among college graduates, has reached intolerable levels. Armed robbery and crime constitute a present danger to the economy. These impediments must be more determinedly addressed to enhance Nigeria's chances for growth and development.

DEPENDENCIES

Nigeria has no territories or colonies.

BIBLIOGRAPHY

Aborisade, Oladimeji, and Robert J. Mundt. *Politics in Nigeria.* New York: Longman, 1999.

Achebe, Chinua. *The Trouble with Nigeria.* London: Heinemann, 1983.

Adejumobi, Said, and Abubakar Momoh, editors. *The Political Economy of Nigeria Under Military Rule: 1984–1993.* Harare: Sape Books, 1995.

Forrest, Tom. *Politics and Economic Development in Nigeria.* Updated edition. Boulder, CO: Westview, 1994.

Ihonvbere, Julius. *Nigeria: The Politics of Adjustment and Democracy.* New Brunswick, NJ: Transaction Books, 1994.

Library of Congress. *Nigeria: A Country Study.* <http://memory .loc.gov/frd/cs/ngtoc.html>. Accessed August 2001.

Oyewole, Anthony, and John Lucas. *Historical Dictionary of Nigeria.* Second edition. London: Scarecrow, 2000.

Palmer, Monte. *Comparative Politics: Political Economy, Political Culture, and Political Independence.* Itasca, IL: E.E. Peacock, 1997.

Soyinka, Wole. *The Open Sore of a Continent: A Personal Narrative of the Nigerian Crisis.* New York: Oxford Univ., 1996.

Theen, Rolf H.W., and Frank L. Wilson. *Comparative Politics: An Introduction to Seven Countries.* Fourth edition. Upper Saddle River, NJ: Prentice Hall, 2001.

U.S. Central Intelligence Agency. *World Factbook 2000.* <http:// www.odci.gov/cia/publications/factbook/index.html>. Accessed August 2001.

U.S. Department of State. *FY 2001 Country Commercial Guide: Nigeria.* <http://www.state.gov/www/about_state/business/ com_guides/2001/africa/nigeria_ccg2001.pdf>. Accessed August 2001.

—*F. Ugboaja Ohaegbulam*

RWANDA

Republic of Rwanda
Republika y'u Rwanda

CAPITAL: Kigali.

MONETARY UNIT: Rwanda Franc (RFr). One Rwanda franc equals 100 centimes. There are coins of 1, 5, 10, 20, and 50 francs and notes of 100, 500, 1,000, and 5,000 francs.

CHIEF EXPORTS: Coffee, tea, hides and skins, cassiterite, pyrethrum.

CHIEF IMPORTS: Food, machinery and equipment, steel, petroleum products, cement and construction material.

GROSS DOMESTIC PRODUCT: US$5.9 billion (purchasing power parity, 1999 est.).

BALANCE OF TRADE: Exports: US$70.8 million (f.o.b., 1999 est.). Imports: US$242 million (f.o.b., 1999 est.).

COUNTRY OVERVIEW

LOCATION AND SIZE. The Republic of Rwanda is a landlocked country located in central Africa. It is bordered on the east by the Democratic Republic of the Congo, with which it shares the shores of Lake Kivu; on the north by Uganda; on the west by Tanzania; and on the south by Burundi. Rwanda is a small country with an area of 26,338 square kilometers (10,169 square miles). Comparatively, Rwanda is about the size of the state of Maryland. The capital city of Kigali is in the center of the country.

POPULATION. Rwanda's population was estimated at 7,229,129 in 2000. Already the most densely-populated country in Africa, Rwanda's population is growing at a rate of 3 percent annually, according to the U.S. State Department. At this rate the population is expected to reach 11.2 million by 2012, despite the fact that huge numbers of Rwandans are dying from AIDS-related illnesses. In 2000, there were approximately 34.78 births per 1,000 people. The fertility rate in Rwanda is high. An average Rwandan mother gives birth to 5 children in her lifetime. But this statistic is tempered by the fact that approximately 12 percent of Rwandan babies die at birth. The average

Rwandan's life expectancy is equally dismal; on average, Rwandan males live to 38.58 years old and the average female has a life expectancy of 40.13 years.

Rwanda is populated by 3 ethnic groups: Hutu (84 percent), Tutsi (15 percent), and Twa, or Pygmoid (1 percent). Rwandans are predominantly Christian. Some 65 percent of the population is Roman Catholic, while 9 percent is Protestant. About 25 percent of the population practices indigenous and other beliefs, with only 1 percent being Muslim. Rwanda has 3 official languages: Kinyarwanda, French, and English. Kiswahili (an offshoot of Swahili) is spoken primarily in the country's commercial centers. Rwanda is one of the most densely populated countries in Africa, with 317 persons per square kilometer on average (or 820 people per square mile).

OVERVIEW OF ECONOMY

The single biggest factor in Rwanda's recent economic history is the 1994 genocide (see Politics, Government, and Taxation). In that year, Rwanda's ethnic majority, the Hutus, committed genocide against the Tutsi minority. The casualties of that genocide numbered more than half a million Tutsis. The genocide devastated Rwanda's already fragile economy by further impoverishing its population and unraveling its social fabric. The economy shrank by 50 percent within a year of the genocide, and per capita incomes dropped to US$80 a year.

Since the 1994 genocide, however, Rwanda has made significant headway in rehabilitating its economy. Annual **gross domestic product** (GDP) growth rates hit 37 percent in 1995, 12 percent in 1996 and 1997, and 10 percent in 1998. **Inflation** fell from its 1994 highs and government revenues increased. Agricultural production reached pre-war levels by 1998, though there is little new investment in this sector. Moreover, nearly 40 percent of the

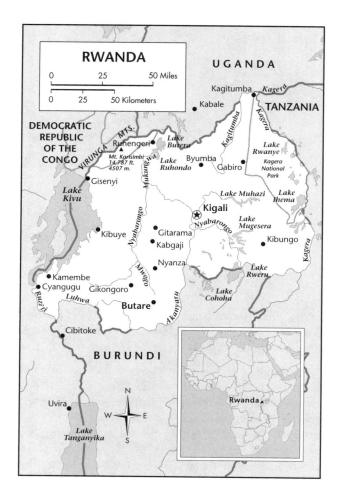

RWANDA

0   25   50 Miles
0   25   50 Kilometers

UGANDA

Kagitumba   Kagera

TANZANIA

Kabale

DEMOCRATIC
REPUBLIC
OF THE
CONGO

VIRUNGA MTS.

Ruhengeri

Lake
Bulera

Mt. Karisimbi
14,787 ft.
4507 m.

Lake
Ruhondo   Byumba

Gabiro

Lake
Rwanye

Kagera
National
Park

Gisenyi

Lake
Kivu

Lake Muhazi   Lake
Ihema

★ Kigali

Lake
Mugesera

Kibuye   Gitarama
Kabgaji

Nyabarongo

Kibungo

Nyanza

Kamembe
Cyangugu   Gikongoro

Lake
Rweru

Lake
Cohoha

Butare

Cibitoke

BURUNDI

Uvira

N
W   E
S

Rwanda

Lake
Tanganyika

industries operating in 1994 have not resumed operations. Economic growth slowed in 1999, thanks to low prices for Rwanda's major exports and rising world oil prices.

Today, Rwanda remains a poor country dependent on agricultural production and foreign aid. It is primarily a rural country and about 90 percent of its population works in subsistence agriculture, and 65.3 percent of the population lived below the poverty line in 1998. Its main exports, coffee and tea, account for 70 percent of exports. Rwanda receives 75 percent of its budgetary requirements from foreign aid organizations. The Rwandan government, the International Monetary Fund (IMF), and the World Bank have agreed to a **privatization** program that is expected to invigorate Rwanda's economy. Future growth in Rwanda's economy, however, will depend on continued political stability, assistance from the IMF and the World Bank, and the strengthening of world coffee and tea prices.

POLITICS, GOVERNMENT, AND TAXATION

Rwanda's politics have long been colored by conflicts between the nation's 2 dominant ethnic groups, the

Hutus and the Tutsis. In 1959, the Hutu ethnic majority toppled the ruling Tutsi king. After the king fled, the Hutus killed thousands of Tutsis, and more than 150,000 Tutsis fled into exile in neighboring countries. The children of these exiled Tutsis eventually formed a rebel group, the Rwandan Patriotic Front (RPF), and in 1990 returned to Rwanda to wage war against the Hutu government. This war, along with the assassination of Rwanda's Hutu President Juvenal Habyarimana and certain economic upheavals, compounded ethnic tensions which erupted in 1994. The Hutus massacred more than half a million Tutsis and some moderate Hutus (some estimates indicate that the number of dead was closer to 1 million). That same year, the RPF defeated the FAR (the Hutu regime's army) and the Interhamwe (the Hutu militia group that spearheaded the Tutsi genocide) and took military control of the country. The Tutsi ascension to power sparked a massive exodus of Hutus from Rwanda. Once defeated, the Hutus feared Tutsi retribution and approximately 2 million Hutu refugees, including armed members of the ex-FAR and Interhamwe, poured into the Democratic Republic of the Congo (the Congo) and trickled into Burundi, Tanzania, and Uganda. Most of these refugees have since returned to Rwanda. But the ex-FAR and the Interhamwe remain in the Congo and continue to threaten Rwanda's stability.

In 1991, the primarily Hutu Rwandan government ratified a constitution that provided for a multiparty democracy, a limited executive term, and independent legislative and judicial branches. In 1994, however, the Rwandan Hutu government collapsed and the Tutsi RPF seized power. Once it assumed control, the RPF prohibited all political parties that were determined to have participated in the Tutsi genocide. A multiparty Transitional National Assembly was installed to preside over a 5-year transition from military to civilian rule. In 1995, the Transitional National Assembly adopted a new constitution that was essentially a combination of the 1991 constitution and peace agreements signed after the 1994 war. In 1999, the government extended the transition period for another 5 years because ethnic tensions remained too high to hold elections.

Though still in the transition period, Rwanda held special elections in 2000 that gave Major General Paul Kagame of the RPF the presidency. Kagame received 81 of 86 votes from members of the National Assembly, who represent a variety of political parties. Kagame is expected to rule until regular elections can be held.

There are at least 4 factors that impede Rwanda's economic growth. First, Rwanda's economy depends far too much on foreign aid and will continue to do so for the near future. Currently, 75 percent of the Rwandan government's budget is financed by foreign aid. Second, the government expends a considerable percentage of its resources reintegrating the returning refugees into the folds of Rwandan society. This expenditure continues to divert from the Rwandan economy resources that could improve the country's **infrastructure**. Third, the government also spends much of its resources supporting rebel groups at war in the Congo. This funding could be diverted to invest in the economy. Fully 25.6 percent of the government's budget went toward the support of the Rwandan Patriotic Army in 2000, according to the U.S. State Department. Finally, Rwanda's prison population has swelled to 100,000, and the government expends considerable sums to house the inmates who were convicted of perpetrating the 1994 genocide.

INFRASTRUCTURE, POWER, AND COMMUNICATIONS

Rwanda has a fairly good road system with approximately 14,900 kilometers (9,258 miles) of roads. For the most part, the primary roads are well maintained. But feeder roads have deteriorated due to the war, excessive loads by heavy-duty trucks, and a 1997 flood. Currently, though, the World Bank is providing financing for road rehabilitation and new construction in certain parts of the country.

Rwanda lacks a railroad system, although it is linked to the Ugandan-Kenya railroad system by road. Since Rwanda is landlocked, most of its international trade is transported through the Kenyan port of Mombasa. Rwanda has several airports, but the main international airport is in Rwanda's capital, Kigali.

The cost of electricity in Rwanda is exorbitant. Electricity in Rwanda costs 3 to 4 times that of neighboring countries. It therefore costs businesses more money to manufacture goods and as a result, the manufacturing sec-

tor has failed to attract significant foreign investment. To address this problem, the Rwandan water and energy utility company, Electrogaz, will be privately managed as early as 2001. Eventually, the Rwandan government intends to privatize Electrogaz. The Rwandan government, in conjunction with the **private sector**, is considering alternate sources of energy, such as harnessing the reserves of methane gas found in Lake Kivu.

Rwandatel, the government-owned telephone company, is the sole wire-based telephone company operating in Rwanda and is also the exclusive Internet service provider. There were only 15,000 main telephone lines in use in 1995, primarily in the capital area. To date, Internet service has proven unreliable and expensive. Thus, the Rwandan government intends to establish an agency that will privatize Rwandatel and **liberalize** the telecommunications sector. MTN Rwandacell provides mobile phone service to certain areas of the country. Additionally, 2 radio stations and 1 television station operate from Kigali.

ECONOMIC SECTORS

Rwanda's economy is dominated by the agricultural sector, which contributes 44 percent of GDP and 70 percent of exports, and employs 9 out of 10 of the country's workers. In 1998, agricultural exports accounted for US$36.5 million. Most of Rwanda's population is engaged in some form of subsistence agriculture, producing goods for their own consumption and not for sale.

Roughly 10,000 workers are employed in the industrial sector, which represents 20 percent of the country's GDP. The industrial sector is composed of small- to medium-sized companies, whose capital rarely exceeds US$1 million and which produce primarily food-related

Communications

Country	Telephones[a]	Telephones, Mobile/Cellular[a]	Radio Stations[b]	Radios[a]	TV Stations[a]	Televisions[a]	Internet Service Providers[c]	Internet Users[c]
Rwanda	15,000 (1995)	N/A	AM 0; FM 3; shortwave 1	601,000	2	N/A	1	1,000
United States	194 M	69.209 M (1998)	AM 4,762; FM 5,542; shortwave 18	575 M	1,500	219 M	7,800	148 M
Dem. Rep. of Congo	21,000	8,900	AM 3; FM 12; shortwave 1 (1999)	18.03 M	20 (1999)	6.478 M	2	1,500 (1999)
Burundi	16,000	619	AM 2; FM 2; shortwave 0	440,000	1 (1999)	25,000	1	2,000

[a]Data is for 1997 unless otherwise noted.
[b]Data is for 1998 unless otherwise noted.
[c]Data is for 2000 unless otherwise noted.

SOURCE: CIA *World Factbook 2001* [Online].

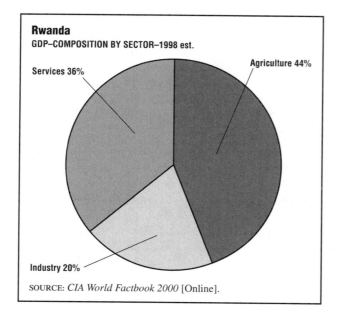

Rwanda
GDP–COMPOSITION BY SECTOR–1998 est.

Services 36%

Agriculture 44%

Industry 20%

SOURCE: *CIA World Factbook 2000* [Online].

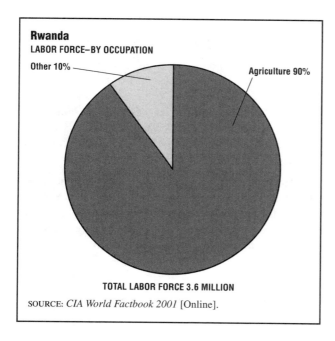

Rwanda
LABOR FORCE–BY OCCUPATION

Other 10%

Agriculture 90%

TOTAL LABOR FORCE 3.6 MILLION

SOURCE: *CIA World Factbook 2001* [Online].

products. After the war, the industrial sector came to a halt. Since then, the Rwandan industrial sector has only been able to resume 40 percent of its pre-war levels. The services sector represents just 36 percent of GDP. Financial services are weak, and tourism nearly nonexistent thanks to the country's reputation for violence.

AGRICULTURE

The Rwandan people depend on subsistence agriculture for survival, but do produce several key crops for export. The crop that generates the most foreign exchange

is coffee. In 1999, about 14,500 metric tons of coffee were produced. Most coffee is grown on small farms by independent farmers. Tea is the other major export, and Rwanda also produces pyrethrum, plantains, maize, soybeans, sugar cane, wheat, beans, cassava, sweet potatoes, and sorghum. The country has approximately 980,000 goats, 500,000 cattle, 270,000 sheep, and 80,000 pigs.

INDUSTRY

MANUFACTURING. The manufacturing sector primarily produces beer, soft drinks, hoes, cigarettes, soap, wheelbarrows, cement, plastic pipe, mattresses, textiles, and roofing materials. Most manufacturing is geared toward **import substitution**—providing goods that must otherwise be imported. Like every other sector, industry came to a halt in 1994, but had returned to 75 percent of its capacity by mid-1997.

MINING. After agricultural products, minerals generate the most foreign exchange. Rwanda has significant reserves of cassiterite (tin ore), wolfram (tungsten ore), gold, and beryl. But due to a drop in the global price of cassiterite in 1986, this metal ceased to be mined. In 1987, the wolframite mines suffered the same fate. Since 1991, some cassiterite and wolframite began to be exported, but not at their pre-1987 and 1991 levels. The mining of other mineral ores was also gravely disrupted by the 1994 genocide and have also yet to reach their pre-1994 levels of production.

Efforts have been made to explore the possibility of producing methane that is emitted from Lake Kivu, but these have yet to reach their potential. Because it is a mountainous country with many rivers, Rwanda has the capacity to produce hydroelectric power, and is currently exploring hydroelectric projects with neighboring Burundi and the Democratic Republic of the Congo.

SERVICES

Most tourists go to Rwanda to see its mountain gorillas. However, Rwanda's tourism came to a halt during the 1994 war. There is hope that if Rwanda continues to benefit from its current levels of stability, the hotel and restaurant industry (the primary beneficiaries of tourism) will grow as tourism resumes its pre-war levels.

The banking system has been liberalized by the government, and there are few barriers to the flow of foreign exchange. Rwanda has a central bank and 5 commercial banks, 1 development bank, and a credit union system. In 1999, the Rwandan parliament passed a new set of liberalization measures that in part ensure that the private banks operate under the close supervision of the National Bank of Rwanda. All in all, the progress is encouraging, given Rwanda's recent history and the continuing con-

Trade (expressed in billions of US$): Rwanda		
	Exports	Imports
1975	.042	.099
1980	.072	.243
1985	.131	.298
1990	.110	.288
1995	.054	.237
1998	.063	.287

SOURCE: International Monetary Fund. *International Financial Statistics Yearbook 1999.*

Exchange rates: Rwanda	
Rwandan francs per US$1	
Jan 2001	432.24
2000	389.70
1999	333.94
1998	312.31
1997	301.53
1996	306.82

SOURCE: CIA *World Factbook 2001* [ONLINE].

flict in the neighboring Congo. **Retail** services improved in the late 1990s as returning Rwandan refugees opened a variety of small enterprises.

INTERNATIONAL TRADE

Rwanda's main export partners are Brazil, Germany, Belgium, Pakistan, Spain, and Kenya. Most of Rwanda's coffee and tea are shipped to Germany and other European countries. Rwanda's main import partners are Kenya, Tanzania, the United States, the Benelux countries, and France. Rwanda imported motor vehicles, textiles, fuels and machinery. In 1998, Rwanda generated US$58 million in exports, but imports cost Rwanda more than US$240 million that same year.

Tea and coffee continue to be the country's most important exports. In 1999, they represented 70 percent of Rwanda's exports. Lately, Rwandan businesses have been exploring other agriculturally-based exports that would be equally suited to the country's small farms, steep slopes, and cool climates. The feasibility of many of these new proposals to expand the agriculture industry is limited by the country's high transportation costs.

Although Rwanda's primary partners have been African and European countries, recently there have been significant purchase imports from the United States. Northrop Grumman sold a US$16 million commercial radar system and Lucent Technologies made a sale of US$25 million for a wireless air loop telephone system. It remains to be seen whether Rwandan-U.S. trade will continue.

MONEY

The local currency is the Rwandan franc, and it is allowed to float freely on the world currency market. The **exchange rate** in 1998 was 312 Rwandan francs for 1 U.S. dollar. The National Bank of Rwanda is the country's central bank and determines **monetary policy** for the country. Inflation, which had been extremely high fol-

lowing the 1994 war, has since been stabilized and was about 5 percent in 2000.

POVERTY AND WEALTH

Rwanda is, by all measures, a poor country. The 1994 war obliterated the country's economy, social fabric, human resource base, and institutions. Almost 90 percent of the population lives on less than US$2 per day and half of its population lives on less than US$1 per day. Government statistics indicated that 65.3 percent of the people lived below the poverty line in 1998.

Though the Rwandan government reports that 87 percent of the population lived within 2 hours walking distance of a health care facility in 1996, the quality of the Rwandan people's health is quite poor. Life expectancy is low, and malnutrition is high. Malaria and respiratory diseases—which are rarely the cause of death in more developed countries—are the biggest killers in Rwanda. Not only are the people unhealthy, they are also poorly educated. According to government reports, only 46 percent of Rwandan teachers are qualified, teaching materials are poor, and drop-out rates are high. Only 7 percent of eligible students were enrolled in secondary schools in 1998.

In an effort to curb Rwanda's poverty, the IMF, the African Development Bank (ADB), and the World Bank have taken certain steps to assist Rwanda in its efforts towards economic recovery. Thus, in 1998 the IMF approved

GDP per Capita (US$)					
Country	1975	1980	1985	1990	1998
Rwanda	233	321	312	292	227
United States	19,364	21,529	23,200	25,363	29,683
Dem. Rep. of Congo	392	313	293	247	127
Burundi	162	176	198	206	147

SOURCE: United Nations. *Human Development Report 2000; Trends in human development and per capita income.*

Distribution of Income or Consumption by Percentage Share: Rwanda

Lowest 10%	4.2
Lowest 20%	9.7
Second 20%	13.2
Third 20%	16.5
Fourth 20%	21.6
Highest 20%	39.1
Highest 10%	24.2

Survey year: 1983–85
Note: This information refers to expenditure shares by percentiles of the population and is ranked by per capita expenditure.

SOURCE: *2000 World Development Indicators* [CD-ROM].

the Poverty Reduction and Growth Facility, the ADB approved a structural adjustment credit of US$20 million, and the World Bank agreed to provide US$75 million to Rwanda. These efforts are designed to reduce rural poverty, pave the way for private sector growth, and promote prospects for national reconciliation by opening up economic opportunities to all Rwandans.

WORKING CONDITIONS

The Rwandan constitution permits professional associations and labor unions, and the Rwandan government generally respects this right. Rwanda has no uniform minimum wage, and wages vary in accordance with the position. In any event, the vast majority of wages paid to workers in Rwanda are insufficient to support a decent standard of living for a worker and his or her family. The majority of families supplement their earnings by working in subsistence agriculture. Pressured by labor unions, the Transitional National Assembly has considered creating a new labor code to provide protections for workers but, as with much else in Rwanda, completion of this work awaits greater political and economic stability.

Women make up 54 percent of the Rwandan population, but discriminatory practices in education and employment have meant that women bear a disproportionate brunt of the poverty in the country. The government has plans to craft laws to protect the rights of women, but these laws are still pending as of 2001.

COUNTRY HISTORY AND ECONOMIC DEVELOPMENT

1894. The first European, German Count Von Geotzen, visits what is present-day Rwanda.

1918. Following World War I, Rwanda becomes a protectorate of the League of Nations under Belgian rule.

1926. The Belgian colonizers issue identity cards distinguishing the Tutsis from the Hutus.

1959. The Hutus rebel against the Belgian colonizers and the Tutsi elite, forcing the Tutsi monarch and more than 150,000 Tutsis to flee the country.

1961. Rwanda is established as a republic. The Party of the Hutu Emancipation Movement (PARMEHUTU) wins a majority of the seats in the National Assembly, and the assembly votes against the return of the Tutsi king.

1962. Belgium grants Rwanda independence, and the PARMEHUTU party changes its name to the Democratic Republican Movement whose leader, Gregoire Kayibanda, becomes the country's president.

1963. Exiled Tutsis unsuccessfully attempt to take over Rwanda, and the Hutus respond by massacring the Tutsis.

1973. General Juvenal Habyarimana topples President Kayibanda, accusing him of favoring southern Hutus, and suspends all political activities.

1975. Habyarimana creates the National Revolutionary Movement for Development (MRND) as the country's lone political party.

1978. President Habyarimana is given another 5-year term in single-party elections and a new constitution is ratified. Habyarimana is reelected in 1983 and 1988.

1989. Coffee prices plummet, famine increases, and the country turns to the World Bank for assistance. Following a World Bank reform plan, Rwanda liberalizes trade, divests state enterprises, devalues the Rwandan franc, and reduces government **subsidies**.

1990. Central African nations and Belgium send troops to Rwanda to help the Habyarimana regime defend itself against an attack from a rebel group of Tutsi exiles from Uganda.

1991. A new constitution is ratified that states Rwanda is a multiparty democracy.

1992. The price of coffee continues to plummet and Rwandan coffee trees are uprooted because coffee growers are unable to earn a living. The World Bank imposes more privatization, with proceeds going to service Rwanda's **external debt**. Ethnic tensions between Hutus and Tutsis rise.

1994. President Habyarimana dies after his plane is shot down. The Hutus set out to massacre all Tutsis within the country, and hundreds of thousands of Tutsis are killed. An external Tutsi rebel group, the Rwandan Patriotic Front, takes control of Rwanda, and forms the Transitional Government of National Unity to oversee a return to normalcy.

1996. The Rwandan government tacitly supports a rebel, Laurent Kabila, from Zaire (now the Democratic Republic of the Congo) to assist in securing Rwanda's border from the Interhamwe and ex-FAR operating from the Congo. Rwanda backs Kabila's efforts to overthrow the government of the Congo. At the same time, huge numbers of refugees who had fled during 1994 return to the country.

1998. President Kabila expels Rwanda's forces from the Congo and Rwanda in turn supports rebel groups in the Congo seeking Kabila's ouster.

2000. Major General Paul Kagame, a Tutsi, is elected president of Rwanda in a special parliamentary vote, but the government is still considered to be in transition.

FUTURE TRENDS

After the 1994 war and genocide, the Rwandan government focused on establishing peace within its territory and **repatriating** refugees, mostly from the Congo. The Rwandan economy, as a result of the war, had reached rock bottom. In 1995, the GDP rebounded by 37 percent after the cessation of hostilities allowed the Rwandan citizenry to return to its normal affairs. This normalization of the Rwandan economy continued in 1996 and resulted in a GDP growth of 15.8 percent. That year, the agricultural sector grew by 10 percent, livestock production by 17 percent, and the manufacturing sector by 25 percent. In 1998, Rwanda set upon an ambitious privatization program encouraged by the World Bank and also signed an Enhanced Structural Adjustment Facility with the IMF, both of which were designed to provide order to the economy and encourage economic growth. This same year, Rwanda's economy grew by 9.5 percent and in 1999 by 5.9 percent. Unfortunately, the country experienced a drought which caused extensive crop failure in 2000. The economy, however, is still expected to grow by at least 5.8 percent for the next 3 years. After the 1994 war, inflation had risen to 64 percent. Since then, inflation has come down to around 5 to 7 percent. Admirably, by 1998, the country's GDP surpassed its pre-war level.

Rwanda faces 2 major threats to its continued economic progress: its support of the rebel groups at war with the government of the Congo, and HIV/AIDS. With respect to the first threat, the IMF blames Rwanda's poor coffee production on the fact that Rwanda has diverted indispensable resources needed for coffee production to fund the rebel groups operating in the Congo. Particularly, the IMF contends that unless funding for the rebel groups ceases, Rwanda will be unable to finance the replacement of the aging Arabica trees with newer high-yield trees, and if that is not done, Rwandan coffee production will continue to fall. Both the IMF and the European Union have warned Rwanda that if it does not keep its military expenditures below 2 percent of GDP, they may curtail their funding. With respect to the second threat, 11 percent of the rural Rwandan population is infected with the AIDS virus and that number is growing exponentially. If the Rwandan government fails to implement effective prevention and treatment programs, Rwanda may begin to experience very severe strains on its labor and budgetary expenses.

Prior to 2000, Rwanda had fallen behind in some of its external debt repayments in some bilateral agreements. But as of 2000, Rwanda was not in **arrears** to either the World Bank or the IMF. Based on this good credit, the IMF has approved a 3-year program with total disbursements of US$56.3 million. Equally important to Rwanda's continued progress is the fact that the IMF and the World Bank have stated that Rwanda qualifies for **debt relief** under the Highly Indebted Poor Countries program. But these donors, however, made clear that this debt relief is contingent on Rwanda disentangling itself from the Congo war.

DEPENDENCIES

Rwanda has no territories or colonies.

BIBLIOGRAPHY

Action Programme for the Development of Rwanda, 2001–2010. Kigali: Government of Rwanda, 2001.

Economist Intelligence Unit. *Country Profile: Rwanda.* London: Economist Intelligence Unit, 2001.

Official Website of the Republic of Rwanda. <http://www.rwanda1.com/government/rwandalaunchie.html>. Accessed September 2001.

Rwanda: The Embassy of the Republic of Rwanda, Washington, D.C. <http://www.rwandemb.org>. Accessed September 2001.

The Rwandan Economy Website. <http://www.rwanda1.com/economy>. Accessed September 2001.

U.S. Central Intelligence Agency. "World Factbook 2000: Rwanda." <http://www.odci.gov/cia/publications/factbook/geos/rw.html>. Accessed February 2001.

U.S. Department of State. *Background Notes: Republic of Rwanda, March 1998.* <http://www.state.gov/www/background_notes/rwanda_0398_bgn.html>. Accessed February 2001.

U.S. Department of State. *FY 2001 Country Commercial Guide: Rwanda.* <http://www.state.gov/www/about_state/business/com_guides/2001/africa/index.html>. Accessed February 2001.

—Michael David Nicoleau and Raynette Rose Gutrick

SÃO TOMÉ
AND PRÍNCIPE

Democratic Republic of São Tomé and Príncipe
República Democrática de São Tomé e Príncipe

COUNTRY OVERVIEW

LOCATION AND SIZE. São Tomé and Príncipe is located in the Gulf of Guinea 290 kilometers (180 miles) west of Gabon, which is located on the western edge of Africa. The 2 mountainous main islands of the republic are São Tomé and Príncipe; other rocky islets include Caroco, Pedras, and Tinhosas off Príncipe Island, and Rolas off São Tomé Island. The islands are the tips of an extinct volcanic mountain range and make up one of Africa's smallest countries. The country has an area of 1,001 square kilometers (386.5 square miles). The coast line is 209 kilometers (130 miles). Comparatively the area of São Tomé is more than 5 times of the size of Washington, D.C. The capital city of the country, São Tomé, is located on the northeastern coast of the island of São Tomé.

POPULATION. The population of São Tomé and Príncipe was estimated at 159,883 in July 2000. In 2000, the birth rate stood at 42.98 per 1,000, which is quite high. The death rate in the same year was 7.76 per 1,000, giving an annual average population growth rate of 3.16 percent. The life expectancy at birth is 65.25 years for total population, 63.84 years for males and 66.7 years for females. The population density in 1997 was 135.5 per square kilo-

meters (351 per square mile). Ninety-five percent of the country's population lives on the island of São Tomé and 46 percent of the population lived in urban areas in 1996. São Tomé and Príncipe is a country of young people with 48 percent of the population below the age of 14, and just 4 percent of the population older than 65.

The country's population is very diverse and represents mainly descendants from different parts of the African continent. Ethnic groups include mestico, angolares (descendants of Angolan slaves); forros (descendants of freed slaves); servicais (contract laborers from Angola, Mozambique, and Cape Verde); tongas (children of servicais born on the island); and Europeans (primarily Portuguese). Roughly 80 percent of the islanders are Christians, with representatives of the Roman Catholic, Seventh-Day Adventist, and Evangelical Protestant faiths. The official language of the republic is Portuguese; however, Lungwa São Tomé (a Portuguese creole) and Fang (a Bantu language) are widely used as well.

OVERVIEW OF ECONOMY

Presently São Tomé and Príncipe is in the process of diversifying its economy, which was dependent on cocoa production since the 19th century. After achieving independence in 1975 the nation adopted a **socialist** economy, imposing state control over major sectors of economy. The islands were mainly producing cocoa on the state-owned farms, and cocoa remains the main export commodity. Fishing and forestry are also important economic activities of São Toméans. The islands have no mineral resources with the exception of oil discovered in its territorial waters in 1998. The manufacturing sector is mainly limited to production of textiles, beer, soft drinks, and soap to cover the local demand. The country imports up to 90 percent of its food requirements, machinery, and petroleum products.

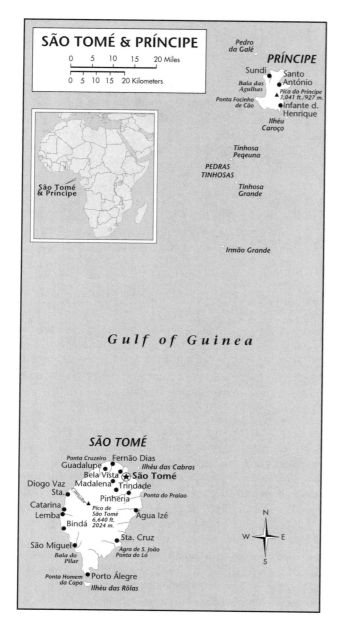

SÃO TOMÉ & PRÍNCIPE

0   5   10   15   20 Miles

0   5 10 15   20 Kilometers

São Tomé & Príncipe

Gulf of Guinea

PRÍNCIPE

Pedro da Galé

Sundi
Santo António
Baía das Agulhas
Pico da Príncipe 3,041 ft./927 m.
Ponta Focinho de Cão
Infante d. Henrique
Ilhéu Caroço

Tinhosa Peqeuna

PEDRAS TINHOSAS

Tinhosa Grande

Irmão Grande

SÃO TOMÉ

Ponta Cruzeiro Fernão Dias
Guadalupe *Ilhéu das Cabras*
Bela Vista ★ São Tomé
Diogo Vaz Madalena Trindade
Sta. *Pinheria* *Ponta do Praia*
Catarina *Pico de São Tomé 6,640 ft. 2024 m.*
Lemba Água Izé
Bindá
São Miguel Sta. Cruz
Baía do Pilar *Agra de S. João Ponta do Ló*
Ponta Homem da Capa Porto Álegre
Ilhéu das Rôlas

In the early 1980s São Tomé and Príncipe proclaimed itself a non-aligned state and started establishing trade links with non-socialist countries. In attempting to diversify its economy in the early 1990s, São Tomé requested international financial assistance. This economic development assistance was offered to the republic under conditions of economic **liberalization**, **privatization**, administrative reforms, and changes in the financial sector. During the 1990s the government increasingly relied on external sources to finance its liberalization program designed by the International Monetary Fund (IMF) and the World Bank.

According to a World Bank report, in 1999 São Toméan outstanding debt reached US$296 million, compared to US$135 million in 1989. This made about

US$1,851 of debt per person, including infants, in 1999. The country is one of the largest recipients of aid per capita in the world; nonetheless, corruption and mismanagement undermined the administration of aid. The country sees its economic future in the development of offshore oil reserves and the expansion of tourism, which is not yet fully established. Beginning in 1993 the nation also sought to establish **free trade zones** to attract foreign investors and further develop the country's shipping and manufacturing sectors.

POLITICS, GOVERNMENT, AND TAXATION

São Tomé and Príncipe became a colony of Portugal in 1522 and was administered by Portugal for the next several hundred years. A liberation movement emerged in the 1960s, resulting in the creation of the Movement for the Liberation of São Tomé and Príncipe (MLSTP) in 1972. Based in Gabon and led by Dr. Manuel Pinto da Costa, the MLSTP led the country to independence following a military coup in Portugal in 1974. The new Portuguese administration oversaw the peaceful transition to independence over the course of the next year.

After declaring independence on 12 July 1975, Dr. Manuel da Costa became the country's first president. The ruling MLSTP party adopted a socialist economic program, providing state ownership and direction of all the islands' industries. There were several unsuccessful coups and attempts to overthrow the regime of President da Costa, yet da Costa maintained close links with the **communist** bloc countries amid worsening economic conditions.

The severe drought of 1982 prompted President da Costa to change his priorities in international relations. In 1984 the president proclaimed São Tomé and Príncipe a nonaligned state. This meant that the government adopted a strategic and political position of neutrality towards the major powers aligned with the United States and the U.S.S.R. Most of the Soviet, Cuban, and Angolan advisers had to leave the country. New international links were established with neighboring African states and Portugal. The initial attempts to reduce state control over the economy halted after the minister of Planning and Commerce and the minister of Foreign Affairs and Co-Operation were dismissed.

In August 1990 a referendum indicated that 72 percent of the electorate (90.7 percent of participating voters) favored a newly drafted constitution. The new constitution declared the republic as a sovereign, independent, unitary, and democratic state. The MLSTP lost its dominating role as the new constitution allowed a multi-party system. At new National Assembly elections on 20 January 1991 the MLSTP was defeated. It obtained only 21 seats in the 55-seat **unicameral** National Assembly, while the opposition Party for Democratic Convergence (PCD) secured 33 seats. The remaining seat was won by the Partido Democratico de São Tomé e Príncipe—Coligacao Democratico de Oposicao (PDSTP-CODO). Miguel Trovoada of the PCD was chosen as president and retained that role in elections in 1996.

Members of the National Assembly are elected for 5-year terms in free and fair multi-party elections. The president of the republic is elected to a 5-year term by direct election. The president names the prime minister from a name submitted by the party holding a majority in the National Assembly. The prime minister then names the 14 members of the cabinet. In 2001 Miguel Trovoada was the president and Guilherma Posser da Costa was the prime minister. The next presidential election will be held in July of 2001 and the next legislative election will be held in 2003.

There are 4 types of taxes imposed by the government on imported goods: an 8 percent transaction tax; import **duties** ranging from 0 percent on basic foodstuff and pharmaceuticals to between 6 and 50 percent on alcoholic drinks and 10 and 66 percent on petroleum products; a 3.5 percent customs duty; and a consumption **excise tax**, which varies significantly on different types of goods (from 0 percent on basic foodstuff to 250 percent on tobacco) and is levied on the after-tax value on goods.

In the late 1980s, the new government requested international assistance in order to improve the economic situation. The new economic policy included economic liberalization, currency **devaluation**, price liberalization, and privatization. Drastic economic measures imposed by the IMF and the World Bank as part of the economic recovery programs led to a significant decline in the living standards of people. According to the *EIU Country Report*, **inflation** ballooned from 35.5 percent in 1996 to 68.5 percent in 1997. However, the annual **inflation rate** was reduced to 10.5 percent in 1999, and the annual GDP growth rate grew from 1.0 percent in 1997 to 3.0 percent in 2000.

INFRASTRUCTURE, POWER, AND COMMUNICATIONS

São Tomé and Príncipe have a limited network of 320 kilometers (198 miles) of roads, two-thirds (218 kilometers, or 135 miles) of which is paved. There were 4,581 light vehicles registered in 1994, 561 heavy vehicles, 299 tractors, and 815 motorcycles. There is no public transportation on the islands and no rail network.

There are 2 main seaports: 1 at São Tomé city and another at Santo Antonio on Príncipe island. The republic has 10 ships, but Dutch and Portuguese ships serve the links with Gabon, Portugal, and the Netherlands. The seaports are managed by the state. Although the seaports have been modernized, the maritime shipping of goods is irregular and total shipping traffic is limited due to the absence of a deep-water seaport. In 2000, there were plans to build a deep-water seaport at Agulhas Bay on Príncipe island.

There are 2 main airports, in São Tomé and Santo Antonio. Both have been recently modernized. The US$16 million modernization of the international airport in São Tomé was financed by the African Bank of Development and was completed in 1992. The airports are owned jointly by the government (35 percent), Portugal (40 percent), and France (25 percent). Domestic and regional lines are served by Portugal, Angola, and Gabon. The country's lone airline, Air São Tomé e Príncipe, owns only 1 airplane.

Communications

Country	Telephones[a]	Telephones, Mobile/Cellular[a]	Radio Stations[b]	Radios[a]	TV Stations[a]	Televisions[a]	Internet Service Providers[c]	Internet Users[c]
São Tomé & Príncipe	3,000	6,942	AM 2; FM 4; shortwave 0	38,000	2	23,000	2	500
United States	194 M	69.209 M (1998)	AM 4,762; FM 5,542; shortwave 18	575 M	1,500	219 M	7,800	148 M
Nigeria	500,000 (2000)	26,700	AM 82; FM 35; shortwave 11	23.5 M	2 (1999)	6.9 M	11	100,000
Equatorial Guinea	4,000 (1996)	N/A	AM 0; FM 2; shortwave 4	180,000	1	4,000	1	500

[a]Data is for 1997 unless otherwise noted.
[b]Data is for 1998 unless otherwise noted.
[c]Data is for 2000 unless otherwise noted.
SOURCE: CIA *World Factbook 2001* [Online].

Electricity production in 1998 of 15 million kilowatt hours (kWh) comes from 2 main sources, imported fossil fuel (which generates up to 47 percent of total power) and hydroelectric power (up to 53 percent) generated from the nation's abundant water supply. However, only 53 percent of households have electricity and there are regular power cuts.

Local telephone service is served by the former state-owned Companhia Santomense de Telecomunicacoes (CST), over half of which has been sold to Radio Marconi of Portugal. There were 3,000 telephones lines in 1995. The international lines were improved with international financial assistance. CST tried to compete with Swedish Bahnhof Internet in providing Internet services in the country. In July 1999 Bahnhof Internet became the owner of the country's top Internet domain and it planned to introduce a satellite connection to the Internet. In 1997 the island nation had 2 television stations serving some 23,000 sets.

ECONOMIC SECTORS

The São Toméan economic sectors are influenced by its size and geographical position. The agricultural sector is mainly export-oriented and devoted to cocoa production, so that the country relies heavily on imports of food. Agricultural production is extremely sensitive to weather and prices in the international market; therefore, part of the government's policy of economic diversification is further development of fishing and tourism. Tourism is a growing sector and has been considered a priority for future development. The industrial sector is very limited. All told, agriculture contributes 23 percent of GDP in 1997, industry contributed 19 percent, and services contributed 58 percent.

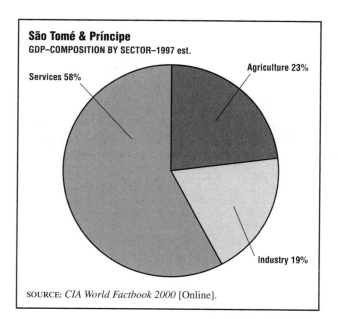

São Tomé & Príncipe
GDP–COMPOSITION BY SECTOR–1997 est.

Services 58%
Agriculture 23%
Industry 19%

SOURCE: *CIA World Factbook 2000* [Online].

AGRICULTURE

São Tomé and Príncipe is an agricultural country. According to the World Bank, in 1997 the agricultural sector contributed 23.3 percent of the GDP and provided employment for 39.6 percent of the economically active population. The agricultural sector mainly produces cocoa, which constituted 86 percent of export revenues in 1997. It also produces coffee, copra, coconuts, and palm oil. Since almost all agricultural production of the country is export-oriented, it has to import foodstuff. By the mid-1990s it imported almost 90 percent of its food requirements. The government accepted a program to develop **smallholder** farms since 1993 in order to diversify agricultural production. However, inadequate training, poor road quality, and limited access to markets hinder this development.

FISHING. Fishing is another important economic activity of São Toméans. The annual total catch of fish is estimated at about 3,000 tons. About 90 percent of the total local catch is provided by 2,300 fishermen. The country's 160,000 square kilometer Exclusive Economic Zone (EEZ) has a potential to produce about 12,000 tons of fish per year. The EEZ—created by the United Nations Convention of the Law of the Sea and completed in 1982—allows coastal nations to claim a territorial sea of up to 12 nautical miles and an exclusive economic zone of up to 200 nautical miles. The government uses this potential to receive its second largest source of foreign exchange by issuing fishing licenses to foreign fishing fleets. The government has prioritized the development of this sector as part of its economic diversification policy, but awaits significant foreign investments for development to be realized.

FORESTRY. The country had considerable forest resources, but these are in the process of being depleted. In 1995 São Toméans produced 8,500 cubic meters of trunks and 3,150 cubic meters of processed timber. Severe deforestation of the country speaks for itself: the rain forest cover dropped to 28 percent of the land area and about 30 percent of the rain forest is secondary forest. New legislation was introduced in the 1990s to protect the rain forest. The government also plans to create national parks to protect the land, which should contribute to plans to boost tourism.

INDUSTRY

São Toméan industry is very small. It includes manufacturing, power generation, and light construction. In 1997 this sector contributed 18.7 percent of the GDP and employed 15.8 percent of economically active population. There are no mineral resources on the island except the discovery of oil in the territorial waters (in the Gulf of Guinea) in 1998, the development of which will depend on agreements with Gabon, Nigeria, and Equatorial Guinea.

Small manufacturing plants that produce only items for local consumption such as beer, textiles, soap, and bread represent the manufacturing sector. Most of the enterprises were under state control in the 1970s and 1980s. While the state would like to privatize these and all other industries, it is awaiting significant investments of capital and management expertise before it can relinquish control.

SERVICES

The services sector contributed about 58 percent of the GDP and employed 33.6 percent of economically active population in 1997. The banking system in the republic is underdeveloped and notorious for its corruption scandals. In 1999 there were several arrests in Belgium when some individuals tried to cash in false bonds. After the arrests the government was forced to dismiss the governor of the Banco Central de São Tomé e Príncipe, the bank's administrator, and its administrative board.

TOURISM. A big potential for the country lies within the fast-growing tourism sector. Fantastic mountain scenery, breathtaking beaches, and unique species of flora and fauna are big attractions for tourists. However, high airfares, the extreme isolation of the islands, and underdeveloped **infrastructure** discourage potential tourists, although there were considerable improvements in telecommunications and hotel accommodations in recent years. This sector attracts the largest portion of foreign investments. While in the early 1980s there was only 1 hotel, in 1996 there were already 9 hotels and 9 guesthouses with a total of 520 beds. In 1996, 2,000 tourists visited the country bringing US$2 million in revenue; in 1998 there were about 6,000 foreign visitors who brought US$4 million.

INTERNATIONAL TRADE

São Toméan international trade relies mostly on the export of cocoa that gives up to 86 percent of the earnings. According to *The CIA World Factbook,* it also exports copra, coffee, and palm oil to the Netherlands (51 percent), Portugal (6 percent), and Germany (6 percent). Exports totaled US$4.9 million in 1999.

The country depends heavily on food imports, mainly from Portugal. It also imports machinery, electrical equipment, and petroleum products. The main import partners are Portugal (26 percent), France (18 percent), Angola, Belgium, and Japan. Angola is the main source of petroleum products. Imports in 1999 totaled US$19.5 million.

Trade (expressed in billions of US$): São Tomé & Príncipe		
	Exports	Imports
1975	.007	.011
1980	.017	.019
1985	.006	.010
1990	.004	.021
1995	.005	.029
1998	N/A	N/A

SOURCE: International Monetary Fund. *International Financial Statistics Yearbook 1999.*

Exchange rates: São Tomé and Príncipe	
dobras (Db) per US$1	
2001	N/A
Dec 2000	2390.04
1999	7,119.0
1998	6,883.2
1997	4,552.5
1996	2,203.2

SOURCE: CIA *World Factbook 2001* [ONLINE].

MONEY

The value of the São Toméan dobra has decreased steadily against the U.S. dollar with the implementation of the economic adjustment program and the devaluation of currency. Throughout the late 1990s the dobra collapsed 5-fold within 4 years. In 1995 US$1 was equal to 1,420.3 dobras; by 1999 that figure rose to 7,200 dobras. Though the diminishing value of the dobra was meant to spur exports, it also caused high inflation in the country, which translated in a higher cost of goods for São Toméans. Before the start of economic reforms in the 1990 the inflation rate was about 44.8 percent (1989); it went down to 27.4 percent in 1992 and up again to 68.2 percent in 1997.

POVERTY AND WEALTH

São Tomé and Príncipe is an agricultural country with the majority of its population living in rural areas and plantations with poor quality roads, no electricity, and little access to medical help and education. The deeply indebted government of São Tomé and Príncipe cannot afford to spend more on health and education for its people. Spending on health declined over the years and constitutes slightly more than 10 percent of total expenditures. In 1992 all São Toméan hospitals and medical centers had 556 beds and 66 practicing doctors. Although the life

GDP per Capita (US$)

Country	1975	1980	1985	1990	1998
São Tomé and Príncipe	N/A	N/A	N/A	365	337
United States	19,364	21,529	23,200	25,363	29,683
Nigeria	301	314	230	258	256
Equatorial Guinea	N/A	N/A	352	333	1,049

SOURCE: United Nations. *Human Development Report 2000; Trends in human development and per capita income.*

expectancy is relatively high for an African country, there are about 40,000 cases of malaria infection per year as well as numerous cases of respiratory and diarrheal diseases. There were also 32 registered AIDS cases, although it is estimated that the actual figure is higher.

The education sector receives about 10–15 percent of total budget expenditures. There were 69 primary and 10 secondary schools in 1997. Although the average adult literacy rate was 73 percent in 1991, one-third of the population between the ages of 6 and 20 never went to school. The network of secondary and tertiary institutions is inadequate; there are also shortages of school equipment, textbooks, and properly trained teachers. Although there is some foreign financial assistance directed into education, it cannot cover all of the problems.

WORKING CONDITIONS

The crawling growth of wages for workers could not keep up with the growing inflation, and the real value of wages has plummeted significantly since 1987. Constant demonstrations of angry people prompted the government to increase the wages in spite of criticism from the IMF. The **public-sector** wages were increased by 200–300 percent in 1997 and the teachers' wages were up by 100 percent in 1998. A threat of a strike came from the civil servants' union (Sindicato da Funcao Publica), who demanded an increase in minimum monthly wages from 40,000 dobras ($6) to 350,000 dobras ($52.50). Just finding a job in the country is difficult, however, for estimates of unemployment run as high as 50 percent.

COUNTRY HISTORY AND ECONOMIC DEVELOPMENT

c. 1471. Portuguese explorers discover uninhabited islands of São Tomé and Príncipe.

1522. The islands become a Portuguese colony, and are eventually populated with slave labor from the African continent.

1800s. Two **cash crops**—cocoa and coffee—are introduced to the islands.

1876. Slavery is officially abolished.

1951. São Tomé and Príncipe become an overseas province of Portugal.

1975. São Tomé and Príncipe achieve independence from Portugal and select Manuel Pinto da Costa as president.

1984. São Tomé is proclaimed a nonaligned state, ending its special relationship with other socialist states.

1987. The constitution is amended to allow universal adult voting.

1990. A new constitution is approved by referendum and allows multi-party politics.

1991. First multi-party elections.

1994. Príncipe is granted political and administrative autonomy.

FUTURE TRENDS

São Tomé has a history of coups, demonstrations, and strikes by people whose expectations for economic improvement are crushed by economic stagnation, high inflation, low salaries, and constant disagreements between the legislature and the president. The government's attempts to attract international financial aid in the 1990s resulted in accepting a "shock therapy" approach to economic reorganization, which led to the further deterioration of the quality of life in the country. However, IMF projections on poverty reduction efforts suggest that inflation may be reduced to 3 percent annually and that GDP may grow by 4 percent as early as 2001. Should these projections prove true, and should the government succeed in its 2 great economic projects—offshore oil extraction and the expansion of tourism—it is possible that São Tomé and Príncipe may correct its longstanding economic woes. The single biggest question is whether the cash-poor country can attract enough foreign investment to allow it to realize its dreams.

DEPENDENCIES

São Tomé and Príncipe has no territories or colonies.

BIBLIOGRAPHY

Assembleia Nacional São Tomé and Príncipe. <http://www.parlamento.st>. Accessed August 2001.

Economist Intelligence Unit. *Country Profile: São Tomé and Príncipe.* London: Economist Intelligence Unit, 2000.

Hodges, T., and M. Newitt. *São Tomé and Príncipe: From Plantation Colony to Microstate.* Boulder: Westview Press, 1998.

International Financial Statistics Yearbook, 1999. Washington, D.C.: International Monetary Fund, 2000.

Siebert, Gerhard. *Comrades, Clients and Cousins: Colonialism, Socialism and Democratization in São Tomé and Príncipe.* Leiden, the Netherlands: Leiden University, 1999.

U.S. Department of State. *Background Notes: São Tomé and Príncipe, March 1997.* <http://www.state.gov/www/background_notes/sao_tome_0397_bgn.html>. Accessed August 2001.

—Alfia Abazova

SENEGAL

Republic of Senegal
République du Sénégal

CAPITAL: Dakar.

MONETARY UNIT: Communauté Financière Africaine franc (CFA Fr). There are coins of 1, 2, 5, 10, 25, 50, 100, and 500 CFA francs, and notes of 50, 100, 500, 1,000, 5,000, and 10,000 CFA francs.

CHIEF EXPORTS: Fish, groundnuts (peanuts), petroleum products, phosphates, cotton.

CHIEF IMPORTS: Foods and beverages, consumer goods, capital goods, petroleum products.

GROSS DOMESTIC PRODUCT: US$16 billion (purchasing power parity, 2000 est.).

BALANCE OF TRADE: Exports: US$959 million (f.o.b., 2000). Imports: US$1.2 billion (f.o.b., 2000).

COUNTRY OVERVIEW

LOCATION AND SIZE. A relatively small country located in West Africa, Senegal has a total area of 196,190 square kilometers (75,748 square miles), making it slightly smaller than the state of South Dakota. Water composes 4,190 square kilometers (1,618 square miles) of this area, while the coastline, which borders the North Atlantic Ocean, stretches for 531 kilometers (330 miles). Senegal is bordered to the north by Mauritania, to the east by the Republic of Mali, to the south by Guinea and Guinea-Bissau, and to the west by the Atlantic Ocean. The country of Gambia juts out below the central part of the Senegalese coast, creating a finger-like enclave that penetrates deep into Senegal. Dakar, the capital of Senegal, is located on the northern coast.

POPULATION. In July 2000 the population of Senegal was estimated at 9,987,494. The growth rate was estimated at 2.94 percent per year, with a birth rate of 37.94 births per 1,000 people, and a death rate of 8.57 deaths per 1,000 people. The population of Senegal is young, with 45 percent under 14 years of age, 52 percent be-

tween the ages of 15 and 64, and only 3 percent above 65. A young population can benefit the economy because there are fewer elderly people to care for. Yet it creates pressure on the economy to continually expand to create new employment opportunities for new entrants to the **labor force**. In 2000, the World Bank stated that 125,000 people were expected to join the Senegalese labor force every year, creating a major impediment to the country's developmental efforts. Therefore, the Senegalese government has adopted a population control policy designed to limit the birthrate of Senegalese women. The importance of reducing Senegal's high fertility (5.21 children born per woman) will be a difficult challenge for a country that is socially conservative and resistant to using birth control.

Like many African countries, the people of Senegal are ethnically diverse. Of the many ethnic groups that make up the Senegalese population, 43.3 percent are Wolof, 23.8 percent Pular, 14.7 percent Jola, 3 percent Mandinka, 1.1 percent Soninke, and 1 percent European and Lebanese. Several smaller ethnic groups compose the remaining 9.4 percent of the population. The country is mostly Muslim, with 92 percent of the population followers of Islam. Followers of several indigenous religions constitute about 6 percent of the population, while the remaining 2 percent are Christian, mostly Roman Catholic. French is the official language of the country, though many people speak indigenous languages such as Wolof, Pulaar, Jola, or Mandinka.

OVERVIEW OF ECONOMY

Throughout the latter part of the 19th century, the area that now comprises the country of Senegal, along with several other regions in West Africa, came under the colonial domination of France. As a French colony

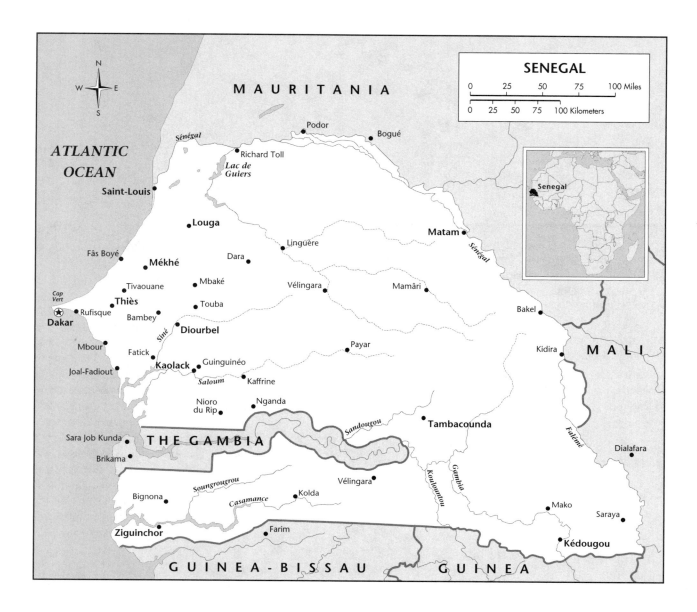

until 1960, Senegal based its economy on the exportation of peanuts. Though the dominance of the peanut industry led to a monocultural economy, the administrative apparatus constructed by the French created a demand for a locally educated elite to occupy these positions. The national elite that developed, and which has identified with French history and culture, took control of Senegal after independence in 1960.

Though Senegal has remained dependent on its peanut exports, the economy has diversified since independence. In the late 1960s and 1970s the state contributed to economic diversification by establishing public enterprises to fuel industrial growth. By 1974 there were 87 such enterprises but the government's emphasis on industry brought bias against the agricultural sector. The state controlled the purchasing of all agricultural produce to feed the masses of people flocking from rural to urban areas in search of employment. Under this state-controlled system, peasant farmers were paid for their produce at prices lower than its real worth.

In the late 1970s, the prices paid on the international market by importers of peanuts and phosphate increased, helping to improve the situation of the peasants. Phosphate was Senegal's second most important export. The prosperity that accompanied the elevation in international prices for Senegal's major exports was short-lived, however. Deterioration in the world price of peanuts, along with an increase in world prices for oil, a resource that Senegal imported heavily, led to an economic crisis in 1978.

By the early 1980s, Senegal was undergoing a first wave of reforms of structural adjustment as a condition of receiving badly needed loans from both the International Monetary Fund (IMF) and the World Bank (WB). Structural adjustment, as the name implies, meant that

Senegal was obliged to change certain "structures" within its economy, which the IMF and the WB viewed as inefficient to economic prosperity. The state was criticized for playing too great a role in the economy, creating corrupt enterprises (involving bribery in return for contracts) that drained state funding.

Many of Senegal's major exports, including peanuts, cotton, and fish, come from the agricultural sector. The modern, or non-agricultural, sector, which includes chemical industries, phosphates, petroleum refining, manufacturing, and tourism, is concentrated in Dakar and along the coastal belt. Senegal imports foods, beverages, **capital goods**, **consumer goods**, and unrefined petroleum products (such as crude oil). Because of historical ties between the 2 countries, France remains Senegal's largest trading partner.

Senegal has a huge **trade deficit**. In 2000 export revenue equaled US$959 million, while the costs of imports totaled US$1.3 billion. The country depends heavily on foreign assistance, which represented about 42.8 percent of the government's budget in 1994. Besides France, the European Union (EU) and Japan are major donor countries. The United States Agency for International Development (USAID) provides about US$30 million annually in assistance. Senegal has borrowed heavily, both from international financial institutions such as the WB and the IMF, and from commercial banks. In 1998 the country's debt amounted to US$3.4 billion.

Unemployment has been a long-standing economic problem for the people of Senegal. Though figures vary, several official estimates during the 1980s placed the unemployment rate between 20 and 30 percent. The CIA *World Fact Book* estimates that about 40 percent of all urban youth are unemployed. This situation has contributed to deep-seated urban problems such as juvenile delinquency and drug addiction.

POLITICS, GOVERNMENT, AND TAXATION

Senegal is a democracy where people can vote in elections at age 18. They elect a president every 7 years as the head of state who, in turn, appoints a prime minister to head a government. The Council of Ministers, or cabinet, is appointed by the prime minister in consultation with the president. The **unicameral** legislature, the National Assembly, has 140 members who serve a 5-year term. The judiciary has 3 parts: the Constitutional Court, the Court of Appeal, and the Council of State. The legal systems are based on French civil laws and are in need of strengthening as an institution. There is respect in both theory and practice for civil liberties, including freedom of speech, press, association, movement, and democratic electoral procedures. The military, on which the state spent US$68

million in 1997, includes an army, airforce, navy, and a national security police force that is non-political and highly professional.

Senegal is recognized as one of the most democratic and politically stable countries on the continent of Africa. Unlike many other African states, Senegal has never experienced revolution or a military coup, yet, as Frederic C. Schaffer argues in his book *Democracy in Translation: Understanding Politics in an Unfamiliar Culture*, Senegal's democracy is imperfect. Since its independence, a single-party rule has dominated, and the government has been accused of being corrupt and authoritarian. Furthermore, discontent in the rural Casamance region has led to an ongoing internal rebellion by the Movement of Democratic Forces of the Casamance (MFDC). The MFDC represents forces in the Casamance who feel marginalized and neglected by government policies.

After Senegal gained independence in 1960, the Senegalese government was headed by the Socialist Party (PS) until the presidential elections of March 2000. The current president, Abdoulaye Wade, represents the Democratic Party, though the Socialist Party still dominates the National Assembly. The Senegalese Socialist Party promotes a mixed economy in which both the market and the state play significant roles, unlike other **socialist** parties in the developing world that adhere to the **communist** ideals of complete state control of the economy. Before the 1980s, the PS insisted on a much greater economic role for the state, but as the Senegalese economy has become more **liberalized**, support for state control has diminished.

The WB and the IMF have made demands on Senegal to liberalize its economy in return for loans they have granted since the 1980s. They argue that state controls in the economy have proved inefficient because of the inability of **parastatals** (state-owned enterprises) to compete internationally with their privately-owned foreign counterparts. Many such enterprises have been **privatized**, although the state still dominates the telecommunications, transport, mining, and electric power industries. The state remains the country's largest employer and consumer.

While the Senegalese Democratic Party (PDS) makes up the largest opposition party, there are many other political parties, 26 in all, representing ideologies across the political landscape. According to the U.S. State Department *Country Commercial Guide*, opposition parties are personality-driven, relying on the charisma of their leaders rather than concrete ideas. Most parties differ little from the ruling PS about economic matters.

Taxation is the chief source of government revenue. In 1997 92.8 percent of revenue came from taxes, broken down as follows: 28.1 percent from income and property tax, 36.7 from taxes on goods and services, 25.2 percent from import tax, and 9.1 percent from taxes on petroleum products. Personal **income tax** is progressive, meaning those who earn more money must pay a higher percentage of tax than those who make less money. There are 10 tax brackets, or categories of taxable income. Those who make less than 600,000 CFA francs are not obligated to pay income tax.

Because of economic contraction in the early 1990s, the inability of many firms to compete and survive in a freer market led to a shrinking tax base for the government. Government was forced to rely on strict revenue measures, such as heavy taxation on petroleum imports. According to the World Bank, this caused harmful results to companies that depend on petroleum imports, forcing many to close or join the **informal economy**.

INFRASTRUCTURE, POWER, AND COMMUNICATIONS

For a developing nation, Senegal has a well organized **infrastructure** compared to most other African countries. The World Bank estimated that in 1995 there were 507 kilometers (315 miles) of paved road per million people. The CIA *World Fact Book 2001* notes that there are 14,576 kilometers (9,058 miles) of highway, 4,271 kilometers (2,653 miles) of which are paved. Although the railway system is somewhat antiquated, it carries more than 3 million tons of cargo per year. The railway network, which extends across 906 kilometers (563 miles), links the major cities to Dakar and provides services between Senegal and Mali. The port in Dakar is one of the few African ports with a floating dry dock, a container terminal, and container service. Despite the wide range of services, port charges are high and service is inefficient. There are also ports and harbors in Kaolack, Matam, Podor, Richard Toll, Saint-Louis, and Ziguinchor.

According to the U.S. Department of State *Country Commercial Guide*, the airport at Dakar is one of the principal international airports in West Africa, handling a variety of aircraft on its 2 runways. The airport serves more than 24 international airlines, handling 1.5 million passengers per year and moving more than 20,000 metric tons of international airfreight. There are direct flights to Europe and North America, along with frequent flights to several African countries. Secondary airports are located in the regions of Saint-Louis, Tambacounda, and Ziguinchor. In total, there were 20 airports in 1999.

The parastatal Senelec supplies electricity in Senegal, though the electric power market is open to foreign investment. France has invested heavily in this sector of the economy. Senegal produces 1.2 billion kilowatt hours (kWh) of electricity per year, all of which is created domestically by fossil fuel. Therefore, the country has no need to import electricity from abroad. To meet the rapidly growing demand for increased capacity, Senelec is actively seeking upgrades to its existing power-generating capabilities.

The telecommunications sector is dominated by Sonatel, another parastatal. In 1996 there were only 11 phone lines per 1000 people, compared to 640 phone lines per 1000 people in the United States. Access to the Internet is severely restricted. In 1996 there were 0.31 Internet hosts per 1000 people, but in the United States there were 442.11 Internet hosts per 1000 people. Sonatel hopes to modernize the telecommunications industry by digitizing its current network and installing a fiber optic network and cellular telephone system. As in the case of the electricity market, France has also invested heavily in telecommunications. The competitive advantage of French firms in this sector relates, in part, to concessional funding (funds are granted in exchange for specific contracts) given by the French government to the Senegalese government for the modernization of the telecommunications network.

ECONOMIC SECTORS

Senegal's economic sectors reflect the traditional nature of the society. Since most Senegalese live in the countryside, the agriculture sector provides employment for most of the population. Moreover, agricultural products comprise Senegal's most important exports. Because

Communications

Country	Newspapers	Radios	TV Sets[a]	Cable subscribers[a]	Mobile Phones[a]	Fax Machines[a]	Personal Computers[a]	Internet Hosts[b]	Internet Users[b]
	1996	1997	1998	1998	1998	1998	1998	1999	1999
Senegal	5	142	41	N/A	2	N/A	11.4	0.28	30
United States	215	2,146	847	244.3	256	78.4	458.6	1,508.77	74,100
Nigeria	24	223	66	N/A	0	N/A	5.7	0.00	100
Guinea	N/A	47	41	0.0	3	0.4	2.6	0.00	5

[a]Data are from International Telecommunication Union, *World Telecommunication Development Report 1999* and are per 1,000 people.
[b]Data are from the Internet Software Consortium (http://www.isc.org) and are per 10,000 people.

SOURCE: World Bank. *World Development Indicators 2000.*

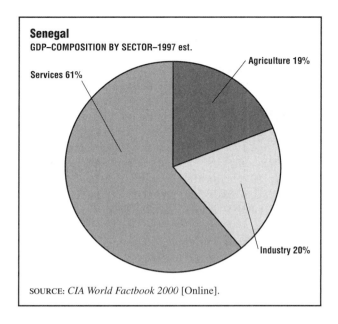

Senegal
GDP–COMPOSITION BY SECTOR–1997 est.

Services 61%

Agriculture 19%

Industry 20%

SOURCE: *CIA World Factbook 2000* [Online].

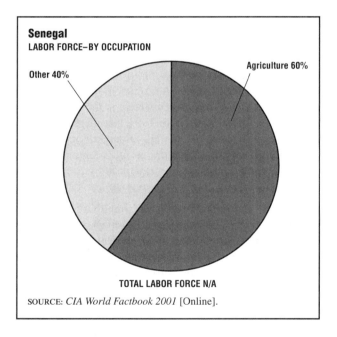

Senegal
LABOR FORCE–BY OCCUPATION

Other 40%

Agriculture 60%

TOTAL LABOR FORCE N/A

SOURCE: *CIA World Factbook 2001* [Online].

husbandry, fishing, and forestry. It accounts for about 19 percent of the country's GDP. The most important agricultural activity in Senegal is peanut production. Other important primary products produced for the domestic market include millet, corn, sorghum, rice, cotton, tomatoes, green vegetables, cattle, poultry, pigs, and fish. Besides peanuts, primary exports include fish and cotton.

With agricultural production playing such a dominant role in the Senegalese economy, the country is susceptible to destructive natural forces such as declining rainfall and **desertification**. Countries that rely heavily on agriculture are similarly vulnerable, but the problems are particularly severe in Senegal, a semi-arid country in which rainfall can vary considerably from year to year. Moreover, only 12 percent of all land is arable (capable of supporting agriculture). The prices of agricultural commodities in the international market are similarly dependent upon natural forces. If there were to be heavy rainfall in all peanut-producing countries, the international supply of peanuts would be high, leading to a decrease in the international price for peanuts because of the abundant supply. Since it is impossible to predict the situation in any given year, fluctuating prices are a constant threat and source of insecurity for agricultural nations like Senegal.

Groundnut production takes up 42 percent of all cultivated land, providing income for more than 1 million people. Each year, Senegal produces thousands of metric tons of peanuts, with output depending on rainfall. In 1990, about 703,000 metric tons were produced, while output in 1997 was much less at 545,000 metric tons. Senegalese research authorities found oscillating patterns of rainfall over a 40-year period on the groundnut basin. In 1989 the level of rainfall was 7,785 millimeters (30.9 inches), while in 1999 it was only 507 millimeters (20 inches). Furthermore, the sector continues to suffer from a shrinking market, with world demand for peanuts showing a steady decline. Production is also being affected by natural environmental factors, such as soil depletion. Exports of peanut products provided US$20 million in income in 1994.

The Senegalese government has made efforts to reduce dependence on groundnuts by diversifying cash and food crops, by expanding cotton, rice, sugar, and market-garden produce. While the output of each crop has risen sharply over the past 20 years, the annual average output of rice (150,000 tons) fails to meet even domestic demand, which runs at about 500,000 tons. Since rice is the major staple of the urban population, Senegal is forced to import rice from abroad, mostly from the Far East. Several small and medium-sized development projects, supported by foreign aid, were adopted throughout the 1990s to increase the area of irrigated land that is needed to grow rice. The traditional food sector, which consists

these products are generally worth less than manufactured goods or services, the industrial and service sectors generate a larger percentage of **gross domestic product** (GDP) than the agricultural sector. While agriculture provided 19 percent of GDP in 1997, the industrial sector and the services sector provided 20 percent and 61 percent, respectively, in 1997.

AGRICULTURE

The agricultural sector occupies the largest percentage of the population, employing 60 percent of the Senegalese labor force. The sector includes farming, livestock

of millet, sorghum and maize, has increased its overall output since the mid-1970s, though fluctuations because of the level of rainfall are the norm.

FISHING. The fishing industry is one of the most important areas of primary sector activity in Senegal. In 1994 the industry accounted for 8.5 percent of the GDP, employed 200,000 persons, provided 27.3 percent of total exports, and earned US$240 million. Favorable world prices and competitive pricing because of the 1994 currency **devaluation** boosted fishing exports. The output of fishing, or "fish-catch," reached 486,800 metric tons in 1997. This figure demonstrates the exceptional growth of the fishing industry in recent years, considering that total output for 1991 was only 387,800 metric tons. According to the U.S. State Department *Country Commercial Guide*, the development of the fishing sector is hampered by an aging and outmoded fleet, the threat of over-fishing (thereby depleting supply), and stiff competition from South Asia in international fish markets.

Livestock and forestry are less important contributors to the country's GDP. Forestry has shown little growth over the years, comprising only 0.8 percent of the GDP in 1991 and marginally less in 1998 (0.6 percent of the GDP). Livestock has figured more prominently. In 1991 it included 6.9 percent of the GDP and 7.0 percent in 1998.

INDUSTRY

The secondary economic sector, that is, the sector that converts primary goods into finished products and is more commonly referred to as industry, accounted for 20 percent of Senegal's GDP in 1997. The 2 major industrial activities are mining and manufacturing.

MINING. Mining output in Senegal is primarily calcium phosphates. In 1994 phosphate and phosphate products accounted for 19 percent of total merchandise export earnings, producing US$162 million in export revenue. While Europe has traditionally been the major importer of Senegalese phosphates, the U.S. State Department *Country Commercial Guide* notes that new markets in Asia and Africa have recently developed. Despite its importance as an exporting industry, however, phosphates have not played a large role domestically. Phosphate mining accounts for less than 2 percent of Senegal's GDP. The industry provides important jobs, but only about 2,000 are available. Production of phosphates has also decreased over the past several years. In 1991 phosphate production reached 1,546 metric tons, whereas figures for 1998 were much less at 1,087 metric tons. This reflects diminishing reserves of phosphates and illustrates how environmental or geographical factors can influence a country's economy.

MANUFACTURING. Manufacturing is an important component of the secondary sector, accounting for 12.5 percent of GDP. Senegalese industries process a range of commodities that includes food, textiles, wood products, chemicals, construction materials, machinery, equipment, electricity, and water. Food ranks as the most important economic contributor, accounting for 43.1 percent of all industrial manufacturing output. Food production consists of fish canning, oil milling, and sugar refining. Textiles, along with clothing and leather, account for 12.3 percent of all manufacturing output. Senegal's textile industry is the most important in black francophone (French-speaking) Africa, with 4 cotton-ginning mills and spinning, weaving, dyeing, and printing plants. Chemical industries are the third largest contributor and account for 11.4 percent of output. Senegal produces refined petroleum, fertilizers, pesticides, plastic, and rubber materials. Industrial production grew 7 percent in 1998, indicating that industrial manufacturing offers important prospects for future economic growth.

SERVICES

The tertiary or service sector is the most productive sector in the Senegalese economy. It accounted for 61 percent of the GDP in 1997. Commerce, which is centered in Dakar and other urban areas, is the largest component of tertiary activity. In 1991 commerce made up 22.7 percent of the GDP, though the contribution diminished slightly by 1998, accounting for 21.1 percent of the GDP. Commerce included the buying and selling of commodities and services, and banking and finance.

TOURISM. Known for its mild climate, multiple beaches, and great sport fishing, Senegal has long been a tourist destination for European travelers, particularly the French. The high season runs from December to February, when Senegalese weather is most inviting. In recent years, the tourist industry has skyrocketed. In 1991 about 269,300 tourists visited Senegal, contributing 37.9 billion CFA francs to the economy. By 1997 the number of visitors reached 341,500 and contributed 80 billion CFA francs to the economy. Tourism is now one of Senegal's major sources of foreign currency earnings, which are vital for meeting the country's import bills. Although most tourists are French, there has been a rise in vacationers from other European countries and from North America. Most of the impetus towards growth in the tourism industry has come from the **private sector**. The government has hardly invested in tourism over the past 10 years and sold off many state-owned hotels to the private sector.

FINANCIAL SERVICES. As a member of the West African Economic and Monetary Union (UEMOA), Senegal shares its currency, the CFA franc, with 6 other member countries: Benin, Togo, Mali, Côte d'Ivoire, Burkina

Faso, and Niger. The CFA franc is issued by the West African Central Bank. The commercial banking sector has a long history in Senegal, which has 8 banks, all of them established prior to the 1990s. The largest banks are French, reflecting the historical link between the French and Senegalese economies. The Société Generale de Banques du Senegal (SGBS), the largest commercial bank, with total deposits and borrowing equaling 152,099 million CFA francs, is an affiliate of the Société Generale de Banques of France. The Senegalese government does not own any shares in the bank. The other commercial banks are owned by private and foreign (French) shareholders, the major exception being the Caisse Nationale de Crédit Agricole du Senegal.

RETAIL. Besides a few large French-owned import-export firms that are involved in retailing, there are many competitive small-scale traders specializing in the wholesale and **retail** distribution of fabrics and consumer goods. In the past, Lebanese merchants were the interface between French trading companies and the Senegalese population. They are gradually being replaced by Senegalese merchants selling popular consumer goods, such as textiles and electronics. There are also a limited number of larger retail stores, such as supermarkets, which deal in imported goods. Since the currency devaluation in 1994, however, these stores are threatened by the high costs of imports.

Because of the few employment opportunities offered in the formal economy, many Senegalese have turned to the informal sector to survive. The informal sector remains unregulated and untaxed because it operates outside the administrative framework of the government. The sector's activities are not criminal, but "extra-legal," meaning they are legitimate and not controlled. Informal activities range from selling fruit on street-corners to selling sophisticated high-tech stereo equipment. There are about 30,000 small businesses in the informal sector, employing about 57,000 persons, according to 1995 estimates. Sandaga, a sprawling unregulated market in the heart of Dakar, is the capital's principal distribution center for manufactured goods such as textiles, footwear, cosmetics, food, and electronic equipment.

INTERNATIONAL TRADE

Senegal suffers from a trade deficit. In 1991 the value of the country's exports equaled 79.6 billion CFA francs, although the value of imports equaled 100 billion CFA francs. In 1997 the value of exports grew far greater, equaling 177.8 billion CFA francs. Yet, the value of imports continued to outpace exports, growing to about 226.4 billion CFA francs. In 2000, the trade deficit reached US$341 million on exports of US$1.3 billion and imports of US$959 million.

Trade (expressed in billions of US$): Senegal		
	Exports	Imports
1975	.461	.583
1980	.477	1.052
1985	.562	.826
1990	.762	1.220
1995	.969	1.243
1998	N/A	N/A

SOURCE: International Monetary Fund. *International Financial Statistics Yearbook 1999.*

Senegal relies heavily on **primary commodities** such as groundnut products, phosphates, fish, and cotton for its export revenue. Though France remains Senegal's largest trading partner, its share of Senegal's exports has declined steadily over the past decade. In 1990, about 34.4 percent of Senegal's exports went to France. By 1999, however, this figure had declined to 17 percent. Other important trading partners include India (17 percent), Italy (12 percent), Spain (6 percent), Mali (6 percent), and Côte d'Ivoire (4 percent). Over the years the amount of trade to the major industrialized European countries has dropped, shifting instead to Asian or other African countries. A recent publication by the United Nations Committee on Trade and Development (UNCTAD 2000) indicates that the industrial countries are importing less from the African continent. UNCTAD attributes this decline to the inability of African countries to compete with Latin American and Asian countries for the markets of the developed world. Senegal now exports predominantly to other developing countries. Many of these countries are African, the most significant of which are Cameroon, Côte d'Ivoire, Mali, Mauritania, and Nigeria. Developing countries purchased 67.6 percent of Senegal's exports in 1998 (January-June). This figure doubled over an 8-year period from 1990, when developing countries only accounted for 34.3 percent of all Senegalese imports.

Trade between Senegal and its West African neighbors has been facilitated through 2 regional trading organizations: the Economic Community of West African States (ECOWAS), which consists of 16 member-states, and the West African Economic and Monetary Union (UEMOA). The latter is a more integrated regional trading arrangement so that the 7 francophone states that share the same currency enjoy closer economic relationships and cooperation. UNCTAD suggests that most of the recent increase in trade between West African countries can be attributed to increased demand for primary commodities by the larger countries in the region.

Although Senegal exports primarily to developing countries, it continues to import most of its foreign goods from industrialized nations. France provided a majority of imports in 1999, with 30 percent. Other major importers are Nigeria (7 percent), Italy (6 percent), Thailand (5 percent), Germany (4 percent), and the United States (4 percent). Senegal imports from industrial countries because it requires many capital and consumer goods that it cannot produce itself. Imported capital goods are important to manufacturing industries, while luxury consumer goods are in high demand by Senegal's wealthy elite. Since neighboring African countries lack the modern industrialized economies necessary to produce high quality capital and consumer goods, Senegal must look to the developed world for such commodities.

MONEY

Throughout the 1980s and early 1990s, Senegal suffered extreme economic difficulties characterized by sustained **recession** and under-utilized capacity (which means that the working age population was not used to its full potential). One of the symptoms of the troubled Senegalese economy was a chronic **balance of payments** deficit. The WB and the IMF, therefore, contested that Senegal should devalue its currency, which would lower the price of its exports and make its products more attractive to the international markets. Devaluation would make the Senegalese economy more competitive and help to rectify the balance of payments problem.

On the eve of the devaluation in January 1994, the Senegalese currency, the Communauté Financière Africaine franc (CFAF), was valued at 50 CFA francs to 1 French franc. Devaluation converted this figure to 100 CFA francs to 1 French franc. Since 1 January 1999, the CFAF has been fixed to the euro (the currency of the EU countries) at a rate of 655.957 CFA francs per euro, a rate which reflects the devaluation of 1994. This connection causes the value of the CFA franc to adjust to the value of the euro in international foreign exchange markets. In January 2000 the CFA franc-dollar exchange was 647.25 CFA francs to 1 U.S. dollar.

Although WB contends that devaluation stimulated growth in the export-oriented sectors of the Senegalese economy, and in the economy as a whole, it has also brought negative results. Devaluing the **exchange rate** increases the amount of currency needed to pay for imports. For the urban poor, who are dependent upon imported food, the cost of food has escalated. Since the urban poor are already malnourished, devaluation has been detrimental to the nation's well-being. Moreover, Senegal continues to run a balance of payments deficit, despite its more competitive position in the international market.

POVERTY AND WEALTH

Like many African countries, poverty is rampant in Senegal. Also, **GDP per capita** has actually declined over the past 25 years. The GDP per capita in 1975 was US$609 and by 1998 it had fallen to US$581 (at 1995 U.S. dollar exchange rates). In the same year, the GDP per capita in the United States was US$29,683. The United Nations Development Programme (UNDP), which classifies countries according to their human development index score (HDI), ranked Senegal 155th out of 174 countries in 1998, while the United States ranked third. The HDI is a composite index that examines specific figures on education, health, and standard of living. Senegal's low ranking reflects the country's low development in these areas, consistent with its overall poverty.

GDP per Capita (US$)					
Country	1975	1980	1985	1990	1998
Senegal	609	557	561	572	581
United States	19,364	21,529	23,200	25,363	29,683
Nigeria	301	314	230	258	256
Guinea	N/A	N/A	N/A	532	594

SOURCE: United Nations. *Human Development Report 2000;
Trends in human development and per capita income.*

Exchange rates: Senegal	
Communauté Financière Africaine francs per US$1	
Jan 2001	699.21
2000	711.98
1999	615.70
1998	589.95
1997	583.67
1996	511.55

Note: From January 1, 1999, the CFA Fr is pegged to the euro at a rate of 655.957 CFA Fr per euro.

SOURCE: CIA *World Factbook 2001* [ONLINE].

Distribution of Income or Consumption by Percentage Share: Senegal	
Lowest 10%	2.6
Lowest 20%	6.4
Second 20%	10.3
Third 20%	14.5
Fourth 20%	20.6
Highest 20%	48.2
Highest 10%	33.5

Survey year: 1995
Note: This information refers to expenditure shares by percentiles of the population and is ranked by per capita expenditure.

SOURCE: *2000 World Development Indicators* [CD-ROM].

Household Consumption in PPP Terms

Country	All food	Clothing and footwear	Fuel and power[a]	Health care[b]	Education[b]	Transport & Communications	Other
Senegal	46	13	13	3	15	3	7
United States	13	9	9	4	6	8	51
Nigeria	51	5	31	2	8	2	2
Guinea	29	18	5	2	9	16	21

Data represent percentage of consumption in PPP terms.
[a]Excludes energy used for transport.
[b]Includes government and private expenditures.

SOURCE: World Bank. *World Development Indicators 2000.*

The people of Senegal, like many of the poor across the world, spend much of their money on getting the necessities of life, such as food. The UNDP estimates that food averages 52 percent of Senegalese household consumption compared to the United States, where food only accounts for 8 percent of household consumption. For this reason, the Senegalese are vulnerable to increases in the price of basic foods. Because food is the highest priority, little money is left over to pay for other necessities such as clothes and shelter. The poor make up most of the urban population and live in run-down areas or makeshift shanty towns thrown together on land that is not paid for. Saving to escape the conditions of poverty is not an option, since the poor must spend all their money to survive.

The poverty of most of the Senegalese people stands in marked contrast to the wealth of the country's small elite. After independence, the elite comprised a few Senegalese businessmen in the private sector, influential politicians, government ministers, university professors, and political **cadres** (in this case, members of the Socialist Party) who worked for parastatals. As Sheldon Gellar notes in his book *Senegal: An African Nation Between Islam and the West*, the elite group is predominantly male, urban, highly educated, politically connected, and able to afford European-style living standards. Perks include the ownership of cars, modern appliances, nice villas or apartments, the provision of good schooling and higher education for their children, and opportunities to travel abroad. In the rural areas, Muslim clerics, known as marabouts, make up a wealthy agricultural elite. Gellar also notes that structural adjustment plans have increased the inequality between the Senegalese elite and the masses. While the standard of living for the poor has declined, the nation's wealthy continue to prosper.

WORKING CONDITIONS

Senegal maintains a comprehensive labor code that defines legal regulations about workers' rights and employer obligations. According to the U.S. Department of State *Country Report on Human Rights in Senegal (1998)*, most Senegalese workers fall outside the laws of the labor code because they work in the informal or agricultural sectors. The law only applies to the non-agricultural formal sector. Moreover, certain regulations, such as those relating to safety standards in the work place, are neither adequately monitored nor enforced by the government. Because most workers are unskilled and uneducated and there are few employment opportunities in the economy, workers usually find themselves unable to contest violations of labor code standards. Thus, working conditions are often sub-standard.

Under the Senegalese constitution, the minimum age for employment is 16 years for apprenticeships and 18 years for all other activities. The government has strictly enforced this article of the constitution in the formal sector, though child labor is common in the agriculture and informal sectors. Most families in these sectors are so disadvantaged that all family members must work, regardless of age.

After independence, Senegal ratified the International Labor Convention No. 87, regarding freedom of association and protection of the right to organize. Senegal also ratified convention No. 48, which provides rights to organize and bargain collectively. Senegal has a long history of organized trade unions. Nearly all workers in the industrial sector of the economy are unionized. The principal labor unions are the National Confederation of Senegalese Workers (CNTS) and the National Union of Autonomous Labor Organizations of Senegal (UNSAS). The CNTS is an umbrella union that organizes individual unions into a collective framework. The PS established it in 1968 after the National Union of Senegalese Workers was dissolved due to its opposition to government policies. Under President Leopold Senghor's program of "responsible participation," CNTS leaders were given important party and government posts. Despite being allied with the PS, the union has often disagreed with government policies. In 1986, changes in the labor code provided more room for employers to lay off workers and caused a great deal of agitation from CNTS supporters.

In recent years, trade unions and political persuasions united to protest government policies. In September 1993, the Intersyndicale (a broad trade union coalition headed by the CNTS that also includes independent unions and those close to the major opposition parties) led a one-day general strike to protest the government's decision to cut state employee salaries by 15 percent. The decision to cut the salaries was made in compliance with IMF and WB demands for greater cutbacks in government spending. UNSAS, the second most important union in the coalition, broke away from Intersyndicale after the organization decided to negotiate with the government following the general strike. UNSAS has supported a less compromising stance towards unpopular government policies, making it difficult for the union to work with its less militant counterparts.

COUNTRY HISTORY AND ECONOMIC DEVELOPMENT

4TH CENTURY A.D. The first centralized state in what becomes the Senegal region, the Tekrur kingdom, develops in the Senegal River valley.

1040. Zenaga Berbers from the north establish an Islamic monastery, probably along the Senegal River. The monastery subsequently became the base of the Almoravids, who converted many of the region's people to Islam.

13TH CENTURY. The Tekrur kingdom falls under the dominance of the Mali Empire, which is centered to the east. During the same period, the Jolof kingdom arises on the northwestern savanna, conquering the Wolof inhabitants. Thereafter, various Muslim states and kingdoms rise and fall in the northern grasslands and central savannas of present-day Senegal, contributing to a tradition of centralized states and rigid social hierarchies.

1444. Portuguese navigators become the first Europeans known to visit the area of present-day Senegal and Gambia. Until the end of the 16th century, the Senegambian region is the most important source of slaves for the transatlantic slave trade.

1659. The French establish a slave-trading post on the island of Saint-Louis at the mouth of the Senegal River, while the British establish a base around the Gambia River. These divisions later result in the independent nations of English-speaking Gambia and French-speaking Senegal.

1840s. Peanuts become the major trade commodity of interest for the French operating in Senegambia. In the coming decades France conquers the Wolof and Serer states in order to exert greater control over the peanut trade.

1886. With the decisive conquest of Cayor State, the French more or less control all of present-day Senegal, with the exception of the Casamance, which was not fully subjugated until the 1920s.

1890–1919. Beginning in the 1890s, a Senegalese urban elite that identifies with French culture and customs develops. In 1914, these elites are given the vote, and the urban areas in Senegal are allocated 1 seat in the French National Assembly. Blaise Diagne becomes the first African deputy. In 1919, he founds the Republican Socialist Party, the first western-style political party in the region.

1929. Lamine Gueye, Diagne's major political opponent, founds the Senegalese Socialist Party, with links to the French Socialist Party.

1930s. The decline in global demand for peanuts as a result of the global economic depression leads to increased hardship and poverty in Senegal.

1945. The French government extends the vote to rural Senegal, which gains a seat in the French assembly alongside that of the urban areas. Gueye wins the election for the urban seat while his protégé, Leopold Sedar Senghor, wins the rural seat. Senghor later breaks with the socialists and founds his own party, the Senegalese Democratic Bloc (BDS).

1956–59. France permits limited self-government within its African colonies. In 1957, the socialists merge with the BDS to form the Senegalese Progressive Union (UPS), which subsequently wins a strong majority in the 1959 national elections. Popular demands for complete independence from France increase, and the UPS negotiates with the French government for independence as part of a Mali Federation.

1960. On 4 April, the Mali Federation, which combines present-day Senegal and Mali, becomes independent, but the federation is short-lived. Rivalry between Senegal and Mali soon leads to its dissolution, and in August 1960, Senegal becomes an independent state with Leopold Senghor as president.

1962. A power struggle between President Senghor and Prime Minister Mamadou Dia leads to the latter's imprisonment and the banning of opposition parties.

1968. Lack of political debate leads to student protests and union strikes, which are routinely crushed by the army.

1970–75. The rapid rise in the cost of imported oil, combined with drought in the Sahel region, creates an economic crisis.

1973. The West African Economic Community (CEAO) of 7 francophone states is established to facilitate trade between member states.

1975. Senegal joins the Economic Community of West African States (ECOWAS), an organization of 16 West African states designed to facilitate trade and development between members.

1976. The government releases Dia from prison, and a new constitution permits 3 political parties.

1977. Senghor wins the first contested presidential elections since 1963.

1980. As Senghor's popularity declines due to economic stagnation, the president announces his resignation.

1981. Senghor's protégé, Abdou Diouf, takes office. Under the auspices of the World Bank and the International Monetary Fund, Diouf gradually replaces the Socialist Party's ideology of state-led "African Socialism" with a free-market oriented policy. Senegal and Gambia proclaim a regional alliance, the Senegambian Confederation.

1984. Discontent in the rural Casamance region of Senegal leads to the beginning of an internal rebellion by the Movement of Democratic Forces of the Casamance (MFDC).

1989. The Senegambian Confederation is disbanded due to Gambian fears of absorption into Senegal.

1994. The West African Economic and Monetary Union (UEMOA) is established to replace the CEAO. The CFA franc, the common currency of UEMOA, is devalued by nearly 100 percent.

2000. Abdoulaye Wade, from the Democratic Party, is elected president, making him the country's first non-socialist president since the country gained independence in 1960.

FUTURE TRENDS

Like many African countries and developing nations, Senegal enters the 21st century with deep-seated economic difficulties. Several economic plans and strategies that have been pursued by the Senegalese government since independence have failed to generate sustained economic development. Mass unemployment, continued dependence on agricultural exportation for foreign revenue, a widening trade deficit, and chronic poverty continue to characterize the Senegalese economic situation. The recent emphasis on privatization and free-market competition has thus far failed to break the pattern. Structural adjustment plans have helped to contain macro-economic instability (in the form of **inflation**), but they have not improved the impoverished conditions of the masses. Structural adjustment and the emphasis on the free-market has created greater inequality and increased hardship for the poor.

However, the situation in Senegal is not entirely bleak. On the political front, the victory of a Democratic Party candidate in the 2000 presidential elections indicated that Senegal might be progressing toward a more open and less authoritarian democracy. Economically, the various regional integration schemes developed in West Africa may provide an impetus for Senegal and other West African nations to experience economic growth. By providing preferential access to member states, such regional schemes can cushion West African nations against competition from the more competitive outside world.

DEPENDENCIES

Senegal has no territories or colonies.

BIBLIOGRAPHY

Economist Intelligence Unit. *Country Profile: Senegal.* London: Economist Intelligence Unit, 2001.

Gellar, Sheldon. *Senegal: An African Nation between Islam and the West.* Boulder: Westview Press, 1995.

International Monetary Fund. "Senegal and the IMF." *International Monetary Fund.* <http://www.imf.org>. Accessed January 2001.

Schaffer, Frederic C. *Democracy in Translation: Understanding Politics in an Unfamiliar Culture.* Ithaca: Cornell University Press, 1998.

Senegal Tourism Office. <http://www.senegal-tourism.com>. Accessed October 2001.

UNCTAD. *African Development in a Comparative Perspective.* New York: Africa World Press, Inc. 2000.

United Nations. *Human Development Report 2000.* New York: Oxford University Press, 2000.

U.S. Central Intelligence Agency. *World Factbook 2001.* <http://www.odci.gov/cia/publications/factbook/index.html>. Accessed September 2001.

U.S. Department of State. *FY 2000 Country Commercial Guide: Senegal.* <http://www.state.gov/www/about_state/business/com_guides/2000/africa/senegal00.html>. Accessed October 2001.

World Bank Group. "Senegal." *World Bank Group.* <http://www.worldbank.org>. Accessed October 2001.

—Neil Burron

SEYCHELLES

CAPITAL: Victoria.

MONETARY UNIT: Seychelles rupee (SRe). There are coins of 1, 5, 10, 20, and 50 cents. One Seychelles rupee equals 100 cents.

CHIEF EXPORTS: Fish, cinnamon bark, copra, petroleum products (re-exports).

CHIEF IMPORTS: Machinery and equipment, food products, petroleum products.

GROSS DOMESTIC PRODUCT: US$590 million (purchasing power parity, 1999 est.).

BALANCE OF TRADE: **Exports:** US$91 million (f.o.b., 1998). **Imports:** US$403 million (c.i.f., 1998).

COUNTRY OVERVIEW

LOCATION AND SIZE. The Seychelles are a group of islands in the Indian Ocean about 925 kilometers (575 miles) northeast of Madagascar. The country consists of 115 small islands with a total land area of 455 square kilometers (176 square miles) and a total coastline of 491 kilometers (305 miles). The territory of the Seychelles is about 2.5 times the size of Washington, D.C. The country consists of 2 groups of islands, the largest being the Mahe group in the northern part of the archipelago, comprised of 40 granite rock islands (the largest are Mahe, Praslin, La Digue, Silhouette, Fregate, and North) with hilly interiors rising up to 900 meters (2,953 feet). The other group consists of about 65 small coral islands spread over a wide area of ocean south of the Mahe group. Mahe Island, with a total area of 153 square kilometers (59 square miles) is home to the capital city Victoria (pop. 40,000, 1997). The strategic importance of the Seychelles group is derived from its location in the Indian Ocean on the sea route from South Africa to the Indian subcontinent, which was a major route before the Suez Canal was opened in 1869.

POPULATION. The population of the Republic of Seychelles was estimated at 79,326 in July 2000, an increase

of around 16 percent from 68,598 in 1987. In 2000 the birth rate stood at 17.99 per 1,000 and the death rate at 6.74 per 1000. The estimated population growth rate is 0.49 percent, a low rate attributed mainly to the high **emigration** rate of 6.3 per 1,000. Life expectancy at birth is 64.87 years for males and 76.12 years for females. It is expected that the country's population will reach 100,000 by 2020.

The diverse population is composed of 3 major ethnic groups: French settlers, freed slaves of African descent, and Indians brought to work on the plantations. Creoles (mixture of Asian, African, and European) make up 89.1 percent of the population, Indians make up 4.7 percent, and Malagasy (from Madagascar) make up 3.1 percent. There are also small minorities of Chinese (1.6 percent) and European (1.5 percent) origin. Some 29 percent of the population is below the age of 14, and 6 percent is older than 65. A majority of the country's inhabitants, 56.1 percent, lives in urban areas.

Limited natural resources and scarce land forces the government of the Seychelles to limit inflow of immigrants and to control population growth. In the 1980s there was sizable emigration of the people from islands due to economic difficulties and political instability. In the early 1990s many of them returned home when the Seychelles government significantly **liberalized** the political and economic environment and allowed opposition parties.

OVERVIEW OF ECONOMY

Tourism, agriculture and fishing, and industry are the 3 main sectors of the Seychelles economy. The current structure of the country's economy was formed during the 1970s and 1980s and underwent drastic changes in the 1990s. Despite government efforts to encourage agricultural and industrial development, tourism remains the

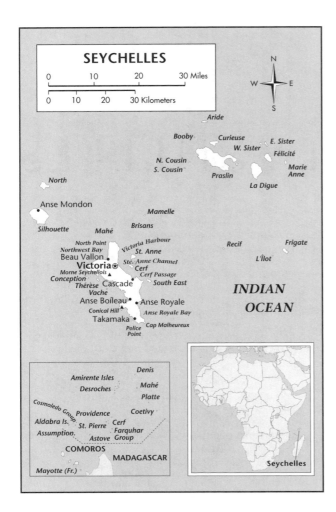

SEYCHELLES

0   10   20   30 Miles

0   10   20   30 Kilometers

Aride

Booby   Curieuse
                    W. Sister   E. Sister
                                          Félicité
         N. Cousin
         S. Cousin   Marie
                    Praslin   Anne
North   La Digue

Anse Mondon

                    Mamelle

Silhouette   Brisans
         Mahé
         North Point
         Northwest Bay   Victoria Harbour   Recif   Frigate
         Beau Vallon   St. Anne
         Victoria⊛   Ste. Anne Channel   L'îlot
         Morne Seychellois Cerf
         Conception   Cerf Passage
         Thérèse Cascade   South East
         Vache
         Anse Boîleau• •Anse Royale   INDIAN
         Conical Hill   •Anse Royale Bay   OCEAN
         Takamaka•
                    •Cap Malheureux
              Police
              Point

                    Denis

         Amirente Isles   Mahé
         Desroches   Platte

Cosmoledo Group Providence   Coetivy
Aldabra Is.   St. Pierre   Cerf
Assumption.   Farquhar
         Astove   Group

         COMOROS

                    MADAGASCAR
Mayotte (Fr.)   Seychelles

dominant sector in the country's economy. It provides most of the country's revenue and employment, and it maintains a positive image of the archipelago as an exotic and desirable destination.

France acquired the uninhabited islands in 1756 and populated them with French settlers and slaves from the African continent. In 1814, after the Napoleonic wars in Europe, Great Britain established its control over the Seychelles, administering them from Mauritius. The islands were important to British trade routes, due to their strategic location halfway between the Cape of Good Hope (South Africa) and the Indian subcontinent. This strategic importance diminished somewhat after the opening of the Suez Canal in 1869. In 1903 the Seychelles became a Crown Colony, but its extremely limited resources and remote location isolated the country from the major events of the 20th century.

Since the 1970s, 2 factors have impacted the economic and social life of the Seychelles: mass-market international tourism—an international airport opened in 1971—and independence in 1976, which ushered in a period of centralized planning. A government led by

France Albert Rene introduced state control over major sectors of the economy, and the first centralized 5-year plan was introduced in 1985, modeled after the **socialist** economies of Eastern Europe. This plan created around 30 **parastatals** (state-controlled enterprises) covering all sectors of economic activities. With the demise of the Soviet Union and of state socialism in the early 1990s, the Seychelles government initiated elements of a free-market economy under the guidance of the International Monetary Fund (IMF) and World Bank. Most state enterprises, with the exception of public utilities and transport, were **privatized**, and the government attempted to increase foreign investments by developing the country as an international "offshore" financial-services center. The economic development program in the 1980s and 1990s increasingly relied on external borrowing, although the country managed to reduce its total **external debt** from US$474 million in 1979 to US$166 million in 1989. In 1999 the external public debt was estimated by the IMF at US$188.5 million (31 percent of the GDP), compared with US$153 million (26 percent of the GDP) in 1997. These figures are very high for a small country of 79,000 people, leading to fiscal and external imbalances and to the growing burden of external debt servicing.

POLITICS, GOVERNMENT, AND TAXATION

Since achieving independence from the United Kingdom in 1976, the Seychelles political scene has been dominated by the intense competition between 2 political parties and personalities, the right-centrist Seychelles Democratic Party (SDP) and the leftist Seychelles People's United Party (SPUP). Immediately after independence, Sir James Mancham of the SDP became the first president and France Albert Rene of the SPUP became prime minister. The coalition unraveled after a 1977 coup by Rene that forced Mancham into exile. In 1979, the constitution of 1976 was replaced by a significantly revised one that replaced the multiparty system with a one-party state. The SPUP, renamed to the Seychelles People's Progressive Front (SPPF), became the only political party in the country. Rene was elected president in 1979 and survived several coup attempts. In a dramatic political turn, the one-party political system was abandoned in 1992 under a new constitution that restored multiparty rule and saw Mancham return from exile to lead the SDP once more. Support of the SDP gradually declined with the rise of another opposition party, the Seychelles National Party (SNP, formerly the United Opposition), led by Wavel Ramkalawan. In elections for the 35-seat legislature in 1998, the SPPF won 61.7 percent of the vote, SNP won 26.1 percent, and the SDP won only 12.1 percent. Rene also won reelection as president. Despite this political tumult, elections and transitions of power have been peaceful.

Under President Rene, Seychelles introduced a socialist economy with state control over economic activities and 5-year national development plans, though the government also sought financial assistance from England and France. The main aims of the government policy were the diversification of the national economy, development of agricultural and manufacturing industries, the production of goods for domestic consumption and for export, and increase of **hard currency**. Most tax revenues in the Seychelles are derived from the net income or profit of a business. This tax is paid by resident and non-resident business owners on a graduated scale that ranges from 0 percent of the first SRe24,000 of income up to 40 percent of higher levels of income. Imported products, including alcohol and cigarettes, are also taxed. In 1998 trade taxes accounted for 44 percent of total revenues.

INFRASTRUCTURE, POWER, AND COMMUNICATIONS

The Seychelles has a well-established **infrastructure** in the northern Mahe group of islands, but not in the remoter group of coral islands to the south. After independence, the government made considerable efforts to expand its infrastructure in order to attract upper-middle-class tourists from Europe and North America. The concentration of the population in the capital of Victoria and in the few main islands made this task easy. In 1999, the major islands were served by a network of 424 kilometers (263 miles) of roads, of which 370 kilometers (230 miles) were paved. The country restricts car ownership through an annual quota system for auto imports. It is estimated that the total number of registered vehicles reached 9,394 in 1999. None of the islands have railways, and the islands' public transportation system relies on a bus fleet.

The country has 6 airports with paved runways and 8 with unpaved runways. The international airport at Pointe Larue was opened in 1971. The national air carrier, Air Seychelles, regularly flies to Frankfurt, London, Milan, Paris, Rome, and Zurich in Europe, as well as to Dubai, Johannesburg, Mauritius, Nairobi, and Singapore. It operates a small fleet of 4 light aircraft servicing the inter-island routes and a fleet of Boeing aircraft for inter-continental flights. The islands are also served by some international air-carriers, including the British Airline, Kenya Airways, Aeroflot, Air Mauritius, and others. The main port and harbor is Victoria. The state-controlled operator uses ferries to link Mahe with Praslin and La Digue. Private schooners are also available for trips to some islands.

The Seychelles has no oil, gas, or coal resources and relies solely on imported petroleum. Only Mahe, Praslin, and La Digue islands have electricity; total power production was around 125 million kW in 1998, and there was a plan to build a new 50 mW thermal station.

Telecommunication services in the Seychelles have been under intensive reconstruction since the early 1990s. According to the local authorities, there were 19,635 telephone lines and a rapidly growing number of mobile phone subscribers (16,316 in 1999), although the CIA *World Factbook* lists considerably lower numbers of phone usage. The country had 1 Internet service provider (ISP) hosting 818 accounts in 1999.

ECONOMIC SECTORS

Economic development in the Seychelles is limited by its geographic isolation, lack of natural resources, and a small population. The country heavily relies on international tourism from European and North American countries. The number of tourists arriving to the Seychelles

Communications

Country	Telephones[a]	Telephones, Mobile/Cellular[a]	Radio Stations[b]	Radios[a]	TV Stations[a]	Televisions[a]	Internet Service Providers[c]	Internet Users[c]
Seychelles	19,635	16,316 (1999)	AM 1; FM 2; shortwave 2	42,000	2	11,000	1	5,000
United States	194 M	69.209 M (1998)	AM 4,762; FM 5,542; shortwave 18	575 M	1,500	219 M	7,800	148 M
South Africa	5.075 M (1999)	2 M (1999)	AM 14; FM 347; shortwave 1	13.75 M	556	5.2 M	44	1.82 M
Mauritius	223,000	37,000	AM 5; FM 9; shortwave 2	420,000	2	258,000	2	55,000

[a]Data is for 1997 unless otherwise noted.
[b]Data is for 1998 unless otherwise noted.
[c]Data is for 2000 unless otherwise noted.

SOURCE: CIA *World Factbook 2001* [Online].

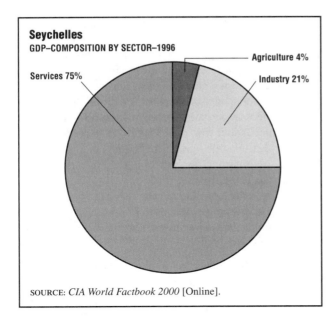

Seychelles
GDP–COMPOSITION BY SECTOR–1996

Services 75%

Agriculture 4%

Industry 21%

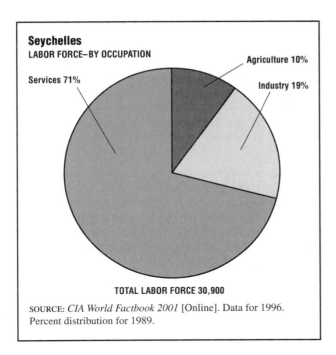

Seychelles
LABOR FORCE–BY OCCUPATION

Services 71%

Agriculture 10%

Industry 19%

TOTAL LABOR FORCE 30,900

an average annual rate of 2.8 percent. Services accounted for 68 percent of GDP in 1999, however, and employed 57 percent of the population in 1998. During the 1990s, the agricultural sector experienced a gradual decline and by 1999 contributed only 3.2 percent of GDP. Large investments into expansion of the manufacturing and other sectors led to considerable **balance-of-payment** deficits and foreign-exchange shortages.

AGRICULTURE

Agriculture and forestry have limited importance for the Seychelles, accounting for just 3.2 percent of GDP in 1999 and providing employment for 7 percent of the labor force (including fisheries). The country produces copra, cinnamon bark, and tea for export in very small quantities and depends on the world prices on these products. The country exported 214 tons of cinnamon bark and 236 tons of green leaf tea in 1999. However, it has to import cereals and some other foodstuff in order to meet the consumer needs of the local population and tourists. During the last few years there was an attempt to expand fruit and vegetable production for the local market. The government has also invested considerably in forestry in order to increase the country's lumber resources for domestic consumption.

Fishing is an important sector of the Seychelles economy. The country's **exclusive economic zone** extends 320 kilometers (200 miles) beyond its coastal area, which provides control of over 1 million square kilometers (386,100 square miles) of the Indian Ocean. The local population is engaged in catching fish for local consumption and for export while the government benefits from licensing fishing in its territorial waters and from payments by foreign vessels. In 1987 the first tuna-canning factory was opened in the country. Exports of canned tuna have been growing steadily, from SRe169 million in 1996 to SRe541.5 million (US$102 million) in 1999. The prawn-producing sector expanded rapidly in the early 1990s with its exports reaching SRe34.1 million (US$6.5 million) by 1998. Liberalization and opening of the country's economy attracted some foreign investments in the 1990s. In 1995 the U.S.-based H. J. Heinz Company established control over the tuna-processing plant and pledged US$15.4 million in investments and 900 jobs.

INDUSTRY

The industrial sector in the Seychelles is small and domestically oriented, accounting for 28.8 percent of the GDP and providing employment for 23 percent of the labor force in 1999, according to *Seychelles in Figures 2000*. During the 1980s the government heavily invested in the manufacturing sector, and by 1999 the country

rose steadily from the 1970s until the middle of the 1990s, and declined slightly afterwards. While employment in tourism-related industries dominates **private sector** employment, the largest single employer is the government, which employed 9,989 people, or 32 percent of the **labor force**, in 1999.

Manufacturing, which in 1999 accounted for 28.8 percent of total GDP according to *Seychelles in Figures 2000*, is the fastest-growing sector of the national economy, with an average annual growth rate of 4.8 percent between 1979 and 1989, while services were growing at

was producing beer (6,000 tons), soft drinks (10,500 tons), cigarettes (70 million), and some other consumer products.

Mining has played an insignificant role in the national economy, although some experts believe that the seabed around the Seychelles is rich in various natural resources. However, the current development technologies do not allow exploration or extraction of these natural resources that could yield commercially viable profits.

SERVICES

TOURISM. Since the 1970s, tourism has dominated the national economy as its single most important sector, providing direct employment (hotels and restaurants) for 3,829 people or 12.4 percent of the workforce, according to *Seychelles in Figures 2000*. Including secondary employment, these figures rise to 9,797 people or 32 percent of the workforce. In 1998 an estimated 128,000 tourists visited the country, contributing SRe584 million (US$111 million) to the economy. The island nation offers a total of over 4,700 hotel rooms. The Seychelles promotes itself as the "Dream Destination," offering upmarket services to international visitors seeking the charms of a tropical island paradise, mainly from France, Germany, and Britain. The government plans to redefine the national tourism strategy in 2001.

FINANCIAL SERVICES. The services sector was controlled by the state throughout the 1980s, until the economic and financial liberalization in the 1990s. The Central Bank of Seychelles (CBS) is fairly efficient according to international standards, although it lacks independence from the government. The largest local bank is the Development Bank of Seychelles. In 1999 there were also 4 international banks in the country: Barclays Bank (UK), Banque Française Commerciale-Ocean Indien (France), Bank of Baroda (India), and Habib Bank (Pakistan). In 1995 the government established the Seychelles International Business Authority (SIBA) and opened the Seychelles International Trade Zone (SITZ) in an attempt to develop the country as an international "offshore" financial-services center.

RETAIL. The **retail** sector is developed to meet the demands of foreign tourists. This sector is dominated by small and medium-sized retail shops where visitors and local consumers can buy a wide variety of products and souvenirs.

INTERNATIONAL TRADE

The Seychelles' international trade has fluctuated considerably after the country achieved independence in 1976 due to its sensitivity to world prices and economic conditions in main trade-partner countries. The country incurs **trade deficits** because it imports all machinery and

Trade (expressed in billions of US$): Seychelles		
	Exports	Imports
1975	.006	.032
1980	.021	.099
1985	.028	.099
1990	.056	.186
1995	.053	.233
1998	N/A	N/A

SOURCE: International Monetary Fund. *International Financial Statistics Yearbook 1999.*

equipment, and a wide range of **consumer goods**, including foodstuffs, and fuel. The government addresses the problem by imposing certain restrictions on imports through the Seychelles Marketing Board (SMB) and by promoting self-sufficiency.

The country's economy is so small that the construction of even a single plant or hotel might significantly improve the country's statistics: the opening of a tuna-canning plant in 1987 boosted exports by 160 percent. Britain is the Seychelles' traditional primary trading partner, followed by France, Germany, and South Africa. In 1998 exports reached US$91 million, while imports reached US$403 million. The trade balance deficit was US$312 million. The Seychelles' government is working to improve the **current-account balance** deficit with assistance from the IMF.

MONEY

The Seychelles rupee has been remarkably stable since 1979, when it was linked to the IMF's special drawing rights (SDR). This fixed link was abandoned only in 1997 in favor of a free **exchange rate**. The exchange rate for the Seychelles rupee rose slowly from 4.762 per U.S. dollar in 1995 to Sre5.306 in 1999. The average rate of consumer **inflation** was around 6.5 percent in 1999, compared to 2.6 percent in 1998.

Exchange rates: Seychelles	
Seychelles rupees (SRe) per US$1	
Nov 2000	6.0397
2000	5.6009
1999	5.3426
1998	5.2622
1997	5.0263
1996	4.9700

SOURCE: CIA *World Factbook 2001* [ONLINE].

GDP per Capita (US$)					
Country	1975	1980	1985	1990	1998
Seychelles	3,600	4,882	4,957	6,297	7,192
United States	19,364	21,529	23,200	25,363	29,683
South Africa	4,574	4,620	4,229	4,113	3,918
Mauritius	1,531	1,802	2,151	2,955	4,034

SOURCE: United Nations. *Human Development Report 2000;
Trends in human development and per capita income.*

POVERTY AND WEALTH

The Seychelles has one of the highest standards of living when it is compared to countries in continental Africa. In 1999 the **GDP per capita** was equivalent to US$7,500 (estimated at **purchasing power parity**). During the first 2 decades after independence in 1976, the government attempted to reduce social polarization through state control over economic activities and by creation of the parastatals. Education has been accessible to the majority of the population, and the literacy rate is 84.2 percent. However, since the middle of the 1990s there has emerged evidence of increasing diversification of incomes and social polarization.

WORKING CONDITIONS

In 1999 the Seychelles labor force consisted of 30,786 people, according to *Seychelles in Figures 2000,* and the unemployment rate was around 11.0 percent. The labor market is heavily regulated, which requires all those working or seeking work to register with the government. Permission from the National Workers' Union is required for all dismissals or changing of jobs. In recent years, however, there has been some liberalization of the labor market, especially in conjunction with the opening of the Seychelles International Trade Zone in 1995. The government-controlled parastatals traditionally provided employment for almost half of the economically active population, although their role decreased in the late 1990s. Independent trade unions have been allowed since November 1993.

COUNTRY HISTORY AND ECONOMIC DEVELOPMENT

1756. France takes over the uninhabited islands.

1814. Great Britain establishes control, administering from Mauritius.

1903. The Seychelles become a Crown Colony.

1964. The socialist-oriented Seychelles People's United Party (SPUP) is established.

1976. Republic of Seychelles declares its independence within the Commonwealth. The first constitution is introduced.

1976. Sir James Mancham of the right-center Seychelles Democratic Party (SDP) becomes president.

1977. France Albert Rene stages a coup.

1977. The SPUP is renamed the Seychelles People's Progressive Front (SPPF).

1979. Second constitution is introduced, making the Seychelles a one-party political system; Rene is elected president; Seychelles rupee is linked to the IMF's special drawing right (SDR).

1981. Attempted overthrow of socialist government by mercenaries disguised as tourists.

1985. The first 5-year National Development Plan (NDP One) is introduced.

1986. Attempted coup by former Minister of Defense.

1991. Return to multiparty political system.

1993. Third constitution is adopted; Mancham returns from exile after legislative elections.

1995. Economic Development Act (EDA) introduced in attempt to attract offshore financial services; establishment of the Seychelles International Trade Zone (SITZ).

1997. Abandonment of the fixed link between the Seychelles rupee and the IMF's special drawing right (SDR).

1998. Rene and his supporters win in legislative elections.

FUTURE TRENDS

Despite the steady economic growth since the 1970s, and the contributions of tourism to revenues, the economic future of the Seychelles is far from certain. As a niche market in the tourism industry, it has to compete with neighboring Mauritius, Madagascar, and Comoros, which offer cheaper tourist services. Decay of the barrier reefs due to global warming might lead to the erosion of many small islands. The country needs to further diversify its economy by reducing its over-dependence on the tourism sector while preserving its standards of living and its political stability.

DEPENDENCIES

Seychelles has no territories or colonies.

BIBLIOGRAPHY

Gabbay, Rony, and Robin N. Ghosh. *Economic Development in a Small Island Economy: A Study of the Seychelles Marketing Board.* Perth (Australia): Academic Press International, 1992.

Economist Intelligence Unit. *Country Report: Seychelles.* London: Economist Intelligence Unit, November 2000.

Scarr, Deryck. *Seychelles since 1770: History of a Slave and Post-Slavery Society.* Trenton, NJ: Africa World Press, 2000.

Seychelles International Business Authority. *Seychelles: Your International Business Centre.* <http://www.siba.net>. Accessed July 2001.

Statistics and Database Administration Section MISD. *Seychelles in Figures 2000.* <http://www.seychelles.net/misdstat>. Accessed July 2001.

U.S. Central Intelligence Agency. *The World Factbook, 2000.* <http://www.cia.gov/cia/publications/factbook>. Accessed June 2001.

—Alfia Abazova, MILS

SIERRA LEONE

Republic of Sierra Leone

CAPITAL: Freetown.

MONETARY UNIT: Leone (Le). One leone equals 100 cents. Leone notes are available in denominations of 1, 2, 5, 10, 20, 50, 100, 500, 1,000, 2,000, and 5,000. Coins are in denominations of Le50 and 100.

CHIEF EXPORTS: Diamonds, rutile, cocoa, coffee, fish.

CHIEF IMPORTS: Foodstuffs, machinery and equipment, fuels and lubricants, chemicals.

GROSS DOMESTIC PRODUCT: US$2.7 billion (purchasing power parity, 2000 est.).

BALANCE OF TRADE: Exports: US$65 million (f.o.b., 2000 est.). Imports: US$145 million (f.o.b., 2000 est.).

COUNTRY OVERVIEW

LOCATION AND SIZE. Sierra Leone is located in West Africa, bordering the North Atlantic Ocean, with an area of 71,740 square kilometers (27,925 square miles) and a total coastline of 402 kilometers (250 miles). The country shares a border with Guinea in the north and east and with Liberia in the southeast. In comparative terms, Sierra Leone is in area about half the size of the U.S. state of Illinois. Freetown, the capital city, is located in the western part of the country.

POPULATION. The population of Sierra Leone was estimated in 2000 to be roughly 5.2 million. Exact figures for the country are impossible to find because a civil war has ravaged the country since 1991. Since the beginning of the war, it is estimated that some 2.5 million people have been displaced as refugees, mostly to Guinea and Liberia. Sierra Leone has an annual population growth rate of 3.6 percent, a birth rate of 45.6 per 1,000, and a death rate of 19.58 per 1,000, according to 2000 estimates.

Most of the population (99 percent) is of indigenous African descent. There are roughly 18 different native African ethnic groups. The largest, the Mendes and the Temnes, each make up roughly 30 percent of the entire population. The other groups account for about 39 percent, with the Krio (or Creole), Lebanese, and Indians making up about 1 percent. The Krio are descendants of freed slaves from Britain, North America, the Caribbean and re-captives from slave ships, who were settled in Freetown when it became a British colony in 1808.

Although English is the official language, it is only spoken by government officials and a limited number of educated Sierra Leoneans. Mende and Temne are spoken in the south and north, respectively. Krio, a mix of English and African languages, is spoken by the Krio, who make up an estimated 10 percent of the population. Although a small percentage of the population speaks Krio, the language is understood by an estimated 95 percent of the population, according to the World Factbook.

The population of Freetown was estimated at over 1.2 million in 1994. Many rural people fled to the city to escape the rebel Revolutionary United Front (RUF) that is responsible for a campaign of terror involving hundreds of random amputations (cutting off of hands, legs, ears, etc.), rapes, murders, and lootings.

OVERVIEW OF ECONOMY

Sierra Leone is an extremely impoverished country with an economy primarily based on agriculture and mining. Although the country is richly endowed with natural resources and minerals—especially diamonds—a decade-long civil conflict has brought most production to a near standstill. Sierra Leone has large areas of fertile land, but the vast majority of farmers engage only in subsistence farming. Of the cash crop agricultural production that continues during the internal conflict, the most significant

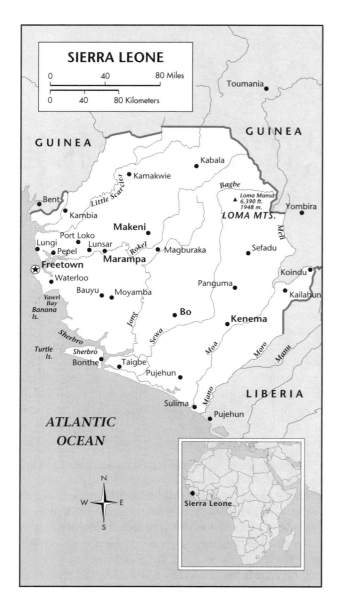

SIERRA LEONE

0   40   80 Miles

0   40   80 Kilometers

GUINEA

GUINEA

Toumania

Kabala

Kamakwie

Bagbe

Little Scarcies

Loma Mansa
6,390 ft.
1948 m.

Yombira

Bent

LOMA MTS.

Kambia

Makeni

Port Loko

Lungi   Lunsar   *Rokel*

Pepel   Magburaka   Sefadu

Marampa

Freetown

Waterloo   Panguma   Koindu

Bauyu   Moyamba   Kailahun

*Yawri
Bay*
Banana
Is.   *Jong*

Bo

Sewa   Kenema

Moa

Sherbro   *Moro*

Turtle   *Mano*

Is.   Sherbro   *Manu*

Bonthe   Taigbe

Pujehun

LIBERIA

Sulima

Pujehun

ATLANTIC
OCEAN

N
W   E
S

Sierra Leone

products are palm kernels, palm oil, cocoa and coffee, and food crops including rice (the main food crop), cassava, corn, millet, and peanuts.

Sierra Leone has vast deposits of diamonds, gold, rutile, and bauxite. Diamonds make up the country's principal export. However, diamonds have become more of a curse than a blessing for Sierra Leone. The civil war that has been raging for the past 10 years has mainly been a struggle for control of the diamond fields. Illicit diamond mining has provided money for the rebels to continue the war, and has made it difficult to realize peace in the country.

The country's economy has been steadily declining since the 1960s, with severe stagnation and **recession** since the early 1980s. Between 1980 and 1990, the World Bank put the country's average GDP growth rate at 0.6

percent, decreasing to -3.3 percent between 1990 and 1996, and falling to -3.6 percent in 1996. The civil war is the main reason for the steady decline. Although a brief ceasefire in the late 1990s brought hope to the economy, the resumption of fighting by 1999 caused more damage to the country. The *World Factbook* estimated that **gross domestic product** (GDP) at **purchasing power parity** was US$2.7 billion in 2000. The disruption of the war has reduced Sierra Leone to one of the poorest countries in the world.

POLITICS, GOVERNMENT, AND TAXATION

Sierra Leone gained its independence on 27 April 1961 as a constitutional monarchy within the British Commonwealth. When its first leader, Sir Milton Margai, passed away in 1964, the competitive political struggles between the Sierra Leone People's Party (SLPP) led by Albert Margai, and the All People's Congress (APC) led by Siaka Stevens, heightened the ethnic cleavages (divisions) within the country. Since independence, the recurrent political divide has been expressed regionally in the Krio descendants of the original Freetown settlers and the indigenous people of the hinterland (interior of the country); the Temne-dominated northern province and the Mende-dominated region of the southeast; an economically powerful immigrant Lebanese and Afro-Lebanese group and the indigenes; and a traditional group of native rulers and a modern, mostly urban, Western-educated elite.

The SLPP held power until the general elections of 1967, which were won by the APC. The 1967 coup d'état (take-over of the government), however, prevented the APC from governing until April 1968 when a counter-coup restored civilian rule. In 1971, Sierra Leone was proclaimed a republic and a new republican constitution was adopted in which the head of state, Siaka Stevens, became executive president. In a new constitution adopted in 1978, Sierra Leone became a 1-party state, although it had been in practice a 1-party state as far back as 1973. In 1985, Siaka Stevens handed over power to the commander of the armed forces, Major-General Joseph Momoh.

As president, Joseph Momoh initially announced sweeping reforms. He also implemented IMF donor prescriptions (policies and regulations) aimed at **privatization**, attracting foreign investments, and urging more efficient domestic revenue collection. He worked with the IMF to resume stabilization (efforts to strengthen the economy) programs that had been interrupted during the Siaka Stevens regime. Other changes targeted the export of gold, diamonds, and fish products, which severely undermined the privileged position of Lebanese and Afro-

Lebanese merchants who had long **monopolized** these economic activities. For example, foreign firms like LIAT Construction and Finance Corporation were given the authority to redirect production and profits through the formal (legal) economy to the benefit of the entire nation. The Lebanese population and politicians engaged in private mining of diamonds were discouraged from doing so through tougher restrictions and laws. Tougher laws such as longer prison sentences and stiff fines were also passed to curb smuggling of minerals, as well as more vigorous searches by customs officers at airports and at border crossings. The aim was to increase revenue collection by the government, and end the dominance of the informal (illegal) economy of smuggling, corruption, and private mining of minerals by influential groups in the country.

During the early years of President Momoh's tenure, he seemed to have ensured government control of the economy, especially in the area of diamonds. For example, in 1986–87, official diamond exports were 280 percent higher than 1985–86 figures. Similarly, foreign reserve holdings of the Bank of Sierra Leone rose to $7.6 million by the end of 1986, from a mere $196,000 in November 1985 when Momoh assumed the presidency.

The sweeping economic reforms angered the influential business community and resulted in an attempted coup in March 1987. Perhaps due to the fear of another coup attempt, the enforcement of drastic economic reforms slowed down after March 1987. A financial crisis in the 1980s, coupled with misrule and government corruption, as well as the difficulties caused by the effects of a civil war in neighboring Liberia, led to a coup d'état in April 1992. The coup was led by a group of young army officers, who selected 27-year old Captain Valentine Strasser to be the head of state. Captain Strasser led the country's Military Supreme Council of State until he was deposed in January 1996 because of his opposition to national elections that would hand over power to a civilian government.

Ahmed Tejan Kabbah of the SLPP won the elections held in February 1996 and set about forming a government of national unity. Another coup in 1997 overthrew the elected government, which went into exile in Guinea. The rebels then controlled the country until 1998, when the elected government was returned to power with the help of armed forces from Nigeria. Although a peace agreement was signed between the warring parties in 1999, fighting continues between the government and the rebels.

Corruption at all levels has destroyed the effectiveness of taxation in Sierra Leone. Individuals with strong ties to politicians often evade taxation—they end up not paying taxes either because they bribe the tax officials or threaten them with loss of their jobs. The strong political, economic, and ethnic ties based on favoritism, bribery, and corruption, among top members of the ruling political party use up state resources and thereby deprive the bureaucracies of funds for national development. According to William Reno in his book *Corruption and State Politics in Sierra Leone,* President Stevens is said to have used up to 70 percent of state revenues for "preferred (untaxed) concessions in diamond mining areas to political allies who were essential to his effort to resist local demands for greater revenue allocations."

INFRASTRUCTURE, POWER, AND COMMUNICATIONS

The civil war has disrupted any improvements to the country's **infrastructure** for nearly a decade. The road system is in serious need of repair, as the lack of resources has led to neglect. The small railway system is used very infrequently because the mines it leads to have been closed. Air transport in Sierra Leone is focused on the International Airport at Lungi, which, prior to the war, served many airlines, such as KLM, British Airways, and the regional airlines.

Communications

Country	Newspapers	Radios	TV Sets[a]	Cable subscribers[a]	Mobile Phones[a]	Fax Machines[a]	Personal Computers[a]	Internet Hosts[b]	Internet Users[b]
	1996	1997	1998	1998	1998	1998	1998	1999	1999
Sierra Leone	4	253	13	0.0	0	0.5	N/A	0.14	2
United States	215	2,146	847	244.3	256	78.4	458.6	1,508.77	74,100
Nigeria	24	223	66	N/A	0	N/A	5.7	0.00	100
Cote d'Ivoire	17	164	70	0.0	6	N/A	3.6	0.25	20

[a]Data are from International Telecommunication Union, *World Telecommunication Development Report 1999* and are per 1,000 people.
[b]Data are from the Internet Software Consortium (http://www.isc.org) and are per 10,000 people.

SOURCE: World Bank. *World Development Indicators 2000.*

Electricity supply is very unreliable in Freetown. There are constant outages as the old generators break down. However, it is estimated that the nearly-completed Bumbuna hydroelectric power project will be capable of providing electricity to most of the country. Its completion is dependent on the end of the war.

Sierra Leone's ports have provided important access to trade. The Port of Freetown has been an important center of trade for many countries. The natural harbor at the mouth of the Sierra Leone River is one of the world's finest; it affords 21 square kilometers (8 square miles) of anchorage for large ships. Bonthe and Pepel are 2 additional ports used in the export of goods.

The telephone system in Sierra Leone is not an advanced or extensive system. In 1997, Sierra Leone had roughly 17,000 main telephone lines in use, and in 1999 there were 650 mobile telephones. The telephone system was enhanced by a satellite earth station which offered up to 70 channels. Despite the limited resources available, Sierra Leone has made considerable progress in expanding its links with neighboring countries through the Pan-African Telecommunications Network (PANAFTEL) since independence. External services are handled by Sierra Leone External Telecommunications Services (SLET).

ECONOMIC SECTORS

Sierra Leone, since the mid-1980s, has been considered by the United Nations as the country most seriously affected by adverse economic conditions. Sierra Leone is virtually a failed state characterized by a severe decline in educational, health, transportation, and other services.

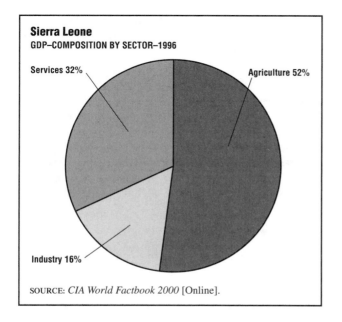

Sierra Leone
GDP–COMPOSITION BY SECTOR–1996

Services 32%
Agriculture 52%
Industry 16%

SOURCE: *CIA World Factbook 2000* [Online].

The **private sector** dominates the country's free market economy, with subsistence agriculture contributing the most. Agriculture made up the greatest portion of GDP in 1999: 43 percent, according to the *World Factbook*. The country could be self-sufficient in foodstuffs, but the destabilizing effects of the civil war has driven most farmers of cash crops from the land.

Diamond mining is the nation's most important source of foreign currency, but its percentage contribution to total foreign earnings has declined from 65 percent in the mid-1970s to less than 20 percent in the 1990s. The decline is the result of a combination of smuggling, unfavorable prices for developing country commodities, depletion of resources, and the effects of the war. The *World Factbook* reported that industry contributed 26 percent of GDP in 1999 and services contributed 31 percent.

AGRICULTURE

Since over 60 percent of the population of Sierra Leone is usually engaged in agriculture, during the 1970s efforts were made by the government to increase productivity in food crops and achieve self-sufficiency, especially in rice production. However, the government's emphasis on cash crops, and overall poor agricultural planning tends to relegate agriculture to a secondary role. Rice accounts for approximately 40 percent of the value of the output of food crops. Other food crops include cassava, millet, sorghum, peanuts, beans, and corn, among others. Livestock (cattle, goats, and sheep) and fishing are also of importance to the economy.

According to *Background to Sierra Leone,* a 1980 publication of the Sierra Leone government, agricultural development was a priority in the 1970s. Accordingly, the government launched a series of Integrated Agricultural Development Projects (IADPs) aimed at maximizing agricultural production in individual regions of the country. The projects included a detailed study of a region's agricultural need and potential, as well as assistance to small farmers. Farmers were encouraged to use fertilizers and equipment together with advice on improved methods of cultivation. However, the economic dislocation of the 1980s, coupled with the war of the 1990s, have effectively undermined progress in agricultural development. Little has been done to improve the sector at the beginning of 2000.

INDUSTRY

MINING. Sierra Leone is endowed with many mineral resources. Prospects for minerals began in 1926 and reserves of iron, gold, diamonds, platinum, chromite, bauxite, and rutile (a titanium ore) were quickly found. The first diamond was discovered in 1930 and mining began 2 years later. Bauxite mining began in 1963 and reserves are estimated at nearly 50 million tons with a high alumina content of 55 to 56 percent. Exploitation of the estimated 170 million tons of rutile started in 1967. The country has one of the world's largest deposits of rutile. At the height of production in the 1970s, Sierra Leone was ranked as the fourth largest producer of gem diamonds in the world.

The country's civil unrest has caused serious problems in the mining sector. All mining permissions have been suspended since January 2000. Although diamonds and rutile have historically played major roles in Sierra Leone's economy, the war has caused legitimate mining production to virtually cease and has increased smuggling of diamonds from the country. In addition, the exploration of potentially valuable amounts of gold and bauxite in the country has been interrupted.

MANUFACTURING. Sierra Leone's manufacturing sector is one of the smallest in all of Africa. Manufacturing industries are very few and still in a stage of infancy in Sierra Leone due to the lack of financial support available during the civil strife. The manufacturing businesses are mainly raw materials processors and light manufacturers for the domestic market. Items processed are mostly palm kernels and rice. Other manufacturing industries produce a variety of goods including salt, knitwear and other clothing, paint, oxygen, plastic footwear, nails, soap and cosmetics, and a wide range of furniture. Sierra Leone also has a refinery for imported petroleum. The continuing trouble in this sector is indicated in the small number of new manufacturing businesses that opened recently. In 1998, only 0.5 percent of the country's new businesses were involved in manufacturing or construction, according to the Sierra Leone News Agency.

SERVICES

TOURISM. Prior to the outbreak of the war in 1991, serious tourist development took place. The center of attraction was the Cape Sierra district bordered by Lumley Beach. Many modern hotels catered to the tourist population. In 1978, the Bintumani Hotel was built, equipped with 300 beds and a conference center. The Cape Sierra Hotel and the Mammy Yoko Hotel are also located in the Lumley Beach area. Within the city, the main hotels are Brookfields and the Paramount. However, many of these hotels have been damaged by the war or have been transformed as lodgings for soldiers.

Sierra Leone is also home to historic Bunce Island, once a slave trading post. Freetown itself is part of the Freetown Peninsula endowed with unspoiled beaches, na-

ture trails, and historic buildings. The number of tourists has been dramatically reduced because of the war.

FINANCIAL SERVICES. Sierra Leone was chosen as the site for the West African Clearing House, which was established in Freetown in 1975. Banking was first introduced to the country in 1898 by the then Bank of West Africa, which later became the Standard Bank of Sierra Leone. It was followed in 1917 by Barclays. The nation's first indigenous commercial bank, the Sierra Leone Commercial Bank, Ltd., was opened in 1973 and is entirely government-owned. Sierra Leone's banking system is supervised by the Bank of Sierra Leone, which serves as the central bank and therefore controls, maintains, and regulates the nation's money supply and foreign reserves.

Of major importance to the nation's economic growth is the National Development Bank, founded in 1968. Its function is to provide finance in the form of loans or **equity** capital to many development projects in agriculture, agro-based industry, and industry. However, the ongoing civil strife, especially the 1997 coup d'état that toppled the civilian government of President Tejan Kabbah, seriously dislocated these financial services. Barclays Bank, for example, ceased operations in the country, and the Treasury Building was severely damaged by fire.

RETAIL. Sierra Leone is a land of petty traders and street **hawkers**. Many indigenous people engage in **retail** with items as varied as food commodities, clothing, and building materials, among others. According to *Background to Sierra Leone,* over 8 percent of the country's working population is engaged in retail and wholesale distribution.

INTERNATIONAL TRADE

Over the years, the value of Sierra Leone's exports has steadily declined as the value of imports has risen, forcing the country to bear the burden of an increasing **trade deficit**. In 1998 exports were valued at $17 million, and imports totaled $92 million. The *World Factbook* estimated that exports had increased to US$65

Trade (expressed in billions of US$): Sierra Leone		
	Exports	Imports
1975	.118	.185
1980	.224	.427
1985	.130	.151
1990	.138	.149
1995	.025	.135
1998	N/A	.095

SOURCE: International Monetary Fund. *International Financial Statistics Yearbook 1999.*

million and imports to US$145 million by 2000. Chief trading partners for exports are the United States, Britain, Belgium, Italy, the Netherlands, and Germany. Leading sources for imports are the United States, Britain, Italy, Nigeria, the Netherlands, Indonesia, and Germany. Despite some successful efforts to increase the output of agricultural productivity and diversify exports, Sierra Leone's balance of visible trade has still been unfavorable. The balance of trade has also suffered from an increase in short-term debts, and the deterioration of terms of trade related to the sharp increases in the price of petroleum products and manufactured goods from the industrial world. These increases exceeded those of agricultural produce, diamonds, and bauxite.

Prior to the war, the domestic market was favored by the growing tourist trade, while the policy of non-discriminatory **tariffs** served the interests of consumers by keeping prices relatively low. The National Trading Company set up in 1971 with government financial assistance, also ensured the maintenance of competitive prices on the home market, and the promotion of indigenous enterprise in commerce.

MONEY

The value of the leone has been declining since the early 1980s. The leone was formerly linked to the pound sterling. Its value is now determined largely by the export earnings of the country. Since the country does not earn a great deal from its external trade, the IMF and the World Bank constantly encourage the country to reduce government spending in order to maintain a balanced budget. The Sierra Leone economy has undergone several IMF economic and financial policies aimed at improving the value of the leone in relation to other currencies of the world. A stronger leone is supposed to translate into a stronger economy. However, the outcome has often been high **inflation** (a weak currency in terms of **exchange rates**) and a great deal of leone fluctuations, mostly downwards.

Exchange rates: Sierra Leone	
leones (Le) per US$1	
Jan 2001	1,653.39
2000	2,092.13
1999	1,804.20
1998	1,563.62
1997	981.48
1996	920.73
SOURCE: CIA *World Factbook 2001* [ONLINE].	

GDP per Capita (US$)					
Country	1975	1980	1985	1990	1998
Sierra Leone	316	320	279	279	150
United States	19,364	21,529	23,200	25,363	29,683
Nigeria	301	314	230	258	256
Dem. Rep. of Congo	392	313	293	247	127
SOURCE: United Nations. *Human Development Report 2000; Trends in human development and per capita income.*					

POVERTY AND WEALTH

Sierra Leone, like many developing states, is a land of gaping inequalities where national income is concerned. According to *The World Development Report, 1999–2000,* in 1989 the richest 10 percent of the population had 43.6 percent of the national income, whilst the poorest 20 percent of the population had 1.1 percent of the national income. The access to national income and resources tends to be heavily weighted in favor of ruling party leaders, cabinet ministers, and those with political ties to the president.

According to Earl Conteh-Morgan and Mac Dixon-Fyle, authors of *Sierra Leone at the End of the Twentieth Century,* by the mid-1980s, the level of poverty in the country was such that "state hospitals and clinics suffered heavily through a lack of supplies, modern equipment, and motivated employees. This sector also suffered nonpayment of inadequate government salaries. The consequence was that many officials were forced to corruption diverting drugs and medical equipment or putting them into private use." In other words, Sierra Leone, by the mid-1980s was already a failed state. Central government ministers and bureaucracies simply centralized and monopolized important functions, and thereby public revenues. In the process, they deprived the local authorities of adequate revenues and responsibilities nec-

Distribution of Income or Consumption by Percentage Share: Sierra Leone	
Lowest 10%	0.5
Lowest 20%	1.1
Second 20%	2.0
Third 20%	9.8
Fourth 20%	23.7
Highest 20%	63.4
Highest 10%	43.6
Survey year: 1989	
Note: This information refers to expenditure shares by percentiles of the population and is ranked by per capita expenditure.	
SOURCE: *2000 World Development Indicators* [CD-ROM].	

Household Consumption in PPP Terms

Country	All food	Clothing and footwear	Fuel and power[a]	Health care[b]	Education[b]	Transport & Communications	Other
Sierra Leone	47	9	9	3	13	8	12
United States	13	9	9	4	6	8	51
Nigeria	51	5	31	2	8	2	2
Liberia	N/A	N/A	N/A	N/A	N/A	N/A	N/A

Data represent percentage of consumption in PPP terms.
[a]Excludes energy used for transport.
[b]Includes government and private expenditures.
SOURCE: World Bank. *World Development Indicators 2000.*

essary to nurture grassroots local development and a democratic culture. The lack of funds and the continued centralization of authority by the central government meant that such basic but necessary functions as garbage collection, maintenance of public toilets, and supervision and maintenance of public markets, were eventually abandoned. Even Freetown, the capital, suffered a decrease in the scope of service deliveries. In the 1980s, it was described by many observers as increasingly developing into overgrown and overcrowded shantytowns with crumbling buildings, open drains, and deteriorating, chaotic roads.

By the late 1980s and long before the eruption of civil strife, political and economic deterioration in Sierra Leone had become extreme. Between 1980 and 1985 incomes per capita declined by an average of roughly 6 percent per annum. The **inflation rate** reached 80 percent by the end of the 1980s. Loss of morale and significant economic deprivation was the consequence for government workers, teachers, and others dependent on government salaries. Often deprived of salaries for months on end, many resorted to **informal economic** activities as a way to supplement their meager or nonexistent incomes. The most popular form of economic activity became petty trading for the mass of people, and the more influential obtained import licenses and involved their relatives in trading activities. Private vehicles were often used for commercial purposes, either as taxis or to transport goods.

Deterioration and dilapidation was not just confined to the roads and streets, but were found in the classrooms as well. Teachers lacked even chalk for writing on the board. Windows, roofs, and furniture not only deteriorated, but were, in many schools, absent. As a result, the quality of education decreased substantially from the primary level to college. The consequence for higher education has been a massive brain drain of lecturers and school teachers to neighboring African states, to international organizations, and to the West.

WORKING CONDITIONS

Since the early 1980s, the Sierra Leone **labor force** has been shrinking due to a combination of factors such as worsening economic conditions that affected most developing countries in the 1980s, the decline in the price of raw materials in the world market, misrule in the form of embezzlement of funds by government officials, and the effects of IMF conditions such as the freeze on hiring and the laying off of thousands of civil servants, in order to reduce the size of government.

In 1981, before the downward slide into massive unemployment, the country had an estimated 1.369 million workers with most found in agriculture (65 percent), followed by industry (19 percent), and services (16 percent). However, in 1985 there were only 65,000 wage earners. The struggle for good working conditions by trade union activists has been an integral part of relations between government and labor. Trade unionism began in Sierra Leone as early as 1914 with the formation of a union among temporary customs workers. In 1971 an act of Parliament guaranteed the right of workers to industrial action upon due notification. According to law, minimum pay rates and maximum hours should be regulated every 2 years and the government is committed to upholding the right of workers to form unions and bargain for better pay and good working conditions. Politicians have often undermined the effectiveness of labor unions through co-optation of the leaders—bribing the leaders, or enticing them with better job offers, so that they drop their demands for pay raises and better working conditions. In the early 1980s, for example, both the leaders of the Sierra Leone Labor Congress (SLLC), and the president of the Sierra Leone Teachers' Union (SLTU) were appointed members of parliament in order to separate them from the unions, which would, in turn, end their activism. Working conditions are still far from ideal. Government employees get meager salaries, and often go unpaid for several months. The uncertainty of government jobs means that many workers engage in petty trading in order to survive.

COUNTRY HISTORY AND ECONOMIC DEVELOPMENT

1495. Portuguese establish a fort on the site of modern Freetown, a base for traders in gold, ivory, pepper, and slaves.

1672. British Royal African Company establishes 2 trading depots, 1 on Bunce Island and 1 on York Island.

1787. The first settlers (freed slaves) arrive from Britain and establish a self-governing "Province of Freedom."

1808. Freetown becomes a British colony.

1896. The British impose a protectorate on the hinterland of the country (the interior of the country was declared an overseas territory of the British Crown).

1926. Prospecting for minerals starts, and by 1930 employs over 16,000 workers.

1949. Sierra Leone Produce Marketing Board (SLPMB) set up to exert government control over agricultural marketing and production.

1960. Development of Industries Act passes as a result of the government's construction of the Wellington Industrial Estate in the suburbs of Freetown.

1961. Sierra Leone becomes an independent nation within the British Commonwealth.

1963. Central Bank of Sierra Leone set up.

1971. Sierra Leone becomes a republic, casting off the last vestige of colonialism, with Siaka Stevens as the first executive president.

1978. Sierra Leone becomes a republican 1-party state on 14 June 1978, with the All People's Congress (APC) as the sole party.

1980s. The continent-wide African economic crisis affects Sierra Leone, adversely resulting in high inflation and chronic unemployment.

1991. The internal economic dislocation (massive unemployment and high inflation), coupled with the spillover of the Liberian civil war, plunges Sierra Leone into civil strife perpetuated by the Revolutionary United Front (RUF) rebels.

1999. The RUF and the Sierra Leone government sign the Lome Peace Accord that allows the deployment of over 12,000 UN peacekeeping troops in the country.

2000. Despite the peace accord, internal fighting continues.

FUTURE TRENDS

Sierra Leone entered the last decade of the 20th century as a failed state, culminating in the outbreak of civil strife in 1991. The anarchy has resulted in massive suffering, displacement of people, and deaths in the hundreds of thousands. However, if the Lome Peace Accord is successfully implemented and future governments manage the mineral and agricultural wealth of the country wisely, Sierra Leone could become another Singapore. Britain is currently engaged in training a new army and a new police force for the country. Although the United Nations' peacekeeping operation has experienced some difficulties, including some of their troops being taken hostage by rebels, it is still hoped that the peacekeeping mission will help to bring an end to the civil strife.

DEPENDENCIES

Sierra Leone has no territories or colonies.

BIBLIOGRAPHY

Background to Sierra Leone. Freetown: State House, 1980.

Conteh-Morgan, Earl, and Mac Dixon-Fyle. *Sierra Leone at the End of the Twentieth Century: History, Politics, and Society.* New York: Peter Lang, 1999.

Human Rights Watch. <http://www.hrw.org>. Accessed December 2000.

Reno, William. *Corruption and State Politics in Sierra Leone.* New York: Cambridge University Press, 1995.

Sierra Leone News Agency (SLNA). *Business Page: Trade and Industry Overview.* <http://www.sierra-leone.gov.sl/business/trade_overview1.htm>. Accessed October 2001.

United Nations High Commissioner for Refugees. *Background Paper on Refugees and Asylum Seekers From Sierra Leone.* Geneva: UNHCR, 1998.

U.S. Central Intelligence Agency. *The World Factbook 2001.* <http://www.odci.gov/cia/publications/factbook/index.html>. Accessed October 2001.

—*Earl Conteh-Morgan*

SOMALIA

CAPITAL: Mogadishu.

MONETARY UNIT: Somali shilling (SH). One shilling equals 100 cents. There are coins of 1, 5, 10, and 50 cents and 1 shilling, and notes of 5, 10, 20, 100, 500, and 1,000 shillings. The self-declared Republic of Somaliland introduced its own currency, the Somaliland shilling, in 1995. U.S. dollars are the most widely used currency.

CHIEF EXPORTS: Livestock, bananas, fish, hides and skins, myrrh.

CHIEF IMPORTS: Petroleum products, foodstuffs, fertilizers, machinery and parts, transport equipment, manufactured goods.

GROSS DOMESTIC PRODUCT: US$4.3 billion (purchasing power parity, 1999 est.).

BALANCE OF TRADE: **Exports:** US$187 million (f.o.b., 1998 est.). **Imports:** US$327 million (f.o.b., 1998 est.).

COUNTRY OVERVIEW

LOCATION AND SIZE. Somalia, formerly known as the Somali Democratic Republic, is a coastal country covering a land area of 637,657 square kilometers (246,199 square miles) and a water area of 10,320 square kilometers (3,985 square miles), with a land-bordered circumference of 2,366 kilometers (1,470 miles). It has a coastline of 3,025 kilometers (1,880 miles) stretching along the Indian Ocean to the southeast and along the Gulf of Aden in the southern mouth of the Red Sea to the north. These coastal features give the region the name the Horn of Africa. To the north, Somalia faces the Arabian Peninsula with which it has had centuries of commercial and cultural interaction. To the northwest it shares a border with the Republic of Djibouti (58 kilometers, or 36 miles), to the west by Ethiopia (1,626 kilometers, or 1,010 miles) and southwest by Kenya (682 kilometers, or 424 miles).

The capital is Mogadishu, which in 1987 had a population of 1 million, followed by the other major towns of Hargeysa, with 400,000; Kismaayo, with 200,000;

Marka, with 100,000; and Berbera, with less than 100,000. Since the 1991 outbreak of civil strife, the northern region—formerly a British colony—has formed an internationally unrecognized de facto autonomous country, Somaliland, with Hargeysa as its capital.

Somalia is principally desert. There is a monsoon in the northeast from December to February, with moderate temperatures in the north but very hot in the south. From May to October the southwest monsoon brings irregular rainfall. Between monsoons it is generally very hot and humid. Somalia is divided into 3 main topographical regions. The northern region is somewhat mountainous with high plateaus ranging from 900 meters (2,953 feet) above sea level to peaks at 2,450 meters (8,038 feet) above sea level in the northeast. The second region extends south and west to the Shabeelle river and hosts a plateau elevated to a maximum of 685 meters (2,247 feet) above sea level. The third region lies between the Jubba and Shabeelle rivers and is a low agricultural land that also extends into a low pastureland lying southwest of the Jubba river toward the Kenyan border. The country's main drainage is provided by the Shabeelle and Jubba rivers, which originate in Ethiopia and flow toward the Indian Ocean, although the Shabeelle dries before reaching the ocean. These rivers are not navigable by commercial vessels, but they do supply irrigation. Despite its long coastal shoreline, Somalia has only 1 natural harbor, at Berbera.

POPULATION. Determining the population of Somalia has long been a difficult task. According to the February 1975 population census, the population of Somalia was 3,253,024 (excluding adjustment for undercounting), while the February 1986 census recorded it at 7,114,431, implying a doubling of the population over the decade. According to the United Nations (UN) estimates, the midyear population increased from 7,875,000 in 1985 to 10,217,000 in 1997. However, the *CIA World Factbook* estimated the population in 2000 as 7,253,137. All such estimates were derived by extrapolating from official censuses taken in 1975 and 1986 by the Somali government. Such estimates are complicated by the large number of nomads and by refugee movements in a country that has been racked by war and famine for a decade.

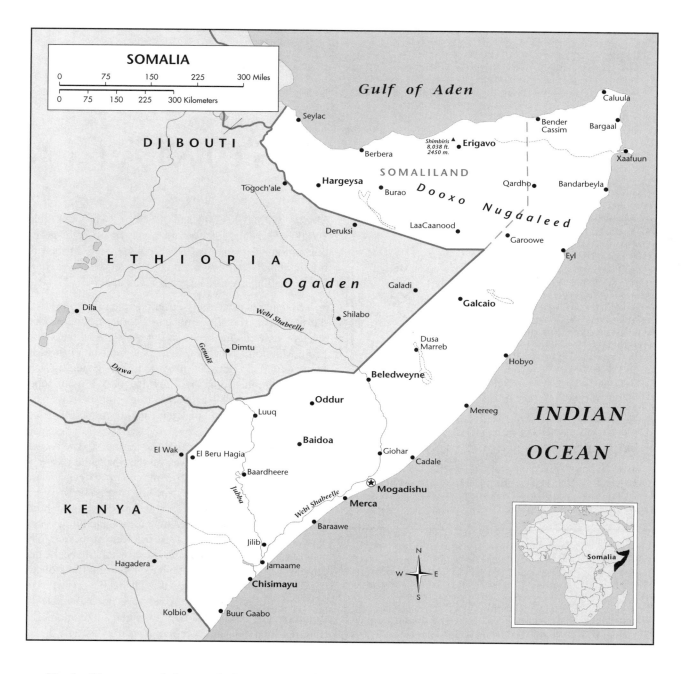

Nearly 50 percent of the population are nomadic, moving mainly in the central and northern areas, where drought is an ever-present threat. Almost all the nomadic clans are accustomed to grazing on both sides of the border with Ethiopia. About 28 percent of the population are settled farmers, mostly in the southern areas between the Jubba and Shabeelle rivers. The population profile was estimated in 2000 as 44 percent in the 0–14 years age group, 53 percent between 15 and 64 years, and 3 percent in the 65 years and over age group.

Before the 1991 civil conflict, population density averaged 12 people per square kilometer (31 per square mile) but was unevenly distributed. The areas of greatest rural density were the settled zones adjacent to the Jubba and Shabeelle rivers, a few places between them, and several small areas in the northern highlands. The most lightly populated zones were in northeastern and central Somalia, but there were some other sparsely populated areas in the far southwest along the Kenyan border.

OVERVIEW OF ECONOMY

Most economic activity was disrupted by the breakdown of the Somali state in 1991. Before this disaster, Somalia was one of the world's poorest countries, but it had been making modest progress despite the absence of mineral or hydro resources and limited fertile agricultural land. The breakdown of the state and the immersion of the country in nearly a decade of civil war has devastated the economy and distanced the country from the international community.

Agriculture is the country's most important sector, comprising some 60 percent of the GDP, with livestock accounting for about two-thirds of the value of agricultural output and about two-thirds of export earnings. Livestock is produced mainly by nomadic groups who make up perhaps 50 percent of the total population. Bananas are also exported. Sugar, sorghum, and corn are the other main agricultural crops. Fish are harvested by small-scale methods for local consumption. The industrial sector has always been small, at around 10 percent the GDP, and its output has probably contracted faster than the rest of the economy, so it now produces perhaps 5 percent of the GDP. It comprises some agricultural processing, but the simple manufactures, such as soap, soft drinks, and **consumer goods**, have almost all closed down as the result of the ongoing conflict. The lack of security has impeded international aid programs, and there is continual fear of food shortages throughout the country and famine when harvests fail through drought. In normal circumstances the people are industrious and enterprising, and many Somalis have fled to neighboring countries where they have established successful enterprises, particularly in the transport sector, remitting money back to Somalia, which has been an important feature of the population's survival over the past decade.

Somalia was formerly a **socialist**-oriented economy that was undergoing market-oriented structural adjustments until 1991. These policies were designed to allow more sectors of the economy to have production, sales, and prices determined by the market, rather than regulated by the government. Major features of the program were to allow the **exchange rate** to be determined by supply and demand for foreign exchange, to allow banks to set interest rates for both depositors and borrowers, to end controls on prices of commodities, and to transfer state-owned enterprises to private ownership. **Privatization** of wholesale-trade and financial sectors was largely completed by 1991, and although economic growth was sporadic and uneven across the sectors, average living standards were being maintained in the face of a population growth rate of around 2.9 percent a year. Since the overthrow of President Siad Barre in 1991, however, the country has had no viable central government, and national economic planning has been haphazard or nonexistent.

POLITICS, GOVERNMENT, AND TAXATION

The Somali people have a strongly established common culture, but the Somalis are divided into a number of clans. Most Somalis identify themselves first with their clan and then with the Somali people. These divided loyalties have given rise to Somalia's current problems.

The Somali Republic was formed on 1 July 1960 as the result of a merger of British Somaliland, which became independent from the United Kingdom on 26 June 1960, and Italian Somaliland, which became independent from an Italian-administered United Nations trusteeship on July 1, 1960. A coalition government was formed by the Somali Youth League (SYL) and the 2 leading northern political parties, with Dr. Abd ar-Rashid Ali Shirmake, a leading SYL politician and member of the Darod clan, as first prime minister, and a single legislative body.

The initial problems of combining the previous colonial administrations were eased by shared Somali cultural ties, and for the first years of the country's existence internal conflicts among clans were secondary to ongoing efforts to extend the boundaries of the new state to include Somali communities in Ethiopia, French Somaliland (present-day Djibouti) and northern Kenya. Liberation movements were established for this cause in each of the neighboring territories. It soon became obvious that these efforts were bound to fail, however, and political efforts turned to addressing the problems of Somali peoples resident in other countries—and to internal conflict.

Abd ar-Rashid Ali Shirmake was elected president in 1967, but in October 1969 he was assassinated in the course of factional violence, leading to a coup d'etat. A Supreme Revolutionary Council (SRC) formed an army and police officers announced that it had acted to preserve democracy and justice and to eliminate corruption and clanism and that the country was to be renamed the Somali Democratic Republic to symbolize these aims. Army commander and president of the SRC Major General Jalle Mohamed Siad Barre became head of state. For nearly 30 years Barre led Somalia as a socialist state, but economic stability was continually disrupted by internal dissent and by troubled relations with neighboring Ethiopia. On 27 January 1991, the United Somali Congress (USC) ousted the regime of Siad Barre, and the country descended into anarchy and widespread banditry based on clan feuding.

Since the overthrow of the Barre regime, politics in the country have been in a state of chaos. Clan-based political parties have seized different areas of the country and have fought each other over control of disputed regions. No one clan has a national base of support. While chaos has been the norm in much of Somalia throughout the decade, some orderly government has been established in the northern part. In May 1991, the elders of clans in former British Somaliland established the independent Republic of Somaliland, which, although not recognized by any government, maintains a stable existence, aided by the overwhelming dominance of the ruling clan and the economic **infrastructure** left behind by British, Russian, and American military assistance programs. In 1998 neighboring Puntland, in the northeast of the country, declared its autonomy and has also made progress towards reconstructing a legitimate, representative government.

Over the course of Somalia's troubled decade, several foreign relief efforts have been attempted in the country. From 1993, a 2-year UN humanitarian effort (primarily in the south) was able to alleviate famine conditions, but when the UN withdrew in 1995, having suffered significant casualties, order still had not been restored. In February 1996, the European Union (EU) agreed to finance the reconstruction of the port of Berbera in Somaliland. Since then, other aid projects have been undertaken by the EU and by an Italian non-government organization.

In August 2000, delegates at a 3-month peace conference in Djibouti formed the National Transitional Assembly and elected Abdulkasim Sala Hassan as the new president of Somalia. Although the new administration has made progress in creating the beginnings of an army to establish law and order and has taken up residence in Mogadishu, Somalia still faces real difficulties. The warlords of the various feuding clans are unwilling to give up their positions as powerful and feared leaders controlling substantial resources gathered through protection, looting, and extortion. They are heavily armed, and they need to be offered a way to show support for the fledgling government. Another challenge for the new government is the problem of its relations with the administrations in Somaliland and Puntland. An agreement to allow these areas to secede would allow them to gain international recognition and thus aid, while allowing the rest of former Somalia to the south to concentrate on its internal security problems.

Somalia once had a 4-tier court system based on Western models. Under Barre, separate National Security Courts operated outside the ordinary legal system and under direct control of the executive and were given broad jurisdiction over offenses defined by government as affecting state security. These were abolished in 1991, and no organized court system exists in the country. The Republic of Somaliland uses the pre-1991 penal code.

With no effective government, there is no formal taxation. However, warlords exact payments from businesses in return for not harassing them and provide some protection against the predations of others. Surprisingly, some observers report that the lack of government has contributed to positive developments in the economy, as entrepreneurs have been freed to develop their business free from government intervention and bureaucracy. Most economic transactions are conducted in U.S. dollars, thus easing the problems of the utter instability of the Somali shilling.

INFRASTRUCTURE, POWER, AND COMMUNICATIONS

Somalia has a deteriorating infrastructure that has seen little improvement in the last decade. One paved road extends from Berbera in north through Mogadishu to Kismaayo. Roads of all categories totalled 22,100 kilometers (13,733 miles) in 1996, of which 2,608 (1,621 miles) kilometers were paved. Many of the improved earth roads were frequently impassable in rainy seasons. Highway infrastructure is insufficient to open up isolated areas or to link the regions. The country has no railroads.

Somalia has 8 paved civilian airfields and fewer than 20 additional widely-scattered gravel airfields. The international airport is at Mogadishu. In 1990 a domestic service linked Mogadishu with 7 other Somali cities

Country	Telephones[a]	Telephones, Mobile/Cellular[a]	Radio Stations[b]	Radios[a]	TV Stations[a]	Televisions[a]	Internet Service Providers[c]	Internet Users[c]
Somalia	N/A	N/A	AM 0; FM 0; shortwave 4	470,000	1	135,000	1	200
United States	194 M	69.209 M (1998)	AM 4,762; FM 5,542; shortwave 18	575 M	1,500	219 M	7,800	148 M
Dem. Rep. of Congo	21,000	8,900	AM 3; FM 12; shortwave 1 (1999)	18.03 M	20 (1999)	6.478 M	2	1,500 (1999)
Ethiopia	157,000	4,000 (1999)	AM 5; FM 0; shortwave 2 (1999)	11.75 M	25 (1999)	320,000	1	7,200

Communications

[a]Data is for 1997 unless otherwise noted.
[b]Data is for 1998 unless otherwise noted.
[c]Data is for 2000 unless otherwise noted.

SOURCE: CIA *World Factbook 2001* [Online].

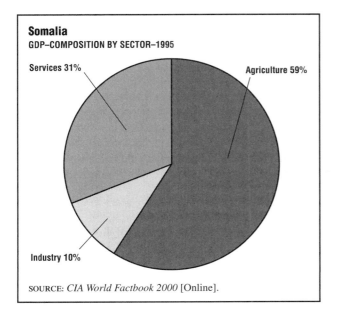

Somalia
GDP–COMPOSITION BY SECTOR–1995

Services 31%

Agriculture 59%

Industry 10%

SOURCE: *CIA World Factbook 2000* [Online].

served, in part, by Somali Airlines, which owned 1 Airbus 310 in 1989. There was no scheduled service in existence in 1992.

Electricity is produced entirely from diesel and petrol powered generators, with all the fuel imported. In 1998, it was estimated that 265 million kilowatt hours (kWh) were supplied, all from privately-owned generators. There is some hydroelectric potential on Somalia's rivers, but thus far it has remained unexploited and is likely to remain so until Somalia's security and stability become better established. Poor people, and most of the population outside the towns, rely on wood for cooking and kerosene oil-lamps for light.

There are 4 major ports—deepwater facilities at Berbera, Mogadishu, and Kismaayo and a lighterage (for transportation of goods on flat-bottomed barges) port at Marka—and a minor port at Maydh. A port modernization program that was launched in the latter half of 1980s with U.S. aid significantly improved cargo handling capabilities at Kismaayo and increased the number of berths and deepened the harbor at Berbera.

The public telecommunications system was completely destroyed or dismantled by the civil war factions; all relief organizations depend on their own private systems. Recently, local cellular telephone systems have been established in Mogadishu and in several other population centers. International connections are available from Mogadishu by satellite.

ECONOMIC SECTORS

Somalia's economy is mainly based on **subsistence agriculture** comprising livestock herding and to a lesser extent a simple form of hoe-agriculture. Attempts to in-

troduce modern techniques of animal husbandry and agriculture have been only partially successful. Agriculture was estimated to comprise of 59 percent of the GDP in 1995—with livestock alone contributing 41 percent of the GDP—services 31 percent, and industry 10 percent. Current estimates are that a higher proportion of GDP comes from agriculture, with services slightly reduced, and a much diminished role for industry.

AGRICULTURE

The Somali economy is traditionally based principally on the herding camels, sheep, and goats, with cattle more prevalent in the southern region. Agriculture still provides for the subsistence needs of 75 percent of the population and furnishes a substantial export trade in live animals, skins, clarified butter, and canned meat. After independence in 1960, exports of these items rose dramatically and, until 1988, outstripped the other main export, bananas, which accounted for 40 percent of the total value of exports in that year. In 1982 exports of livestock products accounted for about 80 percent of Somalia's total export earnings. In 1989, livestock products accounted for 49 percent of the GDP. However, Somali agriculture is at the mercy of periodic droughts, the worst of which have led to high levels of famine and starvation.

Before 1972 fishing along the Somali coast was mainly a small-scale subsistence activity, but by 1980 it was coming to be recognized as one of the country's leading economic activities. During the 1974–75 drought, some 12,000 nomads were settled and encouraged to organize themselves into fishing co-operatives, which showed considerable promise. Although fish production

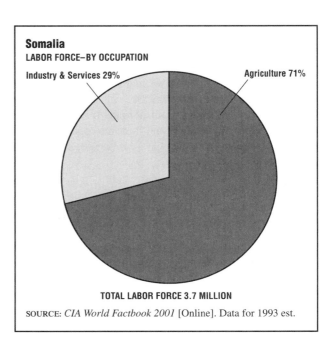

Somalia
LABOR FORCE–BY OCCUPATION

Industry & Services 29%

Agriculture 71%

TOTAL LABOR FORCE 3.7 MILLION

SOURCE: *CIA World Factbook 2001* [Online]. Data for 1993 est.

more than doubled, fish was still not a significant feature of the Somali diet.

INDUSTRY

Prior to 1991, there was a small manufacturing sector, based primarily on the processing of agricultural products, and consisting of a few large state enterprises, hundreds of medium-sized private firms, and thousands of small-scale informal operations. Large-scale enterprises were dedicated mainly to the processing of sugar, milk, and hides and skins. Overall manufacturing output declined during 1980s as a result of inefficient state enterprises failing under market conditions. Manufacturing activity was further curtailed by civil war and collapse of the Somali state. By 1990 manufacturing ceased to play a significant role in economy and is currently about 5 percent of GDP.

At 0.3 percent of the GDP in 1988, mining's contribution to the economy was negligible, despite substantial deposits of gypsuman hydrite, quartz and piezoquartz, uranium, and iron ore. Gold deposits are suspected but not confirmed.

SERVICES

In the south of the country banking is re-emerging in the form of private ventures. The Barakaat Bank of Somalia, for example, was established in Mogadishu in October 1996 by a group of small businessmen who also run a telephone company and postal and computer services. Similarly, the Somalia-Malaysian Commercial Bank was opened in Mogadishu in April 1997 by a group that also runs the Somali Telecommunications Service. In most other parts of the country financial services are provided by less formalized money-changers.

Somalis living outside the country are currently the most significant source of foreign investment. In Somaliland, a central bank has been established (Central Bank of Somaliland), but no other formal financial institutions exist. Informal facilitators typically charge 5–10 percent commission on transfers from abroad. In August 1999 the Central Bank of Puntland became operational in Boosaaso.

Somalia's retail trade, which was hit hard by the civil war, is supplied largely by the informal sector. Mogadishu's main market, Bakara, offers a wide range of consumer goods and weaponry. Tourism is non-existent.

INTERNATIONAL TRADE

Up-to-date reliable information on the international trade of Somalia is hard to discover, thus much of what is presented here is based on the structure before 1991. Somalia's foreign trade deficit, which was almost en-

tirely financed by foreign aid, increased to around US$300 million in 1987. The trade balance remained negative throughout 1980s and early 1990s. The last reliable reported figures were for 1990, when exports were US$130 million and imports US$360 million. Surprisingly, there has not been much material change in the decade since those statistics were released: estimates for 1998 were that exports were US$87 million and imports US$327 million. The main difference is that prior to 1991, the trade deficit was met by aid receipts, while currently it is covered by remittances from the Somali diaspora.

Export composition has remained largely unchanged, consisting of mainly agricultural raw materials and food products with livestock and bananas the principal items, followed by hides and skins, fish and fish products, and myrrh. The major destination for Somali exports is Saudi Arabia, with 57 percent, followed by the United Arab Emirates (15 percent), Italy (12 percent), and Yemen (8 percent) in 1997.

Somalia's principal imports are food, transportation equipment, heavy machinery, manufactured consumer goods, cement and building materials, fuels, iron and steel. Djibouti was the main supplier of imported goods in 1997 with 20 percent, followed by Kenya (11 percent), Belarus (11 percent), India (10 percent), Saudi Arabia (9 percent), and Brazil (9 percent).

MONEY

The Somali shilling is the currency issued by the government prior to 1991. It has depreciated sharply since then: in 1989 the rate was SH252 to US$1, and by 1999 the rate was SH2,600 to US$1. It is most surprising that the currency is still in circulation at all as, until 2000, there has been no government to enforce the currency as legal tender (the acceptance of the currency in making payments). U.S. dollars are widely used for anything other than small transactions.

Exchange rates: Somalia	
Somali shillings per US$1	
Nov 2000	11,000
Jan 1999	2,620
Nov 1997	7,500
Jan 1996	7,000
Jan 1995	5,000
Jul 1993	2,616

Note: The Republic of Somaliland, a self-declared independent country not recognized by any foreign government, issues its own currency, the Somaliland shilling.

SOURCE: CIA *World Factbook 2001* [ONLINE].

GDP per Capita (US$)

Country	1996	1997	1998	1999	2000
Somalia	600	N/A	600	600	600
United States	28,600	30,200	31,500	33,900	36,200
Dem. Rep. of Congo	400	N/A	710	710	600
Ethiopia	N/A	530	560	560	600

Note: Data are estimates.

SOURCE: *Handbook of the Nations*, 17th, 18th, 19th and 20th editions for 1996, 1997, 1998 and 1999 data; CIA *World Factbook 2001* [Online] for 2000 data.

The self-declared Republic of Somaliland started issuing its own currency, the Somaliland shilling (SoSh), in January 1995, which was set at SoSh80 to US$1.

POVERTY AND WEALTH

Without official data or coordinated collection and collation of available information, it is hard to give realistic indications of the situation. However, the **UN Development Program**'s 1994 Human Development Report ranked Somalia 165th out of 173 countries in terms of its Human Development Index, which combines income levels with educational attainments and life expectancy. According to the World Bank, health standards in Somalia before the 1991 were among the worst in the world. It was estimated that there was 1 doctor for every 20,000 people (in the United States it was 1 doctor for every 470 people), and 1 nurse for every 1,900 persons (in the United States it was 1 nurse for every 70 persons). Only 2 percent of births were attended by a health professional, whereas in the United States nearly 100 percent of births were so attended. In 1990 average life expectancy at birth was 46 years, the infant mortality was about 123 per 1,000 live births (in the United States it is 7 per 1,000). The adult literacy rate was 27 percent.

WORKING CONDITIONS

Despite a series of wage increases over the previous 3 years, in January 1990 salaries for the highest-grade public employees were still only SH8,000 (US$16) per month and the lowest grade received SH1,200 (US$2.40). Consequently all civil servants needed additional sources of income to meet their basic needs. In the absence of a central government, the civil service has ceased to function after 1991.

Subsequently the 75 percent of the population in the rural areas were engaged in a desperate struggle to survive. Those in the urban areas were better off, and the thugs involved in the looting and extortion that go hand-in-hand with clan fighting have enjoyed relatively high living standards, albeit accompanied by high risks.

COUNTRY HISTORY AND ECONOMIC DEVELOPMENT

1840. European colonization of the Horn of Africa begins, and the traditional area of the Somali people is divided among 5 states: the British Somaliland protectorate, Italian Somalia, French Somalia (present day Djibouti), the Ethiopian province of Ogaden, and northeastern Kenya.

1886. Britain declares a protectorate over northern Somalia.

1936. Italy establishes a colony in the southern region, Italian Somaliland.

1941. The Italian colony is captured by British forces and placed under military administration during World War II.

1950. Italian Somaliland becomes the UN Trust Territory of Somalia and is placed under Italian administration for a 10-year transitional period prior to independence.

1959. The Trust Territory's first general elections based on universal adult suffrage are held. The Somali Youth League (SYL) wins 83 of the 90 seats in the Legislative Assembly.

1960. British Somaliland becomes independent on 26 June. On 1 July the former Italian Somaliland unites with the former British Somaliland as the Somali Republic. A coalition government is formed by the SYL and the 2 leading northern parties, with Dr. Abd ar-Rashid Ali Shirmake, a leading SYL politician and member of the Darod clan, as the first prime minister.

1964. SYL secures majority seats in Assembly elections. However, a split in the party leads to appointment of a new Darod prime minister, Abd ar-Razak Hussein, leaving the party seriously divided.

1967. Shirmake is elected president and forms a government.

1969. Shirmake is assassinated in the course of factional violence; Major General Mohamed Siad Barre of the Supreme Revolutionary Council (SRC) becomes president.

1972. Mass literacy campaign is launched, leading to the adoption of Somali as the national language.

1974. Somalia joins Arab League.

1975. Land is **nationalized**: farmers receive holdings on 50-year renewable leases from the state.

1976. Under Soviet influence, the Somali Socialist Party is established. Siad Barre **restructures** the Western Somali Liberation Front (WSLF) and allows it to operate inside Ethiopia in an effort to claim Ethiopian territory.

1977. Somalia and the Soviet Union break off relations when the Soviet Union backs Ethiopia in the ongoing conflict between Somalia and Ethiopia. Somali forces retreat from Ethiopia, and Somalia seeks to align itself with Western countries.

1980. The United States is permitted to use air and naval facilities at Berbera.

1986. Siad Barre is re-elected president, but his regime is soon faced with unrest in the northeast and northwest of the country.

1989. Forces opposed to Barre form the United Somali Congress (USC) in exile, in Rome, Italy. The USC military wing, headed by Gen. Mohamed Farah Aideed, sets up base in Ethiopia. Siad Barre announces that opposition parties can contest elections scheduled before the end of 1990 and that he would relinquish power.

1990. After an insurgency in the northwest, the USC captures Mogadishu. Siad Barre flees with the remnants of his army and the USC attempt to take power, but the country descends into clan-based civil war. The self-declared "Republic of Somaliland" declares independence.

1991. A UN force led by the United States tries to establish peace in Mogadishu.

1994. United States withdraws troops after a gunbattle with Somali gunmen leaves hundreds dead or wounded.

1995. The United Nations withdraws from Somalia. General Aideed is elected president by his USC faction but is not recognized by anyone else. Somaliland introduces its own currency.

1996. Aideed is killed by cross-fire during a skirmish. Leadership of USC passes to Aideed's son, Hussein Mohamed Aideed.

1997. Autonomy is declared for the northeastern province of Puntland.

2000. Delegates (excluding any official representatives form Somaliland and Puntland) meet in Djibouti, form a National Transitional Assembly, and elect Abdulkasim Sala Hassan as president, but clan-based fighting continues in Mogadishu.

FUTURE TRENDS

Economic progress in Somalia depends on the re-establishment of peace, security, and stability. Otherwise there will be no significant investment, qualified and talented Somalis will continue to make their lives elsewhere, and the bulk of the population will continue in a wretched struggle for survival.

There are some international observers who argue that the relatively stable areas of Somaliland and Puntland in the north should be allowed to secede and receive recognition from the international community so that they can receive aid and begin to make steady progress. There is great opposition to this move, however, in the south, and it seems that such acts will only be internationally acceptable if they are agreed to by all parties (as with the secession of Eritrea from Ethiopia). The priority of the new government will be to establish its authority in the south, and the autonomy of Somaliland and Puntland will be allowed to continue in the immediate future. But the future of Somaliland and Puntland in the new Somalia will have to be addressed at some stage.

Despite the creation of a new army, it will be immensely difficult for the new government of President Hassan to establish law and order in the face of hostility from the clan-based militias, who have declared that they do not recognize the new government. The militias cannot be crushed by force, and some place must be found for them in the new order in Somalia if peace is to be established. As of 2001 the country remains in a state of terrible disorder.

DEPENDENCIES

Somalia has no territories or colonies.

BIBLIOGRAPHY

Cousin, Tracey L. "Somalia: The Fallen Country." *ICE Case Studies.* <http://www.american.edu/projects/mandala/TED/ice/somwar.htm>. Accessed September 2001.

Economist Intelligence Unit. *Country Profile: Somalia.* London: Economist Intelligence Unit, 2001.

Hodd, M. "Somalia." *The Economies of Africa.* Aldershot: Dartmouth, 1991.

Samatar, S. S. *Somalia: A Nation in Turmoil.* Manchester: Minority Rights Group International, 1995.

U.S. Central Intelligence Agency. *World Factbook 2000.* <http://www.odci.gov/cia/publications/factbook/index.html>. Accessed August 2001.

U.S. Department of State. *Background Notes: Somalia, July 1998.* <http://www.state.gov/www/background_notes/somalia_0798_bgn.html>. Accessed September 2001.

—Allan C. K. Mukungu

SOUTH AFRICA

Republic of South Africa
Republiek van Suid-Afrika

CAPITAL: Pretoria (administrative); Cape Town (legislative); Bloemfontein (judicial).

MONETARY UNIT: South African rand. One rand equals 100 cents. There are coins of 1, 2, 5, 10, 20, and 50 cents and 1 rand. There are notes of 2, 5, 10, 20, 50, 100, and 200 rand.

CHIEF EXPORTS: Gold, diamonds, other metals and minerals, machinery, equipment.

CHIEF IMPORTS: Machinery, foodstuffs and equipment, chemicals, petroleum products, scientific instruments.

GROSS DOMESTIC PRODUCT: US$369 billion (purchasing power parity, 2000 est.).

BALANCE OF TRADE: **Exports:** US$30.8 billion (f.o.b., 2000 est.). **Imports:** US$27.6 billion (f.o.b., 2000 est.).

COUNTRY OVERVIEW

LOCATION AND SIZE. South Africa is situated at the southern tip of the continent of Africa. Ranging from west to east across its northern border are the neighboring countries of Namibia, Botswana, and Zimbabwe; Mozambique lies to the east, as does the small nation of Swaziland, which is nearly encircled by South Africa. Another small nation, Lesotho, lies entirely within the borders of South Africa, in the east central region. Total land borders measure 4,750 kilometers (2,952 miles). South Africa has a coastline of 2,954 kilometers (1,836 miles), with the cold Atlantic Ocean on the west coast and the Indian Ocean on the east coast. The area of the Republic of South Africa is approximately 1,219,912 square kilometers (471,008 square miles), making it slightly less than twice the size of the state of Texas, or slightly bigger then Holland, Belgium, Italy, France, and Germany combined. The capital of Pretoria is located in the northeast central area of the country. Other major cities include Cape Town, Port Elizabeth, and Durban on the coast, and Johannesburg, Soweto, and Bloemfontein in the interior of the country.

POPULATION. The last official census taken in South Africa in 1996 revealed a population 40,582,573 people. In 2001, estimates are that the population of South Africa has grown to 43,586,097. The population of South Africa can be divided into the following main racial groups: Africans (blacks), whites, coloreds (mixed-race descendants of early white settlers and indigenous people), and Asians. The general indication is that the proportion of Africans has slowly been increasing and the proportion of whites decreasing. The proportion of Asians and coloreds has remained quite constant. In 1996, Africans made up 76.6 percent of the population, whites made up 10.9 percent, coloreds 8.9 percent, and Asians 2.6 percent; the remaining 0.9 percent represented a variety of races.

The population growth rate for the entire population is a very low 0.26 percent. The birth rate in South Africa was estimated at 21.12 per 1,000 people in 2001, and the birth rate was estimated at 16.77 per 1,000 people. It is likely that the fertility and mortality figures could change due to the HIV/AIDS epidemic. The spread of HIV/AIDS in South Africa was very rapid in the 1990s. United Nations (UN) estimates indicate that currently 1 in 8 adult South Africans is infected with HIV. The epidemic has exacted tremendous social and economic costs. By affecting the population's most productive age group, it hampers the labor supply.

About 64 percent of the South African people live in urban centers, and that number is expected to grow because more people move to urban areas every year. The migration rate creates increasing demands on municipal services such as sanitation, water provision, safety, security, as well as schools, hospitals, and recreational facilities.

The population of South Africa is young, with 32 percent of people between the age of 0 and 14, 63 percent between 15 and 64, and only 5 percent over the age of

65. Life expectancy is fairly low, at 48.09 years for the entire population, 47.64 for males and 48.56 for females.

OVERVIEW OF ECONOMY

Emerging from a long period when it was a pariah nation because of its racial policies, South Africa is an attractive emerging economy that is both modern and diversified. Paradoxically, the country still exhibits many of the characteristics of a less developed nation, including a distorted distribution of wealth and a thriving **informal sector** economy whose interactions are outside the law. The agricultural, industrial, and service sectors are well developed, however, and government plans to improve services and economic access to the poor and

dispossessed offer the promise of modernizing the lagging elements of the economy.

The dominant forces which shaped South Africa's economy in the modern era exhibited themselves in 8 main periods. From 1910 to 1922, British influence dominated in economic and political terms, and a racially-segregated community was structured. When economic nationalism was born from 1922 to 1933, white mineworkers and farmers tried to establish a **welfare state** in South Africa. Between 1933 and 1948 English political power dominated again, and industrialization in South Africa occurred with less government interference. From 1948 to 1960 was the period of Afrikaner ascendancy (Afrikaners were the descendants of the original Dutch and German settlers). Between 1960 and 1973, black urbanization became important as a strong social force, and attempts were made to impart further institutional force to apartheid (the nation's official policy of racial segregation) via the homeland policies of President Verwoerd. The sixth period, between 1973 and 1984, was characterized by industrialization and the realization that the racial policy was economically damaging to the country. The seventh period stretches from 1984 to 1994, and can be seen as a period of transition during which economic growth decreased, mainly due to economic **sanctions** placed on South Africa by many nations. The eighth period started when apartheid ended and a democratic election took place in April 1994. The new government elected at this time initiated economic reforms intended to establish South Africa as a dynamic and more internationally competitive economy.

The free elections of 1994 became possible thanks to changes that had been occurring for years, as the government slowly removed many of the barriers to black political and economic participation. A new constitution, approved in 1993, followed by a plea by African National Congress (ANC) president Nelson Mandela (the nation's foremost black political leader) for foreign nations to lift sanctions led to a pledge of US$850 million in economic aid for South Africa by the International Monetary Fund (IMF). International financing sources saw the IMF funding as a signal to international investors that South Africa was a safe place in which to invest. International investment bankers and large Wall Street investment companies began trading with South Africa, thus opening the way to the current economic era.

The development of the South African economy has seen a long-term transfer from production based on agriculture to production based on industries. Once this transition had been made there was a period of sustained accumulation of physical and human capital. Consumers' spending patterns changed from spending on basic items and essential goods to spending on diverse manufactured and luxury items.

The nation's geography and topography have a significant influence on the country's economic development. The fact that South Africa has vast mineral resources is one of the reasons for its economic survival. In many cases, the country possesses large percentages of the world's known reserves of certain minerals, for example 88 percent of platinum group metals, 83 percent of manganese, and 72 percent of chromium reserves.

Since its early history, South Africa was shaped by its location on major global trade routes. In fact the country's oldest city, Cape Town, grew from a catering station for passing ships, established almost 350 years ago by the Dutch East India Company. Given that relationships between South Africa and other African countries have improved, the country's location on the African continent has earned it the title, "Gateway to Africa." South Africa has a rich variety of natural assets, making it an important **eco-tourist** destination. The wide variety of habitats accommodate numerous animal species.

South Africa has vast farmlands and climatic conditions that are ideal for agricultural activities. Even though South Africa has an erratic climate, its relatively large supply of arable land and modern methods employed in commercial agriculture are major reasons why it is largely self-sufficient in food supply.

Despite many good economic indicators in South Africa, though, the crime rate has risen to unacceptable levels. Particularly the high occurrence of violent crimes has led to the widespread belief that the police, judicial system, and correctional services are unable to cope with the problem. Large-scale **black-market** activities further fuel the crime wave in South Africa. Affirmative action, high taxes, and the rising crime rate have contributed to a renewed skills drain as many highly trained workers leave the country, a movement of workers the government needs to stop in order to preserve and develop the tax base. The loss of economically active persons in professional, technical, and managerial positions is particularly discomforting. Moreover, in South Africa, AIDS is a fast growing problem. More than 3.2 million South Africans are infected and living with the disease, with an estimated 1,500 infections taking place everyday. This health crisis is slowing South Africa's economic development because it decreases the number of people who can work.

POLITICS, GOVERNMENT, AND TAXATION

The political system of South Africa was reshaped following the 1994 elections. The African National Congress (ANC), which won the elections, governed under an interim constitution with the Inkatha Freedom Party (IFP) in what was known as the Government of National Unity (GNU). The GNU created a new constitution, which was signed into law by President Nelson Mandela on 3 February 1997. Under the new constitution, the South African Parliament has 2 houses, a National Assembly and a National Council of Provinces. The National Assembly has 400 members who are elected under a system of "list **proportional representation**." Voters cast their ballot for a party, which in turn selects the actual members. The National Council of Provinces has 90 members, 10 each from the 9 provinces. Of the 10 delegates from each province, 6 are permanent and 4 are rotating.

The executive president is selected by the ruling party in the National Assembly. The president then selects a cabinet of 28 ministers who must be approved by the National Assembly. The judicial system is topped by a constitutional court and a supreme court of appeals, which rule on constitutional and nonconstitutional matters, respectively. The 1997 constitution provides for a bill of rights which protects the basic human rights of all South African citizens. Because of the high crime rate the general feeling in South Africa is that the legal/court system is insufficient. This belief causes economic instability, which discourages foreign investors from investing in the country. Due to low long-term foreign investments, the growth of the South African economy has slowed.

South Africa has many political parties but is dominated by just a few. In the 1999 elections, the African National Congress gained the vast majority of the seats in parliament, with 266. The ANC formed a coalition with the Inkatha Freedom Party, which gained 34 votes. The Democratic Party (DP), with its 38 seats, and the New National Party, with its 28 seats, formed an opposition coalition called the Democratic Alliance. In 1999 the ANC's Thabo Mbeki was elected president.

As the ruling and most powerful party in South Africa, the ANC has had to balance a number of difficult challenges in managing the economy. On the one hand, the ANC wished to honor the alliance it made with the South African Communist Party (SACP) and labor federation COSATO for the purposes of the 1994 election. This alliance would imply that government policies will be characterized by **Marxist** tendencies, favoring the **nationalization** of industry, collective ownership of land, equalization of after-tax income, and direct intervention in the economy. However, the realities of trying to rule over a modern economy while at the same time addressing the problems of decades of racial inequity have pushed the ANC in other directions. The ANC has since dropped its commitment to nationalizing industries and has in fact **privatized** a number of state-owned firms. Reflecting its still growing commitment to a free market economy, the ANC has committed itself to maintaining

fiscal discipline, an anti-inflationary **monetary policy**, and a stable **exchange rate**, and the relaxation of exchange controls. The ANC also hopes to lower import **tariffs**, to expand tax incentives, and to privatize some **public sector** assets. Perhaps the more pressing of the jobs before the government, however, are the dual tasks of providing for the nation's many impoverished or economically disadvantaged people and dealing with the growing problem of violence and corruption.

The ANC government supports an open economy and has attempted to enter into a variety of trade agreements to ease international trade. The openness of the economy makes the country highly dependent on events in the outside world. This fact was clearly illustrated by the Asian economic crisis and by the increased price of oil after 1999; both events affected the South African economy negatively.

The government **levies** a variety of taxes, which together amounted to 24.1 percent of the GDP in 2000–01. The largest share (43 percent) of tax revenues come from individuals, who pay a progressive **income tax** that ranges from 18 to 42 percent. Corporate taxes contributed 10 percent of the total. **Indirect taxes**, such as customs and excise **duties**, a **value-added tax**, a fuel levy, and stamp duties and fees, account for 40 percent of revenues. The government has committed itself to lowering the tax burden on individuals in the coming years.

INFRASTRUCTURE, POWER, AND COMMUNICATIONS

Compared to the rest of Africa, South Africa has a good **infrastructure**, including a highly developed network of some 358,596 kilometers (222,831 miles) of roads (only 17 percent of which are paved, however) and 21,431 kilometers (13,317 miles) of rail track. There are a number of international and national airports; a highly developed system of bulk water supply; a power supply **parastatal**, ESCOM, that supplies

Communications

Country	Newspapers	Radios	TV Sets[a]	Cable subscribers[a]	Mobile Phones[a]	Fax Machines[a]	Personal Computers[a]	Internet Hosts[b]	Internet Users[b]
	1996	1997	1998	1998	1998	1998	1998	1999	1999
South Africa	32	317	125	N/A	56	3.5	47.4	33.36	1,820
United States	215	2,146	847	244.3	256	78.4	458.6	1,508.77	74,100
Nigeria	24	223	66	N/A	0	N/A	5.7	0.00	100
Namibia	19	144	37	N/A	12	N/A	18.6	11.73	6

[a]Data are from International Telecommunication Union, *World Telecommunication Development Report 1999* and are per 1,000 people.
[b]Data are from the Internet Software Consortium (http://www.isc.org) and are per 10,000 people.
SOURCE: World Bank. *World Development Indicators 2000.*

roughly half of Africa's electricity at rates that are among the cheapest in the world; a telephone utility company, TELKOM, that provides services for about 4 million main telephones and network links for one of the fastest growing cellular telephone industries in the world; and broadcasting services. However, the infrastructure in the areas occupied by the black majority is generally undeveloped or badly maintained. The Spatial Development Initiative (SDI) program provides the **private sector** with unique opportunities to exploit the potential of under-utilized areas by identifying public-private partnerships in bulk and municipal infrastructure projects.

South Africa's modern and extensive transport system plays a very important role in the national economies of several other African states. A number of countries in Southern Africa use the South African transport infrastructure to trade. Private motorcars are an important mode of personal travel. In 1998, there were some 6.55 million registered motor vehicles, of which more than 3.8 million were motorcars. Minibus-taxis provide a vital service to nearly 50 percent of South Africa's commuters. More than 480 taxi associations are operating throughout the country. SPOOR-NET, the largest railroad operator in Southern Africa, has 3,500 locomotives and 124,000 wagons. There are 30 international airports, where the necessary facilities and services exist to accommodate international flights. About 15 million passengers use these airports every year. SAA, Com Air, Sun Air, SA Express, and SA Air Link operate scheduled international air services within Africa and to Europe, Latin America, and the Middle and Far East.

Telecommunications, the lifeline of modern business and industry, is one of the fastest growing industries in South Africa. With a growth rate of 45 percent prompted largely by the introduction of cellular telephones and the partial privatization of TELKOM, this sector is a vital component in the strategy to modernize and increase international competitiveness.

South Africa has approximately 5.3 million installed telephones and 4.3 million installed exchange lines. This figure represents 39 percent of the total lines installed in Africa. By November 1998, more than 1.5 million South Africans were using the Internet with service providers increasing their customer base by 10 percent a month. A 1-channeled television service was introduced on 5 January 1976. Currently, the South African Broadcast Corporation (SABC) offers 3 television channels in 11 languages. It also operates 2 pay-television channels, broadcasting into Africa by satellite. About 14 million adults watch SABC television daily, making South Africa the country with by far the largest television audience on the continent.

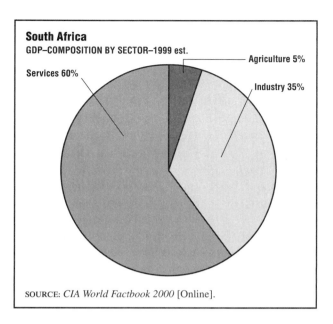

South Africa
GDP–COMPOSITION BY SECTOR–1999 est.

Services 60%
Agriculture 5%
Industry 35%

SOURCE: *CIA World Factbook 2000* [Online].

ECONOMIC SECTORS

In the primary sector South Africa's abundant natural resources, especially in the mining and agriculture-based categories, provide noteworthy opportunities for companies to add value prior to export. Export earnings associated with the **value added** to primary products represented 29 percent of total exports in 1995, as compared to 21 percent in 1988, indicating that South African companies are learning to extract more economic value from their natural resources. On average, the contribution of the primary sector to the GDP grew at less than 1 percent per year from 1960 to 1985, and at a negative rate

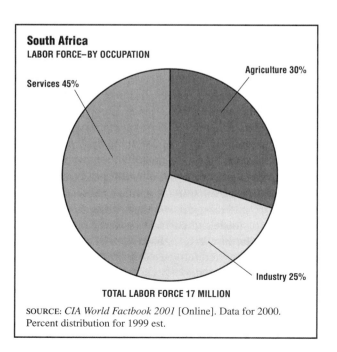

South Africa
LABOR FORCE–BY OCCUPATION

Services 45%
Agriculture 30%
Industry 25%

TOTAL LABOR FORCE 17 MILLION

SOURCE: *CIA World Factbook 2001* [Online]. Data for 2000. Percent distribution for 1999 est.

after 1980. However, forecast assumptions yield a positive growth rate for the next 10 years. This sector (agriculture, forestry, fishing, mining, and quarrying) contributed 12 percent to the GDP in 1997.

The secondary sector had stronger growth than the primary sector in the period after 1960. However, due to economic adversity during the struggle against apartheid, the average annual growth rate was only 0.5 percent. This sector (manufacturing electricity, gas, water, and construction) contributed 31 percent to GDP in 1997. Although the tertiary sector showed slower growth than the primary and secondary sectors in the entire period since 1960, its growth was higher after 1980, propped up by government spending. It is expected that this sector will grow at an average rate of about 3.0 percent per year to 2005.

The tertiary sector (trade, catering, accommodation, transport, storage, and communications) is expected to grow at roughly the same rate. The lackluster domestic demand should be countered by the rapidly expanding tourist industry. Rising tourism should boost passenger transport, while technological improvements should continue providing impetus to the communications industry.

Financial and business services have been growing at above-average rates and should continue to do so as the traditional and informal sectors become more formalized and make use of these services. Community and social services and general government services are unlikely to show high real growth, due to the expected tight fiscal situation.

AGRICULTURE

In monetary terms, agriculture's share of the economy has long since been outstripped by those of the mining and secondary industries. In 1960, agriculture contributed 11.1 percent of the GDP, down from about 20 percent in the 1930s. By 1999, however, agriculture's share of the GDP had dropped to 5 percent. Despite the farming industry's declining share of the GDP, it remains vital to the economy, development, and stability of the Southern African region. The various sectors of the industry employ approximately 1 million people, or 30 percent of the workforce.

Agriculture in South Africa has changed radically in recent years. Formerly, it was a highly regulated sector with **subsidies** and financial concessions available to farmers. But farming has been **deregulated** since the 1980s, and the agricultural sector is now expected to respond to free market conditions. Farmers seek the most competitive suppliers and purchasers and are increasingly using the South African Futures Exchange to exchange futures contracts and hedge prices for their products.

South Africa has what is known as a dual agricultural economy. On the one hand, there is a well-developed commercial sector; on the other hand, the majority of people engaged in agriculture are involved in subsistence-oriented practices in rural areas. In the predominantly white-controlled commercial sector, applied research and improved farm management have nearly doubled agricultural production during the past 30 years. Currently, South Africa is not only self sufficient in virtually all major agricultural products but in a normal year is also a net food exporter, making it 1 of 6 countries in the world capable of exporting food on a regular basis. Because South Africa's summer harvest season coincides with winter in the Northern Hemisphere, the country is well positioned to supply agricultural goods to a number of wealthy countries in the more developed world.

South Africa has developed 1 of the largest man-made forestry resources in the world. These plantations cover more than 1.4 million hectares with exports accounting for 35 percent of total **turnover** of forestry products. The 2 private pulp and paper manufacturers rank among the largest companies of their kind in the Southern hemisphere.

About 13 percent of South Africa's surface area can be use for crop production. Some 1.3 million hectares are under irrigation. The most important factor limiting agricultural production is the availability of water. Rainfall is distributed unevenly across the country. Almost 50 percent of South Africa's water is used for agricultural purposes.

The largest area of farmland is planted in maize, followed by wheat and, on a lesser scale, sugar cane and sunflowers. About 15,000 farmers produce maize, mainly in the northwest, the northwestern, northern, and eastern Free State, the Mpumalanga Highveld and KwaZulu-Natal midlands. Local consumption of maize amounts to approximately 6.5 million tons, and surplus maize is usually exported. Wheat is produced in the winter rainfall areas of the western Cape and the eastern parts of the Free State. The 1998–99 season yielded 1.5 million tons. Barley is produced mainly on the southern coastal plains of the western Cape, accounting for more than 98 percent of locally produced barley. The 1998–99 season yielded 215,100 tons. Sorghum is cultivated mostly in the drier parts of the summer rainfall areas. Groundnuts are grown in the northern province, Mpumalanga, the northern Free State, and the northwest.

South Africa is the world's tenth largest producer of sunflower seeds with an annual harvest of between 186,300 and 780,000 tons. South Africa is also the world's tenth largest sugar producer. The bulk of the sugar crop is cultivated on the frost-free coastal areas and the KwaZulu-Natal midlands. However, about 10 percent is grown under irrigation in the southern parts of

Mpumalanga. Deciduous fruit trees are grown mainly in the western Cape, as well as in the Langkloof Valley in the eastern Cape. This industry's export earnings represent 21 percent of the country's total earnings from agricultural exports.

South Africa's wine and spirits industry is one of the most developed in the world. About 4,500 grape producers had 103,300 hectares of land under cultivation, making South Africa the 20th largest wine growing area in the world. The average size of the country's harvest is around 900 million liters, ranking it seventh in the world. Exports of South African wine grew from 23 million liters in 1991, to 50 million liters in 1994, and to 100 million liters in 1998. The industry provides income to 3,000 cooperative cellar staff and 45,000 farm workers.

Citrus production is largely limited to the irrigated areas of the northern province, Mpumalanga, the eastern and western Cape and KwaZulu-Natal. Pineapples are grown in the eastern Cape and northern KwaZulu-Natal. Other subtropical crops such as avocados, mangos, bananas, litchis, guavas, pawpaws, grenadillas, and macadamia and pecan nuts are produced mainly in Mpumalanga and the northern province. About 40 percent of the country's potato crop is grown in the higher-lying areas of the Free State and Mpumalanga. About two-thirds of the country's total potato crop is produced under irrigation. In terms of gross income to the grower—apart from potatoes—tomatoes, onions, green mealies, and sweet corn are probably the most important crops.

Cotton, produced mainly in the northern province, constitutes 74 percent of the natural fiber and 42 percent of all fiber processed in South Africa. About 75 percent of local production is harvested by hand. Virginia tobacco is produced mainly in Mpumalanga and the northern province. There are more than 1,000 growers in the country who produce an annual average of 33 million kilograms on about 24,000 hectares of land. The crop represents 173 different grades of Virginia and 5 different grades of Oriental tobacco.

Rooibos tea is an indigenous herbal beverage produced mainly in the Cederberg area of the western Cape. There are some 280 producers, and about 580 tons of tea are exported annually. Ornamental plants are produced throughout the country. They include nursery plants, cut flowers, and potted plants. The industry creates jobs for about 15,000 people. Proteas are the country's top export flowers.

Livestock is farmed in most parts of South Africa, though the numbers vary according to climatic conditions. The 1998 estimates for head of cattle and sheep are 13.8 million and 29.3 million, respectively. South Africa normally produces 85 percent of its meat requirements while 15 percent is imported from Namibia, Botswana,

and Swaziland. In 1998, 1.7 million heads of cattle were slaughtered, and the gross value of the red meat industry was estimated to be about R4,954 million. Most sheep are fine-wooled Merinos (50 percent). The Dorper, a highly productive, locally-developed mutton breed for arid regions, and the Merino account for most of South Africa's mutton production. Marketing of wool is free of any intervention. The indigenous meat-producing Boer goat accounts for about 40 percent of all goats, and the angora goat, used for mohair production, for the remaining 60 percent. South Africa has about 3,500 angora farmers. Compared with the extensive cattle and sheep industries, the poultry and pig industries are more intensive and are located on farms near metropolitan areas. The predominant pig breeds are the South African landrace and the large white. South Africa accounts for 80 percent of world sales of ostrich products, including leather, meat, and feathers. In October 1997, Parliament approved legislation to allow the export of breeding ostriches and fertile eggs, which was previously forbidden. Dairy farming also occurs throughout South Africa.

The volume of agricultural production has been erratic in the last decade primarily because of severe droughts. The country is, however, still self-sufficient as far as most primary foods are concerned, with the exception of wheat, oilseeds, rice, tea, and coffee.

INDUSTRY

In 1999, industry provided approximately 30 percent of the GDP and employed 25 percent of the workforce.

MINING. South Africa has a natural competitive advantage in both mining and adding value to mined products thanks to its immense concentrations of reserves of important minerals, its low cost coal-based electricity supply, its excellent infrastructure, developed skills and technology base, and the entrepreneurial abilities of its people. South Africa's mineral wealth is found in its diverse and extensive geological formations. The unique Witwatersrand Basin contains a considerable portion of the world's gold reserves, as well as uranium, silver, pyrite, and osmiridium. It also yields some 98 percent of South Africa's gold output. The Bushveld Complex, a sill-like geological feature occupying about 50,000 square kilometers (19,300 square miles), contains more than half of the world's chrome ore and platinum-group metals (PGMs). It also contains vanadium, iron, titanium, copper, nickel, and fluorspar. South Africa holds the world's largest reserves of ores of manganese (possessing 80 percent of the total world reserves), chromium (68 percent), PGMs (56 percent), vanadium (45 percent), gold (39 percent), and alumino-silicates (37 percent). It is also the leading holder of reserves of ores of vermiculite, andalusite, zirconium, titanium, antimony, fluorspar, and phosphate rock.

As a result of this large reserve base, South Africa is the world's leading producer of PGMs, vanadium, and vermiculite, contributing about 50 percent of the world's total of these commodities. South Africa is also the largest world supplier of alumino-silicates, chrome ore, ferrochromium, and gold, for which its contribution ranges between 20 and 60 percent.

The domestic market for most of these minerals is relatively small, so South Africa's mineral industry is strongly export-oriented. For example, South Africa provides 96 percent of world exports of vermiculite, 76 percent of vanadium, 55 percent of alumino-silicates, 53 percent of ferrochromium, 47 percent of PGMs, 41 percent of chrome ore, and 27 percent of manganese ore and ferro-manganese. For these commodities, as well as for gold, it is also the world's largest exporter. The more notable imports into South Africa in 1997 were diamonds, precious metals, alumina, certain ferro-alloys, nickel, coking coal, phosphate rock, sulphur, magnesite, and magnesia. With some gold mines exceeding a depth of 3,000 meters (10,000 feet), the South African mining industry has become a world leader in developing deep-level mining technology.

In 1997, some 695 mines and quarries employed about 552,000 people, many of whom are workers from neighboring countries, representing about 10.5 percent of all workers in the non-agricultural, formal sectors of the economy. More than R18.1 million was paid out in wages. Over the past 5 years, South Africa's goldmines have been plagued by low productivity, diminishing reserves in some mines, and labor unrest. More than 25,000 workers have lost their jobs through retrenchments in the industry since 1987. On 8 July 1999, the gold price slumped to US$257.20 per ounce, the lowest in 20 years. During 1998, 370 miners were killed, and during 1997–98, 6,064 were injured in mine accidents. Through the Rand Mutual Assurance Company, the mining industry provides care and compensation in the case of accidents. The medical infrastructure of the industry includes group hospitals in all the mining areas, as well as clinics and stations on mines for emergency treatment. The Mine Health and Safety Act of 1996 was put into operation on 15 January 1997 to protect mine workers.

ENERGY. The energy sector is critical to the South African economy, contributing about 15 percent of GDP and employing about 250,000 people. South Africa's energy resource base is dominated by coal. Many of the deposits can be exploited at extremely favorable costs, and as a result, a large coal-mining industry has developed. In fact, South Africa ranks as the world's fifth largest coal producer. In addition to the extensive use of coal in the domestic economy, large amounts are exported. South Africa is the second largest exporter of steam coal. South Africa produces 5,000 to 1 million tons of coal per month.

About 55 percent of South African coal-mining is done underground. The coal-mining industry is highly concentrated, with 3 companies, namely Ingwe, Amcoal, and Sasol, accounting for 80 percent of local production.

South Africa has 1 nuclear power station in operation. The Eskom nuclear power station, Koeberg, is located in the western Cape and operates 2 reactors with a capacity of 1,840 megawatts. Nuclear power contributed 6.87 percent of the country's electricity supply in 1999; the remainder was supplied by fossil fuels, both coal and petroleum.

South Africa consumed some 21 billion liters of liquid fuels in 1998. About 36 percent of the demand is met by synthetic fuels (synfuels) produced locally, largely from coal and a small amount from natural gas. The rest is met by products refined locally from imported crude oil. Sasol is the largest petrochemical corporation in the country. Apart from limited gas and oil reserves in the Mossel Bay area, the country does not have significant commercially exploitable gas or crude oil reserves. In addition to coal gas and liquid petroleum gas, South Africa produces about 1,237,000 tons of gas and 250,000 tons of condensate liquid fuels.

South Africa, which supplies two-thirds of Africa's electricity, is one of the 4 cheapest electricity producers in the world. About 92 percent of South African electricity is produced from coal, with generation dominated by the utility Eskom. It is the world's fifth largest electricity utility, with an installed generating capacity of about 39,870 MW. All told, South Africa produced 186.903 billion kilowatt hours (kWh) of electricity in 1999.

MANUFACTURING. Exports of manufactured goods experienced growth between 1988 and 1995. The driving forces behind this growth included the introduction of the General Export Incentive Scheme (GEIS) and consecutive phases of the motor industry development scheme; the real depreciation of the Rand; excess manufacturing capacity as a result of **recessionary** conditions forced on the domestic markets after 1985; and the opening up of international markets as sanctions subsided from the early 1990s. The average annual growth rates in the real output of the manufacturing subgroups from 1995 to 2005 are expected to vary between 0.5 percent in the cases of tobacco products and leather products to 7.5 percent in the case of plastic products. Other industries with good growth potential are industrial chemicals, rubber products, and paper.

The basic iron and steel industry is relatively important within South African manufacturing. There are unprecedented opportunities for growth and prosperity in the global steel industry across the globe, the common thread being privatization and free market focus. The already privatized South African steel industry will have to position itself to compete in the global steel economy and to provide goods for the increasingly segmented market. Possibilities are links with overseas producers and greater specialization, which will bring about greater exports as well as imports of steel products.

SERVICES

TOURISM. In the context of the country's economic and political transformation, tourism has been accepted by the government, business, and labor as one of the key drivers for job growth, wealth creation, and economic empowerment. After years of isolation, South Africa has emerged as a highly attractive tourist destination.

There are some major strengths operating in South Africa's favor which can facilitate further growth in tourism. Among the top tourist attractions are Victoria and Alfred Waterfront in Cape Town, Cape Point, Table Mountain, the wine region in the western Cape, and numerous other attractions. South Africa attracts more tourists than any other country in Africa. The country's scenic beauty and wildlife remain the biggest attractions for international tourists. Tourism is the fourth biggest industry in South Africa, supporting some 1,200 hotels, 2,000 guesthouses, and 8,000 restaurants. Between January and August 1998, there were 871,414 foreign visitors to South Africa. During 1998, economic conditions, in particular the devalued rand, made South Africa one of the cheapest places in the world to visit.

According to a report released in September 1998 on the direct and indirect effect of tourism on South Africa's economy, the tourism industry provided jobs to more than 737,600 people. It was estimated that the number could increase to 1.25 million by the year 2010.

The fastest growing segment of tourism in South Africa is ecological tourism (eco-tourism), which includes nature photography, bird-watching, botanical studies, snorkeling, hiking, and mountain climbing. Village tourism is becoming increasingly popular, with tourists wanting to experience South Africa in the many rural villages across the country.

With tourism currently contributing approximately 5 percent of GDP against an international norm of between 8 and 9 percent, the potential for significant growth in international tourism and its contribution to GDP is immense.

FINANCIAL SERVICES. South Africa has a well-developed financial system. Legislation governing the financial sector has been streamlined to meet international norms and provides for the introduction of major foreign financial institutions into the local market. The banking industry in South Africa currently has 55 banks, including 12 branches of foreign banks, and 4 mutual banks are registered with the Office of the Registrar of Banks. Furthermore, 60 foreign banks have authorized representative offices in South Africa. Several major groups dominate the South African banking sector: ABSA Group Limited, Standard Bank Investment Corporation Limited, First National Bank Holdings Limited, and Nedcor Limited. These groups maintain extensive branch networks across all 9 provinces and together hold 70 percent of the total assets of the banking sector.

The major banks offer a wide range of services to both individual and corporate customers. A single relationship banking, with its emphasis on universal banking, instead of isolated services, has gained importance. Nevertheless, several banks specialize in providing merchant banking services, securities underwriting, or services in other niche areas.

On 31 December 1998, the 55 registered banking institutions collectively employed 123,272 workers. Their offices (including both branches and agencies) totaled 3,251, that is, approximately 1 office for every 13,000 inhabitants. If the 2,442 post offices through which the Postbank offers its services are included, banking services are provided at some 5,693 offices throughout the country, or 1 location for every 7,500 inhabitants.

Several new banks have been registered, and competition has intensified, both among banks and between banks and other financial service providers. As a result, the assets held in the banking sector have expanded rapidly, from R39 billion in 1980 to R654 billion in December 1998.

The Johannesburg Stock Exchange (JSE), formed in 1887 and a member of the Federation of International Stock Exchanges since 1963, is the tenth largest stock exchange in the world by **market capitalization**. The South African Futures Exchange (SAFEX), established in 1990, trades in **equity** futures contracts, options on equity futures, and a variety of other futures contracts.

The growing momentum in the field of public-private partnerships in project financing and the emergence of powerful black economic empowerment groups continue to drive innovation and efficiency in this sector.

Including the contributions of other services, the services industry provided 65 percent of the GDP in 1999 and employed 45 percent of the workforce.

INTERNATIONAL TRADE

South Africa's trade and industrial policy is moving away from a highly protected, inward looking economy towards an internationally competitive economy, capitalizing on its competitive and comparative advantages. For years, South Africa's ability to trade with the outside world was severely limited by the sanctions placed on

Trade (expressed in billions of US$): South Africa

	Exports	Imports
1975	8.719	8.226
1980	25.525	19.598
1985	16.293	11.319
1990	23.549	18.399
1995	27.860	30.555
1998	26.322	29.268

SOURCE: International Monetary Fund. *International Financial Statistics Yearbook 1999.*

the country by most developed countries as a punishment for South Africa's commitment to apartheid. With the end of apartheid in the early 1990s, international trade has expanded dramatically so that in 2000 international trade constituted 16 percent of the GDP.

South Africa's economy is still largely reliant on the export of primary and intermediate commodities to industrialized countries. However, manufactured goods account for about 70 percent of exports to Africa. Net gold exports are responsible for a large part of foreign exchange earnings. Earnings from this source, however, fluctuate with the shifting international gold price. Imports mainly consist of **capital goods**, raw materials, semi-manufactured goods (approximately 76 percent of total trade imports), and consumer commodities.

South Africa maintains formal trade relations with various countries by means of treaties, trade agreements, and membership in international trade institutions. The centerpiece of South Africa's foreign economic policy is the Southern African Development Community (SADC), comprising Angola, Botswana, the Democratic Republic of Congo (DRC), Lesotho, Malawi, Mauritius, Mozambique, Namibia, Seychelles, South Africa, Tanzania, Zambia, and Zimbabwe. The government's key policy objective is to strengthen trade and investment linkages between South Africa and the other SADC countries.

Trade with SADC countries increased dramatically during the period 1988 to 1997. At present, the ratio of South Africa's exports to imports to SADC countries stands at 6:1. Exports to the region are concentrated in high value-added sectors, such as minerals and base metals, chemicals, machinery, transport equipment, and food and beverages. The most important SADC purchaser of South African exports is Zimbabwe, followed by Mozambique, Zambia, Mauritius, Malawi, Angola, and Tanzania. Zimbabwe is also the largest source of imports, followed by Malawi, Angola, Zambia and Mozambique. The member states of the SADC are negotiating a Free Trade Agreement (FTA) to strengthen trade, investment, and industrial linkages within the region.

Europe is the biggest source of trade for South Africa. In fact, 7 out of 10 of South Africa's top trading partners are European countries. Britain is South Africa's largest single trading partner. British exports to South Africa were worth R14 billion in 1998 while South African exports to Britain totaled R22 billion. Trade between Germany and Africa rose in 1997: German exports to South Africa were valued at DM5.9 billion in 1997, while German imports from South Africa were up almost 16 percent to R9 billion in 1998. There has been a steady increase in bilateral trade between France and South Africa, and at the end of 1998, France was the fifth largest supplier of goods to South Africa. South African exports to France totaled more than R2 billion. Bilateral trade between South Africa and Switzerland is worth R6.384 billion a year. Almost 400 Swiss companies are represented in South Africa. Italy is one of the top 5 major trading partners of South Africa, with the 2-way trading relations amounting to R8 billion in 1997. In March 1999, South Africa concluded an historic trade agreement with the European Union (EU) that will result in the abolition of tariffs on more than 90 percent of trade between the 15 EU countries and South Africa within 12 years.

The United States is another of South Africa's largest trading partners. South Africa is a beneficiary of the U.S. Generalized System of Preferences (GSP), which grants duty-free treatment for more than 4,650 products. South Africa's exports to the United States increased from R5.2 billion in 1993 to R14.8 billion in 1998. South Africa also has important trading relations with Japan, South Korea, and countries in South America.

In 2000 South Africa enjoyed a **trade surplus** of US$3.2 billion on exports of US$30.8 billion and imports of US$27.6 billion.

MONEY

The South African rand was a very strong currency until the early 1980s. Due to political unrest the rand declined slowly but was controlled artificially by the government. After the first democratic elections in April

Exchange rates: South Africa

rand (R) per US$1	
Mar 2001	7.60
2000	6.93983
1999	6.10948
1998	5.52828
1997	4.60796
1996	4.29935

SOURCE: CIA *World Factbook 2001* [ONLINE].

1994, the value of the rand dropped dramatically. In 1996 the South African rand was valued at R4.30 per U.S. dollar, but by May 2001 the rand was valued at R7.90 per U.S. dollar. The very weak rand causes imports to South Africa to be very expensive and almost unaffordable. However, the devalued rand does make it far easier to export South African products, which seem a bargain to foreign buyers.

The South African financial sector is very modern and can be compared with the best banking systems in the world. The central bank in South Africa is the South African Reserve Bank. The South African Reserve Bank is responsible for monetary policy, and for ensuring that the South African money and banking system is sound, meets the requirements of the community, and keeps abreast of developments in international finance.

South Africa has one of the oldest stock exchanges in the world. The Johannesburg Stock Exchange (JSE) was established on 8 November 1887. The JSE provides a market where securities can be freely traded under a regulated procedure. It not only channels funds into the economy but also provides investors with returns on investments in the form of dividends. All buying and selling of stocks on the JSE is done via computer.

POVERTY AND WEALTH

Due to South Africa's history of apartheid, a period when blacks were oppressed both politically and economically, the country's poverty and wealth profile is highly skewed to favor the white population. According to a study conducted in 1995, whites in South Africa, with per capita income of US$32,076, made 11.8 times more per capita than blacks (who had a per capita income of US$2,717), 5.1 times more than people of mixed-race (with an income of US$6,278), and 2.5 times more than Asians (with an income of US$12,963). In fact, South Africa has one of the most unequal distributions of wealth and income in the world. Recent research indicates that 40 percent of the households with the lowest income in South Africa earn less than 6 percent of total income, while the 10 percent with the highest income earn more

Distribution of Income or Consumption by Percentage Share: South Africa	
Lowest 10%	1.1
Lowest 20%	2.9
Second 20%	5.5
Third 20%	9.2
Fourth 20%	17.7
Highest 20%	64.8
Highest 10%	45.9

Survey year: 1993–94
Note: This information refers to expenditure shares by percentiles of the population and is ranked by per capita expenditure.

SOURCE: *2000 World Development Indicators* [CD-ROM].

than half the total income. The average income of the top-earning 20 percent of the households is 45 times that of the bottom earning 20 percent.

The general population has high expectations of improvement in their quality of life, particularly concerning housing, education, healthcare, jobs and income. These expectations are the result of election promises by the ANC alliance, formalized in the so-called Reconstruction and Development Program (RDP). The RDP came into being as an ANC election document in the run-up to the 1994 election, and reflected the party's then dominant commitment to state intervention in the economy. According to the U.S. Department of State's *Background Notes: South Africa,* "The RDP was designed to create programs to improve the standard of living for the majority of the population by providing housing—a planned 1 million new homes in 5 years—basic services, education, and health care."

In 1996, as the government shifted to embrace free-market economic practices, it announced new plans to deal with poverty under a market-driven plan called *Growth, Employment and Redistribution: A Macroeconomic Strategy.* This plan took the a more market-based approach to economic improvement, using fiscal and trade policy to create jobs and lending less direct government aid to the impoverished.

WORKING CONDITIONS

South Africa has 17 million economically active people but a high unemployment rate of 30 percent in 2000. The unemployment problem is mainly related to structural factors, such as the high rate of population growth and the existence of large sectors of the economy that are poorly developed. The new government has pledged to reduce inequality in the job market by means of affirmative action in favor of non-whites, the disabled, and women. It has begun with a vigorous program of affirmative action in the public sector. A strong influx of

GDP per Capita (US$)					
Country	1975	1980	1985	1990	1998
South Africa	4,574	4,620	4,229	4,113	3,918
United States	19,364	21,529	23,200	25,363	29,683
Nigeria	301	314	230	258	256
Namibia	N/A	2,384	2,034	1,948	2,133

SOURCE: United Nations. *Human Development Report 2000; Trends in human development and per capita income.*

illegal aliens from neighboring countries, particularly since 1990, has added to the rapid growth rate of the domestic population and the high unemployment rate. According to news reports, the ranks of squatters and criminals have been swelled by illegal aliens.

Affirmative action policies, high tax rates, and the rising crime rate have all helped to drive more highly skilled workers out of the country. The net loss of economically active persons in professional, technical, and managerial positions is very disturbing. Exact figures are difficult to determine, however, because many South Africans leave the country permanently without stating it clearly.

Both governments elected since 1994 have taken steps to secure and protect the rights of workers, especially black workers, in the South African economy. Among the rights listed in the Bill of Rights in the 1996 constitution were provisions guaranteeing workers the right to fair labor practices, the right to collective bargaining, the right to strike, and other labor friendly practices. Since that time, the government has created a number of laws friendly to workers, including a Labor Relations Act (which sets parameters for workplace bargaining and entrenches the right to strike); the Basic Conditions of Employment Act (which prescribes the maximum number of hours in a work week, leave, and overtime pay provisions, etc.); the Employment Equity Act (which sets out to eliminate discrimination in the workplace on the basis of gender, race, or disability); and the Skills Development Act (which aims to improve the general skills level throughout industry).

According to the U.S. Department of State *Country Commercial Guide for FY2000: South Africa,* "In 1997 there were 3.4 million union members in South Africa, or nearly 35 percent of the economically active population" (with the latter using a lower figure of 9.8 million workers used by the International Labor Organization). "The largest labor federation, the 1.8 million-strong Congress of South African Trade Unions (COSATU), is in a formal alliance with the African National Congress (ANC) and the South African Communist Party (SACP)." Many union leaders play a prominent role in government, contributing to the generally labor friendly reputation of the government. Unions have used strike threats to persuade employers to pay higher wages, and unions are particularly strong in the mining and industrial sectors. However, the recent tendency of the government to favor free market solutions to economic problems has led to tensions with organized labor.

COUNTRY HISTORY AND ECONOMIC DEVELOPMENT

1652. The first Dutch settlement is established on the Cape of Good Hope by the Dutch East India Company.

In the coming decades, French Huguenots, the Dutch, and Germans establish settlements along the coast. Eventually, they go to war with indigenous peoples to establish their claims to the land.

1795–1803. First British occupation of the Cape, leading to tensions between the British and the Afrikaners, the name for the original European settlers in the area.

1806. Second British occupation of the Cape occurs.

1814. Holland cedes the Cape to Britain.

1836. Afrikaner farmers, known as Boers, undertake a "Great Trek" to establish settlements in the South African interior. They battle the native Zulus for control of the area. The Zulus retain control of some parts of the interior until 1879.

1847–49. British immigrants arrive in Natal, and soon sugar is grown in the area.

1852–54. The independent Boer Republics of Transvaal and Orange Free State are created, straining relations with the ruling British.

1869. Diamonds are discovered near Kimberley.

1880–81. The first Anglo-Boer War is fought between British troops and Afrikaner settlers (Boers).

1886. Gold is discovered in the Witwatersrand region of the Transvaal.

1887. Johannesburg Stock Exchange (JSE) is established

1899–1902. The second Anglo-Boer War breaks out, with the British gaining control of the Boer republics.

1910. The 2 republics and British colonies become the Union of South Africa, a self-governing dominion of the British Empire with Louis Botha as prime minister.

1912. Native blacks establish the South African Native National Congress (SANNC), which later becomes the African National Congress (ANC), to protest the creation of laws and practices based on color.

1927. Compulsory segregation is announced.

1930. White women get to vote.

1948. The victory of the National Party (NP) in all-white elections leads to the creation of a strict policy of white domination and racial separation known as "apartheid."

1950–52. Passage of strict racial laws.

1960s. Following protests in the town of Sharpeville that leave 69 black protestors dead and hundreds injured, the ANC and the Pan-African Congress (PAC) are banned and ANC leader Nelson Mandela is imprisoned in 1962 on charges of treason. From this time onward the ANC functions as an illegal but powerful op-position force for black rights in South Africa.

1961. The nation leaves the British Commonwealth and becomes the independent Republic of South Africa.

1984. Revisions to the constitution give colored and Asian people a limited role in the national government, but power remains in white hands.

1990. Following years of mounting black protest and increasing sanctions against South Africa because of apartheid, President F.W. De Klerk announces the un-conditional release of Nelson Mandela from prison and the legalization of the ANC, PAC, and other anti-apartheid groups.

1991. The so-called "pillars of apartheid"—the Group Areas Act, Land Acts, and Population Registration Act—are officially rescinded.

1994. First democratic elections take place in April under a new constitution. The ANC wins a majority in the legislature and elects Nelson Mandela as president.

1996. National Party pulls out of the Government of National Unity (GNU). First official census occurs in post-apartheid South Africa.

1999. In the country's second democratic elections the ANC increases its majority in the legislature and se-lects Thabo Mbeki as president.

FUTURE TRENDS

South Africa's GDP is expected to grow at a mod-est rate of 3.0 percent a year in the decade from 1996 to 2005, well higher than the 1.7 percent annual growth reg-istered in the years of economic adversity from 1975 to 1995. However, economic problems inherited from that period and the challenges of the political transformation will prevent the growth rate from reaching levels associ-ated with more vigorous growth.

South Africa should enjoy a high level of **foreign direct investment** in the coming years, especially in comparison to the near total lack of such investment dur-ing the years when it was an outcast nation due to its apartheid policies. Years of underinvestment in infra-structure and housing among disadvantaged communi-ties, coupled with government social spending targets set in the RDP, are likely to lead to a relatively high aver-age growth rate of 6.5 percent in government expendi-tures. Even though unemployment is expected to in-crease, labor unions are likely to persist in demanding wage and salary increases to compensate them for **infla-tion** in the recent past. Both exports and imports are likely to be stimulated by trade **liberalization**.

Long-term interest rates are expected to remain high because of inflation and continued deficit spending by the government. Monetary discipline and the globaliza-tion on the money market will also keep upward pres-sure on short-term interest rates. The current political transformation makes it very difficult to forecast trends in the financial system, however.

As with any major political and economic transition, problems of adjustment are evident in the incidence of crime and violence in the major metropolitan centers. The concerns of foreign visitors are shared by all South Africans and are addressed by a comprehensive national crime prevention strategy focusing on all components of the criminal justice system. Solutions are also provided by the resurgence of urban renewal and re-development projects in the inner city areas of Johannesburg, Durban, and Cape Town, public works and programs in under-developed areas, and community development projects linking the youth to meaningful income generating op-portunities.

Against the background of a rapidly transforming na-tional economy, striving to expand and increase its com-petitive edge in world markets, the South African gov-ernment has implemented a variety of incentive programs aimed at easing and accelerating the transition to com-petitive and sustainable manufacturing industries. These programs are geared to provide support for training and education, technology development, competitive prices for manufacturing inputs, and investment in competitive machinery and equipment.

A level of economic liberalization has accompanied South Africa's political transformation and is reinforced by a **restructured** civil society. The new constitution pro-vides a solid foundation for political stability as a key cornerstone to long-term real economic growth.

DEPENDENCIES

South Africa has no territories or colonies.

BIBLIOGRAPHY

Arnold, Guy. *The New South Africa.* New York: St. Martin's Press, 2000.

Bond, Patrick. *Elite Transition: From Apartheid to Neoliberalism in South Africa.* London and Sterling, VA: Pluto Press, and Pietermaritzburg, South Africa: University of Natal Press, 2000.

Du Toit, J., and A. J. Jacobs. *Southern Africa: An Economic Profile.* South Africa: Southern Book Publishers, 1995.

Economist Intelligence Unit. *Country Profile: South Africa.* London: Economist Intelligence Unit, 2001.

Ginsberg, Anthony Sanfield. *South Africa's Future: From Crisis to Prosperity.* New York: St. Martin's Press, 1998.

National Treasury. <http://www.treasury.gov.za>. Accessed October 2001.

Naude, W. A., and E.P.J. Kleynhans. *Economic Development Decisions and Policy: A South African Manual.* Potchefstroom, South Africa, 1999.

South Africa Government Online. <http://www.gov.za>. Accessed October 2001.

South African Embassy, Washington, D.C. USA. <http://usaembassy.southafrica.net>. Accessed October 2001.

South Africa Yearbook. Cape Town: The Rustica Press, N'dabeni, 1999.

Statistics South Africa. *Stats in Brief.* Pretoria, South Africa, 2000.

U.S. Central Intelligence Agency. *World Factbook 2001.* <http://www.odci.gov/cia/publications/factbook/index.html>. Accessed September 2001.

U.S. Department of State. *Background Notes: South Africa, April 2000.* <http://www.state.gov/www/background_notes/southafrica_0004_bgn.html>. Accessed October 2001.

U.S. Department of State. *Country Commercial Guide FY 2000: South Africa.* <http://www.state.gov/www/about_state/business/com_guides/2000/africa/southafrica00.html>. Accessed October 2001.

WEFA. *South Africa Long Term Economic Outlook, 1996–2005.* WEFA Group, Pretoria, South Africa, 1996.

WEFA. *South African Macroeconomic Outlook.* WEFA Group, Pretoria, South Africa, 2001.

Whiteford, A., D. Posel, and T. Kelatwang. *A Profile of Poverty Inequality and Human Development.* Pretoria, South Africa: Human Research Council, 1995.

World Economic Forum. *The Africa Competitiveness Report, 2000/2001.* Oxford: Oxford University Press, 2000.

—Wilma Viviers, A. Tromp, and L. Campbell

S U D A N

Republic of the Sudan
Jumhuriyat as-Sudan

CAPITAL: Khartoum.

MONETARY UNIT: Sudanese dinar (SDD). One Sudanese dinar equals 100 piastres. There are bills of 10, 25, 50,100 and 1,000SDD.

CHIEF EXPORTS: Cotton, sesame, livestock, groundnuts (peanuts), oil, gum arabic.

CHIEF IMPORTS: Foodstuffs, petroleum products, manufactured goods, machinery and transport equipment, medicines and chemicals, textiles.

GROSS DOMESTIC PRODUCT: US$35.7 billion (purchasing power parity, 2000 est.).

BALANCE OF TRADE: Exports: US$1.7 billion (f.o.b., 2000 est.). **Imports:** US$1.2 billion (f.o.b., 2000 est.).

COUNTRY OVERVIEW

LOCATION AND SIZE. Sudan is located in North Africa. Sudan borders the following countries: Central African Republic (1,165 kilometers, 724 miles), Chad (1,360 kilometers, 845 miles), Democratic Republic of the Congo (628 kilometers, 390 miles), Egypt (1,273 kilometers, 791 miles), Eritrea (650 kilometers, 404 miles), Ethiopia (1,606 kilometers, 998 miles), Kenya (232 kilometers, 144 miles), Libya (383 kilometers, 238 miles), and Uganda (435 kilometers, 270 miles). Sudan is the largest country on the African continent; its total area is 2,505,810 square kilometers (966,710 square miles), making the country slightly larger than one-quarter the size of the United States. The 853-kilometer (530-mile) long coastline borders the Red Sea and lies between Egypt and Eritrea. The Sudan's capital, Khartoum, is located in the central part of the country, on the Nile river.

POPULATION. The population of Sudan was estimated at 35,079,814 in July 2000 and represents a net growth of 2.84 percent in comparison with 1999. Estimates increased to 36,080,373 by July 2001. The birth rate stood at 37.89 per 1,000 and the death rate at 10.04 death per 1,000 in 2001. In 1975, the total population was estimated

at 16 million, in 1998 at 28.3 million, in 2001 at 36.1 million, and in 2015 it should reach 39.8 million.

The Sudanese population is highly diverse, consisting of about 19 different ethnic groups and almost 600 subgroups. Most of the inhabitants are of black African origin (52 percent), 39 percent are Arabs, 6 percent Beja, and 3 percent foreigners and other small national groups. Cultural conflicts between the black Africans, who live mostly in the south, and the Arabics, who live mainly in the north, have been the source of many internal struggles within the country. The official language is Arabic, which is spoken by about 60 percent of the population. An estimated 115 tribal languages are spoken as well, including Nubian, Ta Beawie, Nilotic, and Nilo-Hamitic. English and several Sudanic languages are also spoken.

The population is relatively young: while 45 percent are younger than 14 years old, only about 2 percent are older than 65. A majority of the population (69 percent) lives in the rural regions, while 31 percent live in the urban areas. The average population density is 9.8 per square kilometer (25.4 per square mile). The highest density is in the western and some southern provinces of the country, while the northern part of the country is rarely inhabited.

Population development and assessment is complicated by a continuing civil war and famine. Many people fall victim to the conflict or die as a result of the famine or diseases, and some of them escape to find asylum in Chad or Uganda. The average life expectancy is estimated at 55.85 years for men and 58.08 years for women. The literacy rate is 58 percent for men and 35 percent for women.

OVERVIEW OF ECONOMY

For the past 2 decades, Sudan has suffered from a violent civil war, chronic political instability, devastating

SUDAN

| 0 | 125 | 250 | 375 Miles |
| 0 | 125 | 250 | 375 Kilometers |

drought, weak world commodity prices, decreases in **remittances** from abroad, and counterproductive economic policies. Agriculture is the largest portion of the economy, accounting for 39 percent of the **gross domestic product** (GDP) and employing nearly 80 percent of the workforce. Other important areas of the **private sector** include trading and the processing of agricultural products. Sluggish economic performance over the past decade, attributable to declining annual rainfall, has kept per capita income at low levels. A large **foreign debt** and huge **arrears** continue to cause economic difficulties.

In 1990, the International Monetary Fund (IMF) took the unusual step of declaring Sudan non-coopera-

tive because of its nonpayment of arrears to the Fund. After Sudan backtracked on promised reforms in 1992–93, the IMF threatened to expel Sudan from the Fund. To avoid expulsion, the Sudanese government agreed to make token payments on its arrears, to **liberalize exchange rates**, and to reduce **subsidies**. By 2000, the government had partially implemented these measures. The government has also tried to develop the oil sector, and, working with foreign partners, the country is now producing approximately 150,000 barrels per day. But the continuing civil war and the country's growing international isolation has inhibited growth in the nonagricultural sectors of the economy.

In addition to civil strife, Sudan has an economy which suffers from the country's geographic location. Sudan belongs to the Sahel belt of Africa along the Sahara Desert, which comprises some of the poorest countries in the world. The dry climate in the central parts of the country makes economic and agricultural performance difficult. The main agricultural activities concentrate, therefore, in Khartoum, Port Sudan, or around the Nile River.

In 1999, the government changed its economic behavior and started implementation of IMF programs, including **privatization** and economic liberalization. It decreased subsidies on some products, which consequently led to a 30 percent increase in the price of chicken and beef and a 20 percent increase in the price of oil and petrol. **Foreign direct investments**, mainly from rich Arab countries, have enabled oil pipelines and extraction accessories construction, producing an estimated oil income for 2000 of US$300 million. The reforms have sparked the economy. The GDP growth was predicted to be 7 percent in 2000.

The privatization program was expected to include some of the largest state-controlled companies, including the state airlines Sudan Air, the state energy giant NEC, the irrigation system Al-Gezira, the sugar factories, and the maritime transport providers. French energy company, Electricité de France, has already expressed its interest in NEC, and 1 consortium (group) from South Korea was pursuing the purchase of the irrigation system. The future regulation of the private sector remains unclear. The legislature has not laid firm regulations for the private sector and some financial experts fear that that may limit the activities of private companies and allow **monopolies** in some sectors. The uncertainty surrounding the legislation for the private sector has stalled foreign investment in the country.

POLITICS, GOVERNMENT, AND TAXATION

Before independence in 1956, Sudan had been a British-Egyptian condominium (under the common governance of both countries). Since independence, Sudan's political situation has been very unstable. Sudan experienced several coups d'etat and conflicts. There is a clear difference between the predominantly Arab and Muslim north side and the predominantly African south, which has a population of mainly Christians and followers of indigenous religions. The cultural differences between the groups has led to an ongoing conflict within the country.

Since independence, the northern population has dominated politics, filling more governmental posts and gaining official authority. Shortly after independence, southerners, upset by the strict Islamic penal code (which included amputations for stealing and public beatings for

alcohol possession) that had been added to the country's laws and the deterioration of the economy, began a civil war to gain independence for the south.

The country experienced its first coup d'etat in 1958, another in 1964, and yet another in 1969. The coup of 1969 brought Jaafar al-Nimairi to power and started Sudan's cooperation with the countries of the **Communist** block. Nimairi shaped Sudan's government around the idea of National **Socialism** and patterned his administration after his idol Abd al-Nasser in Egypt. Nimairi established the Arab Socialist Union and included the Communist Party in a government coalition. He also gave a great deal of autonomy to the south. In 1971, Communists tried to overtake the government, but Nimairi remained in power with help of the army.

Until this conflict, all the revolutions and coups d'etat in Sudan were bloodless. This one changed the course. Nimairi had the Communist leaders executed. He also turned away from the Communist block and sought better cooperation with the rich oil-producing countries of the Persian Gulf, mainly Saudi Arabia. Under Nimairi, Sudan actively tried to attract more foreign direct investment (FDI) and studied which areas of the economy should be targeted. Agricultural production, especially grains, topped the list for FDI; some even expected that Sudan could become the main grain supplier for all Arab countries. Sudan's first oil deposits were also found, which led to conflicts with the south over the proposed oil revenues distribution.

But economic growth did not come to Sudan; by the 1980s, the economy had deteriorated and the living standards of the vast majority of the population plunged to very low levels. In addition, in 1983 Nimairi again changed his ruling policy, this time to a radical Islamism and Islamic fundamentalism. He tried to implement the Islamic legislative system "Sharia in praxis," which included such extreme punishments as cutting off a hand for theft or stoning to death for fornication. He also canceled autonomy for the south.

Civil war erupted, displacing nearly 2 million people. The war practically split the country in 2. The larger northern part of Sudan remained under the official control of the Muslim pro-governmental army. The south was controlled by the Sudan People's Liberation Army led by John Garang. But the division was unstable, and by 1985, another coup removed Nimairi's regime from power. The new government was led by Sadiq al-Mahdi, an Oxford University graduate and an intellectual. Al-Mahdi sought normalization of the political situation and revitalization of the economy. However, he did not succeed in finding compromise with the rebelling south, and another coup overthrew his administration in 1989.

The 1989 coup installed a one-party system led by the National Islamic Front (NIF). Umar al-Bashir became the official head of the state and prime minister. Hasan al-Turabi became the second most important political figure since 1989 as the leader of the NIF and the spiritual Islamic leader of the country. The new regime was marked by a hard dictatorship, prohibition of any political activities that would not be in accordance with official propaganda, suppression of any opposition, and support for international terrorism.

The only country that continues to have good relations with Sudan is Iran, its main financial supporter. Sudan has served as a vanguard and loyal agent of Iranian interests in the region. Through Sudan, many extremist Islamic and fundamentalist movements were supported in neighboring Egypt, Ethiopia, Uganda, and other countries. Therefore, the relations with those countries deteriorated, and Sudan remained totally isolated. The country once granted asylum to the international terrorist leader Osama bin Laden. The extremist Islamic and fundamentalist leadership of the country forced the population to follow its religious instructions and introduced hard Islamic laws which led to uprisings among other religious groups and sharpened the fights for independence in the south. Sudanese leaders introduced more violence to the country when they blamed neighboring countries (Egypt, Ethiopia, Eritrea, and Uganda) for giving support to the Sudan People's Liberation Army, which led to border conflicts with those countries.

By the 1990s, Sudan was so isolated that its economic situation became unsustainable. In addition, some changes in the Iranian political scene occurred that led to policy changes towards Sudan. The new Iranian government did not want to be connected with Sudan's support for international terrorism and pressed the Sudanese government to change its political course. In 1996, the terrorist Osama bin Laden was expelled from Sudan. Negotiations with the opposition leaders, including former country leaders Sadiq al-Mahdi and Jaafar al-Nimairi, started. However, the political change was not sufficient. In 1997, the United States imposed economic **sanctions** that forbid U.S. companies from investing in Sudan.

In 1998, the NIF was reorganized as the National Congress (NC) and the country adopted a new constitution and legislature allowing political activities and official registration of other parties. This new legislature came into force in 1999 and other political parties were formed at that time, including the National Democratic Alliance (NDA; the Alliance consists of the Umma Party and Democratic Unionist Party), Sudan People's Liberation Movement (SPLM), Sudan People's Liberation Army (SPLA), Muslim Brothers, People's Social Party, and the Liberation Party.

This change in the policy brought about conflict between the president Umar al-Bashir and the religious leader and chairman of the parliament, Hasan al-Turabi.

In December 1999, Umar al-Bashir dismissed the parliament and declared a state of emergency. Al-Turabi summoned protest demonstrations, but with little success. Al-Turabi was excluded from the official policy and formed his own opposition group called the Popular National Congress.

In December 2000, there were presidential and parliamentary elections. Umar al-Bashir gained 86 percent of the votes and the ruling National Congress of President Umar al-Bashir won 97 percent of the seats. Nevertheless, most of the opposition representatives, including al-Turabi, boycotted the elections, saying the elections were manipulated and rigged. The political situation is, in spite of Bashir's victory, still not clear or stable. Negotiations with the south, for example, have not been fruitful.

Until the recent time, the government had a dominant role in the country's economy. All key sectors were totally controlled by the state authorities, with the exception of some small activities and agriculture. The taxation policy of the government was always very unstable and obscure. The state budget has been in permanent deficit. Financial experts, however, expect this to change now that the government has started a privatization and liberalization process.

INFRASTRUCTURE, POWER, AND COMMUNICATIONS

The **infrastructure** is at a relatively low level because of the bad economic situation and internal conflicts. Some parts of the country (mainly in the south) are cut off from the modern world, leaving some villages totally isolated. The total railways length is 5,500 kilometers (3,418 miles). However, because of the conflict in the south and long time neglect, the quality of the rail tracks is very poor. Therefore, only about one-fifth of its length could be used. Narrow single track railways from the beginning of this century are prevailing. The main railway leads from Wadi Halfa through Khartoum to El Obeid, from Khartoum to Port Sudan and from El Obeid to Nyala in the southern part of the country. In 1997, new railways were finished connecting Muglad and Abu Jabra. All railways are managed by the state-run Sudan Railways Corporation.

There are 50,000 kilometers (31,070 miles) of roads in Sudan, but the quality is commonly very poor. Many of the roads are located in the desert and are not passable during the rainy seasons. Only the road connecting Khartoum and Port Sudan is covered by asphalt. Bus connections are between these 2 cities and Kassala. Gravel roads connect Khartoum with Port Sudan, Atbara, Dongola, and Gedarif. The connections are commonly very bad and transport facilities very old. The Iranian gov-

Communications

Country	Newspapers	Radios	TV Sets[a]	Cable subscribers[a]	Mobile Phones[a]	Fax Machines[a]	Personal Computers[a]	Internet Hosts[b]	Internet Users[b]
	1996	1997	1998	1998	1998	1998	1998	1999	1999
Sudan	27	271	87	0.0	0	0.6	1.9	0.00	5
United States	215	2,146	847	244.3	256	78.4	458.6	1,508.77	74,100
Egypt	40	324	122	N/A	1	0.5	9.1	0.28	200
Dem. Rep. of Congo	3	375	135	N/A	0	N/A	N/A	0.00	1

[a]Data are from International Telecommunication Union, *World Telecommunication Development Report 1999* and are per 1,000 people.

[b]Data are from the Internet Software Consortium (http://www.isc.org) and are per 10,000 people.

SOURCE: World Bank. *World Development Indicators 2000.*

ernment is financing the construction of connections between Rabak and Juba. Taxi services are available in big cities, but donkeys and camels are often used in villages. To improve the infrastructure, the government opened road construction to the private sector in 1998. According to contracts with Saudi Arabia, 250 kilometers (155 miles) of new roads between Khartoum and Port Sudan should be finished in 20 years. Another project, which should bring 126 kilometers (78 miles) of roads between Khartoum and Wad Medani in 20 years, involves the cooperation of the United Arab Emirates.

Besides roads and railways, water is also an important transport route in Sudan. The Nile River is the main source of some 5,310 kilometers (3,300 miles) of water transportation routes. There are some ports, including Khartoum, along the Nile and others, including Port Sudan and Sawakin, along the Red Sea. The main sea port is Port Sudan. The country has 4 merchant marine ships.

Sudan Airways owns 2 Boeing 707s, 2 Boeing 737–200s, 4 Fokkers, and 3 Airbus planes. Major airports are in Khartoum and Port Sudan, and there are some minor airports throughout the country. Of the country's 61 airports, 12 have paved runways. There is 1 heliport.

Sudan has not established a comprehensive power supply for the country. Khartoum uses 87 percent of the country's energy. The country's own energy producing power is not sufficient and is complicated by the conflict in the south. Sometimes, the opposition groups have stopped the power stations providing Khartoum with energy and have endangered the city. Hydroelectric power stations in Roseires, Sennar, and Khaslun Al Gibra provide 250 megawatts (MW), 15MW and 12MW of electric energy. The capacity changes during the year. Dips in power supply are caused by river pollution from heavy materials and mud in the raining seasons that requires turbines to be repaired. When the hydroelectric plants slow their production for repairs, heating plants located around Khartoum supply energy, but their total capacity

is only 150MW. The government plans construction of 2 new hydroelectric power stations. The Merowe project located 300 kilometers (186 miles) north of Khartoum should have 10 generators, each of them producing 110MW. The Kajbar project should supply 80MW. In addition, a heating plant that will produce 200MW is planned to be built near Khartoum. Negotiations regarding possible non-traditional power station construction are being held with some German companies. Such power stations could use solar or wind energy.

The telephone system in Sudan is well equipped by regional standards, but barely adequate and poorly maintained by modern standards. There were about 75,000 fixed telephone lines in use (serving 6,000 inhabitants) in the 1990s, but the *World Factbook* estimated that there were 400,000 by 2000. About 40 percent of the fixed lines are in Khartoum. Cellular communications started in 1996, and there were about 3,000 mobile phones by the end of the 1990s and nearly 20,000 by 2000. In 1997, an agreement between the Sudanese government and French company Alcatel for telephone net modernization was signed. A Sudan-South Korean consortium (including Sudatel and Daewoo companies) is constructing mobile phone facilities for Khartoum, Omdurman, and Wad Medani. The target is to gain 1.5 million users by 2003.

Other means of communication include radio, television, and computers. There are 7.55 million radios in use and 2.38 million televisions (141 per 1,000 people). There were 12 AM stations, 1 FM, 1 shortwave, and 3 television stations in 1997. There was only 1 Internet service provider by 2000, and only 2 of every 1,000 inhabitants owned a personal computer.

ECONOMIC SECTORS

Sudan belongs to a group of the poorest and least developed countries in the world. Its economy is very sluggish and underdeveloped. Sudan's civil war and political instability have caused havoc on the country's

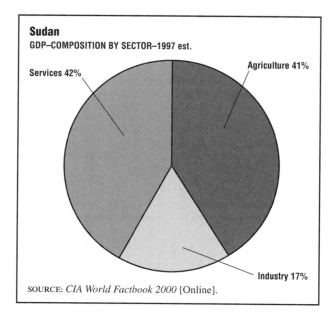

Sudan
GDP–COMPOSITION BY SECTOR–1997 est.

Services 42%

Agriculture 41%

Industry 17%

SOURCE: *CIA World Factbook 2000* [Online].

it succeeds in breaking international isolation, mitigating the inner conflict, and attracting more investment, the country could experience significant growth. There were plans for developing the petrochemical and chemical industry, improving textile manufacturing, and attracting tourism. But by 2001, little progress had been made.

AGRICULTURE

The agricultural sector is the most important economic sector in the country. It created 39 percent of the GDP, employed about 80 percent of population, and contributed 80 percent of the country's exports in the late 1990s. Cotton is the main agriculture export item, although its export volumes have been decreasing recently. The lack of any marketing or developed market policy is evident. The government has suggested the end of export taxes in order to promote more agriculture products in the future. Other agricultural products include sesame seeds, sorghum, and gum arabic.

Sudan's climatic conditions, mainly the rainy seasons, enable double annual harvests (in July and November) in the southern parts of the country. Most of the agricultural activities are concentrated near the Nile River. The Al Gezira irrigation system that is located between the White and the Blue Nile Rivers (both rivers merge to form the Nile River) is the most important agriculture project and, according to some statistics, is also the largest artificially irrigated region in the world. As the irrigation system has been put in place, sorghum, wheat, and groundnuts have been planted instead of cotton in an effort to make Sudan self-sufficient in foodstuffs.

economic sectors. There are labor shortages for almost all the categories of skilled employment. The most recent **labor force** estimation is from 1996 and measured the workforce at 11 million. Of that 11 million, 4 percent (or 440,000) were officially registered as unemployed. Some estimate that the real unemployment rate is nearly 30 percent, however. Most of the population survives on **subsistence agriculture**. Industry is limited to some textile and foodstuffs manufacturing facilities, which operate at very low standards.

Since the late 1990s, the government has been trying to improve the economic prospects of the country. If

Animal husbandry represents a very important part of the national economy, as well. Its production increased during recent years as a result of better veterinary treatment, better credit policy, and higher prices in the market.

Fishing is another important sector of the national economy. The average yearly production averages around 33,000 tons, from which sea fish represent about 1,500 tons. Perch is the most important fresh-water fish, which is caught mostly in the Nile River.

INDUSTRY

Sudanese industry accounted for an estimated 17 percent of GDP in 1998. The small size of the country's industrial sector is a result of chronic problems, including lack of skilled labor force, raw materials, and investments. These problems are most apparent in the textile and foodstuff industries, as well as in the production of sugar. If these problems were resolved, Sudan could dramatically reduce its reliance on imports.

About 80 percent of the industrial sector is privately-owned. The main industries are: tannery and leather pro-

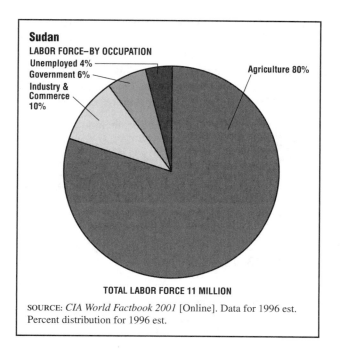

Sudan
LABOR FORCE–BY OCCUPATION

Unemployed 4%
Government 6%
Industry & Commerce 10%

Agriculture 80%

TOTAL LABOR FORCE 11 MILLION

SOURCE: *CIA World Factbook 2001* [Online]. Data for 1996 est. Percent distribution for 1996 est.

duction, weaving mills, spinning mills, gum arabic production, paper mills, minerals, ores, and raw materials extraction. The tannery industry creates 6 percent of the country's exports. It contains production of raw furs for export and local market, furs for the footwear industry, belts production, and artificial leathers. There are 7 big tanneries and 290 traditional manufacturers in Sudan. The furs and leathers are manufactured in 72 factories, and the yearly production of shoes amounts to 12 million pairs.

The textile industry is the oldest one in the country. Weaving and spinning mills are supported by the government that has spread the motto, "Let's wear what we produce ourselves." There is a large gap between production and consumption, however. Production amounts to 2,000 tons of combed cotton yarn: 235 million meters of textile fabrics, 5 million pieces of clothing, 1 million cover blankets, and 400 tons of cotton bandages yearly. By the end of the 1990s, plans were in place to increase investment incentives that would boost production capacities, to invest in new technologies, and to build spare parts factories. In 1999, an agreement with a Chinese consortium was signed that could lead to a new cooperation in textile factories reconstruction.

Sudan is the biggest producer of arabic gum that is extracted from the resin of Senegalese acacia trees. Its production covers 80 percent of the world consumption. The gum is used in foodstuffs, the chemical industry, cosmetics, pharmaceuticals, and lithography.

Sudan has 2 paper mills producing 2 tons of paper every year. Because Sudan has access to all the materials necessary for production (wood, papyrus, and other raw materials) and a cheap labor force, it is expected that investments in this sector will grow in the future.

Foodstuffs production include sugar, beef, poultry, fish, and others. Sugar production is very important to Sudan. Sudan is the third largest producer of sugar in Africa, after South Africa and Egypt. The yearly production is estimated at 450,000 tons in the late 1990s, up from 100,000 tons in 1980. The government plans enlargement of crop fields near the Nile River. The biggest country producer is White Nile Sugar Co. The Kenana Sugar Company is an excellent example of how the government wants **joint ventures** and investments to spur growth in the industrial sector. The growth of the Kenana Sugar Company prompted the government to open its state-owned Sudanese Sugar Company to private investment at the beginning of the millennium.

There are large deposits of copper, gold, chrome, iron ore, lead, wolfram, zinc, uranium, diamonds, marble, talc and plaster. The gold production is estimated at 6 tons yearly and is realized by 2 joint ventures: first, Sudan-Chinese and, second, Sudan-French. Total gold deposits are expected to contain 37 tons. Copper extraction

is to be set in the future in cooperation with the British Western Cordofan.

Oil deposits were found in the 1960s and 1970s and Sudan started its extraction in the 1980s. Most of the oil deposits are located in the southern part of the country. Disputes over how the oil revenues would be used fueled the civil conflict and made construction of extraction facilities and a pipeline difficult. Many times, opposition groups have blasted some of the pipelines and cut production.

Oil extraction and export in Sudan has benefitted from cooperation with foreign companies. Foreign oil consortiums from China, Malaysia, Canada, Qatar, and Austria are operating in the country. (The United States has imposed sanctions against the country so large U.S. oil companies have withdrawn from Sudan.) A pipeline from the oilfields in the south to Port Sudan along the Red Sea was completed in 1998, and the country exported its first oil in 1999. The yearly oil production is expected to reach 1 million barrels in 2005. This result, however, depends also on the political climate and evasion from attacks. Besides this there are still some unchecked fields where new deposits are expected. Oil refineries are already established in Port Sudan, El Obeid, and Abu Gabra.

A petrochemical factory is being built 30 kilometers (19 miles) south of Khartoum in cooperation with China. Its yearly production should be 2.5 million tons. Gas deposits were detected in the Red Sea shelves, where 7 sources are being drilled.

SERVICES

The service sector's contribution to the GDP suffered in the early and mid-1990s but appeared to be improving by the end of the decade. In 1996, services accounted for 40.6 percent of the GDP, but services in 1999 accounted for only 34.4 percent. By 1998, services had increased to 44 percent of the GDP, according to the *World Factbook.* Services include commerce and commerce services, restaurants and hotels, finance and insurance, transport and communications, and government offices.

TOURISM. Revenues from tourism could play a more important role in the future, but their contribution to the state budget is now very poor because of the low quality and standards. To increase revenues, the government, in coordination with the International Monetary Fund, has privatized many accommodations and tourist facilities. The government plans to enlarge usage of the Red Sea for special tourism activities, including wind surfing and diving possibilities. There are plans for the construction of new hotels, restaurants, and camps as well as tourist agencies. The Nile River could also be used for water sports.

The country has a total hotel capacity of 17,990 beds. The total number of hotels is 45, with another 48 in construction. There are 3 tourist resorts, 8 youth hostels, and 2 tourist camps. There are 3 five-star hotels in Khartoum (the Hilton, Grand Holiday Villa, and Palace), 1 four-star hotel (Meridien), and 5 three-star hotels. Khartoum and Port Sudan have the most accommodations.

Development of the tourism sector is complicated by the conflict in the south of the country and the unstable political situation. The government had difficulty attracting tourists and had difficulty getting Sudan added to the lists of world famous tourist places. Although the number of tourists is expected to grow in the future, Sudan could hardly attract as many tourists as neighboring Egypt at the end of 1990. Without a more stable political climate, Sudan will not be able to attract increasing numbers of tourists.

INTERNATIONAL TRADE

Sudan has long had an adverse foreign trade balance. Foreign trade has been negatively influenced by the civil war and international isolation. In August 1999, Sudan started exporting oil. Nearly 70 percent of the oil production is exported. In 1999–2000, the country experienced its first **trade surplus**. That surplus rose to US$500 million in 2000 on exports of US$1.7 billion and imports of US$1.2 billion.

Foodstuffs are the most important import into Sudan. But steel and alloy products were the main industrial items having been imported to Sudan. Their imports accounted for US$76.6 million. Spare parts import accounted for US$88.3 million, audio and video devices for US$43.1 million, refrigerators for US$112.2 million, personal cars for US$30.2 million, lorries and trucks for US$38.7 million, and buses for US$6.8 million.

Export and import policy has recently been liberalized. In the past, the country was isolated, and foreign trade was highly restricted. Since the early 1990s, trade

Exchange rates: Sudan	
Sudanese dinars per US$1	
Jan 2001	257.44
2000	257.12
1999	252.55
1998	200.80
1997	157.57
1996	125.08
SOURCE: CIA *World Factbook 2001* [ONLINE].	

policy has been more open. All import prohibitions were removed with the exception of alcoholic beverages, drugs, hazard playing machines, weapons, and ammunition. Foreign trade has been especially encouraged in 2 **free zones**: the Red Sea Free Trade Zone and the Al Gaili Free Zone.

MONEY

The Sudanese dinar has declined in value as a consequence of the civil war and political instability in the country. Until the late 1990s, the Sudanese pound (an old currency) was commonly used as well. In July 1999, the Sudanese Central Bank made the formal declaration that all dealings in the Sudanese pound should stop.

The Central Bank—Bank of Sudan—regulates the **liquidity** of other banks and governs the financial aspects of national development programs. The bank has 11 branches. Although the banking system has been centralized in the past, changes in the economic policy of the country has led some to expect that the banking sector will be liberalized in the future. There are 29 other banks in Sudan with a total of 671 offices.

Sudan has 1 stock exchange, the Khartoum Stock Exchange, which was started in 1994, even though plans for a Sudanese stock exchange began in 1962. The Khartoum Stock Exchange is one of the only stock exchanges to work under the rules of the Islamic *Sharia*. One of the primary objectives of the stock exchange is to promote savings and to infuse the private sector with the capital it needs to grow. There are 8 brokers for the stock exchange.

POVERTY AND WEALTH

Sudan is one of the poorest countries of the world. Most of the population lives in unbelievably hard conditions. One of the Sahel countries, Sudan is located in the Sahara desert. Hard climate conditions and lack of natural resources were always responsible for the poor life conditions. But the country's political instability and internal conflict has increased the poverty.

Trade (expressed in billions of US$): Sudan		
	Exports	Imports
1975	.438	.887
1980	.543	1.576
1985	.374	.771
1990	.374	.619
1995	.556	1.219
1998	.596	1.915
SOURCE: International Monetary Fund. *International Financial Statistics Yearbook 1999.*		

GDP per Capita (US$)

Country	1975	1980	1985	1990	1998
Sudan	237	229	210	198	296
United States	19,364	21,529	23,200	25,363	29,683
Egypt	516	731	890	971	1,146
Dem. Rep. of Congo	392	313	293	247	127

SOURCE: United Nations. *Human Development Report 2000;
Trends in human development and per capita income.*

The southern parts of the country are practically isolated and it is very hard to estimate the level of poverty in those territories, although it is known that many people are dying of hunger or diseases. It is difficult for international aid or health-care organizations to provide care for southern Sudanese because of the civil war.

Most of the population is nourished from subsistence agriculture. Food is so scarce that during droughts lives are endangered. The isolationist policies of the totalitarian regime deprived the country of foreign direct investment, as well. The result was that only sporadic international humanitarian aid reached some of the poorest regions for many years. Historically, the United States has been the most important donor of financial aid to the south.

To escape the difficult conditions, many people have fled the country. The people of relative wealth in Sudan live in Khartoum, Port Sudan, and near the Nile River, where the conditions are a bit better. Only small groups of people loyal to the regime would be considered "rich."

According to the *Human Development Report 2000*, 26.6 percent of the population is not expected to survive to more than 40 years of age. Comparatively, in Egypt the number is only 9.9 percent and in China 7.7 percent. The early death of so many Sudanese can be traced to the violence but also the lack of basic necessities. About 27 percent of the population do not have access to safe water (in Egypt, 13 percent); 30 percent have no access to health services (in Egypt, 1 percent). For children under the age of 5, 34 percent are underweight (in Egypt, 12 percent). The *World Factbook* estimated that the **GDP per capita** at **purchasing power parity** in 2000 was US$1,000. All of these numbers underscore the difficulty of most people's lives in Sudan.

WORKING CONDITIONS

The working conditions in Sudan are very difficult to measure. Although the *World Factbook* estimated the unemployment rate to be 4 percent in 1996, some believe the real unemployment is much higher, perhaps even 30

percent. Estimating unemployment is impeded by the lack of official registration, the fact that women are isolated in their homes as housekeepers, and the isolation of southern regions.

Sudanese nationals once made up a very skilled workforce. Since the British colonial era, education has been given a high priority. Many Sudanese succeeded at the best British schools and universities. Sudanese were known as intelligent and educated people. Unfortunately, during the years of political instability and conflicts, education deteriorated and most of the skilled people fled the country. There are no chances for skilled people to succeed in Sudan. The salaries are very low and political loyalty is the main criterion for creating a successful career. You can find more Sudanese intellectuals, doctors, engineers, and specialists in New York; Washington, D.C.; London; or Paris than in Khartoum or other parts of Sudan.

Of the Sudanese in Sudan, 80 percent work in agriculture, 10 percent in industry and commerce, and about 6 percent in government offices. Working conditions in the rural areas are very undeveloped and resemble medieval times. Children also commonly work.

COUNTRY HISTORY AND ECONOMIC DEVELOPMENT

7TH CENTURY. The territory is conquered by Arab fighters and added to the Arab-Islamic empire.

1820–21. Mohammed Ali conquers the areas and incorporates it with Egypt. Gold extraction and slavery flourish.

1885–98. Mohammed Ahmed al-Mahdi, an Islamic spiritual leader, brings independence to Sudan.

1898. Sudan is conquered and proclaimed a Egyptian-British condominium. The British dominate the ruling of the government.

1956. Independence is declared.

1958–64. Ibrahim Abbud becomes president. Abbud prohibits political parties and starts the Islamisation of the country. Arabic is introduced as an official language, replacing English. First conflicts with the south begin. In 1964, Abbud resigns after mass protests.

1964–69. Relative stability, prosperity, and parliamentary democracy come to Sudan.

1969. Jaafar al-Nimairi organizes a coup d'etat. Nimairi grants wide autonomy to the south but follows socialistic and nationalistic policy influenced by the Communist countries.

1971. Communists try to overthrow the government, but Nimairi's forces defeat them, and Nimairi orders the leaders to be executed. Nimairi breaks off relations with the Communist countries in favor of cooperation with conservative Islamic oil producing countries of the Persian Gulf.

1983. Nimairi introduces Islamic law into the civil legal system. Autonomy for the south is terminated and the economy deteriorates. The civil war starts.

1985–89. Sadiq al-Mahdi, descendant of the legendary Mohammed Ahmed al-Mahdi, overthrows Nimairi. Al-Mahdi's regime brings relative stability and some economic growth to Sudan. But Al-Mahdi is unable to stop the conflict in the south.

1989–99. Umar al-Bashir overthrows al-Mahdi's regime and institutes a dictatorship. Hasan al-Turabi, the Islamic spiritual leader and chairman of the parliament, becomes the second most important state official. Together, al-Bashir and al-Turabi enforce one of the worst totalitarian regimes in the world. Strict Islamic laws and fundamentalist rules are implemented. Sudan supports international terrorism. The civil war rages in the south. Sudan is practically isolated internationally.

1996. Bashir is popularly elected as president of Sudan.

2000. Bashir is popularly elected for a second term as president.

FUTURE TRENDS

The future of Sudan is uncertain. Even though Bashir won 2 democratic elections, the opposition to his government seems to be growing. His main opponent, Turabi, boycotted the elections in 2000 and is actively seeking coalitions with other strong leaders, including Sadiq al-Mahdi and John Garang. The coalition of more parties and more autonomy for the south is necessary for any kind of positive development in the future.

Sudan has an urgent need for foreign direct investment. Without it, Sudan will hardly be able to survive. Sudan needs to stop its isolationist policies and seek cooperation with other countries. Even though the government is seeking such changes, it is unlikely that much improvement will happen under the current government. It is more likely that the government of Sudan will change and open the country to relative democracy and a more open economy.

Sudan has experienced some positive changes: it has improved relations with its neighbors, mainly Egypt and Libya, and mutual cooperation agreements have been signed with these countries. In addition, the country has started to cooperate with the International Monetary Fund, and the economy is implementing liberalization and privatization policies. Sudan's focus on these policies combined with more oil extraction and exploration are the most encouraging trends for future.

DEPENDENCIES

Sudan has no territories or colonies.

BIBLIOGRAPHY

Africa: South of the Sahara. European Publications Ltd., 1997.

Anderson, G. Norman. *Sudan in Crisis: The Failure of Democracy.* Gainesville, Florida: University Press of Florida, 1999.

Bank of Sudan. <http://bankofsudan.org>. Accessed October 2001.

Economist Intelligence Unit. *Country Profile: Sudan 1999–2000.* London: Economist Intelligence Unit, 2000.

International Historical Statistics: Africa, Asia and Oceania 1750–1993. Macmillan Reference Ltd., 1999.

International Monetary Fund. *International Financial Statistics Yearbook 2000.* London: International Monetary Fund, 2000.

Kok, Peter Nyot. *Governance and Conflict in the Sudan 1985–1995: Analysis, Evaluation and Documentation.* Berlin: Deutsches Orient Institut, 1996.

Sidahmed, Abdel Salam. *Politics and Islam in Contemporary Sudan.* London: St. Martin's Press, 1996.

"Sudan." *WTC Corps.* <http://www.wtc-corps.org/resources/sudan.htm>. Accessed October 2001.

U.S. Central Intelligence Agency. *World Factbook 2001.* <http://www.odci.gov/cia/publications/factbook/index.html>. Accessed September 2001.

World Bank. *Human Development Report 2000.* London: World Bank, 2000.

World Bank. *World Development Indicators 2000.* London: World Bank, 2000

—Tomas Strnad

SWAZILAND

CAPITAL: Mbabane (administrative and judicial) and Lobamba (royal and parliamentary).

MONETARY UNIT: The lilangeni (E); the plural is emalangeni. One lilangeni equals 100 cents. There are coins of 1, 2, 5, 10, 20, and 50 cents, and 1 lilangeni, and notes of 2, 5, 10, 20, and 50 emalangeni. The lilangeni is on par with the South African rand, which is also accepted as legal tender in the country.

CHIEF EXPORTS: Sugar, citrus, canned fruit, soft drink concentrates, textiles, wood pulp, cotton yarn, refrigerators.

CHIEF IMPORTS: Manufactured goods, machinery, transport equipment, food, chemicals, fuels.

GROSS DOMESTIC PRODUCT: US$4.44 billion (purchasing power parity, 2000 est.).

BALANCE OF TRADE: Exports: US$881 million (f.o.b., 2000). Imports: US$928 million (f.o.b., 2000).

COUNTRY OVERVIEW

LOCATION AND SIZE. Swaziland is a small landlocked country in southern Africa, with an area of 17,363 square kilometers (6,704 miles), extending 176 kilometers (109 miles) north to south and 135 kilometers (84 miles) east to west. By comparison, it is slightly smaller than the state of New Jersey. It shares a border of 105 kilometers (65 miles) to the east with Mozambique and is otherwise surrounded by South Africa, with which it shares a total border of 430 kilometers (267 miles). It is divided from east to west into 4 well-defined regions: the High-Veld, Middle-Veld, and Low-Veld, and the Lubombo plain and escarpment. Their height ranges from the High-Veld in the west which rises to 1,850 meters (6,070 feet) and the Low-Veld which stands at only 300 meters (985 feet) above sea level. The country is traversed by rivers and streams, making it one of the most well-watered areas of southern Africa.

POPULATION. In 2001, the population was estimated at 1,101,343. The population has risen from 906,000 in 1997, and from 712,313 in 1986. The population grew at 2.9 percent annually between 1970–90 and 2.8 percent between 1990–97, while life expectancy in 2001 was 60 years (though the CIA World Factbook reports a figure of 38.62 years). The population growth rate in 2001 was 1.83 percent, based on a birth rate of 40.12 per 1,000 and a death rate of 21.84 per 1,000, all based on 2001 estimates. About 33 percent of the population live in urban areas. It is a relatively young population with more than half of the population below 20 years of age.

Around 90 percent of the population are Swazi (although there are around 70 district groups), and most of the rest are Zulu, Tonga, Shangaan, European, and people of mixed descent. Large numbers of Mozambicans fled to Swaziland to escape the civil war in their country, but repatriation was completed in 1993 following a return to peace in Mozambique. About 77 percent of Swazi are Christian, with the rest practicing Islam or traditional faiths. English is an official language and the language of government and business, and is widely spoken alongside siSwati, the other official language.

OVERVIEW OF ECONOMY

Swaziland has one of the highest per capita income levels in Africa, although it is, after the Gambia, the smallest state on the mainland of the continent. According to the CIA World Factbook, Swaziland's gross domestic product (GDP) per capita in 2000 was estimated at US$4,000 at purchasing power parity, high enough to rank Swaziland as a middle-income country.

Swaziland experienced slow growth in the 1980s and early 1990s, a period much influenced by world recession and then political changes in South Africa, but there were still increases in the gross national product (GNP) per head of 2.3 percent a year over the period 1980 to 1993. Swaziland has, over the longer period, had one of the most liberal policies towards foreign and private investment in all of Africa. Its vulnerability lies in heavy

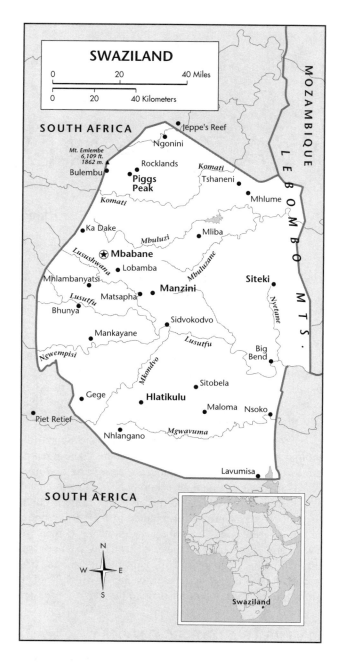

SWAZILAND

MOZAMBIQUE

SOUTH AFRICA

Jeppe's Reef
Ngonini
Mt. Emlembe
6,109 ft.
1862 m.
Rocklands
Komati
Bulembu
Piggs
Peak
Tshaneni
Komati
Mhlume
Ka Dake
Mbuluzi
Mliba
Mbabane
Lusushwana
Lobamba
Mbuluzane
Mhlambanyatsi
Siteki
Matsapha
Manzini
Lusutfu
Bhunya
Nyetane
Sidvokodvo
Mankayane
Lusutfu
Mkondvo
Big
Bend
Ngwempisi
Sitobela
Gege
Hlatikulu
Maloma
Nsoko
Piet Retief
Mgwavuma
Nhlangano
Lavumisa

SOUTH AFRICA

N
W E
S

Swaziland

export dependence on soft drink concentrate and sugar cane and on the strong economic links with South Africa which provides imports, an export market, investment, and employment.

Since the late 1980s the country's economic situation has improved noticeably. The economy has grown more rapidly and foreign investment expanded. A significant part of the food produced is now sold to the European Union (EU). This improvement—initially a direct consequence of trade **sanctions** against South Africa which forced the EU to turn to Swaziland as an alternative source of food supplies—has allowed the manufacturing sector to increase in importance, contributing 20

percent of the GDP by 1991 and helping the country raise its economic growth rate to 3.5 percent per year.

There is a dual administration of Swaziland's official resources. The communal land resources (known as Swazi National Land or SNL) and the minerals, are managed by Tibiyo Taka Ngwane, an independent institution created by Royal Charter in 1968 and not responsible to Parliament. The non-communal land and all the other resources are subject to the legislation of Parliament.

Swaziland is committed to a free market economy and private ownership: **nationalization** is illegal. The Swaziland Investment Promotion Authority was set up in 1997 to encourage the growth of private business. Investment accounted for 34 percent of the GDP in 1997, and **foreign direct investment** was 5.7 percent of the GDP, both very high figures. The government wants to encourage the expansion of industrial sites. The Swaziland stock exchange was established in 1990 and by the late 1990s had 6 companies listed and a **market capitalization** of US$129 million.

POLITICS, GOVERNMENT, AND TAXATION

Swaziland, a British protectorate since 1867, became independent on 6 September 1968. The Kingdom of Swaziland is an absolute monarchy. The king appoints the prime minister and the council of ministers (cabinet) and can legislate by decree. A new constitution was launched in 1968. However, in 1973 the king repealed the constitution, abolishing Parliament and all political parties.

A system of government with elections for local councils, who then chose their representatives in the National Assembly, was introduced in 1978, creating a 2-tier form of representative government which was reformed in 1993 to allow the introduction of secret ballots and the direct election of National Assembly members. The vote was granted to all citizens over the age of 21 who were not insane or had not committed serious crimes. There are 30 senators, of whom 20 are appointed by the king and 10 elected by the National Assembly. The National Assembly consists of 65 deputies, of whom 55 are directly elected from candidates nominated by the local councils and 10 appointed by the king.

In 1998 government revenues amounted to 27 percent of the GDP. The most recent year for which tax revenue data are available is 1987, when taxes on income, profits, and capital gains generated 38 percent of government revenue, domestic taxes on goods and services 11 percent, export **levies** and import **duties** 42 percent, other taxes 1 percent, and non-tax revenue 7 percent.

The corporate **income tax** is 37.5 percent. Small mining companies with net income below the equivalent of around US$2,500 are taxed at 27 percent. There is a withholding tax of 15 percent on dividends paid overseas, and dividends paid to residents are taxed at 10 percent. There are tax breaks for companies producing for export, and for companies with staff training programs.

INFRASTRUCTURE, POWER, AND COMMUNICATIONS

Swaziland has a good road network with 3,000 kilometers (1,864 miles) of roads, 28 percent of which were paved by 1997. In 1997, there were 78,900 motor vehicles licensed, 4,320 of which were government-owned. Rail service is for freight only. The Kadaka-Goba line links up with Mozambique's Maputo line (providing Swaziland with access to the sea), and since 1986 there has been a direct heavy-duty connection between Mpaka and South Africa. Matsapha International Airport is 8 kilometers (5 miles) from Manzini. The national airline, Royal Swazi National Airways Corporation, operates flights throughout the region.

Swaziland generates its power from coal and hydropower. Oil and the coal used for domestic energy generation are imported from South Africa. Swaziland Electricity Board imports over 80 percent of its electricity from South Africa and generates the balance from diesel and hydropower. In 1998 Swazis consumed 198 million kilowatt hours (kWh) of electricity. On-site power generation takes place at the large sugar and wood pulp plants (from waste sugar cane or scrap wood), but they only generate for their own needs. Wood is still an important fuel for the rural population.

English language dailies are *The Times* of Swaziland and *The Swami Observer*. There were 27 daily newspapers in 1996. The Swaziland Broadcasting Service runs several radio stations, broadcasting in siSwati and English. There is a television channel, run by the Swaziland

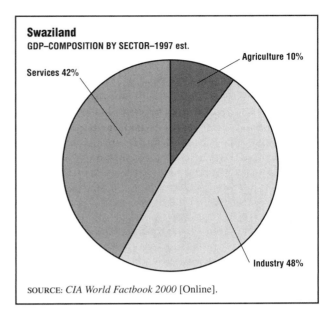

Swaziland
GDP–COMPOSITION BY SECTOR–1997 est.

Services 42%
Agriculture 10%
Industry 48%

SOURCE: *CIA World Factbook 2000* [Online].

Television Authority (STA), which covers 80 percent of the population and 60 percent of the country. STA has a **monopoly** in the TV rentals market. There were 170 radios and 23 TV sets per 1,000 people in 1996.

All the main population centers have post offices. International direct dialing is available. The telephone network comprises 14 digital, 5 analog, and 3 manual exchanges. There were 33,500 telephone main lines in use in 2000, in addition to 20,000 cellular phones.

ECONOMIC SECTORS

The economy of Swaziland depends on soft drinks concentrates and sugar cane for export revenue and on South Africa, which provides significant trade investment and employment. However, Swaziland has one of the best

Communications

Country	Telephones[a]	Telephones, Mobile/Cellular[a]	Radio Stations[b]	Radios[a]	TV Stations[a]	Televisions[a]	Internet Service Providers[c]	Internet Users[c]
Swaziland	33,500 (2000)	30,000 (2000)	AM 7; FM 6 (2000)	155,000	10 (2000)	21,000	3	4,000
United States	194 M	69.209 M (1998)	AM 4,762; FM 5,542; shortwave 18	575 M	1,500	219 M	7,800	148 M
South Africa	5.075 M (1999)	2 M (1999)	AM 14; FM 347; shortwave 1	13.75 M	556	5.2 M	44	1.82 M
Lesotho	20,000	1,262 (1996)	AM 1; FM 2; shortwave 1	104,000	1 (2000)	54,000	1	1,000

[a]Data is for 1997 unless otherwise noted.
[b]Data is for 1998 unless otherwise noted.
[c]Data is for 2000 unless otherwise noted.

SOURCE: CIA *World Factbook 2001* [Online].

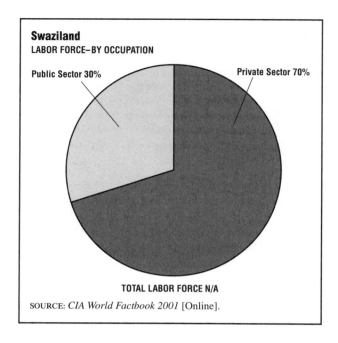

Swaziland
LABOR FORCE–BY OCCUPATION

Public Sector 30%

Private Sector 70%

TOTAL LABOR FORCE N/A

SOURCE: *CIA World Factbook 2001* [Online].

business environments in Africa as a result of its liberal policies towards foreign and private investment since independence. In 2000, the composition of Swaziland's GDP was as follows: agriculture, 10 percent; industry, 46 percent; and services, 44 percent.

AGRICULTURE

Agriculture's share of the GDP fluctuates with the fortunes of the harvest, accounting for 10 percent of the GDP in 2000, 13 percent in 1998, and 11 percent in 1994. The chief products are sugar, wood pulp, maize, citrus, and pineapples. About 44 percent of land is held on a free-hold basis (that is, the ownership is for an indefinite period in which the owner is free to buy and sell the land), mainly by non-Swazis. Large estates controlled mainly by Europeans produce the sugar, citrus fruits, and forestry products that dominate exports. The remainder of the land, known as Swazi Nation Land (SNL), is farmed on a small-scale by 70 percent of the population, in many cases on a part-time basis. The land is held in trust by the king. All Swazis are entitled to land, which is allocated by the chiefs according to traditional procedures.

Sugar used to be the mainstay of the economy until it was overtaken by fruit concentrates. However, it remains the country's largest source of employment. Maize, the country's staple food, and cotton are the main products of SNL farmers. Large-scale cotton production is being introduced as the Royal Swaziland Sugar Corporation begins to diversify into this crop. Oranges and grapefruit are grown for export on large estates, mainly controlled by Europeans, and mainly in the Low-Veld area.

Unbleached wood pulp is 1 of Swaziland's main export earners. Plantations cover 6 percent of the country, mainly in the High-Veld. Nearly two-thirds of this is made up of Usutu forest, one of the largest man-made forests in the world. The Usutu forest consists mainly of pine and eucalyptus and alone provides about 12 percent of the world supply of wood pulp. The Usutu pulp company is the country's largest employer. Indigenous industry produces mining and construction timber and furniture from local wood, some of which is exported.

Cattle are the traditional sign of wealth, and 80 percent of the cattle population remains in the hands of Swazi **smallholders**. The traditional nature of cattle raising has led to the slow development of the meat industry, as there is a strong resistance to offering cattle for slaughter. Domestic milk production is increasing and beef, tinned and frozen, is exported to the EU and South Africa.

INDUSTRY

The industrial sector is dominated by agro-industries involving local sugar, wood pulp, citrus and other fruit, cotton, and meat. Swaziland has been successful in attracting investment from Coca-Cola (which opened a concentrate plant in 1986) and Cadbury (which opened a new sweets factory in 1989). These, combined with continued investment from the Far East (4 Taiwanese-owned textile plants were opened in 1986), and investments in the mid-1990s in refrigerator production, means that the manufacturing sector continues to grow. However, there has been some domestic unrest caused by low wages.

Mining has fallen in importance since the 1960s, contributing only about 1 percent of the GDP in 1997–98. High-grade iron ore was exhausted by 1978, and health concerns have reduced the world demand for asbestos. Asbestos mining (by a **joint venture** between the government and a South African Company, HVL Asbestos) is nevertheless the principal mining activity. Production was 27,700 tons in 1998, and most of this was exported. Deposits are mainly in the High-Veld.

The diamond mine at Dvokolwako closed at the end of 1996. A new coal mine at Maloma in the south of the country opened in 1993 which produces mainly anthracite for export to Europe (203,100 tons in 1997 and 410,000 tons in 1998). It replaced the now closed Mpaka Mine as the main source of coal. Stone is quarried at 3 centers, and production is increasing. Local construction and roads industries take all stone production.

SERVICES

The services sector is very significant to the Swazi economy, comprising 44 percent of the GDP in 2000, up from 37 percent in 1994. Government services accounted for 20 percent of the GDP in 1996–97, and amounted for the majority of services production. **Private sector** services were dominated by tourism giant, Swazi Spa Holdings (a subsidiary of Sun International, a South African Hotel group). Tourism is mostly on a package-tour basis, and most visitors come from South Africa. The attractions are wildlife, splendid scenery, and casino facilities. Tourist arrivals numbered 322,000 in 1997, generating receipts of about US$7 million.

INTERNATIONAL TRADE

With a small economy, Swaziland does not have enough domestic demand to provide a basis for a wide range of production. Therefore, it must import a variety of goods. Imports typically outweigh exports, as they did in 2000 when imports were valued at US$928 million and exports at US$881 million.

The country's main exports are soft drink concentrate, sugar, citrus, canned fruit, textiles, wood pulp and refrigerators; the main imports are manufactured **consumer goods**, machinery, transport equipment, food, chemicals, and fuels. South Africa was far and away the dominant trading partner, taking 65 percent of exports and providing 84 percent of imports in 1998. Other major export destinations were the European Union (EU) (12 percent), Mozambique (11 percent), and the United States (5 percent). Other major importers were the EU (5 percent), and Japan and Singapore (2 percent each).

MONEY

The lilangeni is maintained at par with the South Africa rand, as it is in the de facto rand area involving Swaziland, South Africa, Namibia, and Botswana. The rand was on par with the U.S. dollar in the early 1980s, but has since lost value, very rapidly at times in the latter 1990s. In mid-2001, the lilangeni stood at E8.27:US$1. In March 1995, a 2-tier financial system (which allowed a different **exchange rate** for certain transactions) was

Exchange rates: Swaziland	
emalangeni (E) per US$1	
Jan 2001	7.7803
2000	6.9056
1999	6.1087
1998	5.4807
1997	4.6032
1996	4.2706

Note: The Swazi lilangeni is at par with the South African rand; emalangeni is the plural form of lilangeni.

SOURCE: CIA *World Factbook 2001* [ONLINE].

ended with the abolition of the financial rand, making the currency more vulnerable to international reaction to political developments in South Africa.

POVERTY AND WEALTH

Swaziland is a lower middle-income country, with a **GDP per capita** in 2000 of US$4,000 using the purchasing power parity conversion factor (which makes allowance for the low price of certain basic commodities in Swaziland). There are no figures for the incidence of poverty, but the number of under-weight children would suggest around 14 percent below the dollar-a-day poverty line. Most of those in poverty obtain their livelihoods from the agriculture sector, and they do not have enough income to provide the barest minimums of food, clothing, and shelter. Income is very unequally distributed, with the poorest 20 percent receiving 2.7 percent of total income in 1998, and the richest 20 percent receiving 64 percent. The poorest groups in the rural areas live in traditional dwellings with timber frames and mud walls, thatched roofing, and a beaten earth or polished cow dung floor. Water comes from a well, sanitation is by pit latrine, cooking is done over a wood fire, and lighting comes from a kerosene lamp.

The poor in the urban areas live in shanty dwellings constructed from timber, plastic sheeting, cardboard and

Trade (expressed in billions of US$): Swaziland		
	Exports	Imports
1975	.199	.180
1980	.369	.623
1985	.180	.324
1990	.557	.663
1995	.957	1.105
1998	N/A	N/A

SOURCE: International Monetary Fund. *International Financial Statistics Yearbook 1999.*

GDP per Capita (US$)					
Country	1975	1980	1985	1990	1998
Swaziland	1,073	1,046	1,035	1,446	1,409
United States	19,364	21,529	23,200	25,363	29,683
South Africa	4,574	4,620	4,229	4,113	3,918
Lesotho	220	311	295	370	486

SOURCE: United Nations. *Human Development Report 2000; Trends in human development and per capita income.*

Distribution of Income or Consumption by Percentage Share: Swaziland

Lowest 10%	1.0
Lowest 20%	2.7
Second 20%	5.8
Third 20%	10.0
Fourth 20%	17.1
Highest 20%	64.4
Highest 10%	50.2

Survey year: 1994
Note: This information refers to income shares by percentiles of the population and is ranked by per capita income.
SOURCE: *2000 World Development Indicators* [CD-ROM].

rusty scrap metal sheets. Water is obtained from a communal tap, sanitation is by pit latrine, cooking is done over charcoal, and kerosene lamps provide light. The wealthier groups live in modern houses with cement block walls and tin roofs, with electricity, piped water, and either a sewage system or a septic tank.

The UN's Human Development Index, which combines measures of income, health, and education, put Swaziland at 112 out of 174 countries in 1998, and this placed it in the medium human development category, one of the few African countries to achieve this status. Thus Swaziland has a level of development with relatively few of its population in poverty (more than 50 percent are in poverty in some countries), and has good basic education provisions, with 95 percent of children in primary school and 85 percent in secondary school, and sound health facilities which allow a life expectancy of 60 years (in the rest of Africa it is 49 years).

WORKING CONDITIONS

In 1997, about 113,000 people were employed in Swaziland: 57 percent in the private sector, 28 percent in the **public sector**, and 15 percent in the **informal sec-**

tor. An additional 13,000 Swazis worked as miners in South Africa. About 22 percent of the **labor force** is recorded as unemployed. However, the unemployment rate has little meaning in Africa, for it relates to those registering as looking for jobs in the urban areas as a percentage of the formal labor force. The largest part of the labor force in Swaziland, 60 percent, is in the agricultural sector, much of it in small-scale family farms outside the formal sector.

With no social security provisions, those without work or support from families or charities cannot survive. For much of the year in **subsistence farming** there is relatively little work to do, and what work there is is shared among the family members. During planting and harvesting, there is more work to be done, and everyone is more fully occupied, but even in these periods, there may be more than enough labor to do the tasks, and the work is again shared. Everyone sharing the work appears to have an occupation in agriculture, but in fact workers are not engaged full time for all the year, and hence there is some disguised unemployment.

There is a Federation of Trade Unions in Swaziland. Minimum wage levels are set, but the level is low, particularly for female agricultural workers, to avoid creating unemployment.

COUNTRY HISTORY AND ECONOMIC DEVELOPMENT

1867. Swaziland formally becomes a British protectorate.

1961. The Union of South Africa breaks relations with Britain and toughens racial segregation policies (known as apartheid). Britain accelerates the decolonization process in the region, and Swaziland is granted internal autonomy.

1868. Swaziland gains independence from Britain. King Sobhuza II is recognized as head of state and governs with 2 legislative chambers.

Household Consumption in PPP Terms

Country	All food	Clothing and footwear	Fuel and power[a]	Health care[b]	Education[b]	Transport & Communications	Other
Swaziland	25	7	9	6	13	8	32
United States	13	9	9	4	6	8	51
South Africa	N/A	N/A	N/A	N/A	N/A	N/A	N/A
Lesotho	N/A	N/A	N/A	N/A	N/A	N/A	N/A

Data represent percentage of consumption in PPP terms.
[a]Excludes energy used for transport.
[b]Includes government and private expenditures.
SOURCE: World Bank. *World Development Indicators 2000*.

1972. Swaziland holds its first parliamentary elections; the traditionalist Imbokodvo National Movement wins.

1973. King Sobhuza II declares the constitution unworkable, dissolves parliament, and prohibits political parties and trade unions. The Royal Defence Forces are reactivated.

1977. Elections to Parliament are held under the local council system.

1982. King Sobhuza II dies. The powers of head of state are transferred to Queen Mother Dzeliwe, who is named regent. In a power struggle, traditionalists gain the upper hand.

1983. Prime Minister Prince Mabandla Dlamini, head of the liberal faction, is dismissed and replaced by conservative Prince Bhekimpi Dlamini. The Queen Regent is presented with document transferring most of her power to the Liqoqo, a traditional advisory body. On her refusal to sign, she is ousted in favor of Ntombi, mother of the heir apparent, Prince Makhosetive. Ntombi is installed as Regent, and power rests with the Liqoqo.

1986. Prince Makhosetive is installed as King Mswati III at the age of 18, and the Liqoqo is abolished.

1987. King Mswati III dissolves parliament in September, 1 year early. In November, elections are held and a new cabinet is appointed.

1992. In February the People's United Democratic Movement (PUDEMO) declares itself an opposition party, which is illegal.

1993. More than 50 opposition activists are arrested, including leaders of PUDEMO and the Swaziland Youth Congress (SWAYOCO). The local council system of indirect elections ends, and direct elections are held.

1996. PUDEMO announce plans for a campaign of protests and civil disobedience following the government's failure to respond to demands for the installation of a multi-party system and for the adoption of a constitution that would restrict the monarch to symbolic role in government.

1997. In mid-October the Swaziland Federation of Trade Unions (SFTU) calls for countrywide strikes in support of demands for democratic reform after talks with the government fail to produce any agreement. Support for strikes is low as a result of the limited success of earlier strikes.

FUTURE TRENDS

The Swaziland economy will for the foreseeable future continue to be heavily reliant on the South African economy as well as regional economic organizations such as the Southern African Customs Union and the Southern African Development Cooperation. Its small size and landlocked location make any changes in economic partnerships difficult to envisage. Even with greater regional integration, the dependence on South Africa will continue as South Africa has the largest manufacturing sector in southern Africa, as well as sophisticated financial expertise, and the ability to provide effective management for its investments in neighboring states.

Nevertheless, to exploit the benefits of regional integration and maintain economic stability, Swaziland is being pressured to speed-up its **privatization** program, upgrade **infrastructure**, and improve the regulation of the financial sector. The political maneuverings have to date been seen as having little effect on the economy. However, there is no doubt that Swaziland will receive more aid and international cooperation if the awaited constitutional review recommends a bill of rights, the introduction of a multiparty democratic system, and the reversion of the king to the role of constitutional monarch.

DEPENDENCIES

Swaziland has no territories or colonies.

BIBLIOGRAPHY

Commonwealth Secretariat. "Swaziland." *The Commonwealth Yearbook 2000.* Birmingham, UK: Stationery Office, 2000.

Economist Intelligence Unit. *Country Profile: Swaziland.* London: Economist Intelligence Unit, 2001.

Hodd, Michael. "Swaziland." *The Economies of Africa.* Aldershot: Dartmouth, 1991.

Swaziland. <http://www.magma.ca/~mali/swaziland/main.htm>. Accessed September 2001.

U.S. Central Intelligence Agency. *World Factbook 2001.* <http://www.odci.gov/cia/publications/factbook/index.html>. Accessed September 2001.

U.S. Department of State. *Background Notes: Swaziland, August 2000.* <http://www.state.gov/www/background_notes/swazi_0008_bgn.html>. Accessed September 2001.

—Allan C. K. Mukungu

TANZANIA

CAPITAL: Dodoma. In 1996, the capital was officially moved from Dar es Salaam to Dodoma. The National Assembly now meets regularly in the new capital, though most government ministries are still located in Dar es Salaam. Slowly, government ministries are being relocated to Dodoma.

MONETARY UNIT: Tanzanian shilling (TSh). One shilling equals 100 cents. Coins include 5, 10, 20, and 50 cents and 1, 5, 10, and 20 shillings. Notes include 10, 20, 50, 100, 200, 500, and 1,000 shillings.

CHIEF EXPORTS: Coffee, manufactured goods, cotton, cashew nuts, minerals, tobacco, sisal.

CHIEF IMPORTS: Consumer goods, machinery and transportation equipment, industrial raw materials, crude oil.

GROSS DOMESTIC PRODUCT: US$23.3 billion (purchasing power parity, 1999 est.).

BALANCE OF TRADE: **Exports:** US$828 million (f.o.b., 1999 est.). **Imports:** US$1.44 billion (f.o.b., 1999 est.).

COUNTRY OVERVIEW

LOCATION AND SIZE. A relatively large country located in East Africa, Tanzania has a total area of 945,087 square kilometers (364,900 square miles), rendering it slightly larger than twice the size of California. The area of Tanzania includes the islands of Mafia, Pemba, and Unguja; the latter 2 form a semi-autonomous region called Zanzibar that is part of an official union with the republic of Tanzania. With a coastline that spans 1,424 kilometers (883 miles), the eastern part of Tanzania borders the Indian Ocean, while to the north lies Kenya, to the northeast Uganda, Rwanda, and Burundi, to the west Zaire, to the southwest Zambia, and, finally, to the south, Malawi and Mozambique. The former capital of Tanzania, Dar es Salaam, is situated slightly to the north of the central point along the coastline of the Indian Ocean. The new

capital, Dodoma, is located slightly to the north of the center of the country.

POPULATION. In 1975, the total population of Tanzania stood at 15.9 million. Since then, the population has grown exponentially, reaching a total of 35.3 million in July 2000. Joe Lugalla, author of *Crisis, Urbanization, and Urban Poverty in Tanzania: A Study of Urban Poverty and Survival Politics,* attributes the rapid population growth to increased life expectancy, a high birth rate accompanied by a declining rate in infant mortality, better health care, the availability of clean water, and better nutrition. With a birth rate of 40.17 births per 1,000 people and a death rate of 12.88 deaths per 1,000 people, the current population growth rate, estimated at 2.3 percent (1997), is still quite significant. Indeed, by 2015, the population will reach approximately 47.2 million. In order to contain this growth, the Tanzanian government adopted an official population policy in 1992. The policy, which came into effect in 1995, emphasizes measures designed to increase the general standard of living of the population. It is argued that one of the major causes of population growth is poverty, as families are obliged to have large families in order to increase familial income. The age structure of Tanzania is relatively young, with 45 percent of the population aged between 0 and 14 years, 52 percent aged between 15 and 64 years, and only 3 percent aged 65 years and over. More than 80 percent of the population of Tanzania resides in rural areas.

In terms of ethnicity, 99 percent of the population of mainland Tanzania is of native African descent—95 percent of which belong to one of the more than 130 tribes that form part of the Bantu group of people. The remaining 1 percent consists of those of Asian, European, and Arab descent. The population of Zanzibar is slightly more diverse, with a higher percentage of Arab and mixed

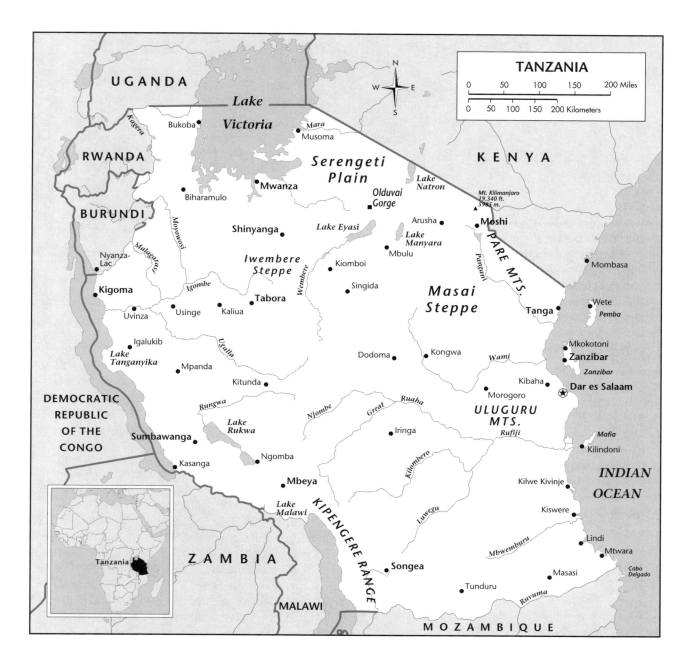

Arab and native African people. Conversely, religion in Zanzibar is more homogeneous (less diverse), with 99 percent of the population adhering to Islam. On the mainland, 45 percent of the population is Christian, 35 percent Muslim, and 20 percent categorized as adherents to indigenous religious systems (ones that are unique to the region). The official languages of the country are English and Kiswahili, the latter being a Bantu-based language with strong Arabic influences. The first language of most people, however, is usually one of the numerous local Bantu languages that are commonly spoken. English is quite prevalent in the business community, and Arabic is widely spoken in Zanzibar. Kiswahili, incidentally, has become the common language of central and eastern Africa.

One of the most daunting problems that the population of Tanzania confronts is the high incidence of HIV/AIDS. According to data released by the European Union on 2 December 2000—World AIDS Day—it is estimated that 1.3 million people in Tanzania have AIDS. This figure does not include the number of people that are afflicted with HIV, the condition that almost inevitably causes the fatal AIDS disease. That same day, President Mkapa announced the formation of the Tanzanian National AIDS Commission (TanAIDS), which will seek to implement the country's national strategy to respond to the HIV/AIDS epidemic. Of course, as in many African countries, the success of an AIDS policy, however well concocted, will depend on the ability of the government to address the structural conditions that facilitate the spread of HIV/AIDS, such as poverty and inequality.

OVERVIEW OF ECONOMY

The area that now comprises Tanzania came under the colonial dominance of Britain and Germany in the late 1880s and early 1890s. Britain assumed complete control of the area, which, at the time, was called Tanganyika, following the allied defeat of Germany in World War I. As a British colony, the economy of Tanganyika was based primarily on the production of **cash crops**, such as coffee, tea, and sisal, designated for consumption in the markets of the British metropole (the colonial power).

In 1961, Tanganyika achieved independence under the leadership of the Tanganyika African National Union (TANU), headed by Julius Nyerere. In 1964, Zanzibar, which was also a British colony, joined Tanganyika as a semi-autonomous island in a political union called the republic of Tanzania. As president of the republic, Nyerere worked with the TANU party to create a **socialist** society and economy. Policies directed towards realizing socialism in the economic sphere revolved around the complete public ownership of the economy, including all firms, factories, and industries. After 1967, the government also controlled the regulation, production, marketing, and distribution of agricultural cash crops, the country's major source of economic activity.

According to Khapoya, the author of the *African Experience,* the government's practice of economic control lost popular support with the intrusive "villagization" policies, in which numerous communities of rural Tanzanians were forced off their sacred ancestral lands and into new "development villages" that were better served with roads and other **infrastructure**. The development of a strong social sector, financed chiefly through aid from the Scandinavian countries, did not offset the resentment felt by many Tanzanians as a result of the villagization policies. Peasant resentment translated into a decline in productivity, which, in conjunction with the soaring increase of oil prices in the late 1970s, placed severe strains upon the Tanzanian economy.

To add to these problems, Tanzania was forced to spend US$500 million on a war effort aimed at repelling an invasion launched by neighboring Ugandan dictator Idi Amin in 1979. As a result of these economic strains, the Tanzanian government was obliged to borrow heavily from both foreign commercial banks and International Financial Institutions (IFIs), such as the World Bank and the International Monetary Fund (IMF).

By the early 1980s, the IFIs demanded that Tanzania implement a **Structural Adjustment Program** (SAP) designed to decrease the role of the government in the economy while increasing the role of the free market, in order to reschedule its debts and qualify for continued foreign aid. Though Nyerere himself refused to accept the SAP, his resignation as president in 1985 opened the way for his successor, Ali Hassan Mwinyi, to accept and implement the SAP reforms in 1986. Ten years later, an Enhanced Structural Adjustment Facility (ESAF) arrangement was made with the IMF, which focused on a major **privatization** campaign of selling state-owned enterprises to the **private sector**.

The economy of Tanzania continues to be based primarily on agricultural activity. Since the value of agricultural goods, which constitute Tanzania's major exports, is lower than the value of manufactured and consumer products, which comprise the country's major imports, the country runs a severe **balance of trade** deficit. The trade deficit, in turn, means that Tanzania must continue to borrow money in order to pay for its imports. In 1999, for example, the total debt stood at US$7.7 billion. According to the U.S. Department of State, the servicing of the debt absorbs about 40 percent of total government expenditures. In addition to loans, Tanzania is dependent upon foreign aid. In 1997 alone, Tanzania received US$963 million in aid. Most of Tanzania's exports are directed towards the markets of the European Union (EU), while aid also comes predominately from the countries of the EU.

POLITICS, GOVERNMENT, AND TAXATION

The legislative branch of the Tanzanian government consists of a **unicameral** National Assembly elected by popular vote. There is also a House of Representatives in Zanzibar, which makes laws specifically for the semi-autonomous island. The executive branch of the government consists of a president, who is both chief of state and head of government, and a cabinet, whose members are appointed by the president from among representatives in the National Assembly. Zanzibar elects a president who is head of government for matters internal to the island. The legal system is based on English common law, while the judicial branch of the government comprises a Court of Appeal, and a High Court, whose judges are appointed by the president. The army is considered more or less apolitical (not involved in politics), and the country has never experienced a coup d'etat (political overthrow).

Throughout most of Tanzania's post-independence history, the country has been a one-party democracy, dominated by the Chama Cha Mapinduzi (CCM, or the "Revolutionary Party"). The CCM emerged in 1977, following the consolidation of TANU and the Afro-Shirazi

Party, the ruling party in Zanzibar. Prior to the merger, candidates of the respective parties possessed the sole right to compete for electoral office. Similarly, until 1992, when the state decided to introduce a multi-party system, all persons wishing to hold electoral office had to be members of the CCM party.

In 1973, the TANU government announced its decision to relocate the capital from Dar es Salaam to Dodoma—an urban bastion of TANU/CCM support. The official reason given to explain the move related to Dodoma's central geographical position in the country and thus its symbolic national importance. The move did not take effect until 1996, however, when an appropriate building to house the National Assembly was finally constructed.

Under the leadership of Nyerere, the ideology of TANU and its CCM postdecessor was a particular variant (version) of African socialism called Ujamaa, which emphasized the central role of the extended family. According to Nyerere, prior to the colonial period in Africa, African communities based on networks of extended families were relatively egalitarian and free of exploitative relationships. Although Nyerere's argument may have actually been a romanticization of the past, it nonetheless served to inform the Ujamaa vision of a return to the communal egalitarian ethos of the past within a context of a partially modern (industrial) socialist society.

The first general multi-party elections in Tanzania were held in October-November 1995. The CCM candidate, Benjamin W. Mkapa, won the presidential election, while the CCM party gained a majority of seats in the parliamentary elections. Mkapa, reelected for a second term in 2000, has more or less abandoned the old socialist ideology of the party, promoting, rather, a free market economy in line with the structural reforms supported by the World Bank and the IMF. With 244 seats in the National Assembly out of a total of 269, the CCM continues to dominate Tanzanian politics. The 2 major opposition parties, the Chama Cha Demokrasia na Maendeleo (CHADEMA) and the Civic United Front (CUF), respectively have 4 and 15 seats. While the former is more or less a centrist party that advocates constitutional democratic reform, the latter is a regionalist party from Zanzibar.

Though many observers, such as the U.S. State Department, have declared Tanzania an island of political stability in East Africa, the reelection of the CCM in the House of Representatives in Zanzibar has engendered considerable political violence. The CCM's victory in the 2000 elections was marred (tainted) by electoral irregularities that led to the re-running of polls in 16 constituencies. International observers condemned the format of the ballots that were used and the CUF denounced the elections as illegitimate. Since the elections took place,

clashes between police and CUF supporters have occurred in Zanzibar and Pemba, leaving at least 30 people dead.

In terms of government revenue, import **duties** are the major source of government income, accounting for 31.7 percent of total revenue in the 1996 **fiscal year**. Consumption taxes are the second most important, while **income taxes** are the third, accounting, respectively, for 26.8 percent and 24.3 percent of total revenue during the same period.

There are a total of 12 income tax brackets, leading to a steeply **progressive taxation** system in which those that earn low incomes pay a lower percentage of income tax than those that earn higher incomes. For example, the lowest tax bracket, which consists of people that earn less than 20,000 shillings per month, are exempted from taxation because their incomes are considered too low, whereas the highest tax bracket, comprised of individuals who earn more than 700,000 shillings per month, pay 35 percent of their income to taxes. At the same time, however, the high sales taxes and **excise taxes** levied on goods and services, which form part of consumption taxes, strongly affect the poor. Excisable goods, for instance, such as alcoholic beverages and petroleum products, are subjected to excise tax rates as high as 30 percent.

INFRASTRUCTURE, POWER, AND COMMUNICATIONS

According to the U.S. State Department, infrastructure in Tanzania is extremely poor. In terms of the road network, for instance, only 3,704 kilometers (2,296 miles) of a total of 88,200 kilometers (54,684 miles) of highway is paved. Paved highways link Dar es Salaam to Tunduru, Dodoma, Tanga, and Arusha. The remaining 84,496 kilometers (52,388 miles) of highway is unpaved, making it extremely difficult to reach certain areas from Dar es Salaam, such as Lindi and Mtwara, during the rainy season. At the same time, many rural roads are virtually impassable, as seasonal washouts are commonplace. Although the road network has suffered as a result of many years of government debt-related negligence, funds allocated for road maintenance and rehabilitation have increased in the past 10 years.

With a combined total of 3,569 kilometers (2,213 miles) of railway track, there are 2 railway systems that operate independently in Tanzania. In addition to operating the internal railway network, the Tanzania Railways Corporation (TRC) connects the country with Uganda, Kenya, Burundi, and Rwanda. Many parts of the TRC railway network are in need of major repairs. The Tanzanian/Zambian Railway Authority (TAZARA), in contrast, connects the port of Dar es Salaam with Zambia. Following the end of apartheid (the system of racial segregation in South Africa that prompted many countries to

Communications

Country	Newspapers	Radios	TV Sets[a]	Cable subscribers[a]	Mobile Phones[a]	Fax Machines[a]	Personal Computers[a]	Internet Hosts[b]	Internet Users[b]
	1996	1997	1998	1998	1998	1998	1998	1999	1999
Tanzania	4	279	21	0.0	1	N/A	1.6	0.05	25
United States	215	2,146	847	244.3	256	78.4	458.6	1,508.77	74,100
Dem. Rep. of Congo	3	375	135	N/A	0	N/A	N/A	0.00	1
Kenya	9	104	21	N/A	0	N/A	2.5	0.19	35

[a]Data are from International Telecommunication Union, *World Telecommunication Development Report 1999* and are per 1,000 people.
[b]Data are from the Internet Software Consortium (http://www.isc.org) and are per 10,000 people.

SOURCE: World Bank. *World Development Indicators 2000.*

restrict economic ties with the country), the amount of income generated by TAZARA, in addition to the port of Dar es Salaam, has drastically declined as a result of new competition with the South African Railway system and the South African ports of Durban and Port Elizabeth.

There are a total of 11 airports in Tanzania with paved runways. Dar es Salaam International Airport, Kilimanjaro International Airport, and the Zanzibar Airport handle international air traffic. Several international airlines provide transportation to countries around the world, while the Tanzanian airline, Air Tanzania, has regional and domestic routes across Southern Africa.

The Tanzanian Electric Supply Company (TANESCO) supplies the country with electricity, 95 percent of which is derived from hydroelectric power. As a result of this dependency, power shortages often occur in times of regional drought. The government has taken measures to diversify energy sources, including support for projects to develop the Songo Songo natural gas reserve and the Mchuchuma coal fields.

Telecommunications infrastructure in Tanzania is considerably underdeveloped. With only 4.5 telephone mainlines per 1,000 people (est. 1999), telephone services are highly unpredictable and extremely expensive. The situation contrasts sharply with the United States, where there are 640 telephone lines per 1,000 people (est. 1996). In conjunction with the international donor community, the Tanzanian government has sought to ameliorate the situation through increased investment for telecommunications infrastructure. In 1999, the international donor community commenced sponsorship of a 5-year, US$250 million program to rehabilitate and expand the existing telephone network.

ECONOMIC SECTORS

Agriculture is by far Tanzania's most important economic sector, in terms of both employment provision and contribution to GDP. Unfortunately, the large degree of dependency on this sector renders the Tanzanian economy particularly vulnerable to adverse weather conditions and unfavorable prices in international **primary commodity** markets. The exceptionally low level of industrial development makes the negative economic impacts associated with agricultural dependency all the more severe.

Industry and mining are relatively small areas of economic activity, though many observers, such as the U.S. State Department, believe that the mining sector offers important prospects for economic growth.

AGRICULTURE

As the pillar of both the domestic and the export economy, the agricultural sector in Tanzania engages 80 percent of the **labor force**, which equaled approximately 13.495 million in 1999, while providing 49 percent of the

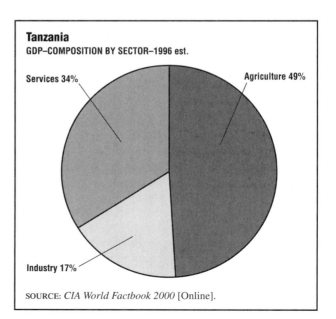

Tanzania
GDP–COMPOSITION BY SECTOR–1996 est.

Services 34%
Agriculture 49%
Industry 17%

SOURCE: *CIA World Factbook 2000* [Online].

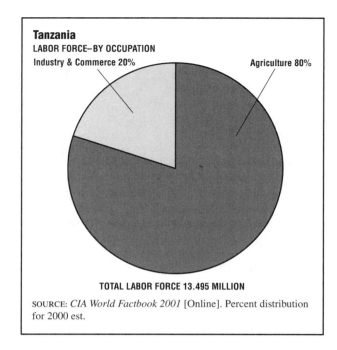

Tanzania
LABOR FORCE–BY OCCUPATION

Industry & Commerce 20%

Agriculture 80%

TOTAL LABOR FORCE 13.495 MILLION

SOURCE: *CIA World Factbook 2001* [Online]. Percent distribution for 2000 est.

a dispute has emerged between cashew producers and cashew exporters over the government-set prices. While the former supports the prices, the latter argues they are unreasonable. The Economist Intelligence Unit (EUI) argues that the quasi-official prices are detrimental to agricultural growth, as they cause confusion and conflict. At the same time, however, the government argues that they apply pressure on private purchasers to pay fair prices for different crops. Despite the pressures of **deregulation** in the agricultural sector, the government has not made plans to abandon the quasi-official pricing system.

The February 2001 Tanzania Country Report issued by the EIU forecasts that GDP growth in Tanzania will equal 5.3 percent in 2001 and 5.9 percent in 2002. Not surprisingly, this growth will be led by the production of traditional agricultural commodity exports. While growth in GDP represents a positive development, the cash crop basis of this growth renders it largely unsustainable. In other words, Tanzania is currently experiencing a period of favorable production conditions, which, due to the volatile (frequently changing) nature of the weather, are guaranteed to change, for better or worse.

Production patterns in Tanzania and other agriculturally based developing nations oscillate (rapidly increase and decrease) dramatically, according to the shifting weather conditions in a given harvest year. In the past 10 years, for instance, maize production in Tanzania has varied considerably, ranging from a high of 2,638 produced tons in 1995–96, to a low of 2,107 tons in 1996–97. Though maize production is largely for domestic consumption, the same unstable patterns of production characterize agricultural crops designated for exportation, as both are subject to the debilitating effects of drought and flooding during the rainy season.

The volatile prices of agricultural commodities on international markets exacerbate (make worse) the instability of countries such as Tanzania that are highly dependent upon cash crop exports. For example, in any given year, the international prices of a commodity such as coffee can increase or decrease considerably, depending upon how much or how little all coffee-producing countries collectively produce. If there is a large international coffee harvest, prices will diminish, as competition will increase. The same holds true in the opposite direction.

Another major inhibiting factor working against the sustainability of growth generated by agricultural production relates to the small amount of existing arable land in Tanzania. Only 4 percent of all land is arable, with only 1 percent suitable for permanent crops. To make matters worse, Tanzania currently confronts issues of soil degradation, deforestation, and **desertification**. For all these reasons, it is imperative that Tanzania develop the other sectors of its economy.

country's GDP (est. 1996). Agricultural products include coffee, sisal, tea, cotton, pyrethrum, cashew nuts, tobacco, cloves, corn, wheat, cassava, bananas, and vegetables. Livestock production includes cattle, sheep, and goats. Agricultural output remains predominately based on **small holder** production, as opposed to estate cultivation, though the latter does account for some sisal, tea, coffee, tobacco, rice, wheat, and wattle (construction material made of tied-together poles or sticks) production. Cash crops, such as coffee, tea, cotton, cashews, sisal, cloves, and pyrethrum account for the vast majority of export earnings. Maize, paddy, wheat, and cassava are produced for domestic consumption.

In terms of agricultural exports, coffee constitutes the most important cash crop. According to the IMF, coffee accounted for 17.7 percent of Tanzania's total exports in 1996. At 16.3 percent of total exports, cotton was the second most important cash crop, followed by cashew nuts (12.7 percent), tobacco (6.4 percent), tea (2.9 percent), and sisal (0.7 percent). In Zanzibar, the major cash crop is cloves, 90 percent of which are produced on the island of Pemba. The major importers of Tanzania's agricultural exports consist of the EU countries, especially the United Kingdom, Germany, and the Netherlands.

In the past, the agricultural sector was completely controlled by the government. While **liberalization** of the sector has rapidly occurred, there are still government marketing boards that set quasi-official (semi-official) prices for certain crops. Purchasers are not forced to abide by the set prices, but often feel compelled to because most peasants normally support the prices the government establishes. This has led to some conflict, and most recently

INDUSTRY

MINING. Accounting for approximately 17 percent of GDP (est. 1996), industry plays a small, albeit important role in the Tanzanian economy. As a subdivision of industry, the mining sector alone constitutes about 5 percent of GDP. At the same time, however, both industry in general and mining in particular engage a relatively small percentage of the labor force. Indeed, the industrial sector combined with the commercial sector provides employment for only 20 percent of the labor force.

The country is endowed with a wide variety of mineral deposits, including gold, diamonds, salt, gypsum, gemstones, iron ore, natural gas, phosphates, coal, nickel, and cobalt. Many of these minerals are exported to other countries, and mining, excluding petroleum products, accounted for 7.3 percent of export earnings in 1996. In the same year, petroleum products comprised 2.1 percent of export earnings.

As in the case of agricultural produce, however, mining output and output of refined minerals seems to oscillate considerably from year to year. In 1989, for example, 617,000 tons of petroleum products were produced, whereas in 1992, 3 years later, this figure plummeted to 55,900 tons. Similarly, 3,200 tons of aluminum were produced in 1993, while this figure dropped to 1,100 in 1995. According to the U.S. State Department, some of the impediments that prevent effective exploitation of mineral resources include a lack of capital, poor infrastructure, bureaucratic inefficiency, and limited technology.

Under the auspices of the IMF and World Bank sponsored SAPs, Tanzania has enthusiastically promoted **foreign direct investment** in the mining sector, effectively reversing its strong regulatory policies. Though few foreign mining firms are actually in operation, many **multinational corporations** (MNCs) (firms that operate in several countries) are beginning to look upon prospects in Tanzania favorably. Recently, there have been several developments with a Canadian company, Tanganyika Oil, which owns 75 percent of an oil concession in Mandawa, 250 kilometers (155 miles) south of Dar es Salaam.

Some critics, such as Chachage Seithy L. Chachage, author of the essay "New Forms of Accumulating in Tanzania: The Case of Gold Mining," which appeared in *Mining and Structural Adjustment: Studies on Zimbabwe and Tanzania,* severely criticize Tanzania's new policy of openness. Chachage argues that the government is on the path of creating an "economy of plunder," in which the benefits of the country's rich minerals will accrue to foreigners rather than Tanzanians. At the same time, the government is in an extremely difficult position, as it lacks the resources to exploit the mineral reserves itself. This incapacity is largely related to the limited money the government has to invest in economic projects because of the large burden imposed by **debt servicing**.

MANUFACTURING. According to the U.S. Department of State, Tanzania's industrial, or manufacturing sector, is one of the smallest in Africa. The main industrial activities include producing raw materials, **import substitutes**, and processed agricultural products. Specific areas of activity include production of cement, soft drinks, corrugated iron sheeting, food processing, chemicals, leather products, and textiles.

Once again, manufacturing activities seem to oscillate in their respective output capacities. In 1991, for example, 85.2 million square meters of textiles were produced, whereas 5 years later, in 1995, the output had deteriorated to 33.4 million square meters. The production of iron sheets similarly suffered decline. In 1993, for instance, 25,800 tons of iron sheets were produced, while in 1996, the figure dropped to 6,400 tons. Production of cement is one area of industrial activity that has escaped this negative pattern. Notwithstanding a huge increase in output in 1991, production has increased at a steady pace, growing from 589,100 tons in 1989, to 725,800 tons in 1996.

One of the major factors contributing to industrial instability relates to persistent power shortages caused by low rainfall. Since Tanzania is almost entirely dependent upon hydroelectricity, low rainfall translates into low water levels in hydroelectric dams. In November 2000, the Ministry of Energy and Minerals was obliged to announce the temporary introduction of power rationing, intended to reduce electricity consumption by about 35 percent until the beginning of the next rainy season in January 2001.

Government involvement in the industrial sector, as in all spheres of economic activity, has steadily declined since the early 1990s. The Presidential Parastatal Sector Reform Commission (PSRC), an integral component of the SAPs, continues to scrutinize **parastatals** and push for privatization. By June 1998, 201 firms of the 398 parastatals singled out by the PSRC experienced privatization. It is argued that private firms are more efficient and competitive than parastatals, as they must depend on profit rather than guaranteed government financing in order to continue operation.

SERVICES

TOURISM. Tanzania's tourism sector, which, according to the U.S. State Department, is growing at a rate of more than 8 percent per annum (est. 1999), is one of the country's most important sources of foreign currency. Currently, most of the tourism sector investment is concentrated in the northern part of the country in the so-called

Northern Safari Circuit (Ngorongoro Crater, Serengeti Plains, and Lake Manyara). There, a number of internationally acclaimed hotels provide services to tourists from around the world, particularly Europeans.

Numerous government initiatives have sought to increase investment in the Southern Circuit (Selous Game Reserve, Mikumi and Ruaha National Parks) as well. Though service facilities and infrastructure in this area are poor, the area's diverse wildlife renders it an ideal location for further tourist development. The international donor community has helped finance the rehabilitation of infrastructure in the Southern Circuit, thereby complementing efforts put forward by the Tanzanian government. The government, for its part, recently established the Tanzanian Tourism Board (TTB) to oversee tourist development in the country, though it has renounced its previous policy orientation of controlling the tourist market.

FINANCIAL SERVICES. Legislation passed in August 1991 led to a fundamental **restructuring** of the banking system in Tanzania. Prior to the legislation, the government exercised a complete **monopoly** over the banking sector. Under the old system, the Bank of Tanzania acted as the central bank, while the government-run National Bank of Commerce (NBC) accounted for over 75 percent of the country's financial transactions. Although the Bank of Tanzania has retained its functions, which include the administration of the exchange control, the NBC has been subdivided with the creation of a separate National Micro-finance Bank (NMB). Both the NBC and the NMB are in the process of being privatized.

Since the banking legislation was passed, several private banks have registered with the Bank of Tanzania. In addition to some domestic financial institutions, numerous foreign banks have established operations, including Citibank of New York, Stanbic Bank of South Africa, Standard Charter Bank of Great Britain, EuroAfrican Bank, Akiba Commercial Bank, and Exim Bank.

INTERNATIONAL TRADE

Despite numerous Structural Adjustment Programs designed to increase exports and encourage growth and investment, Tanzania has suffered from a chronic negative **balance of payments** since the late 1970s. Moreover, instead of progressively diminishing, the balance of payments deficit has actually increased. Indeed, in the past 5 years, the country's deficit has grown from US$297.5 million in 1997, to US$528.5 million in 1999.

Tanzania's major exports include coffee, cotton, tea, sisal, tobacco, cashew nuts, and minerals. Together, agricultural exports accounted for 56.8 percent of all exports in 1996, while manufactured products only constituted 16.5 percent of exports. In the same year, the countries of

Trade (expressed in billions of US$): Tanzania		
	Exports	Imports
1975	.374	.780
1980	.511	1.252
1985	.247	1.324
1990	.415	1.027
1995	.639	1.619
1998	.674	1.454

SOURCE: International Monetary Fund. *International Financial Statistics Yearbook 1999.*

the EU collectively purchased the largest percentage share of Tanzanian exports (42 percent). Interestingly, however, Tanzania's dependence on Europe as a market for exports has substantially declined, as other regions, such as Asia and Africa, have become more important. In 1989, Africa accounted for 4.2 percent of all exports, while Asia accounted for 22.9 percent. By 1996, these figures respectively rose to 11.5 percent and 27.4 percent.

Tanzanian imports range the gamut of products, including machinery, transport and equipment (**capital goods**); oil, crude oil, petroleum products, industrial raw materials (**intermediate goods**); and finally, textiles, apparel, and food and foodstuffs (**consumer goods**). In 1996, capital goods comprised 36 percent of imports, intermediate goods 38 percent, and consumer goods 26 percent. Countries of the European Union are the major sources of imports, though their importance has declined considerably as the importance of Asian and African countries have concomitantly increased. In 1989, the EU (then the European Community) accounted for 58.4 percent of Tanzanian imports, Africa 3.9 percent, and Asia 13 percent. By 1996, the figures respectively changed to 42 percent, 11.5 percent, and 27.4 percent. Important African and Asian trading partners (for both exports and imports) include Japan, India, Hong Kong, China, Singapore, Kenya, Zambia, and Burundi.

One of the major criticisms of the IMF/World Bank sponsored SAPs is that trade liberalization will lock countries like Tanzania into a pattern of sustained agricultural exportation at the expense of industry and commerce. At the most basic level, reduction of barriers will mean countries with emerging manufacturing industries will have to compete with much more competitive and efficient manufacturing industries from abroad. The result could be a long-term structural entrenchment of the only economic area in which Tanzania and similar countries can compete internationally: the agricultural sector. This is disadvantageous because international terms of trade accord higher prices to products that contain **value added** (meaning that they undergo a degree of manufacturing), such as capital goods, than those that contain less or no value added, such as agricultural commodities. Thus, a country like Tanzania that depends, in large part, upon agricultural exports and higher value added imports, will suffer from a negative balance of trade.

This seems to be precisely the situation in Tanzania, where even the pro-trade Economist Intelligence Unit attributes the recent deficit increase to weak international commodity prices for coffee and tea, 2 of the country's most important exports. The free trade rationale that all countries will benefit by individually trading that which they produce more efficiently than their counterparts conspicuously overlooks this crucial dilemma.

At the same time, however, trade liberalization at the regional level may offer positive benefits for participating countries as it can potentially enable them to realize the gains of competition and specialization in an environment characterized by a more level playing field. In other words, if 2 countries such as Tanzania and Mozambique partake in free trade, the competition will be more even, thereby enabling each to exchange a wide array of products, including manufactures and industrial commodities. This, in turn, will facilitate increased production capacity, preparing them to compete more effectively at a global level. Currently, Tanzania is a member of 2 separate regional trading arrangements (RTAs): the East African Community and the Southern African Development Community. The former includes Tanzania, Kenya, and Uganda; the latter comprises Tanzania, Zaire, Zambia, Malawi, and Mozambique.

MONEY

The value of the Tanzanian currency, the shilling, is determined by a free **floating exchange rate** system based on supply and demand in international foreign exchange markets. This means that if the shilling is in high demand in international exchange markets, its value will accordingly increase in relation to other currencies. The value of the shilling, like many other currencies, is normally expressed against the value of the U.S. dollar. Over

the past several years, this value has steadily depreciated. In 1995, for example, the **exchange rate** was 574.76 shillings for 1 U.S. dollar. In January 2000, the exchange rate rose to 798.9 shillings for 1 U.S. dollar.

According to the Economist Intelligence Unit, one of the major factors behind the depreciation of the shilling relates to the decline in international commodity prices for the agricultural cash crops on which the export economy depends. The EIU forecasts a further depreciation of 5.1 percent in 2001, increasing to 12.4 percent in 2002. The poor will doubtlessly experience the ramifications of the depreciation process more than any other group, as a devalued shilling means that more money will be needed to purchase needed imports from abroad, such as food and other consumer products.

POVERTY AND WEALTH

Although a small segment of Tanzanians with secure access to employment in the public and business sectors enjoy a relatively high standard of living, the vast majority of Tanzanians live in poverty. Indeed, the **United Nations Development Programme**'s (UNDP) human development index (HDI) listings, which arranges countries according to their overall level of human development, ranks Tanzania 156th out of a total of 174 nations. The HDI, a composite index (one that assesses more than one variable) that measures life expectancy at birth, adult literacy rate, school enrollment ratio, and **GDP per capita**, is indicative of a country's general social and economic well-being. As such, Tanzania's HDI ranking demonstrates that the country is one of the poorest and least developed in the world.

Under the socialist policies of Julius Nyerere, the Tanzanian government focused heavily on achieving social **equity** through the development of a strong health and education sector. Inequality in the early years of Ujamaa was mainly the result of the colonial legacy in which some peasants were connected to the cash crop export economy while others were not. Those that lived in areas favorable for cash crop production enjoyed a slightly higher standard of living than their subsistence peasant

Exchange rates: Tanzania	
Tanzanian shillings (TSh) per US$1	
Dec 2000	803.34
2000	800.41
1999	744.76
1998	664.67
1997	612.12
1996	579.98
SOURCE: CIA *World Factbook 2001* [ONLINE].	

GDP per Capita (US$)					
Country	1975	1980	1985	1990	1998
Tanzania	N/A	N/A	N/A	175	173
United States	19,364	21,529	23,200	25,363	29,683
Dem. Rep. of Congo	392	313	293	247	127
Kenya	301	337	320	355	334
SOURCE: United Nations. *Human Development Report 2000; Trends in human development and per capita income.*					

Distribution of Income or Consumption by Percentage Share: Tanzania

Lowest 10%	2.8
Lowest 20%	6.8
Second 20%	11.0
Third 20%	15.1
Fourth 20%	21.6
Highest 20%	45.5
Highest 10%	30.1

Survey year: 1993
Note: This information refers to expenditure shares by percentiles of the population and is ranked by per capita expenditure.

SOURCE: *2000 World Development Indicators* [CD-ROM].

counterparts. Though Nyerere's social policies were generous, they were unsustainable in a context of economic crisis and negligible growth. Moreover, many critics, such as Enos S. Bukuku, the author of *The Tanzanian Economy: Income Distribution and Economic Growth,* argue that Nyerere's development policies promoted the modern, nascent industrial sector, at the expense of agriculture. The result was actually increased poverty in the countryside, and the creation of a few highly skilled and highly paid jobs associated with the parastatals and policies of import substitution industrialization.

Today, the cleavage (division; in this case economic) between the general peasantry and those with higher-paying jobs in the urban centers persists, though this type of inequality is characteristic of most countries that are still in the throes of the development process. According to the CIA *World Factbook,* the poorest 10 percent of the Tanzanian population consume a marginal 2.9 percent of total national consumption, while the richest 10 percent consume 30.2 percent. In 1998, the GNP per capita in Tanzania was estimated at a paltry US$220, whereas the GNP per capita in the United States was US$29,240 in the same year.

Social policy in Tanzania is currently guided by the so-called "Vision 2025," a comprehensive framework emphasizing 7 priority areas linked to overall poverty reduction. In 2000–01, the Tanzanian government allocated its budget amid these 7 priority areas as follows: education (23.2 percent), health (8.4 percent), roads (6.4 percent), agriculture (1.0 percent), judiciary (1.0 percent), water (0.6 percent), and HIV/AIDS (0.6 percent). While the government's coherent strategy is a welcomed development, the IMF notes that it needs work in some areas, including education, promotion of agricultural/rural development, gender strategies, and a more comprehensive approach to HIV/AIDS and the environment.

The vast majority of Tanzanians spend their meager incomes on the basic necessities of life, such as food, rent, clothing, fuel, and transportation. Very little is spent on entertainment and recreation, which are considered luxuries for those that live in considerable poverty. To make matters worse, in the past 10 years the increase in the GNP per capita has been grossly outweighed by mounting **inflation,** which means that Tanzanians are having an increasingly difficult time purchasing the commodities essential for human existence. The UNDP estimates that the annual growth rate in GNP per capita between 1990 to 1998 was 0.4 percent, while the average annual rate of inflation during the same period was 24.3 percent.

WORKING CONDITIONS

The Tanzanian labor force stood at 13.495 million in 1999. Although recent statistics on the level of unemployment are unavailable, a 1991 statistical abstract produced by the Tanzanian Bureau of Statistics stated that the unemployment rate in rural and urban areas was 2.2 percent and 10.6 percent, respectively. The higher unemployment rate in the urban areas results from both a lack of economic prospects and a much higher rate of population growth. This latter factor, in turn, stems chiefly from a high rate of rural to urban migration, caused, in large part, by the migrant perception that urban employment is generally higher paying.

Household Consumption in PPP Terms

Country	All food	Clothing and footwear	Fuel and power[a]	Health care[b]	Education[b]	Transport & Communications	Other
Tanzania	67	6	5	4	12	6	0
United States	13	9	9	4	6	8	51
Dem. Rep. of Congo	N/A	N/A	N/A	N/A	N/A	N/A	N/A
Kenya	31	9	21	2	8	3	26

Data represent percentage of consumption in PPP terms.
[a]Excludes energy used for transport.
[b]Includes government and private expenditures.

SOURCE: World Bank. *World Development Indicators 2000.*

Confronted with the reality of limited opportunity in the urban areas, however, many migrants are obliged to find work in the **informal sector** of the economy, which consists of the wide range of activities that are unregulated and untaxed by the government. Those that work in the informal sector do not enjoy the various employment protections afforded by the government. On the contrary, many informal sector participants, considered nuisances, confront harassment and intimidation by police and government officials. Joe Lugalla, author of *Crisis, Urbanization, and Urban Poverty in Tanzania: A Study of Poverty and Survival Politics,* argues that the informal sector is vital for the livelihoods of the urban poor and that government restrictions and harassment are therefore regressive. Instead, the government could encourage informal activity by abolishing restrictions such as requirements to operate in fixed premises and other bureaucratic restrictions which prevent licensing for certain activities.

The right of association for workers in the formal sector is recognized by the Tanzanian Constitution, though the government-created Tanzanian Federation of Trade Unions (TFTU) is the only trade union organization in the country. The TFTU, which represents 60 percent of workers in industry and government, is comprised of 11 independent trade unions that have the right to separate from the federation and collect their own dues. If this were to happen, however, 5 percent of the dues must be legally contributed to the TFTU.

All workers are permitted to join unions, but "essential" workers are not permitted to strike. In total, only 25 percent of Tanzania's wage earners are organized in trade unions, with most agricultural workers remaining unorganized. Moreover, the right to strike is only granted following complicated and protracted mediation and conciliation procedures. According to the U.S. Department of State, frustrated workers have staged impromptu, illegal, wildcat strikes and walkouts pending resolutions. The Tanzanian's Security of Employment Act of 1964 prohibits discriminatory activities by employers against union members and employers found guilty of such activities are legally required to reinstate workers.

The Tanzanian Constitution prohibits forced labor and work by children under 12 years of age in the formal wage sector in both rural and urban areas. At the same time, children are permitted to work on family farms or in herding domestic livestock. Young persons between the ages of 12 and 15 may engage in industrial employment but only between the hours of 6 a.m. to 6 p.m. Government enforcement of the minimum working age and of regulations governing the rights of young workers, however, is highly inadequate and has reportedly declined with increased privatization. Approximately 3,000 to 5,000 children engage in seasonal employment on various cash crop plantations. They are often paid less than their adult counterparts and are subjected to hazardous and detrimental conditions, especially on sisal plantations. An additional 1,500 to 3,000 children work in unregulated gemstone mines, while thousands assist their parents in unregulated piecework manufacturing in the informal sector. The ugly reality is that for many families suffering from acute poverty, children must work simply in order for the household to survive.

Although there is a legal minimum wage in Tanzania, which equals approximately US$30 per month, it is not always sufficient to provide an adequate standard of living for a worker and family. Consequently, many workers must depend on the extended family, or a second, or even third, job. There is no standard legal workweek for non-government employees, though most employers retain a 6-day, 44- to 48-hour workweek. An occupational health and safety factory inspection system is managed by the Ministry of Labor and Social Welfare and Youth Development to monitor implementation of the several laws that regulate safety in the workplace. Its effectiveness is severely limited. Workers have the right to take an employer to court through their TFTU branch for failure to comply with health and environmental standards, though they cannot remove themselves from dangerous situations without jeopardizing their employment.

COUNTRY HISTORY AND ECONOMIC DEVELOPMENT

EARLY CENTURIES A.D. Bantu farmers migrate to Southern Africa from the west and south, largely displacing the original ethnic groups that used a click-tongue language similar to that of South Africa's Bushmen and Hottentots.

8TH-12TH CENTURY. Arab, Persian, and Indian traders and immigrants build several highly developed cities and trading states along the coast, including Kibaha, a settlement that held ascendancy until the Portuguese destroyed it in the early 1500s.

1498-1506. The Portuguese explore the East African coast and claim control over the entire area. Control is nominal, however, and the Portuguese are driven out by the early 18th century.

MID-19TH CENTURY. European exploration of the interior begins, led by German missionaries and English explorers.

1840. Sultan Seyyid Said of the Omani Arabs moves his capital from Muscat to Zanzibar, promoting a lucrative trade in slaves and ivory.

1876. The British succeed in forcing Said to abolish the slave trade.

1884. Karl Peters, head of the Society for German Colonization, concludes a series of treaties with chiefs from the interior, establishing a German protectorate over the area.

1886–1890. Anglo-German agreements are negotiated that delineate British and German spheres of influence in the interior. Also, Zanzibar becomes a British protectorate, administered through an Arab sultan.

1905–07. The Maji Maji rebellion against European rule erupts, resulting in a total of 120,000 African casualties from fighting or starvation.

1918. The United Kingdom assumes complete control of Tanganyika.

1954. Julius Nyerere establishes the nationalistic Tanganyika African National Union (TANU).

1956. The Afro-Shirazi Party is founded in Zanzibar, led by Abaid Karume.

1959. The United Kingdom agrees to grant Tanganyika internal self-government and Nyerere becomes chief minister of the new government.

1959. Tanganyika achieves full independence and soon after becomes a republic within the Commonwealth with Nyerere as president.

1963. Zanzibar achieves independence.

1964. Tanganyika forms a union with Zanzibar, thereby creating the United Republic of Tanzania and embarking on a path towards the realization of socialism based on the ideology of *Ujamaa*.

LATE 1970s. Soaring oil prices in conjunction with Ujamaa's villagization policies seriously undermine the economy.

1977. TANU and the Afro-Shirazi Party merge into the Chama Cha Mapinduzi.

1977. Idi Amin's Ugandan invasion of Tanzania costs the Tanzanian government US$500 million to repel, exacerbating the severe economic situation.

1985–86. Nyerere is succeeded by Ali Hassan Mwinyi, who accepts the International Monetary Fund's and World Bank's Structural Adjustment Package (SAP) in order to qualify for further borrowing and a rescheduling of debt payments. The SAP focuses on acquiring **macroeconomic** stability, privatizing the economy, and export promotion.

1995. The first multi-party elections are held, resulting in a CCM victory.

1995. The Enhanced Structural Adjustment Facility is negotiated with the IMF, emphasizing rapid privatization of parastatals.

FUTURE TRENDS

Like many African states and other developing countries, Tanzania has adopted 2 diametrically opposed models of economic organization that have mutually failed to launch the country on a path of sustainable economic development. Indeed, the socialist policies advanced by Nyerere under the rubric of Ujamaa created a weak economy heavily dependent upon aid and loans from foreign countries, international financial institutions, and commercial banks. The free-market policies advanced by Nyerere's successors under the auspices of the IFI-sponsored SAPs have equally failed to rectify the endemic economic crisis.

While a degree of macroeconomic stability has been achieved, especially in the realm of containing inflation, a growing negative balance of payments, a continued dependence on the exportation of weak agricultural commodities, a mammoth debt, and an enormous degree of poverty continue to characterize the economic situation in Tanzania. If nothing else, the major lesson that can be drawn from the Tanzanian experience is that solutions to economic problems based on unbending principles of ideology are bound to fail in one way or another.

While the Tanzanian government continues to base its policies on free market panaceas (cure-alls), the recent IMF and World Bank's Heavily Indebted Poor Countries Initiative (HIPCI), which reduces the debt-servicing obligations of Tanzania and other heavily indebted poor countries, may enable the government to spend more money on needed social services. The aim of the HIPCI is in fact to accomplish exactly that, with the ultimate intention of creating a more educated labor force and thus a more skilled economy. This is certainly a step in the right direction, though it is doubtful that such a measure will succeed on its own.

DEPENDENCIES

Tanzania has no territories or colonies.

BIBLIOGRAPHY

Bukuku, Enos S. *The Tanzanian Economy: Income Distribution and Economic Growth.* Westport: Praeger Publishers, 1993.

Chachage, Chachage Seithy L. "New Forms of Accumulating in Tanzania: The Case of Gold Mining." In *Mining and Structural Adjustment: Studies on Zimbabwe and Tanzania.* Uppsala: Nordiska Afrikainstitutet, 1993.

Economist Intelligence Unit. *Country Report: Tanzania, Comoros, February 2001.* London: Economist Intelligence Unit, 2001.

International Monetary Fund. *IMF Staff Country Report, Tanzania: Statistical Appendix.* <http://www.imf.org>. Accessed January 2001.

Lugalla, Joe. *Crisis, Urbanization, And Urban Poverty in Tanzania: A Study of Poverty and Survival Politics.* Lanham: University Press of America, 1995.

UNDP. *Human Development Report 2000.* New York: Oxford University Press, 2000.

U.S. Department of State. *FY 1999 Country Commercial Guide: Tanzania.* <http:www.state.gov/www/about_state/business/ com_guides/1999/Africa/Tanzania99.html>. Accessed May 2001.

U.S. Department of State. *Background Notes: Tanzania.* <http: www.state.gov/www/background_notes/tanzania_0008_bgn .html>. Accessed May 2001.

World Bank Group. *Tanzania: Competitiveness Indicators.* <http:// wbln0018.worldbank.org/psd>. Accessed January 2001.

—Neil Burron

TOGO

Togolese Republic
République Togolaise

CAPITAL: Lomé.

MONETARY UNIT: Communauté Financière Africaine franc (CFA Fr). The CFA franc is tied to the French franc at an exchange rate of CFA Fr50 to Fr1. One CFA franc equals 100 centimes. There are coins of 5, 10, 50, 100, and 500 CFA francs, and notes of 500, 1,000, 2,000, 5,000, and 10,000 CFA francs.

CHIEF EXPORTS: Ginned cotton, coffee, cocoa, phosphate.

CHIEF IMPORTS: Consumer goods, foodstuffs, petroleum products.

GROSS DOMESTIC PRODUCT: US$8.6 billion (purchasing power parity, 1999 est.).

BALANCE OF TRADE: Exports: US$400 million (f.o.b., 1999 est.). **Imports:** US$450 million (f.o.b., 1999 est.).

COUNTRY OVERVIEW

LOCATION AND SIZE. The Togolese Republic is situated in West Africa. It is a narrow rectangle of land which extends north from the Bight of Benin, on which it has a small coastline of 50 kilometers (31 miles). To the west lies Ghana, to the east is Benin, and Burkina Faso borders on the north. It has a land area of 56,785 square kilometers (21,925 square miles), making it slightly smaller than West Virginia. Lomé, the capital city, is situated on the coast and is the only city with an international airport.

POPULATION. In mid-1999 the United Nations estimated Togo's population at 4.5 million. With an average annual population growth of 2.6 percent, the population is projected to grow by the year 2025 to 8.5 million. Some 31 percent of the population lives in towns, which have an urban growth rate of 4.8 percent. Togo has a young age profile, with half the population aged less than 14 years. Life expectancy in Togo is 48.8 years. Although infant mortality is down from 110 per 1,000 births in 1980 to 70 in 1995, it remains high. (In the United States,

by way of comparison, the rate is 7 per 1,000 births). Fertility rates remain high, with an estimated average of 6.05 children born per woman. The country's workforce stands at 1.74 million and this comprises about 41.7 percent of the population.

The largest ethnic group, the Ewe, live predominantly in the south and on the coast, and have cross-border ties to Ghana. Also in the south live the Mena and the Ana. The Kabre people are concentrated in the Kozah and Binah prefectures of the Kara region in the north. The Losso and Tchokossi live in north Lamba. The Bassar inhabit Central Kotokoli and Kotokoli, and have strong links to northern Ghana. The population is 10 percent Muslim, one-third Christian, and the remainder follow traditional beliefs.

OVERVIEW OF ECONOMY

Togo is a small economy in terms of the total value of its output. This is because the population is small, at around 4.5 million, and the **GDP per capita** in 1999 was very low at US$1,700 a year (by way of comparison the U.S. figure is US$33,900 per capita). The population is growing rapidly, at 3.4 percent a year, which adds to the problems of generating higher incomes. Most people (66 percent of the total) depend on agriculture for their livelihoods, mostly from small family farms. The economy of Togo has not performed well in recent years. Output has increased less rapidly than population, and average living standards have fallen. The agriculture sector has performed better than industry and services, however, and agricultural output per person has increased in recent years.

Togo is by all accounts a severely underdeveloped country. Low income levels mean that most income is devoted to subsistence, and more than 80 percent of GDP

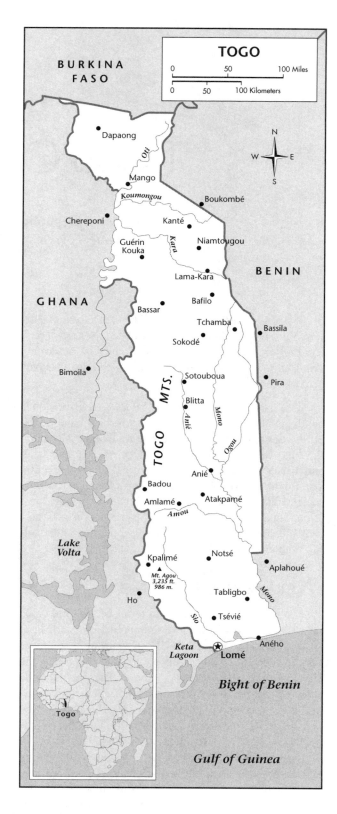

TOGO

dex, and the problems in both these areas helped place Togo 145th out of the 174 countries listed by the Human Development Index in 1998.

There are, however, some bright spots in Togo's economic picture. Mineral exploration in 1998 showed oil deposits in Togo waters, which may be exploited if shown to be viable. Hoping to attract investment, the government inaugurated what it calls an "industrial **free zone**" (actually, a free trade zone) with fiscal benefits in exchange for company guarantees on export levels and employment. And electricity imports fell after the completion in 1988 of a hydroelectric dam, built in conjunction with Benin.

In 1994, Togo embarked upon a strategy to achieve currency and other fiscal stabilization in consultation with the IMF. This program has been delayed due to political instability. The IMF has also since been very critical of the government's loss of momentum in tightening public finances. In the lead-up to the election in 1998 the government overspent, which meant the **budget deficit** grew to 6.7 percent of GDP, well outside the IMF guidelines of 3 percent of GDP. There is pressure to establish effective control of the budget and to reduce **public sector** wages, with spending reallocated to poverty alleviation and other high priority issues. Despite efforts to rationalize and broaden the tax system, heavy deficits were still recorded. In the 2000 budget many cutbacks were made. Health spending decreased by 16.3 percent, defense spending decreased by 17.7 percent, presidential office spending decreased by 32.7 percent, and expenditures by the prime minister's office decreased by 51.1 percent. However, the government is still dependent on foreign aid to cover the US$40 million deficit.

Togo is a member of the CFA Franc Zone, with its currency linked by a **fixed exchange rate** to the French franc. This provides a convertible currency with other countries that share the CFA franc and **exchange rate** stability. However, in order to achieve this, Togo has agreed to give control of its **monetary policy** to the regional central bank of the CFA Franc Zone, the Banque Centrale des Etats de l'Afrique de l'Ouest (BCEAO). Since more rapid **inflation** makes it difficult to maintain the fixed exchange rate, the money supply is under the control of the BCEAO. The BCEAO changed its 1980s policy of expansion and started to restrict credits to the private and government sectors in the early 1990s, which meant a slowdown in the growth of the money supply. As inflation fell after a 1994 **devaluation** of the currency, BCEAO was able to ease its monetary policy by reducing interest rates from 19.5 percent (1994) to 6 percent (1997). In 1998 BCEAO raised interest rates to 6.25 percent and increased commercial bank minimum **reserve ratios** (which restrict the banks' ability to lend) to forestall inflation. In 1999 the CFA franc became tied to the

goes to private consumption. Savings (7 percent of GDP) and investment (13 percent of GDP) are both low. But underdevelopment is more than just a matter of income levels. The United Nations (UN) includes education and health as well as income in its Human Development In-euro (the European Union's common currency) at a rate that reflected the euro's relationship to the French franc. A smooth transition meant that the BCEAO was able to cut interest rates to 5.75 percent, making it easier for people and business to borrow money.

Steady economic growth in the 1970s (averaging about 4 percent) gave way to low growth in the 1980s, with GDP growth becoming less than population growth, leading to a reduction in GDP per capita. Political and social unrest in the early 1990s meant that GDP contracted by 3.7 percent in 1992 and 13.7 percent in 1993. The situation was aggravated by depressed world commodity markets and an economic crisis in the West African Franc Zone.

After a return to relative domestic normality and devaluation in 1994, the economy had a positive, if patchy, recovery. **Real GDP** increased by 16.7 percent in 1994 (albeit from a very low base), 6.8 percent in 1995, and by 9.7 percent in 1996. Growth fell back to 4.3 percent in 1997, but it became negative in 1998 (at -1.3 percent) due to the energy crisis. GDP growth rallied in 1999, on the back of a good harvest, to 3.5 percent. This improvement partly reflected higher phosphate production, but manufacturing, which is still state dominated, suffered due to weak demand and inefficiency.

On average, consumer inflation is normally around 5 percent or less. In 1994 the CFA devaluation caused inflation to rise to approximately 40 percent, although it fell back down over the next 2 years. Inflation then rose again to 8.7 percent in 1998 due to an increase in the **value-added tax** (VAT), higher oil and food prices, and increased government spending. By 2000, however, inflation had settled to the targeted 3 percent, and is expected to remain at this level.

POLITICS, GOVERNMENT, AND TAXATION

Politics have been dominated since 1967 by President Gnassingbé Eyadema, Africa's longest-serving head of state. Despite the introduction of a multi-party system in 1992 and elections in 1994, democracy still seems a long way off. The 1998 elections were boycotted and were deemed flawed by outside observers. A process of national reconciliation was forced on the president by the donor community, and talks with opposition groups resumed with a promise of a re-run of elections in 2000. Most bilateral and multilateral aid remains frozen, and the country has had a poor human rights record.

Togoland was originally a German protectorate from 1884 until the end of World War I. Britain and France split Togoland after the war and ruled under a League of Nations mandate. The western sector was controlled by

Britain as part of the Gold Coast, which went on to become Ghana. French Togo became independent in 1960. The first leader, Sylvanus Olympio, was assassinated in 1963, and the army appointed a civilian, Nicolas Grunitzky, to rule. Four years later the army overthrew Grunitzky, and Colonel Eyadema took over control of the government. Eyadema formed the Rassemblement du Peuple Togolese (RPT) party in 1971 and drew civilian **technocrats** into government. Cabinet reshuffles in the late 1970s were designed to add legitimacy to the military regime.

A constitution based on universal suffrage was introduced in 1979, but the RPT remained the only legal party. After demonstrations and international pressure, Eyadema called a national conference in April 1991. A transitional government was appointed with opposition representation and was led by a lawyer, Joseph Koffigoh. However, the new government came under attack from the president's armed forces. Trade unions and opposition parties launched a general strike in 1992 which lasted for 9 months. A quarter of a million Togolese took shelter in neighboring countries from massacres perpetrated by the armed forces. The presidential election in 1993 was held amid further violence. The opposition boycotted the presidential election, only a third of the electorate voted, and all international observers (with the notable exception of France) rejected Eyadema's victory.

There was a legislative election in 1994. Two opposition parties gained 43 seats out of 81 in the assembly and hence the majority. The pro-Eyadema parties gained 37 seats, with Koffigoh's party winning only 1 seat. The major opposition party, the Union of Forces for Change (UFC), boycotted the election. Eyadema maintained supremacy by convincing the opposition leader, Edem Kodjo, to form an RPT-dominated government. In 1996 Kodjo was thrown out and a technocrat with links to Eyadema took control.

In the lead-up to the 1998 election there were opposition protests, social unrest, and military repression, although not nearly on the same scale as in the early 1990s. After chaos on election day, during which vote-counting stopped, the multi-party election was abandoned and Eyadema was proclaimed the winner. However, this led to violent demonstrations in Lomé. All 5 major opposition party leaders supported the claim of Gilchrist Olympio (son of the former leader and head of the UFC) that he won with 59 percent of votes. International observers condemned the result.

Legislative elections were held again in 1999. There is a National Assembly of 81 seats, with members elected for 5-year terms. The main opposition parties boycotted the election and the RPT gained all but 3 seats. There was much international pressure, including European Union threats to strike Togo off the Lomé Convention (a

European Union aid program which compensates certain African and Pacific countries when the prices of their export products fall on world markets). This led to the government and opposition having reconciliation talks, mediated by the European Union and other bodies. A framework agreement was signed in July 1999 to hold a new election by March 2000, with an independent electoral commission. Disagreements have delayed this election, which may not take place until late 2001.

Eyadema remains in power with the support of the army. He has stated that he will not run in the 2004 election, although he has been known in the past to change his mind.

Government revenue comprises around 30 percent of GNP. Of this, about a third comes from taxes on incomes, profits, and capital gains, and a further third from customs **duties**. Of the rest, about 15 percent comes from **indirect taxes** on goods and services, and 14 percent is generated by government enterprises (mainly the surpluses from the phosphate sector).

INFRASTRUCTURE, POWER, AND COMMUNICATIONS

Togo's main port and growing road transport sector have an important role in the sub-regional economy. The commercial and transport sector earns 35 percent of Togo's GDP. Togo has 9,600 kilometers (5,965 miles) of roads, 1,600 kilometers (994 miles) of which are paved. The World Bank has introduced a US$200 million transport **infrastructure** program, which was instituted in 1997. Parts of the 700 kilometer (435 miles) north-south road (the main road to Burkina Faso) have already been rehabilitated. The main east-west road which links Togo to Benin and Ghana also has money earmarked for rehabilitation. The railway network is limited and needs modernizing. There are 275 kilometers (171 miles) of track leading from Lomé to Blitta, and 262 kilometers (163 miles) from Kpalimé to Aného.

Lomé's deep-water port has benefitted from undercapacity in other countries and competes successfully within the region. In the 1970s the port grew rapidly, reflecting increased trade with Niger, Burkina Faso, and Mali. Togo's social upheaval and a general regional economic downturn has led to a trade slump, with **re-exports** dropping from 2.7 million metric tons to 1.1 million metric tons in 1993. Under a government **privatization** program, new installations are planned, including computerization to speed up loading and unloading in order to make the port competitive.

Telecommunications are operated by Togo Telecom, which is a **parastatal**. Togo Telecom sought to increase the number of telephone lines in the country from 21,500 in 1998 to 30,400 in 2000. The company has been slated for privatization since 1997. One of its subsidiaries, Togocellulaire, manages the digital network, which had 6,000 subscribers by the end of 1998.

Apart from the government-run *Togo Presse*, there are several outspoken opposition newspapers. Since 1998 privately-owned television and radio stations have been allowed to operate alongside the parastatals.

In a US$400 million agreement with Nigeria, Ghana, and Benin in 1999, Togo hopes to find a solution to its energy supply problems. A gas pipeline will supply industry and power stations in recipient countries, which should reduce Togo's dependence on Ghana's unpredictable hydroelectricity supply. The pipeline should be in operation by 2002, and is funded by ECOWAS, the World Bank, the United States, and Italy, and will be managed by Chevron Oil of the United States. The problems of Togo's dependency on Ghana for energy were highlighted in 1998, when it received less than 5 percent of its requirements for electricity, severely disrupting the economy.

CEET, the Togolese electricity company, still relies heavily on Ghana. The hydroelectric dam that is jointly owned by Togo and Benin has produced output only sporadically. In 1996 CEET produced 35.1 million kilowatt-

Communications

Country	Newspapers	Radios	TV Sets[a]	Cable subscribers[a]	Mobile Phones[a]	Fax Machines[a]	Personal Computers[a]	Internet Hosts[b]	Internet Users[b]
	1996	1997	1998	1998	1998	1998	1998	1999	1999
Togo	4	218	18	N/A	2	4.1	6.8	0.17	15
United States	215	2,146	847	244.3	256	78.4	458.6	1,508.77	74,100
Nigeria	24	223	66	N/A	0	N/A	5.7	0.00	100
Benin	2	108	10	N/A	1	0.2	0.9	0.04	10

[a]Data are from International Telecommunication Union, *World Telecommunication Development Report 1999* and are per 1,000 people.
[b]Data are from the Internet Software Consortium (http://www.isc.org) and are per 10,000 people.

SOURCE: World Bank. *World Development Indicators 2000*.

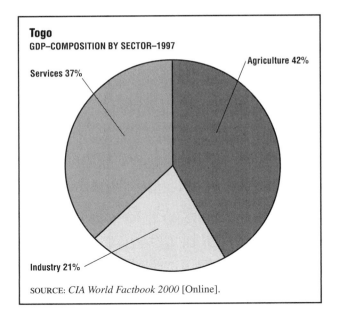

Togo
GDP–COMPOSITION BY SECTOR–1997

Agriculture 42%
Services 37%
Industry 21%

SOURCE: *CIA World Factbook 2000* [Online].

hours, but 349.3 million kilowatt hours (kWh) were required. CEET has also been earmarked for privatization.

ECONOMIC SECTORS

The agricultural sector provided 42.1 percent of Togo's GDP in 1997, and was responsible for 65 percent of employment. Core food crop production and livestock rearing make up most of the sector's output. Togo is self-sufficient in beans, ground nuts, yams, cassava, and sweet potatoes. Roughly 20 percent of cereals are imported. Export crops—including cotton, coffee, and cocoa—account for 20 percent of agricultural output.

The industrial sector is dominated primarily by phosphate production, which is the principal foreign exchange earner. The sector provided 21 percent of GDP in 1997 and employed 5 percent of the active population. Industry in Togo is also involved in agro-processing, construction, and energy. The government has recently set up a small Export Processing Zone in Lomé, which is designed to lure foreign companies who can take advantage of relaxed labor laws and hold large foreign exchange accounts.

The services sector (which includes commerce, transport, and tourism) provided 37 percent of GDP and 30 percent of employment in 1997.

AGRICULTURE

Agriculture is the most important sector to most Togolese. It employs two-thirds of the active population, who predominantly work on small land holdings. Food crops (mainly cassava, yams, maize, millet, and sorghum) account for two-thirds of production, and are mostly used domestically. Togo's **cash crops** are mainly cocoa, coffee, cotton, and to a lesser extent, palm oil. These cash crops provide a valuable return for small farmers, and they provide 40 percent of exports. Some foodstuffs need to be imported. The main imported foodstuff is rice, although production has increased 6-fold since the mid-1980s. Production increased by 9.1 percent in 1999 due to good weather, although depressed world prices for exports affected Togo (especially in cotton).

Agricultural exports are dominated by cotton. The cotton production sector employs 230,000 people, predominantly small farmers. Cultivation has expanded rapidly since the mid-1980s. Output has quadrupled from the 1985–1986 season to 200,000 metric tons in 1998, stabilizing at 190,000 metric tons in the 1999–2000 season. About 163,420 hectares were under cotton cultivation during the 1999–2000 season. Soil degradation is likely to become a problem.

Most farmers are under contract to the state-owned marketing board, Sotoco. In 1995 Sotoco lost its **monopoly** on processing and the external marketing of cotton, and a private company, Sicot, was given export and processing rights. Sotoco still has a dominant purchasing position and is the sole provider of fertilizers and pesticides. Several new ginning plants opened in the late 1990s, and they should be running at full capacity by early 2001.

Cocoa and coffee production appear less important than cotton, but unrecorded cross-border trade distorts the figures. Togo's production of these 2 commodities is small compared to its neighbors, producing 13,000 metric tons of coffee and 9,000 metric tons of cocoa in 1998.

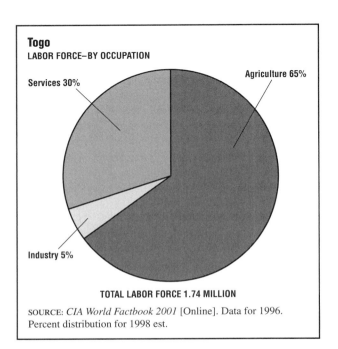

Togo
LABOR FORCE–BY OCCUPATION

Services 30%
Agriculture 65%
Industry 5%

TOTAL LABOR FORCE 1.74 MILLION

SOURCE: *CIA World Factbook 2001* [Online]. Data for 1996. Percent distribution for 1998 est.

The state-owned OPAT was in charge of marketing, processing, and exporting until 1996, when private companies were introduced.

INDUSTRY

Togo is the world's fourth-largest phosphate producer. Phosphate is a mineral used to produce fertilizers. Reserves are estimated at 260 million metric tons of first-class phosphate and 1 billion metric tons of carbonate phosphate. Deposits were found in 1952 not far from Lomé. The good geological characteristics and geographical position led to a low cost for extraction.

Established in 1974, the parastatal OTP has a monopoly on phosphates. Annual production was around 3.3 million metric tons in 2000, and OTP employed 2,200 people. After expansion during the 1980s, the industry suffered in the 1990s. In 1993 production was only 1.79 million metric tons, and prices bottomed at US$33 per metric ton, putting the company on the verge of bankruptcy. The devaluation of the CFA franc in 1994 restored the profitability of the phosphate industry. In 1997 output was 2.69 million metric tons, which realized US$110 million, though production fell in 1998 to 2.24 metric tons. Although the industry looks good in the short term, it is likely to face growing international competition, especially as world phosphate fertilizer demand is falling. After World Bank negotiations, 40 percent of the OTP is to be privatized, mainly to outside investors.

The overvaluation of the CFA franc in the early 1990s hit the industrial sector hard. In addition, it was not helped by the political instability of the early 1990s, when industry's GDP contribution fell by a fifth. Once order was restored, and following the devaluation in 1994, industry's GDP contribution grew by 26 percent, and 20 percent in 1995, before settling to around 5 percent growth in 1997. Industrial activity recovered in 1998 after 2 bad years, despite the 1994 devaluation boost. The privatized construction sector led the recovery. In November 1999, the International Finance Corporation (IFC), the agency of the World Bank which lends to the **private sector**, announced a US$6 million loan to the building materials sector.

A duty-free "Export Processing Zone" was launched in 1989, and now includes 41 industrial units, which involve a US$50 million investment and 7,000 new jobs. It has attracted international interest, predominantly French, and advantageous terms for foreign investors if they export 80 percent of their production and give jobs to Togolese.

SERVICES

A recent World Bank report shed doubt on the stability of Togo's banks, once thought to be amongst the most stable in West Africa, following the crises of the 1990s, during which period many banks suspended activities. The commercial banks, already faced with falling deposits and increased lending, also had to absorb public sector deficits in the early 1990s. Weak capital flows and stagnant exports led to a US$24 million decrease in bank assets by 1990–94. Credit grew by US$12 million in the same period, reflecting increased lending, while the government indebtedness increased by US$19 million. This meant that banks had to borrow heavily from BCEAO. The 2 state-owned banks fared the worst, and accounted for 74 percent of all lending and 62.5 percent of all deposits. The rest of the sector is shared between a variety of foreign banks, including French and Belgian interests.

In 1993, the hotel industry included 4,163 beds and employed 1,309 people. During the problems of the 1990s, hotel occupancy dropped to less than 20 percent of capacity. International arrivals halved, and visitors stayed on average only 3.5 nights. The 80,000 arrivals were a record in 1996, although many of these were business travelers and returning Togolese. Several state-owned hotels have been slated for privatization, and the government has allowed foreign leasing of the more prestigious hotels.

INTERNATIONAL TRADE

For the past 20 years Togo has had a net **trade deficit**, reaching $50 million in 1999, with exports at US$400 million and imports at US$450 million. Exports and imports both contracted in 1992 and 1993, but in 1994 the currency devaluation boosted agricultural exports, which meant that the trade deficit fell to $37 million from US$111 million in 1993. The main destinations for exports in 1994 were France, Benin, Ghana, and Canada, while imports came from France, Germany, Côte d'Ivoire, and China.

In 1998 trade revenue from cotton and cocoa fell, despite an increase in the volume exported, due to unfavorable world prices. However, phosphate exports increased both in terms of volume and revenue collected.

Trade (expressed in billions of US$): Togo

	Exports	Imports
1975	.126	.174
1980	.338	.551
1985	.190	.288
1990	.268	.581
1995	.208	.386
1998	N/A	N/A

SOURCE: International Monetary Fund. *International Financial Statistics Yearbook 1999.*

Exchange rates: Togo

Communauté Financière Africaine francs per US$1

Jan 2001	699.21
2000	711.98
1999	615.70
1998	589.95
1997	583.67
1996	511.55

Note: From January 1, 1999, the CFA Fr is pegged to the euro at a rate of 655.957 CFA Fr per euro.

SOURCE: CIA *World Factbook 2001* [ONLINE].

Re-exports increased in 1998 (as in every year since 1994), and accounted for 20 percent of exports in 1998. France is historically the main importer of goods, but the suspension of aid led to a decrease in French imports and an increase in Chinese imports. However, the published data underestimate cross-border trade with Benin, Ghana, and Nigeria, much of which goes unrecorded.

MONEY

Togo is part of the 8-member Union Economique et Monetaire Ouest-Africaine (UEMOA) and uses the CFA franc. The BCEAO issues currency notes and regulates credit expansion throughout the region. The CFA franc was pegged to the French franc at a 50:1 exchange rate from 1948, but was overvalued in the late 1980s; the 1994 devaluation dropped the value to a 100:1 exchange rate. With France having joined the European Monetary Union, the CFA franc is now valued at CFA Fr 655.959 to 1 euro.

POVERTY AND WEALTH

Togo is a poor country; GDP per capita stood at $1,700 in 1999, and 32 percent of the population was thought to be living below the poverty line (according to 1987–89 estimates).

GDP per Capita (US$)

Country	1975	1980	1985	1990	1998
Togo	411	454	385	375	333
United States	19,364	21,529	23,200	25,363	29,683
Nigeria	301	314	230	258	256
Benin	339	362	387	345	394

SOURCE: United Nations. *Human Development Report 2000; Trends in human development and per capita income.*

Education provisions have deteriorated in Togo in recent years. The one university, the University of Benin, was established in 1970. Originally designed for 6,000 students, it currently is trying to cope with 17,000, which has led to many campus demonstrations. A second university is planned in Clara, Eyadema's hometown, but its development is at a standstill due to the political situation.

Education has suffered during the 1990s due to demographic pressures and the freeze on hiring civil servants. A World Bank-sponsored scheme to provide 6,000 primary-level educators is under way. Despite these problems, Togo has traditionally had good education standards for a sub-Saharan African country. The **United Nations Development Program** (UNDP) put adult literacy in Togo at 53.2 percent in 1997, with 82.3 percent of primary school age children attending school and 58.3 percent of children of the appropriate age attending secondary school. The government provided 24.7 percent of the money required for education. However, gender imbalances are rife throughout the education system. Roughly 43 percent of males and only 31 percent of females are literate in Togo, according to the U.S. Department of State.

Togolese health care has struggled due to a lack of resources and population growth. The number of AIDS cases is expected to increase up to 2005, when the number of new cases is expected to stabilize and then begin a slow fall, although this depends on the success of AIDS education programs. In 1993 there were 6 doctors and 31 nurses per 100,000 population, and this figure is unlikely to change in the near future. Regional disparities are huge, as 50 percent of all medical staff work in the capital. Infant mortality stands at 78 deaths per 1,000 live births, and 125 children per 1,000 die before the age of 5. The maternal mortality rate stands at 640 per 100,000. In 1997 there were 185 AIDS cases per 100,000.

WORKING CONDITIONS

A Labor Tribunal is provided for in Togo's judicial system. The Collectif des Syndicates Independents (CSI) was founded in 1992 and is a coordinating body for labor organizations. The other main trade union in Togo is the Confederation Nationale des Travailleurs de Togo (CNTT), which was affiliated with the RPT party until 1991. The trade unions can be militant in Togo, as was shown in a 9-month general strike in 1992.

In the 1990 budget a mere US$1.2 million was spent on social security and welfare. Togo has no minimum wage. The **labor force** was estimated at 2 million in 1998, of which 40 percent were women. Unemployment figures have little significance in Togo. There are very few people with no work at all, but few people work at what is considered **full employment**, and much work is informal or subsistence labor. There are no unemployment benefits, and those who do not work tend to rely on support from charities or their families. Many people would like a modern sector job, but eke out an existence on family farms or in casual **informal sector** activities in the urban areas.

COUNTRY HISTORY AND ECONOMIC DEVELOPMENT

1884–1919. Togoland is a German protectorate.

1919. Britain and France take Togoland from Germany during World War I; they split the country—with France ruling French Togoland—and rule under a League of Nations mandate.

1960. On April 27, the newly named Republic of Togo becomes independent, and Sylvanus Olympio is elected president under a provisional constitution.

1963. President Olympio is assassinated by army officers, and Nicolas Grunitzky leads a provisional government as prime minister and, later, as president.

1967. President Grunitzky's government is overthrown by the military, and Colonel Etienne Gnassingbé Eyadema takes control.

1972. Eyadema is reelected to the presidency in a national referendum in which he is the only candidate.

1979. Eyadema is reelected once more in elections in which he is the only candidate. A new constitution provides for a national assembly which will consult with the president, but Eyadema holds all the power.

1991. Facing pressure from pro-democracy protestors, Eyadema agrees to a transitional government leading up to free elections. Kokou Joseph Koffigoh is selected as prime minister, and Eyadema's powers are limited.

1992. Fearing that Eyadema will not relinquish power, trade unions and opposition parties launch a general strike, which lasts for 9 months and decimates Togo's economy.

1993. Presidential elections are held, but alleged fraud keeps many opposition parties and voters away. Eyadema wins with 96 percent of the votes and declares the success of democracy in Togo.

1994. Multiparty legislative elections are held, giving parties opposed to Eyadema's RPT control in the legislature. Edem Kodjo is named prime minister but has little power in a country that is still dominated by Eyadema.

1994. The CFA franc is devalued, leading to a surge in exports for Togo.

1998. Presidential elections are again boycotted by the opposition and deemed flawed by outside observers. Eyadema retains presidency.

1999. CFA franc becomes tied to the euro. Legislative elections are won by Eyadema's RPT.

FUTURE TRENDS

It is very difficult to have economic progress without a platform of political stability, as both domestic and foreign investors are unwilling to risk their resources unless they are confident that they will be secure. In the Togolese context, the lack of consensus over the operation of the political system between the government and the opposition parties is the main worry for international donors and the business community. Until these matters are resolved, Togo cannot expect to make progress in improving the living standards of its people.

Disagreements between the opposition and the ruling parties may lead to such a delay that new legislative elections (to replace the elections in 1999, widely seen as flawed) may not be carried out until the end of 2001. European Union aid will resume if new elections are seen to be free and transparent. It is likely that the United States and the IMF will follow suit. The government plans to restore stability to public finances, including the banking and financial sectors, and to revive the privatization process. Real GDP is expected to grow to 3.5 percent in 2001, and 3.8 percent in 2002, thanks to external assistance. Assuming a satisfactory harvest and a downturn in oil prices, inflation is forecast to fall to 2 percent in 2001 and 1.5 percent in 2002. Aid inflow means Togo's economy can be expected to improve between 2001 and 2002.

Following international pressure, a national independent electoral commission will oversee the 2001 election. The president has strengthened his international position through the presidency of the Organization of African Unity (OAU). A joint UN and OAU investigation is underway into the murder of political opponents in the 1998 election.

Though there has been little increase in revenue, a decrease in public expenditures has resulted in a lower deficit. In 2000 the economy was recovering from the 1998 **recession**, helped by an agricultural upturn and by the fact that the OAU summit was held in Lomé. Cotton output is estimated to have fallen to 110,000 metric tons in 2000 due to uneven rainfall, but cereal and coffee production both increased in the 2000–2001 season. The new Togo, Benin, and Nigeria power scheme should improve Togo's power situation.

DEPENDENCIES

Togo has no territories or colonies.

BIBLIOGRAPHY

Economist Intelligence Unit. *Country Profile: Togo.* London: Economist Intelligence Unit, 2001.

Hodd, Michael. *The Economies of Africa.* Dartmouth: Aldershot, 1991.

Togo. <http://www.republicoftogo.com/english/index.htm>. Accessed September 2001.

U.S. Central Intelligence Agency. *World Factbook 2000.* <http://www.odci.gov/cia/publications/factbook/index.html>. Accessed August 2001.

U.S. Department of State. *Background Notes: Togo, October 1997.* <http://www.state.gov/www/background_notes/togo_9710_bgn.html>. Accessed September 2001.

U.S. Department of State. *FY 2000 Country Commercial Guide: Togo.* <http://www.state.gov/www/about_state/business/com_guides/2001/africa/index.html>. Accessed September 2001.

Welcome to the Republic of Togo (official home page). <http://www.afrika.com/togo>. Accessed September 2001.

—*Jack Hodd*

TUNISIA

Republic of Tunisia
Al-Jumhuriyah at-Tunisiyah

CAPITAL: Tunis.

MONETARY UNIT: Tunisian dinar (TD). One Tunisian dinar equals 1,000 millimes. The notes in circulation are 5, 10, 20, and 30 dinars, and there are coins of 5, 10, 20, 50, 100, and 500 millimes, and 1 dinar.

CHIEF EXPORTS: Textiles, machinery, electrical equipment, phosphates, chemicals, olive oil, hydrocarbons.

CHIEF IMPORTS: Textiles, mechanical and electrical equipment, vehicles, petroleum and derivatives, iron and steel, plastics, cereals.

GROSS DOMESTIC PRODUCT: US$52.6 billion (purchasing power parity, 1999 est.).

BALANCE OF TRADE: Exports: US$5.750 billion (1998). **Imports:** US$8.338 billion (1998).

COUNTRY OVERVIEW

LOCATION AND SIZE. Situated in northern Africa, Tunisia is bordered by Algeria on the west and Libya on the southeast and by the Mediterranean Sea on the north, where it has a coastline of 1,148 kilometers (713 miles). Tunisia has an area of 163,610 square kilometers (63,169 square miles), making it slightly larger than the state of Georgia. Its capital city of Tunis is located on the country's northern coastline.

POPULATION. Tunisia's population was estimated at 9,593,402 in 2000, compared with 8,790,000 in the 1994 census. In 2000 the birth rate was 17.38 births per 1,000 population while the death rate was 4.98 deaths per 1,000 population. The population is expected to reach 11.2 million by 2015 with a projected annual population growth rate of 1.17 percent.

The Tunisian population is almost entirely of Arab descent (98 percent). Europeans make up 1 percent of the population, and Jewish and other ethnic groups make up the rest. Tunisia's population is young: 30 percent of the people are below the age of 14, and only 6 percent are older than 65. The population is increasingly concentrated along the eastern coast, with 43 percent either living in the capital city or on the mid-eastern and northeastern coasts. There has been a large population shift from the countryside to the cities due to increased job opportunities in the urban areas; since 1984, 86 new towns have been created.

Tunisia was the first Arab country to initiate nationwide birth-control programs. Since the creation of the Department of Family Planning and Population in 1966, the birth rate has fallen sharply, from 3 percent in 1966 to 1.17 percent in 2000. This drop is the result of an increase in the standard of living, widespread access to education, and improved health care. The number of women who are entering the **labor force** increased by 12 percent in 2000, and women's rights are actively promoted.

OVERVIEW OF ECONOMY

When Tunisia achieved its independence from France in 1956, a 1-party state was established by President Habib Bourguiba. During his 31-year tenure, economic policy focused on state ownership and high levels of protection from outside competition. At this time the economy was based primarily on agriculture, oil, and phosphates. Although this degree of government control led to inefficiency and waste, the economy remained stable due to revenue from the export of oil and phosphates during the 1960s and 1970s. The collapse of the price of oil in the 1980s meant that Tunisia could no longer rely on oil as its principal source of foreign exchange. Tunisia's agricultural and tourism sectors deteriorated simultaneously. Under advice from the International Monetary Fund (IMF), Tunisia promptly adopted a 3-pronged program of structural adjustment: to reduce the size of the **public sector**, to reduce **tariff** barriers, and to create a stable **macroeconomic** climate.

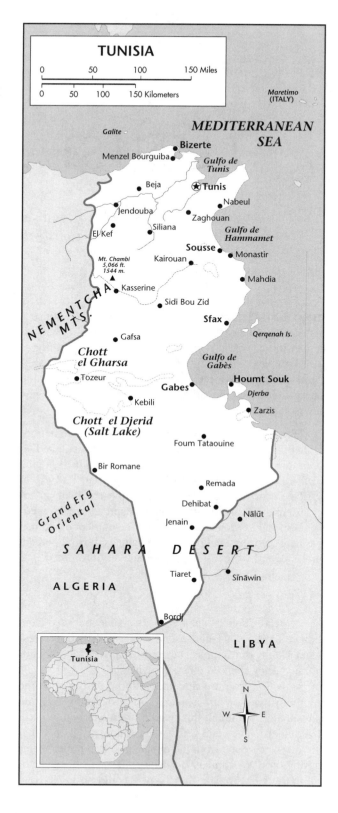

Maretimo (ITALY)

Galite

MEDITERRANEAN SEA

Bizerte

Menzel Bourguiba

Gulfo de Tunis

Beja

★Tunis

Nabeul

Jendouba

Zaghouan

El Kef

Siliana

Gulfo de Hammamet

Sousse

Monastir

Kairouan

Mt. Chambi
5,066 ft.
1544 m. ▲

Kasserine

Mahdia

Sidi Bou Zid

Sfax

Qerqenah Is.

Gafsa

Chott el Gharsa

Gulfo de Gabès

Tozeur

Houmt Souk

Gabes

Djerba

Kebili

Zarzis

Chott el Djerid
(Salt Lake)

Foum Tataouine

Bir Romane

Remada

Dehibat

Nālūt

Jenain

SAHARA DESERT

ALGERIA

Tiaret

Sīnāwin

Bordj

LIBYA

Tunisia

N
W E
S

Following the adoption of the adjustment program in 1986, the Tunisian economy has shifted from being largely state-controlled to being based on market principles. The economy is now diverse, with a large services

sector, a healthy tourism industry, and a growing manufacturing sector. Despite these improvements, the Tunisian government is still faced with a serious unemployment problem. In 2001, there were 480,000 unemployed Tunisians, or 15.4 percent of the workforce.

As the economy improved, the amount Tunisia received in Official Development Assistance more than halved, from US$559 million in 1990 to US$278 million in 1995. Since 1996, the European Union has been the main source of assistance, with France, Italy, and Germany as the main donors. Tunisia's **external debt** remains high, having risen from US$3.5 billion in 1980 to US$11.078 billion in 1998. Most of this debt is owed to private creditors, and the Tunisian government has issued international bonds (financial notes promising repayment of a given amount by a given date, plus interest).

POLITICS, GOVERNMENT, AND TAXATION

After gaining independence from France on 25 March 1956, Tunisia became a republic headed by President Habib Bourguiba, who promptly assumed the title, "president for life." Since his ascension to office, Tunisia has been largely a 1-party state. The president's left-wing party, the Socialist Destourien Party (PSD), is dominated political life and punished its opponents with censorship and imprisonment. The 1960s saw a short-lived **socialist** experiment that finally gave way to increased economic **liberalization** in the 1970s under the influence of Prime Minister Hedi Nouira. By the middle of the 1980s, the state started to face serious problems as the ailing Bourguiba became increasingly unable to effectively rule the country. Bourguiba's presidency was marked by serious economic instability towards the end of the 1980s, followed by serious civil unrest. A party called the Islamic Movement (MTI), an effective organization with a large base of support, challenged the government's stability. In response to this movement, the president appointed General Zine al-Abidine Ben Ali, a former head of the security services, to be the minister of the interior. His main task was to dismantle the MTI. Following thousands of arrests and the successful dismantling of the MTI, the president appointed Ben Ali the prime minister.

According to the terms of the Tunisian Constitution and based on the opinion of a team of medical doctors who declared Bourguiba unfit to govern, Prime Minister Zine El Abidine Ben Ali assumed the **duties** of president on 7 November 1987. Ben Ali started to dismantle the old oppressive regime by allowing increased freedom of the press, releasing political prisoners, and legalizing political parties. The PSD party was renamed the Rassemblement Constitutionnel Democratique (RCD) and legislation was passed implementing a multi-party system.

Today there are 6 legal opposition parties in Tunisia, but most of them lack the necessary resources to be effective, and they are still prohibited from criticizing government policies. President Ben Ali's government has brought with it economic and political stability, focusing extensively on health care, women's rights, and education. Despite these reforms, Tunisia is still essentially a 1-party state.

The principle source of revenue for the Tunisian government is taxation. According to the EIU Country Profile, more than 50 percent of government revenues come from **direct taxation** and 40 percent from domestic or foreign borrowing. In 2000, the corporate rate of taxation in Tunisia was set at 35 percent, except for those businesses involved in the fishing, agriculture, or handicraft industries, which are taxed at a 10 percent rate. Normal business expenditures such as depreciation (the decline in value of a physical asset as it is used over time), social security contributions, and costs are deductible. Due to generous government incentives, exporting businesses are exempt from all major taxes in Tunisia. Personal **income tax** is paid on a progressive basis ranging from 15 to 35 percent. Non-residents have to pay tax only on income earned from Tunisian sources. There is a 17 percent **value-added tax** (VAT) on sales that is applicable to most items and transactions.

INFRASTRUCTURE, POWER, AND COMMUNICATIONS

Since 1995 the Tunisian government has invested heavily in the country's **infrastructure**. There are 20,000 kilometers (12,428 miles) of good-quality roads linking all parts of the country; 18,226 kilometers (11,326 miles) of these roads are paved. Having such roads is a considerable feat given that Tunisia is a large country with differing and often inhospitable terrain. There is only 1 modern highway in the country, but a second (from Tunis to Bizerte) is under construction and is expected to be completed by 2002. After 1996, there was a rapid growth in the number of licensed vehicles, which has led to heavy congestion and pollution. The government has made plans to modernize the railway system that is operated by a company called SNCFT. The railways have traditionally transported phosphates and fertilizers, although the number of passengers has been increasing by about 5 percent a year. Still, the SNCFT ran at a loss throughout 2000. There are a total of 2,168 kilometers (1,347 miles) of rail lines in the country.

There are 6 international airports in Tunisia: Tunis-Carthage, Monastir-Skanes, Jerba-Zarzis, Tozeur-Nefta, Tabarka, and Gafsa. The national airline, Tunisair, flies to many European and Middle Eastern countries with the exception of Israel. In turn, most European and Middle Eastern carriers fly into Tunis. The Tunis-Carthage airport has a capacity of 4.5 million passengers a year. There are 8 commercial seaports and 22 smaller ports within Tunisia, known for their inefficient customs officers and bad links to railways and roads.

Tunisians receive their electricity from the state-owned company, Société Tunisienne de l'Electricité et du Gaz (STEG), which can produce 1,974 megawatts of power at full capacity. More than 90 percent of the country's electricity is generated by this company. There are 29 radio stations and 19 television stations. Telecommunications services in Tunisia are poor, rates are high, and Internet use is not common. According the EIU Country Profile 2000, the country had only 30,000 Internet users at the beginning of 1999 and only 2 government-controlled Internet service providers.

ECONOMIC SECTORS

The Tunisian economy is a diverse one with services contributing 60 percent of **gross domestic product** (GDP) in 1998 and industry contributing 28 percent. In the 1960s and 1970s, when there was heavy state control, oil and phosphates were central to the economy. These sectors have diminished in importance since the 1980s with increases in the manufacturing of textiles and

Communications

Country	Newspapers	Radios	TV Sets[a]	Cable subscribers[a]	Mobile Phones[a]	Fax Machines[a]	Personal Computers[a]	Internet Hosts[b]	Internet Users[b]
	1996	1997	1998	1998	1998	1998	1998	1999	1999
Tunisia	31	223	198	N/A	4	3.4	14.7	0.06	30
United States	215	2,146	847	244.3	256	78.4	458.6	1,508.77	74,100
Egypt	40	324	122	N/A	1	0.5	9.1	0.28	200
Libya	14	233	126	0.0	3	N/A	N/A	0.00	7

[a]Data are from International Telecommunication Union, *World Telecommunication Development Report 1999* and are per 1,000 people.
[b]Data are from the Internet Software Consortium (http://www.isc.org) and are per 10,000 people.

SOURCE: World Bank. *World Development Indicators 2000*.

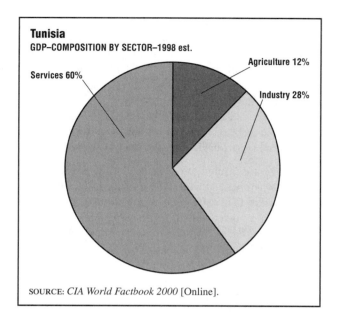

Tunisia
GDP–COMPOSITION BY SECTOR–1998 est.

Services 60%

Agriculture 12%

Industry 28%

SOURCE: *CIA World Factbook 2000* [Online].

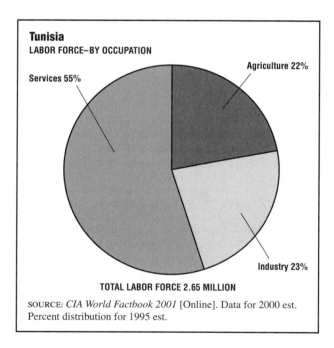

Tunisia
LABOR FORCE–BY OCCUPATION

Services 55%

Agriculture 22%

Industry 23%

TOTAL LABOR FORCE 2.65 MILLION

SOURCE: *CIA World Factbook 2001* [Online]. Data for 2000 est.
Percent distribution for 1995 est.

electrical equipment. The agricultural industry employs nearly a quarter of the labor force, but its output is dependent upon the weather; during drought years this sector's contribution to GDP can fall from 16 percent to 12 percent, the contribution in 1998.

AGRICULTURE

Agricultural output is central to the Tunisian economy, accounting for 12 to 16 percent of the GDP, depending on the size of the harvest. This sector provided jobs for 22 percent of the country's labor force in 1998.

The 2 most important export crops are cereals and olive oil, with almost half of all the cultivated land sown with cereals and another third planted with more than 55 million olive trees. Tunisia is one of the world's biggest producers and exporters of olive oil, and it exports dates and citrus fruits that are grown mostly in the northern parts of the country. The center of the country is used largely to raise cattle, the Sahel region is famous for its olive groves, and the southern part of the country is known for its date production. Tunisia remains one of the few Arab countries which is self-sufficient in dairy products, vegetables, and fruit and almost self-sufficient in red meat. Since the 1980s, agricultural output has increased by about 40 percent, and exports of food have risen considerably. At the beginning of 2000 the government entered into talks with the European Union seeking a free-trade agreement for its agricultural goods. The remainder of Tunisia's agricultural production consists of several smaller export products including tomatoes, peppers, artichokes, melons, onions, potatoes, sugar beets, almonds, apricots, and wine.

Tunisia's labor-intensive agricultural sector uses very low levels of fertilizers and pesticides. Because farms are not highly mechanized, plowing a field may take 5 times longer than in the United States. Most of the land is split into very small farms making production much less efficient. Some 80 percent of farms are smaller than 20 hectares, and only 3 percent are larger than 50 hectares. Transportation and storage facilities are poor, leading to high levels of waste. Severe droughts, like the one experienced in 2000, have proven to be enormously costly.

Annual agricultural production can vary significantly from year to year due to Tunisia's unpredictable and largely irregular rainfall patterns. Almost all of Tunisia's water is used in irrigation, and the government is seeking more efficient methods that will conserve water. Its national plan aims to increase water resources from 2.1 to 3.5 cubic meters billion per year by building 21 large dams, 203 hillside dams, 547 reservoirs, and 1,580 deep wells by the end of 2001.

The fishing industry employs 25,000 people and catches an average of 93,000 tons of fish a year. However, coastal fishing has declined dramatically since 1995 due to pollution and the depletion of fish stocks. Fish is Tunisia's second most important food export after olive oil, and the government has made strong efforts to improve processing and storage facilities in order to match European standards. The government has also invested heavily in the upgrading of its ports and the improvement of its fleets.

INDUSTRY

OIL. The production of oil in Tunisia began in 1966 when 2 main oil fields in the southern part of the country were tapped: El Borma and Ashtart. Over the years, many smaller oil fields have been discovered, and by 2000 there were 28 known oil deposits. In 1999, just over 4 million tons of crude oil was produced, and it is estimated that Tunisia has 55 million tons (400 million barrels) of total oil reserves. In spite of the fact that Tunisia has fairly small oil reserves compared with those of other countries in the region, overseas companies still consider it worth the risk to prospect for oil because the tax laws are favorable to even the smallest of discoveries. In 1999 more than US$100 million was invested in exploration, with some 40 separate explorations being carried out in 2000. Petroleum products, such as motor fuels, fuel oil, and liquefied petroleum, are not being produced to full capacity because of the small size of the state-owned refinery at Bizerte on the northern coast.

GAS. Prior to 1966, gas was largely imported via the TransMediterranean pipeline that transports Algerian gas to Italy. In that year, British Gas invested US$600 million into the Miskar field in the Gulf of Gabès, a site that produced 168 million cubic feet of gas per day in 2000, a figure that was forecast to rise to 230 million in 2001. Given plans by British Gas to invest an additional US$450 million in 2001, it is likely that this industry will continue to grow and become increasingly important.

PHOSPHATES. Tunisia is one of the world's largest producers of phosphates, which are found mainly in mines in the southern part of the country. **Private-sector** activity is limited in this industry which is dominated by the state-owned Compagnie des phosphates de Gafsa. A reduction in exports, falling world gas prices, and rising labor costs led to financial difficulties within the company in the mid-1990s, but it recovered with the upturn in world prices. In 1999, about 8 million tons of phosphates were produced. Tunisia also has reserves of other important minerals including iron ore, lead, zinc, and sea salt. The production of iron ore has been steadily declining since 1993 as reserves neared depletion.

MANUFACTURING. Manufacturing accounts for 20 percent of Tunisia's GDP and employs 20 percent of the country's labor force in 5 different sectors: textiles, food processing, mechanical and electrical industries, construction materials, and chemicals. Almost one-third of the manufacturing sector is involved in the production of textiles, a sector that grows an average of 6 percent a year. In 1999 the textile industry accounted for 6.7 percent of the GDP. Some 1,800 firms are involved in textile production, 700 of which are partly or totally owned by foreign companies. Textile exports were valued at more than 3 billion Tunisian dinars in 1999, a figure equal to 23 percent of total exports; however, the sector is heavily dependent on Europe for its raw materials and faces the challenge of increased competition from Asia.

Manufacturing overall continues to perform better than any other sector, having grown an average of 5.2 percent a year since the early 1990s. However, product quality is variable, and much of the labor force is underskilled. Manufacturing is dependent upon imports of raw materials, spare parts, and **capital goods** and is challenged by increasing competition within its European export markets. Tunisia signed an association agreement with the European Union in 1995 which will lead to free trade in industrial goods with Europe by 2008. In 1996, the government initiated a project aimed at industrial modernization.

SERVICES

TOURISM. Employing 270,00 people, the tourism sector is of vital importance to the Tunisian economy, contributing 6.2 percent to the GDP each year and 16 percent to foreign exchange earnings. In 1999 Tunisia welcomed 4,832,000 tourists, three-quarters of whom were French, German, Italian, or British. In the wake of the Gulf War (1990–91) the number of tourists fell sharply, and in 1995 there was a brief downturn due to an economic decline in the European Union. The sector has been growing steadily since that date. Important Tunisian tourist destinations include the historic site of Carthage and the many locations in the desert where the film *Star Wars* was shot.

The government has identified the need to attract tourists from Central and Eastern Europe. Development has slowly started to expand beyond the principal resort areas, and more moderately priced restaurants are beginning to open. Tunisia is becoming increasingly popular as a multi-seasonal destination because of its range of climatic conditions, its popular skiing resorts, and its attractive beaches. It still remains heavily dependent on the European market. Compared to the rest of north Africa, revenue per tourist remains fairly low: US$340 compared with US$468 in Morocco and US$850 in Egypt (all 1999 figures). This low amount is mostly due to the lack of opportunities for tourists to spend their money.

FINANCIAL SERVICES. The financial-services industry is largely regulated by the Central Bank of Tunisia. In 1999 there were 8 development banks, 2 merchant banks, 13 commercial banks, and 8 **offshore banks**. The banking system continues to be highly inefficient, holding large amounts of debt. In 2001 the sector is planning to open itself up to foreign competition following agreements signed with the European Union and the World Trade Organization.

The financial markets in Tunisia are composed of a semi-**privatized** stock exchange (partly owned by the government and partly owned by the private sector) known as the Bourse des Valeurs Mobilières (BVM), plus various bond and stock/bond funds. The government opened the BVM in 1990 primarily to encourage foreign investment, but it has not succeeded in its aim due to the overvaluation of stock, illiquidity (unavailability of hard money), and a lack of investor confidence. In response, the government privatized the managing company, BVM, and set up a state-controlled watchdog, a central share depository, and a guarantee fund. In 2001, there were 23 mutual funds, 87 investment funds, and 25 risk capital funds totaling US$1.24 billion.

INTERNATIONAL TRADE

In the 1960s and 1970s, Tunisia's chief exports were oil and mining products; after the 1980s, the chief exports became manufactured or processed goods. The export of textiles grew significantly in the 1990s and amounted to 43 percent of total exports in 1999. Olive oil, chemicals, shoes, and leather goods are also increasingly important exports. Given that the manufacturing industry is the largest, many **intermediate goods** such as textiles, machinery, and electrical equipment are needed in the process, and these materials have to be imported. The European Union, Tunisia's principal trading partner, buys 81 percent of Tunisian exports and provides 71 percent of its imports. France alone accounted for 26.3 percent of total Tunisian trade in 1999.

Tunisia has kept substantial large external **trade deficits** that have amounted to over US$2 billion since 1995. In 1999 the trade deficit stood at US$2.5 billion on exports of US$5.8 billion and imports of US$8.3 billion. These serious deficits are due to 5 main causes: a sharp drop in traditional exports such as crude oil and phosphates; Tunisia's need to import most of its capital equipment; the practice of converting raw and semi-processed imports into end products for **re-export**; long-standing deficits in energy and agricultural trade balances; and an increase in **disposable income** that has led to a surge in the number of imports of **consumer goods**.

Exchange rates: Tunisia	
Tunisian dinars (TD) per US$1	
Jan 2001	1.3753
2000	1.4667
1999	1.1862
1998	1.1387
1997	1.1059
1996	0.9734
SOURCE: CIA *World Factbook 2001* [ONLINE].	

Tunisia took steps toward free trade by joining the World Trade Organization (WTO) and by signing an association agreement with the European Union in July, 1995. Tunisia will have to increase its exports and put an end to its trade deficit, a daunting task given that Tunisian exports have very low **value-added** status (increase in the market value of a product at a particular stage of production). Plans are underway to solve this problem by encouraging the domestic manufacture of intermediate goods that Turkey is forced to import in order to produce goods for export. The government has implemented several measures to ease this process, such as doing away with the red tape that hampers exports and allowing exporters improved access to credit.

MONEY

The goal of the Tunisian central bank is to maintain a stable dinar so that the economy can function competitively abroad. Since the end of 1995 the government has gradually devalued the dinar against the U.S. dollar, French franc, Italian lira, and German mark to help Tunisian exporters be competitive abroad. In July 2000 US$1 was equal to 1.186 Tunisian dinars, and 1 EU euro was equal to 1.265 Tunisian dinars.

In 1996 a foreign exchange crisis occurred when Tunisia's foreign-currency reserves fell to alarmingly low levels. This problem was an important reason for the adoption of the IMF **structural adjustment program**. Since 1995 foreign reserves have fluctuated between US$1.6–2.2 billion and in January 2000 rose to an all-time high of US$2.3 billion.

POVERTY AND WEALTH

The distribution of income in Tunisia, like that in many developing countries, is quite unequal. The top 20 percent of the people in Tunisia earn 46.3 percent of the country's total income while the 20 percent at the bottom of the scale earn only 5.9 percent of income. The majority of wealthy Tunisians live in Tunis and are able

Trade (expressed in billions of US$): Tunisia		
	Exports	Imports
1975	.856	1.424
1980	2.198	3.540
1985	1.738	2.757
1990	3.526	5.542
1995	5.475	7.903
1998	5.750	8.338
SOURCE: International Monetary Fund. *International Financial Statistics Yearbook 1999.*		

GDP per Capita (US$)

Country	1975	1980	1985	1990	1998
Tunisia	1,373	1,641	1,771	1,823	2,283
United States	19,364	21,529	23,200	25,363	29,683
Egypt	516	731	890	971	1,146
Nigeria	301	314	230	258	256

SOURCE: United Nations. *Human Development Report 2000; Trends in human development and per capita income.*

Distribution of Income or Consumption by Percentage Share: Tunisia

Lowest 10%	2.3
Lowest 20%	5.9
Second 20%	10.4
Third 20%	15.3
Fourth 20%	22.1
Highest 20%	46.3
Highest 10%	30.7

Survey year: 1990
Note: This information refers to expenditure shares by percentiles of the population and is ranked by per capita expenditure.

SOURCE: *2000 World Development Indicators* [CD-ROM].

to purchase the most expensive imported goods from up-scale shops. Still, unlike many less developed capitals in the Middle East, there is a real sense of community in Tunis and a desire to create an egalitarian society.

When President Zine El Abidine Ben Ali came into office in 1987, about 22 percent of the Tunisian population was living below the poverty line, impelling him to declare an all-out war on poverty in his inaugural speech. In 1992 he created the National Solidarity Fund whose goal was to promote 1,144 disadvantaged regions throughout the country, at an estimated cost of US$500 million. Since 1996, more than US$300 million has already been raised. Created in 1998, the Tunisian Solidarity Bank has also offered thousands of micro-credit loans (loans of very small amounts to help get a small business started, for example) to young graduates and small business owners.

Currently, the 6 percent of the population who are under the poverty line receive heavy **subsidies** from the government. Tunisia's first involvement with the World Bank in 1960, an education project, is testimony to the country's commitment toward the reduction of poverty and the redistribution of wealth. Various indicators also show a substantial improvement in the living standards of all Tunisians over the past 20 years. Average life expectancy increased from 67 in 1984 to 72.4 years in 1999. The annual rate of population growth dropped from 1.7 percent in 1994 to 1.1 percent in 2000. The per capita in-

come increased from 952 dinars in 1986 to 2,644 dinars in 1999.

WORKING CONDITIONS

In 1999 the labor force stood at 3.3 million, a substantial increase from the 1995 figure of 2.84 million. Some 22 percent of the labor force is employed in agriculture, 23 percent in industry, and 55 percent are in services. The public sector employs around 25 percent of the labor force. The official unemployment rate in 2000 was 15.4 percent, leaving the number of people without a job at 480,000. It is likely that the real rate of unemployment is significantly higher than the official figure, with some estimates putting it as high as 20 or 25 percent. About half of the unemployed are under the age of 25, many of whom are unskilled. The country has a national literacy rate of over 70 percent, and about 90 percent of the workforce under the age of 35 is literate. Although job-training programs and secondary educational institutions produce many skilled workers, many young people still cannot expect to find jobs with high-paying salaries. According to the EIU Country Profile, 70,000 jobs will need to be created outside agriculture to create **full employment**. There is also a large **underground**

Household Consumption in PPP Terms

Country	All food	Clothing and footwear	Fuel and power[a]	Health care[b]	Education[b]	Transport & Communications	Other
Tunisia	28	8	8	3	12	8	34
United States	13	9	9	4	6	8	51
Egypt	44	9	7	3	17	3	17
Libya	N/A	N/A	N/A	N/A	N/A	N/A	N/A

Data represent percentage of consumption in PPP terms.
[a]Excludes energy used for transport.
[b]Includes government and private expenditures.

SOURCE: World Bank. *World Development Indicators 2000.*

economy whose production is estimated at 15 percent of the GDP, and in which workers have no legal protections against adverse working conditions.

According to law, Tunisian workers have the right to form labor unions, and about 30 percent of the workforce is unionized. There is 1 national labor confederation, the General Union of Tunisian Workers (UGTT), to which all unions belong. Wages and working conditions are agreed upon through collective bargaining between the UGTT and the employers' association, and these agreements apply to about 80 percent of the public sector. The Labor Code sets a standard 48-hour workweek for most sectors and requires one 24-hour rest period. The industrial minimum wage is 170 dinars (US$155) per month for a 48-hour workweek and 149 dinars (US$136) for a 40-hour workweek. The agricultural minimum wage is 5.20 dinars (US$4.74) per day. The law prohibits forced child labor and sets the minimum age for employment in manufacturing at 16 years. The minimum age for light work in agriculture and some other non-industrial sectors is 13 years. The law also requires children to attend school until age 16.

COUNTRY HISTORY AND ECONOMIC DEVELOPMENT

1574. Tunisia becomes part of the Ottoman Empire.

1705. Husseinite Dynasty is established.

1881. French Protectorate is established on 12 May 1881. Anti-colonial resistance, led mostly by the Neo-Destour party, persists for most of the 75 years of French domination.

1956. Independence from France is declared on 20 March.

1957. The Republic of Tunisia is proclaimed. Habib Bourguiba becomes the first president on 25 July.

1959. The first Constitution of the Republic of Tunisia is adopted on 1 June.

1960. First Tunisian project is funded by the World Bank.

1963. The French evacuate Bizerta, their last base in the country.

1966. The production of oil begins.

1986. The International Monetary Fund's Structural Adjustment Program is adopted.

1987. Prime Minister Zine El Abidine Ben Ali succeeds the ailing President Bourguiba.

1990. Tunisia becomes a member of GATT.

1994. President Ben Ali is re-elected and an opposition party accedes to Parliament for the first time.

1995. Tunisia becomes the first country south of the Mediterranean to sign an association free-trade agreement with the European Union.

1995. Tunisia joins the WTO.

1998. The Tunisian Solidarity Bank starts to offer thousands of micro-credit loans to young graduates and small businesses.

1999. After the first-ever contested presidential elections, President Ben Ali is re-elected to a third term by an overwhelming majority. The Democratic Constitutional Rally keeps its majority in the Chamber of Deputies, but the opposition gains 20 percent of the 182 seats. The number of women in Parliament increases to 21.

FUTURE TRENDS

The international community recognizes that Tunisia has made serious and successful attempts at economic reform. As of 2000 more than 800 foreign companies were investing in the country. The World Bank has recommended that Tunisia speed up the sales of its publicly-owned companies, but this process has been overshadowed by an aggressive campaign to free up 93 percent of import-related businesses from state control and a major regional free-trade agreement. Having become a member of the World Trade Organization, Tunisia has also shown its serious commitment to free trade. Although Tunisia has moved somewhat slowly, especially in the telecommunications sector, the reforms that it has undertaken since 1990 have been far-reaching. Currently, Tunisia needs to concentrate on privatization to ensure continued and increased efficiency.

DEPENDENCIES

Tunisia has no territories or colonies.

BIBLIOGRAPHY

Economist Intelligence Unit. *Country Profile: Tunisia.* London: Economist Intelligence Unit, 2000.

McMahon, Janet. "Tunisia: Progress through Moderation." *Washington Report on Middle East Affairs.* <http://www .washington-report.org/backissues/0499/9904019.html>. Accessed July 2001.

Morrisson, Christine, and Talbi Bechir. *Long-Term Growth in Tunisia.* OECD, 1996.

Salem Norman. *Habib Bourguiba and the creation of Tunisia.* London: Croom Helm, 1984.

Tunisie: Site du Gouvernement. <http://www.ministeres.tn>. Accessed May 2001.

Tunisia Online. <http://www.tunisiaonline.com>. Accessed May 2001.

U.S. Central Intelligence Agency. *World Factbook 2000.* <http://www.odci.gov/cia/publications/factbook/index.html>. Accessed July 2001.

U.S. Department of State. *FY 2000 Country Commercial Guide: Tunisia.* <http://www.state.gov/www/about_state/business/com_guides/index.html>. Accessed May 2001.

World Bank. *Republic of Tunisia: Towards the 21st Century.* 2 vols. Report No. 14375 TUN. Washington, D.C.: World Bank, 1995.

World Bank. *World Development Report 2000.* Washington, D.C.: World Bank, 2000.

—Salamander Davoudi

UGANDA

Republic of Uganda

CAPITAL: Kampala

MONETARY UNIT: Uganda Shilling (USh). The largest Ugandan note in circulation is USh10,000 and the smallest is USh50. Recently introduced coins come in denominations of 50, 100, 200, and 500. There are plans to discontinue all notes in these denominations.

CHIEF EXPORTS: Coffee, cotton, tobacco, tea.

CHIEF IMPORTS: Petroleum products, machinery, textiles, metals, transportation equipment.

GROSS DOMESTIC PRODUCT: US$24.2 billion (purchasing power parity, 1999 est.).

BALANCE OF TRADE: Exports: US$471 million (f.o.b., 1999). Imports: US$1.1 billion (f.o.b., 1999).

COUNTRY OVERVIEW

LOCATION AND SIZE. A landlocked state in Eastern Africa, west of Kenya and east of the Democratic Republic of the Congo (former Zaire), Uganda has an area of 236,040 square kilometers (146,675 square miles) and a total land boundary of 2,698 kilometers (1,676 miles). Comparatively, the area occupied by Uganda is slightly smaller than the size of Oregon. Uganda's capital city, Kampala, is located in the country's southeast on the shore of Lake Victoria, Africa's largest lake and the source of the river Nile. Lake Victoria is also bordered by Kenya and Tanzania.

POPULATION. The population of Uganda was estimated at 22,459,000 in 2000 by the United Nations Economic Commission for Africa, an annual average increase of 2.5 percent from the 1995 population of 19,689,000. In 2000 the birth rate stood at 48.04 per 1,000 while the death rate was at 18.44 per 1,000. With similar annual growth rate, the population is likely to stand at 34,762,000 in 2015 and 66,305,000 by 2050. Although population per square kilometer was only 241 in 1999 (93 per square

mile), the above projected population growth could create a future crisis of land and resources.

The Ugandan population is primarily of African descent, consisting of thirteen principal ethnic groups, although there are actually 49 such groups in total. The rest of the population is made up of Asians and Europeans (around 1 percent) and a fluctuation of refugees escaping from crises in neighboring countries—most recently from Sudan, Rwanda, and the Democratic Republic of the Congo. It is important to note that Uganda had a large number of Asian citizens at independence in 1962; however, the majority of them were forcibly expelled under the regime of General Idi Amin (1971–78) in a racist attempt to "Africanize" the country.

Uganda's population is very young, with 51 percent below age 14 and just 2 percent of the population at 65 or older. A majority of Ugandans—86 percent—lived in rural areas in 2000. The urban population was 7 percent of the total population in 1965, rising to 14 percent in 2000 (5 percent of the population is centered in and around Kampala). It should be noted that it is difficult to be precise about population distributions because of frequent fluctuation between urban and rural areas as workers move to find seasonally-based employment.

Uganda is commonly conceived to be the epicenter of the HIV/AIDS epidemic; in fact HIV/AIDS in Uganda is commonly accepted to be a pandemic (the occurrence of a disease over a whole country). It is estimated that 110,000 Ugandans died from AIDS in 1999, and it has been the most common form of death of young adults since the late 1980s. It is important to understand that these deaths resonate beyond their own profound significance due to the socio-economic effects of HIV/AIDS. For example, the drawn-out nature of death from AIDS requires a large amount of care and attention. Therefore, large numbers of, predominantly, women who could be productively employed are spending their time caring for

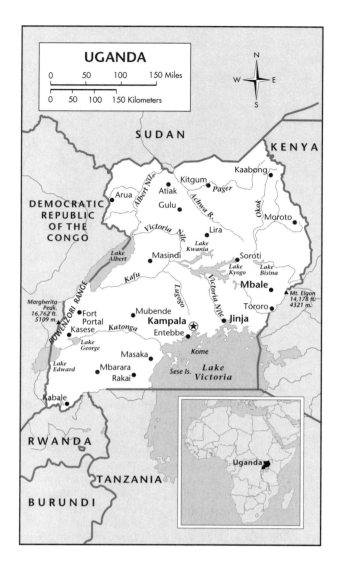

UGANDA

0   50   100   150 Miles

0   50   100   150 Kilometers

SUDAN

KENYA

Kaabong

Kitgum

DEMOCRATIC
REPUBLIC
OF THE
CONGO

Arua   Atiak   *Pager*

Gulu

Okok

Moroto

Victoria Nile   Lira

Achwa R.

Lake
Kwania

Masindi

Soroti

Lake   Lake
Kyoga   Bisina

Lake
Albert

Kafu

Lusoso

Mbale

Margherita
Peak.
16,762 ft.
5109 m.

*Fort
Portal*

Mubende

Kampala ⊛

▲ Mt. Elgon
14,178 ft.
4321 m.

Tororo

Victoria Nile

Jinja

Kasese   *Katonga*   Entebbe

Lake
George

Masaka

Kome

Lake
Edward

Mbarara
Rakai

Sese Is.

Lake
Victoria

Kabale

RWANDA

TANZANIA

BURUNDI

Uganda

the dying. In addition, by 1999 the cumulative number of orphans created due to AIDS since the pandemic began reached 1,700,000. This raises the problem of the development and guidance of Uganda's children. However, the Ugandan government was one of the first in Africa to promote public education programs and openness about HIV/AIDS. As a result of this proactive policy, Uganda is one of Africa's success stories for reducing HIV/AIDS; for example, 10,235 AIDS cases were reported in 1990 but only 1,406 in 1998.

OVERVIEW OF ECONOMY

Uganda's economy is dominated by the production of agricultural goods, which employs some 82 percent of the workforce. These goods range from crops grown mainly for subsistence purposes such as plantains, maize, beans, and potatoes, and exported **cash crops** such as coffee, tea, and tobacco. The reliance of the national economy on cash crops for foreign exchange is a legacy of

Uganda's colonial period when it was made a British protectorate (1894–1962) during the "scramble for Africa" by the imperialist European powers. In other words, the country's productive structure remains dominated by what the British colonial administration had forcefully demanded Ugandans produce.

At independence in 1962 Uganda was one of Africa's most economically promising states and was widely cited as the "Pearl of Africa." It was self-sufficient in food, its manufacturing sector produced basic inputs and **consumer goods**, and its transportation **infrastructure** was one of the best in the continent. Its key exports—coffee and cotton—were in global demand as the world economy was registering substantial growth built on the import demands of the United States, Western Europe, and parts of Northeast Asia. Health services were among the best in Africa, and schools, although in limited supply, were of a generally high quality.

However, from the beginning of President Idi Amin's regime in 1971 to the National Resistance Movement's (NRM) adoption of free market reforms in 1987, the official economy fell deeper and deeper into crisis under the strain of spasmodic civil wars and short-sighted economic programs such as the **nationalization** of certain industries and the expulsion of the Asian population. In 1960 cotton provided 40 percent of Uganda's export revenue (because cotton is a less volatile crop than coffee, its production had acted as a good counterbalance to **foreign exchange reserves** earned through exports). However, the harvesting of goods such as cotton and sugar declined considerably during the period 1971–1987 so that even in 2000 they were a minimal part of Uganda's agricultural production. The instability of the economy and the Uganda shilling between 1971–1987 led to the rise of the **informal sector**. The NRM had inherited an economy that had had the worst growth rate of all African countries between 1962–1987. The country's reliance on coffee production has left the economy highly vulnerable to the continual flux of international coffee prices.

Under the influence of the International Monetary Fund (IMF) and the World Bank, the NRM embraced free market reforms in 1987; these included the **privatization** of industry and services, the **devaluation** of the Uganda shilling (USh), and the **liberalization** of the **exchange rate** system. Since then Uganda has become one of the most economically liberal countries in the world. Due to a combination of free market reform, the large amount of post-conflict national reconstruction required, and the relative degree of security maintained by the NRM, the economy has enjoyed consistently high rates of GDP growth since the late 1980s. By the late 1990s external donors such as the IMF and European Union (EU) promoted Uganda as one of the key success stories of free market reform in Africa. For instance, evidence suggests that the stabilization of the Uganda shilling has created an economic environment suitable for the growth of the country's manufacturing sector and, more broadly, the diversification of export production into "non-traditional goods" such as fish products and cut flowers.

The reduction of the drain on state revenue since the banking sector was partially denationalized has contributed to the successful balancing of the national current account. The privatization of **parastatals** and the reduction of state spending by means of downsizing social services and the **public sector** have, similarly, lessened government spending. Because of the social stability throughout most of Uganda in the 1990s the incidence of tourism is increasing very quickly after having been heavily reduced by the violence permeating the country from 1971 to 1986.

Yet Uganda still suffers from considerable economic difficulties. The economy is dependent on the continued flow of aid from external donors. Total **external debt** has risen from US$0.689 billion in 1980 to US$3.708 billion in 1997, and the country remains entirely dominated by the unpredictability of the production and international prices of coffee. During the Amin period and the economy's decline, corruption within the government and society as a whole became very common in order to satisfy greed amongst the rich and survival for the poor. In 2000 corruption still saturated the government and the **private sector** despite efforts to curtail its influence. Similarly, by 2000 the informal sector remained of considerable size. However, the liberalization of the exchange rate system and the subsequent evening out of informal and official prices have sent the informal sector into decline.

POLITICS, GOVERNMENT, AND TAXATION

Like most African countries, the territory known as Uganda was an arbitrary creation of the European colonial powers. The borders cut across and brought together a whole range of ethnic and linguistic groups. Since gaining independence from Britain in 1962, the history of Uganda's politics and government falls into 4 broad periods.

The first period was opened at the country's independence with multi-party elections which brought the Uganda People's Congress (UPC) to power, led by Prime Minister Milton Obote. However, the Obote regime soon opted for a more authoritarian leadership. By using its base of support in the north of the country and the military to discard Uganda's traditional kingdoms and check its historical rivals in the south (who had been the country's elite during the colonial administration), Obote became the self-appointed executive president.

The second period began in 1971 when Obote was ousted from government by one of his key pillars of support, the military, led by Idi Amin. This was a major turning point for Uganda as Amin's 8 years of rule (1971–1979) saw the economy and political process collapse. Amin's regime used fear and racism as central instruments of policy and social control; over 300,000 people were murdered by the regime, and the vast majority of the country's 88,000 Asians were forcibly expelled and their land and other assets divided amongst Amin's followers. Economically, this was a disaster. After this policy had been enacted, the redistributed assets were placed in the hands of people who were inexperienced and lacked established business networks; this led to the decline of the productivity and efficiency of Uganda's business sector. Moreover, as Uganda's citizens became less confident in the stability of the formal economy due to Amin's unpredictable rule, they increasingly began to turn to the informal sector, thereby bypassing the state and its revenue-collecting authorities. In sum, the economy became less productive and more reliant upon the informal sector, both drastically reducing state taxation revenue. As state revenue was so depleted, the government began borrowing from international lenders at such a rate that Uganda became heavily indebted. These factors, in combination with the deteriorating terms of trade for Uganda's products on international markets after the decline of world economy in the 1970s, explain why the Ugandan economy was in dire crisis by the end of Amin's regime.

The third broad period of Uganda's political history began when Amin was finally overthrown in 1979 by a coalition of domestic forces under the banner of the Uganda National Liberation Front (UNLF) and the neighboring Tanzanian army. This led to an 8-year period of crisis and uncertain rule that plagued the country. After Amin's defeat, a string of 3 limited and short-term governments followed, led by the UNLF, President Binaisa, and President Lule, respectively. This period was one in which the economy was devastated further by continued widespread disruption, huge military expenditures, and the effects of the international rise of oil prices in 1979. This quick succession of regimes culminated in the corrupt and widely disputed multiparty elections of 1980 that reinstated Obote as president. Commonly known as Obote II, this period was characterized by 2 central dynamics. First, Obote attempted to address the country's considerable economic woes by approaching the IMF and the World Bank for financial aid. This aid was dependent upon Uganda liberalizing the economy with the hope that free market forces would make it more competitive in the world economy. Second, the social effects of this reform were negative, which in combination with the corrupt and heavy-handed rule of Obote II, culminated in growing popular support for the

National Resistance Movement (NRM) led by Yoweri Museveni that was waging a guerrilla war from its support-base in Uganda's south.

The fourth key period of Uganda's political history began when the NRM took state power in 1986; the NRM remained in power in early 2001. With Museveni as president the NRM had seized power on the back of a set of left-progressive, anti-imperialist policies. However, because of the legacy left by Amin and his successors, the country was in a state of severe social, economic, and institutional crisis. Consequently, by 1987 the NRM was forced to go back on its initial left-progressive developmental policies simply because there was insufficient revenue to pursue such an approach. In fact, like Obote II, the NRM applied to the IMF and World Bank for aid that was conditional upon adopting free market reform.

Although Uganda's economy is claimed by many to have been in a relatively good state of health since the opening to free market forces from 1987 onwards, the political situation is somewhat more ambiguous. The country remains a "no party democracy." Museveni stresses that the NRM is not a political party but a national "movement" of a broad coalition of societal and political forces. As a result, while Uganda maintains a high level of press freedom (especially in comparison with most other African countries), political parties are illegal. A referendum in July 2000 saw 90 percent of voters favoring the continuation of the "no party system" which seems to have justified the NRM's political stance.

However, a level of contention remains about this system's legitimacy as the 2 most prominent opposition parties, Uganda People's Congress (UPC) and Democratic Party (DP), boycotted the referendum. Furthermore, the U.S.-based human rights group Human Rights Watch claimed in a 1999 report that, due to the illegal nature of organized opposition, the country has "a restricted political climate." Contemporary indications of discontent in Uganda are clearly illustrated by a series of violent insurgencies by dissident groups such as Joseph Kony's Lord's Resistance Army in the north and the Allied Democratic Forces (ADF) in the southwest. In order to counter these rebellions, the army now has permanent barracks in these volatile areas.

Presidential elections were held at the beginning of March 2001. Museveni won an easy victory with 69.3 percent of the votes compared to the 27.8 percent of his closest competitor, the politically progressive former army colonel, Dr. Kizza Besigye. Although Museveni's victory was tainted by accusations of intimidation, fraud, and violence (an estimated 5–15 percent of votes cast could have been compromised), this margin of potential electoral corruption still gave Museveni a sufficient mandate to hold onto the presidency.

Since 1998 Uganda has been at war in neighboring Democratic Republic of the Congo (DRC) to depose the Kabila regime first led by Laurent Kabila (who was assassinated in January 2001) and then by his son Joseph. This is a very complex war involving Rwanda, which supports a separate but similar anti-Kabila faction, and Angola, Zimbabwe, and Namibia, which all support the DRC government. The war is a considerable drain on the government's already sparse revenue; the Ministry of Defence received 33 percent of all ministerial allocations in the 1999–2000 budget. Yet by March 2001, Uganda was beginning to withdraw some troops from the DRC; however, this conflict has subsided and re-ignited before.

A key reform promoted by the IMF and World Bank was the **restructuring** of Uganda's taxation regime. One of the intentions was to lower the dependence on trade taxes, which reduced incentives for production, and to rely instead on **indirect taxes** on goods and services. Indirect taxes provided an average of 79.8 percent of total revenue between 1990–1998. Taxes on income and profits have steadily increased from 9.8 percent of total revenue in 1989 to 15.2 percent in 1998. Yet, of total taxes, about 50 percent still emanates from indirect taxes on only 4 products—petroleum, cigarettes, beer, and soft drinks. In fact, Uganda's tax revenue to GDP ratio is fifty percent below the African average.

The Uganda Revenue Authority (URA) was established to address the priority of improving government tax-collecting abilities. However, it is claimed that almost immediately after the creation of the URA its officials were involved in the major embezzlement of the funds it was set up to collect. In addition, throughout the government departments in 1997–98, US$120 million in tax revenue and government spending was unaccounted for. Due to these high levels of ingrained corruption, low levels of household income, and a small proportion of waged (thus taxable) labor, the majority source of government revenue still emanates from external donors. Of the government's estimated total financial requirement for 2000, US$1.467 billion was expected to come from domestic resources, whereas US$2.255 billion was required in external aid. It is due to regular deficits such as this that Uganda's external debt as a percentage of GNP has risen from 35.5 percent in 1985 to 58.2 percent by 1998.

INFRASTRUCTURE, POWER, AND COMMUNICATIONS

Uganda is a landlocked country served by a network of 27,000 kilometers (16,800 miles) of roads, although only 1,800 kilometers (1,100 miles) are paved and 4,800 kilometers (2,900 miles) of the remainder are suitable for all-weather purposes. This road network supplied Uganda's total 25,900 passenger cars and 42,300 com-

Communications

Country	Newspapers	Radios	TV Sets[a]	Cable subscribers[a]	Mobile Phones[a]	Fax Machines[a]	Personal Computers[a]	Internet Hosts[b]	Internet Users[b]
	1996	1997	1998	1998	1998	1998	1998	1999	1999
Uganda	2	128	27	N/A	1	0.1	1.5	0.06	25
United States	215	2,146	847	244.3	256	78.4	458.6	1,508.77	74,100
Dem. Rep. of Congo	3	375	135	N/A	0	N/A	N/A	0.00	1
Kenya	9	104	21	N/A	0	N/A	2.5	0.19	35

[a]Data are from International Telecommunication Union, *World Telecommunication Development Report 1999* and are per 1,000 people.

[b]Data are from the Internet Software Consortium (http://www.isc.org) and are per 10,000 people.

SOURCE: World Bank. *World Development Indicators 2000.*

mercial vehicles in 1995. With funding from a range of external donors, Uganda launched an ongoing road rehabilitation project in 1987 with the principal aims of providing improved access of agricultural products to markets within the country and a regional network to link Rwanda, the east of the Democratic Republic of the Congo, and Uganda with the port of Mombasa in Kenya. A 22-kilometer (13-mile) road linking Uganda to Rwanda was opened in 2000.

The nation's rail system had lacked sufficient investment since decolonization, but the state-owned Uganda Railways Corporation's (URC) 1,241 kilometers (770 miles) of railroad has benefitted from a rejuvenation project since 1995. This includes plans by the government to partially privatize the operation of the network. The URC has US$350 million in assets and a US$20 million annual **turnover**, and, due to the trebling of freight traffic between 1989 and 1995, the URC network has the potential of becoming highly profitable.

The Entebbe International Airport is Uganda's major airport, which is situated 35 kilometers (22 miles) from Kampala. Although there are another 28 airports throughout the country, the vast majority are unpaved. Uganda's landlocked status makes it dependent upon the port services of neighboring countries, such as Mombasa in Kenya and Dar-es-Salaam in Tanzania. Rail links to the port of Durban in South Africa are growing in importance. The country's situation in the "Great Lakes" region means that it boasts 5 large lakes and 2 major rivers that are frequently used for transportation purposes. The use of waterways has benefitted from an extensive program of government investment and external aid.

The vast and varied waterways in Uganda are also highly beneficial for the production of hydroelectricity. A parastatal, Uganda Electricity Board (UEB), utilizes this natural resource to produce enough power to satisfy the country's needs and also to export 115 million kWh of electricity in 1998. UEB commands assets worth over

US$600 million and has an annual turnover in the region of US$70 million. The government intends to grant concessions to the private sector for the operation of parts of UEB upon its disintegration into separate operators maintaining the generation, transmission, and distribution of electricity.

In 2000 there were 2 national telecommunications operations in the country, Uganda Telecomm Limited (UTL) and Mobile Telephone Network Uganda (MTN). A third operator, Celtel Uganda, supplies additional mobile telephone services. Although as many as 12 Internet service providers had been licensed to provide both Internet e-mail and Internet services by early 2001, only 4 are actually in operation.

ECONOMIC SECTORS

Uganda's economic sectors reflect the legacy of colonial structures, the country's position as a land-

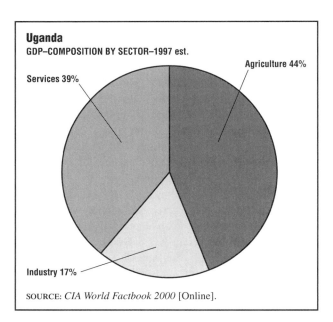

Uganda
GDP–COMPOSITION BY SECTOR–1997 est.

Agriculture 44%
Services 39%
Industry 17%

SOURCE: *CIA World Factbook 2000* [Online].

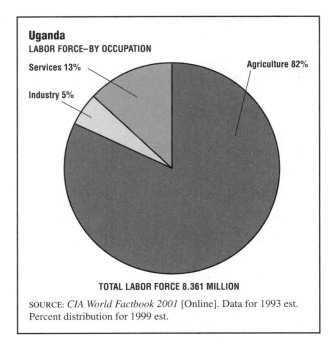

Uganda
LABOR FORCE–BY OCCUPATION

Services 13%

Industry 5%

Agriculture 82%

TOTAL LABOR FORCE 8.361 MILLION

SOURCE: *CIA World Factbook 2001* [Online]. Data for 1993 est.
Percent distribution for 1999 est.

AGRICULTURE

The agricultural sector is dominant in Uganda's economy. Whilst this sector grew at an annual average of only 3.7 percent over 1990–99 compared to the far more impressive growth of the industrial and service sectors, the importance of agriculture in Uganda's economy outweighs all other sectors put together. The agricultural sector employs 82 percent of the workforce, accounts for 90 percent of export earnings, and provided 44 percent of GDP in 1999. Moreover, the farmers in Uganda's 2.5 million **smallholdings** and scattered large commercial farms provide the majority of their own and the rest of the country's staple food requirements. Uganda is able to rely on agriculture due to the country's excellent access to waterways, fertile soils, and, (relative to many other African nations) its regular rainfall, although it does still suffer from intermittent droughts such as in 1993–94.

Uganda's key agricultural products can be divided into cash crops, food crops, and horticultural produce. The most important cash crops are coffee, tea, cotton, tobacco, and cocoa. Uganda is second only to Kenya as Africa's largest producer of tea, exporting US$17.06 million of tea in 1996 and $39 million by 1998. Unmanufactured tobacco exports provided US$9.5 million in 1998, over 25 percent more than in 1996. The export of cocoa beans hit a recent high in 1996 with US$1.07 million in export receipts, but this had declined to $0.87 million in 1998. The primary food crops, mainly for domestic consumption, include plantains, cassava, maize, millet, and sorghum. Total cereal production was 1.76 million metric tons in 1998, which provided US$17.82 million of exports in 1998. This gain was in part negated as imports of cereals were $30.9 million in the same year. The more recent development of cultivating horticultural produce includes fresh flowers, chilies, vanilla, asparagus, and medicinal plants. At the beginning of 2001 it is unclear how well horticultural production will prosper but it does indicate the economy's potential diversity. The fact that vanilla production is the third largest in Africa, providing US$930,000 in export receipts in 1998, is a success in itself.

The economy of northeast Uganda is dominated by pastoralism (cattle farming). Although agricultural production is apparent in some areas, this is normally a mixture known as "agro-pastoralism" (integrated cattle and crop farming). It should be noted that pastoralism is in decline due to the constant cattle raids by guerrilla groups such as the Lord's Resistance Army based in southern Sudan, as well as government and aid agency intervention which encourages the fencing off of land to discourage the traditional free-roaming of cattle.

COFFEE. Coffee is by far the most important factor in the nation's entire economy. Uganda is one of the largest pro-

locked territory, its politically tumultuous past, and the widespread lack of foreign investment in sub-Saharan Africa as a whole. Uganda is highly dependent on agricultural exports in order to provide much-needed foreign currency, and its underdeveloped industry and services necessitate an increasing level of imports. Consequently, in 1997 the government was in 5.7 percent deficit as a percentage of GDP (excluding external aid). In addition, Uganda lacks a significant internal market for domestically produced goods because of low household incomes. In light of these factors it is unlikely that the economy will reduce its primary dependence on the export-based growth strategy of producing goods such as coffee in the medium-term future; nonetheless, it does remain a leader in international coffee markets.

In order to address these geographical, historical, and material problems, the Ugandan government is attempting to diversify its economic sectors to produce more manufactured goods for domestic, regional, and international consumption to reduce the dependence of the economy on foreign aid and imports. With the continued financial support of the IMF, World Bank, EU, and United States for Uganda's free market reforms there is a genuine possibility that the economy's present diversification will contribute to its current growth rate—one of the fastest in the world. Uganda had an average GDP annual growth rate of 7.2 percent over 1990–99, which constitutes a growth rate of agriculture of 3.7 percent, of services at 8.1 percent and industry at 12.7 percent. This consistent growth of various sectors suggests a dynamic economy.

ducers of coffee in sub-Saharan Africa and exported 197,200 metric tons in 1998, second only to Côte d'Ivoire. This provided US$314 million in export earnings. Although this was a drop in earnings from the 1996 level of $396.2 million, the 1996 harvest had provided 81,511 metric tons more than in 1998. The country's high altitude, relatively high rainfall, and mild climate are suited to the growing of coffee. Robusta coffee is grown in areas near Lake Victoria and in some Western districts. Arabica coffee is grown in the volcanic regions in Mbale and Kapchorwa where the cooler, higher altitude provides the increased rainfall necessary for the growth of this more profitable crop. The dual process of the devaluation of the Ugandan Shilling and its flotation was intended to provide an incentive to producers to take advantage of more competitive exports and thus expand their production of exportable goods. On face value this process was a success as producer prices dramatically increased. For example, coffee farmers received a 182 percent rise in the price paid for their product, and there was an annual average growth of coffee exports of 6.5 percent between 1990–1997.

However, the apparent growth of Uganda's coffee exports does not take account of smuggling into the country from neighboring countries such as the war-torn Democratic Republic of Congo whose farmers often do not receive as good a price for their crops as those in Uganda. Furthermore, increased productivity was based upon an increase in the area cultivated rather than on higher yields. When there is a rise in available cultivated land it acts as an increased drain on the country's environmental resources. The 50 percent projected rise of the population by 2015 more than likely will increase competition, and perhaps conflict, over ever-decreasing land plots.

Regarding improvements to the agricultural sector, farmers simply lack the access to capital (*see* Services rubric below) in order to mechanize production and increase agricultural productivity. Productivity per agricultural worker was an average of US$345 per annum over 1996–1998. In consequence, farmers are unable to take full advantage of increased returns for the export of coffee when they do arise, for instance, during the coffee boom of 1994–95 where the price in U.S. cents to a pound of coffee was 126.83. This failure to improve production is based upon a lack of investment and an assumption of the continuation of the usually relatively low levels paid by the volatile world market for **primary commodities**. For example, in 1999 the price in U.S. cents to a pound of coffee was only 67.65. Considering the long-term maturity of coffee plants, the instability of international markets does not provide much of an incentive for improved efficiency of production. It should also be noted that export crops such as coffee are very susceptible to natural disasters, which further reduces

their economic viability. For instance, a hurricane in 2000 pushed Uganda's national harvest back a year.

INDUSTRY

Industry is very limited in Uganda. The most important sectors are the processing of agricultural products (such as coffee curing), the manufacture of light consumer goods and textiles, and the production of beverages, electricity, and cement. The production of beer in Uganda has increased dramatically in recent years, rising from 215,000 hectoliters in 1988 to 896,000 in 1997. Similarly, cement production has expanded from a low of 15,000 metric tons in 1988 to 290,000 in 1997. Of lesser importance is the production of sawn wood, remaining stable at 83,000 cubic meters from 1994 onwards. However, there is little evidence of the sufficient replanting of trees, which may not only affect this level of production but could have adverse environmental effects such as soil erosion and increased landslides. A key block to the development of Uganda's industrial and commercial sector is corruption. Bribes are commonly demanded to acquire even the most basic services such as an electricity supply and telephones.

Due to increased domestic security, market reform, and tax breaks, Uganda's manufacturing sector is growing. Merchandise exports have expanded from US$147 million in 1990 to US$501 million in 1998. However, merchandise imports have also expanded but at an even greater rate, from US$213 million in 1990 to US$1,414 million in 1998. This imbalance indicates a serious problem with Uganda's economy because, in order to continue the present rate of import of manufactured goods, the government is obliged to borrow ever greater amounts of money from foreign donors which makes the country increasingly indebted.

The privatization of industry is a central dynamic in Uganda's contemporary national economy. This is of central importance considering that government **subsidies** to parastatals were equal to that spent on much needed education between 1994–1998. The Privatization Unit of the Ministry of Finance has plans to open a number of industries to the private sector. For example, the largest dairy processor in the country, the government-owned Dairy Corporation, which has an annual turnover of US$12 million, is undergoing full privatization. Copper mining used to be a mainstay of the economy in the 1960s to mid-1970s with an output of up to 18,000 metric tons per annum. Due to the country's civil unrest and the decline of copper prices on international markets, the 90 percent government-owned Kilembe Mines Ltd. mining activity has been inactive since 1982. The planned privatization of this enterprise should end government subsidies to this company and is hoped to lead to the reinvigoration of Uganda's copper production.

SERVICES

The export of Uganda's commercial services has grown dramatically from US$21 million in 1990 to US$165 million in 1998. Yet at the same time the import of commercial services has grown from US$195 million in 1990 to US$693 million in 1998. This imbalance, similar to that of manufactured goods, contributes to the deficit of Uganda's **balance of payments**. Therefore, in order to maintain this level of imports, Uganda is forced to borrow more money from external donors, thus leading to the deepening of the country's public debt and the consequent drain of debt interest payments upon an already limited government revenue.

TOURISM. Due to the severe insecurity permeating Uganda through the 1970s and most of the 1980s, tourism was a very limited sector. Today, the majority of Uganda is entirely safe for tourists and the country has a lot to offer, such as a number of beautiful reserves and national parks, vast lakes, rare and endangered wildlife, relatively untouched rural communities, and safe cities. By 1995, 159,899 tourists provided receipts of US$188 million; by 1997 receipts from tourism rose to US$227 million. However, it should be noted that internal tourism expenditures drew out almost as much money as was brought in to the country, with US$137 million being spent by Ugandans abroad in 1997.

FINANCIAL SERVICES. Uganda's banking system had been in disarray throughout the 1970s and 1980s, in part due to an almost full government **monopoly** of this sector. The 2 most important national banks, the state-owned Bank of Uganda (BOU) and the Cooperative Bank, had received automatic **liquidity** support from the Uganda Central bank (UCB) up until the early 1990s—that is, the UCB would supply banks with money to prevent their financial collapse even if they had been making irresponsible and irretrievable loans, often to allies of the various political regimes. As a result, the UCB's **non-performing loans** accounted for 75 percent of its total loan portfolio. Uganda's most important financial mechanism was bankrupted.

In order to make the UCB less of a drain on state revenue, the IMF and World Bank encouraged its privatization, a 48 percent cut in personnel, and a reduction of branches from 190 to 85. The improved stability of the banking sector has encouraged people to save, and a 1995 IMF report claimed that bank deposits grew from 4 percent of GDP in 1989–90 to 5.8 percent in 1993–94. However, due to the economy's severe underdevelopment, low incomes, and low opportunities for lending, there is limited incentive for private-sector banks to operate. Even though the economy has been substantially liberalized, foreign banks have failed to reinvest or to re-establish themselves, or to innovate their practices in Uganda, in part due to the fact that more than half of commercial banks made losses in 1994.

The privatization of the banking system has reduced the availability of basic banking services, in particular for rural farmers. In 1972 there was one branch per 34,000 people; by the mid-1990s this figure was 164,000. This means that the most important sector of the economy, namely agriculture, receives insufficient investment to improve productivity. Primarily due to fraudulent practice by employees, 3 of Uganda's national banks collapsed in 1999, namely the Cooperative Bank, International Credit Bank, and Greenland Bank. This has given foreign-owned banks such as Stanbic, Barclays, Standard Chartered, and Trans Africa Bank increased footing in those areas they deem commercially viable, thus providing greater competition against the remaining national banks.

INTERNATIONAL TRADE

Uganda is becoming increasingly dependent on the import of capital through loans and grants, the import of services, and of manufactured goods. The value of imports was consistently double the value of exports throughout the 1990s, and in 1999 the ratio of imports to exports came close to being 3 times in size. Apart from cash-crops such as tea and coffee (*see* Agriculture rubric above), Uganda's principal exports in 1998 were US$39.9 million of fish and fish products, US$47.4 million of iron and steel, and US$47.2 million worth of electrical machinery and supplies. It should be noted that the EU banned the import of fish from Uganda between 1999 and mid-2000 as some supplies were poisonous; although this ban has now been lifted this event seems likely to effect future sales. The main recipient of these exports in 1998 was the EU, which received 50.9 percent of the total; broken down individually, the key countries were the Netherlands, which imported 6.3 percent, Switzerland (6.2 percent), Germany (5 percent), and Belgium (3.7 percent). Other key export-partners are the United States which regularly receives around 25 percent, and Kenya which received 4.6 percent in 1998.

Uganda's imports in 1998 consisted of US$130.3 million of road vehicles, US$111.6 million of petroleum,

Trade (expressed in billions of US$): Uganda		
	Exports	Imports
1975	.026	.200
1980	.345	.293
1985	.387	.327
1990	.147	.213
1995	.461	1.058
1998	.512	1.409

SOURCE: International Monetary Fund. *International Financial Statistics Yearbook 1999.*

US$72.4 million in cereals, and US$53.65 million of medical goods and pharmaceuticals. These imports were predominantly sourced from the EU, which supplied 17.3 percent (the United Kingdom being the main partner, providing 5.6 percent), neighboring Kenya supplied 12.3 percent, Japan 4.5 percent, and India 4.1 percent. The countries of East Africa have been trying to create a meaningful intra-regional trade organization since the 1960s. The signing of the East African Cooperation (EAC) treaty between Uganda, Tanzania, and Kenya in 1999 was a continuation of this historic aim; however, in practice little has been done to reduce **tariffs**. Uganda is also a member of the Common Market for Eastern and Southern Africa (COMESA), which in 1996 introduced an 80 percent tariff reduction on trade within COMESA countries; by 2001 Uganda was one of the only members to implement this reduction in full.

MONEY

Uganda's monetary and financial sector has gone through dramatic change since the government adapted free market reform from 1987 onwards. Two of the most important reforms were the devaluation of the Uganda shilling (USh) and the liberalization of the exchange rate system. In order to make national exports cheaper and more competitive on world markets the USh was devalued by 77 percent in 1987; after subsequent minor devaluations, it was again substantially reduced by 41.2 percent in 1989. The liberalization of the exchange rate system was undertaken in a number of stages, culminating in the establishment of a unified inter-bank market for foreign exchange and the commercialization of all foreign exchange transactions, which were to be undertaken by commercial banks and foreign exchange bureaus.

By 1994 the government accepted the obligations of Article VIII, Sections 2, 3, and 4 of the IMF's Articles of Agreement, which maintained a commitment to a free and open exchange system. The Uganda shilling had become a competitive monetary unit, open to the speculation of international currency markets. This resulted in its depreciation from USh100 per U.S. dollar in 1987, to

USh965 in 1994. Although these policies had initial inflationary consequences (as late as 1991–92 annual average **inflation** was 42 percent), by 1994–95 the USh had stabilized at only 5 percent; considering that inflation had hit 1,000 percent during the Amin era, this is a considerable government success. Uganda's capital markets are based on 2 main organizations: the Uganda Securities Exchange (USE), and its regulator, the Capital Markets Authority (CMA). In June 1997 the USE was licensed to operate as an approved stock exchange and began formal trading operations in January 1998. In 2001 there were only 4 listed securities trading on the exchange: 2 corporate bonds and 2 companies, Uganda Clays Limited and British American Tobacco, Uganda.

POVERTY AND WEALTH

With an average **GDP per capita** of US$332 in 1998, Uganda is one of the poorest countries in the world. The vast majority of Ugandans are farmers on small plots of land which are used for subsistence agriculture or for the cultivation of cash crops such as coffee and tea. However, most of this land is owned by landlords such as chiefs or government functionaries who seldom reinvest in the productive capacity of the village as they can simply rely on rents. This disparity of the ownership of the means of production is reflected by vast inequalities in the distribution of income. The poorest 20 percent of the country controls only 6.6 percent of the wealth, whereas the richest 20 percent benefit from 46.1 percent. In fact, 69 percent of the population lives on less than US$1 a day and the majority of this limited income (63 percent) is spent on food. As a result, in a country whose government spends only 1.9 percent of its GDP on health, the majority of Ugandan citizens struggle to acquire even the most basic health care. There are only 4 doctors and 28 nurses per 100,000 people. Nonetheless, the government has helped to reduce the infant mortality rate from 110 deaths per 1,000 births in 1970 to 84 by 1998.

Most Ugandans have to work 2 or 3 jobs simply to survive, often even to secure a standard of living below the poverty threshold. Moreover, one or more of these jobs are often within the informal sector which draws tax-

Exchange rates: Uganda	
Uganda shillings (USh) per US$1	
Feb 2001	1,700
2000	1,644.5
1999	1,454.8
1998	1,240.2
1997	1,083.0
1996	1,046.1
SOURCE: CIA *World Factbook 2001* [ONLINE].	

GDP per Capita (US$)					
Country	1975	1980	1985	1990	1998
Uganda	N/A	N/A	227	251	332
United States	19,364	21,529	23,200	25,363	29,683
Dem. Rep. of Congo	392	313	293	247	127
Kenya	301	337	320	355	334
SOURCE: United Nations. *Human Development Report 2000; Trends in human development and per capita income.*					

Distribution of Income or Consumption by Percentage Share: Uganda

Lowest 10%	2.6
Lowest 20%	6.6
Second 20%	10.9
Third 20%	15.2
Fourth 20%	21.3
Highest 20%	46.1
Highest 10%	31.2

Survey year: 1992–93
Note: This information refers to expenditure shares by percentiles of the population and is ranked by per capita expenditure.
SOURCE: *2000 World Development Indicators* [CD-ROM].

ation revenue away from the government. With the increased unemployment levels associated with the privatization and reduction of employment opportunities in the public service, the army, and former parastatals, workers have become an increasingly flexible and less expensive factor of production. Consequently, trends after 1991 have been in the direction of increased inequality, both between rural and urban areas but also in intra-urban terms, as wages did not increase anywhere near as fast as the rise of profits.

The labor surplus and the desperate need for employment has meant that employers can offer almost whatever they want for wages as they know that they will fill their vacancies. As Susan Dicklitch observes in her book, *The Elusive Promise of NGOs in Africa,* even the middle class, the traditional bastion of democracy and agitator for change, like the working class are "often too busy trying to eke out a living" to fulfil their historic political role. However, if Uganda's GDP continues its 7 percent annual growth of recent years, if President Museveni's anti-poverty strategy promoted in March 2000 is effective, and if the country continues to benefit from the proposed US$2.3 to US$2.5 billion in external aid, then there is hope that the standard of living for the majority may improve.

WORKING CONDITIONS

Uganda's **labor force** is the sixth largest in sub-Saharan Africa, totaling 8.4 million workers in 1993. Yet, as 51 percent of the population is below the age of 14, it is difficult for a government with such limited revenue to provide sufficient education and vocational training for the mass of Uganda's youth. The majority of the nation's workforce is thus unskilled. However, in part by increasing public expenditure on education from 1.5 percent of GDP in 1990 to 2.6 percent in 1997, the government has been successful in attacking illiteracy. The 49 percent of the population over 15 years of age who were

illiterate in 1985 had been reduced to 36 percent by 1997—9 percent better than the African average. The problem of an unskilled workforce has been accentuated by the AIDS pandemic. Because it is likely that a trained teacher or doctor will contract HIV, it is necessary to train 2 or even 3 people to ensure the supply of even one skilled employee.

Labor migration is very common in Uganda. Areas of high unemployment (in districts such as Kabale) were forcibly created by the British colonial administration in order to facilitate the movement of cheap labor from these districts to "industrial" districts such as Buganda and Ankole to work in mines, towns, factories, and plantations. While migratory labor had been relatively well paid before 1986 (people could save part of their wages to buy products such as bicycles and other "luxuries"), due to high inflation and the liberalization of the Uganda shilling imports are far more expensive and workers struggle to even feed their families. Workers are unable to return to their respective districts with basic tools to improve or buy their own land. Hence, there is a growing landless peasantry that is subject to a cycle of laboring simply in order to buy food and basic essentials.

Uganda's trade unions were given legal recognition by the British colonial administration in 1952. In 1993 the unionization of public services was legally permitted, which brought the number of trade unions in Uganda to 17. All unions are legally obliged to affiliate with the highly centralized National Organization of Trade Unions (NOTU) which is part of a tripartite negotiating structure involving the Federation of Ugandan Employers (FUE) and the Minister of Labor. Although the government supports workers' rights conventions promoted by the International Labor Organization (ILO), trade unions are ineffective in Uganda. This is in part due to a lack of unity amongst workers as they work 2 or 3 jobs, and are subject to ethnic, regional, and gender divides. Also, trade unions and other workers' movements have had their powers reduced by the government, and individual workers are often tied to large commercial farms by the provision of normally very poor accommodation, a small plot of land for subsistence, and low wages. Though meager, without these limited resources the worker is lost, hence the space for challenging employers is limited. In light of this situation, although the power of trade unions has been historically low in Uganda, it is no surprise that they are now a virtually non-existent lobby group.

COUNTRY HISTORY AND ECONOMIC DEVELOPMENT

c. 1850. Arab traders make first non-African contact within the territory of Uganda and promote Islam.

1862. Explorer John Hanning Speke is the first European to enter Uganda.

1885. Uganda is designated as a British sphere of influence at the Treaty of Berlin.

1890. A small British military force arrives in Uganda.

1894. Britain declares Uganda a protectorate.

1962. Uganda achieves independence from Britain, and Milton Obote becomes prime minister in multiparty elections.

1971. General Idi Amin forcibly seizes power.

1972. The country's Asian population is expelled, and British companies are taken under government control.

1979. Tanzanian army with Ugandan dissidents under the banner of the Uganda National Liberation Front (UNLF) oust Idi Amin.

1980. Corrupt multi-party elections reinstate Milton Obote as president.

1986. National Resistance Army enters Kampala and forms a government as the National Resistance Movement (NRM), led by President Yoweri Kaguta Museveni.

1987. The NRM government adapts free market reform and starts to receive aid from the IMF and World Bank.

1998. Uganda starts its involvement in the war in the Democratic Republic of the Congo.

2000. A flawed national referendum maintains the "no-party" political system.

2001. Presidential elections held in March.

FUTURE TRENDS

At the outset of 2001, Uganda has the potential to diversify its economy, and there are signs that alternatives to the present substantial reliance on the export of coffee are arising. But in the face of continually falling coffee prices on international markets, in order to prosper in the 21st century diversification of the economy is essential. Unless there is a serious unforeseeable crisis Yoweri Museveni will remain as president at least until 2006, and Uganda will continue on its path of free market reform. This reform will continue to be backed-up by substantial aid from the World Bank, the IMF, the EU and other donors.

There will be an intensification of the privatization of parastatals. The revenue freed-up from previously subsidizing parastatals may allow the government to spend a greater proportion of GDP on essential public services such as education and health. Without investment in these areas an unhealthy and poorly educated workforce will constrain improved social and economic development. GDP growth for 1999–2000 was 5.4 percent, a considerable decline from the highs of 7 percent in 1995 and 1996. This is some indication of the economy's growth beginning to stabilize after the essential reconstruction work undertaken from 1987 onwards. In light of this evidence, it is likely that annual GDP growth will remain at around 5 percent or less for the next 5 years. A continued drain on government resources is Uganda's involvement in the ongoing war in the Democratic Republic of the Congo (DRC). At the beginning of 2001 Museveni was faced with a dilemma between withdrawing and allowing the potential for increased destabilizing attacks upon Uganda by forces based in the DRC or to remain involved in an unpopular and expensive war.

DEPENDENCIES

Uganda has no territories or colonies.

BIBLIOGRAPHY

Ahikire, J. "Worker Struggles, the Labor Process, and Control in United Garments Industry Limited." In *Uganda: Studies in Living Conditions, Popular Movements, and Constitutionalism,* edited by M. Mamdani and J. Oloka-Onyango. Vienna: JEP, 1994.

Bank of Uganda. <http://www.bou.or.ug>. Accessed February 2001.

Belshaw, D., and P. Lawrence. "Agricultural Tradables and Economic Recovery in Uganda: The Limitations of Structural Adjustment in Practice." *World Development.* Vol. 27, No. 4, 1999.

Brownbridge, M. *Financial Repression and Financial Reform in Uganda.* Sussex: Institute of Development Studies, 1996.

Common Market for Eastern and Southern Africa. <http://www.comesa.int>. Accessed March 2001.

Dicklitch, S. *The Elusive Promise of NGOs in Africa: Lessons from Uganda.* Basingstoke: Macmillan, 1998.

Economist Intelligence Unit. *Country Report: Uganda, 1999.* London: EIU, 1999.

Food and Agriculture Organization. *FAO Yearbook: Trade 1998.* Rome: FAO, 1999.

Human Rights Watch. "Uganda Silences Political Parties with Harassment and Oppression." *Press Release.* Kampala: HRW, 12 October 1999. Reprinted online at <http://www.hrw.org>. Accessed February 2001.

International Monetary Fund. *International Financial Statistics Yearbook 2000.* Washington DC: IMF, 2000.

Isegawa, M. *Abyssinian Chronicles.* New York: Alfred A. Knopf, 2000.

Jamal, V. "Changing Poverty Patterns in Uganda." In *Developing Uganda,* edited by M. Twaddle and H. B. Hansen. Oxford: James Currey, 1998.

Lamont, T. "Economic Planning and Policy Formulation in Uganda." In *Uganda: Landmarks in Rebuilding a Nation,* edited by P. Langseth, J. Katorobo, E. Brett, and J. Munene. Kampala: Fountain, 1995.

Mamdani, M. "Analysing the Agrarian Question: The Case of a Buganda Village." In *Uganda: Studies in Labor,* edited by M. Mamdani. Dakar, Senegal: CODESRIA, 1996.

Mehran, H., P. Ugolini, J. Briffaux, G. Iden, T. Lybek, S. Swaray, and P. Hayward. "Financial Sector Development in Sub-Saharan African Countries." *IMF Occasional Article 169.* Washington DC: IMF, 1998.

Mitchell, B.R. *International Historical Statistics: Africa, Asia and Oceania 1750–1993,* third edition. London: Macmillan, 1998.

The Monitor. <http://www.monitor.co.ug>. Accessed March 2001.

Munene, J. C. "Organisational Pathology and Accountability in Health and Education in Rural Uganda." In *Uganda: Landmarks in Rebuilding a Nation,* edited by P. Langseth, J. Katorobo, E. Brett, and J. Munene. Kampala: Fountain, 1995.

Museveni, Y. K. *Sowing the Mustard Seed: The Struggle for Freedom and Democracy in Uganda.* London: Macmillan, 1997.

Nadzam, B., ed. *Countries of the World and Their Leaders Yearbook 2001.* Farmington Hills, MI: Gale Group 2001.

Ocan, C. "Pastoral Crisis and Social Change in Karamoja." In *Uganda: Studies in Living Conditions, Popular Movements, and Constitutionalism,* edited by M. Mamdani and J. Oloka-Onyango. Vienna: JEP, 1994.

Rutanga, M. "A Historical Analysis of the Labor Question in Kigezi District." In *Uganda: Studies in Labor,* edited by M. Mamdani. Dakar, Senegal: CODESRIA, 1996.

Sharer, R. L., H. R. De Zoysa, and C. A. McDonald. *Uganda: Adjustment with Growth, 1987–94.* Washington DC: IMF, March 1995.

Tukahebwa, G. B. "Privatization as a Development Policy." In *Developing Uganda,* edited by M. Twaddle and H. B. Hansen. Oxford: James Currey, 1998.

Uganda Home Pages Ltd. <http://www.uganda.co.ug>. Accessed February-March 2001.

United Nations. *Statistical Yearbook, Forty-Fourth Issue, 1997.* New York: United Nations, 1999.

United Nations. *UNAIDS (Joint United Nations Program on HIV/AIDS).* <http://www.unaids.org/hivaidsinfo/statistics/june00/fact_sheets/pdfs/uganda.pdf>. Accessed March 2001.

United Nations Development Program (UNDP). *Human Development Report 2000.* New York: Oxford University Press, 2000.

United Nations Economic Commission for Africa. <http://www.uneca.org>. Accessed February 2001.

Upham, M., editor. *Trade Unions of the World,* fourth edition. London: Cartermill, 1996.

U.S. Central Intelligence Agency. *World Factbook 2000.* <http://www.odci.gov/cia/publications/factbook/index.html>. Accessed February 2001.

World Bank. *African Development Indicators 2000.* Washington DC: World Bank, 2000.

———. *Sub-Saharan Africa: From Crisis to Sustainable Growth.* Washington DC: World Bank, 1989.

———. *Uganda: The Challenge of Growth and Poverty.* Washington DC: World Bank, 1996.

———. *World Development Indicators 2000.* Washington DC: World Bank, 2000.

———. *World Development Report: From Plan to Market.* New York: Oxford University Press, 1996.

———. *World Development Report: Poverty.* New York: Oxford University Press, 1990.

———. *World Development Report 1997: The State in a Changing World.* New York: Oxford University Press, 1997.

———. *World Development Report 2000/2001: Attacking Poverty.* New York: Oxford University Press 2000.

—Liam Campling

ZAMBIA

Republic of Zambia

CAPITAL: Lusaka.

MONETARY UNIT: Zambian kwacha (K). One Zambian kwacha is equal to 100 ngwee. Coin denominations include 1, 2, 5, 10, 20, and 50 ngwee and notes include 1, 2, 5, 10, 20, 50, 100, and 500 kwacha.

CHIEF EXPORTS: Copper, cobalt, lead, and zinc.

CHIEF IMPORTS: Crude oil, manufactured goods, machinery, transport equipment, and foodstuffs.

GROSS DOMESTIC PRODUCT: US$3.325 billion (1999). [CIA *World Factbook* estimates GDP at purchasing power parity at US$8.5 billion (1999 est.).]

BALANCE OF TRADE: Exports: US$1.057 billion (1998). **Imports:** US$1.140 billion (1998). [CIA *World Factbook* reports exports to be US$900 million (f.o.b., 1999 est.) and imports to be US$1.15 billion (f.o.b., 1999 est.).]

The HIV/AIDS epidemic is a considerable problem in Zambia with 19 percent of the working age population infected. It is estimated that 99,000 Zambians died from AIDS in 1999 whilst those with HIV infection who were still alive at the end of 1999 numbered 870,000. These deaths and levels of infection are not only important in themselves but have extremely negative social and economic costs. The drawn-out nature of death from AIDS means that many of the population (predominantly women) who could be productively employed have to provide long-term care for the dying. In addition, by 1999 the cumulative number of orphans created since the epidemic began in the mid-1980s reached 650,000. This raises the problem of the development and guidance of Zambia's children.

COUNTRY OVERVIEW

LOCATION AND SIZE. A landlocked state located in southern Africa, east of Angola, Zambia has an area of 752,614 square kilometers (290,584 square miles) and a total land boundary of 5,664 kilometers (3,520 miles). Comparatively, Zambia is slightly larger than Texas. Zambia's capital city, Lusaka, is located in the southern center of the country's territory.

POPULATION. The United Nations Economic Commission for Africa estimated Zambia's population at 9,133,000 in 2000, a notable rise from the 1995 level of 8,081,000. In 2000 the birth rate stood at 41.9 births per 1,000 population while the death rate was 22.08 deaths per 1,000. With similar annual growth rates, the population will stand at 13,201,000 in 2015 and 21,965,000 in 2050. Zambians of African descent constitute 98.2 percent of the population, and 1.1 percent are European. In 1998, 39 percent of Zambians lived in urban habitats—one of the highest levels of urbanization in Africa.

OVERVIEW OF ECONOMY

The mining of copper dominates Zambia's national economy. A central legacy of the colonial period (1899–1964) was the exploitation of Northern Rhodesia's (modern Zambia) vast copper deposits, first, by the British South Africa Company (BSAC) who administered the territory until 1924 and, second, by the British government. The need for copper miners meant that a high percentage of Zambia's male workforce was, often forcibly, encouraged to leave their **subsistence farms** and work in the mines. This led to the neglect of the agricultural sector and Zambia's reliance on copper exports—a trend that continued to affect the national economy by 2001.

At independence in 1964, Zambia's economy was highly skewed; most regions outside of the "line of rail" (the railway that serviced the mining sector) were highly underdeveloped. However, the newly elected United National Independence Party's (UNIP) policy of actively developing the economy meant that the manufacturing and agricultural sectors increased in importance, and the sup-

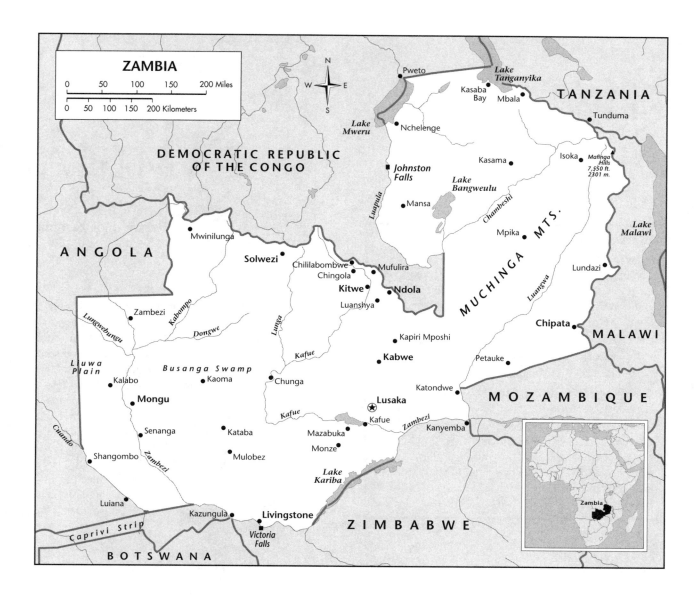

ply of health and education services to the population dramatically improved.

The UNIP, led by President Kenneth Kaunda, promoted a brand of so-called "humanist" **socialism** which was the ideological justification for the creation of a large number of **parastatals** in Zambia. The important reasons for this policy were the Unilateral Declaration of Independence (1965) by the neighboring white-supremacist Rhodesia (modern Zimbabwe), which threatened Zambia's supply lines, and the fact that the foreign owners of Zambia's enterprises often invested their profits abroad. In addition, parastatals were seen by the Zambian government as a mechanism to develop and diversify the economy.

By the late 1970s, parastatals employed a third of the official **workforce** and consisted of over 330 enterprises whose activities criss-crossed Zambia's economy with areas such as mining, transport, agriculture, construction, tourism, trade, and finance. Partly due to the parastatal

system, Zambia's manufacturing output rose by more than 160 percent between 1965 and 1975, and the level of domestic power generated grew by more than 350 percent. However, the parastatals, and the economy as a whole, continued to rely on colonial structures in that they were dependent on foreign capital, expertise, technology, imports, and markets. In addition, parastatals (along with the government and civil service) were rife with corruption and inefficiency as many could not function without large government **subsidies**. This simply meant that the Zambian form of parastatals was inherently unsustainable.

In order to continue to subsidize state spending on parastatals and social services, UNIP continually borrowed from the International Monetary Fund (IMF) to support the economy's **balance of payments** deficits. By the early 1980s the IMF began to impose conditions of free market reform for continued lending. These reforms consisted of the stabilization of the economy and a degree of economic **liberalization**. However, the effects of these reforms on the incomes and employment of Zambia's workers were negative. By 1987, widespread social protest and discontent persuaded Kaunda to drop the IMF-sponsored reform.

In 1991 the UNIP government was defeated during multiparty elections by the Movement for Multi-Party Democracy (MMD). The MMD immediately institutionalized a radical program of free market reform in order to secure continued external aid and to satisfy Zambia's business class. Parastatals were **privatized**, the kwacha was devalued, and the **exchange rate** was liberalized. As well as reducing consumer incomes, these reforms caused a considerable amount of financial uncertainty, and a number of domestic banks collapsed. Moreover, even though the government had benefitted from increased revenue through the privatization of 85 percent of its parastatals by 1998, the national balance of payments remained in deficit.

In comparison to Zambia's traditional reliance on copper and cobalt at independence, by the 1990s the economy had significantly diversified. In 1999, non-traditional exports such as processed foods, copper rods, and textiles constituted 39.4 percent of export earnings. However, the growth of the national economy and government revenue was still determined by the unstable prices of **primary commodities**, particularly copper and cobalt, in world markets.

CRIME. It is important to note that Zambia is a key transhipment point for the global illegal drug trade. A significant quantity of heroin and cocaine bound for Europe and for distribution throughout the rest of Southern Africa passes through Zambia. This illicit trade is supported by the fact that Zambia is a regional **money-laundering** center that acts as an excellent facility for those dealing in drugs to disguise the illegal source of their profits.

DEBT. **External debt** is a huge drain on Zambia's economy. Due to government subsidies of parastatals and investment in public health and education, by 1980 Zambia was one of sub-Saharan Africa's most indebted countries; it owed $3.261 billion. By 1997, the **national debt** had risen to $6.758 billion. This increased indebtedness was predominantly caused by an annual average government deficit of 10.72 percent of GDP between 1989 and 1998. Although the national balance of payments had been improving over the latter half of the 1990s, by 2000 the government remained fully dependent upon external aid in order to function.

POLITICS, GOVERNMENT, AND TAXATION

Like most of sub-Saharan Africa's countries, Zambia was a false creation of European imperialism during the "scramble for Africa" during the late 1800s. The territory of Zambia (formerly Northern Rhodesia) cut across dozens of ethnic groupings, chiefdoms, and languages and pulled these different societies together under an increasingly centralized colonial state. Colonial rule in Zambia (1899–1964) was a period of "divide and rule" where different chiefdoms were played off each other by the BSAC and the British government, respectively. (Although specific African leaders would often use colonial power to achieve their own ends).

When vast copper reserves were discovered in the mid-1920s the country was mobilized to mine this valuable mineral to enrich the colonial powers, whilst the rest of the economy was neglected. As Marcia Burdette noted in her *Zambia: Between Two Worlds,* the colonial administration transformed Zambia into "a mineral-exporting enclave with a vast underdeveloped hinterland." Due to the growing nationalist militancy of the African population, independence was achieved in 1964. Zambia's post-colonial politics can be divided into 3 periods, each of which corresponds to the establishment of a new republic and constitution.

THE FIRST REPUBLIC. The First Republic (1964–1972) was formed at independence in 1964. In multiparty elections in 1964 the United National Independence Party (UNIP) defeated its main rival, the African National Congress (ANC). The socialist-"humanist" orientation of the government (led by President Kenneth Kaunda) was bolstered by a large revenue supplied by high international copper prices, which allowed the opening of health and education services to the black population. The UNIP could boast a considerable success; by 1972 Zambia's hospitals had grown by 50 percent and health clinics doubled, whilst the availability of education services also dramatically increased. In order to administer the growing **public sector** the civil service expanded dramatically and acted as a mechanism for the UNIP ruling elite to award the party faithful. Due to the lack of a significant business sector, civil servants became the nation's upper class.

THE SECOND REPUBLIC. The Second Republic (1972–1990) was established in 1972. Known as the "one party-participatory democracy," it was a one-party state ruled by the UNIP. All other political parties were banned, and Kaunda's dominant role in the UNIP and the government assured him an uncontested rule. However, the Second Republic ran into serious difficulties due to corruption within the civil service, government, and parastatal sector, and declining government revenue caused by the falling price of copper. The government began to borrow heavily to support the vast state expenditure and the country became highly indebted.

Discontent grew throughout the country over the 1980s because of rapidly declining incomes and rising prices, partly caused by an IMF economic liberalization program (which was subsequently dropped in 1987). The culmination of worker militancy, student protests, and growing opposition within the ruling class was the formation of the Movement for Multi-Party Democracy (MMD) led by Frederick Chiluba (a key trade union figure). Mounting economic crisis and political pressure led Kaunda to sign a new constitution in 1990, putting an end to one-party rule.

THE THIRD REPUBLIC. The Third Republic adopted a multi-party parliamentary democracy. Peaceful presidential and parliamentary elections were held in 1991 wherein Chiluba received 76 percent of votes cast. After this defeat Kaunda stepped down from office and ended his 27 years of leading the country. Relatively free and fair elections were held again in 1996 and the MMD won a landslide victory for the second time. In 2001, the MMD continued to pursue free market economic reform. The global dominance of free market **capitalism** since the 1990s and, perhaps, the success of the pro-business MMD has led the UNIP to drop its socialist orientation and adopt "capitalism with a social conscience."

The Zambia Revenue Authority (ZRA) was set up in 1994 to increase government revenue—which had been historically low—and to reduce the economy's growing dependence on external aid, which is essential in supporting Zambia's most basic necessities. The ZRA had reported considerable success in its role. For example, **value-added tax** (VAT) was introduced in 1995 and by the turn of the century it constituted 20 percent of all tax revenue. In order to provide increased incentives for domestic and international business the levels of these various revenue-collecting mechanisms had been progressively reduced in the 1990s. Nonetheless, even in light of these pro-business tax reductions, ZRA revenue collections still grew from K421 billion in 1994 to K954 billion in 1997.

INFRASTRUCTURE, POWER, AND COMMUNICATIONS

Of Zambia's 66,935 kilometers (41,500 miles) of roads, relatively few are of good quality and paved except for those routes linking Lusaka to main border posts. The publicly-owned Zambia Railways (ZR) controls most of the 2,169 kilometers (1,345 miles) of national rail **infrastructure**. Rail routes to regional seaports are very important because Zambia is landlocked. The railway track linking Zambia to the seaport of Dar es Salaam in Tanzania is jointly run by the Tanzania-Zambia Railway Authority (TZRA), which is not part of ZR. Other seaports used for Zambia's imports and exports are Beria in Mozambique, Durban in South Africa, and Walvis Bay in Namibia. Lusaka International is Zambia's primary airport; the main secondary airports are based at Ndola, Livingstone, and Mfuwe. All of these airports are run by the publicly-owned National Airport Corporation (NAC).

The state-owned Zambia Electricity Supply Corporation (ZESCO) produced 8.16 billion kilowatts (kWh) of electricity in 1998 using hydropower. Of this, 1.2 billion kWh was exported. However, the use of commercial energy within the country declined by an annual average of 1.7 percent between 1980 and 1997, whereas the use of traditional fuels as a percentage of total energy use rose from 37.4 percent in 1980 to 73.1 percent in 1996. This increased reliance on traditional energy sources, mainly wood, means that Zambia's environment is threatened by deforestation which, in turn, creates soil erosion and a subsequent decrease in arable land.

The state-owned Zambia Telecommunications Company (ZAMTEL) is the national provider of telecommunication services (predominantly telephone lines). ZAMTEL is planned to be partially privatized. Although generally adequate, Zambia's telecommunications can be unreliable, particularly during rainy seasons. A cellular telephone service is available in Lusaka and

Communications

Country	Newspapers	Radios	TV Sets[a]	Cabl subscribers[a]	Mobile Phones[a]	Fax Machines[a]	Personal Computers[a]	Internet Hosts[b]	Internet Users[b]
	1996	1997	1998	1998	1998	1998	1998	1999	1999
Zambia	12	121	137	N/A	1	0.1	N/A	0.48	15
United States	215	2,146	847	244.3	256	78.4	458.6	1,508.77	74,100
South Africa	32	317	125	N/A	56	3.5	47.4	33.36	1,820
Dem. Rep. of Congo	3	375	135	N/A	0	N/A	N/A	0.00	1

[a]Data are from International Telecommunication Union, *World Telecommunication Development Report 1999* and are per 1,000 people.
[b]Data are from the Internet Software Consortium (http://www.isc.org) and are per 10,000 people.

SOURCE: World Bank. *World Development Indicators 2000.*

other built-up areas. Fax machines are widely used, and the Internet is becoming an increasingly popular means of communication for those few who are fortunate enough to have access.

ECONOMIC SECTORS

Zambia's economic sectors reflect 3 key constraints. First, the influence of colonial rule created a reliance on mining (in particular, copper) and a failure to fully exploit the agricultural sector. Second, the small size of the population means that domestic markets are limited. Third, its landlocked status reduces the competitiveness of exports as they are subjected to the **tariffs** of neighboring countries and high transportation costs.

However, for such an underdeveloped country, Zambia has been relatively successful in diversifying its economy. Although copper exports continue to be of primary importance, the export of **cash crops** such as cotton and tobacco, as well as refined sugar, provide a high level of revenue and employment. However, all of these goods are highly sensitive to fluctuations in international market prices. The manufacturing sector produces a large quantity of textiles for export and there is a growth in the production of cut flowers. Within the industrial sector, the mining of gems and other minerals, as well as the production of cement, engineering products, and chemicals, helped balance out the economy's reliance on the mining of copper and cobalt.

AGRICULTURE

Zambia's main agricultural exports are cotton, sugar, and cut flowers. Agricultural exports increased signifi-

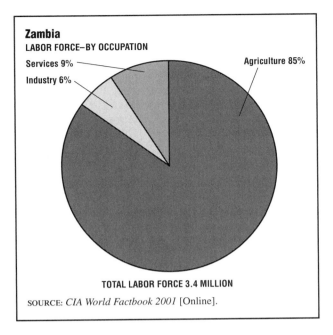

Zambia
LABOR FORCE–BY OCCUPATION

Services 9%
Industry 6%
Agriculture 85%

TOTAL LABOR FORCE 3.4 MILLION

SOURCE: *CIA World Factbook 2001* [Online].

cantly between 1993 and 1998 from US$27.2 million to US$89.7 million. However, Zambia's agricultural sector has historically lacked significant infrastructure and productive investment. This means that the sector is highly underdeveloped whilst offering considerable potential if large investment was supplied. For example, neighboring Zimbabwe, which is of a comparable size and climate to Zambia, exported US$1,157 million of agricultural goods in 1998. The key problem with Zambia's failure to fully exploit its agricultural production to a similar extent as Zimbabwe is that agricultural imports have significantly outweighed agricultural exports throughout the 1990s. This represented another imbalance on the national balance of payments and a serious drain of foreign currency reserves that have to be used to pay for imports.

COTTON. Cotton is one of Zambia's most important cash crops. Although it is partly produced on large commercial farms by expatriates and some African commercial farmers, like most of Zambia's cash crops, the vast bulk of cotton output comes from small subsistence farmers. Even though the price of cotton plummeted between 1998–1999, export earnings from this crop rose from US$22.8 million to US$41.4 million, partly due to companies holding back 1998 stocks in the hope that prices would rise. The production of cotton also supports Zambia's large domestic textile industry.

Another key cash crop is tobacco. In 1998 Zambia exported US$9.5 million of tobacco, an impressive rise from the 1988 level of US$3.8 million. However, like most primary commodities, tobacco exports are subject to the continuing change and instability of international market prices. In 1960 1 metric ton of tobacco fetched US$8,391; by 1999 this had fallen to US$2,922. Also of

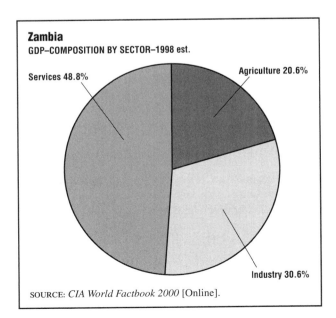

Zambia
GDP–COMPOSITION BY SECTOR–1998 est.

Services 48.8%
Agriculture 20.6%
Industry 30.6%

SOURCE: *CIA World Factbook 2000* [Online].

note is the farming of coffee. In 1999 coffee provided US$8.7 million in exports; these earnings would have been higher if the world market leader, Brazil, had not almost doubled its normal output.

SUGAR. Sugar is a dominant agricultural export, accounting for 70 percent of all export earnings in the processed food sub-sector in 1999 (other key goods in this sub-sector are stock feeds, marigold meal, mealie-meal, and wheat flour). Sugar exports have increasingly benefitted from initiatives by the European Union which, under the Lome Convention, agreed to buy 13,000 metric tons from the Zambia Sugar Company in 2000. However, processed food exports suffered a decline from the 1998 level of US$49.4 million to US$33 million in 1999. This is because of serious instability in the Democratic Republic of the Congo which was the recipient of roughly 40 percent of Zambia's processed food exports.

A recent agricultural development of huge significance is the production of floricultural goods (mainly cut flowers). Despite low prices at Dutch auctions in 1999 (the Netherlands is the key trading point for flowers in Europe), Zambia's floricultural products fetched US$42.8 million in export earnings. In addition, in 1999 horticultural production (mainly fruit and vegetables) earned US$23.8 million. However, there appears to be a certain imbalance here as Zambia exports vast amounts of fruit and vegetables whilst remaining a net importer of food for domestic consumption.

The major food crops produced in Zambia for domestic consumption are cassava, maize, and wheat. Maize used to be one of the most important food goods in Zambia with 1,845,000 metric tons being produced in 1989, but by 1998 this had declined to 650,000 tons. However, over the same ten-year period the consistent growth of cassava production (from 290,000 tons to 817,000 tons) and of wheat (from 10,000 tons to 70,000 tons) partly canceled out the decrease of maize output. Nonetheless, the total domestic production of these 3 basic food crops was 608,000 tons less in 1998 than in 1989. This decline of domestic food production often means that Zambians have to pay more for their essential nutritional requirements with a negative knock-on effect on the standard of living.

INDUSTRY

MINING. National copper and cobalt reserves are by far the most important factor in Zambia's national economy. Zambia is the world's fourth largest producer of copper and, due to the ongoing civil war in the cobalt-rich Democratic Republic of the Congo, it has been the leading producer of cobalt in the late 1990s. In 1996 total copper exports amounted to US$568 million and cobalt exports US$193 million.

Copper is subject to the constant fluctuation and uncertainty of international market prices. In 1960 the price for a metric ton of copper was US$3,271; at its height in 1970 it was US$5,629. Yet from the mid-1970s onwards it consistently declined to only US$1,519 by 1999. For example, even though Zambia produced 12,700 tons more copper in 1993 than in 1988, it received US$219.4 million less in export receipts. But, in total, copper production has steadily declined from a 1970 high of 700,000 metric tons to only 250,000 tons in 1999. More importantly, it is estimated that, at the ongoing level of production, the nation's economically viable copper reserves will be exhausted by 2010.

By 2000 the giant parastatal mining company, Zambia Consolidated Copper Mines (ZCCM), had been fully privatized. The **private sector** successors (principally the mining giants Anglo America, Avmin, and the Glencore/First Quantum consortium) had begun to invest hundreds of millions of dollars in Zambia's mines. In combination with the fact that Zambia has the largest non-exploited underground copper reserve in the world, private sector investment means that the mining sector may continue to provide considerable export earnings to the national economy well into the 21st century.

In the 1960s and 1970s Zambia also mined and refined a significant amount of lead and zinc. The high point for the production of these minerals was in 1974 when 27,000 tons of lead and 58,000 tons of zinc were produced; however, by 1993 these levels had dropped dramatically to 3,000 tons and 5,000 tons, respectively. Yet, lead and zinc in combination with gold, silver, and platinum provided US$12.3 million in export earnings in 1998. (In 1999 this fell to only US$3.3 million, but this was due to the modernization and rehabilitation of mines.) The export of gemstones has grown in importance and provided US$13.8 million of exports in 1999 to the main market of East Asia.

MANUFACTURING. Unusual for an economy in sub-Saharan Africa, Zambia exports more manufactured goods than it imports—with US$180 million exported in 1997 and US$116 million imported (although as a whole the economy generally remains in deficit). The principal manufacturing exports are textiles, engineering products, and building materials.

Zambia's textile industry is considered to have vast competitive potential in the region due to relatively cheap labor costs and a high level of domestic cotton production. But the dumping (the sale of a good on a foreign market at a price below marginal cost) of foreign textiles on the Zambian market by regional competitors has negated the growth of domestic textile production. Zambia's export earnings from textile products (80 percent of which is cotton yarn) declined from US$42.4 million in 1998 to US$37 million in 1999. This is principally due to a fall in the price of cotton yarn over this period as the quantity of exports remained stable. The principal destinations for textile products were the EU countries, which consumed 80 percent, and regional African countries with 15 percent.

In 1999, the main engineering products manufactured in Zambia were copper rods (73.4 percent), electrical cables (13.7 percent), and copper wire (11.2 percent). The export of these engineering products declined by 26.7 percent between 1998 and 1999 to US$23.2 million. This is mainly because of a fall in international demand due to the slow recovery of the industrialized economies in East Asia after the 1996–97 world financial crisis. Similarly, the export of building manufactures (such as cement and roofing sheets) declined in 1999 to US$10.2 million. Again, this was due to the ongoing civil war in the Democratic Republic of the Congo, traditionally the main destination of these goods.

SERVICES

TOURISM. Zambia has a great deal to offer adventurous tourists. It provides a sample of relatively "untouched" Africa with authentically wild national parks, stunning scenery, and the Victoria Falls and Zambezi River (2 of Southern Africa's main tourist spots), which it shares with Zimbabwe.

Zambia's tourism sector has benefitted from the serious social and political instability in neighboring Zimbabwe (which was traditionally a preferred destination). As a consequence, and also due to considerable public and private investment in tourist facilities, the level of tourists visiting Zambia rose from 87,000 in 1980 to 362,000 in 1998. This created an increase in tourism receipts from US$20 million to US$75 million, although it should be noted that Zambian nationals vacationing abroad spent US$59 million in 1998.

FINANCIAL SERVICES. In the 1960s the Zambian government **nationalized** several non-bank financial institutions (such as insurance companies) and set up the Zambia National Commercial Bank to compete with existing private commercial banks. But due to political interference and the inefficient allocation of loans, this system of public banking was unsuccessful. With the aim of improving efficiency in the banking sector through the discipline of free market competition, Zambia liberalized interest rates between 1992 and 1995. This created a considerable amount of financial turmoil and instability. In 1995, Zambia's third largest bank, Meridien Bank, collapsed along with 2 other local banks. In addition, due to a new regulation requiring banks to have at least US$140 million in working capital, and because of the insufficient experience of domestic banks in operating in a liberalized economy, 5 other banks had their licenses withdrawn by the Bank of Zambia (the central bank) by 1998.

Despite free market reform, by the late 1990s there was still considerable evidence of political leaders and their allies defaulting on loans and interfering in the affairs of Zambia's banks. In addition, not only has new regulation and economic liberalization failed to significantly increase confidence in the banking sector (which remains fragile as 30 percent of total loans are non-performing), the Economist Intelligence Unit maintained in 1997 that "too many banks [are] chasing the little profit available." This has led to the increased domestic dominance of huge multinational banks such as Barclays and Citibank, thereby displacing less powerful national banks such as the National Savings and Credit Bank of Zambia and the publicly owned Zambia National Commercial Bank.

INTERNATIONAL TRADE

From 1991 Zambia became a net importer of goods, importing US$83 million more than it exported in 1998. The national balance of payments generally remained in deficit throughout the 1990s. In order to address this imbalance the government relied on external aid to prop up the economy; this in turn has led to a deeper indebtedness and a rise of annual debt repayment levels. In 1993, Zambia's main imports were US$144 million of crude oil (it is refined domestically into petroleum oils), and US$30 million in fertilizer. The main sources of Zambia's imports in 1996 were South Africa (US$303 million), Saudi Arabia (US$107 million), the UK (US$81 million), neighboring Zimbabwe (US$67 million), and Japan (US$19 million).

Historically, Zambia's main exports are copper and cobalt, which in total provided US$761 million in export earnings in 1996. However, there has been a huge expansion of non-traditional exports (NTEs) such as sugar, cotton, copper rods, textiles, cut flowers, gemstones, and cement since independence in 1964. In 1999, the European Union was the largest market for Zambia's NTEs, which

Trade (expressed in billions of US$): Zambia		
	Exports	Imports
1975	.810	.929
1980	1.298	1.116
1985	.784	.545
1990	1.309	1.220
1995	1.040	.700
1998	N/A	N/A

SOURCE: International Monetary Fund. *International Financial Statistics Yearbook 1999.*

consumed US$117.4 million (38.54 percent) of total NTE earnings. Within the EU the largest market was the Netherlands which accounted for US$40.6 million of such goods as cut flowers and live fish. The UK was the second largest EU market and imported US$37.4 million of specialty vegetables, cotton yarn, and coffee. Germany consumed US$21.3 million in cotton yarn and cut flowers.

The Common Market for Eastern and Southern Africa (COMESA) was Zambia's second largest regional market for NTEs in 1999 and imported US$81.8 million. Some of the principal NTEs sold in this region were sugar, petroleum oils, cement, food, and electricity. The main 3 markets and their percentage of COMESA's imports were the Democratic Republic of the Congo (41.93 percent), Malawi (18.66 percent), and Zimbabwe (12.86 percent). However, due to war in the Democratic Republic of the Congo and social unrest in Zimbabwe, 1999 exports to these countries fell. The key market for Zambia's copper rods, gemstones, and tobacco was East Asia, accounting for US$10.3 million.

MONEY

Since the liberalization of the kwacha in the early 1990s Zambia has suffered from a permanently high level of **inflation**. In part due to the influx of imports to modernize Zambia's recently privatized copper mines, the kwacha lost 40 percent of value to the U.S. dollar in 2000. Zambia's inflation has resulted in its coinage being more valuable as pieces of metal than at face value. In consequence, notes are the population's source of cash. Due to expensive and scarce credit facilities, Zambia's domestic trade is generally undertaken using cash.

Zambia has a single stock exchange, the Lusaka Stock Exchange (LuSE). The LuSE opened in 1994. By 1997 it had benefitted from increased trading volumes, and its capitalization value was US$502 million. At the outset of 2000 it listed 15 companies. The national Securities and Exchange Commission (SEC) regulates Zambia's stock market.

GDP per Capita (US$)					
Country	1975	1980	1985	1990	1998
Zambia	641	551	483	450	388
United States	19,364	21,529	23,200	25,363	29,683
South Africa	4,574	4,620	4,229	4,113	3,918
Dem. Rep. of Congo	392	313	293	247	127

SOURCE: United Nations. *Human Development Report 2000; Trends in human development and per capita income.*

POVERTY AND WEALTH

Zambia is a country defined by extreme poverty. By 2000, over 70 percent of the population lived on less than 1 dollar a day (the figure 10 years before was 50 percent) and 64 percent of this income was spent on essential food. This is in a country whose public expenditure on health as a percentage of GDP fell from 2.6 percent in 1990 to 2.3 percent in 1998, and where external aid per capita fell from US$119.7 in 1992 to US$36.1 in 1998. In addition, the daily per capita supply of calories fell from 2,173 in 1970 to 1,970 in 1997, and the daily supply of protein declined by 19.2 percent and fat by 27.1 percent over the same period. Consequently, 3 in 5 of Zambian children were malnourished by 2001. Along with the impact of the HIV/AIDS epidemic, these factors have contributed to a declining life expectancy for the average Zambian from 47.3 years in the early 1970s to 40.1 in the late 1990s.

There are vast disparities in living conditions between Zambia's rural and urban habitants. For example, whilst 64 percent of the urban population have access to safe water, only 27 percent of the rural population are so fortunate. Moreover, 46 percent of the urban population live below the poverty line compared to a massive 88 percent in rural areas. In more general terms, the disparity of wealth between Zambia's rich and poor is also con-

Exchange rates: Zambia	
Zambian kwacha (K) per US$1	
Jan 2001	4,024.53
2000	3,110.84
1999	2,388.02
1998	1,862.07
1997	1,314.50
1996	1,207.90

SOURCE: CIA *World Factbook 2001* [ONLINE].

Distribution of Income or Consumption by Percentage Share: Zambia	
Lowest 10%	1.6
Lowest 20%	4.2
Second 20%	8.2
Third 20%	12.8
Fourth 20%	20.1
Highest 20%	54.8
Highest 10%	39.2

Survey year: 1996
Note: This information refers to expenditure shares by percentiles of the population and is ranked by per capita expenditure.

SOURCE: *2000 World Development Indicators* [CD-ROM].

Household Consumption in PPP Terms

Country	All food	Clothing and footwear	Fuel and power[a]	Health care[b]	Education[b]	Transport & Communications	Other
Zambia	52	10	8	2	11	3	14
United States	13	9	9	4	6	8	51
South Africa	N/A	N/A	N/A	N/A	N/A	N/A	N/A
Dem. Rep. of Congo	N/A	N/A	N/A	N/A	N/A	N/A	N/A

Data represent percentage of consumption in PPP terms.
[a]Excludes energy used for transport.
[b]Includes government and private expenditures.

SOURCE: World Bank. *World Development Indicators 2000.*

siderable. The poorest 60 percent of the population share 25.2 percent of the nation's wealth, whereas the wealthiest 10 percent benefit from 39.2 percent of the wealth. Incomes have not grown as fast as inflation which, in combination with the introduction of user fees for health and education services, means that a majority of Zambians cannot afford to provide themselves with even basic social services.

WORKING CONDITIONS

Of a labor force of 4 million the average Zambian works for 45 hours a week. However, this official figure does not take account of those who work outside of the official sector and embark upon such activities as subsistence farming on small plots of land and petty trading. Zambia has been a member of the International Labour Organisation since independence in 1964, yet it only ratified Conventions 87 (Freedom of Association and Protection of the Right to Organize) and 98 (Right to Organize and Collective Bargaining) as late as 1994. Zambia's trade unions are obliged to join the highly centralized Zambia Congress of Trade Unions (ZCTU). The ZCTU is a very powerful organization and by withdrawing its support from the UNIP in 1990, it almost assured the MMD's electoral success in 1991. Six of 7 ZCTU leaders joined the 1991 MMD government, including President Chiluba who had been the ZCTU's chairman. However, the ZCTU is highly critical of the MMD, in particular its pro-business policies such as the liberalization of the economy which has resulted in a decline of living standards for Zambia's workers. There is also tension within the ZCTU. In 1995 3 of its twenty affiliate trade unions broke away with the intention of setting up a competing center body.

COUNTRY HISTORY AND ECONOMIC DEVELOPMENT

1899. The British South African Company (BSAC) assumes control over Zambia (then Northern Rhodesia).

1924. British government takes over Zambia's administration.

1964. Zambian independence and the beginning of the First Republic. The United National Independence Party (UNIP) wins multi-party elections, and Kenneth Kaunda becomes president.

1965. Unilateral Declaration of Independence in Rhodesia (modern Zimbabwe) threatens Zambia's supply routes.

1972. The one-party state of the Second Republic is formed.

1987. A series of riots against declining incomes ends an IMF-sponsored free market reform program.

1990. Kaunda agrees to the formation of the Third Republic.

1991. Multi-party elections are won by the Movement for Multi-Party Democracy led by Frederick Chiluba. The MMD embarks on a program of IMF-sponsored free market reform.

1996. The MMD wins a second round of elections.

2000. The former parastatal Zambia Consolidated Copper Mines (ZCCM) is fully privatized.

FUTURE TRENDS

The Zambian government projects that the privatization of the giant mining parastatal (ZCCM) will lead to the increased efficiency of copper production, improved export earnings, and a subsequent influx of foreign exchange in order to correct the economy's sizeable balance of payments deficit. The proposed privatization of other major parastatals in the telecommunications, electricity, and transport sectors is expected to produce similar results. In part due to this adaptation of free market reform, Zambia's external creditors seem likely to write off US$670 million of debt in 2001, continue to reschedule the repayments of a large proportion of debt, and extend the level of credit available to the government by US$4.5 billion in order to prop up the economy. However, signs of a global **recession** in early 2001 indicate that the world market for Zambia's exports may become less profitable. This will have a severely negative impact on the country's population and the growing non-traditional export sector, and make the repayment of outstanding debt unfeasible.

DEPENDENCIES

Zambia has no territories or colonies.

BIBLIOGRAPHY

Africa Institute. *Africa A-Z: Continental and Country Profiles.* Pretoria, Republic of South Africa: Africa Institute of South Africa, 1998.

Africa South of the Sahara 2001. 30th edition. London: Europa, 2000.

Africa: the South. London: Lonely Planet, 1997.

Arnold, G. *The Resources of the Third World.* London: Cassell, 1997.

Burdette, M.M. *Zambia: Between Two Worlds.* Boulder: Westview, 1988.

Central Intelligence Agency. *World Factbook 2000.* <http://www.odci.gov/cia/publications/factbook/index.html>. Accessed February 2001.

Chikulo, B. C. and O. B. Sichone. "Introduction: Creation of the Third Republic." In *Democracy in Zambia: Challenges for the Third Republic,* edited by O. B. Sichone and B. C. Chikulo. Harare: SAPES Books, 1996.

Common Market for Eastern and Southern Africa (COMESA). <http://www.comesa.int>. Accessed March 2001.

Export Board of Zambia (EBZ). <http://www.ebz.co.zm/country_profile>. Accessed March 2001.

Food and Agriculture Organisation. *FAO Yearbook: Trade, Volume 52, 1998.* Rome: FAO, 1999.

International Monetary Fund. *International Financial Statistics Yearbook 2000.* Washington, D.C.: IMF, 2000.

Mehran, H., P. Ugolini, J. Briffaux, G. Iden, T. Lybek, S. Swaray, and P. Hayward. "Financial Sector Development in Sub-Saharan African Countries." *IMF Occasional Article 169.* Washington, D.C.: IMF, 1998.

Mitchell, B.R. *International Historical Statistics: Africa, Asia and Oceania 1750–1993.* 3rd edition. London: Macmillan, 1998.

Mulenga, C. "Structural Adjustment and the Rural-Urban Gap." *Institute of African Studies Working Papers.* University of Zambia: Institute of African Studies, 1993.

Mwanakatwe, J. M. *End of Kaunda Era.* Lusaka: Multimedia, 1994.

Nadzam, B., ed. *Countries of the World and Their Leaders Yearbook 2001.* Two volumes. Farmington Hills, Michigan: Gale Group, 2001.

Republic of Zambia Revenue Authority (ZRA). <http://www.zra.org.zm>. Accessed March 2001.

Turok, B. "The Penalties of Zambia's Mixed Economy." In *Development in Zambia: A Reader,* edited by B. Turok. London: Zed, 1979.

United Nations. *Statistical Yearbook: 44th issue, 1997.* New York: United Nations, 2000.

United Nations. *UNAIDS (Joint United Nations Program on HIV/AIDS).* <http://www.unaids.org/hivaidsinfo/statistics/june00/fact_sheets/pdfs/zambia.pdf>. Accessed March 2001.

United Nations Conference on Trade and Development (UNCTAD). *UNCTAD Commodity Yearbook 1995.* New York: United Nations, 1995.

United Nations Development Program (UNDP). *Human Development Report 2000.* New York: Oxford University Press, 2000.

United Nations Economic Commission for Africa. <http://www.uneca.org>. Accessed March 2001.

United States Department of State. *Country Commercial Guide: Zambia, Fiscal Year 2001.* <http://www.state.gov./www/about_state/business/com_guides/index.html>. Accessed February 2001.

Upham, M., ed. *Trade Unions of the World.* 4th edition. London: Cartermill, 1996.

World Bank. *African Development Indicators 2000.* Washington DC: World Bank, 2000.

——. *World Development Indicators 2000.* Washington DC: World Bank, 2000.

——. *World Development Report: From Plan to Market.* New York: Oxford University Press, 1996.

——. *World Development Report: Poverty.* New York: Oxford University Press, 1990.

——. *World Development Report 1993: Investing in Health.* New York: Oxford University Press, 1993.

——. *World Development Report 1997: The State in a Changing World.* New York: Oxford University Press, 1997.

——. *World Development Report 2000/2001: Attacking Poverty.* New York: Oxford University Press, 2000.

—Liam Campling

ZIMBABWE

Republic of Zimbabwe

CAPITAL: Harare.

MONETARY UNIT: Zimbabwe Dollar (Z$). Z$1 equals 100 cents. Coins are in denominations of 1, 5, 10, 20, and 50 cents and Z$1 and 2. Paper currency is in denominations of Z$2, 5, 10, 20, 50, and 100.

CHIEF EXPORTS: Tobacco, gold, ferro-alloys, nickel, cotton, clothing, textiles, agricultural food crops.

CHIEF IMPORTS: Machinery, transport equipment, manufactured goods, chemicals, fuels.

GROSS DOMESTIC PRODUCT: US$28.2 billion (purchasing power parity, 2000 est.).

BALANCE OF TRADE: Exports: US$1.8 billion (f.o.b., 2000 est.). Imports: US$1.3 billion (f.o.b., 2000 est.).

COUNTRY OVERVIEW

LOCATION AND SIZE. The Republic of Zimbabwe is a landlocked country in southern Africa, covering an area of 390,757 square kilometers (150,872 square miles), of which land occupies 386,670 square kilometers (1,929 square miles), and water occupies 3,910 square kilometers (1,509 square miles). Zimbabwe is bounded on the north and northwest by Zambia (797 kilometers), southwest by Botswana (813 kilometers), Mozambique (1,231 kilometers) on the east, South Africa (225 kilometers) on the south, and Namibia's Caprivi Strip touches its western border at the intersection with Zambia. The country is slightly larger than Montana.

Zimbabwe sits astride the high plateaus between the Zambezi and Limpopo rivers, its main drainage systems. Much of the country is elevated, 21 percent being more than 1,200 meters (3,937 feet) above sea level. The topography consists of 4 relief regions. The high veld (an open, grassy expanse) rises above 1,200 meters and extends across the country from the northeast narrowing towards the southwest. The middle veld, lying between 900 and 1,200 meters (2,953 and 3,937 feet) above sea level, flanks the high-veld, mostly extending towards the northwest. The low veld stands below 900 meters (2,953 feet) and occupies the Zambezi basin in the north and the more extensive Limpopo and Sabi-Lundi basins in the south and southeast. The eastern highlands have a distinctive mountainous character, rising above 1,800 meters (5,906 feet), and include Mount Inyangani (sometimes called simply Inyangani), standing at 2,592 meters (8,504 feet) above sea level.

POPULATION. The census of 1992 indicated a population of 10.41 million, and by mid-2000 the estimate was 11.34 million. The population has been growing at a rate estimated at 2.6 percent a year from 1990 to date, and this implies a fertility rate of 3.8 children per woman. The population is youthful, with only 3.5 percent over the age of 65, 39.6 percent in the 0 to 14 age group, and 56.8 percent in the 15 to 64 age group.

The country's population is diverse and was estimated in the mid-1980s to include—besides the indigenous people—some 223,000 people of European descent as well as 37,000 Asians and people of mixed ethnic backgrounds—all of them the legacy of the colonial era. The indigenous people accounted for more than 98 percent of the population in the mid-1997 estimates, and were comprised mostly of 2 broad ethnic or linguistic groups: the Ndebele and Shona. The Shona comprised 71 percent and Ndebele 16 percent of the population in 1997. There are, in addition, several other minor ethnic groups such as the Hlengwe, Sena, Sotho, Tonga, and Venda who constituted the other 11 percent. English, Shona, and Sindebele are the official languages universally taught in schools.

Urban growth has been rapid in recent years. Over the 1982–92 period, the population of Harare, the capital, is reported to have almost doubled from 656,000 to 1,189,103, while that of Bulawayo, the second-largest

city, increased from 413,800 to 621,742 over the same period. The urban poor, operating within the highly competitive **informal sector** are now a large and increasing part of the urban social structure.

OVERVIEW OF ECONOMY

Since independence, Zimbabwe's primary goal has been redressing the socio-economic imbalances and **restructuring** the economy while maintaining growth and avoiding alienating its white population, whose skills are of vital importance to its economy. Unlike many countries in post-independent sub-Saharan Africa, Zimbabwe did not tread the **nationalization** path, rather choosing to purchase shares in various enterprises.

Zimbabwe has a relatively diversified economy with good **infrastructure**, strong manufacturing and agricultural sectors, a vigorous financial services sector, and extensive mining. Agriculture, which in 1997 contributed 28 percent of **gross domestic product** (GDP), is the mainstay of the economy and a major determining factor in its growth. It is diversified and well-developed in terms of food production, **cash crops**, and livestock. Its growth, however, has been erratic since independence in 1980. Periods of rapid economic growth have been interrupted by agricultural slumps caused largely by drought in 1992, when about 80 percent of the maize crop and an estimated 1.7 million cattle were lost, and another drought in 1995.

Zimbabwe's mining sector is diversified, currently producing over 40 different minerals. These include gold, platinum, nickel, coal, copper, silver, emeralds, graphite, granite, cobalt, quartz, kaolin, and mica. Gold is the primary source of revenue in the mining sector.

Zimbabwe produces a wide variety of manufactured goods for both local and export markets. Manufacturing is centered in the 2 major urban centers, Harare and Bulawayo. Developed within a **protectionist policy**, the sector enjoyed certain **tariff** barriers in the period from 1965 to 1979. It faced stiff competition, mostly from South Africa, after 1990 when the barriers were progressively removed.

One of the most pressing issues affecting the Zimbabwean economy concerns land redistribution. Due to costs and delays in sourcing financing, Zimbabwe has been behind schedule in the redistribution of land to landless rural families as promised in the war of liberation. This culminated in the 1999–2000 land crisis in the run-up to the 2000 elections, when war veterans began occupying white-owned farms. This precipitated a crisis in the farming sector that is yet to be resolved.

The export position has been generally strong, with **trade surpluses** recorded in most years except during the droughts of 1992 and 1995. Government policy aims to encourage foreign investment and expand exports—a policy it has pursued since the 1990 **structural adjustment programs** (SAP). However, export-led growth, the reduction of government **budget deficits**, and low levels of **inflation** have proved to be elusive goals. **Real GDP** grew at an average annual rate of 3.6 percent between 1980 and 1990, but halved to 1.8 percent annually between 1990 and 1997. By 1995, GDP was shrinking at -0.7 percent, but by 1996 the economy was growing again at a 7.6 percent growth rate. But in 2000 and 2001, the output of the economy is thought to have contracted once more, and living standards have fallen markedly. Inflation was high through the 1990s, averaging 22.4 percent annually between 1990 and 1997, ranging from a peak of 42 percent in 1992 to a low of 19 percent in 1997. In 1999, with the political crisis, inflation had risen to 166 percent a year and currently continues to be very high.

POLITICS, GOVERNMENT, AND TAXATION

Zimbabwe is a former British colony; it was known as Southern Rhodesia during British rule, and was established in 1890. Gold discoveries sparked an influx of white farmers, mostly from Britain and South Africa. The most powerful of the gold seekers was Cecil Rhodes (after whom Rhodesia was named), the eccentric owner of the De Beers mining company, which he had bought for its diamond concessions in Africa. The massive migration of white Europeans and land acquisition by these groups produced economic and political consequences still reverberating in the country more than a century later.

In 1953, Southern Rhodesia was united by the British government with Northern Rhodesia (present-day Zambia) and Nyasaland (present-day Malawi) into a Central African Federation, against opposition from Africans in all 3 regions. Due to the strength of African opposition in Northern Rhodesia and Nyasaland, the Federation was disbanded in 1963. Whites in Southern Rhodesia formed the Rhodesia Front (RF), dedicated to upholding white rule and demanding full independence from the United Kingdom and the retention of the existing minority-rule constitution. Prime Minister Ian Smith introduced a Unilateral Declaration of Independence (UDI) in November 1965 and renamed the territory "Rhodesia."

African nationalist opposition had split in 1963 into 2 resistance groups: the Zimbabwe African People's Union (ZAPU), led by Joshua Nkomo, and the breakaway Zimbabwe African National Union (ZANU), led by Rev. Ndabaningi Sithole and later Robert Mugabe. Repressive measures by the Smith government galvanized ZAPU and ZANU into a guerilla (non-conventional, stealthy) war to overthrow it. ZAPU's operations, based in Zambia and backed by the Soviet Union, were mainly confined to majority Ndebele areas. ZANU, on the other hand, linked with the People's Republic of China and a guerilla group fighting the Portuguese in Mozambique. They concentrated on infiltration and rural mobilization in Shona-speaking areas in the northeast, and later in eastern and central areas of the country.

From 1976, a common struggle was waged under the banner of the Patriotic Front (PF), an uneasy alliance of ZAPU and ZANU, backed by neighboring African states. This struggle, coupled with international economic **sanctions** (with the exception of South Africa), led to declining white morale, forcing the Smith regime into the 1979 "Internal Settlement"—a multi-racial government under the leadership of Bishop Abel Muzorewa, a Methodist minister and black nationalist. This paved the way for all parties to the conflict to participate in talks which led to the February 1980 elections and the emergence of the independent state of Zimbabwe on 18 April 1980.

In the elections, Mugabe's ZANU-PF won 57 of the 80 "common-roll" (reserved for black Africans) seats in the house, receiving 63 percent of the vote. Nkomo's ZAPU-PF won 20 and Bishop Muzorewa's United African National Council (UANC) won 3 seats. Mugabe's ZANU has retained power in Zimbabwe ever since.

The constitution of the Republic of Zimbabwe took effect at independence. Amendments to the constitution must have the approval of two-thirds of the members of the House of Assembly, the country's **unicameral** (single chamber) parliament. The executive president (Mugabe) is both head of state and head of the government, as is the U.S. president. The House of Assembly has 150 members, of whom 120 are directly elected by universal adult suffrage, 12 are nominated by the president, 10 are traditional chiefs, and 8 are provincial governors.

In 1997, government expenditure was 36 percent of GDP, which is high by African standards. Government revenue was 31 percent of GDP, and the budget deficit was 5.1 percent of GDP, significantly above the International Monetary Fund (IMF) guideline of 3 percent. Subsequently, the deficit has been substantially above this level, the money supply has expanded rapidly, and the rate of inflation has accelerated.

Corporate tax rates are moderate at 37.5 percent, although the government discriminates against foreign corporations by imposing an additional 8.4 percent. Most government revenue is raised from taxes on income, profits, and capital gains (45 percent). Taxes on goods and services generated 26 percent of revenue, trade taxes on exports and imports garnered 19 percent, and other non-tax income (mainly licenses and surpluses of state-owned enterprises) accounted for 9 percent.

INFRASTRUCTURE, POWER, AND COMMUNICATIONS

Zimbabwe is a landlocked country with a well-developed road network that was comprised in 1996 of 18,338 kilometers (11,395 miles) of roads, of which 8,692 (5,401 miles) are paved. The closest seaport is Beira in Mozambique.

Zimbabwe has a direct railway link with Zambia, which connects it to the Tanzanian port of Dar es Salaam through the Tazara railway. The railway system also connects Zimbabwe to the Mozambican ports of Beira and Maputo as well as 2 South African ports. It comprises 2,759 kilometers (1,714 miles) of track, of which 313 kilometers (194 miles) is electrified. Another link is planned between Beitbridge and Bulawayo, the second largest city in Zimbabwe. The National Railways of Zimbabwe (NRZ), which operates the rail service, is under reform in preparation for **privatization**.

Zimbabwe has 2 state-controlled airlines—the passenger carrier Air Zimbabwe and freight carrier Affretair—which are experiencing financial difficulties resulting from poor management and political interference.

This has enabled a private company, Zimbabwe Express Airlines, to emerge and capture a substantial share of the market. A new international airport is being built at Harare.

Zimbabwe Electricity Supply Authority (ZESA) has the sole responsibility for power generation and distribution. The search for national energy self-sufficiency in the early 1980s led to an emphasis on coal and other thermoelectric projects (78 percent of supply) and the hydroelectric power from the Kariba dam (22 percent). Although the second stage of the Hwange thermal power station, commissioned in 1987, raised the total capacity to 2,071 megawatts (mw), supply has failed to keep up with demand, leading to imports from Mozambique and South Africa. All oil and gas is imported. A pipeline from Port Beira in Mozambique to Mutare which was built before the 1965 declaration of independence did not become operational until 1982, and was extended to Harare only in 1993. Ethanol, produced since 1980 from sugarcane, is blended with gasoline for domestic sale. Imports of fuel are **monopolized** by the National Oil Corporation of Zimbabwe (Noczim), which has been mired in scandals and run at a loss for several years, partly due to lack of authority to raise prices in line with the depreciation of the Zimbabwe dollar.

Zimbabwe's domestic communication system consists of microwave radio relay links, land lines, radiotelephone communication stations, fixed wireless local loop installations, and a substantial mobile cellular phone network. Internet connection is available in Harare and planned for all major towns and for some of the smaller ones. International communication is through satellite earth stations including 2 Intelsat and 2 international digital gateway exchanges (in Harare and Gweru).

Zimbabwe's telephone system was once one of the best in Africa, but now suffers from poor maintenance with more than 100,000 outstanding requests for connection despite an equally large number of installed but unused lines. The Posts and Telecommunications Cor-

Communications									
Country	Newspapers	Radios	TV Sets[a]	Cable subscribers[a]	Mobile Phones[a]	Fax Machines[a]	Personal Computers[a]	Internet Hosts[b]	Internet Users[b]
	1996	1997	1998	1998	1998	1998	1998	1999	1999
Zimbabwe	19	93	30	N/A	4	N/A	9.0	1.19	20
United States	215	2,146	847	244.3	256	78.4	458.6	1,508.77	74,100
South Africa	32	317	125	N/A	56	3.5	47.4	33.36	1,820
Dem. Rep. of Congo	3	375	135	N/A	0	N/A	N/A	0.00	1

[a]Data are from International Telecommunication Union, *World Telecommunication Development Report 1999* and are per 1,000 people.
[b]Data are from the Internet Software Consortium (http://www.isc.org) and are per 10,000 people.

SOURCE: World Bank. *World Development Indicators 2000*.

poration (PTC), despite investing heavily in the digitization of its network using fiber-optic technology, has failed to satisfy demand. By 1997 there were 212,000 telephone lines in use. In addition, there are about 20,000 fixed telephones with wireless local loop connections. There were 70,000 mobile cellular phones in 1999. The PTC has since lost its monopoly rights to cellular phone operators such as Eocene, which won the right to establish a cellular phone network in 1997 after more than 4 years of legal battles.

Zimbabwe has a well-diversified media. The press is relatively free but dominated by the state-controlled Zimbabwe Newspapers, which operates 2 dailies, the *Herald* and *Bulawayo Chronicles,* as well as their sister papers, the *Sunday Mail* and the *Sunday News.* Since 1999, when the *Daily News,* backed by investors from the United Kingdom and South Africa, was launched, the market share of Zimbabwe Newspapers has been significantly reduced. Other independent papers include weeklies such as the *Financial Gazette,* the *Zimbabwe Independent,* and the *Standard,* which mainly serve as opposition voices and are highly critical of the government. A number of monthlies including *Motto, Horizon,* and *Parade* are estimated to have a readership approaching 1 million each.

Radio and television are run by the state-owned Zimbabwe Broadcasting Corporation (ZBC), but variety is provided by channels from South Africa. In 1998, however, journalists critical of the government were removed and the state-controlled media have since largely provided government propaganda. In the wake of the outbreak of the land-reform crisis, which the independent media blamed on the government for instigating in the run-up to the 2000 elections, the government has announced plans to curtail the rights of the independent press.

ECONOMIC SECTORS

Zimbabwe's economy is well-developed, consisting of diversified sectors such as manufacturing, commercial farming, productive small-scale family farming, and exploitation of various mineral resources. Agriculture generated about 88 percent of GDP in 1997, one-third of which came from communal farmers, and mining was about 13 percent of GDP. These 2 sectors generally determine the state of health of the economy because of their impact on export revenue. Agriculture alone employs about 66 percent of the total **labor force**. Tobacco and gold, followed by tourism receipts, dominate export earnings. Although manufacturing's relative importance has declined over the years, it is still a significant sector, contributing about 18 percent of GDP in 1998. The services sector has risen in significance, contributing more than 58 percent of GDP in 1998, mostly as a result of in-

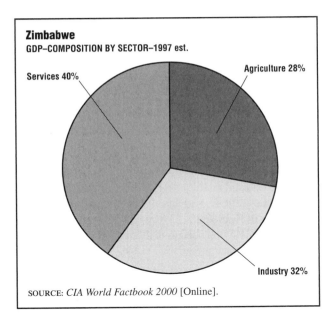

Zimbabwe
GDP–COMPOSITION BY SECTOR–1997 est.

Services 40%

Agriculture 28%

Industry 32%

SOURCE: *CIA World Factbook 2000* [Online].

creased spending on education and health, and an expansion of tourism in the 1980s. The latest figures the CIA *World Factbook* released were for 1997 and estimated agriculture at 28 percent, industry at 32 percent, and services at 40 percent of GDP.

AGRICULTURE

Zimbabwe has a well-developed and diversified agricultural sector, producing food crops, cash crops, and livestock. Although agriculture accounted for only 28 percent of GDP in 1998, it engaged about 66 percent of

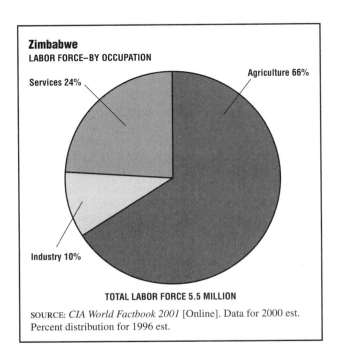

Zimbabwe
LABOR FORCE–BY OCCUPATION

Services 24%

Agriculture 66%

Industry 10%

TOTAL LABOR FORCE 5.5 MILLION

SOURCE: *CIA World Factbook 2001* [Online]. Data for 2000 est. Percent distribution for 1996 est.

the labor force in 1996. Some 27 percent of formal sector employment was in the agriculture sector in 1997. Agriculture's share of GDP has been fluctuating from 17 percent in 1985, 12 percent in 1990, 14 percent in 1996, and 28 percent in 1998, depending on the impact of drought and the level world prices for export crops.

Zimbabwe produces much of its own food, except in years where drought affects maize and wheat production. The staple food crop is maize, and other cereal crops include barley, millet, sorghum, and wheat. In spite of the high concentration of arable farmland in the commercial sector, **smallholder** production share of agricultural output rose from 9 percent in 1983 to 25 percent in 1988, and 50 percent in 1990. Tobacco is the largest export crop (23 percent of merchandise exports in 1997) and Zimbabwe is among the world's biggest exporters. The other main exports are sugar and cotton and in years of surplus maize is exported. Horticulture is growing rapidly and Zimbabwe is now the world's third-largest exporter of roses.

Zimbabwe is one of a few sub-Saharan African countries allowed to export beef to the European Union. Exports began in 1985; however, Zimbabwe could not keep up with its quota, and exports have dwindled over the years. Total exports were 9,500 metric tons in 1996. Sheep, goats, pigs, and poultry are also extensively farmed. About half the country's timber is produced by the Forestry Commission. Rough-sawn timber is exported to Botswana and South Africa. High quality timber is exported mainly to the United Kingdom. In 1994, Zimbabwe's forestry sector produced 29,000 cubic meters of non-coniferous sawn wood, 3,000 cubic meters of non-coniferous sawn logs and veneer logs, and 1.8 million cubic meters of industrial round wood.

INDUSTRY

In 1998, Zimbabwe was the world's thirteenth-largest producer of gold, which is the country's biggest mineral export. Mining contributed 13 percent of GDP in 1997 and generated US$900 million of export revenue in 1995 (amounting to 45 percent of total value of exports), up from US$623 million in the previous year. About 90 percent of mining production is exported. In 1997, gold constituted 14 percent of the value of exports, followed by ferro-alloys at 7 percent, then nickel, and asbestos. Coal is mined for domestic power generation as well as for export, iron ore to supply the steel industry, and phosphate rock for fertilizer production.

Mineral deposits are dispersed throughout the country, but it is the Great Dyke, which runs for hundreds of kilometers from northeast to southwest, that contains the most extensive concentration of mineral deposits. In the 1980s, the state tried unsuccessfully to wrest control of mining from the main mining companies. Anglo-American Corporation controlled nickel and chrome mining, Rio Tinto Zimbabwe mined nickel and gold, Turner and Newall concentrated on asbestos, Lonrho on gold and copper, and Ashanti Goldfields mined gold. In an effort to control **transfer pricing**, all minerals except gold are required to be marketed through the state's Zimbabwe Minerals Marketing Corporation, but this organization's future has recently been questioned.

Zimbabwe has one of the largest, most diversified, and integrated manufacturing sectors in sub-Saharan Africa, partly due to **import substitution** policies implemented after the 1965 declaration of independence. The Zimbabwe Steel Corporation (Zisco) is the only full-fledged sub-Saharan Africa steel producer outside South Africa, producing from its Kwekwe plant alone more than 700,000 metric tons annually. Other major industries include Zimbabwe Alloys, which produces ferro-chrome for export; a number of heavy engineering companies working for the mining industry and railways; Dunlop Zimbabwe which makes tires and tubes; car and truck assembly plants; a large pulp and paper firm; and several plastics companies. The removal of protective measures under the 1990 Enhanced Structural Adjustment Program (ESAP) has caused manufacturing's output to contract and its share of GDP to decline to about 18 percent in 1997 from around 25 percent in the 1970s. However, about 40 percent of Zimbabwe's exports are classified as manufactured products, and the recent decline in the value of the Zimbabwe dollar will serve to make Zimbabwean manufactures more competitive at home and overseas.

Although several new buildings have been erected in Harare in recent years, the construction industry has been depressed since the boom of the early 1970s, and its share of GDP has fallen from 5 percent in the 1970s to 3 percent in 1997 as a result of a virtual freeze on large-scale developments. On the other hand, employment in the sector has increased by more than 50 percent to about 80,000 as construction of low-cost, labor-intensive dwellings for Africans has expanded.

SERVICES

The central bank, the Reserve Bank of Zimbabwe (RBZ), acts as banker to the government, issues currency and government loans, controls foreign reserves, serves as lender of last resort to commercial banks, and handles revenue from gold exports. The RBZ is also responsible for banking sector supervision, although it lacks the necessary legislative framework and statutory power to monitor banks adequately. The Ministry of Finance is responsible for issuing banking licenses.

Zimbabwe has a growing tourism industry, and hunting safaris in particular have expanded in recent years.

The government favors upmarket tourism, especially **eco-tourism** and safari holidays. There are a number of world-class hotels in the country, including the historic Victoria Falls Hotel. The total number of visitors has grown at an annual rate of 20 percent since 1990 when there were about 635,000, to over 2 million visitors in 1998. Tourism generated an estimated US$125 million in 1998, making it the third-largest foreign exchange earner after tobacco and gold. But the continuing political unrest and violence has hurt the tourism industry, with the number of overseas visitors plunging 35 percent during the first 6 months of 2000 compared to the same period in 1999.

The distribution sector features a large number of South African **retail** chains. As a result of import substitution policies, these companies rely on domestic suppliers of processed food, clothing, furniture, and light **consumer goods**.

INTERNATIONAL TRADE

Exports of goods and services grew by about 6.3 percent a year between 1965 and 1997, and manufactured exports accounted for more than 32 percent of total merchandise exports in 1997. Zimbabwe's export partners vary significantly from year to year. In 1996, the most important were South Africa, Botswana, Lesotho, and Swaziland (38 percent of imports and 12 percent of exports)—all members of the Southern African Customs Union. The United Kingdom was also an important trading partner (9 percent of imports and 12 percent of exports), as was Japan (5 percent of imports and 6 percent of exports), Germany (6 percent of imports), and the United States (5 percent of imports). Zimbabwe's membership in the Common Market for Eastern and Southern Africa (COMESA) has, in theory, provided access to new markets in regional trade. In practice, however, Zimbabwean exporters have been somewhat disappointed due to constraints in foreign exchange availability with the potential partners. The historic change of government in South Africa has enabled investment and trade between

the 2 countries, but the overall result has been that South Africa has taken an even larger share of Zimbabwe's domestic market following the recent increase in trade **liberalization**.

MONEY

Before 1994, the value of the Zimbabwe dollar was determined by the Reserve Bank of Zimbabwe (RBZ) on the basis of a trade-weighted basket of foreign currencies. Although there were large **devaluations** in 1982, 1991, and 1993, high domestic inflation frequently caused monthly adjustments of 1 to 2 percent. As part of the 1990 Enhanced Structural Adjustment Program (ESAP), the Zimbabwe dollar was floated, allowing companies to retain export earnings in foreign currencies, and restrictions were removed on holding the currency abroad and on investing on the Zimbabwe stock exchange. However, the RBZ reserves the right to intervene in the foreign exchange market (buying the Zimbabwe dollar when its price begins to fall, and selling when its price rises) to maintain a stable **exchange rate**. However, the price of the Zimbabwe dollar has been subject to a falling trend, and the RBZ has been unable to stabilize the exchange rate because it has lacked the foreign exchange to make purchases. The Zimbabwe dollar has lost considerable ground against the U.S. dollar since independence, depreciating from an average rate of Z$0.64=US$1 in 1980 to Z$38.15=US$1 in 1999. This depreciation has worsened since November 1997, owing to economic and political instability that prompted a run on the currency, depreciating it to Z$55.05=US$1 by mid-2001.

POVERTY AND WEALTH

It was estimated in 1991 that 14 percent of the population was below the U.S. dollar-a-day poverty line (this line is based on the income required to provide the absolute minimum nutrition, clothing, and shelter). This means that 16 percent of children under age 5 are malnourished (the figure is 1 percent for the United States) and life expectancy is 53 years (in the United States it is

Exchange rates: Zimbabwe	
Zimbabwean dollars (Z$) per US$1	
Jan 2001	54.9451
2000	43.2900
1999	38.3142
1998	21.4133
1997	11.8906
1996	9.9206
SOURCE: CIA *World Factbook 2001* [ONLINE].	

Trade (expressed in billions of US$): Zimbabwe		
	Exports	**Imports**
1975	.932	.932
1980	1.415	1.448
1985	1.113	.896
1990	1.726	1.847
1995	2.119	2.660
1998	N/A	N/A
SOURCE: International Monetary Fund. *International Financial Statistics Yearbook 1999.*		

GDP per Capita (US$)

Country	1975	1980	1985	1990	1998
Zimbabwe	686	638	662	706	703
United States	19,364	21,529	23,200	25,363	29,683
South Africa	4,574	4,620	4,229	4,113	3,918
Dem. Rep. of Congo	392	313	293	247	127

SOURCE: United Nations. *Human Development Report 2000;
Trends in human development and per capita income.*

Distribution of Income or Consumption by Percentage Share: Zimbabwe

Lowest 10%	1.8
Lowest 20%	4.0
Second 20%	6.3
Third 20%	10.0
Fourth 20%	17.4
Highest 20%	62.3
Highest 10%	46.9

Survey year: 1990–91
Note: This information refers to expenditure shares by percentiles of the
population and is ranked by per capita expenditure.

SOURCE: *2000 World Development Indicators* [CD-ROM].

---

77 years). Estimates in 1999 suggest that the deteriorating economic conditions, particularly the disruption of agriculture by the violent occupation of farms by landless Zimbabweans, has increased the dollar-a-day poverty level to 60 percent of the population. Most of those in poverty are in the rural areas, relying on small-scale agriculture for their livelihoods. They suffer because of poor land, inadequate rainfall, and insufficient income to purchase good seeds, fertilizer, or farm machinery. With the economic deterioration, increasing numbers of urban dwellers are finding themselves in poverty. There is a huge income distribution disparity. In 1990, the poorest 10 percent of the population received 1.8 percent of total income, while the richest 10 percent received 46.9 percent.

The national social security authority had about 840,000 employed persons registered with it in 1995. **Subsistence farmers** and informally employed people do not participate in pension, sickness benefits, or other formal welfare schemes, but rely on traditional community support structures.

WORKING CONDITIONS

Since independence in 1980, the government has tried unsuccessfully to reduce the wide income gap between the rich and poor in Zimbabwe. The Minimum Wage Act of 1980 established a minimum wage of Z$85 (US$133) per month for workers who qualified under the Industrial Conciliation Act, and Z$67 (US$105) for others in industry. Minimum wages were set at Z$58 (US$91) per month for mine workers and Z$30 (US$47) per month for agricultural and domestic workers. In 1982, minimum wages were again raised.

Although minimum wages were subsequently raised several times after independence and **real wages** rose significantly between 1980 and 1982, they have fallen since. Attempts were made in the 1980s to introduce wage controls, but these were widely circumvented by private industry. The landscape has since changed and collective bargaining now appears to be the norm, although tight regulation of the right to strike action has provoked workers to engage in wildcat (a strike not officially sanctioned by a union) actions. Since 1997, however, the Zimbabwe Congress of Trade Unions (ZCTU) has gained prominence, organizing successful strikes against new taxes and **levies** in 1997–98 and pushing for an increase in the minimum salary to Z$2,000 per month (about US$36 at current exchange rates).

Growth in employment was considerably slower than the population's increase after independence. In the late 1980s, about 40,000 jobs a year were being created, enough to accommodate only 20 percent of young people who had left school to find work. The percentage of total population formally employed fell from 18 percent in 1965 to 11 percent in 1997. There have also been ma-

---

Household Consumption in PPP Terms

Country	All food	Clothing and footwear	Fuel and power[a]	Health care[b]	Education[b]	Transport & Communications	Other
Zimbabwe	20	10	21	3	15	9	22
United States	13	9	9	4	6	8	51
South Africa	N/A	N/A	N/A	N/A	N/A	N/A	N/A
Dem. Rep. of Congo	N/A	N/A	N/A	N/A	N/A	N/A	N/A

Data represent percentage of consumption in PPP terms.
[a]Excludes energy used for transport.
[b]Includes government and private expenditures.

SOURCE: World Bank. *World Development Indicators 2000.*

jor sectoral shifts in employment since independence, with employment rising particularly rapidly in the education, health, and other services, while the number of people working in manufacturing has declined.

COUNTRY HISTORY AND ECONOMIC DEVELOPMENT

1890. Southern Rhodesia becomes a British colony.

1953. Britain unites Southern Rhodesia with Northern Rhodesia (present-day Zambia) and Nyasaland (present-day Malawi) into a Central African Federation (CAF), which is opposed by Africans in all 3 territories.

1962. Whites in Southern Rhodesia hostile to British softening of stance towards CAF vote into office the newly formed Rhodesian Front (RF), dedicated to upholding white rule and demanding full independence from the United Kingdom.

1963. British government recognizes African hostility to federation and concedes independence of territories, breaking up the federation. African Nationalist opposition splits into the Zimbabwe African People's Union (ZAPU), led by Joshua Nkomo, and the breakaway Zimbabwe African National Union (ZANU), led by the Rev. Ndabaningi Sithole and subsequently by Robert Mugabe.

1965. Ian Smith is appointed leader of the RF and prime minister of Southern Rhodesia. Smith implements a Unilateral Declaration of Independence (UDI), renaming the country "Rhodesia."

1976. African opposition launches combined struggle against the Smith regime, backed by neighboring African states (excluding South Africa).

1979. Smith regime develops an internal settlement under which the black-led government of Bishop Abel Muzorewa is instituted.

1980. Democratic elections give Mugabe's ZANU-PF a majority in the house, Nkomo's ZAPU-PF wins 20 seats, and Muzorewa's United African National Congress (UANC) wins 3 seats.

1982. All ZAPU-PF members of cabinet dismissed from government. Dissidents from ZAPU's former guerrilla army and others perpetrate numerous indiscriminate acts of violence.

1984. Army unit is accused of atrocities against civilians.

1985. The RF is reconstituted as Conservative Alliance of Zimbabwe (CAZ). First general elections are held in the summer.

1987. The reservation of 20 white seats in Parliament and 10 in the Senate is abolished.

1988. Mugabe and Nkomo sign agreement to merge ZANU-PF and ZAPU-PF into ZANU-PF with a commitment to establish a 1-party state with a **Marxist**-Leninist doctrine. Open public and parliamentary criticism of corrupt government officials mounts as unemployment and inflation rise. Plans to establish a 1-party state result in student protests.

1988. House votes to abolish upper chamber of parliament, the Senate. The single chamber is enlarged from 100 to 150 seats.

1990. ZANU-PF Central Committee refuses to endorse a 1-party state.

1991. The Enhanced Structural Adjustment Program (ESAP) is adopted. The constitution is amended to restore corporal and capital punishment and deny recourse to the courts in cases of seizure of land by the government, amidst fierce criticism from the judiciary and human rights campaigners.

1992. In May, a non-party Forum for Democratic Reform (FDR), led by former Chief Justice Enoch Dumbutshena and supported by some prominent Zimbabweans, is formed. Four parties form an informal alliance, the United Front (UF), with the aim of defeating the government at the 1995 general elections.

1993. In February, divisions appear in the UF alliance.

1994. Bishop Muzorewa returns to active politics and merges UANC with the Zimbabwe Unity Movement (ZUM). Later in the year, he founds a new opposition grouping, the United Parties (UP). Economic **recession** leads to widespread industrial unrest.

1995. The government wins the April general election, despite widespread discontent.

1996. Mugabe is returned to office with 93 percent of the votes cast in an election with a 32 percent voter turnout.

1997. Corruption becomes a prominent issue with allegations of official contracts being unfairly tendered and embezzlement of public resources to construct private homes for civil servants, ministers, and Mugabe's wife. In October, Mugabe announces acceleration of the national land resettlement program in an attempt to revive his declining popularity.

1998. Unprecedented food riots erupt in most of the country's urban areas in response to rises in the price of the staple food, maize meal. In April, government officials are reported to have misused funds intended to assist veterans of the struggle for independence. A new party, Zimbabwe Union of Democrats (ZUD), is launched with Margaret Dongo as leader. The opposition protests the government's decision to send troops to the Democratic Republic of the Congo.

1999. In July Mugabe acknowledges existence of corruption within the government. Joshua Nkomo dies at age 81. In September, Morgan Tsvangarai joins other prominent citizens in establishing the Movement for Democratic Change. Tsvangarai calls for electoral reform prior to 2000 parliamentary elections. World Bank and other donors suspend financial assistance.

2000. After delays in implementing a land reform program with compensation for white farmers, the government encourages war veterans to occupy farms, and considerable violence erupts. Elections are contested in which ZANU-PF wins 62 seats, the Movement for Democratic Change 57 seats, and ZANU-Ndonga 1 seat.

FUTURE TRENDS

Zimbabwe faces a wide variety of political and economic problems. The agricultural sector has been dealt a severe blow through the land occupation by war veterans frustrated by 20 years of delay in receiving land allotments for their military service. However, the government-sanctioned violent takeover of many white-owned farms has all but destroyed Mugabe's international reputation along with Zimbabwe's agricultural output. Thus, it is unlikely there will be a resolution to the conflict while Mugabe remains in power, particularly since the international community will withold funds for an orderly transfer with compensation for the white farmers until he is gone. For now, the economic prospect is bleak, with a steady attrition of white farmers and falling agricultural output, and exports provoking crises as food and fuel fall into short supply. Tourism has virtually ceased, incomes are plummeting, and inflation is likely to continue at hyper-inflation levels. With a change in government, there will be a challenge in consolidating earlier progress in developing a market-oriented economy. Support from the IMF will resume once the government shows some determination in meeting budgetary targets.

DEPENDENCIES

Zimbabwe has no territories or colonies.

BIBLIOGRAPHY

Economist Intelligence Unit. *Country Profile: Zimbabwe.* London: Economist Intelligence Unit, 2001.

Embassy of Zimbabwe. <http://www.zimembassy-usa.org>. Accessed October 2001.

Green, Richard, editor. *Commonwealth Yearbook.* London: Her Majesty's Stationery Office, 2000.

Hodd, M. "Zimbabwe." In *The Economies of Africa.* Aldershot: Dartmouth, 1991.

U.S. Central Intelligence Agency. *World Factbook 2000.* <http://www.odci.gov/cia/publications/factbook/geos/zi.html>. Accessed December 2000.

U.S. Central Intelligence Agency. *World Factbook 2001.* <http://www.odci.gov/cia/publications/factbook/index.html>. Accessed October 2001.

World Bank. *World Bank Africa Database 2000.* Washington DC: World Bank, 2000.

ZDNews.com. "Zimbabwe's Troubled Tourist Industry." <http://www.zwnews.com/issuefull.cfm?ArticleID=37>. Accessed September 2001.

"Zimbabwe." In *Africa South of the Sahara.* London: Europa Publications, 2000.

—Allan C. K. Mukungu

GLOSSARY

Advance Tax: A percentage of the previous year's tax bill which is paid at the beginning of the new fiscal year and later credited back at its end.

Agribusiness: Agricultural and livestock production on a large scale, often engaged in by large, multinational companies; also used to refer to the companies themselves.

Arrear: Usually plural, **arrears**. Unpaid, overdue debt.

Bad Loan: An unrecoverable loan; the amount cannot be reclaimed by the lender.

Balance of Payments: The measure of all the money coming into a country and all the money leaving the country in a given period, usually a year. The balance of payments includes merchandise exports and imports, the measure of which is called the **balance of trade**, as well as several other factors.

Balance of Trade: A measure of the value of exports and imports, not including services. When imports exceed exports, there is a trade deficit. When exports exceed imports, there is a trade surplus.

Bank of Issue: The bank that is given the right to issue and circulate currency in a country.

Barter System: An exchange of goods and/or services for other goods and/or services, rather than for money.

Bear Market: A sustained period of negative growth in the stock market.

Bicameral: A legislative body consisting of two houses or chambers.

Black Market: An informal market in which buyers and sellers can negotiate and exchange prohibited or illegal goods (such as exchanging local money for foreign currency). Black markets often exist to avoid government controls. *See also* **Informal Sector.**

Budget Deficit: A government budget deficit occurs when a government spends more money on government programs than it generates in revenues. Governments must borrow money or print currency to pay for this excess spending, thus creating potential financial difficulties. *See also* **Budget Surplus.**

Budget Surplus: A government budget surplus occurs when a government generates more revenues than it spends on government programs. Governments can adjust to surpluses by lowering tax rates, paying down the national debt, or stockpiling the money. *See also* **Budget Deficit.**

Cadre: A group of important and influential members of political parties who direct the actions of that party.

Capital Adequacy: The state of a bank having enough capital to maintain its loans and operating costs.

Capital Flight; also called **Capital Outflow:** Money sent abroad because investors fear that economic conditions within a country are too risky.

Capital Good: A manufactured good used in the production of other goods. For example, factories or machinery used to produce goods are considered capital goods.

Capitalism: An economic system based on the private ownership of the means of production and on an open system of competitive markets. It is assumed that producers in a capitalist system can use their skills and capital in the pursuit of profit.

Capital Outflow: *See* **Capital Flight.**

Cash Crop: An agricultural good produced for direct sale on the market.

Centrally-planned Economy: An economy in which the government exerts a great deal of control over economic planning, including the control of production, the allocation of goods, distribution, and prices. Common in **socialist** countries.

c.i.f.: Abbreviation of **cost, insurance, and freight**; a method of determining the value of imports or exports that includes cost, insurance, and freight in determining the total amount.

Commonwealth of Independent States (CIS): A loose union of 12 of the former republics of the Soviet Union, excluding Estonia, Latvia, and Lithuania.

Communism: An economic system in which the means of production and distribution are held in common by all members of the society, and in which the rewards are distributed based on need. In actual communist countries, the state usually controls all the capital and land, and the economy is centrally planned. *See also* **Centrally-planned Economy.**

Consumer Good: A product sold directly to the end user, or consumer, such as food and clothing.

Crawling Peg: A fixed **exchange rate** between two currencies which is adjusted incrementally based on the movement of an economic indicator such as inflation.

Currency Board: An arrangement whereby a currency's value is fixed in some proportion to a strong foreign currency and such an exchange rate is guaranteed by the country's foreign exchange reserves.

Current Account Balance: The portion of the **balance of payments** that includes merchandise imports and exports (known as the **balance of trade**) plus imports and exports of services.

Debt Relief: Partial or full forgiveness of debts, offered to impoverished countries by lenders, usually after it becomes clear that continued payment on such debt is likely to ruin the country's economy.

Debt Service: Payment of interest on a loan or other debt. Debt servicing can be very expensive and debilitating for developing countries.

Deflation: Falling prices across an economy, expressed as a percentage per year. *See also* **Inflation.**

Dependency Ratio: The ratio of **pensioners** to the number of people employed.

Deregulation: A lessening of government restrictions on the economy.

Desertification: The progressive drying of the land.

Devaluation: An act by the government or central bank which decreases the official price of a nation's currency. When a currency is devalued, it can result in the country's exports becoming cheaper and more attractive.

Direct Tax: A tax levied directly on individuals or companies, such as income and property taxes. *See also* **Indirect Tax.**

Disposable Income: Those parts of a household income not needed for essentials such as food, healthcare, or housing costs. Disposable income may be saved, invested, or spent on non-essential goods.

Duty: A tax imposed on imported goods. *See also* **Indirect Tax.**

E-commerce: Economic activity conducted on the Internet.

Ecotourism: Tourism to natural and cultural areas which tries to minimize environmental impacts.

Embargo: A prohibition by a government against some or all trade with a foreign nation. *See also* **Sanctions.**

Emerging Market: A country with still evolving economic, social, and political structures that shows evidence of moving toward an open market system.

Emigration: To leave one's country to live elsewhere.

Enterprise Entry: The creation of new, predominantly small and medium size enterprises.

Enterprise Exit: The removal of businesses from an economy, either through bankruptcy or downsizing.

Equity: The value of all the shares in a company.

Estate Tax: A tax on inherited property and wealth.

Exchange Rate: The rate at which one country's currency is exchanged for that of another country.

Exchange Rate Mechanism (ERM): A mechanism set up in 1978 to handle fluctuations in the **exchange rates** of various European currencies. Each currency in the ERM may fluctuate only within agreed limits against any other currency.

Exchange Rate Regime: The mode of determining the **exchange rate** between the national currency and other major foreign currencies. In a fixed exchange rate regime, a currency is fixed or "pegged" to the currency of another, usually very stable currency, such as that of the United States. In a **floating** or flexible exchange rate regime, governments allow the value of their currency to be determined by supply and demand in the foreign exchange market.

Excise Tax: A tax on the sale or use of certain products or transactions, sometimes luxury or non-essential items.

Exclusive Economic Zone (EEZ): The area extending from a country's coastline over which that country has exclusive control of its resources.

External Debt: The total amount of money in a country's economy owed to enterprises and financial institutions outside the country.

Fiduciary: Related to a trust or trusteeship.

Fiscal Policy: The programs of a national government relating to spending on goods, services, **transfer payments**, and the tax system.

Fiscal Year: Any period of 12 consecutive months for which a company or a government calculates earnings, profits, and losses.

Fixed Exchange Rate: *See* **Exchange Rate Regime.**

Floating Exchange Rate: *See* **Exchange Rate Regime.**

Floor Price: The minimum price for a good or service which normally cannot be further reduced due to political, economic, or trade considerations.

f.o.b.: Abbreviation of **Free on board**; a method of determining the value of exports or imports that considers the value of goods excluding the cost of insurance and freight charges.

Foreign Debt: *See* **External Debt.**

Foreign Direct Investment (FDI): The total value of investment by foreign entities in a country, usually expressed on an annual or cumulative basis.

Foreign Exchange Reserves: The amount of money a country has in its treasury consisting of currency from foreign countries.

Free Market System: An economic system based on little government intervention and the freedom of private association and control of goods. *See also* **Capitalism.**

Free Trade Zone: Also called **Free Zone.** An industrial area where foreign companies may import, store, and sometimes export goods without paying taxes.

Full Employment: The level of employment at which a minimal amount of involuntary unemployment exists. It is considered the maximum level of employment in an economy.

Fully Convertible Currency: A currency that can be freely traded in international foreign exchanges for units of another currency.

GDP per Capita: Gross domestic product divided by the number of people in a country. GDP per capita is a convenient way to measure comparative international wealth.

Gini Index: An index used to measure the extent to which the distribution of income within an economy deviates from perfectly equal distribution. A score of 0 would mean perfect equality (with everyone having the same level of wealth) and 100 would signify perfect inequality (with a few extraordinarily wealthy people and the large majority living in dire poverty).

Glut: An excess of goods in a particular market, which typically causes the price of that good to fall.

Grey Economy: Economic activity that takes place in both the formal and **informal economy,** meaning that some but not all economic activity is reported to authorities such as tax collectors.

Gross Domestic Product (GDP): The total market value of all goods and services produced inside a country in a given year, which excludes money made by citizens or companies working abroad.

Gross National Product (GNP): The total market value of all goods and services produced in a year by a nation, including those goods produced by citizens or companies working abroad.

Guarantor: An institution or individual that guarantees to pay the debts of another institution or individual in the case of bankruptcy.

Guest Worker: Persons from a foreign country who are allowed to live in a host country so long as they are employed. Many guest workers send **remittances** to their native country.

Hard Currency: Money that can be exchanged on the foreign market and is stable enough to purchase goods from other countries.

Hawking: Selling wares, often pirated goods, in the **informal sector.**

Holding Company: A company that owns or controls several other companies.

Immigration: To move into a country that is not one's native country.

Import Substitution: A policy which calls for the local production of goods that have traditionally been imported. The goal of import substitution is to lessen a country's dependence on foreign suppliers.

Income Tax: A **direct tax** on an individual's earned income.

Indirect Tax: A tax which is not paid directly, but is passed on as part of the cost of an item or service. For instance, **tariffs** and **value-added taxes** are passed on to the consumer and included in the final price of the product. *See also* **Direct Tax.**

Inflation: A persistent increase in the average price of goods in an economy, usually accompanied by declining purchasing power of the national currency.

Inflation Rate: The rate at which prices rise from one period to the next.

Informal Sector: Also called **Informal Economy.** The part of an economy that lies outside government regulations and tax systems. It usually consists of small-scale and usually labor-intensive activities; it often includes illegal activities. *See also* **Black Market.**

Infrastructure: The system of public facilities, services, and resources in a country, including roads, railways, airports, power generation, and communication systems.

Intermediate Good: A good used as an ingredient or component in the production of other goods. For instance, wood pulp is used to produce paper.

Internally Displaced Person: A person fleeing danger (such as war or persecution) who has not crossed international boundaries. Those who relocate to another country are called "refugees."

Joint Sector: An economic sector in which private enterprise and the government invest jointly.

Joint Venture: A special economic initiative or company formed by a foreign firm and a domestic company, usually in a developing state. The domestic partner often holds a majority interest, thus allowing the host country to control the amount and kind of foreign economic activity. Can also be a simple joint operation by two or more companies.

Labor Force: Also called **Workforce**. The total number of people employed in a country plus the number of people unemployed and looking for a job.

Labor Mobility: The ability and readiness of workers to move to regions or sectors of higher growth within a country or economy.

Levy: A tax based on the assessed value of personal property and/or income.

Liberal Economy: An economy in which markets operate with minimal government interference and in which individual choice and private ownership are the guiding forces.

Liberalization: The opening of an economy to free competition and a self-regulating market, with minimal government-imposed regulations or limitations.

Liquidity: Generally, the amount of money on hand. When related to government, it refers to the amount of money in circulation.

Macroeconomics: Economic issues large enough to impact the nation as a whole.

Market Capitalization: The total market value of a company, expressed by multiplying the value of a company's outstanding shares by the current price of the stock.

Marxism: A set of economic and political theories based on the work of 19th century theorists Karl Marx and Friedrich Engels that holds that human history is a struggle between classes, especially those who own property and those who do not (the workers). Marxism provided the theoretical basis for the economic systems of modern **communism** and **socialism.**

Microcredit: The lending of small amounts of startup capital to the very poor as a way of helping them out of poverty. The World Bank and other aid agencies often make mircrocredit loans to small-scale entrepreneurs in the developing world.

Monetary Policy: A government policy designed to regulate the money supply and interest rates in an economy. These policies are usually determined by the central bank or treasury in order to react to or to anticipate inflationary trends and other factors that affect an economy. They are said to be "tight" when interest rates are raised and other measures are implemented in an effort to control inflation and stabilize currency values.

Monetized Economy: An economy based on money as opposed to barter.

Money Laundering: A method used by criminal organizations to hide income gained from illicit activities, such as drug smuggling, by manipulating banks to provide a legitimate explanation for the source of money.

Monopoly: A company or corporation that has exclusive control over the distribution and availability of a product or service.

Multinational Corporation (MNC): A corporation which has economic ties to or operations in two or more countries.

National Debt: The amount of money owed to lenders by a government. The debt occurs when a government spends more each year than it has raised through taxes. Thus, to spend more than it has, the government must borrow money from banks or through the issuance of bonds.

Nationalization: The movement of privately-owned (and usually foreign-owned) companies into government ownership. Companies have often been nationalized by the developing countries whose government argued that the foreign firms involved did not pay their fair share of the profits to the host country and unfairly exploited it in other ways.

Nomenklatura: The elite members of the Communist Party in communist nations, who were often given privileges not extended to ordinary citizens.

Nomenklatura Privatization: A system of **privatization** in communist nations that openly or covertly transferred ownership of state assets to the **nomenklatura.**

Non-performing Loan: A delinquent loan or one in danger of going into default.

Offshore Banking: Banking operations that offer financial services to people and companies from other countries, usually with associated tax benefits. Offshore banking operations are often suspected as a cover for **money laundering** or other illegal financial activities.

Overheated Economy: An economy that is growing at a very high annual rate, which leads to low interest rates, a high borrowing rate, and an abundance of money in the economy—all of which can lead to **inflation.**

Parastatal: A partly or wholly government-owned enterprise.

Participation Rate: The ratio between the labor force and the total population, which indicates how many people are either working or actively seeking work.

Pensioner: A retired person who lives off a government pension.

Price Control: Artificial limitation on the prices of goods set by the government, usually in a **centrally-planned economy.**

Price Index: An index that shows how the average price of a commodity or bundle of goods has changed over a period of time, usually by comparing their value in constant dollars.

Primary Commodity: A commodity, such as a particular crop or mineral, which is a natural rather than manufactured resource.

Private Sector: The part of an economy that is not directly controlled by the government, including businesses and households.

Privatization: The transition of a company or companies from state ownership or control to private ownership. Privatization often takes place in societies that are making a transition from a **socialist** or mixed-socialist economy to a **capitalist** economy.

Procurement: The purchase of goods or services by the government.

Progressive Taxation: An income taxation system in which tax rates rise in accordance with income levels. Thus, a person making a large salary will be taxed at a higher rate than someone who makes less money.

Proportional Representation: An electoral system whereby the number of legislative seats allocated to a particular political party is decided in proportion to the number of votes that party won in an election.

Protectionist Policy: A government policy used to protect local producers from competition from imported foreign goods. Countries may erect various trade barriers such as **tariffs** or quotas in an effort to protect domestic firms or products.

Public Sector: The part of the economy that is owned and operated by the government.

Purchasing Power Parity (PPP): The purchasing power parity method attempts to determine that relative purchasing power of different currencies over equivalent goods and services. For example, if it costs someone in the United States US$300 to buy a month's worth of groceries, but it costs someone in Ghana only US$100 to buy the same amount of groceries, then the person in Ghana can purchase three times as much for the same amount of money. This means that though the average citizen of Ghana may earn less money than the average citizen of the United States, that money buys more because goods and services cost less in Ghana. The PPP calculation attempts to account for these differences in prices and is used to calculate **GDP** and **GDP per capita** figures that are comparable across nations. Note: GDP figured at purchasing power parity may be three or more times as large as GDP figured at **exchange rate** parity.

Pyramid Scheme: Fraudulent investment strategy involving a series of buying and selling transactions that generate a paper profit, which, in turn, is used to buy more stocks. They were prevalent in Eastern Europe following the fall of the Soviet Union, and preyed on the average citizen's lack of understanding of **free-market** investment transactions.

Real GDP: The **gross domestic product** of a country expressed in constant prices which are determined by a baseline year. Real GDP thus ignores the effects of inflation and deflation and allows for comparisons over time.

Real Wage: Income measured in constant dollars, and thus corrected to account for the effects of inflation.

Recession: A period of negative growth in an economy, usually defined as two consecutive quarters of negative **GDP** growth. A recession is characterized by factors such as low consumer spending, low output, and high unemployment.

Re-export: An imported good that does not undergo any changes (e.g., not turned into a new product) before being exported.

Relative Income Poverty: This is a measure of the overall equality in income among employed workers. Relative income poverty is high when a high percentage of the sum of total income is concentrated in the hands of a small percentage of the working population, and it is low when income is more equally spread among all workers.

Remittance: Money that is sent back to people, usually relatives, living in the home country of a national working abroad.

Repatriation: Taking money out of a foreign country in which it had been invested and reinvesting it in the country where it originated.

Reserve Ratio: The percentage of a bank's assets in reserve against the possibility of customers withdrawing their deposited funds. Some governments impose a minimum percentage, usually enforced by a central bank in proportion to the total amount of currency in circulation.

Restructuring: A catch-all phrase for turning around a company, involving cutting costs, restoring finances, and improving products.

Retail: The sale of goods and services to individuals in small amounts.

Sanction: A penalty, often in the form of a trade restriction, placed on one country by one or several other countries as a penalty for an action by the country under sanctions. Sanctions are designed to force the country experiencing them to change a policy, such as its human rights practices.

Shadow Economy: Economic interactions that are invisible to standard accounting and taxing procedures. See **Informal Economy.**

Sharecropper: A farmer who works someone else's land in exchange for a share of the crops they produce.

Smallholder: A farmer who has only a very small farm or plot of land.

Social Security Tax: A **direct tax** levied partly on the worker and partly on the employer in order to provide funds for a nation's **social welfare system.**

Social Welfare System: A set of government programs that provides for the needs of the unemployed, aged, disabled, or other groups deemed in need of government assistance.

Socialism: An economic system in which means of production and distribution are owned by the community, and profits are shared among the community. Countries with socialist economies put a premium on centralized control over an economy rather than allowing market forces to operate, and tend to have a relatively equal distribution of income.

Solvency: Financial stability.

Statist Economic Policy: A policy in **capitalist** or quasi-capitalist countries that favor state control or guidance of companies or sectors of the economy that are thought to be vital.

Strategic Industry: An industry considered extremely important to the well being of a country.

Structural Adjustment Program (SAP): A set of economic programs and policies aimed at stabilizing the overall structure of a troubled economy. Structural adjustment programs are often required by international lending agencies such as the World Bank and the International Monetary Fund. These programs often involve devaluing the currency, reducing government spending, and increasing exports.

Structural Unemployment: Unemployment caused by a mismatch between the needs of employers and the skills and training of the labor force.

Subsidy: A payment made by a government to an individual or company that produces a specific good or commodity. Some countries subsidize the production of certain agricultural crops, while others may subsidize mass transit or public art.

Subsistence Farming: Farming which generates only enough produce to feed the farmer's family, with little or nothing left over to sell.

Tariff: An **indirect tax** that is applied to an imported product or class of products.

Tax Haven: A place where investors shield their money from the national taxes of their own country. *See also* **Offshore Banking.**

Tax Holiday: A period of time in which businesses or investors enjoy exemptions from paying taxes. Tax holidays are offered as a lure to investment or business development.

Technocrat: Government official who is expert in specialized—usually technological—areas.

Trade Deficit: *See* **Balance of Trade.**

Trade Surplus: *See* **Balance of Trade.**

Transfer Payment: Cash paid directly to individuals by a government, usually as part of a **social welfare system.**

Transfer Pricing: A method used by foreign firms to overprice their overseas costs and thereby reduce their local tax liabilities.

Treasury Bill: Also called a **T-bill**. A guaranteed government investment bond sold to the public. They usually reach maturity after short periods, for example, three months or six months.

Trickle Down: An economic theory that contends that tax relief and other governmental incentives should be given primarily to the highest income earners in a society, on the assumption that their increased economic investment and other activity will provide benefits that "trickle down" to the lower- and middle-income wage-earners.

Turnover: The measure of trade activity in terms of the aggregated prices of all goods and services sold in the country during a year.

Two-tier Economy: An economy where skilled or educated workers enjoy a high standard of living, but unskilled workers are trapped in poverty.

Underemployment: A situation in which people are not reaching their economic potential because they are employed in low-paying or part-time jobs. For example, an engineer who is working in a fast food restaurant would be said to be experiencing underemployment.

Underground Economy: Economic transactions that are not reported to government, and therefore not taxable. **Informal sectors** and **black markets** are examples of underground economic activity.

Unicameral: A legislative body consisting of a single house or chamber.

United Nations Development Program (UNDP): The United Nations' principal provider of development advice, advocacy, and grant support.

Value Added: The increase in the value of a good at each stage in the production process. When a company adds value to its products it is able to gain a higher price for them, but it may be liable for a **value-added tax.**

Value-added Tax (VAT): A tax levied on the amount of **value added** to a total product at each stage of its manufacture.

Vertical Integration: Control over all stages of the production and distribution of a certain product. For example, if one company owns the mines, the steel plant, the transportation network, the factories, and the dealerships involved in making and selling automobiles, it is vertically integrated.

Voucher Privatization: A system for selling off state-owned companies in which citizens are given "vouchers" which they may invest in such companies. This system was devised to allow all citizens the opportunity to invest in formerly state-owned businesses; however, in practice many citizens invest their vouchers in voucher funds, which are professionally managed investment groups who amass vouchers in order to exert control over the direction of companies.

Welfare State: A government that assumes the responsibility for the well-being of its citizens by providing institutions and organizations that contribute to their care. *See also* **Social Welfare System.**

Workforce: *See* **Labor Force.**

INDEX

Page numbers appearing in bold-face indicate major treatment of entries. A page number accompanied by an italicized "t" indicates that there is a table on that page, while a page number accompanied by an italicized "f" indicates there is a figure on that page.

A

Abacha, Sani, **I:**352
Aboriginal lands, Australia, **III:**17
Abubakar, Abdulsalami, **I:**352–353
Acquired Immune Deficiency Syndrome (AIDS). *See* AIDS and HIV
Advertising industry, Lebanon, **III:**331
Affirmative action, South Africa, **I:**427–428
Afghani (money), **III:**8
Afghanistan, **III:1–10**
African National Congress (South Africa), **I:**420
African Party for the Independence of Cape Verde, **I:**69
"Agenda 2000," Spain, **IV:**439–440
Aging populations
  Japan, **III:**239
  Romania, **IV:**375
  United Kingdom, **IV:**501
  United States, **II:**375–376
Agriculture
  Afghanistan, **III:**5–6
  Albania, **IV:**4
  Algeria, **I:**6–7
  Andorra, **IV:**12–13
  Angola, **I:**17
  Antigua and Barbuda, **II:**4–5
  Argentina, **II:**14, 15–16
  Armenia, **IV:**20
  Australia, **III:**16
  Austria, **IV:**31, 36
  Azerbaijan, **III:**28
  The Bahamas, **II:**28

Bahrain, **III:**35
Bangladesh, **III:**47–48
Barbados, **II:**36–37
Belarus, **IV:**40–41
Belgium, **IV:**53–54
Belize, **II:**44–45
Benin, **I:**24–25
Bhutan, **III:**61
Bolivia, **II:**54–55
Bosnia and Herzegovina, **IV:**66
Botswana, **I:**32
Brazil, **II:**67–69
Brunei Darussalam, **III:**68
Bulgaria, **IV:**75–76
Burkina Faso, **I:**41–42
Burma, **III:**78–79
Burundi, **I:**50
Cambodia, **III:**89
Cameroon, **I:**60–61
Canada, **II:**83–84
Cape Verde, **I:**70
Central African Republic, **I:**78–79
Chad, **I:**87
Chile, **II:**98–99
China, **III:**101
Colombia, **II:**113–114
Comoros, **I:**94
Congo, Democratic Republic of the, **I:**103–104
Congo, Republic of the, **I:**112
Costa Rica, **II:**125–126
Côte d'Ivoire, **I:**122
Croatia, **IV:**88
Cuba, **II:**137–138
Cyprus, **III:**120
Czech Republic, **IV:**99
Denmark, **IV:**111
Djibouti, **I:**130–131
Dominica, **II:**146–147
Dominican Republic, **II:**155
Ecuador, **II:**164–165
Egypt, **I:**141
El Salvador, **II:**175
Equatorial Guinea, **I:**154–155
Eritrea, **I:**162–163

Estonia, **IV:**121–122
Ethiopia, **I:**172–173
Fiji, **III:**130–131
Finland, **IV:**132–133
France, **IV:**143, 147–148
French Antilles and French Guiana, **II:**185–186
French Polynesia, **III:**138
Gabon, **I:**182–183
The Gambia, **I:**190
Georgia, **IV:**159
Germany, **IV:**171
Ghana, **I:**199–200
Greece, **IV:**184–185
Grenada, **II:**194–195
Guatemala, **II:**203
Guinea, **I:**209
Guinea-Bissau, **I:**219
Guyana, **II:**213
Haiti, **II:**221
Honduras, **II:**229
Hong Kong, **III:**149
Hungary, **IV:**199–200
Iceland, **IV:**209
India, **III:**165
Indonesia, **III:**178–179
Iran, **III:**194–195
Iraq, **III:**207–208
Ireland, **IV:**219–220
Israel, **III:**217–218
Italy, **IV:**235–236
Jamaica, **II:**239
Japan, **III:**231
Jordan, **III:**244–245
Kazakhstan, **III:**256–257
Kenya, **I:**228
Kiribati, **III:**268
Korea, North, **III:**276
Korea, South, **III:**287
Kuwait, **III:**299–300
Kyrgyzstan, **III:**309
Laos, **III:**319
Latvia, **IV:**249
Lebanon, **III:**330
Lesotho, **I:**238–239

Agriculture (*continued*)

Liberia, **I:**247

Libya, **I:**255

Liechtenstein, **IV:**258

Lithuania, **IV:**268

Luxembourg, **IV:**280

Macau, **III:**338

Macedonia, **IV:**288

Madagascar, **I:**264–265

Malawi, **I:**272–273

Malaysia, **III:**349

Maldives, **III:**363

Mali, **I:**280–281

Malta, **IV:**296

Marshall Islands, **III:**370

Mauritania, **I:**289

Mauritius, **I:**296–297

Mexico, **II:**250–251

Micronesia, **III:**379

Moldova, **IV:**304–305

Monaco, **IV:**312

Mongolia, **III:**386

Morocco, **I:**307

Mozambique, **I:**318

Namibia, **I:**331

Nauru, **III:**393

Nepal, **III:**401–402

Netherlands, **IV:**321–322

Netherlands Antilles and Aruba, **II:**266

New Zealand, **III:**413

Nicaragua, **II:**273–274

Niger, **I:**341

Nigeria, **I:**349–350, 356–357

Norway, **IV:**336

Oman, **III:**422–423

Pakistan, **III:**436–437

Palau, **III:**448

Panama, **II:**283–284

Papua New Guinea, **III:**456

Paraguay, **II:**296

Peru, **II:**308–309

Philippines, **III:**466

Poland, **IV:**349

Portugal, **IV:**364–365

Puerto Rico, **II:**318

Qatar, **III:**478

Romania, **IV:**380

Russia, **IV:**394–395

Rwanda, **I:**368

St. Kitts and Nevis, **II:**326

St. Lucia, **II:**334

St. Vincent and the Grenadines, **II:**342–343

Samoa, **III:**485–486

San Marino, **IV:**408

São Tomé and Príncipe, **I:**376

Saudi Arabia, **III:**498–499

Senegal, **I:**385–386

Seychelles, **I:**396

Sierra Leone, **I:**404

Singapore, **III:**511

Slovakia, **IV:**415

Slovenia, **IV:**424–425

Solomon Islands, **III:**522

Somalia, **I:**413

South Africa, **I:**422–423

Spain, **IV:**439–440

Sri Lanka, **III:**532–533

Sudan, **I:**436

Suriname, **II:**350

Swaziland, **I:**444

Sweden, **IV:**452

Switzerland, **IV:**465–466

Syria, **III:**543

Taiwan, **III:**557–559

Tajikistan, **III:**570

Tanzania, **I:**453–454

Thailand, **III:**583–584

Togo, **I:**467–468

Tonga, **III:**597–598

Trinidad and Tobago, **II:**358

Tunisia, **I:**476

Turkey, **III:**609–610

Turkmenistan, **III:**625

Tuvalu, **III:**634

Uganda, **I:**488–489

Ukraine, **IV:**479–480

United Arab Emirates, **III:**641

United Kingdom, **IV:**494

United States, **II:**369–370

Uruguay, **II:**385–386

Uzbekistan, **III:**652

Vanuatu, **III:**660

Venezuela, **II:**395

Vietnam, **III:**669

Yemen, **III:**680

Yugoslavia, **IV:**514–515

Zambia, **I:**499–500

Zimbabwe, **I:**509–510

See also specific crops and agro-industries

AIDS and HIV

Botswana, **I:**29

Burma, **III:**73

Burundi, **I:**47

Central African Republic, **I:**75, 91–92

Ethiopia, **I:**167–168

Gabon, **I:**179

Kenya, **I:**223

Lesotho, **I:**235, 241

Malawi, **I:**269

Mozambique, **I:**313

Niger, **I:**343

Rwanda, **I:**371

South Africa, **I:**417

Tanzania, **I:**450–451

Thailand, **III:**593

Togo, **I:**469

Uganda, **I:**483–484

Zambia, **I:**495

Aircraft and aerospace industry

Canada, **II:**85

France, **IV:**148–149

United States, **II:**368

Airports and airlines

Afghanistan, **III:**4

Algeria, **I:**5

Argentina, **II:**13

Australia, **III:**15

Azerbaijan, **III:**27

Bangladesh, **III:**46

Belgium, **IV:**52

Bolivia, **II:**53

Brazil, **II:**66

Burkina Faso, **I:**40

Burma, **III:**76–77

Cameroon, **I:**59

Cape Verde, **I:**69

Central African Republic, **I:**78

China, **III:**99

Colombia, **II:**112

Denmark, **IV:**109

Djibouti, **I:**130

Dominican Republic, **II:**154

Egypt, **I:**139

Ethiopia, **I:**171

Gabon, **I:**181

The Gambia, **I:**189

Germany, **IV:**169

Greece, **IV:**185–186, 187

Guinea-Bissau, **I:**218

Honduras, **II:**228

Hong Kong, **III:**148

Iran, **III:**193

Iraq, **III:**206

Ireland, **IV:**218

Italy, **IV:**233

Jamaica, **II:**238

Japan, **III:**230

Kenya, **I:**227

Korea, South, **III:**286

Lesotho, **I:**237–238

Liberia, **I:**246

Libya, **I:**253

Luxembourg, **IV:**278

Madagascar, **I:**264

Malawi, **I:**271–272

Malaysia, **III:**348

Mauritania, **I:**288

Mauritius, **I:**295

Mexico, **II:**249

Micronesia, **III:**377

Namibia, **I:**330

Netherlands Antilles and Aruba, **II:**265

New Zealand, **III:**412

Niger, **I:**340

Nigeria, **I:**355

Norway, **IV:**335

Oman, **III:**421–422

Pakistan, **III:**434

Peru, **II:**307

Philippines, **III:**464

Poland, **IV:**348

São Tomé and Príncipe, **I:**375

Saudi Arabia, **III:**497

Senegal, **I:**384

Seychelles, **I:**395

Singapore, **III:**510

Solomon Islands, **III:**521

Somalia, **I:**412–413

Spain, **IV:**437, 441

Sri Lanka, **III:**531

Sudan, **I:**435

Sweden, **IV:**450

Switzerland, **IV:**463

Taiwan, **III:**556

Tanzania, **I:**453

Thailand, **III:**581

Tonga, **III:**596

Tunisia, **I:**475

Turkey, **III:**607

Turkmenistan, **III:**624

Ukraine, **IV:**478

United States, **II:**368

Uruguay, **II:**384

Vanuatu, **III:**659, 661

Zimbabwe, **I:**508

Albania, **IV:1–7**

Algeria, **I:1–11**

All-China Federation of Trade Unions, **III:**109

Alma-Ata Declaration, **III:**254, **IV:**391

Althingi, **IV:**207

Alumina. *See* Aluminum production; Bauxite mining

Aluminum production

Bahrain, **III:**36

Mozambique, **I:**319

Tajikistan, **III:**571

Venezuela, **II:**396

Andean Community of Nations, **II:**311

Andorra, **IV:9–15**

Angkor Wat complex, **III:**87, 90

Angola, **I:13–20**

Animal husbandry. *See* Livestock and meat production

Antigua and Barbuda, **II:1–8**

ARBED conglomerate, **IV:**276, 280

Argentina, **II:9–23**

Aristide, Jean-Bertrand, **II:**219

Armenia, **IV:17–24**

Arms exports, Ukraine, **IV:**481

Aruba. *See* Netherlands Antilles and Aruba

Asia-Pacific Regional Operations Center Plan, **III:**555–556

Asian Clearing Union, **III:**199

Asian financial crisis of 1997

Hong Kong, **III:**144

Indonesia, **III:**175, 182

Japan, **III:**227, 239

Korea, South, **III:**282, 283, 288, 289

Macau, **III:**338

Malaysia, **III:**346, 351, 353

Philippines, **III:**462

Singapore, **III:**512–514

Thailand, **III:**581, 588–589

Vietnam, **III:**667

Assoumani, Azali, **I:**92

ASTRA satellites, **IV:**281

Australia, **III:11–23**

Austria, **IV:25–36**

Automated teller machines, Portugal, **IV:**366–367

Automobile industry

Argentina, **II:**16

Belgium, **IV:**55

Brazil, **II:**69

Canada, **II:**85

Germany, **IV:**172

Iran, **III:**197

Italy, **IV:**236–237

Japan, **III:**232

Portugal, **IV:**366

Spain, **IV:**440

Sweden, **IV:**452

Taiwan, **III:**559–560

Thailand, **III:**585

United Kingdom, **IV:**495

United States, **II:**370

Uzbekistan, **III:**652–653

Automobile service industry, Poland, **IV:**351

Azerbaijan, **III:25–32**

B

Ba'ath Party (Iraq), **III:**205, 211

The Bahamas, **II:25–31**

Bahrain, **III:33–39**

Baht (money), **III:**587

Balance of trade. *See* International trade

Balboa (money), **II:**286

Banana and plantain production

Belize, **II:**45

Cameroon, **I:**61

Costa Rica, **II:**125

Dominica, **II:**146, 149

Ecuador, **II:**164–165

Grenada, **II:**194–195

Guatemala, **II:**203

Honduras, **II:**229

Jamaica, **II:**239

Panama, **II:**284

St. Lucia, **II:**331–332, 334

St. Vincent and the Grenadines, **II:**342

Bangladesh, **III:41–55**

Bangladesh Nationalist Party, **III:**44

Banking. *See* Financial services; Money

Barbados Labour Party, **II:**34

Barbuda. *See* Antigua and Barbuda

Barter arrangements, Russia, **IV:**392

al-Bashir, Umar, **I:**434

Basque terrorism, **IV:**434–435, 445

Bauxite mining

Guinea, **I:**210

Jamaica, **II:**239–240

Suriname, **II:**350

Bazaar merchants, **III:**190, 197–198

Beef production

Brazil, **II:**68

Spain, **IV:**439

Vanuatu, **III:**660

Belarus, **IV:37–45**

Belgium, **IV:47–61**

Belgium-Luxembourg Economic Union (BLEU), **IV:**57

Belize, **II:41–48**

Benetton, **IV:**237

Benin, **I:21–28**

Bermuda, **IV:**502–503

Betel nut production, Taiwan, **III:**557–558

Bhumibol Adulyadej, King, **III:**579

Bhutan, **III:57–64**

bin Laden, Osama. *See* Laden, Osama bin

Biotechnology and pharmaceutical industries

Cuba, **II:**138

Iceland, **IV:**210

Singapore, **III:**511

United Kingdom, **IV:**495

Birr (money), **I:**175

Birth rates. *See* Country overviews

Biya, Paul, **I:**57–58

Black market, Peru, **II:**305

BLEU. *See* Belgium-Luxembourg Economic Union (BLEU)

Bokassa, Jean Bedel, **I:**77

Bolívar (money), **II:**398

Bolivia, **II:49–61**

Bologna Declaration, **IV:**190

Bolshevik Revolution, **IV:**390

Bonaire. *See* Netherlands Antilles and Aruba

Bond market, Poland, **IV:**354

Bonded labor, Pakistan, **III:**442

Bongo, Omar, **I:**180–181

Bonyad (Iranian religious foundations), **III:**190

Border disputes
  Ethiopia and Eritrea, **I:**129, 132
  Honduras and Nicaragua, **II:**231, 234
  See also War and civil unrest

Bosnia and Herzegovina, **IV:63–81**

Botswana, **I:29–35**

Bovine spongiform encephalopathy. *See* Mad cow disease

"Brain drain"
  Canada, **II:**80, 91
  Nigeria, **I:**360
  Sudan, **I:**439
  Suriname, **II:**347, 352

Brazil, **II:63–75**

Breton Woods economic system, **II:**373

Brewing and beverage production
  Burundi, **I:**51
  Cameroon, **I:**62
  See also Wine and spirits production

British Virgin Islands, **IV:**503

Brunei Darussalam, **III:65–72**

"Bubble economy," Japan, **III:**227

Budgets. *See* Economic overviews and trends

Bulgaria, **IV:71–81**

Bundesrat
  Austria, **IV:**28
  Germany, **IV:**168

Burkina Faso, **I:37–45**

Burma, **III:73–83**

Burundi, **I:47–53**

Business and managerial services, Thailand, **III:**585

C

Callejas, Rafael Leonardo, **II:**227

Cambodia, **III:85–93**

Cameroon, **I:55–66**

Canada, **II:77–91**

Canning industry, Maldives, **III:**363

Cape Verde, **I:67–73**

Capital flight, Russia, **IV:**398–399

Cardoso, Fernando Henrique, **II:**74

Caribbean Departments of France. *See* French Antilles and French Guiana

Cash crops. *See* Agriculture; *specific crops*

Cashew nut production
  Guinea-Bissau, **I:**219
  Mozambique, **I:**318, 319

"Casino economics," Finland, **IV:**129

Caspian Pipeline Consortium, **III:**256, 257–258

Caste systems
  India, **III:**161
  Nepal, **III:**405

Cayman Islands, **IV:**503

Cedi (money), **I:**201

Cellular telephones. *See* Telecommunications

Cement production
  Egypt, **I:**142
  Turkey, **III:**611

Central African Republic, **I:75–82**

Cereal crops. *See* Agriculture

CFA franc (money)
  Benin, **I:**22, 26
  Burkina Faso, **I:**43
  Cameroon, **I:**63
  Central African Republic, **I:**80
  Chad, **I:**89
  Congo, Republic of the, **I:**113
  Côte d'Ivoire, **I:**124
  Equatorial Guinea, **I:**155
  Gabon, **I:**184
  Guinea-Bissau, **I:**216, 220
  Mali, **I:**282
  Niger, **I:**343
  Senegal, **I:**388
  Togo, **I:**464, 469

CFPF (money), **III:**139–140

Chad, **I:83–90**

Chad-Cameroon Oil Production and Pipeline project, **I:**65, 85

Chaebols, **III:**283

Chama Cha Mapinduzi, **I:**451–452

Channel Islands, **IV:**501–502

Chechnya, **IV:**388

Chemical industry
  Argentina, **II:**17
  Armenia, **IV:**20–21
  Belarus, **IV:**41
  Belgium, **IV:**54–55
  Denmark, **IV:**112

Finland, **IV:**134

Germany, **IV:**173

Hungary, **IV:**200

Lithuania, **IV:**269

Netherlands, **IV:**322

Poland, **IV:**350

Romania, **IV:**381

Singapore, **III:**512

Switzerland, **IV:**466

Turkey, **III:**611

Chernobyl nuclear accident (1986), **IV:**38

Child labor
  Bangladesh, **III:**53
  Burma, **III:**82
  China, **III:**110–111
  Congo, Democratic Republic of the, **I:**106
  Egypt, **I:**147
  Hong Kong, **III:**155–156
  Malaysia, **III:**355
  Pakistan, **III:**442–443
  Panama, **II:**287
  Philippines, **III:**471
  Sri Lanka, **III:**536–537
  Tanzania, **I:**459
  United Arab Emirates, **III:**645
  See also Working conditions

Child prostitution, Thailand, **III:**590

Chile, **II:93–106**

China, **III:95–114**
  See also Hong Kong; Taiwan

"Chunnel," **IV:**492

Citizens Union of Georgia, **IV:**157

Citizenship issues, Andorra, **IV:**14

Ciudad del Este (Paraguay), **II:**293, 298

Civil unrest. *See* War and civil unrest

Clan structure, Uzbekistan, **III:**649–650

Closed economies. *See* Economic overviews and trends

CLT (company), **IV:**281

Co-princes of Andorra, **IV:**11

Coal mining
  Afghanistan, **III:**7
  Australia, **III:**17
  France, **IV:**149
  Germany, **IV:**172
  Japan, **III:**233
  Niger, **I:**341
  Poland, **IV:**349
  Romania, **IV:**380
  South Africa, **I:**424

Coca leaf production
  Bolivia, **II:**51–52

Colombia, **II:**113–114
Peru, **II:**309
Cocoa production
Brazil, **II:**68
Cameroon, **I:**60
Côte d'Ivoire, **I:**122
Ecuador, **II:**165
Equatorial Guinea, **I:**154
Ghana, **I:**199
Togo, **I:**467–468
Coconut products
Marshall Islands, **III:**370
Micronesia, **III:**376
Samoa, **III:**486
Sri Lanka, **III:**533
Vanuatu, **III:**660
Coffee production
Angola, **I:**17
Brazil, **II:**68
Burundi, **I:**50
Cameroon, **I:**60
Central African Republic, **I:**79
Côte d'Ivoire, **I:**122
Ecuador, **II:**165
El Salvador, **II:**175
Equatorial Guinea, **I:**154
Ethiopia, **I:**172
Guatemala, **II:**203
Honduras, **II:**229
Kenya, **I:**228
Rwanda, **I:**371
Togo, **I:**467–468
Uganda, **I:**488–489
Colombia, **II:107–120**
Colón Free Trade Zone, **II:**285
Colón (money), **II:**128–129
Colonies. *See* Dependencies
Colorado Party (Paraguay), **II:**294
Common Agricultural Policy of the
European Union, **IV:**235
Commonwealth of Independent
States, **III:**626–627
Communications. *See* Publishing;
Telecommunications
Communist Party
China, **III:**97–98
Moldova, **IV:**302, 307–308
Comoros, **I:91–97**
Computer hardware and software
production. *See* Information
technology
Computer use. *See*
Telecommunications
Confederation of Bolivian Workers,
II:59
Confederation of the United Workers
of Bolivian Peasants, **II:**59

Congo, Democratic Republic of the,
I:99–107
Congo, Republic of the, **I:109–115**
Conservative Party (United
Kingdom), **IV:**491
Construction
Antigua and Barbuda, **II:**5
Azerbaijan, **III:**29
The Bahamas, **II:**29
Belgium, **IV:**55
Belize, **II:**45
Brunei Darussalam, **III:**69
Canada, **II:**85
Chile, **II:**101
Croatia, **IV:**88
Czech Republic, **IV:**99
Denmark, **IV:**112
Djibouti, **I:**131
Egypt, **I:**142
El Salvador, **II:**176
Finland, **IV:**134
French Antilles and French Guiana,
II:186
Greece, **IV:**185–186
Hong Kong, **III:**150–151
Iraq, **III:**209
Ireland, **IV:**221
Japan, **III:**232–233
Jordan, **III:**245–456
Korea, North, **III:**277
Korea, South, **III:**289
Laos, **III:**320
Lebanon, **III:**331
Libya, **I:**256
Liechtenstein, **IV:**259
Malta, **IV:**296
Morocco, **I:**309
Netherlands, **IV:**322–323
Nicaragua, **II:**275
Panama, **II:**284
Paraguay, **II:**297
Poland, **IV:**350
Puerto Rico, **II:**318
Saudi Arabia, **III:**500
Slovakia, **IV:**416
Turkey, **III:**611–612
United Arab Emirates, **III:**642–643
United Kingdom, **IV:**495
United States, **II:**371
Uruguay, **II:**386
Venezuela, **II:**397
Vietnam, **III:**670
Zimbabwe, **I:**510
Conté, Lansana, **I:**207
Convergence and Union Party
(Spain), **IV:**436
Cooperatives, Philippines, **III:**470

Copper mining
Chile, **II:**99–100
Congo, Democratic Republic of the,
I:104
Papua New Guinea, **III:**457
Uganda, **I:**489
Zambia, **I:**495, 500
Copra. *See* Coconut products
Copyright infringement and pirating
Bangladesh, **III:**50
Malaysia, **III:**352
Peru, **II:**305
Taiwan, **III:**561
Córdoba (money), **II:**276
Corn. *See* Maize production
Corporacion Minera Boliviana, **II:**55
Corporacion Nacional del Cobre de
Chile, **II:**100
Corruption
Algeria, **I:**3
Benin, **I:**22
Cameroon, **I:**57
Chad, **I:**85
Congo, Democratic Republic of the,
I:101
Egypt, **I:**137
Georgia, **IV:**156
India, **III:**170
Indonesia, **III:**175
Italy, **IV:**232
Lebanon, **III:**327
Liberia, **I:**245
Nigeria, **I:**348–349, 360–361
Pakistan, **III:**431
Romania, **IV:**378, 384
Sierra Leone, **I:**403
Uganda, **I:**485
Ukraine, **IV:**477
Yemen, **III:**679
Costa, Manuel da, **I:**374
Costa Rica, **II:121–132**
Côte d'Ivoire, **I:117–126**
Cottage industries, Nepal,
III:402–403
Cotton production
Benin, **I:**24, 25
Cameroon, **I:**61
Central African Republic, **I:**79
Chad, **I:**87
Côte d'Ivoire, **I:**122
Egypt, **I:**141
Mali, **I:**280–281
Mozambique, **I:**318
Pakistan, **III:**436
Paraguay, **II:**294, 296
Peru, **II:**309
Tajikistan, **III:**570

Cotton production (*continued*)

Togo, **I:**467

Turkey, **III:**609

Turkmenistan, **III:**625

Uzbekistan, **III:**652

Zambia, **I:**499

Country overviews

Afghanistan, **III:**1, 9–10

Albania, **IV:**1, 7

Algeria, **I:**1–2, 10

Andorra, **IV:**9–10, 14–15

Angola, **I:**13, 19–20

Antigua and Barbuda, **II:**1, 7–8

Argentina, **II:**9–10, 21–22

Armenia, **IV:**17, 23

Australia, **III:**11, 22–23

Austria, **IV:**25–26, 35–36

Azerbaijan, **III:**25, 31

The Bahamas, **II:**25–26, 31

Bahrain, **III:**33, 38–39

Bangladesh, **III:**41–42, 53–54

Barbados, **II:**33–34, 39

Belarus, **IV:**37–38, 44

Belgium, **IV:**47–48, 59–61

Belize, **II:**41, 47–48

Benin, **I:**21, 27

Bhutan, **III:**57–58, 63

Bolivia, **II:**49–50, 59–60

Bosnia and Herzegovina, **IV:**63, 68–69

Botswana, **I:**29, 34

Brazil, **II:**63, 73–74

Brunei Darussalam, **III:**65, 71–72

Bulgaria, **IV:**71, 80–81

Burkina Faso, **I:**37, 44–45

Burma, **III:**73, 83

Burundi, **I:**52–53, 147

Cambodia, **III:**85, 91–92

Cameroon, **I:**55, 65

Canada, **II:**77–78, 89–91

Cape Verde, **I:**67–68, 72–73

Central African Republic, **I:**73, 81

Chad, **I:**83, 89–90

Chile, **II:**93–94, 105–106

China, **III:**95–96, 111–113

Colombia, **II:**107–109, 118–119

Comoros, **I:**91–92, 96–97

Congo, Democratic Republic of the, **I:**99, 106–107

Congo, Republic of the, **I:**109, 114–115

Costa Rica, **II:**121, 130–131

Côte d'Ivoire, **I:**117–118, 125–126

Croatia, **IV:**83, 92–93

Cuba, **II:**133, 141–142

Cyprus, **III:**115–116, 123–124

Czech Republic, **IV:**95, 102–103

Denmark, **IV:**105, 116

Djibouti, **I:**127, 133–134

Dominica, **II:**143, 149

Dominican Republic, **II:**151, 158

Ecuador, **II:**168–169

Egypt, **I:**135–136, 147–148

El Salvador, **II:**171, 179

Equatorial Guinea, **I:**152, 156

Eritrea, **I:**159, 165

Estonia, **IV:**119, 124–125

Ethiopia, **I:**167–168, 177

Fiji, **III:**127–128, 133

Finland, **IV:**127, 138

France, **IV:**141–143, 153–154

French Antilles and French Guiana, **II:**181–182, 189–190

French Polynesia, **III:**135–136, 140–141

Gabon, **I:**179, 185

The Gambia, **I:**187, 192–193

Georgia, **IV:**155, 162–163

Germany, **IV:**165–167, 177–178

Ghana, **I:**195, 203–204

Greece, **IV:**179–180, 191–192

Grenada, **II:**191, 197

Guatemala, **II:**199–200, 207

Guinea, **I:**205, 212

Guinea-Bissau, **I:**215, 221

Guyana, **II:**209, 215–216

Haiti, **II:**217, 223

Honduras, **II:**225, 233

Hong Kong, **III:**143–144, 156–157

Hungary, **IV:**195, 203–204

Iceland, **IV:**205, 212–213

India, **III:**159–161, 170

Indonesia, **III:**173–174, 184

Iran, **III:**187–189, 201–202

Iraq, **III:**203, 211–212

Ireland, **IV:**215, 225

Israel, **III:**213–214, 221–222

Italy, **IV:**227–228, 242–243

Jamaica, **II:**235, 244

Japan, **III:**225, 237–238

Jordan, **III:**241, 248–249

Kazakhstan, **III:**251–252, 262–263

Kenya, **I:**223, 233–234

Kiribati, **III:**265, 270

Korea, North, **III:**273, 279

Korea, South, **III:**281, 293–294

Kuwait, **III:**297, 302

Kyrgyzstan, **III:**305, 312–313

Laos, **III:**315–316, 323

Latvia, **IV:**245–246, 252–253

Lebanon, **III:**325–326, 333–334

Lesotho, **I:**235–236, 241

Liberia, **I:**243, 249–250

Libya, **I:**251, 258

Liechtenstein, **IV:**255–256, 261

Lithuania, **IV:**263, 272–273

Luxembourg, **IV:**275–276, 283–284

Macau, **III:**335, 340

Macedonia, **IV:**285, 291

Madagascar, **I:**261, 267

Malawi, **I:**269, 275

Malaysia, **III:**343–344, 355–356

Maldives, **III:**359, 365

Mali, **I:**277, 283–284

Malta, **IV:**293, 298

Marshall Islands, **III:**367, 372–373

Mauritania, **I:**285, 291

Mauritius, **I:**293, 299–300

Mexico, **II:**245–246, 257–258

Micronesia, **III:**375, 381

Moldova, **IV:**301, 307

Monaco, **IV:**309–310, 314

Mongolia, **III:**383, 389

Morocco, **I:**303, 311–312

Mozambique, **I:**313–314, 323–324

Namibia, **I:**327, 334

Nauru, **III:**391, 395

Nepal, **III:**397, 407

Netherlands, **IV:**315–317, 327–328

Netherlands Antilles and Aruba, **II:**261–263, 269–270

New Zealand, **III:**409, 417–418

Nicaragua, **II:**271, 277

Niger, **I:**337, 344

Nigeria, **I:**347–348, 361–362

Norway, **IV:**331–333, 339–340

Oman, **III:**419, 426–427

Pakistan, **III:**429–431, 443

Palau, **III:**445, 449–450

Panama, **II:**279–280, 287–288

Papua New Guinea, **III:**453, 459

Paraguay, **II:**291–292, 301

Peru, **II:**303–304, 313–314

Philippines, **III:**461, 471–472

Poland, **IV:**343–344, 356

Portugal, **IV:**359–361, 371–372

Puerto Rico, **II:**315–316, 320

Qatar, **III:**475, 481

Romania, **IV:**375, 384–385

Russia, **IV:**387–388, 401

Rwanda, **I:**365, 370–371

St. Kitts and Nevis, **II:**323, 328–329

St. Lucia, **II:**331, 337

St. Vincent and the Grenadines, **II:**339, 345

Samoa, **III:**483, 488

San Marino, **IV:**405, 409–410

São Tomé and Príncipe, **I:**373, 378

Saudi Arabia, **III:**491, 503–504

Senegal, **I:**381, 390–391

Seychelles, **I:**393, 398

Sierra Leone, **I:**401, 408

Singapore, **III:**507–508, 515–516

Slovakia, **IV:**411, 419

Slovenia, **IV:**421, 428–429

Solomon Islands, **III:**519, 524–525

Somalia, **I:**409–410, 415–416

South Africa, **I:**417–418, 428–429

Spain, **IV:**431–432, 444–445

Sri Lanka, **III:**527–528, 537

Sudan, **I:**431, 439–440

Suriname, **II:**347, 352

Swaziland, **I:**441, 446–447

Sweden, **IV:**447–448, 456–457

Switzerland, **IV:**459–460, 471–472

Syria, **III:**539, 548–549

Taiwan, **III:**551–552, 564–565

Tajikistan, **III:**567, 574

Tanzania, **I:**449–451, 459–460

Thailand, **III:**577, 591–592

Togo, **I:**463, 470

Tonga, **III:**595, 600

Trinidad and Tobago, **II:**355, 361

Tunisia, **I:**473, 480

Turkey, **III:**603, 617–618

Turkmenistan, **III:**621, 628–629

Tuvalu, **III:**631–632, 636

Uganda, **I:**483–484, 492–493

Ukraine, **IV:**475, 484–485

United Arab Emirates, **III:**636, 645

United Kingdom, **IV:**487–489, 499–501

United States, **II:**363–365, 376–377

Uruguay, **II:**381, 389

Uzbekistan, **III:**647, 655–656

Vanuatu, **III:**657, 663

Vatican City, **IV:**505, 509

Venezuela, **II:**391, 400–401

Vietnam, **III:**665, 673–674

Yemen, **III:**677, 683

Yugoslavia, **IV:**511, 517–518

Zambia, **I:**495, 503

Zimbabwe, **I:**505–506, 513–514

Croatia, **IV:83–94**

Crop production. *See* Agriculture; *specific crops*

Crude oil. *See* Oil and gas industry

Cuba, **II:133–142**

Curaçao. *See* Netherlands Antilles and Aruba

Currency. *See* Money

Customs and duties. *See* International trade

Cyprus, **III:115–125**

Czech Republic, **IV:95–103**

D

Dairy production

Belgium, **IV:**54

Brazil, **II:**68–69

Netherlands, **IV:**321–322

New Zealand, **III:**413

Poland, **IV:**349

Dalasi (money), **I:**191

Data processing and telemarketing

Barbados, **II:**37

Grenada, **II:**195

Date production, Algeria, **I:**6

Debt

Algeria, **I:**3

Angola, **I:**15

Antigua and Barbuda, **II:**2

Argentina, **II:**11

Armenia, **IV:**18

Australia, **III:**13

Bangladesh, **III:**43

Barbados, **II:**34

Belgium, **IV:**50

Benin, **I:**26

Bhutan, **III:**58

Brazil, **II:**65

Bulgaria, **IV:**73

Burundi, **I:**48

Cameroon, **I:**57

Comoros, **I:**93

Congo, Republic of the, **I:**115

Croatia, **IV:**85

Cuba, **II:**135

Denmark, **IV:**107

Egypt, **I:**138

Finland, **IV:**129

Guyana, **II:**210

Jordan, **III:**242–243

Korea, South, **III:**283

Lithuania, **IV:**270

Malta, **IV:**294

Mexico, **II:**247, 254

Netherlands Antilles and Aruba, **II:**263, 268

Nicaragua, **II:**273

Nigeria, **I:**350

Pakistan, **III:**431, 441

Portugal, **IV:**363, 367

Spain, **IV:**434

Syria, **III:**541

Thailand, **III:**579

Uganda, **I:**485

Ukraine, **IV:**478

Uruguay, **II:**383

Venezuela, **II:**398

Vietnam, **III:**672

Zambia, **I:**497

See also Economic overviews and trends

Defense spending. *See* Politics and government

Deforestation and desertification

Burkina Faso, **I:**42

Burma, **III:**78

Central African Republic, **I:**91

Comoros, **I:**94

Côte d'Ivoire, **I:**122

Ethiopia, **I:**172–173

Laos, **III:**320

Malaysia, **III:**349–350

Nepal, **III:**402

Panama, **II:**284

Poland, **IV:**349

Senegal, **I:**385

Thailand, **III:**584

Democratic Labour Party (Barbados), **II:**34

Democratic Party (United States), **II:**366

Democratic Progressive Party (Taiwan), **III:**554–555

Democratic Republic of the Congo. *See* Congo, Democratic Republic of the

Denar (money), **IV:**290

Denmark, **IV:105–118**

Dependencies

Denmark, **IV:**117–118

Israel, **III:**223

United Kingdom, **IV:**501–503

United States, **II:**378–379

Depression. *See* Economic overviews and trends

Deregulation. *See* Economic overviews and trends

Derg regime (Ethiopia), **I:**169, 175–176

Desalinization plants, United Arab Emirates, **III:**640

Devaluation of currency. *See* Money; *specific currencies*

Diamond mining

Angola, **I:**17

Botswana, **I:**30–31, 34

Central African Republic, **I:**78, 79

Congo, Democratic Republic of the, **I:**104

Ghana, **I:**200

Guinea, **I:**210

Lesotho, **I:**239

Liberia, **I:**247

Sierra Leone, **I:**404

Diamond processing and trading

Belgium, **IV:**54

Israel, **III:**218

Dinar (money)

Algeria, **I:**32

Bahrain, **III:**37

Iraq, **III:**210

Dinar (money) (*continued*)
  Kuwait, **III**:301
  Libya, **I**:257
  Sudan, **I**:438
Direct marketing
  Slovenia, **IV**:426
  Switzerland, **IV**:467
Dirham (money)
  Morocco, **I**:310
  United Arab Emirates, **III**:643–644
Discrimination
  Canada, **II**:89
  China, **III**:110
  Croatia, **IV**:92
  Georgia, **IV**:162
  Japan, **III**:237
  Thailand, **III**:590
  United States, **II**:376
Djibouti, **I**:**127–134**
Dobra (money), **I**:377
Doi moi, **III**:667, 668, 670–671
Dollar-a-day poverty line, **I**:26
Dollar (money)
  Antigua and Barbuda, **II**:6
  Australia, **III**:20, 394
  The Bahamas, **II**:30
  Barbados, **II**:38
  Brunei Darussalam, **III**:70
  Canada, **II**:87
  Fiji, **III**:132
  Guyana, **II**:214
  Hong Kong, **III**:153
  Jamaica, **II**:42
  Kiribati, **III**:269
  Liberia, **I**:248–249
  Namibia, **I**:333
  Singapore, **III**:513–514
  Solomon Islands, **III**:524
  Tuvalu, **III**:635
  United States, **II**:166–167, 177, 286, 319, **III**:371, 380, 448–449
  Zimbabwe, **I**:511
Dominica, **II**:**143–150**
Dominica Freedom Party, **II**:144–145
Dominica Labor Party, **II**:144–145
Dominican Republic, **II**:**151–159**
Dram (money), **IV**:22
Drought and water shortages
  Afghanistan, **III**:5–6
  Cyprus, **III**:116
  India, **III**:165
  Jordan, **III**:245
  United Arab Emirates, **III**:640
  Uzbekistan, **III**:652
Drug policy, Netherlands, **IV**:326
Drug trafficking

Afghanistan, **III**:6
The Bahamas, **II**:26
Bangladesh, **III**:43–44
Bolivia, **II**:51–52
Burma, **III**:74–75
Colombia, **II**:110, 113–114
Jamaica, **II**:239
Malaysia, **III**:345
Pakistan, **III**:436, 442
Peru, **II**:309
Singapore, **III**:508
Zambia, **I**:497
Dutch Antilles. *See* Netherlands Antilles and Aruba
Duties and customs. *See* International trade
Duty-free status, Andorra, **IV**:10–11

E

Eastern Caribbean dollar (money)
  Dominica, **II**:148
  Grenada, **II**:196
  St. Kitts and Nevis, **II**:327
  St. Lucia, **II**:335–336
  St. Vincent and the Grenadines, **II**:344
E-commerce
  Portugal, **IV**:367
  Sweden, **IV**:453
"Economic citizenship," Dominica, **II**:147–148
Economic Cooperation Organization, **III**:627
Economic overviews and trends
  Afghanistan, **III**:2–3, 5, 10
  Albania, **IV**:1–2, 4, 7
  Algeria, **I**:2–3, 5–6, 10
  Andorra, **IV**:10–11, 12, 15
  Angola, **I**:13–15, 16–17, 20
  Antigua and Barbuda, **II**:1–2, 4, 8
  Argentina, **II**:10–11, 14–15, 22–23
  Armenia, **IV**:17–18, 19–20, 23
  Australia, **III**:11–13, 15–16, 23
  Austria, **IV**:26–27, 30–31, 36
  Azerbaijan, **III**:25–26, 28, 31
  The Bahamas, **II**:26, 28, 31
  Bahrain, **III**:33–34, 35, 39
  Bangladesh, **III**:42–44, 46–47, 54–55
  Barbados, **II**:34, 35–36, 39
  Belarus, **IV**:38–39, 40, 44–45
  Belgium, **IV**:48–50, 52–53, 61
  Belize, **II**:41–42, 44, 48
  Benin, **I**:21–22, 24, 27
  Bhutan, **III**:58, 60, 63
  Bolivia, **II**:50–51, 54, 60
  Bosnia and Herzegovina, **IV**:63–65, 66, 69
  Botswana, **I**:29–31, 31–32, 34–35

Brazil, **II**:63–65, 67, 74
Brunei Darussalam, **III**:65–66, 67–68, 72
Bulgaria, **IV**:71–73, 75, 81
Burkina Faso, **I**:37–39, 41, 45
Burma, **III**:73–75, 77–78, 83
Burundi, **I**:47–48, 49–50, 53
Cambodia, **III**:85–87, 88, 92
Cameroon, **I**:55–57, 59–60, 65–66
Canada, **II**:78–80, 82–83, 91
Cape Verde, **I**:68, 70, 73
Central African Republic, **I**:75–77, 78, 81–82
Chad, **I**:83–85, 86–87, 90
Chile, **II**:94, 98, 106
China, **III**:96–97, 100–101, 113–114
Colombia, **II**:109–110, 112–113, 119
Comoros, **I**:92, 94, 97
Congo, Democratic Republic of the, **I**:99–101, 103, 107
Congo, Republic of the, **I**:109–110, 112, 115
Costa Rica, **II**:122–123, 124–125, 131
Côte d'Ivoire, **I**:118–119, 121, 126
Croatia, **IV**:83–85, 87–88, 93
Cuba, **II**:134–135, 137, 142
Cyprus, **III**:116–117, 118–120, 124
Czech Republic, **IV**:95–97, 98–99, 103
Denmark, **IV**:105–107, 110–111, 116–117
Djibouti, **I**:127–129, 130, 134
Dominica, **II**:144–145, 145, 149–150
Dominican Republic, **II**:151–153, 154–155, 158–159
Ecuador, **II**:162, 164, 169
Egypt, **I**:136–137, 140, 148
El Salvador, **II**:171–173, 174, 179–180
Equatorial Guinea, **I**:151–153, 154, 156–157
Eritrea, **I**:156–157, 162, 165
Estonia, **IV**:119–120, 121, 125
Ethiopia, **I**:168–169, 171–172, 177–178
Fiji, **III**:128, 130, 133–134
Finland, **IV**:127–129, 131–132, 138–139
France, **IV**:143–144, 146–147, 154
French Antilles and French Guiana, **II**:182–183, 184–185, 190
French Polynesia, **III**:135–137, 138, 141
Gabon, **I**:180, 182, 185–186
The Gambia, **I**:187–188, 189–190, 193
Georgia, **IV**:155–157, 158–159, 163
Germany, **IV**:167, 170–171, 178
Ghana, **I**:195–197, 198–199, 203

Greece, **IV:**180–181, 183–184, 192

Grenada, **II:**191–192, 194, 197

Guatemala, **II:**200–201, 202–203, 207–208

Guinea, **I:**205–207, 209, 212–213

Guinea-Bissau, **I:**215–217, 218–219, 221

Guyana, **II:**209–210, 212–213, 216

Haiti, **II:**217–219, 220–221, 223–224

Honduras, **II:**225–226, 228–229, 233–234

Hong Kong, **III:**144–145, 148–149, 157

Hungary, **IV:**195–197, 199, 204

Iceland, **IV:**205–207, 208, 213

India, **III:**161–162, 164–165, 170–171

Indonesia, **III:**174–175, 178, 184

Iran, **III:**189–191, 194, 202

Iraq, **III:**203–205, 207, 212

Ireland, **IV:**215–217, 219, 225–226

Israel, **III:**214–215, 217, 222–223

Italy, **IV:**229–230, 234–235, 243

Jamaica, **II:**235–236, 238–239, 244

Japan, **III:**225–228, 230–231, 238–239

Jordan, **III:**241–243, 244, 249

Kazakhstan, **III:**252–253, 255–256, 263–264

Kenya, **I:**224–225, 227–228, 234

Kiribati, **III:**265–266, 268, 270–271

Korea, North, **III:**273–274, 275–276, 279

Korea, South, **III:**281–284, 287, 294–295

Kuwait, **III:**297–298, 299, 302

Kyrgyzstan, **III:**305–307, 308, 313

Laos, **III:**316–317, 318–319, 323

Latvia, **IV:**246–247, 248–249, 253–254

Lebanon, **III:**326–327, 329–330, 334

Lesotho, **I:**236–237, 238, 241–242

Liberia, **I:**243–244, 246–247, 250

Libya, **I:**251–253, 254–255, 258–259

Liechtenstein, **IV:**256, 258, 261

Lithuania, **IV:**263–265, 267–268, 273

Luxembourg, **IV:**276–277, 279, 284

Macau, **III:**335–336, 337–338, 341

Macedonia, **IV:**285–286, 288, 291

Madagascar, **I:**261–262, 264, 267

Malawi, **I:**270, 272, 275–276

Malaysia, **III:**344–345, 348–349, 356

Maldives, **III:**359–360, 362–363, 365–366

Mali, **I:**278–279, 280, 284

Malta, **IV:**293–294, 295–296, 298–299

Marshall Islands, **III:**367–368, 369–370, 373

Mauritania, **I:**285–287, 288–289, 291–292

Mauritius, **I:**293–294, 296, 300

Mexico, **II:**246–248, 250, 258

Micronesia, **III:**375–377, 378–379, 381–382

Moldova, **IV:**301–302, 304, 307–308

Monaco, **IV:**310, 312, 314

Mongolia, **III:**383–385, 386, 390

Morocco, **I:**303–305, 306–307, 312

Mozambique, **I:**315, 317–318, 324

Namibia, **I:**327–329, 331, 334–335

Nauru, **III:**391–392, 393, 395–396

Nepal, **III:**398–399, 401, 407–408

Netherlands, **IV:**317, 320–321, 328–329

Netherlands Antilles and Aruba, **II:**263, 265, 270

New Zealand, **III:**409–411, 412–413, 418

Nicaragua, **II:**271–272, 273, 277

Niger, **I:**337–339, 341, 344–345

Nigeria, **I:**348–351, 355–356, 362

Norway, **IV:**333, 336, 340

Oman, **III:**419–420, 422, 427

Pakistan, **III:**431–432, 435–436, 443–444

Palau, **III:**445–446, 447–448, 450

Panama, **II:**280–281, 283, 288–289

Papua New Guinea, **III:**453–454, 456, 459

Paraguay, **II:**292–293, 295–296, 301–302

Peru, **II:**304–305, 308, 314

Philippines, **III:**461–463, 465, 472–473

Poland, **IV:**344–345, 348–349, 356–357

Portugal, **IV:**361, 364, 372–373

Puerto Rico, **II:**316, 317–318, 320–321

Qatar, **III:**475–476, 478, 481–482

Romania, **IV:**375–377, 379–380, 385

Russia, **IV:**389–390, 393–394, 401–402

Rwanda, **I:**365–366, 367–368, 371

St. Kitts and Nevis, **II:**324, 325–326, 329

St. Lucia, **II:**331–332, 333–334, 337

St. Vincent and the Grenadines, **II:**339–340, 342, 345–346

Samoa, **III:**483–484, 485, 488–489

San Marino, **IV:**405–406, 407–408, 410

São Tomé and Príncipe, **I:**373–374, 376, 378

Saudi Arabia, **III:**492–494, 497–498, 504–505

Senegal, **I:**381–383, 384–385, 391

Seychelles, **I:**393–394, 395–396, 398

Sierra Leone, **I:**401–402, 404, 408

Singapore, **III:**508–509, 510–511, 516

Slovakia, **IV:**411–413, 414–415, 419–420

Slovenia, **IV:**421–423, 424, 429

Solomon Islands, **III:**519–520, 522, 525

Somalia, **I:**410–411, 413, 416

South Africa, **I:**418–419, 421–422, 429

Spain, **IV:**432–435, 438–439, 445

Sri Lanka, **III:**528–529, 532, 537–538

Sudan, **I:**431–433, 435–436, 440

Suriname, **II:**347–348, 349, 352–353

Swaziland, **I:**441–442, 443–444, 447

Sweden, **IV:**448–449, 451–452, 457–458

Switzerland, **IV:**460–461, 465, 472

Syria, **III:**539–541, 542–543, 549

Taiwan, **III:**552–553, 556–557, 565–566

Tajikistan, **III:**567–568, 569–570, 574–575

Tanzania, **I:**451, 453, 460

Thailand, **III:**577–579, 582–583, 592–593

Togo, **I:**463–465, 467, 470

Tonga, **III:**595–596, 597, 600–601

Trinidad and Tobago, **II:**355–356, 357–358, 361–362

Tunisia, **I:**473–474, 475–476, 480

Turkey, **III:**604–605, 608, 618

Turkmenistan, **III:**621–622, 624–625, 629

Tuvalu, **III:**632, 634, 636

Uganda, **I:**484–485, 487–488, 493

Ukraine, **IV:**475–477, 479, 485

United Arab Emirates, **III:**637–639, 640–641, 645–646

United Kingdom, **IV:**489–490, 493–494, 501

United States, **II:**365–366, 368–369, 377–378

Uruguay, **II:**382–383, 385, 389

Uzbekistan, **III:**647–649, 651–652, 656

Vanuatu, **III:**657–658, 659–660, 663

Vatican City, **IV:**505–507, 509

Venezuela, **II:**391–393, 394–395, 401

Vietnam, **III:**665–667, 669, 674–675

Yemen, **III:**677–679, 680, 683

Yugoslavia, **IV:**512–513, 514, 518

Zambia, **I:**495–497, 499, 503–504

Zimbabwe, **I:**506–507, 509, 513–514

See also specific economic sectors

Ecuador, **II:161–170**

Education

    Bangladesh, **III:**52–53

Education (*continued*)

　Belgium, **IV:**58–59

　Benin, **I:**26

　Bhutan, **III:**63

　Botswana, **I:**34

　Burkina Faso, **I:**44

　Burma, **III:**82, 83

　Burundi, **I:**52

　Cape Verde, **I:**72

　Colombia, **II:**117

　Comoros, **I:**93

　Congo, Republic of the, **I:**114

　Croatia, **IV:**91

　Djibouti, **I:**133

　Ecuador, **II:**167

　Egypt, **I:**146

　El Salvador, **II:**178

　Eritrea, **I:**164

　Georgia, **IV:**162

　Greece, **IV:**189–190

　Guatemala, **II:**206

　Guinea, **I:**211

　Guinea-Bissau, **I:**221

　Hong Kong, **III:**154–155

　Indonesia, **III:**183

　Iran, **III:**201

　Japan, **III:**236

　Korea, North, **III:**278

　Korea, South, **III:**292

　Liberia, **I:**249

　Luxembourg, **IV:**283

　Madagascar, **I:**267

　Malaysia, **III:**355

　Mexico, **II:**256

　Micronesia, **III:**380

　Netherlands Antilles and Aruba, **II:**269

　Niger, **I:**344

　Paraguay, **II:**292

　Peru, **II:**312

　Poland, **IV:**355

　Romania, **IV:**383

　São Tomé and Príncipe, **I:**378

　Saudi Arabia, **III:**503

　Sierra Leone, **I:**407

　Singapore, **III:**514

　Sudan, **I:**439

　Thailand, **III:**589, 591

　Togo, **I:**469

　Venezuela, **II:**399

　Vietnam, **III:**674

　Yemen, **III:**682

Egypt, **I:135–149**

"8-7 Plan," China, **III:**108

Ejidos, **II:**251

El Salvador, **II:171–180**

Elections. *See* Politics and government

Electricity. *See* Energy production and consumption; Hydroelectric power

Electronics manufacturing

　Belgium, **IV:**55

　Canada, **II:**85

　Estonia, **IV:**122

　Finland, **IV:**133–134

　Germany, **IV:**173

　Hong Kong, **III:**150

　Japan, **III:**232

　Malaysia, **III:**350–351

　Netherlands, **IV:**322

　Singapore, **III:**512

　Thailand, **III:**585

Emigration. *See* Country overviews; Expatriate and overseas workers

Employment. *See* Labor force; Poverty and wealth; Working conditions

Employment Promotion Measures law (Taiwan), **III:**563

Employment Services Act (Taiwan), **III:**563

Empty Quarter, **III:**499

Energy production and consumption

　Afghanistan, **III:**5

　Albania, **IV:**3

　Algeria, **I:**5

　Angola, **I:**18

　Antigua and Barbuda, **II:**4

　Argentina, **II:**14

　Armenia, **IV:**19

　Australia, **III:**15

　Austria, **IV:**29

　Azerbaijan, **III:**27

　The Bahamas, **II:**27

　Bahrain, **III:**35

　Bangladesh, **III:**46

　Barbados, **II:**35

　Belarus, **IV:**40

　Belgium, **IV:**52

　Belize, **II:**44

　Benin, **I:**24

　Bhutan, **III:**60, 61

　Bosnia and Herzegovina, **IV:**66

　Botswana, **I:**31

　Brazil, **II:**66–67

　Bulgaria, **IV:**74

　Burkina Faso, **I:**41

　Burma, **III:**77

　Burundi, **I:**49

　Cambodia, **III:**88

　Cameroon, **I:**59

　Canada, **II:**81

　Cape Verde, **I:**70

　Central African Republic, **I:**77

　Chad, **I:**86

　Chile, **II:**97

　China, **III:**99–100

　Colombia, **II:**112

　Comoros, **I:**93

　Congo, Democratic Republic of the, **I:**103

　Congo, Republic of the, **I:**111

　Costa Rica, **II:**124

　Côte d'Ivoire, **I:**121

　Croatia, **IV:**87, 88–89

　Cuba, **II:**137

　Czech Republic, **IV:**98

　Denmark, **IV:**109–110, 112

　Djibouti, **I:**130

　Dominican Republic, **II:**154

　Egypt, **I:**139

　El Salvador, **II:**174

　Equatorial Guinea, **I:**154

　Eritrea, **I:**162

　Estonia, **IV:**121

　Ethiopia, **I:**171

　Fiji, **III:**130

　Finland, **IV:**131

　France, **IV:**146

　French Antilles and French Guiana, **II:**184

　Gabon, **I:**182

　The Gambia, **I:**189

　Georgia, **IV:**157–158

　Germany, **IV:**169–170

　Ghana, **I:**198

　Greece, **IV:**183

　Guatemala, **II:**202

　Guinea, **I:**208

　Guinea-Bissau, **I:**218

　Haiti, **II:**220

　Hong Kong, **III:**148, 151

　Hungary, **IV:**198

　Iceland, **IV:**209–210

　India, **III:**163–164, 165–166

　Indonesia, **III:**178

　Iran, **III:**193

　Iraq, **III:**207

　Ireland, **IV:**219

　Israel, **III:**216

　Italy, **IV:**234

　Jamaica, **II:**238

　Japan, **III:**230

　Jordan, **III:**244

　Kazakhstan, **III:**257

　Kenya, **I:**227

　Kiribati, **III:**268

　Korea, North, **III:**275

　Korea, South, **III:**286

　Kuwait, **III:**298–299

Kyrgyzstan, **III:**307–308
Laos, **III:**318, 320
Latvia, **IV:**248
Lebanon, **III:**329
Liberia, **I:**246
Libya, **I:**252
Liechtenstein, **IV:**258
Lithuania, **IV:**267
Luxembourg, **IV:**277
Macau, **III:**337
Macedonia, **IV:**287
Madagascar, **I:**264
Malawi, **I:**271–272
Malaysia, **III:**348
Maldives, **III:**362
Mali, **I:**280
Malta, **IV:**295
Marshall Islands, **III:**369
Mauritania, **I:**288
Mauritius, **I:**295–296
Mexico, **II:**249
Micronesia, **III:**378
Moldova, **IV:**303–304
Mongolia, **III:**386
Morocco, **I:**306
Mozambique, **I:**317
Namibia, **I:**330, 332
Nepal, **III:**400–401
Netherlands, **IV:**320
Netherlands Antilles and Aruba,
　II:265
New Zealand, **III:**412
Niger, **I:**340–341
Nigeria, **I:**355
Norway, **IV:**335
Pakistan, **III:**434
Palau, **III:**447
Panama, **II:**283
Paraguay, **II:**295, 296–297
Peru, **II:**307–308
Philippines, **III:**465
Poland, **IV:**348
Portugal, **IV:**363–364
Puerto Rico, **II:**317
Qatar, **III:**477
Romania, **IV:**379
Russia, **IV:**393, 395–396
Rwanda, **I:**367
São Tomé and Príncipe, **I:**376
Saudi Arabia, **III:**497
Senegal, **I:**384
Seychelles, **I:**395
Sierra Leone, **I:**404
Singapore, **III:**510
Slovakia, **IV:**414
Slovenia, **IV:**424
Solomon Islands, **III:**521

Somalia, **I:**413
South Africa, **I:**424
Spain, **IV:**437
Sri Lanka, **III:**531
Sudan, **I:**435
Suriname, **II:**349
Swaziland, **I:**443
Sweden, **IV:**451
Switzerland, **IV:**463–464
Syria, **III:**542
Tajikistan, **III:**569, 571
Tanzania, **I:**453
Thailand, **III:**582
Togo, **I:**466–467
Trinidad and Tobago, **II:**357
Tunisia, **I:**475
Turkey, **III:**608
Turkmenistan, **III:**624
Uganda, **I:**487
Ukraine, **IV:**479
United Arab Emirates, **III:**640
United Kingdom, **IV:**493, 495
United States, **II:**368, 371
Uruguay, **II:**384–385
Uzbekistan, **III:**650–651
Vanuatu, **III:**659
Venezuela, **II:**394
Vietnam, **III:**668, 670
Yemen, **III:**679–680
Yugoslavia, **IV:**514
Zambia, **I:**498
Zimbabwe, **I:**508
England. *See* United Kingdom
Enhanced Structural Adjustment
　Facilities, Burkina Faso, **I:**38
Enterprise exit processes, Lithuania,
　IV:273
Environmental issues
　Australia, **III:**17, 23
　Belgium, **IV:**51
　Canada, **II:**84
　China, **III:**113–114
　Denmark, **IV:**109, 111
　El Salvador, **II:**178
　Finland, **IV:**134, 139
　French Antilles and French Guiana,
　　II:186
　Kiribati, **III:**267
　Maldives, **III:**360
　Micronesia, **III:**382
　Nauru, **III:**393
　Philippines, **III:**466
　Russia, **IV:**394
　Taiwan, **III:**559
　Thailand, **III:**593
　Uruguay, **II:**385–386
　Yugoslavia, **IV:**515

See also Deforestation and
　desertification
Equatorial Guinea, **I:151–157**
Eritrea, **I:159–165,** 169–170
Escudo (money), **I:**71
Estonia, **IV:119–125**
Estrada, Joseph, **III:**462–463
ETA (terrorist group), **IV:**434–435,
　445
Ethiopia, **I:167–178**
Ethiopian People's Revolutionary
　Democratic Front, **I:**170
Ethnic groups. *See* Country
　overviews
Ethnic violence. *See* Terrorism; War
　and civil unrest
EU. *See* European Union
Euro (money)
　Andorra, **IV:**14
　Austria, **IV:**34
　Belgium, **IV:**57
　Finland, **IV:**136
　France, **IV:**149, 151
　French Antilles and French Guiana,
　　II:188
　Germany, **IV:**175
　Italy, **IV:**239
　Netherlands, **IV:**325
　Portugal, **IV:**368
European Monetary Union
　Denmark, **IV:**107, 117
　Finland, **IV:**139
　Italy, **IV:**230
　Netherlands, **IV:**325, 328
　Spain, **IV:**434, 441
　Sweden, **IV:**449–450, 457–458
European Union
　agricultural reforms, **IV:**171
　Andorra, **IV:**10–11, 15
　Armenia, **IV:**19
　Austria, **IV:**27
　Belgium, **IV:**49–50, 51, 57, 61
　Cyprus, **III:**124
　Czech Republic, **IV:**103
　Denmark, **IV:**109
　Estonia, **IV:**125
　Finland, **IV:**129–130, 133, 139
　food bans, **IV:**33
　France, **IV:**144, 150
　French Antilles and French Guiana,
　　II:188
　Greece, **IV:**181, 187
　Iceland, **IV:**206–207, 211
　insurance industry, **IV:**56
　Ireland, **IV:**217–218, 219
　Italy, **IV:**235
　Latvia, **IV:**253–254

European Union (*continued*)
Liechtenstein, **IV:**261
Lithuania, **IV:**265, 270
Luxembourg, **IV:**278, 281–282, 284
Macedonia, **IV:**286
Malta, **IV:**293, 299
Mexico, **II:**254
Monaco, **IV:**314
Netherlands, **IV:**324, 325
Norway, **IV:**333, 334
Poland, **IV:**345
Portugal, **IV:**361, 372–373
preferential treatment, banana
industry, **II:**331, 339–340, 342
Romania, **IV:**377, 385
Slovenia, **IV:**422
Spain, **IV:**439, 445
Sweden, **IV:**448–449
Switzerland, **IV:**461, 462, 472
Ukraine, **IV:**482
United Kingdom, **IV:**501
university standardization, **IV:**190
See also International trade
Exchange rates. *See* Money; *specific currencies*
Exclusive Economic Zones
Cape Verde, **I:**70
Maldives, **III:**363
Namibia, **I:**331
New Zealand, **III:**414
São Tomé and Príncipe, **I:**376
Vanuatu, **III:**660–661
Expatriate and overseas workers
Indonesia, **III:**183–184
Kuwait, **III:**302–303
Philippines, **III:**471
Tonga, **III:**595–596
United Arab Emirates, **III:**638, 645
Yemen, **III:**679
Export Processing Zones
Bangladesh, **III:**49
Mauritius, **I:**293–294, 297
Exports. *See* International trade
Extremist group activity. *See* Terrorism
Eyadema, Gnassingbé, **I:**465, 466

F

Facusse, Carlos Flores, **II:**227
Fahd, King, **III:**495
Fanmi Lavalas Party (Haiti), **II:**219
Farmland. *See* Agriculture; Land reform
Faroe Islands, **IV:**117–118
Federal Reserve, United States, **II:**366, 373–374
Fertilizer production, Poland, **IV:**350

Fianna Fáil Party (Ireland), **IV:**217
FIAT (company), **IV:**236–237
Fiji, **III:127–134**
Financial services
Afghanistan, **III:**7
Albania, **IV:**5
Algeria, **I:**7–8
Antigua and Barbuda, **II:**5
Argentina, **II:**17
Armenia, **IV:**21
Australia, **III:**19
Austria, **IV:**32–33
Azerbaijan, **III:**29
Bahrain, **III:**36–37
Bangladesh, **III:**49
Barbados, **II:**37
Belarus, **IV:**42
Belgium, **IV:**55–56
Belize, **II:**45–46
Benin, **I:**25
Bhutan, **III:**62
Bolivia, **II:**56, 57
Bosnia and Herzegovina, **IV:**67
Botswana, **I:**32–33
Brazil, **II:**70–71
Brunei Darussalam, **III:**69–70
Bulgaria, **IV:**76
Burkina Faso, **I:**43
Burma, **III:**80
Cambodia, **III:**90
Cameroon, **I:**62
Canada, **II:**86
Cape Verde, **I:**71
Central African Republic, **I:**79
Chad, **I:**88
Chile, **II:**102
Colombia, **II:**114–115
Congo, Democratic Republic of the, **I:**104
Congo, Republic of the, **I:**113
Costa Rica, **II:**127
Côte d'Ivoire, **I:**123
Cyprus, **III:**121–122
Czech Republic, **IV:**100
Denmark, **IV:**113
Dominica, **II:**147
Egypt, **I:**143
El Salvador, **II:**176
Eritrea, **I:**163
Estonia, **IV:**122
Ethiopia, **I:**174
Fiji, **III:**131
Finland, **IV:**135
France, **IV:**149
French Polynesia, **III:**139
Georgia, **IV:**160
Germany, **IV:**174

Ghana, **I:**200
Greece, **IV:**188
Grenada, **II:**195
Guinea, **I:**210
Guinea-Bissau, **I:**220
Honduras, **II:**230
Hong Kong, **III:**151
Hungary, **IV:**200–201
Iceland, **IV:**210, 211
India, **III:**166
Indonesia, **III:**180
Iran, **III:**197
Iraq, **III:**209
Ireland, **IV:**221
Israel, **III:**218
Italy, **IV:**238
Jamaica, **II:**241
Japan, **III:**233–234
Jordan, **III:**246
Kazakhstan, **III:**258–259
Kenya, **I:**230
Kiribati, **III:**269
Korea, North, **III:**277
Korea, South, **III:**289
Kuwait, **III:**300
Kyrgyzstan, **III:**309
Laos, **III:**321
Latvia, **IV:**250
Lebanon, **III:**331
Lesotho, **I:**240
Liberia, **I:**248
Libya, **I:**256
Liechtenstein, **IV:**259
Lithuania, **IV:**269
Luxembourg, **IV:**280–281
Macau, **III:**339
Macedonia, **IV:**288–289
Madagascar, **I:**265
Malawi, **I:**273
Malaysia, **III:**351, 353
Mali, **I:**281
Malta, **IV:**297
Marshall Islands, **III:**371
Mauritania, **I:**289
Mauritius, **I:**297
Mexico, **II:**253
Moldova, **IV:**305
Monaco, **IV:**313
Morocco, **I:**309
Mozambique, **I:**320
Namibia, **I:**332
Nauru, **III:**394
Nepal, **III:**403
Netherlands, **IV:**323
Netherlands Antilles and Aruba, **II:**267
New Zealand, **III:**415

Nicaragua, **II**:275
Niger, **I**:342
Nigeria, **I**:358
Norway, **IV**:337
Oman, **III**:424
Pakistan, **III**:439
Palau, **III**:448
Panama, **II**:284–285
Paraguay, **II**:298
Peru, **II**:310–311
Philippines, **III**:469
Poland, **IV**:351–352
Portugal, **IV**:366–367
Puerto Rico, **II**:319
Qatar, **III**:479
Romania, **IV**:381
Russia, **IV**:396–397
Rwanda, **I**:368–369
St. Kitts and Nevis, **II**:327
St. Lucia, **II**:335
St. Vincent and the Grenadines, **II**:343
Samoa, **III**:487
San Marino, **IV**:408–409
São Tomé and Príncipe, **I**:377
Saudi Arabia, **III**:501
Senegal, **I**:386–387
Seychelles, **I**:397
Sierra Leone, **I**:405
Singapore, **III**:512–513
Slovakia, **IV**:416
Slovenia, **IV**:425
Solomon Islands, **III**:523
Somalia, **I**:414
South Africa, **I**:425
Spain, **IV**:440–441
Sri Lanka, **III**:534
Suriname, **II**:350–351
Sweden, **IV**:452–453
Switzerland, **IV**:466
Syria, **III**:546
Taiwan, **III**:560
Tajikistan, **III**:571–572
Tanzania, **I**:456
Thailand, **III**:586
Togo, **I**:468
Tonga, **III**:598
Trinidad and Tobago, **II**:360
Tunisia, **I**:477
Turkey, **III**:612–613
Turkmenistan, **III**:626
Uganda, **I**:490
Ukraine, **IV**:481–482
United Arab Emirates, **III**:642
United Kingdom, **IV**:496
United States, **II**:371–372, 373
Uruguay, **II**:386

Uzbekistan, **III**:653
Venezuela, **II**:397
Vietnam, **III**:670
Yemen, **III**:681
Yugoslavia, **IV**:515
Zambia, **I**:501
Zimbabwe, **I**:510
See also Money
Fine Gael Party (Ireland), **IV**:217
Finland, **IV:127–140**
First era, Sri Lanka economy, **III**:529
First Republic, Zambia, **I**:497
Fishing and aquaculture
Algeria, **I**:7
Angola, **I**:17
Antigua and Barbuda, **II**:5
Argentina, **II**:15–16
Austria, **IV**:32
The Bahamas, **II**:28
Bahrain, **III**:36
Bangladesh, **III**:48
Belgium, **IV**:54
Brunei Darussalam, **III**:68
Burkina Faso, **I**:42
Burma, **III**:79
Cambodia, **III**:89
Canada, **II**:84
Cape Verde, **I**:70
Chile, **II**:99
China, **III**:102
Comoros, **I**:94
Côte d'Ivoire, **I**:122
Croatia, **IV**:88
Cyprus, **III**:120
Denmark, **IV**:111
Djibouti, **I**:131
Dominica, **II**:147
Dominican Republic, **II**:155
Equatorial Guinea, **I**:154–155
Eritrea, **I**:163
Fiji, **III**:131
France, **IV**:143, 148
French Antilles and French Guiana, **II**:185–186
The Gambia, **I**:190
Greece, **IV**:184
Guinea, **I**:209
Guinea-Bissau, **I**:219
Honduras, **II**:229
Hong Kong, **III**:149–150
Iceland, **IV**:209
Indonesia, **III**:179
Iran, **III**:195
Ireland, **IV**:220
Jamaica, **II**:239
Japan, **III**:232

Kiribati, **III**:268, 270
Korea, North, **III**:276
Korea, South, **III**:288
Kuwait, **III**:300
Libya, **I**:255
Madagascar, **I**:265
Maldives, **III**:363
Mali, **I**:281
Marshall Islands, **III**:370
Micronesia, **III**:376, 381–382
Morocco, **I**:307–308
Namibia, **I**:331
Netherlands, **IV**:322
New Zealand, **III**:414
Nicaragua, **II**:274
Oman, **III**:423
Pakistan, **III**:437
Palau, **III**:448
Peru, **II**:309–310
Philippines, **III**:466
St. Vincent and the Grenadines, **II**:343
Samoa, **III**:486
São Tomé and Príncipe, **I**:376
Senegal, **I**:386
Seychelles, **I**:396
Solomon Islands, **III**:522–523
Somalia, **I**:413–414
Spain, **IV**:440
Sri Lanka, **III**:533
Sudan, **I**:436
Suriname, **II**:350
Taiwan, **III**:558, 559
Thailand, **III**:584
Tonga, **III**:598
Tunisia, **I**:476
Tuvalu, **III**:634
United Arab Emirates, **III**:641
United Kingdom, **IV**:494
United States, **II**:370
Uruguay, **II**:385–386
Vanuatu, **III**:660–661
Vietnam, **III**:669
Yemen, **III**:680–681
Five year plans, Saudi Arabia, **III**:493
"Flag of convenience"
Liberia, **I**:248
Panama, **II**:282–283
Vanuatu, **III**:659
"Flatted factories," Hong Kong, **III**:150
Flemish-Walloon disputes, **IV**:48
Flexible work schedules, United Kingdom, **IV**:499
Flotas, **II**:53
Folketing, **IV**:107

Food bans, Austria, **IV**:33

Food processing
   Argentina, **II**:16
   Armenia, **IV**:21
   Bangladesh, **III**:49
   Cameroon, **I**:62
   Finland, **IV**:134
   Ireland, **IV**:221
   Italy, **IV**:237
   Maldives, **III**:363
   Pakistan, **III**:438
   Thailand, **III**:584–585
   Uzbekistan, **III**:653

Food service. *See* Retail, wholesale, and food services

Food shortages. *See* Agriculture; Poverty and wealth

Forced labor. *See* Working conditions

Ford-Volkswagen joint venture, Portugal, **IV**:366

Foreign aid. *See* Economic overviews and trends; Politics and government

Foreign debt. *See* Debt

Foreign direct investment. *See* Economic overviews and trends; International trade

Foreign exchange adjustment centers, China, **III**:106

Forestry
   Argentina, **II**:16
   Austria, **IV**:31
   Bangladesh, **III**:48
   Belgium, **IV**:54
   Belize, **II**:45
   Bhutan, **III**:61
   Brunei Darussalam, **III**:68, 79
   Burkina Faso, **I**:42
   Cambodia, **III**:89
   Cameroon, **I**:60
   Central African Republic, **I**:79
   Chile, **II**:99
   China, **III**:101–102
   Congo, Republic of the, **I**:112
   Côte d'Ivoire, **I**:122
   Croatia, **IV**:88
   Denmark, **IV**:111
   Equatorial Guinea, **I**:154
   Fiji, **III**:130–131
   Finland, **IV**:133, 139
   France, **IV**:148
   Gabon, **I**:183
   Germany, **IV**:171
   Ghana, **I**:200
   Guinea-Bissau, **I**:219
   Hungary, **IV**:200
   Indonesia, **III**:179
      Ireland, **IV**:220
      Japan, **III**:231–232
      Korea, South, **III**:287–288
      Laos, **III**:319–320
      Latvia, **IV**:250
      Liberia, **I**:247
      Lithuania, **IV**:269
      Luxembourg, **IV**:280
      Malaysia, **III**:349–350
      New Zealand, **III**:413–414
      Nicaragua, **II**:274
      Pakistan, **III**:437
      Panama, **II**:284
      Papua New Guinea, **III**:456
      Peru, **II**:309
      Samoa, **III**:486
      São Tomé and Príncipe, **I**:376
      Solomon Islands, **III**:522
      South Africa, **I**:422
      Suriname, **II**:350
      Swaziland, **I**:444
      Thailand, **III**:584
      United Kingdom, **IV**:494
      United States, **II**:370
      Vanuatu, **III**:660
      Vietnam, **III**:669

Forza Italia, **IV**:231

Franc (money)
   Congo, Democratic Republic of the, **I**:105
   Madagascar, **I**:266
   Rwanda, **I**:369
   See also CFA franc (money)

"Franc Zone." *See* CFA franc (money)

France, **IV**:141–154

Franchising, Austria, **IV**:33

Franco, Francisco, **IV**:432–433

Free trade agreements and zones. *See* International trade

French Antilles and French Guiana, **II**:181–190

French Polynesia, **III**:135–141

Frente de Libertacao de Mocambique (Mozambique), **I**:315, 316

Frente Farabundo Marti para la Liberacion Nacional (El Salvador), **II**:173

Friendship Bridge (Laos), **III**:317–318

Fruit production
   Belize, **II**:44
   Chile, **II**:98–99
   New Zealand, **III**:413
   Taiwan, **III**:558
   Turkey, **III**:609–610

Fujimori, Alberto, **II**:306

Furniture manufacturing
   Belgium, **IV**:55
   Malaysia, **III**:351
   Taiwan, **III**:560

G

Gabon, **I**:179–186

The Gambia, **I**:187–193

Gambling
   The Bahamas, **II**:29
   Macau, **III**:336, 339

García, Alán, **II**:306

Garment industry
   Bangladesh, **III**:49
   Cambodia, **III**:89
   Italy, **IV**:237

Gas. *See* Oil and gas industry

Gasoline stations, Poland, **IV**:351

Gayoom, Maumon Abdul, **III**:361

Gaza Strip, **III**:213, 223

Gbagbo, Laurent, **I**:119

GDP. *See* Gross Domestic Product (GDP)

General Confederation of Greek Workers, **IV**:191

Genetic research, Iceland, **IV**:210

Geographic information. *See* Country overviews; Maps

Georgia, **IV**:155–163

Geothermal energy, Iceland, **IV**:209–210

Germany, **IV**:165–178

Ghana, **I**:195–204

Gini index. *See* Poverty and wealth

Glassmaking, Belgium, **IV**:54

Gold mining
   Burkina Faso, **I**:42
   Congo, Democratic Republic of the, **I**:104
   French Antilles and French Guiana, **II**:186
   Ghana, **I**:200
   Guinea, **I**:210
   Kyrgyzstan, **III**:309
   Papua New Guinea, **III**:457
   Solomon Islands, **III**:523
   South Africa, **I**:424
   Suriname, **II**:350
   Uzbekistan, **III**:652

Gorbachev, Mikhail, **IV**:391

Gourde (money), **II**:222

Government. *See* Politics and government

Great Britain. *See* United Kingdom

Greece, **IV**:179–193

Green Party (Ukraine), **IV**:477

Greenland, **IV**:117

Grenada, **II:191–198**

Grenadine Islands. *See* St. Vincent and the Grenadines

Gross Domestic Product (GDP)

Afghanistan, **III:**5*f*, 8*t*

Albania, **IV:**4*f*, 6*t*

Algeria, **I:**6*f*, 9*t*

Andorra, **IV:**14*t*

Angola, **I:**16*f*, 19*t*

Antigua and Barbuda, **II:**4*f*, 6*t*

Argentina, **II:**14*f*, 20*t*

Armenia, **IV:**19*f*, 22*t*

Australia, **III:**15*f*, 20*t*

Austria, **IV:**30*f*, 34*t*

Azerbaijan, **III:**28*f*, 30*t*

The Bahamas, **II:**28*f*, 30*t*

Bahrain, **III:**36*f*, 37*t*

Bangladesh, **III:**46*f*, 51*t*

Barbados, **II:**36*f*, 38*t*

Belarus, **IV:**40*f*, 43*t*

Belgium, **IV:**52*f*, 58*t*

Belize, **II:**44*f*, 46*t*

Benin, **I:**24*f*, 26*t*

Bhutan, **III:**60*f*, 62*t*

Bolivia, **II:**54*f*, 57*t*

Bosnia and Herzegovina, **IV:**66*f*, 68*t*

Botswana, **I:**32*f*, 33*t*

Brazil, **II:**67*f*, 72*t*

Brunei Darussalam, **III:**68*f*, 71*t*

Bulgaria, **IV:**75*f*, 78*t*

Burkina Faso, **I:**41*f*, 44*t*

Burma, **III:**77*f*, 81*t*

Burundi, **I:**50*f*, 52*t*

Cambodia, **III:**89*f*, 91*t*

Cameroon, **I:**59*f*, 64*t*

Canada, **II:**82*f*, 88*t*

Cape Verde, **I:**70*f*, 72*t*

Central African Republic, **I:**78*f*, 80*t*

Chad, **I:**86*f*, 88*t*

Chile, **II:**98*f*, 104*t*

China, **III:**100*f*, 107*t*

Colombia, **II:**112*f*, 116*t*

Comoros, **I:**94*f*, 95*t*

Congo, Democratic Republic of the, **I:**103*f*, 105*t*

Congo, Republic of the, **I:**112*f*, 114*t*

Costa Rica, **II:**124*f*, 129*t*

Côte d'Ivoire, **I:**121*f*, 124*t*

Croatia, **IV:**87*f*, 90*t*

Cuba, **II:**137*f*, 139*t*

Cyprus, **III:**118*f*, 119*f*, 123*t*

Czech Republic, **IV:**98*f*, 101*t*

Denmark, **IV:**110*f*, 114*t*

Djibouti, **I:**130*t*, 133*t*

Dominica, **II:**146*f*, 148*t*

Dominican Republic, **II:**154*f*, 157*t*

Ecuador, **II:**164*f*, 167*t*

Egypt, **I:**140*f*, 145*t*

El Salvador, **II:**175*f*, 178*t*

Equatorial Guinea, **I:**154*f*, 156*t*

Eritrea, **I:**162*f*, 164*t*

Estonia, **IV:**122*f*, 123*t*

Ethiopia, **I:**171*f*, 176*t*

Fiji, **III:**130*f*, 132*t*

Finland, **IV:**131*f*, 137*t*

France, **IV:**146*f*, 152*t*

French Polynesia, **III:**138*f*, 140*t*

Gabon, **I:**182*f*, 184*t*

The Gambia, **I:**190*f*, 192*t*

Georgia, **IV:**158*f*, 161*t*

Germany, **IV:**170*f*, 176*t*

Ghana, **I:**199*f*, 201*t*

Greece, **IV:**184*f*, 189*t*

Grenada, **II:**194*f*, 196*t*

Guatemala, **II:**203*f*, 205*t*

Guinea, **I:**209*f*, 211*t*

Guinea-Bissau, **I:**219*f*, 220*t*

Guyana, **II:**212*f*, 214*t*

Haiti, **II:**220*f*, 222*t*

Honduras, **II:**228*f*, 232*t*

Hong Kong, **III:**149*f*, 154*t*

Hungary, **IV:**199*f*, 202*t*

Iceland, **IV:**209*f*, 211*t*

India, **III:**164*f*, 168*t*

Indonesia, **III:**178*f*, 182*t*

Iran, **III:**194*f*, 199*t*

Iraq, **III:**207*f*, 210*t*

Ireland, **IV:**219*f*, 223*t*

Israel, **III:**217*f*, 220*t*

Italy, **IV:**234*f*, 240*t*

Jamaica, **II:**238*f*, 242*t*

Japan, **III:**231*f*, 236*t*

Jordan, **III:**244*f*, 247*t*

Kazakhstan, **III:**255*f*, 260*t*

Kenya, **I:**227*f*, 231*t*

Kiribati, **III:**268*f*, 269*t*

Korea, North, **III:**276*f*, 278*t*

Korea, South, **III:**287*f*, 292*t*

Kuwait, **III:**299*f*, 301*t*

Kyrgyzstan, **III:**308*f*, 311*t*

Laos, **III:**318*f*, 322*t*

Latvia, **IV:**249*f*, 251*t*

Lebanon, **III:**329*f*, 332*t*

Lesotho, **I:**238*f*, 240*t*

Liberia, **I:**246*f*, 249*t*

Libya, **I:**254*f*, 257*t*

Liechtenstein, **IV:**260*t*

Lithuania, **IV:**267*f*, 271*t*

Luxembourg, **IV:**279*f*, 282*t*

Macau, **III:**338*f*, 340*t*

Macedonia, **IV:**288*f*, 290*t*

Madagascar, **I:**264*f*, 266*t*

Malawi, **I:**272*f*, 274*t*

Malaysia, **III:**348*f*, 354*t*

Maldives, **III:**362*f*, 365*t*

Mali, **I:**280*f*, 282*t*

Malta, **IV:**296*f*, 298*t*

Marshall Islands, **III:**370*f*, 372*t*

Mauritania, **I:**288*f*, 290*t*

Mauritius, **I:**296*f*, 299*t*

Mexico, **II:**250*f*, 255*t*

Micronesia, **III:**378*f*, 380*t*

Moldova, **IV:**304*f*, 306*t*

Monaco, **IV:**314*t*

Mongolia, **III:**386*f*, 388*t*

Morocco, **I:**307*f*, 310*t*

Mozambique, **I:**317*f*, 322*t*

Namibia, **I:**331*f*, 333*t*

Nauru, **III:**394*t*

Nepal, **III:**401*f*, 405*t*

Netherlands, **IV:**320*f*, 326*t*

Netherlands Antilles and Aruba, **II:**265*f*, 269*t*

New Zealand, **III:**412*f*, 416*t*

Nicaragua, **II:**274*f*, 276*t*

Niger, **I:**341*f*, 343*t*

Nigeria, **I:**355*f*, 360*t*

Norway, **IV:**336*f*, 339*t*

Oman, **III:**422*f*, 425*t*

Pakistan, **III:**435*f*, 441*t*

Palau, **III:**449*t*

Panama, **II:**283*f*, 286*t*

Papua New Guinea, **III:**456*f*, 458*t*

Paraguay, **II:**295*f*, 300*t*

Peru, **II:**308*f*, 312*t*

Philippines, **III:**465*f*, 469*t*

Poland, **IV:**348*f*, 354*t*

Portugal, **IV:**365*f*, 369*t*

Puerto Rico, **II:**317*t*

Qatar, **III:**478*f*, 480*t*

Romania, **IV:**379*f*, 383*t*

Russia, **IV:**393*f*, 399*t*

Rwanda, **I:**368*f*, 369*t*

St. Kitts and Nevis, **II:**325*f*, 328*t*

St. Lucia, **II:**334*f*, 336*t*

St. Vincent and the Grenadines, **II:**342*f*, 344*t*

Samoa, **III:**485*f*, 488*t*

San Marino, **IV:**409*t*

São Tomé and Príncipe, **I:**376*f*, 378*t*

Saudi Arabia, **III:**498*f*, 502*t*

Senegal, **I:**385*f*, 388*t*

Seychelles, **I:**396*f*, 398*t*

Sierra Leone, **I:**404*f*, 406*t*

Singapore, **III:**511*f*, 514*t*

Slovakia, **IV:**414*f*, 418*t*

Slovenia, **IV:**424*f*, 427*t*

Solomon Islands, **III:**522*f*, 524*t*

Somalia, **I:**413*f*, 415*t*

South Africa, **I:**421*f*, 427*t*

Spain, **IV:**438*f*, 442*t*

Gross Domestic Product (GDP)
(*continued*)
Sri Lanka, **III:**532*f,* 535*t*
Sudan, **I:**436*f,* 439*t*
Suriname, **II:**350*f,* 352*t*
Swaziland, **I:**443*f,* 445*t*
Sweden, **IV:**451*f,* 455*t*
Switzerland, **IV:**465*f,* 470*t*
Syria, **III:**543*f,* 547*t*
Taiwan, **III:**556*f,* 563*t*
Tajikistan, **III:**570*f,* 573*t*
Tanzania, **I:**453*f,* 457*t*
Thailand, **III:**582*f,* 588*t*
Togo, **I:**467*f,* 469*t*
Tonga, **III:**597*f,* 599*t*
Trinidad and Tobago, **II:**358*f,* 360*t*
Tunisia, **I:**476*f,* 479*t*
Turkey, **III:**608*f,* 615*t*
Turkmenistan, **III:**624*f,* 627*t*
Tuvalu, **III:**635*t*
Uganda, **I:**487*f,* 491*t*
Ukraine, **IV:**479*f,* 483*t*
United Arab Emirates, **III:**640*f,* 644*t*
United Kingdom, **IV:**493*f,* 498*t*
United States, **II:**368*f,* 374*t*
Uruguay, **II:**385*f,* 387*t*
Uzbekistan, **III:**651*f,* 654*t*
Vanuatu, **III:**659*f,* 662*t*
Venezuela, **II:**394*f,* 399*t*
Vietnam, **III:**669*f,* 672*t*
Yemen, **III:**680*f,* 682*t*
Yugoslavia, **IV:**514*f,* 517*t*
Zambia, **I:**499*f,* 502*t*
Zimbabwe, **I:**509*f,* 512*t*
See also Economic overviews and
trends; *specific economic sectors*
"Gross National Happiness," Bhutan,
III:58
Groundnut production
The Gambia, **I:**190
Senegal, **I:**385
Group of Four, **II:**231
Guadalcanal, **III:**523
Guadeloupe. *See* French Antilles and
French Guiana
Guam, **II:**378
Guaraní (money), **II:**299
Guatemala, **II:199–208**
Guatemalan Republic Front, **II:**201
Guei, Robert, **I:**120
Guinea, **I:205–213**
Guinea-Bissau, **I:215–222**
Gum arabic production
Chad, **I:**87
Sudan, **I:**437
Guyana, **II:209–216**

H
Haider, Jörg, **IV:**28
Haiti, **II:217–224**
Haj, **III:**501
Hamad, Sheikh, **III:**447
Hans Adam II, Prince, **IV:**257
Heads of state. *See* Politics and
government
Health and social welfare programs
Bangladesh, **III:**52
Belgium, **IV:**58
Bhutan, **III:**62–63
Brunei Darussalam, **III:**71
Canada, **II:**88–89
Chile, **II:**104
Costa Rica, **II:**129
Croatia, **IV:**91
Denmark, **IV:**108–109
Ecuador, **II:**167
El Salvador, **II:**178
Finland, **IV:**138–139
Georgia, **IV:**162
Germany, **IV:**165–166, 176–177
Greece, **IV:**189
Hong Kong, **III:**154
Ireland, **IV:**224
Japan, **III:**236
Jordan, **III:**247–248
Kazakhstan, **III:**261–262
Malaysia, **III:**354
Oman, **III:**425
Pakistan, **III:**442
Peru, **II:**312
Philippines, **III:**470
Poland, **IV:**354–355
Romania, **IV:**383
Spain, **IV:**443
Sweden, **IV:**447–448, 455–456
Taiwan, **III:**562–563
Thailand, **III:**558, 559
Turkey, **III:**616
Venezuela, **II:**399–400
See also Poverty and wealth;
Working conditions
High-speed railway, Taiwan, **III:**556
Histadrut, **III:**221
History. *See* Country overviews
HIV. *See* AIDS and HIV
Holocaust victim assets, Switzerland,
IV:469
The Holy See. *See* Vatican City
Honduras, **II:225–234**
Hong Kong, **III:143–158**
"Horizon 2000," Lebanon, **III:**328
Horticulture
Kenya, **I:**228

Netherlands, **IV:**322
South Africa, **I:**423
Spain, **IV:**439
Taiwan, **III:**558
Zambia, **I:**500
Houphouet-Boigny, Felix, **I:**119
House of Commons, United
Kingdom, **IV:**490
House of Lords, United Kingdom,
IV:490
Household consumption
Albania, **IV:**6*t*
Antigua and Barbuda, **II:**7*t*
Argentina, **II:**20*t*
Armenia, **IV:**22*t*
Australia, **III:**21*t*
Austria, **IV:**35*t*
Azerbaijan, **III:**30*t*
The Bahamas, **II:**30*t*
Bahrain, **III:**38*t*
Bangladesh, **III:**52*t*
Belarus, **IV:**44*t*
Belgium, **IV:**58*t*
Belize, **II:**47*t*
Benin, **I:**26*t*
Bolivia, **II:**58*t*
Botswana, **I:**34*t*
Brazil, **II:**73*t*
Bulgaria, **IV:**79*t*
Cameroon, **I:**64*t*
Canada, **II:**88*t*
Chile, **II:**104*t*
Congo, Republic of the, **I:**114*t*
Côte d'Ivoire, **I:**125*t*
Croatia, **IV:**91*t*
Czech Republic, **IV:**102*t*
Denmark, **IV:**115*t*
Dominica, **II:**149*t*
Ecuador, **II:**168*t*
Egypt, **I:**146*t*
Estonia, **IV:**124*t*
Fiji, **III:**133*t*
Finland, **IV:**137*t*
France, **IV:**152*t*
Gabon, **I:**184*t*
Georgia, **IV:**161*t*
Germany, **IV:**176*t*
Greece, **IV:**190*t*
Grenada, **II:**197*t*
Guinea, **I:**212*t*
Hong Kong, **III:**154*t*
Hungary, **IV:**202*t*
Iceland, **IV:**212*t*
Indonesia, **III:**183*t*
Ireland, **IV:**224*t*
Israel, **III:**221*t*
Italy, **IV:**241*t*

Jamaica, II:243t
Japan, III:237t
Jordan, III:248t
Kazakhstan, III:261t
Kenya, I:232t
Korea, South, III:292t
Kyrgyzstan, III:312t
Latvia, IV:252t
Lebanon, III:333t
Lithuania, IV:272t
Luxembourg, IV:283t
Macedonia, IV:290t
Madagascar, I:267t
Malawi, I:275t
Mali, I:283t
Mauritius, I:299t
Mexico, II:256t
Moldova, IV:307t
Mongolia, III:389t
Morocco, I:311t
Nepal, III:406t
Netherlands, IV:327t
New Zealand, III:417t
Nigeria, I:360t
Norway, IV:339t
Oman, III:426t
Pakistan, III:442t
Panama, II:287t
Peru, II:313t
Philippines, III:470t
Poland, IV:355t
Qatar, III:481t
Romania, IV:383t
Russia, IV:400t
St. Kitts and Nevis, II:328t
St. Lucia, II:337t
St. Vincent and the Grenadines, II:345t
Senegal, I:389t
Sierra Leone, I:407t
Singapore, III:515t
Slovakia, IV:418t
Slovenia, IV:427t
Spain, IV:443t
Sri Lanka, III:536t
Swaziland, I:446t
Sweden, IV:456t
Switzerland, IV:470t
Tajikistan, III:573t
Tanzania, I:458t
Thailand, III:588t
Trinidad and Tobago, II:361t
Tunisia, I:479t
Turkey, III:616t
Turkmenistan, III:628t
Ukraine, IV:483t
United Kingdom, IV:499t

United States, II:375t
Uruguay, II:388t
Uzbekistan, III:655t
Venezuela, II:399t
Vietnam, III:673t
Yemen, III:683t
Zambia, I:503t
Zimbabwe, I:512t
Housing. See Poverty and wealth
Hryvnya (money), IV:482
Human Immunodeficiency Virus (HIV). See AIDS and HIV
Human Rights and Democracy Movement (Tonga), III:596
Human rights violations
Afghanistan, III:3–4, 9
Burma, III:75
Equatorial Guinea, I:153
Oman, III:426
Saudi Arabia, III:503
Turkmenistan, III:629
Hungary, IV:195–204
Hurricane Keith, II:48
Hurricane Lenny and Hurricane Georges, II:324, 326
Hurricane Mitch
Honduras, II:225–226, 229, 232, 233
Nicaragua, II:274
Hussein, King, III:243
Hutu-Tutsi conflict, I:365, 366
Hydrocarbons. See Oil and gas industry; Petrochemical industry
Hydroelectric power
Angola, I:18
Bhutan, III:60, 61
Bosnia and Herzegovina, IV:66
Burundi, I:49
Central African Republic, I:77
Chile, II:97
Comoros, I:93
Congo, Democratic Republic of the, I:103
Congo, Republic of the, I:111
Côte d'Ivoire, I:121
Ethiopia, I:171
Ghana, I:198
Kenya, I:227
Kyrgyzstan, III:307–308
Laos, III:318
Nepal, III:400–401
Paraguay, II:295, 296–297
Sri Lanka, III:531
Sudan, I:435
Tajikistan, III:571
Tanzania, I:453, 455
Uganda, I:487

I
Ibn Saud, III:494–495
Ibrahim, Anwar, III:346–347
Iceland, IV:205–213
Ikhwan al-Muslimin, I:138–139
Illegal immigration, Spain, IV:445
Illiteracy. See Education; Poverty and wealth
Immigration. See Country overviews; Expatriate and overseas workers
Imports. See International trade
Income distribution
Algeria, I:9t
Australia, III:21t
Austria, IV:34t
Bangladesh, III:52t
Belarus, IV:43t
Belgium, IV:58t
Bolivia, II:58t
Brazil, II:72t
Bulgaria, IV:79t
Burkina Faso, I:44t
Burundi, I:52t
Cambodia, III:91t
Canada, II:89t
Central African Republic, I:80t
China, III:107t
Colombia, II:117t
Costa Rica, II:129t
Côte d'Ivoire, I:124t
Croatia, IV:91t
Czech Republic, IV:101t
Denmark, IV:115t
Dominican Republic, II:157t
Ecuador, II:167t
Egypt, I:146t
El Salvador, II:178t
Estonia, IV:124t
Ethiopia, I:176t
Finland, IV:137t
France, IV:152t
The Gambia, I:192t
Germany, IV:176t
Ghana, I:202t
Greece, IV:189t
Guatemala, II:206t
Guinea, I:211t
Guinea-Bissau, I:221t
Guyana, II:214t
Honduras, II:232t
Hungary, IV:202t
India, III:168t
Indonesia, III:182t
Ireland, IV:223t
Israel, III:220t
Italy, IV:240t

Income distribution (*continued*)

Jamaica, **II:**242*t*

Japan, **III:**236*t*

Jordan, **III:**248*t*

Kazakhstan, **III:**261*t*

Kenya, **I:**232*t*

Korea, South, **III:**292*t*

Kyrgyzstan, **III:**311*t*

Laos, **III:**323*t*

Latvia, **IV:**251*t*

Lesotho, **I:**241*t*

Lithuania, **IV:**271*t*

Luxembourg, **IV:**282*t*

Madagascar, **I:**266*t*

Malaysia, **III:**354*t*

Mali, **I:**282*t*

Mauritania, **I:**291*t*

Mexico, **II:**255*t*

Moldova, **IV:**306*t*

Mongolia, **III:**389*t*

Morocco, **I:**310*t*

Mozambique, **I:**322*t*

Nepal, **III:**405*t*

Netherlands, **IV:**326*t*

New Zealand, **III:**416*t*

Nicaragua, **II:**276*t*

Niger, **I:**343*t*

Nigeria, **I:**360*t*

Norway, **IV:**339*t*

Pakistan, **III:**441*t*

Panama, **II:**287*t*

Papua New Guinea, **III:**458*t*

Paraguay, **II:**300*t*

Peru, **II:**312*t*

Philippines, **III:**469*t*

Poland, **IV:**354*t*

Portugal, **IV:**370*t*

Romania, **IV:**383*t*

Russia, **IV:**399*t*

Rwanda, **I:**370*t*

St. Lucia, **II:**336*t*

Senegal, **I:**388*t*

Sierra Leone, **I:**406*t*

Slovakia, **IV:**418*t*

Slovenia, **IV:**427*t*

South Africa, **I:**427*t*

Spain, **IV:**442*t*

Sri Lanka, **III:**536*t*

Swaziland, **I:**446*t*

Sweden, **IV:**455*t*

Switzerland, **IV:**470*t*

Tanzania, **I:**458*t*

Thailand, **III:**588*t*

Trinidad and Tobago, **II:**360*t*

Tunisia, **I:**479*t*

Turkey, **III:**615*t*

Turkmenistan, **III:**628*t*

Uganda, **I:**492*t*

Ukraine, **IV:**483*t*

United Kingdom, **IV:**498*t*

United States, **II:**375*t*

Uruguay, **II:**388*t*

Uzbekistan, **III:**654*t*

Venezuela, **II:**399*t*

Vietnam, **III:**673*t*

Yemen, **III:**682*t*

Zambia, **I:**502*t*

Zimbabwe, **I:**512*t*

See also Poverty and wealth

Income tax. *See* Taxation

India, **III:159–171**

Indochina, **III:**666–667

Indonesia, **III:173–185**

Industry. *See* Manufacturing; *specific industries*

Infant mortality. *See* Poverty and wealth

Infitah policy, Egypt, **I:**138

Inflation. *See* Economic overviews and trends; Money

Informal economy. *See* Retail, wholesale, and food services; Working conditions

Information technology

Bulgaria, **IV:**76

Costa Rica, **II:**127

Hong Kong, **III:**144, 157

Mauritius, **I:**297

Singapore, **III:**515

Sweden, **IV:**452

Taiwan, **III:**559

United States, **II:**372

Infrastructure. *See* Airports and airlines; Energy production and consumption; Pipelines; Ports and waterways; Public transportation; Railroads; Roads; Telecommunications; Transportation industry

Insurance industry

Belgium, **IV:**56

China, **III:**106

Egypt, **I:**144

France, **IV:**149

Hong Kong, **III:**151–152

Japan, **III:**234

Korea, South, **III:**289–290

Luxembourg, **IV:**281

Taiwan, **III:**562

Interest rates. *See* Debt; Economic overviews and trends; Money

International Monetary Fund (IMF). *See* Economic overviews and trends; Money

International trade

Afghanistan, **III:**7–8, 7*t*

Albania, **IV:**5

Algeria, **I:**8, 8*t*

Andorra, **IV:**13

Angola, **I:**18

Antigua and Barbuda, **II:**6, 6*t*

Argentina, **II:**18–19, 18*t*

Armenia, **IV:**21–22, 21*t*

Australia, **III:**19–20, 19*t*

Austria, **IV:**33, 33*t*

Azerbaijan, **III:**29, 29*t*

The Bahamas, **II:**29–30, 29*t*

Bahrain, **III:**37, 37*t*

Bangladesh, **III:**50, 50*t*

Barbados, **II:**37–38, 38*t*

Belarus, **IV:**42–43, 42*t*

Belgium, **IV:**56–57

Belize, **II:**46, 46*t*

Benin, **I:**25–26, 25*t*

Bhutan, **III:**62, 62*t*

Bolivia, **II:**56–57, 56*t*

Bosnia and Herzegovina, **IV:**67

Botswana, **I:**33, 33*t*

Brazil, **II:**71, 71*t*

Brunei Darussalam, **III:**70, 70*t*

Bulgaria, **IV:**77, 77*t*

Burkina Faso, **I:**43, 43*t*

Burma, **III:**80–81, 80*t*

Burundi, **I:**51, 51*t*

Cambodia, **III:**90, 90*t*

Cameroon, **I:**63, 63*t*

Canada, **II:**86–87, 86*t*

Cape Verde, **I:**71, 71*t*

Central African Republic, **I:**79–80, 80*t*

Chad, **I:**88–89, 88*t*

Chile, **II:**102–103, 102*t*

China, **III:**104–105, 104*t*

Colombia, **II:**115–116, 115*t*

Comoros, **I:**95, 95*t*

Congo, Democratic Republic of the, **I:**104–105, 104*t*

Congo, Republic of the, **I:**113, 113*t*

Costa Rica, **II:**127–128, 127*t*

Côte d'Ivoire, **I:**123–124, 123*t*

Croatia, **IV:**89–90, 89*t*

Cuba, **II:**138–139

Cyprus, **III:**122, 122*t*

Czech Republic, **IV:**100–101, 100*t*

Denmark, **IV:**113–114, 113*t*

Djibouti, **I:**132, 132*t*

Dominica, **II:**148, 148*t*

Dominican Republic, **II:**156, 156*t*

Ecuador, **II:**166, 166*t*

Egypt, **I:**144, 144*t*

El Salvador, **II:**176–177, 177*t*

Equatorial Guinea, **I:**155, 155*t*

Eritrea, **I:**163–164

Estonia, **IV:**123

Ethiopia, **I:**174–175, 174*t*

Fiji, **III:**131–132, 132*t*

Finland, **IV:**135–136, 135*t*

France, **IV:**150–151, 150*t*

French Antilles and French Guiana, **II:**187–188, 187*t*

French Polynesia, **III:**139, 139*t*

Gabon, **I:**183–184, 183*t*

The Gambia, **I:**191, 191*t*

Georgia, **IV:**160

Germany, **IV:**174–175, 175*t*

Ghana, **I:**201, 201*t*

Greece, **IV:**187–188, 187*t*

Grenada, **II:**195–196, 196*t*

Guatemala, **II:**204, 204*t*

Guinea, **I:**210–211

Guinea-Bissau, **I:**220, 220*t*

Guyana, **II:**213–214, 214*t*

Haiti, **II:**222, 222*t*

Honduras, **II:**230–231, 231*t*

Hong Kong, **III:**152–153, 153*t*

Hungary, **IV:**201, 201*t*

Iceland, **IV:**210–211, 211*t*

India, **III:**167, 167*t*

Indonesia, **III:**181, 181*t*

Iran, **III:**198–199, 198*t*

Iraq, **III:**209–210

Ireland, **IV:**222–223, 222*t*

Israel, **III:**219–220, 219*t*

Italy, **IV:**238–239, 238*t*

Jamaica, **II:**241–242, 241*t*

Japan, **III:**235, 235*t*

Jordan, **III:**246–247, 246*t*

Kazakhstan, **III:**259, 259*t*

Kenya, **I:**230–231, 230*t*

Korea, North, **III:**277

Korea, South, **III:**290–291

Kuwait, **III:**300–301, 301*t*

Kyrgyzstan, **III:**310, 310*t*

Laos, **III:**321–322, 321*t*

Latvia, **IV:**250–251

Lebanon, **III:**332, 332*t*

Lesotho, **I:**240

Liberia, **I:**248, 248*t*

Libya, **I:**256, 256*t*

Liechtenstein, **IV:**259–260

Lithuania, **IV:**269–270

Luxembourg, **IV:**281–282

Macau, **III:**339, 339*t*

Macedonia, **IV:**289

Madagascar, **I:**265–266, 265*t*

Malawi, **I:**273–274, 274*t*

Malaysia, **III:**352–353, 352*t*

Maldives, **III:**364, 364*t*

Mali, **I:**282, 282*t*

Malta, **IV:**297, 297*t*

Marshall Islands, **III:**371

Mauritania, **I:**290, 290*t*

Mauritius, **I:**297–298, 298*t*

Mexico, **II:**253–254, 253*t*

Micronesia, **III:**379–380

Moldova, **IV:**305

Monaco, **IV:**313

Mongolia, **III:**388, 388*t*

Morocco, **I:**309, 309*t*

Mozambique, **I:**320–321, 320*t*

Namibia, **I:**332

Nauru, **III:**394

Nepal, **III:**403–404, 403*t*

Netherlands, **IV:**324–325, 324*t*

Netherlands Antilles and Aruba, **II:**267–268, 268*t*

New Zealand, **III:**415, 415*t*

Nicaragua, **II:**275, 275*t*

Niger, **I:**342–343, 342*t*

Nigeria, **I:**359, 359*t*

Norway, **IV:**337–338, 338*t*

Oman, **III:**424–425, 424*t*

Pakistan, **III:**440, 440*t*

Palau, **III:**448

Panama, **II:**285–286, 285*t*

Papua New Guinea, **III:**457, 457*t*

Paraguay, **II:**298–299, 298*t*

Peru, **II:**311, 311*t*

Philippines, **III:**467–468, 467*t*

Poland, **IV:**352–353, 352*t*

Portugal, **IV:**368, 368*t*

Puerto Rico, **II:**319, 319*t*

Qatar, **III:**479–480, 480*t*

Romania, **IV:**382, 382*t*

Russia, **IV:**397, 397*t*

Rwanda, **I:**369, 369*t*

St. Kitts and Nevis, **II:**327, 327*t*

St. Lucia, **II:**335, 335*t*

St. Vincent and the Grenadines, **II:**343–344, 344*t*

Samoa, **III:**487, 487*t*

San Marino, **IV:**409

São Tomé and Príncipe, **I:**377*t*

Saudi Arabia, **III:**501–502, 501*t*

Senegal, **I:**387–388, 387*t*

Seychelles, **I:**397, 397*t*

Sierra Leone, **I:**405–406, 405*t*

Singapore, **III:**513, 513*t*

Slovakia, **IV:**417

Slovenia, **IV:**426

Solomon Islands, **III:**523–524, 524*t*

Somalia, **I:**414

South Africa, **I:**425–426, 426*t*

Spain, **IV:**441, 441*t*

Sri Lanka, **III:**534–535, 534*t*

Sudan, **I:**438, 438*t*

Suriname, **II:**351, 351*t*

Swaziland, **I:**445, 445*t*

Sweden, **IV:**454, 454*t*

Switzerland, **IV:**467–468, 467*t*

Syria, **III:**546–547, 547*t*

Taiwan, **III:**560–561, 561*t*

Tajikistan, **III:**572, 572*t*

Tanzania, **I:**456–457, 456*t*

Thailand, **III:**586–587, 586*t*

Togo, **I:**468–469, 468*t*

Tonga, **III:**599, 599*t*

Trinidad and Tobago, **II:**359, 359*t*

Tunisia, **I:**478, 478*t*

Turkey, **III:**613–614, 613*t*

Turkmenistan, **III:**626–627

Tuvalu, **III:**635

Uganda, **I:**490–491, 490*t*

Ukraine, **IV:**482, 482*t*

United Arab Emirates, **III:**643, 643*t*

United Kingdom, **IV:**497, 497*t*

United States, **II:**372–373, 373*t*

Uruguay, **II:**387, 387*t*

Uzbekistan, **III:**653–654, 653*t*

Vanuatu, **III:**661–662, 662*t*

Venezuela, **II:**397–398, 398*t*

Vietnam, **III:**671–672, 671*t*

Yemen, **III:**681–682

Yugoslavia, **IV:**516, 516*t*

Zambia, **I:**501–502, 501*t*

Zimbabwe, **I:**511, 511*t*

Internet service. *See* Telecommunications

Investment. *See* Economic overviews and trends; International trade

Investment trust companies, South Korea, **III:**289

Iran, **III:187–202**

Ireland, **IV:215–226**

Iron and steel production

Belgium, **IV:**54

Brazil, **II:**69, 70

Iran, **III:**196

Luxembourg, **IV:**276, 279, 280

Pakistan, **III:**438

Qatar, **III:**479

South Africa, **I:**424–425

Turkey, **III:**611

Venezuela, **II:**396

Irrigation

Egypt, **I:**131

Iran, **III:**194

Laos, **III:**320

Oman, **III:**423

Sudan, **I:**436

Syria, **III:**543

Tunisia, **I:**476

Turkmenistan, **III:**625

Islamic Revolution of 1979, Iran,
   III:190, 191, 192
Islamic Salvation Front (Algeria),
   I:4
Isle of Man, **IV:**501–502
Israel, **III:213–223**
Italy, **IV:227–243**

J

Jamaica, **II:235–244**
Jamaica Labour Party, **II:**236–237
Japan, **III:225–239**
Job protection, Croatia, **IV:**92
Jordan, **III:241–249**
Judicial systems. *See* Politics and
   government
Jute production, Bangladesh,
   III:47–48, 48
JVP (Sri Lanka), **III:**530

K

Kabila, Joseph, **I:**101, 102, 107
Kabila, Laurent, **I:**101–102
Kashmir, **III:**171
Kava production, Vanuatu, **III:**660
Kazakhstan, **III:251–264**
Kenya, **I:223–234**
Kenya African National Union,
   I:225–226
Kenya Railways Corporation, **I:**226
Kerekou, Mathieu, **I:**22–23, 27
Khatami, Mohammed, **III:**192, 202
Khmer Empire, **III:**86
Khmer Rouge, **III:**87
Khomeini, Ayatollah Ruhollah,
   III:191, 192
Kibbutzim, **III:**217
Kidnappings, Yemen, **III:**681
Kiribati, **III:265–271**
Korea, North, **III:273–279**
Korea, South, **III:281–295**
Kuna (money), **IV:**90
Kuomintang, **III:**554
Kurds, **III:**205–206, 210–211
Kuwait, **III:297–303**
Kwacha (money), **I:**502
Kyat (money), **III:**81
Kyrgyzstan, **III:305–313**

L

Labor force
   Afghanistan, **III:**5*f*
   Albania, **IV:**4*f*
   Algeria, **I:**6*f*
   Andorra, **IV:**13*f*
   Angola, **I:**16*f*

Antigua and Barbuda, **II:**4*f*
Argentina, **II:**14*f*
Armenia, **IV:**20*f*
Australia, **III:**16*f*
Austria, **IV:**31*f*
Azerbaijan, **III:**28*f*
The Bahamas, **II:**28*f*
Bahrain, **III:**36*f*
Bangladesh, **III:**47*f*
Barbados, **II:**36*f*
Belgium, **IV:**53*f*
Belize, **II:**44*f*
Bhutan, **III:**61*f*
Brunei Darussalam, **III:**68*f*
Burkina Faso, **I:**41*f*
Burma, **III:**78*f*
Burundi, **I:**50*f*
Cambodia, **III:**89*f*
Cameroon, **I:**60*f*
Canada, **II:**82*f*
Chad, **I:**87*f*
Chile, **II:**98*f*
China, **III:**100*f*
Colombia, **II:**113*f*
Comoros, **I:**94*f*
Congo, Democratic Republic of the,
   I:103*f*
Costa Rica, **II:**125*f*
Cuba, **II:**137*f*
Cyprus, **III:**119*f*
Denmark, **IV:**110*f*
Djibouti, **I:**131*f*
Dominica, **II:**146*f*
Dominican Republic, **II:**154*f*
Ecuador, **II:**164*f*
Egypt, **I:**140*f*
El Salvador, **II:**175*f*
Eritrea, **I:**162*f*
Estonia, **IV:**122*f*
Ethiopia, **I:**171*f*
Fiji, **III:**130*f*
Finland, **IV:**132*f*
France, **IV:**146*f*
French Antilles and French Guiana,
   II:185*f*
French Polynesia, **III:**138*f*
Gabon, **I:**182*f*
The Gambia, **I:**190*f*
Georgia, **IV:**158*f*
Germany, **IV:**170*f*
Ghana, **I:**199*f*
Greece, **IV:**184*f*
Grenada, **II:**194*f*
Guatemala, **II:**203*f*
Guinea, **I:**209*f*
Guinea-Bissau, **I:**219*f*
Haiti, **II:**221*f*

Honduras, **II:**229*f*
Hong Kong, **III:**149*f*
Hungary, **IV:**199*f*
Iceland, **IV:**209*f*
India, **III:**165*f*
Indonesia, **III:**178*f*
Iran, **III:**194*f*
Ireland, **IV:**219*f*
Israel, **III:**217*f*
Italy, **IV:**234*f*
Jamaica, **II:**238*f*
Japan, **III:**231*f*
Jordan, **III:**244*f*
Kazakhstan, **III:**256*f*
Kenya, **I:**227*f*
Korea, North, **III:**276*f*
Korea, South, **III:**287*f*
Kuwait, **III:**299*f*
Kyrgyzstan, **III:**308*f*
Laos, **III:**319*f*
Latvia, **IV:**249*f*
Lebanon, **III:**330*f*
Lesotho, **I:**238*f*
Liberia, **I:**247*f*
Libya, **I:**254*f*
Liechtenstein, **IV:**258*f*
Lithuania, **IV:**268*f*
Luxembourg, **IV:**279*f*
Macau, **III:**338*f*
Malawi, **I:**272*f*
Malaysia, **III:**349*f*
Maldives, **III:**362*f*
Mali, **I:**280*f*
Mauritania, **I:**288*f*
Mauritius, **I:**296*f*
Mexico, **II:**250*f*
Micronesia, **III:**379*f*
Moldova, **IV:**304*f*
Morocco, **I:**307*f*
Mozambique, **I:**317*f*
Namibia, **I:**331*f*
Nepal, **III:**401*f*
Netherlands, **IV:**321*f*
Netherlands Antilles and Aruba,
   II:265*f*
New Zealand, **III:**413*f*
Nicaragua, **II:**274*f*
Niger, **I:**341*f*
Nigeria, **I:**356*f*
Norway, **IV:**336*f*
Pakistan, **III:**436*f*
Panama, **II:**283*f*
Papua New Guinea, **III:**456*f*
Paraguay, **II:**296*f*
Philippines, **III:**465*f*
Poland, **IV:**348*f*
Portugal, **IV:**365*f*

Puerto Rico, **II:**318*f*

Romania, **IV:**379*f*

Russia, **IV:**394*f*

Rwanda, **I:**368*f*

St. Lucia, **II:**334*f*

St. Vincent and the Grenadines, **II:**342*f*

Samoa, **III:**485*f*

San Marino, **IV:**408*f*

Saudi Arabia, **III:**498*f*

Senegal, **I:**385*f*

Seychelles, **I:**396*f*

Singapore, **III:**511*f*

Slovakia, **IV:**415*f*

Somalia, **I:**413*f*

South Africa, **I:**421*f*

Spain, **IV:**439*f*

Sri Lanka, **III:**532*f*

Sudan, **I:**436*f*

Swaziland, **I:**444*f*

Sweden, **IV:**451*f*

Switzerland, **IV:**465*f*

Syria, **III:**543*f*

Taiwan, **III:**557*f*

Tajikistan, **III:**570*f*

Tanzania, **I:**454*f*

Thailand, **III:**582*f*

Togo, **I:**467*f*

Tonga, **III:**597*f*

Trinidad and Tobago, **II:**358*f*

Tunisia, **I:**476*f*

Turkey, **III:**608*f*

Turkmenistan, **III:**625*f*

Uganda, **I:**488*f*

Ukraine, **IV:**479*f*

United Arab Emirates, **III:**641*f*

United Kingdom, **IV:**493*f*

United States, **II:**369*f*

Uzbekistan, **III:**651*f*

Vanuatu, **III:**660*f*

Venezuela, **II:**395*f*

Zambia, **I:**499*f*

Zimbabwe, **I:**509*f*

See also Working conditions

Labor Inspection Law (Taiwan), **III:**563–564

Labor Insurance Act (Taiwan), **III:**563

Labor Safety and Health Law (Taiwan), **III:**563

Labor Standards Law (Taiwan), **III:**563

Labor strikes and work stoppages. *See* Unions

Labour Party (United Kingdom), **IV:**491

bin Laden, Osama, **I:**434

Lagos, Ricardo, **II:**95

Land holdings. *See* Agriculture; Land reform and redistribution

Land reform and redistribution

Iran, **III:**194–195

Nepal, **III:**402

Taiwan, **III:**552–553

Thailand, **III:**589

Zimbabwe, **I:**507

Landmines, Angola, **I:**15

Laos, **III:315–324**

Lari (money), **IV:**161

Latvia, **IV:245–254**

Leather industry

Pakistan, **III:**438–439

Sudan, **I:**436–437

Lebanon, **III:325–334**

Lempira (money), **II:**231–232

Lesotho, **I:235–242**

Lesotho Highlands Water Development Project, **I:**239–240

"Letter box" companies

Liechtenstein, **IV:**256, 259

Monaco, **IV:**310

Leva (money), **IV:**78

Lhotshampa movements, Bhutan, **III:**59, 63

Liberal Democracy of Slovenia, **IV:**423

Liberation Tigers of Tamil Elam (Sri Lanka), **III:**530

Liberia, **I:243–250**

Libya, **I:251–259**

Liechtenstein, **IV:255–262**

Life expectancy. *See* Country overviews; Poverty and wealth

Lignite mining, Poland, **IV:**349–350

Lilangeni (money), **I:**445

Liquor monopoly, Sweden, **IV:**453–454

Lira (money)

Cyprus, **III:**122

Malta, **IV:**297

Turkey, **III:**614

Literacy. *See* Education; Poverty and wealth

Lithuania, **IV:263–274**

Livestock and meat production

Afghanistan, **III:**6

Argentina, **II:**15

Belgium, **IV:**53

Belize, **II:**45

Benin, **I:**24–25

Brazil, **II:**67

Burma, **III:**79

Cameroon, **I:**61

Chad, **I:**87

Djibouti, **I:**131

Ethiopia, **I:**172

Gabon, **I:**182–183

Ghana, **I:**199

Greece, **IV:**184–185

Guinea, **I:**209

Ireland, **IV:**220

Jordan, **III:**245

Lesotho, **I:**239

Libya, **I:**255

Luxembourg, **IV:**280

Mali, **I:**281

Mexico, **II:**251

Mongolia, **III:**387

Netherlands, **IV:**322

New Zealand, **III:**413

Nicaragua, **II:**274

Pakistan, **III:**437

Russia, **IV:**395

South Africa, **I:**423

Spain, **IV:**439

Sri Lanka, **III:**533

Swaziland, **I:**444

Taiwan, **III:**558

Thailand, **III:**583–584

Turkey, **III:**610

Uganda, **I:**488

United Kingdom, **IV:**494

Uruguay, **II:**385

Livestock diseases, United Kingdom, **IV:**494

Living standards. *See* Poverty and wealth

Lukashenka, Alyaksandr, **IV:**39, 44

Lumber and forest products. *See* Forestry

Lusaka Peace Accord, **I:**102

Luxembourg, **IV:275–284**

M

Macau, **III:335–341**

Macedonia, **IV:285–291**

Machinery production

Germany, **IV:**172–173

Romania, **IV:**381

Mad cow disease, **IV:**439

Madagascar, **I:261–267**

Maize production

South Africa, **I:**422

Tanzania, **I:**454

Majlis, **III:**191

Malawi, **I:269–276**

Malaysia, **III:343–357**

Malaysian Development Agency, **III:**350

Maldives, **III:359–366**

Mali, **I:277–284**

Malnutrition. *See* Poverty and wealth

Maloti (money), **I**:240

Malta, **IV:293–299**

Manufacturing

    Afghanistan, **III**:7

    Albania, **IV**:4–5

    Algeria, **I**:7

    Angola, **I**:18

    Antigua and Barbuda, **II**:5

    Argentina, **II**:16

    Armenia, **IV**:20–21

    Australia, **III**:17–18

    Austria, **IV**:32

    Azerbaijan, **III**:29

    The Bahamas, **II**:28–29

    Bahrain, **III**:36

    Bangladesh, **III**:48

    Barbados, **II**:37

    Belarus, **IV**:41

    Belize, **II**:45

    Benin, **I**:25

    Bhutan, **III**:61

    Bolivia, **II**:55

    Bosnia and Herzegovina, **IV**:67

    Botswana, **I**:32

    Brazil, **II**:69–70

    Brunei Darussalam, **III**:69

    Bulgaria, **IV**:76

    Burkina Faso, **I**:42

    Burma, **III**:79

    Burundi, **I**:51

    Canada, **II**:84, 85

    Cape Verde, **I**:71

    Chad, **I**:88

    China, **III**:102, 103

    Colombia, **II**:114

    Congo, Democratic Republic of the, **I**:104

    Congo, Republic of the, **I**:113

    Costa Rica, **II**:126

    Côte d'Ivoire, **I**:123

    Croatia, **IV**:88

    Cuba, **II**:138

    Cyprus, **III**:120–121

    Czech Republic, **IV**:99

    Denmark, **IV**:111–112

    Djibouti, **I**:131

    Dominica, **II**:147

    Dominican Republic, **II**:155–156

    Egypt, **I**:142

    El Salvador, **II**:176

    Equatorial Guinea, **I**:155

    Eritrea, **I**:163

    Ethiopia, **I**:173

    Fiji, **III**:131

    France, **IV**:148–149

    French Antilles and French Guiana, **II**:186

    Gabon, **I**:183

    The Gambia, **I**:190–191

    Georgia, **IV**:159

    Germany, **IV**:171–172

    Ghana, **I**:200

    Greece, **IV**:185

    Grenada, **II**:195

    Guinea, **I**:210

    Haiti, **II**:221

    Honduras, **II**:230

    Hong Kong, **III**:150

    Hungary, **IV**:200

    India, **III**:165

    Indonesia, **III**:179–180

    Iran, **III**:196

    Iraq, **III**:209

    Ireland, **IV**:220–221

    Israel, **III**:218

    Italy, **IV**:236–237

    Jamaica, **II**:240

    Japan, **III**:232

    Jordan, **III**:248

    Kenya, **I**:229

    Korea, North, **III**:277

    Korea, South, **III**:288–289

    Kyrgyzstan, **III**:309

    Laos, **III**:320

    Latvia, **IV**:250

    Lebanon, **III**:330

    Lesotho, **I**:239

    Liberia, **I**:247–248

    Libya, **I**:255–256

    Liechtenstein, **IV**:258

    Lithuania, **IV**:268–269

    Macau, **III**:338–339

    Macedonia, **IV**:288

    Madagascar, **I**:265

    Malawi, **I**:273

    Malaysia, **III**:350

    Maldives, **III**:363

    Mali, **I**:281

    Marshall Islands, **III**:370

    Mauritania, **I**:289

    Mauritius, **I**:297

    Mexico, **II**:251–252

    Moldova, **IV**:305

    Monaco, **IV**:312

    Mongolia, **III**:387

    Morocco, **I**:308

    Mozambique, **I**:319–320

    Namibia, **I**:332

    Nepal, **III**:402

    Netherlands, **IV**:322

    Netherlands Antilles and Aruba, **II**:266

    New Zealand, **III**:414

    Nicaragua, **II**:274

    Niger, **I**:342

    Nigeria, **I**:357–358

    Norway, **IV**:337

    Oman, **III**:424

    Pakistan, **III**:437, 438–439

    Palau, **III**:448

    Papua New Guinea, **III**:457

    Paraguay, **II**:296, 297

    Peru, **II**:310

    Philippines, **III**:466–467

    Poland, **IV**:350–351

    Portugal, **IV**:365–366

    Puerto Rico, **II**:318

    Qatar, **III**:479

    Romania, **IV**:380–381

    Rwanda, **I**:368

    St. Kitts and Nevis, **II**:316

    St. Lucia, **II**:334–335

    St. Vincent and the Grenadines, **II**:343

    Samoa, **III**:486

    São Tomé and Príncipe, **I**:377

    Saudi Arabia, **III**:500

    Senegal, **I**:386

    Seychelles, **I**:396–397

    Sierra Leone, **I**:405

    Singapore, **III**:511–512

    Slovakia, **IV**:416

    Solomon Islands, **III**:523

    Somalia, **I**:414

    South Africa, **I**:424–425

    Spain, **IV**:440

    Sri Lanka, **III**:533

    Sudan, **I**:436–437

    Suriname, **II**:350

    Swaziland, **I**:444

    Sweden, **IV**:452

    Switzerland, **IV**:466

    Syria, **III**:545

    Tanzania, **I**:455

    Thailand, **III**:584–585

    Tonga, **III**:598

    Trinidad and Tobago, **II**:359

    Tunisia, **I**:477

    Turkey, **III**:610–611

    Turkmenistan, **III**:625–626

    Uganda, **I**:488

    Ukraine, **IV**:480–481

    United Arab Emirates, **III**:642

    United Kingdom, **IV**:495

    United States, **II**:370–371

    Uruguay, **II**:386

    Vanuatu, **III**:661

    Venezuela, **II**:396–397

    Vietnam, **III**:670

    Yemen, **III**:681

    Yugoslavia, **IV**:515

Zambia, **I**:500–501

See also specific industries

Maps

Afghanistan, **III**:2

Albania, **IV**:2

Algeria, **I**:2

Andorra, **IV**:9

Angola, **I**:14

Antigua and Barbuda, **II**:1–2

Argentina, **II**:10

Armenia, **IV**:18

Australia, **III**:12

Austria, **IV**:26

Azerbaijan, **III**:26

The Bahamas, **II**:26

Bahrain, **III**:34

Bangladesh, **III**:42

Barbados, **II**:33

Belarus, **IV**:37

Belgium, **IV**:48

Belize, **II**:42

Benin, **I**:22

Bhutan, **III**:58

Bolivia, **II**:50

Bosnia and Herzegovina, **IV**:64

Botswana, **I**:30

Brazil, **II**:64

Brunei Darussalam, **III**:66

Bulgaria, **IV**:72

Burkina Faso, **I**:38

Burma, **III**:74

Burundi, **I**:48

Cambodia, **III**:86

Cameroon, **I**:56

Canada, **II**:78

Cape Verde, **I**:67

Central African Republic, **I**:73

Chad, **I**:82

Chile, **II**:94

China, **III**:96

Colombia, **II**:108

Comoros, **I**:92

Congo, Democratic Republic of the, **I**:100

Congo, Republic of the, **I**:110

Costa Rica, **II**:122

Côte d'Ivoire, **I**:118

Croatia, **IV**:84

Cuba, **II**:134

Cyprus, **III**:115

Czech Republic, **IV**:96

Denmark, **IV**:106

Djibouti, **I**:128

Dominica, **II**:144

Dominican Republic, **II**:152

Ecuador, **II**:161

Egypt, **I**:136

El Salvador, **II**:172

Equatorial Guinea, **I**:152

Eritrea, **I**:160

Estonia, **IV**:120

Ethiopia, **I**:168

Fiji, **III**:127

Finland, **IV**:128

France, **IV**:142

French Antilles and French Guiana, **II**:182

French Polynesia, **III**:136

Gabon, **I**:180

The Gambia, **I**:188

Georgia, **IV**:156

Germany, **IV**:166

Ghana, **I**:196

Greece, **IV**:180

Grenada, **II**:192

Guatemala, **II**:200

Guinea, **I**:206

Guinea-Bissau, **I**:216

Guyana, **II**:210

Haiti, **II**:218

Honduras, **II**:226

Hong Kong, **III**:143

Hungary, **IV**:196

Iceland, **IV**:206

India, **III**:160

Indonesia, **III**:174

Iran, **III**:188

Iraq, **III**:204

Ireland, **IV**:216

Israel, **III**:214

Italy, **IV**:228

Jamaica, **II**:236

Japan, **III**:226

Jordan, **III**:242

Kenya, **I**:224

Kiribati, **III**:266

Korea, North, **III**:274

Korea, South, **III**:282

Kuwait, **III**:298

Kyrgyzstan, **III**:306

Laos, **III**:315

Latvia, **IV**:246

Lebanon, **III**:326

Lesotho, **I**:236

Liberia, **I**:244

Libya, **I**:252

Liechtenstein, **IV**:256

Lithuania, **IV**:264

Luxembourg, **IV**:276

Macau, **III**:336

Macedonia, **IV**:286

Madagascar, **I**:262

Malawi, **I**:270

Malaysia, **III**:344

Maldives, **III**:360

Mali, **I**:278

Malta, **IV**:294

Marshall Islands, **III**:368

Mauritania, **I**:286

Mauritius, **I**:294

Mexico, **II**:246

Micronesia, **III**:376

Moldova, **IV**:302

Monaco, **IV**:310

Mongolia, **III**:384

Morocco, **I**:304

Mozambique, **I**:314

Namibia, **I**:328

Nauru, **III**:392

Nepal, **III**:398

Netherlands, **IV**:316

Netherlands Antilles and Aruba, **II**:262

New Zealand, **III**:410

Nicaragua, **II**:272

Niger, **I**:338

Nigeria, **I**:348

Norway, **IV**:332

Oman, **III**:420

Pakistan, **III**:430

Palau, **III**:446

Panama, **II**:280

Papua New Guinea, **III**:454

Paraguay, **II**:292

Peru, **II**:304

Philippines, **III**:462

Poland, **IV**:344

Portugal, **IV**:360

Puerto Rico, **II**:315

Qatar, **III**:476

Romania, **IV**:376

Russia, **IV**:388

Rwanda, **I**:366

St. Kitts and Nevis, **II**:323

St. Lucia, **II**:332

St. Vincent and the Grenadines, **II**:340

Samoa, **III**:484

San Marino, **IV**:406

São Tomé and Príncipe, **I**:374

Saudi Arabia, **III**:492

Senegal, **I**:382

Seychelles, **I**:394

Sierra Leone, **I**:402

Singapore, **III**:507

Slovakia, **IV**:412

Slovenia, **IV**:422

Solomon Islands, **III**:520

Somalia, **I**:410

South Africa, **I**:418

Spain, **IV**:432

Maps (*continued*)
Sri Lanka, **III:**528
Sudan, **I:**432
Suriname, **II:**348
Swaziland, **I:**442
Sweden, **IV:**448
Switzerland, **IV:**460
Syria, **III:**540
Taiwan, **III:**553
Tajikistan, **III:**568
Tanzania, **I:**450
Thailand, **III:**578
Togo, **I:**464
Tonga, **III:**596
Trinidad and Tobago, **II:**356
Tunisia, **I:**474
Turkey, **III:**604
Turkmenistan, **III:**622
Tuvalu, **III:**631
Uganda, **I:**484
Ukraine, **IV:**476
United Arab Emirates, **III:**638
United Kingdom, **IV:**488
United States, **II:**364
Uruguay, **II:**382
Uzbekistan, **III:**648
Vanuatu, **III:**658
Vatican City, **IV:**506
Venezuela, **II:**392
Vietnam, **III:**666
Yemen, **III:**678
Yugoslavia, **IV:**512
Zambia, **I:**496
Zimbabwe, **I:**506
Maquila industry
El Salvador, **II:**176
Guatemala, **II:**206
Honduras, **II:**230
Mexico, **II:**250, 252
Marcos, Ferdinand, **III:**461–462
Marijuana production, Jamaica, **II:**239
Markka (money), **IV:**136
Marshall Islands, **III:367–373**
Martinique. *See* French Antilles and French Guiana
Mass transit. *See* Public transportation
Mauritania, **I:285–292**
Mauritius, **I:293–301**
Mauritius Trust Fund, **I:**300
Mayotte, **I:**92, 97
Mekong River bridges, Laos, **III:**317–318
MERCOSUR
Argentina, **II:**18–19
Paraguay, **II:**298–299, 302

Uruguay, **II:**382
Metals manufacturing
Belgium, **IV:**54
Chile, **II:**100–101
Kazakhstan, **III:**258
Romania, **IV:**381
Spain, **IV:**440
See also Iron and steel production
Mexico, **II:245–259**
Micronesia, **III:375–382**
Migratory labor, Uganda, **I:**492
Military. *See* Politics and government
Milosevic, Slobodan, **IV:**513
Minimum wage. *See* Poverty and wealth; Working conditions
Mining and mineral processing
Albania, **IV:**5
Argentina, **II:**16–17
Armenia, **IV:**20
Australia, **III:**16–17
Austria, **IV:**32
Azerbaijan, **III:**29
Belize, **II:**45
Benin, **I:**25
Bolivia, **II:**55
Brazil, **II:**70
Burma, **III:**79
Burundi, **I:**50–51
Cambodia, **III:**89–90
Cameroon, **I:**62
Canada, **II:**84–85
Chad, **I:**88
Chile, **II:**100
China, **III:**102–103
Colombia, **II:**114
Costa Rica, **II:**126
Côte d'Ivoire, **I:**123
Cyprus, **III:**120
Czech Republic, **IV:**99
Ecuador, **II:**165
Egypt, **I:**142
El Salvador, **II:**175–176
Equatorial Guinea, **I:**155
Eritrea, **I:**163
Ethiopia, **I:**173
Fiji, **III:**131
France, **IV:**149
French Antilles and French Guiana, **II:**186
Gabon, **I:**183
Georgia, **IV:**159
Germany, **IV:**172
Greece, **IV:**185
Guatemala, **II:**204
Honduras, **II:**229–230
Hungary, **IV:**200

India, **III:**166
Indonesia, **III:**180
Iran, **III:**196
Iraq, **III:**209
Israel, **III:**218
Jamaica, **II:**239–240
Japan, **III:**233
Jordan, **III:**245
Kazakhstan, **III:**258
Kenya, **I:**229
Korea, North, **III:**276–277
Korea, South, **III:**288
Laos, **III:**320
Lebanon, **III:**330
Libya, **I:**255
Madagascar, **I:**265
Malawi, **I:**273
Malaysia, **III:**350
Mali, **I:**281
Mauritania, **I:**289
Mexico, **II:**251
Mongolia, **III:**387
Morocco, **I:**308
Namibia, **I:**331–332
Netherlands, **IV:**323
New Zealand, **III:**414
Nicaragua, **II:**275
Niger, **I:**342
Nigeria, **I:**357
Pakistan, **III:**438
Panama, **II:**284
Papua New Guinea, **III:**456–457, 459
Paraguay, **II:**297
Peru, **II:**310
Poland, **IV:**349–350
Romania, **IV:**380
Rwanda, **I:**368
Saudi Arabia, **III:**500
Seychelles, **I:**397
Sierra Leone, **I:**404–405
Slovakia, **IV:**416
Solomon Islands, **III:**523
South Africa, **I:**423–424
Spain, **IV:**440
Sri Lanka, **III:**533
Sudan, **I:**437
Suriname, **II:**350
Swaziland, **I:**444
Syria, **III:**544
Tajikistan, **III:**571
Tanzania, **I:**455
Turkey, **III:**612
Ukraine, **IV:**480
United Kingdom, **IV:**495
United States, **II:**371
Vanuatu, **III:**661
Venezuela, **II:**396

Vietnam, **III**:670

Yugoslavia, **IV**:515

Zambia, **I**:500

Zimbabwe, **I**:510

See also Oil and gas industry; *specific types of mining*

Moldova, **IV:301–308**

Monaco, **IV:309–314**

Moncloa Pacts, **IV**:433

Money

Afghanistan, **III**:8, 8*t*

Albania, **IV**:5–6, 6*t*

Algeria, **I**:8, 8*t*

Andorra, **IV**:13–14, 13*t*

Angola, **I**:18–19, 18*t*

Antigua and Barbuda, **II**:6, 6*t*

Argentina, **II**:19, 19*t*

Armenia, **IV**:22, 22*t*

Australia, **III**:20, 20*t*

Austria, **IV**:34, 34*t*

Azerbaijan, **III**:29–30, 30*t*

The Bahamas, **II**:30, 30*t*

Bahrain, **III**:37, 37*t*

Bangladesh, **III**:50–51, 50*t*

Barbados, **II**:38, 38*t*

Belarus, **IV**:43, 43*t*

Belgium, **IV**:57–58, 57*t*

Belize, **II**:46, 46*t*

Benin, **I**:26, 26*t*

Bhutan, **III**:62, 62*t*

Bolivia, **II**:57, 57*t*

Bosnia and Herzegovina, **IV**:67–68, 68*t*

Botswana, **I**:33, 33*t*

Brazil, **II**:71–72, 72*t*

Brunei Darussalam, **III**:70, 70*t*

Bulgaria, **IV**:78, 78*t*

Burkina Faso, **I**:43, 43*t*

Burma, **III**:81, 81*t*

Burundi, **I**:51–52, 51*t*

Cambodia, **III**:90–91, 90*t*

Cameroon, **I**:63, 63*t*

Canada, **II**:87–88, 87*t*

Cape Verde, **I**:71–72, 71*t*

Central African Republic, **I**:80, 80*t*

Chad, **I**:89, 89*t*

Chile, **II**:103, 103*t*

China, **III**:105–107, 105*t*

Colombia, **II**:116, 116*t*

Comoros, **I**:95, 95*t*

Congo, Democratic Republic of the, **I**:101, 105, 105*t*

Congo, Republic of the, **I**:113, 113*t*

Costa Rica, **II**:128–129, 128*t*

Côte d'Ivoire, **I**:124, 124*t*

Croatia, **IV**:90, 90*t*

Cuba, **II**:139, 139*t*

Cyprus, **III**:122–123, 123*t*

Czech Republic, **IV**:101, 101*t*

Denmark, **IV**:109, 114, 114*t*

Djibouti, **I**:132–133, 132*t*

Dominica, **II**:148, 148*t*

Dominican Republic, **II**:157, 157*t*

Ecuador, **II**:166–167, 166*t*

Egypt, **I**:145, 145*t*

El Salvador, **II**:177, 177*t*

Equatorial Guinea, **I**:155–156, 156*t*

Eritrea, **I**:164, 164*t*

Estonia, **IV**:123, 123*t*

Ethiopia, **I**:175, 175*t*

Fiji, **III**:132, 132*t*

Finland, **IV**:136, 136*t*

France, **IV**:151–152, 151*t*

French Antilles and French Guiana, **II**:188, 188*t*

French Polynesia, **III**:139–140, 140*t*

Gabon, **I**:184, 184*t*

The Gambia, **I**:191, 191*t*

Georgia, **IV**:160–161, 160*t*

Germany, **IV**:175, 175*t*

Ghana, **I**:201, 201*t*

Greece, **IV**:188, 188*t*

Grenada, **II**:196, 196*t*

Guatemala, **II**:204–205, 205*t*

Guinea, **I**:211, 211*t*

Guinea-Bissau, **I**:220, 220*t*

Guyana, **II**:214, 214*t*

Haiti, **II**:222, 222*t*

Honduras, **II**:231–232, 231*t*

Hong Kong, **III**:153–154, 153*t*

Hungary, **IV**:201, 201*t*

Iceland, **IV**:211, 211*t*

India, **III**:167–168, 167*t*

Indonesia, **III**:181–182, 181*t*

Iran, **III**:199, 199*t*

Iraq, **III**:210, 210*t*

Ireland, **IV**:223, 223*t*

Israel, **III**:220, 220*t*

Italy, **IV**:239, 239*t*

Jamaica, **II**:241*t,* 242

Japan, **III**:235–236, 236*t*

Jordan, **III**:247, 247*t*

Kazakhstan, **III**:259–260, 259*t*

Kenya, **I**:231, 231*t*

Kiribati, **III**:269, 269*t*

Korea, North, **III**:278, 278*t*

Korea, South, **III**:291, 291*t*

Kuwait, **III**:301, 301*t*

Kyrgyzstan, **III**:310–311, 311*t*

Laos, **III**:322, 322*t*

Latvia, **IV**:251, 251*t*

Lebanon, **III**:332, 332*t*

Lesotho, **I**:240, 240*t*

Liberia, **I**:248–249, 248*t*

Libya, **I**:257, 257*t*

Liechtenstein, **IV**:260, 260*t*

Lithuania, **IV**:270–271, 270*t*

Luxembourg, **IV**:282, 282*t*

Macau, **III**:339–340, 340*t*

Macedonia, **IV**:289–290, 289*t*

Madagascar, **I**:266, 266*t*

Malawi, **I**:274, 274*t*

Malaysia, **III**:353–354, 353*t*

Maldives, **III**:364, 364*t*

Mali, **I**:282, 282*t*

Malta, **IV**:297, 297*t*

Marshall Islands, **III**:371, 371*t*

Mauritania, **I**:290, 290*t*

Mauritius, **I**:298–299, 298*t*

Mexico, **II**:253–255, 254*t*

Micronesia, **III**:380, 380*t*

Moldova, **IV**:305–306, 306*t*

Monaco, **IV**:313, 313*t*

Mongolia, **III**:388, 388*t*

Morocco, **I**:310, 310*t*

Mozambique, **I**:321–322, 321*t*

Namibia, **I**:333, 333*t*

Nauru, **III**:394, 394*t*

Nepal, **III**:404, 404*t*

Netherlands, **IV**:325, 325*t*

Netherlands Antilles and Aruba, **II**:269, 269*t*

New Zealand, **III**:416, 416*t*

Nicaragua, **II**:276, 276*t*

Niger, **I**:343, 343*t*

Nigeria, **I**:359, 359*t*

Norway, **IV**:338, 338*t*

Oman, **III**:425, 425*t*

Pakistan, **III**:440–441, 441*t*

Palau, **III**:448–449, 449*t*

Panama, **II**:286, 286*t*

Papua New Guinea, **III**:457–458, 457*t*

Paraguay, **II**:299, 299*t*

Peru, **II**:311–312, 311*t*

Philippines, **III**:468–469, 468*t*

Poland, **IV**:353–354, 353*t*

Portugal, **IV**:368–369, 368*t*

Puerto Rico, **II**:319, 319*t*

Qatar, **III**:480, 480*t*

Romania, **IV**:382, 382*t*

Russia, **IV**:397–399, 398*t*

Rwanda, **I**:369, 369*t*

St. Kitts and Nevis, **II**:327, 327*t*

St. Lucia, **II**:335–336, 336*t*

St. Vincent and the Grenadines, **II**:344, 344*t*

Samoa, **III**:487, 487*t*

San Marino, **IV**:409, 409*t*

São Tomé and Príncipe, **I**:377, 377*t*

Saudi Arabia, **III**:502, 502*t*

Money (*continued*)

Senegal, **I:**388, 388*t*

Seychelles, **I:**397, 397*t*

Sierra Leone, **I:**406, 406*t*

Singapore, **III:**513–514, 514*t*

Slovakia, **IV:**417, 417*t*

Slovenia, **IV:**426–427, 426*t*

Solomon Islands, **III:**524, 524*t*

Somalia, **I:**414–415, 414*t*

South Africa, **I:**426–427, 426*t*

Spain, **IV:**441–442, 442*t*

Sri Lanka, **III:**535, 535*t*

Sudan, **I:**438, 438*t*

Suriname, **II:**351, 351*t*

Swaziland, **I:**445, 445*t*

Sweden, **IV:**454–455, 455*t*

Switzerland, **IV:**468–470, 468*t*

Syria, **III:**547, 547*t*

Taiwan, **III:**561–562, 562*t*

Tajikistan, **III:**572, 572*t*

Tanzania, **I:**457, 457*t*

Thailand, **III:**587, 587*t*

Togo, **I:**469, 469*t*

Tonga, **III:**599, 599*t*

Trinidad and Tobago, **II:**359–360, 360*t*

Tunisia, **I:**478, 478*t*

Turkey, **III:**614–615, 614*t*

Turkmenistan, **III:**627, 627*t*

Tuvalu, **III:**635, 635*t*

Uganda, **I:**491, 491*t*

Ukraine, **IV:**482, 482*t*

United Arab Emirates, **III:**643–644, 643*t*

United Kingdom, **IV:**491, 497–498, 498*t*

United States, **II:**373–374, 374*t*

Uruguay, **II:**387, 387*t*

Uzbekistan, **III:**654, 654*t*

Vanuatu, **III:**662, 662*t*

Venezuela, **II:**398, 398*t*

Vietnam, **III:**672, 672*t*

Yemen, **III:**682, 682*t*

Yugoslavia, **IV:**516, 516*t*

Zambia, **I:**502, 502*t*

Zimbabwe, **I:**511, 511*t*

Money laundering

Antigua and Barbuda, **II:**5

El Salvador, **II:**172–173

Liechtenstein, **IV:**257, 259, 260

Nauru, **III:**394

Netherlands Antilles and Aruba, **II:**267

St. Vincent and the Grenadines, **II:**343

Switzerland, **IV:**469

Mongolia, **III:383–390**

Mongolian People's Revolutionary Party, **III:**385

Montenegro. *See* Yugoslavia

Morales, Ramon, **II:**227

Morocco, **I:303–312**

Moshavim (Israeli settlements), **III:**217

Motherland Party (Turkey), **III:**606

Movement for a Democratic Slovakia, **IV:**413

Movement for Democracy (Cape Verde), **I:**69

Movement for the Liberation of São Tomé and Príncipe, **I:**374–375

Movement of the National Revolution Party (Bolivia), **II:**52

Mozambique, **I:313–325**

Mubarak, Hosni, **I:**138

Multi-Fibre Agreement, **I:**298

Musharraf, Pervez, **III:**433

The Muslim Brotherhood. *See* Ikhwan al-Muslimin

Musveni, Yoweri, **I:**486

Mutawaa'in, **III:**496

Myanmar. *See* Burma

N

NAFTA. *See* North American Free Trade Agreement (NAFTA)

al-Nahyan, Shaykh Zayid, **III:**639

Naira (money), **I:**359

Nakfa (money), **I:**164

Namibia, **I:327–335**

Nasser, Gamal Abdel, **I:**137–138

National Agricultural Information Service, **III:**558

National banks. *See* Money

National Confederation of Senegalese Workers, **I:**389–390

National debt. *See* Debt

National Liberation Front (Algeria), **I:**3–4, 9

National Resistance Movement (Uganda), **I:**486

National Union for the Total Independence of Angola, **I:**13–14, 15

Nationalism, Bhutan, **III:**59

Nationalist Movement Party (Turkey), **III:**606

Nationalist Party (Taiwan), **III:**554

Nationalrat, Austria, **IV:**28

Native peoples. *See* Country overviews

Natural gas. *See* Oil and gas industry

Nauru, **III:391–396**

Nepal, **III:397–408**

Nepali Congress Party, **III:**399

Netherlands, **IV:315–329**

Netherlands Antilles and Aruba, **II:261–270**

Netpin, **IV:**367

Neutrality, Switzerland, **IV:**462

Nevis. *See* St. Kitts and Nevis

New Democratic Party (Egypt), **I:**138

New Economic Policy (Malaysia), **III:**346, 354

New National Party (Grenada), **II:**193

"New Order," Indonesia, **III:**176, 177

New Party (Taiwan), **III:**555

New Zealand, **III:409–418**

Newspapers. *See* Publishing

Nguema, Francisco Macias, **I:**153

Nicaragua, **II:271–278**

Nickel mining, Cuba, **II:**138

Niger, **I:337–345**

Nigeria, **I:347–363**

Nike, Inc., **III:**673

al-Nimairi, Jaafar, **I:**433

Nokia, **IV:**133–134

North American Free Trade Agreement (NAFTA)

Canada, **II:**83, 87

El Salvador, **II:**176, 177

Honduras, **II:**230

Mexico, **II:**247, 254

United States, **II:**373

North Korea. *See* Korea, North

Northern Ireland, **IV:**501

Northern League Party (Italy), **IV:**231

Norway, **IV:331–341**

Nova kwanza (money), **I:**18

Nuclear power

China, **III:**99–100

South Africa, **I:**424

Ukraine, **IV:**479

Nut production, Turkey, **III:**610

Nutmeg production, Grenada, **II:**195

O

Obote, Milton, **I:**485

ODP-MT Party (Burkina Faso), **I:**39

"Offsets" program, United Arab Emirates, **III:**642

Offshore banking. *See* Financial services

Oil and gas industry

Afghanistan, **III:**6–7

Algeria, **I:**2, 5–6, 7

Angola, **I:**14, 17–18

Azerbaijan, **III:**27, 28–29

Bahrain, **III:**33, 36, 39

Bangladesh, **III:**48

Benin, **I:**25

Bolivia, **II:**55

Brunei Darussalam, **III:**67–68, 69

Burma, **III:**79–80

Cameroon, **I:**61–62, 65–66

Central African Republic, **I:**78

Chad, **I:**88

Chile, **II:**101

China, **III:**103

Colombia, **II:**114

Congo, Democratic Republic of the, **I:**104

Congo, Republic of the, **I:**113, 115

Croatia, **IV:**89

Denmark, **IV:**112

Ecuador, **II:**165

Egypt, **I:**141–142

Equatorial Guinea, **I:**152, 154, 155

Gabon, **I:**183

India, **III:**163, 164, 165–166

Indonesia, **III:**180

Iran, **III:**190–191, 195–196, 198

Iraq, **III:**205, 207, 208–209, 210

Israel, **III:**218

Japan, **III:**233

Jordan, **III:**245

Kazakhstan, **III:**255, 256, 257, 263

Kuwait, **III:**300

Libya, **I:**251–252, 255

Malaysia, **III:**350

Mexico, **II:**251

Mongolia, **III:**387

Namibia, **I:**331

Netherlands, **IV:**323

Netherlands Antilles and Aruba, **II:**266

Nigeria, **I:**350, 357

Norway, **IV:**336–337, 340

Oman, **III:**420, 423–425, 427

Pakistan, **III:**438

Qatar, **III:**475–476, 478–479, 480

Romania, **IV:**380

Russia, **IV:**395–396, 397

Saudi Arabia, **III:**492–493, 499–500, 504

Singapore, **III:**512

South Africa, **I:**424

Syria, **III:**544–545

Tajikistan, **III:**571

Trinidad and Tobago, **II:**358–359

Tunisia, **I:**476–477

Turkmenistan, **III:**626

United Arab Emirates, **III:**637, 640–641, 641–642

United Kingdom, **IV:**495

Uzbekistan, **III:**650, 652

Venezuela, **II:**393, 395–396, 397–398

Vietnam, **III:**670

Yemen, **III:**677, 681

Oil embargo of 1973, **III:**495

Oilseed production

Belarus, **IV:**41

Pakistan, **III:**437

Olive production, Italy, **IV:**236

Oman, **III:419–427**

OPEC. *See* Organization of Petroleum Exporting Countries (OPEC)

Open economies. *See* Economic overviews and trends

Opium production

Afghanistan, **III:**6

Pakistan, **III:**436, 442

Orange production

Brazil, **II:**68

Costa Rica, **II:**126

Organic farming, Austria, **IV:**36

Organization for Economic Development and Cooperation, **III:**480

Organization of Petroleum Exporting Countries (OPEC), **III:**497–498

Organized crime

Hungary, **IV:**197

Slovakia, **IV:**413

Orphanages, Romania, **IV:**383–384

P

Pa'anga (money), **III:**599

Pacific Financial Community franc. *See* CFPF (money)

Pakistan, **III:429–444**

Pakistan Telecommunications Corporation, **III:**435

Palau, **III:445–451**

Palestinian National Authority, **III:**213, 223

Palm oil production

Benin, **I:**24, 25

Costa Rica, **II:**126

Malaysia, **III:**349

Panama, **II:279–289**

Panama Canal, **II:**280–281, 285, 288

Panhellenic Socialist Movement (Greece), **IV:**182

Paper mills

Brazil, **II:**69

Sudan, **I:**437

Papua New Guinea, **III:453–459**

Paraguay, **II:291–302**

Partido Democrático de Guinea Ecuatorial (Equatorial Guinea), **I:**153

Partido Revolucionario Institucional (Mexico), **II:**247–248

Party of Social Democracy (Romania), **IV:**377

Passport sales, Marshall Islands, **III:**371

Peanuts. *See* Groundnut production

Pearl harvesting, French Polynesia, **III:**138

Pensions. *See* Poverty and wealth

People First Party (Taiwan), **III:**555

"People Power" revolutions, Philippines, **III:**462, 463

People's Democratic Party (Ukraine), **IV:**477

People's National Movement (Trinidad and Tobago), **II:**356–357

People's National Party (Jamaica), **II:**236–237

People's Party (Austria), **IV:**27–28

People's Republic of China. *See* China

People's United Party (Belize), **II:**42–43

Peron, Juan, **II:**11

Persian Gulf War, **III:**203–204, 206

Peru, **II:303–314**

Peseta (money), **IV:**442

Peso (money)

Argentina, **II:**19

Colombia, **II:**116

Cuba, **II:**139

Dominican Republic, **II:**157

Mexico, **II:**253–254

Philippines, **III:**468

Uruguay, **II:**387

Peter's Pence, **IV:**506

Petrochemical industry

Belarus, **IV:**41

Iran, **III:**196–197

Kuwait, **III:**300

Qatar, **III:**479

Thailand, **III:**585

Petróleos de Venezuela, **II:**396

Philippines, **III:461–473**

Philips (company), **IV:**322

Phosphates mining

Jordan, **III:**245

Morocco, **I:**308

Nauru, **III:**391–392, 393, 395–396

Senegal, **I:**386

Togo, **I:**468

Tunisia, **I:**477

Tuvalu, **III:**632

Pipelines

Chad-Cameroon Oil Production and Pipeline project, **I:**65, 85

Pipelines (*continued*)
  Netherlands, **IV:**320
  Russia, **IV:**393
  Turkmenistan, **III:**624
  See also Oil and gas industry
Plan Colombia, **II:**169
Plastics manufacturing, Hong Kong,
  III:150
Poland, **IV:343–357**
Politics and government
  Afghanistan, **III:**3–4
  Albania, **IV:**2–3
  Algeria, **I:**3–4
  Andorra, **IV:**11–12
  Angola, **I:**15
  Antigua and Barbuda, **II:**2–3
  Argentina, **II:**11–13
  Armenia, **IV:**18–19
  Australia, **III:**13–14
  Austria, **IV:**27–29
  Azerbaijan, **III:**26–27
  The Bahamas, **II:**26–27
  Bahrain, **III:**34–35
  Bangladesh, **III:**44–45
  Barbados, **II:**34–35
  Belarus, **IV:**39
  Belgium, **IV:**50–51
  Belize, **II:**42–43
  Benin, **I:**22–23, 27
  Bhutan, **III:**58–59
  Bolivia, **II:**52
  Bosnia and Herzegovina, **IV:**65
  Botswana, **I:**31
  Brazil, **II:**65–66
  Brunei Darussalam, **III:**66–67
  Bulgaria, **IV:**73
  Burkina Faso, **I:**39–40
  Burma, **III:**75–76
  Burundi, **I:**48–49
  Cambodia, **III:**87
  Cameroon, **I:**57–58
  Canada, **II:**80–81
  Cape Verde, **I:**68–69
  Central African Republic, **I:**77
  Chad, **I:**85
  Chile, **II:**95–96
  China, **III:**97–98
  Colombia, **II:**110–111
  Comoros, **I:**92–93
  Congo, Democratic Republic of the,
    I:101–102
  Congo, Republic of the, **I:**110–111
  Costa Rica, **II:**123
  Côte d'Ivoire, **I:**119–120
  Croatia, **IV:**85–86
  Cuba, **II:**135–136
  Cyprus, **III:**117

  Czech Republic, **IV:**97
  Denmark, **IV:**107–108
  Djibouti, **I:**129–130
  Dominica, **II:**144–145
  Dominican Republic, **II:**153
  Ecuador, **II:**162–163
  Egypt, **I:**137–139
  El Salvador, **II:**173
  Equatorial Guinea, **I:**153
  Eritrea, **I:**161
  Estonia, **IV:**120
  Ethiopia, **I:**169–170
  Fiji, **III:**128–129
  Finland, **IV:**129–130
  France, **IV:**144–145
  French Antilles and French Guiana,
    II:183–184
  French Polynesia, **III:**137
  Gabon, **I:**180–181
  The Gambia, **I:**188–189
  Georgia, **IV:**157
  Germany, **IV:**167–168
  Ghana, **I:**197
  Greece, **IV:**182
  Grenada, **II:**192–193
  Guatemala, **II:**201–202
  Guinea, **I:**207–208
  Guinea-Bissau, **I:**217–218
  Guyana, **II:**210–211
  Haiti, **II:**219
  Honduras, **II:**226–227
  Hong Kong, **III:**145–147
  Hungary, **IV:**197
  Iceland, **IV:**207–208
  India, **III:**162
  Indonesia, **III:**175–176
  Iran, **III:**191–192
  Iraq, **III:**205–206
  Ireland, **IV:**217–218
  Israel, **III:**215–216
  Italy, **IV:**231–232
  Jamaica, **II:**236–237
  Japan, **III:**228–229
  Jordan, **III:**243
  Kazakhstan, **III:**253–254
  Kenya, **I:**225–226
  Kiribati, **III:**267
  Korea, North, **III:**274–275
  Korea, South, **III:**284–285
  Kuwait, **III:**298
  Kyrgyzstan, **III:**307
  Laos, **III:**317
  Latvia, **IV:**247–248
  Lebanon, **III:**327–328
  Lesotho, **I:**237
  Liberia, **I:**244–245
  Libya, **I:**253

  Liechtenstein, **IV:**256–257
  Lithuania, **IV:**265–266
  Luxembourg, **IV:**277–278
  Macau, **III:**336–337
  Macedonia, **IV:**286–287
  Madagascar, **I:**262–263
  Malawi, **I:**270–271
  Malaysia, **III:**345–347
  Maldives, **III:**360–361
  Mali, **I:**279
  Malta, **IV:**294–295
  Marshall Islands, **III:**368–369
  Mauritania, **I:**287
  Mauritius, **I:**294–295
  Mexico, **II:**247–248
  Micronesia, **III:**377
  Moldova, **IV:**302–303
  Monaco, **IV:**310–311
  Mongolia, **III:**385
  Morocco, **I:**305–306
  Mozambique, **I:**315–316
  Namibia, **I:**329
  Nauru, **III:**392
  Nepal, **III:**399–400
  Netherlands, **IV:**318–319
  Netherlands Antilles and Aruba,
    II:263–264
  New Zealand, **III:**411
  Nicaragua, **II:**272–273
  Niger, **I:**339–340
  Nigeria, **I:**351–353
  Norway, **IV:**333–334
  Oman, **III:**421
  Pakistan, **III:**432–433
  Palau, **III:**446–447
  Panama, **II:**281–282
  Papua New Guinea, **III:**454–455
  Paraguay, **II:**293–294
  Peru, **II:**306–307
  Philippines, **III:**463–464
  Poland, **IV:**345–347
  Portugal, **IV:**361–362
  Puerto Rico, **II:**316
  Qatar, **III:**477
  Romania, **IV:**377–378
  Russia, **IV:**390–392
  Rwanda, **I:**366–367
  St. Kitts and Nevis, **II:**324
  St. Lucia, **II:**332
  St. Vincent and the Grenadines,
    II:340–341
  Samoa, **III:**484
  San Marino, **IV:**406–407
  São Tomé and Príncipe, **I:**374–375
  Saudi Arabia, **III:**494–496
  Senegal, **I:**383
  Seychelles, **I:**394–395

Sierra Leone, **I:**402–403
Singapore, **III:**509
Slovakia, **IV:**413
Slovenia, **IV:**423
Solomon Islands, **III:**520–521
Somalia, **I:**411–412
South Africa, **I:**419–420
Spain, **IV:**435–436
Sri Lanka, **III:**529–530
Sudan, **I:**433–434
Suriname, **II:**348–349
Swaziland, **I:**442–443
Sweden, **IV:**449–450
Switzerland, **IV:**461–462
Syria, **III:**541
Taiwan, **III:**553–554
Tajikistan, **III:**568
Tanzania, **I:**451–452
Thailand, **III:**579–580
Togo, **I:**465–466
Tonga, **III:**596
Trinidad and Tobago, **II:**356–357
Tunisia, **I:**474–475
Turkey, **III:**605–606
Turkmenistan, **III:**622–623
Tuvalu, **III:**632–633
Uganda, **I:**485–486
Ukraine, **IV:**477–478
United Arab Emirates, **III:**639
United Kingdom, **IV:**490–492
United States, **II:**366–367
Uruguay, **II:**383–384
Uzbekistan, **III:**649–650
Vanuatu, **III:**658
Vatican City, **IV:**507
Venezuela, **II:**393
Vietnam, **III:**667–668
Yemen, **III:**679
Zambia, **I:**497–498
Zimbabwe, **I:**507–508
Pope, status of, **IV:**507
Popular Movement for the
    Liberation of Angola, **I:**13, 15
Popular Party (Spain), **IV:**435–436
Population control policies
    Bangladesh, **III:**41–42
    China, **III:**95–96
    Egypt, **I:**135–136
    India, **III:**159–161
    Indonesia, **III:**174
    Jamaica, **II:**235
    Nepal, **III:**397
    Peru, **II:**304
    Solomon Islands, **III:**519
    Tunisia, **I:**473
Population demographics. *See*
    Country overviews; Poverty and
    wealth

Portillo, Alfonso, **II:**201
Ports and waterways
    Argentina, **II:**13
    Australia, **III:**15
    Azerbaijan, **III:**27
    The Bahamas, **II:**27
    Bangladesh, **III:**46
    Belgium, **IV:**52
    Benin, **I:**23
    Bolivia, **II:**53
    Burma, **III:**76
    Cameroon, **I:**59, 62
    Canada, **II:**82
    Cape Verde, **I:**69
    Central African Republic, **I:**77
    Chile, **II:**97
    China, **III:**99
    Côte d'Ivoire, **I:**120–121
    Cuba, **II:**136
    Djibouti, **I:**130, 132
    Ecuador, **II:**164
    French Antilles and French Guiana,
        II:184
    Gabon, **I:**181
    The Gambia, **I:**189
    Germany, **IV:**169
    Ghana, **I:**198
    Honduras, **II:**228
    Hong Kong, **III:**148
    Indonesia, **III:**177
    Iran, **III:**193
    Italy, **IV:**233
    Jamaica, **II:**238
    Japan, **III:**230
    Kenya, **I:**226–227
    Kiribati, **III:**268
    Korea, South, **III:**286
    Latvia, **IV:**248
    Liberia, **I:**246
    Malaysia, **III:**348
    Mauritania, **I:**288
    Mauritius, **I:**295
    Micronesia, **III:**377–378
    Morocco, **I:**306
    Mozambique, **I:**317
    Namibia, **I:**330
    Netherlands, **IV:**319–320
    Netherlands Antilles and Aruba,
        II:264–265
    Nigeria, **I:**355
    Norway, **IV:**335
    Pakistan, **III:**434
    Panama, **II:**282–283
    Paraguay, **II:**292–293, 294–295
    Peru, **II:**307
    Philippines, **III:**464
    Poland, **IV:**347

Russia, **IV:**393
São Tomé and Príncipe, **I:**375
Saudi Arabia, **III:**497
Sierra Leone, **I:**404
Singapore, **III:**508, 510
Somalia, **I:**413
Spain, **IV:**437
Sri Lanka, **III:**531
Sudan, **I:**435
Taiwan, **III:**556
Thailand, **III:**581–582
Togo, **I:**466
Turkey, **III:**607
Tuvalu, **III:**633–634
Uganda, **I:**487
Ukraine, **IV:**478
United Kingdom, **IV:**492
United States, **II:**368
Vanuatu, **III:**659
Portugal, **IV:359–373**
"Positive non-intervention," Hong
    Kong, **III:**146
Postage stamp sales, Vatican City,
    IV:507
Postal Savings System of Taiwan,
    III:562
Postal service, Poland, **IV:**348
Poultry production, Brazil, **II:**69
Pound (money)
    Cyprus, **III:**122
    Egypt, **I:**145
    Lebanon, **III:**332
    United Kingdom, **IV:**497
Poverty and wealth
    Afghanistan, **III:**8–9
    Albania, **IV:**6
    Algeria, **I:**9
    Andorra, **IV:**14
    Angola, **I:**19
    Antigua and Barbuda, **II:**6–7
    Argentina, **II:**19–20
    Armenia, **IV:**22
    Australia, **III:**20–22
    Austria, **IV:**34
    Azerbaijan, **III:**30–31
    The Bahamas, **II:**30
    Bahrain, **III:**37–38
    Bangladesh, **III:**51–52
    Barbados, **II:**38
    Belarus, **IV:**43
    Belgium, **IV:**58
    Belize, **II:**46–47
    Benin, **I:**26
    Bhutan, **III:**62–63
    Bolivia, **II:**57–58
    Bosnia and Herzegovina, **IV:**68
    Botswana, **I:**33–34

Poverty and wealth (*continued*)

Brazil, **II**:72–73

Brunei Darussalam, **III**:70–71

Bulgaria, **IV**:78–79

Burkina Faso, **I**:44

Burma, **III**:81–82

Burundi, **I**:52

Cambodia, **III**:91

Cameroon, **I**:63–64

Canada, **II**:88–89

Cape Verde, **I**:72

Central African Republic, **I**:80–81

Chad, **I**:89

Chile, **II**:103–104

China, **III**:107–108

Colombia, **II**:116–117

Comoros, **I**:95–96

Congo, Democratic Republic of the, **I**:105

Congo, Republic of the, **I**:113–114

Costa Rica, **II**:129–130

Côte d'Ivoire, **I**:124–125

Croatia, **IV**:90–91

Cuba, **II**:139–140

Cyprus, **III**:123

Czech Republic, **IV**:101–102

Denmark, **IV**:114–115

Djibouti, **I**:133

Dominica, **II**:148–149

Dominican Republic, **II**:157

Ecuador, **II**:167

Egypt, **I**:145–146

El Salvador, **II**:178

Equatorial Guinea, **I**:156

Eritrea, **I**:164

Estonia, **IV**:123–124

Ethiopia, **I**:175–176

Fiji, **III**:132

Finland, **IV**:136–137

France, **IV**:152–153

French Antilles and French Guiana, **II**:188–189

French Polynesia, **III**:140

Gabon, **I**:184–185

The Gambia, **I**:191–192

Georgia, **IV**:161–162

Germany, **IV**:176–177

Ghana, **I**:201–202

Greece, **IV**:188–189

Grenada, **II**:196

Guatemala, **II**:205–206

Guinea, **I**:211

Guinea-Bissau, **I**:220–221

Guyana, **II**:214–215

Haiti, **II**:222–223

Honduras, **II**:232

Hong Kong, **III**:154

Hungary, **IV**:201–202

Iceland, **IV**:211–212

India, **III**:168–169

Indonesia, **III**:182–183

Iran, **III**:199–200

Iraq, **III**:210–211

Ireland, **IV**:223–224

Israel, **III**:220–221

Italy, **IV**:240–241

Jamaica, **II**:242–243

Japan, **III**:236–237

Jordan, **III**:247–248

Kazakhstan, **III**:260–262

Kenya, **I**:231–232

Kiribati, **III**:269–270

Korea, North, **III**:278

Korea, South, **III**:291–292

Kuwait, **III**:301

Kyrgyzstan, **III**:311–312

Laos, **III**:322

Latvia, **IV**:251–252

Lebanon, **III**:332–333

Lesotho, **I**:240–241

Liberia, **I**:249

Libya, **I**:257–258

Liechtenstein, **IV**:260

Lithuania, **IV**:271–272

Luxembourg, **IV**:282–283

Macau, **III**:340

Macedonia, **IV**:290

Madagascar, **I**:266

Malawi, **I**:274–275

Malaysia, **III**:354

Maldives, **III**:364–365

Mali, **I**:282–283

Malta, **IV**:297

Marshall Islands, **III**:371–372

Mauritania, **I**:290–291

Mauritius, **I**:299

Mexico, **II**:255–256

Micronesia, **III**:380

Moldova, **IV**:306

Monaco, **IV**:313–314

Mongolia, **III**:388–389

Morocco, **I**:310–311

Mozambique, **I**:322–323

Namibia, **I**:333

Nauru, **III**:394–395

Nepal, **III**:404–406

Netherlands, **IV**:326

Netherlands Antilles and Aruba, **II**:268–269

New Zealand, **III**:416–417

Nicaragua, **II**:276

Niger, **I**:343

Nigeria, **I**:359–361

Norway, **IV**:338–339

Oman, **III**:425–426

Pakistan, **III**:441–442

Palau, **III**:449

Panama, **II**:286–287

Papua New Guinea, **III**:458

Paraguay, **II**:299–300

Peru, **II**:312

Philippines, **III**:469–470

Poland, **IV**:354–355

Portugal, **IV**:369–370

Puerto Rico, **II**:319–320

Qatar, **III**:480–481

Romania, **IV**:382–384

Russia, **IV**:399

Rwanda, **I**:369–370

St. Kitts and Nevis, **II**:327–328

St. Lucia, **II**:336

St. Vincent and the Grenadines, **II**:344–345

Samoa, **III**:487–488

San Marino, **IV**:409

São Tomé and Príncipe, **I**:377–378

Saudi Arabia, **III**:502–503

Senegal, **I**:388–389

Seychelles, **I**:398

Sierra Leone, **I**:406–407

Singapore, **III**:514–515

Slovakia, **IV**:418

Slovenia, **IV**:427–428

Solomon Islands, **III**:524

Somalia, **I**:415

South Africa, **I**:427

Spain, **IV**:442–443

Sri Lanka, **III**:535–536

Sudan, **I**:438–439

Suriname, **II**:351–352

Swaziland, **I**:445–446

Sweden, **IV**:455–456

Switzerland, **IV**:470–471

Syria, **III**:547–548

Taiwan, **III**:562–563

Tajikistan, **III**:573

Tanzania, **I**:457–458

Thailand, **III**:587–589

Togo, **I**:469

Tonga, **III**:599–600

Trinidad and Tobago, **II**:360

Tunisia, **I**:478–479

Turkey, **III**:615–616

Turkmenistan, **III**:627–628

Tuvalu, **III**:635

Uganda, **I**:491–492

Ukraine, **IV**:483

United Arab Emirates, **III**:644

United Kingdom, **IV**:498–499

United States, **II**:374–375

Uruguay, **II**:387–388

Uzbekistan, **III:**654–655

Vanuatu, **III:**662

Vatican City, **IV:**508–509

Venezuela, **II:**398–400

Vietnam, **III:**672–673

Yemen, **III:**682

Yugoslavia, **IV:**516–517

Zambia, **I:**502–503

Zimbabwe, **I:**511–512

Power. *See* Energy production and consumption

President Chain Store Group, **III:**560

Presidential guard, Burkina Faso, **I:**40

Príncipe. *See* São Tomé and Príncipe

Privatization. *See* Economic overviews and trends; *specific industries and services*

Privatization Fund, Croatia, **IV:**86

Procurement, Belgium, **IV:**51

Progressive Socialist Party (Ukraine), **IV:**477

Psychological trauma of Afghan children, **III:**8–9

Public transportation

Greece, **IV:**187

Hong Kong, **III:**147–148

Mexico, **II:**248–249

Slovakia, **IV:**414

Sweden, **IV:**450–451

Publishing and printing

Burkina Faso, **I:**40

Côte d'Ivoire, **I:**121

Greece, **IV:**183

Hungary, **IV:**198–199

Lesotho, **I:**237

Singapore, **III:**512

Zimbabwe, **I:**509

Puerto Rico, **II:315–321**

Pula (money), **I:**33

Pulse production, Turkey, **III:**609

Puntland, **I:**416

Q

Qadhafi, Muammar, **I:**252

Qat production, Yemen, **III:**680

Qatar, **III:475–482**

Quality of life. *See* Poverty and wealth

Québec independence, **II:**91

Quetzal (money), **II:**205

R

Rabuka, Sitiveni, **III:**129

Radio. *See* Telecommunications

Railroads

Algeria, **I:**5

Australia, **III:**14–15

Azerbaijan, **III:**27

Bangladesh, **III:**45–46

Benin, **I:**23

Bolivia, **II:**53

Burkina Faso, **I:**40

Burma, **III:**76

Cameroon, **I:**59, 62

Chile, **II:**96

China, **III:**99

Congo, Republic of the, **I:**111

Côte d'Ivoire, **I:**120–121

Djibouti, **I:**131–132

Egypt, **I:**139

Eritrea, **I:**161–162

Ethiopia, **I:**170–171

Gabon, **I:**181

Georgia, **IV:**157

Greece, **IV:**187

Guinea, **I:**208

Iran, **III:**192–193

Ireland, **IV:**218

Italy, **IV:**233

Jamaica, **II:**237–238

Kenya, **I:**226

Malaysia, **III:**347–348

Mexico, **II:**249

Namibia, **I:**330

Nigeria, **I:**354–355

Pakistan, **III:**434

Peru, **II:**307

Poland, **IV:**347

Russia, **IV:**392

Saudi Arabia, **III:**497

Spain, **IV:**436

Taiwan, **III:**556

Tanzania, **I:**452–453

Thailand, **III:**581

Turkey, **III:**607

Turkmenistan, **III:**623–624

Uganda, **I:**487

United States, **II:**367

Vietnam, **III:**668

Zimbabwe, **I:**508

Rand (money), **I:**426–427

Re-exporting of goods

Paraguay, **II:**297–298

United Arab Emirates, **III:**643

Recession. *See* Economic overviews and trends

Redenomination, Russia, **IV:**398

Reform programs. *See* Economic overviews and trends; Money; Politics and government

Religious affiliation. *See* Country overviews

RENAMO movement, Mozambique, **I:**315, 316

Repelita I - VI development plans, Indonesia, **III:**175

Replacement level, Armenia, **IV:**17

Republic of China. *See* Taiwan

Republic of the Congo. *See* Congo, Republic of the

Republican Party (United States), **II:**366

Republican People's Party (Turkey), **III:**606

Restaurants. *See* Retail, wholesale, and food services

Retail, wholesale, and food services

Algeria, **I:**8

Antigua and Barbuda, **II:**6

Argentina, **II:**17–18, 18

Australia, **III:**18–19

Austria, **IV:**33

Bangladesh, **III:**49–50

Barbados, **II:**37

Belgium, **IV:**56

Bolivia, **II:**56

Bosnia and Herzegovina, **IV:**67

Brazil, **II:**71

Brunei Darussalam, **III:**70

Bulgaria, **IV:**77

Cambodia, **III:**90

Cameroon, **I:**63

Canada, **II:**85–86

Central African Republic, **I:**79

Chad, **I:**88

Chile, **II:**102

China, **III:**103, 104

Colombia, **II:**115

Costa Rica, **II:**127

Cuba, **II:**138

Czech Republic, **IV:**100

Denmark, **IV:**112

Dominican Republic, **II:**156

Ecuador, **II:**166

Egypt, **I:**144

Eritrea, **I:**163

Estonia, **IV:**123

Ethiopia, **I:**174

Fiji, **III:**131

Finland, **IV:**134

French Antilles and French Guiana, **II:**187

French Polynesia, **III:**139

Germany, **IV:**173–174

Ghana, **I:**201

Hong Kong, **III:**152

Hungary, **IV:**200

Indonesia, **III:**181

Iraq, **III:**209

Retail, wholesale, and food services
(*continued*)
Ireland, **IV:**222
Italy, **IV:**238
Jamaica, **II:**241
Japan, **III:**234
Kazakhstan, **III:**258
Kiribati, **III:**269
Korea, North, **III:**277
Korea, South, **III:**290
Laos, **III:**320–321
Lebanon, **III:**331
Lesotho, **I:**240
Liechtenstein, **IV:**259
Luxembourg, **IV:**281
Macau, **III:**339
Macedonia, **IV:**289
Madagascar, **I:**265
Malawi, **I:**273
Malaysia, **III:**351–352
Mexico, **II:**253
Moldova, **IV:**305
Monaco, **IV:**313
Mongolia, **III:**388
Morocco, **I:**309
Mozambique, **I:**320
Namibia, **I:**332
Nepal, **III:**403
Netherlands, **IV:**324
Netherlands Antilles and Aruba,
II:267
New Zealand, **III:**415
Nicaragua, **II:**275
Niger, **I:**342
Nigeria, **I:**358–359
Norway, **IV:**337
Paraguay, **II:**298
Peru, **II:**311
Philippines, **III:**467
Poland, **IV:**351, 352
Portugal, **IV:**367
Qatar, **III:**479
Romania, **IV:**381–382
St. Vincent and the Grenadines,
II:343
Samoa, **III:**487
Senegal, **I:**387
Seychelles, **I:**397
Sierra Leone, **I:**405
Singapore, **III:**513
Slovakia, **IV:**416
Slovenia, **IV:**425–426
Solomon Islands, **III:**523
Somalia, **I:**414
Sri Lanka, **III:**533–534
Suriname, **II:**351
Sweden, **IV:**453–454

Switzerland, **IV:**467
Taiwan, **III:**560
Tajikistan, **III:**571
Thailand, **III:**585–586
Tonga, **III:**598
Trinidad and Tobago, **II:**359
United Arab Emirates, **III:**642
United Kingdom, **IV:**496
United States, **II:**372
Uzbekistan, **III:**653
Venezuela, **II:**397
Vietnam, **III:**671
Yemen, **III:**681
Yugoslavia, **IV:**515–516
Zimbabwe, **I:**511
Reunification
Germany, **IV:**167
Korea, **III:**284, 294
Revenues. *See* International trade;
Taxation
Revolutionary Party (Tanzania). *See*
Chama Cha Mapinduzi
Rice production
Bangladesh, **III:**47
Burma, **III:**78
Egypt, **I:**141
Guinea, **I:**209
Laos, **III:**319
Malaysia, **III:**349
Pakistan, **III:**436
Taiwan, **III:**557
Vietnam, **III:**669
Río Muni. *See* Equatorial Guinea
Riyal (money)
Oman, **III:**425
Saudi Arabia, **III:**502
Yemen, **III:**682
Roads
Afghanistan, **III:**4
Albania, **IV:**3
Algeria, **I:**5
Angola, **I:**15
Antigua and Barbuda, **II:**3
Argentina, **II:**13
Australia, **III:**14
Azerbaijan, **III:**27
Bangladesh, **III:**45
Belize, **II:**43
Benin, **I:**23
Brazil, **II:**66
Brunei Darussalam, **III:**67
Bulgaria, **IV:**74
Burkina Faso, **I:**40
Burma, **III:**76
Burundi, **I:**49
Cameroon, **I:**59
Central African Republic, **I:**77

Chad, **I:**86
Chile, **II:**96–97
China, **III:**99, 113
Colombia, **II:**111
Costa Rica, **II:**124
Côte d'Ivoire, **I:**120
Dominican Republic, **II:**154
Egypt, **I:**139
El Salvador, **II:**173–174
Eritrea, **I:**161–162
Ethiopia, **I:**170
The Gambia, **I:**189
Guinea, **I:**208
Honduras, **II:**227–228
Iceland, **IV:**208
Iran, **III:**192
Ireland, **IV:**218
Israel, **III:**216
Italy, **IV:**233
Jamaica, **II:**237
Japan, **III:**229
Kenya, **I:**226
Korea, South, **III:**286
Kuwait, **III:**298
Laos, **III:**317
Latvia, **IV:**248
Lebanon, **III:**328
Libya, **I:**252
Macau, **III:**337
Madagascar, **I:**263
Malawi, **I:**271
Malaysia, **III:**347
Mauritania, **I:**288
Mauritius, **I:**295
Mexico, **II:**248
Micronesia, **III:**377
Morocco, **I:**306
Mozambique, **I:**316
Namibia, **I:**330
Netherlands, **IV:**319
Nicaragua, **II:**273
Nigeria, **I:**354
Oman, **III:**421
Pakistan, **III:**433–434
Paraguay, **II:**295
Peru, **II:**307
Philippines, **III:**464
Poland, **IV:**347
Romania, **IV:**378
Russia, **IV:**392–393
Rwanda, **I:**367
São Tomé and Príncipe, **I:**375
Saudi Arabia, **III:**496–497
Seychelles, **I:**395
Singapore, **III:**509–510
Slovakia, **IV:**414
Solomon Islands, **III:**521

Somalia, **I:**412

Spain, **IV:**436–437

Sri Lanka, **III:**531

Sudan, **I:**434–435

Tajikistan, **III:**569

Tanzania, **I:**452

Thailand, **III:**581

Togo, **I:**466

Tunisia, **I:**475

Turkey, **III:**607

Turkmenistan, **III:**624

Uganda, **I:**486–487

United States, **II:**367

Vietnam, **III:**668

Yemen, **III:**679

Romania, **IV:375–386**

Rubber production

Cameroon, **I:**61

Côte d'Ivoire, **I:**122

Liberia, **I:**247

Sri Lanka, **III:**533

Ruble (money)

Belarus, **IV:**43

Russia, **IV:**398

Tajikistan, **III:**572

Rupee (money)

Mauritius, **I:**298

Nepal, **III:**404

Seychelles, **I:**397

Russia, **IV:387–403**

Russian financial crisis of 1998, **IV:**389–390, 400

Rwanda, **I:365–371**

S

Sadat, Anwar, **I:**138

St. Kitts and Nevis, **II:323–329**

St. Kitts and Nevis Labour Party, **II:**324

St. Lucia, **II:331–338**

St. Lucia Labour Party, **II:**332

St. Vincent and the Grenadines, **II:339–346**

Sales taxes. *See* Taxation

Salt mining, Cape Verde, **I:**71

Samoa, **III:483–489**

San Marino, **IV:405–410**

Sanitation. *See* Poverty and wealth

Sankara, Thomas, **I:**39

São Tomé and Príncipe, **I:373–379**

Sasso-Nguesso, Denis, **I:**111

Al Saud family, **III:**494–495

Saudi Arabia, **III:491–505**

Schilling (money), **IV:**34

Scotland. *See* United Kingdom

Second era, Sri Lanka economy, **III:**529

Second Republic, Zambia, **I:**497–498

Seko, Mobutu Sese, **I:**100–101

Senegal, **I:381–391**

Serbia. *See* Yugoslavia

Service industries. *See* Financial services; Retail, wholesale, and food services; Tourism

Seychelles, **I:393–399**

Sheep production, New Zealand, **III:**413

Shell corporations, Bahamas, **II:**29

Shilling (money)

Kenya, **I:**231

Somalia, **I:**414

Tanzania, **I:**457

Uganda, **I:**491

Shipbuilding

Finland, **IV:**133

Netherlands, **IV:**322

Norway, **IV:**337

Shipping industry

Greece, **IV:**186–187

Malta, **IV:**296

Norway, **IV:**335

"Shock therapy" economic policy

Poland, **IV:**345

Russia, **IV:**397–398

Shrimp farming, Ecuador, **II:**165

Sierra Leone, **I:401–408**

Silver mining

Bolivia, **II:**51

Mexico, **II:**251

Singapore, **III:507–517**

Sino-British Joint Declaration, **III:**144

Sint Eustatius. *See* Netherlands Antilles and Aruba

Sint Maarten. *See* Netherlands Antilles and Aruba

Slovak Nationalist Party, **IV:**413

Slovakia, **IV:411–420**

Slovenia, **IV:421–430**

Soap production, Dominica, **II:**147

SOCATEL (company), **I:**77, 79

Social class and status. *See* Caste systems; Discrimination; Poverty and wealth

Social Democratic Party

Austria, **IV:**27–28

Finland, **IV:**129

Ukraine, **IV:**477

Social partnership, Austria, **IV:**28–29

Social welfare. *See* Health and social welfare programs; Poverty and wealth; Working conditions

Soglo, Nicephore, **I:**23

Solomon Islands, **III:519–525**

Som (money), **III:**310–311

Somalia, **I:409–416**

Somaliland, **I:**411–412, 417

Somoni (money), **III:**572

South Africa, **I:417–430**

South African Customs Union, **I:**33

South African Development Community, **I:**321, 426

South Korea. *See* Korea, South

Southeastern Anatolian Project, **III:**610

Soviet Union

dissolution of, **IV:**391

economic system, **IV:**389

relations with Cuba, **II:**134

relations with Finland, **IV:**128–129, 135

relations with Latvia, **IV:**246–247

relations with Lithuania, **IV:**264

Soybean production

Brazil, **II:**68

Paraguay, **II:**294, 296

Spain, **IV:431–446**

Spanish Socialist Workers Party, **IV:**433–434, 435

Spice production, Comoros, **I:**94

Squash production

Tonga, **III:**598

Vanuatu, **III:**660

Sri Lanka, **III:527–538**

Standard of living. *See* Poverty and wealth

State Law and Order Restoration Council (Burma), **III:**75

State-owned enterprises

China, **III:**105–106

Finland, **IV:**130

Steel. *See* Iron and steel production

Stock exchanges

Antigua and Barbuda, **II:**6

Argentina, **II:**19

Armenia, **IV:**22

Australia, **III:**20

Bahrain, **III:**37

Bangladesh, **III:**51

Belgium, **IV:**57

Benin, **I:**25

Bolivia, **II:**57

Botswana, **I:**33

Brazil, **II:**72

Burkina Faso, **I:**43

Canada, **II:**88

China, **III:**106–107

Congo, Republic of the, **I:**113

Costa Rica, **II:**127

Stock exchanges (*continued*)

Croatia, **IV:**90

Czech Republic, **IV:**101

Denmark, **IV:**114

Egypt, **I:**144

Finland, **IV:**136

Germany, **IV:**175–176

Greece, **IV:**188

Hong Kong, **III:**154

India, **III:**166

Indonesia, **III:**182

Iran, **III:**197, 199

Iraq, **III:**210

Israel, **III:**218–219

Italy, **IV:**239–240

Jamaica, **II:**42

Jordan, **III:**246

Kenya, **I:**230

Korea, South, **III:**291

Latvia, **IV:**250

Lebanon, **III:**331

Lithuania, **IV:**271

Luxembourg, **IV:**282

Malaysia, **III:**353–354

Mexico, **II:**255

Moldova, **IV:**306

Morocco, **I:**309

Nepal, **III:**404

Netherlands, **IV:**325

New Zealand, **III:**416

Nicaragua, **II:**276

Norway, **IV:**338

Oman, **III:**424

Papua New Guinea, **III:**458

Paraguay, **II:**299

Philippines, **III:**469

Poland, **IV:**353–354

Portugal, **IV:**368–369

Qatar, **III:**479

Romania, **IV:**382

Saudi Arabia, **III:**501

Singapore, **III:**514

Slovakia, **IV:**417

Slovenia, **IV:**427

South Africa, **I:**425

Spain, **IV:**442

Sri Lanka, **III:**535

Sudan, **I:**438

Sweden, **IV:**454

Taiwan, **III:**562

Thailand, **III:**587

Tunisia, **I:**477–478

Turkey, **III:**615

Turkmenistan, **III:**627

Ukraine, **IV:**482–483

United Arab Emirates, **III:**644

United Kingdom, **IV:**497

United States, **II:**374

Uzbekistan, **III:**654

Venezuela, **II:**398

Zambia, **I:**502

Sudan, **I:431–440**

Suez Canal (Egypt), **I:**143

Sugar production

Barbados, **II:**36

Belarus, **IV:**41

Belize, **II:**44

Burkina Faso, **I:**42

Costa Rica, **II:**125

Cuba, **II:**137–138

Ecuador, **II:**165

Fiji, **III:**130

Guatemala, **II:**203

Jamaica, **II:**239

Mauritius, **I:**296

Panama, **II:**284

St. Kitts and Nevis, **II:**326

Sudan, **I:**437

Trinidad and Tobago, **II:**358

Zambia, **I:**500

"Sunshine Policy," South Korea, **III:**284

Suriname, **II:347–353**

Swaziland, **I:441–447**

Sweden, **IV:447–458**

Switzerland, **IV:459–473**

Syria, **III:539–549**

T

Taiwan, **III:551–566**

See also China

Tajikistan, **III:567–575**

Taka (money), **III:**50–51

Tala (money), **III:**487

Taliban, **III:**3–4, 6

Tanganyika African National Union (Tanzania), **I:**451–452

Tanzania, **I:449–461**

Tariffs. *See* International trade; Taxation

Taro production, Samoa, **III:**486

Tax evasion, Italy, **IV:**232–233

Tax havens

Andorra, **IV:**13

The Bahamas, **II:**26, 29

Denmark, **IV:**108–109

Luxembourg, **IV:**277

St. Kitts and Nevis, **II:**327

St. Lucia, **II:**335

Vanuatu, **III:**661

Taxation

Afghanistan, **III:**4

Albania, **IV:**3

Algeria, **I:**4–5

Antigua and Barbuda, **II:**3

Australia, **III:**13–14

Austria, **IV:**29

Azerbaijan, **III:**27

The Bahamas, **II:**27

Bangladesh, **III:**45

Barbados, **II:**35

Belarus, **IV:**39

Belgium, **IV:**50–51

Belize, **II:**43

Bhutan, **III:**59

Bolivia, **II:**52

Botswana, **I:**31

Brazil, **II:**66

Brunei Darussalam, **III:**67

Bulgaria, **IV:**73–74

Burkina Faso, **I:**40

Burma, **III:**76

Burundi, **I:**49

Cambodia, **III:**87

Canada, **II:**80–81, 91

Chad, **I:**85

Chile, **II:**95–96

China, **III:**98

Colombia, **II:**111

Comoros, **I:**93

Congo, Democratic Republic of the, **I:**102

Costa Rica, **II:**123, 131

Côte d'Ivoire, **I:**120

Croatia, **IV:**86

Cuba, **II:**136

Czech Republic, **IV:**97

Djibouti, **I:**129

Dominican Republic, **II:**153

Egypt, **I:**139

El Salvador, **II:**173

Eritrea, **I:**161

Estonia, **IV:**120–121

Ethiopia, **I:**170

Fiji, **III:**129

Finland, **IV:**130

France, **IV:**145

French Antilles and French Guiana, **II:**183–184

French Polynesia, **III:**137

The Gambia, **I:**189

Georgia, **IV:**157

Germany, **IV:**168

Ghana, **I:**197

Greece, **IV:**183

Grenada, **II:**193

Guatemala, **II:**202

Guinea, **I:**208

Guyana, **II:**211

Haiti, **II:**219

Honduras, **II:**227

Hong Kong, **III:**146–147

Hungary, **IV:**197

Iceland, **IV:**208

India, **III:**162

Indonesia, **III:**177

Iraq, **III:**206

Ireland, **IV:**217

Italy, **IV:**232–233

Jamaica, **II:**237

Japan, **III:**229

Kazakhstan, **III:**254

Kenya, **I:**226

Kiribati, **III:**267

Korea, North, **III:**275

Korea, South, **III:**285

Kyrgyzstan, **III:**307

Laos, **III:**317

Latvia, **IV:**248

Lebanon, **III:**328

Libya, **I:**252

Lithuania, **IV:**266

Luxembourg, **IV:**278

Macau, **III:**337

Malawi, **I:**271

Malaysia, **III:**347

Maldives, **III:**361

Mali, **I:**279

Malta, **IV:**295

Marshall Islands, **III:**369

Mauritania, **I:**287

Mauritius, **I:**295

Mexico, **II:**248

Micronesia, **III:**377

Monaco, **IV:**311

Morocco, **I:**305–306

Mozambique, **I:**316

Namibia, **I:**330

Nepal, **III:**400

Netherlands Antilles and Aruba, **II:**264

New Zealand, **III:**411

Nigeria, **I:**353–354

Norway, **IV:**334

Oman, **III:**421

Pakistan, **III:**433, 439

Palau, **III:**447

Panama, **II:**282

Papua New Guinea, **III:**455

Peru, **II:**307

Philippines, **III:**463–464

Poland, **IV:**346

Portugal, **IV:**362–363

Puerto Rico, **II:**315–317

Romania, **IV:**378

Russia, **IV:**391, 392

St. Kitts and Nevis, **II:**324

St. Lucia, **II:**333

St. Vincent and the Grenadines, **II:**341

Samoa, **III:**484

São Tomé and Príncipe, **I:**375

Saudi Arabia, **III:**496, 502

Senegal, **I:**383–384

Sierra Leone, **I:**403

Singapore, **III:**509

Slovakia, **IV:**413

Slovenia, **IV:**423

Solomon Islands, **III:**521

Somalia, **I:**412

South Africa, **I:**420

Spain, **IV:**436

Sri Lanka, **III:**530–531

Suriname, **II:**349

Swaziland, **I:**442–443

Sweden, **IV:**450

Switzerland, **IV:**462–463

Syria, **III:**541–542

Taiwan, **III:**55

Tajikistan, **III:**569

Tanzania, **I:**452

Thailand, **III:**580

Tonga, **III:**596

Trinidad and Tobago, **II:**357

Tunisia, **I:**475

Turkmenistan, **III:**623

Tuvalu, **III:**633

Uganda, **I:**486

Ukraine, **IV:**477–478

United Kingdom, **IV:**491

United States, **II:**163, 367

Uzbekistan, **III:**650

Vanuatu, **III:**658

Vatican City, **IV:**407

Venezuela, **II:**393

Vietnam, **III:**668

Yemen, **III:**679

Zambia, **I:**498

Zimbabwe, **I:**508

Taylor, Charles, **I:**245

Tea production

Bangladesh, **III:**48

Burundi, **I:**50

Kenya, **I:**228

Sri Lanka, **III:**532–533

Technology. *See* Information technology; Telecommunications

Technology Development Center, Finland, **IV:**128, 130

Telecommunications

Afghanistan, **III:**4, 4*t*

Albania, **IV:**3–4, 3*t*

Algeria, **I:**5, 5*t*

Andorra, **IV:**12, 12*t*

Angola, **I:**16, 16*t*

Antigua and Barbuda, **II:**3*t*, 4

Argentina, **II:**13–14, 13*t*

Armenia, **IV:**19, 19*t*

Australia, **III:**14*t*, 15

Austria, **IV:**29–30, 30*t*

Azerbaijan, **III:**27*t*, 28

The Bahamas, **II:**27, 27*t*

Bahrain, **III:**35, 35*t*

Bangladesh, **III:**45*t*, 46

Barbados, **II:**35, 35*t*

Belarus, **IV:**39*t*, 40

Belgium, **IV:**51*t*, 52

Belize, **II:**43, 43*t*

Benin, **I:**23*t*, 24

Bhutan, **III:**60, 60*t*

Bolivia, **II:**53–54, 53*t*

Bosnia and Herzegovina, **IV:**66*t*

Botswana, **I:**31*t*

Brazil, **II:**66*t*, 67

Brunei Darussalam, **III:**67, 67*t*

Bulgaria, **IV:**74–75, 74*t*

Burkina Faso, **I:**40*t*, 41

Burma, **III:**76*t*, 77

Burundi, **I:**49*t*

Cambodia, **III:**88, 88*t*

Cameroon, **I:**58*t*, 59, 62–63

Canada, **II:**81, 81*t*

Cape Verde, **I:**69, 70*t*

Central African Republic, **I:**77, 77*t*, 79

Chad, **I:**86, 86*t*

Chile, **II:**96*t*, 97–98

China, **III:**99*t*, 100

Colombia, **II:**111*t*, 112

Comoros, **I:**93, 93*t*

Congo, Democratic Republic of the, **I:**102*t*, 103

Congo, Republic of the, **I:**111, 111*t*

Costa Rica, **II:**124, 124*t*

Côte d'Ivoire, **I:**120*t*, 121

Croatia, **IV:**86*t*, 87

Cuba, **II:**136–137, 136*t*

Cyprus, **III:**118, 118*t*

Czech Republic, **IV:**97*t*, 98, 100

Denmark, **IV:**109*t*, 110, 113

Djibouti, **I:**130, 130*t*

Dominica, **II:**145, 145*t*

Dominican Republic, **II:**153*t*, 154

Ecuador, **II:**163–164, 163*t*

Egypt, **I:**139*t*, 140

El Salvador, **II:**174, 174*t*

Equatorial Guinea, **I:**153*t*

Eritrea, **I:**161*t*, 162

Estonia, **IV:**121, 121*t*, 122

Ethiopia, **I:**170*t*

Fiji, **III:**129*t*, 130

Telecommunications (*continued*)

Finland, **IV**:131, 131*t*, 135

France, **IV**:145–146, 145*t*

French Antilles and French Guiana, **II**:184, 184*t*

French Polynesia, **III**:137*t*

Gabon, **I**:181–182, 181*t*, 183

The Gambia, **I**:189, 189*t*

Georgia, **IV**:158, 158*t*

Germany, **IV**:169*t*, 170

Ghana, **I**:198, 198*t*

Greece, **IV**:183, 183*t*

Grenada, **II**:193–194, 193*t*

Guatemala, **II**:202, 202*t*

Guinea, **I**:208–209, 208*t*

Guinea-Bissau, **I**:218, 218*t*

Guyana, **II**:212, 212*t*

Haiti, **II**:220, 220*t*

Honduras, **II**:227*t*, 228

Hong Kong, **III**:147*t*, 148

Hungary, **IV**:198, 198*t*

Iceland, **IV**:208, 208*t*

India, **III**:163*t*, 164

Indonesia, **III**:177*t*, 178

Iran, **III**:193–194, 193*t*

Iraq, **III**:206*t*, 207

Ireland, **IV**:218–219, 218*t*

Israel, **III**:216–217, 216*t*

Italy, **IV**:233*t*, 234

Jamaica, **II**:237*t*, 238

Japan, **III**:230, 230*t*

Jordan, **III**:243*t*, 244

Kazakhstan, **III**:254*t*, 255

Kenya, **I**:226*t*, 227

Kiribati, **III**:267*t*, 268

Korea, North, **III**:275, 275*t*

Korea, South, **III**:286, 286*t*

Kuwait, **III**:299, 299*t*

Kyrgyzstan, **III**:308*t*

Laos, **III**:317*t*, 318

Latvia, **IV**:248, 248*t*

Lebanon, **III**:329, 329*t*

Lesotho, **I**:237*t*, 238

Liberia, **I**:246, 246*t*

Libya, **I**:253, 253*t*

Liechtenstein, **IV**:257*t*

Lithuania, **IV**:266*t*, 267

Luxembourg, **IV**:277, 278*t*, 279, 281

Macau, **III**:337, 337*t*

Macedonia, **IV**:287, 287*t*

Madagascar, **I**:263*t*, 264

Malawi, **I**:271*t*, 272

Malaysia, **III**:347*t*, 348

Maldives, **III**:362, 362*t*

Mali, **I**:279*t*, 280

Malta, **IV**:295, 295*t*, 297

Marshall Islands, **III**:369, 369*t*

Mauritania, **I**:287*t*, 288

Mauritius, **I**:295, 295*t*, 297

Mexico, **II**:249–250, 249*t*

Micronesia, **III**:378, 378*t*

Moldova, **IV**:303*t*, 304

Monaco, **IV**:312*t*

Mongolia, **III**:385*t*, 386

Morocco, **I**:306, 306*t*

Mozambique, **I**:316*t*, 317

Namibia, **I**:330–331, 330*t*

Nauru, **III**:393*t*

Nepal, **III**:400*t*, 401

Netherlands, **IV**:319*t*, 320, 323–324

Netherlands Antilles and Aruba, **II**:264*t*, 265

New Zealand, **III**:412, 412*t*

Nicaragua, **II**:273*t*, 275

Niger, **I**:340, 340*t*

Nigeria, **I**:354*t*, 355

Norway, **IV**:335–336, 335*t*

Oman, **III**:421*t*, 422

Pakistan, **III**:433*t*, 434–435

Palau, **III**:447, 447*t*

Panama, **II**:282*t*, 283

Papua New Guinea, **III**:455–456, 455*t*

Paraguay, **II**:295, 295*t*

Peru, **II**:307*t*, 308

Philippines, **III**:464*t*, 465, 467

Poland, **IV**:347*t*, 348

Portugal, **IV**:363*t*, 364

Puerto Rico, **II**:317, 317*t*

Qatar, **III**:477, 477*t*

Romania, **IV**:378*t*, 379

Russia, **IV**:392*t*, 393

Rwanda, **I**:367, 367*t*

St. Kitts and Nevis, **II**:325*t*

St. Lucia, **II**:333*t*

St. Vincent and the Grenadines, **II**:341, 341*t*

Samoa, **III**:485*t*

San Marino, **IV**:408*t*

São Tomé and Príncipe, **I**:375*t*, 376

Saudi Arabia, **III**:496*t*, 497

Senegal, **I**:384, 384*t*

Seychelles, **I**:395, 395*t*

Sierra Leone, **I**:403*t*, 404

Singapore, **III**:510, 510*t*

Slovakia, **IV**:414, 414*t*

Slovenia, **IV**:424, 424*t*

Solomon Islands, **III**:521–522, 521*t*

Somalia, **I**:412*t*, 413

South Africa, **I**:420*t*, 421

Spain, **IV**:437–438, 437*t*, 441

Sri Lanka, **III**:531, 531*t*

Sudan, **I**:435, 435*t*

Suriname, **II**:349, 349*t*

Swaziland, **I**:443, 443*t*

Sweden, **IV**:450*t*, 451

Switzerland, **IV**:463*t*, 464–465

Syria, **III**:542, 542*t*

Taiwan, **III**:555*t*, 556

Tajikistan, **III**:569, 569*t*

Tanzania, **I**:453, 453*t*

Thailand, **III**:581*t*, 582

Togo, **I**:466, 466*t*

Tonga, **III**:596–597, 597*t*

Trinidad and Tobago, **II**:357*t*

Tunisia, **I**:475, 475*t*

Turkey, **III**:607–608, 607*t*

Turkmenistan, **III**:623*t*, 624

Tuvalu, **III**:632, 633*t*, 634

Uganda, **I**:487, 487*t*

Ukraine, **IV**:478, 478*t*

United Arab Emirates, **III**:639*t*, 640

United Kingdom, **IV**:492*t*, 493, 496

United States, **II**:367*t*, 368

Uruguay, **II**:384, 384*t*

Uzbekistan, **III**:650*t*, 651

Vanuatu, **III**:659*t*

Vatican City, **IV**:508

Venezuela, **II**:394, 394*t*

Vietnam, **III**:668–669, 668*t*

Yemen, **III**:680, 680*t*

Yugoslavia, **IV**:514, 514*t*

Zambia, **I**:498–499, 498*t*

Zimbabwe, **I**:508–509, 508*t*

Telephones. *See* Telecommunications

Television. *See* Telecommunications

Territories. *See* Dependencies

Terrorism

Algeria, **I**:4

Egypt, **I**:138, 140, 143

Libya, **I**:252–253

Saudi Arabia, **III**:495–496

Spain, **IV**:434–435, 445

Syria, **III**:549

Uzbekistan, **III**:649

Yemen, **III**:681

Terry, Fernando Belaúnde, **II**:306

Textile industry

Belgium, **IV**:55

Brazil, **II**:69

Burkina Faso, **I**:42

Cameroon, **I**:62

Chile, **II**:100

Georgia, **IV**:160

Guatemala, **II**:204

Iran, **III**:197

Ireland, **IV**:221

Italy, **IV**:237

Lithuania, **IV**:269

Pakistan, **III**:438

Peru, **II:**309, 310
Poland, **IV:**350
Sudan, **I:**437
Taiwan, **III:**560
Turkey, **III:**610–611
Zambia, **I:**500–501
Thailand, **III:577–593**
Thanarat, Sarit, **III:**580
al-Thani, Sheikh Hamad bin Khalifa.
   See Hamad, Sheikh
Third Republic, Zambia, **I:**498
Tigrayan Peoples' Liberation Front
   (Ethiopia), **I:**170
Timber. *See* Forestry
Tin mining, Malaysia, **III:**350
Tobacco production
   Brazil, **II:**68
   Cuba, **II:**138
   Malawi, **I:**272–273
   Pakistan, **III:**437
   South Africa, **I:**423
   Turkey, **III:**609
   Zambia, **I:**499–500
Tobago. *See* Trinidad and Tobago
Togo, **I:463–471**
Tonga, **III:595–601**
Torre, Haya de la, **II:**306
Total Independence of Angola,
   I:13–14, 15
Tourism
   Albania, **IV:**5
   Algeria, **I:**8
   Andorra, **IV:**10, 13
   Angola, **I:**18
   Antigua and Barbuda, **II:**5
   Argentina, **II:**18
   Armenia, **IV:**21
   Australia, **III:**18
   Austria, **IV:**32
   The Bahamas, **II:**29
   Bahrain, **III:**36
   Bangladesh, **III:**49
   Barbados, **II:**37
   Belarus, **IV:**42
   Belgium, **IV:**56
   Belize, **II:**45
   Benin, **I:**25
   Bhutan, **III:**61–62
   Bolivia, **II:**51, 55–56
   Bosnia and Herzegovina, **IV:**67
   Botswana, **I:**32
   Brazil, **II:**70
   Brunei Darussalam, **III:**69
   Bulgaria, **IV:**76–77
   Burkina Faso, **I:**43
   Burma, **III:**80
   Burundi, **I:**51

Cambodia, **III:**87, 90
Canada, **II:**86
Cape Verde, **I:**71
Chile, **II:**97, 101–102
China, **III:**103–104
Colombia, **II:**115
Comoros, **I:**95
Costa Rica, **II:**126–127
Côte d'Ivoire, **I:**123
Croatia, **IV:**87, 89
Cuba, **II:**135, 138
Cyprus, **III:**121
Czech Republic, **IV:**100
Denmark, **IV:**112
Dominica, **II:**143–144, 147, 150
Dominican Republic, **II:**156
Ecuador, **II:**166
Egypt, **I:**142–143
El Salvador, **II:**176
Equatorial Guinea, **I:**155
Eritrea, **I:**163
Estonia, **IV:**122–123
Ethiopia, **I:**173
Fiji, **III:**131
France, **IV:**149–150
French Antilles and French Guiana,
   II:187
French Polynesia, **III:**139
The Gambia, **I:**191
Georgia, **IV:**159–160
Germany, **IV:**173
Ghana, **I:**201
Greece, **IV:**186
Grenada, **II:**195
Guatemala, **II:**204
Guinea, **I:**210
Guyana, **II:**213
Haiti, **II:**221
Honduras, **II:**230
Hong Kong, **III:**152
Hungary, **IV:**200
Iceland, **IV:**210
India, **III:**166–167
Indonesia, **III:**180–181
Iran, **III:**198
Ireland, **IV:**221–222
Israel, **III:**218
Italy, **IV:**237–238
Jamaica, **II:**240–241
Japan, **III:**234–235
Jordan, **III:**246, 249
Kazakhstan, **III:**258
Kenya, **I:**229–230
Kiribati, **III:**269, 270
Korea, North, **III:**277
Korea, South, **III:**290
Kyrgyzstan, **III:**309–310

Laos, **III:**321
Latvia, **IV:**250
Lebanon, **III:**331
Lesotho, **I:**240
Libya, **I:**256
Liechtenstein, **IV:**259
Lithuania, **IV:**269
Luxembourg, **IV:**281
Macau, **III:**339
Macedonia, **IV:**289
Madagascar, **I:**265
Malawi, **I:**273
Malaysia, **III:**345, 351
Maldives, **III:**363–364
Mali, **I:**281
Malta, **IV:**296–297
Marshall Islands, **III:**371
Mauritius, **I:**297
Mexico, **II:**252
Micronesia, **III:**379, 382
Monaco, **IV:**313
Mongolia, **III:**388
Morocco, **I:**308–309
Namibia, **I:**332
Nauru, **III:**393–394
Nepal, **III:**403
Netherlands, **IV:**324
Netherlands Antilles and Aruba,
   II:266–267, 269
New Zealand, **III:**414–415, 418
Nicaragua, **II:**275
Niger, **I:**342
Nigeria, **I:**358
Norway, **IV:**337
Oman, **III:**424
Pakistan, **III:**439–440
Palau, **III:**448, 450
Panama, **II:**285
Paraguay, **II:**298
Peru, **II:**310
Philippines, **III:**467
Poland, **IV:**352
Portugal, **IV:**367
Puerto Rico, **II:**318–319
Qatar, **III:**479
Romania, **IV:**381
Russia, **IV:**396
Rwanda, **I:**368
St. Kitts and Nevis, **II:**316–317
St. Lucia, **II:**335
St. Vincent and the Grenadines,
   II:343
Samoa, **III:**486–487
San Marino, **IV:**408
São Tomé and Príncipe, **I:**377
Saudi Arabia, **III:**500–501
Senegal, **I:**386

Tourism (continued)
Seychelles, **I**:397
Sierra Leone, **I**:405
Singapore, **III**:512
Slovakia, **IV**:416–417
Slovenia, **IV**:425
Solomon Islands, **III**:523
South Africa, **I**:425
Spain, **IV**:440
Sri Lanka, **III**:534
Sudan, **I**:437–438
Suriname, **II**:350
Swaziland, **I**:445
Sweden, **IV**:454
Switzerland, **IV**:466–467
Syria, **III**:545–546
Tanzania, **I**:455–456
Thailand, **III**:585
Togo, **I**:468
Tonga, **III**:598
Trinidad and Tobago, **II**:359
Tunisia, **I**:477
Turkey, **III**:612
Tuvalu, **III**:635
Uganda, **I**:490
Ukraine, **IV**:481
United Arab Emirates, **III**:642
United Kingdom, **IV**:496
United States, **II**:372
Uruguay, **II**:386–387
Uzbekistan, **III**:653
Vanuatu, **III**:661
Vatican City, **IV**:506–507
Venezuela, **II**:397
Vietnam, **III**:671
Yemen, **III**:681
Yugoslavia, **IV**:515
Zambia, **I**:501
Zimbabwe, **I**:510–511
Trachoma, **III**:425
Trade deficits. *See* Debt;
International trade
Trade unions. *See* Unions
Transnistria region, **IV**:303
Transportation industry
Belgium, **IV**:55
Colombia, **II**:115
Croatia, **IV**:89
Denmark, **IV**:113
Finland, **IV**:134–135
Greece, **IV**:186–187
Hong Kong, **III**:152
Korea, South, **III**:290
Libya, **I**:256
Niger, **I**:342
Ukraine, **IV**:481
See also specific modes of
transportation

Trinidad and Tobago, **II**:355–362
Truck taxes, Switzerland, **IV**:463
True Path Party (Turkey), **III**:606
Tughrik (money), **III**:388
Tunisia, **I**:473–481
"Turbot War," **IV**:440
Turkey, **III**:603–619
Turkish Republic of Northern
Cyprus. *See* Cyprus
Turkmenistan, **III**:621–629
Turks and Caicos Islands, **IV**:503
Tutsi-Hutu conflict, **I**:365, 366
Tuvalu, **III**:631–636
"Twinning" program, Netherlands,
IV:324

U
Uganda, **I**:483–494
Ujamaa, **I**:452
Ukraine, **IV**:475–485
Underemployment. *See* Working
conditions
Unemployment. *See* Economic
overviews and trends; Labor
force; Poverty and wealth;
Working conditions
Union Generale des Travailleurs
Algeriens (Algeria), **I**:9–10
Unions
Algeria, **I**:9–10
Antigua and Barbuda, **II**:7
Argentina, **II**:20
Armenia, **IV**:23
Austria, **IV**:35
Azerbaijan, **III**:31
Bangladesh, **III**:53
Belize, **II**:47
Bolivia, **II**:59
Brazil, **II**:73
Brunei Darussalam, **III**:71
Bulgaria, **IV**:80
Burkina Faso, **I**:44
Burma, **III**:82
Cameroon, **I**:65
Canada, **II**:89
China, **III**:109
Colombia, **II**:117–118
Costa Rica, **II**:130
Côte d'Ivoire, **I**:125
Czech Republic, **IV**:102
Denmark, **IV**:115–116
Djibouti, **I**:133
Dominican Republic, **II**:158
Ecuador, **II**:168
Egypt, **I**:147
El Salvador, **II**:178
Finland, **IV**:137–138

France, **IV**:153
Georgia, **IV**:162
Ghana, **I**:202
Greece, **IV**:191
Guatemala, **II**:206
Honduras, **II**:232
Hong Kong, **III**:155
Hungary, **IV**:203
Iceland, **IV**:212
India, **III**:169
Iran, **III**:200–201
Iraq, **III**:211
Ireland, **IV**:224
Israel, **III**:221
Italy, **IV**:241–242
Japan, **III**:237
Kazakhstan, **III**:262
Kenya, **I**:233
Kiribati, **III**:270
Korea, North, **III**:278
Korea, South, **III**:293
Lebanon, **III**:333
Luxembourg, **IV**:283
Macau, **III**:339
Malaysia, **III**:355
Mauritania, **I**:291
Mauritius, **I**:299
Morocco, **I**:311
Mozambique, **I**:323
Nepal, **III**:406
Netherlands, **IV**:326–327
Niger, **I**:344
Nigeria, **I**:361
Panama, **II**:287
Paraguay, **II**:294, 300
Peru, **II**:313
Poland, **IV**:355–356
Portugal, **IV**:370
Romania, **IV**:378, 384
Senegal, **I**:389–890
Sierra Leone, **I**:407
Singapore, **III**:515
South Africa, **I**:428
Spain, **IV**:444
Sri Lanka, **III**:537
Sweden, **IV**:456
Syria, **III**:548
Taiwan, **III**:564
Tanzania, **I**:459
Thailand, **III**:580
Togo, **I**:469
Turkey, **III**:617
Uganda, **I**:492
United Kingdom, **IV**:499
United States, **II**:376
Uruguay, **II**:389
Zambia, **I**:503

United Arab Emirates, **III:637–646**

United Democratic Party (Belize), **II:**42–43

United Kingdom, **IV:487–503**

United Left (Spain), **IV:**436

United National Independence Party (Zambia), **I:**495–496, 497

United Nations Human Development Index. *See* Poverty and wealth

United States, **II:363–379**
    aid to Egypt, **I:**137
    aid to Palau, **III:**450
    Panama Canal, **II:**280–281
    relations with Paraguay, **II:**298
    relations with Puerto Rico, **II:**316–317
    relations with Saudi Arabia, **III:**504–505

United Workers' Party (St. Lucia), **II:**332

Unwritten constitution, United Kingdom, **IV:**490

Uranium mining
    Australia, **III:**17
    Niger, **I:**342

Urban-rural inequalities
    age gap, Belarus, **IV:**44
    population distribution, Finland, **IV:**136–137
    poverty, Bangladesh, **III:**51
    poverty, China, **III:**107–108
    poverty, Laos, **III:**322
    poverty, Zambia, **I:**502–503

Uruguay, **II:381–390**

U.S. Virgin Islands, **II:**378–379

Utilities. *See* Energy production and consumption

Uzbekistan, **III:647–656**

V

Value-added tax. *See* International trade; Taxation

Vanuatu, **III:657–663**

Vatican Bank, **IV:**508

Vatican City, **IV:505–509**

Vatu (money), **III:**662

Vegetable production
    Taiwan, **III:**558
    Turkey, **III:**609–610

Venezuela, **II:391–401**

Venture-capital firms, Sweden, **IV:**453

Vicuñas, **II:**308–309

Vieira, Joao, **I:**217

Vietnam, **III:665–675**

Virgin Islands. *See* British Virgin Islands; U.S. Virgin Islands

Virtue Party (Turkey), **III:**606

"Vision 2025," Tanzania, **I:**458

Volkswagen-Ford joint venture, Portugal, **IV:**366

W

Wages. *See* Poverty and wealth; Working conditions

Wahid, Abdurrahman, **III:**176

Wales. *See* United Kingdom

Wangchuck, Jigme Dorji, **III:**59

Wangchuck, Jigme Singye, **III:**59

War and civil unrest
    Afghanistan, **III:**2, 3–4
    Algeria, **I:**4
    Angola, **I:**15, 20
    Bolshevik Revolution, **IV:**390
    Bosnia and Herzegovina, **IV:**63, 65
    Burkina Faso, **I:**45
    Burundi, **I:**48, 49
    Chechnya, **IV:**388
    Colombia, **II:**119
    Congo, Democratic Republic of the, **I:**101, 102, 107, 486
    Congo, Republic of the, **I:**111
    El Salvador, **II:**171, 173
    Fiji, **III:**128, 129
    Israeli-Palestinian conflict, **III:**215
    Lebanon, **III:**326–327
    Moldova, **IV:**303
    Nigeria, **I:**351
    Persian Gulf War, **III:**203–204, 206
    Rwanda, **I:**365, 366
    Solomon Islands, **III:**520–521
    Somalia, **I:**412
    Sudan, **I:**433
    Tajikistan, **III:**568
    Uganda, **I:**486
    Vietnam, **III:**667
    Yugoslavia, **IV:**512–513
    See also Border disputes; Terrorism

Water utilities
    Chile, **II:**97
    Micronesia, **III:**378
    See also Irrigation

Wealth. *See* Poverty and wealth

West Bank, **III:**213, 223

Western Sahara, **I:**306

Wheat production
    Egypt, **I:**141
    Pakistan, **III:**436

Wine and spirits production
    Chile, **II:**99
    Italy, **IV:**236
    Luxembourg, **IV:**280
    New Zealand, **III:**413
    South Africa, **I:**423

Spain, **IV:**439

See also Brewing and beverage production

Wool production, Peru, **II:**308–309

Worker mobility, United Kingdom, **IV:**499

Working conditions
    Afghanistan, **III:**9
    Albania, **IV:**6–7
    Algeria, **I:**9–10
    Andorra, **IV:**14
    Angola, **I:**19
    Antigua and Barbuda, **II:**7
    Argentina, **II:**20–21
    Armenia, **IV:**22–23
    Australia, **III:**22
    Austria, **IV:**35
    Azerbaijan, **III:**31
    The Bahamas, **II:**30–31
    Bahrain, **III:**38
    Bangladesh, **III:**52–53
    Barbados, **II:**39
    Belarus, **IV:**44
    Belgium, **IV:**59
    Belize, **II:**47
    Benin, **I:**27
    Bhutan, **III:**63
    Bolivia, **II:**58–59
    Bosnia and Herzegovina, **IV:**68
    Botswana, **I:**34
    Brazil, **II:**73
    Brunei Darussalam, **III:**71
    Bulgaria, **IV:**79–80
    Burkina Faso, **I:**44
    Burma, **III:**82–83
    Burundi, **I:**52
    Cambodia, **III:**91
    Cameroon, **I:**64–65
    Canada, **II:**89
    Cape Verde, **I:**72
    Central African Republic, **I:**81
    Chad, **I:**89
    Chile, **II:**104–105
    China, **III:**108–110
    Colombia, **II:**117–118
    Comoros, **I:**96
    Congo, Democratic Republic of the, **I:**105–106
    Congo, Republic of the, **I:**114
    Costa Rica, **II:**130
    Côte d'Ivoire, **I:**125
    Croatia, **IV:**92
    Cuba, **II:**140–141
    Cyprus, **III:**123
    Czech Republic, **IV:**102
    Denmark, **IV:**115–116
    Djibouti, **I:**133

Working conditions (*continued*)

Dominican Republic, **II:**157–158

Ecuador, **II:**168

Egypt, **I:**146–147

El Salvador, **II:**178–179

Equatorial Guinea, **I:**156

Eritrea, **I:**164–165

Estonia, **IV:**124

Ethiopia, **I:**176–177

Fiji, **III:**132–133

Finland, **IV:**137–138

France, **IV:**153

French Antilles and French Guiana, **II:**189

French Polynesia, **III:**140

Gabon, **I:**185

The Gambia, **I:**192

Georgia, **IV:**162

Germany, **IV:**177

Ghana, **I:**202

Greece, **IV:**190–191

Grenada, **II:**197

Guatemala, **II:**206–207

Guinea, **I:**212

Guinea-Bissau, **I:**221

Guyana, **II:**215

Haiti, **II:**223

Honduras, **II:**232–233

Hong Kong, **III:**155–156

Hungary, **IV:**202–203

Iceland, **IV:**212

India, **III:**169–170

Indonesia, **III:**183–184

Iran, **III:**200–201

Iraq, **III:**211

Ireland, **IV:**224–225

Israel, **III:**221

Italy, **IV:**241–242

Jamaica, **II:**243

Japan, **III:**237

Jordan, **III:**248

Kazakhstan, **III:**262

Kenya, **I:**232–233

Kiribati, **III:**270

Korea, North, **III:**278–279

Korea, South, **III:**292–293

Kuwait, **III:**301–302

Kyrgyzstan, **III:**312

Laos, **III:**322–323

Latvia, **IV:**252

Lebanon, **III:**333

Lesotho, **I:**241

Liberia, **I:**249

Libya, **I:**258

Liechtenstein, **IV:**260–261

Lithuania, **IV:**272

Luxembourg, **IV:**283

Macau, **III:**340

Macedonia, **IV:**290–291

Madagascar, **I:**266–267

Malawi, **I:**275

Malaysia, **III:**354–355

Maldives, **III:**365

Mali, **I:**283

Malta, **IV:**298

Marshall Islands, **III:**372

Mauritania, **I:**291

Mauritius, **I:**299

Mexico, **II:**256–257

Micronesia, **III:**380–381

Moldova, **IV:**306–307

Monaco, **IV:**314

Mongolia, **III:**389

Morocco, **I:**311

Mozambique, **I:**323

Namibia, **I:**333–334

Nauru, **III:**395

Nepal, **III:**406–407

Netherlands, **IV:**326–327

Netherlands Antilles and Aruba, **II:**269

New Zealand, **III:**417

Nicaragua, **II:**276

Niger, **I:**344

Nigeria, **I:**361

Norway, **IV:**339

Oman, **III:**426

Pakistan, **III:**442–443

Palau, **III:**449

Panama, **II:**287

Papua New Guinea, **III:**458–459

Paraguay, **II:**300–301

Peru, **II:**313

Philippines, **III:**470–471

Poland, **IV:**355–356

Portugal, **IV:**370

Puerto Rico, **II:**320

Qatar, **III:**481

Romania, **IV:**384

Russia, **IV:**400

Rwanda, **I:**370

St. Kitts and Nevis, **II:**328

St. Lucia, **II:**336–337

St. Vincent and the Grenadines, **II:**345

Samoa, **III:**488

San Marino, **IV:**409

São Tomé and Príncipe, **I:**378

Saudi Arabia, **III:**503

Senegal, **I:**389–890

Seychelles, **I:**398

Sierra Leone, **I:**407

Singapore, **III:**515

Slovakia, **IV:**418–419

Slovenia, **IV:**428

Solomon Islands, **III:**524

Somalia, **I:**415

South Africa, **I:**427–428

Spain, **IV:**443–444

Sri Lanka, **III:**536–537

Sudan, **I:**439

Suriname, **II:**352

Swaziland, **I:**446

Sweden, **IV:**456

Switzerland, **IV:**471

Syria, **III:**548

Taiwan, **III:**563–564

Tajikistan, **III:**573–574

Tanzania, **I:**458–459

Thailand, **III:**590–591

Togo, **I:**469–470

Tonga, **III:**600

Trinidad and Tobago, **II:**361

Tunisia, **I:**479–480

Turkey, **III:**616–617

Turkmenistan, **III:**628

Tuvalu, **III:**635–636

Uganda, **I:**492

Ukraine, **IV:**483–484

United Arab Emirates, **III:**645

United Kingdom, **IV:**499

United States, **II:**375–376

Uruguay, **II:**388–389

Uzbekistan, **III:**655

Vanuatu, **III:**663

Venezuela, **II:**400

Vietnam, **III:**673

Yemen, **III:**682

Yugoslavia, **IV:**517

Zambia, **I:**503

Zimbabwe, **I:**512–513

See also Labor force

World Bank. *See* Economic overviews and trends

World Trade Organization (WTO). *See* Economic overviews and trends; International trade

X

Xylitol, **IV:**134

Y

Yemen, **III:**677–684

Yugoslavia, **IV:**511–518

Z

Zambia, **I:495–504**

Zimbabwe, **I:505–514**

Zimbabwe African National Union, **I:**507

Zimbabwe African People's Union, **I:**507

Zinc mining, Namibia, **I:**332

Zloty (money), **IV:**353